Lecture Notes in Computer Science 2532

Edited by G. Goos, J. Hartmanis, and J. van Leeuwen

Lecture Notes in Computer Science 2533
Edited by G. Goos, J. Hartmanis, and J. van Leeuwen

Springer-Verlag Berlin Heidelberg GmbH

Yung-Chang Chen   Long-Wen Chang
Chiou-Ting Hsu (Eds.)

Advances in Multimedia Information Processing – PCM 2002

Third IEEE Pacific Rim Conference on Multimedia
Hsinchu, Taiwan, December 16-18, 2002
Proceedings

 Springer

Series Editors

Gerhard Goos, Karlsruhe University, Germany
Juris Hartmanis, Cornell University, NY, USA
Jan van Leeuwen, Utrecht University, The Netherlands

Volume Editors

Yung-Chang Chen
National Tsing Hua University
Department of Electrical Engineering
Hsinchu, Taiwan
E-mail: ycchen@ee.nthu.edu.tw

Long-Wen Chang
Chiou-Ting Hsu
National Tsing Hua University
Department of Computer Science
Hsinchu, Taiwan
E-mail:{lchang/cthsu}@cs.nthu.edu.tw

Cataloging-in-Publication Data applied for

Bibliographic information published by Die Deutsche Bibliothek
Die Deutsche Bibliothek lists this publication in the Deutsche Nationalbibliografie;

detailed bibliographic data is available in the Internet at <http://dnb.ddb.de>.

CR Subject Classification (1998): H.5.1, H.3, H.5, C.2, K.6, H.4, I.4, I.3

ISSN 0302-9743
ISBN 978-3-540-00262-8   ISBN 978-3-540-36228-9 (eBook)
DOI 10.1007/978-3-540-36228-9

http://www.springer.de

© Springer-Verlag Berlin Heidelberg 2002
Originally published by Springer-Verlag Berlin Heidelberg New York in 2002

Typesetting: Camera-ready by author, data conversion by PTP-Berlin, Stefan Sossna e. K.
Printed on acid-free paper   SPIN 10871500   06/3142   5 4 3 2 1 0

Preface

The 2002 IEEE Pacific Rim Conference on Multimedia (PCM 2002) is the third annual conference on cutting-edge multimedia technologies and was held at Tsing Hua University, Hsinchu, Taiwan, December 16–18, 2002. Hsinchu City, located about 70 km to the south of Taipei, is known as Taiwan's Silicon Valley, where hundreds of successful hi-tech companies, two major national universities, several research centers, and the Industrial Technology Research Institute (ITRI) are clustered to form and reinforce the "Science-Based Industrial Park." The conference complemented this wonderful setting by providing a forum for presenting and exploring technological and artistic advancements in multimedia. Technical issues, theory and practice, and artistic and consumer innovations brought together researchers, artists, developers, educators, performers, and practitioners of multimedia from the Pacific Rim and around the world.

The technical program featured a comprehensive program including keynote speeches, tutorials, special sessions, regular paper presentations, and technical demonstrations. We received 224 papers and accepted 154 of them. We acknowledge the great contribution from all of our committee members and paper reviewers who devoted their time to reviewing submitted papers and providing valuable comments for the authors.

PCM 2002 could never have been successful without the support and assistance of several institutions and many people. We sincerely appreciate the support of the National Science Council and the Ministry of Education of Taiwans, ROC. The financial sponsorships from the Institute of Applied Science & Engineering Research of Academia Sinica, Sunplus Technology Co., Ltd., the Institute for Information Industry, Chunghwa Telecom Laboratories, AIPTEK International, Inc., the MOE Program for Promoting Academic Excellence of Universities, and Opto-Electronics & Systems Lab/ITRI are also gratefully acknowledged. Our sincere gratitude goes to our advisory committee chairs: Prof. Sun-Yuan Kung of Princeton University, Dr. Bor-Shenn Jeng of CHT Labs of Taiwan, and Prof. H.Y. Mark Liao of Academia Sinica of Taiwan. Deep thanks go to the IEEE Signal Processing Society and the Circuits and Systems Society for technical co-sponsorship.

December 2002   Yung-Chang Chen
                                                        Long-Wen Chang
                                                        Chiou-Ting Hsu

IEEE
Networking
the World™

Third IEEE Pacific Rim Conference

on Multimedia

Advisory Committee Chairs:
Sun-Yuan Kung   Princeton University, USA
Bor-Shenn Jeng   Chunghwa Telecom Labs, Taiwan
H.Y. Mark Liao   Academia Sinica, Taiwan

Conference Chair:
Yung-Chang Chen   National Tsing Hua University

Program Chair:
Long-Wen Chang   National Tsing Hua University

Poster/Demo Chair:
Shang-Hong Lai   National Tsing Hua University

Tutorial/Special Session Chair:
Chung-Lin Huang   National Tsing Hua University

Local Arrangements Chair:
Chaur-Chin Chen   National Tsing Hua University

Publicity Chair:
Fenn-Huei Simon Sheu   National Tsing Hua University

Proceedings Chair:
Chiou-Ting Hsu   National Tsing Hua University

Registration Chair:
Tai-Lang Jong   National Tsing Hua University

USA Liaison:
Jenq-Neng Hwang   University of Washington

Japan Liaison:
Kiyoharu Aizawa   University of Tokyo

Korea Liaison:
Yo-Sung Ho   Kwangju Institute of Science and Technology

Hong Kong Liaison:
Bing Zeng   Hong Kong University of Science and Technology

Web Master:
Chao-Kuei Hsieh   National Tsing Hua University

Organizers

National Tsing Hua University, Taiwan

Sponsors

IEEE Circuits and Systems Society

IEEE Signal Processing Society

National Science Council, Taiwan

Ministry of Education, Taiwan

Institute of Applied Science & Engineering Research, Academia Sinica

Sunplus Technology Co., Ltd.

Institute for Information Industry

Chunghwa Telecom Laboratories

AIPTEK International Inc.

MOE Program for Promoting Academic Excellence of Universities (MOE 89-E-FA04-1-4)

Opto-Electronics & Systems Laboratories, Industrial Technology Research Institute

Table of Contents

Mobile Multimedia

Digital Watermarking and Data Hiding

Motion Analysis

Multimedia Retrieval Techniques

Image Processing

Multimedia Security

Image Coding

Multimedia Learning

Audio Signal Processing

Wireless Multimedia Networks

Multimedia Processing Techniques

Image Segmentation

Multimedia Streaming

Multimedia Systems in Internet

Distance Education with Multimedia Techniques

Internet Security

Computer Graphics and Virtual Reality

Object Tracking Techniques

Face Analysis

MPEG 4

Leveraging Information Appliances: A Browser Architecture Perspective in the Mobile Multimedia Age

Toshihiko Yamakami

ACCESS, 2-8-16 Sarugaku-cho, Chiyoda-ku, Tokyo, 101-0064 JAPAN
yam@access.co.jp

Abstract. As the mobile handsets emerges as Internet ready devices, network enabled are among the most useful and visible aspects of the Internet. A wide variety of information appliances are ready for Internet access and advances in network technologies accelerate this trend. Such devices cope with constraints that do not exist in PC. The mobile multimedia services require improvements in embedded network software engineering. The issues in embedded network software engineering are presented. A framework of new network software architecture is presented. Implications towards mobile multimedia are discussed.

1 Introduction

Mobile handsets, game consoles, digital TVs, and car navigation systems start to be network ready. Internet with information appliances is quickly emerging and penetrating into the every-day life [3]. It is predicted that these network devices will outnumber the PCs in the near future. There is a successful example of wireless Internet services in Japan, which is NTT DoCoMo's i-mode. It obtains more than 34 million subscribers in 30 months since the launch of February 1999. This rapid penetration of the mobile Internet became social phenomena of the mobile Internet revolution, which is creating new life and communication style and new industries including contents services, B-to-B services, and wireless Internet communities.

In this paper, the author presents the network software architecture to cope with the mobile multimedia as well as implications for mobile multimedia from the lessons learned in the mobile Internet experience.

2 Emerging Information Appliances

2.1 Challenges in the Internet Ready Information Appliances

To realize the concept 'accessing the Internet anytime, anywhere', mobile phone handsets are the best candidate for the nearest, wearable, and easy-to-use Internet terminal to general people.

Y.-C. Chen, L.-W. Chang, and C.-T. Hsu (Eds.): PCM 2002, LNCS 2532, pp. 1–8, 2002.

Wireless networking infrastructure is becoming ready for high-speed Internet access from mobile devices.

To cope with the new requirements in the mobile Internet, there are three issues to be resolved:

- design of services
- design of enabling technologies
- implementation of enabling technologies

Design of services need the value chain creation to stimulate the service deployments to match the end users' demands. The time has come to apply various standard Internet technologies to wireless networking and wireless devices such as mobile phones. In addition, it needs the consideration of context-aware and culture-aware service development because the mobile Internet needs the transition of social life style for end users.

Design and implementation of enabling technologies need the in-depth considerations of the constraints in information appliances. The information appliances have distinguished features as follows:

- Small display space
- Small memory capacity
- Low-power CPU
- Simple and easy button operation
- Narrow bandwidth and low-speed network

It is always a challenge to cope with the wide variety of hardware and software requirements in information appliances. The diversity is the challenge for technology providers and content providers.

2.2   Compact NetFront Experience in the Mobile Internet

Micro browser software is the key technology in order to develop the Internet-accessible devices, by which end users can browse all kinds of information and exchange e-mails. ACCESS has been active in the design and implementation of enabling technologies since the first design of NetFront for TV in 1995. In 1997, mobile handsets were considered as poor devices unable to catch up the advances in Internet. With the development of Compact HTML[1] and appropriate browser implementations, it is proved that the subset of the Internet can be enabled on mobile handsets. This is the starting point of the mobile multimedia Internet. It should be noted that the design and implementation of enabling technologies should be synchronized with the service creation. Compact HTML is easy to use for content providers. In addition, the contents of it can be shared among different information appliances, like game consoles, digital TVs and network enabled FAX.

HTML is a common knowledge for content providers, therefore, it boosted the content generation. In addition, it did not require any special authoring environment.

Due to the memory restriction, the code size of Compact NetFront was only 300K bytes. It should be robust to the wireless environment. Therefore, the fault-tolerant parser was implemented. In addition, it should be neutral to the underlying network and operating system environments. It was necessary to cope with the diversity in information appliances.

Compact NetFront has the following features:

- Small memory footprint: ROM 300KB/RAM 150KB
- Compact HTML support
- Optimized for low power CPU: 5-15 MIPS
- Direct key assignment - accesskey attribute
- Telephony URL support (tel: xxx-xxxx-xxx)
- CPU/OS and communication protocol independent

Portability is a key issue in developing Compact NetFront. It can be implemented on top of light transport protocol stacks designed for PDC (Personal Digital Cellular Telecommunication System) packet network or on HTTP and TCP/IP over the PHS network. The diversity in information appliances drives the requirements of compactness and high portability.

2.3 Lessons Learned in the Early Stage in Mobile Internet

In August 2002, the mobile Internet users using micro browsers in handsets reached 55 million. With the limited capability and tightly coupled with the use scenes and contexts, it is important that the information appliances should be excellent products without Internet capability. In addition, content and service development aware of the user contexts are critical for capturing regular end-users.

With the information appliances, the end users are demanding. Easy-to-use and clear value prepositions in user contexts are necessary to help users to convert to the network enabled mobile people.

2.4 A Browser Perspective in Mobile Multimedia Enabling Technologies

With the advances in the mobile Internet, the implementation technologies are significantly improved. In the past, color capabilities, SSL capability for security, Java capabilities were considered almost prohibiting. The market demands and additional technological improvements in hardware and software overcame these difficulties. With these advances in technology implementations, it is important to create a common platform for mobile multimedia processing. There are no underlying technologies common in information appliances. The diversity in the local environment is significant in the information appliances. The only shared feature for them is network connectivity, therefore, it is natural to make a scalable browser as a common application platform in the network ready information appliance environment. It is scalable and extensible to underlying operating environments, network environments, user interface components, and multimedia capabilities. Without such a platform, the hard-to-fix-bugs embedded network environment is hard to provide a stable mobile multimedia environment. It should be cope with the possible radical changes in the home network environments.

3   A Connected World by Leveraged Information Appliances

The rapidly changing home network environment leads to another vision with full of network ready information appliances. The connected world in the future multimedia information appliance era is depicted in Fig. 1.

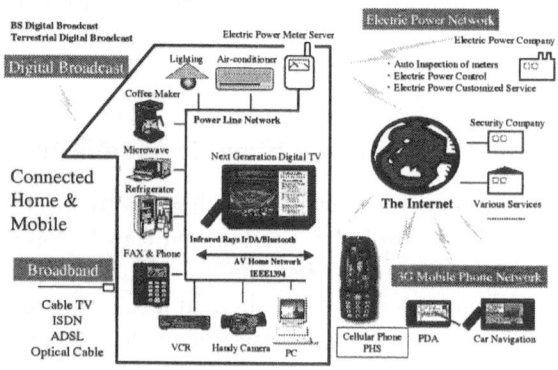

Fig. 1. A Connected World: Multimedia in Information Appliances

The home network environment will witness a radical change in the next few years from high speed cellular network to digital broadcasting. The technology that can embed multimedia Internet facility into a mobile handset enables a wide range of Internet features to embed a wide range of information appliances. The emerging network environment is expected to improve the service connectivity in the home environment.

4   A Scalable and Extensible Network Software Architecture: NetFront 3.0

This emerging new network environment needs new network software architecture. Compact NetFront is very portable on a wide variety of information appliance, it put the highest priority on the compactness especially targeted to the mobile handsets in the early stage. The NetFront 3.0 architecture is an extension of Compact NetFront for mobile handsets and NetFront 2.0 for game consoles and other devices.

The NetFront 3.0 Software Architecture is presented in Fig. 2.

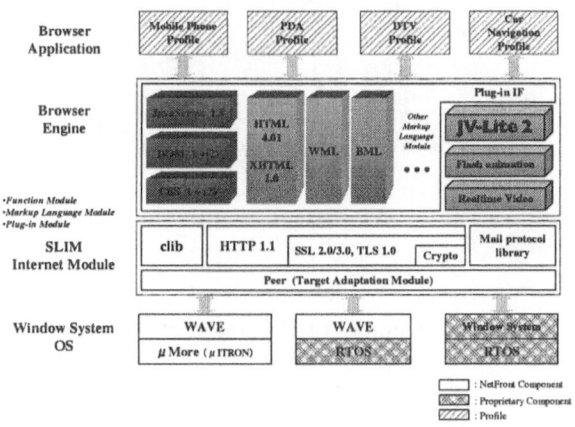

Fig. 2. The NetFront 3.0 Software Architecture

The original NetFront architecture focused on the compactness. The markup parsing part, the processing part and the user interface part were integrated to implement the minimum footprint. The increasing demands on the information appliances and the complexity of multimedia Internet requires a new platform to improve the software productivity. The new platform provides an integrated environment for a wide range of profiles from a mobile handset profile to an auto-motive profile. It also features the original strength of the NetFront architecture: the minimum requirements for operating systems, the separation of user inter-face, and the inclusion of the C library to facilitate the porting. It also provides the feature to integrate the mail environment and the web access environment, which is necessary for the coming multimedia integrated environment. This new architecture supports the three most important standards for mobile phones; Compact HTML (used in i-mode, the most successful wireless Internet service), WML [5] (markup language used in WAP services), and XHTML Basic [2] (re-garded as the new global standard). It uses HTTP and Wireless TCP/IP on the top of physical underlying bearer network layer such as GSM/GPRS, CDMA, W-CDMA, and etc. Also Java and other extension features can be plugged into our browser.

Examples of NetFront 3.0 features are shown in Fig. 3. The enhanced layout capability of XHTML and CSS, the frame capability, and the CSS capability to over wrap images and texts are shown. The full convergence of Internet standards is necessary to promote the new mobile multimedia services.

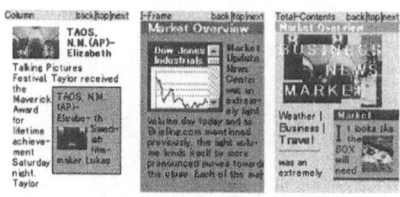

Fig. 3. Examples of NetFront 3.0 Features

5   Towards Mobile Multimedia

5.1   A New Platform for Connectivity

The browser perspective in the Internet era is depicted in Fig. 4. The unified application interface and user interface environment implemented on PCs are not available for the information appliance environments. Each information appliance is tuned to the special use context. Considering the wide variety of requirements in mobile handsets, game consoles, automotives and digital TVs, this

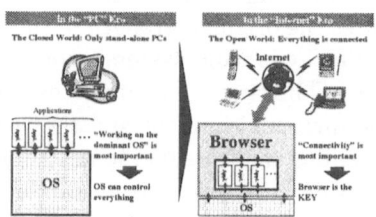

Fig. 4. A Browser Perspective in the Internet Era compared to the PC Era

diversity will continue for a considerable duration. In order to leverage the information appliances, it is crucial to provide an integrated application platform that can cope with a wide range of multimedia application on a wide range of information appliances. The connectivity provided by browsers is a key to the emerging the Internet with network ready information appliances.

5.2   The Mobile Internet Service Evolution Phases

With the rapid growth of the mobile Internet in Japan, there are lessons learned in many aspects. The Internet service needs careful consideration of value-chain to continuously feed the value-added services to the end users. The end users are very demanding and they pay attention to the new platform only when they are satisfied with the services. For this purpose, it is important to create a standard platform to open the reuse opportunities for tools and contents.

The past experience in game consoles, TVs, and PDAs have taught us that information appliance users are demanding. Poor design appliances with Internet capabilities did not have any chance to survive. It is important to keep the high product quality to make additional network capabilities usable for end users. For example, the early stage mobile handset with micro browsers were required to keep the same cost, same weight, same size and same battery life to cope with the end users' demands. It took two years for service deployments after the initial Compact NetFront development was completed. It was also important to make the device service ready so that the number of services ready for use reaches a certain level. Also, the advances of mobile Internet in Japan give us important lessons.

The service-oriented viewpoints are critical in large-scale deployment of mobile multimedia services. The information appliances have severe constraints both in display and input, therefore, it is important to capture the context-aware services. In addition, the careful consideration to the organizational or social cultures to fit in is important. With the constraints forced in the information appliances, it is important to capture the context-aware communication cultures. Communication can provide the very customized content for each user, which is a critical factor in information appliances.

Various multimedia factors need the break-though in the implementation technologies. Any additional CPU power needs additional battery power, which is critical in the mobile environment. It needs time to redesign various components to fit in the multimedia environment which needs more CPU power to process, for example, color, SSL and Java. A combination of various hardware and software implementation techniques is necessary to deploy the real mobile multimedia services.

The mobile Internet service evolution phases in Japan have been as follows:

- mobile Internet service (mail, web access, integrated telephony in web
- color display (color web access)
- application download (Java)
- camera-equipped handsets (image mail)
- multimedia messaging (integrated multimedia service environment)

It is interesting to observe that service feature and visual feature appear in turn with an interval of 6-12 months. By the end of August 2002, the camera-equipped mobile handset share reached 10%, which means more than 7 million handsets were equipped with a camera. After this hardware revolution phase, it will be followed by the next feature enhancement stage. The stage changes are triggered by the life style changes and education propagation in end users. It indicates that the deployment of new use of the mobile Internet needs a significant cost of user education and identifying the new service demands in the social dynamism.

The restrictions inherited in information appliances put significant limitations of realization of multimedia service contexts. In the coming mobile multimedia era, the limitations still put burdens to technology providers and content providers. It is very insightful that Grudin mentioned [4]:

> *Software today does not help us partition our digital worlds effectively. We must organize them ourselves. ... Yet information overload is a major concern: we cannot handle, "everything, everywhere, all the time". We need to partition our digital worlds.*

With the mobile multimedia capabilities, it is crucial to capture the social and contextual aspects of end user Internet world.

6   Conclusion

It is important to foresee the emerging mobile Internet environment. The rapid penetration of the mobile Internet shows the potential of new Internet ready information appliances to make use of the mobile multimedia services. To provide a stable mobile multimedia Internet, scalable, extensible, and flexible embedded network software architecture, NetFront 3.0 is discussed. Implications for large-scale deployment of mobile multimedia services are presented.

References

1. Kamada, T.: Compact HTML for Small Information Appliances W3C Submission, W3C Note, (Feb., 1998) (available at http://www.w3.org/TR/1998/NOTE-compactHTML-19980209)
2. Baker, M., Ishikawa, M., Matsui, S., Stark, P., Wugofsky, T., Yamakami, T.: XHTML™ Basic, W3C Recommendation, (Dec. 2001) (available at http://www.w3.org/TR/xhtml-basic)
3. Cerf, V. Beyond the Post-PC Internet CACM, Vol. 44, No. 9, (Sep. 2001) 34–37
4. Grudin, J. Participating digital worlds: focal and peripheral awareness in multiple monitor use ACM CHI 01, ACM Press, (2001) 458–465
5. WAP Forum™ Wireless Markup Language Version 1.3, WAP-191-WML-20000219-a (Feb. 2000) (available at http://www.wapforum.org/)

Seamless Service Handoff for Ubiquitous Mobile Multimedia

Ken Ohta[1], Takashi Yoshikawa[1], Tomohiro Nakagawa[1], Yoshinori Isoda[1], Shoji Kurakake[1], and Toshiaki Sugimura[1]

Multimedia Laboratories, NTT DoCoMo, Inc., 3-5, Hikari-no-oka, Yokosuka, Kanagawa, 239-8536, JAPAN
{ken, takashi, nakagawa, isoda, kurakake, sugimura}@mml.yrp.nttdocomo.co.jp

Abstract. To realize a ubiquitous multimedia environments utilizing mobile devices with multimedia appliances over heterogeneous access networks, we design and implement a service handoff (HO) system which supports two kinds of mobility; vertical HO between 3G Cellular and wireless LAN, and media redirection from mobile devices to multimedia applicances. To overcome inherently high setup latency of Cellular and multimedia appliances, which causes severe media disruption and throughput degradation, we propose a proactive service HO method with a soft HO mechanism based on a geographical resource map. Location-aided HO using the map allows the system to initiate HO in advance for concealment of setup latency. We evaluate HO performance on a testbed.

1 Introduction

High-speed network access environments for mobile multimedia are being realized as third generation (3G) Cellular services[1] and hot spot(wireless LAN) services are spreading. As mobile hosts (MH) such as handsets and PDAs, however, are severely constrained in terms of size and cost, their internal I/O capability (i.e. display, speakers, and camera) is restricted and should be improved to realize high-quality multimedia applications. In ubiquitous environments, we will be surrounded by multimedia appliances such as TVs and video cameras which can provide their media I/O capability as *external I/O* to MHs through the Internet. MHs can provide high-quality mobile multimedia services, e.g. mobile video phone, music on demand by external I/O.

A user usually have a preference and policy on the choice of access networks and I/O devices, and their availability is location dependent. Therefore we have built an integrated service handoff system for two kinds of mobility; vertical HO[3] between 3G Cellular and Wireless LAN (WLAN) services and media HO between internal and external I/O. HO systems should offer low-latency, efficient HO procedures in order to support gap-sensitive continuous media applications, and to minimize network and host overheads. However, the high setup latency of Cellular and external I/O causes serious media disruption and throughput

Y.-C. Chen, L.-W. Chang, and C.-T. Hsu (Eds.): PCM 2002, LNCS 2532, pp. 9–16, 2002.

degradation during HO. Furthermore, MHs performes repeated HO, called the ping-pong effect[2], when passing the edge of service areas.

This paper proposes a proactive service HO method based on a resource map. The map identifies proactive HO control area using geographical information such as room entrances and passages, and allows an MH to make proactive and efficient HO decisions. There are two main benefits: suppressing setup latency by initiating HO in advance, and avoiding unnecessary HO. We build and evaluate a service HO system testbed that includes location systems based on the use of RFID tags and video camera signals.

2   Related Works

Conventional HO systems consist of two major parts: the HO decision algorithm and the HO signaling/routing protocol. Typical HO decision algorithms are based on wireless link quality metrics such as RSS(Received Signal Strength) with hysterisis and dwell timer. The neural-network-based method[2] and LAH(Location-aided Handover)[6] are other schemes to eliminate the ping-pong effect. LAH makes HO decision according to the user location acquired by GPS and a geographical cell database which stores a user population, call dropping rate, HO statistics, and so on. As signaling/routing protocols, IP micro mobility protocols[4] localize HO signaling by a hierarchial network structure to decrease HO lantency and control traffic. Multicasting packets to multiple access points(AP), called soft HO, and buffering at APs are popular approaches to implementing low-latency, smooth HOs[3][4].

A RSS-based vertical HO to Cellular is triggered when RSS of WLAN link is deteriorated. However, due to the high latency of Cellular setup (about 10sec), the MH suffers the low throughput offered by the degraded WLAN link; the tedious functions include dial-up connection, authentication, and IP address setup. The proposed proactive method exploits geographical resource maps to initiates HO before WLAN link degradation. Proactive HO control is a practical solution since it is hard to reduce the setup time of commercial cellular services.

The mobile computing fields generally refer to media HO in terms of service mobility or personal mobility[12][13] across heterogeneous networks(GSM, PSTN, WLAN), which involves migration between different devices. Mobile People Architecture[7] and ICEBERG[8] deploy agents on networks for user tracking, media conversion(e.g. FAX to jpg), and forwarding among the heterogeneous networks according to user preference. Though they do not support media HO during sessions, SIP-based mobility[9] and the mobile-agent-oriented approach[5] have achieved dynamic session mobility. They, however, do not address low latency, stable, smooth HO for continuous media. High setup latency of external I/O, caused by authentication, negotiation, and device initialization functions, causes serious media disruption on disconnected external I/O. For example, when the user enters the service area of external audio I/O, audio output is not performed, and user voice input to the I/O is lost during HO. We propose proactive HO control with a soft HO mechanism for media continuity.

3   Service Handoff System

Network architecture of the service HO system is presented in Fig. 1. The MH is a user terminal equipped with WLAN and 3G Cellular network interfaces(I/F) to access the Internet. Client programs, e.g. video phone, and a mobility support agent, which is responsible for HO procedures, are running on the MH. The agent is informed of the user's position by an outdoor /indoor location system (LS). We assume that the MH gets new IP addresses of sites in foreign networks by DHCP. This architecture does not assume MobileIP support on hosts and networks. The CH is the correspondent host on which server or peer-client programs are running, for example, a music on demand server and a video phone client. External I/O services are provided by NAs (Networked Appliances) like TVs and acoustic speakers hooked into the Internet.

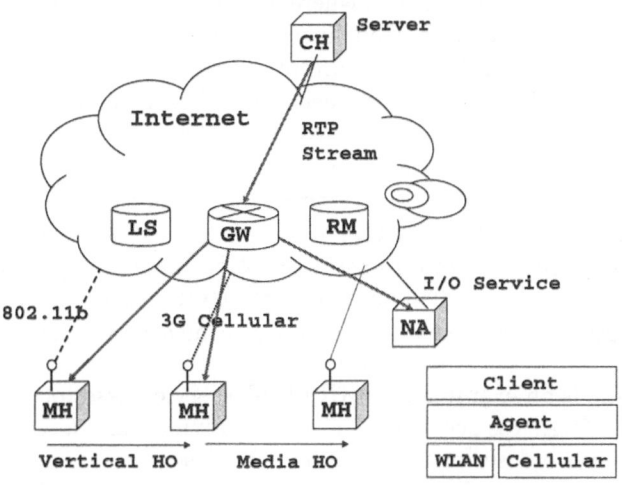

Fig. 1. Network Architecture of Service HO System

This paper focuses on RTP-based realtime multimedia service. Gateways (GW) are deployed between a client and a server to redirect RTP media streams from the server to external I/O and from external I/O to the server. An agent on an MH sends a redirection request(RREQ) with IP address and port specification of external I/O to perform media HO. It can also perform vertical HO by specifying an IP address of WLAN or Cellular I/F in a RREQ. The GW supports a soft HO mechanism that uses multicasting RTP stream to both WLAN and Cellular I/Fs or both internal and external I/Os.

Several reasons why we adopt the GW-based redirection architecture include media HO support, low deployment cost(no server modification), and transcoding at GWs to adapt the contents to MH capability, e.g. screen size, and connection speed[2]. As MobileIP is not suitable for media HO across different devices, application-level routing like this gateway and SIP-based mobility[9] is needed.

3.1   Resource Map

The resource map is a location-based service database generated by service descriptions containing a valid and ready range of each service. Service descriptions are specified manually by service providers, developers, and users. Agents receives them from services directly or indirectly via a service directory(Resource Map server ;RM) through a service discovery protocol such as SLP, Jini, UPnP[1], UDDI, and Bluetooth SDP. A ready range is a proactive HO control area based on geographical information such as room entrances and passages, while a valid range is an effective service area based on wireless link quality and a position of NAs. Fig. 2 presents two examples of a ready and valid range. It depicts the service area of a WLAN service by a 802.11b access point(AP) and an external audio output service by surround speakers (NA). The solid color areas indicate the area in which WLAN link quality is good and users can utilize the speakers available. The shaded area indicates where link quality is adequate but low. The solid color areas enclosed with solid lines are valid ranges. The area enclosed with dotted lines except valid ranges are ready ranges.

A range is a number of polygons, each described as a series of points (longitude, latitude). Height is also specified. Our design of the resource map was inspired by the EasyLiving geometric model [10]. In the model, objects such as users, devices, and services are described using coordinates, direction, position relative to other objects, and range(service area, device size) as figures, e.g. circles and polygons. As making a range description manually is time-consuming, we plan to develop a manual map tool with a GUI like a drawing tool, and an automatic map generation tool according to measured RSS when MHs are moving arround.

The following is an example of an UPnP-like service description for a WLAN service. A type of wireless access I/F, a service provider, and a ready/valid range are specified. Service description for audio output services is similarly specified; "Audio Output" as serviceType, device capability(e.g. the number of speakers), and dynamic resource information like average throughput.

```
<?xml version="1.0"?>
<root> <device>
    <deviceType>802.11b Access Point</deviceType>
    <manufacturer>ABC Company</manufacturer>
... Various Device Info: model, S/N, url...
    <serviceType>802.11b WiFi Service</serviceType>
    <serviceProvider>XYZ ISP</serviceProvider>
    <validRange> <pointList>
      <point> <x>x1</x> <y>y1</y> </point> <point> <x>x2</x> ...
      <point> <x>xn</x> <y>yn</y> </point>
    <pointList>
    <zTop>z0</zTop> <zBottom>z1</zBottom>    </validRange>
    <readyRange>.. pointList, zTop, zBottom.. </readyRange>
... Various Service Info. Authentication, Current Performance...
```

---

[1] Universal Plug and Play Forum, http://upnp.org/

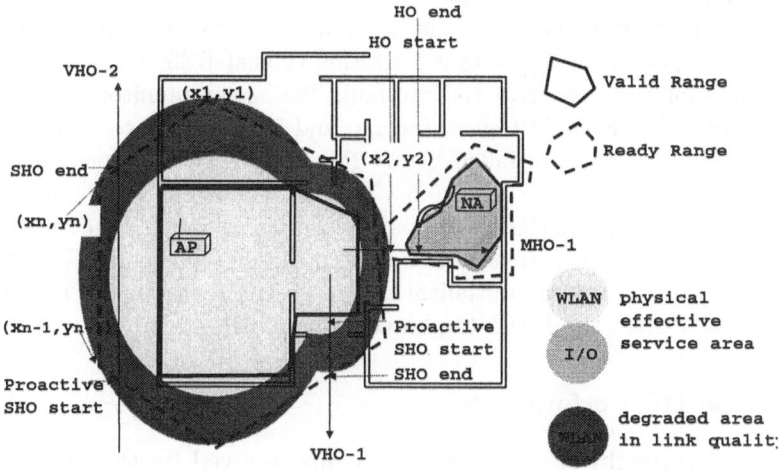

Fig. 2. Resource Map

3.2   Proactive HO Control

An agent on an MH periodically queries the RM about service descriptions available to its user by specifying service types, e.g. types of wireless network I/Fs and media I/O. The user and clients on the MH request service types and preference to the agent through a GUI, API, or configuration files. The agent makes HO decision between preferred and default services. Default services are high-availability backup services like Cellular and internal I/O.

When the MH is outside an area of preferred services, it continues to use or performs a HO to default services. Upon entering (leaving) the ready range of a preferred service, it initiates a soft HO to the preferred (default) service while maintaining the default (preferred) service. Within the valid range of preferred services, it uses only the preferred services.

4   Testbed

We built a service HO system testbed according to the network architecture(Fig.1) and the service deployment (Fig. 2). We implemented a follow-me audio streaming application. The music player client on the MH and the 128Kbps-MP3 streaming server on the CH communicates through RTSP and RTP. The GW and agent acts as RTSP/RTP proxy between the client and server. The GW provides SOAP methods for redirection control; SoftHOstart() and SoftHOend().

The agent queries the RM about service descriptions every thirty seconds and the RFID-tag-based LS or camera-based LS about user location every second. The former enables continuous tracking, while the latter achieves discrete tracking depending on deployment of RFID tag readers. The readers are carefully placed along passages so that the valid and ready range can be distinguished.

We also developed an agent that performs typical RSS-based vertical HO as a reference for the proactive HO method. The agent monitors WLAN I/F speed through a Windows API every second, and initiates HO to Cellular when it detects that the speed has fallen below 2Mbps. WLAN I/F speed decreases from 11Mbps to 2Mbps when link quality is poor. The agent for a conventional media HO method controls HO by comparing user location with the service area of external I/O. In a setup phase of the audio service, authentication by user ID and password and volume initialization are executed through SOAP. In the following experiments, the RFID-tag-based LS was utilized.

4.1   Vertical HO Performance

We measured throughput of the RTP streams received by the MH when a tester walked along the VHO-1 and VHO-2 paths in Fig.2. Throughput is plotted as packet rate (pkt/s); each packet occupies 1312 bytes. In Fig.3, the RSS-based

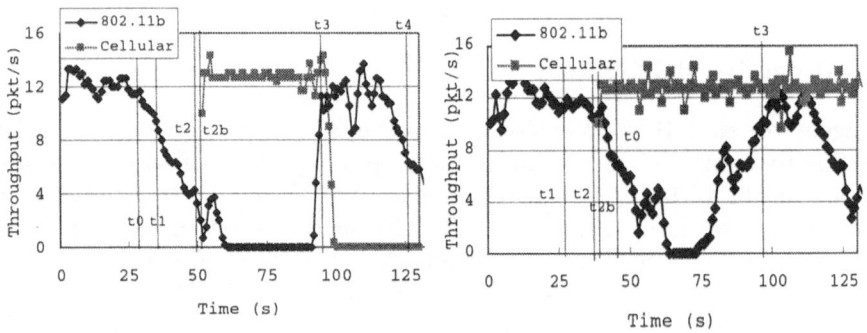

Fig. 3. RSS-based (left) vs. Proactive Vertical HO (right)

method detected a drop in WLAN I/F speed and initiated a HO at t1, although throughput began falling at t0. It established the cellular connection at t2 and received the stream through it at t2b after redirection messaging. Throughput degradation is observed during the decision phase (t0-t1) and the HO phase (t1-t2b). When skirting the WLAN area, it detected a recovery in WLAN I/F speed and disconnected the Cellular link at t3. It, however, tried to reestablish a Cellular connection at t4 due to immediate WLAN degradation. This unwarranted HO caused throughput fluctuation and media stream disruption.

When entering the ready range, the proactive HO method started and completed a HO to Cellular at t1 and t2, respectively. Although WLAN throughput began falling from t0, throughput and media continuity were maintained by Cellular connection. Despite the recovery of the WLAN signal at t3, it maintained the Cellular, because it was still in the ready range. We confirmed the proposed method contributed to stable HO control. However, we observed that some ping-pong effect remained when the user roamed about the boundary of the ready range. That suggests the need for guidelines; the boundary of a ready range should not be set in such a roaming area. We observed by these experiments that ninety percent of vertical HO to cellular took no more than 16 seconds. Service providers can set ready ranges based on these results.

4.2   Media HO Performance

Fig.4 shows the throughput of the conventional and proactive HO methods when walking repeatedly along MHO-1 in both directions. The conventional method initiates HO at t1 from the internal I/O through the cellular I/F to the external I/O when entering the service area. Due to setup latency, a media disruption was perceived during media HO.

In contrast, the proactive HO method started a soft HO at t1 upon entering the ready range. Media disruption was not observed since both internal and external I/O were already outputting audio data before the tester entered the valid range at t2. Although RTP streaming to the internal I/O through Cellular was stopped at t2, it was resumed before the tester left the ready range because of proactive HO control triggered at t3. We confirmed that proactive HO control and soft HO mechanism achieved media continuity.

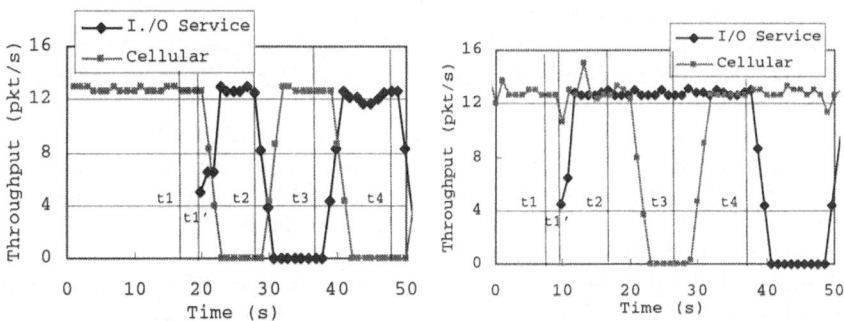

Fig. 4. Conventional Location-based vs. Proactive Media HO

5   Conclusion

We developed an integrated service handoff system for vertical HO between 3G Cellular and Wireless LAN and media HO between internal and external I/O. To support low-latency, efficient HO, we proposed a proactive service HO method based on a resource map that specifies proactive HO control areas. We confirmed that the method achieved seamless service migration without throughput degradation or user-perceived media disruption. Future directions for research include policy-based handoff control for various network I/Fs and I/O services, transcoding to support heterogeneous devices, and media synchronization for audio and video output of multiple I/O services on different devices.

References

1. Special Issue on IMT-2000: Standard Efforts of the ITU. *IEEE Pers. Communications*, Vol. 4, No. 4, pp. 8–40, 1997.
2. K. Pahlavan, P. Krishnamurthy, Ahmad Hatami, Mika Ylianttila, Juha pekka Makela, Roman Pichna, and Jari Vallstrom. Handoff in hybrid mobile data networks. *IEEE Personal Communications Magazine*, April 2000.
3. Mark Stemm and Randy H. Katz. Vertical handoffs in wireless overlay networks. *Mobile Networks and Applications*, Vol. 3, No. 4, pp. 335–350, 1998.
4. Andrew T. Campbell, Javier Gomez, Sanghyo Kim, and Chieh-Yih Wan. Comparison of IP micromobility protocols. *IEEE Wireless Communications*, pp. 72–77, February 2002.
5. J. Bacon, J. Bates, and D. Halls. Location-oriented multimedia. *IEEE Personal Communications*, Vol. 4, No. 5, pp. 48–57, 1997.
6. Pavlos Fournogerakis, Sofoklis Kyriazakos, and George Karetsos. Enhanced handover performance in cellular systems based on position location of mobile terminals. In *IST Mobile Communications Summit 2001*, September 2001. http://quadromsl.com/mcs2001/congreso.nsf.
7. P. Maniatis, M. Roussopoulos, E. Swierk, M. Lai, G. Appenzeller, X. Zhao, and M. Baker. The Mobile People Architecture. *ACM Mobile Computing and Communications Review (MC2R)*, July 1999.
8. H.J. Wang, B. Raman, C. Chuah, R. Biswas, R. Gummadi, B. Hohlt, X. Hong, E. Kiciman, Z. Mao, J.S. Shih, L. Subramanian, B.Y. Zhao, A.D. Joseph, and R.H. Katz. ICEBERG: An Internet-core network architecture for integrated communications. *IEEE Personal Communications, (Special Issue on IP-based Mobile Telecommunication Networks.)*, 2000.
9. M. Handley, H. Schulzrinne, E. Schooler, and J. Rosenberger. SIP: session initiation protocol, May 1999. IETF Request for Comments (Proposed Standard) 2543.
10. B. Brumitt, J. Krumm, B. Meyers, and S Shafer. Ubiquitous computing and the role of geometry. *IEEE Personal Communications*, August 2000.
11. B. Brumitt, B. Meyers, J. Krumm, A. Kern, and S Shafer. Easyliving: Technologies for intelligent environments.
12. H. Chu and S. Kurakake. ROAM(Resource-aware application migration) system. The 5th World Multi-Conference on Systemics, Cybernetics and Informatics (SCI 2001), July 2001.
13. H. Song, H. Chu, N. Islam, S. Kurakake, and M. Katagiri. BrowserState Repository Service. International Conference on Pervasive Computing (Pervasive 2002), pp.253-266, August 2002.

Design of Secure Mobile Application
on Cellular Phones

Masahiro Kuroda[1], Mariko Yoshida[1,2], Shoji Sakurai[2], and Tatsuji Munaka[2]

[1] Yokosuka Radio Communications Research Center,
Communications Research Laboratory,
3-4 Hikarino-oka, Yokosuka, Kanagawa, 239-0847 Japan
{marsh, ymariko}@crl.go.jp
[2] Information Technology R&D Center,
Mitsubishi Electric Corporation
5-1-1 Ofuna, Kamakura, Kanagawa, 247-8501 Japan
{saku, munaka}@isl.melco.co.jp

Abstract. Cellular data services have become popular in Japan. These services are based on the first generation security model for cellular phones. The model has server authentication, data encryption, application integrity check and user authentication. This paper discusses the security functions and evaluates the security features of an application on cellular phones. The evaluation shows that real usage is important to identify security related functions needed for wide range of users. We raise those issues in this paper. We also discuss the enhanced security model targeted for next generation cellular phones and describe topics for future research.

1 Introduction

The advance of the mobile computing infrastructure enables "anytime, anywhere" information services. In Japan, more than 33 million i-mode cellular phones are shipped and more than 50 thousand i-mode sites are available. Recently announced cellular phones can download applications, such as bank services and corporate services, from Internet sites and execute them on the phones. DoCoMo's high-end cellular phones have these capabilities and 14 million devices were shipped by the summer of the year 2002. KDDI's phones also have these functions and are getting popular in the market.

Cellular network is the main wireless network in the current market and other wireless communications will augment the network to satisfy various user requirements spanning in house, campus, metropolitan and regional cells. IEEE802.11(a)(b) [1,2] will be the first additional wireless communications and other emerging wireless communication systems, such as HAPS[3] and UWB[4], will come up in the future. The next generation wireless network will be an integration of these wireless communications to cellular networks and services will be provided by a combination of ser-

Y.-C. Chen, L.-W. Chang, and C.-T. Hsu (Eds.): PCM 2002, LNCS 2532, pp. 17-24, 2002.
© Springer-Verlag Berlin Heidelberg 2002

vice entities, such as wireless network operators, phone manufacturers and service providers.

A common security platform provides for end users' ease-of-use and satisfies the security/management policies of all the service entities. The platform also provides data confidentiality and integrity to users. Threats that exist in wired networks, such as network node attacks, network intrusions, malicious code downloading, information tampering, masquerading, denial-of-service attacks and password sniffing, are expected in wireless networks. The platform needs to equip security features against these threats.

This paper focuses on the security of cellular phones capable of downloading applications from Internet. The phones support SSL as a default and provide secure data transfer. Users can use a service with password protection. We discuss the first generation security model used for mobile devices, such as cellular phones and PDAs, and the enhanced model. We design an application using the current security model and raise issues for the design of the next generation cellular phones.

The rest of this paper is organized as follows. In Section 2, we discuss the current security model and also the enhanced security model targeted for the next generation cellular phones. In Section 3, we explain a design of a nomadic mail system for cellular phones and clarify real issues. In Section 4, we conclude with the summary and future perspective of the mobile security platform

2   Secure Mobile Platform Model

The popularity of application downloading for cellular phones raises the importance of the wireless security. In this section, we discuss about current and enhanced security models for Java enabled cellular phones.

2.1   MIDP1.0 Security Model

The MIDP1.0 (Mobile Information Device Profile 1.0) [5] was standardized to pursue interoperability between Java enabled cellular phones. The MIDP1.0 specification defines user interfaces, networking, persistent storage support and other miscellaneous functions such as timers and exceptions. The specification is defined based on the basic Java execution environment CLDC1.0 (Connected, Limited Device Configuration 1.0) [6] that defines an application execution environment to control access to APIs and functions, such as memory stick access and short-range communication. The DoCoMo's Java enabled phones, on the other hand, are not based on MIDP1.0 but have a similar application execution environment, since the phones were shipped before the MIDP1.0 specification was fixed. The DoCoMo's profile, called DoJa profile, also works on the CLDC1.0 and offers the same security model to MIDP1.0. The security model constrains each application to use only Java libraries defined by CLDC1.0 and MIDP1.0 / DoJa and to operate in a sandbox.

The security model addresses three levels of security. The primary level, known as virtual machine security, ensures that a maliciously-coded class file does not malfunction on devices. The second level is application level security, which means that an application in a phone can access only Java libraries, system resources and other components that the phone allows it to access. The last level is an end-to-end security that guarantees the secure data path from a cellular phone to an entity providing the service. Typical means is the SSL encryption and current phones have this function as a default.

This security model is based on application downloading. We explain the procedure to download and run an application and describe the security features for this model.

In this model, we make following assumptions. A user subscribes a service in advance. A phone has several root certificates and checks if a received certificate is genuine and is still valid when it receives a certificate from a service. The root certificates are used only for SSL authentication. We here define an application as a program running in a phone and providing a service to a user. The application runs in a sandbox of a MIDP 1.0 compliant phone, meaning that it can access only libraries that have been defined by the configuration CLDC1.0, profile MIDP1.0 / DoJa profile and manufacturer specific classes supported by the phone. In other words, a Java application cannot access any libraries or resources that are not part of predefined functions. The application can communicate only with the server that it is downloaded from. The application cannot have a digital signature since the feature is not provided in MIDP1.0.

We explain the procedure to execute an application focusing on security (Fig. 1). (1)A service provider develops an application and installs it into a server. (2)A user connects to the service to download the application. (3)The service may authenticate the user prior to downloading. (4)No verification is done for downloading by the network operator. (5)During downloading, the phone checks the integrity of the application and ensures that the application is not tampered with. It then installs the application locally. (6)The user starts the downloaded application. (7)If SSL is used, the server sends its certificate to the phone and the phone verifies the certificate during SSL handshake. (8)The application communicates with the service running on the server. Communications may be encrypted using SSL. (9)The application may prompt the user to log into the service on the server. If the user is authenticated, the phone executes the body of the application. (10)The application runs within a sandbox so that it can access only predefined resources. (11)The user exits the application, which causes the user to log out of the service and the application to disconnect from the service. Go back to (6) when the user wants to run the application again. (12)The user deletes the application from the phone. Go back to (2) when the user wants to run the application again.

In this model, security features are user authentication with user ID and password, verification that checks if the application is not tampered with, server authentication using a certificate and data encryption by SSL as shown in Fig. 1. These features satisfy the minimum security requirements. In some implementation, SSL is used as an enhanced user authentication in this model. There is no access control mechanism for an application so that the application is not allowed to access any restricted resources in the phone.

There are three entities, a phone manufacturer, a network operator and a service provider in this model. An application is controlled by two entities, a phone manufacturer and a service provider, in terms of security enforcement. It is the phone manufacturer's choice which root certificates are installed, but if the service provider requests the manufacturer to install the service provider's root certificate, the phone automatically authenticates the service provider with no intervention of the phone manufacturer. The security depends on the subject of the root certificates in the phone, as the certificates are pre-installed in this model.

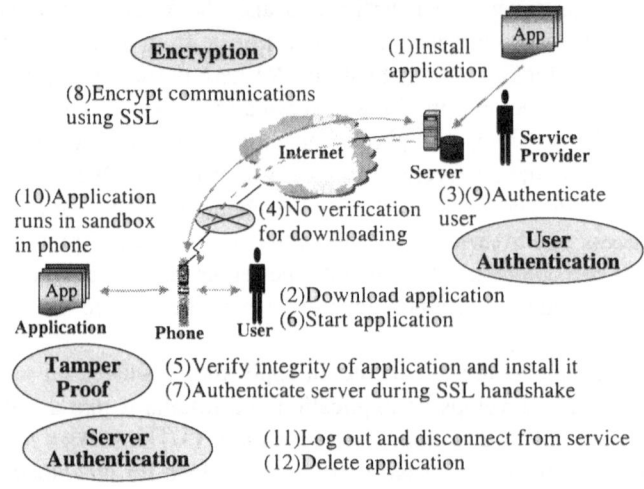

Fig. 1. Application download and security in MIDP1.0

2.2 MIDP2.0 Security Model

The MIDP2.0 [7] is the enhancement of the MIDP1.0 and follows the same application download mechanism. The model introduces the concept of trusted applications that are allowed to use restricted APIs. When a phone determines that an application is trusted, a protection domain is created and accesses to resources, such as Java libraries and local resources, are allowed in the protection domain indicated by the policy in the phone.

In this model, security features added to MIDP1.0 are user authentication with an external device, such as SIM / USIM and a biometrics module, server authentication with a digital signature and access control for an application to local resources in a phone. A phone can have a detachable device like SIM / USIM and store a root certificate in it as well as a user ID for a network operator. A phone can also have a protection domain for each application and enforce access controls to each domain. Combining the detachable device with the domain, the phone can change its access control policy when the network provider is changed. A phone manufacturer basically installs flexible security policy into a phone, which allows all accesses to the phone manufacturer domain, all accesses to network operators, and all accesses to service providers. Network operators, whereas, want to restrict access and protect their networks. To accommodate these different strategies, we need some offline or automatic negotiations as for the security policy. This is an important issue for services on the next generation cellular phones.

3   Security of Mobile Application "Nomad"

Nomad is a nomadic email system based on IMAP4 protocol [8]. It allows a phone user to access a mail server managed by a service provider at anytime from anywhere. A user can send or receive emails using an email account assigned by the service provider that the user subscribes to, not an email account of a wireless network operator (Fig. 2). Nomad is a three-tired application, and consists of a Nomad client executed in a cellular phone and a Nomad proxy running in an application server maintained by the service provider. The Nomad client communicates with the proxy using an email protocol called "IMAP4Light", which we proposed as a light weight IMAP4 based protocol for cellular phones. The proxy converts the IMAP4Light protocol to the IMAP4 protocol and accesses the IMAP4 mail server. The current version of the Nomad is implemented on the DoJa profile, DoJa2.0.

Features of IMAP4Light Protocol. The design principle of the IMAP4Light protocol is to reduce the commands executed on a phone and to eliminate unnecessary data transfer between a Nomad client and a Nomad proxy because of limited resources in a cellular phone.

We describe briefly the protocol to show that an application for a phone needs to keep small and cares security. IMAP4 supports many primitive commands. We select essential commands for IMAP4Light as basic commands, which are LOGIN, LIST, FETCH, DELETE, SELECT and LOGOUT. In wireless network, header overhead cannot be ignored and turn around time is much longer than in wired networks. It is expensive to send many commands over a wireless network. We thus define action oriented commands, LOGINLIST, LISTALL and FETCHALL, to execute multiple IMAP4 commands as one IMAP4Light command. For example, LOGINLIST command replaces LOGIN, LIST folder, FETCH header, FETCH body and STORE flags commands.

We also add REPLY and FORWARD commands in order to eliminate unnecessary data transfer. A unique ID for a replied or forwarded message is specified and the message itself is not included in these commands. The message is not downloaded from the proxy to the client and is appended in the proxy to send the mail server on behalf of the client.

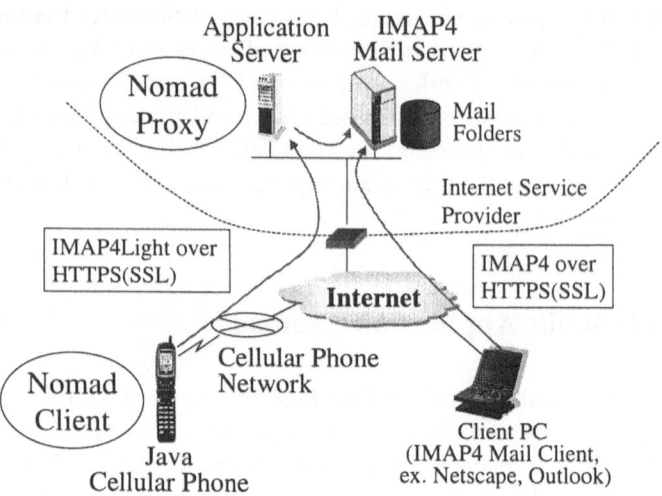

Fig. 2. Nomad architecture

How a Nomad Client Works. We will describe the procedure how a user accesses his/her mail folders in a mail server from a phone.

(1)A Nomad client is installed into an application server maintained by a service provider. The client does not have a digital signature. (2)A user tries to download the client. In DoJa2.0, URL to download the application and URL to which the application connects are the same, including the port number. The Nomad communications are encrypted when downloaded by SSL. When the phone tries to establish a SSL session, a warning message is displayed in the phone screen to confirm that he user agrees to connect an unauthenticated server (Fig. 3) during SSL handshake. This is because a root certificate corresponding to the Nomad service provider is not included in the pre-installed root certificates. The certificate of the application server is not authenticated. If the user selects "YES", the phone proceeds to establish an SSL encrypted session with the application server. After a session is established, the Nomad proxy authenticates the user by a basic authentication with user ID and password. Only when the user inputs his/her correct user ID and password, the downloading is started. No verification is done for downloading by a network operator. The phone verifies the integrity of the downloaded client. (3)When the phone finishes downloading, it installs the Nomad client. In DoJa2.0, the phone also keeps the application server's certificate received during SSL handshake for the information. The phone does not check the integrity of the client since the integrity is verified when it is downloaded from the application server. Then, the phone prompts the user to set permissions for accessing resources requested by the client. The DoJa2.0 only allows the application to connect the downloaded server. (4)When the user starts the client for the first time, the client prompts the user to set a 4 digit PIN code, user ID and password. The PIN code is used to activate the client in the phone, and user ID and password is used to log into the mail server. Once the user sets the PIN code, the user inputs the PIN code only. If the PIN code is wrong, a failure counter in the client is incremented, and when the counter exceeds a specified limit, the client is invalidated and cannot be executed again. In addition, the client deletes the recorded user ID and password in the phone. (5)The client runs within a sandbox in the phone as a service provider's application. The client can access its program area in a flash memory and use the area for caching mails for off line operations. Cached mails contain only plain texts because of the limitation of the memory allocated for the application.

Fig. 3. Warning message for an unauthenticated server

(6)When the client connects to the proxy, the warning message, the same as the one displayed during downloading, is displayed for the same reason. If the user selects "YES", the phone establishes a SSL session with the application server. After the establishment, the Nomad client sends a login request including user ID and password. This request is passed to the mail server through the proxy, and then a response is sent back to the client from the mail server via the proxy. In this case, all the exchanged data for the mail access are encrypted by SSL between the client and the proxy. (7)When the user exits the client, the client sends a logout request to the proxy, which is passed to the mail sever. Go back to (5) when the user wants to run the client again. (8)When the user deletes the client, all the cached data on the memory are also deleted.

Security Related Issues for Nomad. There are three security issues for Nomad. Firstly, a user is informed by a warning message as shown in Fig. 3, though SSL is used for data encryption. This confuses the user if the received certificate is forged or if the communication cannot be encrypted. This problem is solved if a root certificate is allowed to update after manufactured time. Secondary, the user inputs a simple 4 digit PIN code for ease-of-input instead of a recommended type password. The reason is that the input mode needs to be changed every time the next character is not in the same input mode. Lastly, the Nomad client needs to manage cached mail kept in the program area of a phone. An application is responsible to manage memory and program area assigned for its use in MIDP1.0. The phone needs to manage these transactions according to the security domain and delete cached data automatically when the application is exited.

4 Conclusion and Future Directions

Cellular data services have become popular in Japan. In this paper, we discussed the first generation security model MIDP1.0 available in the market and the design of a typical secure application in this model. The reason we discussed the security implementation on current phones is to clarify that security related issues are not security functions themselves but how security functions are provided to a wide range of users. Security features should be easy to use, otherwise, the user misuses them. In this sense, we raised the user notification during SSL session setup and the input of the user ID and password for limited configuration devices, though they are not issues for desktop PC users. We can solve the SSL problem in the MIDP2.0 model since a root certificate can be installed after manufactured time by the provisioning functionality. As for the login issue, we can improve it by controlling the character input mode in the application but it is still cumbersome for a user to input a password. We should have a user authentication that will not force extra operations for mobile users, such as voice biometrics.

We will design and evaluate a secure platform to accommodate plug-in modules, such as a voice biometrics module and personal authentication module based on the MIDP2.0 model. Some cellular phones already have hardware interfaces to plug-in a memory stick to play MP3 music and to store still images, but these interfaces are not standardized for secure access. By adding a secure plug-in interface to the next model, we can enhance the usage of cellular phones.

References

1. IEEE 802.11 (a), ISO/IEC 8802-11:1999/Amd 1:2000(E),
2. IEEE 802.11 (b), Supplement to 802.11-1999
3. Wu, G., Miura, R., Hase, Y.: A Broadband Wireless Access System Using Stratospheric Platforms, IEEE Globecom 2000, November 2000
4. Scholtz, R. A., Win, M. Z.: Impulse Radio, Invited Paper, IEEE PIMRC 1997, Helsinki
5. Connected Limited Device Configuration (CLDC), http://java.sun.com/aboutJava/communityprocess/final/jsr030/index.html
6. Mobile Information Device Profile (MIDP), http://java.sun.com/aboutJava/communityprocess/final/jsr037/index.html
7. Mobile Information Device Profile (MIDP) 2.0, http://jcp.org/jsr/detail/118.jsp
8. Crispin, M. R., "INTERNET MESSAGE ACCESS PROTOCOL - VERSION 4 rev1", RFC 2060, December 1996.

Ubiquitous Displays for Cellular Phone Based Personal Information Environments

Kiyoharu Aizawa, Kentaro Kakami, and Koji Nakahira

University of Tokyo, Dept. of Elec. Eng. & Frontier Informatics
7-3-1 Hongo, Bunkyo, Tokyo, 113-8656, Japan
{aizawa, k-kakami, nakahira}@hal.t.u-tokyo.ac.jp
http://www.hal.t.u-tokyo.ac.jp

Abstract. Cellular phone is one of the most popular personal information device. Cellular phones with Internet services such as i-mode are in wide use in Japan. The communication bandwidths are growing even further under 3G technology. However, the interfaces are still poor; displays of cellular phones will remain small in view of their portable size and power consumption. In this paper, we propose a "ubiquitous display" that can be used in combination with cellular phones. The user operates the cellular phone and the ubiquitous display shows any content that requires a large screen space.

1 Introduction

Mobile communication is growing very quickly. Two decades ago, the cellular phone was about 1000g in the weight and 1000 cc in the volume, and it was only used in a car. Now its weight and volume are much less than 100g and 100cc, respectively, and people carry cellular phones in their pockets. In addition to the traditional speech communication, Internet accessible cellular phones such as i-mode are in wide use in Japan. More than 50 million Internet accessible cellular phones are currently being used [1]. A small terminal worn by a person provides a personal mobile information environment that has "anytime anywhere" connectivity to the Internet. The cellular phone further evolves; a digital camera and GPS are started being installed together, while the size is kept unchanged (See Fig.1). Camera-installed cellular phone is booming and nearly 10 millions are already being used. Considering this quick growth of the technology used for mobile communications, highly functional celluar phones must be one of the most important interfaces for personal information environments.

However, there is a weakness. Because the cellular phone must have low power consumption and be physically small, the display is very limited in size. With the larger bandwidth available in third generation (3G) mobile communication, the small display is a critical problem for effective interfacing. Contents that require larger screen space, such as a large data list, images or video, are not well suited to the small screen sizes of the cellular phone In addition, such larger data flows are costly under the current packet- based charging system.

Y.-C. Chen, L.-W. Chang, and C.-T. Hsu (Eds.): PCM 2002, LNCS 2532, pp. 25–32, 2002.

Fig. 1. A Internet accessible cellular phone with a camera and GPS (CASIO [2])

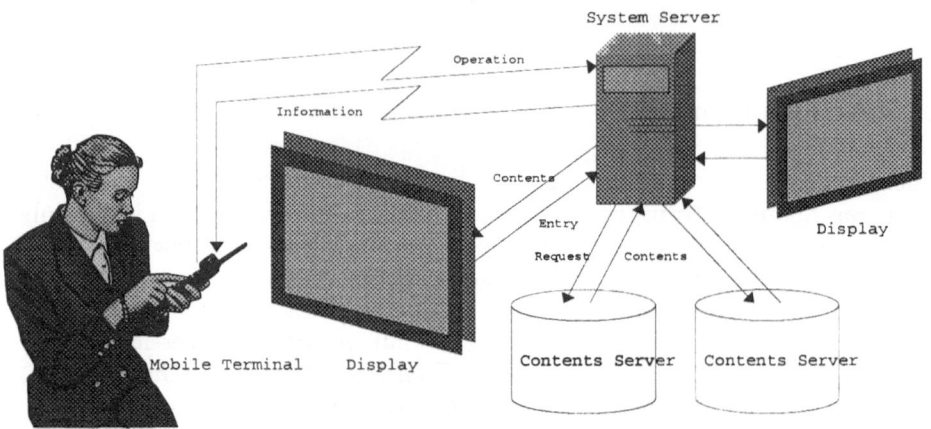

Fig. 2. Ubiquitous Display System

A separate display such as HMD could be worn as the conventional wearable computers [3]. However, such a separate display sacrifices compactness of the cellular phone. In this paper, we propose a "ubiquitous display system", to be used in combination with cellular phones[4]. The displays are intended to be placed in many locations, for example office, streets or shopping malls. They are controlled by the operation of the user's cellular phone. The user can access the system and show the contents on the large display instead of on the cellular phone. The ubiquitous display will function as an effective interface for larger data flows. In the following sections, an outline of the proposed system is given and a prototype of the system is described.

Active poster is a similar proposal[5]. Bluetooth or IrDA are proposed to allow the system to identify the user, and the system actively displays information personalized for the user. Our proposal differs in that we use generic cellular phones and the fundamental function of the display is to passively receive requests from the user. The display also has some advanced functions: for example, it can push messages to the cellular phone that makes request to the display.

2   Ubiquitous Display

The ubiquitous display shows the required information when it receives commands from the cellular phone. The system configuration is shown in Fig.2. The functions are described below.

We propose that ubiquitous displays should be located at such places as streets,malls and shopping areas where people have good access to the mobile network. The displays are connected to their PCs (local servers) and then to the system server via the wired network. The display could be set up so that it usually shows advertisements, and shows what the user wants to see only when the user makes a request in front of the display. The cellular phone functions as a remote controller for the display. Requests are made via the mobile network to the system server, and the requested content is delivered to the system server and then to the display PC via the wired network, and shown on the display. (Hereafter, the ubiquitous display including its PC (local server) is referred to as the display or display PC.)

The system server plays the role of gateway between ubiquitous displays and cellular phones. It receives a request from the cellular phone and sends a request to the display. After the system server receives a response from the display, it sends the data to the display. It also sends control information to the cellular phone.

The cellular phone sends a request to the system server with the ID number of the display to be used. An HTML browser is used for this operation. Thus, an operation on the cellular phone allows the user to view any Internet content on the display. The cellular phone shows control information to guide the operation.

The advantages of the system are summarized below.

- Large screen display
  By removing the limitation of the small two-inch display of the cellular phone, complex contents including long lists or images can be displayed on the large screen.
- Virtual bandwidth expansion
  As the display system downloads any large volumes of data via the wired network, users will not be concerned about the lower bandwidth and the charges for mobile communication. Hence, they will feel more comfortable downloading and showing video and images on the display.

- Cellular phone as a controller
  No special devices are necessary as the system uses only existing technologies.
  The displays and the cellular phones are in wide common use.
- Security and adaptation
  The user can be identified by the cellular phone. Security is assured by the
  use of the cellular phone. Adaptation of the contents to the individual user
  will be possible based on user identification.

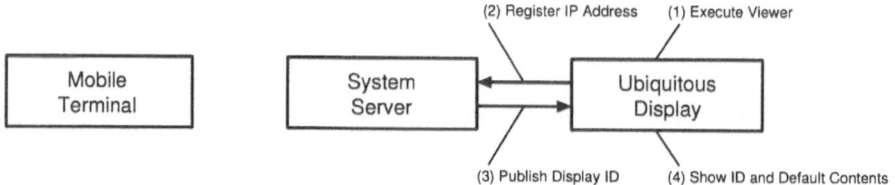

Fig. 3. Registration of Display

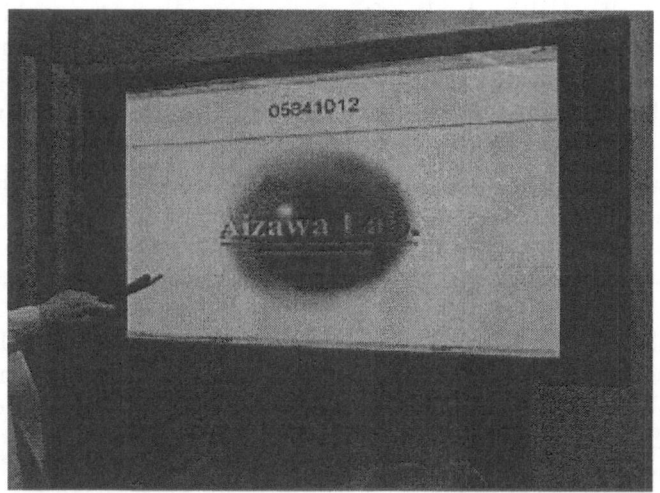

Fig. 4. Initial screen of the ubiquitous display with the ID number

3   Display of HTTP Contents

A prototype system of the ubiquitous display was developed that shows arbitrary
HTTP contents under the control of the cellular phone. Its procedure is described
in detail.

3.1   Registration of a Display

The procedure for controlling the display of the HTTP contents is shown in Fig. 3. At the beginning, the display registers with the system server. The system server registers the IP address of the display and assigns an ID number to the display. The ID number is randomly generated by the system server. The ID is shown on the screen of the display. The initial ID screen of the prototype is shown in Fig. 4.

As a security measure, the ID number is reset and a new ID number is assigned after a certain period of time, so that the display cannot be used easily by a user who is not present in front of the display.

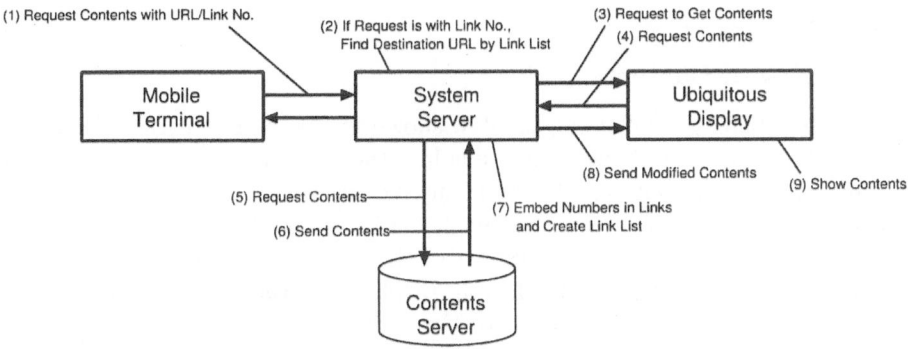

Fig. 5. Procedure to show contents

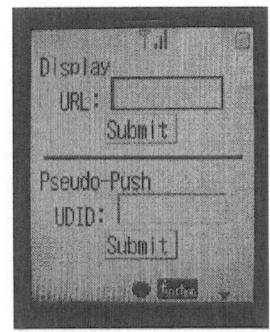

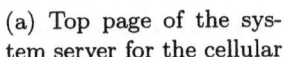

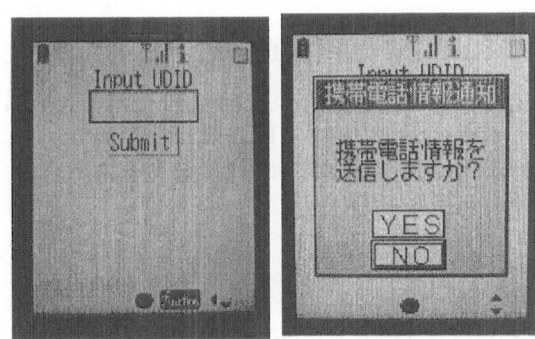

(a) Top page of the system server for the cellular

(b)ID number submission (left) and confirmation (right)

Fig. 6. Cellular phone screen

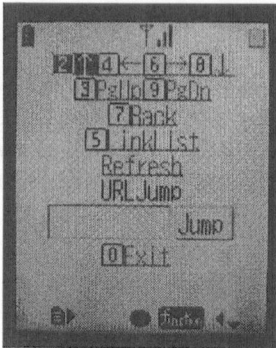

Fig. 7. Control screen of the cellular phone

3.2 Display of Contents

Contents are displayed following the flow shown in Fig. 5. The user makes a call on the cellular phone and the system displays the introductory Web page of the system server on the cellular phone. Then, the system server requests the user to send the URL to be shown on the display (Fig. 6(a)). Next, the system server requests the user to send the ID number of the display (UDID) (Fig. 6(b)).

After the system server checks that the display with the requested ID is ready, the system server sends the request to the display. Based on the request from the system server, the display acquires the contents via the system server. The display requests the system server to download the contents from any server on the Internet. Then, the system server modifies the contents in such a way that the URL of the description $< A \; href="URL"/A >$ is numbered for control by the cellular phone, and sends the modified contents to the display. A list of correspondences between the numbers and the URLs is temporarily kept in the system server.

3.3 Control by the Cellular Phone

Instructions for controlling the display, formatted in HTML, are shown on the cellular phone. The control HTML is shown in Fig. 7. The major control functions of the cellular phone are listed below.

- Scroll
- Show link list
- Choose a link
- Refresh
- Direct URL jump
- Terminate

As an example of function operation, on pushing the scroll function button on the cellular phone, the scroll command is sent to the server and finally transmitted to the display, and the window of the display is scrolled.

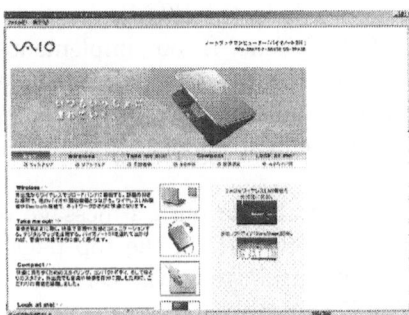
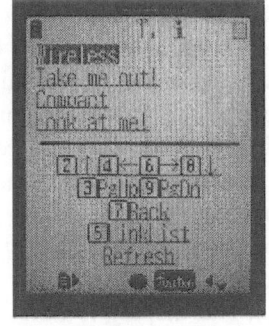

(a) HTML file with an embedded menu

(b) The menu that appears on the cellular phone

Fig. 8. Menu embedded in HTML, and the menu that appears on the cellular phone

Fig. 9. Pseudo push: the message sent by the display

To jump to a link in the HTML content, the links in the page can be extracted and shown on the cellular phone. They are numbered by the server and the number list is kept in the server. By choosing one of them, a new page can be shown on the display. A URL can also be entered directly from the cellular phone through the control HTML.

On pressing the termination button, the system server dissolves the correspondence between the cellular phone's display and its buttons, and shows the end message on the display. If the user does not terminate, the server terminates if, for instance, it does not receive a message from the cellular phone for some period of time.

3.4   Advanced Functions of the System

In addition to the control described above, the system has additional control functions, summarized below.

- Embedded menu

  The system allows use of embedded keywords in the HTML contents that show a compact menu only on the cellular phone. In our implementation, a special tag "mobilemenu" is provided for this purpose. For example, the HTML page in Fig. 8(a) contains an embedded menu for the cellular phone and the menu in Fig. 8(b) is shown on the cellular phone.

- Pseudo push

  In our system, the display is designed to be able to push a message to the cellular phone. When the user enters the display ID in the top page (Fig. 6(a)), the display is able to send a specific message to the cellular phone. For example, when we send the display ID for the initial screen of Fig. 4, a control screen such as Fig. 9 is shown on the cellular phone. This function can send a special message to the users who come to use the display.

- Access control

  In our first prototype, only one user is allowed to use the display at a time. The display is available for others after the current user finishes. To prevent improper use from a remote place, the ID number of the display is regularly changed in a random way. Timeout control is also adopted to limit overlong use.

  Simultaneous access by multiple users will be potentially achievable by showing multiple windows on the display. Control of such multiple access is a problem for the next implementation.

4   Conclusion

In this paper, a ubiquitous display system is proposed for a cellular phone to improve its human interface. The display can be placed anywhere and the screen of the display is controlled by cellular phones, which are widely used. The prototype system that we developed is described. In that system, HTML contents can be navigated by using the buttons of the cellular phone. Such displays are considered to have wide application when the displays are set in streets, malls, and other places where many people use cellular phones. Further investigation is required to improve the control by the cellular phone.

References

1. http://www.johotsusintokei.soumu.go.jp/newdata/ics_data.xls
2. http://www.casio.co.jp/k-tai/a3012ca
3. The PC goes ready-to-wear, IEEE Spectrum, pp.34-39, Oct. 2000
4. K. Kakami and K. Aizawa, Ubiquitous display system linking with mobile terminals,IEICE Technical Report MVE 2001-146 Mar. 2002 (in Japanese).
5. K. Suzuki and R. Honda, An effective advertisement using Active Posters, IPSJ Technical Report, Human Interface, 92-11, Jan. 2001 (in Japanese).

Context-Aware Service Delivery to Mobile Users

Hiroaki Nakamura and Madoka Yuriyama

Tokyo Research Laboratory, IBM Japan, Ltd.
1623-14 Shimotsuruma, Yamato-shi, Kanagawa-ken 242-8502 Japan
{hnakamur,yuriyama}@jp.ibm.com

Abstract. We can deliver context-aware services to mobile users by dynamically computing the groups each user belongs to and providing the user with the
services associated with the selected groups. Recent progress in XML technology has enabled us to describe the information needed for such processing precisely and flexibly. We analyzed the problems in applying XML technology to
context-aware service delivery and studied solutions. In particular we have developed (1) an algorithm for optimizing the performance of our XML-based
matching engine, and (2) tools for editing user profiles and service descriptions
flexibly.

1 Introduction

Advances in new information devices, such as cellular phones, intelligent appliances,
and electronic billboards in public areas, are changing the way users interact with
computers. Mobile users are expecting to access information services everywhere at
any time. Services to be provided to such mobile users must be automatically personalized to users' needs because (1) users frequently change their situations, and (2) the
capability of the new devices are limited compared with traditional PCs. Therefore an
infrastructure to support such services has to be able to predict users' needs using their
contextual information, such as current locations, activity histories, devices, preferences, and ages, and select services that are most suitable to the target users.

Context-aware service delivery can be achieved using a system equipped with the
following functions:

1. Accept a service description that specifies the group of potential target users,
2. Compute the groups a user belongs to using his or her contextual information, and
3. Deliver to the user the services associated with the selected groups.

A group specification for a service is a condition of user contexts. For example, given
a group condition "age > 20", then a person who is 25 years old will be included in this
group, but a person who is 17 will not. A group condition can be a complex one like
"(age > 20) and (location = 'Tokyo')". Multiple group conditions can have overlap like
A:"age > 20" and B:"age > 30", where a person whose age is 35 will be included in

Y.-C. Chen, L.-W. Chang, and C.-T. Hsu (Eds.): PCM 2002, LNCS 2532, pp. 33–40, 2002.

both A and B. Since a user's context is subject to change, the groups of the user have to be computed dynamically exactly when they are required.

The benefits of this approach are:

- Service providers can deliver services only to their intended users without identifying individual users, and
- Users can access the services that best match their situations without knowing anything about the services.

We first present the overall architecture of the system we are developing for providing context-aware services to mobile users. We then explain the mechanism of the core of the system and discuss the technical issues we face in making the system practical for real applications. We also describe our solutions to the problems.

2 System Overview

Figure 1 shows the overall architecture of the system for providing context-aware services to mobile users [1]. The system consists of one Mobile Resource Management (MRM) server and multiple local stations.

MRM Server: This server manages user profiles and service delivery conditions. A user profile contains two types of context: one is static context, such as a list of user preferences provided by each user in advance, and the other is dynamic context, such as a current location captured by the system when needed. Service delivery conditions come from the service providers, and they are used to specify the groups of target users. We use a framework for multi-agent systems [2] so that we can manage user profiles and service delivery conditions flexibly and efficiently.

Local Stations: A mobile user receives services using a local station as an interface to the system. A local station first identifies a user by an ID device the user is carrying, such as a ticket with an RF-ID or bar code, an IC card, or a PDA with a Bluetooth connection. After a user is identified, the local station sends to the server the ID of the user as well as other dynamic contexts including a current time, current location, ID device type, and local station type (which suggests the activity of the user). Then the local station accepts from the server the services that best match the user contexts, and provides the user with those services though a variety of output methods such as public displays, printers, kiosk terminals, and user PDAs. When a user accesses the system directly through the Internet, the functions of the local stations are handled by the MRM server.

Matching Engine: The core component of the MRM server is the matching engine that dynamically computes the connections between users and services. It takes a user profile and the entire set of service delivery conditions, filters the services against the user's personal information, and outputs a list of the service most appropriate to the specific user. We will discuss the mechanism of this component in more detail in the next section.

Applications: The system we are building is a middleware system in that individual applications are developed on top of the common components. To study the feasibility of the architecture of our system as middleware, we have developed some applications. One application is an airport information system that allows travelers carrying tickets with RF-IDs to receive flight schedules and airport guides through public displays without any action to control the system. Another application is a CD advertisement system that pushes promotion pictures as well as sample tunes to users' PDAs. The information delivered to users is selected according to the registered preferences and purchase histories of the users.

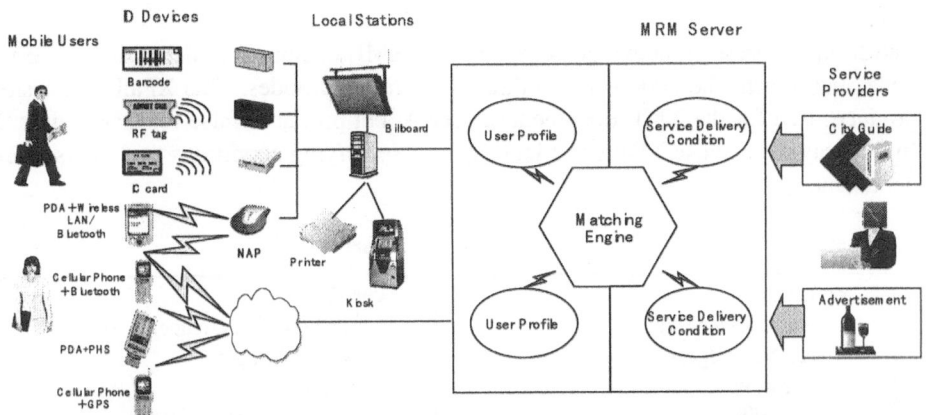

Fig. 1. Overview of the Mobile Resource Management (MRM) System

3 XML-Based Matching Engine

One significant issue in developing a matching engine is the choice of the language for describing user profiles and service delivery conditions. We want to be able to describe various aspects of user profiles in a simple language so that we can handle many types of application in a uniform way. On the other hand, we cannot precisely define the language constructs in advance because different applications require different notations for expressing the same information (for example, location data can have many forms). Thus the language for our purpose must be simple yet extensible.

We use XML (Extensible Markup Language) to represent user profiles. XML is a concise language, but it allows us to freely enhance its expressive power. We can add any new tags for any required purposes. Other advantages of XML are that it is already a popular language in the software industry, and that many XML tools are already available. Figure 2 shows examples of user profiles in XML. Note that the document tags or structures are not fixed. We can modify and extend them freely.

To describe the service delivery conditions that specify target users, we use XPath (XML Path Language) [3]. Although XPath was originally just a language for addressing parts of an XML document, we can use it as a language for specifying conditions that check whether specific parts are included in a XML document. Suppose we have the following XPath expression and apply it to the XML documents in Figure 2:

/profile/interests[sport='Swimming']

The XML document for user A evaluates false because no part of the document matches the XPath expression, while the one for user B evaluates true because it includes a part that matches the XPath expression.

/profile/interests[count(*) >= 3]

The XPath expression above goes inside of an XML document, reaches an "interests" node, and returns the node if it has three or more child nodes. This XPath expression produces true for the XML document of user A, but produces false for that of user B. In this way we can use XPath as a language for specifying conditions that filters XML documents.

User A

```
<profile>
    <name>Alan</name>
    <age>35</age>
    <location>
        <x>58</x>
        <y>38</y>
    </location>
    <interests>
        <sport>Soccer</sport>
        <music>Classical</music>
        <book>History</book>
    </interests>
</profile>
```

User B

```
<profile>
    <name>Betty</name>
    <age>19</age>
    <location>
        <city>Kyoto</city>
        <x>58</x>
        <y>34</y>
    </location>
    <interests>
        <sport>Swimming</sport>
        <music>Pop</music>
    </interests>
</profile>
```

Fig. 2. User Profiles in XML

4 Technical Issues

In building the middleware system equipped with the matching engine, and sample applications on top of the system, we found that we had to address the following problems in order to make the system applicable to real world requirements:
- The matching engine must work efficiently even if we have a very large number of services (which are specified in XPath). A naive implementation would require response time proportional to the number of possible services, which is prohibitive for our purpose because we want to maintain as many services as possible for better personalization.

- We need to be able to modify and extend user profiles and service delivery conditions easily. In addition, since the structures and individual item types of user profiles vary with applications, the tools for editing user profiles and service delivery conditions must be adaptive to the changes in the types of applications.

We will address these issues in Sections 5 and 6.

5   Optimization of the Matching Engine

The key function of the matching engine is to evaluate a large set of XPath expressions against a single XML document so that it can find the subset of XPath expressions that match the document. However if we evaluate each XPath expression separately, the amount of time required to obtain the result would increase in proportion to the number of XPath expressions, which would prevent us from applying our system to large-scale service delivery.

To solve this problem, we have developed an algorithm for evaluating multiple XPath expressions efficiently [4]. The basic idea of the algorithm is to create an appropriate data structure from a given set of XPath expressions, and eliminate duplicated processes among the expressions using the data structure. Given the following XPath expressions:

P1: /profile/demographics/age[text()<20]
P2: /profile/interests/sport[text()='Soccer']
P3: /profile/demographics/age[text()>=40 and text()<50]

We first break them into steps as follows:

P1': profile + demographics + age + [text() < 20]
P2': profile + interests + sport + [text() = 'Soccer']
P3': profile + demographics + age + [text()>=40 and text()<50]

All expressions share the step "profile", and P1' and P3' also share the next step "demographics". We then construct a data structure as shown in Figure 3.

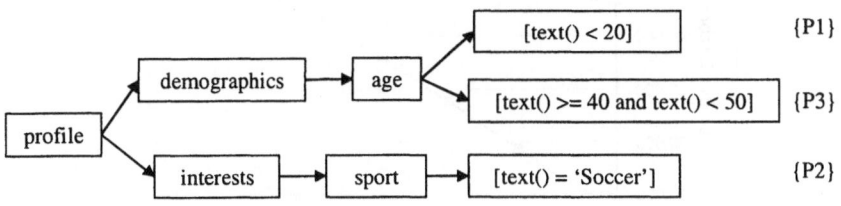

Fig. 3. Data Structure Expressing XPath Expressions

After the complete data structure is obtained, we evaluate the XPath expressions as follows:

1. Apply the top level step to an XML document and get the resulting node set.
2. Apply one of the next steps to each node in the previous step's result.
3. Concatenate the results and get a new resulting node set.
4. Repeat 2 and 3 while any steps remain.

The point of the algorithm is that it computes the result of a common subexpression at most once and thus it reduces the amount of time to evaluate the entire set of XPath expressions.

In addition to the method above, we use other techniques to optimize XPath evaluations including:
• Compute predicates using hash tables and binary search trees.
• Eliminate duplications of operator arguments.

See [4] for more details of our algorithm.

We implemented our algorithm in Java 1.4 and measured its performance. We used CPExchange [5] as the DTD to define user profiles, and generated XML documents using IBM's XML Generator [6]. The size of each of the created XML documents was 10 KB. We also implemented an XPath generator that takes a DTD as input and produces XPath expressions as output. We fixed the depth of the generated XPath expressions at 6, and generated random data. We measured the time for evaluations as the number of XPath expressions increased. We evaluated each set of XPath expressions by (1) a straightforward method without our algorithm, (2) the method using only the step optimization, and (3) the method that uses all of our optimization techniques. The experiment was conducted on an IBM ThinkPad T21 (Mobile Pentium 800 MHz) running Windows 2000 professional.

The results of the experiment are shown in Figure 4. As we expected, Method (1) had the worst performance. Method (2) provided some improvements, but it took time proportional to the number of XPath expressions. Method (3) provided the best performance. In particular, the time for evaluation did not increase linearly.

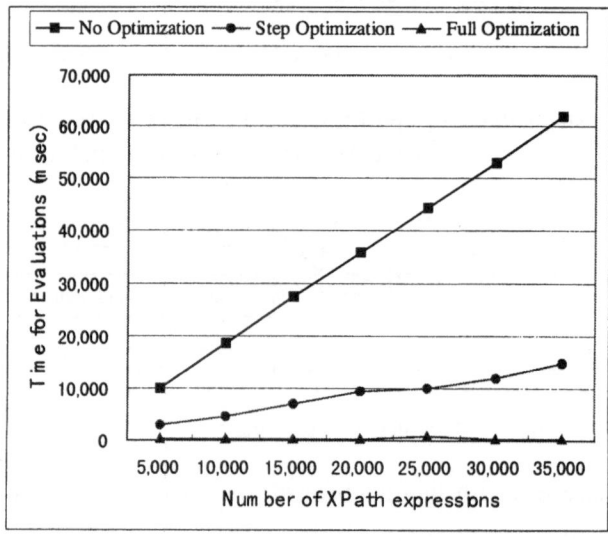

Fig. 4. Performance Evaluation

6 Flexible Profile Editors

Since user profiles and service delivery conditions are provided by non-specialist users, it is not practical to force users to write raw data in XML or XPath. Instead profiles and conditions should be edited with generally used software tools such as Web browsers. However, we selected XML and XPath to hold the data because they can capture a wide variety of data types and structures in unified frameworks. Therefore the tools for editing profiles and conditions must be highly customizable so that we can take advantage of the underlying data representations.

To fulfill these requirements, we built a user profile editor as shown in Figure 5. The design goal of the system is that the functions of the profile editor can be managed by using an auxiliary definition file. By changing this file, we can adapt the editor to any kind of user profiles. The system works as follows:

(1) Generate from the definition file a stylesheet for extracting parts of the profile data.

(2) Extract data from an existing user profile and produce an intermediate file in XML.

(3) Generate an input form in HTML using the current profile data as default values.

(4) Convert the user input into an intermediate XML document.

(5) Generate a stylesheet for updating the user profile.

(6) Update the user profile.

Using similar techniques, we also built a tool for editing service delivery conditions.

An additional benefit of this architecture is that we can provide a user with the profile editor most suitable to the user's context by selecting a definition file using our matching engine. For example, we can customize the screen size of an editor according to the information about the device a user is using.

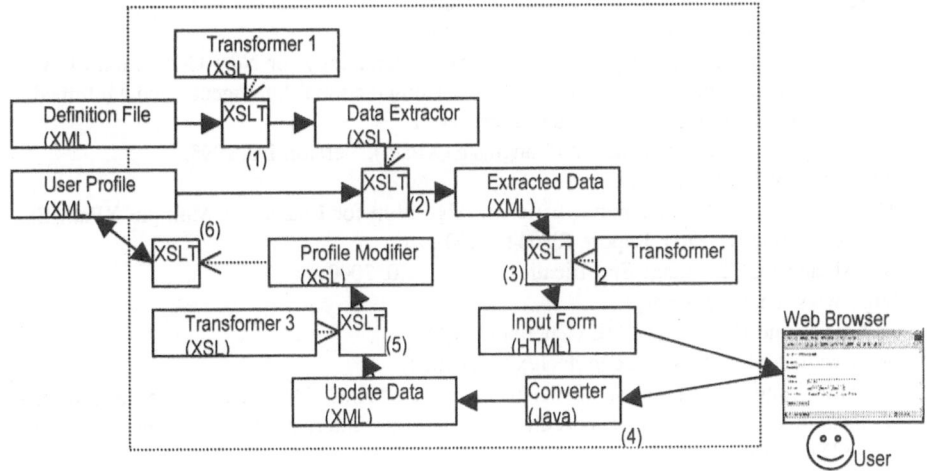

Fig. 5. Structure of the User Profile Editor

7   Concluding Remarks

We have addressed some issues in providing context-aware services using XML technology. Recently, systems for selecting XML documents using XPath-based filters are attracting attention [7][8]. Those systems assume that users will specify the contents of published XML documents, while ours assume that service provides will specify the users and the users need no knowledge about the services. However, we can use the techniques developed in those systems (such as Prefiltering in [7]) to improve our algorithm further.

To make our system more practical, we also have to address some other issues we did not cover in this paper. For example, we have to develop a method to report the behavior of the matching engine. From outside of the system, we can see which services are delivered to a specific user, but we cannot see why those services are selected. We can improve the quality of service selection if we can monitor the dynamic aspects of the matching engine.

Acknowledgements. We would like to thank Masayuki Numao, Norishige Morimoto, Tatsuo Miyazawa, Ryoji Honda, Kazuhiro Suzuki, Lai Jin, and Taiga Nakamura for their helpful comments and advice. Shohji Mishina contributed to the implementation of the profile editors.

References

1.   IBM Japan: Mobile Resource Management, 2002.
     http://www.trl.ibm.com/projects/mrm/index_e.htm
2.   Gaku Yamamoto and Hideki Tai: Agent Server Technology for Next Generation of Web Applications, 4th International Conference on Computational Intelligence and Multimedia Applications, IEEE Computer Society Press, 2001.
3.   J. Clark and S. DeRose: XML Path Language (XPath): Version 1.0, 1999.
     http://www.w3.org/TR/xpath.html
4.   M. Yuriyama and H. Nakamura: Efficient Algorithm for Evaluating Multiple XPath Expressions, IBM Research Report, RT0445, 2002.
5.   IDEAlliance: CPExchange Specification Version 1.0, 2000.
     http://www.cpexchange.org/
6.   A. L. Diaz and D. Lovell: XML Generator, 1999.
     http://www.alphaworks.ibm.com/tech/xmlgenerator
7.   M. Altinel and M. J. Franklin: Efficient Filtering of XML Documents for Selective Dissemination of Information, Proceedings of the 26th International Conference on Very Large Databases, 2000.
8.   C. Chan, P. Felber, M. Garofalakis, and R. Rastogi: Efficient Filtering of XML Documents with XPath Expressions, Proceedings of the 18th International Conference on Data Engineering, 2002.

The Design and Implementation of Network Service Platform for Pervasive Computing

Hiroyuki Morikawa

Department of Frontier Informatics, The University of Tokyo
7-3-1 Hongo Bunkyo-ku Tokyo 113-0033 Japan
mori@mlab.t.u-tokyo.ac.jp
http://www.mlab.t.u-tokyo.ac.jp

Abstract. Two major properties will characterize networks in the future: '3C everywhere' and 'physical interaction'. These two properties promises a computing infrastructure that seamlessly and ubiquitously aids users in accomplishing their tasks and that renders the actual computing devices and technology largely invisible. This paper begins by sketching pervasive computing scenarios. Next, we delve deeper into some key technical challenges. The following section presents our technological developments: STONE, SLSOCKET, and Personal Mesh. Our design goal is distributed transparency, service consistency, and context-awareness.

1 Introduction

The proliferation of terms such as ubiquitous computing, pervasive computing, sentient computing, proactive computing, autonomic computing, and context-aware computing, shows the importance of creation of environments saturated with computing and communication capability, yet gracefully integrated with human users. The importance is rapidly increasing with the current trend toward universal presence of mobile computing, computer networks, and wireless communications in everyday life. The target of these kinds of new computing is to enable networked devices to be aware of their surroundings and peers, and to be capable to provide services to and use services from peers effectively.

Two major properties will characterize networks in the future: '3C everywhere' and 'physical interaction' [1].

3C Everywhere

Computing everywhere: Embedded processors are embedded into every object such as PDAs, cellular phones, monitors, sensors, robots, vehicles, and wearable computers. Even today, 98% of processors are said to be embedded into information appliances, vehicles, and robots as invisible computers. Embedded processors will go anywhere in the future networks.

Content everywhere: Files, data, and application software will be ubiquitous in the networks. Today, we have a distributed database in the form of web. As the cost and the capacity of hard disks become cheaper and larger, the amount of contents

Y.-C. Chen, L.-W. Chang, and C.-T. Hsu (Eds.): PCM 2002, LNCS 2532, pp. 41-49, 2002.

will significantly increase. If 10^9 users have a 1 terabyte hard disk, we can provide 10 zettabyte (10^{21})-order distributed database on the network.

Connectivity everywhere: Everything is connected to a network of some form and work in coordination with other devices, services, and network-enabled entities. Every device will be networked together to satisfy a certain needs of a user.

Physical Interaction:

In the future, computation will be human-centered. It will enter the human world, handling our goals and needs and helping us to do more while doing less. Here, the use of context will yield incredible power. Context means knowing a great deal more about the user and even simple things like the time of day or location of the user. As we deepen the integration of the virtual and physical worlds, we will extend the power of computation.

Thus, a major distinguishing characteristic of future networks is that they interact strongly with physical world. They sense the physical world (e.g., its temperature, air quality, soil factors, or engine vibrations), they communicate and process those sensory date, and in real time they cause physical actions to be taken. While most traditional computers tend to interact directly with human operators, future networks will interact more directly with the physical world. Sensor network is developing into something like a nervous system for the earth, a skin for the earth [2].

With '3C everywhere' and 'physical interaction', pervasive computing and ubiquitous computing promises a computing infrastructure that seamlessly and ubiquitously aids users in accomplishing their tasks and that renders the actual computing devices and technology largely invisible [3,4]. Networking will follow a similar evolution to electrification. A century ago, electrification had as its major applications light and mechanical power. Both light and power followed a clear evolution to mobility (battery-operated flashlights and power tools), ubiquity (virtually every room has electric outlets and appliances), and embeddedness (small electric motors within many products). Networking will follow the same course to have an impact on productivity and standards of living.

In this paper, we begin by sketching pervasive computing scenarios. Next, we delve deeper into some key technical challenges. The following section presents our technological developments: STONE, SLSOCKET, and Personal Mesh.

2 Application Scenarios

As no one could predict the WWW in the 1980s, predicting future applications is considered to be quite difficult. Note that the following scenarios are just for purposes of illustration and not limitation.

World News Service: Alice's house is equipped with a home sensor network system (Fig.1). When she moves from a bedroom to living room, the sensor network detects the change of her location and temperature around her, and controls the lighting and air conditioner. In addition, a world news program which she saw in the bedroom is automatically displayed on her nearest monitor in the living room.

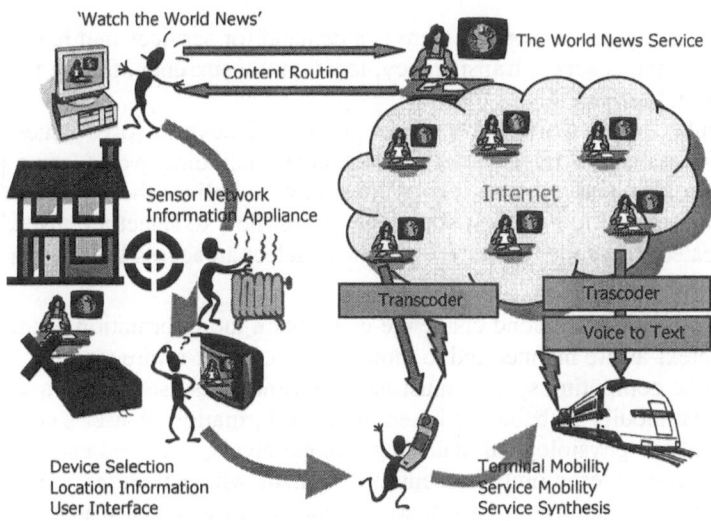

Fig. 1. World news service scenario

When she moves outside, a world news program is displayed onto a PDA screen. As the display size of a PDA is small and the bandwidth of a wireless link is not enough, transcoder is dynamically linked to modify the news source format to meet the requirements of screen size and bandwidth.

When she gets on a train where voice output is undesirable, voice output of a PDA is shut off, and the display mode is switched to news video and text. Here, in addition to transcoder, a voice-to-text conversion proxy is dynamically linked to display the voice data in text on a PDA screen.

APLICOT: Information alliances can be considered as an integration of functions. For example, a cellular phone consists of a display function, a ten-key input function, a voice input and output function, a wireless communication function, a CPU function, and a memory function. APLICOT (appliance conductor) creates a new service by combining several functions on the network. By dynamically combining functions of each device, it is possible to build 'instant disco' where the sound output of a CD player is fed to the lights in the ceiling, and to control television with cellular phones. A salient feature of APLICOT is a dynamic creation of services.

3   Challenges

Practical realization of above application scenarios will require us to solve many difficult design and implementation problems.

Service Discovery: A first challenge is how to cope with a large variety of resources being ubiquitous in the network. Here, resources include computing, content, and network resources which are provided to users as network applications.

In a '3C everywhere' environment, billions of resources will be ubiquitous in the Internet with the penetration of CDN (content delivery network) technologies, peer-to-peer technologies, and global-scale distributed storage technologies. In addition, increasing level of connectivity provides many ways of accessing to the network. As the resources become widespread, there is a demand for services that have distributed transparency such as access transparency, location transparency, failure transparency, and replication transparency.

In particular, in the world news service above, we have to solve issues of how to describe and manage a huge variety of resources including world news programs, transcoder proxies, and voice-to-text proxies, how to deliver the request of 'watch a world news program' to a nearest streaming server, how to select a transcoder among many replicated transcoder proxies, and how to select an access link among available communication links.

Context Awareness: A second challenge is to obtain the information needed to function in a context-aware manner and to implement a context-aware system.

A pervasive computing system must be cognizant of its user's state and surroundings, and must modify its behavior based on this information. A user's context can be physical location, physiological state (e.g., temperature), and personal history. Context-awareness enables mobile presentation system where pictures are always displayed on a nearest monitor to a speaker, and personalized search where search results are actively adapted to the context of query issuer like the time of day or location.

In particular, in the world news scenario above, voice output of a PDA is shut off, and the display mode is switched to news video and text. Here, the detection of context such as 'in a train' and migration of user interfaces as well as user applications are necessary.

Service Synthesis / Service Mobility: A third challenge is to dynamically combine a variety of resources in the network. Service synthesis is performed in the world news scenario above: detecting the voice-to-text conversion proxy and synthesizing a new service, a source server (voice input) to conversion proxies to a PDA screen (text output). APLICOT is for synthesizing service by combining functions of each device.

Likewise, mobility requires 'service mobility' support in addition to 'terminal mobility' support. Service mobility is the capability of service being transported from one device to another by finding equivalent functions. For example, in the world news scenario above, it is important to maintain 'world news service' when Alice goes forth the house by switching display device from a monitor in the living room to a PDA screen.

Service synthesis and service mobility are significant components for achieving a consistent service in ever-changing environment by collecting necessary functions and combining them dynamically in response to changes in time and place. A user can enjoy a service throughout the session without knowing the changes in functional components.

4 STONE

We are developing a network service platform, STONE (Service Synthesizer on the Net), that dynamically synthesizes a desired context-aware service from a set of resources. STONE achieves service discovery, context aware, service synthesis, and service mobility in a unified way using a naming service [5,6].

Fig. 2 depicts the STONE architecture. STONE has three major components: a functional object, a service resolver, and a service graph.

The functional object is the most basic element of a service, and has the mechanisms required for providing the requested service by being dynamically linked to another functional object. Functional objects may be either hardware or software, and include display, camera, speaker, microphone, various types of transcoders and proxies, and streaming videos. A 'synthesized' service is a string of functional objects such as the dynamic combination of functions of the source of world news, a transcoder, and a display.

Here, even if there is a change in the environment around the functional object or user, the service can be maintained and be transparent to mobility or failure as long as the functions composing the service can be maintained (distribution transparency is achieved). Alternatively, the service provided can be tailored to the environment by modifying one function into a more appropriate function as the environment changes, (context-awareness is achieved).

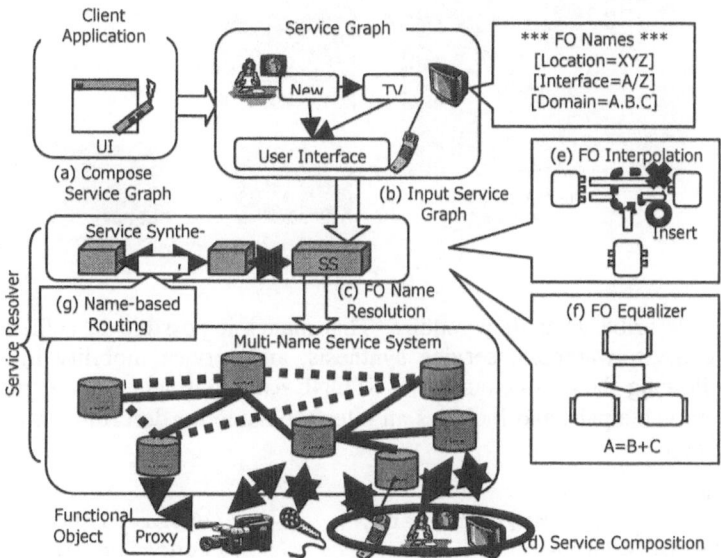

Fig. 2. STONE architecture

STONE achieves such distributed transparency and context-awareness through appropriate naming of functional objects. Networking systems are traditionally organized using a layering model composed of application, transport/network, and link layers. This model is useful in clearly defining the responsibilities and restrictions of software that exists at each level. To be implemented fully, a layer needs a naming scheme, a way to resolve those names, and a way to route communications. In the Internet, naming types used in each layer include MAC addresses in link layers, IP addresses in network layers, and URLs and email addresses in the application layers. In STONE, we extend the model to include a new layer in the top.

STONE adopts location-independent naming for describing *what* users and/or applications are looking for, not *where* to find it. Current naming types of IP addresses and URLs specify the network location of server and client machines: they are location-dependent naming. The advantage of location-independent naming is to be able to achieve distributed transparency such as access transparency, location transparency, failure transparency, and replication transparency. Also, location-independent naming allows nodes that provide a function to precisely describe what they provide

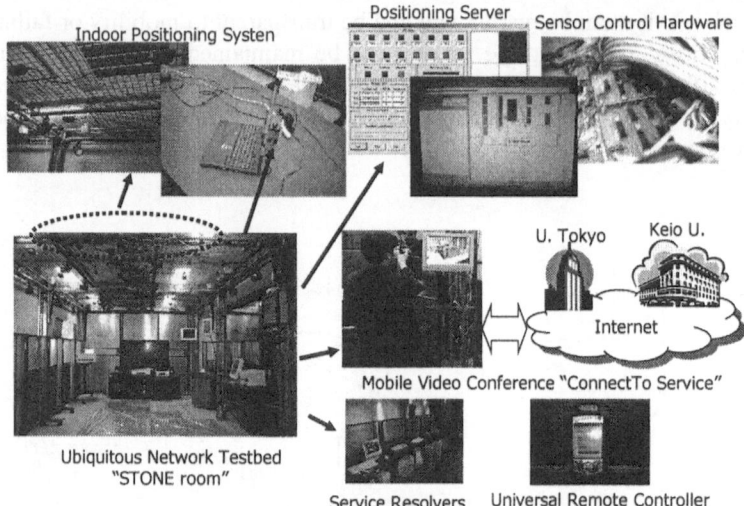

Fig. 3. STONE room.

and users to describe what they require. This makes it possible to achieve service discovery, context-awareness, service synthesis, and service mobility in a unified way. The following shows an example of STONE naming. Every name is represented as an attribute-value pair, and includes an interface name for describing a function of a functional object.

```
[FO Name =
   [Location=x.y.z@myhome.net],          //Physical Location
   [InterfaceName=                       //Function Description
     [Output Interface = Rendered Video],
     [Input Interface = MPEG4/IP],
     [Relation = Convert Input Interface to Output Inter-
face],
       [Ctrl Interface = Display Control/GUI]
   ]
]
[Access Pointer List= [Address=xx.xx.xx.xx:yy],   //IP+Port
]
```

Location-independent naming imposes a scalability problem, since it often has a flat name space (on the contrary, location-dependent naming such as DNS has a hierarchical name space). The introduction of interface names in STONE naming mitigates the scalability problem by grouping interface names to form a two-level hierarchy.

The service resolver network overlaid on the Internet is then used to route request to the appropriate locations by maintaining a mapping between interface descriptions and their network locations. Service revolver network is a logical and overlay network, and finds and connects functional objects with the use of interface names. As an IP router routes a data by examining a destination IP address, a service resolver routes a data by examining an interface name.

The service graph specifies the service request of a client such as 'I like to see the camera images of room 409 on a nearest monitor'. The service graph may be created by the client, or may be downloaded from the network. It describes the interconnection between functional objects (to connect a camera output function with a monitor input function), and a context script to specify context-awareness explicitly (to select a nearest monitor output function). When a user issues a service graph, STONE system finds suitable functional objects and synthesizes a requested service by combining several functional objects dynamically in a context-aware manner.

We have implemented STONE's component in a testbed room and built several application prototypes including mobile video conference, universal remote controller, 'connect to' service, and 'media kitchen' service as shown in Fig. 3 In a STONE testbed room, locating of objects as well as people can be performed with an indoor positioning system which we have developed to implement a 'location-aware' service [7].

5 SLSOCKET and Personal Mesh

SLSOCKET (Session Layer Socket) and Personal Mesh are projects for developing mobile Internet architecture to be able to achieve service consistency when a user moves and context changes. While STONE approaches the service consistency from naming viewpoint, SLSOCKET and Personal Mesh focus on mobility support.

SLSOCKET: Today's Internet architecture was developed without the consideration of mobility. V. Cerf wrote [8] "TCP's dependence upon the network and host addresses for part of its connection identifiers makes dynamic reconnection difficult." The result is that when the underlying IP address of one of the communication peers changes, the end-to-end TCP connection is unable to continue because it has bound to the network-layer identifier, wrongly assuming is permanence for the duration of the connection.

Towards supporting mobility in the Internet, we have developed session-layer mobility support [9]. Session layer mobility support uses a 'session ID' as a communication identifier instead of an IP address and a port number of a communicating peer. A session ID is invariant with any changes in all the layers below the session layer, and only updating the association with the changed socket is necessary.

The one of the benefits of session-layer mobility is to support service mobility for a user to flexibly choosing (or combining) appropriate devices and applications according to the on-the-spot needs. Fig. 4 shows the scenario: 'A is walking on the way to her office while talking about a product with her client B through a VoIP cellular phone. In a while, A has arrived at his office, and laptop computer becomes available which is connected to the Internet by wired LAN and equipped with a microphone, a camera, and speakers. Given this circumstance, A decides to start a video call using her laptop computer, so that the detailed information of the product can be shown to the client B. Session-layer mobility support allows the migration of services across the devices.

In addition to service mobility support, session-layer mobility provides the fol-

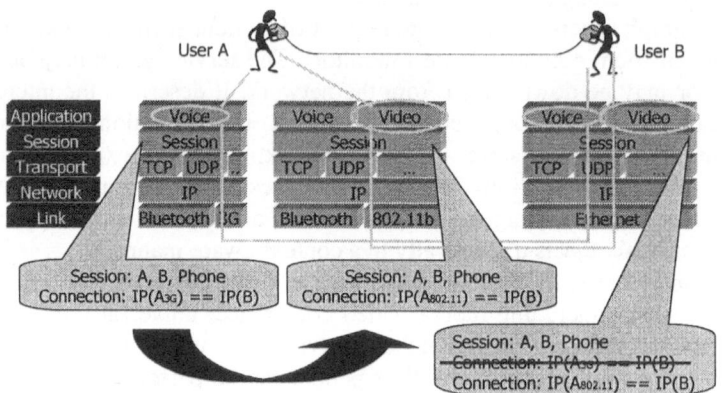

Fig. 4. Service mobility and session-layer mobility support

lowing desirable effects: the elimination of lower-layer dependence, the separation of naming space and communication space, adaptability to the changes in the network, and authentification at the service level. We believe that session-layer mobility support can be regarded as a viable solution in '3C everywhere' environment.

Personal Mesh: Network interfaces to be used by the personal devices will be diversified as much as the personal devices are. Personal Mesh is the sharing mechanism of access links among several personal devices. For example, consider the situation where there are several devices around a user including a 3G phone with a 3G link, a desktop computer with a wired link, and a laptop computer with a wireless LAN link and PHS link. Personal Mesh allows the 3G phone to use the wireless LAN link connected to the laptop computer via short-range communication such as Bluetooth.

Towards this, we implemented virtual interface [10]. Virtual interface distinguishes Personal Mesh from the mere aggregation of the personal devices. The devices share the information on the additional network interfaces, if any, with each other, and virtual network interfaces are created as if the interface is on the device, allowing more desirable route to the Internet to be used.

References

1. Morikawa, H.; New Generation Internet Architecture. ITE Magazine. Vol.55, No.12 (2001) 1609-1615
2. 21 Ideas for the 21st Century. Business Week (1999)

3. Weiser, W.: The Computer for the 21st Century. Sci. Amer. Vol.265, No.3 (1991) 94-104
4. Norman, D.: The Invisible Computer. MIT Press (1998)
5. Minami, M., Sugita, K., Morikawa, H., Aoyama, T.: A Design of Internet Application Platform for Ubiquitous Computing Environment. IEICE Trans. Comm. (2002)
6. Minami, M., Morikawa, H., Aoyama, T.: The Design and Evaluation of an Interface-based Naming System for Supporting Service Synthesis in Ubiquitous Computing Environment. IEICE Trans. Comm. (2002)
7. Shih, S., Minami, M., Morikawa, H., Aoyama, T.: An Implementation and Evaluation of Indoor Ultrasonic Tracking System. IPSJ Technical Report (2001) 2001-MBL-17
8. Cerf, V., Cain, E.: The DoD Internet Architecture Model. Computer Networks, Vol.7 (1983) 850-857
9. Kaneko, K., Morikawa, H., Aoyama, T., Nakayama, M.: End-to-End Mobility Support for Heterogeneous Internet Environments. IEICE Tech. Rep. (2002) MoMuC2002-8
10. Kunito, G., Morikawa, H., Aoyama, T.: A Design and Implementation of Personal Mesh for Heterogeneous Access Link Environments. IEICE Tech. Rep. (2002) IN2001-255

Improved Error Detection Method for Real-Time Video Communication Using Fragile Watermarking

Younghooi Hwang[1], Byeungwoo Jeon[2], and Tai M. Chung[3]

School of ECE, Sungkyunkwan University, Korea
{[1]ungiee, [2]bjeon, [3]tmchung}@ece.skku.ac.kr
http://media.skku.ac.kr

Abstract. This paper proposes a computationally very simple error detection technique using fragile watermarking for real-time video communication. To balance between image quality degradation and error detection efficiency, fragile watermark is embedded only in the least significant bits of selected transform coefficients. The proposed method is workable without an additional bit in video bitstream and can be implemented very efficiently. It will be useful in video communication in error prone environment such as wireless channel.

1 Introduction

Recent rapid growth both in Internet and mobile communication makes diverse multimedia services possible. Among them, video service over various communication channels becomes increasingly proliferate. The video compression standards employ variable-length and predictive coding scheme to remove the redundancy of video data.

Wireless channel is typically noisy and suffers from a number of channel degradations, therefore, it is important to design a video coding and decoding algorithm which can effectively deal with the bit and burst errors due to fading and multi-path reflections [1]. Note that the effect of channel errors on compressed video can be very serious, and sometimes even disastrous. Especially the variable-length coding scheme makes the compressed bitstream extremely vulnerable to channel errors. As a result of the errors, the video decoder loses synchronization with the encoder. Predictive coding technique both in spatial and temporal directions also makes it even worse in that the effects of channel errors in one place propagate through the video sequence. Unless video encoder and decoder are equipped with proper error resilience schemes, video communication system can be totally broken down in a noisy situation.

Many error resilience schemes are available to achieve robust transmission of compressed video data over nosy channels. Generally, these tools are classified into error

---

[2] Corresponding Author
This work was supported in part by the ITRC program (#2000-20000385-000) of the Ministry of Information & Communication of KOREA.

Y.-C. Chen, L.-W. Chang, and C.-T. Hsu (Eds.): PCM 2002, LNCS 2532, pp. 50-57, 2002.

detection, synchronization, data recovery, and error concealment. The MPEG-4 video standard offers such error-resilient tools as resynchronization, data partitioning, and reversible VLC [2]. Note that the success of these techniques relies on how accurately the errors can be detected. This means that a reliable and effective error detection technique is called for in the first place.

The most well-known technique in error detection is the syntax-based error detection scheme [2] which identifies errors by finding abnormalities in decoding such as illegal VLC codeword, more than 64 DCT coefficients in a single block, QP out of range, and inconsistent resynchronization header information, etc. Unfortunately, this conventional scheme is not so accurate: its detection ratio is only 40~60% [3,4]. In this paper, we propose a new error detection method employing a simple fragile watermarking technique to implement more effective and reliable error detection. For this purpose, we embed a special pattern as a fragile watermark in the least-significant bits (LSB) of *selected* non-zero quantized DCT coefficients. The modification in the LSB's of the transformed coefficients certainly causes deterioration in PSNR value [3]. If most LSB's of non-zero quantized DCT coefficients in a coded macroblock (MB) are changed, image quality degradation will be very large [3,4]. In an inter-coded MB, the motion-compensated residual data are known to have the Laplacian distribution [5]. It suggests that *non-zero* quantized DCT coefficients have higher probabilities at odd numbers than at even numbers. Therefore, embedding a special pattern such that the LSB's are all 1 as in [3] can greatly reduce the image quality degradation, but, at the same time, inevitably with lowered error detection rate.

To solve the quality problem, in this paper, we embed a specific pattern just in the LSB's of *last* coded non-zero quantized DCT data in *selected* blocks in an inter-coded macroblock. We use the same method as in [3] in case of intra-coded macroblocks. It is to minimize the image quality loss as much as possible without sacrificing the error detection property too much. The embedding rule is to make the total sum of quantized DCT coefficients in a selected block be even (or odd) by modifying the LSB of the last coded DCT coefficients in the corresponding block. When the decoder receives a VLC codeword for transform coefficients and if the extracted LSB of the corresponding DCT coefficient does not conform to the embedding rule, it can determine that the corresponding MB is erroneous.

The syntax-based error detector cannot always single out an erroneous MB. This is because the preceding erroneous MB's can be decoded (but in a wrong way) without any apparent syntax violation. Note that in this case, the integrity of the decoded data in the same GOB before erroneous MB are doubtful, and, to be on the safe side, one often wishes to discard whole decoded data of the problematic GOB and initiate error concealment routine for the GOB. However, the proposed embedding scheme using fragile watermarking can pinpoint whether each decoded macroblock is erroneous or not. This additional accuracy makes it possible to discard only the erroneous MB's selectively, thus reducing unnecessary degradation of visual quality.

2 Proposed Error Detection Method with Fragile Watermark

Fig. 1 shows the encoder blocks for the proposed error detection scheme using fragile watermarking. The embedding procedure is carried out after DCT and quantization. The "*TCOFF & block selector*" in Fig. 1 selects a block to which watermark should be embedded. Input of the *LSB pattern generator* is selection information of *TCOFF & block selector*, watermarking information, and quantized DCT coefficients. These input information decides whether it modifies least significant bits of the corresponding DCT coefficients in a selected block or not.

Watermark is embedded just in non-zero DCT coefficients, that is to say, the LEVEL data (note that the LEVEL data refers to the non-zero DCT coefficient following zero runs according to a specific scanning direction of choice, for example, zig-zag direction). If it should change the current LSB, the LSB pattern generator selects either +1 or −1 to add to the LEVEL in such a way to reduce the resulting quantization error and the length of resulting VLC codewords. Besides, considering the different coding characteristic of inter-coded and intra-coded MB's, we use different embedding scheme for each of them.

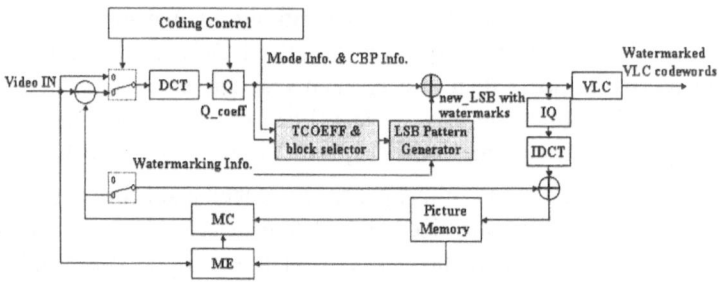

Fig. 1. Encoder with the proposed embedding technique using fragile watermarking

2.1 Error Detection Pattern in an Intra-coded MB

Although there are fewer intra-coded MB than inter-coded ones in a coded bitstream, the compressed data size in an MB is larger than that in an inter-coded one. Therefore, we are able to embed more watermarks in an intra-coded MB in contrast to an inter-coded MB. In an intra-coded MB, we use the embedding rule of Eq. 1 as suggested in [3]: the LSB of each non-zero DCT coefficient is set to 0 if it is at even position in the zia-zag scanning order starting from the DC coefficients, and to 1 if it is at odd position.

$$LSB(Coeff\_position) = \begin{cases} Coeff\_position \bmod 2, \\ \quad \text{when AC \& } (Coeff\_position \geq position\_start) \\ 0, \quad \text{when DC} \end{cases} \quad (1)$$

Here, '*coeff_position*' refers to the position of a given coefficient inside an 8×8 block (0~63) and '*mod*' is the modular operation. To minimize video quality degradation due to insertion of the pattern, no insertion is attempted to the AC coefficients below the position specified by the parameter '*position_start*' (1~63). It is to minimize degradation of visual quality due to the embedding. Note, however, that the DC coefficient is always embedded. We process four luminance and two chrominance blocks in the same way. Embedding the LSB pattern into intra DC and checking its integrity turns out to be quite important in reality since the wrong MB boundary caused by unnoticed error produces totally wrong reconstructed DC values or, sometimes, changes the macroblock type itself. In such instances, its effect in visual quality is utmost deteriorating. The embedded watermark in DC can alarm the decoder of such detrimental errors.

2.2 Error Detection Pattern in an Inter-coded MB

Although the number of inter-coded MB's is more than that of intra-coded ones, their compressed data size is small in comparison with intra-coded MB's. Accordingly, we need to treat them in a slightly different way to take into account the fact that the inter MB's have very fewer number of coded transform coefficients. For this reason, in inter-coded MB's, watermarking pattern is embedded only to LEVEL data of the last coded non-zero quantized DCT coefficient located in the last coded block among four luminance blocks. In a rare case of no coded luminance blocks in an MB, the embedding is performed to the chrominance blocks if they are coded. The reason why we embed preferentially at a luminance block is that the number of non-zero coded transform coefficient in a chrominance block is usually smaller than in luminance blocks, and in order to keep to image quality degradation as small as possible. We first calculate the total sum of quantized DCT coefficients inside a selected block using Eq. 2:

$$S = \sum_{u=0}^{7} \sum_{v=0}^{7} |QF(u,v)| \tag{2}$$

Here, '$QF(u,v)$' refers to the quantized DCT coefficient in a selected block. 'S' is the sum of absolute $QF(u,v)$'s in a corresponding block, and we define the '*Block Parity (BP)*' of a block as Eq. 3.

$$BP = \begin{cases} 1, & S = odd \\ 0, & S = even \end{cases} \quad where \quad S = \sum_{u=0}^{7} \sum_{v=0}^{7} |QF(u,v)| \tag{3}$$

The block parity is '1' if S is odd, and it is '0' if S is even. The block parity is a parameter which decides embedding pattern of watermark. That is to say, we judge whether or not we change the LSB of the last non-zero DCT coefficient in a selected block according to the block parity value. According to the embedding pattern, we propose two methods for inter-coded MB's. The first proposed embedding method for error detection is to make the block parity of a block be 0 by changing the LSB of the last non-zero coefficient appropriately. That is, we embed watermark at the LSB of the last non-zero DCT coefficient in the selected block using Eq. 4:

$$LSB = \begin{cases} 1, & \textit{when Block Parity (BP) before embedding is } 1 \\ 0, & \textit{when Block Parity (BP) before embedding is } 0 \end{cases} \qquad (4)$$

The second proposed embedding method for error detection makes the block parity be '1' in opposition to the first method: we embed watermark at the LSB of the last non-zero DCT coefficient in the selected block so as to make the block parity be '1', using Eq. 5:

$$LSB = \begin{cases} 1, & \textit{when Block Parity (BP) before embedding is } 0 \\ 0, & \textit{when Block Parity (BP) before embedding is } 1 \end{cases} \qquad (5)$$

The performance of these proposed methods is rather different respectively in error detection rate and PSNR. Fig. 2 shows $Prob\{BP=1\}$, the probability that a block has the block parity=1 for various bitrate. $Prob\{BP=0\}$ is equal to $1- Prob\{BP=1\}$. It is obviously seen that this probability is higher than the opposite case (i.e. BP=0) when bitrate reduces. This is because the probability that the magnitude of non-zero level has '1' is the highest of the other magnitude values as in Fig. 3(a). In a low bit rate coding, it is very likely to have only one non-zero quantized transform coefficient in a block. Fig. 3(b) confirms this assertion: it shows $Prob\{Level\_Count\}$, the probability that a block has a given number of non-zero level data. As Figure 3(b) shows, the probability having only one non-zero level in a coded block gradually increases as bitrate decrease, and the only one non-zero level is most likely to be odd number. The two proposed methods are different both in error detection rate and loss of PSNR. The simulation results of these methods are provided in Section 4.

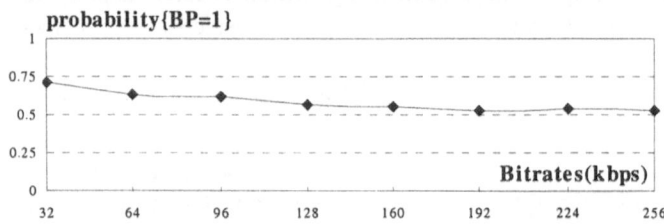

Fig. 2. The Probability of 'Block Parity=1' in a block (Inter-coded MB, foreman 99 frames)

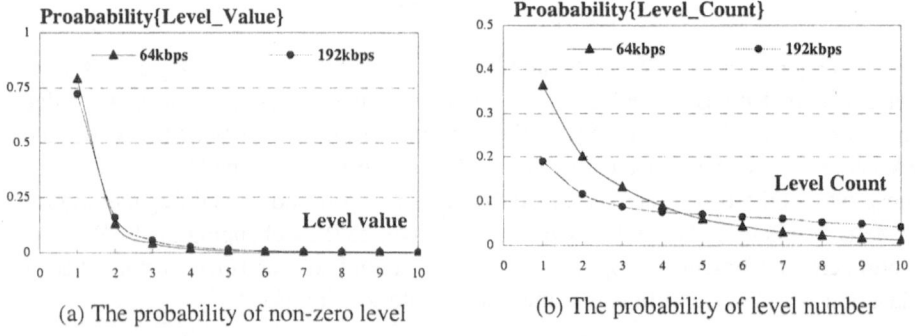

(a) The probability of non-zero level   (b) The probability of level number

Fig. 3. The probability in a coded block (Inter-coded MB, Foreman 99 frames)

2.3 Error Detection and Concealment Method

Fig. 4 shows the proposed error detection. The proposed error detection comprises of two steps. The first step is error detection in a GOB level and it is based on the conventional syntax-based detection. The second step is further scrutinizing each macroblock to filter out any undetected erroneous macroblocks wrongly surviving the first step. The capability of the proposed method pinpointing whether a certain MB is erroneous or not provides additional benefit of executing error concealment at MB level. When it detects any error, it conceals the erroneous MB (in this paper, we just use very straightforward method of copying data by using the MV of the upper MB but more sophisticated method is possible). When the syntax-based error detector finds syntax error and stops decoding, the error concealment routine recovers the remaining (or trashed) MB's in the same GOB.

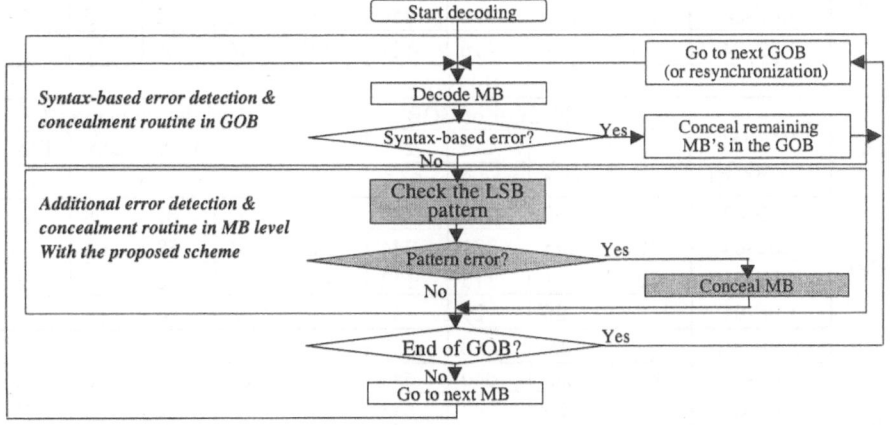

Fig. 4. Flowchart of proposed detection and concealment method

3 Experiment and Discussion

The experiment of the proposed methods is executed with a modified H.263 TMN 3.0 codec using the rate control method of TMN8. To simulate the transmission errors, we insert random bit errors with various bit error rates on variable-length codeword (VLC) parts of the motion vector difference (MVD) data and quantized transform coefficients (TCOEFF) under binary symmetric channel model. We note that under the protection of FEC and interleaving, a real channel can be assumed to be equivalent to a binary symmetric channel [6]. We evaluate the performance of the proposed method in terms of PSNR and error detection rate and compare it with the conventional syntax-based method and the similar previous method [3].

The error detection rates of the conventional syntax-based error detector are shown in Table 1. The test result confirms that just around 46 ~ 68% of the erroneous GOB can be detected. It means that at least 40% of erroneous GOB's go undetected by the syntax–based error detection scheme. Therefore, it is important to check the integrity of each GOB even though it is decoded without apparent syntax error.

Table 1. Number of detected erroneous GOB's by the proposed method (For 100 frames of each Sequence; Average of 10 experiments)

(a) Foreman

Bit Rate	Error rate	Number of GOB					Error detection rate(%)			
		A	B	C	D	E	B/A	C/A	D/A	E/A
64 kbps	PSNR[dB]	·	31.1	30.5	30.5	30.8	·	·	·	·
	1.0E-03	467	229	310	342	337	49	66	73	73
	8.0E-04	386	191	247	283	276	49	64	73	72
	4.0E-04	204	95	127	152	149	47	62	75	73
	1.0E-04	52	27	29	34	35	52	56	65	67
192 kbps	PSNR[dB]	·	36.7	35.8	36.3	36.4	·	·	·	·
	1.0E-03	880	556	653	708	694	63	74	81	79
	8.0E-04	855	494	607	661	645	58	71	77	75
	4.0E-04	611	293	378	459	438	48	62	75	72
	1.0E-04	178	81	116	129	127	46	65	72	71

(b) News

Bit Rate	Error rate	Number of GOB					Error detection rate(%)			
		A	B	C	D	E	B/A	C/A	D/A	E/A
64 kbps	PSNR[dB]	·	35.4	35.0	34.7	35.0	·	·	·	·
	1.0E-03	443	230	268	299	275	52	61	68	62
	8.0E-04	381	195	221	244	241	51	58	64	63
	4.0E-04	207	101	115	132	124	48	56	64	60
	1.0E-04	54	26	29	32	30	48	54	59	56
192 kbps	PSNR[dB]	·	40.9	40.0	40.7	40.7	·	·	·	·
	1.0E-03	852	583	640	680	674	68	75	80	79
	8.0E-04	805	505	597	643	620	63	74	80	77
	4.0E-04	585	316	390	447	427	54	67	76	73
	1.0E-04	176	87	106	128	115	49	60	73	65

A: Number of true erroneous GOB's
B: Number of detected erroneous GOB's by the syntax-based method
C: Number of detected erroneous GOB's by the syntax-based and Park's method
D: Number of detected erroneous GOB's by the syntax-based and the first proposed method using Eq. 4
E: Number of detected erroneous GOB's by the syntax-based and the second proposed method using Eq. 5

Table 1 lists the detection rate of erroneous GOB's by the syntax-based error detection method, previous method [3] and the proposed error detection techniques. The previous method [3] makes all the LSB of the non-zero coefficients in coded block be odd in inter-coded MB's. The proposed embedding techniques are consistently superior to the technique by [3]. The first proposed embedding technique using Eq. 4 ('D' in Table 1) is better than the second technique using Eq. 5 ('E' in Table 1) on error detection efficiency. However, the first embedding method imposes burden because the relative loss of PSNR is great in low bitrate as in Table 1. Therefore, it is quite natural to apply this method in high bitrate, but we had better employ the second proposed embedding technique using Eq. 5 in the channel environment of variable bitrate as well as a low bitrate.

We also compare PSNR values of reconstructed sequence with error free condition without LSB pattern embedding ('B' in Table 1), the previous scheme [3], and the proposed methods. In the experiment, we use 'Pos_start=11' in intra-coded MB in Eq. 1. The comparative result over the various bitrates is provided also in Table 1 which shows superiority of the proposed methods over the previous method [3]. However, the loss of PSNR in the first proposed embedding method is considerably high in low bitrate and is reduced when bitrate increases. The reason for the reduction is because the symbol "End of Block (EOB)" indicating the last coded DCT coefficients in a block is generated more frequently in high frequency region of the transform domain when bitrate increases. It is also obvious that the second proposed embedding method has smaller PSNR loss than the other, since in low bitrate the probability that the block parity is '1' is inherently higher than the other case of being '0'. In such cases, we change the last coded DCT coefficients in a selected block fewer than in high bitrate. Therefore, the second proposed method can keep the loss of PSNR in low bitrate as small as possible.

4 Conclusion

In this paper, we propose an error detection technique using fragile watermarking in order to improve error detection. We are able to keep the deterioration of PSNR value as small as possible and effectively detect transmission errors because the embedding pattern is inserted parsimoniously only to the last coded coefficients of selected block in a macroblock. Another advantage of proposed method is that there is no requirement of additional bit in video bitstream for supporting enhanced error resilience as proposed here and that it can be implemented very efficiently. This method will be useful in error prone environments like wireless channel.

References

1. Raj Talluri: Error-Resilient Video Coding in the ISO MPEG-4 Standards. IEEE Communication Magazine, vol. 26, no. 6 (1998) 112-119
2. Yao Wang, Stephan Wenger, Jiangtao Wen, Aggelos K. Katsaggelos: Error Resilient Video Coding Techniques. IEEE Signal Processing Magazine, vol. 17, no. 4 (2000) 61-82
3. W. Park, B. Jeon: Error Detection and Recovery by Hiding Information into Video Bitstream using Fragile Watermarking. Visual Communications and Image Processing (VCIP) 2002, vol. 4671 (2002) 1-10
4. Minghua Chen, Yun He, Reginald L. Lagendijk: Error Detection by Fragile Watermarking. Proceedings of Picture Coding Symposium (PCS) 2001 (2001) 287-290
5. S. R. Smoot, L. A. Rowe: Study of DCT Coefficient Distributions. Proceedings of SPIE, vol. 1 (1997) 601-605
6. Wee Sun Lee, M. R. Pickering, M. R. Frater, J. F. Arnold: Error Resilience in Video and Multiplexing Layers for Very Low Bit-rate Video Coding Systems. IEEE Journal on Selected Areas in Communications, vol. 15, no. 9 (1997) 1764-1774

Digital Geographical Map Watermarking Using Polyline Interpolation

Kyi Tae Park, Kab Il Kim, Hwan Il Kang, and Seung Soo Han

Next-Generation Power Technology Center, Myong Ji University 449-728, Korea
superz@hanmail.net, {kkl, hwan, shan}@mju.ac.kr

Abstract. This paper presents the watermarking algorithm for copyright protection of the digital geographical map composed of vector format. Most of previously related works had a weak point that degrades the accuracy as the quality of the digital geographical map or is easily destroyed by attacks. The proposed watermarking algorithm preserves the accuracy of vertex and is robust enough against attacks, and also it performs the blind watermarking by extracting the watermark without an original map. Finally, through experiments, this paper shows the proposed method is robust enough against attacks such as the elimination and modification of vertices.

1 Introduction

According to a wide spread of a computer, multimedia contents are converted to a digital form. The conversion to a digital form brings the several conveniences such as edition, modification, and distribution of contents, but it causes a difficulty of the copyright protection. The recently remarkable method for solving this problem is the watermarking. The watermarking is the particular method for a copyright protection by leaving an invisible or inaudible identification that can prove an ownership of digital media contents.

Most of digital contents such as image, video, audio, and etc, can be become the target of the watermarking. In this paper, we try the watermarking for a digital geographical map.

Several previous digital watermarking methods have been proposed. [5] inserts a watermark by moving vertices of spatial data like a contour line but cannot perceive by human eye. [2] increases the robustness against an attack by generalization of square mask of [5] to a rectangular mask. In 3D polygonal model, [6] inserts a watermark by modification of vertex and topology data.

Most of previous methods have chosen the watermark insertion by movement of vertices because the change of topology or structure is weak against attacks. However, it is also not a good idea because the accuracy of the digital map is importance. Therefore, we suggest a robust watermarking algorithm by overlap and interpolation of vector data that can preserve the accuracy of digital map.

Y.-C. Chen, L.-W. Chang, and C.-T. Hsu (Eds.): PCM 2002, LNCS 2532, pp. 58–65, 2002.

2 Basis of Vector Watermarking

The vector data structure is complex and various compared with the raster data structure. It is commonly composed of the spatial and attribute data. The spatial data are space objects like points and lines, and the attribute data describe characteristics of the target or information about data. There are several data structures of digital geographical map such as Whole Polygon, Arc-Node, DIME relational data structure, and etc. In this paper Arc-Node structure is adapted as a main data structure because Arc-Node structure is the most representative structure.

The watermarking methods in Arc-Node structure are as follows.

- Inserts to vertex
- Inserts to topology
- Inserts to structure of vector
- Inserts by overlap or interpolation of data

First method inserts a watermark by moving vertices of spatial data. Therefore, this method has a weak point that the accuracy of data is degraded. Second method inserts a watermark by changing a direction of link between two vertices. This method satisfies an invisibility and unchangeability. However, this method is easily destroyed by sorting the topology. Third method inserts a watermark by changing of object-structure. For example, a polyline is separated to several lines. However, in this method, a watermark is destroyed by the small change of the structure. Finally, last method inserts a watermark by the overlap or interpolation of objects as Fig. 2. This method increases a quantity of data, but it can insert a watermark without the positional change of data.

The overlap of the data brings many increments of data because all information of object are copied. On the other hand, data increment by the interpolation is less than one by the overlap because only vertices are copied. When considering that most of data in the digital map are composed of polyline, the interpolation of data is the very efficient method

3 Proposed Watermarking Algorithm

The proposed algorithm inserts one watermark bit per one block of digital map. First step is dividing the digital map to M areas as Fig. 3 where each area is called cell. A cell has the number of vertices in cell. Second step is sorting these cells by user key for hiding information, and N cells are put together for composing a block. Third step is the frequency transform of these blocks. In this method the frequency transform cannot use characteristics of HAS(Human Audio System) or HVS(Human Visual System) in case of an audio or image. However, the change of a frequency coefficient influences to several cells, otherwise the change of a cell coefficient spreads to several frequency coefficients. Therefore, one frequency coefficient is not largely influenced although a cell coefficient, the number of vertices, is changed by attack such as elimination of objects.

After the frequency transform, frequency coefficients are quantized. In this step a frequency coefficient is quantized to the nearest level equal to a watermark bit where the robustness is decided by quantization width δ (Fig. 4).

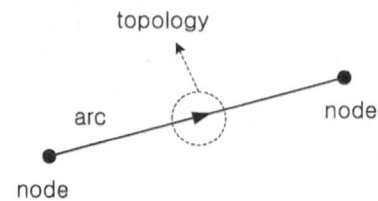

Fig. 1. Arc-Node structure.

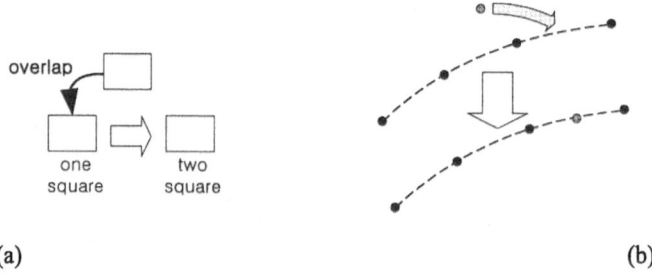

(a)   (b)

Fig. 2. Overlap and interpolation of objects; (a) overlap method, (b) interpolation method

In the embedding process, we assume two conditions. One condition is that there is not data loss by the insertion of the watermark. Other condition is that it is prohibited to insert additional vertices into the cell that the number of vertices is 0 because it is impossible to hide the information in such cell. Two conditions can be expressed concisely as

$$y \geq x \tag{1}$$

$$If\ x = 0, then\ y = 0 \tag{2}$$

where x is the number of input vertices and y is the number of output vertices. One solution satisfied Equation (1) is what shifts y in order to make that all coefficients of y are larger than those of x.

The extraction of a watermark estimates what is a level that a quantized frequency coefficient lies adjacent to. At this time, if the extracted watermark is the image that can be seen by human eye, we can make a subjective evaluation. Besides, we can use NC(Normalized Correlation) for getting objective similarities[1,4] as

$$NC = \frac{\sum_i \sum_j W(i, j)W^*(i, j)}{\sum_i \sum_j W(i, j)^2} \tag{3}$$

where W denotes the original watermark, and W^* denotes the extracted watermark.

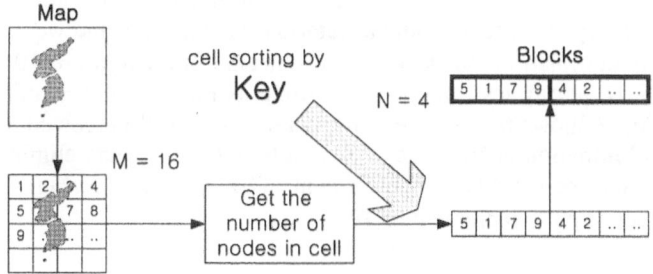

Fig. 3. Division of map and composition of block

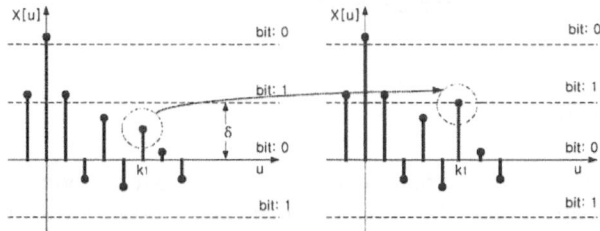

Fig. 4. Quantization of frequency coefficient: Frequency coefficient is quantized to the nearest level, namely, level 1.

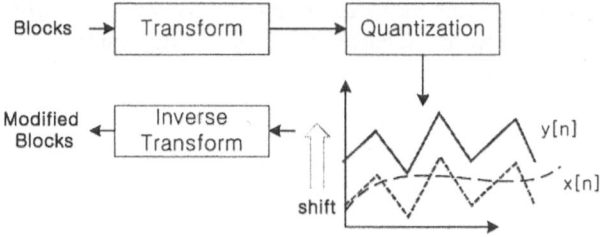

Fig. 5. Insertion of a watermark using quantization of frequency coefficient

4   Experimental Results

Experiments are performed using the digital geographical map of Korea National Geography Institute. Fig. 6 (a) is one part of digital map used and (b) is original watermark.

4.1 Attacks by Elimination of Objects

In this subsection, we test how to extract a watermark against attacks by elimination of objects. Firstly, δ is set to 3 and a watermark is inserted, and we extract watermark after objects elimination attack. Rates of objects elimination are 10, 20, 30, and 50 percent. NC is getting less and less according as rates of objects elimination getting increase. Fig. 7 shows that a watermark is relatively well perceived although the rate of objects elimination is 50 percent. Secondly, rate of objects elimination is fixed to 30 percent, and we get NC with increment of δ from 1 to 5. Fig. 8 shows that NC increases according to increment of δ.

4.2 Attacks by Vertex Moving

Moving of vertices by Gaussian noise is also one kind of attack. This attack adds noises to all vertices. As a result (Fig 9), a watermark is well extracted although a map is gradually distorted by increment of σ.

5   Conclusion

This paper presents the watermarking method for copyright protection of the digital geographical map composed of vector format. The proposed algorithm preserves the accuracy of data, is robust enough against attacks, and consists of the blind watermarking which can extract a watermark without original map. Through experiments, we showed that the proposed method is robust enough against the elimination and modification of vertices.

Acknowledgements. The authors would like to thank the Korea Ministry of Science and Technology and the Korea Science and Engineering Foundation for their support through the ERC program.

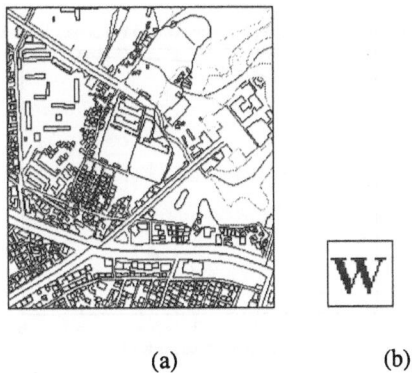

(a)   (b)

Fig. 6. (a) one part of original digital map, (b) original watermark (32*32 binary image)

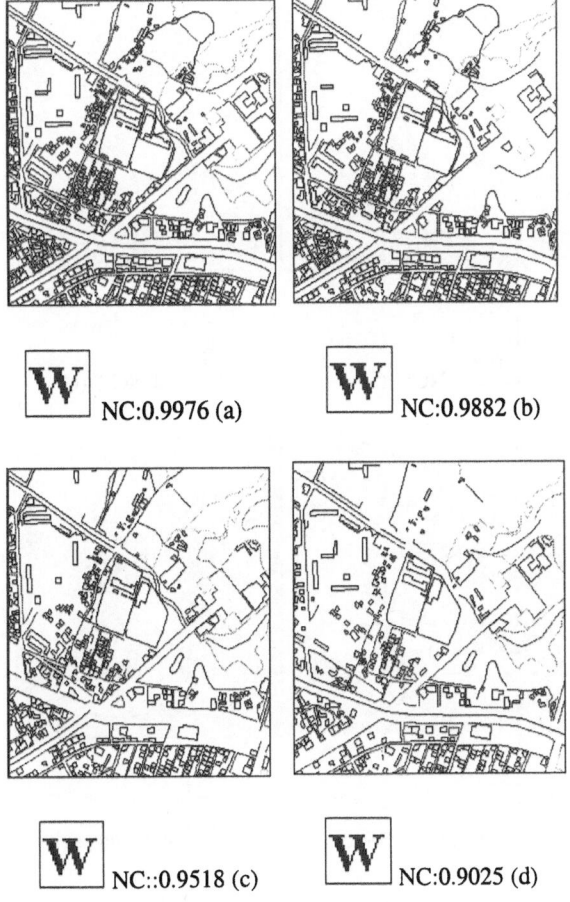

Fig. 7. Extraction of a watermark after attacks by objects elimination: (a)~(d) digital map and extracted watermark when rates of objects elimination are 10, 20, 30, and 50 percent.

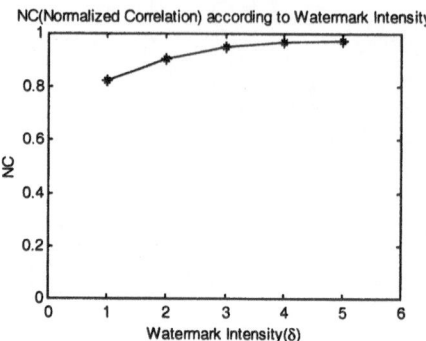

Fig. 8. NC graph according to δ when rate of objects elimination is 30 percent

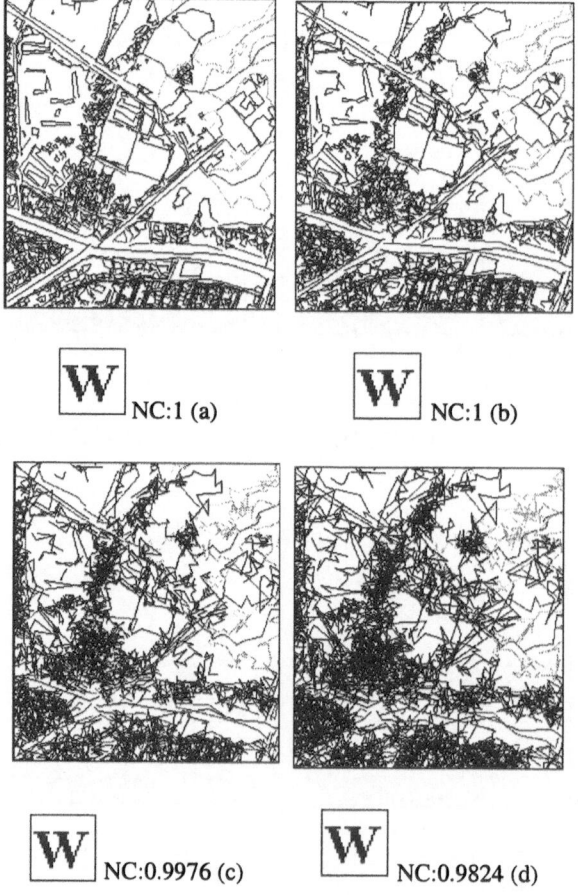

Fig. 9. Extraction of a watermark after attacks by vertex moving: (a)~(d) digital maps with Gaussian noise (σ are 5, 10, 20, and 30) and extracted watermarks from it.

References

[1] Chiou-Ting Hsu and Ja-Ling Wu, "Hidden digital watermarks in images," *IEEE Trans. on Image Processing*, vol. 8 no. 1, pp. 58-68, 1999.

[2] Hwan Il Kang, Kab Il Kim, and Jong-Uk Choe, "A vector watermarking based on the generalized square mask," *In Proc. of the 2001 IEEE International Symposium on Industrial Electronics*, vol. 3, pp. 234-236, 2001.

[3] Ik-pyo Hong, In-taek Kim, and Seung-Soo Han, "A blind watermarking technique using wavelet transform," *In Proc. of the 2001 IEEE International Symposium on Industrial Electronics*, vol. 3, pp. 1946-1950, 2001.

[4] M. Kutter and F.A.P. Petitcolas, "A fair benchmark for image watermarking systems," *In IS&T/SPIE Conf. on Security and Watermarking of Multimedia Contents*, vol. 3657, pp. 226-239, 1999.

[5] M. Sakamoto, Y. Matsumura, and Y. Takashima, "A Scheme of digital watermarking for geographical map data," *Symposium on Cryptography and Information Security*, 2000.

[6] R. Ohbuchi, H. Masuda, and M. Aono, "Watermarking three-dimensional polygonal models through geometric and topological modifications," *IEEE Journal on Selected Areas in Communications*, vol. 16 no. 4, pp. 551-560, 1998.

Watermarking MPEG-4 2D Mesh Animation in Multiresolution Analysis

Shih-Hsuan Yang, Chun-Yen Liao, and Chin-Yun Hsieh

Department of Computer Science and Information Engineering
National Taipei University of Technology
1, Sec.3, Chung-Hsiao E. Rd.
Taipei 106, Taiwan
shyang@ntut.edu.tw

Abstract. Although watermarking techniques have been successfully applied to natural images and videos, little progress is made in the area of graphics animation. In particular, the MPEG-4 dynamic 2D mesh that provides efficient coding for animated graphics data imposes several realistic constraints for watermarking. In this paper, we propose a robust watermarking technique for MPEG-4 2D mesh animation. A multiresolution analysis is applied to locate feature motions of the animated mesh. The watermark signal is inserted based on a spread-spectrum approach by perturbing the extracted feature motions. We have also incorporated a spatial-domain registration technique to restore geometrically transformed mesh data. A variety of attacks, including the affine transformation, smoothing, enhancement and attenuation, and random noise, are used to verify the robustness of the proposed system. Experimental results show that our watermarks can withstand the aforementioned attacks. We also compare the performance of several common integer-to-integer wavelet transforms under the proposed framework.

1 Introduction

In the last decade digital multimedia have proliferated owing to the remarkable growth of PC and Internet. Many content owners, however, are reluctant to offer digital services because their revenues may be jeopardized due to perfect and rapid dissemination of unprotected digital contents. One of the most promising skills proposed for copyright protection is the digital watermarking, which inserts identifiable but usually imperceptible code into the host media. The embedded watermark remains present and detectable when the media are consumed by users, and therefore can be taken for ownership verification.

A digital watermarking system used for copyright protection should satisfy the following requirements [1]:

- Transparency. The perceptual degradation introduced by the watermark should be unnoticeable.
- Robustness. The embedded watermark should remain identifiable unless the attack has rendered the host data useless.

Y.-C. Chen, L.-W. Chang, and C.-T. Hsu (Eds.): PCM 2002, LNCS 2532, pp. 66-73, 2002.

- Security. A watermarking system should be secure in a sense that an unauthorized party is unable to remove the watermark even with full knowledge of the watermarking algorithm.
- Adequate complexity. This issue is critical especially for real-time applications.

Digital watermarking has been extensively developed for images, videos, and audios, either in the original domain or in the transform domain. Among the transformations widely adopted in the literature are the DCT (discrete cosine transform) and the DWT (discrete wavelet transform). Besides the natural image and video data, the synthetic graphics data in terms of the geometric model find many important applications. Two basic attributes, geometry and topology, are associated with a geometric model. In addition to its different constituent components, watermarking of graphics data is more intricate since the perceptual model in this domain is little understood. The pioneering work done by Ohbuchi *et al.* [2] proposes to embed watermarks on geometric or topological primitives including triangle similarity quadruple, tetrahedral volume ratio, and mesh density pattern. Benedens [3] develops a robust watermarking scheme where the watermark is cast on the surface normal distribution of a polygon model. Praun *et al.* [4] develop a general spread-spectrum robust mesh watermarking scheme where the watermark is superimposed upon the original mesh by a set of surface basis functions. In [5], a spectral analysis that derives from the eigen-property of the Kirchhoff matrix is employed for watermarking 3D polygonal meshes. Yin *et al.* [6] propose to use the Burt-Adelson pyramid to obtain the multiresolution representation of a mesh and embed the watermark information in the coefficients of a suitable scale. All the above techniques are performed on a single frame of polygon models and may not be adequate to be directly applied to animated graphics. Kim *el al.* [7] propose a watermarking scheme for the articulated figure, in which the position, orientation, and a rigid transformation of a body segment are specified. They develop a temporal-domain multiresolution framework and insert the watermark by perturbing large detail coefficients. The proposed method is robust against common signal processing and time warping.

In contrast of the former MPEG-1 and MPEG-2 standards that focuses on efficient compression of frame-based natural audio-visual data, the emerging MPEG-4 standard encompasses the synthetic media within an object-based framework [8]. For example, an MEPG-4 dynamic 2D mesh uses a temporal sequence of 2D triangular meshes to tessellate a 2D visual object plane into triangular patches. The dynamic 2D mesh can be used to create 2D animations by mapping texture onto successive meshes. One such example is shown in Fig. 1, in which the frame is composed of three different objects, namely the fish mesh, the fish texture, and the 'MPEG-4' banner.

In this paper, we purpose a robust watermark algorithm for MPEG-4 2D mesh animation. In addition to the possible wide adoption of MPEG-4, the mesh object is chosen because it is regarded as the "lowest common denominator" of surface representations [4]. The proposed approach is most similar to Kim's method [7] since both employ a temporal-domain multiresolution analysis. Instead of focusing on the articulated figure, however, we consider the general 2D triangular mesh animation as the watermarking target and consequently have different embedding and detection procedures. A pyramidal wavelet transform is taken for decomposing the mesh data into a coarse base signal and the detail motion signals. We embed a binary watermark sequence by modifying the motion signals of a proper scale and test the algorithm by a variety of possible attacks. Our watermarking approach is private in the sense that the original mesh is required for watermark extraction. The ownership of the 2D mesh in dispute is verified based on a similarity test of the extracted pattern and the embedded watermark. Similar to other wavelet-based systems, the choice of wavelet filter bases generally affects the system's performance. We evaluate a number of common wavelet bases under the same multiresolution watermarking framework.

Fig. 1. A frame of an MPEG-4 animated 2D mesh.

The rest of the paper is organized as follows. In section 2, we introduce the multiresolution analysis required for MPEG-4 2D mesh animation. Section 3 addresses the proposed temporal-domain watermarking approach. Simulation results are presented next, followed by the conclusion.

2   Multiresolution Analysis for MPEG-4 2D Mesh Animation

2.1   MPEG-4 Dynamic 2D Mesh Coding

A MPEG-4 dynamic 2D mesh consists of a temporal sequence of 2D triangular meshes, called the mesh object planes (MOPs). Each MOP in a sequence has the same topology with time-varying node point locations. The geometry of the first MOP in a sequence is intra-coded, followed by predictive-coded MOPs where only the motion vectors of the node points with respect to the previous MOP are recorded. Mesh node point locations and motion vectors are coded with half pixel accuracy. The triangles and nodes for the initial intra-coded MOP are traversed in a breath-first order that remains unchanged for the subsequent predictive-coded MOPs.

New challenges arise for developing efficient watermarking schemes of the MPEG-4 2D mesh animation due to the following factors:

1. Animation nature

   Most of the previous efforts on polygon watermarking have been focused on single frames, except for the Kim's work. For an animated 2D mesh composed of a group of tightly related MOPs, applying independent watermarking on each MOP is awkward and inefficient.

2. Planar constraint

A 2D model can be regarded as a reduction of a 3D model. Many 3D watermarking techniques employ some features pertinent only for 3D models (such as the surface normals) and therefore cannot be applied to the degenerate 2D case.

3. Quantization effect

The node point locations in an MPEG-4 dynamic 2D mesh are represented with half pixel accuracy while most of the previous work assumes unrestricted precision. The inherent quantization error makes the bulk of known watermarking schemes less effective.

2.2 Temporal-Domain Wavelet Transform

A temporal-domain multiresolution analysis for the MPEG-4 dynamic 2D mesh proceeds as follows. Consider a 2D mesh composed of m MOPs (assuming that m is a power of 2 for simplicity) and having n node points in each MOP. The m node point locations that correspond to the same vertex (i.e., those with the same coding order in MOPs) are gathered, which in turn produce a temporal sequence of 2D vectors denoted as $Z_j(.)$, $j = 1, 2, ..., n$. A p-level pyramidal DWT is performed on each $Z_j(.)$ to generate its $(p + 1)$ subbands. For example, taking 3-level DWT for a sequence of 16 MOPs results in a H1 subband (lowest scale) of 8 frames, a H2 subband of 4 frames, and H3 and L3 subbands (highest scale) of 2 frames. The transformed sequences are arranged in the subband order of L-p, H-p, H-(p-1),..., H1. The L-p subband stands for the base signal while the remaining subbands stand for the motion details at various scales. The high-scale (low-frequency) components reveal the long-term characteristics of a dynamic 2D mesh.

2.3 Choice of Wavelet Filters

The choice of wavelet filter banks generally affects the performance of a transform-based watermarking system. Besides the requirements such as good time-frequency localization, regularity, and orthogonality (or biorthogonality), the linear phase (symmetry) constraint is often imposed to avoid coefficient expansion. As a consequence, the linear-phase biorthogonal wavelets in conjunction with symmetric extensions are widely used in practice. Furthermore, linear-phase biorthogonal wavelet transforms can be efficiently implemented in the lifting framework [9]. In this paper, we consider the reversible integer-to-integer filters given in [10] for performance evaluation. Additional results for Lazy and Haar filters are also included for purposes of comparison.

3 Watermarking Process

3.1 Watermark Embedding

A p-level multiresolution analysis is first performed. Among all the wavelet subbands, we decide to embed the watermark in the highest-scale detail subband, i.e., the H-p subband. The decision is made based on the following observations. Embedding a watermark in the base signal changes the average value and consequently usually results in visible artifacts. On the other hand, a watermark embedded in the low-scale motion details is more vulnerable to attacks since the coefficients in these subbands represent the local and fine characteristics and are usually smaller. In the latter experiments, we vary the value of p to clarify this point. A secret key is used to generate the watermark $\mathbf{w} = \{w(i), i = 1, 2, \ldots, k\}$, a binary M-sequence of length k bits. M-sequences are selected owing to their good correlation properties.

We select k wavelet coefficients with sufficiently large magnitude from the H-p subband. The watermark bit is embedded as follows. Depending on $w(i)$ equal to 1 or 0, we increase or decrease the magnitude of the corresponding wavelet coefficient. To avoid visible degradation, modification of a pre-determined strength is made upon the wavelet coefficient by changing its horizontal or vertical component whichever has a larger magnitude. The keys used to generating the watermark and watermarking locations along with the original mesh are confidentially stored for future watermark verification.

3.2 Mesh Registration

It has been observed that geometric transformations, though hardly affect visual quality, could defeat many watermarking schemes by breaking the synchronization between the watermarked and original data. To circumvent this problem, we employ a mesh registration technique [11] to restore the geometrically transformed data. We assume that the test mesh undergoes an affine transformation $T:(x, y) \rightarrow (x', y')$ specified by the following linear transformation in homogeneous coordinates

$$\begin{bmatrix} x' \\ y' \\ 1 \end{bmatrix} = \begin{bmatrix} \gamma\cos\alpha & -\gamma\sin\alpha & t_x \\ \gamma\sin\alpha & \gamma\cos\alpha & t_y \\ 0 & 0 & 1 \end{bmatrix} \begin{bmatrix} x \\ y \\ 1 \end{bmatrix} \tag{1}$$

where γ is the scaling factor, α is the rotation angle, and (t_x, t_y) is the displacement vector. The four parameters γ, α, and (t_x, t_y) are solved from the least-squares approximation of the mapping from the original unwatermarked mesh to the test mesh.

3.3 Watermark Extraction and Verification

After performing mesh registration, the mesh under suspicion takes the DWT to restore the wavelet coefficients. Each watermark bit is extracted by hard decision, that is, a bit is declared to be 1 (or 0) when the corresponding embedding component is larger or no larger (in magnitude) than that in the original mesh. Collecting all the extracted k bits $\mathbf{v}$, we measure the similarity between $\mathbf{v}$ and the original watermark signal $\mathbf{w}$ by the bit error rate (BER), which is calculated as

$$\text{BER} = \frac{|v_i : v_i \neq w_i|}{k} \qquad (2)$$

where the numerator denotes the number of bits that $\mathbf{v}$ and $\mathbf{w}$ differ.

4 Simulation Results

The proposed system is evaluated against a variety of attacks:
- Affine transformation, rotation, scaling, translation, and a combination of the above
- Temporal smoothing by a low-pass filter with impulse response {1/4, 1/2, 1/4}.
- Enhancement and attenuation by modifying the two lowest-scale subbands by a factor of 1.5 and 0.6, respectively.
- Random noise. 20% of the node points are added with noise with strength equal to 1 pixel or 2 pixels. We will denote the noise strength by N, and so $N = 1$ or $N = 2$. Noise strength greater than 2 will introduce severe visual degradation for mesh animation. One of the attacked meshes is shown in Fig. 2(c).

Define the motion vector $(s^i_{j,x}, s^i_{j,y})$ as

$$(s^i_{j,x}, s^i_{j,y}) = (p^{i+1}_{j,x} - p^i_{j,x}, p^{i+1}_{j,y} - p^i_{j,y}) \qquad (3)$$

where $(p^i_{j,x}, p^i_{j,y})$ represents the coordinate of node point j in the ith MOP. The distortion between two mesh sequences can be calculated by the mean square motion difference (MSMD) given by

$$\text{MSMD} = \frac{1}{n(m-1)} \sum_{i=1}^{m-1} \sum_{j=1}^{n} \left[(s^i_{j,x} - t^i_{j,x})^2 + (s^i_{j,y} - t^i_{j,y})^2 \right] \qquad (4)$$

where $(s^i_{j,x}, s^i_{j,y})$ and $(t^i_{j,x}, t^i_{j,y})$ denote the motion vectors of the two dynamic meshes, m is the number of MOPs, and n is the number of node points each MOP contains.

The evaluation is conducted for "Mesh12", an MPEG-4 conformance testing bitstream for 2D mesh animation. We choose consecutive 128 MOPs from the video where there are 120 node points and 187 triangles on each MOP. The 28th MOP of "Mesh12" is shown in Fig 2(a). The embedded watermark is 127 bits long, and is evenly distributed on the frames of the H-p subband for p-level decomposition. In order to examine the effects of embedding scales and wavelet filters, we test all the filters for decomposition level $p = 2$, 4, and 6. For fair comparison, we adjust the watermark strength to make the watermarked mesh have approximately the same MSMD (= 0.01). Note that the introduced watermark is unnoticeable, as is shown in Fig. 2(b).

The proposed scheme is in general very robust against affine transformation, temporal smoothing, and enhancement and attenuation, where almost all tests yield a zero BER. The BER results for random noise are given in Table 1 and Table 2, where a ten-time average is computed. The resulting MSMD is 0.47 and 1.86 for $N = 1$ and $N = 2$, respectively. Embedding in a higher scale (i.e., a larger p) offers better robustness against random noise. Since the random noise can be regarded as a short-term jamming, a higher-scale watermark persists longer and is thus more resilient. Among all the examined wavelet filters, the trivial Lazy wavelet is especially bad in performance for $N = 2$ whereas all the others make only minor differences.

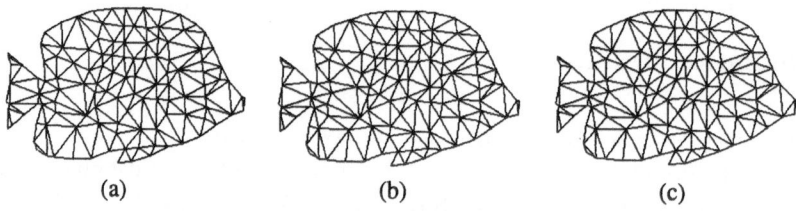

(a)   (b)   (c)

Fig. 2. (a) Original mesh; (b) watermarked mesh (Haar wavelet, $p = 6$); (c) attacked by 20% random noise with strength = 2.

Table 1. BER results for random-noise attacks with $N = 1$

	5/3	5/11C	5/11A	9/7F	9/7M	13/7T	13/7T	Lazy	Haar
$p=2$	0.0205	0.0480	0.0520	0.0449	0.0583	0.0535	0.0417	0.0150	0.0315
$p=4$	$2.36_E\text{-}3$	$3.15_E\text{-}3$	$7.87_E\text{-}4$	0	0	$7.87_E\text{-}4$	0	$3.94_E\text{-}3$	0
$p=6$	0	0	0	0	0	0	0	0	0

Table 2. BER results for random-noise attacks with $N = 2$

	5/3	5/11C	5/11A	9/7F	9/7M	13/7T	13/7T	Lazy	Haar
$p=2$	0.149	0.153	0.119	0.146	0.161	0.148	0.159	0.101	0.115
$p=4$	0.0362	0.0693	0.0417	0.0110	0.0394	0.0142	0.0094	0.119	0.0142
$p=6$	0	0	0	0	0	0	0	0.0756	0

5   Conclusion

In this paper we have realized a robust digital watermarking scheme for MPEG-4 2D mesh animation. We exploit the multiresolution capability of wavelet transform to locate the feature motions of an animated mesh. By embedding the watermark in the salient motion signals within a selected subband, the proposed scheme with spatial-domain registration demonstrates high robustness against a variety of attacks. We have evaluated our system under different selection of embedding scales and wavelet filters. Experimental results show that embedding in a higher scale using nontrivial wavelet transforms gives good performance.

Acknowledgement. This work is supported by the National Science Council, R. O. China, under the contract number NSC 90-2213-E-027-012.

References

1. I. J. Cox, M. L. Miller, and A. J. Bloom, Digital Watermarking, Morgan Kaufmann Publishers, 2002.
2. R. Ohbuchi, H. Masuda and M. Aono, "Watermarking three dimensional polygonal models through geometry and topological modifications," IEEE J. Select. Areas Commun., vol. 16, no. 4, pp. 551-560, May 1998.
3. O. Benedens, "Geometry-based watermarking of 3D models", IEEE Computer Graphics and Applications, vol. 19, no. 1, pp. 46-55, Jan./Feb. 1999.
4. E. Praun, H. Hoppe, and A. Finkelstein, "Robust mesh watermarking," In Computer Graphics (SIGGRAPH'99 Proceedings), pp. 49-56, Aug. 1999.
5. R. Ohbuchi, S. Takahashi, T. Miyazawa, and A. Mukaiyama, "Watermarking 3D polygonal meshes in the mesh spectral domain," Graphics Interface 2001, pp. 9-17, Canada, June 2001.
6. K. Yin, Z. Pan, J. Shi, and D. Zhang, "Robust mesh watermarking based on multiresolution processing," Computers and Graphics, vol. 25, pp. 409-420, 2001.
7. T.-H. Kim, J. Lee, and S. Y. Shin, "Robust motion watermarking based on multiresolution analysis", EUROGRAPHICS 2000, vol. 19, no. 3, pp. 189-198, 2000.
8. ISO/IEC 14496-2, Coding of Audio-Visual Objects: Visual.
9. I. Daubechies and W. Sweldens, "Factoring wavelet transforms into lifting steps," J. Fourier Anal. Appl., vol. 4, no. 3, pp. 247-269, 1998.
10. M. D. Adams and F. Kossentini, "Reversible integer-to-integer wavelet transforms for image compression: performance and analysis," IEEE Trans. Image Processing, vol. 9, no. 6, pp. 1010-1024, June 2000.
11. Y. Chen and G. Medioni, "Object modeling by registration of multiple range images," Image and Vision Computing, vol. 10, pp. 145-155, Apr. 1992

Rotation, Scaling, and Translation Resilient Image Watermarking with Side Information at Encoder

Miin-Luen Day [1,3], I.-Chang Jou[2], and Suh-Yin Lee[1]

[1] Department of Computer Science and Information Engineering, National Chiao-Tung University, Hsin-Chu, Taiwan, R.O.C.
sylee@csie.nctu.edu.tw

[2] Department of Computer and Communication Engineering, National Kaohsiung First University of Science and Technology, Kaohsiung, Taiwan, R.O.C.
icjou@ccms.nkfu.edu.tw

[3] Telecommunication Laboratory, Chunghwa Telecom Co., Chung-Li, Taiwan, R.O.C.
day@cht.com.tw

Abstract. We propose a rotation, scaling and translation (RST) resilient blind image watermarking technique by using Fourier-Mellin transform and informed coding, where watermark detection does not require the existence of the original image. Although the Fourier-Mellin invariant domain is recognized to be nearly RST invariant, which supposedly would make it an ideal space for watermark embedding, however the inverse Log-Polar map (ILPM) could severely destroy the embedded watermark. Therefore a very strong watermark has to be employed to survive the self-destruction process from ILPM, but in turn this leads to a poorly watermarked image. To overcome this problem we introduce the concept of informed coding by embedding a slightly weaker watermark into the image so that both transparency and robustness can be achieved. Experimental results demonstrate that the resulting watermark is robust to a variety of image processing attacks.

1 Introduction

Many watermarking algorithms are good at resisting removal attacks, and more and more algorithms are devoted to combating geometric attacks. This is due to the fact that, attacks such as print-and-scan-process for images and the attacks of the aspect-ratio-changes (for example, changing between 16: 9 (wide-screen and HDTV) and 4:3 (NTSC and PAL) for different movie playing format) will lead to the rotation, scaling and translation problems. Watermarking resisting such geometric attacks is needed for such practical applications.

Inspired by the information theoretic result of Costa's scheme [1], some researchers improve the fidelity/robustness of their watermarking algorithms while some others

Y.-C. Chen, L.-W. Chang, and C.-T. Hsu (Eds.): PCM 2002, LNCS 2532, pp. 74-81, 2002.

derive the optimum watermark capacity bound. Miller [2] proposes an informed coding for correlation-based watermarking application by coding each message with several distinct codes, termed dirty-paper codes. This improves the picture quality by increasing the number of watermark patterns to represent each message. In [3], Lu et al., try to estimate the original image and watermark by using independent component analysis (ICA)-based sparse code shrinkage, in which the side information at the decoder is used. The derived algorithm is resilient to denoising and remodulation attack as well as copy attack. In [4], Tseng et al., propose to watermark on a principal component analysis (PCA)-trained robust watermark space, in which the side information of estimated forged images of the host signal is utilized. By using their optimized second order statistics technique, algorithms such as Cox's, could be significantly enhanced.

2 Proposed Algorithm

In the embedding process (Fig. 1(a)), the original image first goes through Fourier transform, the magnitudes of the coefficients within a specified circular area (whose radius is no more than half the image row size) of the image are then re-sampled in Log-Polar coordinates; once again Fourier transform is applied on the re-sampled coordinates to derive RST invariant Fourier magnitude. The robust watermark chosen from informed coding stage is then embedded into the RST invariant Fourier magnitude. The watermarked image could then be obtained by inversing the transforms of the above processes. In the detection process (Fig. 1(b)), the attacked image first goes through Fourier transform, the magnitudes of the coefficients are then re-sampled in Log-Polar coordinates and once again Fourier transform is applied on the re-sampled coordinates to derive RST invariant Fourier magnitude. Once the feature vector from the middle frequency band of this RST invariant domain is selected, we then compute the correlation coefficients taken between the feature vector and each of N_w predefined reference watermarks. Based on the theory of hypotheses testing, the watermark is present if the resulting maximum correlation value computed is greater than a specific threshold. Otherwise the watermark is absent. The proposed scheme is different from those of [5] and [6]. In [5] only the watermark itself is passing through the RST invariant domain, while [6] extracts features along the log-radius axis of the Log-Polar mapped Fourier spectrum instead of processing in the RST invariant domain. The design goal of our scheme is to embed watermark directly on the geometric invariant Fourier-Mellin domain. No additional features need to be extracted to form a geometric invariant embedding space. Moreover, by informed watermark coding, our scheme could embed a weak watermark signal (meaning one that needs only small perturbations with the host signal) and detect a slightly weaker watermark under the ILPM and the inverse Fourier transform.

2.1 Watermark Generation

The watermark $W = \{x_1, x_2, ..., x_M\}$ consists of a pseudo-random sequence of M real numbers drawn from independent identically normal distributions and determined by a secret key. There are totally N_w watermarks generated.

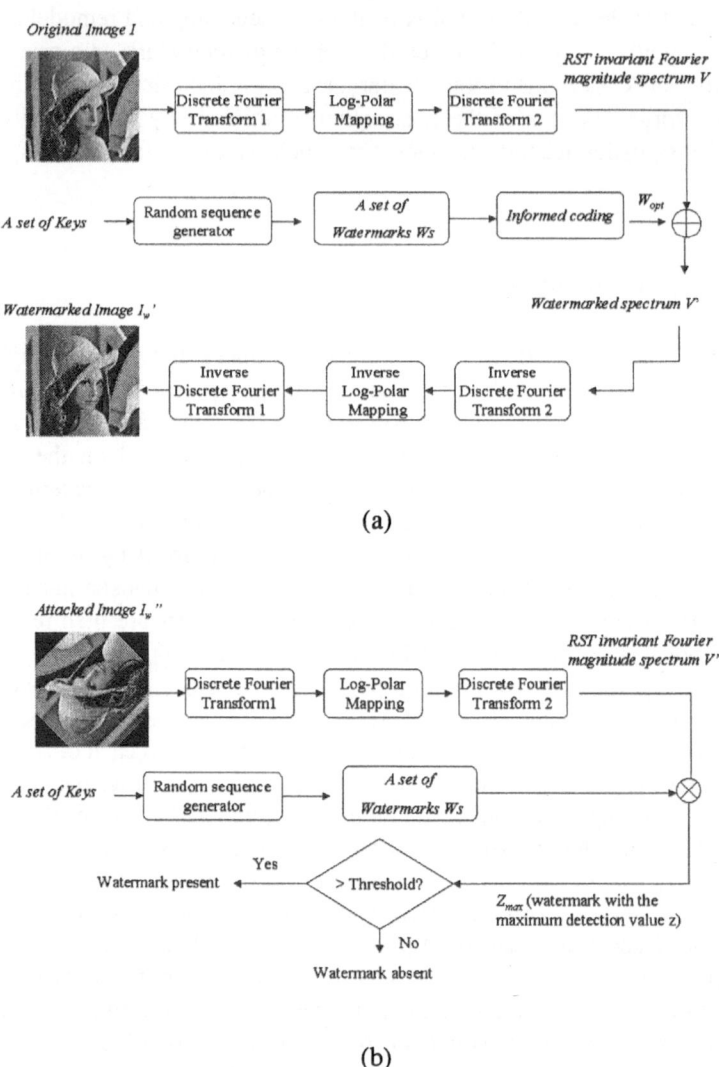

Fig. 1. (a) The flow of proposed watermark embedding scheme, (b) The flow of proposed watermark detection scheme.

2.2 Watermark Embedding

The embedding algorithm consists of the following steps:

1) Take the magnitude of the DFT coefficients of the original image I of size N by N.

2) Perform the Log-Polar mapping of the log magnitude obtained from step (1). Note that the maximal radius ρ is half of the image row size, i.e., $N/2$.

3) Sample uniformly along the log scale and θ axis to obtain a Log-Polar sampled spectrum image of size N_ρ by N_θ.

4) Take the magnitude of the DFT coefficients of these samples. Select M coefficients residing in the middle frequency band to form feature vector V.

5) Informed coding: select the local optimal watermark pattern from a small range of candidate watermark patterns (say $N_w = 1000$). Embed each W_i into V using Eq. (1). Then compute the correlation of each V_i' with each corresponding W_i. Identify the one, say W_{opt}, which has the local optimal correlation among these N_w computed correlation values.

$$V_i' = V(1 + \alpha W_i) ,\qquad\qquad (1)$$

where $i = 1,\dots,N_w$ and α is embedding strength.

6) Embed the selected W_{opt} obtained into the feature vector V using Eq. (2).

$$V' = V(1 + \alpha W_{opt}) .\qquad\qquad (2)$$

7) Take the inverse DFT.

8) Take ILPM. Note that as in step (2) the maximal radius ρ is $N/2$. Some spectrum pixels are not inversely mapped, and these missed pixels are substituted by the original corresponding spectrum pixels obtained in step (1).

9) Take the inverse DFT to get watermarked image I_w'.

2.3 Watermark Detection

The detection algorithm consists of the following steps:

1) Take the magnitudes of the DFT coefficients of the investigated image I_w'' (being attacked from I_w') of size N by N.

2) Perform the Log-Polar mapping of the log magnitude obtained from step (1). Note that the maximal radius ρ is half of the image row size, i.e., $N/2$.

3) Sample uniformly along the log scale and θ axis to obtain a Log-Polar sampled spectrum image of size N_ρ by N_θ.

4) Take the magnitude of the DFT coefficients of these samples. Select M coefficients residing in the middle frequency band to form feature vector V''.

5) Compute the correlation coefficients z_i taken between the feature vector, V'', and each of N_w predefined reference watermarks, $W_1, W_2,..,W_{Nw}$.

$$z_i = \frac{W_i \cdot V''}{M}, \qquad (3)$$

where $i = 1,...,N_w$.

6) The watermark is present if the resulting maximum correlation value (called z_{max}) computed is greater than a specific threshold. Otherwise the watermark is absent.

3 Experimental Results

To evaluate the effectiveness of the proposed method, four standard test images of size 512 x 512 including "Lena", "Barbara", "Goldhill" and "Boat" are used as host signals to embed watermark information. The results used in these experiments are obtained by using parameters $N_\rho = 512, N_\theta = 512, Nw = 1000, M = 45000$ and $\alpha = 0.4$. The watermark strength α determines the tradeoff between the robustness and distortion. Main issues regarding performance evaluation of the proposed method are discussed in the following.

3.1 Fidelity

We observe that for "Lena", the PSNR of reconstructed image through the two rounds of DFT transform is 56.00 dB, while the PSNR of reconstructed image through the two rounds of DFT transform with additional LPM in between is 36.00 dB. As the PSNR of watermarked image through the two rounds of DFT transform with LPM is 34.91 dB, its quality loss of 1.09 dB is rather insignificant compared to the quality loss of 20.00 dB through LPM. Note that the PSNR quality of watermarked image is still at the acceptable quality standard (near 35.00 dB).

3.2 Probability of False Positive

To test the probability of false positive, the images are obtained by manipulating each of the four tested standard images with combinations of rotation ($0°$ to $360°$ with step-size $18°$), scaling (0.8 to 1.2 with step-size 0.5) and translation (0 to 15 with step-size 5) to generate 720 images each and there are 2880 in total. For each of these 2880 watermarked images, the peak correlation value of the mage correlated with 1,000 watermarks is obtained and collected. Yet for original un-watermarked images, all the 2880 x 1000 correlation values for all these 2880 images correlated with 1,000 watermarks are collected.

3.3 Robustness

The correlation ratios of embedded "Lena" under these various crack types including some geometric distorted ones (Table 1.) are summarized in Fig. 2. Note that there is no false alarm reported for all these various crack types by setting threshold $\tau = 4.5$. More extensive tests on the robustness for geometric attacks are again evaluated using the abovementioned 4 sets of 720 images. The probability of recognition rate (P_D) with/without local optimal watermark selection and false positive error detection probability (P_F) for various thresholds are shown in Fig. 3. The performance of proposed invariant watermarking with informed coding is far better than that without using informed coding.

Table 1. The tested crack types

	Crack types
0~5	Translation (50, 50), (100, 100), (150, 150), (200, 200), (75, 150), (150, 75)
6~12	Rotation 45°, 90°, 170°, 185°, 250°, 290°, 345°
13~21	Scale 1.05, 1.10, 1.20, 1.25, 0.90, 0.80, 0.70, 0.60, 0.50
22	Rotation 2° and scaling to size 512 x 512 (stirmark3.1 [7])
23	Rotation 5° and scaling to size 512 x 512 (stirmark3.1)
24	Scale 1.1 and Rotation 45°
25	Scale 1.1 and Rotation 190°
26	Translation (30, 30), Scale 1.1 and Rotation 30°
27	Translation (20, 20), Scale 0.9 and Rotation 45°
28	Cropping 10% and scaling to size 512 x 512 (stirmark3.1)
29	Cropping 5% and scaling to size 512 x 512 (stirmark3.1)
30	Cropping 1% and scaling to size 512 x 512 (stirmark3.1)
31	1_row_1_col removal and scaling to size 512 x 512 (stirmark3.1)
32	1_row_5_col removal and scaling to size 512 x 512 (stirmark3.1)
33	5_row_1_col removal and scaling to size 512 x 512 (stirmark3.1)
34	FMLR (stirmark3.1)
35~41	JPEG Quality factor Q(%) = 30~90 (stirmark3.1)
42~44	JPEG-2000 0.25~1.00 bpp
45	Gaussian filtering 3x3 (stirmark3.1)
46	Sharpening 3x3 (stirmark3.1)
47~49	Median filtering 2x2, 3x3, 4x4 (stirmark3.1)
50~51	Random noise adding 2%, 4%
52~53	Uniform noise adding 10%, 15%
54	Histogram equalization
55	Hybrid

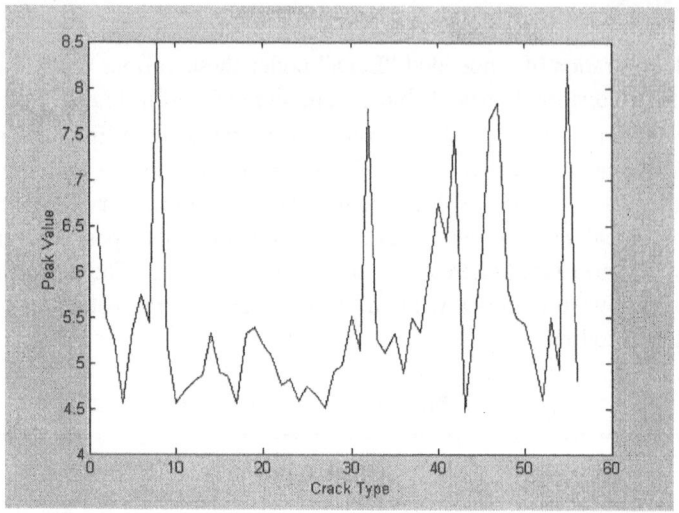

Fig. 2. Peak correlation values of various crack types as shown in TABLE 1 (All are above the threshold $\tau = 4.5$. Note that for "Lena" image, there is no false alarm reported for all the tested 720 images by setting threshold $\tau = 4.5$).

4   Conclusion

We propose in this paper a RST resilient image watermarking technique using Fourier-Mellin transform and informed coding of watermark message. Since the interpolation distortions by LPM /ILPM increase with larger radius, only the specified circular area (whose radius is no more than half the image row size) of the image are LPM transformed, the other portions of the image remain unchanged and thus the transparency of the watermarked image increases. Since both of the ILPM and the inverse Fourier transform could severely destroy the embedded watermark as shown in the simulation experiments, the survived watermark signal embedded in the watermarked host signal becomes pretty small. By employing the informed coding to select a local optimal watermark for embedding, our proposed scheme provides a very good solution to overcome the shortcomings of using heavy watermark in the Fourier-Mellin invariant domain and at the same time reliably detects the survived weak watermark signal.

Acknowledgement. This work was supported in part by the National Science Council under grant 90-2213-E-327-006.

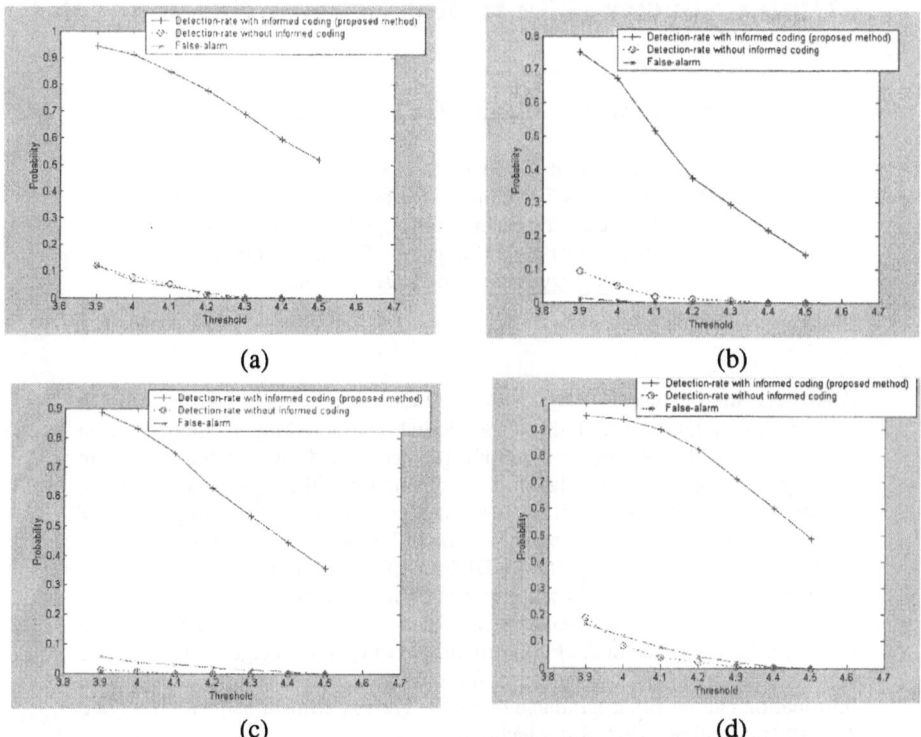

Fig. 3. The comparison of detection probability with/without informed coding and false positive error detection. (a) Lena, (b) Barbara, (c) Goldhill, (d) Boat.

References

1. Max H. M. Costa, Writing on dirty paper, IEEE Transactions on Information Theory (May 1983) 439-431.
2. Matthew L. Miller, Watermarking with dirty-paper codes, in IEEE Int. Conf. Image Processing (ICIP'01), October 2001.
3. Chun-Shien Lu, Hong-Yuan Mark Liao and Martin Kutter, Denoising and copy attack resilient watermarking by exploiting prior knowledge at decoder, IEEE Transactions on Image Processing (March 2002) 280-292.
4. Jengan Tzeng, Wen-Liang Hwang and I-Liang Chern, Enhancing image watermarking methods with/without reference images by optimization on second order statistics, IEEE Transactions on Image Processing (July 2002) 771-782.
5. J. J. K. O'Ruanaidh and T.Pun, Rotation, scale and translation invariant spread spectrum digital image watermarking, Signal Processing 66 (May 1998) 303-317.
6. C.Y. Lin et al., Rotation, scale, and translation resilient watermarking for images, IEEE Transactions on Image Processing (May 2001) 767-782.
7. Fabien A.P. Petitcolas, Ross J. Anderson, Weakness of copyright marking systems, Multimedia and Security Workshop at ACM Multimedia '98. Bristol, U.K., September 1998.

A High Capacity Data Hiding Scheme Based on DFT

Yaxiao Song[1,2], Minghao Cui[1], and Hongxun Yao[1]

[1] Department of Computer Science and Engineering
Harbin Institute of Technology, Harbin 150001, P. R. China
[2] Department of Computer Science, School of Computing
National University of Singapore, Singapore 119260
songyaxiao@hotmail.com

Abstract. In the recent years, with the rapid development of the network multimedia systems, data hiding and digital watermarking techniques have become a feasible solution to copyright protection and data authentication. In this paper, we present a new data hiding scheme for still images. The technique is based on embedding information in the transform domain; the DFT coefficients of the original image are modified to embed information bits. Taking the symmetric property of DFT coefficients into consideration, our scheme makes a tradeoff between imperceptibility and embedding capacity, and achieves a higher data embedding rate than most of the current transform domain embedding methods. Furthermore, not only gray images but also color ones can be used as cover images for covert communications. The hidden information can be either an image or a text. The experiment result shows good performance and prospect of our technique.

1 Introduction

Several data hiding and watermarking methods have been presented in the literature. Confined to methods based on DFT domain, some of them embed information in the magnitude of DFT coefficients [1][2][3], and others in the phase of DFT [4].

The data hiding technique in [1] hides information in the DFT domain by merely modifying the transform coefficient magnitudes. The authors mention that the data embedding rate can reach 1 bit per coefficient. Within our knowledge, most of the current data embedding scheme in transform domain cannot achieve that embedding capacity. In this paper, we propose a new scheme that the embedding capacity is high.

The Discrete Fourier Transform is defined as follows:

$$F(u,v) = \sum_{x=0}^{N_1-1}\sum_{y=0}^{N_2-1} f(x,y)\exp[-2j\pi(\frac{ux}{N_1}+\frac{vy}{N_2})] \tag{1}$$

where $u = 0,1,2,...,N_1 -1$, $v = 0,1,2,...,N_2 -1$, and $N_1 \times N_2$ is the size of the original image.

The inverse Discrete Fourier Transform is

Y.-C. Chen, L.-W. Chang, and C.-T. Hsu (Eds.): PCM 2002, LNCS 2532, pp. 82-88, 2002.

$$f(x, y) = \frac{1}{N_1 N_2} \sum_{u=0}^{N_1-1} \sum_{v=0}^{N_2-1} F(u, v) \exp[j2\pi(\frac{ux}{N_1} + \frac{vy}{N_2})] \tag{2}$$

where $x = 0,1,2,...,N_1 - 1$ and $y = 0,1,2,...,N_2 - 1$.

The 2-D DFT coefficients of a real image are generally complex numbers. As for a matrix of size $N_1 \times N_2$, if both N_1 and N_2 are even, then out of the $N_1 N_2$ DFT coefficients, 4 are real, which are located respectively at $(0,0)$, $(0, \frac{N_2}{2})$, $(\frac{N_1}{2},0)$, and $(\frac{N_1}{2}, \frac{N_2}{2})$, and the others are all complex valued. Similarly, if both N_1 and N_2 are odd, then only one coefficient, $F(0,0)$ is real. If exactly one of N_1 and N_2 is odd, and the other is odd, then there will be 2 real valued DFT coefficients.

Also we should notify the importance of the symmetry of the complex valued DFT coefficients.

$$F(u,v) = F^*(N_1 - u, N_2 - v) \tag{3}$$

To keep the result of the inverse DFT real, when we make changes to the DFT coefficients we have to take the symmetric property into consideration [1]. Altuki and Mersereau [1], and Mahalingam Ramkumar et al [2] independently propose data embedding method using the magnitude coefficients. To keep the inverse DFT result real, the positive symmetry of the magnitude must be kept, i.e.

$$M(u,v) = M(N_1 - u, N_2 - v) \tag{4}$$

where $M(u,v)$ denotes the magnitude of the real and imaginary parts of the (u,v)-th DFT coefficient.

In this way, in order to ensure the symmetry, achieving a data embedding rate of 1 bit per coefficient is impossible. Because only slightly more than half of the $N_1 \times N_2$ coefficients, including several real valued ones (no more than 4) and a half of the complex valued ones, have unique magnitude. That is, only about half of the coefficients can be used to embed data. In anther word, to hide information by quantizing the magnitude of DFT, we can not achieve a data embedding rate higher than 1 bit per 2 coefficients.

Embedding data into the magnitude of DFT coefficients instead of the phase relies on the fact that the phase is much more important than the magnitude [5]. It can be shown by a contrast experiment. See Fig. 1. Here we take the famous "LENNA" 256×256 gray image as an example.

Fig.1 (a) shows the original "LENNA". If we ignore the phase (set the phases of the complex valued coefficients to zero), and use merely the magnitude to reconstruct the original image, we can hardly see any similarity between the received result and the original one. See Fig.1 (b). On the contrary, setting the magnitude to a constant, and keeping their corresponding phases intact, we can still recognize the outline of the figures in the original image. See Fig.1 (c)

(a)

(b)   (c)

Fig. 1. Comparison experiment

Embedding data in the magnitude coefficients ensures high imperceptibility of the data hiding technique. However, in some cases, large data embedding capacity of the data hiding technique is more desired and important. Thus to make a tradeoff between capacity and imperceptibility, we propose a new approach for data hiding based on hundreds of trials and experiments, aiming at higher data embedding rate as well as high security.

Different from the traditional watermarking and data hiding techniques, we embed the data directly in the real and imaginary parts of the DFT coefficients. Section 2 and Section 3 respectively describe our data embedding and extracting scheme. In Section 4, we show an example of our proposed technique. And in Section 5, we give the conclusion and our focus of the future work.

2   Embedding Scheme

In this section, we describe our data embedding system in detail. To increase the security of this system, we keep a secret key for both the encoder and the decoder. Before embedding any information into the original image (the host), we use this secret key to permute the pixels locations of the host.

Let $f(n_1,n_2)$ be some pixel of the original image of size $N_1 \times N_2$, and $\{p_i\}$ be some pseudo random sequence of the size $N_1 N_2$, and the period of the sequence is long enough. Then we rearrange the original pixels so that they are in the order specified by the sequence $\{p_i\}$. The process of the random permutation makes the reordered pixels seemingly uncorrelated.

Let $\tilde{f}(n_1, n_2)$ be some pixel of the rearranged image. We only give the encoder and authorized decoder the secret key $\{p_i\}$. According to the theory of permutation and combination, there are $(N_1 N_2)!$ possible permutations of the original image. Generally $(N_1 N_2)!$ is large enough, so that without knowing the key $\{p_i\}$, to illegally extract the hidden information is impossible.

Next, we take the Discrete Fourier Transform of $\tilde{f}(n_1, n_2)$, and let $\tilde{F}(k_1, k_2)$ denote the DFT coefficient. Let $R_e(k_1, k_2)$ represent the real part of $\tilde{F}(k_1, k_2)$, and $I_m(k_1, k_2)$ represent the imaginary part.

First, we quantize $R_e(k_1, k_2)$ to embed information. Let $A_k = 2k\Delta$, $B_k = (2k+1)\Delta$, $k = 0, \pm1, \pm2, \ldots$, and Δ be the selected quantization step. To embed a binary "1", we round $R_e(k_1, k_2)$ to the nearest odd multiple of Δ, i.e. the nearest A_k; to embed a binary "0", we round $R_e(k_1, k_2)$ to the nearest even multiple of Δ, i.e. the nearest B_k. Thus the real parts of DFT coefficients are modified to hide information.

In many applications, not only the hidden information should be blind to any observer, but also the fact that some information is hidden should be kept secret. However, the quantized coefficient may have some recognizable character, for example, abnormally more real parts of the DFT coefficients are multiples of Δ. To remove this character, so as to further assure the security, we introduce a random quantity into our system. After quantization, we add a random number $rand(R)$ to the quantized coefficients, where $R \leq \Delta/2$. Introducing a random quantity makes the coefficients slightly deviate from multiples of Δ. When Δ is large, adding $rand(R)$ is innocuous to the extracting process.

To ensure high imperceptibility, sometimes it's important to keep the phase of the DFT coefficients unchanged after quantization. To do this, the imaginary parts should be modified as follows:

$$I'_m(k_1, k_2) = I_m(k_1, k_2) \times R'_e(k_1, k_2) / R_e(k_1, k_2) \qquad (5)$$

But in some particular cases, high embedding capacity is require, thus slight changes to the phase is acceptable. So the imaginary parts of DFT coefficients can also be used to embed data. The embedding process is similar to the process for real parts. Let $I'_m(k_1, k_2)$ denote the quantized imaginary part and $\tilde{F}'(k_1, k_2)$ be the quantized DFT coefficient, we have:

$$\tilde{F}'(k_1, k_2) = R'_e(k_1, k_2) + jI'_m(k_1, k_2) \qquad (6)$$

As our former discussion, because of the symmetric property of DFT coefficients, only about half of the $N_1 \times N_2$ coefficients can be used to embed data, and the other half must be modified correspondingly to this half, that is, to keep the conjugate property between $\tilde{F}'(k_1,k_2)$ and $\tilde{F}'(N_1-k_1,N_2-k_2)$. In our method, because we embed data in both real and imaginary parts, so we can achieve a data embedding rate of 1 bit per DFT coefficient.

Next, we take the inverse DFT of $\tilde{F}'(k_1,k_2)$, and use the same sequence $\{p_i\}$ to take an inverse permutation of the pixels and get them back to their former locations. The result image $f'(n_1,n_2)$ is the stego image that has information hidden in.

3 Extracting Scheme

First, authorized observers use the secret key $\{p_i\}$ to scramble pixel locations of the received image. Next, take DFT of the scrambled image. Both the real and the imaginary (if the imaginary parts are also used to embed data) parts are extracted and divided by Δ. Let w_i be the extracted hidden data. If the dividing result is even when rounded to integer, w_i is equal to "1"; otherwise, w_i is equal to "0".

In our data hiding technique, both gray images and color images can be cover images. For the color ones, we basically have two solutions to process them in the similar ways to dealing with gray images. One way is to convert the original image from RGB to YUV format. We can use the conversion formula as following:

$$Y = 0.299 \times R + 0.587 \times G + 0.114 \times B \tag{7.1}$$

$$Cb = -0.1687 \times R - 0.3313 \times G + 0.5 \times B + 128 \tag{7.2}$$

$$Cr = 0.5 \times R - 0.4187 \times G - 0.0813 \times B + 128 \tag{7.3}$$

Thus we can apply our embedding technique to the Y component (the luminance). When the embedding process is completed, we take the inverse DFT, and converse YUV back to RGB format. The formula is:

$$R = Y + 1.402 \times (Cr - 128) \tag{8.1}$$

$$G = Y - 0.34414 \times (Cb - 128) - 0.71414 \times (Cr - 128) \tag{8.2}$$

$$B = Y + 1.772 \times (Cb - 128)$$

(8.3)

The other way is more obvious. The hidden information is embedded directly in the R, G, B components. According to formula (7.1), as well as the different sensitivities of human eyes to colors, we can see that changes in the B components modify the original image to the least extent.

To further increase embedding capacity, we can embed data in not only B but also R and G components. Thus the embedding capacity can be up to 3 times as capacity for gray images.

4 Experiment Results

In this section, we give an example of our data hiding scheme. We use LENNA of size 256×256 as the original image (Fig. 2). And the embedded signal is the logotypes of our Vilab and university (shown in Fig.3). The size of the embedded signal can reach 8k ($\approx 256 \times 256 / 8$) bytes. We select quantization step of $\Delta = 1000$ for gray images. The stego images are shown as Fig.4. Fig.4 (a) shows the stego image embedding data merely into the real parts of the DFT coefficients. Fig.4 (b) shows the stego image embedding data in both real and imaginary parts. And Fig. 5 shows their correspondingly extracted hidden images. See Fig. 5 (a) (b1)(b2).

The sizes of displayed images are one-fourth of the real ones.

Fig. 2. Original Image "LENNA"

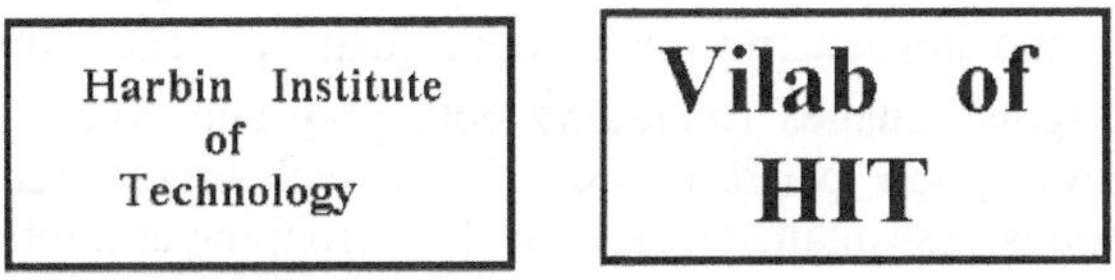

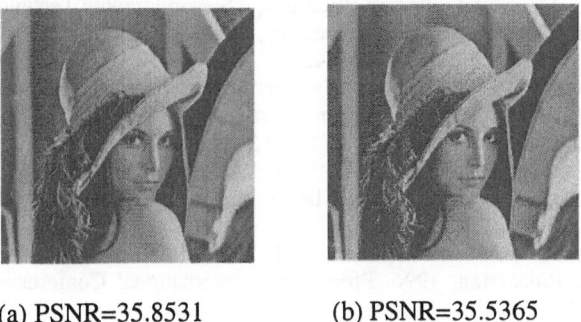

(a)   (b)

Fig. 3. (a) Hidden Image I. (b) Hidden Image II

(a) PSNR=35.8531   (b) PSNR=35.5365

Fig. 4. Stego images

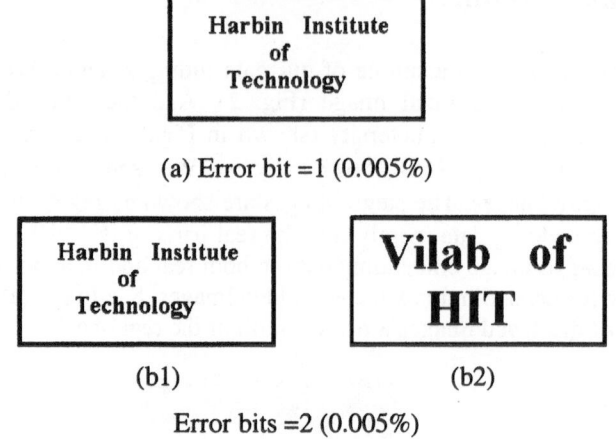

(a) Error bit =1 (0.005%)

(b1)   (b2)

Error bits =2 (0.005%)

Fig. 5. Extracted hidden images

5 Conclusion

This data hiding technique is presented considering an active observer who may have some knowledge of our embedding method. Security is guaranteed by keeping the secret key $\{p_i\}$ and introducing the random quantity. The experiment based on a large pool of original images (including both gray and color images) and hidden information shows good performance of our technique. Our future work will concentrate on robustness against attacks such as cropping and rotation.

References

1. F. Alturki and R. Mersereau, "Secure Blind Image Steganographic Technique using Discrete Fourier Transformation", Image Processing, 2001. Proceedings. 2001 International Conference on, Volume: 2, (2001) 542 -545
2. V. Solachidis and I. Pitas, "Circularly Symmetric Watermarking Embedding In 2-D DFT Domain", Acoustics, Speech, and Signal Processing, 1999. Proceedings, 1999 IEEE International Conference on, Volume: 6, (1999) 3469 -3472
3. M. Ramkumar, Ali N. Akansu and A.A. Alatan, "A Robust Data Hiding Scheme For Images Using DFT", Image Processing, 1999. ICIP 99. Proceedings. 1999 International Conference on, Volume: 2, (1999) 211 -215
4. J.J.K.O. Ruanaidh, W.J. Dowling, and F.M. Boland, "Phase Watermarking of Digital Images", Image Processing, 1996. Proceedings. International Conference on, Volume: 3, (1996,) 239 -242
5. Kenneth. R. Castlman, "Digital Image Processing", Perceptive Scientific Instruments, Inc. Copyright (1996) 667
6. Xiansheng Hua and Qingyun Shi, "To Embde Multiple Watermarks Simultaneously," Acta Scientiarum Naturalium, Unversitatis Pekinensis, Vol. 37, No. 3 (May, 2001)

An Algorithm for Data Hiding Using Median Cut Segmentation

Gareth Brisbane[1], Rei Safavi-Naini[1], and Philip Ogunbona[2]

[1] School of IT and CS, University of Wollongong, NSW 2522, Australia,
{gareth, rei}@uow.edu.au,
[2] Motorola Australia Research Centre, Sydney, Australia,
philip.ogunbona@motorola.com

Abstract. We extend the method proposed by Seppanen et al. in [1] by replacing the k-means algorithm with the median cut algorithm. The median cut algorithm has superior data hiding qualities due to its prismic nature even though the palette is sub-optimal. In addition, considerable savings on computation time are made. The presence of the median cut algorithm in image processing packages implies that this algorithm becomes a simple and integrable tool for steganographic communication.

1 Introduction

1.1 Steganography

Covert communication can be achieved by the clever use of a medium. A history of steganography was documented in [2], including the early creative example of tattooing information on a bald head then allowing the hair to grow back. An informal yet powerful presentation of the problem of steganography was formulated by Simmons in [3], known as the prisoners' problem. In this situation, Alice and Bob are prisoners wishing to escape. They send each other messages in which they try to communicate information, knowing they will be examined. They cannot send encoded messages, so they resort to covertly sending plans (*stego-text*), through innocuous messages, or *cover-text*.

With the advent of digital communication, it is common to represent information in binary form, *e.g.* images and sounds. "Second generation watermarking", coined by Kutter et al. in [4], refers to the practice of watermarking following segmentation, with respect to images. They reason that an attacker will also wish to keep the objects within the image, otherwise the image's aesthetic value will be ruined. Thus, their hidden data is embedded within each segment. Other techniques which watermark segments are [5] and [6].

1.2 Overview of the Original Algorithm

Seppanen et al. propose a process in [1] whereby information can be embedded within segments of a colour image to allow for efficient transmission of information. Their algorithm uses k-means to generate a reduced *palette*, a subset of colours which represents the full set with the intention of minimizing error.

Y.-C. Chen, L.-W. Chang, and C.-T. Hsu (Eds.): PCM 2002, LNCS 2532, pp. 89–96, 2002.

Each colour in the palette represents a segment in 3-dimensional colour space, inside which semantic meaning can be attached to different colour points. The embedding of information is done in the context of a cube, which makes coding simple but is inefficient at representing the true nature of a k-means segment or *Voronoi* region[10]. Additionally, the method is very slow as it is computationally costly, and would not be suitable for general use.

1.3   Our Technique

We have developed a new algorithm which replaces k-means with a more common image processing algorithm, the median cut. Originally published by Heckbert in [7], the problem of representing full colour images in a smaller colour space is usually solved by this process, or an optimization of it, due to its computational simplicity. It is ubiquitous in image processing tools, thus affording the opportunity to integrate steganography into these existing packages. Further heuristics are also used on the algorithm to provide better palette selection and/or speed improvements.

2   Goals of Steganography

There are three major goals in steganography: *imperceptibility; capacity;* and *robustness*[8]. The imperceptibility of an algorithm is a measure of its effectiveness of hiding the stegotext within the covertext. The capacity is defined as the maximum amount of stego-text that can be embedded within a given cover-text. Finally, the robustness refers to the ability of the technique to prevent damage to the stego-text when the cover-text is corrupted, either deliberately or unintentionally. These goals are interdependent, in that they can usually be sacrificed in order to improve the others.

Steganography is primarily concerned with invisibility, then capacity. That is, its key premise is data hiding. For example, in the case of the tattooed man, the success of the communication was that the message went undiscovered. Prior knowledge of the specific location of the information would foil any transmission, even though it may not be decoded correctly. The secondary priority was the amount of information that could be sent. Similarly, when information is embedded in the Least Significant Bit (LSB) of pixels[9], it is easily removed if the attacker suspects its existence.

3   The Original Algorithm

3.1   Methodology

Segmentation using k-means. The segmentation algorithm in [1] uses the *k-means* algorithm to divide a colour image, I, into K segments. All pixels in I have three colour components: red; green; and blue. These are converted into a vector form with those values, *i.e.* $\{P_R, P_G, P_B\}$. Thus, the space of all possible values has three dimensions, all ranging from 0 to 255. As the representation of the pixels has changed into an arbitrary form, they are referred to as *feature vectors*.

The codebook, C, containing K vectors (*centroids*), is initially set to a randomly selected subset of the feature vectors to reduce the time taken in training. Each feature vector is *classified* by determining its closest centroid. The Euclidean distance is used for this measurement: *i.e.* between two vectors $V1$ and $V2$, in K dimensions: $D = \sqrt{\sum_{i=1}^{K}(V1_i - V2_i)^2}$.

When all vectors have been classified, $C'_i = \overline{V_l}, \forall V_l \in C_i$. This procedure is repeated until $\sum_{i=1}^{K}|C'_i - C_i| < \epsilon$. At this point, the solution is within distance ϵ of a local minimum. It is not expected that the global minimum has been found given that there are many ways to represent an image with a set of centroids. C now represents a palette of I.

Embedding. For each segment, S_i, a cube, Q_i, is constructed within S_i such that no point within Q_i is external to S_i (or outside the image space). Beginning with $S_i = C_i$, *i.e.* a cube with length $= 1$, the length is doubled until Q_i does not meet the requirements, then halved.

$\hat{m}$ is the embedded message, where $\hat{m} = m \oplus r$, where m is the intended message, $\oplus$ is XOR, and r is a pseudo-random bit stream. This ensures that the message remains indecipherable, as well as providing a uniformly distributed message which minimizes the amount of error caused by insertion of the message.

As each cube has a length that is radix-2, data is able to be easily encoded. We define L_j to be the length of Q_j and let M be a portion of $\hat{m}$ of length $\log_2 L_j$. For each pixel, P, belonging to S_i, its new location is determined by $C_i - L_i/2 + M$, in each of the red, green and blue dimensions. Therefore P remains in S_i, providing a recoverable message.

Recovery. Both Alice and Bob share C and r. Bob can redetermine each Q_j used in embedding through possession of C, assuming a passive warden. Then for each pixel, $M = P - C_i + L_i/2$, where P belongs to S_i. Thus, $\hat{m}$ can be recovered by concatenation of M. Using r, $m = \hat{m} \oplus r$, completing transmission.

3.2   Analysis

Image quality. The quality of the output images were not recorded by Seppanen. Our own results below in figure 1 give a range of 31dB to 39dB for the parameters they used. The technique that we use for determining the amount of noise is the Peak Signal to Noise Ratio (PSNR), calculated by $\text{PSNR} = 20\log_{10}\frac{255}{\sqrt{\text{MSE}}}$, where MSE is the Mean Squared Error. It can be considered that 40dB represents a visually lossless image, in general. Thus, the technique can be considered to be reasonable, in that visual distortion may be minimal.

Capacity. The quantity of data that is able to be embedded is quite high, ranging from 5 bits per pixel (bpp) to nearly 10 bpp, depending on the distribution

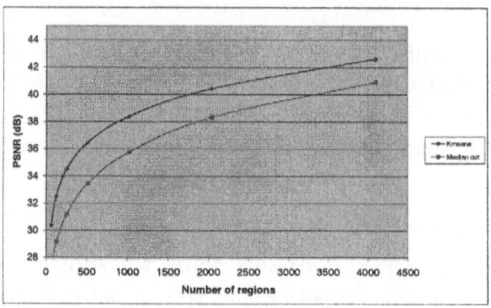

Fig. 1. The quality of the output image after insertion of the watermark in the test images

of colour within the image. Where more colours are present, the size of each segment is larger and more diffuse, allowing greater opportunities to hide data. Images which contain less variation hide less information because of the density of the pixels in the colour space. The images which are used in these tests, are both quite noisy, affording good opportunities for sparse palette construction.

Robustness. The method is known to not be robust at all, given that recovery depends on the pixel order of the scheme. If pixels are incorrectly classified and given that each segment has a different bit rate, it is difficult to ensure that all pixels are correctly reclassified, apart from access to the original image. This precipitates a loss in synchronization. The volume of the segments can be so small that even JPEG compression at 100% quality level causes enough movement to displace pixels from their original segment. Thus, no tests relating to attacks were performed because they are not included in the assumptions of the model.

Speed. The k-means algorithm uses a large amount of time to construct C, as each pixel is repeatedly evaluated for its proximity to all centroids. In addition, the distance calculation is quite slow, owing to the operations of multiplication and square root. It is due to this that it is rarely used for palette selection in image processing despite its excellent performance. This computational complexity implies that the method might not be useful for steganography because the time for segmentation is excessive. Thus, we will measure the speed of the algorithm as a measure to its overall complexity.

4   Our Proposal

4.1   The Median Cut Algorithm

A far more common technique for palette selection is the median cut algorithm, originally developed by Heckbert[7]. This process can also be optimized in various

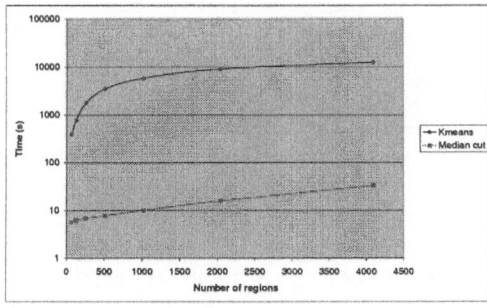

Fig. 2. The length of time required for insertion of the watermark in the test images

ways, such as by quantizing the original image to reduce the number of sorting calculations. As it is able to produce a palette, it can replace k-means for the formation of the segments.

The algorithm begins by constructing a rectangular prism, M_1 say, around the colour space. The length of each dimension is reduced so long as no pixels are excluded from the prism. This constricts the prism to the tightest possible prism around the pixels in the image. Using the longest axis of M_1, the median point is found in that dimension. Then M_1 is divided along that plane, a *median cut*, such that it represents one of those prisms and a new prism, M_2, represents the other prism. Both M_1 and M_2 are constricted again, to minimize the volume required for representation. Then, the prism which has the longest axis over all prisms is selected and split according to the rules above. This continues until K prisms have been formed. Each palette colour is then determined by $C_i = \overline{P_l}, \forall P_l \in M_i$.

The median cut algorithm does not guarantee a local minimum, as k-means does, leading to some ineffeciency. Also, further training is not possible as convergence has occured, while k-means can use additional steps such as simulated annealing. However, the expensive and repetitive distance calculations have been avoided.

4.2   Embedding

Cubes are one of the worst shapes that can be used to represent Voronoi regions[10]. In contrast, the median cut prisms are much better suited to the embedding process due to its similary with the cube. Thus, the inefficiency of palette selection can be considered to be traded against the efficiency of the embedding method. Also, the boundaries of M_i are already known, while the vertices of the cube must be tested for each region with k-means. The embedding process is then performed with the set of cubes, Q, as with k-means.

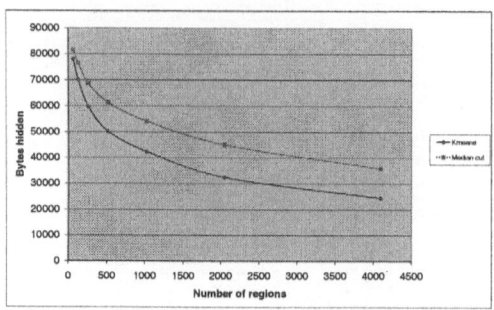

Fig. 3. The capacity of the watermark process in the test images

5   Experiments

5.1   Conditions

The comparison against Seppanen's method needs to contrast any differences between the two techniques. All experiments were performed on a Pentium II-350 with 128 Mb of RAM, on the "peppers" and "mandrill" images. Each image has 256×256 pixels and uses 24 bit colour. For Seppanen's method, 5 tests were performed, and the results averaged. For our method, only 1 test was necessary, because the generation of the palette was entirely determinstic.

We optimized the k-means algorithm slightly in that we did not calculate the square root in our distance calculations, providing a speed improvement of approximately 25%. We implemented the median cut algorithm without any optimizations or heuristics.

5.2   Results

Image quality. Figure 1 displays the improvement in palette selection that the k-means algorithm holds over the median cut algorithm. Because the palette is a better representative of the entire image, the adjustment of pixels within each segment causes less damge to the image. That is, the average distance that pixels move in order to contain information for transmission, is less than that of the median cut algorithm.

Capacity. Despite the inefficiency of the palette selection, the nature of the median cut algorithm being predisposed to hiding information in cubic structures is revealed in figure 3. Initially, there is no difference between the two methods due to the doubling process not providing an advantage when regions are slightly larger. However, as the size of each segment declines, the median cut is better able to handle the cubic substructures than the k-means generated segments. Thus, even as the number of segments becomes quite large and the size of each

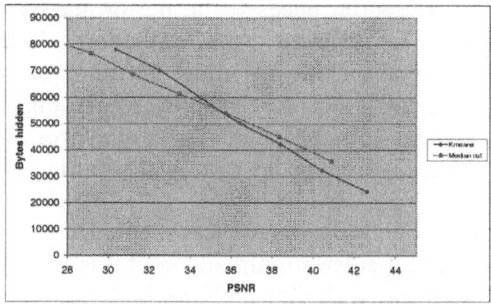

Fig. 4. A comparison of the performance of the two algorithms with the test images

segment is small, it is still easier to fit a cube in the median cut segments than those of the k-means algorithm.

Speed. The difference is speed is demonstrated in figure 2. Although the median cut algorithm appears to increase in an exponential fashion, this probably owes more to inefficient coding than to the algorithm. The embedding portion of the method is relatively quick, so the cost of the algorithm can be attributed to the segmentation component. The improvement in speed is about two orders of magnitude over that of the k-means implementation.

Comparative performance. As the number of segments increases, the median cut algorithm improves with respect to k-means, so that at about 4,000 segments, the performance is 50% better. However, the cost of this is a lower image quality, due to the palette selection. Figure 4 indicates the final result most clearly, that with the tradeoff of palette selection against the increase in capacity, that at about 36dB, the break-even point is reached. Beyond this, it is preferable to use the median cut algorithm over that of k-means, owing to its improvement of the steganographic capacity. At 40dB, the level at which the image quality can be considered visually lossless, a 13% improvement in the bandwidth has been achieved.

6   Conclusion

We have presented an extension of the scheme[1] proposed by Seppanen et al. The original segmentation algorithm of k-means has been replaced with the median cut algorithm. The resultant capacity improvement is 13% at 40dB. In addition, the improvement in speed of the whole process is substantial, by two orders of magnitude at 40dB. There are no drawbacks to this except where extra capacity is of greater importance than image quality.

There are two aspects of this algorithm which need further refinement: security and robustness. Research needs to be performed to determine how well hidden the process is under scrutiny. Also, embedding is inherently fragile as each pixel value contains a specific meaning. Another part of this problem is that the segmentation process needs to reliably return back the data set which was constructed at the time of embedding, or else synchronization will fail. Thus, the use of a compression algorithm, for example, would corrupt the message irretrievably.

Due to the common functionality of the median cut algorithm, as well as optimized versions, existing software already contains most of the capability to encode information with this technique. The embedding algorithm is also simple and unchanged from its predecessor. As a result, it is now plausible to use this technology in existing packages to provide a steganographic service.

References

1. Tapio Seppanen, Kaisu Makela, Anja Keskinarkaus: Hiding information in color images using small color palettes. Information Security, Third International Workshop (2000) 69-81
2. Fabien A. P. Petitcolas, Ross J. Anderson, Markus G. Kuhn: Information hiding - a survey. Proceedings of the IEEE (1999), vol. 87, no. 7 1062-1078
3. Gustavus J. Simmons: The prisoners' problem and the subliminal channel. Advances in Cryptology (1984), Proceedings of CRYPTO 83, 51-67
4. M. Kutter, S. Bhattacharjee, T. Ebrahimi: Towards second generation watermarking schemes. Proceedings of the 6th International Conference on Image Processing (1999), vol. 3, 320-323
5. Gareth Brisbane, Rei Safavi-Naini, Philip Ogunbona: Region-based watermarking by distribution adjustment. Information Security, Third International Workshop (2000) 54-68
6. Athanasios Nikolaidis, Ioannis Pitas: Region-based image watermarking. IEEE Transactions on Image Processing (2001) 1726-1740
7. Paul Heckbert: Color image quantization for frame buffer display. Computer Graphics (1982) 297-303
8. Joshua R. Smith, Barrett O. Comiskey: Modulation and information hiding in images. Workshop on Information Hiding (1996), Isaac Newton Institute, University of Cambridge, vol. 1174
9. R. G. van Schyndel, A. Z. Tirkel, C. F. Osborne: A Digital Watermark. Proceedings of the 1994 International Conference on Image Processing (1994) 86-90
10. J. H. Conway, N. J. A. Sloane: Voronoi regions of lattices, second moments of polytopes, and quantization. IEEE Transactions of Information Theory (1982), vol. IT-28, no. 2, 211-226

An Optimized Spatial Data Hiding Scheme Combined with Convolutional Codes and Hilbert Scan[1]

Zhiyan Du, Yan Zou, and Peizhong Lu

Department of Computer Science and Engineering, Fudan University, Shanghai 200433, China
zydu@fudan.edu.cn, pzlu@fudan.edu.cn

Abstract. This paper presents a new watermarking scheme, which is combined with convolutional codes and Hilbert scan in spatial domain. Our method considerably improves the capacity of watermarks and the robustness of the system as well, compared with the present watermarking systems. Human Visual System (HVS) is applied adaptively in the embedding step. Watermarks are modulated by pseudo-random sequences for precise detection and security purposes. When convolutional code is employed, we adopt soft-decision Viterbi decoding algorithm to achieve lower bit error rate (BER). Our experiments show that choosing suitable convolutional codes can considerably alleviate the trade-off between the capacity and the robustness. This algorithm is also computationally simple so that the information can be extracted without the original image in real time in video watermarking.

1 Introduction

A great deal of research in digital watermark has been carried out for mainly two targets. The first is to enlarge the maximum number of information bits that can be hidden in a host image invisibly. The second is to improve the robustness of watermarks. However, there is a trade-off between the capacity of the information and the robustness of the watermarking system. Some researchers applied error correction codes in watermarking system. But it is still an open problem [1] to find a suitable error correction code to improve the performance of the watermark channel because of the difficulty of designing a compact error correction code to resist all sorts of attacks. Hernandez *et al.* [2] propose a convolutional code watermarking scheme to improve data hiding. It shows that their method performs better than the uncoded one and other error correction code ones do. But they don't discuss how various factors act on BER, such as attacks, distortions, and characters of convolutional codes. And it doesn't measure the capacity explicitly. The number of information bits they use to test robustness is small. K.K.Ying *et al.* [3] introduce a watermarking algorithm in spatial domain which is computationally simple. But their experimental data are not enough to be seen in [3]. Other techniques like in [4] is dealt in transform domain. Hernandez *et al.* in this paper adopts a HVS model which maximizes the admissible

---

[1] Supported by: National Natural Science Foundation of China(10171017), and Special Funds of Authors of Excellent Doctoral Dissertation of China.

Y.-C. Chen, L.-W. Chang, and C.-T. Hsu (Eds.): PCM 2002, LNCS 2532, pp. 97-104, 2002.

amplitude of the watermarks. But their scheme suffers from a heavy computational burden since they have to compute the DCT/IDCT transform and the perceptual mask based on a complex human visual system (HVS) model.

In this paper, we first make a further investigation of Hernandez's scheme in [2]. Then we modify their scheme by using a reasonable bit distribution to obtain an optimized algorithm. A major part of our work is to investigate how the redundancy of a convolutional code affects the capacity and the robustness. For image watermark channel, capacity depends on the watermark strength, on image statistics, and on the way the watermark is embedded [5]. We improve the detection performance of the convolutional code scheme by using Hilbert curve (See Section 4). We conclude in section 5 that all these properties indicate that our scheme can be employed in the broadcasting monitoring and covert communication [6].

2   Watermarking Scheme on Spatial Domain

2.1   Watermark Embedding Algorithm

Watermarking systems in spatial domain are usually considered to have high capacity and low robustness. In this section we present a new watermarking scheme(See Figure 1.) in spatial domain which maintains a moderate capacity and high robustness so as to be used in video monitoring and in video steganography. The bold letter $\mathbf{I}$ denotes the pixel matrix consisting of elements $I(i, j), 0 \leq i < L_x$, $0 \leq i < L_x$, where L_x and L_y are the width and height of the host image.

An N_b-bit information represented by the binary antipodal vector $\mathbf{b} = (b_1, ..., b_{N_b})$, $b_i \in \{-1, 1\}$, $\forall i \in \{1, ..., N_b\}$, is encoded by a convolutional encoder, resulting in the N_c-bit antipodal coded vector $\mathbf{c}$. This codeword is then fed into an interleaver to be disordered. The interleaver spits out a new antipodal vector $\mathbf{c'}$. Then, the vector $\mathbf{c'}$ should be expanded into a $N_{c''}$-bit vector $\mathbf{c''}$, where $N_{c''} = cr \cdot N_c$ and cr is called the expansion window or the spread factor. By a pseudo random sequence $\mathbf{p} = (p_1, ... p_{N_{c''}})$, $p_i \in \{-1, 1\}$, $\forall i \in \{1, ..., N_{c''}\}$, $\mathbf{c''}$ is modulated into vector $\mathbf{p} \cdot \mathbf{c''}$. For the security purpose, the pseudo-random sequence is chosen according to a secret key K. There is a HVS analyzer which calculates the JND mask of the host image. The JND is used to control the watermark strength. Multiplied by the JND, the modulated vector is at last embedded and the watermarked image $\mathbf{I'}$ is obtained:

$$\mathbf{I'} = \mathbf{I} + \mathbf{J} \cdot \mathbf{p} \cdot \mathbf{c''} \tag{1}$$

Bit Distribution. Hilbert scan is a type of space-filling curve which can convert a two-dimensional sequence to a one-dimensional sequence [7]. When the one-dimensional vector $\mathbf{p} \cdot \mathbf{c''}$ is to be scaled by the two-dimensional vector $\mathbf{J}$ during it being embedded into the two-dimensional original image, we follow Hilbert scan as

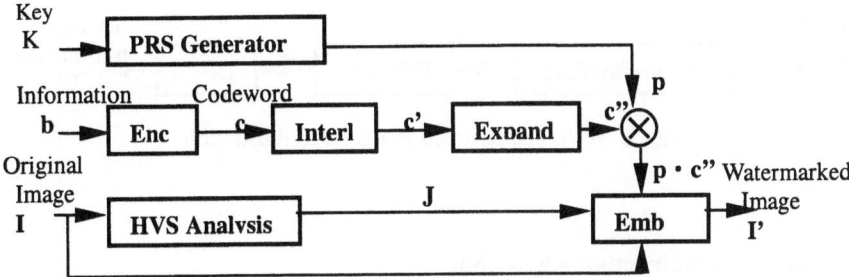

Fig. 1. Watermarking embedding algorithm illustration

the embedding track. For precise extraction, the pixels in one expansion window should be highly related. We find that Hilbert curve can meet this requirement. This curve is also mentioned in [3], but no experiments there show its superiority. In section 4 we will present comparison on the performance between the watermark systems based on Hilbert scan and raster scan.

Perceptual Masking. To maximize the admissible amplitude of the unperceivable information embedded, we simplify the human visual system(HVS) model in [4] and calculate the just noticeable distortion (JND) mask directly in the spatial domain, with blocks of 8x8 pixels. Fist, the original image is divided in blocks of 8x8 pixels. Let $x(k_1, k_2)$ be a function of the characteristic metric of the $[k_1, k_2]^{th}$ block, $0 \le k_1 < B_x$, $0 \le k_2 < B_y$, where B_x and B_y are the width and height of the original image measured in 8x8-pixel blocks. And $J(i, j)$ is the JND of the $[i, j]^{th}$ pixel of the original image, where $0 \le i < L_x$, $0 \le j < L_y$.

$$J(i, j) = l(k_1, k_2) + dif(i, j), \; 8 \times k_1 \le i < 8 \times (k_1 + 1), \; 8 \times k_2 \le j < 8 \times (k_2 + 1) \qquad (2)$$

where $l(k_1, k_2) = P(x(k_1, k_2))$ and P represents a pre-defined function which distributes a basic noise threshold to each block according to its metric value $x(k_1, k_2)$. The set of these basic noise thresholds is obtained according to large quantities of experiments.

For each block the metric function $x(k_1, k_2)$ is obtained by rule (3):

$$x(k_1, k_2) = var(k_1, k_2) + entr(k_1, k_2) \qquad (3)$$

where $entr(k_1, k_2)$ is the entropy of the distribution of the pixels in the block, and $var(k_1, k_2)$ is the variance of the pixel distribution in this block. Then we calculate the additional noise threshold of each pixel in the block according to its own grey level:

$$dif(i, j) = \frac{|c - I(i, j)|^2}{\alpha} \qquad (4)$$

where c is the average grey level of the block in which the pixel $[i, j]$ locates and α is an empirical parameter. The JND threshold of a given pixel is achieved by adding up the additional noise threshold and the basic noise threshold of the block it belongs to. Finally, a JND mask is obtained which has the same size with the original image.

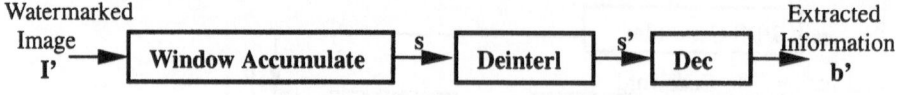

Fig. 2. Watermark extraction algorithm illustration

2.2 Watermark Extraction Algorithm

The extraction algorithm is shown in Figure 2.
We can estimate the codeword bit c'_k by the sign of s_k, where

$$s_k = \sum_{t=k\cdot cr}^{(k+1)\cdot cr-1}(p_t \cdot I'(i,j)) + \Delta \approx cr \cdot J(i,j) \cdot c''_t = cr \cdot J(i,j) \cdot c'_k \tag{6}$$

$$\Delta = -\left(\sum_{t=k\cdot cr}^{(k+1)\cdot cr-1} p_t\right) \cdot E\left(\sum_{t=k\cdot cr}^{(k+1)\cdot cr-1} I'(i,j)\right) \tag{7}$$

The more correlated the pixels in one expansion window are, the more precise equation (6) is. That is why we adopt Hilbert scan to keep correlation between pixels in the same window. Hard-decision extraction will cause loss of valuable information. When convolutional code is employed, we will decode the information by soft-decision which will be introduced in the next section.

2.3 Adaptive Adjustment

In order to obtain better extraction performance, we do adaptive adjustment on the watermark strength, which will enhance the power of information and keep it transparent as well. We investigate whether the sum of a given window $t_k = |s_k|$ is in a proper range and then increase/decrease the JND of each pixel in this window. The critical issue is to define an appropriate range according to the original image itself. The limits in this paper are chosen by experiments. Interesting further research need to be done to find an optimal measure to estimate the limits.

2.4 Additive White Gaussian Noise Model

When we demodulate $cr \cdot J(i,j) \cdot b_t$ by $\sum_{t=k\cdot cr}^{(k+1)\cdot cr-1}(p_t \cdot I'(i,j))$, we know the noise is:

$$e = \sum_{t=k\cdot cr}^{(k+1)\cdot cr-1}(p_t \cdot I(i,j)) \tag{8}$$

If $I(i, j)$ is not constant in a given window, it can be considered as an *iid* random variable. If *cr* is large enough, then *e* is Gaussian according to the central limit theorem because *e* is a sum of many *idd* variables. Thus, the additive white Gaussian noise model can be used to simulate the data hiding channel.

3   Convolutional Codes and Soft-Decision Decoding

Convolutional encoding with Viterbi decoding is a FEC technique that is particularly suited to a channel in which the transmitted signal is corrupted mainly by additive white Gaussian noise [8]. Because the channel model we construct is Gaussian, we can take the advantage of convolutional codes in the watermarking scheme. When the codeword is interleaved and modulated by a pseudo-random sequence and if the expansion window is big enough, all elements of s' have approximately the same mean and variance. Furthermore, these elements are independent. Therefore, the vector s' can be modeled as the output vector of the AWGN channel. Thus, the Signal to Noise Ratio (SNR) of the channel directly affects the bit error rate (BER) of the decoder. In this watermark system, the SNR depends on the amount of hidden information, on the amount of noise, on the compression quality, and on the attacks. Viterbi decoding algorithm has the advantage that it has a fixed decoding time. But the computation grows exponentially as a function of the constraint length. The reasonable constraint length of a convolutional code used in practice is below 10.

4   Experimental Results

All experiments are performed on 512x512 images.

4.1   Capacity Analysis

We studied four kinds of convolutional codes with different constraint lengths by comparing their performance on BER with that of the uncoded scheme(See Figure 3). As we mentioned in section 3, the performance declined when the number of information hidden increases, which results in decrease of SNR. In the range of certain capacity, the convolutional code strategy has remarkable gains. Especially in a range of moderate capacity, its performance is perfect because it keeps the BER zero. And the longer the constraint length is, the better the decoder works. The new scheme achieves higher capacity than that of the uncoded one for a given BER. When constraint length is 9, we can achieve the capacity of around 2bits/100pixels which is about 14 times higher than that of the scheme in [2] (3bits/1000pixels) when the BER is below 10^{-3}. As we discussed in the previous section, Hilbert scan makes the extractor more precise. Also, we find that the BER by Hilbert scan is about 6% lower than that by raster scan.

4.2 Robustness Analysis

Resistance to Gaussian Noise. From Figure 4 we can conclude that in a certain amount range of noise, the convolutional code strategy shows its good performance to resist Gaussian noise. We also notice that the regression curves of convolutional code schemes ascend faster than the uncoded one. And as the constraint length becomes longer, the curve mounts up abruptly. The noise affects the SNR directly so that over a certain threshold (which depends on the number of information bits and the constraint length), the convolutional code shows little superiority. Anyway, our scheme is also considered superior because the threshold itself is big enough below which it can keep the BER considerably low and over which even the uncoded one has a high BER. Especially, when the noise amount is below 10%, our scheme can keep the BER almost zero.

Resistance to Copping. Cropping is a typical attacking method. Our strategy allows strong resistance to cropping attacks. Testing data are shown in the Table 1.

The good resistance is due to the nice performance of convolutional codes and interleavers. These tests are done on the image with its borders cut off like the third one in Figure 5. Even when the image is scraped right on the middle as the right one in Figure 5, the Viterbi detector can still recover the watermark with the BER=0.

Resistance to JPEG Compression. The scheme can resist some JPEG compression of certain quality. In our experiment, the hiding rate is 1 bit per 916 pixels, much higher than that of Hernandez's experiments (which is 1 bit per 5892 pixels). It is interesting that the convolutional code with shorter constraint length has better performance. And when the compression quality is 9 or higher, our new scheme performs much better than the uncoded one does(see Table 2).

4.3 Analysis of Time Cost

Our spatial-domain system is computationally simple. In many occasions, detecting in real time is requested, especially when it applied to video watermark. Table 3 and Table 4 show the time cost of our watermark scheme on a machine with Pentium 800M Hz CPU. Convolutional codes with shorter constraint lengths work faster.

5   Conclusion and Future Work

In this paper, the algorithm combined with Hilbert scan and convolutional code in spatial domain has been investigated. Security and capacity are improved by means of the pseudo-random sequence and the interleaving stage. The original image is not necessary during the decoding process. The adaptive embedding and soft-decision decoding techniques greatly improve the capacity, the robustness and the invisibility of watermarks. This algorithm cost little time on extraction so that it can be applied to video watermark. Its good performance also guarantees it suitable to be used in broadcast monitoring and covert communication due to its good performance.

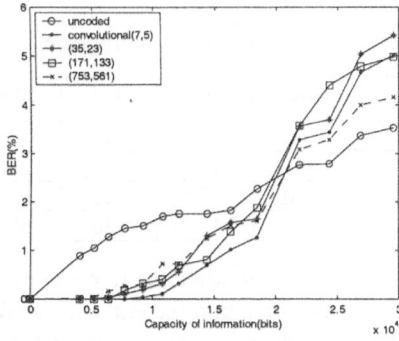
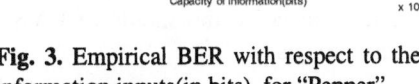
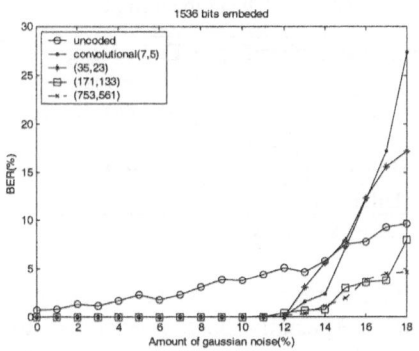

Fig. 3. Empirical BER with respect to the information inputs(in bits), for "Pepper"

Fig. 4. Empirical BER with respect to the of noise(in percentage), for "Pepper"

Fig. 5. From left to right: watermarked image with no distortion, watermarked image with 20% noise, cropped watermarked image and scraped watermarked image

Table 1. Detection BER(%) of five schemes for cropped watermarked image "Peppers" with 1536 information bits

Constraint length	Cut off borders to (pixels) / (amount of image cropped)				
	493x493 (7.28%)	470x463 (16.99%)	450x440 (24.47%)	429x415 (32.09%)	402x394 (39.58%)
uncoded	4.948	9.115	17.253	23.5.3	28.776
3	0	0	0.130	2.865	3.581
5	0	0	0.391	1.042	4.036
7	0	0	0	0.195	6.445
9	0	0	0	1.172	8.333

Table 2. Detection BER(%) of five schemes for compressed watermarked image "Peppers" with hiding rate=1bit/916pixel

constraint length	Compression quality(%compressed)		
	9 (86%)	8 (90%)	7 (93%)
Uncoded	27.273	31.468	47.902
9	4.196	26.923	50.062
7	2.797	9.441	49.674
5	4.196	20.629	36.393
3	1.049	9.505	24.219

Table 3. The embedding time

Means of Embedding	Embedding Time(ms)
Hilbert scan +HVS+adaption	390
Hilbert scan+HVS	390
Hilbert scan only	100
Raster scan+HVS	390

Table 4. The extracting time (ms)

constraint length	The number of information bits			
	1024	2800	3840	5184
3	90	90	100	100
5	90	110	120	140
7	120	170	200	270
9	210	420	580	680

Our further work focuses on designing a better error correction code to resist more attacks, especially the geometrical distortion. Moreover, some parameters, such as the upper&lower bounds of the adaptation process and basic noise thresholds of HVS, have to be estimated adaptively according to different images.

References

1. Stefan Katzenbeisser, Fabien A. P. Peticlolas: Information Hiding Techniques for Steganography and Digital Watermarking. ARTECH HOUSE, INC, Chapter 6, (2000) 91-94
2. Juan R. Hernandez, Jean-Francois Delaigle and Benoit Macq, "Improving Data Hiding by Using Convolutional Codes and Soft-Decision Decoding", *Proceedings of SPIE on Security and Watermarking of Multimedia II*, Vol. 3971, pp.24-47, 2000
3. KangKang Ying, Jiaoying Shi, and Zhigeng Pan, "An image watermarking algorithm with high robustness", *Journal of Software*, vol.5, pp.668-675, Dec, 2001(in Chinese)
4. Juan R. Hernandez, Martin Amado, and Fernando Perez-Gonzalez, "DCT-Domain Watermarking Techniques for Still Images: Detector Performance Analysis and a New Structure", *IEEE Transaction on Image Processing*, vol.9, No.1, pp.55-68, Jan, 2000
5. Mauro Barni, Franco Bartolini, Alessia De Rosa, and Alessandro Piva, "Capacity of Full DCT Image Watermarks", *IEEE transactions on image processing*, vol.9, No.8, pp.1450-1455, August 2000
6. Ingemar J. Cox, Matt L. Miller and Jeffrey A. Bloom, "Watermarking applications and their properties", *Int. Conf. on Information Technology'2000*, Las Vegas, 2000
7. B. Mandelbrot, *The Fractal Geometry of Nature*, Chapter7. W. H. GREEMAN AND COMPANY, 1983
8. J. Hagenauer and P. Hoeher, "A Viterbi algorithm with soft-decision outputs and its applications", *Proc. GlobeCom'1989*, pp.1680-1686, 1989

Research on Technology of Chaos Secrecy Communications in Digital Watermarking

Tanfeng Sun, Lili Cui, and Shuxun Wang

Institute of Communication Engineering, Jilin University,
Changchun, Jilin, China, 130025
tanfengs@yahoo.com.cn Phone:086-0431-5684201

Abstract. In this paper, we present a novel DCSK-based protecting method of watermarks' information security. We apply chaos sequence to encrypt wateramrks' information. It makes watermarks' information more secure than others methods. Then we embedded encrypted sequence into image base on wavelet theory. It make wateramrk' information secure and secret.

As a result, DCSK-based watermarking is more secure in protecting embedded information. Furthermore blind- detection watermarking can be realized. That method possesses research value.

Keyword: Chaos Secrecy Communication; Difference Chaos Shift Key; Watermarking; Wavelet Transformation

1 Introduction

The efficient protection of information is important significance, for commutative net and kinds of multimedia carrier. One side we protect information by kinds of encrypt ways, on the other side it is needed to conceal some important information in protected media to illuminate copyright possession and so on. Information security has been the people's focus all over the world.

Chaos technology has wide application outlook in digital communications field, especially in secret communications. Recently it has become a hotspot theme in communications field. And with more development of technology of chaos communications, it will be one of important technology of communications aspects of 21th century. Digital watermarking is a new technology of information security, which is rapidly developing in recent years. The two technologies have their different advantages in information security. It will create new advantage if they can be integrated.

The advantage of chaos communications is the wonderful encrypt for the content of communications, especially in military affairs paid widely attention to. But the better to encrypt, the easier to arose kings of assaults. And the most advantage of digital watermark is to hide information, and not easy arose vicious assaults. But once the watermarking theory is obtained, the watermarked information will be difficult to survive. Thus in this paper we put forward the new protect technology of information security with integrating the two different technologies to protect important information perfectly.

Y.-C. Chen, L.-W. Chang, and C.-T. Hsu (Eds.): PCM 2002, LNCS 2532, pp. 105-111, 2002.
© Springer-Verlag Berlin Heidelberg 2002

2 Differential Chaos Shift Keying (DCSK)

Following we simply introduce the system frame theory of DCSK:

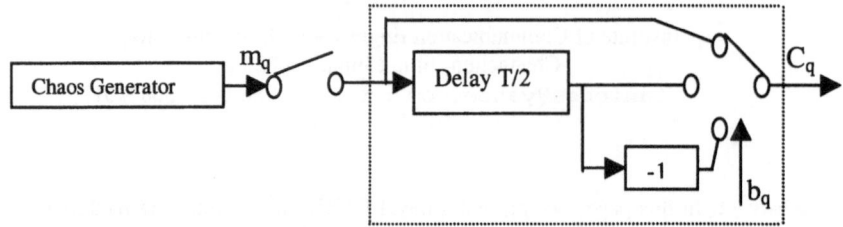

Fig. 1. DCSK modulate system frame figure

In fig1, m_q denotes the chaos sequence that is produced by chaos generator; b_q denotes the information need to be modulated; C_q denotes modulate chaos sequence with information. In fig1 dashed part is DCSK modulate process.

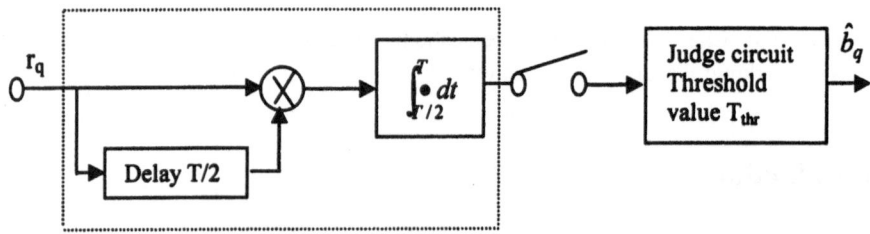

Fig. 2. FM-DCSK modulate and demodulate system frame figure

In fig2, r_q denotes the carrier wave signal arrive sink through channel transmit; $\hat{b}_q$ denotes the estimate of originality information which gained by receive signal demodulated and judged. In fig2 dashed part denotes the process of DCSK demodulate.

According to figure 1, the binary signal $b_q = \{-1, +1\}$ each information code will be replaced by two different sample functions, therefore, the transmit function is

$$C(t) = \begin{cases} m(t), & t_k \leq t < t_k + T/2, \\ b_q m(t - T/2), & t_k + T/2 \leq t < T, \end{cases} \quad (1)$$

At sink, like figure2 show, make correlation judge between the receive signal r_q and the delay $r(t - \dfrac{T}{2})$ during the $\dfrac{T}{2}$, judge circuit gate restrict value is zero. For q-th code, the judge variable is:

$$\hat{b}_q = \int_{T/2}^{T} r_q(t) r_q(t - T/2) dt = \int_{T/2}^{T} [C_q(t) + n(t)][C_q(t - T/2) + n(t - T/2)] dt \quad (2)$$

This paper bring forward the watermark's arithmetic just based on the upwards DCSK idea.

3   Watermarking Based on DCSK

First, we put forward watermark embedded and detected principle frame figure base on this method.

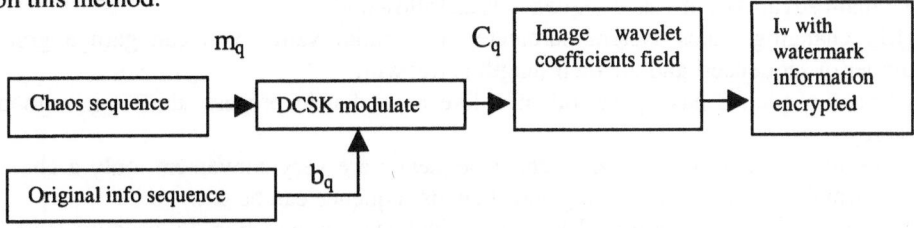

Fig. 3. The theory frame figure watermark embedded, just the model equivalent with DCSK

In fig3, m_q denotes chaos sequence; b_q denotes copyright information; C_q denotes the watermark's information sequence that has been modulated through DCSK; I_w denotes the image embed encrypt watermark info.

In fig4, image I_w' is the gained image after transmit; C_q' is watermark encrypt sequence that is gained from image after wavelet decompose; m_q' is the gained distortion originality chaos sequence after DCSK demodulated; $\hat{b}_q$ is the estimation of original infomation after DCSK demodulated.

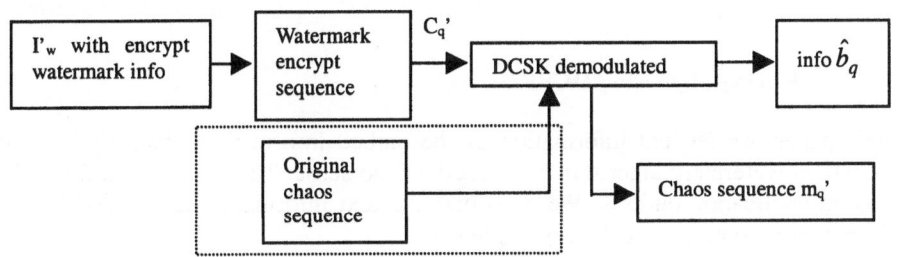

Fig. 4. The principle frame figure of watermark detection

In fig4, the dashed part denotes optional item. During the process of demodulated information, if no original chaos sequence, you can pick up the former half period of code period based on DCSK principle and make it to be chaos sequence and the later period to be information modulate sequence. The two sequences are processed by division calculation, and the estimate value of watermark can be obtained. Another method is utilize the information modulated sequence that has picked up calculate with the original chaos sequence and also estimation of watermark information can be obtained.

Based on watermark embed principle frame, the embed process have the following three parts:

3.1   The Product of Chaos Sequence

In this paper, we put forward using chaos dynamical system to produce real number watermark sequence. Such as, Tent, Logistic, Hybrid equation and so on .
The main advantage of chaos sequence is as following :
(1)By changing chaos system parameter and initial value, you can gain a great number of sequences, and the their length is freewill;
(2)Chaos sequence has no period, just like a stochastic process, thus it has good secrecy;
(3)The product and replication of chaos sequence are very convenient, only a chaos fold formula and an initial value given, a chaos sequence can be got.
This paper adopts Hybrid's chaos dynamical system equation to produce chaos sequence, because it has better self-correlation and mutual-correlation characteristic. And sequence mean value is zero, the chaos dynamical equation as following:

$$
y = \begin{cases}
1 - 2x^2 & -1 \le x < -0.5 \\
1 - 1/2 \cdot (-2x)^{1.2} & -0.5 \le x < 0 \\
1 - 2x & 0 \le x \le 0.5 \\
-(2x - 1)^{0.7} & 0.5 < x \le 1
\end{cases}
\tag{3}
$$

After gaining chaos orbit, by folding the initial value, binary chaos sequence is obtained by dealing with threshold condition.

3.2 Chaos Encrypt by Using DCSK

In this paper, we let text information as the embed information. Recently most of information watermark algorithm embedded has no sense. To embed text information has good application outlook. We transform the text information to be ASCII code, then transform to be [-1, 1] binary sequence.
The chaos sequence and watermark information sequence are produced. The following is DCSK modulation. Watermark information is modulated to be chaos sequence. Just as formula (1) show, m_q denotes chaos sequence, b_q denotes watermark information. C_q denotes chaos carrier wave information after modulated. Up to now, we have finished the modulation process of watermark information, namely the process of information encrypted.

3.3 Embedment of Watermark Information

Now, we need embed chaos sequence with watermark information after modulated into image. We adopt transform field to embed watermark. We adopt Harr wavelet to decompose the image to be 1 level, and then multiply the values of carrier chaos sequence and the coefficients of wavelet which are positive and small, namely equal to sign operation, then resume the image after wavelet invert transform. And now we finish the integrity embed of encrypt watermark information.

3.4 Detection and Resume Watermark Information

Just like fig4, during the detection algorithm, we can resume the watermark information based on different principles.

The first method: At first we obtain distortion chaos carrier sequence by wavelet decompose, then adopt DCSK method to demodulate sequence, that is the former half period and the later half period to calculate, and estimate the original watermark

information $\hat{b}_q$ according to signal consistency.

The second method: we pick up watermark information from chaos carrier signal to compose a new sequence. The new sequence calculates with original chaos sequence, also can estimate original watermark information $\hat{b}_q$.

The first method can be detected blind watermark, but its robust is weak. The second method need the original chaos sequence. It can prove the exist of watermark, but its robust also is weak.

4 Simulation

To detect the performance of this algorithm, Under the condition of no distortion, we select embedded image's watermark information to be "abcdefghijklmnopqrstuvw xyz"26 English letters. Under the condition of compression, we select the embedded information to be "ABCDE"5 English letters. The DCSK modulation code's half-period is 5 signs. In experiment of watermark correlation detection, produce 1000 chaos sequence X_m to detect the image response, in this process X_{500} is original chaos sequence, and the image to be detected is 256x256 Lean image. The initial value of chaos sequence is 0.2. The threshold value T_c is 0.5.

Fig. 5. Left is original image ,right is embedded watermark
Embedded information is "abcdefghijklmnopqrstuvwxyz"

It is a key problem to select watermark detection threshold value. Thus to explain the existence of watermark in this experiment, from probability statistical, present a dynamic detection threshold value. In this arithmetic ,we adopt '4σ' principle to present dynamic threshold value, this will obtain more accurate detection result ,and will discuss at the following experiment. The following results are got from MATLAB simulation.

At the case of no distortion, with the first method, the detection result can detect the information "abcdefghijklmnopqrstuvwxyz". With the second can detect the information "abcdefghijklmnopqrstuvwxyz".

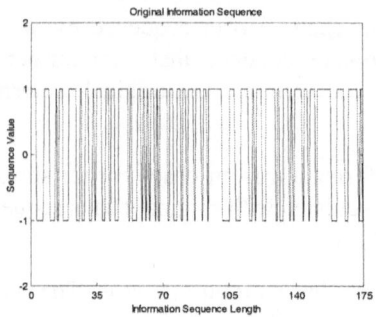 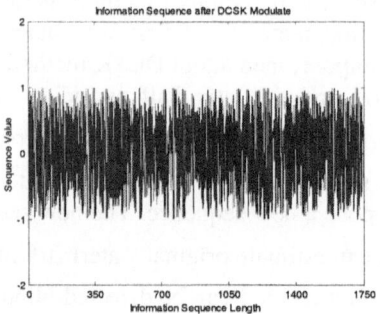

Fig. 6. Original watermark(left), watermark after DCSK modulated (right)
Embedded information "abcdefghijklmnopqrstuvwxyz"

Figure 6 denotes the wave of original information and modulated. Due to chaos sequence is sensitive to initial value , and that make chaos modulation have terribly secret. Hence, utilizing chaos sequence to DCSK modulate original information, the watermark have double protection.

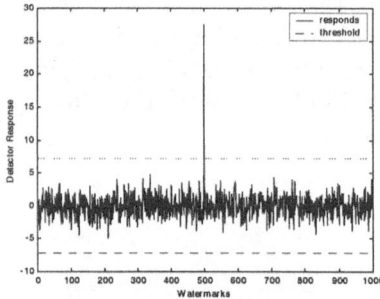 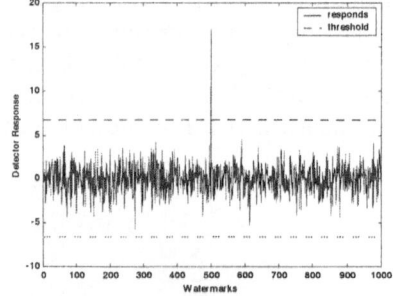

Fig. 7. Left is watermark correlation detection figure under no distortion,
Right is 88% compressed watermark correlation detection figure

As figure 7 has shown, the chaos sequence after DCSK demodulated is correlation inspected with 1000 different initial chaos sequence (include original chaos sequence), the result with no distortion is 27.6. The threshold value is ± 7.15. Under 88% compressed Result is 17.0 and the threshold is 6.7. If under 88%, can't detect exist of watermark, the main reason is the inspect chaos sequence and original sequence are not synchronization. We shall make a further research to find better method.

Resume the compressed information is difficult, so we expand double original information to resume information, and can detect information under 90% compressed. But character number is limit. Under 5,it can be detected, but if above 5,the rate of miscode is high. The next work, reduce rate of miscode is also a critical task.

5 Conclusion

This paper put forward a new digital watermark algorithm based on DCSK. The watermark which has modulated by chaos sequence is embedded into image sub-band, which is obtained from image wavelet decompose, then resume original image by invert-transform. By using DCSK demodulate principle can detect watermarked image, original watermark information can be estimated. We reach the anticipative aim. With a number of experiment data, it proved to be a better algorithm in secrecy performance based on DCSK. It also can realize the blind-detection of common still image watermark.

This algorithm has some issues to be settled. The following is our farther work:

①Analyze capability of chaos sequence and research chaos information coded, rectify coding;

②The research of DCSK modulation and demodulation model and watermark embedded and detection model;

③The synchronization problem of chaos sequence in image;

④The further research on resist-assault.

⑤The further arithmetic research on watermark embedded threshold (DWT).

References

[1]   Michael Peter Kennedy, Geza Kolumban, Digital communications using chaos, Signal Processing 80(2000)1307-1320.

EFBLA: A Two-Phase Matching Algorithm for Fast Motion Estimation

Hsien-Wen Cheng and Lan-Rong Dung

Department of Electrical and Control Engineering
National Chiao Tung University
Hsinchu, Taiwan
jswcheng.ece89g@nctu.edu.tw and lennon@cn.nctu.edu.tw

Abstract. This paper presents a novel matching algorithm for fast motion estimation. The algorithm, called the Edge-matching First Block-matching Last Algorithm (EFBLA), first employs the edge-matching procedure to determine candidate motion vectors and then performs the conventional block matching with the SAD criteria on the candidates. The edge-matching procedure features low computation load and high degree of data reusability; therefore, it requires fewer operations and lower memory size compared with the full search algorithm. As the result of benchmarking and comparing to the full search algorithm, EFBLA may significantly save the computation load by 93.9% while the degradation of PSNR is very little.

1 Introduction

Motion Estimation (ME) has been proven to be effective to exploit the temporal redundancy of video sequences and, therefore, becomes a key component of multimedia standards, such as MPEG standards and H.26X[1]. The most popular algorithm for the VLSI implementation of motion estimation is the block-based full search algorithm [2][3][4][5]. The block-based full search algorithm has high degree of modularity and requires low control overhead. However, the full search algorithm notoriously needs high computation load and large memory size [6]. The highly computational cost has become a major problem on the implementation of motion estimation.

Many papers have proposed different ways to reduce the computation requirement of the full search algorithm. Most of them target on the elimination of impossible motion vectors, such as SEA [7] and LRQ [8], and only perform motion estimation on the possible ones. They have done great jobs on the reduction of block-matching evaluations and further save the computation power and cost. Applying this philosophy, we have developed a two-phase algorithm that is suitable for implementation of motion estimation. The two-phase algorithm contains two steps, one is the edge matching and the other is the block matching. We call the two-phase algorithm the Edge-matching First Block-matching Last Algorithm (EFBLA). Our goal is to decrease the number of block-matching evaluations without degrading the video quality such that the computation load can be significantly reduced. Hence,

Y.-C. Chen, L.-W. Chang, and C.-T. Hsu (Eds.): PCM 2002, LNCS 2532, pp. 112-119, 2002.

how to effectively remove the impossible motion vectors becomes the key to solve the cost-consuming problem of the full search algorithm.

The edge-matching procedure does not require complex computation; it only needs shift operations, quantization, comparison and thresholding. The edge-matching procedure first performs high-pass filtering on a macro-block of the current frame, called a reference block, and then determines edge-pixels that have larger value than threshold. According the distribution of edge-pixels, the procedure will determine the scan direction for high degree of data reusability. Then, we start matching the reference block with macro-blocks of the previous frame, called target blocks. The matching order is based on the scan direction. The matching criterion is unmatched edge-pixel count (UEPC). An unmatched edge-pixel is the pixel of the target block whose low-resolution quantized value is different from that of the corresponding edge-pixel of the reference block. Obviously, the smaller the UEPC value the more similar the target block to the reference block. Thus, the EFBLA only picks the motion vectors with lower UEPC target blocks as the survived motion vectors (SMVs). Following the edge-matching phase, the proposed algorithm begins to perform block matching with the SAD criteria on SMVs. As results of simulating MPEG video clips, the EFBLA requires fewer addition operations than the full search algorithm.

2 Algorithm

Fig.1 illustrates the flow chart of the Edge-matching First Block-matching Last Algorithm (EFBLA). Assume that the macro-block size is N-by-N and the searching window is 2p-by-2p; both coordinates are ranged from –p to p-1. The orientation of the reference block is (x, y).

The first phase of EFBLA contains five steps as described below:

Step 1. Perform basic high-pass spatial filtering [10] on the reference block.

The step 1 first performs the edge enhancement using the high-pass spatial filter mask, as shown in Eq.(1). In eq. (1), the $f_k(x_p, y_i)$ represents the intensity of the pixel at (x_p, y_i) in current frame. Note that $\nabla f_k(u, v)$ expresses the gradient of the pixel at (u, v) and the larger the value of $|\nabla f_k(u, v)|$ the more possible is the pixel on the edge.

$$\nabla f_k(u, v) = \sum_{i=-1}^{1} \sum_{j=-1}^{1} c(i, j) \cdot f_k(u+i, v+j)$$

$$where \begin{cases} c = 8, when \ (i, j) = (0,0) \\ c = -1, \qquad otherwise \end{cases} \qquad (1)$$

$$(u, v) = (x, y) \sim (x + N - 1, y + N - 1)$$

Step 2. Calculate the edge threshold and mark the edge pixels.

The edge threshold is defined as Eq.(2). Basically, the EFBLA considers those pixels with $|\nabla f_k(u, v)|$ greater than Eth are the edge pixels, as shown in Eq.(3). If the pixel at (u, v) is the edge pixel, (u, v) is set to 1; otherwise, $\bullet(uv)$ is set to 0. To increase the accuracy of the edge-matching, the EFBLA also regards the pixels around pixels with $|\nabla f_k(u, v)|$ greater than E_{th} as the edge pixels as well. Thus, the EFBLA employs the edge extension as shown in Eq.(4) to mark the edge pixels.

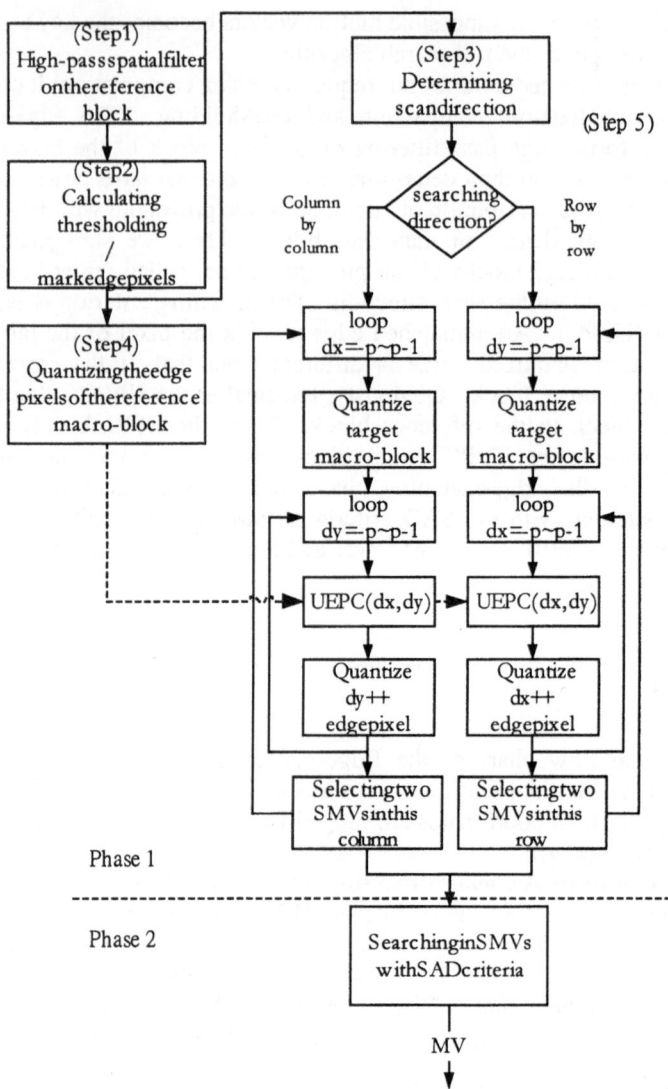

Fig. 1. The flow chart of EFBLA

$$E_{th} = \frac{\max(\nabla f_k(u,v)) + \min(\nabla f_k(u,v))}{2} \quad (2)$$

$$\alpha(u,v) = \begin{cases} 1 & if\ |\nabla f_k(u,v)| > E_{th} \\ 0 & otherwise \end{cases} \quad (3)$$

$$\alpha(u,v) = \begin{cases} 1 & if\ |\nabla f_k(u \pm 1, v \pm)| > E_{th} \\ 0 & otherwise \end{cases} \quad (4)$$

Step 3. Determine the scan direction.

The data reusability is highly dependent on the scan direction because it employs the criteria of unmatched edge-pixel count (UEPC), showed in step 5. For instance, if the edge pixels are widely distributed along with the y-coordinate, searching along with y-coordinate can reuse the data efficiently. Fig.2 shows the impact of the scan direction to the data reusability. Assume that the macro block size is 8-by-8 and the searching position shifts from A to B. The gray and black marks in Fig.2(b)(c) represent the edge pixels when the target block is at the position A. The black and white marks represent the edge pixels when the target block is at the position B. Therefore, the quantized data at the black marks can be reused in matching that uses the criteria of UEPC. Obviously, it just needs to calculate the quantized edge pixels in the white marks, then removes the unmatched edge pixel count in gray marks and plus these in white marks. So the scan direction in Fig.2(b) has higher degree of data reusability than that in Fig.2(c).

The EFBLA has two scan directions: column-by-column and row-by-row, as illustrated in Fig.3. To make the decision of scan direction, this step first determines the span width of edge pixels with x-coordinate, named the x-span, and the span width of edge pixels with y-coordinate, named the y-span. If the x-span is smaller than y-span, the step selects the column-by-column scan as the direction; otherwise, the scan direction will be row-by-row. For the example of Fig.2(a), the value of x-span is equal to four and the y-span is eight, and therefore the scan direction is column-by-column.

Step 4. Quantize the edge pixels of the reference block.

This step quantizes the pixel values at the edge pixels for the low-resolution computation. The philosophy of two-phase motion estimation is to eliminate impossible motion vectors at the lowest computation cost. Hence, the EFBLA utilizes low-resolution computation to perform the edge matching.

Eq.(5) represents the quantization of the reference blocks where $\hat{f}_k(u,v)$ is the value of two most significant bits (MSBs) of $(f_k(u,v) - Avg_k)$, $Q_2(f_k(u,v) - Avg_k)$, and Avg_k is the total pixel average of the reference block. The reason that the step quantizes $(f_k(u,v) - Avg_k)$ instead of $f_k(u,v)$ is because the former has higher variance than later. The higher variance leads to higher degree of accuracy for edge matching.

$$\hat{f}_k(u,v) = Q_2(f_k(u,v) - Avg_k) \ \forall \, \alpha(u,v) = 1$$

$$where \ \ Avg_k = \frac{\displaystyle\sum_{u=x}^{x+N-1} \sum_{v=y}^{y+N-1} f_k(u,v)}{N^2} \tag{5}$$

Step 5. Perform edge matching and generate SMVs.

Upon the completion of the step 3 and 4, the first phase starts to perform edge matching. First, the EFBLA matches the motion vectors along with the scan direction obtained by the step 3. The edge matching employs the criteria of unmatched edge-pixel count (UEPC), as shown in Eq.(6). In Eq.(6), $\hat{f}_{k-1}(u+dx, v+dy)$ is the quantization result of the target block with the motion vector (dx, dy).

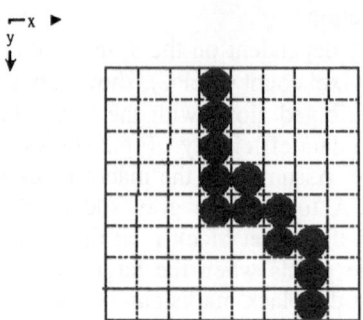

Fig. 2.(a) Edge pixels of reference block

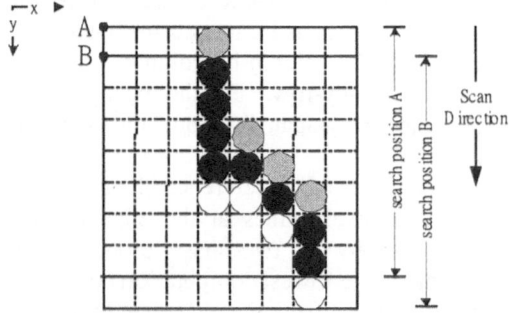

Fig. 2. (b) Efficient searching direction

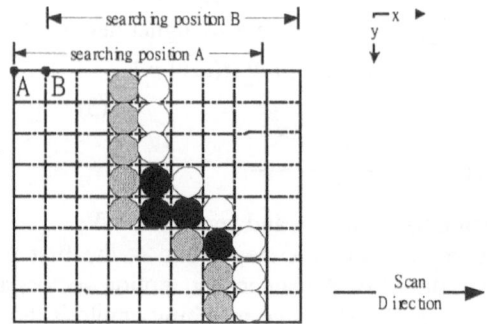

Fig. 2. (c) Inefficient search direction

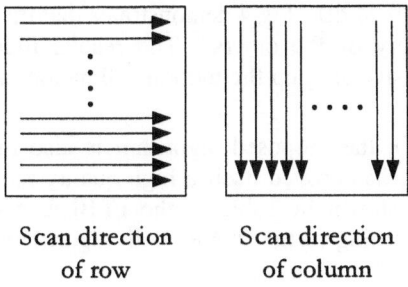

Scan direction   Scan direction
   of row   of column

Fig. 3. Two EFBLA Scan direction of searching

$UEPC(dx,dy)$

$$= \sum_{u=x}^{x+N-1} \sum_{v=y}^{y+N-1} \alpha(u,v) \cdot \delta[\hat{f}_k(u,v), \hat{f}_{k-1}(u+dx, v+dy)] \qquad (6)$$

$where\ \hat{f}_{k-1}(u+dx, v+dy) = Q_2(f_{k-1}(u+dx, v+dy)$

$- Avg_k)\ \ \forall \alpha(u,v) = 1\ and\ \delta[\hat{f}_k, \hat{f}_{k-1}] = \begin{cases} 0, & for\ \hat{f}_k = \hat{f}_{k-1} \\ 1, & otherwise \end{cases}$

Next, the step generates a pair of SMVs for each scan line, either row or column. The motion vectors with the high UEPCs on a scan line are most likely impossible ones. Thus, the EFBLA only picks the motion vectors with lowest two UEPC target blocks as the survived motion vectors (SMVs).

Following the first phase, the EFBLA performs block-matching with SAD criteria on SMVs. Note that the block-matching requires much less evaluations than the traditional full search block-matching because the first phase has eliminated a large amount of impossible motion vectors.

3 Performance Analysis

The proposed algorithm significantly reduces the number of motion vectors that requires costly evaluations. To compare with the other motion estimation algorithms, this paper uses two metrics: computation cost and the peak signal-to-noise ratio (PSNR). Since the major operation of motion estimation algorithms is addition, we approximately consider the total number of additions required for each macro-block as the computation cost.

This paper employs four MPEG video clips, "fish", "weather", "news" and "children", as the testbenches. Each frame has 352 by 288 pixels and each pixel value is 8-bit. The macro-block size is 16 by 16, and the search window ranges from (-16,-16) to (15,15).

Table 1 and 2 show the simulation results for three algorithms: full search algorithm (FS) [1], low-resolution quantization (LRQ) [8] and the proposed algorithm. We simulated 40 frames for each testbench. Obviously, the EFBLA significantly saves up to 93.9% of the computation cost of FS while the PSNR degradation is less than 0.24 dB. Fig.4 demonstrates that the quality of the EFBLA is very close to the quality of the others. The results illustrate that the proposed algorithm is capable of speeding up the motion estimation and having a good quality as well.

Compared with LRQ, the proposed algorithm is also outperformed in terms of computation cost. LRQ has proved itself a high-quality motion estimation with low computation cost. As shown in Table 1, the EFBLA has 7%~15% reduction of computation cost. Regarding to the PSNR, both algorithms are competible to each other.

Table 1. Comparison of the number of operations

	Fish	Weather	News	Children
FS	783,360			
LRQ	57,279			
Proposed	53,263	50,456	47,541	48,797
Reduction vs. FS	93.2%	93.6%	93.9%	93.8%
Reduction vs. LRQ	7.0%	11.9%	17.0%	14.8%

Table 2. Average PSNR (dB)

	Fish	Weather	News	Children
FS	29.5758	32.7005	36.3478	26.3535
LRQ	29.4117	32.6307	36.0524	26.1839
Proposed	29.3986	32.4642	36.2031	26.1330

4   Conclusion

This paper proposes a novel algorithm to significantly speed up the motion estimation by reducing the evaluation of motion vectors. As the result of simulating video clips, the quality degradation is very little comparing with FS, less than 0.24dB. In addition, the algorithm features adaptive choosing for the scan direction; it turns out a high degree of data reusability and low memory requirement.

Acknowledgments. This work was supported in part by Taiwan MOE Program for Promoting Academic Excellent of Universities under the grant number 91-E-FA06- 4-4.

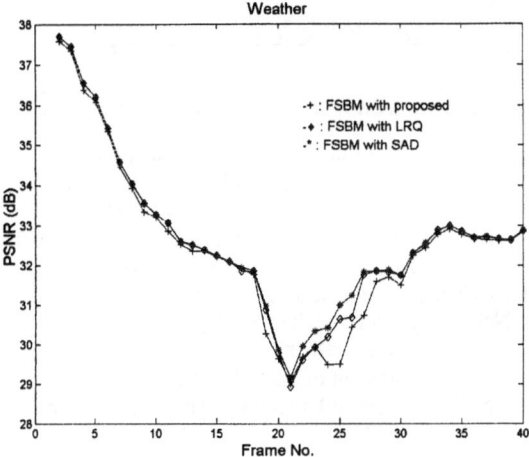

Fig. 4. PSNR of the Weather sequence.

References

1. Peter Kuhn, "Algorithms, Complexity Analysis and VLSI Architectures for MPEG-4 Motion Estimation," Kluwer Academic Publishers, 1999.
2. Jun-Fu Shen, Tu-Chih Wand, and Liang-Gee Chen, "A Novel Low-Power Full-Search Block-Matching Motion-Estimation Design for H.263+," IEEE Trans. on Circuits and Systems for Video Technology, Vol. 11, No. 7, pp. 890-897, July 2001.
3. V. L. Do and K. Y. Yun, "A low-power VLSI architecture for full-search block-matching motion estimation,", IEEE Trans. on Circuits and Systems for Video Technology, Vol. 8, No. 4, pp. 393-398, Aug. 1998.
4. M. Brunig and W. Niehsen, "Fast full-search block matching,", IEEE Trans. on Circuits and Systems for Video Technology, Vol. 11, No. 2, pp. 241-247, Feb. 2001.
5. L. Sousa and N. Roma, "Low-power array architectures for motion estimation,", 1999 IEEE 3rd Workshop on Multimedia Signal Processing, pp. 679-684, 1999.
6. Bo-Sung Kim and Jun-Dong Cho, "VLSI architecture for low power motion estimation using high data access reuse," The First IEEE Asia Pacific Conference on ASIC, AP-ASIC '99, pp162-165, 1999.
7. W. Li and E. Salari, "Sucessive Elimination Algorithm for Motion Estimation," IEEE Transactions on Image Processing, Vol. 4, No. 1, pp. 105-107, Jan. 1995.
8. S. Lee and S. I. Chae, "Motion estimation algorithm using low-resolution quantization," IEE Electronic Letters, vol. 32, no 7, pp. 647-648, Mar. 1996.
9. Takagi A., Nishikawa K. and Kiya H., "Low-bit motion estimation with edge enhanced images for lowpower MPEG encoder," ISCAS 2001, Vol. 2, pp. 505-508, 2001.
10. Rafael C. Gonzalez, and Richard E. Woods, "Digital Image Processing," Addison Wesley, Sep. 1993.

A New Adaptive Return Prediction Search Algorithm for Block Matching

Chih-Lun Fang[1], Wen-Yen Chen[2], Yuan-Chen Liu[3], and Tsung-Han Tsai[4]

[1] Graduate School of Educational Communications and Technology,
National Taipei Teachers College, Taipei, Taiwan
allen@ect.ntptc.edu.tw
[2] Graduate School of Mathematics and Science Education,
National Taipei Teachers College, Taipei, Taiwan
[3] Graduate School of Educational Communications and Technology,
National Taipei Teachers College, Taipei, Taiwan
liu@tea.ntptc.edu.tw
[4] Department of Electrical Engineering,
National Central University, Taoyuan, Taiwan

Abstract. In most block-based video coding systems, some of the fast block matching algorithms use the origin as the initial search center. But the tracking result of these algorithms is not well enough. To improve the accuracy of the fast block matching algorithms, a new adaptive return prediction (ARP) search algorithm is proposed in this paper. The proposed algorithm exploits the temporal correlation and the characteristic of returning phenomenon to obtain one or two predictive motion vectors, and one of the predictive motion vectors are chosen as the initial search center. This predicted search center is found closer to the global minimum, thus the center-biased algorithm can find the motion vector more efficiently. Simulation results show that the proposed algorithm enhances the accuracy of BMA as well as reduces their computational requirement.

1 Introduction

In recent years, the block-matching algorithm (BMA) for motion estimation has been widely applied in various video coding standards, such as CCITT, H.261 [1], H.263 [2], MPEG-1 [3], and MPEG-2 [4]. A straightforward BMA, the full search algorithm (FS), designed to search the best matching block in the previous frame to get the optimal motion vector is time-consuming. Considering the large computation in BMA, it is not capable to meet the requirement of real-time applications. Thus, a lot of fast search algorithms for block motion estimation were proposed in [5]-[10]. Among these fast algorithms, three-step search algorithm (3SS) [5] is applied in various standards and it is recommended by RM8 of H.261 and SM3 of MPEG because of its simplicity and effectiveness.

The block motion displacement in global optimum motion vector distribution is highly biased at the central area, because the block motion field of real video sequence varies slowly. The center-biased method is used in the new three-step search algorithm (N3SS) [6], the four-step search algorithm (4SS) [7], block-based gradient descent search algorithm (BBGDS) [8], and unrestricted center-biased diamond search algorithm (UCBDS) [9], etc. However, most of these fast hierarchical BMAs use the origin point of the searching window as the initial search center and have not

Y.-C. Chen, L.-W. Chang, and C.-T. Hsu (Eds.): PCM 2002, LNCS 2532, pp. 120-126, 2002.
© Springer-Verlag Berlin Heidelberg 2002

exploited the motion correlation of the blocks among the moving object of successive images. To improve accuracy of fast BMAs, the motion correlation between the neighboring frames can be used to predict an initial search center that reflects the motion trend of current frame. Then the final motion vector can be efficiently found by the center-biased BMAs such as the 4SS, BBGDS, and UCBDS.

In this paper, an adaptive return prediction (ARP) block matching algorithm is proposed. The algorithm exploits the temporal correlation [10] and the characteristic of returning origin in real video sequences. By selecting a proper initial search center, the algorithm is capable to estimate larger movements. The main advantages of ARP are to predict the true motion vector accurately and reduce the computational requirement. In this paper, we use this information to predict the initial search center. Experimental results show that the predicted center is closer to the global minimum. Thus, center-biased BMAs such as the 4SS, BBGDS, and UCBDS are used to refine the motion vector.

The rest of this paper is organized as follows. Section 2 discusses the motion vector distribution. The adaptive return prediction block matching algorithm is described in Section 3 Section 4 shows the experimental results and performance comparisons, and conclusions are given in Section 5

2 Motion Vector Distribution

Considering the main characteristics of video sequence, it is found that the most of video sequence has the characteristics that objects move in some small fixed area while the background remains static. This phenomenon is especially suitable for slow motion. Therefore, the distribution of motion vector is highly biased at the central 5x5 area. This can be observed from the distribution of motion displacement (MD) based on the two dimensions full search (2DFS) algorithm for the test sequence of "Salesman". There are nearly 99% MD enclosed in the central 5x5 area, as shown in Fig. 1.

However, there are many errors existing in fast movement images. This can be also observed from the motion vector distribution based on the 2DFS algorithm in another test sequence of "Football" as shown in Fig. 2. In the Football sequence, nearly 68% MD are enclosed in the central 5x5 area and 17% MD are over 7. Thus the 17% search may be trapped in local optima. For this reason, the center-biased search pattern is discomfort in fast movement images. It is needed a proper prediction which makes the predicted search center closer to the real motion vector. Therefore, the center search area should be adapted in the ARP algorithm to find the global minimum with less search points. Fig. 3 illustrates the adaptive return result of the MD distribution started from the prediction point for "Football", nearly 81% MD of "Football" is enclosed in the central 5x5 area and only 6% MD is over 7. Based on the result of the return characteristic of motion vector, we propose a new predictive mode to estimate and search motion vector fast and accurately.

3 Adaptive Return Prediction Block Matching Algorithm

Due to the continuity of motion in the temporal domain, the motion fields of the same macroblock in the natural video sequences may be highly correlated. Therefore, the correlation of successive frames is utilized to estimate the initial motion vector.

However, when the moving object's direction changes abruptly or the motion speed is not steady. It is not effective to estimate the motion from the motion fields in the previous frame. Moreover, the moving object has been left the macroblock or the real motion vector exceeds the search range of block matching that the global minimum will be found in origin possibly. Fig. 4(a)-4(b) and Table 1 illustrate the phenomenon of converted motion vector. Therefore, we use adaptive return origin algorithm to improve search algorithms. The proposed adaptive return prediction block matching algorithm has two stages. The first stage is an initial search center prediction using the temporal correlation and characteristic of returning origin. The second stage is a center-biased fast BMA.

Stage 1) Determination of the Initial Search Center: The motion vectors in horizontal and vertical directions of the k-th macroblock of the previous frame are denoted by x and y, respectively. In logical, if |x|>3 or |y|>3, it seems that the motion vector is bigger and the k-th macroblock will be a fast region. The initial prediction motion vector in current frame is given as Vk=(x,y) or Vk=(0,0), then we choose the smaller SAD point from the motion vector (x,y) and (0,0) as the initial search center. Otherwise, we predict still Vk=(x,y). This process can be formulated as

$$V^k = \begin{cases} (x,y) \text{ or } (0,0), & \text{if } |x|>3 \text{ or } |y|>3 \\ (x,y), & \text{otherwise} \end{cases} \tag{1}$$

where Vk is the motion vector of the k-th macroblock in the current frame.

Stage 2) Refinement of the Motion Vector: After the stage one, if there is temporal correlation or return origin characteristic, the real motion vector should be very close to the initial search center Vk. Thus, center-biased fast BMA's such as 4SS, BBGDS, and UCBDS are chosen to refine the final motion vector. These three algorithms use center-biased checking points patterns in the first step, which increase the chance for finding a global minimum within the central 5x5 area. Fig. 5 is the flowchart of the ARP search algorithms.

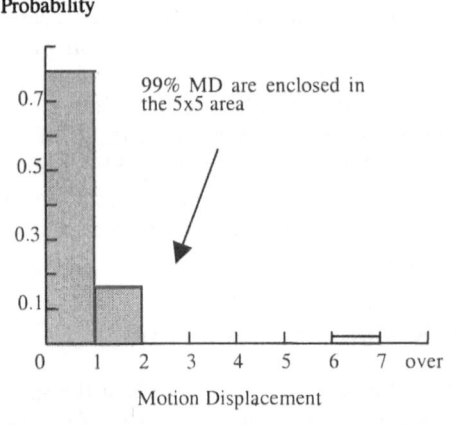

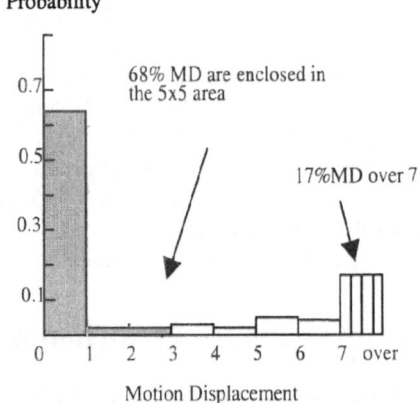

Fig. 1. The MD distribution of "Salesman"   **Fig. 2.** The MD distribution of "Football"

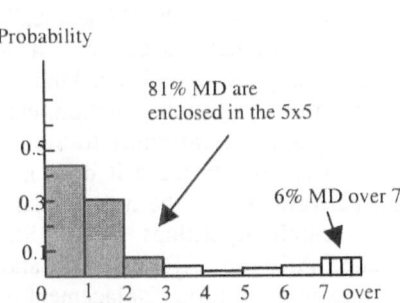

Fig. 3. The MD distribution started from the initial prediction point of "Football"

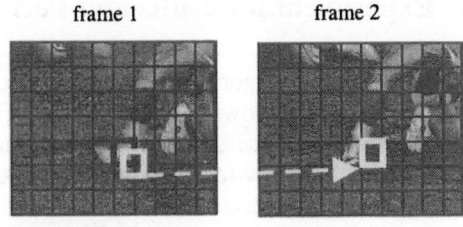

Fig. 4(a). The MV of the 282th macroblock of frame 2 is (7,7).

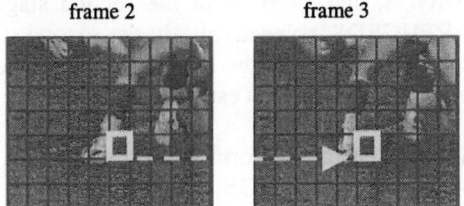

Fig. 4(b). The MV of the 282th macroblock of frame 3 is (0,0).

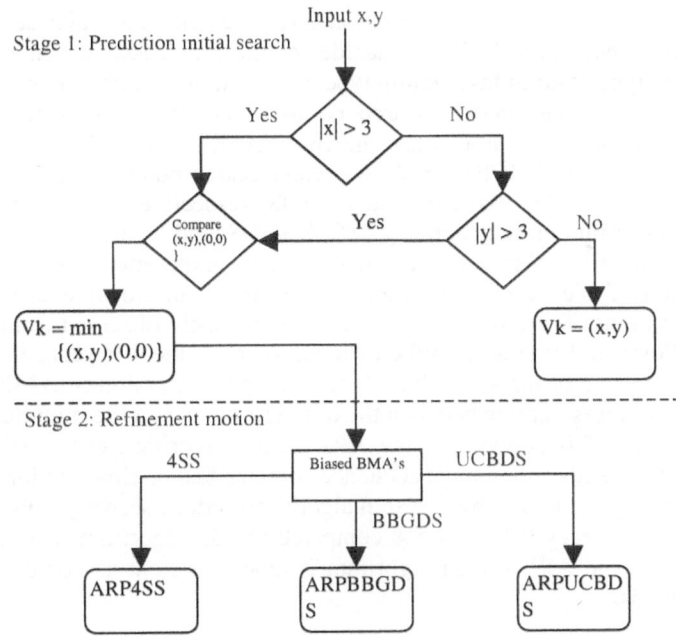

Fig. 5. The flowchart of the ARP search algorithms.

4   Experimental Results and Performance Compairsons

The ARP search algorithm is simulated using four sequences of the "Salesman", "Table Tennis", "Flower Garden", and "Football" of 60 frames, respectively. It is represented that these sequences have been selected to emphasize different kind of motions, such as low-to-high movement, camera zooming and panning motion, etc. The size of each individual frame is 352 x 240 pixels quantized uniformly to 8 bits. The sum-absolute distortion (SAD) matching criterion is used because it does not require any multiplication and can produce similar performance as the mean-square error (MSE). The new adaptive return prediction search algorithms using 4SS, BBGDS, and UCBDS in the second stage are named ARP4SS, ARPBBGDS, and ARPUCBDS, respectively. In the second stage, the maximum motion displacement is set to ±7 pixels and the block size is fixed at 16x16. Only the luminance component is employed for motion estimation.

The statistical performance comparisons of FS, 3SS, 4SS, ARP4SS, BBGDS, ARPBBGDS, UCBDS, and ARPUCBDS in terms of MSE and search points are given in Table 2 and Table 3, respectively. In Table 2, the MSE comparisons show that the ARP4SS, ARPBBGDS, and ARPUCBDS achieved better performance than the original algorithms of 4SS, BBGDS, and UCBDS, respectively. The ARP improvement can be easily observed from these figures, especially in the area where fast motion is involved. In computational requirement, the ARP search algorithm requires only four comparisons to decide for the initial search center in predictive slow motion type. And in fast motion type, the spent on comparison search points had been merged into the average search points of per macroblock to calculate. The results of average search points are shown in Table 3. From Table 3, the ARP4SS, ARPBBGDS, and ARPUCBDS reduce average search points by about 9%, 23%, and 14% compared to 4SS, BBGDS, and UCBDS, respectively. In theory, the average search points of minimum needed by 4SS, BBGDS, and UCBDS are 15.61, 8.30, and 12.07, respectively. Therefore, we can analyze the experimental results to go a step further. From Table 4, we can compare the largest improvable degree of various search algorithms. The ARP improvement can be easily observed from the "MSE to FS" and "Points to Minimum". Where "MSE to FS" is the difference in average MSE between the test algorithms and the full-search algorithm, "Points to Minimum" is the difference in average points between the test algorithms and the minimum need of the test algorithms. This shows that the ARP search algorithm can predict an optimal motion vector whether the image sequence contains fast or slow motion. On the other hand, the average of above ARP search algorithms reduce search points by about 43% and improve accuracy by about 5% compared to 3SS algorithm. No matter how the sequences are, the ARP search algorithm is much efficient as compared with other search methods.

5   Conclusions

Based on the temporal correlation and characteristic of returning origin, new efficient adaptive return prediction search algorithm is proposed in this paper. The algorithm exploits the temporal correlation and the characteristic of returning origin to predict the initial search center and uses center-biased block matching algorithms to refine the final motion vector. Experimental results show that ARP search algorithm combined with 4SS, BBGDS, and UCBDS effectively improves their performance in terms of mean-square error measure with less average searching points. Due to it's accuracy, it can be expected to apply the algorithm to other BMAs to improve the estimation accuracy of the motion vector.

Table 1. Some motion vectors of 2DFS in the Football sequence

macroblock	frame 2	frame3	frame 4	frame 5	frame 6	frame 7	frame 8
76	-4,-4	-5,-3	0,0	0,0	0,-1	0,0	0,0
99	-4,-4	-5,-3	-5,-3	-5,-3	0,-1	2,-2	3,-3
117	-1,-4	4,-7	2,-7	-1,-7	4,-7	0,-7	0,0
124	-2,-7	-1,-6	0,0	-2,-6	-1,-7	0,0	2,-3
153	7,7	3,7	5,7	2,7	3,7	7,7	0,0
176	7,0	4,0	-7,0	-7,0	0,0	2,0	6,0
282	7,7	0,0	0,0	0,-1	0,-1	0,0	2,7
303	1,1	0,1	0,0	0,0	1,7	0,0	0,0
324	-2,6	0,0	0,0	0,-1	0,-1	0,0	0,0

Table 2. Comparison of Average MSE of various algorithms

	Salesman	Tennis	Garden	Football	Average
FS	23.78	111.99	264.24	388.77	197.19
3SS	24.74	151.41	306.59	419.19	225.48
4SS	24.29	132.15	290.72	437.53	221.17
ARP4SS	23.93	124.83	270.57	429.03	212.09
BBGDS	23.97	139.81	279.09	460.18	225.76
ARPBBGDS	23.99	130.18	273.12	442.52	217.45
UCBDS	24.73	142.23	286.49	456.17	227.40
ARPUCBDS	23.96	126.10	270.72	437.13	214.48

Table 3. Comparison of Average search points of various algorithms

	Salesman	Tennis	Garden	Football	Average
FS	202.50	202.50	202.50	202.50	202.50
3SS	22.83	22.93	23.14	22.93	22.96
4SS	16.15	18.42	18.90	18.14	17.90
ARP4SS	15.98	16.18	16.34	16.84	16.33
BBGDS	9.49	13.37	14.32	14.29	12.87
ARPBBGDS	8.71	9.74	9.43	11.88	9.94
UCBDS	13.08	15.31	15.14	17.20	15.18
ARPUCBDS	12.40	12.82	12.76	13.93	12.98

Table 4. Compare the largest improvable degree of various search algorithms in terms of average MSE and search points.

sequences	Salesman		Tennis		Garden		Football	
algorithms	MSE to FS	Points to Minimum	MSE to FS	Points to Minimum	MSE to FS	Points to Minimum	MSE to FS	Points to Minimum
4SS	0.51	0.54	20.16	2.81	26.48	3.29	48.76	2.53
ARP4SS	0.15	0.37	12.84	0.57	6.33	0.73	40.26	1.23
BBGDS	0.19	1.19	27.82	5.07	14.85	6.02	71.41	5.99
ARPBBGDS	0.21	0.41	18.19	1.44	8.88	1.13	53.75	3.58
UCBDS	0.95	1.01	30.24	3.24	22.25	3.07	67.4	5.13
ARPUCBDS	0.18	0.33	14.11	0.75	6.48	0.69	48.36	1.86

References

[1] International Telecommunication Union, "Video codec for audiovisual services at px64 kbits", ITU-T Recommendation H.261, March 1993.

[2] International Telecommunication Union, "Video coding for low bitrate communication ", ITU-T Draft Recommendation H.263, July 1995.

[3] ISO/IEC JTC1/SC29/WG11, "ISO/IEC CD 11172-3:Information technology," MPEG-1 International Standard, 1993.

[4] ISO/IEC JTC1/SC29/WG11, "ISO/IEC CD 13818-3:Information technology," MPEG-2 International Standard, 1995.

[5] T. Koga, K. Ilinuma, A. Hirano, Y. Iijima and T. Ishiguro, "Motion-compensated interframe coding for video conferencing," in Proc. NTC 81, New Orleans, LA, Nov./Dec. 1981, pp. C9.6.1-C9.6.5.

[6] R. Li, B. Zeng, and M. L. Liou, "A new three-step search algorithm for block motion estimation," IEEE Trans. Circuits Syst. for Video Tech., Vol.4, No.4, pp.438-442, Aug. 1994.

[7] L. M. Po and W. C. Ma, "A novel four-step search algorithm for fast block motion estimation," IEEE Trans. Circuits Syst. for Video Tech., Vol.6, No.3, pp.313-317, June 1996.

[8] L. K. Liu and E. Feig, "A block-based gradient descent search algorithm for block motion estimation in video coding," IEEE Trans. Circuits Syst. for Video Tech.,vol. 6, no. 4, pp. 419-422, Aug. 1996.

[9] J. Y. Them, S. Ranganath, M. Ranganath, and A. A. Kassim, "A novel unrestricted center-biased diamond search algorithm for block motion estimation," IEEE Trans. Circuits Syst. for Video Tech.,vol. 8, no. 4, pp. 369-377, Aug. 1998.

[10] Y.-Q. Zhang, S. Zafar, "Predictive block-matching motion estimation for TV coding – Part II: Inter-Frame Prediction", IEEE Trans. Broadcasting, Vol.37, No.3, pp.102-105, September 1991.

A 2-Stage Partial Distortion Search Algorithm for Block Motion Estimation

R. Yu, K.P. Lim, D. Wu, F. Pan, Z.G. Li, G. Feng, and S. Wu

Laboratories for Information Technology
21 Heng Mui Keng Terrace, Singapore 119613,
{rsyu,kplim,djwu,fpan,zglin,gnfeng,swu}@lit.org.sg

Abstract. In this paper, we propose a novel 2-Stage Partial Distortion Search (2S-PDS) algorithm to reduce the computational complexity in block motion estimation algorithms. In this algorithm, an early-rejection stage is introduced where the partial distortion of a decimated pixel block is calculated and compared with its local minimum. A block is rejected without calculating the full distortion of the entire block if the partial distortion is larger. In order to reduce the probability of false rejection, the local minimum is amplified by a pre-defined threshold before the comparison. Experimental results show that the proposed algorithm can reduce the complexity of block motion estimation algorithm significantly with only marginal performance penalty. The proposed algorithm can be used in combination with full-search or other fast search algorithms.

1. Introduction

In low bit rates video coding, the technique of block motion estimation is widely adopted to improve coding efficiency. The basic concept of block motion estimation can be described as follows. For each equal-sized pixel block in the current frame, we look for the block in the previously transmitted frame that is the closest to it, according to a predefined distortion criterion such as Sum of Absolute Error (SAE) or Mean Square Error (MSE). This closest block is then used as a predictor for the present block. The most straightforward way to find the matching block is to use the Full Search (FS) algorithm, where all the candidate blocks inside a search window are matched. Although it gives optimal prediction performance, the computational complexity of FS algorithm is generally too high for practical application.

Numerous search strategies have been proposed to reduce the computation complexity of the block motion estimation procedure. Most search strategies aim to reduce the computational complexity by matching only some of the checking points inside a search window. Typical examples of such approach include 3 Step Search (3SS) [1], 4 Step Search (4SS) [2], Diamond Search (DS) [3], and the Hexagon Search (HS) [4]. Based on the assumption that all pixels in a block move by the same amount, another feasible approach to reduce the computation is to use only a fraction of the pixels in a block in calculating the Block Distortion Measure (BDM). Bierling [5], [6] introduced a hierarchical motion estimation technique in which an

Y.-C. Chen, L.-W. Chang, and C.-T. Hsu (Eds.): PCM 2002, LNCS 2532, pp. 127–134, 2002.

approximation of the motion field is obtained from lowpass-sub-sampled filtered images. Koga *et al.* [7] proposed using 1:2 decimated images without low-pass filtering. Intuitively, using a decreasing number of pixels in the procedure will eventually result in inaccurate estimation. For example, it is reported in [8] that a 1:4 decimation ratio will increase the error entropy by 0.1 bit/pixel and will be considered excessive. In [8], Liu and Zaccarin proposed an efficient method based on pixel decimation that considered only a fourth of the pixels of the total block. The technique is very effective for its quality performance. However, since all the positions in the search window should be considered, it cannot be applied to every search strategy. In [9], [10] and [11] the authors proposed a sequence of adaptive pixel decimation methods in which the patterns of selected pixels varied according to the value of the gradient of the luminance. Although these adaptive methods give slightly better results than [8], the test operations required prevent a global reduction of the computational complexity. Recently, in [12], a technique called Normalized Partial Distortion Search (NPDS) algorithm is proposed where a halfway-stop technique is introduced. In this halfway-stop technique, the distortion from partial pixels is compared with the normalized current minimum distortion obtained with full pixels of a block. Although the normalized process increases the probability of early rejection of non-possible candidate predictor block, it also increases the risk of false rejection. In addition, the employment of normalized current minimum distortion may give inaccurate estimate for blocks with complex textures.

In this paper, we proposed a 2-Stage Partial Distortion Search (2S-PDS) algorithm to reduce the complexity of block motion estimation. In the proposed algorithm, an early-rejection stage is introduced in the BDM calculation where the partial distortion from a portion of the candidate block is first calculated and compared with its current minimum multiplied with a pre-defined threshold $\lambda > 1$. If the partial distortion is larger, this block is not likely to be a matching block and it is rejected without further calculating the full distortion. In general, the probability of false rejection is very small for large value of λ. However, larger λ will generally result in less candidate block being rejected in the early-rejection stage and hence less complexity reduction. In a practical application, the value of λ can be adjusted to determine the trade-off between the performance and the complexity reduction. The proposed algorithm can be used in combined with different block matching algorithms. Simulation results show that the proposed algorithm only introduces marginal performance penalty.

2. 2s-pds Algorithm

We choose the SAE as the matching criterion due to its low computational complexity. We refer to a block of $M \times N$ pixels as block (k, l) where the coordinate (k, l) is the upper left corner of the block and denote the intensity of the pixel with coordinates (i, j) in frame n by $F_n(i, j)$. In the early rejection stage the partial SAE is computed between the block (k, l) of present frame and the block $(k+x, l+y)$ of the previous frame with a pre-defined decimated pattern Φ:

$$\text{SAE}_{partial} = \sum_{(i.j)\in\Phi} \sum \left| F_n(k+i,l+j) - F_{n-1}(k+x+i,l+y+j) \right| \tag{1}$$

Here the pattern Φ is a decimated version of a $M \times N$ block. Some possible decimation patterns Φ with different decimation factors are given in Fig. 1 where the pixels marked with black are used in the SAE calculation.

The full SAE is then given by using all the pixels in the block:

$$\text{SAE}_{full} = \sum_{i=0}^{M-1} \sum_{j=0}^{N-1} \left| F_n(k+i,l+j) - F_{n-1}(k+x+i,l+y+j) \right| \tag{2}$$

The 2S-PDS is then carried out as follows (Fig. 2). For every matching block candidate (x, y) in a particular block matching algorithm, the value of $\text{SAE}_{partial}$ is computed initially. The computed $\text{SAE}_{parital}$ is compared with the current minimum value $\text{SAE}_{partial,min}$ times a pre-defined threshold λ. If $\text{SAE}_{partial} > \lambda \cdot \text{SAE}_{full,min}$, the block (k, l) is rejected without calculating SAE_{full}. In this way, substantial computational saving is achieved since most processing can be completed in this early-rejection stage. In the second stage, SAE_{full} is compared with the current minimum value $\text{SAE}_{full,min}$. The coordinate of that current checking point (x, y) is labeled as the best matching block so far if $\text{SAE}_{full} < \text{SAE}_{full,min}$ and meanwhile the values of $\text{SAE}_{partial}$ and SAE_{full} are recorded as the current minimum values. The search procedure then proceeds to the next checking point as specified by the particular search algorithm used.

Clearly, the value of λ plays a key role that determines the tradeoff between the accuracy of the motion estimation and the computation complexity. In the context of a practical implementation it may be selected experimentally considering the difficulty of finding the theoretically optimal value. It is found in our experiments that a satisfactory tradeoff is yielded for most video contents if λ is selected from 1.1 ~ 1.3. We further note that better results may be achieved if λ is adaptively selected according to certain criteria, such as the content or the motion level of the pixel block being processed. However, the complexity of such an adaptive process may prevent an overall reduction of the computational complexity unless it is implemented with very limited computational cost.

3. Results

We tested the 2S-DPS algorithm with different search strategies including the Full Search (FS), Diamond Search (DS), Hexagon Search (HS) and Four Step Search (FSS). The block size is 16×16 and the search window size is of ±16. We use the 1:9 decimation pattern as in Fig. 1(c) in the calculation of the partial SAE in the 2S-DPS algorithm. BDMs with full block and 1:4 decimated block and the NPDS algorithm

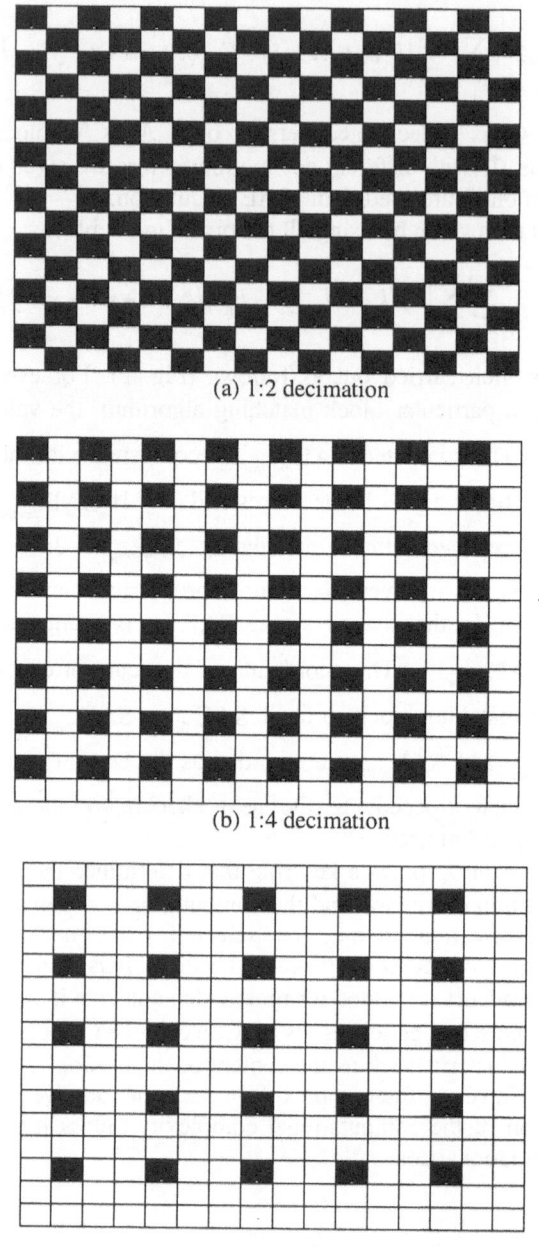

(a) 1:2 decimation

(b) 1:4 decimation

(c) 1:9 decimation

Fig. 1. Different decimation patterns of a 16x16 block with different decimated factors

from [12] are also included in our tests for comparison. MSE is used in our tests as the performance measurement of the quality of the motion estimation and the complexity of a scheme is measured by the ratio of the total number of the operations in BDM calculation of that scheme to that of the BDM with full block. 6 standard MPEG-4 testing sequences (QCIF size) with different motion levels were used. Results of our tests are summarized in Tables 1. From those results it is obvious that 2S-PDS algorithm achieves similar MSE performances to those of the full block method with only 20% ~ 30% of its computational complexity. Note that although the NPDS algorithm achieves lower complexity compared with the 2S-PDS algorithm in most test items, its MSE performance is not acceptable especially in the tests where fast search strategies are used.

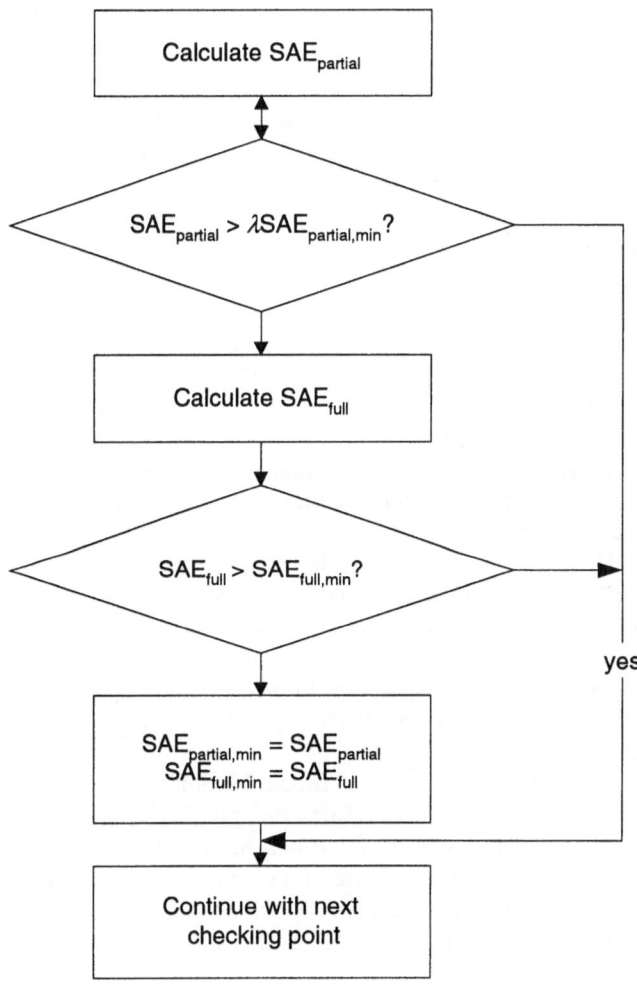

Fig. 2. The 2D-PDS algorithm

4. Conclusions

We have developed a novel 2-Stage Partial Distortion Search algorithm (2S-PDS) for block motion estimation where an early-rejection stage is introduce in the BDM calculation to reduce the computational complexity. Simulation shows that using the proposed 2S-PDS algorithm in combined with full search or other fast block motion estimation algorithms will result in considerable reduction in the computational complexity with only marginal increase in the distortion. The proposed algorithm is therefore suitable for efficient implementations of real-time digital video applications on platforms with limited computational capability.

References

1. R. Li, B. Zeng and M. L. Liou, "A new three-step search algorithm for block motion estimation," *IEEE Tran. on Circuits & System for Video Technology*, vol. 4, pp. 438 –442, Aug. 1994
2. L. M. Po and W. C. Ma, "A novel four-step search algorithm for fast block motion estimation," *IEEE Tran. on Circuits & System for Video Technology*, vol. 6, pp. 313 – 317, June 1996.
3. J. Y. Tham *et al*, "A novel unrestricted center-biased diamond search algorithm for block motion estimation," *IEEE Trans. On Circuits & Systems for Video Technology*, vol. 8, no. 4, pp. 369 – 377, Aug. 1998.
4. C. Zhu *et al*, "A novel hexagon-based search algorithm for fast block motion estimation," *Proc. ICASSP 2001*.
5. M. Bierling and R. Thoma, "Motion compensation field interpolation using a hierarchically structured displacement estimator," *Signal Processing*, vol. 11, no. 4, pp. 387 –404, Dec. 1986.
6. M. Bierling, "Displacement estimation by hierarchical block matching", *SPIE, Visual Commun. Image Processing '99*, vol. 1001, pp. 942 – 951, 1988.
7. T. Koga and *et al*, "Motion Compensated Interframe Coding for Video Conferencing," *Proc. Nat. Telecommun. Conf. 1981*, pp. 5.3.1 – 5.3.5.
8. B. Liu and A. Zaccarin, "New Fast Algorithms for the Estimation of Block Motion Vectors", *IEEE Trans. Circuits and Systems for Video Technology*, vol.3, No. 2, April 1993, pp. 148 – 157.
9. Y. L. Chan and W. C. Siu, "A New Block Motion Vector Estimation Using Adaptive Pixel Decimation," *Proc. ICASSP 1995*, pp. 2257 – 2260.
10. -, "New Adaptive Pixel Decimation for Block Motion Vector Esitmation," *IEEE Tran. Circuits and System for Video Technology*, vol. 6, no. 1, pp. 113 – 118, 1996.
11. Y. L. Chan, W. L. Hui and W. C. Siu, "A Block Motion Vector Estimation Using Pattern Based Pixel Decimation," *Proc. IEEE International Symposium on Circuits and Systems 1997*, pp. 1153 – 1156.
12. C. Cheung and L. Po, "Normalized Partial Distortion Search Algorithm for Block Motion Estimation," *IEEE Tran. Circuits and Systems for Video Technology*, vol, 10, no. 3, pp. 417 – 422, 2000.

Table 1. Performance comparison of BDM with full block and 1:4 decimated block, NPDS algorithm and 2S-PDS algorithm used in combination with different block motion estimation algorithms.

Video Sequence	Full	1:4 decimation	NPDS	2S-PDS		
				$\lambda = 1.1$	$\lambda = 1.2$	$\lambda = 1.3$
	MSE	MSE/ Complexity	MSE/ Complexity	MSE/ Complexity	MSE/ Complexity	MSE/ Complexity
Akiyo	28.13	28.53/ 25%	28.52/ 6%	28.28/ 11%	28.21/ 12%	28.13/ 12%
News	50.56	52.03/ 25%	51.56/ 6%	50.90/ 12%	50.76/ 12%	50.80/ 12%
Hall	46.82	47.91/ 25%	48.27/ 6%	47.23/ 11%	47.00/ 12%	46.90/ 12%
Coast-guard	111.09	117.02/ 25%	115.05/ 7%	112.85/ 13%	112.20/ 14%	112.15/ 16%
Foreman	75.93	81.79/ 25%	80.68/ 6%	78.15/ 11%	77.03/ 12%	77.31/ 13%
Carphone	58.83	62.53/ 25%	61.77/ 6%	60.08/ 12%	59.43/ 12%	59.51/ 13%

(a) Full Search

Video Sequence	Full	1:4 decimation	NPDS	2S-PDS		
				$\lambda = 1.1$	$\lambda = 1.2$	$\lambda = 1.3$
	MSE	MSE/ Complexity	MSE/ Complexity	MSE/ Complexity	MSE/ Complexity	MSE/ Complexity
Akiyo	28.18	28.44/ 25%	28.53/ 13%	28.40/ 19%	28.34/ 21%	28.19/ 22%
News	50.66	52.71/ 25%	51.71/ 14%	51.23/ 20%	51.08/ 22%	50.89/ 25%
Hall	46.93	47.95/ 25%	48.64/ 13%	47.71/ 19%	47.30/ 21%	47.05/ 25%
Coast-guard	119.39	127.14/ 25%	126.14/ 17%	122.61/ 27%	120.95/ 32%	119.21/ 37%
Foreman	80.79	86.10/ 25%	86.31/ 18%	84.40/ 27%	83.05/ 32%	82.24/ 37%
Carphone	58.83	64.53/ 25%	63.40/ 16%	62.68/ 23%	62.28/ 27%	61.61/ 32%

(b) Four Step Search

Video Sequence	Full	1:4 decimation	NPDS	2S-PDS		
				$\lambda = 1.1$	$\lambda = 1.2$	$\lambda = 1.3$
	MSE	MSE/ Complexity	MSE/ Complexity	MSE/ Complexity	MSE/ Complexity	MSE/ Complexity
Akiyo	28.19	28.44/ 25%	28.55/ 15%	28.40/ 21%	28.35/ 23%	28.19/ 25%
News	50.69	52.12/ 25%	51.83/ 16%	51.37/ 22%	51.11/ 25%	50.99/ 28%
Hall	46.91	47.90/ 25%	48.50/ 15%	47.60/ 21%	47.40/ 24%	47.16/ 27%
Coast-guard	118.29	124.85/ 25%	127.14/ 20%	122.26/ 30%	119.74/ 36%	119.00/ 42%
Foreman	80.29	85.49/ 25%	86.70/ 20%	84.10/ 28%	82.85/ 36%	81.25/ 42%
Carphone	60.33	63.53/ 25%	63.31/ 18%	61.58/ 25%	60.94/ 29%	60.58/ 35%

(c) Diamond Search

Video Sequence	Full	1:4 decimation	NPDS	2S-PDS		
				$\lambda = 1.1$	$\lambda = 1.2$	$\lambda = 1.3$
	MSE	MSE/ Complexity	MSE/ Complexity	MSE/ Complexity	MSE/ Complexity	MSE/ Complexity
Akiyo	28.18	28.41/ 25%	28.49/ 14%	28.39/ 20%	28.34/ 22%	28.19/ 24%
News	50.94	52.47/ 25%	51.88/ 15%	51.42/ 21%	51.23/ 23%	51.05/ 27%
Hall	47.03	47.99/ 25%	48.53/ 14%	47.81/ 21%	47.35/ 23%	47.14/ 27%
Coast-guard	120.52	127.99/ 25%	128.01/ 19%	124.53/ 30%	121.94/ 35%	120.88/ 41%
Foreman	82.03	87.24/ 25%	87.64/ 19%	85.30/ 30%	83.64/ 35%	82.86/ 40%
Carphone	60.12	62.95/ 25%	63.38/ 17%	61.42 26%	60.93/ 31%	60.45/ 35%

(d) Hexagon Search

A Fast Block-Matching Motion Estimation Algorithm with Motion Modeling and Motion Analysis

Dong-Keun Lim and Yo-Sung Ho

Kwangju Institute of Science and Technology (K-JIST)
1 Oryong-dong, Puk-gu, Kwangju, 500-712, Korea
{dklim, hoyo}@kjist.ac.kr

Abstract. By modeling the block-matching algorithm as a function of the correlation of image blocks, we derive search patterns for fast block-matching motion estimation. The proposed approach provides an analytical support for the diamond-shape search pattern, which is widely used in fast block-matching algorithms. We also propose a new fast motion estimation algorithm using adaptive search patterns and statistical properties of the object displacement. In order to select an appropriate search pattern, we exploit the relationship between the motion vector and the block differences. By changing the search pattern adaptively, we improve motion prediction accuracy while reducing required computational complexity compared to other fast block-matching algorithms.

1 Introduction

In recent days, there has been an increasing demand for real-time video communication services, such as wireless or internet video conferences. Motion estimation has been widely used to find motion information in various video coding standards and plays an important role in video compression.

A block-matching algorithm (BMA) is adopted in most video coding standards, such as H.261, H.263, MPEG-1, MPEG-2 and MPEG-4, to estimate motion vectors. A brute-force BMA makes an exhaustive search for an optimal block displacement that minimizes a predefined cost function. The full search (FS) BMA requires very expensive computation. Therefore, various fast BMAs have been developed to reduce the computational burden [1-8]. Those fast BMAs employ different heuristic search patterns for improved trade-off between video quality and computational complexity.

In this paper, we derive search patterns for fast block-matching motion estimation analytically, based on the correlation of image blocks. The derived patterns are verified with various test video sequences. The analysis presented in this paper supports the diamond shape search patterns, which are widely used in many fast BMAs [5-8]. We also propose an adaptive search algorithm, which changes search patterns for motion estimation based on statistical properties between the object displacement and block differences. Simulation results are presented to show effectiveness of the proposed motion search algorithm.

Y.-C. Chen, L.-W. Chang, and C.-T. Hsu (Eds.): PCM 2002, LNCS 2532, pp. 135-142, 2002.
© Springer-Verlag Berlin Heidelberg 2002

2 Optimal Search Pattern

2.1 Problem Statement

Since the shape and the size of the search pattern in the fast BMA jointly determine the convergence speed and estimation performance, we analyze search patterns. In the block-matching algorithm, we calculate matching criteria between current and previous blocks in each search pattern. We reduce the displacement between checking positions in several steps to increase motion accuracy.

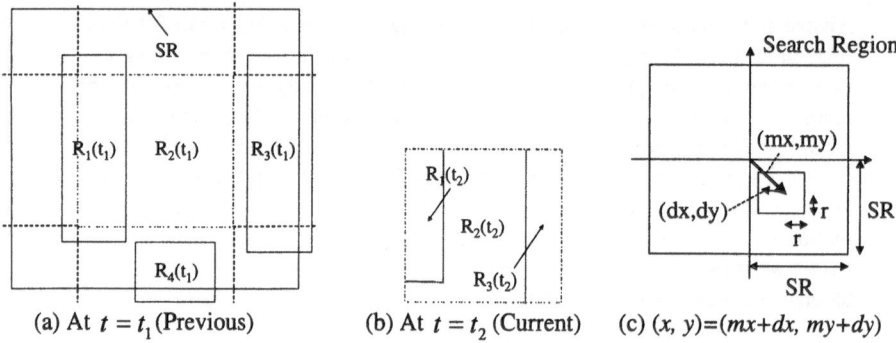

$$\text{(a) At } t = t_1 \text{ (Previous)} \qquad \text{(b) At } t = t_2 \text{ (Current)} \qquad \text{(c) } (x,\ y) = (mx + dx,\ my + dy)$$

Fig. 1. Block Region Diagram

If we assume that a block is partitioned with a limited number of regions of similar characteristics, each region can be represented by a certain value. In Fig. 1, $R_i(t_k)$ means the representative value of region R_i at time k. Let $OA_{(x,y)}(Cost(R_i,\ R_j))$ be an overlapped area with $Cost(R_i,\ R_j)$ when we match a block in the current frame and a block having (x,y) displacement in the search region(SR) in the previous frame.

In order to find the best matched position, we calculate the total cost, $Total-Cost(x,y)$, at each candidate position (x,y) and decide a motion vector, $MV(mx,my)$.

$$TotalCost(x,y) = \sum_{\substack{Ri \in Re\,gion(t=t1) \\ Rj \in Re\,gion(t=t2)}} OA_{(x,y)}(Cost(R_i, R_j)) \tag{1}$$

$$MV(mx, my) = \min_{(x,y) \in SR} TotalCost(x, y) \tag{2}$$

For a simple analysis, we consider an image block whose pixel values are uniform inside the block and the image block is uncorrelated to its background. In this analysis, we use correlation for the following matching criterion.

$$OA_{(x,y)}(Cost(R_i, R_j)) = \begin{cases} 0, & \text{if } i \neq j \\ 1, & \text{if } i = j \end{cases} \tag{3}$$

In Fig. 1(c), r is a small region of 4×4 pixels around the motion vector (mx,my). (dx,dy) indicates the displacement between the optimal search position and the current search position.

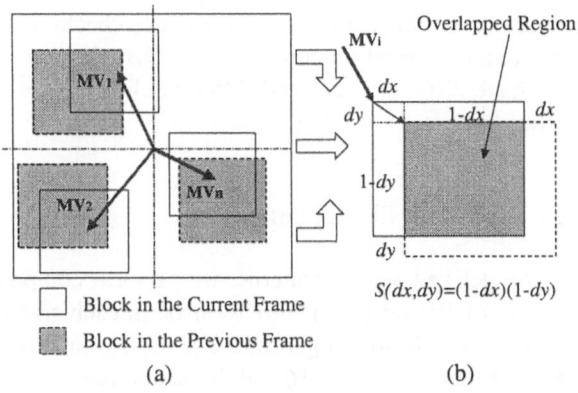

Block in the Current Frame
Block in the Previous Frame

$S(dx,dy)=(1-dx)(1-dy)$

(a)   (b)

Fig. 2. Correlation between Image Blocks.

Although we do not know the direction and the magnitude of the actual object movement, (mx,my) in Fig. 1(c) or MV_i in Fig. 2(a), we can derive analytic search patterns for motion estimation by investigating equi-correlation contours as a function of the distances, dx and dy, between checking positions in the search pattern.

2.2 Derivation of Analytic Search Pattern

The correlation $S(dx,dy)$ between the block and the search region can be calculated as the normalized area of the overlapped region, as shown in Fig. 2(b).

$$S(dx, dy) = (1- | dx |)(1- | dy |), \ 0 \le | dx |, | dy | \le 1 \tag{4}$$

where $|dx|$ and $|dy|$ are normalized by the block size in the horizontal and vertical dimensions, respectively. For $|dx| \ge 1$ or $|dy| \ge 1$, we set $S(dx, dy)=0$.

Similar to the steepest descent algorithm, our search strategy is to find points of the minimal sum of absolute differences on the equi-correlation contours. In practice, we use surrounding motion vectors to predict the current motion vector (mx, my). Around this predicted position, we have small matching errors. We can derive the equi-correlation contours as a function of dx and dy as follows.

If we represent a position (dx,dy) in the block by the following linear relationship

$$dy = c \cdot dx, \ c \in \Re \tag{5}$$

From Eq. (4) and Eq. (5), we can find locations of displacement (dx,dy) having the same correlation value.

$$dx = \frac{(c+1) \pm \sqrt{(c-1)^2 + 4c \cdot S(dx, dy)}}{2c} \tag{6}$$

By varying the value of c both in Eq. (5) and in Eq. (6), we can plot equi-correlation contours in Fig. 3(a). The resulting equi-correlation contours have the same characteristics as the search patterns used in the diamond search [4-5,8] and the advanced zonal search [6-8]. From the analytical equi-correlation contours in Fig. 3(a), we can generate various search patterns. By sampling checking positions from the continuous analytical equi-correlation contours, we chose discrete search points. The diamond shape can have different sizes and different choices of samples to optimize motion characteristics.

2.3 Experimental Results for Search Pattern

In order to verify the derived search patterns, we perform computer simulations on ITU-T test sequences of CIF and ITU-R 601 formats. In each simulation, the original image is used as a reference frame to generate a motion-compensated prediction image. For FS BMA, the block size is 16×16 and the search region is ±7. In other words, we normalize the values such that $0 < |dx|, |dy| < 7/16 \approx 1/2$.

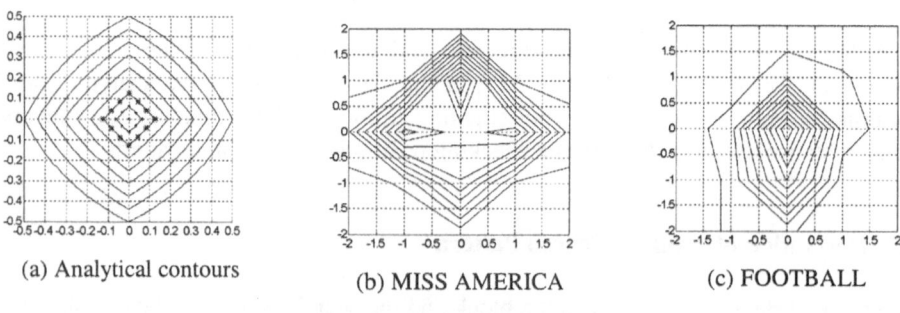

(a) Analytical contours

(b) MISS AMERICA

(c) FOOTBALL

Fig. 3. Motion Distribution

While Fig. 3(a) indicates optimal search patterns for $S(dx,dy) < 1/2$, Fig. 3(b) and Fig. 3(c) show the real motion vector fields for MISS AMERICA and FOOTBALL, respectively, where the axes are normalized. We observe that the derived optimal search patterns and the experimental ones are all diamond-shaped, which implies that our derivation is valid for the optimal search pattern for BMA. To increase the motion estimation accuracy, we may increase the size of diamond shape and the number of checking positions, and modify the diamond shape with rounded sides.

3 Adaptive Motion Search

In teleconferencing video, most image blocks are regarded as stationary. Motion vectors for stationary image blocks are mostly around (0,0). In general, a large object displacement would produce a large block difference (BD) within the search region (SR). We exploit these characteristics for efficient motion search.

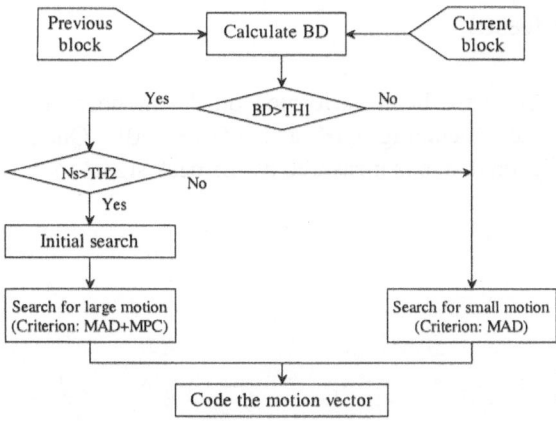

Fig. 4. Adaptive Motion Search Algorithm

Fig. 4 explains the overall procedure of the proposed adaptive motion search (AMS) algorithm, where Ns denotes the number of significant pixels in the block. The threshold values, TH1 and TH2, are determined experimentally.

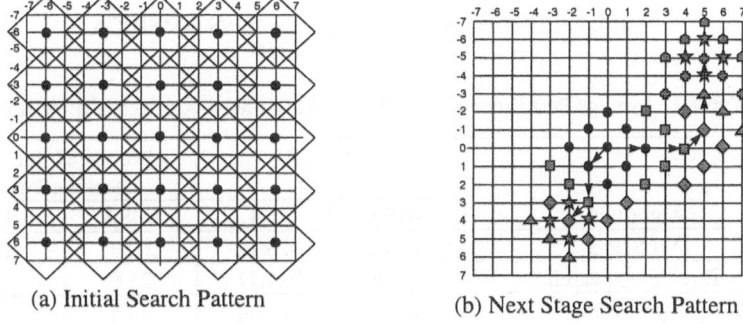

(a) Initial Search Pattern   (b) Next Stage Search Pattern

Fig. 5. Search Patterns for Large Motion

If the block difference is large, we use the initial search pattern, shown in Fig. 5(a). The initial search pattern consists of the uniform lattice that covers the search region. Once the minimum distortion position is selected in the initial search, other positions near this position are examined in the next stages. In Fig. 5(b), we show two diamond search examples [4-5], which explains two different search strategies. Depending on the last position of the minimum distortion, we add three or five new checking positions at each step. This procedure is repeated until we find the minimum distortion in the center of the search pattern or the boundary of search region. The final motion vector is the minimum distortion position among the one-pixel spaced positions around it.

If the block difference is small, the search region is limited to a small local region. The procedure for small motion is similar to that for large motion, while we start with neighboring 3×3 square pixel positions.

4 Simulation Results

Computer simulations have been performed on the monochrome test sequences of different image sizes including CIF and ITU-R 601. Quality of the motion-compensated prediction image is measured by the peak signal-to-noise ratio (PSNR).

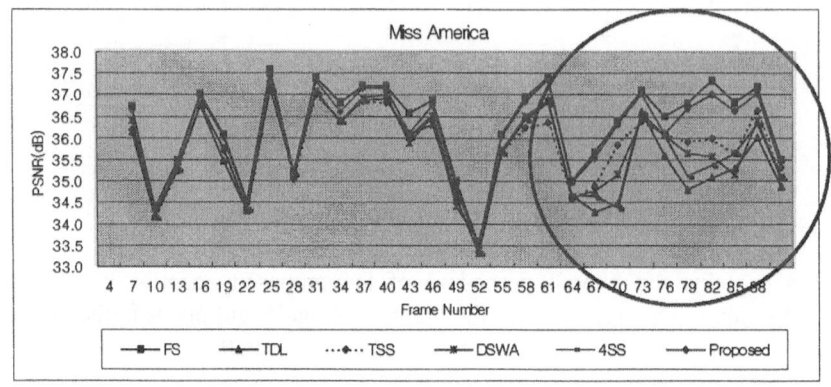

Fig. 6. Performance Comparisons for MISS AMERICA

Table 1. Average Performances of BMAs (MISA: Miss America, FB: Football)

Algorithm	PSNR(dB)		Average Number of Checking Points	
	MISA	FB	MISA	FB
Full Search	36.29	23.12	225.0	225.0
Three Step Search	35.78	21.77	25.0	25.0
4-Step Search	35.81	21.84	20.9	21.9
2-D Log Search	35.62	21.63	16.6	19.3
Dynamic Search	35.77	21.78	19.8	17.8
Adaptive Motion Search(AMS)	36.17	22.99	14.8	29.7

Note: Block Size =16×16, Search Region = ±7

Fig. 6 shows experimental results. The proposed AMS (Adaptive Motion Search) algorithm is compared with FS (full search), TDL (two-dimensional logarithmic search) [1], TSS (three-step search) [1], 4SS (four-step search) [2], and DSWA (dynamic search window adjust and interlaced search) [3] algorithms. From frame number 60 to 85 in Fig. 6, the proposed method provides good prediction while the others fail to estimate large motions. The result is also obvious in FOOTBALL sequence, since it has large motions.

The comparison with popular fast block-matching algorithms are summarized in Table 1, where we note that AMS(adaptive motion search) improves motion prediction accuracy and reduces the average number of checking position (CP).

5   Discussions and Analysis

Diamond search [4-5,8] and zonal search [6-8] have been used in the fast block-matching motion estimation algorithms in the MPEG-4 verification model [8]. Now zonal search was adopted as an informative annex in MPEG-2 IS software [11]. Zonal search can be performed with circular zonal search and diamond zonal search.

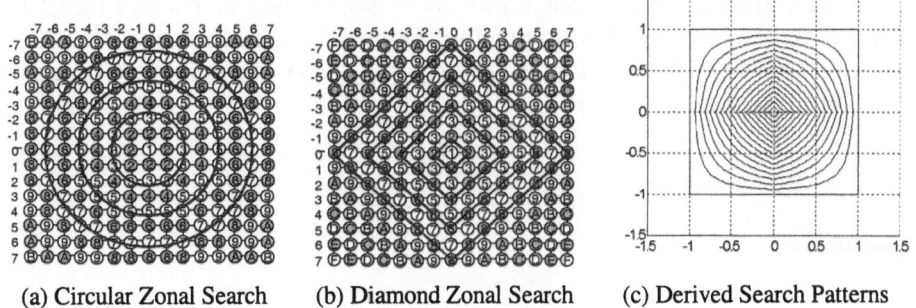

| (a) Circular Zonal Search | (b) Diamond Zonal Search | (c) Derived Search Patterns |

Fig. 7. Comparisons of Search Patterns

Fig. 7 shows the comparison of search patterns. In Fig. 3(a), we show the result for a limited search region to ±7, or 7/16 ≈ 0.5. By limiting the search region to ±15, or 15/16 ≈ 1, we can obtain the derived search pattern in Fig. 7. We can see that the search pattern changes from the diamond shape to the rectangular shape depending on the size of search region. This implies that the diamond shape is advantageous in a small motion, and the circular or the rectangular shape can be used for sequences of large motions.

In general search patterns used in fast block-matching algorithms, checking positions are located at the same distance from the center of the search region. It means that correlations in checking positions located in the same distance from the center of the search region may not always be the same value. Our definition of the search pattern considers the equi-correlation positions since matching criteria are not uniformly distributed according to the distance from the center of search area, but randomly distributed.

6   Conclusions

In this paper, we suggest an idea that the block-matching algorithm can be analyzed with a simplified model. Although our analysis is based on a simplified model, it provides some insights and justifications to the use of diamond search patterns in fast block-matching algorithms. Correlations in checking positions located in the same distance from the center of search region may not always be the same. The derived search pattern is optimal in the sense of equi-correlation positions. We also exploit the relationship between the motion vector and the frame difference of each block to select an appropriate search pattern in each block. As a result, we can improve motion prediction accuracy, while reducing required computational complexity compared to other fast block-matching algorithms.

Acknowledgements. This work was supported in part by the Korea Science and Engineering Foundation (KOSEF) through the Ultra-Fast Fiber-Optic Networks (UFON) Research Center at Kwangju Institute of Science and Technology (K-JIST), and in part by the Ministry of Education (MOE) through the Brain Korea 21 (BK21) project. We would like to thank Professor Ming-Ting Sun at University of Washington for helpful discussions.

References

1.   Musmann, H., Pirsh, P., Grallert, H.: Advances in Picture Coding. Proc. IEEE, vol. 73, no. 4 (1985) 523-548
2.   Po, L.M., Ma, W.C.: A Novel Four-step Search Algorithm for Fast Block Motion Estimation. IEEE Trans. Circuit and Syst. for Video Tech., vol. 6, no. 3 (1996) 313-317
3.   Lee, L.W., Wang, J.F., Lee, J.Y., Shie, J.D.: Dynamic Search-window Adjustment and Interlaced Search for Block-matching Algorithm. IEEE Trans. Circuit and Syst. for Video Tech., vol. 3, no. 1 (1993) 85-87
4.   Tham, J., Ranganath, S., Ranganath, M., Kassim, A.: A Novel Unrestricted Center-biased Diamond Search Algorithm for Block Motion Estimation. IEEE Trans. Circuit and Syst. for Video Tech., vol. 8 (1998) 369-377
5.   Zhu, S., Ma, K.: A New Diamond Search Algorithm for Fast Block Matching Motion Estimation. IEEE Trans. Image Processing, vol. 92 (2000) 287-290
6.   Tourapis, A., Au, O., Liou, M., Shen, G.: An Advanced Zonal Block based Algorithm for Motion Estimation. ICIP'99, vol. 2 (1999) 610-614
7.   Tourapis, A., Au, O., Liou, M.: New Results on Zonal based Motion Estimation Algorithms-Advanced Predictive Diamond Zonal Search. ISCAS, vol.5 (2001) 183-186
8.   Chiang, T., Sun, H.: Report of Ad hoc Group on Encoder Optimization, ISO/IEC/JTC1 /SC29 /WG11 MPEG99/ M5528 (1999)

Video Coding Using Supplementary Block for Reliable Communication[1]

Joo-Kyong Lee, Tae-Uk Choi, and Ki-Dong Chung

Dept. of Computer Science, Pusan National University, Busan, Korea
{jklee,tuchoi,kdchung}@melon.cs.pusan.ac.kr

Abstract. In this paper, we propose a video source coding scheme, called Supplementary Block based Encoding, to protect the propagation of the transmission errors over the network. Unlike the conventional source coding schemes, the proposed coder, for a macroblock in a frame, selects the two best matching blocks among several preceding frames. The best matching block is exploited for motion compensation of the current macroblock. The other block replaces the primary block in case of its loss during transmission at the decoder. This scheme has the advantages of reducing both the frequency and the impact of error propagation in comparision to related research. We implemented the proposed coder by modifying the H.263 standard source code and evaluated the performance through various simulations. The results show that the proposed scheme is more efficient than the H.263 baseline coder for both slow and fast motion video sequences.

1 Introduction

The results from extensive efforts to improve the performance of video coding and delivery have given birth to the international standards such as H.261, H.263, MPEG-1, MPEG-2, MPEG-4, etc. These video coding standards can achieve high coding efficiency by performing motion estimation/compensation and DCT, which eliminate the temporal redundancy between successive frames and spatial redundancy in a frame. However, these coding schemes are susceptible to error propagation over the network when some of the frames are corrupted during transmission.

So far, there have been many researches on the robust transmission over the network, and they could be classified into error concealment schemes, feedback channel schemes and error resilience source coding schemes. In error concealment schemes, the decoder reconstructs a corrupted block using neighboring or preceding blocks [4][5]. Feedback channel techniques utilize the feedback information from the decoder to the coder[6][7]. But these approaches cannot avoid the error propagation during the

---

[1] This work was supported by grant No. R05-2002-000-00354-0
from the Basic Research Program of the Korea Science & Engineering Foundation.

Y.-C. Chen, L.-W. Chang, and C.-T. Hsu (Eds.): PCM 2002, LNCS 2532, pp. 143–150, 2002.

round trip time delay for an ACK/NACK message [8]. In source coding schemes such as RVLC[1], EREC[2] and ISD[3], the coder compresses an original image using synchronization information to confine the corrupted regions by the transmission errors. RVLC is included in the MPEG-4 standard, and ISD is included in the H.263+. In the meantime, other source coding schemes which extend the number of candidate frames or referenced blocks for motion compensation were proposed. M. Budagavi [9] proposed a multiframe block motion compensation, MF-BMC, which selects the best matching block from the several preceding frames to predict the current block at the encoder. This approach has an inherent ability to overcome some transmission errors by referencing different frames. However, this scheme cannot avoid the error propagation if the referenced block is corrupted. C.S Kim[10] proposed Double-vector Motion Compensation(DMC), which performs motion compensation from the weighted superposition of the two preceding frames. If one of the referenced blocks is corrupted during transmission, this approach efficiently suppresses error propagation by reconstructing the current block using the other block. Y. Yu proposed Dynamic Multi-Reference Prediction(DMRP)[11], which is similar to DMC. The difference is that DMRP chooses a pair of blocks located in several previous frames. The diversity of the candidate frames makes the probability of error propagation of DMRP lower than that of DMC. The problem with these last two schemes is that the impact of transmission errors cannot be avoided even if one referenced block is corrupted, since they exploit both blocks for motion compensation[13].

In this paper, we propose a new source coding scheme which avoids error propagation exploiting a supplementary block. This paper is organized as follows. In the next section, we describe the Supplementary Block based Encoding scheme(SBE). In Section 3, we present the results of the simulations. In the last section, we conclude and discuss future research subject.

2 Supplementary Block Based Encoding

SBE(Supplementary Block based Encoding) makes full use of the best matching blocks among several previous frames to compress/decompress, which is the same with MF-BMC, and enhances the error resilience against transmission errors by exploiting the motion vector of the second matching block with minimized overhead. When a transmission error occurs, the decoder reconstructs the compressed block using the second best matching block indicated by the supplementary motion vector.

2.1 Concept

Fig. 1 (a) shows an example of selecting two macroblocks from different frames for a current block in a frame F_n at the encoder. The best matching block, called the primary block, in F_{n-1} is motion-compensated and the second best matching block, called the supplementary block, in F_{n-3} is used when the primary block is corrupted. So, its motion vector is coded into the macroblock header. Fig. 1 (b) shows the process of decoding the original block in F_n using the supplementary block in F_{n-3}, when a transmission error occurs on the primary block in F_{n-1}.

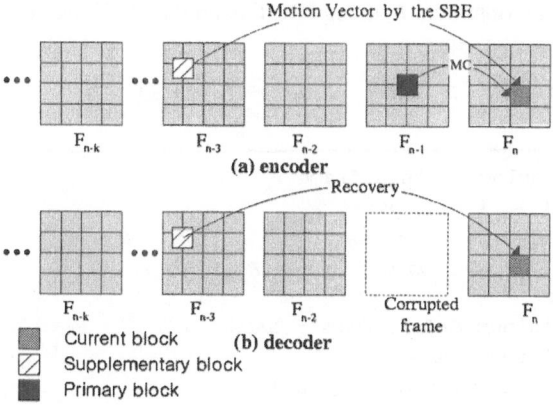

Fig. 1. An example of encoding at the encoder (a) and recovery of the current block at the decoder using a supplementary block (b)

2.2 Coding Process at the Encoder

The first coding process uses the same motion estimation as other video coding schemes except that it performs the estimation from several preceding frames and selects the two best matching blocks. Eq. (1) defines the cost function as Sum of Absolute Difference or SAD to get the differences between the current block and candidate blocks. Let a pixel of the current macroblock B_l in frame F_n be denoted as $F_n(x+u, y+v)$, where (x,y) is the coordinate of the left top corner of B_l and (u,v) is the relative location from (x,y) in B_l. The subscript l, denotes the index of a macroblock in frame F_n. Let a pixel in the kth candidate frame be $F_{n-k}(x+i+u, y+j+v)$ for motion estimation where $-p \square i, j \square p$; p is the search range. Because the motion estimation/compensation process induces a high computing overhead in the video coding system, the number of frames K to be searched should be carefully selected to minimize the overhead.

$$SAD_k(i,j) = \sum_{u=0}^{b-1}\sum_{v=0}^{b-1} |F_n(x+u,y+v)-F_{n-k}(x+i+u,y+j+v)| \, 1 \leq k \leq K, -p \leq i,j \leq p \qquad (1)$$

$$\left. \begin{aligned} sad_k &= \underset{-p \leq i,j \leq p}{Arg \ min} \, SAD_k(i,j), \quad 1 \leq k \leq K \\ S &= \{ sad_1, sad_2, \cdots, sad_K \} \end{aligned} \right\} \qquad (2)$$

Given Eq. (1), we can get sad_k as the minimum of the SAD values and its coordinate (i,j) for frame k (Eq.(2)) and sort K sad_ks by increasing order of the SAD value.

Eq. (3) shows the sorted K sad_ks. $Ssad^1$ is selected for the primary block and $Ssad^2$ for the supplementary block. Let us define B_l^p and B_l^s as the primary block and the supplementary block of current block B_l at the encoder and define $\overline{B}_l$ as the reconstructed block of at the decoder. The encoder performs DCT on the difference between B_l and B_l^p, and the decoder reconstructs B_l using IDCT from the DCT result.

$$Ssad^1 \leq Ssad^2 \leq \cdots \leq Ssad^K, \quad Ssad^k \in S, \quad 1 \leq k \leq K \tag{3}$$

```
for each macroblock B₁ in a frame Fₙ
      SADs ={ }, k = 1, B₁'={ }
      for preceding K frames
            SADs = SADs ∪ min_sad(B₁, Fₙ₋ₖ), k= k+1
      end for
      Bₗᵖ = mininum(SADs), SADs = SADs - Bₗᵖ
      Bₗˢ = minimum(SADs)
      Mode = determin_coding_mode(Bₗᵖ)
      If(Mode == INTER_TYPE)
            B₁'= insert_MV(B₁', B₁ˢ)
            B₁'= B₁'+ DCT(B₁- Bₗᵖ )
      else
            B₁'= intra_coding(B₁)
end for
```

Fig. 2. Coding algorithm at the encoder

2.3 Reconstruction at the Decoder

The decoder adds B_l^p to the IDCT result. In case B_l^p is corrupted during transmission, the decoder reconstructs B_l by replacing B_l^p with B_l^s (see Eq. (4)); this can efficiently suppress error propagation. However, $\overline{B}_l$ would be distorted severely if both the primary block and supplementary block are corrupted. As a matter of fact, the loss probability of both blocks at the same time is rather low because the primary block B_l^p and B_l^s reside in different frames according to Eq. (2) and Eq. (3). When both blocks are corrupted, we cannot apply Eq. (4) to the reconstruction of block B_l. Then, the SBE coder conceals the corruption by copying a block that is located at the same position in the nearest frame available in terms of time sequence.

$$\overline{B}_l = \begin{pmatrix} IDCT + B_l^s \text{ , only if } B_l^p \text{ is corrupted} \\ IDCT + B_l^p \text{ , otherwise} \end{pmatrix} \tag{4}$$

```
for each compressed block B'
      if(B   is uncorrupted)
          B̄ = IDCT(B')+ B
      else if(B is uncorrupted)
          B̄ = IDCT(B')+ B
      else
          B̄ = IDCT(conceal_block(B'))
end for
```

Fig. 3. Decoding algorithm at the decoder

3 Simulation Results

To implement the SBE coder, we modified the H.263 baseline source code by inserting a supplementary motion vector and its frame number. Because some macroblocks are intra-coded according to the coding type decision, they use neither primary block nor supplementary block. SBE codes the first frame as I frame, the others as P frames at the rate of 10 frames per second. We assumed that I frames are not corrupted during transmission. For the sake of convenience, we packetize a GOB(Group of Blocks) in a frame. GOB is a syncronization unit, composed of 11 macroblocks in a QCIF image (176×144) in the H.263 standard. Therefore, a frame can be packetized into 9 packets in QCIF format. We simulated the performance of the SBE with traces from Network Simulater, NS-2. The packet loss rate ranged from 2% to 29% over the Internet. We used the average luminance PSNR as a performance metric. PSNR is used as a measure for the quaility of image or video[12]. In Eq. (5), x_i is the original pixel's value and $\hat{x}_i$ is the reconstructed pixel's value. If the differences between original pixels' value and reconstructed pixels' value are high, PSNR will be low.

$$PSNR[dB] = 10 \cdot \log_{10} \frac{255^2}{\frac{1}{N}\sum_{i=1}^{N}(x_i - \hat{x}_i)^2} \tag{5}$$

At the H.263 decoder, packet loss will be concealed with the previously reconstructed frame available at the decoder. Fig. 4 presents the results of a rate-distortion performance evaluation of SBE and the H.263 standard with various bitrates at packet loss rates(PLR) of 0%, 5% and 15%. At lossless transmission, H.263 shows on average a 0.2dB higher PSNR than that of SBE. At a 5% packet loss rate, SBE shows on average a 1.4 dB higher PSNR for Foreman and a 0.9 dB higher PSNR for Akiyo than those of the H.263 baseline. However, at a 15% packet loss rate, SBE shows just a 0.1 dB higher PSNR for Foreman than that of H.263 and a 1.4dB higher PSNR for Akiyo. According to these experiments, we conclude that while SBE shows higher performance than that of the H.263 standard for slow motion video sequence such as Akiyo, SBE shows high performance at low packet loss rates for fast motion video sequences.

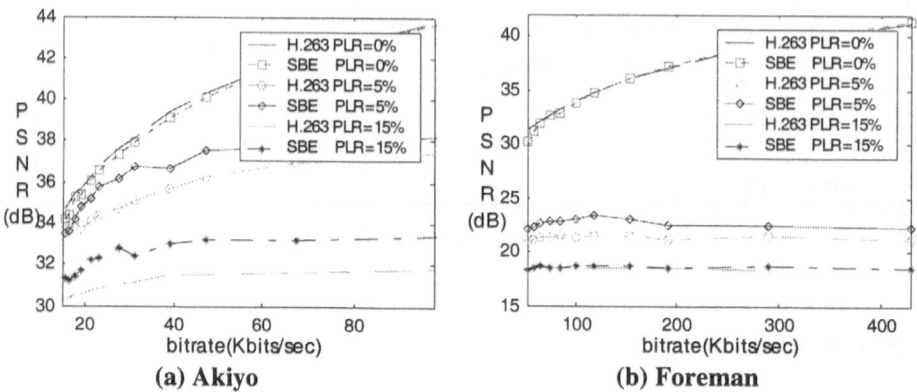

(a) Akiyo   (b) Foreman

Fig. 4. R-D Performance of (a) Akiyo and (b) Forman at various packet loss rates and bitrates.

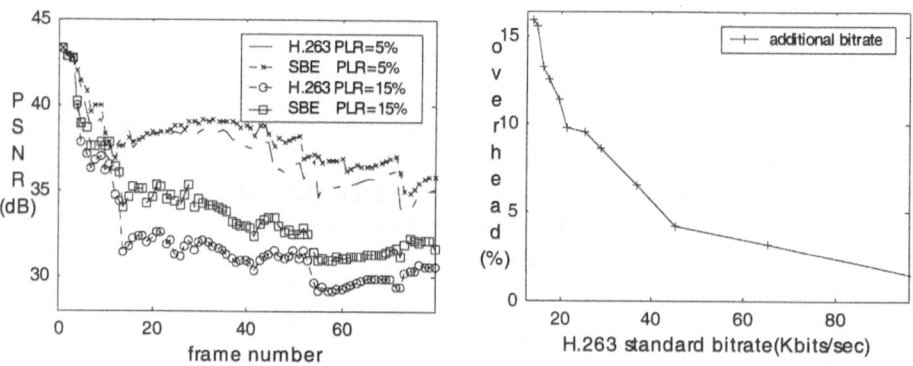

Fig. 5. PSNR for each frame of Akiyo   **Fig. 6.** Overheads of SBE vs. H.263 bitrates

Fig. 5 shows PSNR for each frame of Akiyo at a bitrate of 67.4 Kbps. On the whole, the slopes of SBE are smoother than those of the H.263 standard. At a 16% packet loss rate, SBE outperforms the H.263 standard baseline by a large margin.

Fig. 6 shows the propotion of the additional bits of SBE to the H.263 baseline. The bitrate of the compressed data can be adapted by a quantization value(QV) in video coding. The higher a quantization value is, the lower the bitrate is. In Fig. 6, the overhead goes up to a maximum of 16% at 13.6 Kbits/sec with QV of 2, whereas it goes down to 2% at 96.6Kbits/sec with QV of 3. This is because SBE includes additional information, which takes constant bits regardless of the bitrate change. Because coding efficiency decreases at low bitrates, we need to negotiate between coding efficiency and reconstructed video quality.

In Fig. 7, we calculate PSNR with different packet loss rates ranging from 2% to 29%. Irrespective of different packet loss rates, SBE outperforms the H.263 standard baseline coder. Moreover, SBE shows higher PSNR than that of the H.263 baseline coder with the half bitrate of H.263. As previously stated, motion estimation time takes up a large part of coding process. Fig. 8 shows the performances of reconstructed video sequences with different numbers of candidate frames(FN) for motion estimation. Except for FN of 1, the PSNR shows similar pattern as in Fig. 8. In the end, it is profitable to set the number of candidate frames to 2.

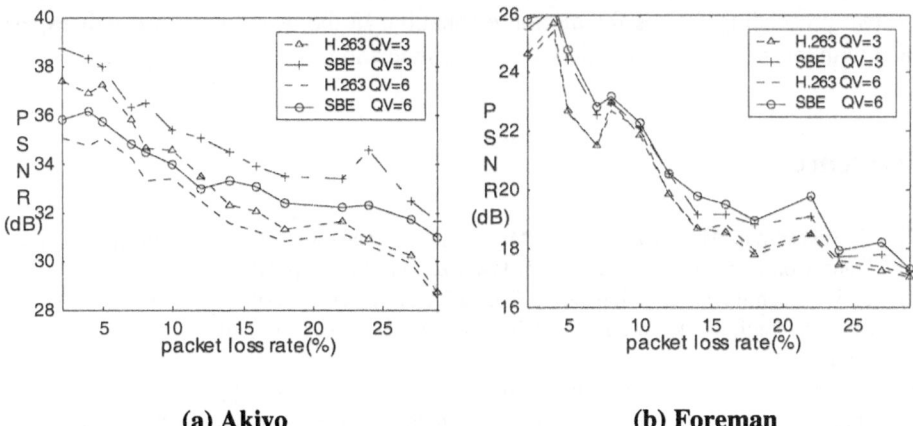

(a) Akiyo   **(b) Foreman**

Fig. 7. Comparision of PSNR of (a) Akiyo and (b) Foreman quantized by 3 and 6 at various packet loss rates.

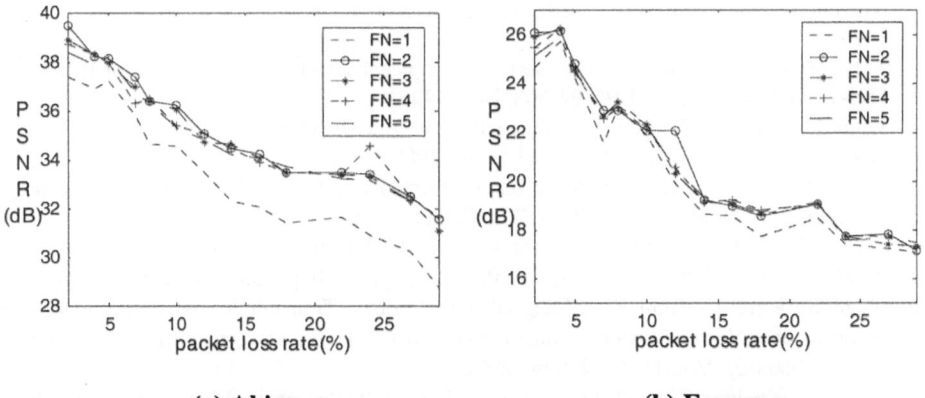

(a) Akiyo   **(b) Foreman**

Fig. 8. Comparision of SBE PSNR of (a) Akiyo and (b) Foreman predicted from 1 to 5 candidate frames at various packet loss rates.

4 Conclusions

In this paper, we propose a video sequence coding scheme called SBE(Supplementary Block based Encoding) to minimize the effects of transmission errors over the network. SBE searches several previous frames to select the best matching block(primary block) and the second best matching block(supplementary block) for the current block to be compressed. The primary block is motion compensated from the current block and the supplementary block is preserved for emerengency such as corruption of the primary block. If the primary block is corrupted, the SBE decoder suppresses the error propagation by exploiting the supplementary block. Through various simulations, we come to the conclusion that the SBE outperforms the H.263 baseline coder for both slow and fast motion video sequences, and, for real time compression, it is useful to use two preceding frames for motion estimation. In the near future, we will experiment with this scheme for mobile video communication.

References

[1] Y. Takashima, M. Wada, and H. Murakami, "Reversible variable length codes", IEEE Trans. Communications., vol. 43, pp. 158-162, Feb./Mar./Apr. 1995

[2] D. W. Redmill, N. G. Kingsbury, "The EREC: An error resilient technique for coding variable-length blocks of data," IEEE Trans. Image Processing, vol. 5, pp. 565--574, Apr. 1996.

[3] S. Wenger, G.Knorr, J. Ott, F. Kossentini: "Error resilience support in H.263+", IEEE Trans. on circuit and System for Video Technology, vol. 8, no. 6 pp. 867-877, Nov. 1998.

[4] S. Aign, "Error concealment for MPEG-2 video", Signal Recovery Techniques for Image and Video Compression and Transmission, A. K. Katsaggelos and N. P. Galatsanos, editors, ch. 8, pp 235-268, Kluwer Academic Publishers, 1998.

[5] H. Sun and W. Kwok, "Concealment of damaged block transform coded images using projections onto convex sets", IEEE Trans. Image Proc., vol. 4, no. 4, pp. 470-477, Apr. 1995.

[6] T. Nakai, and Y. Tomita: "Core Experiments on Feedback channel Operation for H.263+", ITU-T SG15 contribution LBC 96-308, Nov. 1996.

[7] Wada M. Selective Recovery of Video Packet Loss Using Error Concealment. IEEE J. Select. Areas in Commun. 7(5):807-814, June 1989.

[8] B. Girod and N. Farber, "Feedback-based error control for mobile video transmission," Proceedings of the IEEE, pp. 1707--1723, October 1999.

[9] Budagavi, M., Gibson, J.D, "Multiframe Video Coding for Improved Performance over Wireless channels." IEEE Trans. Image Processing. Vol. 10. pp. 252-265, Feb. 2001

[10] Chang-Su Kim, Rin-Chul Kim, Sang-Uk Lee, "Robust Transmission of Video Sequence Using Double-Vector Motion Compensation". IEEE Trans. On circuit and Systems for video technology. Vol. 11, No.9, Sept. 2001

[11] Yang Yu, Xuelong Zhu: Dynamic Multi-reference Prediction in Video Coding for Improved Error Resilience over Internet_, IEEE Pacific Rim Conference on Multimedia 2001, pp. 102-109, Oct. 2001

[12] E. Muller, T. Strutz, "Scalable Wavelet-based Coding of Color images," Proc. of APEIE'98. Vol.10, pp29-35, Sept. 1998.

[13] Joo-Kyong Lee, Tae-Uk Choi, Ki-Dong Chung, "Exploitation of Auxiliary Motion Vector in Video Coding for Robust Transmission over Internet", Proc. of ICIS'02, pp451-456, Aug. 2002.

A Robust, Efficient, and Fast Global Motion Estimation Method from MPEG Compressed Video

Hongliang Li, Guizhong Liu, Yongli Li, and Zhongwei Zhang

School of Electronics and Information Engineering, Xi'an Jiaotong University, Xi'an
710049, China
hllli@mailst.xjtu.edu.cn
liugz@mail.xjtu.edu.cn

Abstract. In the field of content-based visual information, detection of visual
features is a significant topic. In order to process video data efficiently, visual
features extraction is required. Many of the advanced video applications require
manipulations of compressed video data. In this paper, an effective approach
that detects global motion in MPEG compressed images is proposed. First, the
moving background of the current frame is extracted using predictive error dc-
image. Second, a new global motion detecting method based on a 6-parameters
camera motion analysis is proposed in this paper. In the evaluation experiments,
several video test sequences are used to test the proposed algorithm, and compared with an existing method. The experimental results show the efficiency and
robustness of our algorithm in the global motion estimation.

1 Introduction

The identification of scene changes in video sequences is an important task toward
automated content-based analysis and semantic description of video. Generally, a
video is first segmented into temporal "shots," each of which is an uninterrupted sequence of frames generated during a continuous operation and therefore represents a
continuous action in time or space. The boundaries between neighboring video shots
are commonly known as scene changes and the action of segmenting a video into shots
is called scene change detection. Shot transitions can be divided into two categories:
abrupt transitions and gradual transitions. Gradual transitions include camera movements: panning, tilting, zooming and video editing with special effects.

Due to the large amount of data, video sequences are often compressed for efficient
transmission or storage. In order to avoid the unnecessary decompression and recom-
pression operations in indexing and/or searching processes, it is efficient to extract image and video information in the compressed form such as JPEG, MPEG, H.261,
H.263 and HDTV, all based on discrete cosine transform (DCT). Many methods [2]-
[6] have been proposed to perform shot-change detection directly on transform coded
MPEG compressed video by using the features of intensity or color, texture, object
shapes, and spatial layout of interframe motion information. These methods deal with

Y.-C. Chen, L.-W. Chang, and C.-T. Hsu (Eds.): PCM 2002, LNCS 2532, pp. 151-158, 2002.
© Springer-Verlag Berlin Heidelberg 2002

abrupt scene changes fairly well. However it is more difficult to perform the gradual transition-detection.

Recently, Many algorithms [7]-[10] for estimating the global motion have been presented. Tan *et al.* have introduced two methods of estimating camera motion directly from MPEG video without the need for full-frame decompression, and developed a simple annotation system.

In this paper, we proposed an efficient method of global motion detection based on the background extraction from DC coefficients and the camera motion model. This paper is organized as follows. Section 2 gives the algorithm of background estimation. Section 3 presents the computation of a camera motion model. In Section 4, experimental results with various video sequences are analyzed to evaluate the performance of the proposed algorithm. Finally, conclusions will be given in Section 5.

2 Interframe Prediction Error DC Images and Moving Background Estimation

2.1 Interframe Prediction Error DC Image

MPEG-2 [11] extends the MPEG standard in many ways including higher bit-rates and more powerful and efficient compression. In MPEG-2, three "picture types" are defined, as depicted in Fig.1. The picture types define which prediction mode is used to code each block. 'Intra' pictures (I-pictures) are coded without reference to other pictures; Moderate compression is achieved by reducing the spatial redundancy, but not the temporal redundancy. They can be used periodically to provide access points in the bitstream where decoding can begin. "Predictive" pictures (P-pictures) use the

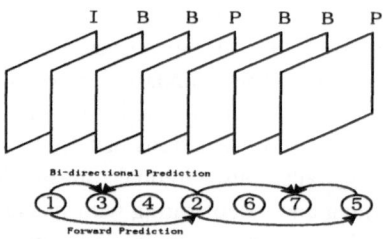

Fig. 1. A typical MPEG coding order

previous I- or P-picture for motion compensation and may be used as references for further prediction. Each block in a P-picture can be either predicted or intra-coded. By reducing spatial and temporal redundancy, P-pictures offer increased compression compared to I-pictures. "Bidirectionlly-predictive" pictures (B-pictures) can use the previous and next I- or P-pictures for motion compensation. Each block in a B-picture can be forward, backward of bidirectionally precdicted or intra-coded. To enable backward prediction from a future frame, the coder reords the pictures from natural "display" order to "bitstream" order so that the B-picture is transmitted after the previous and next pictures it refers to. This introduces a reordering delay dependent on the number of consecutive B-pictures. The different picture types typically occur in a repeating sequence, termed a 'group of pictures' or GOP. A typical GOP in display order is: $I_1 B_2 B_3 P_4 B_5 B_6 P_7 B_8 B_9 P_{10} B_{11} B_{12}$.

DC images are spatially reduced versions of the original images. An image is divided into blocks of 8×8 pixels. The (i, j) pixel of the dc-image is the average value of the block centered at (i, j) of the original image. Fig.2. gives two original frame pictures in the Forman sequence. The corresponding dc-images are shown in Fig.3. (a)-(b).

Fig. 2. The original images of Foreman 1,4.

(a)   (b)   (c)   (d)

Fig. 3. The corresponding dc-images and the error dc-images

In the MPEG compression algorithms the motion compensated prediction techniques are used for reducing temporal redundancies between frames and only the prediction error images—the difference between original images and the motion-compensated prediction images—are encoded using the DCT transform-domain coding. It is apparent that the dc-images of the residual images to be coded are greatly reduced by the motion compensation. For example, Fig.3(c) shows the prediction error dc-image of the frame 4, While Fig.3(d) is the error dc-image between the frames 1,4 without motion compensation.

2.2 Moving Background Estimation

Generally, the apparent motion in most moving sequences taken with a real camera can be attributed to either the camera motion or the movement of the objects in a scene. The motion due to the camera is referred to the global motion, whereas the movement of the objects is called the local motion. The background is defined as the ensemble of pixels that are not subjected to local motion, namely, which only undergo the camera motion. The local motion region is called foreground. Background subtraction based on color or intensity is a commonly used technique to quickly identify foreground elements. Using this method, we perform a binary segmentation of a predictive error dc-image into regions whose motion fields are conforming to or not to the global dominant motion model. Pixels with an absolute value smaller than a truncating threshold are considered background motion; other pixels are classified as foreground. Fig.4 shows a background separation using the technique described above.

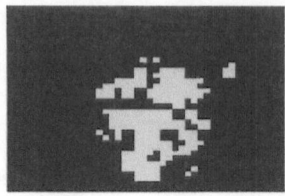

Fig. 4. The background extraction from Foreman 4

3   Global Motion Estimation

In this section, we describe the specific model parameters for our global motion estimation algorithms. Let (X, Y, Z) be a camera coordinate system attached to the camera as shown in Fig.5. The image plane is perpendicular to the Z-axis with its

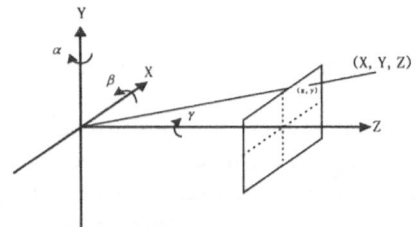

Fig. 5. The camera and the image coordinate systems

center located at the point $(0, 0, f)$, where f is the focal length of the camera. Let (x, y) be the image pixel with respect to the image coordinate system of the image plane. The point at coordinates (X, Y, Z) in the 3-D space is mapped onto (x, y) in the image plane. The corresponding transformation can be defined as: $x = \dfrac{fX}{Z}$, $y = \dfrac{fY}{Z}$. In general, camera movement can be decomposed into the following categories:

- Change of the camera focal length: zooming.
- Rotation of the camera around the Y-axis by an angle α: panning.
- Rotation of the camera around the X-axis by an angle β: tilting.

- Horizontal shift of the image: tracking. The tracking effect can be approximately considered to be identical to that of the panning operation.
- Vertical shift of the image: booming. This effect can be approximately considered to be identical to that of the tilt operation.

Combining the zooming, panning, and tilting described above, we arrive at the following six-parameter model [1][7]:

$$\begin{cases} x_i^{'} = a_0 + a_1 x_i + a_2 y_i + \varepsilon & (a) \\ y_i^{'} = a_3 + a_4 x_i + a_5 y_i + \xi & (b) \end{cases} \tag{1}$$

Here $(x_{i,} y_i)$ denotes the spatial coordinates of the ith pixel in the current frame and $(x_i^{'}, y_i^{'})$ denotes the coordinates of the corresponding pixel in the previous frame; $(a_0, \cdots, a_5)$ are the motion parameters. The coefficients a_1, a_5 indicate the interframe camera zoom factor with $a_1 = a_5 = 1$ no zoom, $a_1 = a_5 < 1$ zoom out, and $a_1 = a_5 > 1$ zoom in. The ratios a_0 / a_1 and a_3 / a_5 are the changes in the camera panning and tilting angles between the two frames scaled by the first focal length. ε and ξ are the random variables, that are assumed to be subjected to the normal distribution $(0, \sigma^2)$.

To compute the model parameters, we use a binary linear regression method. Consider the x coordinate. Let

$$X^{'} = \begin{bmatrix} x_1 \\ x_2 \\ \vdots \\ x_n \end{bmatrix}, \quad X = \begin{bmatrix} 1 & x_1 & y_1 \\ 1 & x_2 & y_2 \\ \cdots\cdots \\ 1 & x_n & y_n \end{bmatrix}, \quad a = \begin{bmatrix} a_0 \\ a_1 \\ a_2 \end{bmatrix}, \quad \varepsilon = \begin{bmatrix} \varepsilon_1 \\ \varepsilon_2 \\ \vdots \\ \varepsilon_n \end{bmatrix} \tag{2}$$

Equation 1(a) can be expressed implicitly by the following equation:

$$X^{'} = Xa + \varepsilon \tag{3}$$

In order to estimate the parameters (a_0, a_1, a_2), the least –squares method can be used. The estimation criterion can be stated as follows:

$$Q = \left\| X^{'} - Xa \right\|^2 = \sum_{i=1}^{n} (x_i^{'} - a_0 + a_1 x_i + a_2 y_i)^2 \tag{4}$$

The optimal values of a_0, a_1 and a_2 can be obtained by solving the following minimization problem:

$$Q = \min \tag{5}$$

The solution to this problem can be obtained by the computation of partial derivative for Q. Let

$$A = \begin{bmatrix} n & \sum_i x_i & \sum_i y_i \\ \sum_i x_i & \sum_i x_i^2 & \sum_i x_i y_i \\ \sum_i y_i & \sum_i y_i x_i & \sum_i y_i^2 \end{bmatrix} \quad B = \begin{bmatrix} \sum_i x_i^{\cdot} \\ \sum_i x_i x_i^{\cdot} \\ \sum_i y_i x_i^{\cdot} \end{bmatrix} \quad \hat{a} = \begin{bmatrix} \hat{a}_0 \\ \hat{a}_1 \\ \hat{a}_2 \end{bmatrix} \qquad (6)$$

The solution $\hat{a}$ to the optimization problem (5) is that of the linear equation.

$$A\hat{a} = B \qquad (7)$$

The parameters a_3, a_4, a_5 can be computed in the same way as derived above.

4   Experimental Results

To verify the performance of the proposed method, simulations are carried out in comparison to the method in [1]. For comparison, we also use the motion vectors from the P-frames. As described in Section 2, we only use the background pixels to evaluate the global motion in order to prevent errors arising from local motions. Therefore, our algorithm can improve the performance of global motion estimation by removing the influence of the outlier pixels corresponding to the local motion. Simulations are done using the sequences *foreman* and *table tennis*. Furthermore, a sequence without global motion is also tested on: *hall monitor*. The test conditions, including the spatial size, the frame rate, the number of frames, the length of GOP, as well as the motion model (zoom, pan, tilt), are summarized in Table I.

Table 1. Video test Sequences

Sequence	Size	Num	Fps	GOP	Zoom	Pan	Tilt
Foreman	352 x 288	300	25	12	No	Right	Down
Table	360 x 240	300	25	12	In	Right	No
Hall	176 x 144	330	25	12	No	No	No

Fig. 6. Local motion in *hall monitor* sequence

We apply our algorithm to the *hall monitor* sequence, which seem to only exhibit persons' movement shown in Fig.6. The results are shown in Fig.7. As is seen, the result of our method shows that no global motion exibits in *hall monitor,* which accord with the camera motion. But the algorithm in [1] tells that this sequence is characterized by a distinct global motion.

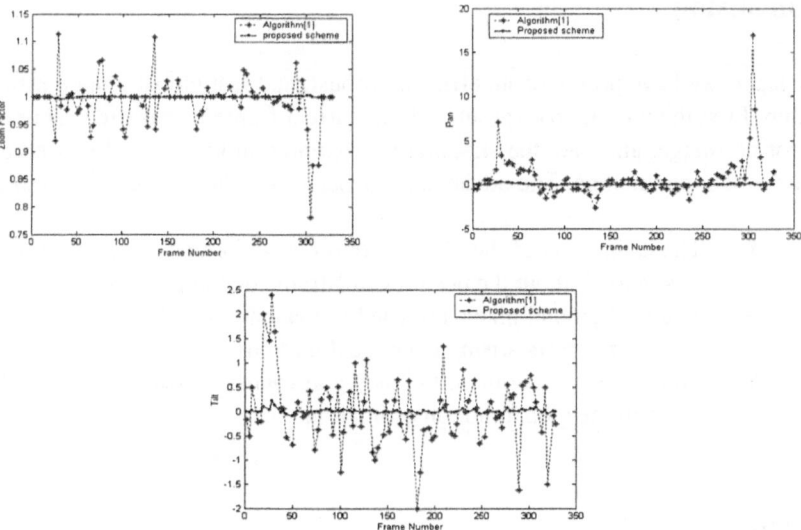

Fig. 7. The estimated zoom, pan, and tilt for *hall monitor* sequence

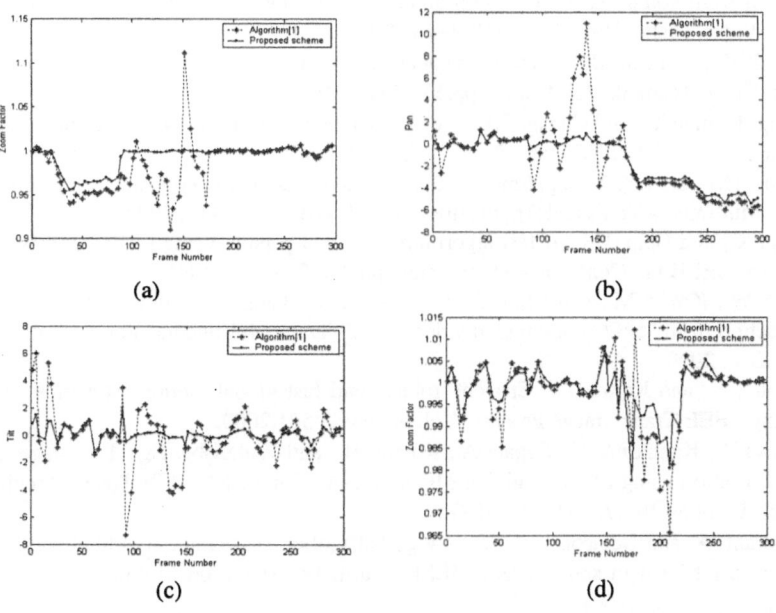

Fig. 8. (a)-(c) The estimated results for *Table tennis*. (d) The estimated zoom for *Foreman* sequence

To test the efficiency of the proposed algorithm on global motion estimation, we apply the algorithm to two video sequences: *table tennis* and *foreman*. The results described in Fig.8 show that our algorithm performs the global motion estimation more effectively and robustly than the algorithm in [1].

5 Conclusion

In this paper, we have presented an efficient, robust, and fast global motion estimation algorithm. First the moving background of the current frame is extracted using predictive error dc-image, and then the six-parameter camera motion model is used to estimate the model parameters. The advantages of our algorithm can be expressed as follows:

- The estimation of the global motion is performed directly from MPEG bitstream without the need for full-frame decompression.
- The background pixels are used to evaluate the global motion in order to prevent errors arising from local motions.
- Simulations show the efficiency and robustness of our proposed algorithm in the global motion estimation.

References

1. Yap-Peng Tan, Saur, D.D., Kulkarni,S.R., and Ramadge, P.J. : Rapid estimation of camera motion from compressed video with application to video annotation. IEEE Tans.Circuits Syst. Video Techo, Vol. 10(1), pp133~145,2000.
2. Yeo, B.-L., and Liu, B. : Rapid scene analysis on compressed video. IEEE Trans. Circuits Syst. Video Technol. Vol. 5, no.6, pp.533-544, 1995.
3. Meng, J., Juan,Y., and Chang, S.F. : Scene change detection in a MPEG compressed video sequence. In IS&T/SPIE Symp.Proc., Vol. 2419,San Jose, 1995.
4. Zhang, H.J., Low, C.Y., and Smoliar, S.W.: Video parsing and browsing using compressed data. Multimedia Tools and Applications, Vol. 1, no1, pp.91-113, 1995.
5. Shen, K., and Delp, E.J.: A fast algorithm for video parsing using MPEG compressed sequences. IEEE Int. Conf. Image Processing, pp.252-255, Oct. 1995.
6. Lee,S.W., Kim,Y.M., and Choi, S.W. : Fast scene change detection using direct feature extraction from MPEG compressed videos. IEEE Trans.Multimedia, Vol. 2, no.4, pp. 240–254, Dec. 2000.
7. Dufaux, F., and Konrad, J.: Effcient, robust, and fast global motion estimation for video coding. IEEE Trans. Image Process, Vol. 9, pp497~501,2000.
8. Jozawa,H., Kamikura, K., Sagata A., Kotera, H., and Watanabe, H. : Two-stage motion-compensation using adaptive global MC and local affine MC. IEEE Trans. Circuits Syst. Video Technol. Vol.7, pp75~85, 1997.
9. Kokaram, A. and Delacourt, P. : A new global motion estimation algorithm and its application to retrieval in sports events. IEEE Fourth Workshop on Multimedia Signal Processing, pp251~256,2001.
10. Giunta, G. and Mascia, U. : Estimation of global motion parameters by complex linear regression. IEEE Trans. Image Process. Vol. 8(11), pp1652~1657, 1999.
11. ISO/IEC 13813: Generic coding of moving pictures and associated audio (MPEG-2).

Querying Image Database by Video Content*

C.H. Wang, H.C. Lin[1]**, C.C. Shih[2], H.R. Tyan[3], C.F. Lin[4], and H.Y. Mark Liao

Institute of Information Science, Academia Sinica, Taipei, Taiwan 115
[1] Department of Information Management, Chang Jung Christian University, Tainan, Taiwan 711
[2] Department of Ecology and Evolution, University of Chicago, USA
[3] Department of Information and Computer Engineering, Chung Yuan Christian University, Chungli, Taiwan 320
[4] Department of Computer Science and Engineering, Yuan Ze University, Chungli, Taiwan 320

Abstract. A content-based image retrieval system using an image sequence as a query is proposed in this study. The proposed system is applied to a fish database in Taiwan, which is collected by the Institute of Zoology, Academia Sinica. Major contribution of this study is threefold: (1) The proposed query-by-an-image-sequence scheme can eliminate the problems caused by non-rigid fish motions, serious deformations, and partial occlusions. (2) In traditional query-by-an-example schemes, queries with different imaging conditions may generate completely different retrieval results, but the proposed query scheme can overcome varying imaging conditions. (3) The proposed fish representation scheme is invariant to translation, scaling, and rotation. Experimental results have proven the effectiveness of the proposed system.

1 Introduction

Content-based image retrieval (CBIR) is a popular research area in recent years. Since the number of digital images grows rapidly, an efficient technique that can be applied to find target images within seconds is urgently required. By content-based techniques, a user can present the content of interest in a query. The contents may be the color, texture, shape, or the spatial layout of a target image. Images that satisfy "perceptual similarity" to the query can be found in the image repertory. For the past decade, several CBIR systems have been proposed, including QBIC (Query By Image Content), Virage, RetrievalWare, Photobook, WebSEEk, Netra, MARS (Multimedia Analysis and Retrieval System), and so on. Detailed surveys on CBIR systems can be found in [1-4].

Among the different types of image contents, the shape feature usually plays an important role due to their relatively unique characteristics. Humans can easily identify an object via its rough shape. This advantage makes the shape feature very

---

* This study was supported partially by the National Science Council, Taiwan, under Grant NSC89-2213-E-001-021, NSC89-2218-E-001-008, and NSC90-2213-E-309-004.
** Corresponding author. E-mail: hclin@mail.cju.edu.tw

Y.-C. Chen, L.-W. Chang, and C.-T. Hsu (Eds.): PCM 2002, LNCS 2532, pp. 159-166, 2002.
© Springer-Verlag Berlin Heidelberg 2002

popular in CBIR systems. Generally speaking, shape-based retrieval systems can be categorized into two classes: contour-based and region-based [5]. Several studies on shape-based retrieval can be found in [6-8].

In this study, we propose a new CBIR system based on the features extracted from an image sequence. We use a fish database of Taiwan that contains more than 2000 fish species as the underlying testbed. By traditional content-based techniques, a user may access an image database using the features extracted from an example (i.e., query by a single image). The query-by-a-single-image scheme may suffer from a number of problems, including (1) the imaging condition for an example is not necessarily identical to that of all database images. Under the circumstances, the features used for matching may be strictly restricted. (2) Since a fish may move in a non-rigid manner, and sometimes it may turn into a bad angle, it is difficult to describe a fish using only one view. Therefore, we use the features extracted from an image sequence to characterize a fish. The proposed system consists of two major phases, including model database construction and matching. The proposed CSS-based fish representation is invariant to translation, scaling, and rotation during the matching. Moreover, the problems caused by non-rigid fish motions, serious deformations, and partial occlusions can also be solved in the proposed system.

2   Model Database Construction Phase

The model database construction phase contains a foreground/background separation process, a CSS-based representation process, and a regularization process. The three processes are respectively described in Sections 2.1, 2.2, and 2.3.

2.1   Foreground/Background Separation

There are about 2450 fish species in Taiwan; images of more than 2000 different species are collected in our database. Note that our database contains only the fish whose length is at least twice larger than the width, and the fish's left view is recorded in the database image. The fish in each database image is first segmented from the background by Sze et al.'s method for foreground/ background separation [8]. A simple boundary tracing method is then used so that the fish is represented as an ordered sequence of boundary points clockwise. We assume that the fish boundary is a closed contour without loops. Finally, the boundary length is normalized to 250 points to eliminate the scale problem during the matching.

2.2   CSS-Based Representation

After the foreground/background separation process, the fish boundary is smoothed gradually by Gaussian functions and its curvature scale space (CSS) image is created [7]. The CSS image contains several arches representing the behavior of curvature zero crossings on the smoothed fish boundary. The intersections of a horizontal line with the arches indicate locations of zero crossings on the smoothed boundary. Note that a zero crossing separates a convex curve from a concave one. As the fish boundary gets smoother and smoother, two neighboring zero crossings may get closer to each other and finally form a complete arch. The location where the two zero crossings meets indicates the maxima point of this arch. The higher the maxima point is, the deeper or wider its corresponding convex (or concave) curve on the fish boundary. In our experiments, maxima points in a CSS image are used to represent a fish boundary.

2.3 Regularization of a Representation

Recall that the length of a fish boundary is normalized to 250 points. Therefore, the fish representation is invariant to translation and scale. However, there are two potential problems that may severely influence the system's performance. First, the representation may be totally different if the starting point is different. Second, a shallow concavity may create a false maxima point and thus reduce the representation accuracy.

In this section, we propose a systematic method to uniquely determine the starting point. The direction toward where the fish moves can be also detected. Let σ denote the spread parameter of a Gaussian function. As σ increases, the fish boundary gets from fine to coarse gradually. When σ is sufficiently large, the fish boundary becomes a convex hull and its curvature function contains only two local maxima. The boundary point with the first local maximum corresponds to the fish tail, whereas the boundary point with the second local maximum corresponds to the fish head. Although the fish may sway its tail fin to move forward, we found that the relative position of the fish head and tail keeps insensitive to the change in a CSS image. Assume that σ_0 is the smallest σ at which all zero crossings vanish from the CSS image. We use $\sigma_i = 1.25\sigma_0$ to smooth the curvature function and obtain a degenerated boundary. The boundary point with the second curvature maximum (i.e., the fish head) can be regarded as the starting point. This point also indicates the direction toward where the fish moves. When the starting point of a fish boundary is determined, its maxima points can be easily circularly shifted to eliminate the rotation problem during the matching.

A shallow concavity is a very wide, but not deep, concave (or convex) curve on a fish boundary. The shallow concavity, as a deep one, may create a very high arch in a CSS image, and thus create a false maxima point. If a raw representation is used during matching, a shallow concavity may be matched with a deep one. The problem of shallow concavities can be overcome by adjusting the height of maxima points within arches [9]. After height adjustment, the new maxima points can eliminate the problem of shallow concavities.

3 Matching Phase

In this section, we detail how the matching phase is executed. In Section 3.1, we introduce our CSS-based motion model for a fish. In Section 3.2, we describe how to use the CSS-based model during matching.

3.1 CSS-Based Motion Model

To build a motion model for a fish, we use a rectangular object shown in Fig. 1(a) as an example. This object is with 232 boundary points. After the Gaussian convolution at $\sigma = 35$, the object boundary degenerates to an ellipse, as shown in Fig. 1(b). The horizontal and vertical lines indicate the long and short axes of the degenerated ellipse, respectively, and the curvature function contains only two local maxima. The two local maxima indicate the long axis of the degenerated ellipse. Before the object rotates around its vertical axis, its projection area is maximal. When the object rotates to 90 degree, its projection area becomes minimal. When the object rotates to 180 or 360 degree, its projection area reaches to the maximum again.

Recall that we only collect fishes whose length is at least twice larger than its width in our database. Therefore, we assume that the bounding parallelogram of a fish can always be a rectangle. After the Gaussian convolution at a specific value of σ, the fish boundary may degenerate to a quasi-ellipse. We also found that, at $\sigma_i = 1.25\sigma_0$, where σ_0 is defined likewise in Section 2.3, the fish boundary degenerates to an easy-to-recognize quasi-ellipse.

Suppose we are observing a moving fish. When the fish is recorded in an image sequence, the fish poses in each image may be different. When moving toward our left, the fish is with its left view. The fish boundary degenerates to a quasi-ellipse at σ_i, and the curvature function contains only two local maxima. However, when turning around, the fish is with its front (or rear) view. The fish boundary may suffer serious deformations or be occluded by other parts of the fish. Therefore, the fish boundary does not degenerate to a quasi-ellipse at σ_i, and the curvature function contains more than two local maxima. Based on the above observation, we propose a CSS-based motion model for a fish, as shown in Fig. 2. The fish poses are classified into three classes, namely the left, right, and front (or rear) views; several fish images taken from different instances are also displayed.

To formalize, let P be the number of local maxima in the curvature function after the Gaussian convolution at σ_i. The value of P can be used to determine the fish pose as follows: If $P = 2$, the fish is with its left or right view, i.e., with its side view. Whereas if $P > 2$, the fish is with its front (or rear) view. In our experiments, the user can use an image sequence grabbed from a moving fish as a query. The images with the side view are used during matching, and those with the front view are considered useless and thus discarded.

3.2 CSS-Based Matching

Assume there are a sequence of k images for a moving fish that are with the left view. After the CSS image creation process, we can obtain k sets of maxima points. The average maxima points (or the average class centers) for the sequence of k images can be derived through the c-means algorithm. The average class centers are used as the representative maxima points for the sequence of k images during matching. Note that if the sequence images of a fish are with the right view, their maxima points should be horizontally flipped in advance because the default view is the left one.

The matching process executed between an image sequence (i.e., the query) and each database image is achieved by comparing the average class centers with maxima points of the fish.

4 Experimental Results

The test image sequence was obtained from Discovery Channel Video KDV-4063 [10]. The number of images was 30 (No. 0-29), each of which was sampled from the video every 0.2 seconds. Fig. 3 shows the 30 images from left to right and top to bottom. The fish in each image was segmented through foreground/background separation. The 30 images can be characterized as follows:

(1) The fish moves leftward (No. 0-3), turns around (No. 4-12), and moves rightward (No. 13-29). Therefore, the fish's left, front, and right views are recorded in the image sequence, which can be used to verify our CSS-based motion model and view classification method. When the fish moves, its position, size, and angle change gradually. These changes can be used to verify the invariance of our CSS-based representation and matching method.
(2) When the fish moves leftward or rightward, the maxima points extracted from the images may change gradually. These images can be used to verify the robustness of the c-means algorithm to serious deformations.

Table 1 summarizes the verification results. For the sake of conciseness, several rows in Table 1 are omitted. The images with the side view (No. 0-3 and No. 13-29) were retained for matching, but those with the front view (No. 4-12) were discarded. According to Table 1, the proposed system can verify fish poses with a very high accuracy.

We now have two image sequences with the side view, namely, No. 0-3 and No. 13-29. For each image in a sequence, we created a CSS image and then extracted maxima points. The maxima points were then regularized through circular shift and height adjustment. For all images in a sequence, the average maxima points were computed through the c-means algorithm. Fig. 4 shows the retrieval results for the test image sequence. The retrieved images were displayed in a descending order of similarity from left to right and from top to bottom. From the experimental results, it is obvious that our system is indeed a superb one.

Table 1. Verification results of the 30 images.

No.	Poses	P	Aspect Ratio	Verification Results
0	Move leftward	2	6.61	Left view
1	Move leftward	2	7.26	Left view
2	Move leftward	2	8.02	Left view
3	Move leftward	2	9.03	Left view
4	Turn around	4	-	Font view
...	...	...	...	...
12	Turn around	3	-	Font view
13	Move rightward	2	5.30	Right view
...	...	...	...	...
29	Move rightward	2	6.98	Right view

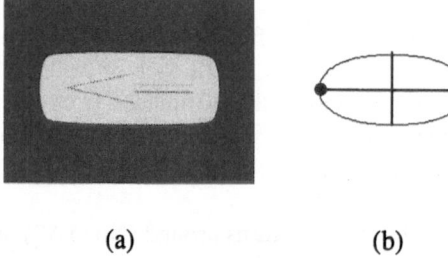

(a)   (b)

Fig. 1. (a) A rectangular object with 232 boundary points; (b) the degenerated ellipse (at $\sigma = 35$) and its two axes.

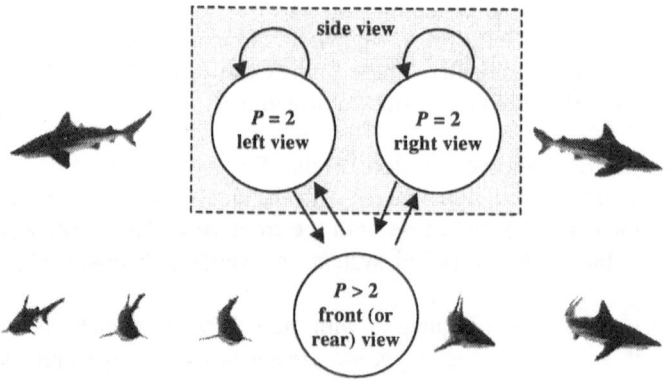

Fig. 2. The CSS-based motion model for a fish.

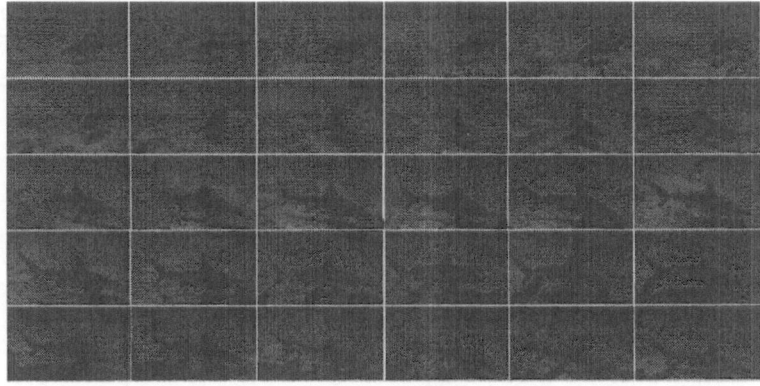

Fig. 3. The 30 test images for a moving fish.

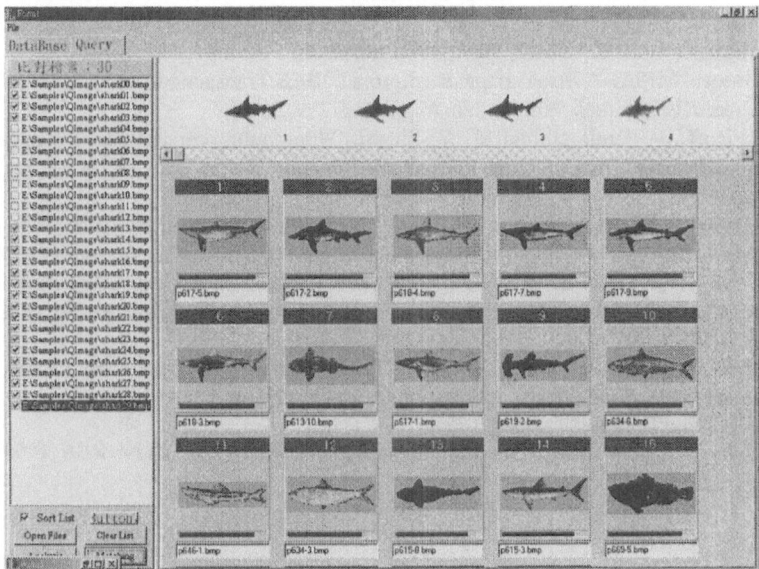

Fig. 4. The retrieval results.

5   Conclusions

A content-based image retrieval system based on an image sequence has been proposed in this study. The proposed system has been tested using a fish database generated in Taiwan. The contribution of this study is threefold. First, our query-by-an-image-sequence scheme can overcome the problems caused by non-rigid fish motions, serious deformations, and partial occlusions. Second, our query scheme can eliminate the problem caused by varying imaging conditions. Third, our CSS-based representation scheme is invariant to translation, scaling, and rotation. Experimental results have strongly supported the above-mentioned claims.

References

1. P. Aigrain, H. J. Zhang, and D. Petkovic, "Content-based representation and retrieval of visual media: a state-of-the-art review," Multimedia Tools and Applications, Vol. 3, No. 3, pp. 179-202, 1996.
2. F. Idris and S. Panchanathan, "Review of image and video indexing techniques," Journal of Visual Communication and Image Representation, Vol. 8, No. 2, pp. 146-166, 1997.
3. Y. Rui, T. S. Huang, and S. F. Chang, "Image retrieval: current techniques, promising directions, and open issues," Journal of Visual Communication and Image Representation, Vol. 10, No. 1, pp. 39-62, 1999.
4. A. W. M. Smeulders, M. Worring, S. Santini, A. Gupta, and R. Jain, "Content-based image retrieval at the end of the early years," IEEE Transactions on Pattern Analysis and Machine Intelligence, Vol. 22, No. 12, pp. 1349-1380, 2000.
5. M. Bober, "MPEG-7 visual shape descriptors," IEEE Transactions on Circuits and Systems for Video Technology, Vol. 11, No. 6, pp. 716-719, 2001.
6. S. Sclaroff, A. Pentland, and R. W. Picard, "Photobook: content-based manipulation of image databases," International Journal of Computer Vision, Vol. 18, No. 3, pp. 233-254, 1996.
7. S. Abbasi, F. Mokhtarian, and J. Kittler, "Curvature scale space image in shape similarity retrieval," Springer Journal of Multimedia Systems, Vol. 7, No. 6, pp. 467-476, 1999.
8. C. J. Sze, H. R. Tyan, H. Y. Mark Liao, C. S. Lu, and S. K. Huang, "Shape-based retrieval on a fish database of Taiwan," Tamkang Journal of Science and Engineering, Vol. 2, No. 3, pp. 163-173, 1999.
9. S. Abbasi, F. Mokhtarian, and J. Kittler, "Scale similarity retrieval using a height adjusted curvature scale space image," International Conference on Visual Information Systems, pp. 173-180, San Diego, CA, USA, 1997.
10. Discovery Channel Video, "Secret of the deep II – sand tigers," KDV-4036, 1999.

An ICA-Based Illumination-Free Texture Model and Its Application to Image Retrieval

Yen-Wei Chen[1,2], Xiang-Yan Zeng[1], Zensho Nakao[1], and Hanqing Lu[3]

[1] Faculty of Engineering, Univ. of the Ryukyus, Okinawa 903-0213, Japan
chen@tec.u-ryukyu.ac.jp
[2] Institute for Computational Science and Eng., Ocean Univ. of Qingdao, Shandong, China
[3] National Laboratory of Pattern Recognition, Chinese Academy of Science, China

Abstract. We propose a novel pixel pattern-based approach for texture classification, which is independent of the variance of illumination. Gray scale images are first transformed into pattern maps in which edges and lines, used for characterizing texture information, are classified by pattern matching. We employ independent component analysis (ICA) which is widely applied to feature extraction. We use the basis functions learned through PCA as templates for pattern matching. Using PCA pattern maps, the feature vector is comprised of the numbers of the pixels belonging to a specific pattern. The effectiveness of the new feature is demonstrated by applications to image retrieval of Brodatz texture database. Comparisons with multichannel and multiresolution features indicate that the new feature is quite time saving, free of the influence of illumination, and has notable accuracy. The applicability of the proposed method to image retrieval has also been demonstrated.

1 Introduction

Texture is a very important feature that can be used to texture segmentation as well as feature representation. To design an effective segmentation algorithm, it is essential to find a texture feature set with good discriminating power. In recent years, the multiresolution and multichannel filtering techniques have been widely used to texture analysis, such as wavelet transforms, and Gabor filters. The substances of multichannel filtering methods are to enhance edges and lines of different orientations in each feature component. Gabor filters can be considered as being orientation and scale tunable edge and line detectors, and the statistics of these microfeatures are often used to characterize the underlying texture information [1,2]. Features are extracted by filtering the texture image with a selected subset of Gabor filter bank and then calculating predefined statistics within small regions of the filtered images. The widely used statistic terms include energy, entropy and variances. The segmentation accuracy is satisfactory if appropriate Gabor filter banks are chosen. However, the statistics are computed from gray scale values and dependent on the illumination.

Y.-C. Chen, L.-W. Chang, and C.-T. Hsu (Eds.): PCM 2002, LNCS 2532, pp. 167–174, 2002.
© Springer-Verlag Berlin Heidelberg 2002

Furthermore, the computation cost is rather high since each component of the feature vector is calculated separately in each filtered image.

In our previous works [3], we have proposed a new feature for texture segmentation that is very simple to calculate and free of the influence of illumination. A gray scale image is first transformed into a pattern map in which edge, line and background pixels are classified by pattern matching. The pixels of the map represent the pattern class, which leads to two advantages:

(1) the pixel values have a much more controllable range than gray scale images;

(2) the pattern classes reflect the edge and line orientations, which is impossible for gray scale values.

Then, the feature vector is created from the pattern map in such a way that the components are the numbers of the pixels belonging to each pattern within a small window. The statistics of this one map is much simpler than that of the multi filtered images, and the calculation time is not related with the number of the components.

In Ref.[3], we have shown that a pattern templates by principal component analysis (PCA) is very effective to obtain the new feature. In this paper, we propose to obtain the pattern templates by Independent Component Analysis (ICA). Compared with PCA (correlation-based transformations), ICA not only decorrelates the signals (2nd-order statistics) but also reduces higher-order statistical dependence. Recent research works have demonstrated that ICA process of nature scene images can result in edge detection [4-6]. We apply ICA to nature scene patches and use the resulting filters as templates for pattern matching to get ICA pattern maps.

2   Texture Segmentation by Multichannel Filtering

In the multichannel filtering method, a texture image $I(x, y)$ is usually convolved with a bank of Gabor filters g with different orientations θ_m and frequencies ω_n :

$$\mathbf{W}_{mn}(x, y) = \mathbf{I}(x, y) \otimes g(x, y, \theta_m, \omega_n) \tag{1}$$

In the filtered images $\mathbf{W}$, statistic terms are calculated in a small window $A = S1 \times S1$. The widely used statistics are mean μ_{mn} and deviation σ_{mn}, and the feature vector is

$$f = \begin{bmatrix} \mu_{00} & \sigma_{00} & \mu_{10} & \sigma_{10} & \cdots & \mu_{mn} & \sigma_{mn} \end{bmatrix} \tag{2}$$

Since a Gabor filter with a specific orientation and frequency enhances only one particular edge feature, the features of an image are generally represented by a set of filtered images. The feature components are calculated separately in the filtered images and so result in costly computation. Also the gray scale features are easily affected by the illumination condition.

3   A New Feature Based on Pattern Maps

In this section, we propose a new feature that is independent of illumination and relatively time saving.

Instead of representing the features in multi-filtered images, we represent the features in one pattern map. A gray scale image is transformed into a pattern map in which edge, and background pixels are classified by pattern matching as Fig. 1.

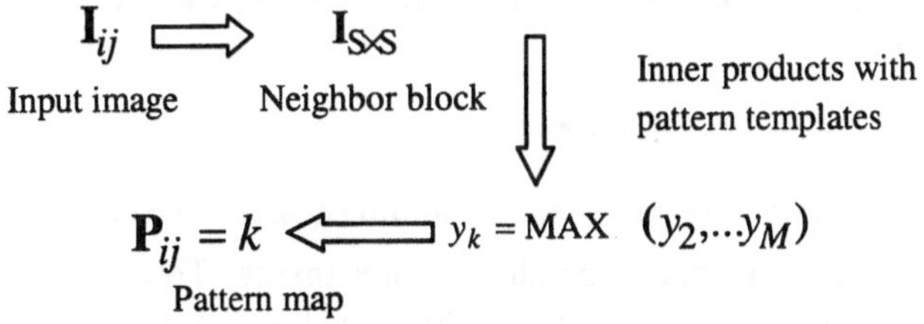

$$\mathbf{I}_{ij} \implies \mathbf{I}_{S \times S}$$

Input image   Neighbor block   Inner products with pattern templates

$$\mathbf{P}_{ij} = k \impliedby y_k = \text{MAX} \ (y_2, \dots y_M)$$

Pattern map

Fig. 1. Pattern matching with templates

The pixels in a pattern map are represented by the classes of the patterns that match the neighbor blocks best. So a pattern map has a rather small and controllable value range. Suppose the number of patterns is M, thus a pattern map is in a range of $[1, M]$. For each pixel $P(x,y)$, the features in a window $S1 \times S1$ can be generated as:

$$f_i(x, y) = \sum_{m=-(S1-1)/2}^{(S1-1)/2} \sum_{n=-(S1-1)/2}^{(S1-1)/2} g_i(m+x, n+y) \quad i=1,\dots M \ ; \tag{3}$$

where the function g is defined as a binary function:

$$g_i(m, n) = \begin{cases} 1 & P(m, n) = i \\ 0 & \text{otherwise} \end{cases} \tag{4}$$

So, the feature f_i is the number of the pixels belonging to the i-th pattern. The feature vector is constructed using f_i as components:

$$F = (f_1, f_2, \dots f_N) \tag{5}$$

4   ICA Filters as Pattern Templates

The pattern templates represent the spatial features in images and should reflect that how the value of one pixel depend on those of its neighbors. Instead of adopting the templates from mathematical formulas, in this work, we proposed to get the pattern templates by independent component analysis of image patches. On this point, there have been some researches on analyzing the inter-relations between neighbor pixels to learn the receptive fields of primary cortex cells [7,8]. We first give the general model of image analysis.

Suppose that each image patch, represented by the vector **x**, is the linear combination of N basis functions as:

$$[x_1, x_2, ..., x_N]^T = s_1 \times [a_{11}, a_{21}, ..., a_{N1}]^T + \cdots + s_N \times [a_{1N}, a_{2N}, ..., a_{NN}]^T \qquad (6)$$

The basis functions are consistent and the coefficients vary with images. Imagine that a perceptual system is exposed to a series of images. We can represent the coding process in matrix form as:

$$\mathbf{x} = \mathbf{As} \qquad (7)$$

where a column of **x** is an image patch, each column of **A** is a basis function a_i, and a column of **s** is the coefficients responding to the image. Thus, the linear image analysis process is to find a matrix **W**, so that the resulting vector **y** (Eq.8) recovers the underlying causes **s**, possibly permuted and rescaled. Each row of **W** is taken as a filter.

$$\mathbf{y} = \mathbf{Wx} \qquad (8)$$

Designing an algorithm to learn **W** depends on what kinds of causes are concerned. If we take the causes as being mutual independent, the Independent Component Analysis (ICA) model can be applied to resolve this problem.

Bell & Sejnowski have proposed a neural learning algorithm for ICA [9]. The approach is to maximize by stochastic gradient ascent the joint entropy, $H(g(\mathbf{y}))$, of the linear transform Eq. (8) squashed by a sigmoidal function g. The updating formula for **W** is:

$$\Delta \mathbf{W} = (\mathbf{I} + g(\mathbf{y})\mathbf{y}^T)\mathbf{W} \qquad (9)$$

where **y**=**Wx**, and $g(y) = 1 - 2/(1 + e^{-y})$ is calculated for each component of **y**. Before the learning procedure, **x** is sphered by subtracting the mean $\mathbf{m}_x$ and multiplying by a whitening filter:

$$\mathbf{x} = [(\mathbf{x} - \mathbf{m}_x)(\mathbf{x} - \mathbf{m}_x)^T]^{-1/2}(\mathbf{x} - \mathbf{m}_x) \qquad (10)$$

In our experiment, the training set was generated of 12,000 8×8 samples from four nature scenes involving trees, leaves and so on. Each row of **W** is taken as a filter, and the resulted 64 filters are displayed in Fig. 2. Olshausen & Field got the similar results by sparseness-maximization network and argued that this is a family of localized, oriented, bandpass receptive fields [6]. However, until now there are few applications of these filters to image processing. One reason is that in many cases not all the filters are necessary and it is difficult to choose an appropriate subset according to specific circumstances.

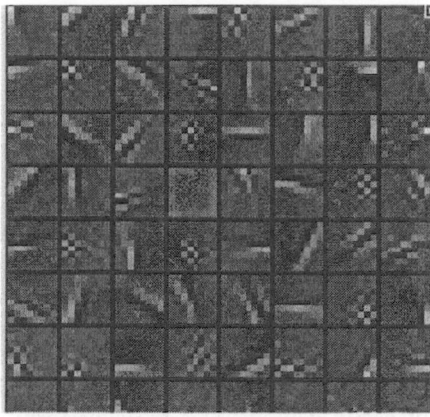

Fig. 2. W of 64 filters obtained by training on whitened data, consisting of Gabor-like oriented filters and checkerboard filters

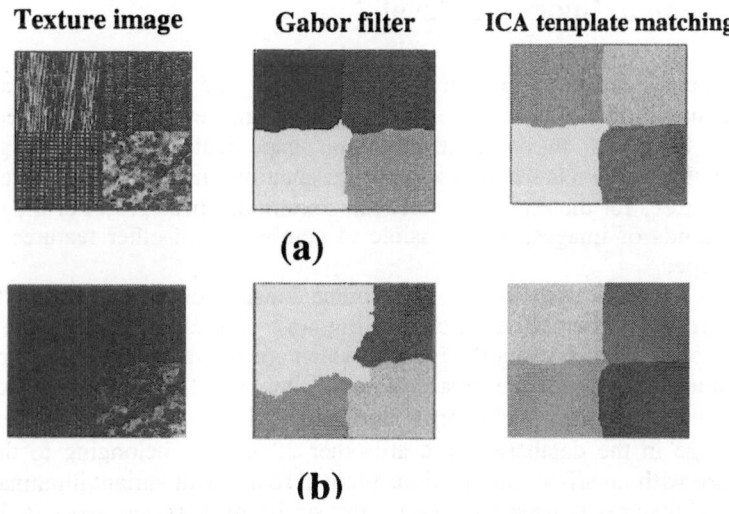

Fig. 3. Texture segmentation results. (a) Invariant illumination; (b) variant illumination.

Typical examples of texture segmentation based on ICA template matching are shown in Fig.3. Figure 3(a) are segmentation results with an invariant illumination, while Fig.3(b) are results with a variant illumination. The segmentation errors and computation time are summarized in Table 1.

Table 1. Comparison of the new feature and Gabor feature

		Gabor filter	ICA Template Matching
Error rate (%)	Invariant illumination	2.32	2.0
	Variant illumination	56.4	2.57
Computation time (sec)		270	13

As shown in Fig.3 and Table 1, the variant illumination will significantly affect the Gabor feature that the error rate is increased up to 56%, while for the proposed ICA feature, the error rate is still 2.6% even with variant illumination. It might be argued that the influence of illumination variation can be removed by normalizing the Gabor features. That is another process and the way to do normalization will still affect the segmentation results. As to the computation cost, the proposed feature is about 13 seconds, while the calculation of each Gabor feature component costs 17 seconds. In case of 8 filters, the computation time for average and variance statistics is 272 seconds. This experiment easily demonstrates the superiority of the new feature to multichannel filtering features.

5 Application to Image Retrieval

The new feature is designed for texture representation, and has many applications in pattern analysis. In this section, it is applied to image retrieval. Content-based image retrieval can be based on color, texture and shape features. To investigate the performance of the new feature for texture representation, in the following, we mainly use texture features for the retrieval of Brodatz texture database [10]. For the retrieval of different kinds of images, it is possible to combine with other features such as color, and shape.

The image database used in this experiment consists of 19 different   textures from   the Brodatz album[10] as shown in Fig.4(a). We also include some variant illumination to the first 10 images (Fig.4(b), which are also added to the database. So thare 29 texture images in the database. Each of the 512×512 images is divided into 16 128×128 nonoverlapping subimages, thus raising the actual database size to 464. For each image in the database, there are other 32 images belonging to the same pattern (16 are with invariant illumination, another 16 are with variant illumination).

Distance of features is used to measure the similarity between textures. For two images i and j, the responding feature vectors are $\mathbf{F}^i = (f_1^{(i)}, ... f_M^{(i)})$ and $\mathbf{F}^j = (f_1^{(j)}, ... f_M^{(j)})$. Then, the distance between the two patterns in the feature space is defined to be:

$$dis(i, j) = \sum_{m=1}^{M} d_m(i, j) \tag{11}$$

where

$$d_m(i,j) = \left| \frac{f_m^{(i)} - f_m^{(j)}}{\alpha(c_m)} \right|$$

(12)

f_m is as defined in section 3.1, and $\alpha(c_m)$ is the standard deviation of f_m over the entire database, and is used to normalize the feature components. M is the number of features.

The retrieval rate is the percentage number of images belonging to the same pattern   as the query image in the top 31 matches.

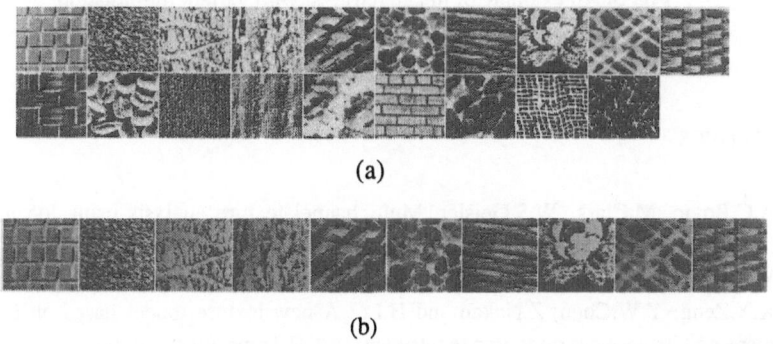

(a)

(b)

Fig. 4. Textures from Brodatz album. (a) Invariant illumiation; (b) variant illumination.

One typical retrieval result is shown in Fig.5. The first one is the query image. The other images are top 31 images with a minimum distance. The retrieval rate is estimated as 87%. The retrieval rate is dependent on the query image, which varies from 50% to 100%. The average retrieval rate is 86.8%. There are no significant influences from the variant illumination.

6 Summary

In this paper, we propose a new ICA-based texture model and its application to image retrieval. The proposed new feature for texture representation that is not only robust to the influence of illumination but most importantly is quite time saving. The proposed method can be used to many applications. An example is given on image retrieval of Brodatz album textures. The applicability of the proposed method has been demonstrated.

This work was partly supported by the Outstanding Overseas Chinese Scholars Fund of Chinese Academy of Science.

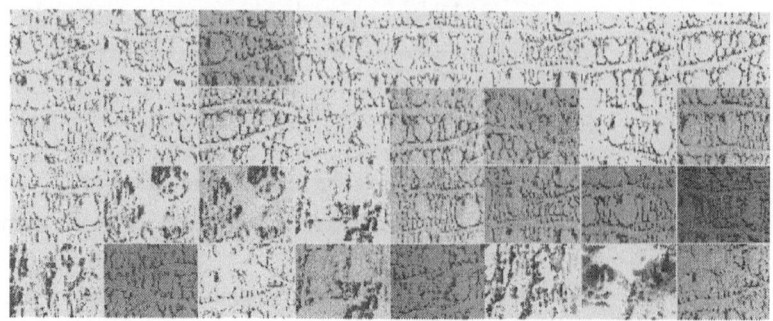

Fig. 5. An example of image retrieval with variant illumination.

References

[1] A.C.Bovic, M.Clark, W.S.Geisler: Multichannel texture analysis using localized spatial filters. IEEE Trans. PAMI, 12 (1990) 55-73.

[2] M.R.Turner: Texture discrimination by Gabor Functions. Biol. Cybern, 55(1986) 71-83.

[3] X.Y.Zeng, Y.W.Chen, Z.Nakao and H.Lu: A new texture model based on PCA pattern maps and its application to image retrieval. IEICE Trans. (2002) in press.

[4] D.J.Field: Relations between the statistics of natural images and the response properties of cortical cells. Journal of the Optical Society of America A, 4(1987) 2379-2394.

[5] A.J.Bell and T.J.Sejnowski: The Independent components of natural scenes are edge filters. Vision research, 37 (1997).

[6] B.A.Olshausen and D.J.Field: Emergence of simple-cell receptive field properties by learning a sparse code for natural images. Nature 381(1996) 607-609.

[7] H.B.Barlow: The coding of sensory messages, Current Problems in Animal Behavior, Cambridge U. Press, Cambridge, (1961) 331-360.

[8] H. B. Barlow "Understanding nature vision, Physical and Biological Processing of Images" Vol. 11 of Spring Series in Information Sciences, Springer-Verlag, Berlin, (1983) 2-14.

[9] A.J.Bell and T.J.Sejnowski: An information maximization approach to blind separation and blind deconvolution. Neural Computation, 7(1995) 1129-1159.

[10] P. Brodatz, Textures: A photographic Album for Artists and Designers, Mineola, NY, Dover, (1966).

A Novel Hierarchical Approach to Image Retrieval Using Color and Spatial Information

Xiuqi Li[1], Shu-Ching Chen[2*], Mei-Ling Shyu[3], Sheng-Tun Li[4], and Borko Furht[1]

[1] Department of Computer Science and Engineering
Florida Atlantic University
Boca Raton, FL 33431, USA
[2] Distributed Multimedia Information System Laboratory
School of Computer Science
Florida International University
Miami, FL 33199, USA
[3] Department of Electrical and Computer Engineering
University of Miami
Coral Gables, FL 33124, USA
[4] Department of Information Management
National Kaohsiung First University of Science and Technology
Juoyue Rd. Nantz District
Kaohsiung 811, Taiwan, R.O.C.

Abstract. A novel hierarchical approach to image retrieval is proposed. First, a color label histogram is used to effectively filter out the images that are not similar to the query image in color. The proposed color label histogram built by categorizing the pixel colors is computationally much more efficient compared to other approaches. Next, the class parameters of those images passing the first filter are used to identify the images similar to the query image in spatial layout. These class parameters are obtained automatically from the proposed unsupervised segmentation algorithm. Moreover, the wavelet decomposition coefficients are used to generate the initial partition for the segmentation algorithm. It doubles the segmentation performance. At the last stage, all images passing two filters are ranked based on the total normalized distance in color and spatial layout. The experiments show the effectiveness and efficiency of our approach.

1 Introduction

Owing to the recent advances in hardware, managing large number of images has become ordinary. This leads to a growing interest in querying images based on the content of the images. Traditionally, images are retrieved using a text-based approach. In this approach, each image is manually annotated and then the retrieval process is converted into retrieval of the keywords in text descriptions

* This research was supported in part by NSF CDA-9711582 and NSF EIA-0220562.

Y.-C. Chen, L.-W. Chang, and C.-T. Hsu (Eds.): PCM 2002, LNCS 2532, pp. 175–182, 2002.
© Springer-Verlag Berlin Heidelberg 2002

of images. There are several inherent problems in such systems. First, manual annotation is often subjective, inaccurate, and incomplete [1]. Secondly, some of the image properties cannot be described using keywords. Because of these reasons, the content-based approach was developed to query images directly based on their visual attributes such as color, texture, shape, layout, object location, etc. without resort to human annotation.

In most of the content-based image retrieval systems, the goal is to find the top N images that are similar to the user query image [1][3]. Because each image has many visual features, similarity comparison based on a single feature is not enough. There have been some hierarchical approaches to content-based image retrieval combining multiple visual features. In [2], a color histogram filter and wavelet-based shape matching were utilized to query and screen objectionable images.

Our approach is different from the previous approaches in three aspects. First, a novel color label histogram is proposed. By categorizing the pixel colors into a set of thirteen colors and by labeling each pixel based on the color category ID, a histogram with only thirteen bins is obtained. It effectively and efficiently captures the global color information. Secondly, a unique unsupervised segmentation algorithm is applied to images to extract the information about the relationship between the pixel intensities and their spatial layout. Thirdly, wavelet decomposition is used to improve the performance of the segmentation algorithm.

The rest of the paper is organized as follows. In section 2, first, an overview of our query framework is given. Then, the color label histogram filter is presented. Next, the unsupervised segmentation parameter filter and the initial partition generation are presented. Finally, the query ranking is described. Section 3 shows the experimental results. Concluding remarks are given in Section 4.

2   Hierarchical Query Framework

Figure 1 illustrates our hierarchical query framework. Before the query, the color label histogram of each image in the image database is extracted offline. The results are stored for later filtering. Each image in the database is also segmented by the SPCPE (Simultaneous Partition and Class Parameter Estimation) algorithm [5][6] offline. The class parameters are generated and stored for later filtering. The query image is processed in the same way as any other image in the database. During the query, the color label histogram and the class parameters of the query image are compared to those of each image in the database. The comparison is performed in two stages. First, a color label histogram filter is used to eliminate all images that are not similar to the query image in color. Those images that passed the color filter are further compared to the query image using the class parameter filter. The second filter uses the class parameters obtained from the SPCPE algorithm to filter out those images that are not similar to the query image in spatial layout. At the end, all images that pass the

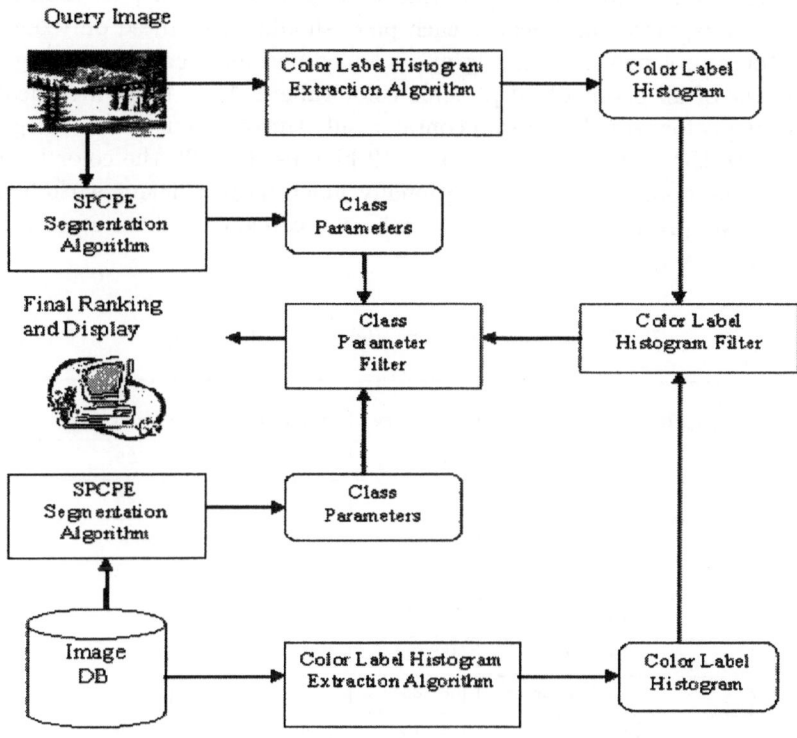

Fig. 1. The hierarchical framework

two filters are ranked based on the total normalized color and class parameter distance and the top six (or fewer) images are displayed in the user interface.

Next, we discuss in more details the color label histogram filter, the unsupervised segmentation parameter filter, and the final query ranking.

2.1   Color Label Histogram Filter

The image color is represented in a 3-channel color space. There are many color spaces, such as RGB, HSV, YUV, YIQ, CIE LAB, and CIE LUV. No color space is dominant in all applications.

In [4], the author used twelve color categories for the representative colors of color regions in an image. All categories are obtained from the experimental results based on the H, S and V value ranges. In our approach, the above categories are modified for our color histogram computation. To reduce the total number of histogram bins, the difference between the bright chromatic pixels and chromatic pixels is ignored. Therefore, bright blue and blue are considered to be in the same color category (BLUE). In addition, each transition slice is counted as a separate bin because each pixel should be counted only once in a color histogram. A new category "gray" is added because a color histogram takes into account of all pixels of all possible color values. After these modifications, the resulting color label histogram contains only thirteen bins (color categories). Compared to the color histogram with 512 bins used in [2], the color label histogram in our approach is computationally much more efficient without much loss of retrieval precision. Table 1 lists each color category and the corresponding H, S, V value ranges.

Table 1. Color category and HSV value ranges

Color category ID	Color category	Hue range	Saturation range	Value range
1	White	Any	< 20	≥ 85
2	Black	Any	Any	< 25
3	Gray	Any	< 20	(25,85]
4	Red	$[350°,25°)$		
5	Red-Yellow	$[25°,45°)$		
6	Yellow	$[45°,65°)$		
7	Yellow-Green	$[65°,85°)$		
8	Green	$[85°,160°)$	≥ 20	≥ 25
9	Green-Blue	$[160°,180°)$		
10	Blue	$[180°,270°)$		
11	Blue-Purple	$[270°,290°)$		
12	Purple	$[290°,330°)$		
13	Purple-Red	$[330°,350°)$		

Histogram comparison between the query image q and the jth image in the database is based on the L_1-*Distance* [1], which is defined as follows:

$$D^{(q,j)}_{colorlabelhist} = \sum_{i=1}^{N} \left| X_i^{(q)} - X_i^{(j)} \right| \tag{1}$$

where X_i is the ith bin and N is the total number of bins.

A threshold value is used by the color label histogram filter to eliminate the images in the database that are not similar to the query image in color.

2.2   Unsupervised Segmentation Class Parameter Filter

Given a gray-scale image, the SPCPE algorithm [5][6] partitions it into s *regions (classes)* that are mutually exclusive and totally inclusive. Each class consists of one or more *segments* that are similar to each other in some sense and may not be spatially contiguous. Therefore, each image is partitioned into s classes and b segments. In the SPCPE algorithm, both the *class parameters* θ and the *partitions* C are considered as random variables. The algorithm estimates C and θ to be that which *maximizes* the *a-posterior probability (MAP)* of the partition variable and class parameter variable given the image data Y. Specifically, the algorithm begins with an initial partition, estimates C and θ iteratively and simultaneously, and stops when the partition cannot be further optimized (the cost function reaches a local minimum).

Initial Partition Generation. The SPCPE algorithm starts with an initial partition and optimizes it using the least square technique and re-labeling rule. It is found in our experiment that the initial partition is very important and different initial partitions lead to different segmentation results. To produce a better result, the wavelet decomposition coefficients [7][8] are used in the initial partition generation. Without loss of generality, assume that there are two classes. The algorithm estimates C and θ, which has the least cost J [5][6].

Our idea of using wavelet transform for initial partition generation is to label pixels as different classes based on the wavelet coefficient values. Images are first decomposed using Haar wavelet at level one. Next, salient points in horizontal, vertical and diagonal subbands are extracted by thresholding. For each of the three subbands, all pixels in the original image that correspond to the salient points in that subband are labeled as one class, and the rest of the pixels are labeled as the other class. This generates three candidate initial partitions. The final initial partition is the one with the least cost J among the three candidates. Compared to the random initial partition generation, the segmentation precision is doubled with the help of the wavelet technique.

Class Parameter Filter. The unsupervised segmentation filter applies the SPCPE algorithm to the query image and all the images in the database to generate the class parameters. Then the filter compares the class parameters of the query image to those of the images passing the color label histogram filter. It filters out the images in its search range whose class parameters are much different from those of the query image.

Class parameter comparison is based on the sum of the Euclidian Distance of each corresponding class parameter between the query image q and the jth image in the search range.

$$D_{classpar}(q,j) = \sum_{m=1}^{NC} \sqrt{\sum_{i=0}^{3} \left(a_{mi}^{(q)} - a_{mi}^{(j)} \right)^2} \tag{2}$$

where NC indicates the total number of classes and a_{mi} is the ith class parameter for class m.

2.3   Final Query Ranking

After passing the above two filters, images are sorted in descending order based on the sum of the normalized color label histogram distance and the normalized class parameter distance. The top six (or fewer) images are returned and displayed in the user interface. It is found that the class parameter distance is much larger than the color label histogram distance. Therefore, the two distances need to be normalized before the sum is computed. Normalization is implemented by dividing each color/parameter distance by the maximum color/parameter distance among all color/parameter distances between the query image and all the images that passed the two filters.

Fig. 2. Initial partition generation for Image 388.

3   Experimental Results

The experiments were conducted on various natural scene images, which were downloaded from yahoo (*www.yahoo.com*) and corbis (*www.corbis.com*). They vary in color and spatial layout. Their sizes are 256x192.

3.1   Experiments on Initial Partition Generation and Filtering Effects

Figure 2 shows the comparison of the initial partition generation effect using the random generation and the wavelet technique for Image 388. The image in the first row is the original image. The left image in the second row is the final segmentation result from a randomly generated initial partition. The right image in the second row is the final segmentation result from an initial partition generated through the wavelet transformation. It can be clearly seen from this figure that the segmentation result using the wavelet initial partition is much better than that of the random initial partition. With the wavelet initial partition, the porch, chairs, and the mountain are identified as the foreground, while the ocean and the sky are identified as the background. However, without using the wavelet initial partition, the top-left section of the porch was wrongly classified as the background, and part of the sky is mistakenly classified as the foreground.

Table 2. Experimental result on the filtering effect

Filter	Avg(%)	Max(%)	Min(%)
Color Filter	80	95	70
Class Parameter Filter	85	90	75

To evaluate the filtering effect, we computed the average, maximum, and minimum percentage of images eliminated from the search range of each filter based on all images in the database. Table 2 shows the experimental result. From Table 2, we can see that the two filters dramatically reduce the number of images that require computation for the following stage. Therefore, the query is speeded up.

QID = 162

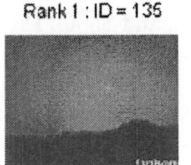

Rank 1 : ID = 135   Rank 2 : ID = 3   Rank 3 : ID = 490

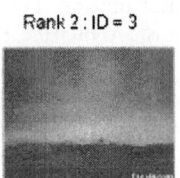

Fig. 3. Query result of Image 162

3.2 Experiment on the Retrieval Performance

The query result of Image 162 is shown in Figure 3. The image in the first row is the query image. The top three similar images and their ranks and image IDs are displayed in the next two rows. There are only three images returned. As can be seen from this figure, the result is quite good. The query image and the top three images contain two major colors: red and black. As for the spatial layout, the query image is very similar to the images with Rank 1 and Rank 2. All of them consist of a top area and a bottom area. The image with Rank 3 is a little bit different. There are several small dark areas on the top half of the image. However, the major areas are still the top and bottom ones.

4 Concluding Remarks

In this paper, a hierarchical framework for content-based image retrieval is proposed. A novel color label histogram, a unique unsupervised segmentation algorithm, and the wavelet technique are integrated in our framework. Before the query process, the color label histogram and the class parameters are extracted from all the images in the database offline.

During the query process, the color label histogram filter and the class parameter filter are used to filter out images that are not similar to the query image in color and spatial layout, respectively. All images passing the two filters are ranked based on the total normalized distance at the final stage. The top six (or fewer) images are returned in the interface. The experimental result demonstrates the effectiveness of our framework.

References

[1] Ma, W., Zhang, H.J.: Content-Based Image Indexing and Retrieval. Handbook of Multimedia Computing, CRC Press (1999)

[2] Wang, J., Wiederhold, G., Firschein O.: System for Screening Objectionable Images Using Daubechies Wavelets and Color Histograms. Proc. of Interactive Distributed Multimedia Systems and Telecommunication Services (1997)

[3] Flicker, M., Sawhney, H., etc.: Query by Image and Video Content: The QBIC System. IEEE Computers, Vol. 28. (1995)

[4] Androutsos, D.: Efficient Indexing and Retrieval of Color Image Data Using a Vector Based Approach. PhD Dissertation. (1999)

[5] Sista, S., Kashyap, R.: Bayesian Estimation For Multiscale Image Segmentation. IEEE International Conference on Acoustics, Speech, and Signal Processing, Phoenix (1999)

[6] Chen, S.-C., Sista, S., Shyu, M.-L., Kashyap, R.: An Indexing and Searching Structure for Multimedia Database Systems. IST/SPIE Conference on Storage and Retrieval for Media Databases. (2000) 262–270

[7] Wavelet Toolbox User's Guide. The Mathworks Inc. (2000)

[8] Daubechies, I.: Ten Lectures on Wavelets. Capital City Press. (1992)

A Semantic Model for Video Description and Retrieval[*]

Chia-Han Lin, Andro H.C. Lee, and Arbee L.P. Chen

Department of Computer Science
National Tsing Hua University
Hsinchu, Taiwan 300, R.O.C.
alpchen@cs.nthu.edu.tw

Abstract. In this paper, a semantic video retrieval system is proposed based on the stories of the videos. A hierarchical knowledge model is used to express the semantic meanings contained in the videos, and a video query language is also provided. The terms of Object, Action and Relation are used to specify rich and complex semantic meanings in a query. Based on the proposed knowledge model, the retrieval system is able to make inferences on the terms appearing in a query, and determine whether a video semantically matches the query conditions. The semantic similarity measurement is also proposed for processing approximate queries.

1 Introduction

Due to the improvement of computer power and the growth of storage space, videos can now be stored in digital formats on computer platforms. Recently, these digital videos are massively distributed and users may want to search for a desired video efficiently. This demand leads to the research of video retrieval.

In the video retrieval system, some approaches [5][9][10] use the text annotation to describe the video content. However, the complicated video content is difficult to describe just by text. Other approaches [3][17] of video retrieval are based on visual features of videos such as the color of the video frame or the shape and the motion trajectory of the objects in videos. Venus [12] is a video retrieval system, which considers the spatial-temporal relationship of objects. Moreover, a video query language is provided for users to specify queries. The hybrid method proposed in [8] combines both the text annotation and visual features to describe the content of video.

In addition to visual characteristics, a video is usually associated with a story, which is more meaningful to humans. Lilac et al. [6] expresses this information in terms of objects, actions and associations. The associations represent the relationships between the objects and the actions. Aguis and Angelides[1] proposed a semantic content-based model for semantic-level querying including objects, spatial relationships between objects, events and actions involving objects, temporal relationships between events and actions. However, it is hard to describe a complex

---

[*] This work was partially supported by the Program for Promoting Academic Excellence of Universities in the Republic of China under the Contract No. 89-E-FA04-1-4

Y.-C. Chen, L.-W. Chang, and C.-T. Hsu (Eds.): PCM 2002, LNCS 2532, pp. 183–190, 2002.
© Springer-Verlag Berlin Heidelberg 2002

story based on the proposed model. Some other researches focus on designing a semantic video query language[2]. More discussions on defining the query language in formal grammar can be found in [5][7]. However, these researches focus on syntax definition rather than the description and organization of semantic meanings.

Some other approaches capture the semantic meaning with some concepts[14] [16]. A video is segmented into several video clips which is described by the associated concepts. In [11], the semantic meaning is captured in concepts with a concept degree to represent the intensity of the concept in a video segment. However, the structure used to express the spatial-temporal relationships of objects is not included.

Both the spatial-temporal relationships and the semantic meaning are important components of a video. A new video retrieval system, which expresses the video content in a semantic way, is proposed in this paper. The events happening in a video such as "moving", "fighting", or "talking" are recorded. We also provide a definable knowledge model to represent the semantic meanings. Finally, a semantic video query language is designed for users to specify queries.

The organization of this paper is as follows. Section 2 presents the modeling of videos. A semantic video query language (SVQL) is proposed in Section 3. Section 4 presents query processing and the semantic similarity measurement. Section 5 concludes this paper and presents future work.

2   Video Modeling

2.1 Knowledge Models

The background knowledge is used to realize the semantic meaning of the video content. In our system, the knowledge can be built as a hierarchical semantic model based on the characteristics of the applications. In this model, three types of knowledge, *Object*, *Action*, and *Relation*, are defined. "Object" represents the objects appearing in the video. "Action" represents an action, such as "moving", of an object. "Relation" is used to describe a relationship between objects, which can be a spatial relation or an implicit semantic relation such as "father of". Each of the three types of knowledge has a corresponding hierarchical semantic tree, which is organized with the object-oriented inheritance relationship to express the relation between different semantic meanings. Fig. 1. is an example of the hierarchical semantic tree for objects.

2.2 Metadata Structures

Some information of a video, such as title and names of actors, can be simply recorded in the metadata. However, some other information, such as the appearance and disappearance of objects, the attributes of objects, or the events happening in the video, may change frequently when a video is played. Such information is recorded with additional duration information.

In the proposed approach, the metadata of videos are recorded in tables. The description for each video is recorded as a row in a table. The format of the tables is defined as follows.

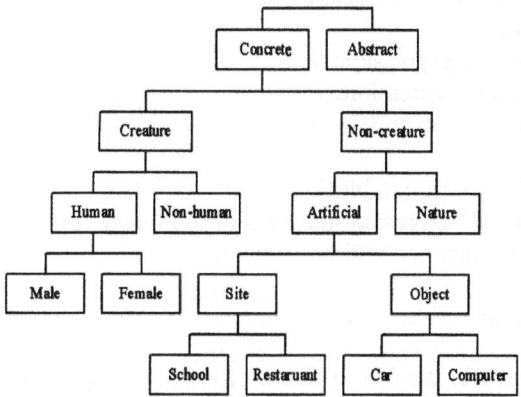

Fig. 1. An example of the hierarchical semantic tree for objects.

Film_Info_table records the production information of a video, such as title and names of actors.

Scene_Concept_table records the values of the concept degree of scene concepts. The scene concept proposed in our previous work[11] is used to express the semantic information of a video segment.

Object_Attribute_table records the values of the object attributes. Since the values may be changed when the video is played, the duration information will be also recorded with the values.

Relation_table records relationships between objects. The object's id and the duration information where the relations hold will be recorded.

Action_table records the actions of a video object or objects. The object's id and the duration information where the actions hold will be recorded.

3   Semantic Video Query Language

Based on the proposed video model, SVQL is proposed for users to specify queries. The variables are declared to represent different objects, actions and relations. Furthermore, these variables can be grouped with a function to form an expression representing an action or a relation. Finally, a sequence of expressions is built to represent a complicated "story", which can be regarded as the query condition. The video clips containing the story will be found and the specified information of the video clips will be returned as the result.

3.1 Syntax

A simplified form of syntax is listed as follows. The formal and detailed definitions in the format of BNF can be found in[13].

```
Find       <target>
Which      Has-
           Object: <var_declaration>
           Action: <var_declaration>
```

Relation: <var_declaration>
Semantic-
<object_expression>,
<doing_expression>,
<relation_expression>
→
next description block...

The clause of "Find" expresses the form of the query result while the clause of "Which" represents the query conditions.

3.2 The <target> Field

There are several ways to display different types of the query result based on the specification of the <target> field. The <target> field has the following possible values:

1.   *Clip*: It indicates that the system should return the video clips matching the expressions in the "Semantic-" part.
2.   *Attribute of FilmInfo*: It indicates that the system should return the value of FilmInfo's attributes for each matched video clip.
3.   *SceneConcept*: Specifying SceneConcept indicates that the system should return the concept degrees of each matched video clip.
4.   *Variables or some attributes of variables*: Specifying attributes of variables indicates that the system should return the values of the attributes. Specifying variables indicates that the system should return the values for each variable's attributes.

3.3 The "Has-" Part

The variables used in the <target> field and the "Semantic-" part are declared in this part as one of the three types: Object, Action and Relation.

3.4 The "Semantic-" Part

This part is used to describe the whole "story." Several types of expressions are provided to describe various semantic meanings. Multiple expressions can be specified and separated by a comma. All expressions in this part are verified to find a suitable query result containing the corresponding semantic meanings. The three different types of expressions are introduced as follows:

<object_expression>

This type of expressions is used to set the constraint of an Object variable's attribute, or to specify a variable as an instance of some class in the corresponding hierarchical semantic tree. Some operators that can be used in this type of expressions are defined as follows:

1.   IS-A operator: "∈"
      The IS-A operator is used to specify that a variable is an instance of some class in the corresponding hierarchical semantic tree.
2.   Attribute operator: "."

Attribute operator is used to specify the attribute of an object. The syntax of using this operator is "<obj>.<attribute>." "<obj>" is a variable name and "<attribute>" is one of the object's attributes.

3. Comparison operator "=", "<", ">", "≠",
    Comparison operator is used to set constraints between attributes and values.

4. Alternative operator: "|"
    This operator is used in the right-hand side of an expression to indicate the "OR" logic, which means if one of these values satisfies the expression, the whole expression holds.
    Here is an example of a sequence of object expressions:

$$x \in \text{"car", } y \in \text{"man,"}$$
$$x.color = \text{"red" | "blue,"}$$
$$y.age = \text{"42"}$$

In this example, x is a car, and y is a man. The color of the car is red or blue. The man is 42 years old.

<doing_expression>

This type of expressions is a function using Object and Action variables as its parameters. It is used to express an action occurring in a video. The two types of functions are introduced below. The parameters of *object1* and *object2* are two variables declared as Object. *Action* is a variable declared as Action.

1. DoingTo(*object1, object2, action*)
    It expresses "*object1* is doing *action* to *object2*."

2. Doing(*object1, action*)
    It expresses "*object1* is doing *action*."

Here is an example following the previous example:

$$m = \text{"drive," } DoingTo(y, x, m)$$

In this example, m is an action of "drive," which means "a man is driving a car."

<relation_expression>

By using this type of functions, the relationships between the variables of Object are described. Since the relation represents the relationship between two objets, the syntax of the function can be expressed as follows:

RelationTo(*object1, object2, relation*)

It expresses "*object1* has a relation of *relation* to *object2*."
Here is an example following the previous example:

$$n = \text{"owner\_of," } RelationTo(y, x, n)$$

In this example, n is a relation of "owner_of" The expression indicates a relation between x and y, which means "a man y is the owner of a car x."

Description Block

The Transition operator "→" is used to connect the expressions in the "Semantic-" part from several groups. Each group of the expressions is considered as a Description Block, which describes one "story." The Transition operator "→" indicates that these stories happen in order.

Here is an example following the previous one:

$$p = \text{"walk," } DoingTo(y, x, p)$$
$$\rightarrow$$
$$y \in \text{"man, } x \in \text{"car," } m = \text{"drive," } DoingTo(y, x, m)$$

The story of these expressions is "At first, a man y walks to a car x, then he drives that car."

3.5 A Complete Query Example

Find a video clip containing the story: "Tom stands to the left of Michael and Michael attacks Tom, Tom asks Michael, "why are you attacking me?" but Michael just runs away.

Find Clip
Which
Has-
   Object: Tom, Michael, dialog
   Action: attack, say, run
   Relation: left
Semantic-
   Tom ∈ "man", Tom.name = "Tom",
   Michael ∈ "man", Michael.name = "Michael",
   left = "left_to", RelationTo(Tom, Michael, left),
   attack = "attack", DoingTo(Michael, Tom, attack),
   →
   say = "say", dialog ∈ "dialog",
   dialog.content = Why are you attacking me? ,
   DoingTo(Tom, say, dialog)
   →
   run = "run", Doing(Michael, run)

4   Query Processing

4.1 Evaluating Expressions

The description for each video is recorded as a row in the metadata table. To process a query, the expressions are evaluated one by one. The matched descriptions can be found after the expression evaluation. If the matched description does not exist for an expression, no result will be found for this query. The video clips containing all matched descriptions will be added to the solution set. After all expressions have been evaluated, the desired target information for each video clip in the solution set will be returned as the query result.

Description Blocks can be connected by the Transition operator. During the query processing, each Description Block is evaluated to find a solution set. The video clips can be selected from the solution sets in order by verifying the temporal relationship of these video clips.

4.2 Reasoning in Semantic Hierarchy

In SVQL, users can declare three types of new variables, Object, Action, and Relation. With the IS-A operator, a variable can be specified as an instance of some class of the corresponding hierarchical semantic tree. A reasoning rule can be defined as follows:

Semantic Class Matching Rule:
Assume A is a variable in a query and B is a candidate description in the database. A and B are declared as of same type. A ∈ A' and B∈ B'. Then B is a matched answer to A if and only if A' = B' or A' is an ancestor class of B'.

For example, based on the hierarchical semantic tree of Object shown in Figure 2, if a variable in the query is "Creature" the description of "Male" in the database will be matched since "Creature" is an ancestor class of "Male."

4.3 Semantic Similarity Measurement

Each variable can be specified to be an instance of some classes in the three semantic hierarchical trees. By Semantic Class Matching Rule, whether the candidate object matches a query variable can be determined. However, in order to allow approximate queries, another approach is designed to calculate the similarity between unmatched classes.

The hierarchical semantic tree is organized with an IS-A relation from top to down. The upper classes are more general and the lower classes are more specific. When considering the issue of semantic similarity measurement, two cases are discussed based on the paths from the root to the two unmatched classes. The first case is that the paths are different. Therefore, if the paths branch earlier, the two classes are more dissimilar. In order to calculate the dissimilarity between two classes, a weight is set for each branch in the hierarchical semantic tree. The weight of the upper branch is higher. The dissimilarity between two classes can be defined as the number of edges from the two classes to the branch plus the weight of that branch.

The other case is the reverse situation described in the Semantic Class Matching Rule: the candidate class and the query class are at the same path, but the candidate class is the ancestor of the query class. The similarity can be measured as the number of edges between the two classes.

Based on these two cases, the Dissimilarity Index Building Algorithm is proposed to calculate the dissimilarity weight of the branches in the hierarchical semantic tree while building the hierarchical semantic model. Moreover the Dissimilarity Measuring Algorithm is proposed to measure the dissimilarity between two classes in a hierarchical semantic tree. By using the algorithm, the dissimilarity degree for each query result can be calculated and can be used to rank the query results. Both algorithms can be found in[13].

5   Conclusion

In this paper, a semantic video retrieval system is proposed. A hierarchical semantic model is designed to express the background knowledge for different applications. Based on the model, the semantic meanings contained in videos are described and recorded in metadata for query processing. A semantic video query language is proposed for users to specify queries. Variables can be declared as objects, actions, or relations, which can be used to describe an event as the query condition. The video clips or desired information can be found from the metadata. During the query processing, a reasoning process is used to parse the semantic meaning of the query and the approximate results can be found based on the proposed similarity measure.

A simple metadata structure is proposed in this approach. Our future work is to design an index structure for the metadata to enhance the query processing performance.

References

[1] Harry W. Agiuo and Marios C. Angelides, "Modeling Content for Semantic-Level Querying of Multimedia," *Multimedia Tools and Applications*, Vol.15, No.1, 2001.

[2] Edoardo Ardizzone and Mohand-Said Hacid, "A Semantic Modeling Approach for Video Retrieval by Content," *Proc. IEEE International Conference Multimedia of Computing and Systems*, 1999.

[3] E. Ardizzone, M. La Cascia and D. Molinelli, "Motion and Color-Based Video Indexing and Retrieval," *Proc. IEEE Pattern Recognition*, pp.135-139 1996.

[4] T. Chua and L. Ruan, "A Video Retrieval and Sequencing System," *ACM Transaction on Information Systems*, 1995.

[5] Cyril Decleir and Mohand-Said Hacid, "A Database Approach for Modeling and Querying Video Data," *Proc. IEEE 15th International Conference on Data Engineering*, 1999.

[6] Lilac A.E. Al Safadi and Janusz R. Getta, "Semantic Modeling for Video Content-Based Retrieval Systems," *Proc. IEEE 23th Australasian Computer Science Conference*, 2000.

[7] M.-S Hacid, C. Decleir, and J. Kouloumdjian, " A database approach for modeling and querying video data," *IEEE Transactions on Knowledge and Data Engineering*, Vol.12, No.5, pp.729-750, Sept.-Oct. 2000.

[8] Mi Hee, Yoon Yong Ik and Kio Chung Kim, "Intelligent Hybrid Video Retrieval System supporting Spatio-temporal correlation, Similarity retrieval," *Systems, Man, and Cybernetics*, 1999.

[9] R. Hielsvold and R. Midtstraum, " Modeling and Querying Video Data," *Proceedings of the 20th International Conference on VLDB*, 1994.

[10] Haitao Jiang, Danilo Montesi and Ahmed K. Elmagarmid, "VideoText Database Systems," *Proceedings of the International Conference on Multimedia Computing and Systems*, 1997.

[11] Jia-Ling Koh, Chin-Sung Lee and Arbee L.P. Chen, "Semantic Video Model for Content-Based Retrieval," *Proc. International Conference on Multimedia Computing and Systems*, 1999.

[12] Tony C.T. Kuo and Arbee L.P. Chen, "Indexing, Query Interface and Query Processing for Venus: A Video Database System," *Proc. International Symposium on Cooperative Database Systems for Advanced Applications*, 1996.

[13] Andro H. C. Lee, "A Semantic Model for Video Description and Retrieval," *Master Thesis, Dept. of Computer Science, National Tsing Hua University*, Taiwan, 2001

[14] Suieet Pradhan, Keishi Tajima, Katsumi Tanaka, "Querying Video Databases based on Description Substantiality and Approximations," *Proceedings of the IPSJ International Symposium on Information Systems and Technologies for Network Society*, September 1997.

[15] T. G. A. Smith and G. Davenport, "The Stratification System: A Design Environment for Random Access Video," *Workshop on Networking and Operating System Support for Digital Audio and Video*, 1992.

[16] Mitsukazu Washisaka, Toshihiro Takada, Shigemi Anyagi and Rikio Onai, "Video/Text Linkage System Assisted by a Concept Dictionary and Image Recognition," *Proceedings of the International Conference on Multimedia Computing and Systems*, 1996.

[17] D. Zhong and S.-F. Chang, "Video Object Model and Segmentation for Content-Based Video Indexing," *Proc. of IEEE International Symposium on Circuits and Systems*, 1997.

A Texture Segmentation Method Using Hierarchical Correlations of Wavelet Coefficients

Michihiro Kobayakawa and Mamoru Hoshi

Graduate School of Information Systems,
University of Electoro-Communications.
1-5-1 Chofugaoka, Chofu, Tokyo 182-8585, Japan
kobayakawa@computer.org, hoshi@is.uec.ac.jp

Abstract. For making an effective and simple region-based image retrieval system, it needs to uniformly realize both image segmentation and retrieval. In this paper, we focus on texture segmentation for region-based texture retrieval, and propose a new texture segmentation method based on the hierarchical correlation between the wavelet coefficients of adjacent level of wavelet decomposition. Firstly, we define a texture feature which is extracted from the hierarchical relations of wavelet coefficients. Secondly, we propose an algorithm for texture segmentation using the texture feature. Lastly, we evaluate the performance of texture segmentations. Experiments show that our method has a good performance for texture segmentation and suggest that the proposed texture segmentation method is applicable to region-based texture retrieval.

1   Introduction

For effectively retrieving images from a large image database, the importance of Content-Based Image Retrieval (CBIR) system is increasing in addition to "query by keywords" [1]. The early CBIR systems have paid attention to "query by image" such as examples, shapes, sketches, textures, colors and so on.

For example, the QBIC system [2] allows us queries by several kind of image contents. We proposed a unifying framework for CBIR system using wavelet transform and made a prototype system which allows us queries by examples, shapes, sketches [3,4], and texture [3,5] on the framework.

The CBIR systems now pay attention to "query by object" or "query by region of an image". To make an effective and simple region-based or object-based image retrieval system, we needs to uniformly realize both segmentation of the regions (objects) and feature extraction of them.

For example, suppose that a user retrieves texture images from a large set of texture images using a query by region of texture in an image. To support such retrieval, the systems have to have two functions for texture analysis: texture segmentation and texture retrieval. Since two functions need texture feature extraction, we support a unifying texture feature extraction method to realize both functions.

Y.-C. Chen, L.-W. Chang, and C.-T. Hsu (Eds.): PCM 2002, LNCS 2532, pp. 191–199, 2002.
© Springer-Verlag Berlin Heidelberg 2002

There are many methods for texture segmentation [6,7,8,9,10] based on the orthonormal wavelet transform. Among them Unser's method [10] applies to both texture classification and segmentation, while other methods are specified to texture segmentation only.

We proposed a texture feature using the hierarchical correlation of wevelet coefficients of adjacent level of decomposition and made a texture retrieval system robust with respect to the size of texture image [3,5].

For realizing query by region of texture on our framework as uniformly as possible, we propose a texture segmentation method using the same texture feature proposed in [3,5], *i.e.*, a texture segmentation method using the hierarchical correlation of wevelet coefficients of adjacent level of wavelet decomposition. To evaluate the performance of the proposed method, we compare the proposed method with Unser's method. Experiments show that the proposed texture feature works well for texture segmentation and suggest that the proposed texture segmentation method is applicable to region-based texture retrieval.

2   Texture Feature Using Hierarchical Correlation of Wavelet Coefficients

The 2-dimensional discrete wavelet transform is computed with scaling functions $\phi_{l,mn}(x,y)$ and wavelet functions $\psi^1_{l,mn}(x,y)$, $\psi^2_{l,mn}(x,y)$, $\psi^3_{l,mn}(x,y)$. Let $\boldsymbol{V}_l$, $\boldsymbol{W}^1_l$, $\boldsymbol{W}^2_l$, $\boldsymbol{W}^3_l$ be the spaces spanned by the functions $\phi_{l,mn}$, $\psi^1_{l,mn}$, $\psi^2_{l,mn}$, and $\psi^3_{l,mn}$, respectively [11].

An image can be expressed by a function $f(x,y)$

$$f(x,y) = \sum_m \sum_n c_{0,mn}\phi_{0,mn}(x,y), \quad \in \boldsymbol{V}_0,$$

where the coefficient $c_{0,mn}$ is given by

$$c_{0,mn} = <f, \phi_{0,mn}> \equiv \int\int_{-\infty}^{+\infty} f(x,y)\phi_{0,mn}(x,y)dxdy.$$

Note that the coefficient $c_{0,mn}$ corresponds to the value of the (m,n) pixel of an image. Therefore, an image (size $2^L \times 2^L$) in the space $\boldsymbol{V}_0$ can be written by a matrix $\boldsymbol{I} \equiv (c_{0,mn})_{m,n=0,\dots,2^L-1}$. Hereafter, we use a function $f(x,y)$ or the corresponding matrix $(c_{0,mn})$, interchangeably.

Let decompose an image $\boldsymbol{O} \in \boldsymbol{V}_0$ (size $2^L \times 2^L$)

$$\boldsymbol{O} \equiv (o_{0,mn}) = (<f, \phi_{0,mn}>), \quad m,n = 0,\dots,2^L-1,$$

into an approximated image $\boldsymbol{A}_1$ of level 1

$$\boldsymbol{A}_1 \equiv (a_{1,mn}) = (<f, \phi_{1,mn}>), \quad \boldsymbol{A}_1 \in \boldsymbol{V}_1, \quad m,n = 0,\dots,2^{L-1}-1,$$

and three detailed images $\boldsymbol{D}^1_1$, $\boldsymbol{D}^2_1$, $\boldsymbol{D}^3_1$ of level 1

$$\boldsymbol{D}^k_1 \equiv (d^k_{1,mn}) = (<f, \psi^k_{1,mn}>), \quad \boldsymbol{D}^k_1 \in \boldsymbol{W}^k_1, \quad m,n = 0,\dots,2^{L-1}-1.$$

Recursively applying the decomposition to the approximated image A_l, we have the images of level $l + 1$ $A_{l+1}, D_{l+1}^1, D_{l+1}^2, D_{l+1}^3$. We can make up a pyramid of the coefficients of the approximated images $\{A_1, A_2, \ldots, A_L\}$, and three pyramids of the coefficients of the detailed images $\{D_1^k, D_2^k, \ldots, D_L^k\}_{(k=1,2,3)}$.

Thus, we can obtain sub-images A_l, $D_l^k{}_{(k=1,2,3)}$ with size $2^L \times 2^L, \ldots, 1 \times 1$.

To represent hierarchical relations, we consider a complete quad tree T of height $L - 1$ where the internal node $n_{l+1,ij}$ of level $l + 1$ has exactly 4 child nodes of level l,

$$n_{l,2i\,2j}, \quad n_{l,2i+1\,2j}, \quad n_{l,2i\,2j+1}, \quad n_{l,2i+1\,2j+1},$$

from left to right in this order. We call this tree "Quad Tree (QT)". Hereafter, we associate the additional information $v_{l,ij}$ with each node $n_{l,ij}$ of quad tree. The associated value $v_{l,ij}$ of node $n_{l,ij}$ is denoted by $\mathrm{Val}(n_{l,ij}; QT)$.

Now, we define the wavelet coefficients vector $c_{l,ij} = (a_{l,ij}, d_{l,ij}^1, d_{l,ij}^2, d_{l,ij}^3)^T$, $l = 1, \ldots, L$; $i, j = 0, \ldots, 2^{L-l} - 1$, where ^{T} denotes the transposition. With each node $n_{l,ij}$, we associate the wavelt coefficients vector $c_{l,ij}$.

Then, we focus on the hierarchical dissimilarity (or descerpency) between the parent node $n_{l+1,mn}$ and his child node $n_{l,ij}$, and define the hierarchical dissimilarity vector between them by

$$g_{l,ij} = c_{l,ij} - c_{l+1,mn}, \quad l = 1, \ldots, L-1; \ i, j = 0, \ldots, 2^{L-l} - 1, \ m = \lfloor \tfrac{i}{2} \rfloor, n = \lfloor \tfrac{j}{2} \rfloor.$$

We describe the correlation among the child nodes $n_{l,2m\,2n}$, $n_{l,2m+1\,2n}$, $n_{l,2m\,2n+1}$, $n_{l,2m+1\,2n+1}$ by the covariance matrix $S_{l+1,mn}$:

$$S_{l+1,mn} = \begin{pmatrix} s_{l+1,mn}^{00} & s_{l+1,mn}^{01} & s_{l+1,mn}^{02} & s_{l+1,mn}^{03} \\ s_{l+1,mn}^{10} & s_{l+1,mn}^{11} & s_{l+1,mn}^{12} & s_{l+1,mn}^{13} \\ s_{l+1,mn}^{20} & s_{l+1,mn}^{21} & s_{l+1,mn}^{22} & s_{l+1,mn}^{23} \\ s_{l+1,mn}^{30} & s_{l+1,mn}^{31} & s_{l+1,mn}^{32} & s_{l+1,mn}^{33} \end{pmatrix},$$

$$l = 1, \ldots, L-1; \quad m, n = 0, \ldots, 2^{L-(l-1)} - 1.$$

where $s_{l+1,mn}^{\delta\gamma}$ is the inner product of the dissimilarity vector of $(\delta + 1)$-th child and that of $(\gamma + 1)$-th child. This matrix $S_{l+1,mn}$ expresses the degree of dissimilarity among the child nodes of the node $n_{l+1,mn}$ through the dissimilarity vectors g_l.

We define the texture vector $f_{l,mn}$ of level l by

$$f_{l,mn} = (s_{l,mn}^{00}, s_{l,mn}^{11}, s_{l,mn}^{22}, s_{l,mn}^{33})^T, \quad l = 2, \ldots, L; \quad m, n = 0, \ldots, 2^{L-l} - 1,$$

where $s_{l,mn}^{00}, s_{l,mn}^{11}, s_{l,mn}^{22}$, and $s_{l,mn}^{33}$ are the diagonal elements of the covariance matrix $S_{l,mn}$. We associate the texture vector $f_{l,mn}$ with each node $n_{l,mn}$ and call the resulting quad tree "Texture Feature Tree (TFT)". The TFT is a basic tree for texture analysis on our framework. The TFT is used not only for the texture image segmentation, but also for the texture retrieval [5].

procedure segmentation(N: the set of nodes of TFT; k: number of classes)
  for $l \leftarrow 2$ *to* L *do*
      apply the k-means algorithm to N_l by using feature vectors f.
      (We have k classes $N_l^1, \ldots, N_l^k$.)
      for $j \leftarrow 1$ *to* k *do*
          compute the mean vector $\mu_l^j \equiv \dfrac{\sum Val(n_{l,mn}^j; TFT)}{\text{the number of nodes of class } j}$
      for $j \leftarrow 1$ *to* k *do*
          associate μ_l^j with each node $n_{l,mn}^j \in N_l^j$,
      for each node $n_{l,mn} \in N_l$ *do*
          compute the hierarchical texture feature vector $t_{l,mn}$ of node $n_{l,mn}$ by

$$t_{l,mn} \equiv (Val(n_{l,mn}; ST), \cdots, Val(n_{l+r,m_r n_r}; ST)),$$
$$m_r = \lfloor \frac{m}{2^r} \rfloor, n_r = \lfloor \frac{n}{2^r} \rfloor, l \geq 2,$$

      where the node $n_{l+r,m_j n_j}$ is the r-th ancestor node of node $n_{l,mn}$.
      apply the k-means algorithm to the set N_l by using hierarchical texture feature
      vectors t_l.

Fig. 1. Procedure of Texture Segmentation (Step 3 – Step 6).

3   Texture Segmentation

This section shows an algorithm for texture segmentation which consists of six steps.

Step 1. Decompose an image into level L by the orthonormal wavelet transform with Haar bases and obtain the wavelet coefficients of the image.

Step 2. Extract the hierarchical correlation of wavelet coefficients and make TFT.

Step 3. Apply the k-means algorithm to the set of nodes N_l of level l of the TFT and classify each node $n_{l,mn}$ into one of k classes. The node of level l classified into class j is denoted by $n_{l,mn}^j$.

Step 4. Compute the mean vector μ_l^j over the nodes of level l and of class j and associate μ_l^j with each node $n_{l,mn}^j$. (We call the resulting tree "Segmentation Tree (ST)".)

Step 5. Compute the hierarchical texture feature vector $t_{l,mn}$ of level l using the values of the nodes on the path from the node $n_{l,mn}$ to its r-th ancestor node of ST, where $r = L - l$ in default. (Note that the hierarchical texture feature vector $t_{l,mn}$ of level l is made from hierarchical structure and relations of wavelet coefficients of the image.)

Step 6. Apply the k-means algorithm to the set of texture vectors $t_{l,mn}$ of level l to classify images corresponding to decomposition level l (size: $2^{L-l} \times 2^{L-l}$).

The procedures from Step 3 to Step 6 are shown in Figure 1. Note that, in Step 6, we get an image which shows the result of segmentation of $2^{L-l} \times 2^{L-l}$ pixels. Each pixel corresponds to a subimage ($2^{L-l} \times 2^{L-l}$) of the original texture image. For example, if we use the hierarchical texture feature vectors of level 3 to segment the original texture image, the size of resulting image is $\frac{1}{2^3 \times 2^3}$ of the size of the original texture image.

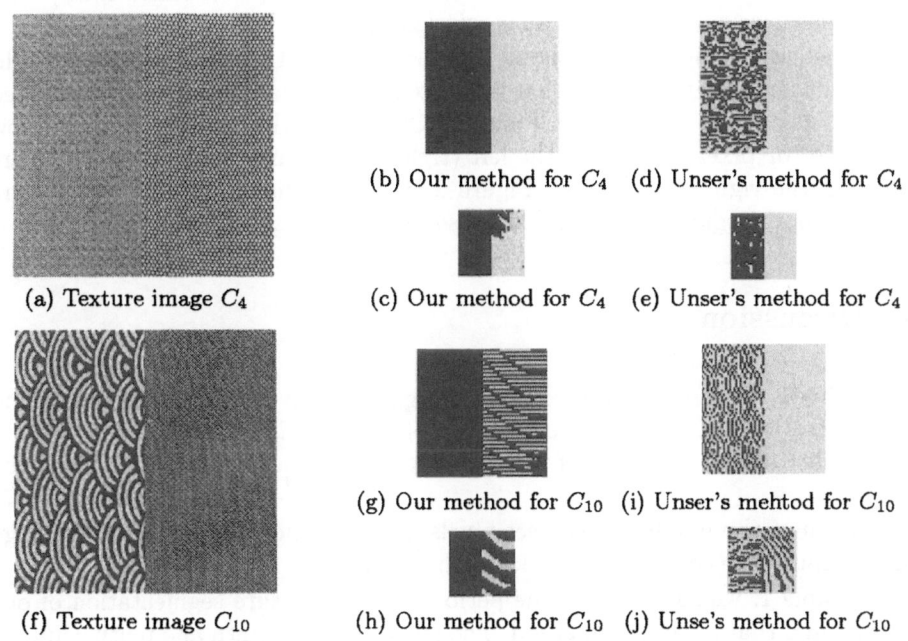

(a) Texture image C_4

(b) Our method for C_4 (d) Unser's method for C_4

(c) Our method for C_4 (e) Unser's method for C_4

(f) Texture image C_{10}

(g) Our method for C_{10} (i) Unser's mehtod for C_{10}

(h) Our method for C_{10} (j) Unse's method for C_{10}

Fig. 2. Results of segmentation for texture images C_4 and C_{10}.

4   Experiment

We apply our texture segmentation method and Unser's method to ten texture images C_i $i = 1, \ldots, 10$ (1024×1024 pixels) consisting of the left and the right rectangle texture regions (512×1024 pixels) to evaluate performance of our texture segmentation method comparing with Unser's method. Both our texture feature and Unser's texture feature are based on the wavelet transform, and are used for texture segmentation and retrieval.

The difference between our method and Unser's method is that we extract hierarchical relations between the wavelet coefficients of adjacent level of wavelet decomposition, while Unser divided an original texture image ($2^L \times 2^L$ pixels) into $2^N \times 2^N$ subimages ($2^{L-N} \times 2^{L-N}$ pixels) and made texture feature from the set of the wavelet coefficients of the subimages (called subimage block).

Figure 2 (a) ((f)) is the texture image C_4 (C_{10}). Figure 2 (b) and (c) ((g) and (h)) show the results of segmentation (we call them classified images) by our method using the hierarchical texture feature vectors of level 3 and of level

4, respectively, where the size of classified images are 64×64 (= 4096) pixels and 32×32 (= 1024) pixels. Figure 2(d) and (e) ((i) and (j)) are the classified images by Unser's method using 64×64 blocks and 32×32 blocks, respectively, where the size of the classified images are 64×64 pixels and 32×32 pixels.

If a pixel of left (right) region of the classified image is classified into yellow (blue) class, we say that the pixel is misclassified (i. e., an error pixel).

For example, Figure 2 (b) shows that no error pixel is found in left and right regions of the classified image, that is, the texture image C_4 is correctly classified into two classes by our method. Figure 2 (c), (g) and (h) ((d), (e) and (i)) show that no error pixel is found in the left (right) region and many error pixels are found in the right (left) region. Figure 2 (j) shows that many error pixels are found in both region, and that texture segmentation failed.

5   Discussion

We evaluate the performance of texture segmentation for texture images using the correct rate R_c. The correct rate R_c of a region is defined by the ratio of the number of correct pixels of the region and the total number of pixels of the region.

We count the number of correct pixels in each region of the classified image and compute the correct rate R_c for each region.

In Table 1, we summarized the performance of texture segmentation of our method and that of Unser's method. The fourth, sixth, eighth and tenth columns in Table 1 show the the correct rates R_c of the left/right region of classified image for texture image C_i. The third, fifth, seventh and ninth columns in Table 1 show correct rates R_c of classified image for C_i (called the total correct rate). The total correct rate of classified image shows a global performance for C_i. The average row A_c denotes the average of the total correct rates of classified images for texture images $C_1, \ldots, C_{10}$, and shows a global performance of texture segmentation for the set of texture images.

For example, applying our method to the hierarchical texture feature vectors of level 3 of texture image C_4, we have the correct rates R_c 1.000 and 1.000 for left and right region of the classified image (Figure 2 (b)), respectively. The total correct rate of the classified image for texture image C_4 is 1.000 (= $\frac{1.000+1.000}{2}$).

Applying Unser's method using 64×64 blocks, we have the correct rates R_c 1.000 and 0.619 for left and right region of the classified image (Figure 2 (d)), respectively. The total correct rate of the classified image for texture image C_4 is 0.810.

From Table 1, we can say that the performance of our method for texture image C_4 is better than that of Unser's method.

Hereafter, we evaluate the performance of texture segmentation of the images $C_1, \ldots, C_{10}$ by using the Table 1.

Firstly, by using the correct rates of the left and the right regions, we discuss how much our method and Unser's method succeed in texture segmentation.

Table 1. Performance of segmentation of our method using the hierarchical texture feature vector of level 3 and 4 and that of Unser's method using 64 × 64 blocks and 32 × 32 blocks. L and R denote the half of left and right regions of the classified image for C_i $(i = 1, \ldots, 10)$.

image		our method				Unser's method			
		R_c of level 3		R_c of level 4		R_c (64 × 64)		R_c(32 × 32)	
C_1	L	0.581	0.998	0.592	1.000	0.541	0.999	0.593	0.592
	R		0.163		0.184		0.082		0.594
C_2	L	0.646	0.836	0.565	0.207	0.495	0.555	0.509	0.506
	R		0.456		0.922		0.438		0.512
C_3	L	0.888	0.776	0.946	0.891	0.693	0.464	0.701	0.438
	R		1.000		1.000		0.922		0.963
C_4	L	1.000	1.000	0.907	1.00	0.810	1.000	0.651	1.000
	R		1.000		0.813		0.619		0.301
C_5	L	0.924	0.869	0.682	0.363	0.501	0.373	0.661	1.000
	R		0.979		1.000		0.628		0.322
C_6	L	1.000	1.000	0.749	1.000	0.524	0.563	0.654	0.307
	R		1.000		0.498		0.485		1.000
C_7	L	0.864	0.728	0.725	0.449	0.697	0.400	0.703	0.406
	R		1.000		1.000		0.993		1.000
C_8	L	0.694	0.988	0.814	0.996	0.569	0.652	0.776	0.986
	R		0.399		0.632		0.485		0.566
C_9	L	0.767	1.000	0.958	1.000	0.415	0.527	0.509	0.467
	R		0.534		0.916		0.302		0.550
C_{10}	L	0.768	0.535	0.971	0.941	0.703	0.405	0.513	0.453
	R		1.000		1.000		1.000		0.572
Average A_c		0.813	0.837	0.791	0.785	0.595	0.594	0.627	0.615
			0.753		0.797		0.595		0.638

Figure 3 shows the correct rates of the fourth, sixth, eighth and the tenth columns in Table 1. The points denote the pairs of correct rates of the left and the right regions of the classified images. The abscissa and ordinate are the correct rate of the left region and that of the right region, respectively.

In Figure 3, the point $(1.0, 0.0)$ indicates that both the left and the right regions are classified into blue class, that is, the texture image is classified into one class. So the point $(1.0, 0.0)$ indicates that the texture segmentation method failed in segmentation. Similarly, the point $(0.0, 1.0)$ indicates that the method failed in segmentation.

The point $(0.5, 0.5)$ indicates that 50% correct pixels and 50% error pixels are found in both the left and the right region, that is, the half of the region is misclassified. So the point $(0.5, 0.5)$ indicates that method failed in segmentation. To say that the performance of texture segmentation is good, it needs that the correct rates of the left and the right regions are higher than 0.5.

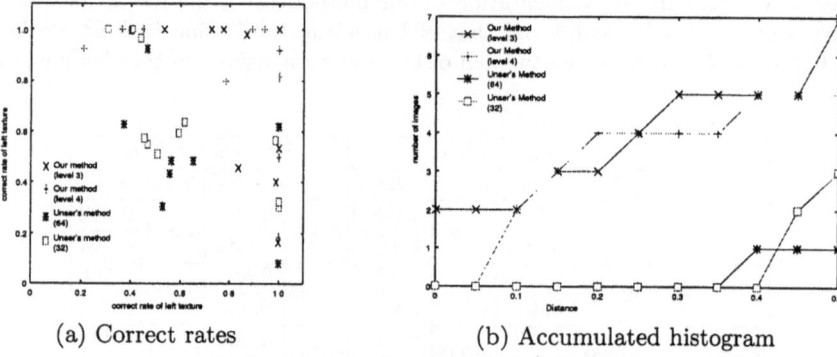

(a) Correct rates   (b) Accumulated histogram

Fig. 3. Correct rates of the left and the right regions and accumulated histogram by the distances.

The point $(1.0, 1.0)$ indicates that no error pixel is found in both the left and the right regions, that is, the texture image is correctly classified into two classes. In other words, the point $(1.0, 1.0)$ indicates that the method completely succeeded in segmentation. Thus, we consider the points in the upper right square in Figure 3 (a). The clsoer a point in the square is to the point $(1.0, 1.0)$, the better performance of texture segmentation is. So we can use the distance between the point $(1.0, 1.0)$ and each point to evaluate the performance of texture segmentation. As the distance, we use maximum metric (L_∞).

We compute an accumulated histogram of the distance. In Figure 3 (b), the lines show the number of images in the distances $0.00, 0.05, 0.10, \ldots, 0.45, 0.50$; the red (green) denotes our method using level 3 (level 4), and the blue (pink) line denotes Unser's method using 64×64 blocks (32×32 blocks).

In the case of our method using level 3 (level 4), we get 7 (5) images in the distance less than 0.5. In the case of Unser's method using 64×64 blocks (32×32 blocks), we get 3 (1) images in the distance less than 0.5. Since the values of red (green) line are always over those of the blue (pink) line, we say that the performance of our method is better than that of Unser's method.

Secondly, by using the total correct rates, we discuss which method is better for texture segmentation. To compare the performance of our method with that of Unser's method, we count the number of images for which the total correct rate of our method is higher than or equal to that of Unser's method.

For 10 (9) images, the total correct rate of our method of level 3 (4) is higher than and equal to that of Unser's method using 64×64 (32×32) blocks.

As for the averages A_c of total correct rates, the average $(\frac{0.813+0.791}{2} = 0.802)$ of our method is higher by 31% $(\frac{0.802-0.611}{0.611} = 0.311)$ than that $(\frac{0.595+0.627}{2} = 0.611)$ of Unser's method.

From the total correct rates, we say that the performance of our method is better than that of Unser's method.

Finally, we discuss which level of the hierarchical texture feature vector is better for texture segmentation. For 5 images, the total correct rate of level 3 is higher than or equal to that of level 4. The average of the total correct rates of level 3 is only 3% higher than that of level 4. Thus, there is little difference between the performance of our method of level 3 and that of level 4.

Experiments show that the proposed texture segmentation method works well.

6   Conclusion

This paper focused on texture segmentation for region-based texture retrieval. We have already proposed a texture retrieval using the hierarchical correlations of wavelet coefficients of adjacent level of wavelet decomposition [3,5]. To realize a unifying region-based texture retrieval system as uniformly as possible, we proposed the unifying texture segmentation using the hierarchical correlation of wavelet coefficients.

We applied our method and Unser's method to ten texture images and compared them to evaluate the performance of our texture segmentation method. Experiments showed that the proposed texture segmentation method had a good performance for texture segmentation. Thus, we have realized two functions based on our texture feature: texture segmentation and retrieval. By using our texture feature, we can realize texture segmentation, texture retrieval and region-based texture retrieval on our unifying framework.

References

1. V. N. Gudivada and V. V. Reghavan, "Content-based image retrieval systems," *IEEE Computer*, vol. 28, pp. 18–22, September 1995.
2. M. Flickner, H. Sawhney, W. Niblack, J. Ashiley, Q. Huang, D. B, M. Gorkani, J. Hafer, L. D, D. Petkovic, D. Steele, and P. Yanker, "Query by image and video content: The QBIC system," *IEEE Computer*, vol. 28, pp. 23–32, September 1995.
3. M. Kobayakawa, "A study on content-based image retrieval using wavelet transform," Doctor thesis, University of Electro Communications, March, 2001.
4. M. Kobayakawa, M. Hoshi, and T. Ohmori, "Interactive image retrieval using wavelet transform," *Proceedings of SCI'99/ISAS'99*, vol. 6, pp. 76–85, 1999.
5. M. Kobayakawa, M. Hoshi, and T. Ohmori, "Robust texture image retrieval using hierarchical correlations of wavelet coefficients," Proceedings of the 15th International Conference on Pattern Recognition, vol. 3, pp. 412–420, 2000.
6. W. J. Jasper and S. J. Garnier, " Texture characterization and defect detection using adaptive wavelets," *Optical Engineering*, Vol. 35, No. 11, 1996.
7. C. Lu, P. Chung and C. Chen, , "Unsupervised texture segmentation via wavelet transform," *Pattern Recognition*, Vol. 30, No. 5, pp. 729–742, 1997.
8. F. Lumbreras, " Wavelet filtering for the segmentation of marble images," *Optical Engineering*, Vol. 35, No. 10, pp. 2864–2872, 1996.
9. R. Porter and N. Canagarajah, "A robust automatic clustering scheme for image segmentation using wavelets," *IEEE Transactions on Image Processing*, Vol. 5, No. 4, pp. 662–665, 1996.
10. M. Unser, " Texture classification and segmentation using wavelet frames," *IEEE Transactions on Image Processing*, Vol. 4, No. 11, pp. 1549–1460, 1995.
11. S. Mallat, *A wavelet tour of signal processing,* Academic Press, 1998.

An Abstraction of Low Level Video Features for Automatic Retrievals of Explosion Scenes

Jongho Nang[1], Jinguk Jeong[1], Sungyong Park[1], and Hojung Cha[2]

[1] Dept. of Computer Science, Sogang University, 1 Shinsoo-Dong, Mapo-Ku
Seoul 121-742, Korea
jhnang@ccs.sogang.ac.kr
[2] Dept of Computer Science, Yonsei University, Seoul 120-749, Korea

Abstract. This paper proposes an abstraction mechanism of the low-level digital video features for the automatic retrievals of the explosion scenes from the digital video library. In the proposed abstraction mechanism, the regional dominant colors of the key frame and the motion energy of the shot are defined as the primary low-level visual features of the shot for the explosion scene retrievals. The regional dominant colors of shot are selected by dividing its key frame image into several regions and extracting their regional dominant colors, and the motion energy of the shot is defined as the edge image differences between key frame and its neighboring frame. Upon the extensive experimental results, we could argue that the recall and precision of the proposed abstraction and detecting algorithm are about 0.8, and also found that they are not sensitive to the thresholds.

1 Introduction

Recently, there have been a limited number of research efforts to retrieve a high level information automatically from the digital video for a specific purpose. A noticeable example of this research is the MoCa system [1,3,4] developed at Universität Mannheim. In this system, the genres of the film are automatically classified as news, tennis, animation, and advertisement by analyzing the low level video features such as motion energy and scene length. Furthermore, a violence scene is automatically detected by analyzing the motion of the objects in the video. All of these researches extract some high level semantic information from the multimedia data by analyzing and comparing the low level video features such as color histogram, object motion, and shot length to the predefined low level features of interesting (or willing to detect) events.

In order to summarize or extract the highlights of the long action movies, the scene with interesting events such as the explosion, the car racing, and the gun fighting should be identified first. Among these noticeable events, the explosion of building or car might be the most interesting events and usually the highlight of the movies that every user wants to retrieve. This paper proposes an abstraction mechanism of the low level features of digital video for the automatic retrieval of explosion scenes from a large video archive. Since the explosions of building or car are always accompanied

Y.-C. Chen, L.-W. Chang, and C.-T. Hsu (Eds.): PCM 2002, LNCS 2532, pp. 200-208, 2002.

with a yellow-tone flame that is changed rapidly, these features could be used to abstract the explosion events. In the proposed abstraction mechanism, the regional dominant color of the key frame, the motion energy of the shot, and the simplicity of the edge image of the shot are selected as the abstraction of shot for automatic explosion retrievals. The proposed automatic explosion scene retrieval algorithm declares a scene has an explosion event if it contains a shot whose regional dominant colors include a yellow-tone color, its motion energy is higher than that of other shots in the scene, and the edge image of its key frame is relatively simple compare to that of other neighboring frame. Upon the extensive experimental results while changing the thresholds used in retrieval algorithm, we could argue that the recall and precision are more than 0.8, and these values are robust to the thresholds. The proposed explosion scene retrieval algorithm could be used to build a digital video library with a high level semantic query capability, and summarize and abstract the digital movies automatically.

2   Abstracting and Retrieval of Explosion Scene

2.1   Characteristics of Explosion Shot

We could extract three characteristics of explosion events by analyzing several explosion scenes in the various movies as shown in Figure 1. First, if there is an explosion of building, car, or bomb in the shot, the frames in the shot contains a lot of yellow-tone pixels because there are always strong yellow-tone flames in the explosion. The whole image or part of the image could be spread with the flames. Secondly, since the flames are changed dynamically while the explosion is progressed, there are always a lot of motions in the shot with explosions. Finally, since the flames veil all other objects in the frame, they are not visible precisely. Although there would be other events that meet above three characteristics or there is an explosion event that does not have above three characteristics exactly, they could be used to effectively identify the explosion events as shown in our experimental results.

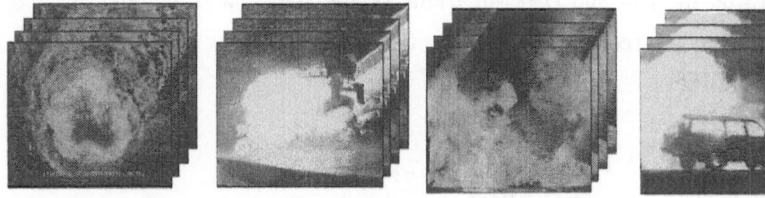

Fig. 1. Some example of explosion shots

2.2   Abstraction Mechanism of Explosion Shot

The low level visual features of shot with explosion event should be carefully selected and properly abstracted in order to retrieve the explosion shots precisely. The low level video features proposed in this paper for automatic explosion scene retrievals are *the regional dominant color* of the shot which reflects the color of the flames, *the motion energy* of the shot which reflects the rapid spread of the flames, and *the simplicity of the edge image* of the shot which reflects the phenomenon that other objects in the shot are hidden by flames.

(1) Abstraction of Color Information

Let us first present how to abstract the color information of the shot for the automatic explosion retrievals. Since to make a color histogram [5] of the all frames requires a lot of the computations, we only check the color histogram of the key frame (1st frame) of the shot. Since the flames in the explosion could be appeared in the whole or the part of the frame image, we divide the key frame image to several regions and check the dominant color of each region separately. The dominant color of region is the highest ranked color in the color histogram of that region. If the number of the regions of the key frame whose dominant color is the yellow-tone exceeds a certain threshold, we suspect that the key frame (or shot) may have an explosion event. Of course, the range of the yellow-tone color is defined as the 48 yellow-tone colors among the 512 quantized RGB color space. Let us formalize the proposed color abstraction mechanism. Assume that the key frame of the shot i, K_i, is divide into m regions. Let Y be a set of 48 yellow-tone colors extracted from the 256 quantized RGB color space, and d_i^j be the dominant color of the j-th region of K_i. We declare that the shot may have an explosion event when its key frame K_i satisfies following condition;

$$\left|\{d_i^j \in Y \mid 1 \le j \le m\}\right| < \alpha \cdot m \tag{1}$$

where α is a threshold ($0 < \alpha < 1$).

(2) Abstraction of Motion Information

The most interesting characteristic of the explosion shot is that there are more object motions than the previous and successive shots in the same scene because the flames are rapidly spread into whole frame in the explosion shot. One way to abstract this object motion information is to compute the total amount of motions in the shot. Let F_j^i and F_{j+k}^i be the j-th and ($j+k$)-th frame of the shot i, and E_j^i and E_{j+k}^i be their binary edge images respectively. Then, the motion energy of the i-th shot, M_i, is defined as follows;

$$D_{j,j+k}^i = MF(E_j^i - E_{j+k}^i) \tag{2}$$

$$M_i = \sum_m \sum_n D_{j,j+k}^i(m,n) \tag{3}$$

where $D_{j,j+k}^i$ is the edge image difference between E_j^i and E_{j+k}^i, $D_{j,j+k}^i(m,n)$ is the pixel value at coordinate (m,n) of $D_{j,j+k}^i$, and MF is a median filter [2] to remove the noise. We declare that the shot may have an explosion event when the motion energy of the shot is β times higher than the average motion energy of the shots in the same scene of n shots. Let M_i be the motion energy of the i-th shot, then above condition could be represented as follows;

$$M_i \geq \beta \cdot \frac{\sum_{j=1}^{n} M_j}{n} \tag{4}$$

If there are at least δ shots that satisfy this condition, we declare that the scene may have an explosion event. This abstraction mechanism is shown in Figure 2 graphically, in which the j-th and $(j+k)$-th frames of the shot are extracted from the shot, and the edge image difference of these frames is computed by subtracting one edge image from the other edge image. The resulting image passes a median filter to remove the noise. The number of remaining pixels in the edge image difference is defined as the abstraction of the motion energy of the shot.

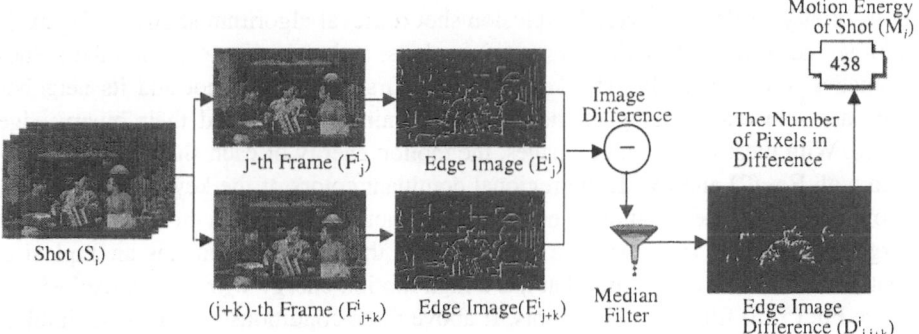

Fig. 2. Abstraction of motion information in shot

(3) Simplicity of the Edge Image

If there is a shot that has a lot of yellow-tone objects with a dynamic movement or camera operations such as panning, above two abstraction mechanisms alone could not retrieve the explosion shot precisely. Fortunately, other characteristic of explosion event could help us to solve this ambiguity. It is the simplicity of the edge image of the frames in the explosion shot. Since the flames are usually spread rapidly in the explosion shot, the other objects in the shot are being hidden rapidly as shown in Figure 1. It means that the binary edge images of the frames in the explosion shot come to be simple as the explosion is being progressed. We could use this information to distinguish the other yellow-tone shots with high motion energy from the explosion shots. In the case of the explosion shot, since the flames come to hide all other objects in the frame rapidly, the difference of the number of edge pixels between frames in the same shot is large enough in addition to a high motion. However, in the case of a dynamic shot without explosion, since all objects are always visible clearly in all frames of the shot, the difference of the number of edge pixels between the frames in the shot is small enough although the motion energy is. This characteristic of explosion could be used to filter out the shots with a relatively high motion energy but not an explosion shot. This condition is represented as follows;

$$G^i_{j,j+k} = \frac{\sum_m \sum_n \left| E^i_{j+k}(m,n) \right|}{\sum_m \sum_n \left| E^i_j(m,n) \right|} \geq \gamma \tag{5}$$

where $G^i_{j,j+k}$ is the edge pixel difference between F^i_j and $F^i_{j,j+k}$ in S^i, $E^i_j(m,n)$ is the pixel value at coordinate (m,n) of the edge image E^i_j, and γ is a threshhold. Eq. (5) needs to compute only 'differences in the number of edge pixels' because the motion energy has already been considered in Eq.(2).

2.3 Retrieval Algorithm

Let us briefly explain an overall explosion shot retrieval algorithm shown in Figure 3. First, we index an MPEG video stream into shots, and grouping them into the scenes automatically or manually. The key frame (or first frame) of shot and its neighbor frame are selected to compute the regional dominant colors and their binary edge images. With these binary edge images, the motion energy of each shot could be computed with Eq. (2) and (3). If the regional dominant colors of the key frame include a yellow-tone color and the motion energy of the shot is higher than the average motion energy of the scene (Eq. (4)), we could declare that the shot contains an explosion event. Since there is also a shot that has a high motion energy without any explosions, we use Eq. (5) to filter out these shots. If above three conditions are satisfied simultaneously, we declare that the shot has an explosion event. These conditions are sufficient and robust enough to retrieve almost all explosion events as shown in the following experiments.

3   Experimental Results and Analyses

We have implemented the proposed abstraction and retrieval algorithm on the top of the digital video library that we are currently building. The performance of the retrieval algorithm presented in Figure 3 depends on the several threshold values[1] such as ;

1. the β in Eq. (4) which represents the number of times that exceeds the average motion energy of the scene to declare an explosion shot,
2. the δ which represents the minimal number of shots which hold the condition in Eq.(4) to declare an explosion scene,
3. the γ value in Eq. (5) which represents the ratio of the number of edge pixels in current and neighboring binary edge images to declare an explosion shot.

---

[1] We divided the frame into 4x4 regions when computing the regional dominant color of the key frames in the experiments. We declare a shot may have an explosion event if more than two regions of the key frame have a yellow regional dominant color. It means that we fix the $\alpha = 0.125$ (2/16) in our experiments.

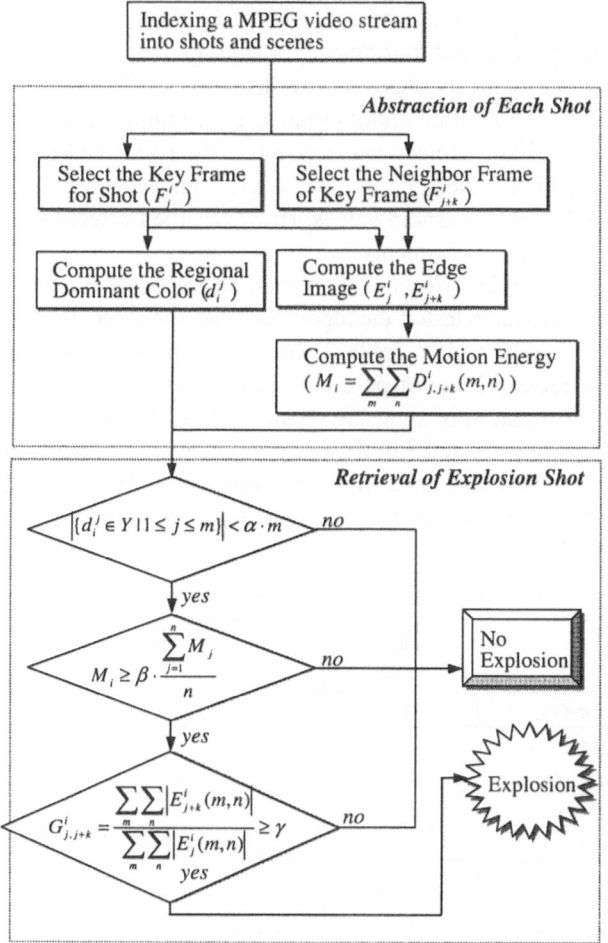

Fig. 3. An explosion shot retrieval algorithm

We have experimented proposed retrieval algorithm with several action movies such as *Lethal Weapon-4, Terminator-1*, and *Platton* each of which has a lot of explosion scenes. Since each movie is too long (about two hours) to store as a single MPEG file, we divide it into two segments so that totally 6 segments of one hour long are used in our experiments. Table 1 shows the performance of the proposed retrieval algorithm with the threshold set that produces the best performance. The threshold values producing the best performances are obtained via an extensive experimental analysis. As shown in this table, the proposed algorithm produces more than 90% performance except *Platoon* movie. Since it is a war movie in Vietnam, the explosion sometimes raises a cloud of dust so that the explosion does not always accompany with the yellow-ton flames. That makes the proposed algorithm sometimes fails to detect the explosion event in *Platoon*. Furthermore, since it is a combat movie at a Vietnam jungle so that there might be a rapid action on a jungle of trees with the yellow leaves, the algorithm sometimes detects it as an explosion event. That is the reason why proposed algorithm produces a false detection in *Platoon*. Except these special cases, the proposed algorithm could produce a very high performance as shown in the "Total (2)" field of the Table 1 that represents the recall and precision values of the experiments excluding these cases. Of course, this relatively high performance might be influenced by the threshold values. However, their effects are not so much as explained in the following experiments.

In order to investigate the effects of the threshold values on the performance of the proposed algorithm, we have tested the algorithm with the same movies while varying the threshold values α, δ, and γ. Table 2 shows the summary of other experiments while varying the threshold values presented in Eq. (1), Eq. (4), and Eq. (5). If we neglect the color information of shot, the recall could be higher since all shots with a high motion energy are extracted, but the precision is lower as shown in the first three rows in Table 2. On the other hand, if we consider the color information, the recall would be somewhat lowered, but the precision would be raised as shown in the last three rows in Table 2.

Table 1. Experimental Results when $\alpha = 0.125$, $\beta = 5$, $\delta = 2$, $\gamma = 200$

Movie Title	Number of Scenes	Number of Explosions	Recall	Precision
Lethal Weapon-4 (1)	16	3	1.00	1.00
Lethal Weapon-4 (2)	16	3	1.00	1.00
Terminator-1 (1)	32	3	1.00	0.75
Terminator-1 (2)	19	6	1.00	1.00
Platoon (1)	18	4	0.00	0.00
Platoon (2)	18	4	0.75	0.75
Total (1)	119	23	0.78	0.86
Total (2)	101	19	0.95	0.90

Table 2. Experimental Results on the Effect of Thresholds to the Performance

Checked Conditions		Recall	Precision
Color is neglected	Eq.(4)	0.98	0.31
	Eq.(5)	0.87	0.33
	Eq.(4) + Eq.(5)	0.87	0.38
Color is considered	Eq.(1) + Eq.(4)	0.78	0.78
	Eq.(1) + Eq.(5)	0.74	0.81
	Eq.(1) + Eq.(4) + Eq.(5)	0.74	0.81

From these experiments, we found that the regional color of the key frame greatly contributes to the precision of the proposed algorithm since it filter out the other shots with rapid changes. The performance of the proposed algorithm is not so sensitive to α if it is in the range of $0.125 \leq \alpha \leq 0.25$. Furthermore, the checking of the differences of edge images (*i.e.* checking the ratio of the number of edge pixels in the binary edge images of two neighboring frames in the same shot) could contribute to the precision of the proposed algorithm because this condition filters out the other shots in which the yellow objects are moved rapidly but not an explosion shot. This phenomenon that the flames rapidly hide the other objects in the frame is a characteristic of the explosion shot that other dynamic shots do not have. However, its effect to the performance of the proposed algorithm is somewhat small.

4 Concluding Remarks

The extracting of a high level semantic information from the digital movie automatically is an important task to build a useful digital video library. However, it has been a very difficult task without a lot of sophisticated artificial intelligence techniques that would not be available in the near future. Recently, there have been some researches to extract a limited number of high level information from the digital video, and these researches usually try to extract a specific information such as dialogues, action, and violence. The explosion shot abstracting and retrieval algorithm proposed in this paper is the one of these research efforts. This paper analyzes the characteristics of the explosion events, and find that, in the explosion shot, the yellow-tone flames are spread into the whole frame rapidly and eventually hide almost all other objects in the frame. Upon these characteristics of the explosion shots, this paper proposes a scheme to abstract them, in which some low level video features such as the regional dominant colors of the key frame, the motion energy of shot, and the binary edge image differences between the neighboring frames in the shot are selected as the abstraction for the explosion shot retrievals. Also an algorithm to automatically retrieve a scene with explosion shots are proposed and experimented. Upon the experimental results, we could argue that the proposed abstraction and retrieval algorithm could find the explosion events from the digital video archives with about 80% recall and precision. Furthermore, its performance is robust to thresholds that are usually dependent on the contents of the movies.

The performance of the proposed scheme could be improved if we also use the audio information of the digital video since the explosion events usually accompany with a very loud sound. The proposed abstraction and automatic retrieval algorithm could be used to summarize the long movies because the explosion event would be the part of the highlight of the movies, and used to build a meta database which contains a high level semantic information.

Acknowledgments. This work was supported from the Korea Science & Engineering Foundation in 2002 (Project Title: *Contents-aware Media Streaming QoS Technologies for Wireless Communication Networks*).

References

[1] S. Fischer, "Automatic Violence Detection in Digital Movies," *Proceeding of SPIE Multimedia Storage and Archiving Systems*, 1996, pp.212-223.

[2] R.C. Gonzalez, *Digital Image Processing*, Addison Wesley, 1993.

[3] http://www.informatik.uni-mannheim.de/informatik/pi4/projects/MoCA/ .

[4] S. Pfeiffer, R. Lienhart, S. Fischer and Wolfgang Effelsberg, "Abstracting Digital Movies Automatically," *Journal of Visual Communication and Image Representation*, Vol.7, No.4, 1996, pp.345-353.

[5] M. Stricker and M. Orengo, "Similarity of Color Images," Proceeding of *SPIE Conference on Storage and Retrieval for Image and Video Databases III*, Vol. 2670, 1996, pp. 381-391.

A Region-Based Image Retrieval System Using Salient Point Extraction and Image Segmentation

Hee-Kyung Lee and Yo-Sung Ho

Kwangju Institute of Science and Technology
1 Oryong-dong Puk-gu, Kwangju, 500-712, Korea
{lhkyung, hoyo}@kjist.ac.kr

Abstract. Although most image indexing schemes are based on global image features, they have limited capability because they cannot capture local variations of the image properly. In order to solve this problem, we propose a new region-based image retrieval system. Since objects are important for image search in a huge database, we first find the important region including an interesting object using image segmentation and salient point extraction. We then find color and texture features in each important region. We have demonstrated that the color and texture information in the important region is very useful for improving performance of the image retrieval system.

1 Introduction

In recent years, there is a rapid increase in the use of digital image collections, which motivates the research on image retrieval [1]. Early research on image retrieval has suggested manually annotated images. However, such text-based image retrieval techniques are impractical mainly because the textural annotation is usually ambiguous and very laborious to make.

An alternative approach to the manual annotation is content-based image retrieval (CBIR) [1], where images are indexed by their visual features, such as color, texture, and shape. Typically, an image index is a set of features that are extracted from the entire image. However, natural images are mainly composed of several parts of different characteristics. Therefore, it is difficult to represent these characteristics only by a few global features. The current CBIR systems, such as QBIC [2], Netra [3], VisualSEEk [4], and Blobworld [5], have focused on image retrieval based on image objects or important regions.

Our aim in this paper is to find important regions using image segmentation and salient point extraction. After salient points are extracted from an input image by the proposed method, image segmentation is performed. If the area of the selected region is large enough, we extract the important region using image segmentation. Otherwise, we use salient points to detect a region of interest (ROI) around distinct objects. We use image features, such as color and texture in the important region and salient points for similarity matching.

Y.-C. Chen, L.-W. Chang, and C.-T. Hsu (Eds.): PCM 2002, LNCS 2532, pp. 209–216, 2002.

2   Salient Point Extraction

2.1   Conventional Methods for Salient Point Extraction

Since salient points in CBIR can represent local properties of the image, they should be related to any visually interesting part of the image. In order to extract salient points from the image, we can employ conventional algorithms for object corner detection. However, they have drawbacks for image retrieval when applied to various natural images, because visual features do not need corners and which may gather in small regions [6]. Therefore, the conventional algorithms do not capture visual features properly from different parts of images.

The idea of previous algorithms for salient point extraction is to find relevant points to represent global variations by looking at wavelet coefficients at finer resolutions. Those algorithms consider the maximum value and search for the highest child. Applying this process recursively, they select a coefficient at the finer resolution. In order to select a salient point from this operation, they choose one point of the highest gradient value among all children [6].

However, they only consider wavelet coefficients of the selected children and their descendants. As a result, they may miss the situation where the coefficient of other child is larger than that of the selected child. Therefore, there are unnecessary salient points in the background.

2.2   The Proposed Method for Salient Point Extraction

In the proposed algorithm, the information is stored in three ordered lists: the list of insignificant sets (LIS), the list of insignificant salient points (LIP), and the list of significant salient points (LSP). The proposed algorithm consists of three passes: initialization, sorting pass, and update of bit planes.

2.2.1 Initialization: In the first step, we calculate the initial bit plane step n in the wavelet transform image X.

$$n = \left\lfloor \max_{\forall (i,j) \in X} (\log_2 |C_{i,j}|) \right\rfloor \qquad (1)$$

In the second step, we determine entries of LIS, LIP and LSP. All coefficients in the lowest subband are used as initial LIS entries, and both LIP and LSP are set to null in this initialization pass.

2.2.2 Sorting Pass: We evaluate the significance [7] of sets in LIS. When a set in LIS is identified to be significant, we evaluate whether the set has only one entry or not. If the set has only one entry, e.g., a pixel, we determine the set as the salient point and the set is moved to LSP. Otherwise, significant evaluation of all children nodes and set partitioning [7] are performed. Each child node is partitioned to four quadrants and the set is removed from LIS. Finally, the four partitioned subsets are added to LIS. Fig. 1 shows the procedure of the LIS sorting pass.

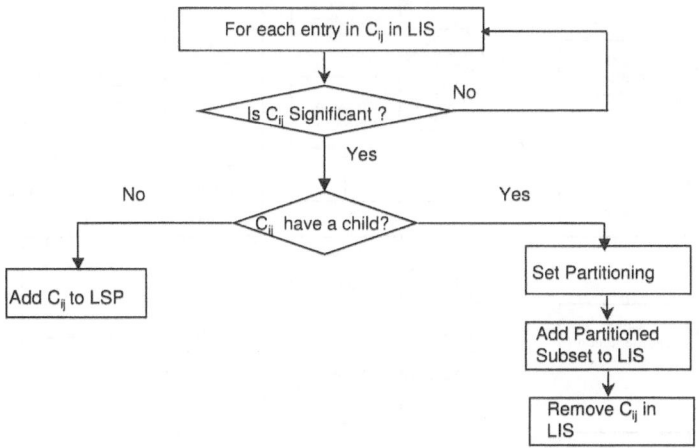

Fig. 1. Procedure for LIS

2.2.3 Update of Bit Planes: After we decrease the bit plane step n by one, we repeat the searching from the sorting pass.

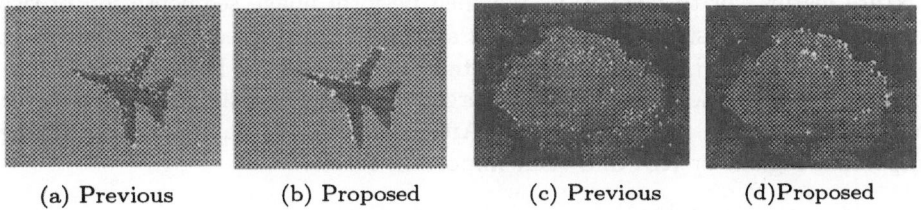

(a) Previous   (b) Proposed   (c) Previous   (d)Proposed

Fig. 2. Comparison of Salient Point Extraction

Fig. 2 shows test results obtained by a conventional method [6] and our proposed algorithm, where the number of salient points is 100. We search for significance of all children using the dispersion principle in the wavelet transform. As shown in Fig. 2, the proposed algorithm can reduce the number of salient points needed to extract the background compared the conventional method. We can obtain extracted results quicker than the conventional recursive method.

3   A Region-Based Image Retrieval System

3.1   Overview of the Proposed System

In this paper, we propose a region-based image retrieval system. Fig. 3 shows the architecture of the proposed system. We can divide it into two parts: database generation and image retrieval.

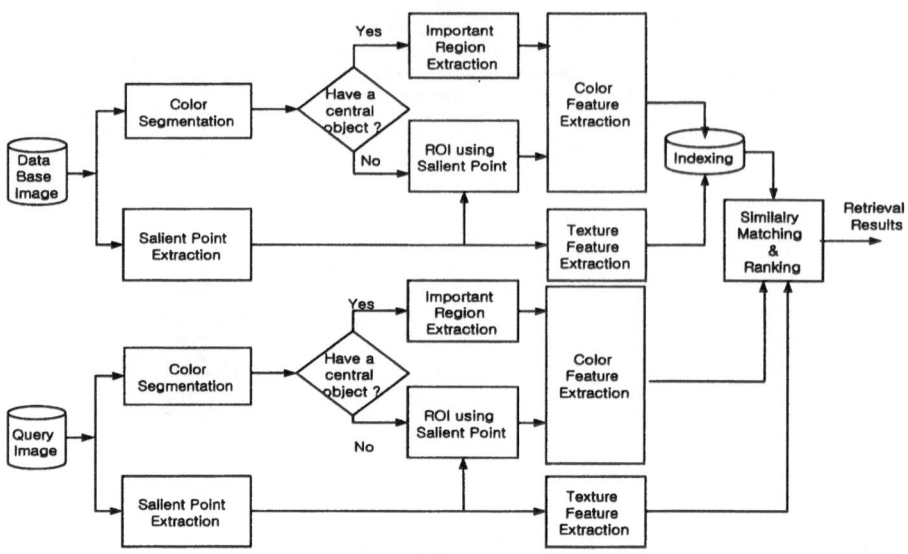

Fig. 3. A Region-based Image Retrieval System

Once salient points are extracted from an input image, they are used to obtain texture features or to form ROI. We then perform image segmentation of two levels [8]. In the first level, we segment an image using three types of adaptive circular filters based on the amount of texture information. In the second level, small patches of the image can be merged into adjacent similar regions by a region merging and labeling method. After image segmentation, we determine important regions or ROI and their important scores.

3.2   Important Region Extraction

Although an image is composed of several regions, all those regions are not equally important for image retrieval. For successful retrieval, we need to find important regions in the image.

In this paper, we propose a new method to search for important regions and extract visually significant features. In general, main objects are located near the center of the scene. Fig. 4(a) shows some examples. We can exploit this property to find important regions by allocating priority levels among different regions. Fig. 5 explains the overall procedure for region extraction.

After image segmentation, we calculate the boundary length and the area of each region. We count the number of pixels that contact with the borders of the image. Then, we check the following condition.

$$\frac{BCL_j}{BL_j} \times 100 \leq Threshold \tag{2}$$

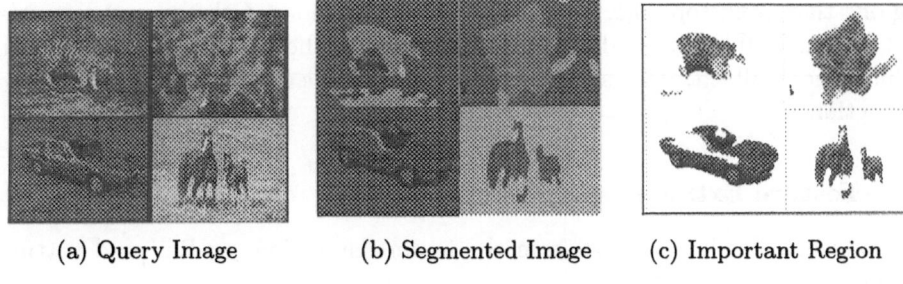

(a) Query Image   (b) Segmented Image   (c) Important Region

Fig. 4. Results of Region Segmentation

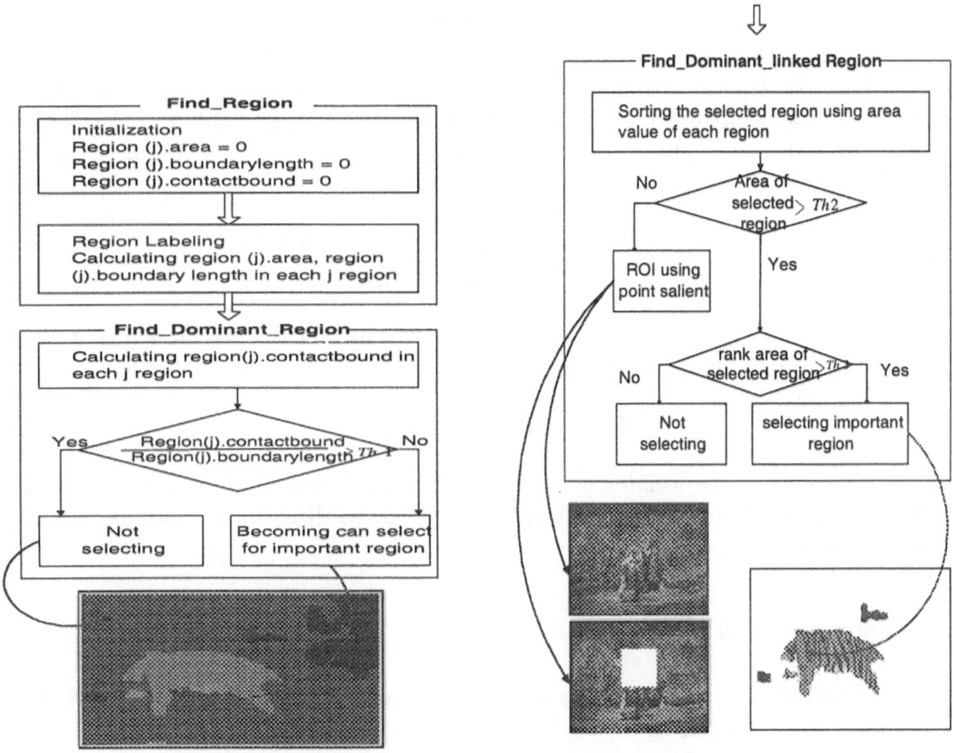

⇩

Find_Region

| Initialization
Region (j).area = 0
Region (j).boundarylength = 0
Region (j).contactbound = 0 |

| Region Labeling
Calculating region (j).area, region
(j).boundary length in each j region |

Find_Dominant_Region

| Calculating region(j).contactbound in
each j region |

Yes — Region(j).contactbound / Region(j).boundarylength $Th1$ — No

Not selecting | Becoming can select for important region

Find_Dominant_linked Region

| Sorting the selected region using area value of each region |

No — Area of selected region $> Th2$ — Yes

ROI using point salient

No — rank area of selected region $> Th3$ — Yes

Not selecting | selecting important region

Fig. 5. Procedure of Important Region Extraction

where BCL_j is the number of pixels contacted with the border, BL_j is the boundary length of each region, and j is the index of the region in the image. *Threshold* is experimentally set to 15%.

When this condition is satisfied, the region becomes a candidate for the important region. We assume that all images in the database have one or more important regions. However, some images, such as landscape, cannot be analyzed because there is no common and central object. If pixels in the selected region are more than $Th2$, 2.5% of the total number of pixels, we adopt the sorted regions that rank top *Th3*, 80% of the selected regions. Otherwise, we form a rectangular ROI box around the object by searching the maximum and minimum values among all extracted salient points. Fig. 4 shows result of important region extraction.

3.3   Feature Extraction

We extract color information from the important regions or ROI and texture features from salient points.

In the first step, we use the salient points to extract directional texture information. After selecting top 50% of the salient points, we examine the texture information of pixels in a neighborhood of 3×3 pixels around each salient point. After the first-step wavelet transform, high frequency sub-images (LH_1, HL_1, HH_1) are upsampled back to the full size. From the full-sized high-frequency images, we calculate X, Y and XY directional magnitude (X_d, Y_d, XY_d) of each salient point. The distance in texture $(d_{Q,T}^T)$ between the query image Q and the database image T is computed by

$$d_{Q,T}^T = |\frac{Yd_Q}{Xd_Q} - \frac{Yd_T}{Xd_T}| + |\frac{XYd_Q}{XYd_Q} - \frac{XYd_T}{XYd_T}| \tag{3}$$

In the second step, we make a color histogram in the extracted important region. The image distance is evaluated by

$$Score = w_1 \cdot H_d + w_2 \cdot D \tag{4}$$

where w_1 and w_2 are weighting factors, set to 0.75 and 0.25 ,respectively. H_d indicates the color histogram distance and D is the directional distance in the texture information.

4   Experimental Results

In order to evaluate performance of the proposed retrieval system, we use the precision factor defined by

$$precision = \frac{detect - falsealarm}{detect} \tag{5}$$

detect means the number of image which is retrieved images and *false alarm* is the number of image which is not related retrieved image with query images. Our database contains 3000 images from COREL (http://corel.digitlriver.com). We have classified the test set into eight groups: Tiger, Bird, Car, Sun, Flower, Lion, Horse, and Sign. Fig. 6 shows Eagle image query from the Bird group and its retrieval results. Matching quality is decreased from the top left to the bottom right.

Fig. 7 compares precision value of different schemes for each query group. While the global color scheme uses only the color histogram, the global moment

Query image

Fig. 6. Retrieved Images from A Query

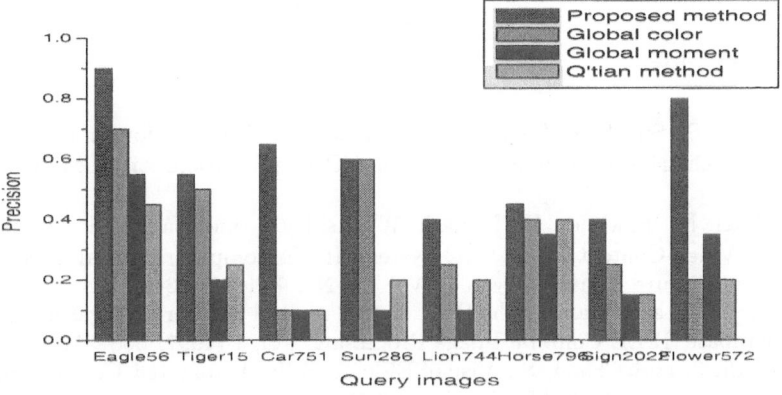

Fig. 7. Performance Comparison

scheme includes the first, second and third moments about the luminance component of the image. Q'tian method [6] is local color indexing using salient point extraction.

When the background of the image is simple, the global color and the global moment schemes perform reasonably well; however, if the image background is complex as in Car and Flower, they do not work well. If the background is complex on the other hand, the proposed algorithm can capture the important region containing a distinct object automatically and correctly. Because the proposed method uses color and texture information in the extracted important region and salient points, we can obtain improved performance compared to other global methods.

5 Conclusions

In this paper, we have proposed a region-based image retrieval system using salient points and important regions. We can find salient points efficiently by removing unnecessary feature points in the background. We extract an important region by capturing the significant object using image segmentation and salient point. Once the important region is determined, we calculate color and texture features and retrieve images by similarity matching. Color and texture features in the important region and salient points enhance retrieval performance significantly, compared to global feature extraction.

Acknowledgement. This work was supported in part by the Korea Science and Engineering Foundation (KOSEF) through the Ultra-Fast Fiber-Optic Networks (UFON) Research Center at Kwangju Institute of Science and Technology (K-JIST), and in part by the Ministry of Education (MOE) through the Brain Korea 21 (BK21) project.

References

1. Chang, S., Smith, J., Beigi, M., and Benitez, A.: Visual Information Retrieval from Large Distributed Online Repositories. Communications of ACM, Vol. 12 (1997) 12–20
2. Flicker, M., Sawhney, H., Niblack, W., Ashley, J. and Yanker, P.: Query by Image and Video Content: The QBIC System. IEEE Computer Special Issue on Content Based Picture Retrieval System, Vol. 28, No. 9 (1995) 23–32
3. Ma, W.Y. and Manjunath, B.S.: Netra: A Tool-box for Navigating Large Image Database. IEEE Conf. on Image Processing, Vol. 1 (1997) 568–571
4. Smith, J. and Chang, S.: VisualSEEk: A Fully Automated Content-Based Image Query System. ACM Multimedia (1996) 87–98
5. Carson, C., Thomas, M., Belongie, S., Hellerstein, J.M. and Malik, J.: Blobworld: A System for Region-based Image Indexing and Retrieval. Int. Conf. Visual Inf. Sys. Vol. 3 (1999) 509–516
6. Tian, Q., Sebe, N., Lew, M.S., Loupias, E. and Huang, T.S.: Image Retrieval using Wavelet-based Salient Points. Journal of Electronic Imaging, Special Issue on Storage, Processing and Retrieval of Digital Media, Vol. 10, No. 4 (2001) 3–11
7. Said, A. and Pearlman, W.A.: A New, Fast, and Efficient Image Codec Based on Set Partitioning in Hierarchical Trees. IEEE Trans. on Circuit and Systems for Video Tech., Vol. 6, No 3 (1996) 243-250
8. Ko, B.C., Lee, H.S. and Byun, H.R.: Region-based Image Retrieval System using Efficient Feature Description. Int. Conf. Pattern Recognition. Vol. 4 (2000) 284–286

Effects of Codebook Sizes, Codeword Dimensions, and Colour Spaces on Retrieval Performance of Image Retrieval Using Vector Quantization

Shyhwei Teng and Guojun Lu

GSCIT, Monash University, Gippsland Campus
Churchill, Vic 3842
AUSTRALIA
shyh.wei.teng@infotech.monash.edu.au

Abstract. Recently, we have proposed an image indexing and retrieval technique that is based on vector quantization. We have already shown that this technique is more effective than the traditional colour-based techniques. Some factors that must be decided during the implementation of the proposed techniques are codebook size, codeword dimension and colour space. In this paper, we investigate how these factors may affect the retrieval performances of the proposed technique.

1 Introduction

With growing utilization of digital image libraries in recently years, content-based image retrieval (CBIR) techniques are developed to allow information to be managed efficiently and effectively. Such techniques use image features such as colour, shape and texture for indexing and retrieval [1-5]. To date, colour-based image retrieval techniques are the most popular and are commonly implemented in many content-based image retrieval applications [6]. Its popularity is mainly due to two reasons. Firstly, compared to shape and texture, it is normally much easier to remember the colour elements in the images. Secondly, colour-based image retrieval techniques relatively are both easier to implement and effective.

In colour-based retrieval techniques, each image in the database is represented by a colour histogram [1, 3, 5]. Traditionally, the histogram H(M) is a vector $(h_1, h_2,..., h_n)$, where each element h_j represents the number of pixels falling in bin j in image M. Each bin denotes an interval of a quantized colour space. During image retrieval, a histogram is found for the query image or estimated from the user's query. A metric is used to measure the distance between the histograms of the query image and images in the database. (If images are of different size, their histograms are normalized.) Images with a distance smaller than a pre-defined threshold are retrieved from the database and presented to the user. Alternatively, the first k images with smallest distances are retrieved.

Recently, we have proposed a retrieval technique that is based on vector quantization (VQ) compressed image data. In concept, it is similar to the technique based on colour histograms. The difference is that in VQ-based technique, a histogram represents the number of blocks using a particular codeword in the

Y.-C. Chen, L.-W. Chang, and C.-T. Hsu (Eds.): PCM 2002, LNCS 2532, pp. 217–228, 2002.

codebook, instead of a particular colour. With such histogram, spatial relationships among the image pixels are captured. Initial studies show that the proposed scheme is more effective than traditional colour-based techniques [7-9].

To implement the proposed technique, we need to determine the appropriate codebook size to ensure the histograms built to index the images are representative of them. We also need to determine the appropriate codeword dimension. This is to ensure information on spatial relationship among the pixels is properly captured in the codewords. Finally, since VQ calculate code vector distances based on colour (pixel values), it is also important for investigate how the use of different colour spaces affect the retrieval performance of the proposed technique.

The following sections are organized as follows. Next section describes the main concepts of image indexing and retrieval based on VQ compressed image data. Section 3, 4 and 5 discuss the potential effects on the retrieval performance using different codebook sizes, codeword dimensions and colour spaces respectively. Section 6 describes the experiment setup. Next, Section 7 presents the experiment results. Finally, Section 8 concludes the paper.

2   Image Indexing and Retrieval Based on Vq Compressed Data

VQ is an established compression technique that has been used for image compression in many areas [10-12]. A vector quantizer can be defined as a mapping Q of K-dimensional Euclidean space R^K into a finite subset Y of R^K, that is:

$$Q: R^K \text{ --} \gg Y,$$

where $Y = (x'_i; i = 1, 2, ... N)$, and x'_i is the ith vector in Y.

Y is the set of reproduction vectors and is called a VQ codebook or VQ table. N is the number of vectors in Y. At the encoder, each data vector x belonging to R^K is matched or approximated with a codeword in the codebook and the address or index of that codeword is transmitted/stored instead of the data vector itself. At the decoder, the index is mapped back to the codeword and the codeword is used to represent the original data vector. In the encoder and decoder, an identical codebook exists whose entries contain combinations of pixels in a block. Assuming the image block size is (n x n) pixels and each pixel is represented by m bits, theoretically, $(2^m)^{n \times n}$ types of blocks are possible. In practice, however, there are only a limited number of combinations that occur most often, which reduces the size of the codebook considerably. This is the basis of vector quantization. If properties of the human visual system are used, the size of the codebook can be reduced further and fewer bits can be used to represent the index of codebook entries. The codebook generation is based on the LBG algorithm [10, 13].

To index an image, the number of occurrences of each index is calculated to obtain an index histogram $H(v_1, v_2, ..., v_i, ..., v_n)$, where v_i is the number of times codeword i is used by the image, and n is the total number of codewords in the codebook. Since each index is unique for each codeword in the codebook and each block of pixels is represented by an index number, this histogram will be able to characterise the major features of the image.

During image retrieval, an index histogram $H(q_1, q_2, ..., q_i, ..., q_n)$ is calculated for the query image. Then the distance between the query image Q and the target image V is calculated as follows:

$$d(Q,V) = \sum_{i=1}^{n} |q_i - v_i|$$

Images can be ranked in an ascending order of calculated distances.

3 Potential Effects of Different Codebook Sizes on Retrieval Performance

The codebook size determines the distortion rate for the compressed image using VQ. A larger codebook contains more distinct codewords, which increases the possibility for each image block of finding a better match codewords during encoding. Thus, VQ compressed images that use larger codebooks are more likely to have a lower distortion rate. Since the histogram built to index each image is based on its VQ compressed image data, less distortion rate should allow more accurate representation of the images. Therefore, theoretically, larger codebook size should lead to more accurate retrieval. However, using a codebook size that is too large can also pose a few issues. Firstly, larger codebook size results in more number of bins in each histogram. The increase of the histogram bins leads to the similarity comparison time to increase exponentially [17]. Thus, larger codebooks decrease the efficiency of the proposed technique. For efficiency purpose, the codebook size should not be greater than 4,096. Secondly, the use of very large codebook size may not improve the retrieval performance. This is because the purpose of a CBIR technique is not only to retrieve database images that are exactly the same as the query image, but it should also retrieve images that are similar to the query. By using codebook size that is very large, very fine details may be captured in the image histograms. Such details may cause the proposed technique to be too discriminative during the similarity comparison, resulting in similar database images not retrieved. Thirdly, the increase in the effectiveness of the retrieval performance may not always be proportional to the increase in the codebook size. This is because the codebook sizes within the efficiency range (4,096 and smaller) are relatively much smaller compared to the number of the distinct original image vectors. Therefore the possibility of having a same set of original image vectors being indexed by a codeword in smaller size codebook and another codeword in the larger size codebook is rather high. Thus, unless there is a very large difference in the codebook size, there may not be a great difference in their retrieval performance. For these reasons, it is important to select a suitable codebook size.

4 Potential Effects of Different Codeword Dimensions on Retrieval Performance

Larger dimension of the codeword allows more information on the spatial relationship among the image neighbouring pixels to be captured when indexing. However, to maintain a constant distortion rate in VQ, the size of a codebook with larger codeword dimension is greater than the size of a codebook with smaller codeword dimension. This is because the combination of colour pixels in a block increases exponentially as the codeword dimension increases. For example, if each pixel consists of 256 colour levels, it is possible to have 256^n combinations of codewords (n is the number of pixels in each codeword). Since Section 3 has illustrated the importance of keeping the codebook at a suitable size for the proposed technique to be both effective and efficient, the codeword dimension must be kept to a size which good amount of information on the spatial relationship among the image neighbouring pixels are captured while the distortion rate of the compress images are kept at a suitable level.

5   Potential Effects of Different Colour Spaces on Retrieval Performance

As the proposed technique mainly uses the image colour information for indexing and retrieval, the effects of different colour spaces on its retrieval performance are investigated next. A colour space is a three dimensional space which defines how colours are represented. There are many colour spaces, which are designed with different sets of characteristics so that they can be effectively used in their respectively areas.

Many of these colour spaces have been used for colour-based image retrieval. However, it is still not clear which colour space is best suited for such applications as there has been no comprehensive testing being carried out using all of these colour spaces on a common large image dataset. Thus to investigate the effects of different colour spaces on the retrieval performance of our proposed technique, we select three commonly used colour spaces with very different characteristics. The three colour spaces are RGB, CIE-LUV and HSV.

RGB colour space is one of the most commonly used colour space in image processing. The three axes in this colour space are Red, Green and Blue. Many devices like colour cameras, scanners and displays are provided with RGB signal input or output. Many image formats, like Windows Bitmap, also store pixels colour data of images in based on this colour space. Image colour data in this colour space therefore can be easily obtained without any colour space conversion. If RGB is used in image retrieval technique, the ease of obtaining the colour data is an advantage as it allows more efficient processing. However, there are some characteristics of RGB that makes image retrieval relatively less effective compared to some other colour spaces. Among these characteristics, the most critical one is that this colour space is not perceptually uniform. Thus distance calculated between colours in this colour space cannot accurately evaluate the perceived differences between them.

The next colour space we will describe is CIE-LUV. CIE-LUV is a colour space which is commonly used for industries considering additive mixing such as colour displays, TV and lighting (where light is emitted). In this colour space, axis L represents luminance, U represents colours approximately red-green and V represents colours approximately yellow-blue. It is also commonly used in image retrieval because it is a uniform colour space, which allows distance calculation between the colours to be more accurate.

Finally, we will describe HSV. HSV is a colour space which is very prominent in computer graphics literature. The three axes of HSV are hue, saturation and value. Hue describes the colours in circular spectrum from red to green to blue and back to red. Saturation describes the vividness or the pureness of the colour and value describes the luminance of the colour. The main characteristic of this colour space is it has good compatibility with human intuition.

6 Experiment Setup

To investigate the effects of different codebook sizes, codeword dimensions and colour spaces have on the retrieval performance of the proposed VQ scheme, we have implemented a web-based image indexing and retrieval system using the proposed VQ scheme. Using the application developed, experiments are carried out using an image dataset of 10,112 general colour images. These images are classified into 60 categories based on their overall appearances.

Recall and precision curves are used to measure image retrieval performance, as commonly done in information retrieval [15, 16].

6.1 Ground Truth

To establish the ground truth for the experiments, 32 images are first selected from the image dataset to serve as query images. For good evaluation purposes, the query images are different in appearance and content. The relevant images from the dataset for each query are established by human judgements in a subject test. There are 35 participants in the subject test. As different participants select a different set of relevant images for each query image, three sets of relevant images are compiled for the 32 query images. The first set comprises of images selected by at least 70% of the participants. The second set comprises of relevant images selected by at least 50% of the participants. The third set comprises of relevant images selected by at least 30% of the participants. We name the relevant image sets GT70, GT50 and GT30 respectively.

6.2 Codebook Generation

60 images (one image from each category) are selected for training the codebooks to be used in the experiments. The codebooks are generated based on:
- codebook sizes of 1,024, 2,048 and 4,096. Codebook size greater than 4,096 are not considered so that the retrieval can be efficient.
- codeword dimensions of 2x2, 4x4, 8x8 and 16x16 pixels block. Since we are considering codebook size not greater then 4,096, dimensions greater than 16x16 can cause the distortion rate to be too high. Thus, dimensions greater than 16x16 are not considered.
- colour spaces of RGB, CIE-LUV and HSV. The choice of colour spaces is based on their difference in characteristics.

Therefore, 36 codebooks of different codebook sizes, codeword dimensions and colour spaces combinations are generated in total.   Images in the dataset are compressed using VQ with each of these codebooks.

7 Experiment Results

The following procedures are used to compile the experiment results using each of the 36 codebooks in the proposed VQ scheme.
1.   Index the images in the image dataset.
2.   Obtain the retrieval results for each of the 32 query images.
3.   Using the retrieval results of the 32 query images, plot the average precision and recall graph based on GT70 as the ground truth. Also plot the curves for GT50 and GT30.
In total, there are 108 average recall and precision curves computed, 36 each for GT70, GT50 and GT30.   We name the 3 sets of curves CB70, CB50 and CB30 respectively.   Each of the 36 average recall and precision curves represents the retrieval performance of the proposed technique using codebook generated from a particular combination of codebook size, codeword dimension and colour space.

Before we evaluate the results, please note that recall and precision curves representing the retrieval performances of IBM QBIC™ colour histogram and colour layout techniques [8] are presented in each of the following figures to serve as a comparison to the proposed VQ scheme.

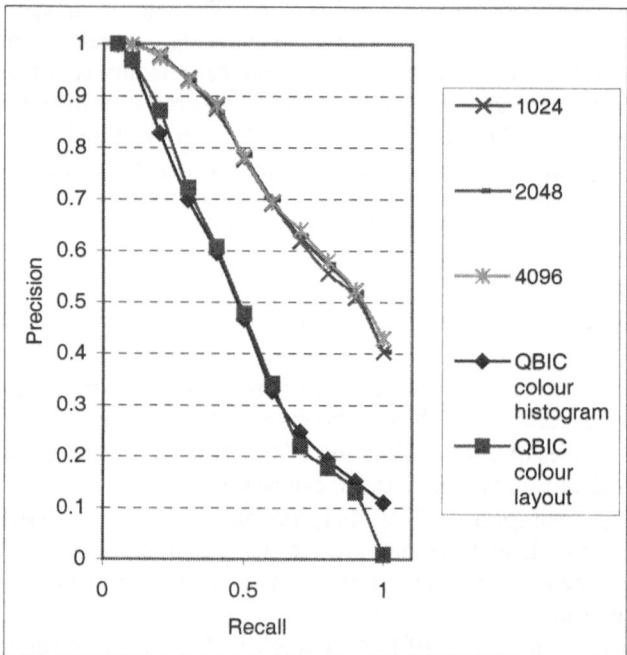

Fig. 1. Average recall and precision curves of VQ scheme using different codebooks. The code-books are generated with common codeword dimension(4x4) and colour space(HSV) but vary in codebook size.

7.1. Evaluation of Experiment Results for Different Codebook Sizes

First we evaluate the effects of different codebook sizes on retrieval performance when the codebooks have common codeword dimension and colour space. The following procedures are carried out on CB70, CB50 and CB30.

1. Group the curves according to the codebook size. Since we are considering codebook sizes 1,024 , 2,048 and 4,096 , 3 groups (each with 12 curves) are obtained.
2. Between the 3 groups, compare curves of codebooks with the same colour space and codeword dimension. Thus, 12 sets of comparison are made.

Since the 12 sets of comparison for CB70, CB50 and CB30 show similar findings, only CB50 is presented.

All the comparison in each of the 12 sets for CB50 shows similar trends. In each set (Figure 1 shows an example), the curves plotted from retrieval results of codebooks with different codebook sizes are of similar position from the origin. This shows that retrieval performances are not greatly affected when the codebook size is increase from 1,024 to 4,096.

Next, to see the overall retrieval performance of different codebook sizes, the average of the curve in each of the 3 groups is plotted. The curves for CB50 in Figure 2 show that the overall retrieval effectiveness of different codebook sizes is similar.

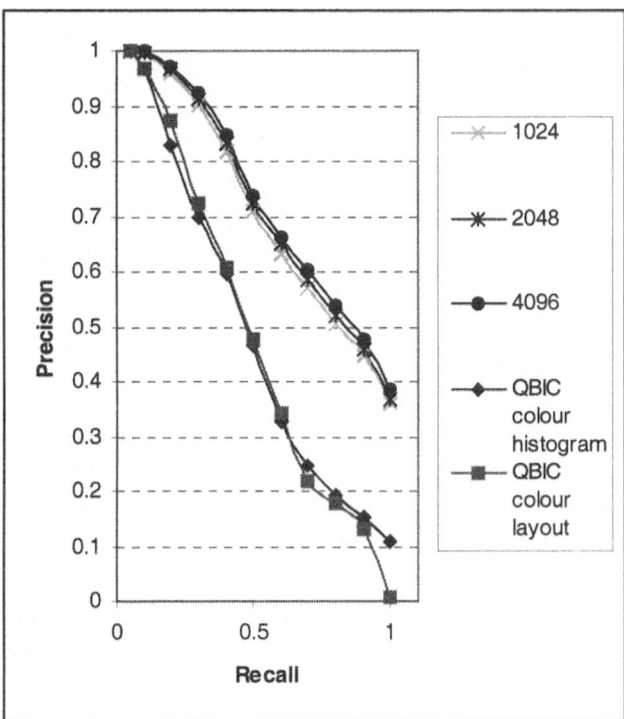

Fig. 2. Curves showing the overall retrieval performance of codebooks with different codebook sizes for CB50.

Such characteristics of the proposed technique illustrated by the findings are ideal for retrieval because with smaller codebook size, not only retrieval performances similar to higher codebook sizes can be achieved, greater retrieval efficiency can also be achieved.

7.2. Evaluation of Experiment Results for Different Codeword Dimensions

To evaluate the effects of different codeword dimensions on retrieval performance, the following procedures are carried out on CB70, CB50 and CB30.
1. Group the curves according to the codeword dimension. Since we are considering codebook dimensions 2x2, 4x4, 8x8 and 16x16, 4 groups (each with 9 curves) are obtained.
2. Between the 4 groups, compare curves of codebooks with the same colour space and codebook size. Thus, 9 sets of comparison are made.
Since the 12 sets of comparison for CB70, CB50 and CB30 show similar findings, only CB50 is presented.

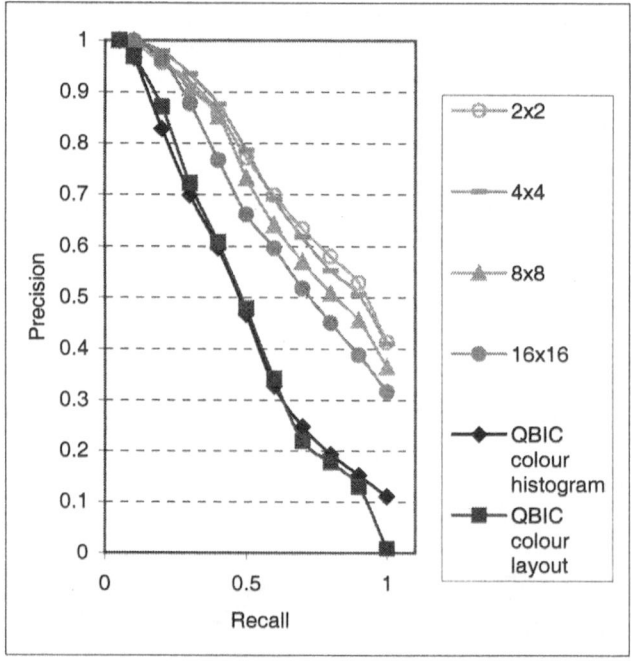

Fig. 3. Average recall and precision curves of VQ scheme using different codebooks. The codebooks are generated with common codebook size (1024) and colour space (HSV) but vary in codeword dimensions.

All the comparison in each of the 12 sets for CB50 shows similar trends. In each set (Figure 4 shows an example), the curves plotted from retrieval results of codebooks with codeword dimensions of 2x2 and 4x4 are furthest from the origin.

This shows that their retrieval performances are better compared to those of dimensions 8x8 and 16x16.

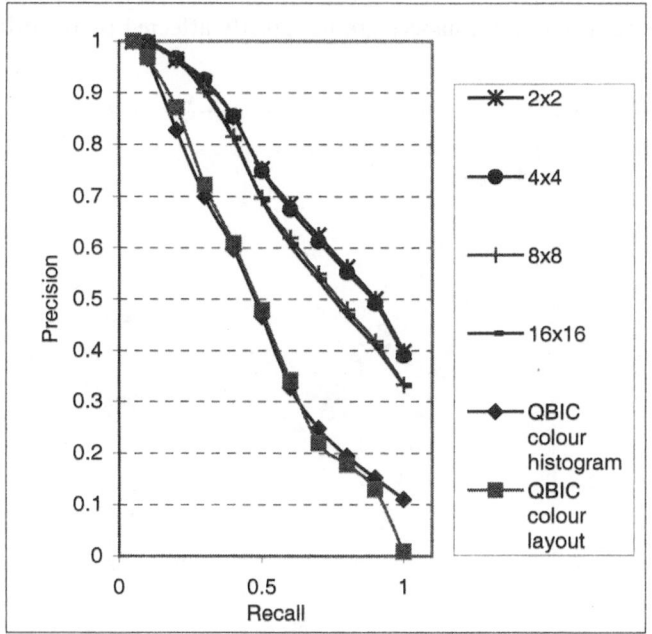

Fig. 4. Curves showing the average retrieval performance of codebooks with different codeword dimensions for CB50.

To evaluate the overall retrieval performance, the average of the curve in each of the 3 groups is plotted. The newly plotted curves (Figure 4) show that the overall retrieval performances of codebooks with different codeword dimensions are of similar trend to those shown in Figure 3. Thus, 2x2 or 4x4 are the optimal codeword dimensions. However, considering the amount of spatial information among neighbouring pixels captured, codeword dimension 4x4 should be more ideal for our proposed technique.

7.3 Evaluation of Experiment Results for Different Colour Spaces

To evaluate the effects of different colour spaces on retrieval performance, the following procedures are carried out on CB70, CB50 and CB30.
1. Group the curves according to the colour space. Since we are considering colour spaces RGB, CIE-LUV and HSV, 3 groups (each with 12 curves) are obtained.
2. Between the 3 groups, compare curves of codebooks with the same codebook size and codeword dimension. Thus, 12 sets of comparison are made.
Since the 12 sets of comparison for CB70, CB50 and CB30 show similar findings, only CB50 is presented.

All the 12 sets of comparison for CB50 show similar trends. In each set (Figure 5 shows an example), the curve plotted from retrieval results of codebook with HSV colour space are slightly above the other 2 curves. The curve of codebook with RGB is relatively nearer to the origin compared to the other 2 curves. However, the differences between the positions of the 3 curves are very little. This shows that the retrieval performances are not greatly affected by the different colour spaces.

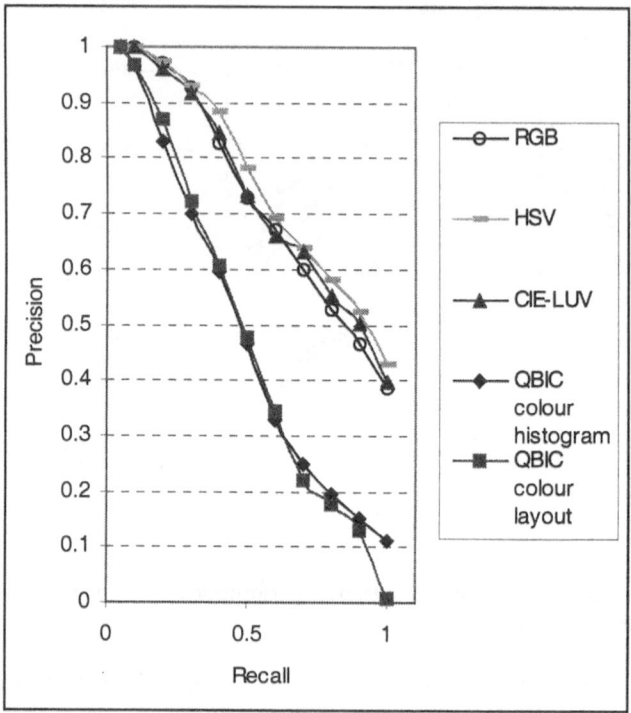

Fig. 5. Average recall and precision curves of VQ scheme using different codebooks. The codebooks are generated with common codebook size (4096) and codeword dimension (4x4) but vary in colour space.

To evaluate the overall retrieval performance, the average of the curve in each of the 3 groups is plotted. The newly plotted curves for CB50 (Figure 6) show that the overall retrieval performances are of similar trend to that in Figure 5. The reason for such retrieval performance is because the number of codewords in the codebook is relatively much smaller compared to the variety of original image blocks. From the way the codebooks are built, the codewords in each codebook are rather distinct from each other. Thus during the indexing process, the deficiency in the characteristics of the colour spaces are not great enough to affect the retrieval performance results.

8   Conclusion

Our work investigates the effects of different codebook sizes, codeword dimensions and colour spaces have on the retrieval performance. Based on the experiment results, we have shown that retrieval performances of our proposed technique are often similar for codebook sizes between 1,024 and 4.096. Thus if retrieval efficiency is very critical, codebook size of 1,024 should be used since this has little effect on the effectiveness compared to codebook size 4,096. The experiment results have also indicated that when codebook size is between 1,024 and 4,096, the codeword dimension has the most effect on the retrieval performance. Based on the experiment results, codeword dimension of 4x4 pixels block is recommended for optimal retrieval performance. Finally, the experiment results show that the use HSV colour space has better retrieval effectiveness in the proposed technique, although the difference is not very significant compared to RGB and CIE-LUV.

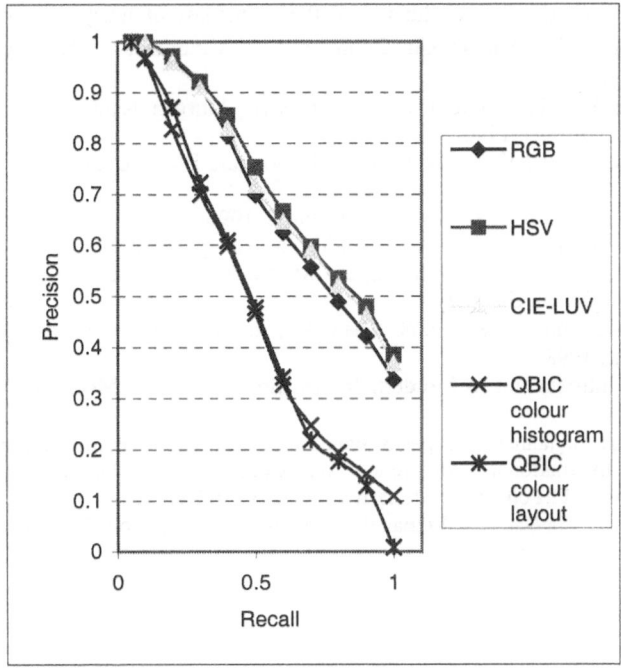

Fig. 6. Curves showing the average retrieval performance of codebooks with different colour spaces for CB50.

References

[1] Y. Gong, H. Zhang and C. Chuan, "An image database system with fast image indexing capability based on colour histograms", Proceedings of IEEE 10's Ninth Annual International Conference, Singapore, 22-26 August 1994, pp.407-411.

[2] S. K. Chan, Content-based Image Retrieval, MSc thesis, National University of Singapore, 1994.

[3] M. J. Swain and D. H. Ballard, "Color indexing", Int. J. Comput. Vision, 7:11-32. 1991.

[4] G. D. Finlayson, Colour Object Recognition, MSc Thesis, Simon Fraser University, 1992.

[5]   W. Niblack et al, "QBIC Project: querying images by content, using colour, texture, and shape" Proceedings of Conference on Storage and Retrieval for Image and Video Databases, 1-3 Feb. 1993, San Jose, California, US, SPIE Vol. 1908, pp.1908-1920.

[6]   V.D. Lecce and A. Guerriero, "An elvalution of the effectiveness of image features for image retrieval", Journal of Visual Communication and Image Representation 10, 1999, pp. 351-362.

[7]   G. Lu and S. Teng, "A Novel Image Retrieval Technique based on Vector Quantization", Computational S. Intelligence for Modeling Control and Automation, February 1999, Australia, pp.36-41.

[8]   S. Teng and G. Lu, "Performance study of image retrieval based on vector quantization", ICCIMADE'01: International Conference on Intelligent Multimedia and Distance Education Conference, 1-3 June 2001, Fargo, ND, USA.

[9]   S. Teng and G. Lu, "An evaluation of the robustness of image retrieval based on vector quantization", IEEE Pacific-Rim Conference on Multimedia 2001, October 24-26, 2001, Beijing, China.

[10] K. Sayood, Introduction to Data Compression, Morgan Kaufmann Publishers, Inc., San Francisco, California, 1996.

[11] A. Gersho and R. M. Gray, Vector Quantization and Signal Compression, Kluwer Academic Publishers, 1992.

[12] H. Abut (ed.), Vector Quantization, IEEE Press, 1990.

[13] S. Teng and G. Lu, "Codebook generation in vector quantization used for image retrieval", International Symposium on Intelligent Multimedia and Distance Education, 2-7 August 1999, Baden-Baden, Germany.

[14] Sangwine S. J. and Horne R. E. N., The colour image processing handbook, Chapman & Hall, London, UK, 1998.

[15] G. Salton, Introduction to Mordern Information Retrieval, McGraw-Hill Book Company, 1983.

[16] G. Lu and A. Sajjanhar, "On performance measurement of multimedia information retrieval systems", International Conference on Computational Intelligence and Multimedia Applications, 9-11 Feb. 1998, Monash University, pp.781-787.

[17] G. Lu, Multimedia Database Management Systems, Artech House, Boston, US, 1999.

A Stochastic Model for Content-Based Image Retrieval

Mei-Ling Shyu[1], Shu-Ching Chen[2], Lin Luo[2], and Chi-Min Shu[3]

[1] Department of Electrical and Computer Engineering, University of Miami,
Coral Gables, FL USA
shyu@miami.edu
[2] Distributed Multimedia Information System Laboratory
School of Computer Science, Florida International University
Miami, FL USA
{chens, lluo0001}@cs.fiu.edu
[3] Department of Environmental and Safety Engineering
National Yunlin University of Science and Technology
Touliu, Yunlin Taiwan, R.O.C.
shucm@yuntech.edu.tw

Abstract. Multimedia data, typically image data, is increasing rapidly across the Internet and elsewhere. To keep pace with the increasing volumes of image information, new techniques need to be investigated to retrieve images intelligently and efficiently. Content-based image retrieval is always a challenging task. In this paper, a stochastic model, called Markov Model Mediator (MMM) mechanism, is used to model the searching and retrieval process for content-based image retrieval. Different from the common methods, our stochastic model carries out the searching and similarity computing process dynamically, taking into consideration not only the image content features but also other characteristics of images such as their access frequencies and access patterns. Experimental results demonstrate that the MMM mechanism together with the stochastic process can assist in retrieving more accurate results for user queries.

1 Introduction

Recently, the volumes of multimedia information are growing rapidly, and it becomes easier to access multimedia data due to the popularity of the Internet. There is a great need for efficient image retrieving methods. Content-Based Image Retrieval (CBIR) is an active research area where the image retrieval queries are based on the content of multimedia data. A lot of research work has been done, which resulted in a number of systems and techniques in both the academic and commercial domains. For example, the QBIC system [2] and Virage's VIR engine [12] are two most notable commercial image retrieval systems, while VisualSEEk [11] and PhotoBook [6] are well-known academic image retrieval systems.

Y.-C. Chen, L.-W. Chang, and C.-T. Hsu (Eds.): PCM 2002, LNCS 2532, pp. 229–236, 2002.

The objective of a CBIR system is to enable the user to efficiently find and retrieve those images he/she wants from the database. Most of the existing CBIR systems retrieve images in the following manner. First, they built the indexes based on the low-level features such as color, texture and shape of the images in the database. The index of a query image is also generated when the query is issued. Secondly, they searched through the whole database and measured the similarity of each image to the query. Finally, the results were returned in a sorted order of the similarity matching level.

In this paper, the Markov model mediator (MMM) mechanism that adopts the Markov model framework and the mediator concept [8,9] is proposed for content-based image retrieval. Markov model is one of the most powerful tools available to the scientists and engineers for analyzing complicated systems. Some research works have been done to integrate the Markov model into the field of image retrieval. Lin et al. [4] used a Markov model to combine the spatial and color information. The hidden Markov model (HMM) was used to parse video data in [14]. In [5], the HMM was employed to model the time series of the feature vector for the cases of events and objects in their probabilistic framework for semantic level indexing and retrieval.

The uniqueness of our model lies in the integration of two relationships when determine the similarity: 1) the relationship between the query and the candidate image; 2) the relationships among all images in the database. A stochastic process that takes into account the image content features and other characteristics of the images is also proposed. Several experiments have been conducted and the experimental results demonstrate that the MMM mechanism together with the stochastic process can assist in retrieving more accurate results for user queries.

The remainder of this paper is organized as follows. Section 2 reviews the key components of the MMM mechanism and introduces the stochastic process for information retrieval. Section 3 presents our experiments and discusses the experimental results. Conclusion and future work are given in Section 4.

2   The Stochastic Model

2.1   Markov Model Mediator (MMM) Mechanism

Markov model mediator, for short, MMM, is a probabilistic-based mechanism that adopts the Markov model framework and the mediator concept. A Markov model is a well-researched mathematical construct that is powerful in analyzing complicated systems [3,7]; while a mediator can collect and report information from time to time [13].

Definition 1: A MMM is represented by a 5-tuple $\lambda = (\mathcal{S}, \mathcal{F}, \mathcal{A}, \mathcal{B}, \Pi)$, where $\mathcal{S}$ is a set of images called states; $\mathcal{F}$ is a set of features; $\mathcal{A}$ denotes the states transition probability distribution; $\mathcal{B}$ is the observation symbol probability distribution; and Π is the initial state probability distribution.

The elements in $\mathcal{S}$ and $\mathcal{F}$ determine the dimensions of $\mathcal{A}$ and $\mathcal{B}$. If there are totally s images in $\mathcal{S}$ and the number of distinct features in $\mathcal{F}$ is f, then the dimensions of $\mathcal{A}$ is $s \times s$ and $\mathcal{B}$ is $s \times f$. The relationships of the images are modeled by the sequences of the MMM states connected by transitions, i.e., each entry (m, n) in $\mathcal{A}$ indicates the relationship between images m and n. A training data set consisting of the access patterns and access frequencies of the queries issued to the database is used to train the model parameters for a MMM.

2.2   Formulation of the Model Parameters

Each MMM has three important probability distributions: $\mathcal{A}$, $\mathcal{B}$, and Π. These distributions are critical for the stochastic process and can be obtained from the training data set.

Definition 2: For the images in database d and their corresponding content features, the training data set consists of the following information:

- A set of queries $Q = \{q_1, q_2, \cdots, q_q\}$ that are issued to the database in a period of time;
- The usage patterns $use_{m,k}$ and access frequencies $access_k$ of the queries.
  - $use_{m,k} = 1$ means that image m is accessed by q_k and 0 otherwise.
  - $access_k$ denotes the access frequency of query q_k per time period.

Definition 3: The relative affinity measurements indicate how frequently two images are accessed together, and is defined as follows.

$$aff_{m,n} = \sum_{k=1}^{q} use_{m,k} \times use_{n,k} \times access_k \qquad (1)$$

Based on the relative affinity measurements obtained from Equation 1, the state transition probability distribution $\mathcal{A}$ is constructed as follows.

$$a_{m,n} = \frac{f_{m,n}}{f_m} \qquad (2)$$

where

$$f_{m,n} = \frac{aff_{m,n}}{\sum_{m \in d} \sum_{n \in d} aff_{m,n}} \qquad (3)$$

$$f_m = \sum_{n} f_{m,n} \qquad (4)$$

Here, $f_{m,n}$ is defined as the joint probability that refers to the fraction of the relative affinity of images m and n in database d with respect to the total relative affinity for all the images in d, and f_m is the marginal probability. $a_{m,n}$ is the conditional probability that refers to the state transition probability for a MMM, where $a_{m,n}$ is the element in the $(m, n)^{th}$ entry in $\mathcal{A}$.

The observation symbol probability $\mathcal{B}$ denotes the probability of observing an output symbol from a state, where the observed output symbols representing the distinct features of the images and the states representing the images in the databases. A temporary matrix $(\mathcal{BB})$ is defined to capture the appearance of features in the images, whose rows are all the distinct images and columns are all the distinct features. The value in the $(p,q)^{th}$ entry is 1 if feature q appears in image p, and 0 otherwise. Then the observation symbol probability distribution $\mathcal{B}$ can be obtained via normalizing $\mathcal{BB}$ per row.

The initial state probability distribution Π indicates the preference of the initial states for queries. For any image $m \in d$, its initial state probability is defined as:

$$\Pi = \{\pi_m\} = \frac{\sum_{k=1}^{q} use_{m,k}}{\sum_{l \in d} \sum_{k=1}^{q} use_{l,k}} \tag{5}$$

2.3   Stochastic Process for Information Retrieval

The desired images are captured through a dynamic programming algorithm that calculates the current edge weights and cumulative weights via a stochastic process. Assume there are N images in the databases, and each query is denoted as $q_k = \{o_1, o_2, \cdots, o_T\}$, where T is the total number of features appeared in the query.

Definition 4: $W_t(i,j)$ is defined as the edge weight of the edge $S_i \rightarrow S_j$ on evaluating the tth feature (o_t) in the query, where $1 \leq i,j \leq N$, $1 \leq t \leq T$, $S_i \in S$ and $S_j \in S$.

Definition 5: $D_t(i,j)$ is defined as the cumulative edge weight of the edge $S_i \rightarrow S_j$ on evaluating the tth feature (o_t) in the query, where $1 \leq i,j \leq N$, $1 \leq t \leq T$, $S_i \in S$ and $S_j \in S$.

Based on Definitions 4 and 5, the dynamic programming algorithm is given as follows. At $t = 1$,

$$W_1(i,j) = \begin{cases} \pi_{S_i} b_{S_i}(o_1) & \text{if } i = j \\ 0 & \text{otherwise} \end{cases} \tag{6}$$

$$D_1(i,j) = W_1(i,j) \tag{7}$$

For $1 \leq t \leq T - 1$, the values of $W_{t+1}(i,j)$ and $D_{t+1}(i,j)$ are calculated using the values of $W_t(i,j)$ and $D_t(i,j)$.

$$W_{t+1}(i,j) = \max_k (D_t(k,i)) a_{S_i,S_j} b_{S_j}(o_{t+1}) \tag{8}$$

$$D_{t+1}(i,j) = (\max_k D_t(k,i)) + W_{t+1}(i,j) \tag{9}$$

where a_{S_i,S_j}, $b_{S_j}(o_k)$ and π_{S_i} are elements in probability distributions $\mathcal{A}$, $\mathcal{B}$ and Π, respectively.

Following are the steps for image retrieval using the dynamic programming algorithm in our proposed stochastic model.

1. For the first feature o_1, calculate $W_1(i,j)$ and $D_1(i,j)$ by Equations 6 and 7.
2. For the rest of the features o_t where $2 \leq t \leq T$, calculate $W_t(i,j)$ and $D_t(i,j)$ according to Equations 8 and 9.
3. Sum up each column in $W_t(i,j)$ and $D_t(i,j)$. That is, calculate $sumW_t(j) = \sum_i W_t(i,j)$ and $sumD_t(j) = \sum_i D_t(i,j)$.
4. Rank the images to the user query based on their corresponding values in $sumD_T(j), \ldots, sumD_1(j)$.
   - First, an image is ranked according to its value in $sumD_T(j)$.
   - If two or more images have the same values, then $sumD_{T-1}(j)$ for these images are compared.

3   Experiments

A testbed of 400 color images with various dimensions is used as the image database for the experiments. One MMM model will be constructed for this image database. The MMM model has three model parameters: $\mathcal{A}$, $\mathcal{B}$, and Π probability distributions. A training data set that consists of the query usage patterns and access frequencies together with the images in the database are required for constructing these model parameters for the MMM model. $\mathcal{A}$ can be obtained according to Equations 1 to 4; $\mathcal{B}$ can be converted from $\mathcal{BB}$; and finally Π can be determined by using Equation 5. In our experiments, we do not use the query-by-example strategy for the queries. However, the query-by-example strategy can be easily implemented and employed in our proposed model.

3.1   Construction of the Model

In our experiments, there are eight typical queries issued to the image database with the same access frequency. Each query accesses one or more features from one or more images in the database. In order to support the semantic level queries, both color information and object location information of the images are exploited as the features of the images for the construction of $\mathcal{B}$.

In our experiments, each image has a 21-bins feature vector: twelve for color descriptions and nine for object location descriptions. Color information is the image's color histogram algorithm in the HSI color space. The whole color space is divided into twelve areas according to combinations of different ranges of hue, saturation and intensity values. These areas are: black, white, red, red-yellow (ry), yellow, yellow-green (yg), green, green-blue (gb), blue, blue-purple (bp), purple, and purple-red (pr). Colors with pixel number less than 5% are ignored. As for the object information of an image, the SPCPE (Simultaneous Partition and Class Parameter Estimation) algorithm proposed in [10,1] is used to extract the object information. Each image is divided into 3×3 regular regions, ordered from left to right and top to bottom as: L1, L2, L3, L4, L5, L6, L7, L8 and L9. The locations of the objects within an image are represented by the locations of their centroids. If there is an object whose centroid falls into the associated

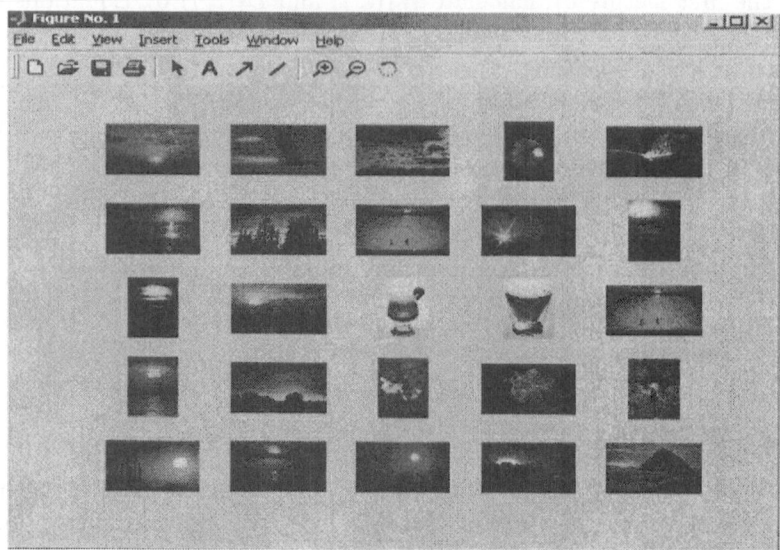

Fig. 1. Snapshot of the query with "red" feature

region, the value 1 is assigned to that location element in the feature vector and the value is 0 otherwise.

Once a query is issued, the stochastic process with the proposed dynamic programming algorithm in Section 2.3 is carried on to retrieve the candidate images that matched the query. The similarity matching degrees of the images with respect to the query are estimated based on the steps described in Section 2.3. The candidate images are sorted decreasingly in accordance with their matching degrees.

3.2   Experiment Results

Experiments have been conducted by issuing various types of queries to the system. We use the snapshot of the query result to illustrate how our proposed model can obtain more accurate retrieval results with respect to a query. In the snapshots, the candidate images are shown with an descending order from *top left* to *bottom right*.

- **Query Type I:** *the number of features in the query = 1.*
In this type of queries, the user specifies only one feature of the desired images, either the color information or the object location information. The system retrieves those images that have this specified feature.

Example: Querying with the "red" color feature.
In this query example, the user wants to retrieve the images that have the red color. Figure 1 shows the snapshot of the window containing the top

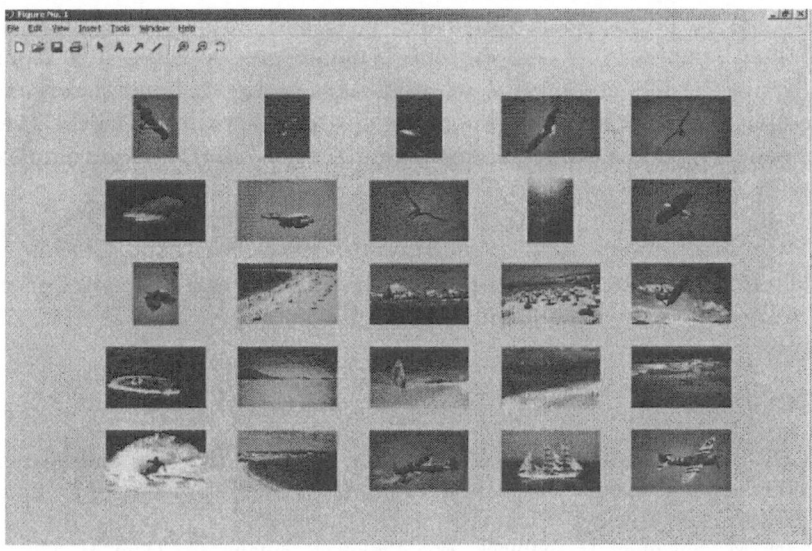

Fig. 2. Snapshot of the query with "white","blue" and "L5" features

25 candidate images. There are quite a few images in our image collection containing the *"red"* color feature. As can be seen from this figure, all the retrieved images have "red" color in them.

• *Query Type II: the number of features in the query* $\geq$ *2.*
This type of queries specifies two or more features including the color features and/or the object location features in the queries.

Example: Querying with the "white", "blue", and "L5" features.
This example shows a three-feature query, including two color features (white and blue) and one object location feature (L5). The snapshot for this query is shown in Figure 2. As can be seen from this figure, all these top 25 images have the "white" and "blue" colors, and have one or more objects at location "L5" within the image, which are the desired features in the query.

4   Conclusion and Future Work

In this paper, the Markov Model Mediator (MMM) mechanism is applied to content-based image retrieval. A stochastic approach based on MMM is used to traverse the database and retrieve the images satisfying the query. This approach performs similarity comparison based on not only the relationship between the query image and the target image, but also the relationships among all the images within the database. Experiments with different numbers of features in the queries were conducted to illustrate how our proposed stochastic-based model works for various types of queries. The experimental results demonstrated that our model can obtain more accurate retrieval results.

The time complexity of the current dynamic programming algorithm is $O(n^2)$. To achieve less complexity, we would like to try to build the dynamic programming algorithm based on the forward variable introduced in the hidden Markov model (HMM) since it has the potential to reduce the time complexity to $O(n)$.

Acknowledgment. For Shu-Ching Chen, this research was supported in part by NSF CDA-9711582.

References

1. Chen, S.-C., Sista, S., Shyu, M.-L., Kashyap, R.L.: An Indexing and Searching Structure for Multimedia Database Systems. IS&T/SPIE Conference on Storage and Retrieval for Media Databases 2000, (2000) 262-270.
2. Flickner, M., Sawhney, H., Niblack, W., Ashley, J., Huang, Q., Dom, B., Gorkani, M., Hafner, J., Lee, D., Petkovic, D., Steele, D., Yanker, P.: Query by Image and Video Content: The QBIC System. IEEE Computer, 28(9) (1995) 23-31.
3. Frank, O., Strauss, D.: Markov Graphs. Journal of the American Statistical Association, 81 (1986) 832-842.
4. Lin, H.C., Wang, L.L., Yang, S.N.: Color Image Retrieval Based on Hidden Markov Models. IEEE Transactions on Image Processing, 6(2) (1997) 332-339.
5. Naphade, M.R., Huang, T.S.: A Probabilistic Framework for Semantic Indexing and Retrieval in Video. IEEE Transactions on Multimedia, 3(1) (2001).
6. Pentland, A., Picard, R.W., Sclaroff, S.: Photobook: Tools for Content-based Manipulation of Image Databases. Proc. Storage and Retrieval for Image and Video Databases II, Vol. 2185, SPIE, Bellingham, Washington (1994) 34-47.
7. Rabiner, L.R., Huang, B.H.: An Introduction to Hidden Markov Models. IEEE ASSP Magazine, 3(1) (1986) 4-16.
8. Shyu, M.-L., Chen, S.-C., Kashyap, R.L.: A Probabilistic-based Mechanism for Video Database Management Systems. IEEE International Conference on Multimedia and Expo (ICME2000), New York (2000) 467-470.
9. Shyu, M.-L., Chen, S.-C., Shu, C.-M.: Affinity-based Probabilistic Reasoning and Document Clustering on the WWW. the 24th IEEE Computer Society International Computer Software and Applications Conference (COMPSAC), Taipei, Taiwan (2000) 149-154.
10. Sista, S., Kashyap, R.L.: Unsupervised Video Segmentation and Object Tracking. IEEE International Conference on Image Processing, Japan (1999).
11. Smith, J.R., Chang, S.F.: VisualSEEK: A Fully Automated Content-based Image Query System. In Proceedings ACM Intern. Conf. Multimedia, Boston (1996) 87-98.
12. http://www.virage.com
13. Wiederhold, G.: Mediators in the Architecture of Future Information Systems. IEEE Computers, (1992) 38-49.
14. Wolf, W.: Hidden Markov Model Parsing of Video Programs. Presented at the International Conference of Acoustics, Speech and Signal Processing, (1997).

Audio Retrieval with Fast Relevance Feedback Based on Constrained Fuzzy Clustering and Stored Index Table

Xueyan Zhao, Yueting Zhuang, Junwei Liu, and Fei Wu

Department of Computer Science and Engineering,
Microsoft Visual Perception laboratory of Zhejiang University
Zhejiang University, Hangzhou, P.R.China
xyzhao2000@263.net   yzhuang@cs.zju.edu.cn   Alvin_Liu@263.net
wufeizheda@263.net

Abstract. Prior work in audio retrieval needs to generate audio templates by supervised learning and find similar audio clip based on pre-trained templates. This paper presents a new and efficient audio retrieval algorithm by unsupervised fuzzy clustering: first, audio features are extracted from compressed domain; second, these features are processed by temporal-spatial constrained fuzzy clustering, and the relevant audio clips can be represented by the clustering centroids; third, we use triangle tree to speedup the similarity measure. Relevance feedback is also implemented during retrieval. Therefore, the result can be adjusted according to users' taste and is consistent with human perception.

Keywords: Audio Retrieval, Time-Spatial Constraint Fuzzy Clustering, Triangle tree, Relevance Feedback

1   Introduction

Audio bears rich semantic information that makes it an important media in multimedia content analysis domain. And audio retrieval is always among the most attractive but difficult problems [1].

Generally speaking, audio retrieval has three strategies: 1) the representation of original audio data; 2) similarity measure between audio clips; 3) mechanism built to make up for the gap between perceptual similarity and lower-level feature similarity [2, 3]. Traditionally, audio templates are trained by supervised learning to recognize different audio clips [4, 5]. But these methods have two limitations: on the one hand, training a template is difficult, because both training samples and training methods have great influence on the final performance. On the other hand, features extracted from the original audio stream are huge. Furthermore, extracting features from uncompressed domain is really time-consuming. With the popularity of the Internet, real-time application becomes more and more important, MPEG has become the de facto compression standard of multimedia. Audio retrieval with uncompressed domain features has to include one additional step: decoding. It cannot be efficiently used at real-time application. Because the coding of MPEG audio is based on

Y.-C. Chen, L.-W. Chang, and C.-T. Hsu (Eds.): PCM 2002, LNCS 2532, pp. 237–244, 2002.

psychoacoustics model. Features extracted from MPEG stream could directly express audio's perceptual contents [6, 7, 8].

In this paper, we propose a new and efficient audio retrieval algorithm by unsupervised fuzzy clustering. Firstly, audio features are extracted from MPEG compressed domain. Secondly, we generate fixed number of centroids for each audio clip by time-spatial constrained fuzzy clustering to represent the clip. Thirdly, similar audio clips are quickly matched by simply measuring centroids' distance. Here, a triangle tree is built to accelerate retrieval speed. Finally, fast relevance feedback [9] is performed to adjust result according to users' act.

The rest of the paper is organized as follows: section 2 introduce feature extraction from compressed domain and centroids generation by temporal-spatial constrained fuzzy clustering; similarity measure, retrieval by triangle tree and fast relevance feedback are presented in section 3; experiment result is analyzed in section 4 and a brief conclusion and direction of future works are mentioned in last section.

2   Audio Features

2.1   Audio Feature Extraction

Since MPEG standard has become one of the most popular ways to store and transport audio data, we extract audio features directly from the compressed MPEG stream.

The original MPEG audio data is segmented into frames of 20ms long[1] with an overlapping ratio of 50%. A root mean square of subband vector is calculated for each frame, as follows: $M[i] = \sqrt{\dfrac{\sum_{i=1}^{32}(S_t[i]^2)}{32}}, i = 1,2,..32$ Where S_t is a 32-dimensional subband vector, M contains all the information we need to compute features. Here, four features are extracted based on $M[i]$: *Centroid*: $C = \dfrac{\sum_{i=1}^{32} iM[i]}{\sum_{i=1}^{32} M[i]}$, Centroid is the balancing point of the vector; *Rolloff*: $R = \arg(\sum_{i=1}^{R} M[i] = 0.85\sum_{i=1}^{32} M[i])$; *Spectral Flux*: Spectral Flux is the Euler distance between normalized M vectors of two successive frames; *RMS*: $RMS = \sqrt{\dfrac{\sum_{i=1}^{32}(M[i]^2)}{32}}$.

2.2   Generate Clustering Centroids

Although extracting features from compressed domain saves a lot of time, it is still not efficient to present an audio clip because a several-minute-long audio clip can be

---

[1] The MPEG audio frame is a block of 576 samples, about 20msec at 22050 Hz

segmented into thousands of frames. Here, clustering is used to solve the problem by simplifying the index mechanism. Traditional clustering is to partition a collection of data points into a number of groups, where the objects within a group keep a certain degree of similarity. Hard clustering assigns each data point (feature vector) to only one of the groups [10]. However,this model does not reflect the real situation, where boundaries between groups might be distinct especially for audio case.

In this paper, fuzzy C-means algorithm is adopted to solve the problem [11] , where a $K \times N$ matrix U is introduced to indicate the degree of membership of all points (feature vectors) to each cluster. Assuming that $\chi = \{\chi_{1l}, \chi_{2l}, \cdots, \chi_{jl}, \cdots, \chi_{Nl}\}$ is an audio clip which is segmented into N frames, and each frame is a 4-dimensional feature vector where $\chi_{jl} (1 \leq j \leq N,$ $1 \leq l \leq 4)$ indicates the lth feature of the jth frame. We also assume $V = \{V_{1l}, V_{2l}, \cdots, V_{il}, \cdots V_{Kl}\}$ to be centroids, where K indicates the number of generated centroids and $K \ll N$. Like χ_{jl}, $V_{il} (1 \leq i \leq K, 1 \leq l \leq 4)$ is also a 4-dimensional vector. The theroy of fuzzy clustering is based on minimization of the following objective function: $J_q (U, V) = \sum_{j=1}^{N} \sum_{i=1}^{K} (u_{ij})^q d^2 (X_{jl}, V_{il})$, Where

$K \ll N$, q is a real number greater than 1, u_{ij} is the degree of membership of χ_j to the ith cluster V_i, $d^2(\chi_{jl}, V_{il})$ is any inner product metric. The parameter q is the weighting exponent of u_{ij} and controls the "fuzziness" of the resulting clusters.

2.2.1   Features Normalization

Because the range of different featurevaries, all x_{jl} are normalized to $\hat{x}_{jl}$ by gaussian distribution: $\hat{x}_{jl} = \dfrac{\chi_{jl} - \mu_l}{3\sigma_l}$

In the end, $\hat{x}_{jl}$ is transformed to [0, 1] by the following shift: $\hat{x}_{jl} = \dfrac{\hat{\chi}_{jl} + 1}{2}$

2.2.2   Fuzzy Clustering

Fuzzy partition is carried out through an iterative optimization of the object funtion:

Step1: Choose initial centroids V_i. Cosine distance between two adjacent frames is calculated and a distance array is arraged in descent order. We choose several frames with maximum distance and mimimum distance to form initial centroids.

Step2: Compute the membership degree of all feature vectors to all the clusters (a):

Step3: Compute new centroids $\hat{V}_i$ (b):

$$u_{ij} = \frac{\left[\dfrac{1}{d^2(X_j, V_i)}\right]^{\frac{1}{(q-1)}}}{\sum\limits_{k=1}^{K}\left[\dfrac{1}{d^2(X_j, V_k)}\right]^{\frac{1}{(q-1)}}} \quad (a) \qquad\qquad \hat{V}_i = \frac{\sum\limits_{j=1}^{N}(u_{ij})^q X_j}{\sum\limits_{j=1}^{N}(u_{ij})^q} \quad (b)$$

Update the degree of memberships u_{ij} with $\hat{u}_{ij}$, according to step2, untill $\max_{ij}\left\|u_{ij} - \hat{u}_{ij}\right\| < \varepsilon$, where ε is a termination criterion between 0 and 1.

We still have to check whether the generated centroids conform to the temporal-spatial constraint. Temporal constraint makes sure that all groups are uniform. And spatial constraint makes sure that none of the centroids are similar with others. If the clustering result does not satisfy the above constraint, a new set of starting centroids is chosen and fuzzy clustering is applied again. When centroids are extracted successfully, an auido clip can be represented by following 4-tuple: *tuple* = (*fuzzycentr oid* , *Cluster* , *weight* , *length*) Audio clips are indexed by the K centroids to perform similarity measure. q and K play important roles on the retrieval. The discussion of them is in section 4.

3   Audio Clip Retrieval and Fast Relevance Feedback

3.1 Similarity Measure

Suppose that $S = \{s_1, s_2, \cdots, s_i, \cdots s_K\}$ is the audio clip example submitted by user, and $T = \{t_1, t_2, \cdots, t_i, \cdots t_K\}$ is one of the retrieved audio clip in database, where K is the number of centroids. The distance between S and T can be calculated as follows:

$$Dis(S,T) \equiv \frac{1}{|S|+|T|}\left[\sum_{s \in S} d(s, g(s,T)) + \sum_{t \in T} d(t, g(t,S))\right]$$

where, $g(s_i, T) \equiv \arg\min_{t \in T} d(s_i, t)$, $g(t_j, S) \equiv \arg\min_{s \in S} d(t_j, s)$ and d is a distance measure, we choose Euclldean distance here.

3.2 Audio Clip Retreival

We can retrieve similar audio clips from database based on user's example and above similarity matching procedure. However, the complexity of this retrieval algorithm is still a bit large, nearly to $O(NK^2)$ (N is the number of audio clips in database, and K is the number of centroids). So the result is decreased linearly with the amount of information available in the database. In order to accelerate the retrieval process, we introduce reference system, being assured that similar audio clips have similar distance to the same reference audio clip.

Definition 1: Assuming V and W are two audio-clips and δ is a samll value. For the reference audio clip $Key_i\,(1 \le i \le m)$, if $\left| Dis(Key_i, B) - Dis(Key_i, C) \right| < \delta$, then we say B is similar to C, where $\{Key_i\}$ is called key-clips.

Then for any two arbitrary audio clips in the database, if the difference of their distances to all key-clips is no more than δ, then they are similar with each other. The distances between each clip in the database and key-clips are pre-computed and stored to speed up retrieval. Complexity of retrieval is reduced to $O(Nm)$ now, where m is the number of key-clips. Yet the above result is not so satisfying. We build a triangle tree to further improve the retrieval efficiency. This data structure is proposed by Andrew P. Berman and Linda G. Shapiro [12] and used in content-based image retrieval. Figure 1 shows the structure of a triangle tree with two levels:

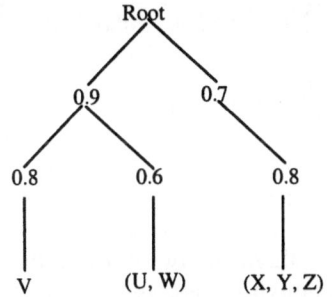

Each layer of the tree stores the distance between audio clips and a specific key-clip, for example, the distance between audio clip V and key1 is 0.9. Suppose an audio clip Q is submitted by user to find similar audio clips. The distance from Q to each key-clips $\{Key_i\}$ $Dis(Key_i, Q)$ $(1 \le i \le m)$ is computed and a depth-first search of the tree is performed. If there is a

Fig. 1. The structure of triangle tree

node P at level 1 with value c that $\left| c - Dis(Key_i, Q) \right| > \delta$, then any stored clips below node P are pruned. When a leaf is reached, we simply measure the distance from Q to every object in the leaf and return those objects whose distance is less than or equal to δ. Therefore, computation time is saved. The number of key-clips controls the depth of the triangle tree. In our experiment, the generation of key-clips is automatic. When a new audio clip R is inserted, it is compared with other current key-clips. If $\min(Dis(Key_i, R)) > \sigma$, audio clip R is recognized as a new key-clip, where δ is a dicision criterion.

3.3 Fast Relevance Feedback

Although fuzzy clustering and triangle tree can speed up audio retrieval, their performance is still limited to less than 55%. The main reason is that audio is represented by low-level features, which merely captures its acoustical contents, but not its semantics. Relevance feedback is used to tackle this problem. Most of the previous relevance feedback research can be classified into two approaches: query point movement and features' re-weighting. Because user themselves are not sure what they intend to retrieve sometimes, the point movement method is used to clarify user' retrieval intention interactively. Suppose $\{Sa_i\}$ ($1 \le i \le m$) are the satisfying results identified by user during one step of relevance feedback, the new query point Qa is generated by fuzzy clustering mentioned above: $Qa = fuzzy\_centroid$ $(Sa_1, Sa_2, \ldots, Sa_m)$ Feature re-weighing is quite simple in our implementation. We can consider each audio clip as a point in a four dimensional space. Because the distance measure between audio clips is linear, if the variance of the satisfying examples is low along a principle axis of a feature, we can deduce that the values on this axis is more important to the retrieval, and a higher weight is assigned to this feature. Weight_Centroid, Weight_Rolloff, Weight_Flux and Weight_RMS are used as the weights of the four audio features. And $User\_prefer =$ $\{up_1, up_2, \cdots, up_i, \cdots up_u\}$ stores the satisfaction degree of the audio clips in retrieval result, where M indicates the number of audio clips. Then new weights can be computed by the following equations.

$$W\_Centroid = \sum_{i=1}^{M}\left(\left(\sum_{K}Weight\_Centroid\right)\times up_i\right)_i \quad W\_Rolloff = \sum_{i=1}^{M}\left(\left(\sum_{K}Weight\_Rolloff\right)\times up_i\right)_i$$

$$W\_Flux = \sum_{i=1}^{M}\left(\left(\sum_{K}Weight\_Flux\right)\times up_i\right)_i \quad W\_Rms = \sum_{i=1}^{M}\left(\left(\sum_{K}Weight\_Rms\right)\times up_i\right)_i$$

But triangle tree can not use the new weights directly during retrieval, because the distance of triangle tree is pre-calculated and stored, new triangle tree must be rebuilt once again for different combination of weights. Here, we only care about the two features with the highest weight, reset a higher weight to them and two other features with lower weights. The experiment shows that it is enough to care about only two relevant features. Therefore, for the four audio features, there are altogether six triangle trees need to be built and pre-stored according to different combination of

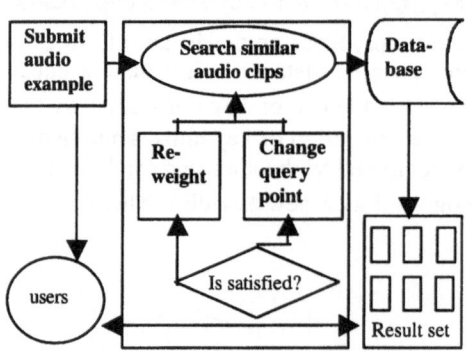

Fig. 2. The relevance feedback of audio retrieval

Table 1. Comparison between retrieval without triangle tree and retrieval with triangle tree

System		A	B	C
Original System	Time(s)	0.311	1.484	9.045
	Returned matches	107	451	2059
New System	Time(s)	0.112	0.236	1.121
	Returned matches	117	489	2132

features and weights. A particular retrieval task may use one of the triangle trees with the specific set of weights. Based on one of six triangle trees, the new similar audio clips would be immediately replied to user according to use's feedback without measuring all of audio clips in database. Therefore, speedup of relevance feedback is achieved. Figure 2 shows the flow of relevance feedback.

Precision(%)

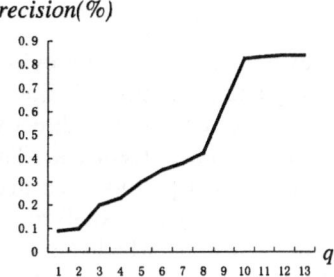

Fig. 3. Influence of q on precision

Precision(%)

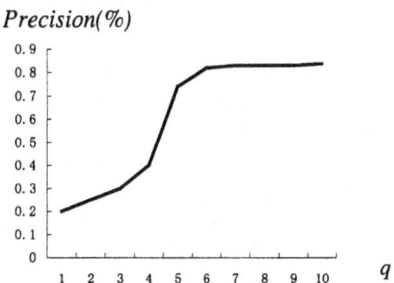

Fig. 5. Influence of *K* on precision

Recall(%)

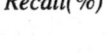

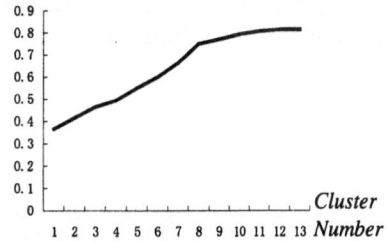

Fig. 4. Influence of q on recall

Recall(%)

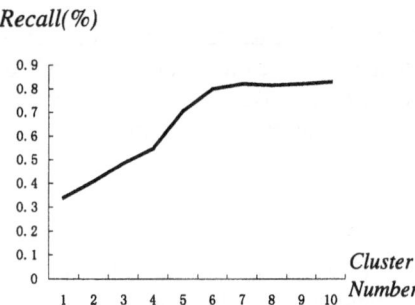

Fig. 6. Influence of *K* on recall

4 Experiment Setup

More than Five thousand of audio clips of all kinds of styles (including MP3 files of music, speech, news, advertise, song, etc) are collected to test the performance of our system. The experiment is implemented by Visual C++ under Windows2000.

In fuzzy clustering, the parameter q controls the "fuzziness" of the resulting clustering, and the parameter K is the number of centroids. Both q and K influence the retrieval result greatly. Here, we compare the performance of different values of q and K on the system and precision/recall is used to measure the result. Figure 3 and figure 4 show the influence of the parameter q. Figure 5 and figure 6 show the influence of the parameter K. It shows that with the increment of values of q and K, precision/recall increased. And when the parameter q is equal to 11 and the parameter K is 6, the best performance is achieved. Both precision and recall exceed 80%. If q and K increase beyond this level, their values will have little influence on the performance. The use of triangle tree accelerates the retrieval. But the process of binning the distances makes the distance matching ambiguous. Comparison between retrieval without triangle tree and retrieval with triangle tree is showed in table 1.

5   Conclusion and Future Work

In this paper, we introduce a new method for audio retrieval. Compared with previous algorithms, this method is based on unsupervised learning and laborious indexing is unnecessary. The audio features are extracted from compressed domain directly. Triangle tree is used to accelerate the retrieval and relevance feedback. The experimental result proves that this method gains a more efficient performance than traditional ones. The future work mainly focuses on the two aspects: 1) Analyze the content carried by audio. Audio contains rich semantic meanings which have no successful model of description. The above four features are insufficient to define an audio clip. 2) The use of triangle tree accelerates the retrieval, but reduces accuracy which is beyond your requirement. New data structure with better performance needs to be explored.

Acknowledgements. This work is sponsored by the National Natural Science Foundation of China, Foundation of Education Ministry for Excellent Young Teacher, College Key Teacher Supporting Plan and Doctorate Research Foundation of the State Education Commission of China.

References

[1]   Y. Wang, Z. Liu and J. Huang, "Multimedia content analysis using audio and visual information," IEEE Signal Processing Magazine. vol. 17, no. 6, pp. 12-36, Nov. 2000. Invited paper in the special issue on joint audio-visual processing.

[2]   Foote J T, An overview of audio information retrieval, Multimedia Systems, 1999 7(1):

[3]   Fei Wu, Yueting Zhuang, Yin Zhang, and Yunhe Pan, "Hidden Markovia Model based Audio Semantic Retrieval", Pattern Recognition and Artificial Intelligence, 14 (1):104-108, 2001

[4]   Jonathan T. Foote, "Content-Based Retrieval of Music and Audio", In C.-C. J. Kuo et al., editor, Multimedia Storage and Archiving Systems II, Proc. of SPIE, Vol. 3229, pp. 138-147, 1997

[5]   Stan Z. Li and GuoDong Guo, "Content-based Audio Classification and Retrieval using SVM Learning", the special session on Multimedia Information Indexing and Retrieval.The First IEEE Pacific-Rim Conference on Multimedia December 13-15, 2000, University of Sydney, Australia.

[6]   ISO/IEC JTC1/SC29, Information Technology-Generic Coding of Moving Pictures an Associate Audio Information-IS 13818 (Part 3, Audio), 1994.

[7]   Slaney M, Lyon R F, "A perceptual pitch detector", In: Proc. Int. Conf. Acoustic, Speech, and Signal Processing 1990 (ICASSP 90).Albuquerque.

[8]   ISO/IEC JTC1/SC29, Information Technology-Coding of Moving Pictures and Associate Audio for Digital Storage Media at up to about 1.5Mbit/s-IS 11172 (Part 3,Audio), 1992.

[9]   Rui.Y, Huang, T. S., Ortega, M., Mehrotra, S., "Relevance Feedback: A Power Tool for Interactive Content-based Image Retrieval", IEEE Trans. on Circuits and VideoTechnology, 1998.

[10] JR.N.Dave and R.Krishnapuram, " Robust clustering method: a unified view", IEEE Transactions on Fuzzy systems, vol.5, no.2, pp.270-293, 1997

[11] N.B.Karayiannis, J.C.Bezdek, " an integrated approach to fuzzy learning vector quantization and fuzzy c-means clustering ", IEEE Trans. on Fuzzy systems, vol 5, no.4, pp 622-628, 1997

[12] Andrew P. Berman, Linda G. Shapiro, " Efficient Content-Based Retrieval: Experimental Results ", http://www.cs.washington.edu/research/imagedatabase/reportfin.htm

Semi-automatic Video Content Annotation

Xingquan Zhu[1], Jianping Fan[2], Xiangyang Xue[3], Lide Wu[3], and
Ahmed K. Elmagarmid[1]

[1]Dept. of Computer Science, Purdue University, IN 47907, USA
[2]Dept. of Computer Science, University of North Carolina at Charlotte, NC 28223, USA
[3]Dept. of Computer Science, Fudan University, Shanghai, 200433, China
{zhuxq, ake}@cs.purdue.edu; jfan@uncc.edu;
{xyxue, ldwu}@fudan.edu.cn

Abstract. Video modeling and annotating are indispensable operations necessary for creating and populating a video database. To annotate video data effectively and accurately, a video content description ontology is first proposed in
this paper, we then introduce a semi-automatic annotation strategy which utilize
various video processing techniques to help the annotator explore video context
or scenarios for annotation. Moreover, a video scene detection algorithm which
joints visual and semantics is proposed to visualize and refine the annotation results. With the proposed strategy, a more reliable and efficient video content description could be achieved. It is better than manual manner in terms of efficiency, and better than automatic scheme in terms of accuracy.

1 Introduction

In recent, advances in computer hardware and networks have made significant progress in the developments of application systems supporting video data. Large scale of
video archive is now available to users as various forms. However, without an efficient and reasonable mechanism for retrieving video data, large archive of video data
remains as merely unmanageable resources of data. Accordingly, various video index
strategies are proposed to describe video content by: (1) *High level indexing*; (2) *Low
level indexing*; and (3) *Domain specific indexing*.

Due to the inadequacy of textual terms in describing video content, many low-
level indexing strategies have emerged [1][7] to parse video content. Unfortunately, all
these strategies alone do not enable a sufficiently detailed representation of video
content. Hence, manual annotation is still widely used.

The simplest way to model video content is using free text to manually annotate
each shot separately. However, since a single shot is separated from its context, the
video scenario information is lost. Accordingly, *Aguierre Smith et. al* [2] implements a
video annotation system using the concept of stratification to assign description to
video footage. Based on this scheme, the *video algebra* [3] is developed to provide operations for the composition, search, navigation and playback of digital video presentation. A similar strategy for evolving documentary presentation is found in [4]. Instead of using textual terms for annotation, *Davis et. al* [5] presents an iconic visual
language based system, however, this user-friendly approach is limited by a fixed vocabulary. Obviously, no matter how efficient a content description structure is, anno-

Y.-C. Chen, L.-W. Chang, and C.-T. Hsu (Eds.): PCM 2002, LNCS 2532, pp. 245-252, 2002.
© Springer-Verlag Berlin Heidelberg 2002

tating videos frame by frame is still a time consuming operation. Hereby, a shot based semi-automatic annotation engine is proposed [6], unfortunately, annotators also have to explore scenarios by browsing shots sequentially. And the problems still remain: (1) no efficient scheme has been developed to explore video scenarios for annotation; (2) keywords at various levels should be organized differently; (3) to minimize annotators' subjectivity and influences of synonymy and polysemy in unstructured keywords, ontologies have been proved to be an efficient way; However, methods above either fail to define their ontology explicitly or do not separate ontology with annotation data to enhance the reusability of annotation data.

To address these problems, a semi-automatic video annotation scheme is proposed in this paper. We first define the content description ontology. Then, video group detection strategy is introduced to help annotators explore video context and scenarios. Based on acquired video group information, the annotator could execute extensive operations to improve annotation efficiency.

2 Video Content Description Architecture

2.1 Video Content Description Ontology

As we know, most videos can be represented by using a hierarchy consisting of five layers (video, scene, group, shots and frames), from top to bottom in increasing granularity for content expression. A flexible and comprehensive content annotation strategy should also describe video content at different layers and with different granularities. Hence, video content description ontology is predefined, as shown in Fig. 1, where four content descriptions, *Video Description* (*VD*), *Group Description* (*GD*), *Shot Description* (*SD*) and *Frame Description* (*FD*), are used to describe video content. They are defined as below:

1. The *VD* addresses the category and specialty taxonomy information of the entire video. There are two descriptors (Video category and Speciality category) contained in *VD*. The description at this level should answer questions like "What does the video talk about?"
2. The *GD* describes the event information in a group of adjacent shots that convey the same semantic information. There are two descriptors (Event and Actor) specified in *GD*. The description at this level should answer the query like " Give me all surgery units among the medical videos?"
3. The *SD* describes the action in a single shot. This action could be a part of an event. e.g., a video shot could show the action "doctor shake hands with patient" in a diagnosis event. There are three descriptors (Object, Action and Location) specified in *SD*. Hence, the *SD* should answer the query like "Give me all units where a doctor touches the head of the patient on the bed".
4. At the lowest level, the frame, the description should address the details of objects in frame(s). There are two descriptors (Object and Status) specified in *FD*. The description should answer query like "What is in the frame(s)?"

The keyword tables of various descriptors are predefined and are still extensible for annotators by adding more instances.

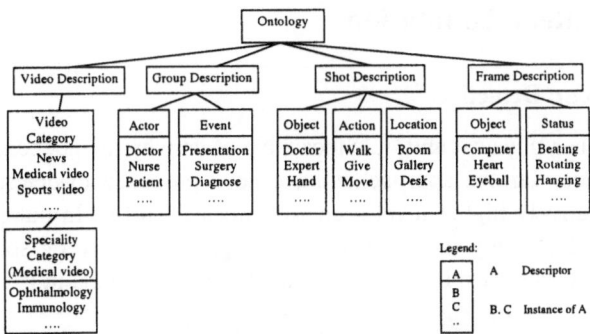

Fig. 1. Video content description ontology

2.2 Shot Based Video Temporal Description Data Organization

To separate the ontology from the description data and integrate video semantics with low-level features, a shot based video description data structure is constructed for each video. Given any video shot S_i, assuming KA indicates the *Keyword Aggregation* (KA) of all descriptors in the ontology, then $KA=\{VD_l, l=1,...,NV_i;\ GD_l, l=1,..NG_i;\ SD_l, l=1,..NS_i;\ FD_l, l=1,..NF_i\}$, where VD_l, GD_l, SD_l and FD_l represent the keywords of VD, GD, SD and FD respectively, and NV_i, NG_i, NS_i and NF_i indicate the number of keywords for each description. To indicate the region where each keyword takes effect, the symbol v_{a-b}^{ID} is used to denote the region from frame a to b in the video with a certain identification (ID). The *Temporal Description Data* (TDD) for shot S_i is then defined as the aggregation of mappings between annotation ontology and temporal frames: $TDD=\{S_i^{ID}, S_i^{ST}, S_i^{ED}, Map(KA, V)\}$, where S_i^{ST} and S_i^{ED} denote the start and end frame of S_i respectively. KA indicates the keyword aggregation of all descriptors, V indicates a set of video streams, $v_{a-b}^{ID} \in V, ID = 1,..,n$, and Map defines the correspondence between annotations and the video temporal information. E.g., $Map(KA_i; v_{a-b}^{ID})$ denotes the mapping between keyword KA_i to region from frame a to b in video with certain identification ID. The advantage of above mapping is that ontology is separated from annotation data. The same video data could be shared and annotated by different annotators for different purposes, and can be easily reused for different applications.

The assembling of *TDD* from all shots forms the *Temporal Description Stream* (*TDS*) of the video. It indicates that all annotation keywords are associated with each shot. The reason we utilize such a data structure is clarified below:

1. A frame based data description structure will inevitably incur large redundancy.
2. Since video shots are usually taken as the basic unit of video processing techniques [1][7][9] the shot based structure will help us integrate low-level features with semantics seamlessly.
3. More keywords can be employed in the *FD* to characterize the changing of shot content. Hence, the details of the video will not be lost.

3 Video Content Annotation

3.1 Video Group Detection

The video shot is a physical unit, it is incapable of conveying independent semantic information. Hence, various approaches have been proposed to determine video units that convey relatively higher level scenario information [9]. In our system, a temporally constrained strategy is employed to merge temporally or spatially correlated shots into groups, as shown in Fig. 2, the details could be found in [9].

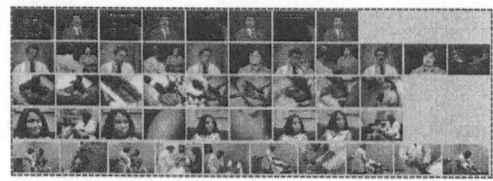

Fig. 2. Group detection results with each row denoting one group

3.2. Unified Similarity Evaluation

In Section 2, we specified that the mapping of each keyword has recorded the frame region where this keyword takes effect. To evaluate the semantic similarity between video shots, this region should be considered since it determines the importance of the keyword in describing the shot content. For *VD*, *GD*, and *SD*, keywords at these levels will have longer (or equal) duration than the current shot. Hence, they will be in effect over the entire shot. However, descriptors in the *FD* may last only one or several frames, to calculate the semantic similarity between shots, the *Effect Factor* of each *FD* descriptor's keyword is calculated first.

Assuming FD_k denotes the kth keyword of *FD*, we suppose there are N mappings associated with FD_k in shot S_i, and the mapping regions are $v_{a_1-b_1}^2,..,v_{a_N-b_N}^2$. Given any two regions $v_{a_i-b_i}^2$, $v_{a_j-b_j}^2$ $(i \neq j, i, j \in N)$ among these mappings, assume operator $\Theta(X,Y)$ denotes the number of overlapped frames between region X and Y. Then, the *Effect Factor* of keyword FD_k corresponding to shot S_i is defined by Eq. (1).

$$EF(FD_k, S_i) = \frac{\sum_{I=1}^{N}(b_I - a_I) - \sum_{m=1}^{N}\sum_{n=m}^{N}\Theta(v_{a_m-b_m}^{ID}, v_{a_n-b_n}^{ID})}{S_i^{ED} - S_i^{ST}}, \quad m, n \in N \tag{1}$$

To evaluate the cross intersection between keywords at various levels, we define $\overline{VDS_k}, \overline{GDS_k}, \overline{SDS_k}, \overline{FDS_k}$ as the aggregation of keywords which have been used to annotate shot S_k in VD, GD, SD and FD respectively. To describe the relationship among series of keywords $(X_1, X_2, .., X_N)$, three operators $\{ \Omega(X_1, X_2, .., X_N),\ \vartheta(X_1, X_2, .., X_N),\ \Psi(X) \}$ are defined:

1. $\Omega(X_1, X_2, .., X_N) = \{X_1 \cup X_2 \cup .. \cup X_N\}$ indicates the union of $X_1, X_2, .., X_N$.
2. $\vartheta(X_1, X_2, .., X_N) = \{X_1 \cap X_2 \cap .. \cap X_N\}$ is the intersection of $X_1, X_2, .., X_N$.
3. $\Psi(X)$ represents the number of keywords in X.

Given any two shots S_i and S_j, assume their TDD are $TDD_i=\{\,S_i^{ID},\ S_i^{ST},\ S_i^{ED},$ $Map(KA,\ V)\}$ and $TDD_j=\{\,S_j^{ID},\ S_j^{ST},\ S_j^{ED},\ Map(KA,\ V)\}$ respectively. Assume also that KAS_i denotes the union of keywords which have been shown in annotating shot S_i. The semantic similarity between S_i and S_j is then defined by Eq. (2):

$$SemStSim\,(S_i,S_j)=W_v\frac{\Psi(\vartheta(\overline{VDS}_i,\overline{VDS}_j))}{\Psi(\Omega(\overline{VDS}_i,\overline{VDS}_j))}+W_G\frac{\Psi(\vartheta(\overline{GDS}_i,\overline{GDS}_j))}{\Psi(\Omega(\overline{GDS}_i,\overline{GDS}_j))}+W_S\frac{\Psi(\vartheta(\overline{SDS}_i,\overline{SDS}_j))}{\Psi(\Omega(\overline{SDS}_i,\overline{SDS}_j))}+W_F\frac{\sum_i\{EF(FD_k,S_i)\cdot EF(FD_k,S_j)\}}{\Psi(\Omega(\overline{FDS}_i,\overline{FDS}_j))} \tag{2}$$

Eq. (2) indicates that the semantic similarity between S_i and S_j is the weighted sum of the cross intersection of keywords at various video content levels.

Based on the semantic similarity in Eq. (2) the overall similarity between S_i and S_j which joint visual features and semantics is given by Eq. (3).

$$StSim(S_i,S_j)=(1-\alpha)\cdot VisStSim(S_i,S_j)+\alpha\cdot SemStSim(S_i,S_j) \tag{3}$$

where $VisStSim(S_i,S_j)$ indicates the visual similarity between shots which is specified in [13]. $\alpha\in[0,1]$ is the weight of the semantic information in similarity measurement, which can be specified by users. Based on Eq. (3), given shot S_i and video group G_j, their similarity can be calculated using Eq. (4).

$$StGpSim\ (S_i,G_j)=Max_{S_j\in G_j}\{StSim\ (S_i,S_j)\} \tag{4}$$

Given group G_i and G_j, assume $\hat{G}_{i,j}$ is the group containing less shot, and $\tilde{G}_{i,j}$ is the other group. $M(X)$ denotes the number of shot in X, then, the similarity between G_i and G_j is given in Eq.(5), with more techniques described in [9].

$$GroupSim\ (G_i,G_j)=\frac{1}{M(\hat{G}_{i,j})}\sum_{i=1;S_i\in\hat{G}_{i,j}}^{M(\hat{G}_{i,j})}StGpSim\ (S_i,\tilde{G}_{i,j}) \tag{5}$$

3.3. Video Scene Detection

After most video groups haven been annotated, we can integrate semantics and visual features to merge similar groups into semantically related units (scenes). And use them to help the annotator visualize and refine annotation results. To attain this goal, the scene detection strategy takes steps below:

1. Given any group G_i, assume GDE_i denotes the aggregation of the event descriptor's keyword which has been used in GD of all shots in G_i.
2. For any neighboring groups G_i and G_j, if $\vartheta(GDE_i,GDE_j)=\varnothing$, these two groups are not merged. Otherwise, go to step 3. I.e., if the event descriptor in two groups is totally different, they cannot be merged into one group.
3. Using Eq. (5) to calculate overall similarity between these two groups; go to step 2 to find all other neighboring groups' similarity. Then go to step 4.
4. Adjacent groups with similarity larger than T_G are merged into a new group. Those reserved and newly generated groups are formed as video scenes.

3.4. Semi-automatic Video Annotation

Some semi-automatic annotation schemes have been implemented in image database [8] by using semantics, visual features and relevance feedback to assist the annotator for annotation. Derived from the same intuition, in this section, a semi-automatic video annotation scheme is presented.

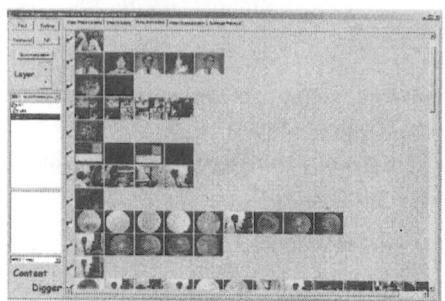 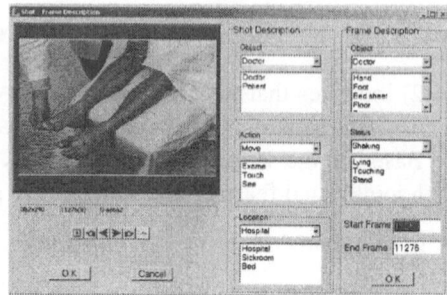

Fig. 3. Video content annotation interface   **Fig. 4.** Shot and frame annotation interface

As the first step, the group detection method is applied to segment temporally or spatially related shots into groups. Then, the groups are shown sequentially for annotation, as shown in Fig.3. Given any group, the annotator has three operations:

1. Annotate a certain shot by double clicking the key-frame of the shot (the result is illustrated in Fig.4.). A series of function buttons such as play, pause, etc. are available to help the annotator determine semantics among the shot and frames.
2. If the annotator thinks that the current group belongs to the same event category, he (she) could specify *GD* and *VD* keywords to the group by clicking the hand-like icon at the left of the group, and select keywords to annotate the group.
3. If the annotator thinks current group contains more than one event category, he (she) can manually separate it into different groups (with each group belonging to only one event category) by dragging the mouse to mask shots in the same event category and click the hand-like icon to assign keywords.

At any annotation state, the annotator can select one or a group of shots as the query to find similar groups for annotation. To do this, the relevance feedback (*RF*) strategy is activated:

1. All selected shot(s) are treated as a video group. The annotator should input keywords to describe them before the retrieval.
2. After the annotator clicks the "Find" button, the similarity evaluation strategy in Eq. (5) is used to find similar groups.
3. At any retrieval stage, the annotator can either annotate retrieved groups separately or mark some of them as feedback examples, and click "RF" button to trigger a *RF* processing. Then, all selected shots are annotated with keywords specified in step 1. The Eq. (6) is used to find other similar groups.

Eq. (6) presents the simplified *RF* model in our system (based on Bayesian formula). Assuming G_i denotes the selected feedback examples in current iteration, for any group G_j in the database, its global similarity $Sim(j)^k$ in the current iteration (k) is determined by its global similarity in the previous iteration $Sim(j)^{k-1}$ and its similarity to current selected feedback examples $GroupSim(G_i, G_j)$. η indicates the influence of the history to the current evaluation, in our system we set $\eta = 0.3$.

$$Sim\,(j)^k = \eta Sim\,(j)^{k-1} + (1-\eta)GroupSim\;(G_i, G_j) \tag{6}$$

By integrating the annotated semantics and visual features related to groups, we can merge the semantically related adjacent groups into scenes to help annotators evaluate and refine annotations results:

1. At any annotation stage, the annotator can click the "Refine" button, the scene detection strategy is invoked to merge adjacent similar groups into scenes.
2. The annotator can specify different values for α to evaluate annotation quality in different situations.

That is, a series of annotation, refinement, annotation, can be recursively executed until a satisfactory result is achieved.

4 Experimental Results

Obviously, the performance of two techniques, video group detection and group similarity assessment, should be evaluated to confirm the efficiency of the proposed semi-automatic annotation strategy. Due to lack of space, we supply only group similarity assessment result; the group detection results could be found in [9]. About 8 hours of medical videos and 4 hours of News programs are used as our test bed. They are first parsed with the shot segmentation algorithm to detect the gradual and break changes [7]. After group detection has been executed on each video, we manually select out groups which have distinct semantic meaning as the test bed, then randomly select one group as the query, all retrieved top-N groups are utilized to evaluate the performance of our group similarity assessment. The results are shown in table 1, with PR and PE define by Eq.(7).

$$PR = SG\;/N; \qquad PE = SG/AG \tag{7}$$

Where AG denotes the number of groups in current video which are similar with the query group; SG indicates the number of groups in top-N retrieved results (we use top-5 return results, thus $N=5$ in our experiment) which are similar with the query.

Table 1. Group similarity evaluation performance (*Top-5*)

Videos type	$\alpha = 0.0$		$\alpha = 0.3$		$\alpha = 0.5$	
	PR	PE	PR	PE	PR	PE
Medicals	0.68	0.71	0.81	0.92	0.72	0.76
News	0.64	0.76	0.79	0.84	0.70	0.73

Table 1 demonstrates that the proposed video group similarity evaluation strategy could be efficiently utilized to help the annotator find interesting video groups. In average, about 65% similar video groups could be retrieved out with only visual features.

By considering semantics, over 80% of similar groups could be retrieved out. However, while α goes higher (e.g. $\alpha=0.5$), the semantics play a more important role in similarity evaluation, accordingly, the retrieval results trend to be consisted with semantically related groups (may not be visually similar).

5 Conclusion

Due to the obvious shortcoming of traditional video annotation strategy, we propose a semi-automatic video annotation framework that employs general video processing techniques to improve the annotation efficiency. We first propose an ontology to describe video content at various levels and with different granularities. Then, the video group detection strategy is utilized to help the annotator explore the video scenario information for annotation. Afterward, the relevance feedback technique and unified video group similarity evaluation scheme are employed to help annotators find the interesting video groups for annotation or visualize the video annotation results. The proposed semi-automatic strategy is better than manual manner in terms of efficiency, and better than automatic scheme in terms of accuracy.

Acknowledgement. Jianping Fan was supported by NSF under contract IIS0208539, Xiangyang Xue was supported by NSF of China under contract 60003017, Chinese National 863 project under contract 2001AA114120, Lide Wu was supported by NSF of China under contract 69935010.

References

1.   S.W. Smoliar; H.J. Zhang, "Content based video indexing and retrieval", *IEEE Multimedia, 1(2), 1994.*
2.   T.G. Aguierre Smith and G. Davenport. "The Stratification System: A Design Environment for Random Access Video". *In 3rd Int'l Workshop on Network and Operating System Support for Digital Audio and Video, 1992.*
3.   R. Weiss, A. Duda, and D. Gifford, " Content-based access to algebraic video", *In IEEE Int'l Conf. on Multimedia Computing and Systems, pp. 140-151, Boston, USA, 1994.*
4.   G. Davenport, M. Murtaugh, "Context: Towards the evolving documentary", *In Proceeding of ACMM Multimedia conference, San Francisco, Nov., 1995*
5.   Marc Davis, "Media streams: An iconic visual language for video annotation", *In IEEE Symposium on Visual Language, pp.196-202, 1993.*
6.   M. Carrer, L. Ligresti, G. Ahanger, T. Little, "An annotation engine for supporting video database population", *Multimedia tools and applications, vol. 5, pp.233-258, 1997.*
7.   J. Fan, W. Aref, A. Elmagarmid, M. Hacid, M. Marzouk, X. Zhu, "MultiView: Multilevel video content representation and retrieval", *Journal of Electronic imaging, 10 (4), 2001.*
8.   X. Zhu, H. Zhang, Liu W., C. Hu, L. Wu, "A new query refinement and semantics integrated image retrieval system with semi-automatic annotation scheme", *Journal of Electronic Imaging, 10 (4). pp.850-860, October 2001.*
9.   X. Zhu, J. Fan, W. Aref, A. Elmagarmid, "ClassMiner: Mining medical video content structure and events towards efficient access and scalable skimming", *In Proc. of ACM SIGMOD Workshop on Data Mining and Knowledge Discovery, June, WI, 2002.*

Shot Classification of Sports Video Based on Features in Motion Vector Field

Xiao-dong Yu, Ling-yu Duan, and Qi Tian

Laboratories for Information Technology,
National University of Singapore, Singapore
{xdyu, lingyu, tian}@lit.a-star.edu.sg

Abstract. In this paper, we present a novel approach for tennis video analysis, which can automatically classify video shots into 5 classes based on MPEG motion vectors and other features. Two types of features have been used: domain-independent features, such as the local motion activity and the persistent camera pan motion, and domain-dependent, such as the motion activity ratio in the court model. Combining these low-level features with domain knowledge of the tennis game, we can categorize the tennis video shots into five classes, which cover majority of the live tennis video shots, and derive semantic annotation for all shot classes. The results can be used in the higher-level video analysis, including structure analysis, table of content extraction for sports video, video summary and personalization. The proposed approach can easily be extended to analyzing other sports.

1 Introduction

With the increasing demand for methods to manage and retrieve the video data effectively, content-based video analysis has attracted much research interests since 1990's. Existing works can be classified into two categories: syntactic approach and semantic approach. Syntactic approaches focus on analysis of low-level features, such as color, texture, edge, objects trajectory, etc.. They mainly address the problems of shot segmentation and shot clustering [1-3]. Although they are usually generic and robust in processing the large variety of the video contents, they provide little semantic information that interests the users . For high-level video analysis, semantic approaches combine with domain knowledge are necessary.

Compared with other videos, sports videos are more suitable for semantic analysis. Sports videos usually have clearly defined temporal/spatial structure and domain rules. Additionally, there are a fixed number of camera views and each scene or story unit usually contains one shot only to cater for the requirement of real-time broadcasting. Thus, there are finite shot classes in sports video that can easily be distinguished.

In this paper, we discuss the application of motion information in sports video analysis. Motion information is abundant in sports videos and was previously exa-

Y.-C. Chen, L.-W. Chang, and C.-T. Hsu (Eds.): PCM 2002, LNCS 2532, pp. 253-260, 2002.
© Springer-Verlag Berlin Heidelberg 2002

mined for event detection in sports videos[4,5]. However, to the best of our knowledge, few studies have explored its application on structure analysis of sports videos.

In this paper, we present a novel approach to classify sports video shots based on features in motion vector field. These features, either domain-independent or domain-dependent, describe some unique characteristics of the specific shot class. Combining with the domain knowledge, we can derive semantic annotation for each shot from these low-level features.

An overview diagram of the proposed approach is shown in Figure 1. The system is composed of three modules. The first module is a MPEG video parser, which extracts motion vectors directly from the MPEG video. The second module is for low-level motion feature computing. Firstly, we estimated the camera motion and local motion. Then, we calculated three motion features from the camera motion parameters and local motion field. In the third module, we classified the video shots by combining the motion features with domain-specific rules of tennis video. In our system, the shot boundaries were selected manually.

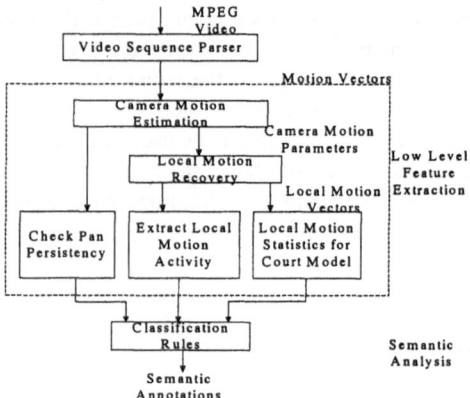

Fig. 1. Overview diagram of tennis shot classification

In Section 2, we first present the classes defined in our approach. Then, the motion features we used are described in Section 3, including their characteristics in different shot classes and measurement. The classification rules are discussed in Section 4. Experimental results and discussions are given in Section 5. Finally, conclusion and future work are summarized in Section 6.

2 Shot Classes in Tennis Video

We define five shot classes for the tennis video based on their contents. They are listed in Table 1.

The court-view-playing shot is a long shot captured by a camera aligned with the center of service line. It covers the scene in which players is playing. Medium-view-player-following shots and close-up-head-tracking shots are two kinds of shots taken during the break of the game. They usually present right before a serve or after a point so they can be used to segment the tennis video into play-break sequence. The site-bird-view shot is a static long shot that is taken far away from the court to give the viewer a panorama of the court. It normally appears before a game begins. The audience shot is taken at the end of a game or after a highlight with a static or panorama shot.

Table 1. Shot classes in tennis video

Shot classes	Court-view-playing	Medium-view-player-following	Close-up-head-tracking	Site-bird-view	Audience
Semantic annotations	Playing	Players' gestures before a serve or after a point	Players' head before a serve or after a point	Game begin	Game end, highlight after a point
Sample Image					

3 Motion Features Extracted from Moton Vector Field

3.1 Camera Motion Estimation and Local Motion Recovery

The motion features in our approach are extracted based on the camera motion and the local motion estimated from the motion vector field.

We employed an affine model [6] with the M-estimator [7] to estimate the camera motion. The affine model is defined as follows,

$$
\begin{bmatrix} u \\ v \end{bmatrix} = \begin{bmatrix} 1 & x & y & 0 & 0 & 0 \\ 0 & 0 & 0 & 1 & x & y \end{bmatrix} \bullet [a_1 \ \ a_2 \ \ a_3 \ \ a_4 \ \ a_5 \ \ a_6]^T \tag{1}
$$

where (x, y) is the coordinate of a macroblock in the current frame, (u,v) is the motion vector associated with this macroblock, $\Xi = (a_1, a_2, a_3, a_4, a_5, a_6)^T$ is the parameters for the affine transformation model.

To estimate the parameters in the affine model, a commonly used approach is to employ the least square estimation (LSE). However, it is proved that the simple LSE is sensitive to the outliers. To reduce the influence of outliers, we apply a robust estimation technique derived form the maximum-likelihood-theory that is called the M-estimator [7]. The principle of the M-estimator is that within an iterative structure, a weight factor $w^{(n)}$ is assigned to each motion vector in the each iteration to reduce the influence of the outliers. The weight factor is calculated as a function of the estimated error $\varepsilon^{(n)}$, which is the n-th motion vector. This process is repeated until the convergence of the parameters.

Once the camera motion parameters are estimated, we recover the local motion by compensating the motion vector field with global motion. A motion vector V can be considered as a sum of two vectors: global motion vector G, from the movement of the camera, and the local motion vector L, from the movement of the moving objects. The local motion L can be recovered from V and G as follows,

$$L = V - G. \tag{2}$$

3.2 Motion Features in Our Approach

The motion features in our approach are local activity, persistent pan and motion ratio in court model. They are all statistical features within a shot.

The local motion activity is extracted from the local motion vectors recovered in (2). Meng and Chang [6] use morphological operations to delete small false objects and to fill noisy spots after thresholding the local motion vectors. However, in our approach, we don't need to identify and track the objects so we do not apply such kind of operations in our system. We measure the amount of local motion activity within a shot by simply normalizing the sum of the magnitude L for all the local motion vectors that exceed the threshold T_L, which is set from experimental study,

$$Lm = \frac{\sum\limits_{\text{for all } L > T_L} L}{H \cdot W \cdot F} \tag{3}$$

where H is the height of the image, W the width of the image, F the frame number within this shot.

The local motion activity L_M is a feature to distinguish between wide-angle shot and telescopic shot. As we observed, there are usually no dominant objects in the wide-angle shots, such as bird-view shots, court-view shots and audience shots, due to the long distance between the camera and the scene; on the other hand, dominant objects normally present in the telescopic shots, such as medium-following shots and close-up shots.

The persistent pan is a cue to discriminate the pan-dominant shots from the others [5]. Pan is common photography technique used in sports video. Pan-dominant shots include medium-following shots and panorama of audience shots. To make our approach robust, we use the direction of pan rather than its amplitude since we found that the later is more sensitive to noise in the motion vectors.

In the pan persistence checking module of our system, we accumulated the number of P-frames in each consistent direction within a shot. The positive number stands for right pan and negative for left. The number will be reset to zero when a different panning direction is encountered. At the end of each shot, we will get a sequence of the P-frame numbers for the persistent pan in this shot. For example, the sequence (-2 10 -2 35 -14 9 -30 25 -21 9) indicates that in this shot, there are 2 consecutive P-frames panning left, followed by 10 consecutive P-frames panning right, then 23 consecutive P-frames panning left, etc. To measure the degree of the persistent pan, we select the largest four number of P-frame, *Pmax(i)*, from the sequence and take the normalized sum of their absolute value, R_A, and the normalized sum of their signed value, R_S, as the features to identify the pan-dominant shots from the others.

$$R_A = \frac{\sum |P_{max}(i)|}{\sum P(i)}, \quad R_S = \frac{\sum P_{max}(i)}{\sum P(i)} \tag{4}$$

The motion ratio in court model R_M is a feature to distinguish between court-view shots, bird-view shots and static audience shots. All three shots have no significant camera motion or dominant objects but the local motion in court-view shots has unique motion pattern that is different from the other two shots. As we have observed, there normally exist relatively large amount of local motion in the top and bottom of the frame due to the movement of the players in court-view shots. Similar to the region model[3], we construct a court model for the court-view shots. In this model, the picture is divided into three horizontal regions: the upper region A and lower region C correspond to the active region for the players and the middle region B correspond to the inactive region near the net. The proposition of the height of three region is H_A: H_B: $H_C = 4:2:4$, which is set experimentally.

We define the motion ratio in court model R_M for a shot as follows,

$$R_M = \frac{\sum\limits_f N_A + \sum\limits_f N_C}{\sum\limits_f (N_A + N_B + N_C)} \tag{5}$$

where N_X is the number of macroblocks whose local motion vector exceeds the threshold T_L in the region X and all sum operations are carried out over all P-frames in one shot.

4 Classification Rules

Our classification rules are based on the domain specific rules in tennis video. Each shot class has its own characters for the motion features described in Section 3. The likelihood of shot class is determined by the likelihood of the motion features related to it.

To measure this kind of likelihood and deal with variations of different features, we map the quantitative values of the features L_M, R_A, R_S, R_M to qualitative scales $\overline{Lm}$, $\overline{R_A}$, $\overline{R_S}$, $\overline{R_M}$ by an ad hoc mapping function F(x, T), which restrict the qualitative scales within 0 to 1. If the likelihood of a shot class is in direct proportion to a certain scale M, we use M to represent this likelihood; otherwise, we use $1-M$ to represent this likelihood with inverse proportion. Table 2 summarizes the relationships between the shot classes and motion feature scales. The overall likelihood for each shot class is the normalized sum of the related likelihoods.

Table 2. Relationship between shot class and motion feature

		Court	Medium	Close-up	Static	Panorama
Local motion activity	Character	Small	Large	Large	Small	Small
	Likeli-hood	$1-\overline{Lm}$	$\overline{Lm}$	$\overline{Lm}$	$1-\overline{Lm}$	$1-\overline{Lm}$
Persis-tent Pan	Character	Interlaced pan left and right	Persistent Pan	No	No	Persistent pan
	Likeli-hood	$1-\overline{R_S}$	$\overline{R_A}$	$1-\overline{R_A}$	$1-\overline{R_A}$	$\overline{R_A}$
Motion ratio in court model	Character	Greater than T_{Rs}	N/A	N/A	Smaller than T_{Rs}	N/A
	Likeli-hood	$\overline{R_M}$	N/A	N/A	$1-\overline{R_M}$	N/A
Overall shot class likelihood		S_{court}	S_{medium}	$S_{close-up}$	S_{static}	$S_{panorama}$

It is found the last two classes in Table 2 are a little different from Table 1. This is because the bird-view shots and static audience shots are the same in the characters of the three motion features. We classify them as static-overview shot while picking up panorama as another shot class.

The ad hoc mapping function F(x, T) is designed to satisfy the following requirements: the quantitative scale is in direct proportion to the qualitative feature; the threshold is a turning point to control the algorithm's sensitivity; if the qualitative feature is much greater/smaller than the threshold, the quantitative scale should close to 1/0.

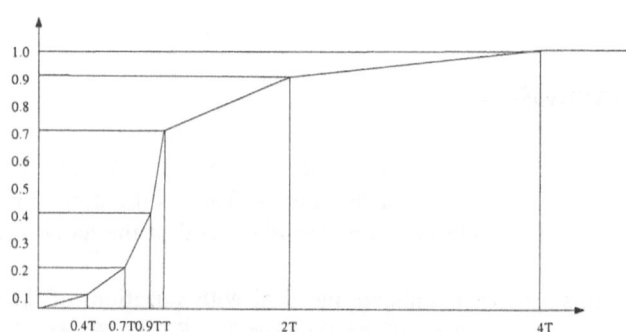

Fig. 2. An ad hoc mapping function F(x, T)

Figure 2 illustrates the ad hoc mapping function we adopted in our approach. It is simple while satisfies all the requirements above. Other types of mapping functions are also applicable. The thresholds in the mapping function are obtained by experimental study: $T_{Lm} = 10$, $T_{Ra} = T_{Rs} = 0.5$, $T_{Rm} = 0.85$.

We select the maximum from the five likelihoods discussed above. If the maximum is much greater than the others, we believe that this shot have a dominant motion characteristics that consistent with certain class so we categorize the shot as this class. If the maximum is undistinguishable or there are more than one maximum, we label the class of this shot as unknown.

5 Experimental Results and Discussion

We have evaluated our approach with four clips from three different games. Table 3 lists the number of correctly classified shots, unclassified shots according to the five pre-defined classes and total shots in each clip.

Table 3. Experimental results

	Wimbledon1	Wimbledon2	Australian	Nasdaq
Length	07'11"	06'26"	08'31"	09'21"
#Total	56	52	67	75
#Correct	50	45	47	51
#Unclassified	2	1	7	9
Accuracy	89%	87%	70%	68%

We found the five classes we defined can cover most tennis shots in all of the test videos. The missed shot classes include close-up of the audience, the commercial shots and some replay shots that cannot be classified as medium-following shots (we have tried to classify some replay shots as medium-following shots as long as they have the similar motion characters with this class).

As long as the accuracy is concerned, the performance for the first two clips are quite satisfactory while for the last two clips the performance is not hot as good as the former. Most errors in the last two clips are caused by model breakdown in the court-view shots. In theory, the local motion in the court-view shots should be very small. But motion vectors are normally random in low-texture area. As the courts of the first two clips are grass courts so there is no such problem. Unfortunately, the courts in the last two clips are synthetic courts that have little texture. So the model based on motion vectors does not perform as well in this case.

6 Conclusion

We have presented a novel approach to classify sports video shots mainly based on features in motion vector field, taking the tennis video as an example. By using features in the compressed domain, great savings have been achieved and real time video analysis can be expected. The proposed approach can also be easily extended to other sports video analysis since sports videos normally have rich motion features and highly structured. The current method adopted for shot classification is based on heuristic rules, however, general learning methods such as supervised learning can be used for the classification and may improve classification results further.

We are working now to improve the accuracy of shot classification by using more features, such as color, edge to cope with the difficult conditions. Furthermore, we are going to build up higher-level semantic annotations by exploring temporal relationship in the tennis video.

References

1. Alan Hanjalic and Hongjiang Zhang, "An integrated scheme for automated video abstraction based on unsupervised cluster-validity analysis", IEEE Transactions on Circuits and System for Video Technology, vol.9, No.8, Dec. 1999
2. Di Zhong, Hongjiang Zhang, Shih-Fu Chang, "Clustering methods for video browsing and annotation", Storage and Retrieval for Still Image and Video Database, IV, vol. SPIE-2670, pp 239-246, Feb. 1996
3. H.J. Zhang, Y. H. Gong, S. W. Smoliar, S. Y. Tan, "Automatic parsing of news video". In Internatinal Conference on Multimedia Computing and Systems, pp. 45--54, 1994
4. G. Sudhir, John, C.M. Lee, Anil K. Jain, "Automatic classification of tennis for high-level content-based retrieval", IEEE International Workshop Content-based Access of Image and Video Database, 1998, pp 81-90
5. Yap-Peng Tan, Drew D. Saur, Sanjeev R. Kulkarni, Peter J. Ramadge, "Rapid estimation of camera motion from compressed video with application to video annotation", IEEE Transactions on Circuits and Systems for Video Technology, vol.10, No.1, Feb. 2000
6. Jianhao Meng, Shih-Fu Chang, "CVEPS – A Compressed Video Editing and Parsing System", Proc. ACM Multimedia 1996, Boston, MA, Nov. 1996
7. Aljoscha Smolic, Michael Hoeynck, Jens Rainer Ohm, "Low-complexity Global Motion Estimation from P-Frame Motion Vectors for MPEG-7 Applications", Proc. ICIP,2000
8. Patrick Bouthemy, Marc Gelgon, Fabrice Ganansia, " A unified approach to shot change detection and camera motion characterization", IEEE Transactions on Circuits and Systems for Video Technology, vol. 9, No. 7, October, 1999

Movie Content Retrieval and Semi-automatic Annotation Based on Low-Level Descriptions

Wenli Zhang[1], XiaoMeng Wu[1], Shunsuke Kamijo[1], Yoshitomo Yaginuma[2], and Masao Sakauchi[1]

[1]Institute of Industrial Science, University of Tokyo,Meguro-ku 4-6-1 Komaba, 153-8505, Japan,
[2]National Institute of Multimedia Education 2-12,WAKABA, MIHAMA-KU, CHIBA, 261-0014, Japan
zhang@sak.iis.u-tokyo.ac.jp

Abstract. In this paper, we present a semantic retrieval and semi-automatic annotation system for movies, based on the regional features of video images. The system uses a 5-dimensional GBD-tree structure to organize the low-level features: the color, area, and minimal bounding rectangle coordinates of each region that is a segment of a key frame. We propose a regionally based "semantic" object retrieval method that compares color, area, and spatial relationships between selected regions to distinguish them from background information. Using this method, movie information can be retrieved for video data containing the same objects based upon object semantics. In addition, a semi-automatic annotation method is proposed for annotating the matched "semantic" objects for further use. A retrieval system has been implemented that includes semantic retrieval and semi-automatic annotation functions.

1 Introduction

In recent years, advances in video technology have made it possible to access huge amounts of video data. In order to deal with these data more efficiently, a framework is required to handle this kind of data source. In our previous work [8], we proposed a framework for movie video data, the *Video Stream Description Language for TV Movie Shows (VSDL-TV)*. In *VSDL-TV*, we defined methods for describing video content according to the video structure, and proposed a set of fundamental operational methods for use with these descriptions. Furthermore, we defined several application-oriented methods that can be stored in *VSDL-TV*, which can be used in combination with our fundamental operational methods. *VSDL-TV* provides a powerful environment for establishing a variety of applications for movie videos. Figure 1 shows an overview of *VSDL-TV*.

The data structure in *VSDL-TV* follows that which is inherent in videos' structure, from scene, to shot, to frame, to object and finally to region. Each video object consists of two parts: *a descriptive part* and *a method part*. In our previous work, we used *D*ynamic *P*attern matching (*DP* matching) to annotate video scenes by referencing matching movie videos and their scripts [7]. As a result, keywords such as a character's name or a location can be extracted from a script for annotation on the corresponding video. The descriptions of the video and scenes, which we call "high-level descriptions", are stored in **XML** (eXtensive Markup Language) format.

Y.-C. Chen, L.-W. Chang, and C.-T. Hsu (Eds.): PCM 2002, LNCS 2532, pp. 261–270, 2002.
© Springer-Verlag Berlin Heidelberg 2002

In this paper, we focus on the layers below a shot and on the "low-level descriptions" extracted from key frames. A shot is a sequence, a set of consecutive frames. To reduce storage space, only a representative frame (called a key frame) from each shot used is stored in the system. Each key frame consists of several segmented regions (Fig. 2). The color, area ratio, and coordinates of the minimal bounding rectangle of a region can be obtained for each segmented region.

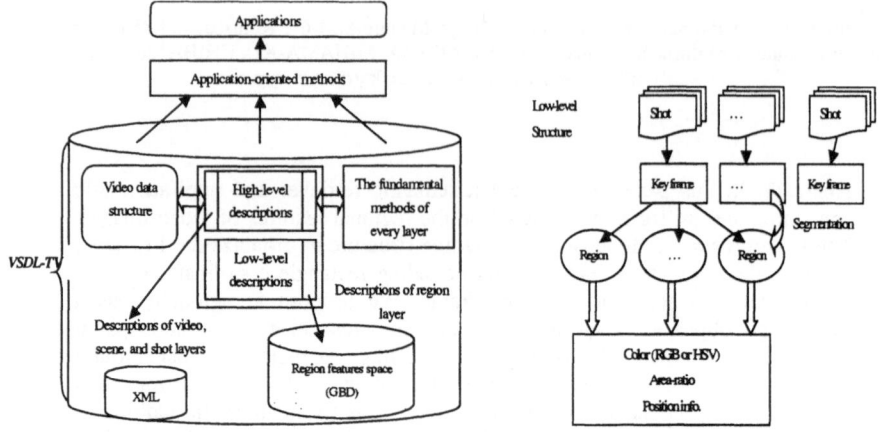

Fig. 1. VSDL-TV overview   **Fig. 2.** Structure of the lower layers

To improve retrieval efficiency, we use an indexing tree structure, a 5-dimensional GBD-tree, to store the following regional features as indices: the color (HVC) and the coordinates of a region's minimal bounding rectangle. In recent years, the K-D-B [2], R [3], SS [10], and SR trees [4] have been proposed for multi-dimensional nearest-neighbor queries. Multi-dimensional tree structures have been used in still-image databases such as QBIC [1] and Visual Seek [12]. However, except for a few systems such as QBIC [1] and VIR [11], little work has been done on video databases. In our research, the GBD-tree [5] was chosen for organizing multi-dimensional feature spaces for the following reasons:

1. Compared with [4] and [10], the GBD-tree is more effective than a tree that has less than five dimensions.
2. The R-tree is a well-known tree structure that has already been used in some image and video databases [1] [12]. Like R-tree, GBD-tree also uses minimal bounding rectangles as an index. However, according to [5], GBD-tree has faster insertion and deletion functions, and performs better at "range retrieval" than R-tree
3. GBD-tree was developed by our research group.

In this paper, we propose a regionally based "semantic" object retrieval method based on a 5-dimensional-feature space that considers color, area ratios and spatial relationships between regions. Images containing varying sizes and locations of the query object can be retrieved using this method. This method, which we have developed as part of our research, differs from other related works [12] [13]. The problem of grouping regions to "semantic" objects is an area of ongoing research. Many related works, such as [13], restrict their attention to regions only. By using our proposed retrieval method, "semantic" objects can be grouped automatically, based upon the regions used for a query. Moreover, a semi-automatic annotation method is proposed for annotating the matched "semantic" objects for further use. A retrieval system has also been implemented that includes semantic retrieval and semi-automatic annotation functions.

The rest of this paper is organized as follows: Section 2 discusses the method used for obtaining the low-level features. Section 3 presents a 5-dimensional feature space using GBD-tree and a regionally based "semantic object" retrieval method. Section 4 proposes a semi-automatic annotation method. Section 5 describes our implementation of the proposed system and Section 6 gives a summary of our work and discusses possible future work.

2   Obtaining the Low-Level Descriptions

There are many image segment methods [15] [16] [17] that can be used to extract features such as the color, texture, shape, and motion of regions. In this paper, we have chosen to use a split-merge segmentation algorithm [9] that was developed by our research group to obtain some of these low-level descriptions. By using the method described in [9], an image can be segmented into several regions. Then, a composite feature of color, area percentage, and position (minimal bounding rectangle) is extracted for each region. This composite feature is given by:

$$(meanH, meanV, meanC, Area\text{-}Rate, X_{min}, Y_{min}, X_{max}, Y_{max}, frame\text{-}number),$$

where *meanH, meanV, and meanC* denote the mean values of hue, value, and chroma for a region, respectively. *Area-Rate* indicates the ratio of a region's area to the whole image. $X_{min}, Y_{min}, X_{max}, Y_{max}$ indicate the coordinates of the minimal-bounding rectangle of a region relative to the top-left vertex of the whole image, and *frame-number* denotes this position of the image on the time axis for a video sequence.

3   Low-Level Features Space

3.1   Indexing Using GBD-Tree

To improve retrieval performance, we use GBD tree[5] to organize the low-level features for the reasons stated in *Section 1*. Using this method, retrieval performance for an image is improved; it is almost ten times better than a similar retrieval request from a linear file [9].

Originally, GBD-tree was proposed for use with very large spatial databases, such as a GIS system; it is a binary and balanced multi-way tree that stores spatial objects as a hierarchy of **minimal bounding rectangle**s (**MBRs**). Figure 3 (a) shows the spatial decomposition. Sub-regions in a GBD-tree are generated only by successive binary divisions, where the dividing axis is selected alternately between the x- and y-axis for two-dimensional cases. Figure 3 (b) shows the tree structure.

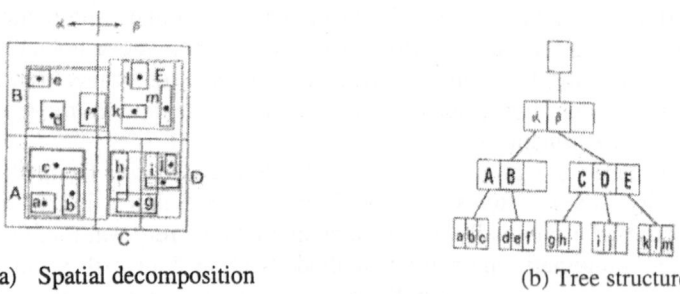

(a) Spatial decomposition   (b) Tree structure

Fig. 3. Outline of a GBD-Tree

Based on GBD-tree, we propose a five-dimensional feature space that includes three-dimensional color information about a region -- hue, value, and chroma -- and the two-dimensional position coordinates of the minimal bounding rectangle of a region. The position coordinates of the **MBR** are the top-left coordinate (X_{min}, Y_{min}) and bottom-right coordinate (X_{max}, Y_{max}). They can be treated as a plane in two-dimensional space. The values of the area-rate and the frame-number are not used as indices. However, they are stored as data objects for future use.

3.2 The "Semantic" Object Retrieval Method

The segmentation and indexing steps are completed by comparing similarities in color, spatial relationships (left, right, up, down, overlap) and area-rate between a query image and the key frames. Then, the "semantic" object (such as a person object) query can be realized. The main focus of our method is on deciding which regions should be used for a semantic object query. The detailed steps are as follows.

- Choose a template key-frame containing the query object (person, car, or other).
- Segment the template key-frame into N major regions, $\{R_1, R2, ..., R_N\}$, and obtain the features of each of these N regions.
- Select the meaningful regions from a segmented template key-frame, $\{R_{m1}, R_{m2}, ..., R_{mn}\}$, where $m1, m2,.., mn \in \{1,..., N\}$ for a query. For example, to query a person object, the selected regions could include those showing a person's hair, face, and body.
- Each key frame in a 5-dimensional feature space that contains a region set of $\{R'_1, R'_2, ..., R'_N\}$, is considered to be a final candidate if it contains regions $\{R'_{k1}, R'_{k2}, ..., R'_{kn}\}$ ($k1, k2,.., kn \in \{1,..., N\}$ that satisfy the following conditions:

(1) The distance of the color: Distance (R_{mi}, R'_{ki}) < Threshold$_{color}$, $mi, ki \in \{m1,..., mn\}$.

$$\text{Distance}(R_{mi,} R'_{ki}) = \sqrt{(H_{R_{mi}} - H_{R'_{ki}})^2 + (V_{R_{mi}} - V_{R'_{ki}})^2 + (C_{R_{mi}} - C_{R'_{ki}})^2}$$

(2) The spatial relationships: The spatial relation of $(R_{mi}, R_{mi+1}) \cong$ the spatial relation of

$(R'_{ki}, R'_{ki+1}))$. Figure 4 shows an example of assessing spatial relationships between

regions.

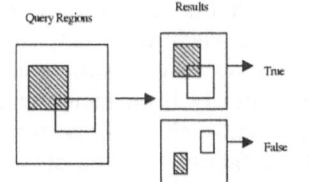

Fig. 4. Spatial relationships between regions

(3) The area ratio between regions:

$$| (Area_{Rmi} / Area_{Rmi+1}) - (Area_{R'ki} / Area_{R'ki+1}) | < Threshold_{Area}, \ mi, ki \in \{m1,...,mn\}$$

For a query operation, the first step is to obtain a set of candidate objects from a search of all of the features of $\{R_j, R2, ..., R_N\}$ in the five-dimensional space by using their color features (H, V, C).. The second step considers the spatial relationships between objects. Finally, the area ratios of the regions in the resulting set are compared to get a secondary candidate set. Since our proposed retrieval method considers the area ratio and the spatial relationships between the regions and detects non-use regions such as background or other noise regions, images containing *varying sizes and locations* of the query object can be successfully retrieved. This is the key difference between our work and other, related works [12] [13]. For the retrieval method proposed in [9], colors, spatial relationships and area-ratios are also employed. However, the query is applied only to the top five regions according to area size. These five regions might be any regions with comparatively large areas, whose "semantic" meaning may not be what is required. Therefore, the method might realize only a partial retrieval of a "non-semantic object".

4 The Semi-annotation Method

The "semantic object" retrieval method improves the processing of region groupings related to an object. Since we retrieve data using regions, we can find regions that match by highlighting matched regions in returned key frames. For example, since we know the coordinates of the minimal bounding rectangle of matched regions, "semantic objects" containing these regions can be determined. Figure 5 shows an example of "semantic object" retrieval.

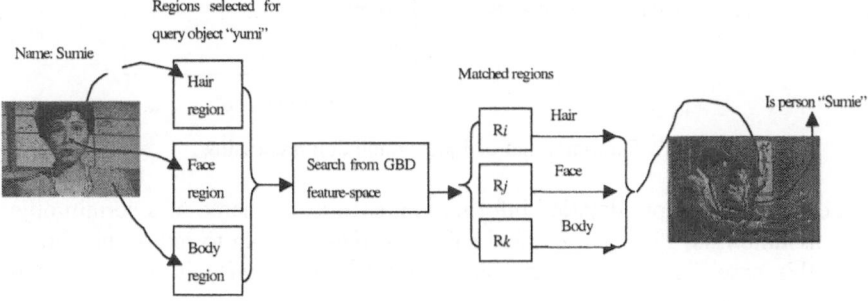

Fig. 5. Example of a "semantic object" grouped by regions.

Therefore, the matched object in Fig. 5, which is contained in the shot, can be annotated with abstract keywords such as object name, object position, etc. For a matched object's annotation, its low level descriptions (color, area, coordinates) that match the query image have already been memorized in a buffer. The high-level descriptions used for annotation, such as a person's name or personal relation information (such as friends or family), can be obtained from the movie data. The position of the person object in the frame can be obtained from the retrieval results. Therefore, the user only needs to select those frames that contain the true query object, ignoring any false ones. This has to be done only once manually using the supplied interface. Subsequently, any annotation requirements will be completed automatically. Thus, we have chosen to call this whole procedure "Semi-automatic annotation". Figure 6 shows the detailed steps of semi-automatic annotation.

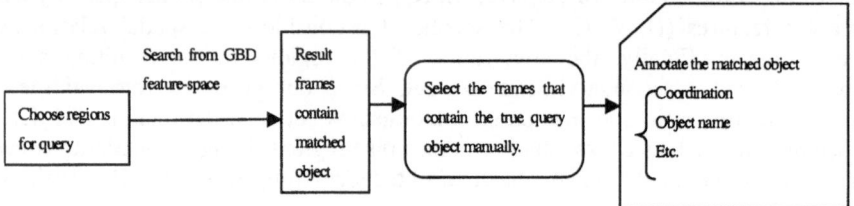

Fig. 6. Semi-automatic annotation steps

In our system, the high-level descriptions of every video structure such as scene, shot, frame, object, and region are stored in XML format. Within the object level, some specified labels such as person, car, and building are used. Processing object annotation adds new items into the XML file. A function called *setAnnotation()* has been implemented for this purpose.

Figure 7 shows an example of the difference in the content of an XML file between "before annotation", Fig. 7(a), and "after annotation", Fig.7 (b). The person object (ex. name is "Yumi") contains two regions, called "Reg1" and "Reg2".

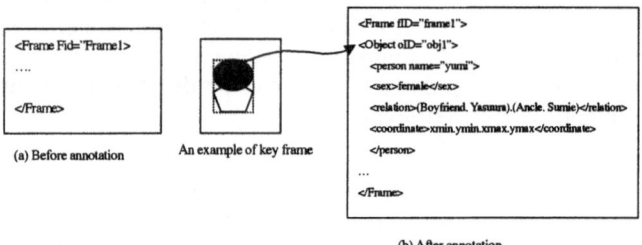

Fig. 7. Semi-automatic object annotation processing

When the user wants more detailed information, such as the name of a certain object (here we assume it is "obj1"), a method called *getWho()* is run to return the value of name, in this case, "Yumi". The method *getObjCoord("yumi")* is used to get the position of the specified object (in this case "Yumi") in the frame.

5   System Implementation

A system that can deal with semantic retrieval and semi-automatic annotation has been built. Figure 8 shows the architecture of the system. The system includes a video database for storage of the movie videos, a key frame database for storage of key frames, a region feature space (GBD-tree) for storage of the low-level features, and a sample-frame database for storage of the template images of typical characters or typical subjects. The system can store seven movies with a total of 10,892 key frames. Visual Café 4.0 was used to create the interface, and some parts of the source were written in C++. Figure 8 shows the architecture of the system.

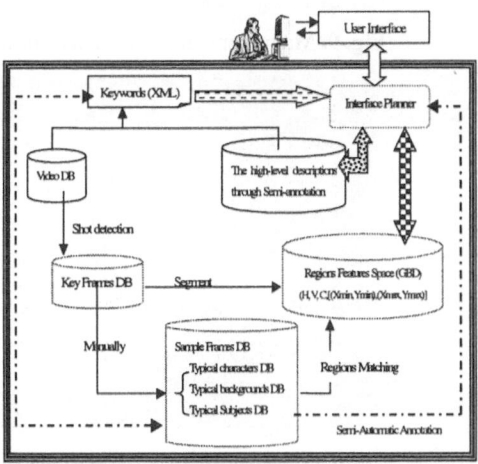

Fig. 8. Architecture of the system

Initially, clear image lists are created of the whole body of the main character, or full-face frames, from every movie (Fig. 9). These image frames are used as template images and are detected manually from the videos and stored in the system in advance. It is also possible to assign a name or other related information to these images. From the interface shown in Fig. 9, the user can choose one template image that contains the query actor. As shown in Fig. 10, for a query on the woman object with green clothes, the user may choose regions with semantic meaning such as hair, face, or body. Based on these three regions, "semantic object" retrieval can be realized. Figure 11 shows a resulting shot containing the green-clothed woman object that appears in thirteen shots in the movie. The test results showed that eight true frames appeared in a total of twelve resulting frames. For annotation, the user must manually select the frames that contain the woman object. Keywords such as name, sex, or her relations, which would be prepared beforehand, can be used for annotation automatically. The interface provides two buttons for the user to decide whether the frame is to be selected for annotation (Fig. 11).

When a movie is replayed over an Internet stream, the user can click on the annotated objects in a movie shot and obtain relevant descriptions of the object. This function can be realized by using the tool *Synchronized Multimedia Integration Language* (*SMIL*)[14]. *SMIL* provides a hyperlink element that allows a hyperlink to be associated with a complete media object in a movie video.

Fig. 9. Main member s' image lists of a movie

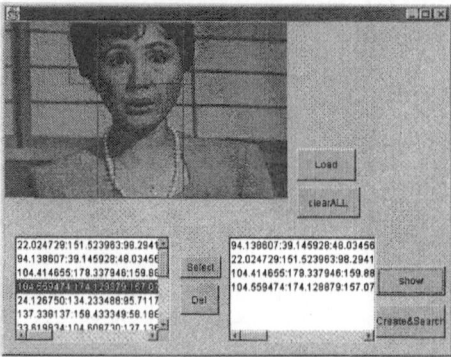

Fig. 10. Select regions for query person objects.

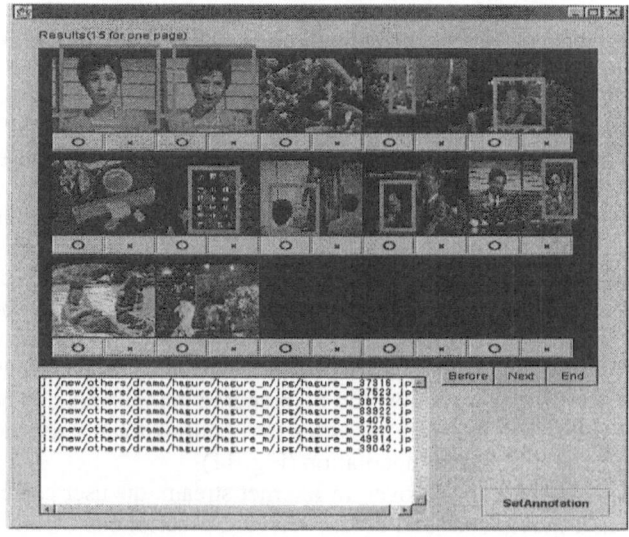

Fig. 11. Interface for Semi-automatic annotation

6 Conclusions and Future Work

In this paper, we have presented a regionally based semantic retrieval and semi-automatic annotation system for movies, with a 5-dimensional feature space indexed by GBD-tree. Presently, only an object in a key frame can be annotated by our proposed method. Future work should consider the possibility of being able to automatically annotate an object that appears in only one shot, by making use of our semi-automatic annotation method. Our future work will also include realization of the semantic utilization system.

Acknowledgement. The authors wish to thank Prof. Yutaka Osawa, and Mr. Teijiro Hayashi of the University of Saitama.

References

[1] M.Flickner, H.Sawhney, W.Niblack, J.Ashley, Q.Huang, B.Dom, M.Gorkani, J.Hafner, D.Lee, D.Petkovic, D.Steele, and P.Yanker,"Query by image and video content: The QBICsystem", IEEE Comput., Mag., vol.28, pp.23-32,Sept.1995

[2] J.T.Robinson,"The K-D-B-tree: a Search Structure for Large Mutidimensional Dynamic Indexes", Proc. ACM SIGMOD, Ann Arbor, USA, pp.10-18, Apr. 1981.

[3] A.Guttman,"R-tree: a Dynamic Index Structure for Spatial Searching", Proc, ACM SIGMOD, Boston, USA, pp.47-57, Jun.1984

[4] D.A.White and R.Jain,"Similarity Indexing with SS-tree". Proc.of the 12th Int.Conf.on Data Engineering. New Orleans, USA. Pp.516-523.Feb.1996.

[5] Y.Osawa, and M.Sakauchi, "A New Type Data Structure with Homogeneous Nodes Suitable for a Very Large Spatial Database", Proc. Of 6th International Conference on Data Engineering, pp.296-303 (Feg.1990).

[7] W.Zhang, Y.Yaginuma, M. Sakauchi, "A Video Movie Annotation System--Annotation Movie with its Script--", International Conf. on Signal Processing of 16th IFIP World Computer Congress, Vol.II, pp.1362-1366, Beijing, China (2000-08)

[8] W.Zhang, Y.Cao, Y.Yaginuma, M.Sakauchi, "Proposal of Movie Video Stream Description Language and its Application", IEEE International Conference on Multimedia and EXPO2001, Tokyo, Japan (2001-08)

[9] Y.cao, Y.Yaginuma, M.Sakauchi, "Partial Image Retrieval Using Color Regions and Spatial Relationships", The Sixth IFIP Working Conference on Visual Database Systems, May 29-31,2002,Brisbane, Australia (Accepted).

[10] N.Katayama, S.Satoh," The SR-tree: An Index Structure for High Dimensional Nearest Neighbor Queries", Proc. Of the 1997 ACM SIGMOD, Tucson, USA, pp.369-380, May 1997.

[11] A. Gupta and R.Jain, "Visual Information Retrieval", Comm. ACM, Vol.40, No.5, pp.71-79, 1997.

[12] John R.Smith and Shih-Fu Chang, "VisualSEEk: a fully automated content-based image query system", ACM Multimedia 96, Boston, MA, November 20,1996.

[13] Shih-Fu Chang, William Chen, Horace J.Meng, Hari Sundaram, and Di Zhong, " A Fully Automated Content-based Video Search Engine Supporting Spatiotemporal Queries", IEEE Transactions on circuits and systems for video technology, Vol.8, No.5, Sep.1998.

[14] http://www.smi.co.jp/web-cm/smil/about.html

[15] D.Comaniciu and P.Meer, "Robust Analysis of Feature Spaces: Color Image Segmentation", Proc. Of IEEE Conf. on Computer Vision and Pattern Recognition, pp750-755, 1997.

[16] Y.Deng, C.Kenney, M.S.Moore, and B.S.Manjunath, "Peer Group Filtering and Perceptual Color Image Quantization", Proc. Of IEEE ISCAS, vol.4, pp.21-24, 1999.

[17] Y.Deng, B.S.Manjunath, and H.Shin, "Color Image Segmentation", Proc. Of IEEE Computer Society Conf. on Computer Vision and Pattern Recognition, pp.446-451, 1999.

An Index Model for MPEG-2 Streams

W.Q. Wang and W. Gao

(Institute of Computing Technology, Chinese Academy of Sciences, BeiJing, P.R.China, 100080)
{wqwang, wgao}@ict.ac.cn

Abstract. The MPEG standards are playing a more and more important role in many multimedia applications now, and will continue in the future. An effective index model is presented for MPEG-1, 2 streams in this paper. Moreover, the algorithm of constructing the index for MPEG-1, 2 streams is designed, as well as the solution to access any frame in the streams rapidly based on the model. The experimental results have shown the index model can provide the power of precisely positioning a frame quickly and can be applied to randomly accessing a frame effectively.

1 Introduction

As the computation power of desktops increases, the cost of storage media decreases, and broadband networks expand, video will become an important media type in digital libraries and bring up many attractive services. To make users freely browse video, the power of very fast accessing any frame is required. Nowadays, though many VCD/DVD software players (WinDVD, PowerDVD, etc.) provide the similar functionality, i.e. VCR, their power of positioning a frame is very limited, since many multimedia applications demand shorter response time and higher precision of positioning a frame to serve thousands of users concurrently. For instance, in a large video database system, which supports the service of content-based browse, the users frequently issue such requests as skipping to another shot, scene or story, and the system must locate and skip precisely to the first frame of that content unit in the shortest response time. In the application context, those software players cannot provide satisfying services. Firstly, their cost of positioning a frame is very high due to byte comparison operations during locating picture headers in MPEG streams. Though [1] presents a method of fast accessing I frames through combining coarse and minute hop during locating picture headers, it is not an optimal solution since byte content comparison still exists. Secondly, the players can only locate I frames when users issue the fast forward or fast backward requests. But it is common that the first frame of content units is a P or B frame.

In the paper, we present an index model for MPEG streams as a solution of fast accessing any frame in MPEG video documents. We observe few researchers have addressed the problem. Through experimental evaluation, we believe it is an effective solution. Based on it the system can access a frame very fast in MPEG documents, no matter what its encoding type is. The time cost of positioning is very low and can be even ignored compared with that in [1]. At the same time, the time cost can be almost

Y.-C. Chen, L.-W. Chang, and C.-T. Hsu (Eds.): PCM 2002, LNCS 2532, pp. 271–278, 2002.

considered as a constant, that is, it is irrelevant to the position of the frame in the MPEG streams.

The remaining part of the paper is organized as follows. Section 2 describes a novel index model in detail, and then some inherent properties are derived. In section 3, two significant algorithms related to the model are described. One is used to generate the index file. The other addresses how to access the specified frame at the lowest time cost, exploiting the index file generated. Section 4 gives some experimental results, to evaluate the performance of the solution. The time complexity of the algorithm to access a frame randomly is further discussed. At the end, we summarize the paper and give some conclusions.

2   The Index Model for MPEG Video Documents

Generally there exist three distinct encoding types of pictures- I, P and B pictures. For MPEG-1 documents, a picture is a frame; for MPEG-2 documents, it may be either a frame or a field. I and P pictures are both called reference pictures. A GOP (Group of Picture) is a set of the consecutive frames between the adjacent I frames [2][3]. We assume the GOP structure of the MPEG video documents to be indexed is always regular. The assumption holds for general MPEG video streams. Here, the "regular" means the GOP structure keeps the same and the number of the B frames between two reference frames is always the same through the whole stream in display order. The formal description of the index model is as follows.

Definition 1. An index X of an MPEG document is a 2-tuple $<G, D>$, where G is a set of the descriptions of global features of the MPEG document, as well as those of the index file. D is a set of the index units in display order.

Definition 2. A sub-group of pictures (SGOP) is a set of all the frames between adjacent reference frames in display order. If the reference frame in the sub-group of pictures is an I frame, we call it I SGOP, or else the SGOP is a P SGOP.

As illustrated in Fig. 1, the GOP in the figure consists of an I SGOP and three P SGOPs. Generally, a GOP is made up of an I SGOP and a number of P SGOPs.

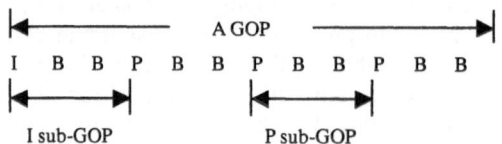

Fig. 1. The conception of sub-GOP

Definition 3. An I or P index unit is a 4-tuple, $<tag, numB, ipPos, dif\_Bs>$, which contains the index information of the corresponding I SGOP and P SGOP. The *tag* is the type of the index unit. The *numB* is the number of the B frames in the SGOP related to the index unit. The *ipPos* contains the position information of the reference frame in the corresponding SGOP. The *dif_Bs* is a set of *numB* elements, and the nth element is the position description of the nth B frame in the SGOP relative to the position of the reference frame.

Definition 4. The component G of an index X is an 8-tuple, $G=<framerate,$ *frames, bRegular, Gop_NP, Gop_NB, BL_GopIdx, BaseFrm, TypeStream>*. The *framerate* is the frame rate of the document. The *frames* is the total frames. The *bRegular* is a tag to indicate whether the GOP structure is regular. We assume it is always true and the field can be used to extend the model in the future. The *Gop_NP* and *Gop_NB* are respectively the number of P and B frames in each GOP. The *BL_GopIndex* is the byte cost to index a GOP. The *BaseFrmNum* is the sequence number of the first I frame in the MPEG document. The *TypeStream* is the type of the MPEG stream, such as the program stream, the video elementary stream, etc.

Normally the value of *BaseFrmNum* is zero. The model also permits it is not zero in some special situation. For instance, it is common for digital TV programs recorded by us through a satellite receiver and other devices. Thus the frames with the sequence number from 0 to *BaseFrmNum* -1 cannot be decoded correctly. Therefore, the index model only constructs the index for the frames with the sequence number from the *BaseFrmNum* to the *frames*. The *TypeStream* is a significant syntax element, since the syntax and semantics of the *ipPos* and *dif_Bs* depends on its value. From the foregoing definitions the following conclusions can be easily derived.

Conclusion 1. The index model can access the specified frame based on time information. The formula (1) can convert time into the sequence number of the frame.

$$Destfrm = CurFrm + TimeLen * framerate \tag{1}$$

Where *CurFrm* and *Destfrm* are respectively the sequence number of the current frame and the target frame, *TimeLen* is the time interval.

Conclusion 2. Given the target frame *Destfrm*, the position *PosIdxI* of the index information of the GOP which *Destfrm* belongs to can be calculated out, using the formula (2) and (3).

$$GopSize = 1 + Gop\_NB + Gop\_NB \tag{2}$$

$$PosIdxI = BL\_GopIdx * \text{INT}(DestFrm - BaseFrm / GopSize) \tag{3}$$

Where the function $\text{INT}(x)$ returns the largest integer that is less than or equal to x.

Conclusion 3. If index units for I and P SGOP have the same byte length *Litem*, the position *PosIdx* of the index information of the SGOP which *Destfrm* belongs to can be derived, based on the formulas (4) to (6), where Mod is the modulus operator.

$$nFrmsItem = Gop\_NB / (1 + Gop\_NP) + 1 \tag{4}$$

$$RmFrms = (DestFrm - BaseFrm)\text{Mod } GopSize \tag{5}$$

$$PosIdx = LItem * \text{INT}(RmFrms / nFrmsItem) + PosIdxI \tag{6}$$

Conclusion 4. If each syntax element in an index unit has the constant byte cost, the position information of the *Destfrm* can be extracted from the index X.

From the foregoing discussion, we know if an index file is generated for an MPEG document based on the index model, the position information of any frame can be extracted with very low computation costs. Since the process does not involve any comparison or search of byte content, it provides a very efficient solution to retrieve the frame position information, no matter what encoding type it is.

3   Implementation and Related Algorithms

3.1 The Algorithm of Constructing the Index File

Based on the index model formulated in the section 2, we designed and implemented an indexing tool for MPEG documents (program streams and video elementary streams). Through scanning the MPEG bit stream, the algorithm locates two kinds of important position information: the start position of video PES header and that of picture header. For video elementary streams, only the position information of picture header is extracted and indexed. Meanwhile, the algorithm makes the transformation from decoding order to display order, so that frame order in index files is display order. The arrangement not only makes it very efficient to retrieve frame position information, but also makes it unnecessary to store the frame sequence numbers in the index files, thus saving the space cost of the index files (the information reflecting the space cost is illustrated in Table 1). The detailed algorithm description is given below.

Algorithm-1 construct the index file for MPEG Documents

Input : the MPEG video document, *mpg_fp*
Output : the index file *mpgidx_fp*
Middle variables:
FwdFrmInfo, BwdFrmInfo, AuxFrmInfo: they are respectively used to store the encode types and position information for forward reference frames, backward reference frames, as well as B frames.
  CurFrmInfo, DisFrmInfo: they are pointers to the significant information of current decoded frame and display frame to be indexed
(1) Initilization. Open *mpg_fp* to read, and a temporary file *tmp_fp* to write. Set *Frames*=0.
(2) Scan the MPEG bit stream, and parse various headers to extract the significant information, such as the frame rate, the stream type, etc. If the MPEG program end code or the end of *mpg_fp* is met, go to (7). When a video PES header is met, its position information is stored in the variable *LastVPESHdrPos*. Repeat the step, until a picture header is met. Then its position is stored in the variable *PicHdrPos*. Parse the picture header to extract the picture coding type and picture structure, and store them in the variables *PicCodingType* and *PicStruct*.
(3) Make the conversion from decoding order to display order and let *CurFrmInfo* point to the correct object.
(4) Write the data *PicCodingType, LastVPESHdrPos* and *PicHdrPos* to the object referred to by *CurFrmInfo*
(5) Make *DisFrmInfo* point to the current display frame. If the current display frame is an I frame, check whether the last GOP is a regular one. If the answer is no, report the failure and go to (9). Otherwise, write the information in the object *DisFrmInfo* into the temporary file *tmp_fp*, according to the predefined syntax.
(6) *Frames=Frames*+1, go to (2).
(7) Close the file *tmp_fp*.
(8) Open the index file *mpgidx_fp* and write the parameters described in the definition 4 into the file *mpgidx_fp*. Then append the whole temporary file to the end of *mpgidx_fp*
(9) Close the files *mpg_fp, mpgidx_fp* and *tmp_fp*. Delete the temporary file *tmp_fp*. The algorithm terminates.

3.2 Randomly Access, and Display a Frame Based on the Index Model

It is significant for many multimedia applications to randomly access and display a video frame. We can exploit index files to quickly position a frame, and make the player tool able to access and display any frame in the stream rapidly and accurately. Fig. 2 shows all the frames in a GOP in their display order. In the MPEG streams, the arrangement of the frame data is not consistent with their display order. When we want to access and display a P or B frame in the GOP, it is required to decode other related frames first. With the help of the index file, the system can quickly locate and decode only those frames requisite for decoding the target frame accurately, and ignore the unrelated B frames. For instance, if B12 is to be accessed and displayed (here, the number behind frame encode types refers to the sequence number of the frame in display order), the system just positions and decodes the frames in the following order: I1, P4, P7, P10, P13, B12.

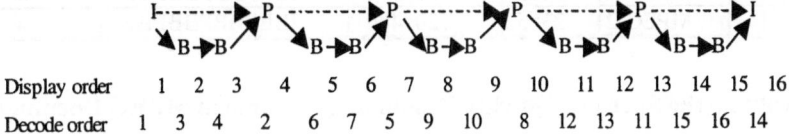

Display order	1	2	3	4	5	6	7	8	9	10	11	12	13	14	15	16
Decode order	1	3	4	2	6	7	5	9	10	8	12	13	11	15	16	14

Fig. 2. Randomly accessing and displaying a frame in the GOP

Algorithm-2 Randomly access, and display a frame based on the index model

> **Input**: the MPEG document mpg_fp, the index file $mpgidx\_fp$,
>   the sequence number $DisFrmNum$ of the target frame
> **Output**: display the target frame
> (1). Open the files mpg_fp and $mpgidx\_fp$ to read. Obtain the related information in the G, and calculate $nFrmsItem$ using the formula (4).
> (2). Calculate the $PosIdxI$ using the formula (2) and (3). Move the file pointer of the $mpgidx\_fp$ to the place specified by the $PosIdxI$, and read an index unit data into the variable $CurIdxer$. Move the file pointer of the mpg_fp to the place specified by $CurIdxer.ipPos$, and decode a frame. Calculate $RmFrms$ using the formula (5)
> (3). Set $LastIdxer=CurIdxer$. If $RmFrms < nFrmsItem$, go to (6).
> (4). Read an index unit data into the variable $CurIdxer$. Move the file pointer of the mpg_fp to the place specified by the $CurIdxer.ipPos$, and decode a frame.
> (5). Set $RmFrms = RmFrms - nFrmsItem$, and go to (3)
> (6). If $RmFrms$ is equal to zero, go to (9).
> (7). Read an index unit data into the variable $CurIdxer$. Move the file pointer of the mpg_fp to the place specified by the $CurIdxer.ipPos$, and decode a frame.
> (8). Move the file pointer of the mpg_fp to the place specified by the $LastIdxer.ipPos + LastIdxer.dif\_Bs[RmFrms-1]$, and decode a frame.
> (9). Display the last decoded frame.

4   Experiments and Analysis

We implemented the algorithms described above, and designed two experiments to evaluate the performance of randomly accessing frames based on the MPEG index files. Several MPEG-1 and MPEG-2 streams with different GOP structures are selected as tested data. The first experiment is carried out on two PCs with PIII-450 CPU, 64M memory, and Pentium 133 CPU, 32M memory respectively. We carry out the second experiment only on the former. The related parameters of the tested streams and the size of the index files generated are tabulated in the Table 1. The statistics show the index file generated is very small and the ratio of its size to that of the corresponding video document is just one of tens of thousands or so.

Table 1. Some feature parameters about the tested streams and their index files

Stream File	Type	File Size (KB)	Frame Dimension	GOP Structure	Index File Size (KB)
A	MPEG-1	47762	352*288	IBBPBBPBB	25
B	MPEG-1	15109	352*240	IBBPBBPBBPBBPBB	12
C	MPEG-2	31237	752*576	IBBPBBPBBPBB	4
D	MPEG-2	23552	720*480	IBBPBBPBBPBB	4

4.1 Evaluate the Speed of Quickly Positioning a Frame in MPEG Documents

In the experiment, the system chooses frame sequence numbers randomly, and then decodes position information from index files. Each operation involves opening the index file, extracting position information and closing the file. After ten thousands of operations, the time cost is recorded. The experimental results are listed in Table. 2. The statistics show that the index model provides a surprisingly fast speed of positioning a frame, which is even 4 times faster than that in [1] under the same computer configuration. Moreover, the speed of positioning frames seems to approximate to a constant. It is independent of frame positions and bit rates of streams.

Table 2. The speed of positioning frames in MPEG streams

File	Operations	Fast Computer[2]		Slow Computer[3]	
		Time cost (s)	Speed (f/s)	Time cost (s)	Speed (f/s)
A	40000	7	5714	99	404
B	80000	15	5333	169	473
C	40000	7	5714	84	476
D	80000	14	5714	189	423

Now we analyze these characteristics theoretically. The algorithm of positioning frames through the index file involves two parts of time cost: the first part ω is consumed by reading the corresponding indexing data for the GOP containing the target frame from hard disks into memory; the other part λ is consumed to compute using the equations (2)~(6) and extract position information from the proper index data block. Because the processing speed of CPU is high faster than the I/O speed of hard disks, i.e., $\omega \gg \lambda$, the total cost $\pi = \omega + \lambda \approx \omega$. Let μ denote the size of disk block units (usually several Ks) read by operating systems each time, and the corresponding time cost is η. In our implementation, the size ρ of the index data corresponding to a GOP is generally tens of bytes at most. Therefore the time cost of extracting position information of a frame is $\pi \approx \omega = 2\eta$ in the worst case, where the index data of the GOP span two disk block units. In the other cases, the cost is $\pi = \eta$. If we assume that access to each frame is of equal probability, the probability of the worst case is proximately $1/\left\lceil \dfrac{u}{\rho} \right\rceil$, and the average time complexity of the algorithm is

$$2\eta / \left\lceil \frac{u}{\rho} \right\rceil + \eta * (1 - 1/\left\lceil \frac{u}{\rho} \right\rceil), \quad \text{i.e.} \quad \eta / \left\lceil \frac{u}{\rho} \right\rceil + \eta \tag{7}$$

If $\mu \gg \rho$, then $\eta / \left\lceil \dfrac{u}{\rho} \right\rceil + \eta$ approximates to η. The analysis result is consistent with observations in the experiment.

4.2 Evaluate the Speed of Randomly Accessing and Displaying Frames

In the experiment, frame sequence numbers are generated randomly for each tested stream. Then, according to the algorithm in section 3.2, the system locates and decodes all the related frames necessary for displaying the target frame, exploiting the index file, and finally the target frame are displayed. We evaluate the performance based on the total time cost after tens of operations in two cases. In the first case (A), the system is constrained to access I frames only. The constraint is canceled in the second case (B). Table 3 tabulates all the experimental results.

Table 3. The experimental results about fast positioning and displaying a frame in MPEG streams on PC with PIII 450 CPU and 64M memory

File	Decoder (f/s)	Operations	Constraints	Time (s)	Speed(f/s)	Ratio
A	31.2	90	Case A	3	30	0.00525
			Case B	7	12.9	0.00226
B	41.2	150	Case A	4	37.5	0.00703
			Case B	13	11.5	0.00201
C	6.5	120	Case A	17	7.1	0.00124
			Case B	59	2	0.00035
D	7.8	60	Case A	7	8.6	0.00151
			Case B	25	2.4	0.00042

The experimental results show it is a satisfying solution to exploit the index model to randomly access and display frames in MPEG documents. When the object randomly accessed is restricted within I frames, we get the performance close to maximum playing power of the decoder for the MPEG-1 steams, and even the better performance for MPEG-2 streams. When the object randomly accessed is any frame type, the performance decreases immensely, compared with the first case. It is because the computing cost for P, B frames is related with their position in a GOP, as well as the structure of the GOP in a given stream. For example, if we want to access and display the last frame in any GOP of the stream Flight.mpg, the system has to decode 7 frames, but only the frame itself is needed to be decoded for an I frame. In the whole process, the decode cost is much higher than other costs (positioning, displaying), and the last column in Table 2 lists the ratio of average positioning time to decoding time. Finally, we must point out that the efficiency of the decoder engine in our experiment is very low, and some famous commercial software can provide over 4 times better performance on average than ours in the same condition. So it can be easily imagined that the support of the index model for the power of randomly accessing any frame will gain further success, with the help of a decoder engine of high performance.

5 Conclusions

This paper presents and discusses an index model for MPEG program streams, which can be extended and used for MPEG transport streams. The algorithm of constructing the MPEG index files based on the model is described in detail, as well as that of randomly accessing and displaying a frame in MPEG documents based on the indexes. The experimental results have shown that the index file can provide an exciting fast system response when the system is required to access a specific frame accurately. Therefore it is preferable for multimedia server-side applications, if they use MPEG documents as their data resources, and serve concurrently to thousands of clients, such as digital libraries, VOD and large video database, as well as the multimedia applications, which exert high requirement of accuracy on browsing and positioning content, such as MPEG oriented non-linear editorial systems. Although the index files consume some storage space, it is just one of tens of thousands of that consumed by the corresponding MPEG documents, so that it can be neglected. Moreover, the higher the bit rate of the MPEG stream is, the less space the index files relatively consumes. Nowadays the price of storage media is becoming lower and lower. Thus the construction and use of the index of MPEG documents is an effective approach to improve the system performance and quality of services in some advanced multimedia applications. The process of generating the index files indeed takes some time, and still needs to scan the whole stream files on the storage media. However, it can be exploited forever, once the index is constructed. Thus, constructing the index for video documents is a good solution especially for those systems, which are required to randomly access some specific frames frequently.

References

[1] W.Q. Chen, W. Gao, "A method of fast searching I pictures in MPEG-2 system stream", Journal of software, pp.520-524. (In Chinese), 1998,7.
[2] International Standard ISO/IEC, 11172, Information technology-coding of moving pictures and associated audio for digital storage media at up to about 1.5Mbits/s, 1993.
[3] International Standard ISO/IEC, 13818, Information technology–generic coding of moving pictures and associated audio, 1995.

MORF: A Distributed Multimodal Information Filtering System

Yi-Leh Wu[1], Edward Y. Chang[1,2], Kwang-Ting Cheng[1,2],
Cheng-Wei Chang[1], Chen-Cha Hsu[1], Wei-Cheng Lai[1], and Ching-Tung Wu[1]

[1] VIMA Technologies, 3944 State Steet, Suite 340, Santa Barbara, CA 93105
[2] Electrical & Computer Engineering, University of California,
Santa Barbara, CA 93106
ywu@vimatech.com, echang@ece.ucsb.edu

Abstract. The proliferation of objectionable information on the Internet has reached a level of serious concern. To empower end-users with the choice of blocking undesirable and offensive Web-sites, we propose a multimodal personalized information filter, named *MORF*. The design of *MORF* aims to meet three major performance goals: efficiency, accuracy, and personalization. To achieve these design goals, we have devised a multimodality classification algorithm and a personalization algorithm. Empirical study and initial statistics collected from the *MORF* filters deployed at sites in the U.S. and Asia show that *MORF* is both efficient and effective, compared to the traditional URL- and text-based filtering approaches.

1 Introduction

Internet is a mixed blessing for home, schools, and workplace. While Internet access has opened up enormous new possibilities, it has also created new hazards in loss of productivity, bandwidth clogging, and corporate or institutional liability. To screen out objectionable information[1], many commercial filtering products have been developed. Most products, however, suffer from low filtering accuracy and lack of personalization capability. In this paper we present *MORF* (Multimodal Objectionable infoRmation Filter), a multimodal (including URL, texts, and images) personalized information filter. *MORF* employs our proposed multimodal classification and personalization algorithms to achieve efficient, effective, and personalized filtering.

The most widely used filters employs the URL-based technique. These filters maintain a "block" list of Web-site addresses. When a user requests a URL, the system checks to see whether the requested URL is on the block list. If yes, the filter refuses the request; otherwise, the request is granted. The drawback of the URL-based techniques is that the block list can quickly become outdated

---

[1] In this paper, unless otherwise stated, objectionable information refers to undesirable and offensive information that can be personally defined; e.g., pornography, hate messages, etc.

Y.-C. Chen, L.-W. Chang, and C.-T. Hsu (Eds.): PCM 2002, LNCS 2532, pp. 279–286, 2002.
© Springer-Verlag Berlin Heidelberg 2002

(according to a report from National Research Counsel, there are 300 to 400 new pornography sites created daily), and hence the filtering accuracy can be low.

The other popular filtering method is based on analyzing the text. A text-based technique analyzes the words in the user's requested content and maintains a list of words that commonly appear at objectionable Web-sites. A text-based filter matches words in the input text with the keywords on the bad-word list. If offensive keywords appear frequently above a tolerable threshold, the Web-site containing the words is regarded as objectionable and blocked. The text-based approach has at least three shortcomings. First, the matching process is language dependent. Second, the lexical meanings of keywords can be ambiguous. For example, some words can be both objectionable and benign depending on their context (e.g. wren tits, wood screws, breast cancer). Third, many objectionable sites (e.g., pornography sites) embed words in images, and therefore, no text is available for text-based analysis.

To overcome the low-accuracy shortcoming of the traditional URL- and text-based approaches while maintaining high filtering efficiency (the filtering activities should not significantly affect network access time and throughput), *MORF* employs a multimodal filtering algorithm. The benefits of this approach can be summarized as follows:

1. High efficiency. The multimodal design improves filtering accuracy (discussed in Section 3) while maintaining high efficiency. If a requested site appears in the URL cache, the filtering decision can be made quickly (in less than one micro second). Otherwise, the site's texts and images are analyzed for accurate site classification and the URL-cache is updated. In addition, *MORF*'s text/image analysis does not consume significant computational resources.
2. High accuracy. *MORF* uses the result of the text analysis to set the *bias threshold* for conducting image analysis. If the text analyzer suspects that the site is objectionable, the image analyzer is set biased toward classifying the site's images as objectionable. The image analyzer serves as a lexical disambiguator. In addition, *MORF* employs a novel *Cross-Bagging* ensemble scheme (discussed in Section 3.1) to achieve accurate image-class prediction. The employment of the multimodal analysis and the novel classifier enables *MORF* to make accurate Web-page classification.
3. Personalization. *MORF* uses the perception-based learning algorithms [1] to adaptively formulate filtering criteria to satisfy different needs of individuals.

The rest of this paper is organized as follows. In Section 2 we depict the components of *MORF* and key system events. In Section 3 we discuss *MORF*'s multimodal classification algorithm (MCA) and its concept-shift algorithm (CSA) for personalization support. Section 4 presents experimental results and some statistics collected from the deployed sites in the United States and Asia. Finally, we present our concluding remarks in Section 5.

2   System Components and Events

Figure 1 presents *MORF*'s functional units including *access point unit, filtering engine, site cache, multimodal classifier, update unit, user interface,* and *report*

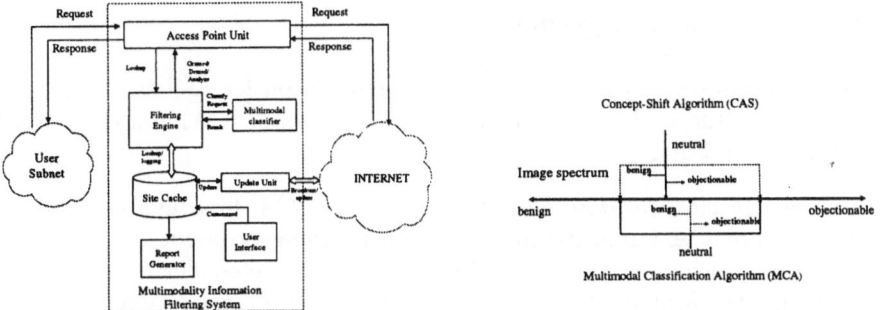

Fig. 2. MCA and CSA.

Fig. 1. System Architecture of our Multimodality Personalized Information Filter

generator. The *access point unit* receives in-coming requests to *MORF*. A received request is forwarded to the *filtering engine*, which decides whether the request should be granted or denied by first looking up in the *site cache* (i.e., the URL cache). If the requested site does not appear in the URL cache, the *filtering engine* 1) queries the *multimodal classifier* to classify the site, 2) updates the site cache, and 3) returns the permit/deny decision. The *update unit* of *MORF* multicasts and synchronizes new URL entries to and from the other *MORF* systems. The *user interface* allows users to provide feedback for personalizing filtering criteria. Finally, the *report generator* generates traffic statistics.

The filtering decision must be made both swiftly and accurately. *MORF* employs three policies to strike a good balance between high filtering accuracy and efficiency.

1. *Presumed pass.* If a request encounters a cache miss, *MORF* first permits the unknown site to be accessed by the user, and at the same time, it classifies the site asynchronously. If the presumed-pass request happens to be objectionable, any subsequent access to that site will be blocked and a log entry made that the objectionable site has been accessed.
2. *Distributed site-cache update.* Each *MORF* periodically multicasts its new entries in the block and bypass lists to its peers. Once a new site is seen and classified by one *MORF*, the new entry is propagated to the other *MORF*s.
3. *Client vs. server deployment.* When filtering accuracy cannot be compromised, *MORF* can be deployed at the client site so that any unseen site is classified synchronously. This synchronous classification does not affect the access performance of the other clients.

The efficiency and effectiveness of *MORF* relies on its multimodal classification and concept-shift algorithms, which we discuss next.

3   Classification Algorithms

To support accurate and personalized site classification for *MORF*, we propose two algorithms, the *multimodal classification algorithm* (MCA) and the *concept-shift algorithm* (CSA).

1. *Multimodal classification algorithm (MCA)*. MCA first analyzes the requested site's text information and then its image content to predict the site's class, either *benign* or *objectionable*. The text classifier returns a score indicating the probability that the requested site is objectionable. This score is used by the image classifier to set the *bias threshold*. The image classifier classifies an image into one of the three categories: *benign*, *neutral*, and *objectionable*. The more the *bias threshold* leans toward the objectionable side, the more likely a neutral image will be classified as an objectionable one. We present MCA in details in Section 3.1.

2. *Concept-shift algorithm (CSA)*. Based on individual subscriber feedback, CSA can further classify the neutral category predicted by MCA into either the *benign* or *objectionable* class. In other words, CSA places a *personalized view* on the neutral category. (Note that without CSA, MCA splits the neutral category into benign and objectionable categories by setting the boundary at the middle of the neutral category.) Due to space limitation, we present the details of CSA in the extended version of this paper [2].

Figure 2 explains how MCA and CSA work. The bottom of the figure shows that the bias threshold of MCA affects the boundary between the benign class (on the left-hand side) and the objectionable class (on the right-hand side) by demarcating a fence in the neutral region. The top of the figure shows that CSA draws a personalized boundary in the neutral region based on individuals' preferences. The MCA provides a default rating for a site, and the CSA sets personalized ratings for individuals. For instance, if a site's texts indicate that the site does not contain objectionable words, the text classifier sets the bias threshold toward benign (the fence in the neutral zone at the bottom thus lies closer to the objectionable side). The site is therefore less likely to be classified as objectionable unless its images provide stronger than usual evidence. The personalized threshold can override the system's default classification. For example, a conservative institute that does not want to take any chances of viewing objectionable content can set a very strict threshold close to or even within the benign boundary.

3.1   Multimodal Classification Algorithm

We employ a novel classification scheme, *Cross-Bagging* ensemble, for MCA. The design goals of the Cross-Bagging ensemble are threefold: fast training time, fast classification time, and high classification accuracy. The MCA consists of three parts: the base classifier, the ensemble scheme, and the text, image and site classifiers. However, due to space limitation, we only discuss the ensemble scheme in this paper. Detailed discussions of the base classifier and the text, image and site classifiers can be found in the extended version of this paper [2].

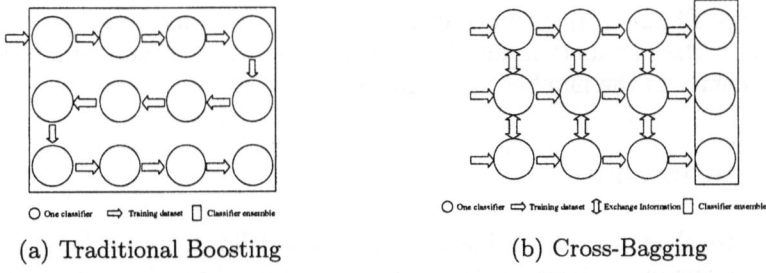

(a) Traditional Boosting   (b) Cross-Bagging

Fig. 3. The difference between traditional Boosting and Cross-Bagging

Cross-Bagging Ensemble. One can employ any base classifiers(e.g., SVMs [3], BPMs [4], etc.) that can perform binary class prediction on text documents or on images. But the classification accuracy of a binary classifier can certainly be improved. Bagging [5] and Boosting [6] are two well-known and extensively validated methods for improving classification accuracy of a base classifier. However, we will explain shortly that a straight adoption of Bagging and Boosting can be computationally intensive, and thus not practical in an on-line application like *MORF*. We therefore propose Cross-Bagging, which intelligently combines Bagging and Boosting to keep the computational cost down.

Bagging employs multiple versions of a base classifier and has been shown successful in reducing classification variance. Boosting adds new classifiers to an ensemble by training the base classifier sequentially to reweighted versions of the training dataset so that the next classifier will focus more on misclassified examples (and less on the correctly classified examples). Bagging adds classifiers that aim to make independent errors, and Boosting adds classifiers that aim to make mutually exclusive errors. Boosting, however, is not computationally feasible for an on-line application such as *MORF*, since it often requires training a large number of classifiers (possibly in the order of thousands), which results in a large ensemble size. A large ensemble size prolongs both training time and classification time. [5,6,7].

Our *Cross-Bagging* scheme aims to improve classification accuracy by intelligently selecting training data for each bag. The key idea of Cross-Bagging lies in the observation that we need only the majority of the ensemble members to vote correctly to make an accurate class prediction. The traditional Boosting method reweights the training population, according to the testing results in the previous round, to train another classifier. Figure 3(a) shows how the traditional Boosting scheme trains a series of classifiers and how a class prediction involves the voting of all classifiers (in the rectangle). Cross-Bagging differs from Boosting in two ways, as depicted in Figure 3(b). First, Cross-Bagging boosts only enough bags to ensure that a misclassified instance will be correctly classified in the next iteration. For instance, suppose we have three bags, A, B, and C, and that instance x_i is misclassified by bags A and B in the current round. We boost x_i in only one of bags A and B in the next training iteration to ensure that the majority will make mutually exclusive errors on x_i and thus can predict x_i correctly. Second, the class prediction of Cross-Bagging is made by the last set of bags. Figure 3(b) shows that only the last set of bags (in the rectangle) is involved in class prediction, and hence the classification time remains constant, independently of the number of rounds of boosting.

4   Experiments

Our empirical study was design to answer the following questions: First, can Cross-Bagging outperform the traditional Bagging scheme in classification accuracy and training time? Second, does a multimodality classifier perform better than single modality classifiers in filtering objectionable Web-sites?

4.1   Experimental Results of Cross-Bagging

The dataset used in our experiments consisted of 20,000 pornographic images as positive examples and 20,000 benign images as negative examples. All images were obtained by crawling the Internet and randomly selected after manually identifying their classes (objectionable/benign). Ten percent (4,000 images) of the entire image population were randomly selected as the testing set and separated from the rest. The remaining 36,000 images were used as the training population

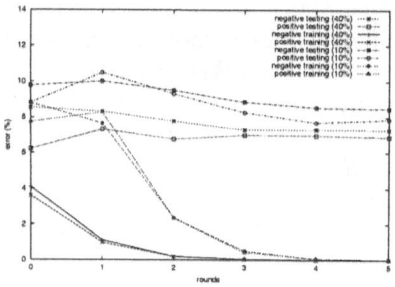

Fig. 4. Training and Classification Error in Cross-Bagging Algorithm

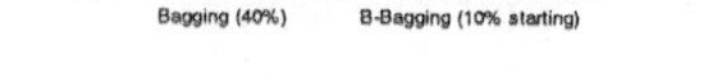

Fig. 5. Training Time Comparison

Figure 4 shows two sets of experimental results of the proposed Cross-Bagging algorithm. One experiment started the training with a training sample ratio of 10% and the other experiment with a sample ratio of 40%. Three bags were used in both experiments. We applied the Cross-Bagging algorithm for five rounds on both experiments. First, Figure 4 shows that the false-positive error (negative examples classified as positive) and the false-negative error (positive examples classified as negative) are comparable in all cases. Second, in Figure 4, the training errors in both experiments decreased logarithmically with each round for the first 3 to 4 rounds. The results show that after a small number of iterations, the training errors become negligible. The testing errors in both cases also decrease accordingly, but at slower rates. The results suggest that the proposed Cross-Bagging algorithm requires only a few training iterations (in our application, three iterations) to achieve accurate class-prediction.

The next experiment compared the training costs of the proposed Cross-Bagging algorithm to those of the traditional Bagging algorithm. Figure 5 shows the training time of the traditional Bagging algorithm and the proposed Cross-Bagging algorithm. A training sample ratio of 40% was used for the traditional Bagging algorithm and a training sample ratio of 10% was used as the starting training set size of the Cross-Bagging algorithm. We ran the Cross-Bagging algorithm for three rounds and compared the total training time with the traditional Bagging algorithm, which runs in a single round. The training time was wall clock time in seconds. Figure 5 shows that the total training time of the proposed Cross-Bagging algorithm is almost 50% less than the training time of the Bagging algorithm.

From the above experiments, we answered the first question raised in the beginning of this section. The proposed Cross-Bagging algorithm requires much less training overhead to achieve comparable accuracy than the traditional Bagging algorithm.

4.2   The Advantage of Multimodality Design

The Web-page filtering accuracy can be increased by using the image classifier as a lexical disambiguator, as discussed in Section 3. The employment of the multimodal analysis and the novel classifier enables the proposed information filtering system to make accurate Web-page classification. The next experiment compared the Web-page filtering accuracy of different filtering techniques discussed in Section 1. This experiment used a 30 days web access logs from MORF testing sites in the United States and Asia. The logs contained a history of 103.2M Web access requests to 25,371 different Web-sites. Out of 25,371 Web-sites, 1,266 sites were considered to be pornographic sites.

We compared the filtering accuracy of URL-based, keyword-based, image-based, and the proposed multimodality techniques on the access requests to the objectionable sites. The result shows that using the URL blocking list alone (from an unnamed commercial filtering software) produced filtering error greater than 50%. The reason for the high filtering error is that the URL-based technique relied on a block list which is often out of date. In contrast, the keyword-base technique produces 33.4% filtering error in this experiment. In this case the high filtering error resulted because many of the objectionable sites contain no keywords. Another reason is that many of those objectionable Web-pages in this experiment were written in languages other than English. The low accuracy of the keyword-based technique strongly suggests the use of information other than text content for filtering purposes. The images-based filtering technique use only images from a site to determine if the site contains objectionable information. The images-based filtering technique produces 13.3% filtering error, which is much lower than the text-based technique, in this experiment. This result suggests that image content is more reliable than text content in the filtering applications because images are less ambiguous to interpret. By employing the multimodality design, our proposed filtering technique can further reduce the classification error. In this experiment, our proposed multimodality filtering system produced the least filtering error, 4.6%, compares to other filtering techniques. This result answers the second question raised in the beginning of this section: the proposed multimodal classification technique does outperform other single modality classifiers in filtering pornographic web-sites.

5   Conclusion

In this paper, we propose a personalizable information filtering system with multimodality design. We depict the components of the filtering system and show how the filtering components interact with each other. The proposed system employs three filtering models— URL, text, and image content—to accurately determine whether a site is objectionable and thus blocks users access to the objectionable sites. We empirically showed that sharing information among different models improves the overall accuracy of classifying web sites with objectionable contents. The proposed multimodality information filtering system is flexible for personalization and is ideal for ISP's, home, schools, libraries, and corporate users to ensure adequate level of filtering criteria in real time.

References

[1] Simon Tong and Edward Chang. Support vector machine active learning for image retrieval. *Proceedings of ACM International Conference on Multimedia*, pages 107–118, October 2001.

[2] Y.-L. Wu, E.Y. Chang, K.-T. Cheng, C.-W. Chang, C.-C. Hsu, W.-C. Lai, and C.-T. Wu. MORF: A distributed multimodal information .ltering system (extended version). *Technical Report, VIMA Technologies*, June 2002.

[3] V. Vapnik. *Estimation of Dependences Based on Empirical Data*. Springer Verlag, 1982.

[4] Ralf Herbrich, Thore Graepel, and Colin Campell. Bayes point machines: Estimating the bayes point in kernel space. *Proceedings of IJCAI Workshop Support Vector Machines*, pages 23–27, 1999.

[5] L. Breiman. Arcing classiffiers. *The Annals of Statistics*, 26(3):801–849, 1998.

[6] Robert E. Schapire, Yoav Freund, Peter Bartlett, and Wee Sun Lee. Boosting the margin: a new explanation for the effectiveness of voting methods. In *Proc. 14th International Conference on Machine Learning*, pages 322–330. Morgan Kaufmann, 1997.

[7] T.G. Dietterich and G. Bakiri. Solving multiclass learning problems via error-correcting output codes. *Journal of Artificial Intelligence Research*, 2:263–286, 1995.

Personalization of Interactive News through J2EE, XML, XSLT, and SMIL in a Web-Based Multimedia Content Management System

SoonNyean Cheong, K.M. Azhar, and M. Hanmandlu

Multimedia University, Faculty of Engineering, Jalan Multimedia, Cyberjaya,
63100 Selangor, Malaysia
{sncheong, azhar.mustapha, madasu.hanmandlu}@mmu.edu.my
http://www.mmu.edu.my

Abstract. This paper describes the design and implementation of a 5 layered web-based multimedia content management system (MCMS) using the Java 2 Enterprise Edition (J2EE). A prototype based on our framework has been implemented in the News On Demand KIOSK Network for organizing, integrating and composing of personalized digital news for interactive broadcasting. The aim of the MCMS project is to provide a collaborative environment among news producers for making them work more effectively despite the time and location constraints. The MCMS generates SMIL document that is structured, profiled and streamed to end-user using XML and XSLT techniques, which form the backbone of digital news broadcasting. The major contributions with regard to the digital MCMS can be summarized as: (1) Support for effective personalization of multimedia news content and presentation styles through the utilization of XML and XSLT. (2) Separation of design and content facilitated by MCMS. This allows journalist and editors to focus on content preparation rather than advanced HTML and SMIL coding. (3) Support for the re-use and re-purpose operations of the same multimedia elements to be part of the other digital news program. (4) Platform independent MCMS allowing an author to access the application everywhere via Internet without any need of additional hardware or software.

1 Introduction

In the past, television had been the most important medium for delivering news to the nations. However, in recent years, World-Wide-Web (WWW) is experiencing a gradual growth as a leading medium for news publication. This is because WWW offers great potential to deliver outstanding features that TV cannot match. These include:

- *Flexibility news show* – News program is broadcasted in a predefined schedule on a TV and if a person is not in front of the TV set, then the information becomes virtually inaccessible. Consumers will have to wait for another time slot

Y.-C. Chen, L.-W. Chang, and C.-T. Hsu (Eds.): PCM 2002, LNCS 2532, pp. 287–294, 2002.
© Springer-Verlag Berlin Heidelberg 2002

to watch the latest news. On the other hand, a well-managed web server will be able to service clients 24 hours a day and stream any news show when being requested at any point in time.

- *Interactivity* – Interactive features in TV set is quite limited to the ability to switch between different channels. As compared to a well-composed website, it can offer the user with a variety of interaction levels such as the ability to search for particular news, selection of languages, feature to select, which item to skip and which item to pursue in more details (hyperlink) and so on.
- *Personalization* – News broadcasted on a TV is the same to all viewers at the same time. Thus, personalization of news program to different users is not achievable through TV, whereas WWW offers the users to define their own profiles for personalization such that different users may experience different look and feel on the same news content.

In view of the qualities features offered by WWW, the Internet bodies, such as W3C [2] and IETF [3] have put in a lot of effort in defining standards that merge World-Wide-Web technology with traditional TV to offer the interactive TV. Although digital news broadcasting in the interactive TV environment seems to be very promising, there are many issues that need to be redesigned, as the workflow in digital news production is much more complicated than in conventional approach. Unlike a person working in a television news publication and dealing with only video element in a television news publication, a digital news producer produces news program by using images, WebPages, animation, video clips and other multimedia gadgets. Most people would agree that multi-style personalization of digital news for different users is desirable. For instance, an investor may be willing to go through long explanation of market analysis in different forms like text, graph, hyper-links, while a layman may only be interested in a summary of local stock market in text form. In order to cater to the user attention span, the publication process will require a tedious multimedia composing and is therefore very time consuming.

Besides, the original target audience for the news was simple, that is everyone! The location of the content (html) was also simple, employing a tree structure where relevant news used to reside in three or four levels deep in static web pages. However, as the information is growing in an exponential manner, many problems are bound to occur while maintaining the content of the news on their website. This is because as the news content authoring and publishing team get bigger involving, in some cases, hundreds of journalists, reporters, web designer and news manager, all need to operate from remote localities.

In view of the above problems, we will present an effective multimedia content management system (MCMS) that adopts a 5 layered architecture using Java 2 Enterprise Edition (J2EE) as this supports collaborative authoring and publishing team within a geographically distributed region and from a diverse functional area for broadcasting personalized interactive news through a website.

1.1 Related Works

1.1.1 Interactive Video

Several digital video systems have been developed for interactive video [4,5,6]. Streaming server developed by Real Network, inc. [7] implements Synchronized Multimedia Integration Language (SMIL) on top of the Real-Time Streaming Protocol and provides a standard way to deliver interactive video on the web. SMIL [8] is a standard developed by the World-Wide Web Consortium for scripting multimedia presentations and is required to develop interactive video on the web.

1.1.2 Content Management System

Some of the open source content management system (CMS) for managing website available today includes Zope and OpenCms [9, 10]. Zope was developed in 1995 in Fredericksburg while OpecCms was deployed since 1994. Both are specializing in content management system for dynamic web-based business application. Some advanced features offered by these systems to ease content management include dynamic and static content publishing, basic workflow and task management, templating mechanism, layout personalization, scheduling system and so on. However, a review of the advertising and marketing literature shows that these systems fall short in the usage and management of multimedia technology like interactive video.

2 Issues in News Authoring and Management

News content is volatile in nature, so to ensure the 'live and growth' of a news website, news content ought to be updated while out-dated news has to be removed consistently. This suggests that the news content providers should be very active. However, the increased activities in news content generation may create many problems if there is a lack of control over the news content management process. Below are some related issues that will cause problems if the content authoring and management process is not properly handled.

> ➢ *Web publishing and control*: News website is surfed by millions of readers around the world everyday. So, all the news published on a news website ought to be reliable and correct. However, misuse of news website by the unauthorized personnel will lead to the publishing of incorrect news on the website. This happens when there is no proper procedures and control over the web publishing process. Thus, before publishing any news on the web, it should be subjected to a review and authorization process to ensure that it is acceptable from a marketing and legal point of view.
> ➢ *Deployment process*: When web editing job is distributed among a group of journalist from different departments the problem of inconsistencies in the look and feel of the news website and variable quality of layout and content would crop up. To solve this, deployment process should clearly separate out the design and content provider group from the web editing team. This will

enable journalists and news template designers to concentrate on their tasks and provide more flexibility to the presentation templates, thus eliminating the inconsistencies of look and feel across the news website.

➢ *Bandwidth*: Since Interactive multimedia news is distributed across the Internet; bandwidth becomes a critical issue as its availability to different user can vary tremendously. Hence, it is impractical to design one-size fit all interactive news. We need a solution that can generate a web structure to provide clients with an easy access to interactive news subject to the bandwidth constraints.

➢ *Personalization*: In this competitive world, organizations are trying to provide value-added services to the clients and one of it is "personalization". The aim of news personalization is to ensure that the right people receive the right news at the right time. For instance, in a multi-racial country like Malaysia consisting of Malays, Chinese and Indian, the clients from each race would prefer to watch the interactive multimedia news show in the language of their origin. As such, an easy to use authoring tool that can support client personalization is needed to provide the same interactive news to different clients with languages of preference.

We tackle the first issue by building a web-based workflow management system that deals with the publishing process including the coordination of tasks, the exchange of data file, media information and task information among the members according to the predefined rules. This will enable reporters, journalists, editors, designers and managers to work together more effectively in a remote environment. Regarding the second issue, XML technique will be used to mark up web content while style languages XSL for presenting the digital news. By using XML, a device independent content can be achieved allowing news publication services to be extended to personal digital assistant (PDA), mobile phone and other digital devices without affecting the content structure. On the other hand using XSL, layout and display of a website can be changed easily by modifying a correspondence style-sheet. The combination of XML and XSL will give a higher flexibility to news content and a better management of website. Concerning the third and fourth issues, we provide an easy way to generate multi-style and multi-lingual digital news through Synchronized Multimedia Integration Language (SMIL). This means that different users can watch the same digital news with different presentation styles and languages of preference.

3   System Architecture

The framework for multimedia content management system presented in this paper is built on top of the J2EE platform [11] that provides a robust scalable system to employees, managers and partners. When deployed, it helps organize content from inception to eventually archiving and deletion of news content. It is built using a 5-layered web-based architecture shown in Fig.1. This architecture consists of a presentation layer, an application logic layer, a persistence layer, a database layer and a streaming platform.

The presentation layer consists of dynamic HTML, which is formed from XML and XSL style sheets and java servlets for content management tools. Application logic layer contains domain-objects and process-objects, which together perform operations on data-objects and provide data for presentation to management and authoring tools on the presentation layer. Digital news is constructed in our system based on XML, XSL and XSLT techniques [12, 13, 14], which are more suitable for description and presentation of hierarchical media structures. The persistence layer possesses the characteristics needed to read, write and delete objects to or from the database. Database layer provides the mechanism for storing news content and user's profiles persistently by using a relational database model. Finally, a streaming server is used to deliver the personalized video content to the user. RealSystem Server Basic from Real Networks is used as a streaming server in our system because it supports SMIL streaming.

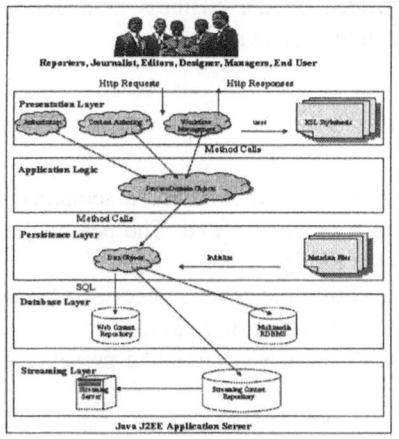

Fig. 1. System Architecture for SMIL-based Multimedia Content Management System

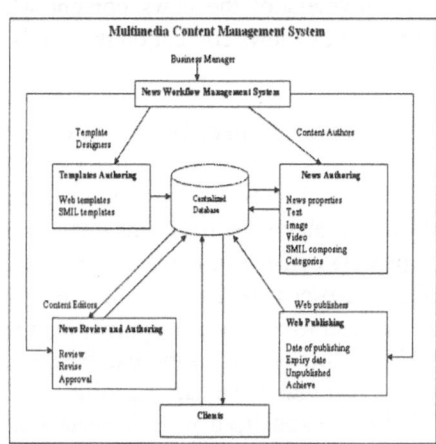

Fig. 2. News Workflow Management system

4 News on Demand Kiosk Network (NODKN)

We have implemented the MCMS framework on NODKN, a collaborative project between Multimedia University and Matshusita. The implementation aspects are discussed in the following sub-sections.

4.1 Operation of Multimedia Content Management System

Business manager within a news publication company will interact with MCMS to define any news event and then use the integrated WFMS shown in Fig. 2 to distribute specific tasks to the employee to complete a news content life cycle. Let, say, a con-

tent author, upon receiving tasks from business manager, will use the MCMS to interact with a centralized database and retrieve any desired information like news report,
photograph, video clip and other relevant materials sent by reporters around the world
to compose digital news by filling up pre-defined templates. During the authoring
process, news content will be segmented according to some categories to provide a
mechanism for searching and for personalization to different users. The template designers, once notified by MCMS, will create a custom template and supply it to the
content author. Thus, there are some dependencies between content authors and template designers. Once the news authoring and templating process has been completed,
content editors will be instructed by the MCMS to review, revise and approve pre-
published news event to ensure that the quality of news is acceptable from the legal
and marketing point of view. Any changes made by the content editor will be saved
for versioning and tracking purposes. This will allow the business manager to perform
any rollback operations whenever necessary. Finally, web publisher would schedule
the deployment of the news content when requested by the business manager and
ensure that the news content on the site is current, appropriate and correct.

4.2 Personalization of Digital News

The MCMS framework is based on a personalization model in which a sequence of
multimedia elements, hyperlinks and presentation styles is profiled. The personalization process consists of the following steps as shown in Fig. 3:
1. The end-user is registered with the server by selecting the news categories of interest subject to bandwidth availability and level of sophistication required.
2. MCMS gets access to the database to retrieve all the news items and presentation
   styles that match the user's profile.
3. MCMS personalized module generates necessary JSP codes to allow a user to retrieve personalized Electronic News Guide, which contains article's name, abstract,
   and URL.

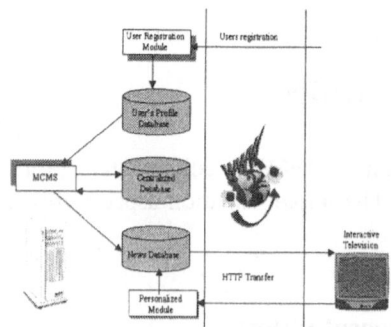

Fig. 3. Digital news personalization process

Fig. 4. A snapshot of composed SMIL based
multimedia interactive news show using
XSLT and XML techniques.

4.3 Multi-styles Authoring System for Interactive News Show

The multi-styles presentation for personalized multimedia interactive news is achieved by using XSLT style sheets that convert multiple XML documents into SMIL files by selecting in a more or less automatic way from a set of suitable presentations according to the user needs. Generally, an interactive news show can be segmented into 2 main sections, the layout section and the body section. Template designers or developers will concentrate on the layout section for the presentation of content dealing with ist type and location. Content authors will compose news content in the body section without worrying about the presentation styles. Personalized interactive news is composed from a sequence of multimedia elements, which matches with the user's profile and groups into sections defined in a selected template. This deployment process will let the employees to publish articles in less time and with more accountability than before.

5 Conclusions

The inherent problem in digital news broadcasting is the lack of content personalization, a proper web publishing and management, centralized deployment process and bandwidth availability. In this paper, we have presented the design and implementation of an effective web-based multimedia content management system (MCMS) using J2EE for interactive broadcasting. The effectiveness of the MCMS is amply demonstrated in the News On Demand Kiosk Network (NODKN). The framework has several novel features as compared to conventional approaches. (1) A web-based workflow management system (WMS) for easy content authoring and profiling. This system facilitates a collaborative environment among contributors in the content production process. (2) MCMS to generate the multi-style and multi-lingual digital news by an easy way through Synchronized Multimedia Integration Language (SMIL). (3) Use of XML and XSLT techniques to provide an effective method to create different presentations of the digital news that is catered to users with different needs and bandwidth. The combination of XML and XSL will give a higher flexibility to news content and a better management of website. As the current system is only tested on computers, we would like to extend the system to cater to other devices such as digital TV, hand phone and PDA in the future.

Acknowledgements. The authors acknowledge the support of Matshusita Electric Industrial Co., Ltd in Japan with thanks for the project NODKN being handled at Multimedia University.

References

1. S.N.CHEONG, AZHAR K.M. and M. HANMANDLU, "Web-based Multimedia Content Management System for Effective News Personalization on Interactive Broadcasting", To be presented in *WSEAS ICOMIV2002*, September 25-28, 2002, Greece.
2. Charles P. Sandbank, "Digital TV in the Convergent Environment", *IEEE Computer Graphics and Applications*, Vol. 21, No. 1, pp. 32-36, 2001.
3. World-Wide-Web Consortium, "Television and the Web Activity Page", At: http://www.w3.org/TV/
4. Real Network, Inc., "Real System RealVideo9 Delivering Unparalleled Quality from Narrowband to HDTV", At: http://docs.real.com/docs/rn/RV9_datasheet.pdf
5. Microsoft Corporation, "Windows Media Services 4.1", At: http://www.microsoft.com/windows/windowsmedia/technologies/services.asp
6. Apple Computer, Inc., "Full Stream Ahead", At: http://www.apple.com/quicktime/products/qtss/
7. Real Networks, Inc., "RealSystem Server Professional", At: http://www.realnetworks.com/products/servers/professional/index.html
8. World-Wide-Web Consortium, "Synchronized Multimedia", At: http://www.w3.org/AudioVideo/
9. Zope Corporation, "ZOPE Commurnity" At: http://www.zope.org/
10. OpenCms, "Features of OpenCms" At: http://www.opencms.org/opencms/opencms/index.html
11. Sun Microsystems Incs., "Java™ 2 Enterprise Edition Developer's Guide", At: http://java.sun.com/j2ee/j2sdkee/techdocs/guides/ejb/html/DevGuideTOC.html
12. World-Wide-Web Consortium, "Extensive Markup Language (XML)", At: http://www.w3.org/XML
13. World-Wide-Web Consortium, "The Extensible Stylesheet Language (XSL)", At: http://www.w3.org/Style/XSL
14. World-Wide-Web Consortium, "XSL Transformations (XSLT)", At: http://www.w3.org/TR/xslt

Deploy Multimedia-on-Demand Services over ADSL Networks

Chih-Cheng Lo and Wen-Shyen E. Chen

Institute of Computer Science
National Chung-Hsing University
Taichung, Taiwan 40227
{loremi, echen}@cs.nchu.edu.tw

Abstract. As the broadband information highway being constructed, many multimedia applications will be realized. Nowadays, customers desired not only purely high-speed Internet access, but also versatile interactive multimedia applications. This article illustrates a multimedia-on-demand (MOD) system that can be provided by incumbent telcos. It provides both multicast and unicast streaming services, including True VOD, Near VOD, Live TV, KaraOK-on-demand (KOD), High-speed Internet access applications, and POTS services.
In this paper, we give an overview of broadband access technologies, including HFC, ADSL, FTTx, MMDS/LMDS, and Satellite access networks, to support a MOD system. We also depict the components of deploying a large-scale MOD system from end to end, from customer premises equipment, video servers, storage system, network system, service management system, DBMS system, to content sources. Finally, we give a complete example to describe the signal flows among the components of the system. As we shall see, deregulation will accelerate the convergence of the telecommunications, cable TV, entertainment, and e-commerce while ADSL is the mainstream technology of access network today and provides a viable solution to the Multimedia-on-Demand services.

1 Introduction

As the Internet revolution progresses, the number of households getting on the Internet has increased exponentially. The activity in the field of broadband services such as VOD, NVOD, Interactive TV, Video conferencing, Datacasting, E-Commerce and Games, etc., have been expanding at a rapid rate. Multimedia-on-demand (MOD), including most of the above services, is emerging to be one of the killer applications in recent broadband services. The market has also expected to capture a significant share of the huge potential revenues contributed by business and residential market [1]. Services of the MOD system include True Video-on-demand, Near Video-on-demand, Live TV, KaraOk-on-demand, and High-speed Internet access services, etc.

MOD can deploy on various network architectures. For incumbent Telcos, use of the ADSL for broadband access is the most popular and rapid solution to promote existing twisted-pair telephone lines toward broadband services to the residential and small businesses. Although in the next few years, we shall see that the increased presence and closer setup of optical fibers in the access network to the customers, ADSL technologies remain to be a viable solution since the connection is readily available [2,3].

A large-scale MOD system comprised many elements that are necessary for the provision of a complete service, including set-top unit, video servers, storage system,

Y.-C. Chen, L.-W. Chang, and C.-T. Hsu (Eds.): PCM 2002, LNCS 2532, pp. 295–302, 2002.

network system, service management system, and content sources, etc. [4,5]. We will discuss those components in more detail in Section 3.

This paper is organized as follows: Section 2 presents the deployment environment. Section 3 presents the system architecture and its components. Section 4 describes signal workflow of the system. Finally, the conclusions are given in Section 5.

2   Services Deployment and Broadband Services

Currently, there are various technologies to deliver multimedia services from a video repository to the customers premise network, such as Hybrid Fiber/Coax (HFC) networks, xDSL, FTTx, MMDS/LMDS, and Satellite access networks [2-4,6,7]. One of the most active debates that are widely discussed in residential broadband deployment is the choice of access network architectures. Nowadays, it is observably, the mainstream access architectures in Taiwan are HFC and ADSL networks, especially the later. There are almost 1,178,000 households ADSL customers versus 235,000 cable modem households as of March 2002. We represent the different access technologies as follows.

● HFC (Hybrid Fiber/Coax) networks

A feasible commercialized deployment providing VOD services can be based on a CATV network. Fig. 1 shows the architecture of the HFC networks. Even it had been provision in many countries such as USA, but it is still a challenge in Taiwan. Since most of CATV networks in Taiwan are still one-way architecture that cannot support interactive application, and the service can only be realized in the future two-way transmission infrastructure. Upgrading the CATV network infrastructure into a two-way HFC (Hybrid Fiber/Coax) network has just started and initially the provider will focus on downtown area for cost consideration.

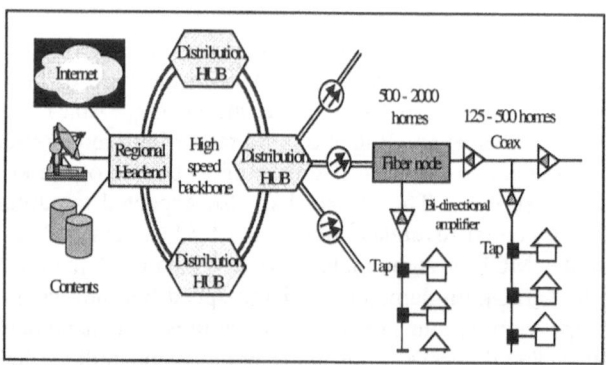

Fig. 1. Architecture of the HFC networks.

● ADSL (Asymmetric Digital Subscriber Loop) networks

Most of the Telcos prefer to capitalize on their existing twisted-pair telephone lines by pushing the evolution of a new technology called digital subscriber line (DSL). xDSL is a generic abbreviation for various flavors of DSL technologies, and ADSL, as shown in Fig. 2, is one of the xDSL families. It is developed by telephone companies to provide the next generation high bandwidth services to the homes and businesses using the existing telephone cabling infrastructure [8]. Typically, ADSL provides a data rate from 1.544 Mbps to 8 Mbps downstream and from 16 Kbps to 640 Kbps upstream, depending upon line length and condition.

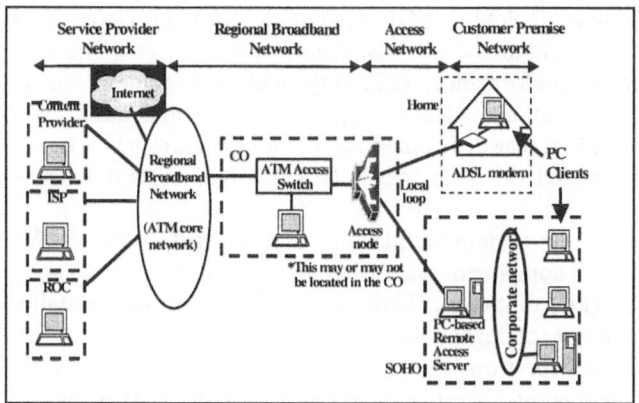

Fig. 2. The end-to-end ADSL-based network architecture.

● Fiber to the Building (FTTB)

Fiber access networks, namely Fiber to the Building (FTTB), Fiber to the Curb (FTTC), Fiber to the Home (FTTH), etc., are referred to the FTTx family. Basically, FTTx is a star-connected network that connects the access networks and customer premises networks directly with optical fibers. It provides interfaces for user terminals as output from optical network unit (ONU) installed at customer premises. Current deployments are trial systems and are at a very early rollout stage. But it will be seen as an emerging technology in the very near future.

● Satellite access networks

The satellite access system such as direct broadcast system (DBS) uses geosynchronous satellites operating in the Ku band. It is downstream with QPSK modulation using satellite transmission in the 10-15 GHz or 2-6 GHz bandwidths with digital television broadcasting. Since it is a one-way service, the return-path network could be telephone line, xDSL, or other wireless services.

● MMDS/LMDS access networks

The Multichannel Multipoint Distribution System (MMDS) and Local Multipoint Distribution System (LMDS) belong to the wireless local loop architecture. It realizes asymmetric wireless network as an alternative to HFC. MMDS occupies 198 MHz of bandwidth in the 2.5 GHz range. The frequency permits long distance distribution to about 50 miles. LMDS occupies up to 1.15 MHz of bandwidth in the 28 GHz range, it is a two-way, high bit rate services. LMDS is a small cell technology, with each cell about 3 to 6 Km in radius.

3   System Architecture

The system we propose [9] can be a commercialized system to serve at least 20,000 customers in the first phase, and will be able to scale up to serve more customers (up to one hundred thousand customers) in the succeeding deployments. Many papers have discussed about deploying VOD systems [2,6,10,11]. Generally speaking, they can be divided into centralized and distributed architectures. The topics of interests include economics, performance, reliability, and management. As compared to a number of VOD operations, such as request batching and multicasting, unicasting, etc., it has been shown that distributed servers architecture has a much lower system cost to offer on-demand video services [12]. This MOD system is deployed with such considerations.

An example of the system architecture is illustrated in Fig. 3. We will describe the functions of each component briefly in the following:

● Set-top Box (STB) or Set-top Unit: The STB is a device installed in customer premises to interconnect legacy A/V equipment to the broadband network. STB accepts MPEG packets from the access network and translates the packets for presentation on an analog TV set or PC monitor. DAVIC [13] specifies this as the A0 interface. Since the operations are designed to be very user friendly, users can browse all services on the screen through an IR (infrared) remote control or remote keyboard with fully VCR-like functionality. The major functions of STU includes receiving the incoming video streams; demodulating, demultiplexing, and decoding the signals; performing the necessary signal conversion, such as D/A transformation for playback on the TV monitor; and sending outgoing control messages [6].

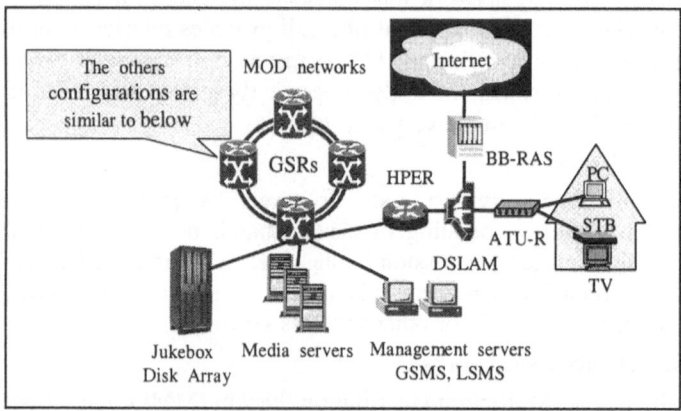

Fig. 3. An example of MOD system architecture.

● Set-top Box Server/User Database: The STB Server is located in the central office to receive the requests from STB in every household, and each one server should serve at least 15,000 customers. The main functions of STB Server are authorization and account management. When a user logs in this system, the system executes the primary account check. If it is a legal user, then the system redirects this session to LSMS (Local System Management Server) or Video Server Gateway (VSG) depends on system configuration.

The user database stores the customer's information for STB server to retrieve, such as customer ID, account information, service class, bandwidth reservation, locality and CPE ID, etc. Each user database can serve more then one STB Server and should adapt the fault-tolerance architecture to make sure the absolute safety of customers' data.

● Access Network/Core Network: The broadband access network is an ADSL- based network architecture. It comprises a Digital Subscriber Line Access Multiplexer (DSLAM), a number of ATU-Rs, and the POTS splitters to construct a broadband access network between central office (CO) and customer premises network. The network uses ATM over ADSL technology to provide the broadband data communication services. The DSLAM uses ATM technology to statistically multiplex the subscriber interface signals into its network interface.

The core network system comprises Gigabit Switch Routers (GSRs) and High Performance Edge Routers (HPERs). The former is constructed by GSRs that transport packets between video servers in the center offices (COs) in a huge bandwidth form STM-1 up to STM-64.

The HPER performs as an edge switch to connect the core and the access network. It also performs many complex functions, such as rich routing protocols, data forwarding or duplication to the customer premises network (CPN), and QoS. It should have high efficiency to handle video stream to prevent locking effect, frame freezing, and frame skipping. The system should support at least 10 Gigabit per second of aggregate switching capacity.

● Video Servers: The video server consists of massive storage and media controllers to store the video (or other services) source in specific compressed format in order to can be requested and accessed by the customers efficiently. In general, there are stored in two formats: MPEG-1 or MPEG-2. For example, a 90 minutes program, using MPEG-1 compression, requires about 1 Gbytes of storage.

The video server is different from a traditional database server in several ways. It performs some basic functions, such as request handling, random access, and user interactions, in addition to admission control, QoS guarantees, and VCR-like functions, including play, pause, resume, fast forward, and rewind. Since the transmission of video data is stream oriented, it needs to be well constructed and offers precise tuning such that programs can be delivered to the end users without any glitches, such as blocked effect, and freeze frame.

● Video Server Gateway/Video Server Database: the video server gateway is one of the most important components in a video system. It performs as a portal of multimedia services. While video server database is cooperating with video server gateway to record the needed information of this system, it adopts an Oracle database to store the massive customers' profile and accounting information. The main functions of a video server gateway are shown in the following:

- ● Detect the state of STB
- ● Provide main menu and send it to the STB for customer to select.
- ● Notify local system management system to reserve or release the bandwidth for program streams.
- ● Dynamically report the bandwidth, video servers loading, massive storage and resources utilization message and status to local system management system.

- Create accounting records, including customer ID, service ID, program ID, starting time, and finish time, etc. The information will be sent to the video server database for billing purpose.

● High-speed Internet access Management System: It consists of the Broadband Remote Access Server (BB-RAS), Remote Authentication Dial In User Services (RADIUS), and routers. When users login in this system for Internet access. The primary functions of BB-RAS are Authentication, Authorization, and Accounting (AAA), Internet roaming, user management, virtual router, etc. The RADIUS server is a database that keeps the detailed profiles and accounting information of the customers. It provides a mechanism of recognizing a user who has registered its rights to access the network source of a service provider and logging the billing record.

● Video Service System: the video service system comprises four components as shown in the following:

- Video input component: The functions of this unit are to digitalize the input analog signal source and encoding to MPEG format to store in the system.
- Video output component: As the services divide into two different types, multicast and unicast. The video output component should provide a mechanism to handle each delivery scheme. Both of them support MPEG-1 and MPEG-2 formats.
- Media storage component: This component consists of massive disk arrays to store at least 500 MPEG-2 movies.
- Media management component: The main functions of this unit are managing all of those medias' on-line, off-line, update, storage control, and monitoring those operations. It also schedules the interval of NVOD services. In addition, it reports the status to the service management system.

● Service Management System: the service management system (SMS) includes three main components:

- Media Management Database Server: The main functions of it are to manage and coordinate each video server database distributed in different central offices.
- Global Service Management System (GSMS): There are only one GSMS in a MOD system, but may be lots of LSMSs located in central offices. The GSMS is responsible to interconnect with legacy systems, e.g., customer ordering system, billing system, and CDRS (Call Detail Record System).
- Local Service Management System (LSMS): The main functions of this component are bandwidth management, supervisory the status of multicast and unicast streaming services, and reply messages to the video server gateway about the status of every local video servers operations.

4   Signaling Control

In addition to construct of each component, there should be the interfaces, signaling flow, and procedures to coordinate the system's operation [14]. The video services will be provided in basic units of streams. The original benefit of streaming media was developed so that viewers do not have to wait a long period of time to download large files. Streaming video is essentially video or image that has been "digitized and compressed" in standardized formats. Streams can originate from a content provider, live source, or an audio feed from a radio station. In either case, a customer needs not to download the file when viewing the stream of a movie. The data is simply being displayed as it arrives by the player and no copy remains on the viewer's hard disk. Users can now view and listen to a streaming video while a media player simultaneously requests packets of information from the host media server and caches these packets of information in the media player's memory buffer. Today's streaming media solutions do not utilize TCP in which web content is delivered, but instead UDP that has been specifically designed for the transmission of multimedia applications.

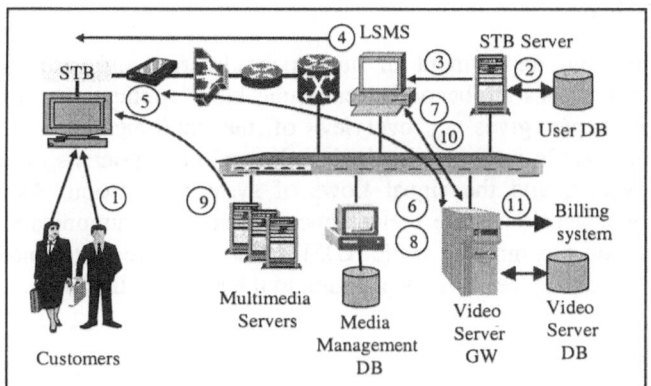

Fig. 4. An example of signaling control flow of the MOD system.

Fig. 4 depicts an example of signaling control flow of this MOD system. Customers are allowed to select programs from a remote control or keyboard. We explain the control flows step by step as follows:
1. When customer wants to enter the MOD system, he/she should enter his/her username and password to initial a request. The STB will pass this request to the STB server.
2. The STB server will make security check according to the information stored in the user database, including customer ID, username, password, privacy information, etc.
3. After the checking phase, if it passes authorization checking, the request flow will be passed to the LSMS; otherwise, the request will be rejected and the customer is notified.
4. The LSMS will reply with a main menu to the STB and it will be displayed on the screen for customer to select the service what he/she wants.
5. The STB get the information from customer and the LSMS will redirect this request flow to the Video server gateway.
6. The video server gateway sends the available programs (movies or other multimedia programs) listing to be shown on the screen for customer to select.
7. After the customer makes a choice, the video server gateway then sends a message to LSMS for requesting a bandwidth and some other resources to delivery that program.
8. If the bandwidth and resources are available, then the video server gateway will notify the STB the location of the video server and where to access this program.

Otherwise, it will reject this request and prompt a notification to the customer to wait a moment or select other services, for example, NVOD instead of TVOD.

9. The STB connects to the video server to receive the video stream.
10. After finishing delivering the program, the stream will be terminated. The video server gateway will notify the LSMS to release the bandwidth and related resources.
11. The video server gateway sends accounting information to the billing system and update the data records in the video server database.

5   Conclusions

Today, as the rapid deployment of high-speed Internet infrastructure, interactive multimedia applications are becoming emerging killer applications of the broadband services. This paper gives an overview of the multimedia-on-demand system, including many visible access technologies, the main components of this large-scale commercial system, and the signal flows of system operation. As we shall see, deregulation will accelerate the convergence of the telecommunications, cable TV, entertainment, and e-commerce while ADSL is the mainstream technology of access network today and provides a viable solution to the Multimedia-on-Demand services.

References

[1]   T-H. Wu and B-C. Cheng, "Distributed Interactive Video system Design and Analysis," IEEE Commun. Mag., pp. 100-108, Mar. 1997
[2]   K. Asatani and Y. Maeda, "Access Network Architectural Issues for Future Telecommunication Networks," IEEE Commun. Mag., pp. 110-114, Aug. 1998
[3]   Y. Maeda and R. Feigel, "A Standardization Plan for Broadband Access Network Transport," IEEE Commun. Mag., pp. 166-172, Jul. 2001
[4]   V. O. K. Li and W. Liao, "Distributed Multimedia Systems," Proceedings of the IEEE, Vol. 85, No. 7, pp. 1063-1108, Jul. 1997
[5]   Chunghwa Telecom, "Telecommunications Technical Specification – Multimedia On Demand System," Jan. 2000.
[6]   Y-H Chang, D. Coggins, D. Pitt, D. Skellern, M. Thapar, and C. Venkatraman, "An Open-Systems Approach to Video-on-demand," IEEE Commun. Mag., pp. 68-80, May. 1994
[7]   Gorge Abe, "Residential Broadband, Second Edition," Cisco Press, 2000.
[8]   C-C Lo andW-S E. Chen, "Toward Broadband Services on Telecommunication Access Network," Proceedings of Taiwan Area Network Conference 2000 (TANET 2000), pp. 134-140, Oct. 2000
[9]   HwaCom Systems Inc. "BM-plaza Introduction," Jun. 2001.
[10] D. Deloddere, W. Verbiest, and H. Verhille, "Interactive Video-on-demand," IEEE Commun. Mag., pp. 82-88, May. 1994
[11] S-H Gray Chen, and F. Tobagi, "Distributed Servers Architecture for Networked Video Services," IEEE/ACM Trans. on networking, Vol. 9, No.2, pp. 125-136, Apr. 2001
[12] C-W Lin, J. Youn, J-Zhou, M-T Sun, and S. Iraj, "MPEG video streaming with VCR functionality," Multimedia Software Engineering, 2000. Proceedings. International Symp. 2000. pp. 146-153
[13] Digital Audio-Visual Council, "DAVIC Specifications 1.4.1," Geneva, Switzer- land, 1998
[14] Thomas D.C. Little, and D. Venkatesh, "Prospects for Interactive Video- on- Demand," IEEE Multimedia Mag., pp. 14-24, 1994

An Experiment on Generic Image Classification Using Web Images

Keiji Yanai

Department of Computer Science, The University of Electro-Communications
1-5-1 Chofugaoka, Chofu-shi, Tokyo 182-8585, JAPAN, yanai@cs.uec.ac.jp

Abstract. In this paper, we describe an experiment on generic image classification using a large number of images gathered from the Web as learning images. The processing consists of three steps. In the gathering stage, a system gathers images related to given class keywords from the Web automatically. In the learning stage, it extracts image features from gathered images and associates them with each class. In the classification stage, the system classifies a test image into one of classes corresponding to the class keywords by using the association between image features and classes. In the experiments, we achieved a classification rate 44.6% for generic images by using images gathered from the World-Wide Web automatically as learning images.

1 Introduction

Due to the recent spread of digital cameras, we can easily obtain digital images of various kinds of real world scenes, so that demand for image recognition of various kinds of real world images becomes greater. It is, however, hard to apply conventional image recognition methods to such generic recognition, because most of their applicable targets are restricted. Therefore, at present, it is impossible to deal with semantics of images of real world scene automatically. Henceforth, it is desired that automatic attaching keywords to images, classification and search in terms of semantic contents of images.

So far, automatic attaching keywords[1] and semantic search[2] for an image database have been proposed. In these works, since learning images with correct keywords were required, commercial image collections were used as learning images, for example, Corel Image Library. However, most of images in commercial image collections are well-arranged images taken by professional photographers, and many similar images are included in them. They are different from images of real world scenes taken by the people with digital cameras.

In this paper, we propose utilizing images gathered from WWW (World-Wide Web) as learning images for generic image classification instead of commercial image collections. In other words, this research is Web image mining for generic image classification. We can easily extract keywords related to an image on the Web (Web image) from the HTML file linking to it, so that we can regard a Web image as an image with related keywords. Web images are as diverse as

Y.-C. Chen, L.-W. Chang, and C.-T. Hsu (Eds.): PCM 2002, LNCS 2532, pp. 303–310, 2002.

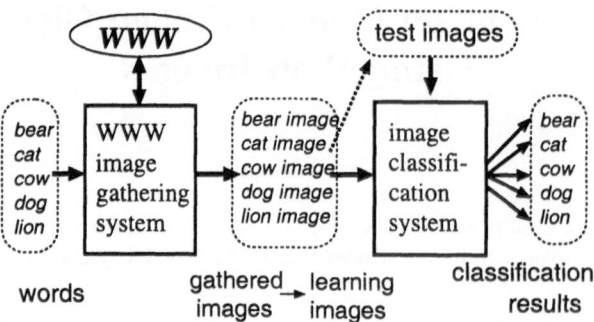

Fig. 1. Image classification by Web images.

real world scene, since Web images are taken by a large number of people for various kinds of purpose.

Image classification by Web images is performed by combination of an image gathering system and an image classification system (Fig.1). First, we gather images related to some kinds of words from the Web by utilizing the Image Collector, which we have proposed in [3]. Next, we extract image features from gathered images and associate image features with words for image classification. Finally, we classify an image into one of classes corresponding to class keywords by comparing its image features with ones of images gathered from the Web in advance.

In this paper, we describe image gathering from the Web, learning and classification. Next, we describe experimental results and conclusions.

2   A Method of Image-Gathering

An image-gathering system gathers images from WWW related to the keywords given by a user. Note that our system is not called an image "search" system but an image "gathering" system, since our system has the following properties: (1) it does not search for images over the whole WWW directly, (2) it does not make a index of the Web images in advance, and (3) it makes use of search results of commercial keyword-based search engines for query keywords. These properties are different from conventional Web image search systems such as WebSeer[4], WebSEEk[5] and Image Rover[6]. These systems search for images based on the query keywords, and then a user selects query images from their search results. These three systems carry out their search in such an interactive manner. Our system is different from those in that our system only needs one-time input of query keywords due to automatic image selection mechanism described later.

Since an image on WWW is usually embedded in an HTML document that explains it, the system exploits some existing commercial keyword-based WWW search engines, and it gathers URLs (Universal Resource Locator) of HTML documents related to query keywords. In the next step, using those gathered URLs, the system fetches HTML documents from WWW, analyzes them, and evaluates the intensity of relation between the keywords and images embedded in HTML documents. If it is judged that images are related to keywords, the image files are fetched from WWW. According to the intensity of relation to the keywords, we divide fetched images into two groups: images in group A having stronger relation to the keywords, and others in group B. For all gathered images, image features are computed. We use a color histogram in the Lu^*v^* color space as image features.

In content-based image retrieval (CBIR), a user provides query images or sketches to the system, because it searches for images based on the similarity of image features between query images and images in an image database. In our image-gathering system, instead of providing query images or sketches, a user only needs to provide query keywords to the system. Then, we select images strongly related to the keywords as group A images, remove noise images from them, and regard them as query images only by examining keywords. Removing noise images is carried out by eliminating images which belong to relatively small clusters in the result of image-feature-based clustering for group A images. Images which are not eliminated are regarded as appropriate images to the query keywords, and we store them as output images. Next, we select images that are similar to the query images from group B in the same way as CBIR, and add them to output images. The detail is described in [3].

3   A Method of Learning and Classification

We make experiments on image classification for images gathered from the Web by image-feature-based search. First, we extract image features from gathered images and associate image features with classes represented by keywords in the learning stage. Next, we classify an image into one of classes corresponding to class keywords by comparing image features in the classification stage.

3.1   Signatures and Earth Mover's Distance

We exploit two kinds of image features for learning and classification: *color signature for block segments*, and *region signature for region segments*. A *signature* describes multi-dimensional discrete distribution, which is represented by a set of vectors and weights. In *case of color signatures*, a vector and a weight correspond to a mean color vector of each cluster and its ratio of pixels belonging to that cluster, respectively, where some color clusters are made in advance by clustering color distribution of an image. Since the number of elements of a signature is variable, it is superior to conventional fixed-size color histograms in terms of expressiveness and efficiency. In case of *region signatures*, a set of feature vectors of regions and their ratio of pixels represents a region signature.

To compute dissimilarity between two signatures, Earth Mover's Distance(EMD) has been proposed[7]. Intuitively, given two signatures, one can be seen as a mass of earth properly spread in the feature space, the other as a collection of holes in the same space. Then, the EMD measures the least amount of work needed to fill the holes with earth. Here, a unit of work corresponds to transporting a unit of earth by a unit of ground distance which is a distance in the feature space. The EMD is based on the transportation problem and can be solved efficiently by linear optimization algorithms.

Formally, let $P = \{(\mathbf{p}_1, w_{p_1}), ..., (\mathbf{p}_m, w_{p_m})\}$ be the first set with m elements, where $\mathbf{p}_i$ is the feature vector and w_{p_i} is its weight; $Q = \{(\mathbf{q}_1, w_{q_1}), ..., (\mathbf{q}_n, w_{q_n})\}$ the second set with n elements; and $d_{ij} = d(\mathbf{p}_i, \mathbf{q}_j)$ the ground distance matrix where d_{ij} is the distance between $\mathbf{p}_i$ and $\mathbf{q}_j$. The EMD between sets P and Q is then

$$\text{EMD}(P, Q) = \frac{\sum_{i=1}^{m} \sum_{j=1}^{n} f_{ij} d_{ij}}{\sum_{i=1}^{m} \sum_{j=1}^{n} f_{ij}} \tag{1}$$

where $\mathbf{F} = [f_{ij}]$, with $f_{ij} \geq 0$ the flow between $\mathbf{p}_i$ and $\mathbf{q}_j$, is the optimal admissible flow from P to Q. In addition, an easy-to-compute lower bound for the EMD between signatures with equal total weights is the distance between their centers of mass.

3.2   Color Signatures

To obtain *color signatures*, first, we normalize the size of learning images into 240×180, and divide them into 16 and 9 block regions as shown in Fig. 2. We make a color signature for each of these 25 block regions. Next, we select some dominant colors by clustering color vectors of each pixel into color clusters by the k-means method. In the experiments, the number of color clusters is 15 or less, and it is decided in order not to make a cluster whose weight is less than 0.005. We make a color signature for each block with elements consisting of a mean color vector of each cluster and its ratio of pixels belonging to that cluster. A mean color vector is represented by the Lu^*v^* color space which is designed in order that Euclid distance between two points in this space matches the human color sense, so that we use Euclid distance as ground distance.

In the classification stage, first, we extract color signatures from each block in an image to be classified (a test image) in the same way as the learning stage after normalizing its size. We obtain 25 sets of signatures for one test image. Next, we search all blocks of learning images of each class for the block with the minimum distance (dissimilarity) to each block of the test image. Here, the distance is computed by the EMD. In the next step, we sum up the minimum distances between the test image and learning images of each class for 25 all blocks. This search and computation is carried out for all the classes. We compare the total distances among all the classes, and we classify the test image into the class whose total distance is the smallest. In the actual implementation, we used lower bound of the EMD to reduce a frequency of computation of the EMD.

3.3   Region Signatures

To obtain *region signatures*, we carry out region segmentation for images instead of dividing images into block segments after normalizing their size (Fig.3). Many methods of region segmentation have been proposed so far. Here, we employ a

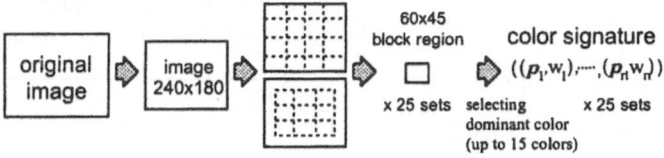

Fig. 2. Color signatures for color segments.

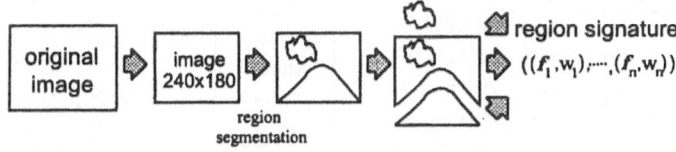

Fig. 3. Region signatures for region segments.

simple segmentation method based on k-means clustering used in [8]. First, we divide a learning image into 4×4 small blocks, and for each block we compute a mean color vector in the Lu^*v^* color space and a texture feature vector, which consists of square means of HL elements, LH elements and HH elements obtained by Daubechies-4 wavelet transform to each 4×4 block. Both vectors are three-dimension, so that a six-dimension feature vector is obtained for each block. Next, we cluster all blocks in a learning image into some regions by the k-means method in the similar way as computing color signatures. In the experiments, the number of color clusters is 15 or less, and it is decided in order not to make a cluster whose weight is less than 0.005. Then, we compute a mean 6-dimension feature vector for each region. In addition, for making a region signatures we extract three more features about shape of a region. We use normalized inertia of order 1 to 3 as three features to describe shape of a region. Finally, we make a region signature with elements consisting of a nine-dimensional feature vector for each region and its ratio of pixels belonging to that region.

In the classification stage, we employ the k-nearest neighbor (k-NN) method to classify a test image into a class. The value of k is decided as 5 by preliminary experiments. We used Euclid distance as ground distance to compute the EMD.

In our method of image classification, image features of not only a target object but also non-target objects such as background included in the image are used as a clue of classification, since non-target objects usually have strong relation to a target object. For example, a cow usually exists with grass field and/or fence in farm, and a lion usually exists in Savannah or zoo. Although the number of combination of a target object and non-target objects is large, we think that we can deal with this largeness by gathering a large amount of image from the Web and using them as learning images. Here, we do not set up "reject", and then all test images are classified into any class.

Table 1. Nine experiments.

no.	num.of classes	num.of images	precision (%)	test images num.	test images src.
1	10	4548	68.2	20	www
2	10	3102	100†	20	www
3	10	500	100‡	10	Corel
4	10	4548	68.2	50	Corel
5	10	3102	100	50	Corel
6	20	5694	61.2	20	www
7	20	3485	100†	20	www
8	20	5694	61.2	20	special
9	20	3485	100†	20	special

†selection of correct images by hand.
‡Corel Image as a learning set

Table 2. Results of image-gathering (left) and classification (right) in experiment no.1

class	num.	pre.	rec.	pre.	F
bear	419	56.4	21.0	31.1	25.1
cat	354	62.0	28.0	60.9	38.4
dog	570	75.7	40.0	23.3	29.4
elephant	506	65.5	25.0	23.1	24.0
tropical fish	275	89.9	22.0	74.6	34.0
lion	504	77.0	45.0	25.2	32.3
penguin	576	57.0	33.5	29.0	31.1
sheep	347	64.0	13.0	34.2	18.8
tiger	405	68.7	24.0	32.2	27.5
whale	592	72.4	66.5	39.0	49.2
total/avg.	**4582**	**68.2**	31.8	37.3	**34.3**
by region sig.			29.4	30.3	**29.8**

4 Experimental Results

We made nine experiments from no.1 to no.9 shown in Table 1.

In the experiment no.1, we gathered images from the Web for 10 kinds of words related to animals shown in Table 2. In the image-gathering processing, about ten thousands URLs were fetched from six major text search engines, Google, InfoSeek, Excite, Lycos, InfoNavi and Goo Japan. The total number of gathered image was 4582, and the precision by subjective evaluation was 68.2%, which is defined to be $N_{OK}/(N_{OK} + N_{NG})$, where N_{OK}, N_{NG} are the number of relevant images and the number of irrelevant images to their keywords. In the left side of Table 2, we show the number and the precision of gathered images.

In the image classification experiment, we regard each of the 10 words as one class. In the right side of Table 2, we show the classification result evaluated by 10-fold cross-validation. In this section, tables describe results by color signatures mainly, and results by region signatures are shown only in the bottom line of each table. In the table, the recall is defined to be M_{OK}/M_{test}, the precision is defined to be $M_{OK}/(M_{OK} + M_{NG})$ and F-measure is the harmonic mean of the recall and the precision, where M_{OK}, M_{NG}, M_{test} are the number of correctly classified images, the number of incorrectly classified images, and the number of test images for each class, respectively. All values are represented in percentage. In the experiment no.1, we obtained 31.0 as the F-measure value.

In the experiment no.2, we select only correct images for each class from gathered images by hand, and the classification experiment was carried out using them. The result is shown in Table 3. Compared to no.1, the F-measure increased. Especially, the result of "whale" was good, since most of "whale" images on the Web were images of "whale watching" scene.

In the experiment no.3, we made a classification experiment not for Web images but for the 500 images of 10 classes picked up from Corel Image Gallery. The classification result evaluated by 10-fold cross-validation is shown in Table

Table 3. Results of image-gathering and classification in experiment no. 2, 3, 4, 5

class	exp. no.2 rec. pre. F	exp. no.3 rec. pre. F	exp. no.4 rec. pre. F	exp. no.5 rec. pre. F
bear	17.1 46.2 25.0	36.0 62.1 45.6	8.0 15.4 10.5	4.0 40.0 7.3
cat	34.3 78.7 47.8	61.2 85.7 71.4	4.1 33.3 7.3	6.1 42.9 10.7
dog	58.6 21.5 31.4	24.0 75.0 36.4	24.0 14.8 18.3	58.0 21.3 31.2
elephant	25.0 32.1 28.1	68.0 69.4 68.7	34.0 34.7 34.3	16.0 25.8 19.8
tropical fish	35.7 62.5 45.5	58.0 93.5 71.6	22.0 61.1 32.4	30.0 46.9 36.6
lion	47.9 35.1 40.5	82.0 77.4 79.6	30.0 19.5 23.6	36.0 27.3 31.0
penguin	47.9 27.3 34.8	50.0 42.4 45.9	26.0 19.7 22.4	48.0 25.5 33.3
sheep	17.1 36.4 23.3	80.0 46.0 58.4	8.0 23.5 11.9	4.0 18.2 6.6
tiger	10.7 60.0 18.2	72.0 69.2 70.6	4.0 7.4 5.2	10.0 45.5 16.4
whale	75.0 55.6 63.8	94.0 53.4 68.1	86.0 32.6 47.3	86.0 40.6 55.1
avg. by color	36.9 45.5 **40.8**	62.5 67.4 **64.9**	24.6 26.2 **25.4**	29.8 33.4 **31.5**
avg. by region	35.4 37.2 **36.2**	67.1 69.2 **68.1**	23.2 20.7 **21.9**	26.0 22.8 **24.3**

3. Since Corel Image Gallery includes many similar images to each other, a high F-measure value, 68.1, was obtained by region signatures.

In the experiment no.4 and no.5, we used the gathered images in the experiment no.1 and no.2 as learning images and the Corel images as test images. The results are shown in Table 3. In no.4 and no.5, we obtained 25.4 and 31.5 as F-measure, respectively. Since "dog", "tropical fish", "lion", "penguin" and "whale" have some typical patterns and both of the gathered images and the Corel images include the images with the typical patterns, their F-measure achieved high values. On the other hand, since "bear", "cat", "elephant", "sheep" and "tiger" had no typical patterns, their F-measures were relatively low.

In the experiment no.6 and no.7, we made an experiment for 20 words (Table 4) which includes many different kinds of words in the same way as the experiment no.1 and no.2. Compared to the expected F-measure, 5.0, in case of the random classification, we obtained much better F-measure, 42.3 and 46.7 shown in Table 5. These results are superior to the result of the experiment no.1 and no.2 for only 10 classes, because all classes used in no.1 and no.2 are related to animals and their learning images include many similar images even between different classes. In case of "apple", "Kinkaku Temple" and "noodle", their result were about 60.0, since their scene have some typical patterns and many of their images were applicable to them. On the other hand, for "house" we obtained only a very low F-measure value, since "house" images had much variation. From these results, difficulty of classification depends on the properties of the class.

It is hard to collect such various kinds of images as images used in the experiment no.6 and no.7 by means of commercial image databases, and it has come to be possible only by image-gathering from the World-Wide Web.

In the experiment no.8 and no.9, we used the gathered images in the experiment no.6 and no.7 as learning images and a special test image set as test images. We make a special test image set by selecting various kinds of 50 typical images for each class from Corel Image Gallery and Web images by hand. The classification results are shown in Table 5. In no.8 and no.9, we obtained 44.6 and 47.0

Table 4. 20 class keywords

20: apple, bear, bike, lake, car, cat, entrance ceremony, house, Ichiro, Ferris wheel, lion, Moai, Kinkaku Temple, note PC, bullet train, park, penguin, noodle, wedding, Mt.Yari

Table 5. Results of experiment no.6, 7, 8, 9

	exp. no.6	exp. no.7	exp. no.8	exp. no.9
class	rec. pre. F	rec. pre. F	rec. pre. F	rec. pre. F
avg. by color	34.9 53.6 **42.3**	35.7 67.8 **46.7**	39.8 50.7 **44.6**	38.5 60.4 **47.0**
avg. by region	34.3 37.7 **35.9**	37.0 45.5 **40.8**	40.1 43.1 **41.5**	42.1 47.9 **44.8**

as F-measure, respectively. These results are comparable to conventional works of generic image recognition. However, unlike them, we provide learning images not by hand, but by gathering images from the World-Wide Web automatically.

5   Conclusions

In this paper, we described experiments on generic image classification using images gathered from the World-Wide Web. While the main targets of the conventional works on knowledge retrieval from the Web are numeric data and text data, we have proposed knowledge retrieval of image data from the Web in this paper. For future works, we plan to make much improvement in classification methods and extraction of image features to obtain more improved classification rate.

References

1. Barnard, K., Forsyth, D.A.: Learning the semantics of words and pictures. In: Proc. of IEEE International Conference on Computer Vision. Volume II. (2001) 408–415
2. Belongie, S., Carson, C., Greenspan, H., Malik, J.: Recognition of images in large databases using a learning framework. Technical Report 07-939, UC Berkeley CS Tech Report (1997)
3. Yanai, K.: Image collector: An image-gathering system from the World-Wide Web employing keyword-based search engines. In: Proc. of IEEE International Conference of Multimedia and Expo. (2001) 704–707
4. Framkel, C., Swain, M.J., Athitsos, V.: WebSeer: An image search engine for the World Wide Web. Technical Report TR-96-14, University of Chicago (1996)
5. Smith, J.R., Chang, S.F.: Visually searching the Web for content. IEEE Multimedia 4 (1997) 12–20
6. Sclaroff, S., LaCascia, M., Sethi, S., Taycher, L.: Unifying textual and visual cues for content-based image retrieval on the World Wide Web. Computer Vision and Image Understanding 75 (1999) 86–98
7. Rubner, Y., Tomasi, C., Guibas, L.J.: The earth mover's distance as a metric for image retrieval. International Journal of Computer Vision 40 (2000) 99–121
8. Wang, J.Z., Li, J., Wiederhold, G.: SIMPLIcity: semantics-sensitive integrated matching for picture libraries. IEEE Transactions on Pattern Analysis and Machine Intelligence 23 (2001) 947–963

An Authoring Tool Generating Various Video Abstractions Semi-automatically

Jongho Nang[1], Jinguk Jeong[1],
Myung-hwan Ha[2], Byunghee Jung[2], and Kyeongsoo Kim[2]

[1] Dept. of Computer Science, Sogang University, 1 Shinsoo-Dong, Mapo-Ku
Seoul 121-742, Korea
jhnang@ccs.sogang.ac.kr
[2] KBS Technical Research Institute, 18 Yoido-dong, Youngdungpo-gu, Seoul 150-790,
Korea

Abstract. Video abstraction is a short version of the original video, and it is used to deliver the summary *or* the highlight of video contents as quickly as possible. According to the objectives of the video abstraction, the set of shots constituting the abstraction should be different. This paper presents an authoring tool that could automatically generate various kinds of video abstractions according to the objectives of the abstraction, and allows the author to easily edit the resulting abstraction manually. In the proposed automatic video abstraction algorithm, a simulated annealing algorithm is used to select the set of shots that simultaneously satisfies several constraints, such as *well-distributed*, *well-fitting*, *high-activities*, and *non-duplicated* (or *concise*), as much as possible. This set of shots could be used as a final video abstraction, or a candidate of the video abstraction that the author could replace with just a drag-and-drop of the key frame of the selected shot on the time-line of target video abstraction.

1 Introduction

Although there have been many researches [2,3,4,7,8,9] to abstract a long video clip to a shorter version automatically, they are usually based on the domain specific heuristics so that their usages would be limited only to the specific domains. For example, the heuristics used to abstract the action movie clips could not be used to abstract the documentary video clips. This problem could be resolved if the abstraction process has reflected the user's requirements for the video abstraction as much as possible, and let the author additionally edit the resulting video abstraction manually.

This paper proposes a subjective video abstraction algorithm that generates various video abstractions according to the user's requirements, and an authoring tool that helps the author to easily edit the generated video abstraction manually. It first analyzes a set of conditions (or constraints) that a good video abstraction should satisfy, and formalizes them as the objective functions. The proposed main constraints that the set of selected shots constituting the abstraction should satisfy are

Y.-C. Chen, L.-W. Chang, and C.-T. Hsu (Eds.): PCM 2002, LNCS 2532, pp. 311–318, 2002.

well-distributed, well-fitting, high-activities, non-duplicated (or *concise*), and so on. Then, this paper formalizes the video abstraction process as a combinatorial optimization problem that selects k shots from the original video clip consisting of n shots while satisfying the above constraints as much as possible. Since this problem is so called an NP-complete ($O(n^2)$), this paper proposes a shot selection algorithm based on the simulated annealing [6] in order to generate a video abstraction, which could satisfy the user's requirements represented by the weights of the objective functions as much as possible, in a polynomial time. After the set of shots are selected, their key frames are placed on the time-line of the video abstraction in the authoring tool and could be replaced by author by just a drag-and-drop operation. We have implemented proposed authoring tool on MS-WINDOWS platform, and this paper explains its main functions with easy-to-use GUI, after presenting the basic idea of proposed video abstraction algorithm together with some experimental results.

2   A Video Abstraction Algorithm

2.1 Problem Definition

The main process to make a video abstraction is to select some important shots from the video clip after it is segmented into a set of shots. Let $V = \{v_i \mid 1 \le i \le n\}$ be the video clip consisting of n shots, and $X = \{x_i \mid x_i \in V, 1 \le i \le k, 1 \le k \le n\}$ be its abstraction consisting of k shots. Then, the video abstraction process is to select the k shots from n shots, and the number of different video abstractions consisting of k shots would be $_nC_k$. Since the range of k would be $1 \le k \le n$ accroding to the target run-time of abstraction, the total number of different video abstractions would be $_nC_0 + {_nC_1} + {_nC_2} + \ldots + {_nC_n} = 2^n$. A good video abstraction would be the one among these 2^n candidates that satisfies the desirable conditions as much as possible. In the proposed abstraction scheme, some low-level visual constraints that a good abstraction should satisfy are idnetified, and the users express their requirements by adjusting the importantces of these constraints. Although this approach could not meet the high level user requirements exactly, the abstraction process could be performed almost automatically while meeting the user's requirements as much as possible. Let us formalize these constraints in the following section.

2.2 Formalizing the Constraints

In the proposed formalization, the start frame number, the end frame number, and the length of shot x_i are represented as S_i, E_i, and L_i, respectively. Let us also assume that the target run-time of the abstraction that is required by the user dynamically is denoted as T.

- *Well-Distributed* (O_1)

This constraint means that the set of shots selected for the abstraction should be uniformly distributed over the whole video in order to provide an impression on the entire video content. It is especially important for the summary-style abstraction. If the intervals between selected shots in X are similar to each other, we can say it is well-distributed abstraction. The average interval between the shots in X, μ, could be computed as follows;

$$\mu = \frac{(S_1 - 0) + (S_2 - E_1) + ... + (E - E_k)}{k+1} = \frac{E - \sum_{i=1}^{k} L_i}{k+1}$$

Since a lower variance implies a higher well-distributed abstraction, its inverse function is defined as an objective function for Well-Distributed constraint, O_1, as follows;

$$O_1(X) = \frac{1}{\text{var}(\mu)} = \frac{1}{|S_1 - \mu| + |(E - E_k) - \mu| + \sum_{i=2}^{k} |(S_i - E_{i-1}) - \mu|}$$

- **Well-Fitting (O_2)**

If the difference between the target run-time of the abstraction (T) and the sum of the run-time of the shots in X $(L = \sum_{i=1}^{k} L_i)$ is small (*i.e.*, $T \approx L$), it could be a good abstraction. This constraint could be formalized as follows using a transcendental function, *sech(x)*, where $C_1 = \frac{2}{T} \ln(2 + \sqrt{3})$.

$$O_2(X) = \frac{2}{e^{C_1(L-T)} + e^{-C_1(L-T)}}$$

- **Not-too-Short (O_3)**

The minimum run-time of a continuous shot should be at least 3.5 seconds to be processed completely by brain [8]. On the other hand, if the shot run-time is greater than 3.5 seconds, the shot has an equal opportunity to be selected as a member of the abstraction. To express this constraint, $f(L_i) = \frac{L_i + C_2 - |L_i - C_2|}{2 \cdot C_2}$ is used to denote the suitability of the shot x_i for the abstraction, where C_2 is fixed as 3.5. The average value of $f(L_i)$ for all shots in X is defined as an objective function for Not-too-Short constraint as follows;

$$O_3(X) = \frac{1}{k} \sum_{i=1}^{k} \frac{L_i + C_2 - |L_i - C_2|}{2 \cdot C_2}$$

- **Highly-Active (O_4)**

If there are a lot of object motions in the shot, it is usually regarded as an important one so that it should be included in the abstraction. It is a commonly used heuristics in the video abstraction researches as in [7, 8, 9]. To express this constraint, *the motion intensity index* of the shot [4] for x_i, $g(x_i)$, is used to represent the degree of activity of the shot. The average motion intensity index of the shot x_i in X is defined as an objective function for Highly-Active constraint as follows;

$$O_4(X) = \frac{1}{k} \sum_{i=1}^{k} |g(x_i)|$$

where $g(x_i) = \dfrac{1}{L} \displaystyle\sum_{j=b}^{e} \sum_{m,n} \left| m_j(m,n) \right|$ and $m_j(m,n)$ is the j-th frame of motion sequence

within the i-th shot unit and L is the length of the analysis window beginning at b-th frame and ending at e-th frame.

- *Concise or Non-Redundancy (O_5)*

In order to include more information in the video abstraction, the similar shots should not be selected repeatedly in the abstraction process. This heuristics has been adopted in a couple of video abstraction researches [1, 2, 8]. We also adopt this heuristics in the proposed scheme, and the degree of the visual differences between the shots in X is used to denote the suitability of X for the video abstraction. Actually, the historgram differences between the key frames of shots are used to compute the visual differences of the shots in X. The overall visual differences between all shots in X could be computed using following equaltion ;

$$O_5(X) = \frac{1}{2} - \frac{1}{2} \cdot \frac{1}{k} \sum_{i=0}^{k-1} \sum_{j=i+1}^{k} \frac{\vec{f}_z^i \cdot \vec{f}_z^j}{\left|\vec{f}_z^i\right| \cdot \left|\vec{f}_z^j\right|}$$

where $\vec{f}_z^i$ is the color histogram of key frame of i-th shot.

- *Shot-Exclusion (O_6)*

If the video abstraction is used as a video trailer, the last part of the video clip should be concealed. In this case, only the shots in the first 80% of the video clips could be the candidates for the video abstraction [7]. In order to express this constraint, the

function, $h(x_i) = \left(\dfrac{E - E_i - \left|E_i - C_3\right|}{2 \cdot (E - C_3)} + \dfrac{1}{2} \right)$, is used to denote the suitability of x_i in X for

the video abstraction, and their average value is defined as an objective function for Shot-Exclusion constraint as follow ;

$$O_6(X) = \frac{1}{k} \sum_{i=1}^{k} h(x_i) = \frac{1}{k} \sum_{i=1}^{k} \left(\frac{E - E_i - \left|E_i - C_3\right|}{2 \cdot (E - C_3)} + \frac{1}{2} \right)$$

where C_3 is the start frame number of last 20% of video clip.

- *Non-Bias (O_7)*

If the run-time of the shot x_i is too long, a relatively small number shots could be included in the video abstraction. To avoid this problem, the shot with too long run-time would be excluded in the video abstraction. To express this constraint, the

difference between the average shot length of the shots in X ($\alpha = \dfrac{1}{k} \cdot \displaystyle\sum_{i=1}^{k} L_i$) and the

longest run length of the shot in X ($\max(L_i)$) is used to denote the suitability of the X for the abstraction. Since less difference implies more suitability, its inverse function is defined as an objective function for Non-Bias constraint as follow;

$$O_7(X) = \frac{1}{\left| \alpha - \max(L_i) \right|}, \forall i \in \{1,...,k\}$$

Since the range of the return values of these objective functions would be different from each other (for example, the ranges would be $[0:\infty]$ for O_1 and O_7, while others are not), they should be normalized to the same range in order to evaluate their suitability precisely. In the proposed scheme, a normalizing function, $f(x) = \dfrac{x}{x+1}$, is used to normalize the objective function values to $[0:1]$. The normalized objective functions could be computed using following equation, and they are used to compute the overall suitability of the X for the abstraction.

$$O'_n(X) = \frac{O_n(X)}{O_n(X) + 1}$$

A good video abstraction would be a set of shots that simultaneously satisfies above constraints as much as possible. However, since the relative importance of the constraints represented by objective functions are dependent on the aims of abstraction, the objective function values should be weighted in computing the overall suitability of X for the abstraction. Thus, the process to make a good abstraction could be formalized by finding a set of shots X that maximizes the weighted sum of the objective functions, $G(X)$, using the following equation;

$$G(X) = \sum_{p=1}^{7} W_p \cdot O'_p(X)$$

where W_p is the weight of the objective function $O'_p(X)$.

2.3 Abstraction Algorithm Using Simulated Annealing

Since the number of possible video abstractions for the video clip consisting of n shots is 2^n, it would be very hard to generate a good video abstraction in a polynomial time as mentioned before. It is a sort of combinatorial optimization problem to find X among 2^n candidates that maximizes the overall objective function $G(X)$. There have been several search algorithms that could find the near-optimal solution of combinatorial optimization problems. Simulated annealing algorithm [6] is one of such search algorithms that could find a sub-optimal solution in a polynomial time. We have used it to find a set of shots X that maximizes the overall objective function $G(X)$, among 2^n candidates.

In order to apply the simulated annealing algorithm to the video abstraction problem, initially a set of shots, X_1, is randomly selected among 2^n candidates, and its overall objective function value $(G(X_1))$ is computed. Then, another set of shots, X_2, is selected again and its overall objective function value $(G(X_2))$ is also computed. If $G(X_2) > G(X_1)$, then X_2 is accepted as a candidate of the good abstraction. Otherwise, X_2 is accepted as the candidate of the good abstraction with the probability of $e^{\frac{-(G(X_2)-G(X_1))}{T}}$, where T is an initial temperature which controls the annealing process. Let the accepted abstraction as the candiate of the good abstraction, and repeat the above process while decreasing the temperature T until it is less than predefined temperature ε. In this annealing process, when T is high enough, the probability of accepting the worse abstraction than current one is also high.

However, as the annealing process is being progressed (i.e., T is being decreased), the probabilty to accept the worse abstraction as the candidate of good abstraction is also decreased. This stochastical annealing process helps to avoid the locally optimal abstraction, and to eventually find a globally near optimal abstraction in a reasonable time.

2.4 Experimental Results and Analyses

Let us show an experimental result on the Korean drama video clip (30 minutes long) consisting of 52,873 frames that are grouped into 239 shots. The target run-time of the abstraction is fixed as 2 minutes (3,600 frames) in this experiment. Note that the total number of possible video abstractions is theoretically 2^{239} in this experiment.

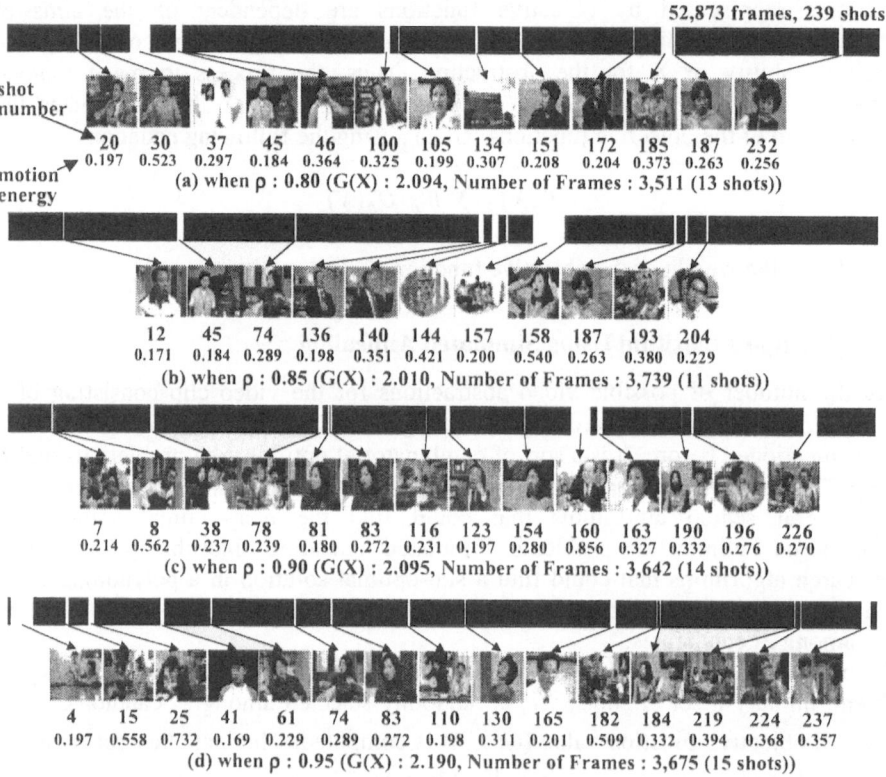

Fig. 1. An example of video abstractions generated with different cooling rates

We have experimented our abstraction algorithm four times while varying the cooling rate (ρ) of simulated annealing. The generated four video abstractions are shown in Figure 1, in which the key frames (or first frames) of the shots in each abstraction are shown with their shot numbers and motion energies. Since the weights of the objective functions to compute $G(X)$ are adjusted to be the same in this experiment, the selected shots equally satisfy the proposed seven constraints as much as possible. For example, the selected shots are uniformly distributed over the whole video, the number of frames in the abstraction is similar to *3,600*, the visually similar shots are seldom selected together, and finally the shots with high motion energies are selected as shown in Figure 1. We can find from this experiment that the visually similar shots (for example, 4th and 5th shot in Figure 1-(b), 5th and 6th shots in Figure 1-(c)) are disappeared as the cooling rate is raised as shown in Figure 1-(d). It is due to the fact that the probability of selecting the visually similar shots are lowered as the cooling rate is raised (slow annealing process) because of the objective function O_5.

3 An Authoring Tool

Although the video abstraction generated by the proposed algorithm could reflect the user's requirements as much as possible by adjusting the weight of the constraints, the resulting abstraction would not be satisfiable because it was generated without a full understanding of the video contents. This problem could be resolved if the selected shots are used as the candidates for the abstraction and replaced with more suitable shots manually by the author, as in the authoring tool presented in this section. In the proposed authoring tool, the video clip is first segmented into a set of shots automatically, the candidate shots for the video abstraction among them are selected using the proposed algorithm, and finally they are edited by the author manually to produce a final video abstraction using the interface as shown in Figure 2. It also provides an user interface to modified the shot boundaries manually, since the automatic indexing algorithm could not find all shot boundaries completely. After the vide clip is segmented into a set of shots, the thumbnail images of the 1st frame of the shots (key frames) are enumerated as shown in Figure 2.

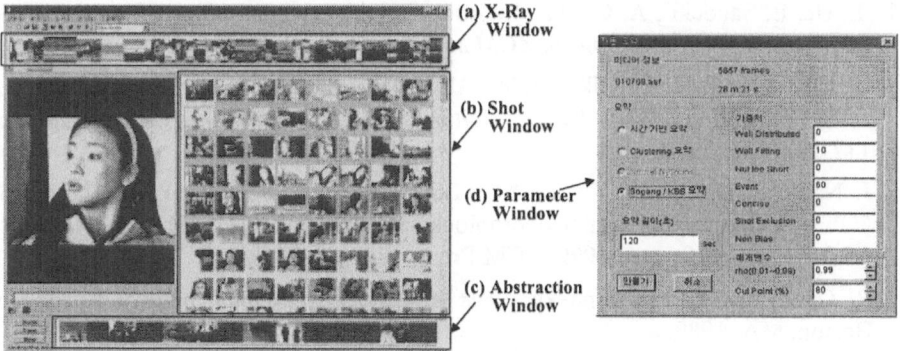

Fig. 2. The User Interface of Authoring Tool

4 Concluding Remarks

As the digital video clips are being used in wide range of applications on Internet or Intranet, the capability to preview the highlight or summary of the long video without viewing the whole video clips becomes an essential feature that a video-based server should provide. However, to automatically abstract (or summarize) the long video clip to a shorter one requires a sophiscated artificial intelligence technology to map the low-level visual/aural features to hight-level semantics. Since this technology would not be available in the near future, this paper proposes other framework that let the user/author express the his/her requirements by the weights of the constraints that a good video abstraction should satisfy, and the abstraction algorithm find a set of shots that satisfies these weighted constraints as much as possible using the searching algorithm based on simulated annealing. Of course, the constraints proposed in this paper would not be the best ones for generating a good video abstraction, and the formalization for these constraints could be also modified. However, although some constraints are modified or formalized with other equations, the proposed abstraction framework could still be used to dynamically generate a video abstraction for various genre of video clips with respect to them. We argue that although the video abstraction generated with the proposed abstraction algorithm could not meet the user's requirements directly, this approach would be a good compromise between the abstraction schemes based on just pattern-matching of pre-defined low-level visual/aural features and the abstraction schemes based on fully understanding of high-level video contents.

References

[1] H. Chang, S. Sull and S. Lee, "Efficient Video Indexing Scheme for Content-Based Retrieval," *IEEE Transaction on Circuits and Systems for Video Technology*, Vol.9, No. 8, pp. 1269-1279, 1999.

[2] A. Hanjalic and H. Zhang, "An Integrated Scheme for Automated Video Abstraction Based on Unsupervised Cluster-Validity Analysis," *IEEE Transaction on Circuits and Systems for Video Technology*, Vol. 9, No.8, pp.1280-1289, 1999.

[3] L. He, E. Sanocki , A. Gupta , J. Grudin, "Auto-Summarization of Audio-Video Presentations," *Proceedings of ACM Multimedia Conference*, pp. 489 - 498, 1999.

[4] J. Nam and A. H. Tewfik, "Video Abstract of Video," *Proceedings of the 3rd IEEE International Workshop on Multimedia Signal Processing (MMSP '99)*, pp. 117-122, Sep. 1999.

[5] J. Nang, S. Hong and Y. Ihm "An Effective Video Segmentation Scheme for MPEG Video Stream using Macroblock Information," *Proceedings of the ACM Multimedia Conference 1999*, ACM Press, 1999, pp.23-26.

[6] R. Otten, and L. van Ginneken, *The Annealing Algorithm*. Kluwer Academic, Boston, MA, 1989.

[7] S. Pfeiffer, R. Lienhart, S. Fischer and W. Effelsberg, "Abstracting Digital Movies Automatically," *Journal of Visual Communication and Image*, Vol. 7, No. 4, pp.345-353, 1996.

[8] J. Saarela and B. Merialdo, "Using Content Models to Builds Audio-Video Summaries," *Proceedings of the Electronic Imaging Conference SPIE'99*, 1999.

[9] M. Smith and T. Kanade, "Video Skimming and Characterization Through the Combination of Image and Language Understanding Techniques," *Proceedings of IEEE Conference on Computer Vision and Pattern Recognition*, pp.775-781, 1997.

Motion Activity Based Semantic Video Similarity Retrieval[†]

Duan-Yu Chen, Suh-Yin Lee, and Hua-Tsung Chen

Department of Computer Science and Information Engineering,
National Chiao-Tung University, 1001 Ta-Hsueh Rd, Hsinchu, Taiwan
{dychen,sylee,huatsung}@csie.nctu.edu.tw

Abstract. *Semantic feature extraction of video shots and fast video sequence matching are important and required for efficient retrieval in a large video database. In this paper, a novel mechanism of similarity retrieval is proposed. Similarity measure between video sequences considering the spatio-temporal variation through consecutive frames is presented. For bridging the semantic gap between low-level features and the rich meaning that users desire to capture, video shots are analyzed and characterized by the high-level feature of motion activity in compressed domain. The extracted features of motion activity are further described by the 2D-histogram that is sensitive to the spatio-temporal variation of moving objects. In order to reduce the dimensions of feature vector space in sequence matching, Discrete Cosine Transform (DCT) is exploited to map semantic features of consecutive frames to the frequency domain while retains the discriminatory information and preserves the Euclidean distance between feature vectors. Experiments are performed on MPEG-7 testing videos, and the results of sequence matching show that a few DCT transformed coefficients are adequate and thus reveal the effectiveness of the proposed mechanism of video retrieval.*

1 Introduction

In the research of video sequence characterization, the most difficult task is to represent video content in a compact form and also to provide enough information to describe rich meaning of video content simultaneously. In the related literatures, video shots are mainly represented by key-frames. Low-level features, like color, texture and shape are extracted from these key-frames for supporting indexing and retrieval. The disadvantage of such strategy is that it ignores the inherent and significant feature – spatial temporal information of consecutive frames through video sequences. Therefore, some researchers take the property of temporal variation of video sequence into account to perform similarity matching.

Wang et al [1] propose a query-by-example system, which extracts features of color, edge and motion and perform similarity measurement of temporal patterns using the method of dynamic programming. Lin et al [2] segment a video shot into subshots and compute the similarity of video shots between corresponding subshots, in which

---

[†] This research is partially supported by Lee & MTI Center, National Chiao-Tung University, Taiwan and National Science Council, Taiwan.

Y.-C. Chen, L.-W. Chang, and C.-T. Hsu (Eds.): PCM 2002, LNCS 2532, pp. 319–327, 2002.

two descriptors are characterized, dominant color histograms and spatial structure histograms. Cheung and Zakhor [3] utilize the HSV color histogram to represent the keyframes of video clips and design a video signature clustering algorithm for video similarity detection. Dimitrova et al [4] represent video segments by the color super-histograms. Roach et al [5] identify and verify cartoons and non-cartoons videos by extracting motion feature in pixel domain. Zhao et al [6] present an approach – nearest feature line in shot retrieval Lines connecting the feature points are further used to approximate the variation in the whole shots. Mohan [8] characterizes the consecutive frames by using the reduced intensity image from DC-images of I, P and B frames. Yeung and Liu [9] select key-frames non-linearly according to the temporal variation of I-frames and perform video sequence matching based on comparison among DC-images of key-frames.

In the previous researches of similarity matching among consecutive frames, most researchers focus on video partition, key-frame selection and low-level feature extraction on the selected key-frames [7]. In the strategy of key-frame matching, the dimensionality of key-frame descriptors is quite high and the high dimensionality of the feature vectors will have efficiency problem in indexing, searching and retrieval of huge volume of video data. Little efforts can accomplish video similarity matching taking high-level temporal variation into consideration throughout video sequences while at the same time they could reduce the dimensionality of the descriptors and preserve the original topology of the high dimensional feature space.

Hence, in this paper, in order to support high-level semantic retrieval of video content, the proposed motion activity descriptor – 2D histogram [10] is exploited to describe video segments considering spatio-temporal relationships among video objects or moving blobs. Furthermore, to retrieve the nearest neighborrs of a query and preserve the local topology of the high dimensional space, the Discrete Cosine Transform is utilized to map the time sequence of high dimensional feature space to lower dimensional space. By applying the Discrete Cosine Transform, original time sequence of feature vector is transformed from time domain to frequency domain. Based on the property of energy concentration of the DCT coefficients, using a few DCT coefficients for indexing of video segments does not affect the retrieval accuracy and is thus adequate for representation of the feature in a video sequence.

The rest of the paper is organized as follows. Representation and matching of video sequences are described in Section 2. Section 3 presents the experimental results. Conclusion and the future works are given in Section 4.

2   Video Sequence Matching

While video segments are characterized by the motion activity descriptors, the Discrete Cosine Transform is applied to map the time sequence of the descriptor into frequency domain. A few DCT coefficients are selected to represent the whole video segment, and the choice of similarity measure is based on the meaning of the DCT coefficients and the characteristic of the motion activity descriptor. The details of the representation of video sequence and the defined similarity measure are illustrated in Subsection 2.1 and Subsection 2.2, respectively.

2.1 Representation of Video Sequences

In order to reduce the dimensionality of the feature vector space, the Discrete Cosine Transform is exploited. The details of the algorithm of video sequence representation are described as follows.

Video Sequence Representation

Input: Consecutive P-frames $\{P1, P2, P3, ..., PN\}$

Output: Sequences of reduced low-dimensional DCT coefficients $\{S1, S2, S3, ..., Sk\}$

1. For each P-frame Pi, detect moving objects by clustering macroblocks, which have similar motion vector magnitude and similar motion direction.
2. For each object,
   Compute its centroid and object size in terms of macroblocks.
3. Set the number of histogram bins to k
4. For each P-frame Pi, compute the X-histogram and Y-histogram according to the horizontal and vertical position of objects, respectively.
5. For each sequence of histogram bin $[Bin_{t,j}^{z}]$, where $t \in [1, N]$, $j \in [1, k]$ and $Z \in \{X, Y\}$, compute the transformed sequence $[Z_{f,j}]$ by utilizing the Discrete Cosine Transform

$$Z_{f,j} = C(f) \sum_{t=1}^{N} Bin_{t,j}^{z} \cos\left(\frac{(2t+1)f\pi}{2N}\right), \text{ where } f \in [1, N]$$

6. Set the number of DCT coefficients to α.
7. For k transformed sequences $[Z_{f,j}]$ of DCT coefficients, Select the DC coefficient and $(\alpha-1)$ AC coefficients to represent a transformed sequence.
8. Generate the k reduced low-dimensional sequences $[Z_{f,j}]$, where $f \in [1, \alpha]$ and $j \in [1, k]$.

2.2 Choice of Similarity Measure

Based on the observation of the Parseval's theorem, the Euclidean distance between two transformed signals $[W_f^X]$ and $[H_f^X]$ of X-histogram ($[W_f^Y]$ and $[H_f^Y]$ of Y-histogram) in frequency domain is the same as their distance in the time domain. Therefore, the L2-norm distance is used as the measure of the distance between two video sequences. Eq. (1) shows the distance measure of the jth X-histogram bin between two transformed sequences $[W_f^X]$ and $[H_f^X]$ ($[W_f^Y]$ and $[H_f^Y]$ of Y-histogram) in frequency domain, where M is the number of the selected DCT coefficients. The total distance of X-histogram $Dist_X(W, H)$ and that of Y-histogram $Dist_Y(W, H)$ is thus defined as the sum of the distance of each bin shown in Eq. (2). Hence, the distance between two video sequences can be defined as the sum of $Dist_X(W, H)$ and $Dist_Y(W, H)$.

$$Dist(W_j^X, H_j^X) = \sum_{c=1}^{M} \left(W_{f,j} - H_{f,j}\right)^2, Dist(W_j^Y, H_j^Y) = \sum_{c=1}^{M} \left(W_{f,j} - H_{f,j}\right)^2 \tag{1}$$

$$Dist_X(W,H) = \sum_{j=1}^{k} Dist(W_j^X, H_j^X) , Dist_Y(W,H) = \sum_{j=1}^{k} Dist(W_j^Y, H_j^Y) \tag{2}$$

However, two video sequences w and h which are regarded as similar is based on the human perception on the spatio-temporal distribution of moving objects, i.e., w and h are considered similar if they confirm to one or more of the following criteria: (1) the number of moving objects of w and h are similar; (2) the variation of spatial distribution in horizontal direction of moving objects in w and h are resembling; (3) the variation of spatial distribution in vertical direction of moving objects in w and h are similar. In order to take these three criteria into account, the distance measure defined in Eq. (2) of video sequences is modified as Eq. (3), where the operator $shr(n,H)$ denotes that each bin in the X-histogram or Y-histogram of the transformed DCT coefficients shifts rights and rotates n bins. The meaning of Eq. (3) is that different video sequences may consist of multiple objects, which may be of similar spatial relationships but with different spatial distribution.

$$Dist_X(w,h) = Min\left(\begin{array}{l} Dist_X(W,H), Dist_X(W, shr(1,H)), \\ Dist_X(W, shr(2,H)),..., Dist_X(W, shr(k-1,H)) \end{array} \right)$$

$$Dist_Y(w,h) = Min\left(\begin{array}{l} Dist_Y(W,H), Dist_Y(W, shr(1,H)), \\ Dist_Y(W, shr(2,H)),..., Dist_Y(W, shr(k-1,H)) \end{array} \right) \tag{3}$$

Therefore, the distance $Dist_X(w,h)$ and $Dist_Y(w,h)$ are considered together for the computation of the total distance $Dist_{total}(w,h)$ between video sequences w and h. The total distance $Dist_{total}(w,h)$ is defined in Eq. (4), where WT_H is the weight of X-histogram (WT_V of Y-histogram), N is the number of P-frames, and $MV_{i,H}$ and $MV_{i,V}$ are the average motion vector magnitude of the X-component and Y-component respectively of inter-coded macroblocks in the ith P-frame. The similarity measure of Eq. (4) is based on the fact that human perception on similarity of video sequences is usually affected by the moving direction of objects in addition to the number of objects. That is, video sequences would be still regarded as similar if their objects move in the same or resembling direction. In general, cameras would pan or tilt while objects move horizontally or vertically. The overall motion in the horizontal and vertical directions of frames are thus computed for weight decision of X-histogram and Y-histogram. While the movement of most regions is in the horizontal (vertical) orientation, it means that the global motion or motion of large object is mainly in the horizontal (vertical) direction. Therefore, the X-histogram needs to be weighted more than the Y-histogram. On the contrary, if most regions move toward the vertical direction, the Y-histogram is assigned more weight than the X-histogram.

The proposed similarity measure would be very effective to differentiate video sequences whose global motion is in distinct orientations, for example, most players in the baseball game run toward vertical direction and the camera would tilt to take the players or to track the baseball while players in football game primarily run horizontally and the camera would pan to focus on the significant events.

$$Dist_{total}(w,h) = WT_H \cdot Dist_X(w,h) + WT_V \cdot Dist_Y(w,h) \tag{4}$$

$$WT_H = \frac{1}{N}\sum_{i=1}^{N}\frac{MV_{i,H}}{MV_{i,H}+MV_{i,V}}, \quad WT_V = 1 - WT_H$$

3   Experimental Results and Discussions

The testing data of experiments is the Spanish news from MPEG-7 test data set and they are segmented into 357 video shots. The content of the Spanish news mainly consists of the shots of anchor person, walking person, football game, bicycle racing and interview. Motion intensity of these shots ranges over low, medium to high, and the size of moving objects varies from small size as the players of football game in the full-court view to large size as the players in the close-up view. The goal of the experiments is to evaluate 1) the effect of the number of bins of the 2D-histogram on the retrieval accuracy, 2) the effectiveness of exploiting individual X-histogram and Y-histogram, and of combining them together, 3) the retrieval performance of DCT-based feature space transformation and dimensionality reduction, and 4) the retrieval performance of the proposed object (moving region)-based motion activity descriptor.

The performance metrics used in the experiments are precision and recall, which are collectively used to measure the effectiveness of a retrieval system. Eq. (5) shows the definition of precision and recall, where "*Retrieve(q)*" means the retrieved video sequences corresponding to a query sequence q, "*Relevant(q)*" denotes all the video sequences in the database that are relevant to a query sequence q and $\|\cdot\|$ indicates the cardinality of the set. Recall is defined as the ratio between the number of retrieved relevant video sequences and the total number of relevant video sequences in the video database, and precision is defined as the ratio between the number of retrieved relevant video sequences and the number of total retrieved video sequences.

$$Recall = \frac{\|Retrieve(q)\cap Relevant(q)\|}{\|Relevant(q)\|}, Precision = \frac{\|Retrieve(q)\cap Relevant(q)\|}{\|Retrieve(q)\|} \tag{5}$$

Details of the experimental results are described in the following Subsections. Subsection 3.1 shows the retrieval performance of the selection of different number of DCT coefficients. Subsection 3.2 exhibits the influence of the number of histogram bins on the retrieval accuracy. In Subsection 3.3, the effectiveness of the object-based motion activity descriptor is demonstrated with its retrieval performance of distinct video clips.

3.1   Decision of the Number of DCT Coefficients

Four representative video shots are selected for testing, in which the motion intensity ranges over low, medium and high and the object size varies from small, medium to

Table 1. Performance comparison of different α settings using four feature descriptors ($\beta = 4$)

Shot Type / Descriptor		Close-Up (CU)	Bicycle Racing (BR)	Walking Person (WP)	Anchor Person (AP)
X-Histogram	Rank #1	2	2	1	5
	Rank #2	3	3	2	3
Y-Histogram	Rank #1	2	2	1	5
	Rank #2	1	3	2	3
2D -Histogram	Rank #1	2	2	1	5
	Rank #2	3	3	2	2
Weighted 2D -Histogram	Rank #1	2	2	1	5
	Rank #2	3	3	2	2

large. The shots of Close-Up (CU) are of high motion intensity, Bicycle Racing (BR) shots are of medium motion intensity, Walking Person (WP) shots are of high motion intensity and Anchor Person (AP) shots are of low motion intensity. The number of frames of these four shots is 203, 596, 187 and 631, respectively. To evaluate the effect of the number of DCT coefficients on the retrieval performance, the number of DCT coefficients α is varied and is tested in the condition that the number of histogram bins β is fixed and descriptors D, X-histogram, Y-histogram, 2D-histogram and the weighted 2D-histogram are utilized, respectively. The value of α means that α DCT coefficients including the DC and (α-1) AC coefficients are used for similarity measurement.

Table 2. Performance comparison among four motion activity descriptors using the different parameter settings of β ($\alpha = 2$)

Shot Type / β Setting		Close-Up (CU)	Bicycle Racing (BR)	Walking Person (WP)	Anchor Person (AP)
$\beta = 4$	Rank #1	X	X	W-2D	W-2D
	Rank #2	W-2D	W-2D	X	2D
$\beta = 6$	Rank #1	W-2D	Y	X	W-2D
	Rank #2	X	W-2D	W-2D	2D
$\beta = 8$	Rank #1	X	W-2D	W-2D	W-2D
	Rank #2	W-2D	2D	2D	2D
$\beta = 10$	Rank #1	W-2D	W-2D	W-2D	X
	Rank #2	2D	2D	2D	2-2D
X: X-Histogram Y: Y-Histogram 2D: 2D-Histogram W-2D: Weighted 2D-Histogram					

3.2 Decision of the Motion Activity Descriptor

The retrieval performance of these four types of shots CU, BR, WP and AP exploiting four descriptors over different number of DCT coefficients ($\alpha=1$, $\alpha=2$, $\alpha=3$ and $\alpha=5$) is shown in Table 1. We can observe that the parameter setting of $\alpha=2$ achieves the best retrieval accuracy. Hence, we infer from the experimental results that two DCT coefficients are adequate for similarity matching of video clips and thus DC

coefficient and an AC coefficient are selected for further experiments.To evaluate the retrieval performance of four motion activity descriptors, X-histogram (X), Y-histogram (Y), 2D-histogram (2D) and weighted 2D-histogram (W-2D), four representative shots in Subsection 6.1 are used and the value of β is varied over 4, 6, 8 and 10, and each of the corresponding performance of the recall-precision pair. The overall performance of these four descriptors over different histogram bins is illustrated in Table 2. We can observe that in most cases the descriptor of weighted 2D-histogram performs better than other descriptor does or at least it's retrieval ranking is 2. Therefore, the weighted 2D-histogram is selected as the motion activity descriptor for further experiments.

3.3 Decision of the Number of Histogram Bins

From the experimental results of Subsection 5.1 and Subsection 5.2, two DCT coefficients one DC and one AC are used and the motion activity descriptor of weighted 2D-histogram is exploited for the decision of the number of histogram bins. To assess the effect of the number of histogram bins β of four different descriptors, the parameter β is varied over 4, 6, 8 and 10. The rank of retrieval performance of each video shot is illustrated in Table 3. We can observe that the retrieval performance of the parameter setting $\beta=8$ is better than others and the worst case is in the parameter setting $\beta=4$. The experimental result reveals that the number of histogram bins should be moderate because the smaller of the number of the histogram bins, the less precise the description of the variation of spatial distribution is. On the contrary, while the number of histogram bins is too large, the descriptor would be very sensitive to the slight change either in the horizontal or vertical directions.

Table 3. Performance comparison of different number of histogram bins (β)

Shot Type / Performance	Close-Up (CU)	Bicycle Racing (BR)	Walking Person (WP)	Anchor Person (AP)
Rank #1	6	8	8	8
Rank #2	10	10	10	10
Rank #3	8	6	6	6
Rank #4	4	4	4	4

3.3 Evaluation of the Retrieval Performance

The retrieval performance of the motion activity descriptor of weighted 2D-histogram is illustrated in Table 4. In the experiment, 30 relevant shots out of 347 ones are selected manually for each shot type, i.e., the similar video shots of each shot type are

Table 4. Retrieval performance of the descriptor of weighted 2D-histogram

Clips / Performance	Close-Up (CU)	Bicycle Racing (BR)	Walking Person (WP)	Anchor Person (AP)
Recall	79%	87%	93%	86%
Precision	81%	84%	90%	77%

Average Recall		Average Precision	
86%		83%	

set as 30. Therefore, the number of returned video shots is set as 30 to evaluate the performance measurement – recall and precision. In Table 4, we can observe that the recall of the four shots is higher than 79% and the recall of the shots of BR, WP and AP is higher than 86%. The worst case is the shot AP shots, of which the precision is 77%. Because the object size of the shots AP is quite large and the motion intensity is low, some medium-size objects of WP shots move closely and the camera catch these objects in the center position of the frame. Therefore, these objects would be detected as a single large object and the corresponding shots are classified as AP. However, although the precision of the shots AP is lower than 80%, the precision of the shots of CU, BR, and WP is higher than 80%. From Table 4, the overall performance of the average recall and the average precision is up to 86% and 83%, respectively.

4 Conclusions and Future Work

In this paper, a novel method of similarity retrieval between video sequences considering the spatio-temporal variation through consecutive frames is proposed. For computation efficiency, videos for all tasks are processed in compressed domain. Furthermore, for bridging the semantic gap between low-level features and the rich meaning that users desire to capture, video shots are analyzed and characterized by the high-level feature of motion activity. The extracted features of motion activity are further described by the object-based 2D-histogram. In order to reduce the dimensions of feature vector space in video sequence matching, Discrete Cosine Transform (DCT) is exploited to map semantic features of consecutive frames to the frequency domain while retaining the discriminatory information and preserving the distance between feature vectors. The energy of DCT transformed sequences is highly concentrated at low indices and experimental results reveal that two DCT coefficients are adequate for achieving good retrieval performance. In addition, the experimental results of sequence matching show that the retrieval performance of the proposed weighted 2D-histogram is better than that of individual X-histogram, Y-histogram and 2D-histogram. The number of histogram bins should be moderate since the object information would be too noisy if the number of histogram bins is too large. On the contrary, if the number of histogram bins is too small, the object-based descriptor cannot reflect the variation of spatial distribution and temporal variation of moving objects through out the video shots. The experimental results demonstrate the good retrieval performance and reveal the effectiveness of the proposed mechanism of similarity retrieval. In the future, we will exploit other features to improve the retrieval accuracy such as the color information - the luminance and the chrominance of moving objects, the orientation of moving objects, and the global motion of camera operations.

References

1. R. Wang, M. R. Naphade, and T. S. Huang: Video Retrieval and Relevance Feedback in The Context of A Post-Integration Model. Proc. IEEE 4th Workshop on Multimedia Signal Processing, pp. 33-38, Oct. 2001.
2. T. Lin, C. W. Ngo, H. J. Zhang and Q. Y. Shi: Integrating Color and Spatial Features for Content-Based Video Retrieval. Proc. IEEE Intl. Conf. on Image Processing, Vol. 2, pp. 592-595, Oct. 2001.
3. S. S. Cheung and A. Zakhor: Video Similarity Detection with Video Signature Clustering. Proc. IEEE Intl. Conf. on Image Processing, Vol. 2, pp. 649–652, Sep. 2001.
4. L. Agnihotri and N. Dimitrova: Video Clustering Using SuperHistograms in Large Archives. Proc. 4th Intl. Conf. on Visual Information Systems, pp. 62-73, Lyon, France, November 2000.
5. M. Roach, J. S. Mason and M. Pawlewski: Motion-Based Classification of Cartoons. Proc. Intl. Symposium on Intelligent Multimedia, Video and Speech Processing, pp. 146-149, Hong Kong, May 2001.
6. L. Zhao, W. Qi, S. Z. Li, S. Q. Yang and H. J. Zhang: Content-based Retrieval of Video Shot Using the Improved Nearest Feature Line Method. Proc. IEEE Intl. Conf. on Acoustics, Speech and Signal Processing, Vol. 3, pp. 1625-1628, 2001.
7. B. S. Manjunath, J. R. Ohm, V. V. Vasudevan and A. Yamada: Color and Texture Descriptors. IEEE Transactions on Circuits and Systems for Video Technology, Vol. 11, No. 6, pp. 703-715, June 2001.
8. R. Mohan: Video Sequence Matching. IEEE International Conference on Acoustics, Speech and Signal Processing, Vol. 6, pp. 3697-3700, May 1998.
9. M. M. Yeung and B. Liu: Efficient Matching and Clustering of Video Shots. Proc. IEEE Int. Conf. on Image Processing, Vol. 1, pp. 338-341, Oct. 1995.
10. D. Y. Chen, S. J. Lin and S. Y. Lee: Motion Activity Based Shot Identification. Proc. 5th Intl. Conf. on Visual Information System, pp. 288-301, Hsinchu, Taiwan, Mar. 2002.

Content-Based Audio Classification with Generalized Ellipsoid Distance*

Chih-Chieh Cheng and Chiou-Ting Hsu

Department of Computer Science, National Tsing Hua University, Taiwan
{br872514, cthsu}@cs.nthu.edu.tw

Abstract. While the size of multimedia database increases, the demand for efficient search for multimedia data becomes more and more urgent. Most recent works on audio classification and retrieval adopt Euclidean distance as their distance measures. However, Euclidean distance is not a perceptual distance measure for some audio features. The purpose of this work is to derive two new distance measures for content-based audio classification, which are based on re-weighting and de-correlating each feature. Weighted Euclidean distance uses a diagonal matrix, which re-weighs the importance of each feature, and generalized ellipsoid distance takes further consideration on correlation between any two features. An audio database of 85 sound clips is used as our training set. The experimental results show that the generalized ellipsoid distance yields the best result and achieves an overall correction rate of classification.

1 Introduction

As the amount of multimedia information increases fast and drastically today, we need efficient tools to search, segment and classify the vast amount of multimedia data, either on the internet or of personal collection. Audio data play an important role in the multimedia applications. For example, for a video sequence, audio data contains the information about scene contents and conversations of actors, etc. However, most of early researches in audiovisual data segmentation and classification only emphasized the use of visual data characteristics and features. Moreover, the amount of audio recordings and broadcasts are growing larger and larger, and thus the demand for an effective archiving and retrieval system becomes indispensable.

Wold et al [9] proposed a boosting work, called "Muscle Fish", of content-based classification for audio data. They used only perceptual features, such as loudness, brightness, pitch, etc. The classification is then achieved using nearest neighbor (NN) rule based on a normalized Euclidean distance. Liu et al [8] analyzed the separability of each feature by intraclass scattering and interclass scattering, and they also chose only perceptual features to represent sound clips. They classified each sound clip by a

---

* This work was supported by MOE Program for Promoting Academic Excellence of Universities under the grant number MOE 89-E-FA04-1-4.

Y.-C. Chen, L.-W. Chang, and C.-T. Hsu (Eds.): PCM 2002, LNCS 2532, pp. 328–335, 2002.

neural network. Foote [10] used 12 MFCCs as features, and those are also known as cepstral features. In their work, they computed the Euclidean distance between any two histograms of MFCCs and used NN rule to classify each sound clip. Li [5] proposed nearest feature line method (NFL), which computes the distance between a sample point to the line formed by two sample points in the training set. It also adopted NN rule to accomplish audio retrieval and classification. An overview of recent works and systems on audiovisual data retrieval and classification is described in [2].

While most of recent works adopt Euclidean as their distance measures, we find some pitfalls with Euclidean distance, especially the performance's dependence on feature selection. In this paper, we propose two new distance measures for content-based audio classification, which are based on re-weighting and de-correlating each feature in order to solve this defect. For feature selection, we only choose perceptual features as in [1, 2, 8, 9]. For classification rule, we use nearest center (NC) to make decision for classification.

The feature selection of this work is described in Section 2. Section 3 illustrates the proposed distance measure and how it works on classification. We demonstrate the performance and analyze the results of our work in Section 4.

2 Feature Extraction

All of our test audio clips are in PCM format and sampled at 11025 Hz. Initially, we divide each audio clip into frames of 512 samples, with 256 samples overlap between adjacent frames. A number of audio features are then extracted from each frame.

To characterize each audio clip, we compute mean and standard deviation of each audio feature over all frames to form a representative feature vector.

Similar to [1], [2] and [8], we extract only perceptual features in our work. Five features, which include time domain and frequency domain features, are chosen to represent each sound clip: energy, zero crossing rate (ZCR), frequency centroid, frequency bandwidth and pitch. We list the features as follows.

- *Total Energy:* The temporal energy of an audio frame is defined by the rms of the audio signal magnitude within each frame.
- *Zero Crossing Rate (ZCR):* ZCR is also a commonly used temporal feature. ZCR counts the number of times that an audio signal crosses its zero axis.
- *Frequency Centroid (FC):* Frequency centroid indicates the weighted average of all frequency components of a frame.
- *Bandwidth (BW):* Bandwidth is the weighted average of the squared differences between each frequency component and its frequency centroid.
- *Pitch Period:* Pitch is a popular audio feature, which measures the fundamental frequency of an audio signal. There are many kinds of approaches to estimate pitch. In this work, we employ temporal domain technique to estimate pitch, and use two correlation functions to accomplish computation: one is autocorrelation function, $R_n(k)$, and the other is average magnitude difference function (AMDF), $A_n(k)$ [3].

In addition to the aforementioned five features, we include one more feature, zero ratio, into our feature set. Zero ratio is defined as the number of non-pitched frames to total number of frames in one audio clip. To form a feature vector for each audio clip, we compute the zero ratio as well as the means and standard deviations of the above-mentioned features over all frames. As the result, we use an 11-dimensional feature vector to characterize each audio clip.

Furthermore, we proceed to normalize each x_i of one 11-dimensional feature vector to be zero-mean and unit-variance over all training set.

3 Proposed Approach

Many related works [1, 5, 9, 10] have adopted several different strategies to classify a query clip. Most of these works simply use Euclidean distance as their distance measure. In this paper, we propose two distance measures for audio classification and will illustrate how these distance measures can be incorporated into audio classification.

Given a well classified audio database, we discuss different distance criteria and their corresponding distortion using NN classification algorithm as follows.

3.1 Distance Measure

In the feature space, each point (vector) represents one sample sound clip in the training set. We then define the distance between any sample point and its class representative point as below [7].

- *Euclidean distance*: This is the most popular distance function adopted by most works. Its function d is defined as

$$d(\mathbf{x}_{ij}, \mathbf{q}_i) = (\mathbf{x}_{ij} - \mathbf{q}_i)^T (\mathbf{x}_{ij} - \mathbf{q}_i), \tag{1}$$

where $\mathbf{x}_{ij}$ is the jth sample point in the ith class and $\mathbf{q}_i$ is the representative of the ith class.
- *Weighted Euclidean distance*: We again assume that there is no correlation between any two different features. But, in one audio class, different features will have different importance to characterize this audio class.

    We just multiply each feature by a weighting to indicate the importance of this feature while computing the distance with Euclidean distance function. Thus, the weighted distance is formulated as:

$$d(\mathbf{x}_{ij}, \mathbf{q}_i) = (\mathbf{x}_{ij} - \mathbf{q}_i)^T \mathbf{D} (\mathbf{x}_{ij} - \mathbf{q}_i), \tag{2}$$

where $\mathbf{D}$ is a diagonal matrix with all weightings on its diagonal entries.
- *Generalized ellipsoid distance*: The other concern, which is omitted in the weighted distance, is the correlation between different features. As we adjust the corresponding weighting of each feature, the weighting may not only affect this feature

but also other features which are correlated with current one. Thus we have to take the inter-feature correlations into account, and eq.(2) is expanded to

$$d(\mathbf{x}_{ij}, \mathbf{q}_i) = (\mathbf{x}_{ij} - \mathbf{q}_i)^T \mathbf{M}(\mathbf{x}_{ij} - \mathbf{q}_i), \tag{3}$$

where $\mathbf{M}$ is a symmetric matrix, and $\mathbf{x}_{ij}$ is the jth sample point in the ith class, $\mathbf{q}_i$ is the representative of the ith class.

Our goal is to find a matrix $\mathbf{M}$ such that, for all audio classes, the distance between each sample point and its representative point is minimized. In other words, we want to find a new distance function which can make all audio classes as compact as possible and all features as independent as possible.

Denote the distortion as summation of distances between the sample point $\mathbf{x}_{ij}$ and its representative point $\mathbf{q}_i$ as [7]:

$$D = \sum_{i=1}^{m} \sum_{j \in class(i)} d(\mathbf{x}_{ij}, \mathbf{q}_i), \tag{4}$$

where m is the number of classes.

We aim to find out a set of optimal class representative $\mathbf{q}$'s and a weighting matrix $\mathbf{M}$ to minimize this distortion which can be formulated as follows:

$$\min_{\mathbf{M}, \mathbf{q}_i} D = \min_{\mathbf{M}, \mathbf{q}_i} \sum_{i=1}^{m} \sum_{j \in class(i)} (\mathbf{x}_{ij} - \mathbf{q}_i)^T \mathbf{M}(\mathbf{x}_{ij} - \mathbf{q}_i), \tag{5}$$

where $\mathbf{M}$ is constrained to

$$\det(\mathbf{M}) = 1. \tag{6}$$

If we define

$$\overline{x}_{ik} = \frac{\displaystyle\sum_{j \in class(i)} x_{ijk}}{N_i}, \tag{7}$$

where N_i is the number of sample points in the class i and x_{ijk} is the kth element of the jth vector in the ith class, and a matrix $\mathbf{C} = [c_{kl}]$ with

$$c_{kl} = \sum_{i=1}^{m} \sum_{j \in class(i)} (x_{ijk} - q_{ik})(x_{ijl} - q_{il}). \tag{8}$$

To minimize eq.(5) using Lagrange multiplier [7], we get

$$\mathbf{q}_i = \overline{\mathbf{x}}_i, \tag{9}$$

and

$$\mathbf{M} = (\det(\mathbf{C}))^{\frac{1}{f}} \mathbf{C}^{-1}, \tag{10}$$

where f is the number of feature dimensions.

For the aforementioned weighted Euclidean distance, which is formulated by a diagonal matrix, we can easily show that it is just a special case of eq.(10) [7].

3.2 Audio Classification

After we obtained a set of optimal class representative q_i's and the matrix M, the distance of a query point (or feature vector) q' to the class i is measured by our derived generalized ellipsoid distance, as eq.(3).

Thus, this method is equivalent to a NC method which is weighted by a weighting matrix M. The decision rule we use here is NN rule. If the distance from the query point q' to class i is smaller than the distance from it to any other classes in the training set, we then classify this query point to the class i.

4 Experimental Result and Analysis

The goal of this experiment is to evaluate and analyze 1) the distortion before and after applying the proposed distance function, 2) the separability of features with and without the weighting matrix, and 3) classification results of different kinds of tests.

An audio database of 85 sound clips are collected from news reports, TV programs and music CD's. All sound clips in this database are of 5 sec mono PCM files and sampled at 11025Hz. They are divided into six classes, as shown in Table 1.

We first define the performance measurement *Correction Rate* as the ratio between the number of correct classifications and the total number of queries.

Table 1. The 85 sounds of 6 classes in the audio database

Sound class i	Number of sound clips N_i	Description
Instrumental music	22	Music of flute, piano, oboe and orchestra
Vocal music	14	Female and male singing without music background
Mixture of instrumental and vocal music	12	Songs of male singing with music background
Female speech	18	Pure speech of female news reporter
Male speech	12	Pure speech of male news reporter
Environmental sound	12	Natural environmental sounds including birdsong, sound of rain, thundering and animal's cry

4.1 The Distortion Analysis

The equation of distortion is defined in eq.(4). In this experiment, the distortion over the whole audio database is computed with three different weighting matrices M – an identity matrix, a diagonal matrix, and a squared matrix, as eq.(10).

The results of this experiment are shown in Table 2. We can see that this result just fits our expectation because our aim is to find a matrix M which minimize the distortion over whole audio database. Because the diagonal matrix doesn't consider the correlation between different features by merely re-weighting all features, the second result is considerably worse than the third result but still better than the first one.

Table 2. Results of applying three different distance functions to compute the average distortions

Distance function	Average distortion D
Euclidean distance (Identity matrix)	440.411394
Weighted Euclidean distance (Diagonal matrix)	418.378917
Generalized ellipsoid distance (Full symmetric matrix)	195.788064

4.2 Intraclass Scattering Analysis

To measure the concentration of each feature and the correlation between any two different features, we define the intraclass scattering matrix of class i [8] as

$$\mathbf{S}_i = \sum_{j \in class(i)} \mathbf{L}(\mathbf{x}_{ij} - \overline{\mathbf{x}}_i)(\mathbf{x}_{ij} - \overline{\mathbf{x}}_i)^T \mathbf{L}^T , \tag{11}$$

where $\mathbf{L}$ is a lower triangular matrix of Cholesky decomposition of the weighting matrix $\mathbf{M}$.

We demonstrate the results of the first class of instrumental music in Table 3, 4 and 5. On the diagonal entries of these three matrices are variances of features in the class of instrumental music. As we expect, the smaller the variances are, the better. A smaller diagonal entry means that this feature has better seperability and is more important. The off-diagonal entries reveal the inter-feature variances and correlations [8]. Of course, they are expected to be as small as possible.

The first test, intraclass with Euclidean distance, obviously has the worst result. The second result of using weighted Euclidean distance seems to be better. Since we aim to decrease the average distortion over the whole database, it is acceptable that some entries in the intraclass scattering matrix of one class become a little larger than the first result. Table 5, which shows the intraclass scattering matrix of using generalized ellipsoid distance, definitely has the best result.

We conclude that, by using the generalized ellipsoid distance, we are able to achieve a near optimal result which concentrates each class to its center point and minimizes its inter-feature correlation.

4.2 Evaluation of Classification

In this test, each sound clip in the database is used as the query in turn [5]. Each time the remaining 84 sound clips are used as the training set. We test the classification using nearest center (NC) rule with three different distance functions.

Table 6 shows correction rates of this experiment. We can find that using generalized ellipsoid results in the best consequence. For the correction rate of each class, generalized ellipsoid distance generally yields a better result, except for the last class. The comparatively poor performance for environmental sound is resulted from our limited sample space and its undistinguishable characteristics.

Table 3. The intra-class scattering result using Euclidean distance. The number on the first row and the first column corresponds to each feature as follows: 1. Mean of Total Energy, 2. Mean of ZCR, 3. Mean of Pitch, 4. Mean of FC, 5. Mean of BW, 6. Variance of Total Energy, 7. Variance of ZCR, 8. Variance of Pitch, 9. Variance of FC, 10. Variance of BW, 11. Zero ratio

	1	2	3	4	5	6	7	8	9	10	11
1	42.76	-0.37	8.13	-1.70	-8.15	35.28	-6.38	2.06	-0.81	0.87	-5.25
2	-0.37	6.43	-5.39	7.53	7.76	-2.08	3.55	-6.97	2.91	2.48	-0.73
3	8.13	-5.39	17.29	-6.60	-7.80	8.63	-3.39	3.50	-0.17	2.51	-10.50
4	-1.70	7.53	-6.60	9.76	10.37	-3.17	4.19	-10.27	3.54	3.51	-2.49
5	-8.15	7.76	-7.80	10.37	13.61	-8.15	6.50	-10.29	5.70	6.67	-1.79
6	35.28	-2.08	8.63	-3.17	-8.15	33.07	-5.22	2.18	0.01	1.41	-5.48
7	-6.38	3.55	-3.39	4.19	6.50	-5.22	4.83	-3.65	4.09	4.49	0.13
8	2.056	-6.97	3.50	-10.27	-10.29	2.18	-3.65	16.42	-4.36	-5.74	8.73
9	-0.81	2.91	-0.17	3.54	5.70	0.01	4.09	-4.36	6.26	9.15	-2.52
10	0.87	2.48	2.51	3.51	6.67	1.41	4.49	-5.74	9.15	15.36	-5.61
11	-5.25	-0.73	-10.50	-2.49	-1.79	-5.48	0.13	8.73	-2.52	-5.61	14.66

Table 4. The intra-class scattering result using weighted Euclidean distance

	1	2	3	4	5	6	7	8	9	10	11
1	27.59	-0.42	6.12	-1.43	-6.33	21.64	-6.32	1.70	-0.67	0.70	-3.94
2	-0.42	12.68	-7.10	11.13	10.55	-2.23	6.15	-10.06	4.20	3.47	-0.95
3	6.12	-7.10	15.18	-6.50	-7.08	6.183	-3.9	3.37	-0.17	2.35	-9.21
4	-1.43	11.13	-6.50	10.80	10.56	-2.55	5.45	-11.11	3.82	3.68	-2.45
5	-6.33	10.55	-7.08	10.56	12.74	-6.02	7.77	-10.23	5.66	6.44	-1.62
6	21.64	-2.23	6.18	-2.55	-6.02	19.31	-4.93	1.71	0.01	1.07	-3.91
7	-6.32	6.15	-3.92	5.45	7.77	-4.93	7.37	-4.64	5.18	5.54	0.15
8	1.70	-10.06	3.37	-11.11	-10.23	1.71	-4.61	17.35	-4.60	-5.89	8.40
9	-0.67	4.20	-0.17	3.82	5.66	0.01	5.18	-4.60	6.60	9.37	-2.42
10	0.70	3.47	2.35	3.68	6.44	1.07	5.54	-5.89	9.37	15.29	-5.23
11	-3.94	-0.95 *	-9.21	-2.45	-2.45	-3.91	0.15	8.40	-2.42	-5.23	12.82

Table 5. The intra-class scattering result using generalized ellipsoid distance

	1	2	3	4	5	6	7	8	9	10	11
1	11.09	1.71	-1.21	2.68	-0.25	4.11	-1.81	0.45	-0.90	0.02	0.29
2	1.71	3.26	-0.88	1.28	1.87	0.29	1.37	-1.30	0.50	1.82	-0.12
3	-1.21	-0.88	6.69	-1.17	-3.21	0.34	-0.67	1.94	-0.17	-1.09	-2.57
4	2.68	1.28	-1.17	2.30	0.19	0.55	0.29	-0.35	-0.67	2.31	0.14
5	-0.25	1.87	-3.21	0.19	3.62	-2.10	1.32	-1.27	0.93	0.27	1.92
6	4.11	0.29	0.34	0.55	-2.10	9.03	-1.57	0.11	-0.01	0.12	-1.90
7	-1.81	1.37	-0.67	0.29	1.32	-1.57	2.57	-1.26	0.28	2.25	-0.85
8	0.45	-1.30	1.94	-0.35	-1.27	0.11	-1.26	7.47	-0.72	-0.44	3.34
9	-0.90	0.50	-0.17	-0.67	0.93	-0.01	0.28	-0.72	1.30	-1.54	0.74
10	0.02	1.82	-1.09	2.31	0.27	0.12	2.25	-0.44	-1.54	6.69	-1.22
11	0.29	-0.12	-2.57	0.14	1.92	-1.90	-0.85	3.34	0.74	-1.22	6.00

Table 6. Correction rate (and number of correct matches) obtained by inside test

Distance / Class	Euclidean Distance	Weighted Euclidean Distance	Generalized Ellipsoid Distance
Instrumental Music	77.27% (17)	81.82% (18)	95.45% (21)
Vocal Music	85.71% (12)	85.71% (12)	85.71% (12)
Mixture	100% (12)	100% (12)	100% (12)
Female Speech	77.78% (14)	83.33% (15)	88.89% (16)
Male Speech	66.67% (8)	66.67% (8)	66.67% (8)
Environmental Sound	100% (12)	91.67% (11)	83.33% (10)
Overall	88.24% (75)	89.41% (76)	92.94% (79)

5   Conclusion

In this paper we propose two new distance measures, weighted Euclidean distance and generalized ellipsoid distance, for content-based audio classification. Weighted Euclidean distance uses a diagonal matrix, which re-weighs the importance of each feature, and generalized ellipsoid distance takes further consideration on correlation between any two features. We perform three different experiments to evaluate this work. The experimental results show that generalized ellipsoid distance yields the best consequence.

References

1. T. Zhang and C.-C. J. Kuo, "Audio Content Analysis for On-line Audiovisual Data Segmantation and Classification," *IEEE Trans. Speech and Audio Processing*, vol. 9, no. 4, May 2001.
2. Y. Wang, Z. Liu, and J.-C. Huang, "Multimedia Content Analysis," *IEEE Signal Processing Magazine*, pp. 12-36, Nov. 2000.
3. A. M. Kondoz, *Digital Speech*, Wiley, 1994.
4. L. Rabiner and B.-H. Juang, *Fundamentals of Speech Recognition*, Englewood Cliffs, NJ: Prentice-Hall, 1993.
5. S. Z. Li, "Content-Based Audio Classification and Retrieval Using the Nearest Feature Line Method," *IEEE Trans. Speech and Audio Processing*, Vol.8, No.5, Sep. 2000.
6. Y. Rui and T. Huang, "Optimizing Learning in Image Retrieval," *Proc. CVPR*, 2000.
7. Y. Ishikawa, R. Subramanya, and C. Faloutsos, "Mindreader: Query databases through multiple examples," *Proc. of the 24th VLDB Conference (New York)*, 1998.
8. Z. Liu, J. Huang, Y. Wang, and T. Chen, "Audio Feature Extraction and Analysis for Scene Segmentation and Classification," *Journal of VLSI Signal Processing 20*, pp.61-79, 1998.
9. E. Wold, T. Blum, D. Keislar, and J. Wheaton, "Content-based classification, search and retrieval of audio," *IEEE Multimedia Mag.*, vol. 3, no.3, pp. 27-36, 1996.
10. J. Foote *et al*, "Content-based retrieval of music and audio," *Multimedia Storage Archiving Syst. II*, vol. 3229, pp. 138-147, 1997.

A Motion-Aided Video Shot Segmentation Algorithm

Wei-Kuang Li and Shang-Hong Lai

Dept. of Computer Science, National Tsing Hua University, Hsinchu, Taiwan
lai@cs.nthu.edu.tw

Abstract. Shot change detection is the initial step of video segmentation and indexing. There are two basic types of shot changes. One is the abrupt change or cut, and the other is the gradual shot transition. The variations of the video feature values in shot transitions are often disturbed by camera or object motions. In this paper, we exploit motion and illumination estimation in a video sequence to detect both abrupt and gradual shot changes. An iterative process is used to refine the generalized optical flow constraints step by step. Two robust measures, the likelihood ratio and the intensity variation monotony in the motion-compensated frames, are used for detecting abrupt changes and gradual transitions. We test the proposed algorithm on a number of video sequences in the TREC 2001 benchmark. The comparisons indicate that the proposed shot segmentation algorithm is competitive against the best existing algorithms.

1 Introduction

A shot is an unbroken sequence of frames and also a basic meaningful unit in a video. It usually represents a continuous action or a single camera operation. Generally, the purpose of a shot segmentation algorithm is to accurately find all the shot boundaries. There are two kinds of shot boundaries (shot changes) [1-2]; namely, abrupt changes and gradual transitions. Abrupt changes usually result from camera breaks, while gradual transitions are produced with artificial editing effects, such as fading, dissolve and wipe.

A number of methods for video shot transition detection have been proposed in the past decade [1-3]. Researchers have proposed many different measures including comparison of pixel values, edge counts, histograms, and compression coefficients to quantify the variation of continuous video frames [1-4]. Most of the methods tend to use simple information from the video to determine various types of shot changes. However, the smooth variations of the video feature values in a gradual transition produced by the editing effects are often confused with those caused by camera or object motions. A feasible solution to overcome this problem is to remove the factors caused by the camera and object motions. In this paper, we explore the possibility to exploit accurate motion and illumination estimation in the video sequence to detect various types of shot changes.

In this paper, we employ a generalized optical flow constraint that includes an illumination parameter to model local illumination changes and iteratively estimate the optical flow as well as the illumination variation parameters in each block. In the iterative estimation process, we refine the generalized optical flow constraint in each step with the currently estimated flow vector updated into the flow constraint to

Y.-C. Chen, L.-W. Chang, and C.-T. Hsu (Eds.): PCM 2002, LNCS 2532, pp. 336–343, 2002.

reduce the Taylor approximation error. A robust measure, which is the likelihood ratio of the corresponding motion-compensated blocks between two consecutive frames, is used for detecting abrupt changes. For the detection of gradual shot transitions, we compute the average monotony of intensity variations on the stable pixels in the images in a twin-comparison framework.

The rest of this paper is organized as follows. An iterative optical flow and illumination change estimation algorithm is proposed in section 2. Section 3 describes the proposed shot change detection algorithm for detecting abrupt changes as well as gradual transitions in video sequences. Some experimental results on different types of video shot changes are presented in section 4. Finally, we conclude this paper in section 5.

2 Optical Flow Estimation

For the sake of efficiency in the computation of optical flow, we first partition an image into smaller n-by-n blocks, and then compute the optical flow vectors only at the centers of these blocks.

To account for brightness variations between frames, we used the generalized optical flow constraint under non-uniform illumination changes proposed by Zhang et al. [5-6]. This generalized optical flow constraint can be written as

$$\frac{\partial I_0(x, y)}{\partial x} u + \frac{\partial I_0(x, y)}{\partial y} v + I_0(x, y) \cdot w + I_0(x, y) - I_1(x, y) = 0 \qquad (1)$$

where w is a constant used for compensating the intensity variation between two corresponding points at consecutive frames.

Following Lucas and Kanade's optical flow computation approach [7], we assume the three unknowns $\hat{u}$, $\hat{v}$, and $\hat{w}$ be constants in a local window. The least-square estimation is to minimize the following energy function.

$$E(u, v, w) = \sum_{(x, y) \in W_{i,j}} \left(\frac{\partial I_0(x, y)}{\partial x} u + \frac{\partial I_0(x, y)}{\partial y} v + I_0(x, y) \cdot w + I_0(x, y) - I_1(x, y) \right)^2 \quad (2)$$

where $W_{i,j}$ is the local neighborhood window centered at the location (i, j).

To alleviate the Taylor approximation error in the above optical flow constraint equation, we have developed an iterative least-square optical flow estimation algorithm that refines the generalized optical flow constraints step by step. The main idea behind this iterative refinement process is to move the block in the image with the newly estimated motion vector and compute the updated flow constraints in a recursive manner. The updated optical flow constraint is given by

$$\frac{\partial I_0(x+u^{(k)}, y+v^{(k)})}{\partial x} \Delta u^{(k)} + \frac{\partial I_0(x+u^{(k)}, y+v^{(k)})}{\partial y} \Delta v^{(k)} + (1+w^{(k)})I_0(x+u^{(k)}, y+v^{(k)}) - I_1(x, y) = 0$$

$$(3)$$

Thus the residual optical flow vector $(\Delta u^{(k)}, \Delta v^{(k)})$ and the illumination factor $w^{(k)}$ are computed by the above least-square estimation procedure with the above updated flow constraint. For the details, please refer to our previous paper [8].

3   Video Shot Change Detection

Our video segmentation system is able to detect both abrupt shot changes and gradual scene transitions including fades and dissolves. Due to the different characteristics of these two types of shot boundaries, we pick one specific measure for each of them separately. For abrupt changes, we use the proportion of unmatched blocks in the image. For gradual transitions, we estimate the accumulated frequency of monotonously increasing or decreasing intensity variation on low-motion pixels. In the next two sections we will describe the two measures separately.

3.1   Abrupt Shot Change Detection

When two shots were separated by an abrupt change, all objects in the previous shot will no longer exist in the current shot. As we applied optical flow computation on two frames across an abrupt shot change, the resulting optical flow vectors just associate the most similar blocks in the neighborhood but do not stand for the motions of objects. Therefore, the similarity of most pairs of corresponding blocks is much less than that of the corresponding blocks in the same shot.

Although we have tried to suppress the effect of camera and object motions by using the motion estimation procedure described in the previous section, it is still not appropriate to evaluate the similarity between two blocks with simple pixel differencing. That is to say, we need a more flexible and reliable measure to describe the difference between two blocks. In this paper, we adopt the likelihood ratio test [9] to compare two blocks k_1 and k_2 at frames i and i+1, respectively, with a likelihood ratio

$$\lambda_k = \frac{\left(\dfrac{\sigma_{k,i} + \sigma_{k,i+1}}{2} + \left(\dfrac{\mu_{k,i} - \mu_{k,i+1}}{2} \right)^2 \right)^2}{\sigma_{k,i} \cdot \sigma_{k,i+1}}, \tag{4}$$

where $\mu_{k,i}, \mu_{k,i+1}$ are the mean intensity, and $\sigma_{k,i}, \sigma_{k,i+1}$ are the variances for the two corresponding blocks k_1 and k_2 in the consecutive frames i and $i+1$. The likelihood ratio is insensitive to slight shift and rotation of pixels in a block. With this measure, we employ the conventional block-based comparison [1] to quantify the difference between two frames to detect abrupt shot changes. Our algorithm for detecting abrupt shot changes is described as follows:

1.   Read two consecutive frames I_{i-1} and I_i. Down-sample and smooth the two images.

2.   Divide the images into many non-overlapped n-by-n blocks.

3. For each block in I_i, first check whether it is fully textured; namely, the sum of absolute gradient magnitudes in a block is greater than a threshold T_g. For the blocks fail to satisfy this condition, they are termed ill-conditioned block.

4. For the well-conditioned blocks, apply the iterative optical flow computation described in section 2 to obtain the motion vectors. Then register every pair of the corresponding blocks at two consecutive frames.

5. For each registered block k in I_i, compute the likelihood ratio λ_k between this block and its corresponding block in frame I_{i-1}.

6. The difference between I_{i-1} and I_i is measured by

$$D(i-1,i) = \frac{\sum_{k=1}^{N} DP(i-1,i,k)}{N}, \quad \text{where } DP(i-1,i,k) = \begin{cases} 1 & \text{if } \lambda_k > T_\lambda \\ 0 & \text{otherwise} \end{cases},$$

and N is the number of well-conditioned blocks determined in step 3.

7. An abrupt shot change is declared between I_i and I_{i-1} if the difference $D(i-1,i)$ is larger than a threshold T_D.

8. Set $i=i+1$. Go to step 1 after all frames are scanned.

3.2 Gradual Shot Transition Detection

Based on many previous works and our experiments, we found that the inter-frame differences, such as histogram deviation and block-based comparison, are not sufficient to distinguish the slight variation in a gradual shot transition from the general inter-frame differences caused by noise, motion, and occlusion. To detect a gradual transition, some video features must be observed for long period of time.

Another view of the dissolve transition can be described as follows. If there exists a dissolve transition between scene A and scene B, an object O_A in scene A will gradually and "continuously" transform into another object O_B in scene B during the dissolve transition. A dissolve transition can be detected if most objects (pixels) in a video sequence monotonously increase or decrease in their intensities for a period of time. A fade-in or fade-out transition can be treated as a special case that one of the two corresponding objects is entirely black.

To make the above approach work well, we need to know the locations of the two corresponding objects O_A and O_B. However, with the random variation of intensities during a dissolve or fading transition, it is very difficult to accurately estimate the locations even with complicated optical flow computation. Fortunately, the optical flow vectors not only provide the information of motions but also the stabilization of a block. In other words, if the magnitude of an optical flow vector is nearly zero, the associated pixels are very possibly static during the gradual transition. In addition, the pixels that are homogeneous in intensity and are ignored by our optical flow computation process may be useful in the determination of gradual shot changes, too.

We choose these two kinds of blocks that are flat or static as the candidates for estimating the degree of intensity variation monotony.

A Stability-Map $F(x, y)$ that is a 2-dimentional Boolean array with the same size of images is maintained to indicate whether a pixel at the location (i, j) is static or flat. The Stability-Map will be updated right after the optical flow computation is completed. An additional Continuity-Map $C(x, y)$, a 2-dimensional integer array, is used to record the frequency of cumulative increase or decrease between consecutive frames. After the optical flow computation of two consecutive frames I_0 and I_1 is accomplished, the static region is indicated on the Stability-Map. For every pixel (i, j) in the static region, if $I_1(i, j) > I_0(i, j)$, then increase $C(i, j)$ by 1. Else if $I_1(i, j) < I_0(i, j)$, decrease $C(i, j)$ by 1. When a dissolve or fading transition occurs, the average of absolute values in the static region of C will monotonically increase. Finally, a twin-comparison algorithm is applied on the consecutive difference of average absolute Continuity-Map to determine a dissolve or fading transition in the sequence.

The gradual transition detection process is given as follows:

1. The preprocessing procedure is the same as step 1~4 of our abrupt shot change algorithm.

2. For each ill-conditioned (homogeneous) block, if the likelihood ratio λ between it and its corresponding block (at the same position in the consecutive frame) is smaller than a threshold T_λ, then assign TRUE to the Stability-Map F for all pixels in the block; else assign FALSE.

3. For each well-conditioned block, assign TRUE to F for all pixels in the block if the length of the motion vector $\sqrt{u^2 + v^2} \approx 0$, else assign FALSE to F for all pixels in the block and the corresponding block associated with (u, v).

4. For each point (i, j) in the flat region, increase the Continuity-Map $C(i, j)$ by 1 if $I_i(i, j) > I_{i-1}(i, j)$, and decrease $C(i, j)$ by 1 if $I_i(i, j) < I_{i-1}(i, j)$. When $I_i(i, j) = I_{i-1}(i, j)$, the map $C(i, j)$ is increased by 1 if $C(i, j) < 0$, otherwise it is decreased by 1.

5. Compute $Cont_i = \dfrac{\sum_{\forall i, j \ni F(i, j) = \text{TRUE}} |C(i, j)|}{N}$ as the variation continuity of this frame i, where N is the number of pixels in the flat region.

6. Set $i=i+1$. Go to step 1 until all frames are scanned.

7. For $i \in [\text{first} + 1, \text{last}]$, apply twin-comparison test [1] on the measure of $Cont_i - Cont_{i-1}$. The periods that pass the twin-comparison test are marked as candidates.

8. For each candidate period, apply our abrupt change detection (described in the last section) on the pair of images at the two boundaries of the period. If the two boundary frames form an abrupt change, a gradual transition is declared detected during the period.

4 Experimental Results

For comparing shot change detection algorithms, there are two commonly used metrics for performance assessment; namely, the recall and precision rates. These two rates are defined as follows:

$$\text{Recall} = \frac{N_c}{N_c + N_m}, \qquad \text{Precision} = \frac{N_c}{N_c + N_f}$$

where N_c denotes the total number of correct detections; N_m is the total number of misses, and N_f represents the total number of false detections.

In our experiments, we tested our video shot segmentation system with the benchmarks adopted by the tenth Text REtrieval Conference (TREC) that was held at the National Institute of Standards and Technology (NIST) in the United States, Nov. 13-16, 2001 [10]. This task was performed on a 5-hour video dataset, which contains MPEG-1 video sequences from "NIST Digital Video Collection, Volume 1" (http://www.nist.gov/srd/nistsd26.htm), the Open Video Project (http://www.open-video.org/), and the BBC. In this paper, we test the proposed shot change detection algorithm on 9 undamaged video sequences obtained from the Open Video Project, which stores publicly available video datasets on internet.

Our experimental results show the Recall and Precision rates for applying the proposed algorithm on each of the nine test video sequences. The accuracy of our system for detecting abrupt change is listed in Table 1. For the testing results on gradual transition detection, the accuracy of our algorithm is summarized in Table 2. In our experiments, the proposed shot change detection algorithm was executed on a PC with a 1500MHZ x86 CPU and 256MB RAM. Excluding decoding time, the time complexity is $45 \, \text{frames}\big/_{\text{sec}}$ in average for a video sequence to be entirely scanned for checking both abrupt and gradual shot changes.

According to the test results of TREC 2001 reported on the NIST web site at http://www-nlpir.nist.gov/projects/trecvid/results.html, the systems of Fudan University and IBM Almaden Research Center produced the best overall performance for abrupt change detection when considering both precision and recall rates. For gradual boundary detection, the three best performed systems are from IBM Almaden Research Center, Microsoft Research in China, and the University of Amsterdam and TNO. They can achieve an average precision/recall rate of roughly 70%. By comparing the experimental results on this subset of video sequences given in Table 1 and 2, we can see that the proposed algorithm is very competitive against the best existing video shot detection algorithms in the world.

Table 1. Accuracy of our system for detecting abrupt shot changes.

Filename	Recall	Precision
Anni005	1.0000	0.7358
Anni009	1.0000	0.6552
Bor03	0.9610	0.9487
Bor08	0.9730	0.9010
Nad31	0.9005	0.9451
Nad33	0.9842	0.9639
Nad53	0.9518	0.9405
Nad57	0.9583	0.9388
Senses111	0.9966	0.9966
Total	0.9678	0.9297

Table 2. Accuracy of our system for detecting gradual transitions.

Filename	Recall	Precision
Anni005	0.7857	0.8800
Anni009	0.8475	0.9259
Bor03	0.9286	0.3824
Bor08	0.7162	0.9298
Nad31	0.7077	0.6866
Nad33	0.9429	0.8049
Nad53	0.8256	0.9467
Nad57	0.8519	0.8846
Senses111	0.4188	0.3500
Total	0.7745	0.8316

5 Conclusions

In this paper, we presented a new shot change detection approach based on accurate motion estimation. For motion vector computation, the generalized optical flow constraint can tolerate illumination variations. The iterative refinement process and extending the range of initial guesses make the Locus-Kanade's method more robust against rapid image motion. Our motion compensation process has overcome the tough problem due to camera and object motion for conventional shot change detection methods. When the disturbance of camera and object motion is alleviated, we can easily compute the variation of a specific object in a video sequence. Thus, an abrupt change can be detected when there do not exist good correspondences for most blocks between consecutive two frames. A gradual transition can also be found by analyzing the variation continuity at low motion pixels.

There are two advantages in our shot change verification scheme. Firstly, the two different measures, one for abrupt changes and the other for gradual transitions, are complementary with each other. This independent property makes the integrated approach much more powerful for making decisions. Secondly, as the motion factors are suppressed, the magnitude of the normalized difference measure will be very small within the same shot but be very large at a shot boundary. This makes it very easy to select a robust global threshold for the verification. The above two characteristics significantly improve the performance of our approach, as demonstrated from the experimental results.

Acknowledgements. This research was jointly supported by the Program for Promoting Academic Excellence of Universities (89-E-FA04-1-4), the Computer Visual Tracking and Recognition project (A311XS1213) funded by MOEA, Taiwan, and the Chinese Multimedia Information Extraction project funded by Academia Sinica, Taiwan.

References

1. Tian, Q., Zhang, H.J.: Video Shot Detection and Analysis: Content-Based Approaches. In: Chen, C. W., Zhang, Y. Q. (eds.): Visual Information Representation, Communication, and Image Processing. Marcel Dekker, New York (1999) 227-253
2. Koprinska, I., Carrato, S.: Temporal Video Segmentation: A Survey. Signal Processing: Image Communication. 16 (2001) 477-500
3. Gargi, U., Kasturi, R., Strayer, S. H.: Performance Characterization of Video-Shot-Change Detection Methods. IEEE Trans. on Circuits and Systems for Video Technology. 10(1) (2000) 1-13
4. Su, C.W., Than, H.R., Liao, H.Y.M., Chen, L.H.: A Motion-Tolerant Dissolve Detection Algorithm. In Proc. IEEE International Conference on Multimedia and Expo. Lausanne, Switzerland (2002)
5. Zhang, L., Sakurai, T., Miike, H.: Detection of Motion Fields under Spatio-Temporal Non-uniform Illumination. Image and Vision Computing. 17 (1999) 309-320
6. Nomura, A.: Spatio-Temporal Optimization Method for Determining Motion Vector Fields under Non-stationary Illumination. Image and Vision Computing. 18 (2000) 939-950
7. Lucas, B.D., Kanade, T.: An Iterative Image Registration Technique with an Application to Stereo Vision. Proc. IJCAI. (1981) 674-679
8. Lai, S.-H., Li, W.K.: New Video Shot Change Detection Algorithm Based on Accurate Motion, and Illumination Estimation. Proc. SPIE: storage and retrieval for media databases. vol. 4676 (2002) 148-157
9. Kasturi, R., Jain, R.: Dynamic Vision. In: Kasturi, R., Jain, R. (Eds.): Computer Vision: Principles, IEEE Computer Society Press, Washington DC (1991) 469-480
10. Voorhees, E. M., Harman, D., Overview of TREC 2001. Proceedings of the Tenth Text Retrieval Conference. (2001)

MPEG IPMP Concepts and Implementation

Cheng-Ching Huang[1], Hsueh-Ming Hang[2], and Hsiang-Cheh Huang[2]

Department of Electronics Engineering, National Chiao-Tung University,
Hsinchu, Taiwan.
[1]cchuang.ee89g@nctu.edu.tw
[2]{hmhang, huangh}@cc.nctu.edu.tw

Abstract. Intellectual Property (IP) protection is a critical element in a multi-media transmission system. Therefore, ISO/IEC MPEG started the IP protection standardization project on MPEG-4 a few years ago. A basic IPMP (Intellectual Property Protection and Management) structure and interface was first defined in its System part. In this paper, we will first outline the MPEG-4 basic IP protection mechanism and then describe our simulation of an MPEG-4 IPMP system. An IP protection application is constructed using the MPEG-4 system software – IM1 (Implementation Model one). This application includes a client-server program, in which a client can request the keys from a server in a secure way using a hierarchical key distribution structure.

1 Introduction

With the rapid development in computer industry and the swift growth of Internet, there is a widespread use of the digital multimedia contents in our daily life. The progress in data compression techniques also makes transmission of multimedia data stream possible. However, Internet is an open environment, therefore, if the user data and information are not protected, it might be illegally used and altered by hackers. To protect privacy and intellectual property (IP) right, people often use cryptographic techniques to encrypt data, and thus the contents protected by encryption are expected to be securely transmitted over the Internet.

One requirement of typical multimedia applications is the demand for real-time transmission. In contrast, conventional security methods are often designed to protect digital data files, which might not be suitable and efficient for real-time applications. To fulfill the demands of both real-time distribution and data security, including the IP protection mechanism into the multimedia standard might be a feasible and effective way to achieve an unambiguous communication environment.

MPEG (Moving Picture Expert Group) is the ISO committee to set up the international standards for multimedia data exchange. MPEG-2 has been applied to digital video broadcasting with some access control specifications [1][2]. IPMP (Intellectual Property Management and Protection), proposed for MPEG-4 standard, aims at pro-

Y.-C. Chen, L.-W. Chang, and C.-T. Hsu (Eds.): PCM 2002, LNCS 2532, pp. 344–352, 2002.
© Springer-Verlag Berlin Heidelberg 2002

tecting the compressed multimedia. In this paper, we will describe and implement a multimedia transmission system using the MPEG-4 IPMP concepts.

This paper is organized as follows. Sec. 2 is an overview of the MPEG-4 System and IPMP standards. Sec. 3 describes the IPMP plug-ins in the MEPG-4 System reference software "IM1." Sec. 4 describes the procedure of constructing the MPEG-4 IP plug-ins and an application example is included. Sec. 5 concludes this paper.

2   MPEG-4 Standard Overview and IPMP Framework

MPEG-4 is an international standard defined by the ISO/IEC committee. Compared to it predecessors, MPEG-4 pays more attention on the following three subjects: (i) real-time streaming, (ii) object-based coding, and (iii) enriched user interaction.

MPEG-4 standards contain 10 parts. The portion related to IP protection is in the first part, Systems. The IPMP framework in ISO/IEC 14496 consists of a normative "interface" that permits an ISO/IEC 14496 terminal to host one or more IPMP sub-systems. An IPMP sub-system is a non-normative component of terminal, which provides several intellectual property management and protection functions. At the moment, MPEG committee is refining and extending the MPEG-4 IPMP specifications. A Message Router mechanism is to be added into the third Amendment of 14496-1.

In the MPEG-4 standards, the IPMP interface consists of IPMP elementary streams and IPMP descriptors. The IPMP elementary streams usually convey time-variant information such as keys associated with the encryption algorithm, which may change very rapidly. IPMP descriptors often convey time-invariant information associated with a given elementary stream or a set of elementary streams. IPMP elementary streams are treated as regular media elementary streams. And the IPMP descriptors are transmitted as part of an object descriptor stream.

Fig.1 shows how an IPMP sub-system works in an MPEG-4 terminal. Almost all the streams may be controlled or accessed by the IPMP sub-system but the Object Descriptor streams shall not be affected by the IPMP sub-systems.

Stream flow controller is a conceptual element that accompanies with every elementary stream. Stream flow controller can take place between the SyncLayer decoder and the decoder buffer. As Fig. 1 indicates, elements of IPMP control can take place at other points in the terminal. For example, they can appear after decoding (as in the case with watermark extractors).

3   IPMP in IM1

IM1 is an MPEG-4 Systems software developed by the MPEG committee. It may be used to verify and demonstrate the functionalities of MPEG-4 [4].

The Systems Core module in IM1 defines the infrastructure to implement MPEG-4 players. It provides the functionality of MediaObject, the base class for all specific node types. The API for Decoder, DMIF and IPMP plug-ins is also supported by IM1. Moreover, the code is written in C++, which is fairly platform-independent [5].

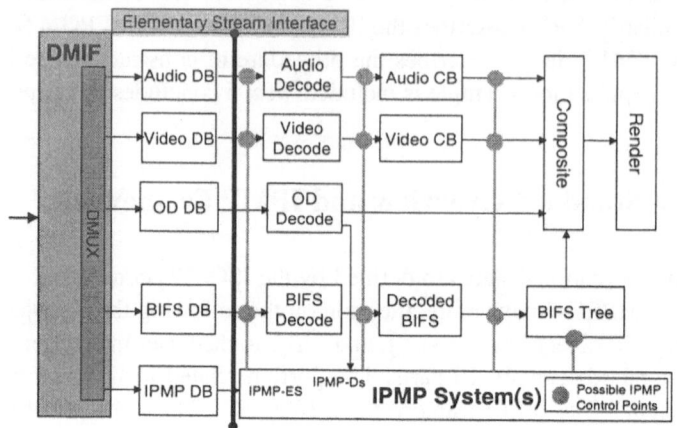

Fig. 1. IPMP sub-system in the ISO/IEC 14496 terminal architecture [3]

3.1 IPMPManager

In IM1, IPMP sub-systems are implemented by extending the IPMPManager class. IPMPManager is an interface between MPEG-4 player and the IPMP sub-system. Each media content access unit goes through the sub-system before it is stored in the decoding buffer. An implementation of IPMPManager can decrypt the encrypted content and thus block the unauthorized access to the media content.

IPMPManagerImp extends the IPMPManager interface, and it provides the major functionality of an IPMP sub-system. Simple implementations need to overload a few setup functions and the *Decrypt()* function, which decrypts one access unit using one IPMP stream. More complex implementations, for instance, when multiple IPMP streams are used to decrypt a single elementary stream, may overload the *Run()* function and implement different data flows by directly accessing the MediaStreams.

IPMP plug-ins interact with the core codes of the player through a special kind of buffer, known as MediaStreams. An IPMPManager object fetches an access unit, which is a kind of media, from one MediaStream object. After decrypting an access unit, it will dispatch one decrypted access unit into an output MediaStream object, which usually is a decoding buffer [6].

3.2 IPMPManagerImp

IPMPManagerImp extends the IPMPManager interface. It is the base class of all the IPMP sub-systems. IPMPManagerImp provides all the needed functions of a regular IPMP sub-system.

Each IPMP sub-system runs on its own thread. An IPMP sub-system is usually attached to three MediaStream objects – the encrypted input stream, the decrypted output stream, and the IPMP stream. According to the SDK [6], the workflow of a typical IPMP sub-system is shown in Fig.2. Our design procedure is modified from that in [6] and is outlined below.

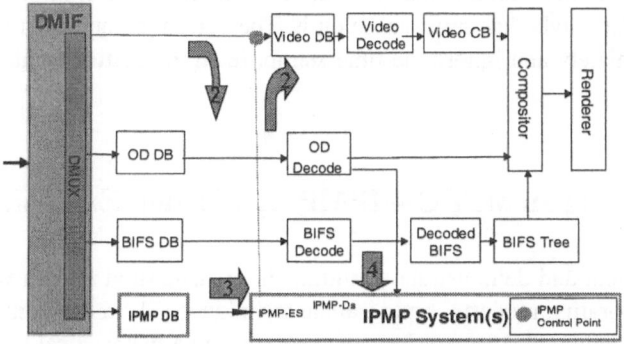

Fig. 2. A typical IPMP sub-system workflow

1. An object derived from IPMPManagerImp is instantiated by the IPMP sub-system module (usually a Dynamic Link Library, or DLL).

2. The application calls *IPMPManager::SetInputStream()* and *IPMPManager::Set*

OutputStream() to attach input and output MediaStreams to the IPMP sub-system.

3. The application calls *IPMPManager::SetIPMPStream()* to attach an IPMP stream to the IPMP sub-system. This function may be called more than once if the elementary stream is protected by multiple IPMP streams.

4. The application calls *IPMPManager::SetDescriptor()* for each IPMP descriptor assigned to the elementary stream.

5. The application calls *IPMPManager::Init()* to initialize the IPMP sub-system and to confirm that the user has access to the protected elementary stream.

6. The application calls *IPMPManager::Start()*, which spawns the IPMP sub-system thread.

7. The IPMP sub-system thread fetches an access unit from the input stream and the corresponding access unit from the IPMP stream. Note that one IPMP access unit can control multiple content access units.

8. The IPMP sub-system calls a private virtual function, *Decrypt()*. This function is overloaded by specific IPMP sub-systems and performs the actual decryption.

9. The output of *Decrypt()* is stored in the output MediaStream.

10. Steps 7-9 are repeated until *IPMPManager::Stop()* is called by the application, or until reaching the end of the input stream.

Some of these steps have been implemented in IPMPManagerImp class, but in some special cases, we need to re-implement them again.

3.3 MediaStream

MediaStream class handles the buffering and synchronization of an elementary stream. It manages the memory buffer and fetch/disfetch access units from the buffer. The stored access unit maybe has time stamp on it. The current solution is to fetch the access unit immediately and ignore the time stamp, fetch the matured unit only, or otherwise suspend.

4   Constructing an MPEG-4 IPMP Application Example

We will implement and demonstrate a multimedia transmission system with MPEG-4 IPMP by incorporating modern cryptographic techniques [7]. In designing the system, we adopt the Conditional Access (CA) concept by using a hierarchical key distribution structure as shown in Fig. 3.

In this system, we encrypt the bitstreams in the TRIF file only. The server generates and embeds the keys in the bitstream. When the keys are correctly retrieved, the decoded and decrypted video sequence can be played properly. Otherwise, the bitstreams cannot be decoded successfully.

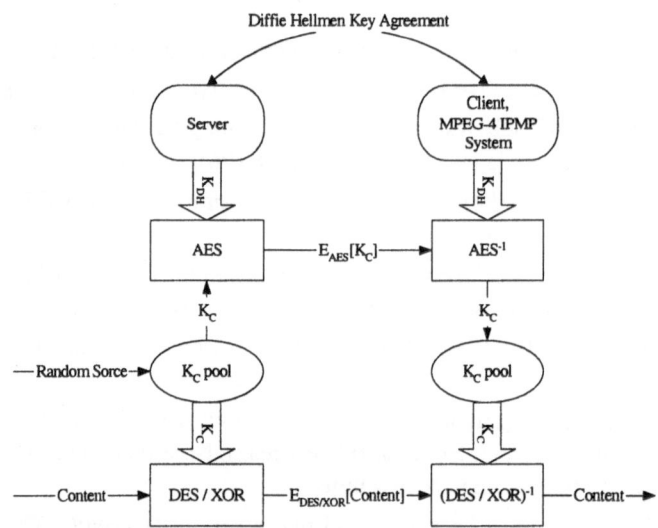

Fig. 3. The hierarchical key distribution structure.

4.1 System Structure and Handshaking Protocol

Our hierarchical key distribution system is illustrated by Fig. 3. At the upper level, we use the Diffie-Hellmen Key Agreement [8] that allows both the client-end and the server-end to securely retrieve the Session Key, K_{DH}, over the Internet. By applying the Advanced Encryption Standard (AES) [9], K_{DH} can serve as a secret key to encrypt K_C, and the encrypted K_c are then transmitted. The use of K_c is to serve as the key for the bottom layer encryptor. In our example, the contents to be encrypted are the compressed video, audio, or image bitstreams. Similar to the CA system in DVB, we achieve the security requirement by changing K_c frequently. The throughput of K_c is so high that we need a K_c pool to generate the keys constantly.

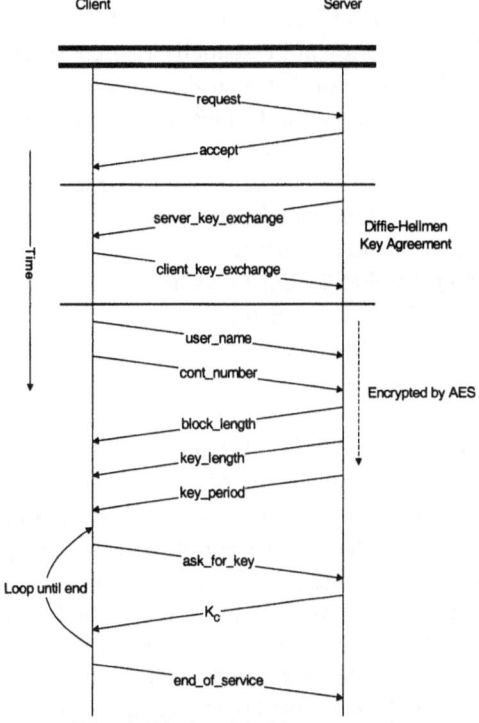

Fig. 4. The handshaking protocol.

One of the most important elements of our system is the handshaking protocol. Fig. 4 shows the basic steps in establishing a connection between the client-end and the server-end. The procedure is stated as follows.

1. Client sends request = 0x31403 (4 bytes).

2. Server sends accept = 0x31403 (4 bytes).

3. Client and server proceed with the Diffie-Hellmen key agreement; all the forthcoming information will be encrypted with AES by this key.

4. Client sends user_name (44 bytes) and cont_number (4 bytes), representing the user name and content number, respectively.

5. Server sends block_length (2 bytes) and key_lengh (2 bytes) to initialize the encryptor, and key_period (1 byte) to tell the bottom layer encryptor the lifetime of K_c.

6. Client sends ask_for_key = 0x5327 (4 bytes) to ask for a new key from the server. Server sends a new K_c to client after receiving ask_for_key.

7. Client sends end_of_service = 0x0 (32 bytes) to terminate the handshaking.

4.2   The Client-End IPMP Plug-In

The player is the "IM1 2D player" executed under the Windows environment. Hence, the IPMP plug-in can be implemented with the DLL file in Windows.

There is one implementation of IPMP plug-in in IM1 core called IPMPNull. It works like a buffer to send the input MediaStream directly to the output side. Based on the existing IPMPNull program, we implement two new IPMP plug-ins in our system: IPMPXOR.dll and IPMPDES.dll. They are essentially two encryption methods. The first plug-in conducts the XOR operation between the received bitstreams and the key at the decryptor, a very simple encryption technique; the second one uses the DES [7] scheme for decryption.

In the MPEG-4 design, the IPMP stream is used to transmit keys. In our example, we transmit the key using TCP/IP, not DMIF, to avoid the incompatibility between our example system and the standard system.

The first step to implement IPMPDES is to create an IPMPDES class, and it inherits a class called "IPMPManagerImp." Then, we implement the *SetDescriptor()* function. The IPMPDescriptor within the TRIF file contains the information of the server location and the content identification number that is to be played. The *SetDescriptor()* function uses the above information to make a connection to the server and to initialize the decryptor locally. Next, we implement the *Decryptor()* function, which can decrypt the received MediaStream, and count the number of times K_c is used.

Figs. 5(a) and 5(b) are the demonstrations of two IM1 2D players. The video sequence is coded in the H.263 format. The bottom-left bitstreams in both figures are decrypted by IPMPXOR, and the ones on the bottom-right are decrypted by IPMPDES. The sequences on the upper side are not protected in both Figs. 5(a) and 5(b). In Fig.5(a), we assume that the key can be reliably transmitted and received. Hence, the two encrypted bitstreams can be decrypted and displayed successfully. In Fig. 5(b), the keys are not retrieved. Thus, the encrypted bitstream cannot be decoded and displayed.

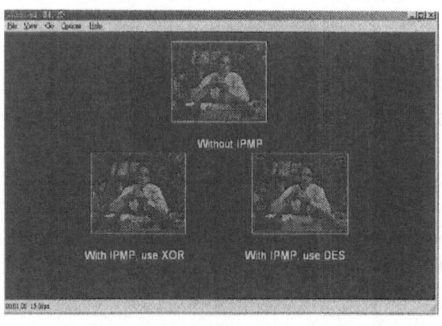 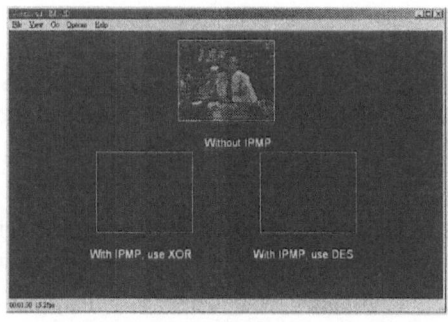

(a)   (b)

Fig. 5. Demonstration of the proposed system: the unprotected bitstreams (*upper*) and the protected bitstreams (*lower*). (a) Correctly retrieved keys, and (b) keys not retrieved.

4.3 The Server-End

The server can be divided into two parts, one is the encryptor and the other part is responsible for sending keys. Fig.6 is a screenshot of the server-end application. We write it in C++ and it is a DOS command-line program. But the GUI is done in Java using the pipes stdin and stdout.

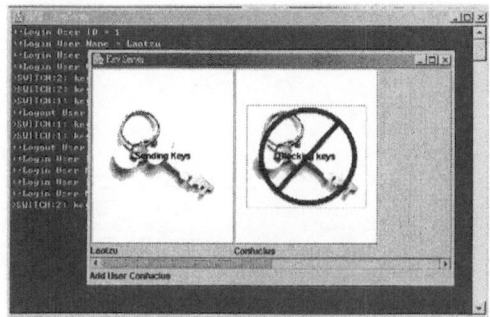

Fig. 6. The server that can turn on/off keys.

5   Conclusions

In this paper, we first briefly describe the MPEG-4 IPMP system concepts. We then analyze the IPMP API in the reference software of the MPEG-4 Systems – IM1. After studying the IM1 Core and its IPMP API, we implement a functional IPMP subsystem by modifying IPMPNull – a prototype of the IPMP sub-system.

We use the hierarchical key architecture to construct an application example, following the MPEG-4 IPMP concepts. Our example simulates the functionalities suggested by the standard. We demonstrate that the MPEG-4 IPMP is a practical way for protecting the multimedia content.

Acknowledgement. This work was supported by National Science Council (Taiwan, ROC) under Grant No. NSC 90-2213-E-009-137.

References

1. ISO/IEC 13818-1 *Generic Coding of Moving Pictures and Associated Audio Information*: *Part 1 Systems* (ISO/IEC JTC1/SC29/WG11 N0801rev), April 1995.
2. H. Benoit, *Digital Television, MPEG-1, MPEG-2 and Principles of The DVB system*, Arnold, 1997.
3. ISO/IEC 14496-1:2000(E) *Coding of Audio-visual Objects: Part 1 Systems* (ISO/IEC JTC1/SC29/WG11 N3850), October 2000.
4. ISO/IEC JTC1/SC29/WG11 N4291, *MPEG Systems (1-2-4-7) FAQ*, Jul. 2001.
5. ISO/IEC JTC1/SC29/WG11 N4709, *MPEG-4 Systems Software Status and Implementation Workplan*, March 2002.
6. ISO/IEC JTC1/SC29/WG11 M3860, *IPMP Development Kit*, Aug. 1998.
7. B. Schneier, *Applied Cryptography, 2nd edition*, John Wiley & Sons, 1996.

8. *PKCS #3: Diffie-Hellman Key-Agreement Standard*, An RSA Laboratories Technical Note, ftp://ftp.rsa.com/pub/pkcs/ascii/pkcs-3.asc.
9. J. Daemen and V. Rijmen, *AES Proposal: Rijndael* (corrected version), http://www.esat.kuleuven.ac.be/~rijmen/rijndael/rijndaeldocV2.zip.

A Visual Model for Estimating Perceptual Redundancy Inherent in Color Image

Chun-Hsien Chou and Kuo-Cheng Liu

Department of Electrical Engineering, Tatung University,
40 Chungshan N. Rd., 3rd Sec., Taipei, Taiwan, 10451, R.O.C.
chou@dsp.ee.ttu.edu.tw, kcliu@gcbc.edu.tw

Abstract. Human eyes are not perfect sensors for perceiving color images shown in 2-D display monitors or represented as photo prints. The maximum extent of variation that is barely noticeable with average human eyes is the error-visibility threshold of the pixel or the so-called just noticeable distortion (JND) of the pixel. In this paper, a color visual model based on characteristics of human visual system (HVS) is proposed to estimate the JND profiles of color images. The contrast masking effect and texture masking effect of color images in uniform color space is measured to optimize the estimation of error-visibility threshold in chromatic channel. A subjective test that compares the perceptual quality of JND-contaminated image with that of the original color image verifies that the validity of the proposed color visual model.

1 Introduction

In the recent year, the topic of image compression [1]-[3] and watermarking technique [5]-[7] based on HVS has become very popular. The effective watermarking technique can be described to insert the maximum information into the host image, but still preserve human transparency. To remove the perceptually insignificant signal from images on the bit rate, at which high reception quality is maintained, is the goal of image compression. Therefore, it is believed that a good human visual model, from which the maximum redundancy of images can be obtained for both of above application, is required.

The surveys exploiting human visual model can be found in [3], [6], [8]-[10]. In [3], a perceptual tuned subband coder is proposed by measuring the JND profile in order to optimize the rate-distortion. In [6], the watermarking scheme based on human visual model was proposed. For generating an imperceptible watermark with maximum modification, JND value of a wavelet based visual model [11] was applied in [7]. According to the local image characteristics of HVS and masking effect [10], Barni et al. [8] give the watermark strength to accomplish the coefficients modulation in wavelet domain. Kutter and Winkler [9] present a perceptual model takes into account the sensitivity and masking behavior of the human visual system by means of a local isotropic contrast measure and a masking model for spread-spectrum watermarking technique. However, the properties of HVS mentioned above are applied to the gray-scale image, no color perceptual model has yet sufficiently integrated the

Y.-C. Chen, L.-W. Chang, and C.-T. Hsu (Eds.): PCM 2002, LNCS 2532, pp. 353-360, 2002.
© Springer-Verlag Berlin Heidelberg 2002

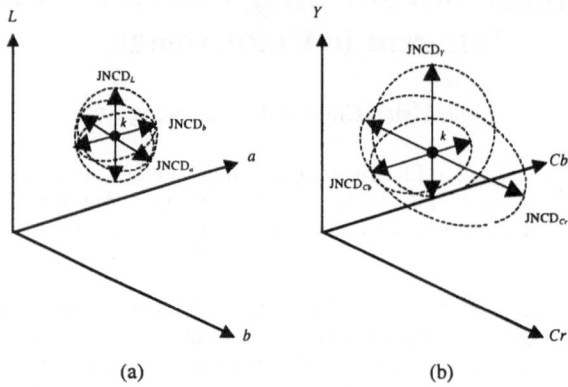

Fig. 1. (a) JNCD in the uniform color space (*Lab* color space); (b) JNCD in the non-uniform color space (*YCbCr* color space).

psychovisual effects to offer a simple and efficient method for evaluate the perceptual redundancies from color images.

Among numerous analyses to HVS, the concept of JND profile addressed by Jayant [1] has been successfully applied to the perceptual coding [7]. Based on the visual model proposed by Chou and Lee [7], the concept of *just noticeable color difference* (JNCD) in uniform color space is incorporated to construct the color visual model. In this paper, a simple but effective color perceptual model is proposed to estimate the JND profile of color image. Firstly, the characteristics of color perceptual redundancy are introduced. Then, the measurement of color perceptual redundancy is conducted by considering the masking effect. Using the concepts in uniform color space, the proposed visual model is depicted to estimate JND profiles of color images in *YCbCr* color space. A fidelity test and conclusion of the paper will be made last.

2   Color Visual Redundancies

In the color space, the JNCD is used to represent the total error-visibility threshold caused by luminance part and chominance part of any color signal. Therefore, the properties of JNCD from the viewpoint of uniform and non-uniform color space are first discussed in the following.

2.1   JNCD in Uniform and Non-uniform Color Space

For any color signal in color spaces, JNCD provides the threshold level of error visibility around that signal, below which reconstruction errors are rendered imperceptible. As shown in Fig. 1(a), the perceptual error thresholds of a color signal k in the uniform color space (*Lab* space), for which the human perception can be defined by simple color difference, are nearly the same in different channels. That is, $JNCD_L$ $=JNCD_a =JNCD_b$. On the other hand, the perceptual error thresholds of a color signal k in the non-uniform color space (*YCbCr* space) are alternative in different channels, that is, $JNCD_y \neq JNCD_{Cb} \neq JNCD_{Cr}$ as depicted in Fig. 1(b).

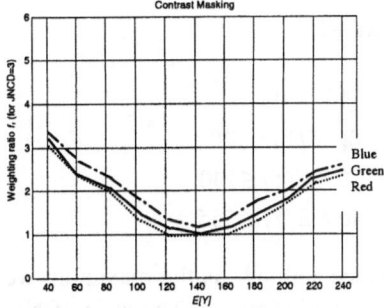
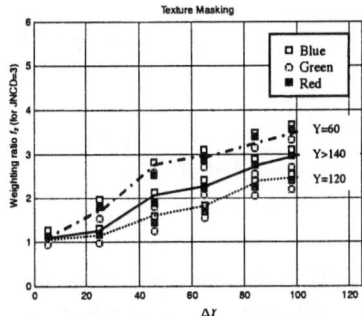

Fig. 2. Weighting curve due to contrast masking. (Left)

Fig. 3. Weighting curve due to spatial. masking (Right)

To quantify the perceptual redundancy further in the uniform color space, the phenomenon of distortion masking which has been widely exploited [8], [9], [11] must be considered. In this paper, the JNCD values which are measured by considering these masking effects are named non-uniform JNCD (NUJNCD) and others are named uniform JNCD (UJNCD).

2.2 Masking Effect

In this paper, there are two experiments to be proceeded to measure the color perceptual redundancy due to masking effect caused by human eyes. One of the experiments to be tested is the one considering the average background luminance behind the pixel. The other is the spatial non-uniformity of the background luminance. The former addresses that effect caused by the inconsistency in sensitivity of the HVS to stimuli of varying levels of contrast. That is, the human visual perception is sensitive to luminance contrast rather than absolute luminance value. The later, which is known as texture masking, focuses on the effect caused by spatial non-uniformity of the background luminance.

The distinction between the UJNCD and NUJNCD in the *Lab* space can be expressed as

$$NUJNCD = s \cdot UJNCD \qquad (1)$$

where s is a weighting function as the masking effect has been employed and UJNCD is set to 3 by empiricism. For simplicity, the NUJNCD of the test stimuli in images is measured under the scenarios by taking account of the average background luminance and luminance gradient mentioned above. Therefore, the model of the weighting function can be expressed as follows:

$$s = \min\{f_1(E[Y]), f_2(\Delta Y)\} \qquad (2)$$

$$f_1(E[Y]) = \begin{cases} -0.0222E[Y] + 3 & \text{for } E[Y] < 127 \\ 0.0125(E[Y] - 130) + 1 & \text{for } E[Y] \geq 127 \end{cases} \qquad (3)$$

$$f_2(\Delta Y) = \alpha(E[Y])\Delta Y + 1 \qquad (4)$$

$$\alpha(E[Y]) = \begin{cases} 0.1 & \text{for } E[Y] \leq 60 \\ 0.03 & \text{for } 60 < E[Y] \leq 100 \\ 0.01 & \text{for } 100 < E[Y] \leq 140 \\ 0.03 & \text{for } 140 < E[Y] \leq 255 \end{cases} \qquad (5)$$

where $E[Y]$ is the average background luminance and ΔY is the maximum weighted average of luminance difference around each pixel in images. The ratio of NUJNCD to UJNCD due to the contrast masking effect is given by f_1, in which the subject test is applied to distinguish noise visibility threshold and the average background luminance. f_2 represents the ratio NUJNCD to UJNCD due to of the texture masking effect. By varying the intensity of the noise, the error visibility threshold due to luminance change is determined when the perturbed edge is just noticeable. Tristimuli are the main tested colors in experiments and the behavior is shown in Fig. 2 and Fig. 3, respectively.

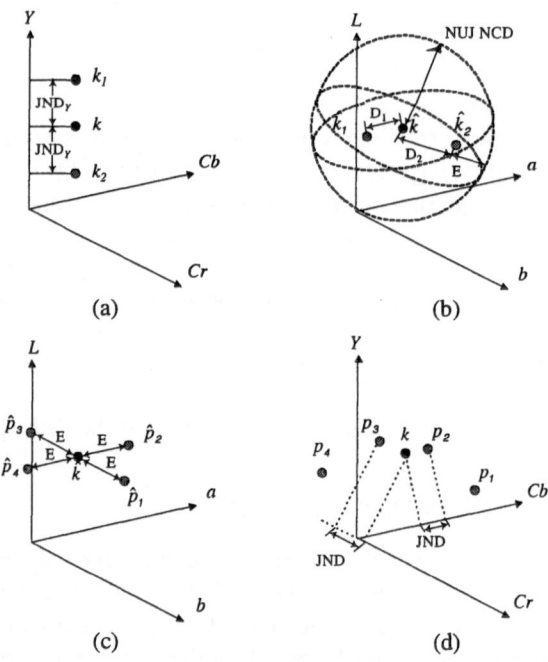

Fig. 4. Diagram of proposed color visual model. (a) color k and the associated JND_Y in *YCbCr* space; (b) color k and the associated NUJNCD in *Lab* space; (c) visibility threshold due to chrominance signals in *Lab* space; (d) the probable visibility threshold due to chrominance signals in *YCbCr* space.

3   The Proposed Color Visual Model

The diagram of the proposed color visual model is composed of four parts and described as follows. Let k be a pixel in the color image presented in the color system of $YCbCr$ where the luminance channel is defined as Y and the chrominance channel is defined as Cb and Cr. As shown in Fig. 4(a), the JND of luminance signals can be obtained by means of the perceptual model conducted in [3] and expressed by JND_Y. The pixels contaminated by adding to and subtracting from k with visibility threshold JND_Y are defined by k_1 and k_2, respectively.

According to the uniformity, the Lab color space provides a nearly perfect invisible distortion sphere for any color signals. Therefore, colors k, k_1 and k_2 are transformed from the $YCbCr$ space to the Lab space and the corresponding transformed colors are given by $\hat{k}$, $\hat{k}_1$ and $\hat{k}_2$. The imperceptual color difference with respect to color $\hat{k}$ in Lab color space caused by JND_Y addition and subtraction in $YCbCr$ space can be expressed as D_1 and D_2, respectively.

$$D_1 = \| \hat{k}_1 - \hat{k} \| \tag{6}$$

$$D_2 = \| \hat{k}_2 - \hat{k} \| \tag{7}$$

where $\|\bullet\|$ means the Euclidean distance. From Fig. 4(b), the indiscernible color difference of $\hat{k}$ induced by chrominance signals can be calculated by referring the UJNCD in Lab space as follows

$$E = \begin{cases} UJNCD - D, & for\ \ UJNCD > D \\ 0, & for\ \ UJNCD \le D \end{cases} \tag{8}$$

where $D = \max\{D_1, D_2\}$. The reason why maximum operator exploited here is to estimate the indiscernible color difference with respect to the chromatic channel more conservatively. Based on the concepts detailed in Sec. 2.2, the UJNCD in Eq. (8) must be replaced by NUJNCD in order optimize the redundancy estimation.

Furthermore, we simply assume that all the indiscernible color difference of $\hat{k}$ due to chrominance signals would spread only in a and b axis. Hence, four pixels $\hat{p}_1$, $\hat{p}_2$, $\hat{p}_3$, and $\hat{p}_4$ contaminated by imperceptual noise caused by chrominance change can be obtained by adding to or subtracting from $\hat{k}$ with E along a and b axis, as indicated in Fig. 4(c). To illustrate the variation of pixel k and contaminated pixels in Cb and Cr channel, the pixels $\hat{p}_1$, $\hat{p}_2$, $\hat{p}_3$, and $\hat{p}_4$ are transformed from Lab space to $YCbCr$ space and are given by p_1, p_2, p_3 and p_4 as depicted in Fig. 4(d). Finally, the JND of pixel k in Cb and Cr channel can be obtained by taking the minimal distance between pixel k and contaminated pixels, respectively. That is

$$JND_{Cb} = \min_{i=1,2,3,4} | Cb_{p_i} - Cb_k | \tag{9}$$

$$JND_{Cr} = \min_{i=1,2,3,4} | Cr_{p_i} - Cr_k |$$ (10)

where (Y_k, Cb_k, Cr_k) and $(Y_{p_i}, Cb_{p_i}, Cr_{p_i})$ are tristmulus values of the color k and p_i in YCbCr color space, respectively.

4 Simulation Results

The following results were obtained with color, 24bpp, 512×512 images. The experiments were intended to test whether the visual quality of images can be maintained or not after contaminating with noises referring to visibility thresholds.

To justify the validity of the proposed color visual model, a subjective test that compares the perceptual quality of the color image contaminated by noises of JND profile with the original color image is conduct. If the JND profiles obtained from the proposed color visual mode are accurate, the perceptual quality of the corresponding JND-contaminated image should be as good as the original image while the PSNR of the contaminated image should be as low as possible. The test image "Banboo" and the contaminated version are shown in Fig. 5(a) and (b), respectively. The Fig. 6 shows the estimated JND profile of the test image, with which the original image is contaminated by randomly adding or subtracting from each pixel with its corresponding JND value. A contaminated image c(x,y) can be obtained as

$$\begin{cases} c_Y(x,y) = p_Y(x,y) + rand(i) \cdot JND_Y(x,y) \\ c_{Cb}(x,y) = p_{Cb}(x,y) + rand(j) \cdot JND_{Cb}(x,y) \\ c_{Cr}(x,y) = p_{Cr}(x,y) + rand(k) \cdot JND_{Cr}(x,y) \end{cases}$$ (11)

$$\text{for } 0 \le x < H, \ 0 \le y < W$$

$$rand(i) = 1 \text{ or } -1, \quad \text{for } 0 \le i < 3 \times H \times W$$

where p(x,y) denotes the pixel at (x,y) and the sub-index indicates the channel where the corresponding pixel located. H and W denote the height and width of the image, respectively. As the image shown in Fig. 5(a) and (b) are displayed on the PC monitor in the dark room, the artifacts between the original and the contaminated image are invisible at a viewing distance of about 6 times the image height. The PSNR of the contaminated image is 32.67dB. In other word, the amount of perceptual redundancy inherent in the color image can be quantified by using our proposed color visual model.

5 Conclusion

A color visual model for JND profile estimation of color images has been developed in this work. In order to reach the optimality for estimating color redundancy, masking effects of local area of images are discussed. On the other hand, to simplify the

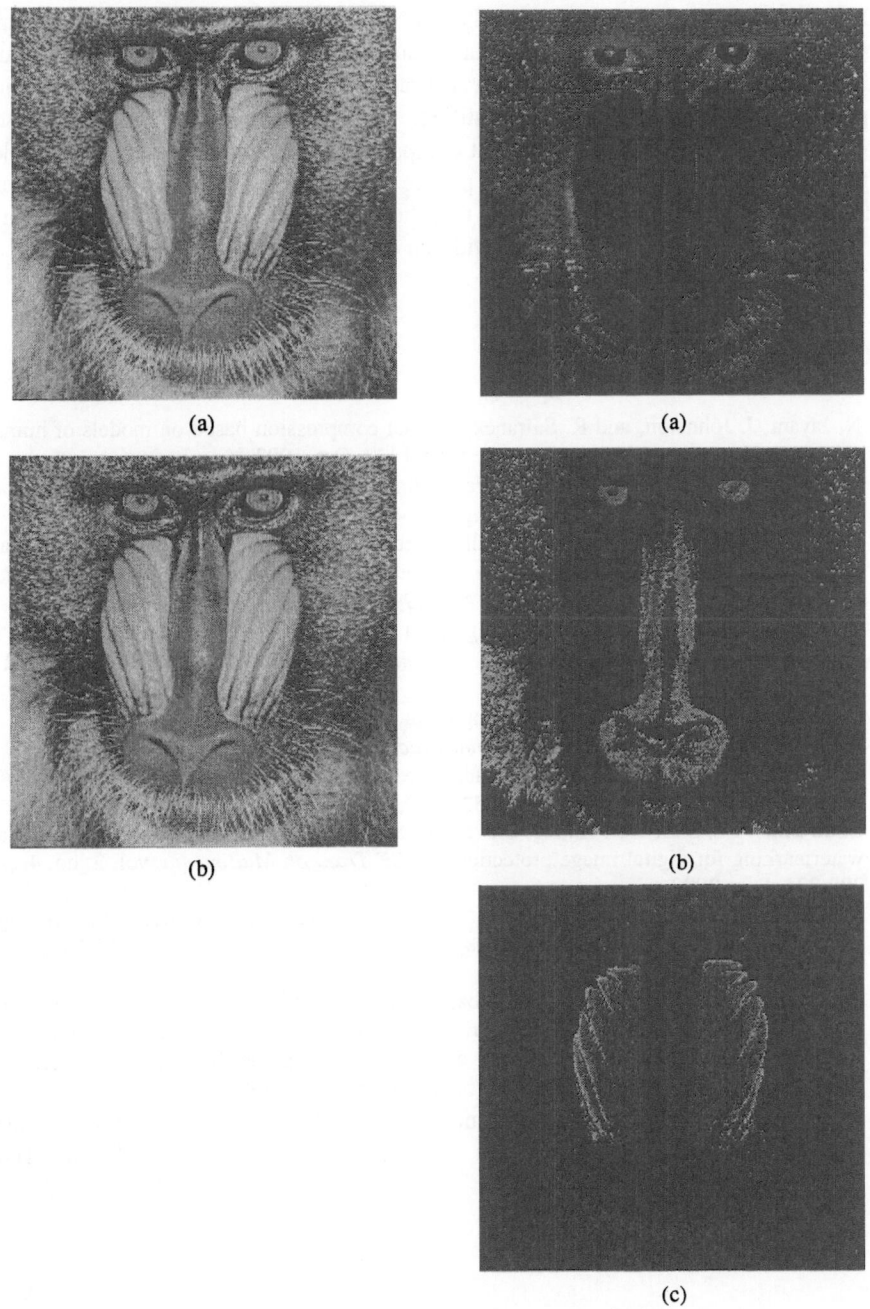

Fig. 5. (a) Original image "Baboon", (b) its color JND-contaminated version (32.67dB). (Left)

Fig. 6. JND profile estimation with color image "Baboon", magnified by a factor 10. (a) Y channel (b) Cb channel (c) Cr channel. (Right)

JND estimation for chrominance signals of color images, the characteristics of uniform color space is adopted. Another important feature of the proposed color visual model is that it can be used to obtain an accurate JND profile pixel by pixel by which the perceptual color redundancy is quantified. To justify the validity of the proposed color visual model, a subjective test that compares the perceptual quality of the color image contaminated by noises of JND profile with the original color image is conducted. The experimental results show that the quality of the JND-contaminated image is perceptual lossless as compared with the original image.

References

1. N. Jayant, J. Johnston, and R. Safranek, "Signal compression based on models of human perception," in *Proc. IEEE*, vol. 81, pp. 1385-1422, Oct. 1993.
2. C. Podilchuk, N. S. Jayant, and N. Farvardin, "Three dimensional subband coding of video," *IEEE Tran. on Image Processing*, vol. 4, pp. 125-139, Feb, 1995.
3. C. H. Chou and Y. C. Li, "A perceptually tuned subband image coder based on the measure of just-noticeable-distortion profile," *IEEE Tran. on Circuits and Systems for Video Technology*, vol. 5, no. 6, pp. 467-476, Apr. 1995.
4. C. H. Chou, "Adaptive transform coding based on removing just noticeable distortion," in *Proc. of SPIE Conf. Visual Commun. and Image Processing*, vol. 2501, pp. 607-618, 1995.
5. C. H. Chou and T. L. Wu, "Embedding color watermarks in color images", in *Proc. of IEEE 4th Workshop on Multimedia Signal Processing*, pp.327 –332, 2001.
6. C. I. Podilchuk and W. Zeng, "Image-adaptive watermarking using visual models," *IEEE J. Select. Areas Commun.*, vol. 16, pp. 525-539, 1998.
7. Chun-Shien Lu, Shih-Kun Huang, Chwen-Jye Sze, and Hong-Yuan Mark Liao, "Cocktail watermarking for digital image protection," *IEEE Tran. on Multimedia*, vol. 2, no. 4, pp. 209-224, Dec. 2000.
8. M. Barni, F. Bartolini, and A. Piva, "Improved wavelet-based watermarking through pixel-wise masking," *IEEE Tran. on Image Processing*, vol. 10, no. 5, pp. 783-791, May. 2001.
9. M. Kutter and S. Winkler, "A vision-based masking model for spread-spectrum image watermarking," *IEEE Tran. on Image Processing*, vol. 11, no. 1, pp.16-25, Jan. 2002.
10. A. S. Lewis and G. Knowles, "Image compression using the 2-D wavelet transform," *IEEE Tran. on Image Processing*, vol. 1, pp. 244-250, Apr. 1992.
11. A. B. Watson, G. Yang, J. A. Solomon, and J. Villasenor, "Visibility of wavelet quantization noise," *IEEE Tran. on Image Processing*, vol. 6, no. 8, pp. 1164-1175, Aug. 1997.

Simultaneous Color Clipping and Luminance Preserving for High Quality Entertainment Movie Coding

Barry G. Haskell and Adriana Dumitras

AT&T Labs – Research
200 Laurel Avenue South, Middletown, NJ 07748, USA
b.haskell@ieee.org, adrianad@ieee.org

Abstract. When processing color images in a luminance-chrominance color space, e.g., YUV or YIQ, it is usually necessary to convert to a primary color space, e.g., RGB, prior to displaying or printing. In some cases the resulting values of R, G, B will be outside the allowable range for the display. The conventional approach to solving this problem is to clip the offending primary color, which can result in color shifts or loss of contrast. In this paper, we attenuate the chrominance instead, resulting in no color shifts, maintenance of luminance and no loss of contrast.

1 Introduction

Many applications that employ conversions from a luminance-chrominance color space to a primary color space, as well as systems that are compliant with the widely used ITU-R BT601 and MPEG standards, make use of color clipping methods to modify the offending pixel values prior to displaying or printing the images. Software [1]-[3] and hardware [4, 5] versions of color clipping methods have been proposed. In [1], a method that employs a color transform look-up table for displaying images such that they look similarly on different display media has been proposed. In this method, the look-up table based transform does not allow the primary color values to exceed the admissible range. In [2], a conversion method from the luminance-chrominance space YUV to the primary color space RGB that employs clipping, look-up tables and computation of trigonometric functions of the conversion coefficients has been proposed. In [3], when one component of the color signal has been clipped, the other components are maintained at values such that the hue is accurately reproduced in the image. In [4], hardware clipping is performed using a color video signal. In [5], a circuit for limiting a color video signal in the primary space has been proposed. The circuit consists of a clipping section, a reference generator and an amplifier.

Clipping of primaries may be performed in the RGB color space, or in the luminance-chrominance space by backward conversion. A version of this idea has been employed in [6], which performs clipping of the saturation values in a different space

Y.-C. Chen, L.-W. Chang, and C.-T. Hsu (Eds.): PCM 2002, LNCS 2532, pp. 361-368, 2002.
© Springer-Verlag Berlin Heidelberg 2002

than the luminance-chrominance space and then converts the resulting picture into a primary space.

Because color clipping may result in color shifts or loss of contrast, which are not acceptable in numerous applications such as entertainment movie coding and high quality color image enhancement, color limitation methods that avoid clipping have been proposed. In [7], a rate of enhancement for each pixel has been computed using adaptive windows. Using this enhancement rate, each pixel value is modified differently such that its resulting value belongs to an admissible range. In [8], an enhancement method for color images that performs histogram modifications and thereby avoids color clipping has been proposed. In [9], a color enhancement method makes use of nonlinear transforms to map the primary R, G, B values of the pixels in the enhanced picture to the admissible range. The transform is assumed to be a rotation of the vector corresponding to each pixel in the RGB color space and the transform coefficients are determined accordingly.

In this paper we propose a method for simultaneous color clipping and luminance preserving. Unlike most of the clipping methods mentioned earlier and unlike those in [3, 6], we do not apply our method in the primary color space. Also, as compared to other color clipping methods, our method features distinct characteristics. First, unlike the clipping methods included in the ITU-R BT601 and MPEG standards, we attenuate the chrominance values while preserving the luminance. Second, unlike the method in [9], which makes use of nonlinear transforms to map the primary R, G, B values of the pixels to the admissible range, our method employs linear transforms that are more efficient. Third, in contrast to methods such as those in [1] and [2], which make use of look-up tables for color conversion and clipping that must be defined apriori, our method does not require setting any coefficients or tables beforehand.

The rest of the paper is divided into three sections. Section 2 provides a detailed presentation of our proposed method. Experimental results using high quality movie sequences and conclusions are included in Sections 3 and 4, respectively.

2 Proposed Method

2.1 Detailed Description

Let us assume that processing is carried out in the luminance-chrominance color space. In this space, each pixel is represented by a luminance component Y and two chrominance components U and V. Before displaying a pixel, the luminance and chrominance components must be transformed to primary colors, e.g., red (R), green (G), and blue (B). The allowable range of primary colors is usually the same as that of the luminance, i.e., $Y_{min} \leq Y \leq Y_{max}$. If the individual primary colors have different ranges then generalization of the methods herein is straightforward. If there are more than three primary colors then generalization of the methods herein is again straightforward.

In most color spaces the conversion to primaries can be described mathematically by

$$R = Y + a_1 U + b_1 V \qquad (1)$$

$$G = Y + a_2 U + b_2 V$$

$$B = Y + a_3 U + b_3 V$$

where a_1, a_2, a_3, b_1, b_2, b_3 are coefficients with suitable values that are specified by the conversion equations. Our goal is to insure that the resulting primary values R, G, B belong to the range $[Y_{min}, Y_{max}]$. First, we compute

$$c = \max_{1 \le i \le 3} (a_i U + b_i V) \qquad (2)$$

$$d = \min_{1 \le i \le 3} (a_i U + b_i V) \qquad (3)$$

Second, if $Y + c > Y_{max}$, then at least one of the primaries R, G, B exceeds the maximum allowable value Y_{max}. In this case we compute c' defined by Eq. (2) using the values U' and V' instead of U and V and then we use c' to reduce the magnitudes of U and V to U' and V', respectively. More specifically, we force the offending primary to have the value Y_{max} by selecting

$$c' = Y_{max} - Y \qquad (4)$$

This is achieved by attenuating U and V by the factor $\dfrac{c'}{c}$, i.e.,

$$U' = U \frac{c'}{c} \quad \text{and} \quad V' = V \frac{c'}{c} \qquad (5)$$

Third, if $Y + d < Y_{min}$, then at least one of the primaries R, G, B is less than the minimum allowable value Y_{min}. In this case we compute d' defined by Eq. (3) using the values U' and V' instead of U and V and then we use d' to reduce the magnitudes of U and V to U' and V', respectively. More specifically, we force the offending primary to have the value Y_{min} by selecting

$$d' = Y_{min} - Y \qquad (6)$$

This is achieved by attenuating U and V by the factor $\dfrac{d'}{d}$, i.e.,

$$U' = U \frac{d'}{d} \quad \text{and} \quad V' = V \frac{d'}{d} \tag{7}$$

Note that in Eq. (7) both d and d' are negative.

2.2 Discussion

The algorithm corresponding to the method discussed in detail in Section 2.1 is illustrated in Fig. 1 and summarized in Table 1. In addition to the processing steps discussed earlier, additional steps are required by the particulars of luminance-chrominance representations presented next.

- *Downsampling*: In some still image and most video processing systems, the chrominance components U and V may be downsampled by two in each direction. Before performing the conversion to primaries, these components must be upsampled by two in each direction such that they have sizes that are equal to that of the luminance component.

- *Digital Luminance-Chrominance Representation*: In some digital representations of luminance and chrominance (Y_d, U_d, V_d), an attenuation and shift are applied to force the color components into a predefined range. For example, for $Y_{min} = 0$, $Y_{max} = 255$ the widely used ITU-R BT601 and MPEG standards define

$$Y = (Y_d - 16) \cdot \frac{255}{219}$$

$$U = (U_d - 128) \frac{255}{224} \tag{8}$$

$$V = (V_d - 128) \frac{255}{224}$$

Before applying our proposed method, a digital luminance-chrominance $Y_d U_d V_d$ representation should be converted to a YUV representation.

We note that, the resulting algorithm in Fig. 1 and Table 1 not only is more efficient than those based on nonlinear transforms, but it may also be slightly more efficient than that based on the linear conversion equations (1) to (8). We also note that no look-up tables for color conversion and coefficients need to be set beforehand.

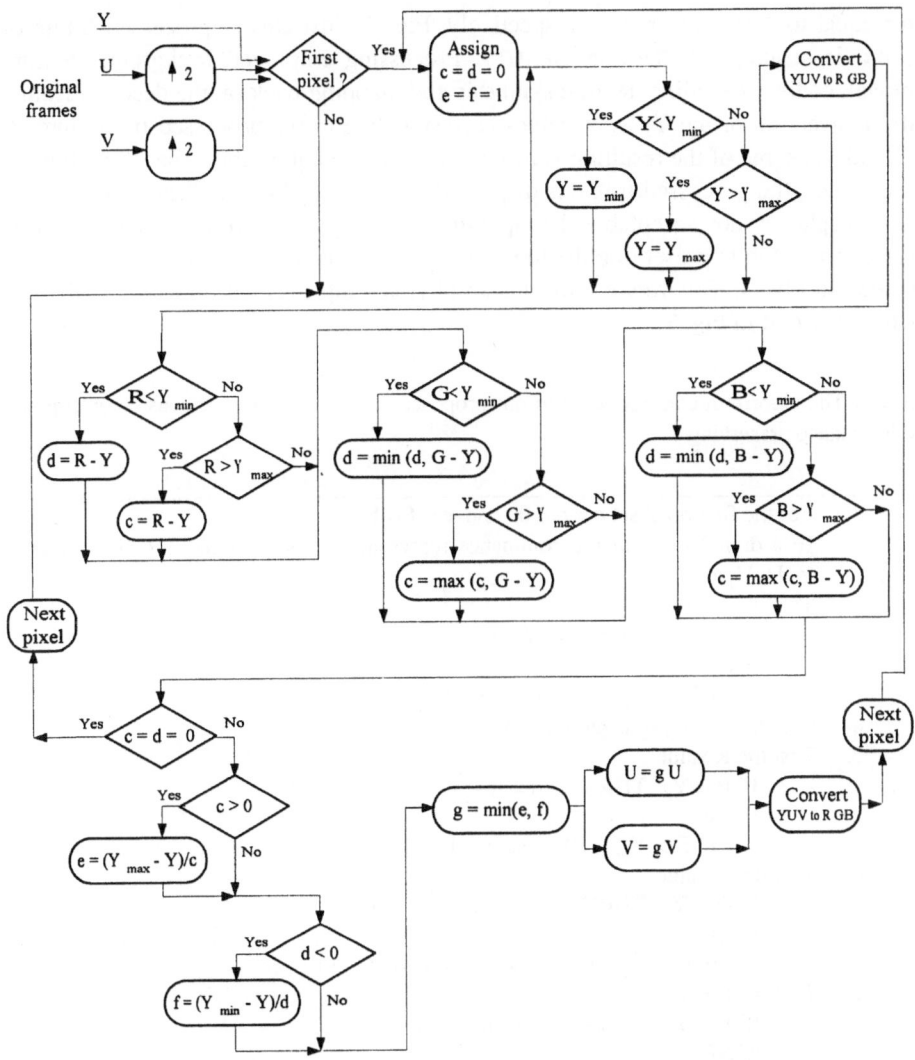

Fig. 1. The block diagram of the proposed color clipping and luminance preserving method

3 Experimental Results

In what follows, we illustrate the performance of our color clipping and luminance preserving method using high quality entertainment movie sequences. In this work, we illustrate our results using 200 color frames from the movie sequence AMERICAN BEAUTY. The frames are represented in YUV format. The size of a luminance (Y) frame is equal to 720 x 352 pixels. The chrominance (U and V) frames have each sizes equal to 360 x 176 pixels, respectively. Fig. 2 illustrates a processed frame of the movie sequence AMERICAN BEAUTY. Processing employed background texture removal, coding, decoding, texture synthesis and mapping back on the decoded frame. After conversion of the Y, U, V values corresponding to the processed frame into R, G, B values, some of the resulting values are outside the admissible range. By clipping these values, the processed frame is displayed as shown in Fig. 2. Clearly, the quality of the display is not acceptable. By applying our proposed method which performs color clipping while preserving the luminance, the processed frame is displayed as illustrated in Fig. 3. This figure indicates an obvious improvement in terms of display quality over that in Fig. 2.

Table 1. The algorithm corresponding to our proposed method for simultaneous color clipping and luminance preserving

1.	For the first pixel set $c = d = 0$ and $e = f = 1$
2.	IF a digital luminance-chrominance representation is available THEN convert Y_d, U_d, V_d to YUV
3.	Test the Y value
	IF $Y < Y_{min}$ THEN set $Y = Y_{min}$
	ELSE
	IF $Y > Y_{max}$ THEN set $Y = Y_{max}$
4.	Calculate R, G, B using Eq. (1)
5.	Test the R value
	IF $R < Y_{min}$ THEN set $d = R - Y$
	ELSE
	IF $R > Y_{max}$ THEN set $c = R - Y$
6.	Test the G value
	IF $G < Y_{min}$ THEN set $d = \min(d, G - Y)$
	ELSE
	IF $G > Y_{max}$ THEN set $c = \max(c, G - Y)$
7.	Test the B value
	IF $B < Y_{min}$ THEN set $d = \min(d, B - Y)$
	ELSE
	IF $B > Y_{max}$ THEN set $c = \max(c, B - Y)$
8.	IF $c = d = 0$ THEN R, G and B are within bounds, and we are done. Go to step 2 to process the next pixel.
	ELSE continue
9.	IF $c > 0$ THEN set $e = \dfrac{Y_{max} - Y}{c}$
	IF $d < 0$ THEN set $f = \dfrac{Y_{min} - Y}{d}$
10.	Set $g = \min(e, f)$
11.	Attenuate U and V by g, i.e, set $U = g U$ and $V = g V$
12.	Recalculate R, G, B using Eq. (1)
13.	Set $c = d = 0$ and $e = f = 1$
14.	Go to step 2 to process the next pixel.

Fig. 2. Processed color frame of the movie sequence AMERICAN BEAUTY with color clipping

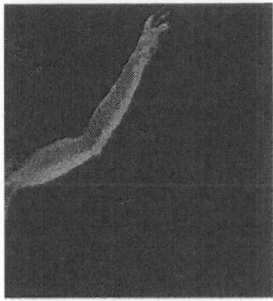

Fig. 3. Processed color frame of the movie sequence AMERICAN BEAUTY with simultaneous color clipping and luminance preserving using our proposed method

4 Conclusions

We have addressed the problem of displaying accurately pictures (images or video frames) that have been transformed from a luminance-chrominance color space such as YUV to a primary color space such as RGB. By attenuating the chrominance and maintaining the luminance, the method proposed in this paper ensures that the R, G, B values are within an allowable range while avoiding color shifts or loss of contrast that are common to other color clipping methods. Experimental results using high quality movie frames show that our method is very effective.

References

[1] A. Ohkubo, "Color Transformation Look-Up Table", patent US62229916, issued May 8, 2001.
[2] R. Stenzel, D. Groff, "Serial Digital Video Processing with Concurrent Adjustment in RGB and Luminance/Color Difference", patent US5737032, issued Apr. 7, 1998.
[3] L.R. Dischert, T.J. Leacock, "Apparatus for Clipping and Limiting Color Signals to Maintain Color Balance", patent US5274439, issued Dec. 28, 1993.

[4] M. Ross, "Color Video Signal Processing Circuits", patent US4096513, issued June 20, 1978.

[5] Hi. Ando, N. Taketani, *et.al.*, "Primary Color Video Signal Output Circuit", patent US6023305, issued Feb. 8, 2000.

[6] C.C. Yang, S.H. Kwok, "Gamut Clipping in Color Image Processing", Proceedings of IEEE International Conference on Image Processing, 2000, pp. 824-827.

[7] N. Liu, Hong Yan, "A Solution to the Dynamic Range Problem of Pixel Values in Color Image Enhancement", Proceedings of the International Symposium on Speech, Image Proc. & Neural Networks, 1994, Hong Kong, pp. 772-775.

[8] P.A. Misna, J.J. Rodriguez, "A Multivariate Contrast Enhancement Technique for Multispectral Images", IEEE Transactions on Geoscience and Remote Sensing, vol. 33, Jan. 1995, pp. 212-216.

[9] K.-M. Kim, C.-S. Lee, Y.-H Ha, "Color Image Enhancement by Highlight-Preserving Vector Transformation and Nonlinear Mapping", Proceedings of IEEE International Conference on Image Processing, 1998, vol. 1, pp. 201-205.

A Dynamic Color Palette for Color Images Coding

Chin-Chen Chang and Yuan-Yuan Su

Department of Computer Science and Information Engineering
National Chung Cheng University Chiayi, Taiwan 621, R.O.C.
{ccc, syy88m}@cs.ccu.edu.tw

Abstract. The Indexed color mode is used mainly in order to lower the number of colors and thus the need for memory space. When the RGB mode is used to describe pixel values, there are totally 16,777,216 colors for each color image; however, an ordinary color image usually does not need so many colors. Generally, 256 colors are enough for common color images; that is, it is usually more than adequate to select 256 representative colors according to the content of the image. However, some images can be so simple in color structure that not so many as 256 colors (e.g. 128 colors, 64 colors) are necessary. In this paper, we shall propose a new scheme that incorporates both CIQBM and Partial LBG. Our new scheme can dynamically adjust the number of colors needed according to the content of the image; in other words, without damaging the image quality, our new scheme will use as few colors as possible to present the color image. As a result, it will reduce the storage demand and save transmission time for images over networks.

Keywords: *Index color, LBG, CIQBM*

1 Introduction

Due to the exploding prosperity of the Internet, growing and growing numbers and amounts of multimedia data of various kinds have been travelling through and across computer networks. Of those tons and tons of multimedia data transmitted on the Internet, most are color pictures and images. In order to speed up the Internet transmitting process, the memory space occupied by color images must be reduced to a minimum without affecting the image quality. Generally, the RGB mode is used where the pixel values are untied with integers from 0 to 255 for the three-color components: red, green, and blue. Therefore, each pixel has 24 bits, and there are 16,777,216 (2^{24}) distinct colors for true-color digital display. On the other hand, the indexed color mode comes in mainly to reduce the number of colors and thus to lower the demand for memory space. The approach of the indexed color is to build up a representative Color Look-Up Table (CLUT), which is also called the palette or codebook. A typical palette supports 256 distinct colors, and every color consists of three RGB color values. Hence, the size of the palette is 256*(8 Bits +8 Bits +8 Bits) = 6144 Bits = 768 Bytes.

Then, every pixel value takes only one byte (8 bits) to point to a particular color located on the palette. Take the image "Peppers" (size: 256×256) for example, if shown as a true-color picture, then the memory space occupied is $256 \times 256 \times 3$ Bytes =196608 Bytes ≒ 196k Bytes. However, if represented with 256 indexed colors, the

Y.-C. Chen, L.-W. Chang, and C.-T. Hsu (Eds.): PCM 2002, LNCS 2532, pp. 369-376, 2002.

memory space occupied would be only $256 \times 256 \times 1$ Bytes + 768 Bytes = 66304 Bytes $\doteqdot$ 65k Bytes. Although the memory space the index color mode takes is only about a third of that taken by the true color mode, the visual difference between the two pictures is not obvious. Therefore, the index color image is more and more frequently transmitted through and across computer networks, dominating the Internet. For instance, one of the most commonplace image file format, GIF, is in the index color image mode. However, for images whose contents are obviously simpler than those of others, a palette of 256 colors seems way too big. Instead, a palette of 128 colors or even 64 colors would be enough to provide the same image quality as a 256-color palette does. As we have discussed, there is no obvious visual difference when the size of color palette is cut down by half with one bit indicating the pixel value reduced. Consequently, besides reducing the use of memory space, the user can also save much of the time spent on Internet transmission. Up to the present time, there seems to have been no such handy schemes as can automatically adjust the size of the color palette so as to give desired image quality with a minimum number of color indices; in other words, so far, to dynamically change the size of the color palette, there seems to be no other way but to do it manually, observing the image quality drop gradually with the naked eye. This obviously is not practical at all.

In this paper, we shall propose a new technique that is able to dynamically adjust the number of index colors in the color palette in accordance with the image content. Without causing any significant harm to the image quality, our new technique manages to reduce the colors needed as far as it can handle and to decide the number of colors that one pixel value requires. Our technique employs 256 colors, and the pixel value it demands takes 8 bits. If the content of the image allows, our new method can adjust the number of index colors down to 64. Therefore, the pixel value that the image requires is 6 bits. This way, the whole memory space can be cut down to only 1/4.

2   Related Works in Color Image Quantization

In this section, we shall introduce some previous works as to color image quantization. Up to the present time, quite a number of color image quantization methods have been proposed for the design of the color palette. A simple solution to color palette generation is to use a predefined color-palette generated off-line [3]; however, by doing so, the image quality would be sacrificed to a considerable degree since the same palette is applied for all images. It is therefore better to optimize the palette for each input image separately.

Joy and Xiang proposed the center-cut algorithm [5]. It uses 3-2-4 bit-cutting to pre-quantize primordial images. Center-cut divides the color cubes along its so-called longest-dimension, and the division plane passes through the center point. The center-cut method is simple and easy to implement. However, the quantization error is not small enough. The median-cut method [6] was proposed by Kruger. It constructs the index color table using the strategy where all the colors in the index color table should represent approximately equal numbers of image pixels. The method recursively subdivides the reduced RGB color space into rectangular color cubes. The median-cut method has the advantage of being simple and easily comprehensible. However, the quantization error is still not small enough.

Orchard and Bouman proposed the binary splitting algorithm [8], which uses a division plane that passes through the mean point of the color set being split and is perpendicular to the principal axis. During the color palette design, it chooses the direction in which the variation cluster is greatest and splits the cluster with a plane perpendicular to that direction and passes through the cluster mean. The ACVRP algorithm was proposed in [7]. It repeatedly uses average color, variance, and radius preserving bisection to quantize color images. It preserves the average color, the variance in each color dimension, and the average color radius of the data set being bisected. Pei and Cheng proposed the dependent scalar quantization (DSQ) algorithm [9]. The DSQ algorithm partitions the color space of an image in a dependent way in order to fully utilize the correlations of the color components. The partitioning follows the binary moment preserving (MP) thresholding technique. In other words, the recursive binary moment preserving (MP) [2][10] thresholding is used to partition the color space by preserving the statistical moments of each color component. The DSQ algorithm is straightforward and simple to implement in comparison with ACVRP. However, the quantization error is still not small enough.

3   The Proposed Scheme

In this paper, we shall propose a new technique that incorporates both CIQBM [1][11] and LBG [4] to capture index colors into the color palette. What's more, our scheme can dynamically adjust the number of index colors according to the original true color image. This way, we cannot only gain good image quality but also save memory space.

3.1   Using CIQBM to Pick Out the Initial Color Points

CIQBM can divide the color space of an original ture color image into k cubes and let every cube have almost the same number of pixels. It can find out the initial color points for the color-palette from the k cubes. From now, every cube has its centroid that is represented by one color point in the initial color-palette of the index color image. To utilize CIQBM to pick out the initial color points for the color-palette of the index color image, two steps have to be executed: the preprocessing for the variances of the RGB color space of the original ture color image, and the decision of how many intervals can be inserted in the RGB color component, respectively. CIQBM uses the Bit Allocation technique [12] to automatically assign a given quota of bits to each component of the color space from the input color image; in other words, a fixed number of bits B_n for one pixel of the index color image must be assigned to the components, b_1, b_2, and b_3. That is, $B_n = b_1 + b_2 + b_3$. The Bit Allocation algorithm assigns fewer bits to the components with smaller variances and more bits to the components with larger variances. Because the pixels in the color space are very roughly distributed for a certain color component of the ture color image, assumably the pixels in that component have a more deepgoing influence on the image than those in more densely grouped components. Hence, CIQBM assigns more bits to the significant components in order to reduce the quantization errors and to keep as many representative parts as possible. Following this principle, an approximate solution to the bit allocation of each component B_i can be found [12].

$$B_i = \frac{B}{T} + \frac{1}{2}\log_2 \frac{\sigma_i^2}{\left[\pi_{j=1}^3 \sigma_j^2\right]^{\frac{1}{3}}} \quad , \quad \text{for } i = 1,2,3. \quad (1)$$

Here, B is the total number of bits of one pixel (here, $N = 8$), σ_i^2 is the variance of the component B_i, and T is the number of RGB components (in here, $T = 3$). Then, we follow the former CIQBM algorithm to divide the RGB components of the color space with 2^{B_i} intervals respectively.

The former CIQBM method can divide the color space into a preset number of cubes and let every cube have almost the same number of pixels. Therefore, if a cube has pixels of a lower density, then the cube must be larger; on the contrary, smaller cubes will have pixels of higher densities. For example, assume P is the total number of pixels in the color space, as displayed in Fig.2. The CIQBM algorithm has to arbitrarily choose a color component (R or G or B) from the color space and divide this color component into 2^{B_1} cubes with every cube possessing approximately $P/2^{B_1}$ pixels. After that, It goes on to choose one color component from the other two and divide this second color component into $2^{B_1} \times 2^{B_2}(= 2^{B_1+B_2})$cubes with every cube possessing approximately $P/2^{B_1+B_2}$ pixels. Finally, It divides the remaining component into $2^{B_1} \times 2^{B_2} \times 2^{B_3}(= 2^{B_1+B_2+B_3})$cubes with every cube containing approximately $P/2^{B_1+B_2+B_3}$ pixels. In this paper, systems with 8 bits/pixel frame buffers can display only 256 colors. In the mean time, let the image size be 256 pixels × 256 pixels, and then P = 65536 pixels. In accordance with the Bit Allocation approach, we set the total number of bits to be 8. That is, the total number of bits allocated to the three components of the color space is eight (R bits + G bits + B bits = 8 bits). For one thing, suppose B (red) gets 3 bits, G (green) gets 3 bits, and R (blue) gets 2 bits. Now, CIQBM chooses B (blue) first and divides this component into $2^3 =$ 8 cubes with every cube containing approximately 65536/8=8192 pixels. Second, it chooses G (green) and divides this component into $8 \times 2^3 = 64$ cubes with every cubes possessing approximately 65564/64 =1024 pixels. Finally, it divides R (red) into $64 \times 2^2 = 256$ cubes with every cube containing approximately 65536/256 =256 pixels. Now, we can figure out the initial color points for the color-palette from the 256 cubes. At the same time, every cube has its centroid that is represented by one color point in the initial color-palette of the index color image.

3.2 Utilizing Partial LBG Skill to Reduce the Number of Index Colors

After the above step, we obtain an initial color-palette containing a number of representative colors, which represents the cubes with almost the same number of pixels in the color space as shown in Fig. 1. Every cube in the color space can be distributed equally; that is, every cube has almost the same number of pixels. Such a way of pixel distribution seems fine, and yet some pixels may not be fully represented. That is to say, sometimes one pixel can belong to cube C_i but is farther away from centroid C_i than from centroid C_j of cube C_j as shown in Fig. 2. Under such circumstances, we use the partial skill of LBG to make some necessary modifications. The LBG algorithm usually acquires good results for color palettes when the initial color points for the color palettes are carefully chosen. However, when a poor initial color-palette is used, the final color-palette might also be poor, and, to make things worse, the LBG algorithm will waste a terrible lot of time. Namely, the performance of LBG is strongly dependent on the initial color-palette. Because we have attained a good initial color-palette by using former CIQBM, little time is needed to carry out the LBG algorithm. According to our experiment, just one cycle of LBG is enough to get a good result. At the same time, some representative colors are lost during the processing of LBG, as shown in Fig. 2. Otherwise, if the number of pixels in some cubes are below the threshold, which is preestablished, then the representative colors will be eliminated too. Hence, the representative colors obtained will eventually be fewer than or equal to those set up previously. In similar conditions, we can lessen the memory space for images too. In Fig. 1 and Fig. 2 right below, the stars stand for the representative colors for every cube, and the dots are the pixels in the color space.

4 Experimental Results

In this section, we shall show the index color images produced by our method, that is the color palette with a dynamically adjustable number of index colors; at the same time, we shall also compare our method with some traditional methods which have to give or set the index colors of a fixed number beforehand. In our experiments, we use Adobe Photoshop Version 5, which is a famous professional image processing software, to translate true color images into index color images. Photoshop processes an index color image with 256 colors at 8 bits per pixel, which is only one third of the memory required by a 24-bit true color image of the same size and resolution (256 pixels×256 pixels). That is, the image becomes an index color image with 256 different colors, and the requirement of storage is only 64 k bytes. However, our method will employ the technique that dynamically adjusts the number of colors according to the content of the image without significantly influencing the image quality. At the same time, we use as few colors as possible. Fig. 3, and Fig. 4 show three sub-figures that are respectively the true color image, the index color image transferred by Adobe Photoshop Version 5, the index color image processed by our method, and the index color table of our method. As the results show, our method requires fewer index colors because it can adjust itself to best fit the content of the color image. Therefore, the index color image produced by our method occupies less memory space. The numbers of colors and PSNR values for the four various test images, each processed by Photoshop and our method, are shown in Table 1. Table 2 shows the number of colors and PSNR value for four various images with threshold, which were set below five pixels in every cube for our experiments.

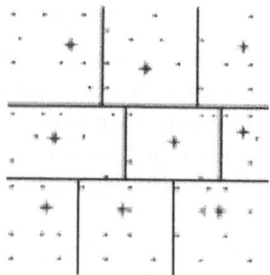

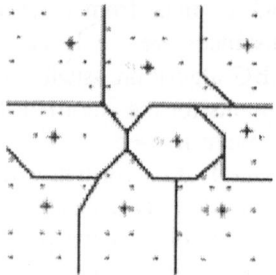

Fig. 1. The 2-D color space of RGB partitioned by the former CIQBM algorithm

Fig. 2. Utilizing LBG to improve the quality further

5   Conclusions

In this paper, we have proposed a new technique to make index color images out of true color images. Our new method can dynamically adjust the number of colors according to the content of the image; furthermore, without influencing the image quality, it only needs a minimum number of colors. Distinct from traditional methods, our new method does not need any preset index colors of a fixed number beforehand. Therefore, our method cannot only gain good image quality but also save much memory space. Compared with the traditional Photoshop algorithm, the proposed approach provides almost the same image quality at the cost of much less memory space.

True color (24 bits per pixel)   256 colors (8 bits per pixel)   188 colors (8 bits per pixel)

Fig. 3. One 8-bit pixel of an index color image with an index color table

True color (24 bits per pixel) 256 colors (8 bits per pixel)   80 colors (7 bits per pixel)

Fig. 4. One 7-bit pixel of an index color image with an index color table

Table 1. The number of colors and psnr values for the four various test images

Images Algorithm	Peppers		Washington		Lighthouse		Violin	
	Colors	APSNR	Colors	APSNR	Colors	APSNR	Colors	APSNR
Photoshop V.5	256	34.67	256	30.48	256	30.05	256	30.02
Our method	186	34.56	106	30.37	72	29.79	58	29.87

Table 2. The number of colors and psnr values for the four various test images with threshold

Images Algorithm	Peppers		Washington		Lighthouse		Violin	
	Colors	APSNR	Colors	APSNR	Colors	APSNR	Colors	APSNR
Photoshop V.5	256	34.67	256	30.48	256	30.05	256	30.02
Our method	188	34.62	111	30.43	80	29.89	63	29.96

References

1. C. C. Chang and Y. Y. Su, "A New Approach of Color Image Quantization Based on Multi-Dimensional Directory," *VRAI' 2002*, Hangzhou, China, pp. 508-514, April 2002.
2. E. J. Delp and O. R. Mitchell, "Image Compression Using Block Truncation Coding," *IEEE Transactions on Communications*, vol. COM-27, pp. 1335-1341, Sept. 1979.
3. J. D. Foley, A. V. Dam, S. k. Feiner, and J. F. Hughes, "Comput. Graphics: Principles and Practice," *Ma Addison-Wesley*, 1990.

4. R. Gray, "Vector Quantization," *IEEE ASSP Mag.*, vol. 1, pp. 4-29, April 1984.
5. G. Joy and Z. Xiang, "Center-Cut for Color-Image Quantization," *The Visual Computations*, vol. 10, pp. 62-66, 1993.
6. A. Kruger, "Median-cut Color Quantization," *Dr. Dobb's Journal*, pp. 46-92, Sept. 1994.
7. Wu-Ja Lin and Ja-Chen Lin, "Color Quantization by Preserving Color Distribution Features," *Signal Processing*, Vol. 78, pp. 201-214, 1999.
8. M. T. Orchard and C. A. Bouman, "Color Quantization of Images," *IEEE Transactions on Signal Processing*, vol. 39, no. 12, pp. 2677-2690, 1991.
9. S. C. Pei and C. M. Cheng, "Dependent Scalar Quantization of Color Images," *IEEE Transactions on Circuits and Systems for Video Technology*, vol. 5, pp. 124-139, April 1995.
10. W. H. Tsai, "Moment Preserving Thresholding: A New Approach," *Computer Vision, Graphics and Image Processing*, vol. 29,pp. 377-393, 1985.
11. J. H. Liou and S. B. Yao, "Multi–dimensional Clustering for Database Organization," *Information Systems*, vol. 2, pp. 187-198, 1997.
12. A. Segall, "Bit Allocation and Encoding for Vector Sources," *IEEE Transactions on Information Theory*, vol. IT-22, pp. 162-169, May 1976.

A Two-Stage Switching-Based Median Filter

Ju-Yuan Hsiao and Shu-Yi Chen

Department of Information Management
National Changhua University of Education
Changhua, Taiwan 500, R.O.C.
hsiaojy@cc.ncue.edu.tw, chensy@mail2000.com.tw

Abstract. In this paper, we proposed a two-stage switching-based median filter for impulsive noise removal. The noise-detection scheme contains a switching mechanism to identify the characteristic of center pixel. The first stage of our scheme is to identify the center pixel is a really uncorrupted pixel or not. If not, in order to increase the accuracy of noise detection, the center pixel is further discriminated as "uncorrupted pixel", "impartial impulsive noise "or "impulsive noise " in the second stage. In the filtering scheme, action of "no filtering" is applied to "uncorrupted pixels". The output of center weighted median and standard median are respectively applied to "impartial impulsive noise" and "impulsive noise".

1 Introduction

The acquisition or transmission of digital images through sensors or communication channels is often corrupted by impulsive noise [1,2,7]. Impulsive noise corrupts pixels to relative high or relative low randomly when it compares to its neighboring pixels. Various restoration techniques have been proposed for removing impulsive noise [2,3,4,7]. However, linear filter usually brings serious blurring of images while eliminating the impulsive nose. In the nonlinear methods, they can suppress the impulsive noise efficiently and preserve the details of image. The standard median (SM) filter is initially proposed nonlinear approach to eliminate impulsive noise. The center weighted median (CWM) filter is an extension from the standard median filter. The SM and CWM filters change the detected pixels unconditionally. Therefore, a proper filtering should be applied to the corrupted pixels and uncorrupted pixels should be kept unchanged.

2 Related Concepts

2.1 Impulsive Noise Model

Impulsive noise appears in the image as dark and light spots. First at all, we should know the impulsive noise model. For an image corrupted by impulsive noise with density of occurrence p can be described as follows:

Y.-C. Chen, L.-W. Chang, and C.-T. Hsu (Eds.): PCM 2002, LNCS 2532, pp. 377-385, 2002.
© Springer-Verlag Berlin Heidelberg 2002

$$X(i,j) = \begin{cases} N(i,j) & \text{with probability } p \\ O(i,j) & \text{with probability } 1-p \end{cases}$$

$N(i,j)$ denotes the impulsive noise and $O(i,j)$ is the original image pixel value. Impulsive noise is one kind of noises in electronic communication, which is happened usually. It changes pixels randomly making their pixel values very different from normal value and surrounding pixels value [3,4,9].

2.2 The Standard Median (SM) Filter

The standard median filter replaces the center pixel with middle value of all pixels in the scanning window. In two-dimensional domain, assume the considered pixel is $X(i,j)$. The corresponding output $Y(i,j)$ from the standard median filter can be defined as[3,5]:

$$Y(i,j) = median\{X(i-s, j-t) | (s,t) \in W, (s,t) \neq (0,0)\}$$

2.3 The Center Weighted Median Filter

The center weighted median filter is an extension of the standard median and it gives more weight to the center pixel of the scanning window. The output of center weighted median filter, in which a weight adjustment is applied to the center pixel $X(i,j)$ within the scanning window, can be defined as[1,3]:

$Y(i,j) = median\{X(i-s,j-t), w \lozenge X(i,j) | (s,t) \in W, (s,t) \neq (0,0)\}$

In the above equations, w is the center weight (usually to be positive and odd) and operator $\lozenge$ denotes the repetition operation. In other words, $w \lozenge X(i,j)$ means that there are totally w copies of $X(i,j)$ among the input sample.

2.4 The Tri-State Median (TSM) Filter

The tri-state median filter incorporates the standard median filter and center weighted median filter into a new one. Given a specified threshold T, the output of tri-state median filter may correspond to three possible cases, the original pixel, the output of standard median filter, or the output of center weighted median filter [2,12].

3   The Proposed Scheme

Intuitively, the filtering should be applied to corrupted pixels only. Apply median filter unconditionally to all the pixels of entire image will remove signal details of those uncorrupted pixels. Therefore, it is desirable that a noise-detection process to discriminate the uncorrupted pixels from the corrupted ones prior to apply nonlinear filter.

In this paper, a two-stage switching-based median filter used to suppress impulsive noise is proposed. Our noise-detection scheme contains a switching mechanism to identify the characteristic of center pixel.

The flow chart of our scheme is shown in Fig. 1.

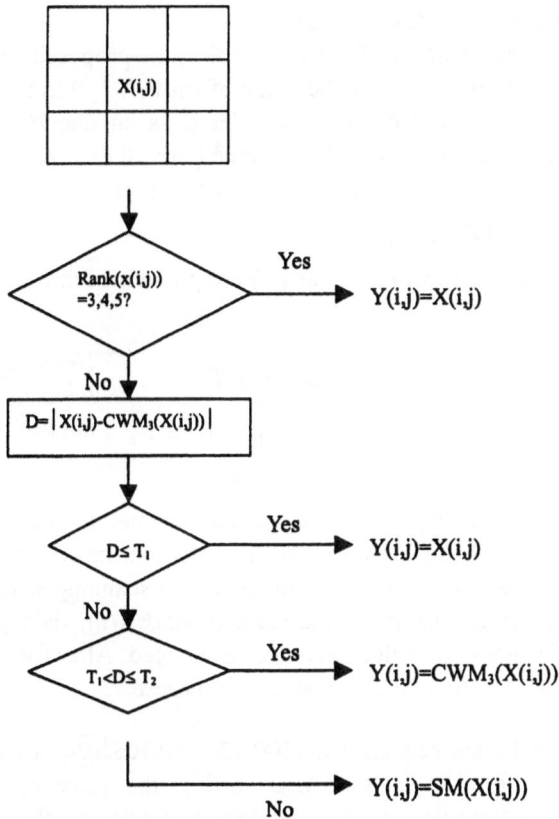

Fig. 1. The flow chart of our scheme

Form a 3×3 scanning window, the center pixel is $X(i,j)$. In this case, it corresponds to a left-to-right, top-to-down mapping from the 3×3 scanning window to the 1-D vector in Fig. 2. $W(i,j)=\{X_1(i,j),X_2(i,j),X_3(i,j),X_4(i,j),X_5(i,j),X_6(i,j),X_7(i,j),X_8(i,j)\}$ $W(i,j)$ is a eight-element vector. It contains the elements of a 3×3 window centered around $X(i,j)$.

$X_1(i,j)$	$X_2(i,j)$	$X_3(i,j)$
$X_4(i,j)$	$X(i,j)$	$X_5(i,j)$
$X_6(i,j)$	$X_7(i,j)$	$X_8(i,j)$

Fig. 2. The scanning window

We sort all the pixel value in the 3×3 scanning window in ascending order. After sorting, each pixel owns a rank number from 1 to 9. We use $rank(X(i,j))$ to denote the rank of $X(i,j)$ in the sorted sequence. The rank order is essential for our scheme. We depend on it to determine the filtering output.

In order to enhance the accuracy of detecting noise, the proposed scheme is based on two-stage noise detection. We verity the value of $rank(X(i,j))$ in the fist stage. If it is equal to 4,5 or 6, the center pixel is considered as an uncorrupted one and left unchanged. In other cases, the more detail detection will be continued in the second stage. We calculate the difference between $X(i,j)$ and $CWM_3(X(I,j))$. Let

$$D=\left|X(i,j)-CWM_3(X(i,j))\right|$$

The output is defined as following: (T_1 and T_2 are predefined threshold values and $T_1 > T_2$.)

$$Y(i,j)=\begin{cases}X(i,j) & ,\text{If } D\le T_1 & \text{Uncorrupted pixel} \\ & & \text{Impartial noise} \\ CWM_3(X(i,j)) & ,\text{If } T_1 < D \le T_2 & \text{Impulsive noise} \\ SM(X(i,j)) & ,\text{If } D > T_2 \end{cases}$$

We use two examples to explain the proposed scheme. In the first example, the sequence is (104,120,110,108,118,114,124,122,135) and the center pixel for filtering is 118. At first, it is necessary to sort all pixels in the scanning window and find the rank of center pixel. In this example, the value of $rank(X(i,j))$ is 5. According to our filtering rules, the center pixel value need not be changed. After filtering, the output is still 118. We only use the first detection stage in this case.

In the second example, the sequence is (100,120,110,108,104,114,124,122,135) and the center pixel for filtering is 104. After sorting, the value of $rank(X(i,j))$ is 2. According to our filtering rules, it is hard to decide whether $X(i,j)$ is noise or not, thus the more detail noise detection and filtering stage (second stage) must be started. In the scanning window, $SM(X(i,j))$ is 114, $CWM_3(X(i,j))$ is 110, $D=\left|104-110\right|$=6. In this case, the pixel value will be changed to three possible values: 104,110 or 114. In this example, T_1 and T_2 are respectively arranged to 10 and 20. After filtering, the center pixel is still 104.

4   Experimental Results

In order to verify the proposed scheme, several commonly used gray level images were tested. Among them, "Airplane", "Boat","Girl","House","Lenna","Peppers" ,"Sailboat", "Tiffany", and "Zelda" are chosen. The size of each test image is 512×512. In Table 1, each test image has 20% corrupted pixels (i.e., p=20%) that is uniformly distributed over the range of [0,255]. In Table 2, each test image has 30% corrupted pixels.

To quantitatively measure the performance of our filtering scheme versus other filters, the mean square error (MSE) standard is utilized following:

$$MSE=(\frac{1}{MN})\sum_{i=1}^{M}\sum_{j=1}^{N}(\ X(i,j)-Y(i,j)\ )^2$$

Where M and N are the height and width of the image; $X(i,j)$ and $Y(i,j)$ are the original and filtered image pixel value, respectively.

The MSE performance of our scheme is comparison with mean filter, 3×3 SM filter, 3×3 CWM$_3$ filter, and TSM filter. The threshold value of TSM filter is 20. Experimental results reveal that the performance of the proposed schemes is better than traditional filters. The feature of our scheme is that if we filter the image twice, we get a better result than just once. That means we obtain the best performance when we run the proposed scheme twice. In our scheme, threshold T_1 and T_2 will influence the filtering performance. In the simulations, the T_1 and T_2 respectively arranged as 10 and 20 will obtain the best performance. Subjective visual comparisons of the noise reduction using test images are presented in Fig. 3,4 and 5. The original image "Lenna" is shown in Fig. 3(a). The noisy image "Lenna" with 20% impulsive noise is shown in Fig.3 (b). The image "Lenna" filtered by Mean filter, SM filter and CWM$_3$ filter are shown in Fig. 3(c), Fig. 3(d) and Fig. 3(e). The image "Lenna" filtered by the first filtering by the proposed scheme is shown in Fig.3 (f). We can see the difference between mean filter and median filter. The mean filter brings serious blurring of images while eliminating the impulsive noise. The image quality after median filter is better than mean filter. In Fig. 4, we show the test image "House" with noise ratio 30%. Generally speaking, each test image corrupted by 20% impulsive noise, the performance is almost superior to previous methods except the images "Boat" and "Sailboat". Due to the variation of pixel intensities of those images is sharper. When the noise ratio is higher, the performance is much better. We compare the results between the first filtering and the second filtering, as shown in Fig. 5 with test images "Pepper" and "Girl". After the second filtering, we can get better image quality than the first filtering.

Table 1. The MSE of the test images with 20% noise pixels

	Airplane	Boat	Girl	House	Lenna	Pepper	Sailboat	Tiffany	Zelda
Noise image	1790.51	1616.93	1577.57	1684.56	1550.40	1693.29	1741.59	2213.05	1498.59
Mean	380.95	346.33	289.01	320.17	280.61	325.07	365.84	499.12	244.33
SM	58.74	89.64	35.03	57.44	41.78	41.76	92.39	39.94	23.05
CWM	49.96	69.68	34.16	52.80	37.85	41.76	70.98	49.24	22.90
TSM	37.45	53.22	22.57	33.88	26.04	29.85	49.31	30.67	16.60
(a)	35.25	53.87	18.66	32.32	23.64	26.61	49.51	28.68	12.78
(b)	33.32	53.35	16.95	30.19	22.38	24.26	48.35	25.49	11.15

(a)The proposed scheme by using 1st filtering
(b) The proposed scheme by using 2nd filtering

Table 2. The MSE of the test images with 30% noise pixels

	Airplane	Boat	Girl	House	Lenna	Pepper	Sailboat	Tiffany	Zelda
Noise image	2718.5	2453.0	2420.5	2513.4	2343.6	2570.0	2627.6	3350.9	2277.44
Mean	655.32	546.01	502.37	537.40	468.30	561.06	608.69	896.04	417.42
SM	98.15	133.05	65.62	84.71	72.14	75.05	135.82	68.87	39.17
CWM	128.85	140.11	98.50	117.85	90.91	116.99	149.63	155.40	70.65
TSM	81.61	99.48	57.70	65.85	54.51	66.68	94.89	79.65	42.03
(a)	77.48	98.37	53.41	64.29	52.72	62.95	94.47	73.41	35.67
(b)	63.32	89.45	39.70	52.85	43.29	49.80	81.20	53.18	25.72

(a)The proposed scheme by using 1st filtering
(b) The proposed scheme by using 2nd filtering

5 Discussions

A noise-detection process should discriminate the uncorrupted pixels from the corrupted ones. The filtering is applied only to the corrupted pixels, and uncorrupted pixels should be kept unchanged. Sun and Neuvo [8], Florencio and Schafer [6] have proposed their switching-based median filter by applying "no filtering" to preserve the normal pixels and SM filter to remove impulsive noise. Based on this opinion, the proposed scheme subdivides each pixel's characteristic such as "uncorrupted pixels"," impartial pixels", or "impulsive noise". The filtering action is like Sun and Neuvo's method and "no filtering" is applied to "uncorrupted pixel". SM filter should remove impulsive noise. How do we process the impartial pixels? In order to keep balance between noise-free and impulsive noise, the impartial pixels will be replaced by the output of CWM_3.

For a 3×3 scanning window, it contains nine pixels. Let $\{X_1, X_2, X_3, ..., X_9\}$ be the pixels value in ascending order, that is, $X_i \leq X_{i+1}$ (i=1,2..8) and denotes X the center pixel value. We are interesting in the relation between the center pixel's sorting order and the output of CWM_3. In this case, $SM = X_{(9+1)/2} = X_5$ and the center pixel has a weight 3.If the order of center pixel is 1,2,or 3, output of CWM_3 is the fourth pixel in sorting order (i.e., Region I in Fig.6). If the order of center pixel is 4,5,or 6, output of CWM_3 is the fifth pixel in sorting order (i.e., Region I in Fig.9). Otherwise, output is the sixth pixel (i.e., Region III in Fig.9). Then, we will discuss the relation among SM, CWM and center pixel X. Let $D_1 = |SM - X|$ and $D_2 = |CWM_3 - X|$. We can find that D_1 is surely greater than or equal to D_2. Therefore, when X is identified as "impartial impulsive noise", the filtering action of center pixel is applied to the output of CWM_3.

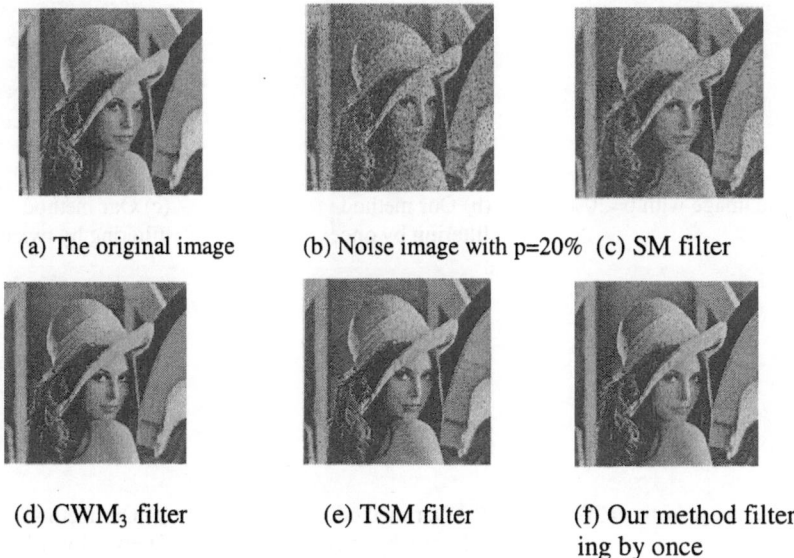

(a) The original image   (b) Noise image with p=20% (c) SM filter

(d) CWM$_3$ filter   (e) TSM filter   (f) Our method filtering by once

Fig. 3. The experimental result of test image "Lenna"

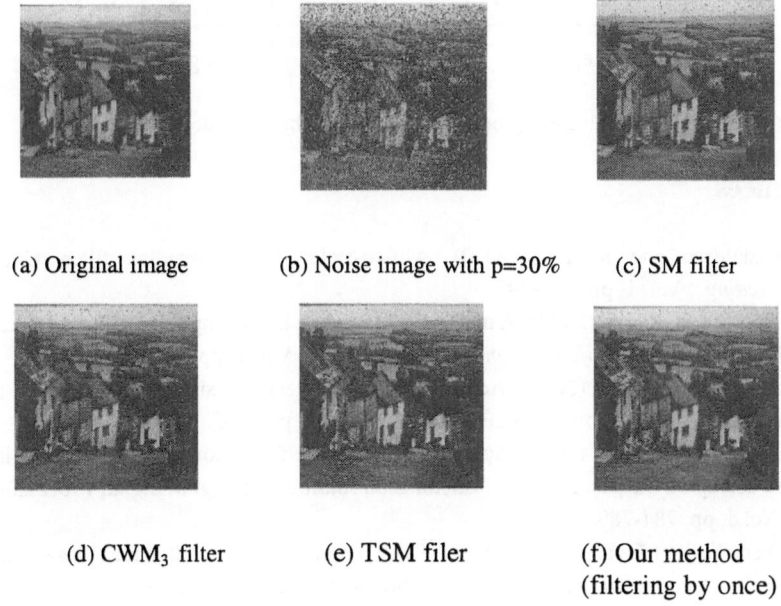

(a) Original image   (b) Noise image with p=30%   (c) SM filter

(d) CWM$_3$ filter   (e) TSM filer   (f) Our method
(filtering by once)

Fig. 4. The experimental result of test images "House"

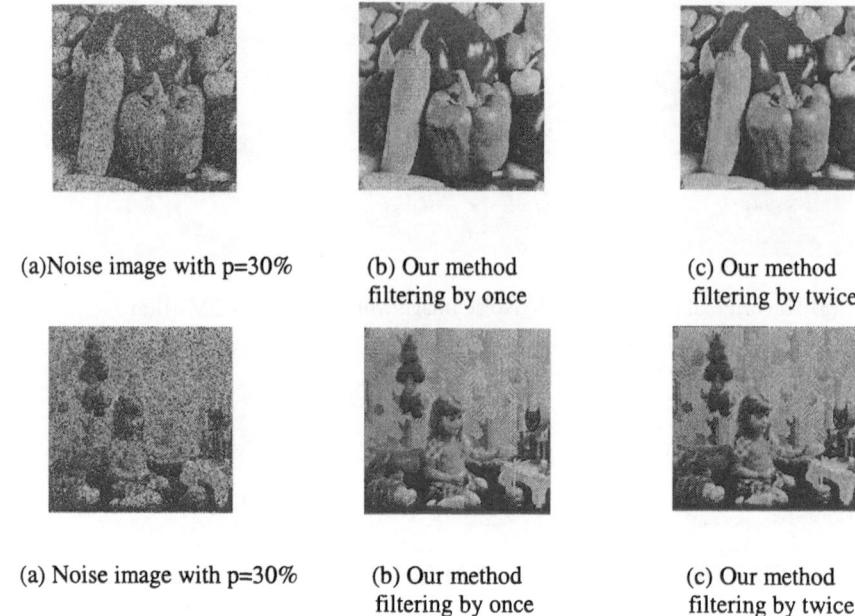

(a)Noise image with p=30%   (b) Our method   (c) Our method
                              filtering by once   filtering by twice

(a) Noise image with p=30%   (b) Our method   (c) Our method
                              filtering by once   filtering by twice

Fig. 5. The experimental result of test images "Pepper" and "Girl"

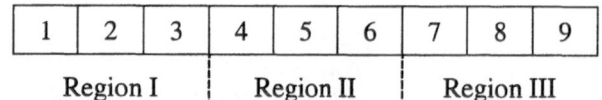

1	2	3	4	5	6	7	8	9

Region I   Region II   Region III

Fig. 6. The sorting order of a pixel and three divided regions

References

1. P. Badulescu and R. Zacin(2000), A two-state switched-median filter, *CAS 2000 Proceedings*, Vol. 1, pp. 289-292.

2. T. Chen and H. R. Wu (2000), A new class of median based impulse rejecting filters, *Proc. 2000 International Conference on Image Processing*, Vol. 1, pp. 916 -919.

3. T. Chen and H. R. Wu (2001), Adaptive impulse detection using center-weighted median filters, *IEEE Signal Processing Letters*, Vol. 8, No. 1, pp. 1 –3.

4. T. Chen and H. R. Wu (2001), Space variant median filters for the restoration of impulse noise corrupted images, *IEEE Transactions on Analog and Digital Signal Processing*, Vol. 48, No. 8, pp. 784-789

5. T. Chen, K. K. Ma, and L. H. Chen (1999), Tri-state median filter for image denoising, *IEEE Transactions on Image Processing*, Vol. 8, No. 12, pp. 1834-1838.

6. D. Florecio and R. W. Schafer (1994), Decision-based median filter using local signal statistics, *Proc. SPIE Sysmp. Visual Communications Image Processing*, Vol. 2308, pp. 268-275.

7. H.L. Eng and K. K. Ma (2001), Noise adaptive soft-switching median filter, *IEEE Transactions on Image Processing*, Vol. 10, No. 2, pp. 242-251.

8. T. Sun and Y. Neuvo (1994), Detail-preserving media based filters in image processing, *Pattern Recognition Letter*, Vol. 15, pp. 341-347

9. C.L. Chiang (2001), The design of some filters for Image denoising, Unpublished Mater Thesis, Institute of Information Engineering, National Chungcheng University, Taiwan, R.O.C.

A Fast and Efficient Noise Reduction Method Suitable for Low Noise Density

Chin-Chen Chang[1], Chih-Ping Hsieh[1], and Ju-Yuan Hsiao[2]

[1]Department of Computer Science and Information Engineering
National Chung Cheng University
Chiayi, Taiwan 621, R.O.C.
{ccc, sjb88}@cs.ccu.edu.tw
[2]Department of Information Management
National Changhua University of Education
Changhua, Taiwan 500, R.O.C.
hsiaojy@cc.ncue.edu.tw

Abstract. A fast and efficient noise reduction method is proposed in this paper. The main idea of the method is to reduce the running time of the standard median filter. The major difference between our method and the standard median filter is the preprocessing work before filtering. We use a simple noise detection scheme to decide which pixel should be processed with the standard median filter. Our noise detection scheme is based on image hiding technology. The experimental results show that our method uses only about a quarter of the running time consumed by the standard median filter. By the experimental results, we shall also show that our method is more suitable for low noise density than other famous median filters like the standard median filter and the center weighted median filter.

Keywords: *Standard median filter, center weighted median filter, tri-state median filter, image hiding*

1 Introduction

Image noise reduction techniques are usually used to reduce the damage done to an image when it is transformed through an electronic channel. The most important issue of noise reduction is the improvement of the image quality.

Quite a number of methods about image noise reduction techniques have been developed and proposed so far, such as the mean filter [1][13], the standard median filter [1][9][11][13][14], the center-weighted median filter [2][10][12], the tri-state median filter [6] and the soft-switching median filter [7][8]. These filters can be classified into two types. One of them includes the filters that use only one filter technology in it, like the mean filter, the standard median filter and the center-weighted median filter. The other type is the filter that integrates more than one filter techniques. It usually incorporates a noise detection scheme and two or more filters in it. The tri-state median filter, for example, includes both the standard median filter and the center-weighted median filter in it and employs a threshold as a simple noise detection scheme. Similarly, the soft-switching median filter uses the standard median filter and the fuzzy weighted [7][8] median filter for noise reduction, and the authors

Y.-C. Chen, L.-W. Chang, and C.-T. Hsu (Eds.): PCM 2002, LNCS 2532, pp. 386–392, 2002.

have also proposed a complex but effective noise detection scheme in the paper. In these examples, we find out that the standard median filter is quite a handy filter technology for noise reduction; therefore, we shall also include it in our method.

As we know, a noise reduction scheme that uses only some certain filter technique but no detection step is usually less competitive in the performance of image quality. For this reason, we think that a good noise detection scheme is needed in our method. Among several noise detection schemes, we decide to use an image-hiding technique in our method as a noise detection scheme. Image hiding [3][4][5] is a technique that can safely transfer a secret image by hiding it in the cover image so as not to be discovered by attackers. In this technique, the hiding and retrieving of the secret image will not do too much damage to the cover image.

The common noise in the Internet is the impulsive noise. This kind of noise usually corrupts pixels into relatively low or high pixel values when we transfer images through an unclear electronic channel. Sometimes natural forces such as lightning strokes can cause this kind of noise, too. The impulsive noise can damage pixels by not only one bit but more. Under such circumstances, we reckon that a good image-hiding technique would be suitable for our noise detection scheme. We shall introduce our noise detection scheme in Section 2, too. In this paper, we shall propose a simple and fast noise reduction scheme suitable for low noise density. We can use only a quarter of the running time needed by the standard median filter but has better performance when the noise density is less than ten percent.

2   The Reviews

2.1   The Median Filters

The standard median filter is the earliest median filter proposed after the mean filter. It has been proved by many researches that the performance of the standard median filter is better than the mean filter when it is used for noise reduction.

We have some examples shown in Fig. 1 and Fig. 2. In Fig. 1(a) and Fig. 2(a), there are two different kinds of pixel values: Fig. 1(a) shows a smooth block and Fig. 2(a) shows an edge block. The results of these two blocks processed by the standard median filter are shown in Fig. 1(b) and Fig. 2(b). Besides that, we also show the results of these two blocks processed by the mean filter in Fig. 1(c) and Fig. 2(c). We can compare these two different filters and find out the advantage of the standard median filter. In the first example of smooth block, the results of the standard median filter and the mean filter are similar. However, in the second example, we can find out the standard median filter can make the pixel values more reasonable than the mean filter does because the mean filter tends to make the central pixel dissonant with its neighbors. For this reason, the standard median filter has been used for noise reduction more often than the mean filter in recent years.

2.2   The Image Hiding Technique

In the embedding phase, the secret image is hidden into the cover image to form a stego-image. In this place, we shall introduce a simple and fast embedding scheme.

As we know, each pixel value in the gray level image system can be represented by eight bits, and these bits can be divide into two parts: the most significant bits (MSBs) and the least significant bits (LSBs). If one most significant bit is changed, the pixel value will also be changed, and the difference will be so large that it will be easily discovered by human eyes. On the other hand, the least significant bit is just opposite to the most significant bit. Knowing how image hiding techniques work, we decide to put the most significant bits of the secret image into the cover image, taking the place of the least significant bits of the cover image. For example, if a given pixel value of the secret image is s, a given pixel value of the cover image is c, and their corresponding pixel value of the stego-image is S. Then s and c can be represented as

$s = s_7s_6s_5s_4s_3s_2s_1s_0$ and $c = c_7c_6c_5c_4c_3c_2c_1c_0$, where $s_i, c_i \in \{0, 1\}$. Here

we define the first three bits as the most significant bits and the others as the least significant bits. We can embed the secret image's pixel in the cover image, taking the

place of its pixel, and make up this stego-image pixel $S = c_7c_6c_5c_4c_3s_7s_6s_5$. With this simple scheme, the secret image can be hidden into the cover image very easily. It is clear that the retrieval procedure is the reversed process of the embedding procedure.

With this image hiding technology, we can design a simple and fast noise detection scheme that is suitable for our reduction method. The details of the noise detection scheme used in our method will be given in Section 3.

155	155	156
155	155	156
155	156	157

155	155	156
155	155	156
155	156	157

155	155	156
155	156	156
155	156	157

(a) Original pixel values   *(b) Output of the median filter (c) Output of the mean filter*

Fig. 1. The difference between the median filter and the mean filter

155	155	50
155	50	50
155	50	50

155	155	50
155	50	50
155	50	50

155	155	50
155	97	50
155	50	50

(a) Original pixel values   *(b) Output of the median filter (c) Output of the mean filter*

Fig. 2. The difference between the median filter and the mean filter

3   The Proposed Scheme

As we have stated, we use an image hiding technique for noise detection in our method. Here, we must explain the reason why we use this image hiding scheme, what it can do, and how it can play the role of a noise detection scheme in the name of an image hiding scheme. The first question is why we use the image hiding technique. As we know, image noise reduction methods need good detection schemes. However, how can these schemes work correctly and fast? Our answer is to hide some data into each pixel of the original image before transmission. After transmission, if the embedded data are unchanged, we can assume that this pixel is not a noise. If not, we can correct the noisy pixel with the standard median filter.

The second question is what the image hiding technique can actually do. In our method, we use the image hiding technique simply to hide the original image into itself. This means that the original image plays two roles in the image hiding technique: both the secret image and the cover image. The embedding sequence, on the other hand, is an important part in image hiding. We use the zig-zag scanning sequence as the embedding sequence, which is a famous sequence used in Discrete Cosine Transform (DCT). The zig-zag sequence is shown in Fig. 3. Our method is to embed the first three most significant bits of the current pixel into the last three least significant bits of the pixel next to the current pixel in the zig-zag sequence. An example of our image hiding procedure is shown in Fig. 4.

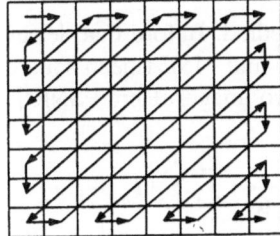

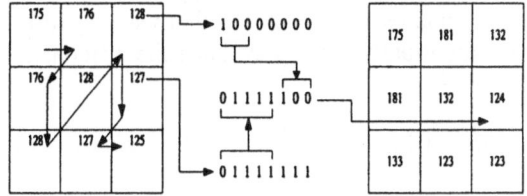

Fig. 3. The zig-zag sequence   **Fig. 4.** An example of our image hiding procedure

The third question we would like to raise here is how the image hiding technique can play the role of a noise detection scheme. We believe that all our readers can easily find out the answer—because we get to recheck the hidden data. When an image has been transferred through any kind of electronic channel, the image may have been corrupted by the impulse noise. With the image hiding scheme, we can extract and check the embedded data to see if they still remain correct after the transference. In our method, the standard median filter will be used to filter the pixels whose hidden data are judged to be corrupted by our image hiding/noise detection scheme. That is to say, if we find out that A's most significant bits are not the same as B's last three least significant bits, the standard median filter will be triggered to process A, where B is the next position of A in the zig-zag sequence.

The most important part is the checking process where the output table (namely the correction table) is produced. In our method, we check whether the pixels are corrupted or not at first, then we target the standard median filter at the pixels that are identified as corrupted pixels. This procedure puts the standard median filter on only when we really need it, which can save us a lot of the running time. In the following, we will introduce the standard median filter used in our method, which is a slightly modified version of the original one. An extra table, i.e. the correction table, is output in the checking process, where all the pixels are recorded as either noise or not. According to the output table, we can aim the standard median filter only at those pixels identified as noise pixels. As Fig. 5 shows, an image block is shown in Fig. 5(a), and the correction table of this block is shown in Fig. 5(b), where the scanning window size is three by three. After the noise detection, all the standard median filter has to do is output the standard median values of the pixel values whose correction bit recorded in the correction table is 1, which means the pixel value is normal and free from noise. In this example, the data input to the standard median filter are 155, 156, 157, 158 and 159, and then the output values from the standard median filter is 157. We must point out that the correction table will not be changed in our filter phase, and this means that we only use the truly correct pixels in the standard median filter. Therefore, in this example, the pixel value 70, judged by the image hiding/noise detection scheme as a noisy pixel, gets the correction bit of zero and crossed out when we are processing the central pixel.

4   Experimental Results

In this part, we shall give the experimental results of our method. Before that, let us define some terms at first. PSNR (peak signal to noise ratio) and MSE (mean square error) are usually used to evaluate the differences between two images. Here PSNR is defined as

$$PSNR = 10\log_{10}\frac{255^2}{MSE}, \text{ and MSE is defined as } MSE = (\frac{1}{H \times W})\sum_{i=1}^{H}\sum_{j=1}^{W}(I_{ij} - I'_{ij})^2 ,$$

where variables H and W denote the height and width of the image, respectively, I and I' denote two different images.

155	156	70
157	28	158
220	128	159

1	1	0
1	0	1
0	0	1

(a) The sub block of a noisy image (b) The corresponding correction table

Fig. 5. An example of our noise detection result

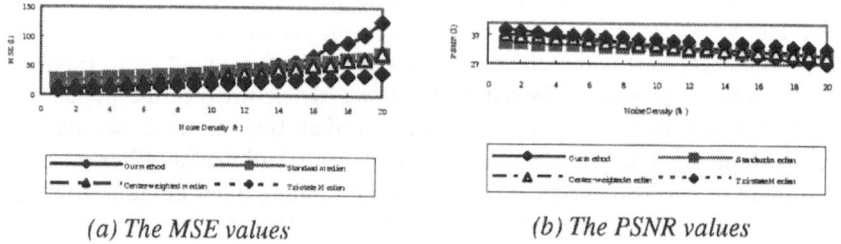

(a) The MSE values   *(b) The PSNR values*

Fig. 6. The comparison of image quality among our method and other filters

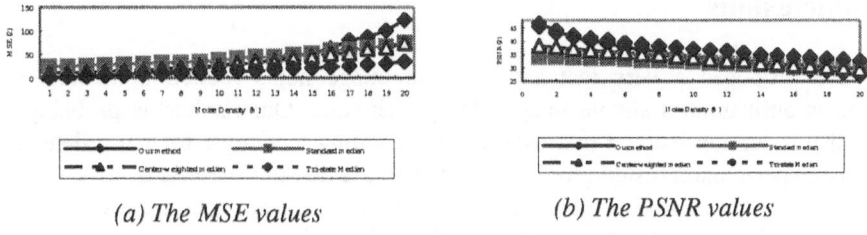

(a) The MSE values   (b) The PSNR values

Fig. 7. The comparison of image quality among our method and other filters

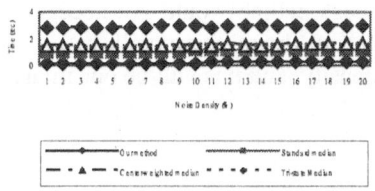

Fig. 8. The comparison of run time between our method and the other filters

The experimental results are shown in Fig. 6 and Fig. 7. In these figures, we also compare our method with some other famous filters. The test image is "Lena," and the image size is 512×512. As to these two figures, there is one thing we have to mention: There are two different PSNR values and two different MSE values in these two figures. This is because we use two different bases for image comparison. The values in Fig. 6 are the comparison between the image processed and the original image after processing by our image hiding scheme, and the values in Fig. 7 are the comparison between the image processed and the image before processing by our image hiding scheme.

The running time of the filters are shown in Fig. 8. Our experimental environment is a Pentium II 400 personal computer. We can find out that the running time of our method is only roughly a quarter of those of the other filters. The reason is that our method does not turn on the standard median filter for all the pixels of the image. Instead, our method only filters the pixels whose pixel values are identified as abnormal. Meanwhile, with our fast noise detection scheme, we can also reduce the damage that the standard median filter does to the pixels whose pixel values are correct. Therefore, the image quality of our method is better than those of the others when the noise density is low. We can find out that our method is better than the standard median filter when the noise density is lower than 13%, better than the center-weighted median filter when the noise density is lower than 10% and better than the tri-state median filter when the noise density is lower than 3%.

By these experimental results, we can prove that our method is a fast and efficient noise reduction method and is very suitable for low noise density. We believe that the noise density should be very low in the ordinary Internet environment. Therefore, we conclude our method is much more suitable than the other filters for electronic communications, especially as it can provide high image quality in a very short time.

5   Conclusions

We have proposed a very fast and efficient image noise reduction method. Our method is built upon a simple image hiding technique. Our method is probably the first noise reduction method that uses an image hiding technique for noise detection. With the experimental results, we have demonstrated that our method is more suitable for the Internet than several other famous filters because our method gives a better performance than the other famous median filters in very short running time in the low noise density situation.

However, it is still frustrating that our method cannot accept high noise density images although we think high noise density is not likely at all to happen in the Internet environment because people would not accept the impulsive noise of more than ten percent. Finally, we hope there will be a more suitable image hiding technique for high noise density, and this will be our future work.

References

1. J. Astola and P. Kuosmanen. "Fundamentals of nonlinear digital filtering," CRC, Boca Raton, FL, 1997.
2. D. R. K. Brownrigg, "The weighted median filter," ACM Communications, Vol. 27, Aug. 1984, pp. 807-818.
3. C. C. Chang and K. F. Hwang, "Hiding images using dynamic bit-replacement and human visual system," to appear in Distributed Multimedia Databases: Techniques and Applications, (Timothy Shih Editor), Idea Group, U.S.A., 2001.
4. C. C. Chang and R. J. Hwang, "A simple picture hiding scheme," Computer Processing of Oriental Languages, Vol. 12, No. 2, 1998, pp. 237-248.
5. C. C. Chang and R. J. Hwang, "Sharing secret images using shadow codebooks," Information Sciences - Applications, pp. 335-345, 1998.
6. T. C. Chen, K.K Ma and L.H Chen, "Tri-state median filter for image denoising," IEEE Transactions on Image Processing, Vol. 8, No. 12, Dec. 1999, pp. 1834-1838.
7. H. L. Eng and K. K. Ma, "Noise adaptive soft-switching median filter for image denoising," IEEE International Conference on Acoustics, Speech, and Signal Processing, vol. 4, 2000, pp. 2175-2178.
8. H. L. Eng and K. K. Ma, "Noise adaptive soft-switching median filter," IEEE Transactions on Image Processing, Vol. 10, No. 2, Feb. 2001, pp. 242 –251.
9. T. S. Huang, Ed., "Two dimensional digital signal processing II: Transforms and Median Filters," Springer-Verlag, New York, 1981.
10. S. J. Ko and Y.H Lee, "Center weighted median filters and their applications to image enhancement," IEEE Transactions on Circuits and Systems, Vol. 38, 1991, pp. 984-993.
11. H. M. Lin and A. N. Willson, Jr., "Median filters with adaptive length," IEEE Transactions on Circuits and Systems, Vol. CAS-35, Jun. 1991, pp. 675-690.
12. T. Loupas, W. N. McDicken and P. L. Allan, "An adaptive weighted median filter for speckle suppression in medical ultrasonic images," IEEE Transactions on Circuits and Systems, Vol. 36, Jan. 1989, pp. 129-135.
13. I. Pitas and A.N Venetsanopoulos, "Nonlinear digital filters: principles and applications," Kluwer, Boston, MA, 1990.
14. A. Rosenfeld and A. C. Kak, "Digital picture processing," Academic Press, New York, Vol. 1, 1982.

A Cross-Type Peak-and-Valley Filter for Error Prevention and Resilience in Image Communications

Chin-Chen Chang[1], Ju-Yuan Hsiao[2], and Chi-Lung Chiang[1]

[1]Department of Computer Science and Information Engineering
National Chung Cheng University
Chiayi, Taiwan 62107, R.O.C.
{ccc, cjl88}@cs.ccu.edu.tw
[2]Department of Information Management
National Changhua University of Education
Changhua, Taiwan 500, R.O.C.
hsiaojy@cc.ncue.edu.tw

Abstract. The peak-and-valley filter has been shown to be a fast and efficient filter in suppressing impulsive noise. In order to find the best filtering route, we have tested several different kinds of scanning orders, such as zigzag scan, Hilbert curve, etc. The result of the tests shows the vertical scanning order is the best one. Next, we have incorporated a simple edge detection scheme into the peak-and-valley filter and then propose a new filter, called the cross-type peak-and-valley filter. Experimental results show that our filter with vertical filtering route outperforms the peak-and-valley filter proposed by Windyga.

Keywords: Impulsive noise, non-linear filter, peak-and-valley filter

1 Introduction

Due to the prevalence of digital technology, many instruments and equipments have been developed to deal with digital images. Every single day, there are more and more digital images transferred on the Internet. Thus, how to recover the quality of digital images when they are corrupted by noises becomes a significant topic. Digital images are often corrupted by impulsive noise when they are transmitted on the communication channel or accessed from storage. Impulsive noise usually results from bit errors that make us get the wrong data. Generally speaking, impulsive noise is either relatively high or relatively low when compared with its neighboring signals. In this paper, we shall focus on the impulsive noise that occurs in image data.

When the impulsive noise occurs on a gray-level image, it usually appears in the form of black or white spots on the image as if some salt-and-pepper were sprinkled on the picture. That is why the impulsive noise is also called the salt-and-pepper noise. In other words, chances are we might not be able to see a real-world image with "pure" salt-and-pepper-noised pixels very often. Consequently, it seems that we still have to find a way to model the impulsive noise as it truly appears to be in our everyday life before we can eventually effectively suppress it.

In order to solve the problem caused by impulsive noise, there are many researches about various kinds of filtering techniques going on at all times. All of

Y.-C. Chen, L.-W. Chang, and C.-T. Hsu (Eds.): PCM 2002, LNCS 2532, pp. 393-400, 2002.
© Springer-Verlag Berlin Heidelberg 2002

them can be classified into two categories. One is the group of linear filters and the other one is of course the group of non-linear filters [1, 15]. The mean filter is a common representative of linear filters. Its principle is "to replace the noisy pixel with the mean value". We define a simple mean filter for the one-dimensional signal as follows:

$$\tilde{X}_i = mean \ \{ X_{i-1}, X_i, X_{i+1}\}, \ i = 2,..., \ n-1,$$

where n is the signal size.

The non-linear filter has been shown to be superior to the linear filter [1]. The linear filter tends to change the value of every pixel, while the non-linear filter replaces the suspect pixel with the one inside the filtering window. As a result, the linear filter ends up making the image more blurred and fuzzy. Nevertheless, although the non-linear filter is generally said to be better than the linear filter, it is also guilty in disturbing some fine details of the image. Therefore, the recent researches about the non-linear filter, including those about the center weighted median (CWM) filter [12], the tri-state median (TSM) filter [4], and the noise adaptive soft-switching median (NASM) filter [6], have been almost exclusively focused on how to preserve more details while suppressing impulsive noise.

The median filter has a fatal flaw, and that is the huge computation time. It needs much time to sort the pixel value to find out the median, which makes it not practical for the live videos on the network. To save it from this flaw, Windyga has proposed the peak-and-valley filter [16]. It is more efficient than the median filter. The performance of the peak-and-valley filter has been shown to be comparable with the median filter. The original peak-and-valley filter is designed for the one-dimensional signal. Thus, how to apply it to image data becomes an interesting topic. In this work, we shall try to discover a better way to make use of the peak-and-valley filter in dealing with image data.

2   Background Review

The peak-and-valley filter is based on min-max operators [16]. In a normal case, most noisy images do not have a high probability of obvious noise appearance. That means the pixels which are in a specific region will have the similar values unique to that specific region. Due to this property, we can replace the noisy pixel with its uncorrupted neighborhood and get the best result. This is basically how the median filter works. The median filter replaces the noisy pixel with the median, which comes from a small region around the noisy pixel itself. Since the noise density is normally not high, how to detect the noisy pixels efficiently becomes a significant topic. As we can imagine, the performance would be bad if we just replaced every pixel with something from its neighbors. The reason is that most pixels are simply uncorrupted. Changing the values of these uncorrupted pixels will destroy the image quality instead of improving it. Since the value of an impulsive-noise-affected pixel is either relatively low or relatively high to its neighbors, we shall make use of this distinction to easily detect noisy pixels. If the pixel value in question is distinctively larger or smaller than all its neighbors, we judge that this pixel is very likely to be a corrupted one and thus needs to be corrected. This is the main concept of the peak-and-valley filter.

However, the peak-and-valley filter that we introduced above is a one-dimensional filter. As the main concern of this work is to discover the best way to apply the peak-and-valley filter to image denoising, the problem turns out to be the space-filling curve problem [8]. If we could find a route to push the filter forward through all the pixels just once and the performance is still acceptable, then we could save half of the computation time since the peak-and-valley filter in [16] goes over all the pixels twice. In this work, we choose the Hilbert curve as one of our space-filling curves.

The Hilbert curve is one of the space-filling curves. In memory of Peano [14], space-filling curves are also called Peano curves. Many variants of space-filling curves were proposed by Hilbert [7]. The Hilbert curve has been applied to image compression [5, 11], image analysis [9] and so on [10]. As implied by the name, each pixel in the two-dimensional image data should be mapped into one point on a one-dimensional space-filling curve. Each point on the Hilbert curve is represented by an integer, which is called the Hilbert order. The Hilbert orders increase along the Hilbert curve. That means we can trace all the pixels in the image along the Hilbert curve by their orders. For example, assume we have two images whose sizes are 2×2 and 4×4, respectively. For an image space (a rectangular space), the origin of the coordinates is defined to be the lower-left corner of the space. An important characteristic of the Hilbert curve is that the points that are adjacent to each other on the Hilbert curve will also be adjacent to each other on the two-dimensional space. Due to this characteristic and locality, the Hilbert curve seems readily able to be applied to image compression and image processing. Meanwhile, Liu and Schrack [13] have developed an encoding formula for producing a Hilbert curve. Assume there is an image whose size is N×N and $N=2^r$. This encoding formula will map a pixel at position (x, y) into a Hilbert order o.

Anyone who is interesting in the Hilbert curve can refer to [13] for more detailed information.

3 Methods and Some Experiments

In this work, we shall show the results of our tests on some representative variants of the peak-and-valley filter. These schemes can be classified into three different kinds according to their own characteristics.

3.1 Method One

The two-dimensional peak-and-valley filter proposed by Windyga [16] needs to move forward through all the pixels in an image twice. We wonder whether it is possible to filter through all the pixels just once without affecting the filtering performance. If we can do that, we can save half of the processing time. In this subsection, we shall introduce four different filtering routes and demonstrate their performance.

3.1.1 Horizontal Direction
This scheme filters through all the pixels along the route as the Horizontal direction. The filtering route in the horizontal direction goes through all the pixels from left to

right, starting from the top line and going down till the bottom. We can actually apply the one-dimensional peak-and-valley filter we mentioned above in this sequence order through all the pixels once.

3.1.2   Vertical Direction

The second proposal of scanning order is the vertical direction. Along this route, we can go through all the pixels in an image from top to bottom, starting from the left side to the right. As mentioned in the last paragraph, we also apply the one-dimensional filter in this filtering sequence. Consequently, we get another variant of the peak-and-valley filter.

3.1.3   Zigzag Scan

Zigzag scan is a well-known sequence in the field of image processing. It is used in many applications, such as JPEG. We can go through all the pixels in an image following the method of zigzag scan and get yet another variant of the peak-and-valley filter.

3.1.4   The Hilbert Curve

We have introduced the Hilbert curve in Section 2. It could be used to map a two-dimensional space on a one-dimensional curve. Taking advantage of this characteristic, we can go through all the pixels in an image along the Hilbert curve. Thus, all the pixels will be filtered just once in this sequence order.

So far, we have introduced four different approaches to filter through all the pixels just once. In this paper, we use the Mean Square Error (MSE) to evaluate the image quality.

Here x_{ij} denotes the original pixel value and $\overline{x}_{ij}$ denotes the filtered pixel value. The size of all the tested images in this paper is uniformly 512×512.

We need to review these schemes in order to find out the reason why the performance is not good. By observing the filtered images, we find that there is some propagation of noisy spots along the filtering route, which comes from the fact that there can sometimes be more than two noisy pixels adjacent to each other along the filtering route. Another important reason is edge blurring. Once the filter crosses some edge, it blurs the edge. This too significantly lowers the image quality. We can explain this blurring by means of Table 1. In Table 1, the average differences between two pixels along the route are shown.

As we know, if there is an edge between two pixels, the difference between these two pixels would be large. The larger the average difference is, the more edges there could probably be. According to this observation, we can visualize why the performance of the zigzag sequence is worse than the others. The average difference of the zigzag sequence is the largest one among the four sequences, and that means there are many edges crossed by the filter of the zigzag sequence.

Although the results of these four filters do not have satisfied our goal, we have still learned some important lessons from them. We find that, if the peak-and-valley filter goes across an edge, it blurs it. Thus, we wonder whether the performance would be better if we include an edge detection scheme into this filter. That is the motivation of the next approach right below.

3.2 Method Two

In this method, we attempt to combine a simple edge detection scheme with the peak-and-valley filter. In [2, 3], a simple edge detection approach has been proposed. This method uses masks for edge detection. To give an instance, we list four masks for edge detection in Fig. 1. The masks in Fig. 1 are examples of 4×4. The numbers listed on the mask are the correspondent coefficients. First, we apply the horizontal edge detection mask, which is listed in Fig. 1 (a). Every pixel in the block is multiplied by its correspondent coefficient on the mask. Then, we sum up the results of these multiplications and get its absolute value. In this example, we will get the result of 1471. If we apply the mask in Fig. 1 (b), we will get 7. Obviously, the result of applying the horizontal edge detection mask is much larger than applying the vertical edge detection mask, which perfectly agrees with the fact that there does exist a horizontal edge in this block.

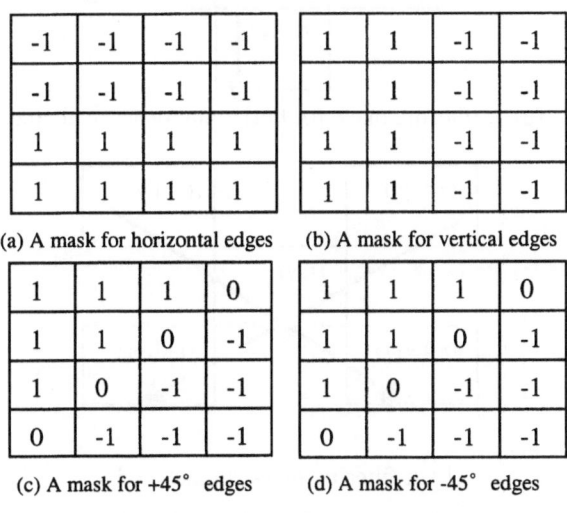

-1	-1	-1	-1
-1	-1	-1	-1
1	1	1	1
1	1	1	1

1	1	-1	-1
1	1	-1	-1
1	1	-1	-1
1	1	-1	-1

(a) A mask for horizontal edges   (b) A mask for vertical edges

1	1	1	0
1	1	0	-1
1	0	-1	-1
0	-1	-1	-1

1	1	1	0
1	1	0	-1
1	0	-1	-1
0	-1	-1	-1

(c) A mask for +45° edges   (d) A mask for -45° edges

Fig. 1. Masks for edge detection

Once we have performed the edge detection scheme, we know where edges are and what kind of edges they are. Then we can start our filtering process. We can apply the filter to every pixel in this block along the horizontal direction route. This time, we do it a little bit differently. When the original filter processes a pixel, it just looks for the information from its predecessor and successor on the route. However, in this modified filter, the filter first processes a pixel as usual, and then the processing direction is rotated by 90 degrees, and this same pixel is then processed in the new direction all over again. As shown in Fig. 2, this new filter goes along the X-axis (X'-axis) first and then processes this pixel again in the direction of the Y-axis (Y'-axis) and then moves on to the next pixel. In Fig. 2, there are two different filtering masks. If the block has horizontal, vertical or no edges, we take the one in Fig. 2 (a). Otherwise, we take the one in Fig. 2(b).

3.3 Method Three

Finally, we try to modify the filter by changing the range of its referenced neighbors and processing orders. We design a filter that processes pixels with the mask shown in Fig. 2 (a). It performs the peak-and-valley filter on the X-axis and then does the same procedure on the Y-axis. We apply this filter along the vertical direction route, which is from top to bottom and then from left to right, through all the pixels. Because of the vertical direction route has the best performance in Table 1. We call this filter the Cross Filter because it goes through every pixel with a cross.

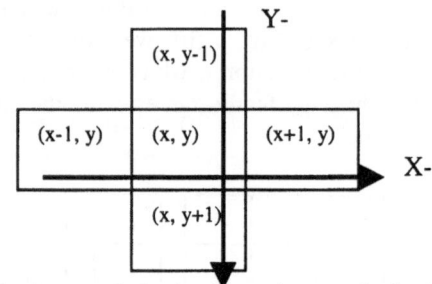

(a) A filtering mask for horizontal or vertical edge

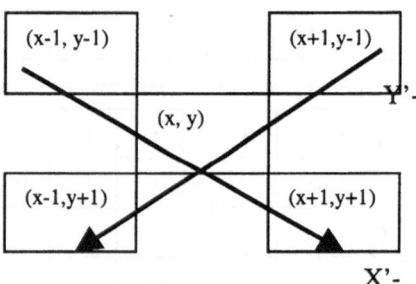

(b) A filtering mask for skew edge

Fig. 2. Filtering masks for edge

The two-dimensional peak-and-valley filter proposed in [16] is a combination of two one-dimensional filters. First, it filters through all the pixels along the horizontal direction route; then, it filters through all the pixels along the vertical direction route. Besides MSE and average differences, we also have some other ways to take the measure of these filters' feet. We take down how much noise is eliminated and attenuated, and these data are shown in Table 2. If a noisy pixel is modified by the filter but not correctly adjusted, the difference between the noisy pixel and its filtered value, called the attenuation value, can indicate the degree of the modification. If the filter spoils a clear pixel, the difference between the clear pixel value and its spoiled value is called the spoiling value. We also show the average attenuation and the average spoiling in Table 2. The Cross Filter we propose here and the filter proposed in [16] have comparable performance.

4   Conclusions and Future Work

In this work, we have tested many variants of the peak-and-valley filter. First, we try to come up with a faster way to process an image. There are four filtering routes proposed and tested. Although the results are not as good as what we expected, they can teach us the lessons we need to improve our approach. In addition, we have also combined a simple edge detection scheme with the filter to preserve details, and it does get an acceptable performance. To further improve the performance, one could use a more precise edge detector. However, there is an inevitable tradeoff between the processing time and the performance, and the balance can only be reached when the filter can adaptively fit the real needs. Finally, we pick up the cross filter after testing the variants above. The *Cross Filter* is simple and works well. Its performance is even better than the scheme in [16].

Table 1. Average differences of four filtering routes

	Horizontal	Vertical	Zigzag	Hilbert curve
Lena	5.30	4.25	5.86	4.79
Boat	7.12	5.63	8.55	6.39
Sailboat	7.81	8.14	9.73	8.02
Zelda	4.04	3.19	4.77	3.64
Pepper	4.43	4.70	5.89	4.57
Tiffany	4.71	3.96	5.15	4.41
Girl	5.10	4.41	6.43	4.77

Table 2. Other performance measurements on image Lena

TTest Images	Noisy Image (20%)	Block size of edge detection mask		
		4×4	8×8	16×16
Lena	1471.787	61.561	56.138	52.726
Boat	1536.141	100.388	96.640	96.727
Sailboat	1644.504	117.264	110.520	112.284
Zelda	1439.265	45.590	40.290	40.243
Pepper	1604.894	68.542	62.144	60.495
Tiffany	2070.020	66.876	70.490	65.263
Girl	1533.429	66.281	60.522	60.028

References

1.   J. Astola and P. Kuosmanen, Fundamentals of Nonlinear Digital Filtering, Boca Raton, FL: CRC, 1997.
2.   C. C. Chang, T. S. Chen and Y. Lin, "An Efficient Edge Detection Scheme of Color Images," Proceedings of the Fifth Joint Conference on Information Sciences, Vol. II, New Jersey, U.S.A., Feb. 2000, pp. 448-455.

3.   C. C. Chang, F. C. Shine and T. S. Chen, "Pattern-based Side Match Vector Quantization for Image Quantization," Imaging Science Journal, Vol. 48, (2000), pp. 63-76.
4.   T. Chen, K. K. Ma and L. H. Chen, "Tri-State Median Filter for Image Denoising," IEEE Trans. Image Proc., Vol. 8, (12), (Dec. 1999), pp. 1834-1838.
5.   K. L. Chung, Y. H. Tsai and F. C. Hu, "Space-filling approach for fast window query on compressed images," IEEE Trans. Image Proc., Vol. 9, (12), (Dec. 2000), pp. 2109-2116.
6.   H. L. Eng and K. K. Ma, "Noise Adaptive Soft-Switching Median Filter," IEEE Trans. Image Proc., Vol. 10, (2), (Feb. 2001), pp. 242-251.
7.   D. Hilbert, "Über die stetige Abbildung einer Linie auf ein Flächen-stück," Math. Ann., Vol. 38, (1891), pp. 459–460.
8.   H. V. Jafadish, "Analysis of the Hilbert curve for representing two-dimensional space," Information Processing Letters, Vol. 62, (1997), pp. 17-22.
9.   F. C. Jian, "Hilbert curves and its applications on image processing," Master Thesis, Department of Electrical Engineering, National Taiwan University, Jun. 1996.
10.   S. Kamata, R. O. Eason and E. Kawaguchi, "An implementation of Hilbert scanning algorithm and its application to data compression," IEICE Transactions on Information and Systems, Vol. E76-D, (4), (Apr. 1993), pp. 420-428.
11.   S. Kamata, M. Niimi and E. Kawaguchi, "A gray image compression using a Hilbert scan," Proceedings of the 13th International Conference on Pattern Recognition, Vol. 3, Aug. 1996, pp. 905-909.
12.   S. J. Ko and Y. H. Lee, "Center Weighted Median Filters and Their Applications to Image Enhancement," IEEE Trans. Circuits Syst., Vol. 38, (9), (Sep. 1991), pp. 984-993.
13.   X. Liu and G. F. Schrack, "Encoding and decoding the Hilbert order," Software-Practice and Experience, Vol. 26, (12), 1996, pp. 1335-1346.
14.   G. Peano, "Sur une courbe qui remplit toute une aire plane," Math. Ann., Vol. 36, 1890, pp. 157–160.
15.   I. Pitas and A. N. Venetsanopoulos, Nonlinear Digital Filters: Principles and Applications, Boston, MA: Kluwer, 1990.
16.   P. S. Windyga, "Fast Impulsive Noise Removal," IEEE Trans. Image Proc., Vol. 10, (2), (Jan. 2001), pp. 173-179.

Adaptive-Hierarchical-Filtering Technique for Image Enhancement

Tsung-nan Lin [1] and Joseph Shu [2]

[1] Department of Electrical Engineering, National Taiwan University, Taipei, Taiwan
tsungnan@cc.ee.ntu.edu.tw
[2] EPSON R&D Inc, San Jose, CA 94303, USA
shu.joseph@erd.epson.com

Abstract. This paper describes a novel adaptive-hierarchical-filtering technique to achieve high-quality image enhancement when the image possesses the artifact of moiré pattern during the reproduction of the image by different computer peripherals such as color copier, or scanners plus printers.
Commercial magazine images are halftoned images. Unacceptable noises and moiré distortion may result when halftone images are copied (i.e., scanned and printed). In this paper, we analyze the formation of moiré patterns in the frequency and spatial domain. Based on the analysis, a set of hierarchical filter is developed to suppress the moiré artifacts and enhance the image adaptively. The hierarchical filter consists of a set of variable-length low-pass filters and high-pass filters. The low-pass filters have a nice inheritance of canceling aliased low frequency components (moiré distortion). High- pass filtering is also applied to sharpen image edges. An image classifier is developed to determine that an edge is either a global true edge (for sharpening enhancement) or a local halftone's micro-structural edge (for LPF for moiré reduction), so that adaptive filter technique can be applied to achieve the smooth transition between sharp edges and smooth halftone regions. Thus, we achieves overall high-quality output images.
Experimental results have been shown the effectiveness of the presented technique that works well on wide combinations of above-mentioned 6 factors, which will be explained during the following sections, for high-quality magazine image reproduction.

1 Introduction

In printing industry, halftoning technology has been almost exclusively used for low-cost massive production of pictures, e.g., magazines, and newspapers. A halftone image is essentially a binary image (i.e., a printable form by a typesetter or a printer) whose picture element (i.e., pixel) is either "0" or "1" corresponding to white and black. A number of black/white pixels form a halftone dot. The perception of gray tone is achieved by varying the halftone dot size. Today, there are increasing needs to scan halftoned images for reproduction for display and/or printing applications such as desktop publishing, newspaper, and Yellow Pages production. However, when a halftoned image is scanned, unacceptable moiré distortion may result

Much research has been done on the analysis and reduction of moiré patterns by various approaches as follows: (1) high frequency scanning (2) low pass filtering, (3)

Y.-C. Chen, L.-W. Chang, and C.-T. Hsu (Eds.): PCM 2002, LNCS 2532, pp. 401–408, 2002.

manipulation of the factors producing moiré patterns, and (4) post-scan image processing algorithms [1-4]. A. Rosenfeld and A. Kak showed that moiré patterns are caused by aliased frequencies produced when sampling images containing periodic structure [2]. T. S. Huang analyzed moiré patterns resulting from ideally sampling an image with uniform halftone dot patterns in the Fourier domain [3]. A. Steinbach and K. Y. Wong extended Huang's model to include the effects of scan aperture size and shape, and the reproduction printing process in the frequency domain [4]. J. Shu, R. Springer, and C. Yeh analyzed moiré formation factors and derived a formula to manipulate these factors to minimize moiré visibility [1]. J. Shu achieved moiré elimination and tone correction using a local tonal compensation technique [5].

However, there is no satisfactory result exist for the problem of halftone image reproduction. In this paper, we make efforts in tackling the problem of moiré suppression. A novel technique has been developed that applies adaptive hierarchical filters to remove moiré patterns adaptively.

2 Moire Analysis

The formation of moiré patterns depends on the following factors: (1) the halftone screen frequency (i.e., number of halftone dots per inch), (2) the scan frequency (i.e., number of scan spots per inch), (3) the angle between the scan direction and the halftone screen orientation, (4) the scanner aperture size and shape, (5) halftoning and printing mechanisms, (for example, error diffusion tends to randomize the moiré patterns, and cluster-dot or line screen show more moiré distortion.) (6) viewing conditions. Different magazine originals on different scanners, printers and copiers produce different moiré noises visually. This causes algorithm development difficult for moiré and noise removal. In addition image sharpening is usually required for enhancing reproduced image edges. However, the image sharpening also enhances moiré distortion and noises. Direct blurring methods can be used to reduce moiré distortion and noises but will greatly degrade the fidelity of image sharpness.

In the spatial domain, moiré patterns can be described as visible "beat" patterns resulting from the incorrect reproduction of halftone dots. As shown in Figure 1, the same size halftone dots before scanning become different size after scanning. The first halftone dot has 160% black pixel coverage and the 2nd halftone dot has 200% black pixel coverage. This error comes from the phase difference between halftone dots and scanned dots, and causes the cyclic change of lighter/darker zones, producing "beat" patterns.

From the uniform sampling theory and its application to halftoned images, we know the following facts: (1) any spatially bounded signal (e.g. size-limited imagery) has an infinite band in the spatial frequency domain; (2) if we digitally sample spatially bounded signals in the ideal sampling situation, aliasing is unavoidable; (3) if the sampled signal contains periodic structures, aliased frequencies may be seen in the output signal reconstructed from these samples; (4) if the sampled signal is from a halftone image, these visible aliased frequencies correspond to moiré patterns.

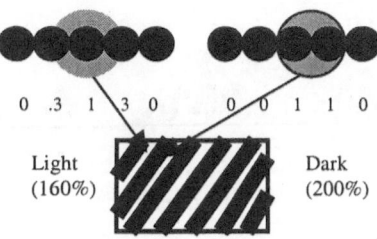

Fig. 1. Spatial Analysis

As shown in Figure 2, in the frequency domain, moiré patterns are seen as aliased frequency components, which result from the scanning of screened art that possesses infinite bandwidth.

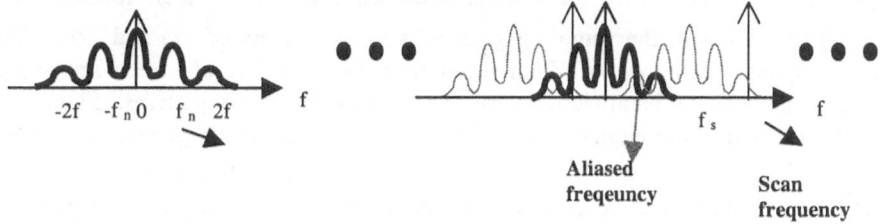

Fig. 2. Frequency Analysis

3 Aliased-Frequency Component Canceling Filtering

The visibility of these aliased frequency components (i.e., moiré patterns) have a relation between scan frequency, screen frequency, and screen angle. We develop a set of low pass filters that have a nice inheritance of canceling aliased frequency components while the filtering processes. [6] [7] show the spectrum of the halftone image consists of the displaced spectra of nonlinearly transformed versions of the original continuous-tone image. The spectra repeat periodically with the halftone grid period. The zeroth-order spectrum is that of the quantized original image. The other spectra correspond to distortions of the original image. Figure 3 displays a schematic frequency relationship in frequency domain between a continuous-tone image and its corresponding halftoned iamge

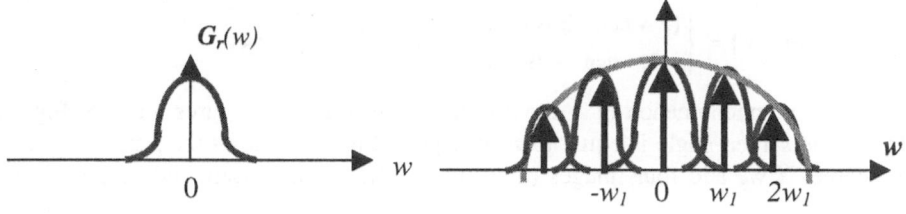

Fig. 3. $G_r(w)$ is the frequency representation of the original continuous image and its transformed version of halftone image in frequency domain.

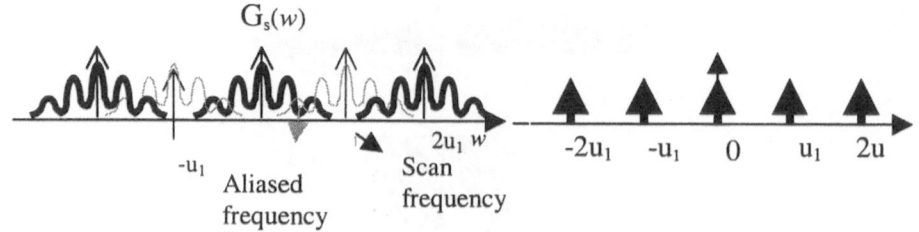

Fig. 4. Frequency Analysis of Scanned Halftone.

$$g_s(r) = [h(r) \otimes a(r)] * \sum \sum \delta(\mathbf{r} - m\alpha_1 - n\alpha_2) \quad (1)$$

$$G_s(\mathbf{w}) = [H(\mathbf{w}) * A(\mathbf{w})] \otimes \sum \sum \delta(\mathbf{w} - k\mathbf{u}_1 - l\mathbf{u}_2) \quad (2)$$

The scanning process can be modeled by Equation(1) which shows the halftone image $h(r)$ convolves with the optical low-pass filter $a(r)$ then follows by a sampling process with the sampling grid defined by vectors of α_1 and α_2. The aliased frequency components which result from the scanning of screen image that possesses the infinite bandwidth cause the artifact of moiré patterns. Figure (4) illustrates the schematic explanation of how scanned halftone image results in moiré patterns. When we add a spatial phase delay d to the scanning process, the sampling dynamics of scanning can be described by Equation (3). The frequency response of the delayed sampling grid is shown in Equation (4). The spatial delay effect becomes a phase shift $e^{-2\pi j\,d\cdot w}$ in the frequency domain. When the delay d is half cycle of the scanning frequency (i.e., $d = \frac{1}{2}\alpha_i, i = 1,2$), the phase shift $e^{-2\pi j\,d\cdot w}$ in frequency components has an alternate sign changes as shown in Figure 5 in the one dimension case. If we add the original scanned image and the scanned image with half cycle phase delay $d = \frac{1}{2}\alpha$, the aliased frequency components can be cancelled each other as illustrated in Figure. 6. The moiré patterns are therefore reduced.

$$S_n(r) = \sum \sum \delta(\mathbf{r} - m\alpha_1 - n\alpha_2 - \mathbf{d}) \quad (3)$$

$$F\{S_n(r)\} = C[\sum \sum \delta(\mathbf{w} - k\mathbf{u}_1 - l\mathbf{u}_2)]\exp\{-2\pi j\mathbf{d}.\mathbf{w}\} \quad (4)$$

$$\exp\{-2\pi\,j\mathbf{d}\cdot\mathbf{w}\} = \begin{cases} 1, & \text{when } k \text{ is even} \\ -1, & \text{when } k \text{ is odd} \end{cases} \left(\text{if } \mathbf{d} = \frac{1}{2}\alpha_i,\right) \quad (5)$$

The same phenomenon in 2-dimensional is illustrated in Figures 7 and 8. Figure 7 shows the screen angle is equal to zero degree. Figure 8 shows the screen angle is any degree. If we add four images (that include the original scan, and scanned with half cycle phase shifts horizontally $(d = \frac{1}{2}\alpha_1)$, vertically $(d = \frac{1}{2}\alpha_2)$, and diagonally($d = \dfrac{1}{2}(\alpha_1 + \alpha_2)$), we can achieve the same effect of canceling aliased frequency components   to achieve the moiré reduction.

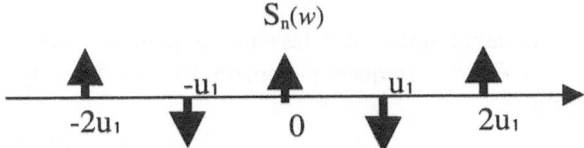

Fig. 5. The phase shift in the frequency domain constitutes the alternate signs when d equals to half of the scan frequency.

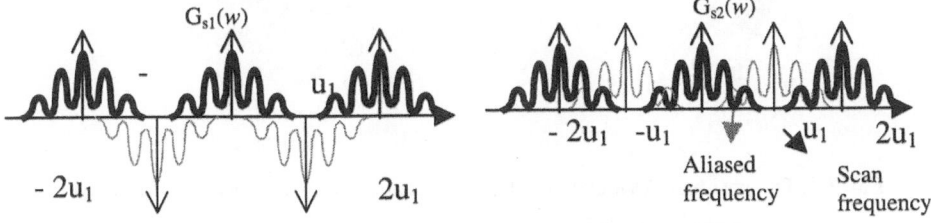

Fig. 6. Halftone of Two Scans with ½ Phase Delay

4   Adaptive Hierarchical Filtering

From above frequency analysis, we know these anti-aliased filters can be constructed with 2x2 averaging filter, as illustrated in Figure. 9.

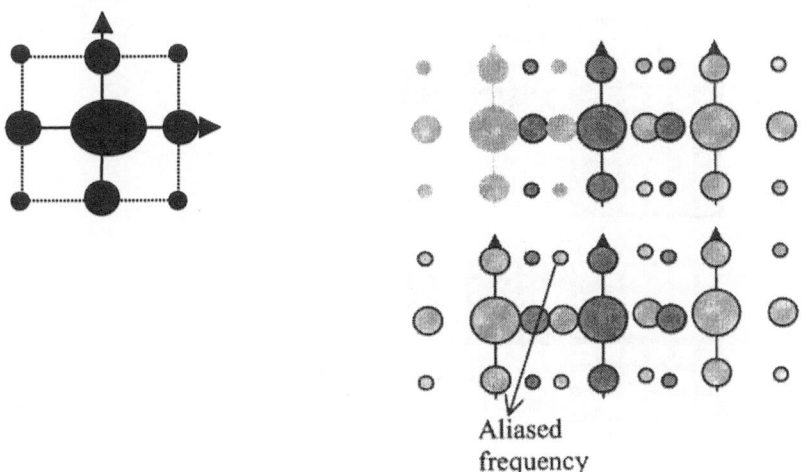

Original

Fig. 7. 2-Dimensional Frequency Analysis of Scanned 0 Degrees Halftones

By the same reasons, 4x4 , 8x8, 16x16 averaging filters can be used which have the nice inheritance of canceling even more aliased low frequency components at the expense of larger size filters in the filtering process. Using the set of filters with size 2x2, 4x4, 8x8, ..., etc., we can construct a set of pyramid of images, as shown in Figure 10.

The higher-level pyramid image has less moiré patterns. Detailed theoretical and analytical proof in Fourier frequency domain for the filtering process has been described as above.

Original   Aliased
                                     frequency

Fig. 8. 2-Dimensional Frequency Analysis of Scanned Non-zero Degrees Halftones

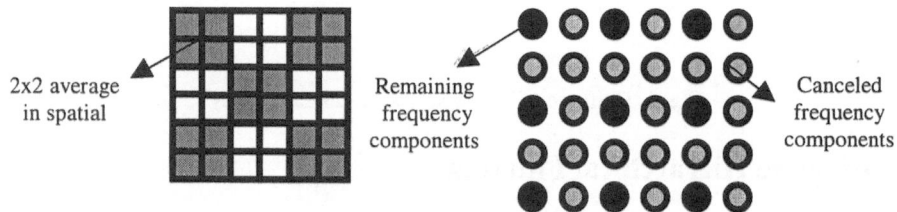

Fig. 9. Anti-aliased 2x2 filtering

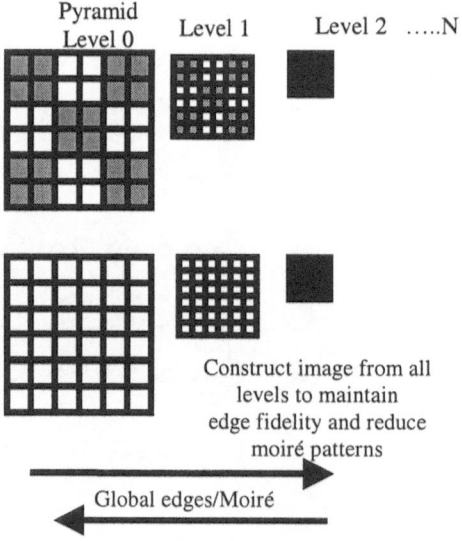

Fig. 10. Anti-aliased pyramid image processing

It illustrated why this set of filters can cancel the aliased low frequency noise components. Thus, the filtering process removes moiré distortion and noises. However, the LPF filtering process causes the penalty of that the image becomes more blurring. In order to maintain the sharpness of the image edges, a set of hierarchical high pass filters is also applied.

An edge classification module is developed to determine that an edge is either a global true edge or a local halftone's micro-structural edge. From the original image, we construct a set of pyramid images.   Image edges in higher layer pyramid are more global edges, while image edges in lower layer pyramid contains more halftone-dot microstructure edges (i.e., noises)

If the edge is a global edge, then the edge is maintained without LPF or is enhanced for sharpening purpose; non-edge and halftone's micro edge are filtered out by stronger LPF; the transition area between two situations above uses weak LPFs to avoid discontinuity between the transition. Thus, we achieves high-quality output images by removing moiré distortion and noises in smooth image regions, and also maintain (or enhance with unsharp masking technique) edge sharpness fidelity by applying the adaptive hierarchical filters according to regions which belong to either image edges or halftone areas.

5   Experimental Result

Figure 11 are 4 halftone image with different LPIs of of 100, 133, 175 and 150 in the clockwise direction. The image is scanned at 100 dpi. We can see different moiré noises visually produced from different LPI images. Not all halftone images generate the same amount of moiré noise; noise becomes stronger when the halftone image is 133 LPI in this example. Figure 12 presents the result processed by the presented technique. In this experiment, the image classification module is constructed based on 2 layers of pyramid images. We can see that the moiré noise of the halftone images is reduced significantly. Another advantage of the proposed algorithm is the processing speed thanks to the design simplicity. Due to the efficiency and effectiveness, the proposed algorithm has been granted the US patent of 6,233,060 [8] and implemented in ASIC and several EPSON imaging products in the market.

6   Summary

In summary, this paper describes a novel technique that achieves high performance in terms of algorithm complexity and computational speed and high quality moiré suppression using an adaptive hierarchical filtering approach. The technique works very well for wide combinations of various screen frequencies, screen angles as well as scan frequencies on various scanners and printers for high-quality magazine image reproduction. Experimental results are shown in Figures 11 and 12. Figure 11 shows the original image scanned and printed at 600 dpi before applying the presented technique. Figure 12 shows the original in Figure 11 is processed by the presented technique. As shown, the presented technique has demonstrated the effectiveness of high-quality moiré suppression with shape edge fidelity results.

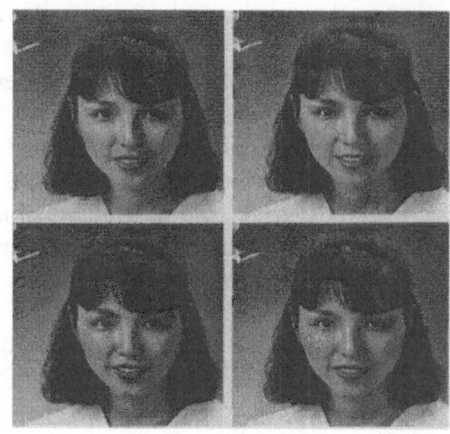

Fig. 11. 4 halftone images with 100, 133, 175, 150 LPIs starting from the left-upper corner in the clockwise direction scanned at 100 dpi.

Fig. 12. Processed Image by the proposed Adaptive-Hierarchical-Filtering Technique

References

[1] J. Shu, R. Springer, and C. Yeh, "Moiré factors and visibility in scanned and printed halftone images," *Optical Engineering* Vol. 28, No. 7, 1989, pp805 - 812.

[2] A. Rosenfeld and A. C. Kak, *Digital Picture Processing*, Chapter 4, 2nd ed., Academic Press, New York, (1981).

[3] T. S. Huang, "Digital transmission of halftone pictures," *Computer Graphics and Image Processing,* Vol. 3, pp 195-202, (1974).

[4] A. Steinbach and K. Y. Wong, "An understanding of moiré patterns in the reproduction of halftone images," *IEEE Computer Society Conference on Pattern Recognition and Image Processing,* pp 545-552, (1979).

[5] J. Shu, "Reproduction of halftone original with moiré reduction and tone adjustment" US Patent No. 4,942,480 July 17, 1990.

[6] D. Kermisch and P. Roetling, "Fourier spectrum of halftone images", Journal of the Optical Society of America A, Vol.65(6), pp. 716-723, (June 1975).

[7] J. Allebach and B. Liu, "Analysis of halftone dot profile and aliasing in the discrete binary representation of images", Journal of the Optical Society of America, Vol. 67(9), pp. 1147-1154, (September 1977).

[8] J. Shu, A. Bhattacharjya, and Tsung-Nan Lin, "Reduction of moire in screened images using hierarchical edge detection and adaptive-length averaging filters", US Patent 6,233,060, May 15, 2001.

A Design Method for Compactly Supported Sampling Function Generator

Koji Nakamura[1], Kazuo Toraichi[1], Kazuki Katagishi[2], Kenji Sayano[1], Akira Okamoto[3], and Yukio Koyanagi[3]

[1] The Center for Tsukuba Advanced Research Alliance, University of Tsukuba
1-1-1 Tennodai, Tsukuba, Ibaraki, 305-8577, Japan
{knakamura, toraichi, sayano}@tara.tsukuba.ac.jp
[2] Institute of Infromation Sciences and Electronics, University of Tsukuba
katagisi@is.tsukuba.ac.jp
[3] Niigata Seimitsu Co., Ltd., Japan,
Shibaohmon116 bldg. 8F, 1-16-3, Shibaohmon, Minato-ku, Tokyo 105-0012, Japan.
okamoto@niigata-s.co.jp, koyanagi@mbk.sphere.ne.jp

Abstract. This paper proposes the design method of a function generator for use in a Digital-to-Analog converter for DVD-Audio. The impulse response of the function generator is a compactly supported sampling function of degree 2 that is expressed in the form of linear combination of quadratic piecewise polynomials function systems. To generate this impulse response, we design the convolution operator that can generate quadratic piecewise polynomials from the basis rectangular function. The function generator is constructed by combining a set of these convolution operators suitably. We further simplify the design of this function generator by making use of a two-scale relation of piecewise polynomials. This function generator can be realized in a small scale circuitry.

1 Introduction

The convolution between a source digital signal and a sampling function has widely been used in reproducing an analog signal in multimedia signal processing. The device that makes possible such FIR-paradigm of signal processing is the Digital-to-Analog converter. We have conducted research on D/A converter for audio signals by applying the Fluency information theory [1], and developed a D/A converter for CD-DA in 1987 [2]. The D/A converter is commonly known as the Fluency DAC [2], and was constructed by convolving the source digital signals with the sampling functions in the signal space spanned by quadratic piecewise polynomials systems [3]. The CD-Player equipped with this D/A converter received the Golden Sound Award in 1988. In recent years, the sampling rate used in digital signal processing has been considerably increased. This led to the introduction of DVD-Audio that is capable of dealing with a maximum sampling rate of above 192 kHz. As such, due to the introduction of DVD-Audio that requires four times the sampling rate of nowadays CD-DA, the request for developing a new Fluency DAC for DVD-Audio was initiated. Because of this necessity, we have been conducting research in order to satisfy this request.

Y.-C. Chen, L.-W. Chang, and C.-T. Hsu (Eds.): PCM 2002, LNCS 2532, pp. 409–416, 2002.

In our previous paper [4], we derived the compactly supported sampling function of degree 2 for applying to the Fluency DAC for DVD-Audio, and examine properties including the frequency response. As the second report on this project in developing the Fluency DAC for DVD-Audio, in this paper we propose a function generator in which the impulse response is the compactly supported sampling function of degree 2 (also known as the C-type sampling function).

In order to design the function generator, we consider two kinds of circuit scheme. We first consider the convolution operator that generates a quadratic piecewise polynomials, because of C-type sampling function is expressed in the form of linear combination of quadratic piecewise polynomials. Then, the function generator is desinged by combining the convolution operator. Next, we consider another circuit scheme in order to simplify the function generator obtained from the above procedure. Here, we apply the two-scale relation of the quadratic piecewise polynomials, and represent the continuous signal by using piecewise polynomials in low resolution.

By using this method, we can simplify the design of the function generator in which impulse response is piecewise polynomials, and their expansion coefficients are calculated by the digital circuit.

The D/A converter whose impulse response is the C-type sampling function has developed into a single IC-chip. Moreover, a DVD-player equipped with this D/A converter has already been developed into an actual product. Both of the DVD-player and the D/A converter have received awards in local contests in Japan on audio equipment at the end of 2000 and 2001.

2   Compactly Supported Sampling Function of Degree 2

In this section, the compactly supported sampling function (also known as the C-type sampling func-tion) that is the impulse response of the function generator will be briefly explained.

In general, the space of all signals that signal processing deals with exists and is considered a sub-space of the typical Hilbert space,

$$L_2(\boldsymbol{R}) \triangleq \{u | \int_{-\infty}^{\infty} |u(t)|^2 dt < +\infty\}, \tag{1}$$

with the inner product expressed as

$$(u, v)_{L_2} \triangleq \int_{-\infty}^{\infty} u(t)\overline{v(t)}dt. \tag{2}$$

Here, $\boldsymbol{R}$ denotes the set of all real numbers.

Let $_{[b]}^{3}\psi(t)$ denotes the quadratic piecewise polynomials that is only 1 time continuously differentiable defined as follows:

$$_{[b]}^{3}\psi(t) \triangleq \int_{-\infty}^{\infty} \left(\frac{\sin \pi f\tau}{\pi f\tau}\right)^3 e^{j2\pi ft} df. \tag{3}$$

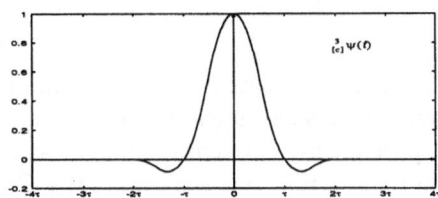

Fig. 1. The waveform of ${}^3_{[c]}\psi(t)$

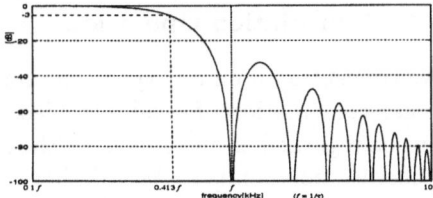

Fig. 2. The frequency response of ${}^3_{[c]}\psi(t)$

Here, τ denotes the sampling interval.

Then, the C-type sampling function derived for applying to the Fluency DAC for DVD-Audio is represented as the following equation [4],

$$
{}^3_{[c]}\psi(t) = -\frac{\tau}{2}\,{}^3_{[b]}\psi(t+\frac{\tau}{2}) + 2\tau\,{}^3_{[b]}\psi(t) - \frac{\tau}{2}\,{}^3_{[b]}\psi(t-\frac{\tau}{2}). \tag{4}
$$

Let ${}^3S_C$ denote a signal space where the function itself is the sampling function in the signal space.

$$
{}^3S_C \triangleq [\,{}^m_{[b]}\psi(t-l\tau)\,]_{l=-\infty}^{\infty}, \quad {}^3S_C \in L_2(R). \tag{5}
$$

And in the interval of $[k, k+1)$, $\forall u \in {}^3S_C$ can be represented in the form of linear combination of four C-type sampling functions with four sampled values as expansion coefficients:

$$
u(t) = \sum_{l=k-1}^{k+2} u(l\tau)\,{}^3_{[c]}\psi(t-l\tau). \tag{6}
$$

Also, in order to be applicable to reproducing DVD-Audio, the C-type sampling function is designed according to the following specifications.

(i). Sampling function should have local support in the time domain.

(ii). The frequency response of the sampling function should be relatively similar to that of the conventional sampling function that was applied to the Fluency DAC for CD-DA [2].

To satisfy the first specification, the C-type sampling function is designed to converge to 0 at both the left and right second sampling points with respect to the origin. Figure 1 illustrates the waveform of the C-type sampling function. Moreover, the frequency characteristics of the C-type sampling function satisfies the second specifications as shown in Figure 2.

3   Function Generator Based on Convolution Operator

In this section, we will design the function generator that generates the C-type sampling function which is formularized in Section 2.

3.1   Convolution Operation

We concentrated on a C-type sampling function that is expressed in the form of linear combination of quadratic piecewise polynomials as shown in Eq.(4). This can be regarded as an element in the signal space of three dimensional quadratic piecewise polynomials. As a design principle for the function generator, the C-type sampling function should be generated by combining quadratic piecewise polynomials.

The quadratic piecewise polynomials can be derived by repeating the convolution of rectangular function twice. In general, it is difficult to realize the convolution integration of rectangular function directly by using analog circuit. As such, we propose an operation that is equivalent to the convolution of rectangular functions in the sense of generating these piecewise polynomials.

We define the functions as given in Eqs. (7) and (8), and discuss the method of generating piecewise polynomials based on their mathematical properties [5],

$$\phi_1(t) \triangleq \begin{cases} 1/\tau, & 0 \leq \tau, \\ 0, & otherwise. \end{cases} \tag{7}$$

$$\phi_m(t) \triangleq \phi_{m-1} * \phi_1(t). \tag{8}$$

Also, the relation between $\phi_3(t)$ and $_{[b]}^{3}\psi(t)$ satisfies the following equation:

$$\phi_3(t) = {}_{[b]}^{3}\psi(t - 3\tau/2). \tag{9}$$

By using the $\phi_m(t)$ defined above, the relation between $\phi_1(t)$ and $\phi_2(t)$, $\phi_2(t)$ and $\phi_3(t)$ can be summarized as the following theorem.

Theorem 1.

$$\frac{1}{\tau} \int_0^t \{\phi_1(t') - \phi_1(t' - \tau)\} \, dt', = \phi_2(t) \tag{10}$$

$$\frac{1}{\tau} \int_0^t \{\phi_2(t') - \phi_2(t' - \tau)\} \, dt'. = \phi_3(t) \tag{11}$$

(Proof)
From Eq.(7), the equation $\frac{1}{\tau}\{\phi_1(t) - \phi_1(t - \tau)\}$ can be expressed as following piecewise polynomials:

$$\frac{1}{\tau}\{\phi_1(t) - \phi_1(t - \tau)\} = \begin{cases} 1/\tau^2, & 0 < t \leq \tau, \\ -1/\tau^2, & \tau < t \leq 2\tau, \\ 0, & otherwise. \end{cases}$$

Then, by integrating the above equation from 0 to t, we can obtain the following result,

$$\frac{1}{\tau} \int_0^t \{\phi_1(t') - \phi_1(t' - \tau)\} dt' = \begin{cases} t/\tau^2, & 0 < t \leq \tau, \\ 1/\tau - t/\tau^2, & \tau < t \leq 2\tau, \\ 0, & otherwise. \end{cases}$$

Furtheremore, when we calculate the convolution $\phi_1 * \phi_1(t)$, the result can be expressed as,

$$\phi_1 * \phi_1(t) = \int_{-\infty}^{\infty} \phi_1(s)\phi_1(t-s)ds = \begin{cases} t/\tau^2, & 0 < t \leq \tau, \\ 1/\tau - t/\tau^2, & \tau < t \leq 2\tau, \\ 0, & otherwise. \end{cases} \quad (12)$$

From Eqs.(12) and (12), we can obtain the following relation.

$$\frac{1}{\tau} \int_0^t \{\phi_1(t') - \phi_1(t'-\tau)\}dt' = \phi_1 * \phi_1(t) = \phi_2(t). \quad (13)$$

Similarly, the equation $\frac{1}{\tau}\{\phi_2(t) - \phi_2(t-\tau)\}$ is integrated from 0 to t, we obtain the following result,

$$\frac{1}{\tau} \int_0^t \{\phi_2(t') - \phi_2(t'-\tau)\}dt' = \begin{cases} \frac{t^2}{(2\tau^3)}, & 0 < t \leq \tau, \\ -\frac{(t-2\tau/3)^2}{\tau^3} + \frac{3}{4\tau}, & \tau < t \leq 2\tau, \\ \frac{(t-3\tau)^2}{\tau^3}, & 2\tau < t \leq 3\tau, \\ 0, & otherwise. \end{cases} \quad (14)$$

Furtheremore, the convolution $\phi_2 * \phi_1(t)$ can be expressed as the following result.

$$\phi_2 * \phi_1(t) = \int_{-\infty}^{\infty} \phi_2(s)\phi_1(t-s)ds = \begin{cases} \frac{t^2}{(2\tau^3)}, & 0 < t \leq \tau, \\ -\frac{(t-3\tau/2)}{\tau^3} + \frac{3}{4\tau}, & \tau < t \leq 2\tau, \\ \frac{(t-3\tau)^2}{\tau^3}, & 3\tau < t \leq 3\tau, \\ 0, & otherwise. \end{cases} \quad (15)$$

From Eqs.(14) and (15), we can obtain the following relation:

$$\frac{1}{\tau} \int_0^t \{\phi_2(t') - \phi_2(t'-\tau)\}dt' = \phi_2 * \phi_1(t) = \phi_3(t). \quad (16)$$

(Q.E.D.)

3.2   Function Generator by Combining Convolution Operator

By referring to the results of the previous subsections, the method for generating quadratic piecewise polynomials can be represented by the following procedure.

(i):   A rectangular function as the input
(ii):   The input is delayed, reversed, and added to the original rectangular function. Then, these functions are integrated. A triangular function is generated as a result.
(iii): By repeating step (ii), a quadratic piecewise polynomials is generated from the triangular function.

Therefore, generating a triangular function from the rectangular function and quadratic piecewise polynomials from the triangular functions are performed using the similar procedure. Figure 3 illustrates the model of convolution operatora and the function generator in which impulse response is C-type sampling function.

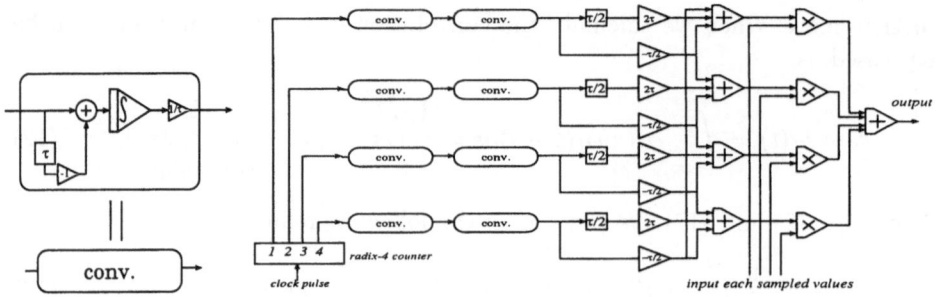

Fig. 3. Configulation of the convolution operator and the function generator

4   Simplicication of the Function Generator

In this section, we will discuss the simplification of the function generator designed in previous section.

In the previous section, the function generator that generates the output continuous signal by convoluting C-type sampling functions and sampled values is designed. However, in order to generate the C-type sampling function, the piecewise polynomials should be shifted to 1/2 of the sampling interval. Due to this requirement, the circuit shown in Figure 3 generates both time of sampling interval and the rectangular pulse that has support of clock interval twice. Therefore, the circuitry of the function generator is complicated digital and analog circuit are intermingled. We discuss the simplification of this function generator based on the following two design principles:

– The continuous output signal should be expressed as piecewise polynomials generated based on clock pulse interval.
– The expansion coefficients of a piecewise polynomials should be calculated in digital circuit.

In order to satisfy the above two purposes, the mathematical properties of the C-type sampling function is considered. Here, the sampling interval $\tau = 1$ to simplify the discussion. Moreover, Let $\psi_0(t)$ denotes the function that is shifted $\frac{3}{[b]}\psi(t)$ to 2 on the time axis. That is, a function $\psi_0(t)$ is considered as the function that responses from $t = 0$. The function $\psi_0(t)$ can be represented as following equation.

$$\psi_0(t) = -\frac{1}{2}\phi_3(t) + 2\phi_3(t - \frac{1}{2}) - \frac{1}{2}\phi_3(t - 1). \tag{17}$$

We consider what form continuous signal $u(t)$ in the interval of $[k, k+1)$

$$u(t) = \sum_{l=k-3}^{k} v_l\psi_0(t - l), \tag{18}$$

can be expanded. Note that: the sampling value which corresponds to $\psi_0(t - k)$ denotes v_k. By substituting Eq.(17) to Eq.(18), we can obtain following expanded expression.

$$u(t) = 2 \sum_{l=k-3}^{k} v_l \phi_3(t - l - \frac{1}{2}) - \frac{1}{2} \sum_{p=k-2}^{k} (v_p + v_{p-1}) \phi_3(t - p) \qquad (19)$$

From above equation, we can found that the number of dimension increases by 3 to 7 in the case of representing continuous signal $u(t)$ by using piecewise polynomials. Then, by applying the two-scale relation [5] of $\phi_3(t)$;

$$\phi_3(t) = \frac{1}{4} \sum_{l=0}^{3} \binom{3}{l} \phi_3(2t - l), \qquad (20)$$

to Eq.(19), $u(t)$ can be rearranged as,

$$u(t) = \sum_{l=k-3}^{k} \sum_{n=0}^{3} \frac{v_l}{2} \binom{3}{n} \phi_3(2t - 2l - 1 - n) - \sum_{p=k-2}^{k} \sum_{q=0}^{3} \frac{v_p + v_{p-1}}{2} \binom{3}{q} \phi_3(2t - 2p - q) \qquad (21)$$

By considering the locally supported property [5] that $\phi_3(t) = 0$ for $t < 0$ or $t > 3$, the above equation can be rearranged as,

$$u(t) = \sum_{l=k-1}^{k} \sum_{p=0}^{1} \left\{ (-1)^{p+1} \frac{v_l}{8} + v_{l-1} + (-1)^p \frac{v_{l-2}}{8} \right\} \phi_3(2t - 2l - p) \qquad (22)$$

Here, we define following coefficients and function.

$$w_{k,l} \triangleq (-1)^{l+1} \frac{v_k}{8} + v_{k-1} + (-1)^l \frac{v_{k-2}}{8}, \qquad (23)$$

$$\hat{\phi}_l(t) \triangleq \phi_3(2t - l). \qquad (24)$$

By using $w_{k,0}$, $w_{k,1}$, and $\hat{\phi}_l(t)$, Eq.(22) can be represented as:

$$u(t) = \sum_{l=0}^{2} w_{k,l} \hat{\phi}_l(t - k) + \sum_{p=0}^{2} w_{k-1,p} \hat{\phi}_p(t - k + 1) \qquad (25)$$

It means that the continuous signal $u(t)$ in $[k, k+1)$ is expressed by using piecewise polynomials $\{\hat{\phi}_0(t - k), \hat{\phi}_1(t - k)\}$ whose expansion coefficients are $w_{k,0}, w_{k,1}$, that calculated at $t = k$, and $\{\hat{\phi}_0(t - k + 1), \hat{\phi}_1(t - k + 1)\}$ whose expansion coefficients are $w_{k-1,0}, w_{k-1,1}$ that calculated at $t = k - 1$.

Figure 4 illustrates the block diagram for obtaining the coefficients $\{w_{k,0} w_{k,1}\}$ from the input sampled value v_k. Also, Figure 5 illustrates the configuration of the function generator that generate continuous signal $u(t)$ by using piecewise polynomials and $\{w_{k,0} w_{k,1}\}$ that is as expansion coefficients. This simplified function generator does not require generating the pulse whose support is twice the clock interval. And this function generator can generate piecewise polynomials by making use of the rectangular function whose support is same as the clock interval, and derive the output continuous signal in the form of linear combination of these functions. Therefore, as shown in Figures 3 and 5, the function generator designed in this section can be realized in a small scale circuitry.

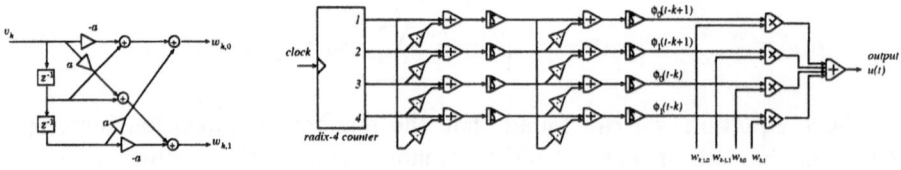

Fig. 4. Block dia- **Fig. 5.** A complete configuration of the function generator in gram for obtaining the case of using piecewise polynomials $\{w_{k,0}, w_{k,1}\}$ from v_k ($a = 1/8$)

5   Conclusions

In this paper, we have introduced the design of the function generator for the Fluency DAC for DVD-Audio. The requirements for realizing the function generator were discussed. We first designed the convolution operator that consecutively generates quadratic piecewise polynomials from input rectangular functions. Then, by combining the convolution op-erators, the function generator in which the impulse response is compactly supported sampling function of degree 2 can be constructed.

Then, we discuss another circuit scheme in order to simplify the designed function generator. Specifically, we make use of the mathematical properties of the C-type sampling function in order to express output continuous signal in the form of linear combination of quadratic piecewise polynomials. Furthermore, we considered their expansion coefficients are calculated by digital circuit. Based on the above methods, we can realize function generator in a small scale circuitry.

References

1. M.Kamada, K.Toraichi, and R.Mori, "Periodic spline orthonormal bases," J. Approx. Theory, vol.55, pp.27-38, 1988.
2. Q. Wang, K. Toraichi, M. Kamada, and R. Mori, "Circuit Design of a D/A Converter Using Spline Functions," Signal Processing, vol.16, no.3, pp.279-288, Mar. 1989.
3. K. Toraichi, M. Kamada, and R. Mori, "Sampling Theorem in the Signal Space Spanned by Spline Functions of Degree 2," Trans. IEICE vol.E68, no.10, pp.660-666, Oct.1985.
4. K. Nakamura, K. Toraichi, K. Katagishi, and S. L. Lee, "Compactly Supported Sampling Function of Degree 2 for Applying to Reproducing DVD-Audio," Proc. IEEE Pacific Rim Conference on Communica-tion, Computer and Signal Processing, Victoria, Can-ada, pp.670-673, Aug. 2001.
5. C. K. Chui, WAVELETS: A Tutorial in Theory and Applications, Academic Press, 1992.

A Smooth Interpolation Method for Nonuniform Samples Based on Sampling Functions Composed of Piecewise Polynomials

Tomoyuki Takahashi[1], Kazuo Toraichi[2], Keisuke Kameyama[2], and
Koji Nakamura[2]

[1] Doctoral Program, Graduate School of Systems and Information Engineering,
University of Tsukuba, Japan
takahasi@wslab.is.tsukuba.ac.jp
[2] Institute of Information Sciences and Electronics, Tsukuba Advanced Reserch
Alliance, University of Tsukuba, Japan
{toraichi, kame, nakamura }@wslab.is.tsukuba.ac.jp

Abstract. Interpolation of nonuniform samples is required for various
cases of signal processing. In such a case, we often use sampling functions to interpolate signals. We show one example of sampling functions
to interpolate signals from nonuniform samples, inheriting the properties of the C-type Fluency sampling functions introduced by Toraichi et
al. The proposed sampling function is locally supported and composed
with piecewise polynomial functions of degree 2 as the C-type Fluency
sampling function. In this paper, we extend the C-type Fluency sampling function and derive the nonuniform sampling function which has a
favorable property such that it can interpolate flat signal from samples
that are constant. By using this sampling function, we get smooth and
small undulate signal from samples of arbitrary.

1 Introduction

In the field of multimedia, we deal with many types of analog signals. When we
need to process them for practical use with computers, they are often encoded.
In case of encoding analog signal or thinning digital data points out, we can
sometimes get the set of data points more efficiently, from *nonuniform encoding*.
For example, local maxima or minima, or some special points are selected leaving
out the unimportant ones. In such cases, or when we have incomplete set of data
points, we need the method to retrieve analog signal from nonuniform data
points.

Various researches for interpolation of nonuniform samples have been reported. One of the typical methods is the cubic spline interpolation [1]. In this
method, we can interpolate from nonuniform samples with piecewise polynomials of degree 3, whose knots are samples themselves. However, large undulation
appears under some conditions of interval of samples. Several methods that solve
this problem have been proposed.

Y.-C. Chen, L.-W. Chang, and C.-T. Hsu (Eds.): PCM 2002, LNCS 2532, pp. 417–424, 2002.

In this paper, as one of the methods to solve this problem, we propose a sampling function to approximate signal from samples. For interpolation from uniform samples, the C-type Fluency sampling function has been derived by Toraichi in [2][3]. The C-type Fluency sampling function is represented by eight piecewise polynomial functions of degree 2. Additionally, it is locally supported, smooth, and one time continuously differentiable. By using the C-type Fluency sampling functions, we can interpolate analog signal by convolving with the sampled data. However, the C-type Fluency sampling function cannot interpolate analog signal from nonuniform samples, because they have been derived under the assumption that the data points are uniformly spaced.

In this paper, we derive a nonuniform sampling function, which has almost the same properties as the C-type Fluency sampling function.

2   The C-Type Fluency Sampling Function

The C-type Fluency sampling function has been derived in [2][3]. The C-type Fluency sampling function is composed with B-spline basis of degree 2. Here, let $\{\phi_l(t)\}_{l=-2}^2$ denote the B-spline basis of degree 2, defined as follows:

$$\phi_l(t) \equiv \int_{-\infty}^{\infty} \left(\frac{\sin \pi f h}{\pi f h} \right)^3 e^{j2\pi f(t-lh)} df, \tag{1}$$

where h and l are, shift interval and the number of shifts, respectively. This means that each basis function is equivalent to $\phi_0(t)$ shifted by lh. The C-type Fluency sampling function is derived in [2] and [3] as,

$$\psi(t) = \sum_{l=-2}^{2} \lambda_l \phi(t - \frac{l}{2}). \tag{2}$$

Here, the values for λ_l have been derived as $\{\lambda_l\}_{l=-2}^2 = \{0, -\frac{1}{2}, 2, -\frac{1}{2}, 0\}$. Explicitly, the C-type Fluency sampling function is represented by the piecewise polynomial functions of,

$$\psi(t) = \begin{cases} -\frac{1}{4}t^2 - t - 1 & [-2, -\frac{3}{2}] \\ \frac{3}{4}t^2 + 2t + \frac{5}{4} & [-\frac{3}{2}, -1] \\ \frac{5}{4}t^2 + 3t + \frac{7}{4} & [-1, -\frac{1}{2}] \\ -\frac{7}{4}t^2 + 1 & [-\frac{1}{2}, \frac{1}{2}] \\ \frac{5}{4}t^2 - 3t + \frac{7}{4} & [\frac{1}{2}, 1] \\ \frac{3}{4}t^2 - 2t + \frac{5}{4} & [1, \frac{3}{2}] \\ -\frac{1}{4}t^2 + t - 1 & [\frac{3}{2}, 2] \end{cases} . \tag{3}$$

Here, $h = \frac{1}{2}$ has been employed, which is the half of the sampling interval.

The C-type Fluency sampling function has some useful properties as follows:

- The sampling function consists of piecewise polynomial functions of degree 2, and is one time continuously differentiable. Due to these properties, the approximate analog signal is smooth and has small undulation.
- It is locally supported. Therefore, truncation errors do not exist.

3   Specifications of the Sampling Function for Nonuniform Samples

In this section, the specifications of the nonuniform sampling function derived in this paper will be listed.

When we derive the nonuniform sampling function, we can give various specifications according to the objectives. In this paper, we try to derive the nonuniform sampling function by extending the C-type Fluency sampling function. Specifications of the nonuniform sampling function basically inherit many among those of the C-type Fluency sampling functions. They are follows:

1. The nonuniform sampling function is locally supported (by 5 samples including the center and 2 samples on each side).
2. The function is composed with eight piecewise polynomial functions, and their knots are placed on the samples and the middle of two adjacent samples.
3. The value at the center sample point is 1, and 0 at the other sample points.
4. The sampling function is one time continuously differentiable.
5. The approximate analog signal has small undulation. Particularly, the interpolation of the constant-valued-samples are flat.

4   Nonuniform Interpolation

Based on the specifications, the nonuniform sampling function is derived.

4.1   The Nonuniform Sampling Function

By the specifications 1 and 2, the nonuniform sampling function y can be represented by the piecewise polynomial functions of degree 2 as,

$$
\begin{cases}
y_1 = a_1 t^2 + b_1 t + c_1 \ [t_{-2}, \frac{t_{-2}+t_{-1}}{2}] \\
y_2 = a_2 t^2 + b_2 t + c_2 \ [\frac{t_{-2}+t_{-1}}{2}, t_{-1}] \\
y_3 = a_3 t^2 + b_3 t + c_3 \ [t_{-1}, \frac{t_{-1}+t_0}{2}] \\
y_4 = a_4 t^2 + b_4 t + c_4 \ [\frac{t_{-1}+t_0}{2}, t_0] \\
y_5 = a_5 t^2 + b_5 t + c_5 \ [t_0, \frac{t_0+t_1}{2}] \\
y_6 = a_6 t^2 + b_6 t + c_6 \ [\frac{t_0+t_1}{2}, t_1] \\
y_7 = a_7 t^2 + b_7 t + c_7 \ [t_1, \frac{t_1+t_2}{2}] \\
y_8 = a_8 t^2 + b_8 t + c_8 \ [\frac{t_1+t_2}{2}, t_2]
\end{cases}
\tag{4}
$$

Here, the values for $\{t_i\} (i = -2, -1, 0, 1, 2)$ are the positions of the five samples, which support the nonuniform sampling function. Next, according to specifications 3 and 4, the following conditions have to be met.

- Coordinates of knots of the piecewise polynomials y,
  $(t_{-2}, 0)$, $(\frac{t_{-2}+t_{-1}}{2}, d_{-2})$, $(t_{-1}, 0)$, $(\frac{t_{-1}+t_0}{2}, d_{-1})$, $(t_0, 1)$, $(\frac{t_0+t_1}{2}, d_1)$, $(t_1, 0)$, $(\frac{t_1+t_2}{2}, d_2)$, $(t_2, 0)$.

– Differential coefficients at the knots of y,

$y_1'(t_{-2}) = 0$, $y_1'(\frac{t_{-2}+t_{-1}}{2}) = y_2'(\frac{t_{-2}+t_{-1}}{2})$, $y_2'(t_{-1}) = y_3'(t_{-1})$,

$y_3'(\frac{t_{-1}+t_0}{2}) = y_4'(\frac{t_{-1}+t_0}{2})$, $y_4'(t_0) = 0$, $y_5'(t_0) = 0$,

$y_5'(\frac{t_0+t_1}{2}) = y_6'(\frac{t_0+t_1}{2})$, $y_6'(t_1) = y_7'(t_1)$, $y_7'(\frac{t_1+t_2}{2}) = y_8'(\frac{t_1+t_2}{2})$, $y_8'(t_2) = 0$.

Then, we can get 26 simultaneous equations.

$$a_1 t_{-2}^2 + b_1 t_{-2} + c_1 = 0 \tag{5}$$

$$a_1(t_{-2} + t_{-1})^2 + 2b_1(t_{-2} + t_{-1}) + 4c_1 = 4d_{-2} \tag{6}$$

$$a_2(t_{-2} + t_{-1})^2 + 2b_2(t_{-2} + t_{-1}) + 4c_2 = 4d_{-2} \tag{7}$$

$$a_2 t_{-1}^2 + b_2 t_{-1} + c_2 = a_3 t_{-1}^2 + b_3 t_{-1} + c_3 = 0 \tag{8}$$

$$a_3(t_{-1} + t_0)^2 + 2b_3(t_{-1} + t_0) + 4c_3 = 4d_{-1} \tag{9}$$

$$a_4(t_{-1} + t_0)^2 + 2b_4(t_{-1} + t_0) + 4c_4 = 4d_{-1} \tag{10}$$

$$a_4 t_0^2 + b_4 t_0 + c_4 = a_5 t_0^2 + b_5 t_0 + c_5 = 1 \tag{11}$$

$$a_5(t_0 + t_1)^2 + 2b_5(t_0 + t_1) + 4c_5 = 4d_1 \tag{12}$$

$$a_6(t_0 + t_1)^2 + 2b_6(t_0 + t_1) + 4c_6 = 4d_1 \tag{13}$$

$$a_6 t_1^2 + b_6 t_1 + c_6 = a_7 t_1^2 + b_7 t_1 + c_7 = 0 \tag{14}$$

$$a_7(t_1 + t_2)^2 + 2b_7(t_1 + t_2) + 4c_7 = 4d_2 \tag{15}$$

$$a_8(t_1 + t_2)^2 + 2b_8(t_1 + t_2) + 4c_8 = 4d_2 \tag{16}$$

$$a_8 t_2^2 + b_8 t_2 + c_8 = 0 \tag{17}$$

$$2a_1 t_{-2} + b_1 = 0 \tag{18}$$

$$a_1(t_{-2} + t_{-1}) + b_1 = a_2(t_{-2} + t_{-1}) + b_2 \tag{19}$$

$$2a_2 t_{-1} + b_2 = 2a_3 t_{-1} + b_3 \tag{20}$$

$$a_3(t_{-1} + t_0) + b_3 = a_4(t_{-1} + t_0) + b_4 \tag{21}$$

$$2a_4 t_0 + b_4 = 2a_5 t_0 + b_5 = 0 \tag{22}$$

$$a_5(t_0 + t_1) + b_5 = a_6(t_0 + t_1) + b_6 \tag{23}$$

$$2a_6 t_1 + b_6 = 2a_7 t_1 + b_7 \tag{24}$$

$$a_7(t_1 + t_2) + b_7 = a_8(t_1 + t_2) + b_8 \tag{25}$$

$$2a_8 t_2 + b_8 = 0 \tag{26}$$

Solving them leaving out the conditions of Eqs.(20) and (24), (that is, leaving out the conditions of one time differentiablilty at the coordinates $(t_{-1}, 0)$ and $(t_1, 0)$) the piecewise polynomial functions y of Eq.(4) are represented as follows:

$$y_1 = \frac{4}{(t_{-1} - t_{-2})^2} \left[d_{-2} t^2 - 2t_{-2} d_{-2} t + t_{-2}^2 d_{-2} \right], \tag{27}$$

$$y_2 = \frac{4}{(t_{-1} - t_{-2})^2} \left[\left\{ d_{-2} + \frac{2(t_{-1} - t_{-2})(2d_{-1} - 1)}{t_0 - t_{-1}} \right\} t^2 \right.$$

$$+ \left. \left\{ -2t_{-1} d_{-2} + \frac{(2d_{-1} - 1)(t_{-2}^2 + 2t_{-1}t_{-2} - 3t_{-1}^2)}{t_0 - t_{-1}} \right\} t \right.$$

$$+ t_{-1}^2 d_{-2} + \frac{t_{-1}(t_{-1}^2 - t_{-2}^2)(2d_{-1} - 1)}{t_0 - t_{-1}} \Bigg], \tag{28}$$

$$y_3 = \frac{4}{(t_0 - t_{-1})^2} \left[(-3d_{-1} + 2)t^2 + \{2(2t_{-1} + t_0)d_{-1} - (3t_{-1} + t_0)\}t \right.$$
$$\left. - 2t_{-1}t_0 d_{-1} - t_{-1}^2(d_{-1} - 1) + t_{-1}t_0 \right], \tag{29}$$

$$y_4 = \frac{4}{(t_0 - t_{-1})^2} \left[(d_{-1} - 1)t^2 - 2t_0(d_{-1} - 1)t + t_0^2(d_{-1} - 1) \right] + 1, \tag{30}$$

$$y_5 = \frac{4}{(t_1 - t_0)^2} \left[(d_1 - 1)t^2 - 2t_0(d_1 - 1)t + t_0^2(d_1 - 1) \right] + 1, \tag{31}$$

$$y_6 = \frac{4}{(t_1 - t_0)^2} \left[(-3d_1 + 2)t^2 + \{2(t_0 + 2t_1)d_1 - (t_0 + 3t_1)\}t \right.$$
$$\left. - 2t_0 t_1 d_1 - t_1^2(d_1 - 1) + t_0 t_1 \right], \tag{32}$$

$$y_7 = \frac{4}{(t_2 - t_1)^2} \left[\left\{ d_2 + \frac{2(t_1 - t_2)(2d_1 - 1)}{t_0 - t_1} \right\} t^2 \right.$$
$$+ \left\{ -2t_1 d_2 + \frac{(2d_1 - 1)(t_2^2 + 2t_1 t_2 - 3t_1^2)}{t_0 - t_1} \right\} t$$
$$\left. + t_1^2 d_2 + \frac{t_1(t_1^2 - t_2^2)(2d_1 - 1)}{t_0 - t_1} \right], \tag{33}$$

$$y_8 = \frac{4}{(t_2 - t_1)^2} \left[d_2 t^2 - 2t_2 d_2 t + t_2^2 d_2 \right]. \tag{34}$$

If we calculate the parameter set $D = \{d_{-2}, d_{-1}, d_1, d_2\}$ satisfying Eqs.(20) and (24), we obtain the additional conditions of,

$$\begin{cases} \frac{2d_{-2}}{t_{-1} - t_{-2}} + \frac{2d_{-1}}{t_0 - t_{-1}} = \frac{1}{t_0 - t_{-1}}, \\ \frac{2d_2}{t_1 - t_2} + \frac{2d_1}{t_0 - t_1} = \frac{1}{t_0 - t_1}. \end{cases} \tag{35}$$

Therefore, the nonuniform sampling function is represented by Eqs.(27), ...,(34), which satisfy Eq.(35).

4.2   Decision of the Parameter Set D

The nonuniform sampling function with the parameter set D has been derived. We have the freedom of choosing the elements of D, as long as the elements of D satisfy Eq.(35),

This nonuniform sampling function is basically supported by five samples. We call this support "Support-2". But if $d_{-2} = d_2 = 0$, the support will reduce to three samples. We call this support "Support-1". In this case, the elements of D are uniquely determined($d_{-2} = d_2 = 0, d_{-1} = d_1 = \frac{1}{2}$). We call the function of "Support-1" as "Function-1".

In the case of "Support-2", We show one example of choosing the elements of D that satisfy Eq.(35), which guarantee specification 5.

Here, as a straightforward extention of the C-type Fluency sampling function, the values of knots of the proposed sampling function are selected so that they are approximately equal to the ones of the C-type Fluency sampling function $(d_{-2}, d_2 = -\frac{1}{16}, d_{-1}, d_1 = \frac{9}{16})$.

From Eq.(35), we get

$$\begin{cases} d_2 = \frac{t_1 - t_2}{t_0 - t_1}(\frac{1}{2} - d_1) \\ d_{-2} = \frac{t_{-1} - t_{-2}}{t_0 - t_{-1}}(\frac{1}{2} - d_{-1}) \end{cases} \quad (36)$$

Substituting Eq.(36) to

$$\begin{cases} J_1 = (\frac{9}{16} - d_1)^2 + (-\frac{1}{16} - d_2)^2 \\ J_2 = (\frac{9}{16} - d_{-1})^2 + (-\frac{1}{16} - d_{-2})^2 \end{cases} \quad (37)$$

and choosing d_1 and d_{-1} to minimize both J_1 and J_2, the elements of D are calculated as

$$\begin{cases} d_1 = \frac{1}{2} + \frac{A+1}{16(A^2+1)} \\ d_{-1} = \frac{1}{2} + \frac{B+1}{16(B^2+1)} \\ d_2 = A(\frac{1}{2} - d_1) \\ d_{-2} = B(\frac{1}{2} - d_{-1}) \end{cases} \quad (38)$$

Here, $A = \frac{t_1 - t_2}{t_0 - t_1}, B = \frac{t_{-1} - t_{-2}}{t_0 - t_{-1}}$. We call the function which has these elements of D as "Function-2". "Function-2" is equal to the C-type Fluency sampling function (Eq.(3)) for uniform samples. It's one of the important properties of "Function-2".

"Function-1" and "Function-2" can interpolate flat signal from samples that are constant. So, these functions satisfy specification 5. We will show it in the following. Here, the segment of the approximation function between two samples will be considered. Four samples are considered in $[x_0, x_3]$ whose coordinates are $\{(x_0, f_0), (x_1, f_1), (x_2, f_2), (x_3, f_3)\}$. The approximation functions in $[x_1, \frac{x_1 + x_2}{2}]$, and in $[\frac{x_1 + x_2}{2}, x_2]$, will be denoted F_1 and F_2, respectively.

- Function-1 $(d_{-2} = d_2 = 0, d_{-1} = d_1 = \frac{1}{2})$

$$F_1 = \frac{4(f_2 - f_1)}{(x_2 - x_1)^2}\{\frac{1}{2}t^2 - x_1 t + \frac{1}{2}x_1^2\} + f_1. \quad (39)$$

If $f_1 = f_2 = \alpha$, then $F_1 = \alpha$. Similarly, $F_2 = \alpha$. Therefore, we can interpolate $F = \alpha$ from nonuniform samples that are constantly α.

- Function-2

$$\begin{aligned} F_1 = \frac{1}{4(x_2 - x_1)^2} & [\{3C(f_0 - f_2) + D(f_1 - f_3) - 8(f_1 - f_2)\}t^2 \\ & + \{2(x_2 + 2x_1)C(f_2 - f_0) + 2x_1 D(f_3 - f_1) + 16x_1(f_1 - f_2)\}t \\ & + (x_1^2 + 2x_1 x_2)C(f_0 - f_2) + x_1^2 D(f_1 - f_3) + 8x_1^2(f_2 - f_1)] + f_1. (40) \end{aligned}$$

Here, $C = \frac{(x_1 - x_2)^2 + (x_0 - x_1)(x_1 - x_2)}{(x_1 - x_2)^2 + (x_0 - x_1)^2}, D = \frac{(x_1 - x_2)^2 + (x_1 - x_2)(x_2 - x_3)}{(x_1 - x_2)^2 + (x_2 - x_3)^2}$. If $f_0 = f_1 = f_2 = f_3 = \alpha$, then $F_1 = \alpha$. Similarly, $F_2 = \alpha$. Therefore, "Function-2" also satisfies specification 5.

5   Experiments

In this section, we will show experiments to interpolate signals from nonuniform samples comparing the proposed nonuniform sampling function and the cubic spline interpolation.

The functions that are used in the experimentations are as follows.

1. The cubic spline function. ("spline")
2. Function-1. ("func-1")
3. Function-2. (Eq.(38)) ("func-2")

Using each function, two sets of nonuniform samples are interpolated, and then the length of each approximated function are calculated.

The results are shown in Figs.(1) and (2). In the Fig.(1), the results of interpolation from nonuniform samples which have random values are shown. In the Fig.(2), the results of interpolation from samples that are constant except for first sample are shown.

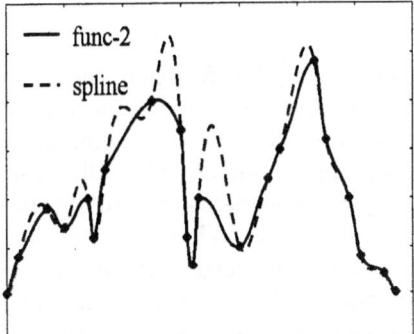 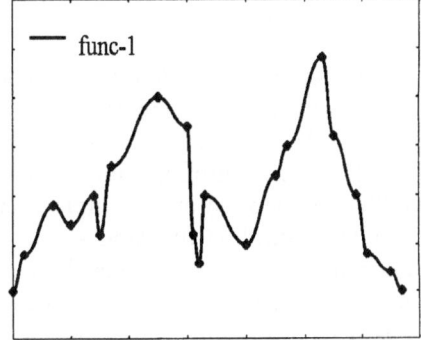

Fig. 1. (left) Samples that are placed random are interpolated with "spline" and "func-2". Each sample is represented by "◇". A solid line expresses the interpolation with "func-2". A dotted line is "spline" interpolation. Looking at "spline" interpolation, larger undulations appear when compared with the interpolation by "func-2". The length of the interpolation with "func-2" is 105.46. The length of "spline" is 145.70. (right) Samples that are placed random are interpolated with "func-1". Here, the differential coefficients at the position of samples are constantly 0. The length is 104.68.

From these results, we can say that the proposed sampling function can interpolate with small undulation, shortness, but still providing the smoothness.

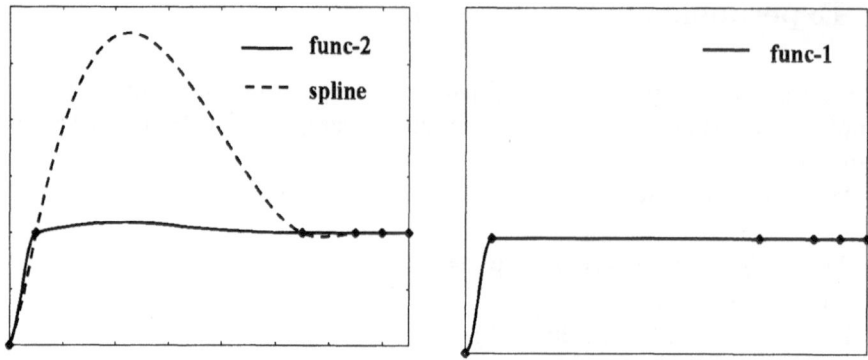

Fig. 2. (left) The set of samples that are constant except for the leftmost sample, are interpolated with "func-2" and "spline". Overshoot and undershoot are smaller for the interpolation with "func-2". The length of the solid line is 2.93. The dotted line's length is 4.92. (right) The set of samples are interpolated with "func-1". Overshoot and undershoot are not observed. The length is 2.91.

6   Conclusions

In this paper, we extended the C-type Fluency sampling function and derived a nonuniform sampling function composed with piecewise polynomial functions of degree 2. It is also locally supported and one time continuously differentiable. The nonuniform sampling function has the parameter set D which allows some flexibility. We showed one example of choosing of the elements of D to obtain the nonuniform sampling function satisfying specification 5. When we interpolated signal from nonuniform samples by our nonuniform sampling function, we could obtain the smooth signal. Comparing the cubic spline interpolation and the proposed sampling function, The proposed one can interpolate signal with small undulation.

The next step of our reserch is to find the method for efficiently choosing the samples, when analog signal is sampled or digital data points are thinned out.

References

1. de Boor C. :A Practical Guide to Splines. Springer-Verlag, 1978.
2. M.Obata, K.Wada, K.Toraichi, K.Mori, M.Ohira. : An approximation of data points by piecewise polynomial functions and their dual orthogonal functions. Trans. Signal Processing 80 (2000) 507-514.
3. K.Nakamura, K.Toraichi, K.Katagishi, and S.L.Lee. : Compactly Supported Sampling Function of Degree 2 for Applying to Reproducing DVD-Audio. Proc. IEEE Pacific Rim Conference on Communication, Computer and Signal Precessing, Victoria, Canada, pp.670-673, Aug.2001.

Motion Vector Based Error Concealment Algorithms

Che-Shing Chen, Mei-Juan Chen, Chin-Hui Huang, and Shih-Ching Sun

Dept. of Electrical Engineering, National Dong Hwa UniversityHualien 974, Taiwan
cmj@mail.ndhu.edu.tw

Abstract. Compressed video bitstream is sensitive to channel errors and may degrade the reconstructed images severely even the bit error rate is small. For combating the impact of errors, several techniques have been developed to protect the bitstream. One approach is adding some protection codes at the encoder, or combining the forward error correction to enhance the robustness of the highly compressed bitstream. Another approach aims at error concealment at the decoder, include to detect error positions and to conceal them using the spatial or temporal correlation. In this paper, we focus on the research of error concealment at the decoder. We propose motion vector based error concealment algorithms to recover the displacement per pixel according to the relation of neighboring motion vectors. We can estimate more accurate displacement per pixel by using the tendency of motion vectors; therefore, the damaged images can be reconstructed more acceptable by human eyes.

1 Introduction

Visual communication becomes an important application for the rapid development of multimedia. Due to the large size of digital video data, the bitstream produced by video data must be compressed to meet the channel bandwidth requirement. For achieving the high compression efficiency, the redundancy of spatial and temporal correlation has to be removed; therefore, the tightly dependency of data in the bitstream is produced by using the prediction code and variable length coding (VLC). Moreover, the transmission channel of network is error-prone. Once a single bit error occurred, the remaining part of the bitstream becomes useless even the decoder received correctly. For avoiding the compressed bitstream suffering from errors, several techniques are developed to protect the bitstream from the errors during transmission via network channel. These approaches include adding some protection codes at the encoder [1-2] or combining the FEC in channel coding stage. Another direction of research is aimed at the error concealment at the decoder. Such researches include how to detect the position of errors occurred in the bitstream; therefore, the detected errors can be recovered by using the correlation in spatial or/and temporal domain.

In this paper, we focus on the error concealment at the decoder. We propose motion vector based error concealment algorithms to recover the damaged blocks. We use the neighboring motion vectors (MVs) to estimate the lost MV. Like the motion field

Y.-C. Chen, L.-W. Chang, and C.-T. Hsu (Eds.): PCM 2002, LNCS 2532, pp. 425-433, 2002.
© Springer-Verlag Berlin Heidelberg 2002

interpolation (MFI) method proposed in [3-4], instead of one MV per block, we estimate the MV per pixel. By tracking the tendency of the movement, we use the consistency and similarity of the neighboring MVs to find some correlation among them. Thus, we can use the relation of neighboring MVs to interpolate the MV at each pixel. The proposed methods get better quality than existing algorithms.In section 2, we describe proposed error concealment algorithms in more details. We show the simulation results in section 3 and make some conclusions in section 4.

2 Proposed Error Concealment Algorithms

In this section, we propose two algorithms. Depending on the property of the neighboring MVs and the tendency of pixels in the damaged block, we introduce several techniques to recover the MVs.

2.1 Rectangular Motion Vector Interpolation

We propose an error concealment method to conceal the error block by finding the motion vector per pixel using the rectangular motion vector interpolation (RMVI) algorithm. Then we employ the displacements to find the estimated values of the pixels and use them to replace the error pixels in the error block.

In RMVI, we use six motion vectors of the neighborhood of the error block. The corresponding position of the neighboring MVs is shown in Fig.1. We describe the algorithm step by step in the following.

Step 1: Calculate the Levels for Interpolation. As Fig.2 shows, we first determine the levels, L_{TL}, L_{TR}, L_{BL} and L_{BR}, respectively. The term "level" is the number of the MVs interpolated by other MVs. We can understand that the closer two motion vectors are to each other, the smaller the difference of the corresponding blocks will be. So the levels have inverse proportion to the difference between the neighboring MVs. Let $L_i = [l_{i1}, l_{i2}]^T$ be the level vector and $V_i = [v_{i1}, v_{i2}]^T$ the seed vector shown as Fig.3. The term "seed vector" is the motion vector used to interpolate other MVs. Each component of level vector can be calculated as follows:

$$l_{1j} = \begin{cases} \dfrac{d(v_{2j},v_{3j})}{d(v_{1j},v_{2j})+d(v_{2j},v_{3j})}N & , \ if \ \ d(v_{1j},v_{2j}) \times d(v_{2j},v_{3j}) \neq 0 \\[4mm] \left(\dfrac{1}{2^{\left\lfloor \frac{d(v_{1j},v_{2j})}{s} \right\rfloor +1}} - \dfrac{1}{2^{\left\lfloor \frac{d(v_{2j},v_{3j})}{s} \right\rfloor +1}} + \dfrac{1}{2} \right)N & , \ otherwise \end{cases} \tag{1}$$

$$l_{2j} = N - l_{1j}$$

where j is a component of vector, N is the width of the lost block, S is the smooth factor, and d(c1,c2)=|c1-c2|.

Smooth factor controls the smoothness of the displacements in error block.

Therefore, L_{TL}, L_{TR}, L_{BL} and L_{BR} can be calculated by Eq.1. The relative MVs are shown as Fig.4.

Step 2: Calculate the Basis Vectors. The basis vectors, B_T and B_B shown in Fig.2, are raw vectors interpolated by seed vectors and will be used to interpolate other motion vectors. Let $B = \{B(x)\}_{x=0}^{N-1}$ be the basis vector with $B(x) = [b1(x),b2(x)]T$ and $Vi = [vi1, vi2]T$ the seed vector shown as Fig.5. Each component of basis vector can be expressed as follows:

$$b_j(x) = \begin{cases} (1 - f(x,l_{1j}))v_{1j} + f(x,l_{1j})v_{2j} & , \quad if \quad 0 < x < l_{1j} \\ (1 - f(x - l_{1j}, l_{2j}))v_{2j} + f(x - l_{1j}, l_{2j})v_{3j} & , \quad if \quad l_{1j} \le x < N \end{cases} \tag{2}$$

where j is a component of vector, L_1 and L_2 are calculated from step 1 and f(·,·) is defined by

$$f(a, L) = \frac{a + 1}{L + 1}, \quad 0 \le a < L \quad and \quad 0 \le L \le N \tag{3}$$

where N is the width of the error block. Therefore, we can get the basis vectors B_T and B_B by Eq.2.

Step 3: Calculate the Displacement of Each Pixel. We use the basis vectors calculated from step 2 as seed vectors to interpolate the MVs between the corresponding upper and lower basis vectors. As shown in Fig.2, let $M(x,y) = [m_1(x,y), m_2(x,y)]^T$ be the displacement at pixel (x,y). Then the displacement $M(x,y)$ at pixel (x,y) can be calculated as follows:

$$M(x, y) = (1 - g(y)) B_T(x) + g(y)B_B(x) \tag{4}$$

where (x,y) are the coordinates as the origin at the top-left corner of the error block and g(·) is defined by

$$g(b) = \frac{b + 1}{M + 1}, \quad 0 \le b < M \tag{5}$$

where M is the height of the error block.

Step 4: Conceal the Error Block. Let $\hat{I}_e$ be the recovered intensity of pixel (x,y) in current error block and I_r the intensity in reference frame. The recovered pixel (x,y) can be expressed by

$$\hat{I}_e(x, y) = I_r(x + m_1(x, y), y + m_2(x, y)) \tag{6}$$

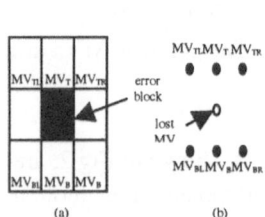

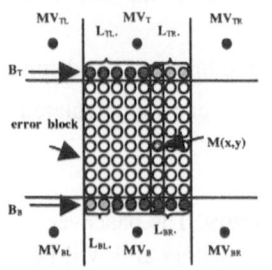

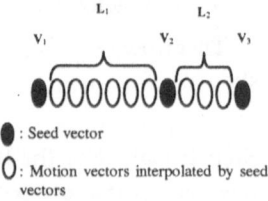

Fig. 1. Position of six neighboring motion vectors used in RMVI

Fig. 2. Illustration of levels, basis vectors and displacements in RMVI

Fig. 3. Relation of level vectors and motion vectors

2.2 Diamond Motion Vector Interpolation

In this subsection, we propose an error concealment method to conceal the error block by finding the motion vector per pixel using the diamond motion vector interpolation (DMVI) algorithm. In DMVI, there are four MVs to be used. The position of the four MVs is shown in Fig.6. In the following, we describe the algorithms in details.

Step 1: Calculate the Estimated MVs. In this step, we will calculate the estimated motion vectors, E_L and E_R shown in Fig.7, by the inverse proportion of distance between neighboring motion vectors. The estimated motion vectors should have the trend to go closer to the direction of similar motion vector. So we can use the relation of distance between neighboring motion vectors to calculate the estimated motion vectors in the error block for the need of interpolation. Let $E = [e_1, e_2]^T$ be the estimated motion vector, $V_i = [v_{i1}, v_{i2}]^T$ the MV shown as Fig.8. Each component of the estimated MV is calculated as follows:

$$
e_j = \begin{cases} \dfrac{d(v_{1j}, v_{2j})v_{3j} + d(v_{2j}, v_{3j})v_{1j}}{d(v_{1j}, v_{2j}) + d(v_{2j}, v_{3j})} & , \quad if \quad d(v_{1j}, v_{2j}) \times d(v_{2j}, v_{3j}) \neq 0 \\ \dfrac{v_{1j} + v_{3j}}{2} & , \quad otherwise \end{cases}
\tag{7}
$$

where j is a component of vector and $d(c1,c2)=|c1-c2|$. We can use the Eq.7 to calculate the estimated MVs, E_L and E_R, respectively. The relative MVs are shown as Fig.9.

Step 2: Calculate the Levels for Interpolation. As shown in Fig.7, we determine the value of levels, L_{LT}, L_{LB}, L_{RT} and L_{RB}, respectively. The levels can be calculated in similar way as defined in Eq.1, but N represents the height of the error block here. The relative MVs are shown as Fig.10.

Step 3: Calculate the Displacement of Each Pixel. As Fig.7 shows, we will calculate the displacement per pixel (x,y). For two estimated motion vectors we get from step 2, two displacements $R_L(y)$ and $R_R(y)$ can be calculated by Eq.2. Similarly, N represents the height of the error block here. The relative MVs are shown as Fig.11.

Finally, we merge the two MVs into one displacement by averaging them. Therefore, the displacement $M(x,y) = (m1(x,y),m2(x,y))T$ at each pixel (x,y) can be expressed by

$$M(x,y) = \frac{R_L(y) + R_r(y)}{2}$$ (8)

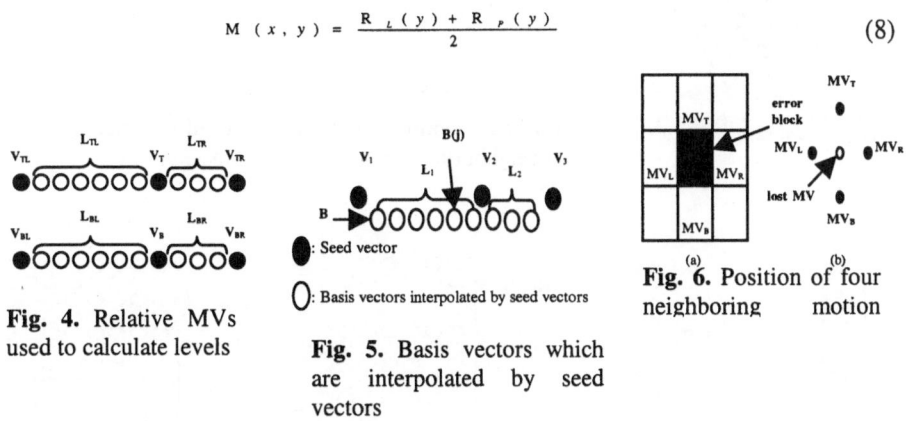

Fig. 4. Relative MVs used to calculate levels

Fig. 5. Basis vectors which are interpolated by seed vectors

Fig. 6. Position of four neighboring motion

Step 4: Conceal the Error Block. The missing pixels of the error block can be concealed by displacement compensation at each pixel (x,y) and can be calculated by Eq.6.

3 Simulation Results

In this section, we will show the simulation results of proposed algorithms. Four QCIF sequences, Football, Flower Garden, Mobile and Foreman are tested. All test sequences are compressed by the H.263 encoder. All startcodes of the GOB header are assumed correctly received by the decoder. The compressed bitstreams are corrupted by different bit error rates (BER) ranging from 0.01% to 0.1%.

We modify the H.263 decoder partially to meet our experimental requirements. No intra frame used except the first frame of a sequence. Error detection is first applied to the decoded bitstream and the position of errors occurred is recorded by the decoder, then the error concealment procedure is turned on after decoding a picture and conceals damaged blocks using error concealment method. In addition, smooth factor, S, is set to 2 in our experiments.

Six temporal error concealment techniques are considered. TR replaces the error block with corresponding block in reference frame. AV averages the neighboring motion vectors of the error block to estimate the lost MV. FBBM is a block-matching based method using the available blocks above and/or below error block to match the best block causing the MAD minimization in reference frame [5]. MFI uses bilinear interpolation to get the motion vector per pixel. RMVI and DMVI are our proposed methods which are described in section 2. The neighboring MV used by error concealment methods is set to 0 if it is not available due to the damaged block or outside the frame.

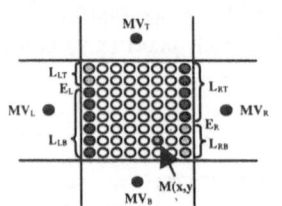

Fig. 7. Illustration of levels, estimated motion vectors and displacements in DMVI

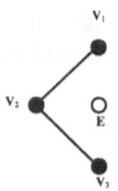

Fig. 8. Relation of the estimated motion vectors and neighboring vectors.

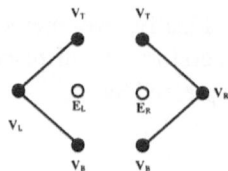

Fig. 9. Relative MVs used to calculate estimated MVs

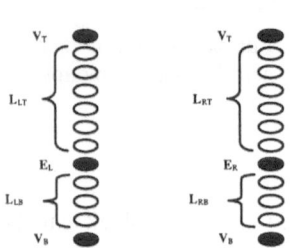

Fig. 10. Relative MVs used to calculate levels

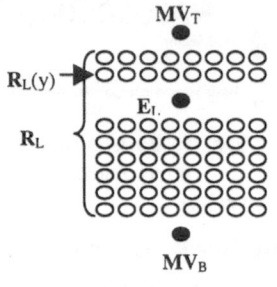

Fig. 11. Two displacements per pixel calculated by estimated MV and neighboring MVs

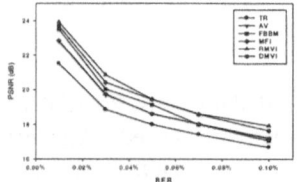

Fig. 12. PSNR comparison of different error concealment methods with different BER for Flower Garden sequence

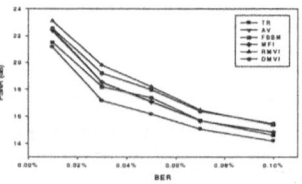

Fig. 13. PSNR comparison of different error concealment methods with different BER for Mobile sequence

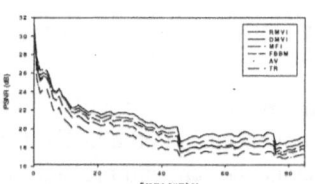

Fig. 14. PSNR comparison of different error concealment methods with BER = 0.03% frame by frame for Flower Garden sequence

Table. 1. Comparison of PSNR (dB) for different sequences and temporal error concealment methods with BER = 0.01%

Sequence / Method	Football	Flower Garden	Mobile	Foreman
No loss	28.51	29.35	28.00	37.24
TR	24.87	21.51	21.16	27.98
AV	25.43	22.82	22.39	29.06
FBBM	25.27	23.53	21.52	29.40
MFI	25.42	22.86	22.47	29.34
RMVI	25.60	23.93	23.12	30.25
DMVI	25.59	23.72	22.56	30.07

Table. 2. Comparison of PSNR (dB) for different sequences and temporal error concealment methods with BER = 0.05%

Sequence / Method	Football	Flower Garden	Mobile	Foreman
No loss	28.51	29.35	28.00	37.24
TR	19.82	18.00	16.18	17.28
AV	20.43	18.62	17.09	19.16
FBBM	20.20	19.14	17.40	22.04
MFI	20.53	18.60	17.09	18.47
RMVI	20.65	19.46	18.21	22.27
DMVI	20.69	19.44	17.98	22.57

The PSNR is used to measure the objective performance of each component (Y, Cb, Cr) for the decoded and concealed sequence. The PSNR of one frame is expressed by

$$PSNR_{avg} = \frac{4 \times PSNR_{Y} + PSNR_{c_b} + PSNR_{c_r}}{6} \quad (9)$$

Table 1. and Table 2. list the PSNR comparison of different error concealment methods and different sequences with BER = 0.01% and BER = 0.05%, respectively. Total PSNR is the average of all PSNRavg calculated from each frame of sequence. Fig.12 and Fig.13 show the PSNR comparison of different error concealment methods with different bit error rates for Flower Garden and Mobile sequences and Fig.14 shows the PSNR comparison of different error concealment methods with BER = 0.03% frame by frame for Flower Garden sequence, respectively. From the results, we can find our proposed methods have better performance than others. Fig.15 and Fig.16 show the subjective comparison of different methods with 0.01% BER for Football and Flower Garden sequences, respectively. We can look at the player of number 41 in Fig.15. The number "41" concealed by our methods can be seen more clearly than other methods. Besides, we can focus on the trunk of the tree in Fig.16. Our proposed methods have better results in recovering the damaged part and acceptable quality by human eyes. That is, the relation among neighboring MVs and pixels in the error block exists.

(a) Decoded image   (b) Error image with   (c) TR   (d) AV
                          error propagation

(e) FBBM   (f) MFI   (g) RMVI   (h) DMVI

Fig. 15. Decoded and concealed frame (Y component) of the 99th frame with BER = 0.01% for Football sequence: (a) the decoded image, (b) error image with error propagation, (c)-(h) the concealed images by TR, AV, FBBM, MFI, and proposed RMVI and DMVI

432   C.-S. Chen et al.

4 Conclusion

Two error concealment methods based on motion vector interpolation are proposed in this paper. For estimating the displacement per pixel, we use the consistency and similarity features of neighboring MVs. When we consider the relation between MVs and pixels in the error block, we can acquire more accurate approximation of the lost MV. Furthermore, these two methods can mitigate the impact of the situation which the interpolated MVs are not directly lying on the path in horizontal and vertical interpolation of the neighboring MVs to the left of, to the right of, above and below the damaged block.

In addition, for further improving the performance of proposed methods, if the lost MVs in the neighborhood of the error block can be estimated by other methods, then use the proposed methods to interpolate the displacement per pixel. This also can improve the quality of the concealed images.

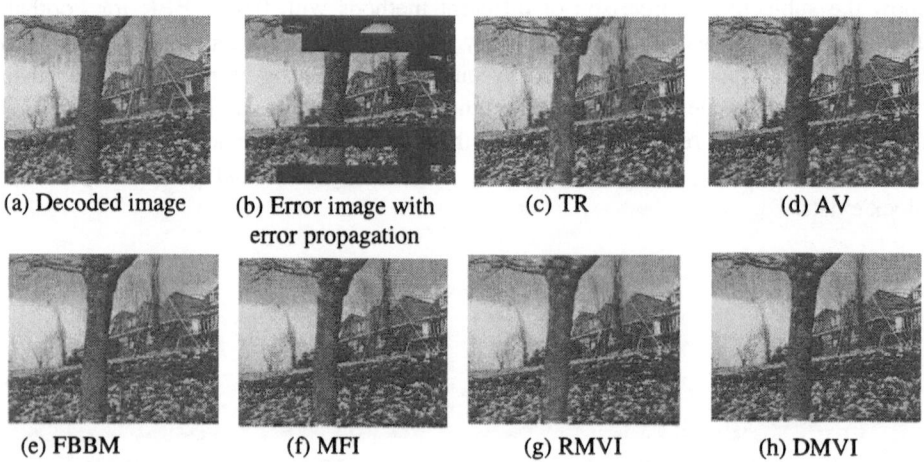

(a) Decoded image   (b) Error image with   (c) TR   (d) AV
                          error propagation

(e) FBBM   (f) MFI   (g) RMVI   (h) DMVI

Fig. 16. Decoded and concealed frame (Y component) of the 16th frame with BER = 0.01% for Flower Garden sequence: (a) the decoded image, (b) error image with error propagation, (c)-(h) the concealed images by TR, AV, FBBM, MFI, and proposed RMVI and DMVI

References

1. D.W. Redmill and N.G. Kingsbury, "The EREC: An error resilient technique for coding variable-length blocks of data," IEEE Trans. Image Processing, vol. 5, pp. 565-574, April 1996.
2. Video coding for low bit-rate communication, recommendation H.263, ITU-T Draft Standard, January 1998.
3. M. E. Al-Mualla, N. Canagarajah and D. R. Bull, "Error concealment using motion field interpolation," in Proc. Int. Conf. Image Processing, vol. 3, pp. 512-516, 1998.

4. M. E. Al-Mualla, C. N. Canagarajah and D. R. Bull, "Motion field interpolation for temporal error concealment," in Proc. IEE-Vision, Image and Signal Processing, vol. 147, no. 5, pp. 445-453, October 2000.

5. S. Tsekeridou, and I. Pitas, "MPEG-2 error concealment based on block-matching principles," IEEE Trans. Circuits and Systems for Video Technology, vol. 10, pp. 646-658, June 2000.

A New Steganalysis Approach Based on Both Complexity Estimate and Statistical Filter[1]

Xiangwei Kong[1], Ting Zhang[1], Xingang You[1], and Deli Yang[2]

[1] Institute of Information, Dalian University of Technology, Dalian, 116023, China
kongxw@dlut.edu.cn; zt_dlut@yahoo.com.cn; xgyou@126.com
[2] Dalian University of Technology, Dalian, 116023, China

Abstract. The development of steganalysis technique becomes more and more important, because steganalysis could be used to detect the fact that terrorists are using steganography to hide their communication from law enforcement. In this paper, we study on the spatial nature difference between cover-images and stego-images, and present an effective approach used for steganography detection. The method we proposed is based on both statistical filter and estimate of bit-plane-complexity, and experimental results by the approach show that it could detect hiding fact more effectively, that is, reveal the facts that there is information embedded in the image.

1 Introduction

Steganography is the art and science to conceal the existence of communication by innocuous cover carriers. That is to say, the essential goal of steganography is to concealing the facts of a hidden message. If not, though the secret content keeps unknown, we still say the steganography system is broken. Many steganography algorithms have been proposed and studied for their imperceptibility, but there has been little attention on the media data properties during hiding information. In fact, the modification of redundant bits may change the media data properties of cover [1]. As a result, statistical analysis can be used to reveal the facts of hiding information. So the ability of minimizing the risk of detection by an adversary is a more important factor to be paid attention to [2]. Steganalysis is the technique of revealing hiding data including breaking covert channels.

Over the past few years, some steganalysis techniques have been proposed in the spatial domain or transform domain [3,4,5,6,7]. Jiri Fridrich developed RQP method to detect LSB embedding in 24-bit color images [3], it works effectively only on high resolution color images stored in an uncompressed format. Later a more reliable and accurate method was proposed through analyzing the capacity for lossless data embedding in the LSBs [4]. Besides, she also introduced a new detection method which is applicable to images originally expressed in the JPEG format [5]. Pfitzmann and

---

[1] This work was supported by National Foundation Research Project (G1999035805)

Y.-C. Chen, L.-W. Chang, and C.-T. Hsu (Eds.): PCM 2002, LNCS 2532, pp. 434–441, 2002.

Westfeld introduced a method based on the statistical analysis of pairs of values exchanged after message embedded, and it provides reliable results for GIF format images when the message placement in it is known (such as sequential) [6]. Niels Provos proposed a statistical test for the JPEG image format. Similar to the one described in [7], the χ^2 -test was used to determine whether the DCT distribution deviate from the norm.

In this paper, we study on the spatial nature difference between cover-images and stego-images, and present an effective approach used for steganography detection. The method we proposed is based on both statistical filter and estimate of bit-plane-complexity.

This paper is organized as follows. In the next section we give an overview of steganalysis. A detailed description of the statistical filter proposed is given in Section 3. The analysis of image complexity is described in Section 4. Experimental results and conclusions are given in Section 5 and in Section 6 respectively.

2 An Overview of Steganalysis

Multimedia can be thought as an excellent container for hidden message, for normally there are some redundant parts that would be allowed the addition of embedded-data while preserving imperceptibility. In this paper, we will focus on images only, which is the most widespread carrier medium.

Hiding information within an image requires modification of redundant bits in the image, in the general, such distortions cannot be sensed by human vision, but it may change media data properties. For example, statistical properties of the cover-image may be changed since information is embedded. As a result, statistical analysis is one kind approach of steganalysis, it may reveal the hiding traces or facts. Perhaps, this is also one of the foundations for steganalysis.

Donovan Artz pointed out that there are two major tools in steganalysis, information theory and statistical analysis [9]. One of the main tools used in information theory is the calculation of entropy.

Figure 1 illustrates the entropies of cover-image and stego-image, and the entropy of a random distributed image is also given for comparison. The steganography software used is Ezstego in Fig. 1(a) and Jsteg-shell in Fig. 1(b). From the figure we may see that image with hidden data has higher entropy than that without, no matter the secret data is embedded in spatial domain or transform domain. It is to say, the uncertainty of image is increased. However, we think this viewpoint would not be exact even be incorrect. Because the pixels would have correlation between each other, how to define it is still unknown, this made the accurate calculation of entropy to be very hard, even impossible [10]. Further more, the calculation of cover entropy in information hiding field should be study more seriously than in traditional information theory application fields.

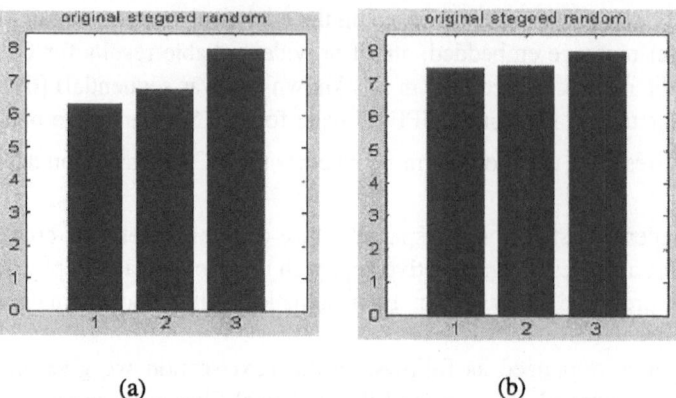

(a)   (b)

Fig. 1. (a) Entropies of cover-image, (b) stego-image

3 The Proposed Statistical Filter

Digital images are categorized as either binary (black-and-white) or multi-valued pictures despite their actual color. For example, we can decompose the intensity of each pixel on a grayscale image into a set of 8 binary-images. In general, we assume 2 or 3 least significant bit-planes in a nature image are completely random and could therefore be replaced [11]. But in fact from Fig.1 we can see, this assumption is somewhat wrong. There is still some usable information in the LSBs, this help us to construct our statistical filter.

Westfeld and Pfitzman present a so called Visual-Attacks method to detect hidden data in palette images [7]. The result depends on the ability of human sight, and it works well only on low complexity images. Inspired by it, we construct a general statistical filter that can be applied to high complexity images in either BMP or GIF format, and the result is drawn by the complexity analysis of filtered image despite of the feeling of human. We present our statistical filter in the following.

(1) For a $M \times N$ image I:

$$I = \{ I_i(x, y), \ 0 \le x < M, 0 \le y < N, \tag{1}$$

$$0 \le i < M \times N, I_i(x, y) \in \{0,1, \dots, 2^L - 1\}\}$$

where L is the bits present for a pixel, as in 256 grey image L=8. We describe the process of extracting the image grey value to construct a palette as:

$$G(I_0, I_1, \dots, I_{n-1}) = D(I(x, y)), n \le 2^L - 1 \tag{2}$$

(2) Then we sort them in an increasing order to get the sort result as:

$$G'(I_0', I_1', \dots, I_{n-1}') = S(G(I_0, I_1, \dots, I_{n-1})) \tag{3}$$

and $0 < G'(I_i') < G'(I_j') < 2^L - 1$.

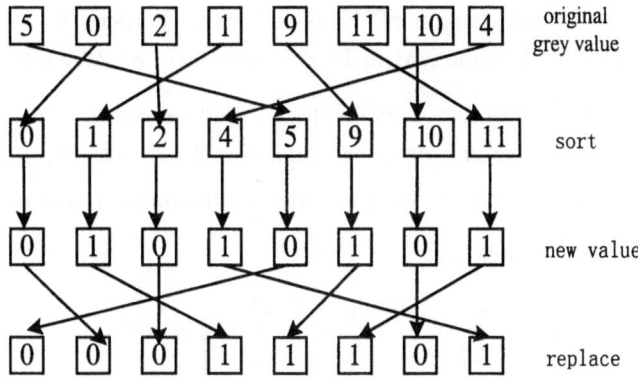

Fig. 2. Illustration of the statistical filter

(3) After that, we give a new value to the sorted palette:

$$G'(I'_j) = \begin{cases} 0, & j \text{ is odd} \\ 1, & j \text{ is even} \end{cases} \tag{4}$$

(4) Replace original image with the new palette to get the filtered result I':

$$I'(x, y) = D^{-1}(G'(I'_0, I'_1, \dots, I'_{n-1})) \tag{5}$$

Since I' is composed of 0 and 1, we can regard it as a binary image. Fig.2 illustrates the process of filtering.

4   Analysis of Complexity

After the image has been filtered, we have got a binary-image I', but how to determine whether there is hidden message in it or not? Unlike the traditional statistical method, the criterion used here is the analysis of image complexity. During vast experiments we found, the filtered results differ greatly between cover-image and stego-image. This inspires us to use it as a criterion.

There is no standard definition of image complexity. Kawaguchi discussed this problem and proposed three types of complexity measures. Here a black-and-white border image complexity was adopted and we modified it to fit our algorithm [12].

The image complexity α is defined by the rate between the length of the black-and-white border and the maximum possible length in the binary image as following:

$$\alpha = \frac{K}{MAX_{B-W}\{I(x, y)\}} \tag{6}$$

where K is the total length of black-and-white border in the image, while $MAX_{B-W}\{ I(x,y) \}$ is the maximally possible length of B-W border. So α has a range from 0 to 1. I' becomes more complex with the increase of α.

To a given image, we calculated the local complexity $\alpha_1, \alpha_2, ..., \alpha_n$ by dividing the image into 16×16 blocks. Then we calculate the mean μ and standard deviation σ^2 for local complexity as

$$\mu = \frac{1}{n}\sum_{i=1}^{n}\alpha_i \quad \sigma^2 = \frac{1}{n^2}\sum_{i=1}^{n}(\alpha_i - \mu)^2 \tag{7}$$

where n is the number of blocks in image.

We can draw the primary decision by comparing μ and σ^2 to the chosen experimental thresholds respectively.

$$r_\mu = \begin{cases} 0 , & \mu < \mu_0 \\ 1 , & \mu \geq \mu_0 \end{cases} \quad r_{\sigma^2} = \begin{cases} 0 , & \sigma^2 \geq \sigma_0^2 \\ 1 , & \sigma^2 < \sigma_0^2 \end{cases} \tag{8}$$

where 0 stands for that there is a hidden message in the image, and 1 means that the image seems to be unmodified.

At last, we get the final result as

$$p = sign\,(\beta_1 \cdot r_\mu + \beta_2 \cdot r_{\sigma^2} - 0.5) \tag{9}$$

where β_i $(i = 1, 2)$ is an experimental factor. We can draw the final conclusion by the value of p, if $p = 1$ then the image is unmodified and if $p = -1$ we can say that the image contains a hidden message in it.

5   Experimental Results

To evaluate the proposed method, we have done a large number of experiments. The testing 80 images are randomly chosen from an image database which contains 300 color scanned images. They are converted into grayscale and down sampled to 300×300 pixels. We call them cover-images.

With the 80 cover-images, we do the steganography process with a steganography tool named Stash-It v1.1 [13]. The message embedded is a piece of text with five to ten percent of the cover-image size, after that we can get 80 stego-images.

Fig. 3(a)-(d) illustrate the proceeding of our algorithm. Cover-image and stego-image are shown in Fig. 3(a) and Fig. 3(b). From which we can see that it is hard to distinguish any visual difference between them. Fig. 3(c) and Fig. 3(d) show the statistical filter result, and the local complexity drawn from them are shown in Fig. 4(a) and Fig. 4(b). From them we can find the difference easily.

Final results are shown in Fig. 5 and Fig. 6, and the beeline in the figure stands for the threshold. Experimental threshold are also listed in table 1. It seems that our method deals with spatial domain steganography technique perfectly well, with the classification accuracy less than 3% false rate. Although we test on BMP format images only, we believe that similar concepts are equally applicable to GIFs since they can lossless convert to each other.

Table 1. Experimental threshold

	μ	σ^2
threshold	0.4271	0.75×10^{-3}

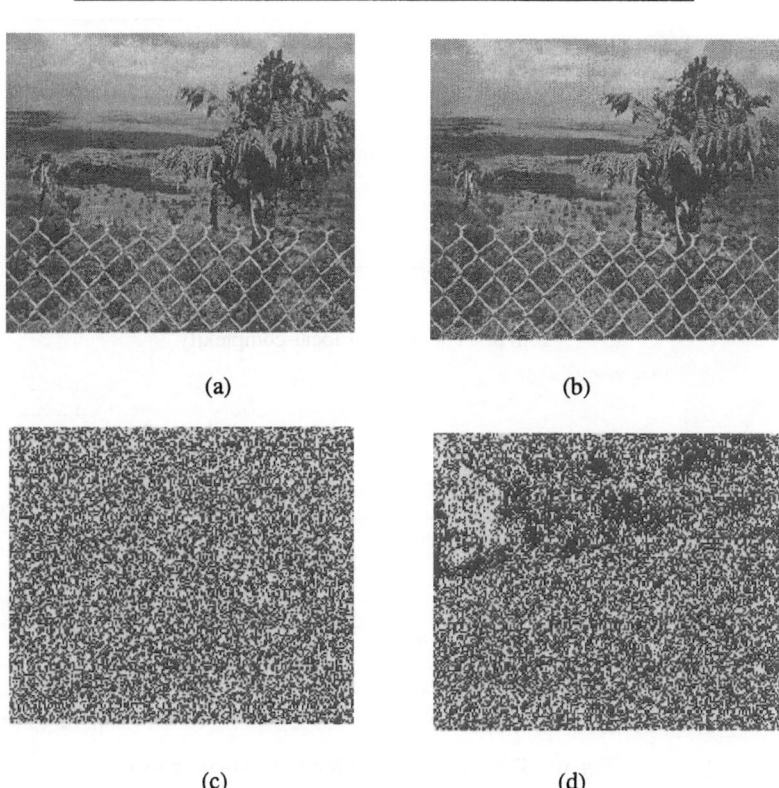

(a)　　　　　　　　　　　(b)

(c)　　　　　　　　　　　(d)

Fig. 3. (a) Cover-image (b) Stego-image (c) Filtered result of cover-image (d) Filtered result of stego-image

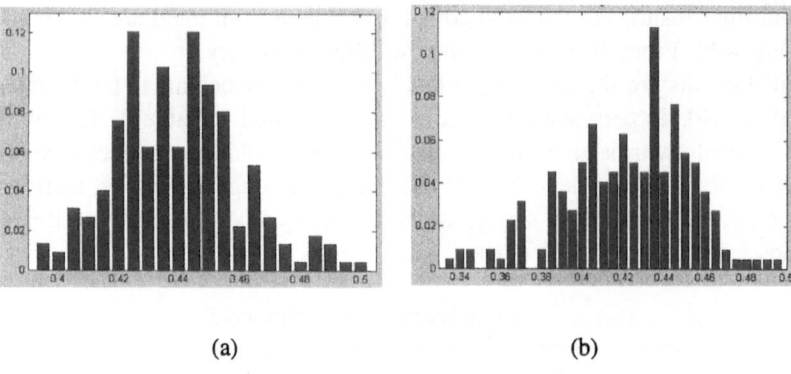

(a)   (b)

Fig. 4. (a) Local-complexity of Fig.3(c),   (b) Local-complexity of Fig.3(d)

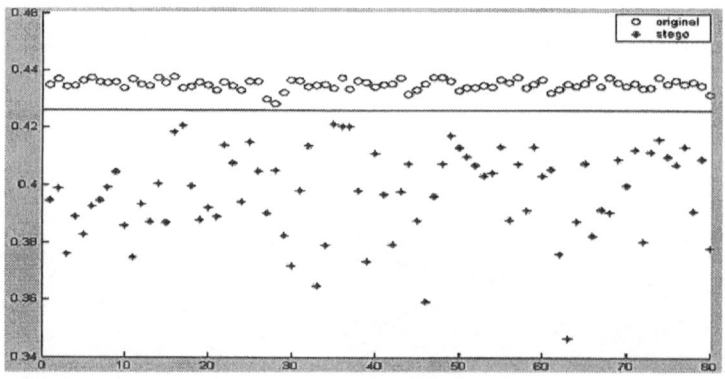

Fig. 5.   The mean of local-complexity

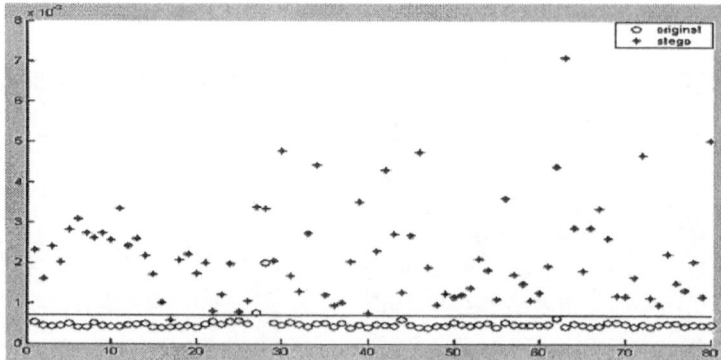

Fig. 6.   The standard deviation of local-complexity

6   Conclusions and Further Works

In this paper, we present a new scheme for image steganalysis. Combining with the statistical filter and complexity estimate, we show that our method works reasonably well on image steganography. In particular, our scheme allows the image to have either high or low complexity. But there is still a disadvantage that we need some images to calculate the threshold. Further more, due to the variety of steganography tools and cover-images, our method is not always effective in all cases. But we also believe that when applying high-order statistical model or changing the filter to transform domain would aid us to develop a more accurate and universal algorithm. This is one of the possible resolving we should focus on in the future.

References

1.   Xingang You, Yunbiao Guo, Linna Zhou: Affections to Image Data Properties in Spatial Domain from Information Hiding, Proceedings of CIHW2000, Beijing, China, 6 (2000) 208-215
2.   R.Chandramouli, Nasir D.Memon: A Distributed Detection Framework for Steganalysis, Proceedings on ACM multimedia Workshops, Los Angeles 10-11 (2000) 123-126
3.   Jiri Fridrich, R. Du, M. Long: Steganalysis of LSB Encoding in Color Image, Proceeding of IEEE International Conf. on Multimedia and Expo, Piscataway, (2000)
4.   Jiri Fridrich, R. Du, M.Goljan, Detecting LSB Steganography in Color and Grey-Scale Images, Magazine of IEEE Multimedia Special Issue on Security,10 (2001) 22-28
5.   Jiri Fridrich, R. Du, M.Goljan: Steganalysis Based on JPEG Compatibility, Special Session on Theoretical Practical Issues in Digital Watermarking and Data Hiding, SPIE Multimedia Systems and Applications, Denver 8 (2001) 20-24
6.   iels. Provos: Defending against Statistical Steganalysis, In 10th USENIX Security Symposium, Washington, DC 8 (2001) 323-335
7.   A.Westfeld, A.Pfitzmann: Attacks on Steganographic Systems,In Proceedings of Information Hiding, Third International Workshop, Dresden, Germany (1999)
8.   Neil F. Johnson, Sushil Jajodia, Steganalysis: The Investigation of Hidden Information, Proceedings of the IEEE Information Technology Conference, Syracuse, New York, USA 9 (1998) 113-116
9.   Donovan Artz, Digital Steganography: Hiding Data within Data, IEEE Internet Computing, 5-6 (2001) 75-80
10.   Lindai Mao, "Analysis of image entropy", Proceedings of CIHW2000, Beijing, China, 6 (2000) 205-208
11.   Yujin Zhang: Image Engineering – image processing and analyzing, Tsinghua University Press, Beijing 10 (1999)
12.   Eiji Kawaguchi, Richard O.Eason: Principle and applications of BPCS- Steganography, The SPIE Conf. On Multimedia Systems and Applications, Boston, Vol.3528, (1998) 464-473
13.   Chris Losinger: Smaller Animals Software, Inc. http://www.smalleranimals.com/stash.htm

Quantization Watermarking Schemes for MPEG-4 General Audio Coding

Shu-chang Liu and Jin-tao Li

Digital Technology Lab, Institute of Computing Technology, CAS,
No.6 Kexueyuan South Road, P.O.Box 2704, 100080, Beijing, PRC
{scliu,jtli}@ict.ac.cn

Abstract. Quantization Watermarking or Quantization Index Modulation is usually used for uniform scalar quantizarion. In this article, the Quantizaion Watermarking extendedly refers to all the watermarking schemes that achieve watermark embedding during quantization process, ignoring the concrete method: scalar or vector quantization. After a brief review of audio watermarking, this paper mainly introduces the watermarking techniques, whose aim is to embed watermark in the quantized MDCT coefficients of AAC or the index value of TwinVQ. Some experimental results show that it works well, for the distortion coming from quantization watermarking is limited within the HAS thresholds, and the embedded watermark is difficult to be removed without significantly audio quality degrading and the key only known by the owner.

1 Introduction

MPEG-4 audio should become the most favorite audio stream over Internet, because of its freedom providing for the network end users. Like as other types of multimedia, copyright protection and multimedia authentication problems must be taken into account during designing its aimed Internet applications. Simultaneously, the flexibility and integration of MPEG-4 audio add the difficulties in realizing copyright protection.

Firstly, MPEG-4 audio integrates many different types of audio coding [1]. As far as we know there is no current watermarking methods can be fit for all kinds of coding tools, to define the most suitable watermarking schemes for each of them according to its characteristics is the basic assignment research on watermarking in MPEG-4 audio. The watermarking scheme may include embedding domain: time or frequency, applied techniques: spread-spectrum or quantization, robustness: robust, semi-fragile or fragile, detection mode: blind or non-blind (public or private), intention: ownership proof, owner identification, device control, transaction tracking, or copy control [2]. This is named *multi-scheme* coexistence problems. Secondly, the same MPEG-4 audio coding stream may be divided into more than one audio object, such as background music and foreground speech. This leads to the multi-ownership identification scenario, since different object could belong to distinct producers. In order to protect all rights and interests of the actors, say, composer, artist, content provider and sub

Y.-C. Chen, L.-W. Chang, and C.-T. Hsu (Eds.): PCM 2002, LNCS 2532, pp. 442-450, 2002.

scriber, one possible solution is to embed different watermarks on the different position or domain during specific coding stage. Here, we called this *multi-watermark* coexistence issues. The following question of *multi-scheme* and *multi-watermark* is mutual conflict between distinct watermarking methods. For instance quantization watermarking is useful information for some applications like as copy control, but it is indeed an incidental distortion in the viewpoint of time- and/or transform-domain watermarking used for ownership proof. Based on Intellectual Property Management and Protection, a framework should be defined to control the whole multi-watermark embedding and detection process, to deal with the mutual conflicts, to analyze and stretch the capacity of the multi-watermarking.

From the ideas listed afore, we began our research on copyright protection mechanism of MPEG-4 audio last year. In this paper watermarking schemes applying to general audio (GA) coding tools are briefly reviewed in section 2. Section 3 and 4 mainly focus on the improved quantization watermarking techniques that is implemented during quantization and inverse quantization process of MDCT coefficients. Some experimental results and evaluations are presented in section 5. And the last section gives the summaries and some future works.

2   Watermarking Schemes Applying to GA Copyright Protection

As I.J. Cox pointed out in [2] that electronic watermarking began with embedding an identification code into music for ownership proof in 1954, and the last 10 years digital watermarking also started from LSB (least significant bits) audio watermarking proposed by L.F. Turner. Although fewer watermarkers make a study of audio watermarking, lots of audio watermarking techniques have been put forward.

The earlier techniques work by placing the hiding information in some human perceptually insignificant regions [3]. For example, LSB replaces the least significant bits of randomly selected audio samples with the bits of watermark, phase coding substitutes the phase of an initial audio segments with a reference phase representing the data [4], in [5] the Fourier transform magnitude coefficients over the frequency band from 2.4kHz to 6.4kHz are replaced by the watermark coded spectral components. Other audio watermark working on some non-sensitivity of HAS should be called statistics-based technique, because their watermark embedding and/or detection are based on statistical characteristic of the time-domain samples [6,7] or the Flourier/DCT domain coefficients [8,9].

The explicitly making-based audio watermarking may include: echo hiding [4], frequency masking hiding, temporal & frequency masking hiding [10,11], if HAS masking effects can be classified into temporal, frequency and echo masking. Echo hiding works by introducing multiple echoes, which differ in three parameters: initial amplitude, decay rate and offset to represent binary one and zero respectively. Unlike echo hiding, the latter two masking-based watermarking algorithms exploit temporal and/or frequency masking to add a perceptually shaped pseudorandom sequence (watermark coded signal) to PCM samples or frequency coefficients.

After I.J. Cox introduced the spread spectrum communication theory into watermarking [12], spread-spectrum (SS) techniques are widely applied in multimedia copyright protection. It certainly includes audio watermarking such as [13], which spread each bit w_i of an SS sequence in frequency (a subband of MCLT samples x_k) and in time (T_0 consecutive MCLT frames) simultaneously. The major problem of SS watermarking is synchronization requirement between the frequencies of the pseudorandom sequences embedded in the content and that is used for detection. The methods of resisting synchronization attack include: frame synchronization [14], synchronization code [13], redundancy synchronization [15], and content synchronization [3].

Brian Chen etc and Joachim J. Eggers etc proposed Quantization Watermarking parallelly, one concentrates more on Quantization Index Modulation [16,17], and the other more on Dithered Quantization [18,19]. In other words, the former utilizes multiply quantizers to quantize the host signal, each quantizer with its associated index. Embedding is realized by modulating the quantilizers' associated index to make the quantilized value be fallen in the corresponding set. The latter adds a dither signal to cover signal before quantization, consequently the watermarking information is embedded in the quantization noise. The hypotheses test or correlation calculations can accomplish watermark detection. A scheme similar to QIM called Parity Modulation [20] was described in M.Ramkumar's PhD Thesis. Mean Quantization-based Fragile Watermarking proposed by Gwo-Jong Yu, Chun-Shien Lu etc [21] belongs to the Dithered Quantization. In fact, quantization-watermarking techniques mentioned afore all make full use the quanization noise hole between distortion perceptual threshold and compression techniques to hiding information in the quantized values, only viewing it from different points. If the extended meaning of Quantization Watermarking refers to all watermarking techniques which embed information bits in quantized value (index) or quantization noise during quantization process, then some watermarking techniques which combine watermark embedding with audio stream encoding process and watermark detection with decoding process can be viewed as Quantization Watermarking. Lintian Qiao etc in [22] introduced a method hiding information in the modulated scalefactors. Jack Lacy etc gave more general description about this method in paper [14]. In another scheme, watermark embedding is performed during vector quantization [23]. It works by changing the number of candidates used for preselection in the search procedure or changing weighting factor used for distortion measure of the conjugate vector quantization. One disadvantage of these algorithms is that they are not standard Quantization Watermarking schemes, and another is private detection.

3   AAC Quantization Watermarking

3.1   AAC Quantization of MDCT Coefficients

AAC Quantization module is divided into three levels: frame loop, rate loop, and distortion loop [1]. The quantizied data *quant*[*i*] are calculated as follows:

$$quant[i] = \mathrm{floor}\left(\left(\frac{\mathrm{fabs}(spectrum[i])}{quantFac[sb]}\right)^{3/4} + M\right) \tag{1}$$

Where i is the index of MDCT coefficients, sb is the index of scalefactor bands, and M is defined to 0.4054, the quantizer step size $quantFac[sb]$ follows:

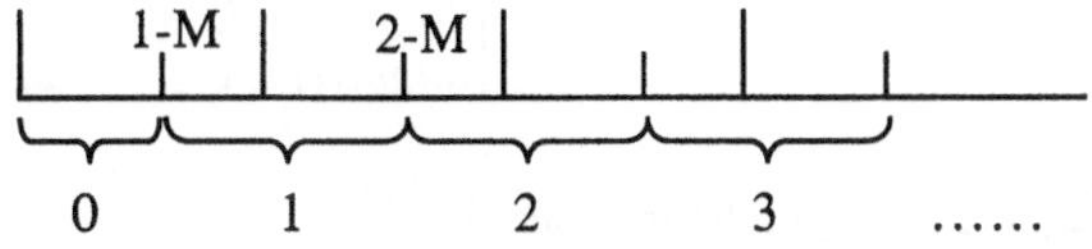

Fig. 1. AAC quantized intervals

$$quantFac[sb] = \mathrm{pow}\left(2,\ scalefactor[sb]/4\right)$$

3.2 Modulation (Embedding) Functions

There are two modulation functions to modulate the parity of $quant[i]$.

$$M(quant[i], w) = \begin{cases} \mathrm{re}(quant[i]) & \begin{array}{l} \mathrm{pa}(quant[i])=\text{even and } w=0 \\ \mathrm{pa}(quant[i])=\text{odd and } w=1 \end{array} \\ \mathrm{disregard} & quant[i]=0 \text{ or } quant[i]=1 \\ \mathrm{ch}(quant[i]) & \begin{array}{l} \mathrm{pa}(quant[i])=\text{even and } w=1 \\ \mathrm{pa}(quant[i])=\text{odd and } w=0 \end{array} \end{cases} \tag{2}$$

$$M(p, quant[i], w) = \begin{cases} \mathrm{re}(quant[i]) & \begin{array}{l} \mathrm{pa}(quant[i])=\mathrm{pa}(p) \text{ and } w=0 \\ \mathrm{pa}(quant[i])\neq\mathrm{pa}(p) \text{ and } w=1 \end{array} \\ \mathrm{disregard} & quant[i]=0 \text{ or } quant[i]=1 \\ \mathrm{ch}(quant[i]) & \begin{array}{l} \mathrm{pa}(quant[i])=\mathrm{pa}(p) \text{ and } w=1 \\ \mathrm{pa}(quant[i])\neq\mathrm{pa}(p) \text{ and } w=0 \end{array} \end{cases} \tag{3}$$

Where w is the current watermark bit, $\mathrm{ch}(quant[i])$ and $\mathrm{re}(quant[i])$ separately represents changing and retaining the parity of $quant[i]$, and $\mathrm{pa}(quant[i])$ returns the parity of $quant[i]$. Function (2) forces the non-zero and non-one $quant[i]$ to be an even integer when $w=0$, and forces it to be odd when $w=1$. Function (3) has one more parameter p, which means the last previous modulated $quant[]$, This function forces the parity of the non-zero and non-one $quant[i]$ to be the same one of p when $w=0$, while forces it to be the opposite one when $w=1$.

3.3 Effects of ch(*quant[i]*)

The operations of ch(*quant[i]*) follows (4), and its meaning is illustrated in Figure 2

$$ch(quant[i]) = \begin{cases} quant[i] + 1 & quant[i] = 2 \\ quant[i] - 1 & qf - quant[i] < 0 \\ quant[i] + 1 & qf - quant[i] \geq 0 \end{cases} \qquad (4)$$

Where $qf = \left(\dfrac{fabs(spectrum[i])}{quantFac[sb]} \right)^{3/4}$ is

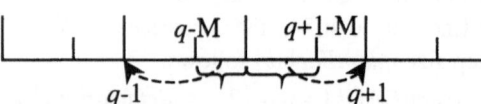

the actual quantized float data. When qf falls in interval $(q\text{-}M, q)$, let *quant[i]* be q-1, and let it be q+1 while qf falls in $[q, q+M]$, where q is the original quantized data (integer).

Fig. 2. Meanings of ch(*quant[i]*)

Another explanation about effects of ch(*quant[i]*) comes from Dither Quantization [22]. Let r be the quantization errors of (fabs(*spectrum[i]*))^(3/4).

$$r = \left(fabs(spectrum[i]) \right)^{3/4} - q * \left(quantFac[sb] \right)^{3/4} = (qf - q) * (quantFac[sb])^{3/4} \qquad (5)$$

Then u that denotes the dither signal adding to fabs(*spectum[i]*)^(3/4) follows:

$$u = \begin{cases} -r & re(quant[i]) \\ -r + (quantFac[sb])^{3/4} & quant[i] + 1 \\ -r - (quantFac[sb])^{3/4} & quant[i] - 1 \end{cases} \qquad (6)$$

In fact u can be others as long as the quantized data conforms to (2) & (3).

3.4 Demodulation (Detection) Functions

According to modulation process, the demodulation functions (7) & (8) can be used for watermark detection, when the original audio is impossible to be got. The watermark detection can also be achieved by hypotheses test or correlation computation, which usually need original cover signal.

$$D(quant[i]) = \begin{cases} disregard & quant[i] = 0 \text{ or } quant[i] = 1 \\ w = 1 & pa(quant[i]) = odd \\ w = 0 & pa(quant[i]) = even \end{cases} \qquad (7)$$

$$D(p, quant[i]) = \begin{cases} disregard & quant[i] = 0 \text{ or } quant[i] = 1 \\ w = 1 & pa(quant[i]) \neq pa(p) \\ w = 0 & pa(quant[i]) = pa(p) \end{cases} \qquad (8)$$

4 Vector Quantization Watermarking

4.1 Vector Quantaization of TwinVQ

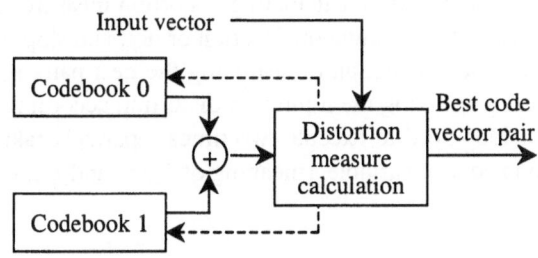

Fig. 3. Conjugate-structure vector quantization scheme

TwinVQ [24] is suitable for low-bit-rate general audio coding. It uses a conjugate-structure vector quantization scheme, which includes separate pre- and main-selection procedures. In pre-selection, a fixed number of candidate code vectors are chosen form codebook, and the best pair giving the minimum distortion measure is chosen during main-selection. Like as embedding watermark bit in *quant[i]*, we can modulate the index pair to hide data.

4.2 Modulation (Embedding) and Demodulation (Detection) Functions

There are also two modulation functions executed during main-selection procedure in this vector quantization-watermarking scheme. Where *sum* = *index1* + *index2*, is the sum of code vector index of codebook1 (*index1*) and the one of codebook2 (*index2*).

$$\mathrm{M}(sum, w) = \begin{cases} \mathrm{pa}(sum) = \text{even} & w = 0 \\ \mathrm{pa}(sum) = \text{odd} & w = 1 \end{cases} \tag{9}$$

$$\mathrm{M}(p, sum, w) = \begin{cases} \mathrm{pa}(sum) = \text{even} & \begin{array}{l} \mathrm{pa}(p) = \text{even and } w = 0 \\ \mathrm{pa}(p) = \text{odd and } w = 1 \end{array} \\ \\ \mathrm{pa}(sum) = \text{odd} & \begin{array}{l} \mathrm{pa}(p) = \text{odd and } w = 0 \\ \mathrm{pa}(p) = \text{even and } w = 1 \end{array} \end{cases} \tag{10}$$

The demodulation functions list below:

$$\mathrm{D}(sum) = \begin{cases} w = 0 & \mathrm{pa}(sum) = even \\ w = 1 & \mathrm{pa}(sum) = odd \end{cases} \tag{11}$$

$$\mathrm{D}(p, sum) = \begin{cases} w = 1 & \mathrm{pa}(sum) \neq \mathrm{pa}(p) \\ w = 0 & \mathrm{pa}(sum) = \mathrm{pa}(p) \end{cases} \tag{12}$$

4.3 Effects of Modulation

Virtually, the Modulation functions change the search process in the main-selection procedure. Before calculating distortion measure [24], judge whether the variable *sum* satisfies the modulation function or not, and skip if it does not meet the condition. The real implementation of searching the best pairs is a dual-for loop. In order to get the best pair giving the minimum distortion according with the *sum* modulation, the dual-for loop need to execute two times separately taking *i_can* and *j_can* as the outer-for loop control variable. (meaning of *i_can* and *j_can* can be refered to [1]).

5 Experiments and Evaluations

The experimental environments was built based on VM of MPEG-4 audio: m4985 and w3309. The randomly selected tested audio clips list in Table 1.

Table 1. Basic information of tested audio clips

Clip Name	Type	Sample rate& Bitrate	File Size (kb)
AR001.AIF	Mono	22050, 176kbps	151
spacemusic.au	Mono	8000, 64kbps	47
San01.WAV	Mono	44100,353kbps	11,653
xuqu.wav	Mono	44100,706kbps	2,960

We modified the AAC quantization and TwinVQ vector quantization module to implement the watermarking scheme discussed above. The results about watermarking capacity of AAC_SYS mode and TVQ_SYS mode were tested in different encoding bitrate, as shown in Table 2 & Table 3. (The frame size is 1024)

Table 2. Capacity of AAC quantization watermarking

Bitrate(kb/s)	24	32	48	96	128
Capacity(b/frame)	11-15	21-35	28-58	60-110	250-370

Table 3. Capacity of TwinVQ quantization watermarking

Core Bitrate	8kps	16kps	24kps	32kps
AR001.AIF	25	55	87	117
spacemusic.au	79	165	250	335
San01.WAV	9	25	40	55
xuqu.wav	9	25	40	55

The advantages of the proposed watermarking scheme are blind-detection, more secure than pure Parity Modulation, and difficult to remove without significantly audio quality degrading. Inevitably they are fragile watermark, but this leads to its fitness for multimedia authentication (integrity assurance), under certain bit error rate of network transmissions, say 10^{-4}.

6 Conclusions

In this paper, the major problems of MPEG-4 audio copyright protection were firstly discussed, and then presented an AAC QW scheme combined with AAC quantization module and a vector QW algorithm implemented in the main-selection procedure of TwinVQ in detail. This is only the beginning of our project; there are a lot of works to do in future, such as more robust QW scheme, IPMP-integrated copyright protection framework, and capacity analysis tools for multi-watermark and multi-scheme.

References

1. ISO/IEC 14496-3. Information Technology–Coding of Audio-visual Objects–Part 3: Audio
2. I.J. Cox, M.L. Miller: The First 50 Years of Electronic Watermarking. Journal of applied Signal Processing. 2 (2002) 126-132
3. C.P. Wu, P.C. Su and C.J. Kuo: Robust and Efficient Digital Audio Watermarking Using Audio Content Analysis. Proceedings of SPIE Vol. 3971. (2000) 382-392
4. W. Bender, D. Gruhl, N. Morimoto and A. Lu: Techniques for Data Hiding. IBM Systems Journal. VOL 35, NOS 3&4 (1996) 313-336
5. J.F. Tilki and A.A. Beex: Encoding a Hidden Digital Signature onto an Audio Signal Using Psychoacoustic Masking. The 7th International Conference on Signal Processing Application & Technology, Boston MA. (1996) 476-480
6. P. Bassia and I. Pitas: Robust Audio Watermarking in the Time Domain. Proceedings of Eusipco-98. (1998) 25–28
7. P. Bassia, I. Pitas and N. Nikolaidis: Robust Audio Watermarking in the Time Domain. IEEE Transactions on multimedia. Vol.3 No.2 (2001) 232-241
8. M. Arnold: Audio Watermarking: Features, Applications and Algorithms. IEEE International Conference on Multimedia and Expo 2000, New York, NY, USA, (2000)
9. In-K. Yeo and H. J. Kim: Modified PatchWork Algorithm: a novel Audio Watermarking Scheme. Proc. of ITCC'01, Las Vegas, NV, (2001)
10. L. Boney, A.H. Tewfik and K.N. Hamdy: Digital Watermarks for Audio Signals. IEEE International Conference on Multimedia Computing and Systems. (1996) 473-480
11. M.D. Swanson, B. Zhu, A.H. Tewfik and L. Boney: Robust Audio Watermarking using Perceptual Masking. Signal Processing. Vol. 66 No.3, (1998) 337-355
12. I.J. Cox, J. Kilian, T. Leighton and T. Shamoon: Secure Spread Spectrum Watermarking for Multimedia. IEEE Transactions on Image Proceedings. Vol.6, No.12, (1997) 1673-1687

13. D. Kirovski and H.S. Malvar: Robust Covert Communication over a Public Audio Channel Using Spread Spectrum. IH Workshop, (2001)
14. J. Lacy, S.R. Quackenbush, A. Reib-man, D. shur, and J. Snyder: On Combining Watermarking with Perceptual Coding. In ICASSP, Vol.6 (1998) 3725-3728
15. R. Tachibana, S. Shimizu, T. Nakamura and S. Kobayashi: An audio watermarking method robust against time- and frequency-fluctuation. Security and watermarking of Multimedia Content, Proceedings of SPIE, Vol.4314. (2001) 104-115
16. B. Chen: Design and Analysis of Digital Watermarking, Information Embedding and Data Hiding System. PhD Thesis, MIT (2000)
17. B. Chen, G.W. Wornell: Quantization Index Modulation: A Class of Provably Good Methods for Digital Watermarking and Information Embedding. IEEE Transaction on Information Theory. Vol.47, No.4 (2001) 1423-1443
18. J.J. Eggers and B. Grid: Quantizaion Watermarking. Proceedings of SPIE Vol. 3971 (2000)
19. J.J. Eggers and B. Girod: Quantization Effects on Digital Watermarks. Signal Processing. Vol.81, No.2 (2000) 239-263
20. M.Ramkumar: Data hiding in Multimedia: Theory and Application. PhD thesis, New Jersey Institute of Technology (NJIT) (2000)
21. G.J. Yu, C.S. Lu, and H.M. Liao: Mean Quantization-based Fragile Watermarking for Image Authentication. Optical Engineering, Vol.40, No.7 (2001) 1396-1408
22. L.T. Qiao and K. Nahrstedt: Non-Invertible Watermarking Methods for MPEG Audio. Research report of CS Department, UIUC, UIUCDCS-R-98-2069. (1998)
23. T. Moriya, Y. Takashima, T. Nakamura and N. Iwakami: Digital Watermarking Schemes Based on Vector Quantization. IEEE Workshop on Speech Coding for Telecomm.. (1997)
24. N. Iwakami, T. Moriya, A. Jin, T. Mori and K. Chikira: Fast Encoding Algorithms for MPEG-4 TwinVQ Audio Tool. ICASSP2001. (2001)

Asymptotic Analyses of Visual Distortions: A New Approach to Defining Transparency*

Nicholas Tran[1] and Lianju Wang[2]

[1] Department of Mathematics & Computer Science,
Santa Clara University, Santa Clara, CA 95053, ntran@math.scu.edu
[2] Building 21 3D11, Lucent Technologies, 1600 Osgood Street,
North Andover, MA 01845, lwang31@lucent.com

Abstract. We define transparent watermarking algorithms as those whose expected distortions of input images are at most $c \log l$, as measured under the average absolute difference metric (l is the range of possible pixel values, and c is a positive constant.) Our definition is based on asymptotic analyses of the expected distortions caused by two prototypical watermarking methods generally considered as transparent: the Patchwork and NEC methods. We also propose some shift-resistant variants of these distortion metrics that incorporate alignment techniques used in DNA string comparisons. Experiments show that these new distortion metrics yield much smaller values when a small number of columns are deleted.

1 Introduction

Two most important criteria in evaluating digital image watermarking systems are: i) *transparency*: how perceptible are the embedded watermarks to the human visual system ?; and ii) *robustness (security)*: how resistant are the embedded watermarks to normal processing and malicious attacks ? Thanks to a large body of experimental research pointing to a multichannel model of human vision (e.g. [4]), the transparency requirement has been solved satisfactorily; modern image watermarking systems can produce watermarks that are acceptably transparent to the human eye. In contrast, most if not all current digital watermarking systems are susceptible to one of three types of robustness attacks, seeking to either damage the embedded watermark, prevent the watermark from being detected, or neutralize the power of the watermark as proof of ownership [3,8].

1.1 A Theory of Watermarking

We seek a formal framework that allows discussions about the transparency and robustness of digital watermarking systems in a precise and *asymptotic* manner[1].

---

* This research is partially supported by the US Air Force Office of Scientific Research under Grant F49620-00-1-03 and matching support from the Kansas Technology Enterprise Corporation.

[1] Our proposal is patterned after historical developments in the field of analysis of algorithms. In the early days, the performance of an algorithm was often reported

Y.-C. Chen, L.-W. Chang, and C.-T. Hsu (Eds.): PCM 2002, LNCS 2532, pp. 451–459, 2002.
© Springer-Verlag Berlin Heidelberg 2002

One approach to obtaining such a subclass is to start with a computational model of the human retina and then define transparent algorithms as those whose inputs and outputs are indistinguishable to the retina model [10]. In this paper we consider a more direct approach, which begins with a definition of transparency based on some distortion metric and then defines transparent algorithms as those whose inputs and outputs are separated by distances less than a certain threshold. Two issues arise immediately: which distortion metric and which threshold function should we use in defining transparency? Clearly, the threshold function depends on the choice of distortion metric, which should correspond perceptually to the human visual system. Currently, computationally simple pixel-based metrics such as mean squared error and signal-to-noise ratio are commonly used to measure image distortions, despite the fact that they are not very accurate. More perceptually realistic metrics have been proposed in [9,6], although they can be expensive to compute.

1.2 New Contributions

Our contributions in this paper are two-fold. First, we propose an asymptotic definition of transparent algorithms based on pixel-based distortion metrics. An algorithm f is transparent if the *expected* average absolute difference between its input and output images is at most $c \log l$, where l is the range of pixel values, and c is a fixed positive constant.

Our definition is based on analyses of the *expected* distortions caused by two prototypical watermarking systems: the Patchwork method [1] in the spatial domain, and the NEC method [2] in the frequency domain. Empirical data have shown that these two systems produce acceptably transparent watermarks. Our analyses derive the expected distortions as measured by three distortions metrics: average absolute difference, mean squared error, and normalized mean square error. Images are $X \times Y$ rectangular arrays of pixels, whose values are integers between 0 and $l-1$ inclusive. The results are given in the form of *upper bounds* in the table below (M is the size of the embedded watermark, $E[\|U\|^2]$ is the expected energy of $X \times Y$ images, and δ and α are parameters specific to the Patchwork and NEC methods respectively). Experimental data we obtained closely approximate these upper bounds. It is important to point out that no assumption is made on the distribution of pixel values, and therefore our results hold in the general setting.

Method	E[A]	E[M]	E[N]
Patchwork	$\sqrt{\dfrac{2\delta^2 M}{XY}}$	$\dfrac{2\delta^2 M}{XY}$	$\dfrac{2\delta^2 M}{E[\|U\|^2]}$
NEC	$\sqrt{\dfrac{E[\|U\|^2]}{XY}}\alpha$	$\dfrac{E[\|U\|^2]\alpha^2}{XY}$	α^2

numerically. Gradually, algorithm designers began reporting running times in asymptotic formulae. Besides giving a global picture of an algorithm's behavior, running time functions ultimately led to the formalization of "fast" algorithms as those computable in polynomial time with a Turing machine.

Secondly, we propose new variants of the average absolute difference, mean squared error, and normalized mean squared error distortion metrics. Based on the concept of string alignment developed for DNA matching, these new variants are resistant to column deletion, a simple but effective attack that produces inflated distortion values from the above metrics. To get around this attack, spaces are inserted into two corresponding rows from the two images in order to maximize the number of matched values. In effect, the modified image is realigned with the original *columnwise* before the usual pixel-by-pixel computations are performed.

The rest of this paper is organized as follows. Section 2 provides definitions of the distortion metrics and some properties of the discrete cosine transforms. Sections 3 and 4 present asymptotic analyses of the transparency of the Patchwork and NEC methods respectively. Our definition of transparent algorithms based on the results of these analyses is given in Section 5. Shift-resistant versions of the distortion metrics are introduced in Section 6. Experimental results appear in Section 7. Section 8 concludes with a discussion about our results and future research.

2   Preliminaries

2.1   Distortion Metrics

Let U be an $X \times Y$ gray-scale image. $\|U\|$, the *Frobenius norm* of U, is defined as $\|U\|^2 = \sum_{x=0}^{X-1} \sum_{y=0}^{Y-1} (u(x,y))^2$. Given two gray-scale images of the same dimensions, we are interested in quantifying their similarity. The analyses in this paper focus on the following three distortion metrics:

1. *Average Absolute Difference:* $A(U,U') = \frac{1}{XY} \sum_{x=0}^{X-1} \sum_{y=0}^{Y-1} |u(x,y) - u'(x,y)|$;
2. *Mean Squared Error:* $M(U,U') = \frac{\|U-U'\|^2}{XY}$;
3. *Normalized Mean Squared Error:* $N(U,U') = \frac{\|U-U'\|^2}{\|U\|^2}$.

Lemma 1 (Relationships between the metrics).

$$\sqrt{\frac{M(U,U')}{XY}} \leq A(U,U') \leq \sqrt{M(U,U')}.$$

2.2   The Discrete Cosine Transform

An image U and its image V under the discrete cosine transform (DCT) are related by the equations $V = PUQ$ and $U = P^T V Q^T$, where

$$p(i,j) = \sqrt{\frac{2}{X}} C(i) \cos\left(\frac{(2j+1)i\pi}{2X}\right); \quad q(i,j) = \sqrt{\frac{2}{Y}} C(j) \cos\left(\frac{(2i+1)j\pi}{2Y}\right).$$

Lemma 2 (Properties of DCT).

1. *(Orthogonality)* $P^T P = I$, and $Q^T Q = I$;
2. *(Energy Conservation)* $\|V\|^2 = \|U\|^2$.

3   Distortion Analysis for the Patchwork Method

The Patchwork method [1] makes the assumption that the expected difference in brightness between two randomly selected pixels is zero. To embed a watermark, M pairs of pixels (a_i, b_i) are randomly selected using a secret key and a pseudo-random number generator. (More precisely, each a_i and b_i is a pair of row and column numbers.) The brightness level of pixel a_i is increased by δ, while the brightness level of b_i is lowered by the same amount.

Theorem 1. *The expected distortions over all $X \times Y$ images caused by inserting a watermark of size M using the Patchwork method with parameter δ satisfy*

$$E[A_p(X, Y, M, \delta)] \le \sqrt{\frac{2\delta^2 M}{XY}};$$

$$E[M_p(X, Y, M, \delta)] \le \frac{2\delta^2 M}{XY};$$

$$E[N_p(X, Y, M, \delta)] \le \frac{2\delta^2 M}{E[\|U\|^2]}.$$

Proof. Let S_M (and T_M) be the sum of M independent Bernoulli random variables each having probability $p = 1/XY$ of assuming the value 1. It is well known that $E[S_M] = Mp$, $Var[S_M] = Mp(1-p)$, and $E[S_M^2] = Mp(Mp+1-p)$. The expected mean squared error for a fixed image U is given by

$$E[M_p(U, M, \delta)] = E[\frac{1}{XY} \sum_{x=0}^{X-1} \sum_{y=0}^{Y-1} \delta^2 (S_M - T_M)^2] = \frac{2\delta^2 M}{XY}(1 - \frac{1}{XY}) \le \frac{2\delta^2 M}{XY}.$$

By Lemma 1, we have $E[A_p(U, M, \delta)] \le \sqrt{\frac{2\delta^2 M}{XY}}$. Since these expressions do not depend on U, they also bound the expected values of M and A over all $X \times Y$ images. Similarly,

$$E[N_p(U, M, \delta)] = \frac{XY}{\|U\|^2} E[M_p(U, M, \delta)] \le \frac{XY}{\|U\|^2} \frac{2\delta^2 M}{XY} = \frac{2\delta^2 M}{\|U\|^2}.$$

We use the Weak Law of Large Numbers to approximate $E[\frac{1}{\|U\|^2}]$:

$$E[N_p(X, Y, M, \delta)] \le E[\frac{2\delta^2 M}{\|U\|^2}] = 2\delta^2 M \cdot E[\frac{1}{\|U\|^2}] \approx \frac{2\delta^2 M}{E[\|U\|^2]}.$$

$\square$

4   Distortion Analysis for the NEC Method

The NEC method spreads a watermark among the most significant DCT coefficients of the input image. The embedding process involves the following steps:

1. generate the watermark W, which consists of M real numbers $w_1, w_2, \cdots, w_M$ using a pseudo-random number generator having the normal distribution $N(0, 1)$;
2. compute the DCT coefficient matrix $V = (v(i, j))$ of a gray-scale image $U = (u(m, n))$ to be watermarked;
3. insert the watermark into the M most significant AC coefficients $v_1, \ldots, v_M$:

$$v_i' = (1 + \alpha w_k)v_i,$$

   where α is a parameter to control the strength of the watermark;
4. calculate the watermarked image U' using the inverse DCT on the modified DCT coefficients V'.

Theorem 2. *The expected distortions over all $X \times Y$ images caused by inserting a watermark of size M using the NEC method with parameter α satisfy*

$$E[A_n(X, Y, M, \alpha)] \leq \alpha \sqrt{\frac{E[\|U\|^2]}{XY}}$$

$$E[M_n(X, Y, M, \alpha)] \leq \frac{\alpha^2 E[\|U\|^2]}{XY}$$

$$E[N_n(X, Y, M, \alpha)] \leq \alpha^2.$$

Proof. By the Orthogonality property of DCT (Lemma 2), the expected mean squared error for a fixed image U is given by

$$M_n(U, M, \alpha) = \frac{1}{XY} \sum_{x=0}^{X-1} \sum_{y=0}^{Y-1} (v(x, y) - v'(x, y))^2 = \frac{1}{XY} \sum_{i=1}^{M} (\alpha w_i v_i)^2.$$

Since each w_i is normally distributed with mean 0 and variance 1, $E[w_i^2] = 1$. Thus

$$E[M_n(U, M, \alpha)] = \frac{1}{XY} \sum_{i=1}^{M} \alpha^2 v_i^2 E[w_i^2] \leq \frac{\alpha^2}{XY} \sum_{x=0}^{X-1} \sum_{y=0}^{Y-1} v^2(x, y) = \frac{\alpha^2}{XY} \|U\|_F^2.$$

The last equality follows from the Energy Conservation property of DCT. The bound on $E[A_n(U, M, \alpha)]$ follows immediately from Lemma 1. Similarly,

$$E[N_n(U, M\alpha)] = \frac{XY}{\|U\|^2} E[M_N(U, M, \alpha)] \leq \frac{XY}{\|U\|^2} \frac{\alpha^2 \|U\|^2}{XY} = \alpha^2.$$

Taking the expected values of M_n, A_n, and N_n over all $X \times Y$ images, we have the theorem.   □

5   A Definition of Transparent Algorithms

Intuitively, the average change in pixel values made by a transparent watermark should be a slow-growing function in terms of l, the range of pixel values, such as $\log l$. It turns out that our analyses and experimental data support the logarithmic function as a reasonable definition of transparency. First, the following lemma is straightforward to show:

Lemma 3. $E[\|U\|^2] \approx l^2/3$ *for* $X \times Y$ *gray-level images* U *whose pixels are independently distributed with either the uniform or Gaussian distribution.*

Applying this lemma to the formula for $E[A_n]$ in Section 4, and setting α to 0.1 as suggested in [2], we have $E[A_n] = (0.1)(256)/\sqrt{3} = 14.8$. Experimental data reported in Table 2 on actual values of A_n range between $9.5 - 13.5$. Similarly, the expected average absolute value for the Patchwork method is $\delta\sqrt{\frac{2M}{XY}}$. Experiments performed on the mandrill.pgm image (see Section 7) with the watermark size $M = XY$ show that the distortion becomes perceptible for $\delta \geq 10$. Thus $A_p \leq \sqrt{(10\sqrt{2})} = 14.1$.

Both theoretical and experimental values for the expected distortions caused by the Patchwork and NEC methods are close to $\log l = \log 256 = 8$. We take this as supporting evidence for the following definition of transparent algorithms:

Definition 1. *An algorithm* f *is* transparent *if its expected distortion of input images as measured by the average absolute difference metric is at most* $c \log l$, *where* l *is the range of pixel values, and* c *is a fixed positive constant.*

6   Shift-Resistant Metrics

Removing a few columns (or rows) from a watermarked image and adding the same number of random columns (or rows) at the end is an effective method of frustrating detection of the watermark. In this section we propose shift-resistant variants of some of the pixel-based distortion metrics. To compute the new metrics, corresponding *rows* of the two images are "aligned" to minimize the number of mismatched *columns*. The distortions based on pixel differences are then computed as before. Discussions on string alignment appear frequently in computational biology literature (e.g. [7]). Our modified definitions of the A, M, and N distortion metrics are given in terms of the best alignment scores between corresponding rows of the two images.

Definition 2. *Let* U_r *and* U_r' *be corresponding rows of pixels of two* $X \times Y$ *images. Define*

- $D_1(U_r, U_r')$ = *the optimal alignment score between* U_r *and* U_r' *where* $score(v_1, v_2) = -|v_1 - v_2|$ *and* $g = -\frac{2l(l+2)}{3(l+1)}$;
- $D_2(U_r, U_r')$ = *the optimal alignment score between* U_r *and* U_r' *where* $score(v_1, v_2) = -(v_1 - v_2)^2$ *and* $g = -\frac{l(l+2)}{3}$;

(Gap values are chosen to be twice the expected difference between two random pixel values under the uniform distribution for the A and M metrics.)

Definition 3. *Let* U *and* U' *be two* $X \times Y$ *images, whose pixel values are between* 0 *and* $l - 1$. *The definition of the A, M, and N metrics are modified as follows:*

- $A'(U, U') = \frac{1}{XY} \sum_{x=0}^{X-1} -D_1(U_x, U_x')$;
- $M'(U, U') = \frac{1}{XY} \sum_{x=0}^{X-1} -D_2(U_x, U_x')$;
- $N'(U, U') = \frac{XY M'(U, U')}{\sum_{x=0}^{X-1} \sum_{y=0}^{Y-1} (U(x,y))^2}$.

Fig. 1. Test images: mandrill, peppers, bowl, and waterfall

7   Experimental Results

We performed various watermarking processes on a small set of images, measured the average distortions using the A, M, and N metrics and compared them against our derived results. The gray-level images `mandrill.pgm` (256×256), `peppers.pgm` (256×256), `bowl.pgm` (178×178), and `waterfall.pgm` (178×178) appear in Figure 1. All computations were done using Octave and the JPEGtool package [5].

In our first test, we watermarked `mandrill.pgm` 1000 times using the Patchwork method with different values for δ and $M = \alpha XY$. The average actual distortions are reported in Table 1 and can be seen to be in close agreement with those predicted by Theorem 1.

Table 1. Distortions for the Patchwork algorithm with different α and δ.

α	δ	M	Th.1	A	Th.1	N	Th.1
0.3	8	38.4	38.4	3.7	4.8	2.1E-3	1.8E-3
0.1	1	0.20	0.2	0.2	0.2	1.1E-5	9.2E-6
0.1	5	5.0	5.0	0.9	1.0	2.7E-4	2.3E-4
0.1	10	20.0	20.0	1.8	2.0	1.1E-3	9.2E-4
0.1	20	80.0	80.0	3.6	4.0	4.3E-3	3.7E-3
0.1	40	315.7	320.0	7.3	8.0	1.7E-2	1.5E-2

In our second test, we ran the NEC algorithm 1000 times on the test images using watermark sizes $M = 100$, 1000, and 10,000 and computed the average distortion values. The results are reported in Table 2. Again, they can be seen to agree closely with the theoretical values predicted by Theorem 2.

Table 2. Averages of actual distortions caused by the NEC method.

	mandrill	peppers	bowl	waterfall	Th. 2
A	10.50	9.51	13.33	11.93	14.74
M	172.73	143.07	277.95	222.38	217.18
N	0.0093	0.0090	0.0099	0.0096	0.01
A	10.56	9.77	13.38	12.099	
M	174.85	150.98	280.32	228.81	
N	0.0095	0.0095	0.01	0.0099	
A	10.63	9.87	13.46	12.21	
M	177.17	153.97	283.67	233.07	
N	0.0096	0.0097	0.01	0.010	

In our third test, we performed the column deletion operation on the test images 10 times and computed the average distortion values using the regular and alignment-based versions of the A and M metrics. The results, reported in Table 3, show significantly lower distortion values for the new metrics:

Table 3. Comparisons of A and M versus A' and M'.

Image	A	A'	M	M'
mandrill	10.96	1.33	494.18	0.67
peppers	4.68	1.33	177.47	0.67
bowl	6.49	1.25	381.45	1.33
waterfall	11.80	1.25	655.34	1.33

8   Conclusions

We defined transparent algorithms as those whose expected distortion of input images is at most $c \log l$, as measured under the average absolute difference metric (l is the range of pixel values.) Our proposal was based on asymptotic analyses of the expected distortions caused by two prototypical watermarking methods generally considered as transparent. We also proposed some shift-resistant variants of these distortion metrics that incorporate alignment techniques used in DNA string comparisons. Directions for future research include carrying out similar analyses for other watermarking algorithms such as low-pass filters and StirMark under the usual as well as more perceptually realistic metrics.

References

1. W. Bender, D. Gruhl, N. Morimoto, and A. Lu. Techniques for data hiding. *IBM Systems Journal*, 35(3-4):313–336, 1996.
2. I. Cox, J. Kilian, F. Leighton, and T. Shamoon. Secure spread spectrum watermarking for multimedia. *IEEE Transactions on Image Processing*, 6(12):1673–1687, Dec 1997.
3. S. Craver, N. Memon, B.-L. Yeo, and M. Yeung. On the invertibility of invisible watermarking techniques. In *Proceedings of International Conference on Image Processing*, pages 540–543, 1997.
4. B. Girod. The information theoretical significance of spatial and temporal masking in video signals. In *Proceedings of SPIE Human Vision, Visual Processing, and Digital Display*, volume 1007, pages 178–187, 1989.
5. D. Hankerson, G. A. Harris, and P. D. Johnson, Jr. *Introduction to Information Theory and Data Compression*. CRC Press, 1998.
6. C. J. v. B. Lambrecht, editor. *Vision Models and Applications to Image and Video Processing*. Kluwer Academic Publishers, 2001.
7. E. W. Myers and W. Miller. Optimal alignments in linear space. *Computer Applications in the Biosciences*, 4(1):11–17, 1988.

8. F. A. P. Petitcolas, R. J. Anderson, and M. G. Kuhn. Attacks on copyright marking systems. In *Proceedings of the 2nd International Workshop on Information Hiding*, pages 218–238, 1998.

9. Y. Rubner and C. Tomasi. *Perceptual Metrics for Image Database Navigation*. Kluwer Academic Publishers, 2000.

10. N. Tran. Hiding functions and computational security of image watermarking systems. In *Proceedings of the 15th IEEE Computer Security Foundations Workshop*, 2002.

An Information Hiding Technique for Binary Images in Consideration of Printing Process

Hsi-Chun Alister Wang

Department of Graphic Arts and Communications
College of Technology, National Taiwan Normal University
hsiwang@cc.ntnu.edu.tw

Abstract. The objective of this research is to propose a data hiding method for printed images. Three digital halftoning techniques – Floyd-Steinberg error diffusion (FSED), multi-scale error diffusion (MSED) and modified multi-scale error diffusion (MMSED) – are implemented in the view of binarization sequence. Microscopic pictures on printed halftone images at different resolutions are presented for visual inspection. A print-and-scanned image with 16 sub-regions of varied dot percentage is used to evaluate the quality of data recovery. The results show that data recovery has better performance at the low dot percentage region and MMSED can provide greater feasibility for data hiding in printed binary images. The proposed method has numerous potential applications in security printing.

1 Introduction

Due to the concerns of copyright and intellectual property in multimedia contents, studies on watermarking or information hiding techniques used in image, audio and other digital media formats have been very active in the recent years [2,5,6]. Information hiding in binary or halftone image is less addressed in the relevant research area because binary image is lack of capacity for hiding data.[1,4,16] Furthermore, applications of binary image are often in printed format, instead of electronic format such as digital image and audio, and the procedure of data recovery need to be handled in a careful manner. Information hiding in binary image is considered much more difficult and challenging.[4,9,15] However, information hiding in binary image is indeed useful in preparing secured document and beating illegally duplicating [5,6].

Halftoning (or analog screening) is a traditional printing process. Due to limited tones which can be reproduced in the output device, a continuous tone image needs to be halftoned into a bi-level format before output device actually displays the image. Since human visual system possesses the ability to integrate the neighboring halftone dots, human eyes then perceive these discrete dots as a continuous-tone image. With the innovation of computer technology, works on digital halftoning have been reported by many researchers [3,8,11,14], and digital halftoning techniques have already substituted the traditional analog screening in the printing industry today.

Digital haftoning can be divided into two categories: ordered dithering and error diffusion. Ordered dithering is performed by an 8x8 or other sized thresholding

Y.-C. Chen, L.-W. Chang, and C.-T. Hsu (Eds.): PCM 2002, LNCS 2532, pp. 460–467, 2002.
© Springer-Verlag Berlin Heidelberg 2002

matrix on a grayscale image to complete the binarization. Error diffusion is a popular algorithm for frequency modulation, and the well-known algorithm is the Folyd-Steinberg Error Diffusion (FSED)[14]. Most of the default halftoning algorithm for ink-jet printers today is based on FSED with certain modifications. Katasavounidis and Kuo [8] proposed a new error diffusion algorithm, multi-scale error diffusion (MSED), which generates an image pyramid and alters the binarization sequence according to the global and local properties of intensity in the original image. Wang *et al.* [15, 16] modified multi-scale error diffusion (MMSED) by reducing the layers of the image pyramid, which leads to a low computational complexity and a progressive halftone image formation.

Studies on information hiding for binary images using digital halftoning technique have been proposed by several researchers [1, 4, 16]. Since most of the binary image applications are in printed format (it is actually in analog format), it is necessary to design a data recovery scheme to recognize printed data. There are always some errors in the recognition. The error correction code is adopted in [4, 6] to increase the recognition accuracy. However, these recognition errors are related to printing process such as output resolutions.

The objective of this research is to design a new information hiding technique for binary images in consideration of printing processes. In section 2, three error diffusion digital halftoning techniques, FSED, MSED and MMSED, are reviewed according to their binarization sequence. Some microscopic pictures on printed images at different resolutions are presented in section 3 for visual inspection. An error analysis for printed image with different dot area percentages is shown in section 4. The proposed information hiding methods by modified multi-scale error diffusion is given in section 5. Conclusions and future works are presented in section 6.

2   Digital Halftoning in the View of Binarization Sequence

Since the concept of error diffusion first proposed by Floyd and Steinberg, it has been a very popular digital halftoning technique. Although many follow-up researches have been done, all the modifications, such as changing the size or the weight of error diffusion masks, are still based on the same structure – serpentine binarization sequence. That is, the binarization sequence is fixed: from the left to the right, then from right to left, as well as from the top to the bottom (Figure 1(a)). Its sequence is independent of the image properties. In view of binarization sequence, Katasavounidis and Kuo's multi-scale error diffusion did make a remarkable change and MSED's binarization sequence is closely related to image properties. Fig.1(a) and Fig. 1(b) demonstrate the binarization sequence by FSED and MSED with 25%, 50%, 75% and 100% completion. The error diffusion masks for FSED and MSED are listed in Table 1 and Table 2.

Fig. 1(b) illustrates the binarization sequence by MSED that follows the "maximum intensity rule", and the binarization sequence is directly related to the intensity properties of the original image. If the region in the original image is darker (e.g. lower-right section), the earlier binarized pixels would appear in this region. Since a full image pyramid is constructed, it may cause the global blocking effect during binarization as shown in the upper-left graph in Fig. 1(b).   Although the computational complexity of MSED is very high, the concept of altering binarization sequence opens a new path of thinking in data hiding in bi-level images in this research.

On the other hand, after modification of MSED with only constructing 4 floors in the image pyramid, the binarization sequence can be shown in Fig. 1(c), as the image is displayed in a more uniform and progressive way. After 50% of binarization, the shape of logotype in the image is already distinguishable.   The other 50% of binarization can be used to encode the hidden data.   Then thousands of different binary images similar to human vision can be generated if we encode different combination of 0s and 1s in the 50-100% binarization. Since only the last 4 layers on the bottom of the supposed image pyramid is calculated, MMSED is also competitive in cutting down computational complexity.

From the view point of traditional printing and photography, the FSED and modified MSED especially convey the following distinguished meanings: The binarization sequence of FSED can be compared to a printout from a laser or inkjet printer – from top to bottom – no matter what the contents of the image is.   On the other hand, for those who have experience in a darkroom to enlarge a black-and-white picture, the way of image formation in the developer is closer to our MMSED algorithm. It may explain why the MSED-based algorithm is better than FSED-based algorithm in the halftone dot distribution, because the halftone image formation by MSED-based algorithm is in a more uniform and natural way.

3   Microscopic Pictures for Visual Inspection

The outcome of the digital halftoning process is a binary image composed of 0s (white) and 1s (black). As the binary data are sent to the printer, it would be helpful to have some idea about the true face of a printed image. Figure 2(a) is the original binary image data at lower-left corner of a 256x256 pixel binary image. Figure 2(b) and 2(c) are enlargements of the lower-left corner of the 256x256 pixel binary images saved at 300dpi and 600dpi (the true output sizes are 0.85"x0.85" and 0.42"x0.42", respectively), and printed at 600dpi by a laser printer. Pictures shown in Figure 2(b) and 2(c), were captured by a high-resolution digital microscope, and the aliasing effect can be negligible. In Figure 2(b), the dot size is larger than it is supposed to be. This phenomenon is known as "dot gain" [13] which will severely affect the quality of an output image. The 0's (in white region) surrounded by black dots in Figure 2(b) are difficult to be recognized. The black dots (1's) in highlight region might be easier to be identified. In figure 2(c), due to the dot gain effect, there is very little chance to recover the correct data. A limit of the amount of data does exist which can be recognized because of the physical restriction of the printing process. In Figure 3, parts of a binary image saved at 75 dpi, 150 dpi and 300 dpi are printed by a 600 dpi laser printer and shown in (a), (b) and (c). The distance between the centers of neighboring dots are 3/75", 3/150" and 3/300", respectively.   In figure 3(a), the dot shape is square (like a pixel). From figure 3(a) to 3(c), the dot shape becomes rounder and rounder, and the dot area coverage is larger and larger. After the visual inspection of the microscopic pictures on halftone dots, it would be worthwhile to understand the mechanism of the false recognition of printed binary data in a systematic way.

4   Print-and-Scanned Image with Varied Dot Percentage

In both Fu and Au's [4] and Wang's works [16], they found that errors do exist in the recognition stage. It has never been carefully addressed how these errors occurred. A 256x256 binary image with 16 different dot percentages is designed in Figure 4. Numbers of black dots and dot area percentages in these 16 regions are listed in Table 3 and Table 4.

There are two duplicated sets of dot percentages at 0.0% and 100.0% which are located at corner positions, and they would serve as the intensity calibration for print-and-scan images under different exposures.   In Figure 4, several line segments with different length and width surrounding the 256x256 binary image are expected to find correct orientation and position of the control points for recognition.

This 256x256 binary data were saved at 75 dpi, 150 dpi and 300 dpi, and a laser printer with 600dpi resolution is used for output. The physical widths of the printed images are 3.41", 1.71" and 0.85", respectively.   Then these printed images were digitized by a 600dpi scanner and the approximated grayscale image sizes are 2200x2200, 1100x1100 and 550x550 in pixels. Figure 5(a), 5(b) and 5(c) are scanned images from the corresponding portions of the three printed images.   To compare Figure 5 (from 600dpi flatbed scanner) and Figure 3 (from high-resolution digital microscope), binary data in Figure 5(c) are beyond distinguishable which is arisen from two issues, dot gain in printing process and low resolution in scanner. In Figure 5(c), every dot is about equivalent to 2 sampling pixels. According to the Sampling Theorem [10,12], "the original signal can be fully reconstructed if the sampling frequency is twice larger than the signal frequency", this sampling rate is on the edge of correct data recovery.

An algorithm has been developed to recognize the 65536 0s (white) or 1s (black) data on the three 256x256 print-and-scanned images.   The four feature points are extracted by line detection and fitting.   The geometrical transformation between 256x256 binary image and print-and-scanned image is constructed by the following equations.

$$U=AX \tag{1}$$

$$A=UX^T(XX^T)^{-1} \tag{2}$$

X and U are the four feature points' coordinates in binary image and print-and-scanned image, and A is the transformation matrix [7, 12]. The corresponding grayscale values can be extracted from the print-and-scanned image, and then a threshold is chosen to finish the recognition. The recognition rate is 100% correct for the 75dpi print-and-scanned image.   The recognition procedure is abandoned for 300dpi print-and-scanned image because the signals are too noisy.   The recognition results from 150dpi print-and-scanned image deserve a detailed study. In Table 5, the recognition error in each region is listed.

The total number of errors is 5722 out of 65536, which is larger than the data reported by Fu and Au. It is due to the threshold selection and feature point positioning. The two numbers inside the parentheses are number of false positives and false negatives. False positive means 0 (white) in the binary image is recognized as 1 (black). False negative means 1 (black) in the binary image is recognized as 0 (white). Combined Tables 3, 4, and 5, the false recognition rate for false positives, false negatives, and overall at varied dot percentages can be calculated and presented in Figure 6. Several interesting findings can be addressed here: (1) In the print-and-scan process, false positives are dominating. (2) In high dot area percentage region, false positives can reach up to 100%. That is, the 0s (white) data cannot be decoded in the shadow region. (3) In low dot percentage region, both false positives and negatives are close to 0%. That is, data encoded in highlight region can be correctly decoded through the print-and-scan process.

Table 1. Error diffusion mask in FSED

	1	-7/16
-3/16	-5/16	-1/16

Table 2. Error diffusion mask in MSED & MMSED

-1/8	-1/8	-1/8
-1/8	1	-1/8
-1/8	-1/8	-1/8

Table 3. Number of black dots in each region

0	3923	3707	4096
3287	2883	2463	2064
1640	1237	825	423
4096	211	102	0

Table 4. Dot percentage in each region

0.0%	97.8%	90.5%	100.0%
80.3%	70.4%	60.1%	50.4%
40.0%	30.2%	20.1%	10.3%
100.0%	5.2%	2.5%	0.0%

Table 5. Numbers of falsely recognized dots

0 (0,0)	172 (172,0)	385 (385,0)	0 (0,0)
781 (781,0)	1086 (1086,0)	1144 (1144,0)	1130 (1129,1)
716 (716,0)	242 (242,0)	35 (34,1)	29 (25,4)
0 (0,0)	1 (1,0)	1 (1,0)	0 (0,0)

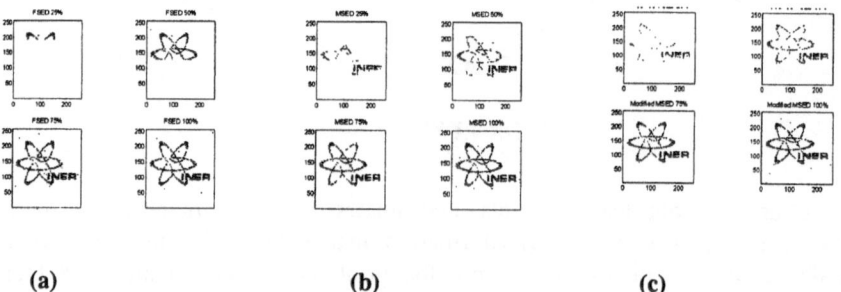

(a)   (b)   (c)

Fig. 1. Schematic diagram of the binarization sequence for (a) FSED, (b) MSED and (c) MMSED.

(a)

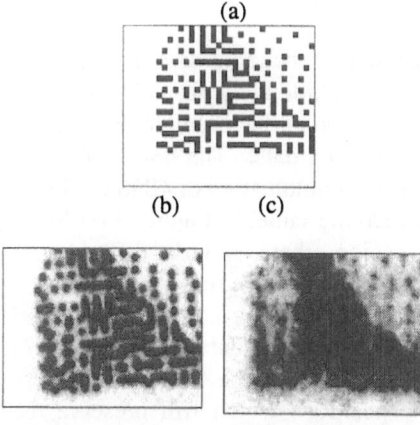

(b)   (c)

Fig. 2. (a) is the original binary image. (b) and (c) are microscopic pictures of 300dpi and 600dpi printed images.

(a)

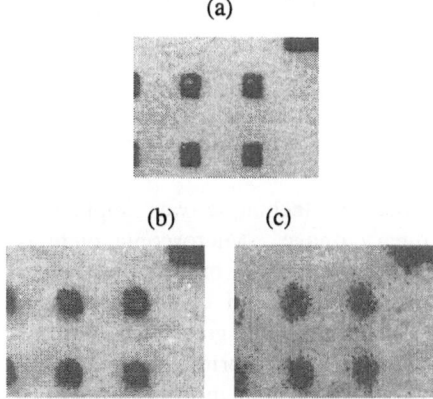

(b)   (c)

Fig. 3. Microscopic pictures of parts of a binary image saved at 75dpi, 150dpi and 300dpi are shown in (a), (b) and (c), respectively.

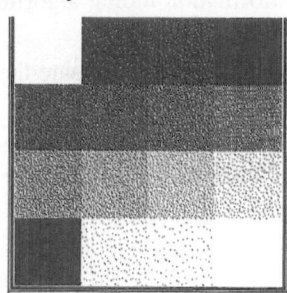

Fig. 4. A 256x256 binary image with 16 sub-regions at different dot percentages

(a)

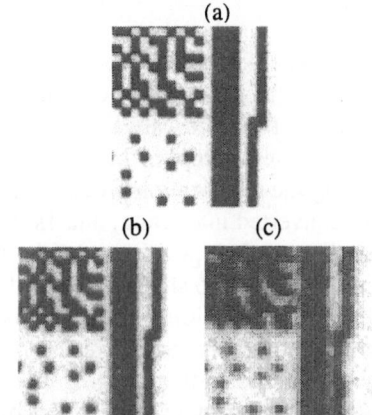

(b)   (c)

Fig. 5. Print-and-scanned images of parts of a binary image saved at 75dpi, 150dpi and 300dpi are shown in (a), (b) and (c), respectively.

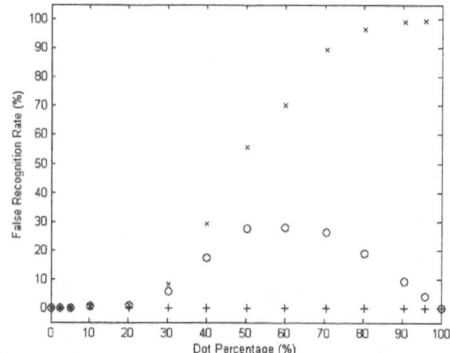

Fig. 6. False recognition rate for false positives ('x'), false negatives ('+'), and overall ('o') at varied dot percentages.

(a)   (b)

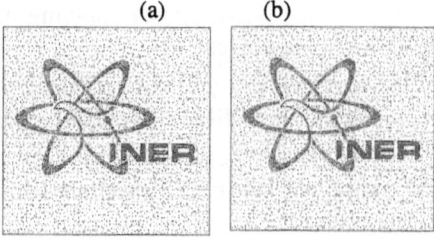

Fig. 7. Data hiding with 4096 0s and 1s by modified multiscale error diffusion. (a) without using pair toggling. (b) using pair toggling.

5 Information Hiding by Modified Multi-scale Error Diffusion

Based on the findings described in the previous section, encoding data by the black dots in the highlight region would be a better choice. While we go back to Figure 1, MSED and MMSED do always complete the binarization at the highlight region. In Figure 7(a), the concept of MMSED is used for encoding data. The last 4096 black dots during the binarization process are encoded as the combination of 4096 0s (black dots are converted into white) and 1s (black dots keep the same) in Figure 7(a). Since almost all encoded positions are in highlight region, there is little difficulty in recognition. The logo shape is retained in the high dot percentage region.

The information hiding algorithm using the MMSED concept is further fine-tuned by pair toggling proposed by Fu and Au (2002). If the encoded data is 1, black dot is assigned to the position according to binarization sequence. If the encoded data is 0, black dot is assigned to one of the neighboring positions which will preserve the summation of dots in the neighboring region. Figure 7(b) shows the results. MMSED data hiding possesses another advantage -- encoding flexibility. No matter how many data bits are to be encoded, the locations in the last part of binarization sequence can always be used. MMSED can assure the optimum data recovery performance because the chosen positions to be encoded are at all times in the lower dot percentage regions.

6 Conclusion

In this paper, a modified multi-scale error diffusion technique was applied to information hiding exclusively for a printed binary image. Microscopic pictures address the importance of "dot gain" effect during the printing process. A binary image with different dot percentages is designed to understand the data recovery performance. The modified multi-scale error diffusion provides great feasibility for encoding, and it assures the optimum data recovery from the printed image. The methods we developed in this research will have great potential in printing security documents such as currency, stamps, ID cards, and other confidential documents. Related future works of this research include:

1) To study the possibility of applying the MMSED information hiding algorithm to color halftone images.

2) To extend the study of dot percentage to spatial frequency and to evaluate the data recognition rate at different spatial frequencies.

3) To include error correction code, such as Reed-Solomon codes, to withstand the uncertainty of substrate properties and surface scratches which may lead to poor recognition rate.

Acknowledgements. This research is supported by the National Science Council of the Republic of China under the grants of NSC89-2320-B-128-002-M08 and NSC90-NU-7-003-001.   Thanks to Y.C. Chen, W.L. Hsieh and L.C. Hwang for taking microscopic images and scanned images.

References

1. Z. Baharav and D. Shaked, Watermarking of dither halftoned images, HP Laboratories Israel, HPL-98-32, May 1999.
2. W. Bender *et al.*, Techniques for data hiding, IBM System Journal, vol 35, Nos 3&4, pp 313-336, 1996.
3. R. Eschback, Editor, Recent progress in digital halftoning, reprinted from IS&T proceedings, 1992-1994, the Society for Imaging Science and Technology, Springfield, VA, 1994.
4. M.S. Fu and O.C. Au, "Data Hiding Watermarking for Halftone Images," IEEE Transaction on Image Processing, 11(4)477-484, 2002.
5. D. Gruhl and W. Bender, Information Hiding to Foil the Casual Counterfeiter, proceedings (Lecture Notes in Computer Science; 1525), 2nd International Workshop on information hiding, pp 1-15, Portland, Oregon, April 1998.
6. D.L. Hecht, Embedded data Glyph technology for hardcopy digital documents, SPIE 2171, pp. 341-352, 1995.
7. B. Jahne, Practical handbook on image processing for scientific applications, CRC Press, New York, 1997.
8. I. Katsavounidis and C.C. Jay Kuo, A multiscale error diffusion technique for digital halftoning, IEEE Transaction on Image Processing, 6(3)483-490, 1997.
9. C.Y. Lin and S.F. Chang, "Distortion Modeling and Invariant Extraction for Digital Image Print-and-Scan Process," Intl. Symp. on Multimedia Information Processing (ISMIP 99), Taipei, Taiwan, Dec. 1999.
10. A.V. Oppenheim, R.W. Schafer, Discrete-time signal processing, Prentice-Hall Inc., New Jersey, 1989.
11. T.N. Pappas, Model-based halftoning of color images, IEEE Transactions on image processing, 6(7)1014-24, 1997
12. W.K. Pratt, Digital image processing, 2nd Ed, John Wiley & Sons, Inc., 1991.
13. Z.A. Prust, Graphic Communications – the Printed Image, Goodheart-Willcox, Tinley Park, IL, 1989.
14. R. Ulichney, Digital Halftoning, MIT Press, Cambridge, MA, 1987
15. H.C. Wang, C.Y.Lin, C.C. Huang, Data Hiding in a binary image by the modified digital halftoning techniques, proceedings, 1999 Conference on Computer Vision, Graphics and Image Processing, pp. 183-190, Taipei, Taiwan, August, 1999.
16. H.C. Wang, Data Hiding Techniques for Printed Binary Images, IEEE International Conference on Information Technology: Coding and Computing (ITCC-2001), proceedings, pp 55-59, Las Vegas, Nevada, April 2001.

Image Watermarking Synchronization by Significant MSB Plane Matching

Shih-Wei Sun, Ta-Te Lu, and Pao-Chi Chang

Electrical Engineering, National Central University, Chung-Li, Taiwan
{swsun, ttlu, pcchang}@roger.ee.ncu.edu.tw

Abstract. We propose a new geometric synchronization method for watermarking. The Significant Most Significant Bit (SMSB) plane is used as the synchronization object. The SMSB of an image is easy to obtain, either in the spatial domain or in the DWT domain, particularly in several image compression techniques, such as SPIHT and JPEG2000. SMSB can be used to represent the feature of the image by its eigen vectors and values with calculating its covariance matrix. In the receiving end, the attacks such as rotation, scaling, translation, and flipping can be detected by comparing the geometric parameters obtained from the sender and calculated from the received image. The simulation results show that the proposed method can successfully re-synchronize the attacked image back to the original format.

1 Introduction

Many watermarking techniques were proposed in recent years, but most of them are still relatively weak to geometric attacks. The existing re-synchronization methods proposed before were part of the embedding/extracting process, and they were not designed to be used independently. Therefore, we propose a general watermark re-synchronization technique independent of the embedding or extracting process. Namely, our method can be used with any present watermarking system to provide the re-synchronization function.

A lot of researchers have worked on the re-synchronization of the image/video. Many DSP techniques, such as DFT [1][2][3][4], log-polar mapping [1][2][3], log-log mapping [1][2][3], have been proposed. Most of them transform the image into the Fourier-based domain for synchronization, in either linear or non-linear such as log scale. The watermark is also embedded in the same domain. These methods are more robust against geometric attacks because they are operated in geometric invariant domains. Clustering algorithms were also applied in re-synchronization. A region-based image watermarking method [5] was proposed by A. Nikolaidis and I. Pitas. It tries to find out closed contour shape regions as the re-synchronization information using K-means algorithm, however, the training complexity is very high.

In this paper, we propose to use the Significant Most Significant Bit plane (SMSB) as the synchronization object. The motivation for using SMSB in this paper is that the signals are easy to obtain in lots of compression techniques, such as SPIHT, JPEG, JPEG 2000, etc. The SMSB can be found both in spatial domain or DWT domain

Y.-C. Chen, L.-W. Chang, and C.-T. Hsu (Eds.): PCM 2002, LNCS 2532, pp. 468–476, 2002.

with spatial/frequency characteristics. After finding the SMSB, we can use the Hotelling transform to get the set of parameters as the extracted features: mean location of SMSB, eigen values, and eigen vectors. Then the set of parameters are sent as the side information to the extracting end. By comparing the set of geometric parameters of the attacked image and the side information from the embedding end, we can use the characteristic functions to determine what the attack is. If the image is rotated, scaled, translated or flipped, the geometric attacks can be detected by calculating the set of parameters to obtain the angle between the eigen vectors, the gain of the eigen values, and the shift of the mean location, etc.

The system architecture is outlined in section 2. The characteristics extraction process is described in section 3. The rotation, scaling, translation, and flipping detections are described in section 4. Section 5 shows the simulation results and discussions. Finally, a conclusion is given in the last section.

2 System Architecture

In the paper, we propose a general SMSB plane matching synchronization method for image watermarking. This method can be easily applied to any existing watermarking system and enhance the system robustness against geometric attacks. The basic block diagram of SMSB synchronization image watermarking system is depicted in Fig. 1.

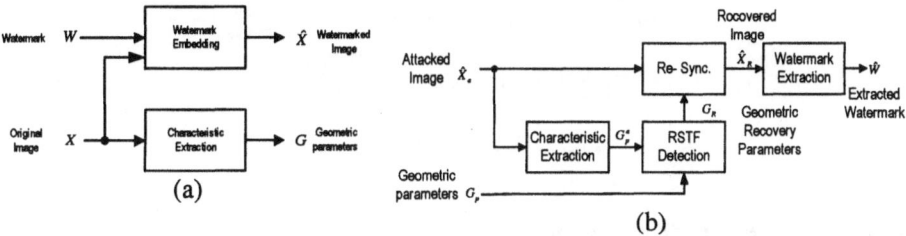

Fig. 1. The block diagram of the proposed SMSB watermarking system (a) the embedding process (b) the extraction process

Fig. 1 (a) shows the watermark embedding process. The proposed synchronization method can be used with any watermark embedding process. The embedding procedure is not affected by the SMSB synchronization method because these operations are running in parallel. The original image X is used in both watermarking embedding and synchronization. While the watermark w is embedded in the image X to produce the watermarked image $\hat{X}$, the characteristic functions of SMSB are calculated from the image X to generate the geometric parameters G. Meanwhile, the calculated geometric parameters G are sent as the side information, probably with the secret key, if it exists. Fig. 1 (b) depicts the extraction process. The attacked image $\hat{X}_a$ may be manipulated by some geometric operations. In general, when suffering geometric attacks, a conventional watermarking system without geometric invariant characteristics cannot extract the watermark w very well due to the synchronization loss.

The system we propose can re-synchronize the attacked image back to its proper position for watermark extraction. The attacked image $\hat{X}_a$ is first processed by the characteristics extraction function, which is the same as the one in Fig.1 (a). The outputs, the geometric parameters G_a, are sent to the rotation, scaling, translation, and flipping (RSTF) detection block. The RSTF detection function is able to determine what the attack is based on the difference between G_a and G. The detection result G_R is used for re-synchronization. The attacked image can be manipulated by the inverse operation of parameter G_R to restore the image back to the original location. After the manipulation, the watermarking extraction process can be continued to extract the watermark $\hat{w}$. The two major blocks for re-synchronization, characteristic extraction and RSTF detection, are discussed in detail in the next two sections.

3   Characteristic Extraction

The characteristic extraction that collects useful characteristics from the image will not degrade image quality. The extracted information is sent as side information to the decoding end and will be used for resynchronization. The block diagram of characteristic extraction is depicted in Fig.2. It consists of three major functions that are described as follows.

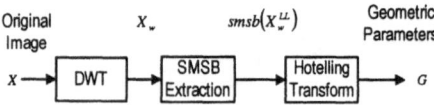

Fig. 2. Characteristic extraction

3.1   Discrete Wavelet Transform (DWT)

The original image X is first normalized to the proper intensity such that the SMSB exists and can be extracted from the LL band of DWT. The normalized image is then 2-D Discrete Wavelet Transformed (DWT) [7] to be the wavelet domain signal X_w. In DWT domain, the LL band signal X_w^{LL} is chosen as the candidate for feature extraction because the LL band contains most energy and information of the original image. The signals in LL band of an $M \times N$ image can be expressed as $X_w^{LL} = \left\{ p(x, y), x = 1,2, \cdots \frac{M}{2^L}, y = 1,2, \cdots \frac{N}{2^L} \right\}$, where L is the decomposition level of DWT, $p(x, y)$ is the pixel value, and (x, y) is the location.

3.2   SMSB Extraction

The Significant Most Significant Bit (SMSB) plane forms an object that contains all pixels with MSB=1. The SMSB plane in LL band of DWT domain contains most energy of an image, and fortunately, in some existing compression techniques, the SMSB plane in DWT domain is offered. For example, SPIHT proposed in [8] and EBCOT included in [9], which is the core of JPEG 2000 image compression standards, the bit plane coding is performed in the DWT domain. As a result, the proposed method is a very practical watermarking re-synchronization method that works with the existing image compression system. The locations of SMSB, denoted as $smsb$, are represented by x-axis and y-axis values, and can be extracted as follows:

$$smsb\left(X_w^{LL}\right) = \left\{msb\left(p(x,y)\right) : if \ msb\left(p(x,y)\right) = 1\right\}, smsb = \left\{smsb\left(q_i(x,y)\right), i = 1,2,\cdots R\right\},$$

where $R = \left\|smsb\left(X_w^{LL}\right)\right\|$, therefore, $q_i(x,y) = [x_i, y_i]^T$.

3.3 Hotelling Transform

In this work, the Hotelling transform [10][11][12] is applied to the SMSB plane $smsb$ to get the geometric parameters, which include the mean vectors m_q, the eigen vectors v, and the eigen values λ as in $C_q = \frac{1}{R}\sum_{i=1}^{R} q_i q_i^T - m_q m_q^T$, where $m_q = \frac{1}{R}\sum_{i=1}^{R} q_i$ and $C_q v_j = \lambda_j v_j$ $(j = 1,2)$. If there is a nontrivial solution, the eigen vectors v_1, v_2 and values λ_1, λ_2 can be found by covariance matrix C_q. The order of eigen values λ_1, λ_2 is in the descent order, i.e., $\lambda_1 \geq \lambda_2$ for convenience. The geometric parameters are denoted as $G : \left\{\bar{m}_q = (m_x, m_y), \vec{v} = (v_1, v_2), \vec{\lambda} = (\lambda_1, \lambda_2)\right\}$ In the extracting end, the same characteristic extraction process is applied to the attacked image to obtain the geometric parameters G_a. By comparing the two sets of geometric parameters G and G_a, one can determine what the attack is on the image.

4 Rotation, Scaling, Translation, and Flipping Detection

After being affected by unknown attacks, the attacked image is pre-processed for re-synchronization. The first step of pre-processing is the SMSB characteristic extraction described in the previous section. The attacked image is transformed into DWT domain and the SMSB of the LL band is obtained. After that, the geometric parameters G_a can be calculated.

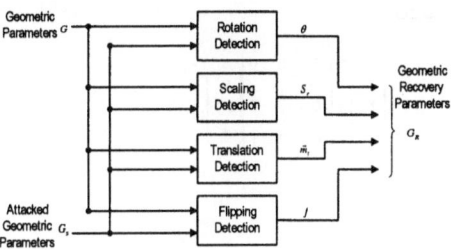

Fig. 3. RSTF detection

The block diagram of RSTF detection is depicted in Fig. 3. By comparing the geometric parameters G and attacked geometric parameters G_a, the geometric recovery parameters G_R, which include θ, s_r, $\bar{m}_t$, and f, can be computed to detect the rotation, scaling, translation, and flipping attacks, respectively. The detection procedures for RSTF attacks are detailed as follows.

4.1 Rotation Detection

Following the definition in [12], the mathematical model for a rotation attack is described in the reference. Based on the eigenanalysis [13], if the eigen vectors with distinct eigen values can be found in a square matrix, then the eigen vectors must be orthogonal. Therefore, eigen vectors v_1, v_2 found in the covariance matrix are orthogonal, that implied that any one of the eigen vectors in v and v^a is enough to calculate the rotation angle : $\theta = \cos^{-1}\dfrac{v_1 \cdot v_1^a}{\|v_1\| \cdot \|v_1^a\|} \cdot \dfrac{180}{\pi}$. After obtaining the rotation angle θ, the attacked image can be restored back to the original angle by rotating back $-\theta$, as in (1) to form the recovery image:

$$\begin{bmatrix} X' \\ Y' \\ 1 \end{bmatrix} = \begin{bmatrix} \cos(-\theta) & \sin(-\theta) & 0 \\ -\sin(-\theta) & \cos(-\theta) & 0 \\ 0 & 0 & 1 \end{bmatrix} \begin{bmatrix} X^a \\ Y^a \\ 1 \end{bmatrix} \tag{1}$$

4.2 Scaling Detection

Similarly, in the scaling case, two groups of eigen values, λ_1, λ_2, λ_1^a, λ_2^a, can be obtained with the relationship $\dfrac{\lambda_1}{\lambda_2} = \dfrac{\lambda_1^a}{\lambda_2^a}$. According to the orthogonal condition and the sorting order, any one of the eigen values can be used to calculate the scaling ratio : $r = \dfrac{\lambda_1^a}{\lambda_1}$, $S_r = S_x = S_y = \sqrt{r}$, where s_r is the scaling ratio. s_x, s_y represent the scaling ratios in x and y coordinates, respectively. After obtaining the scaling ratio s_r, the attacked image can be restored back to the original scale by scaling back $\dfrac{1}{S_r} = \dfrac{1}{S_x} = \dfrac{1}{S_y}$, as in (2) to form the recovery image:

$$\begin{bmatrix} X' \\ Y' \\ 1 \end{bmatrix} = \begin{bmatrix} \dfrac{1}{S_x} & 0 & 0 \\ 0 & \dfrac{1}{S_y} & 0 \\ 0 & 0 & 1 \end{bmatrix} \begin{bmatrix} X^a \\ Y^a \\ 1 \end{bmatrix} \tag{2}$$

4.3 Translation Detection

In the proposed method, the location mean of the SMSB is calculated as before: $m_{smsb} = (m_x, m_y)$. If the image is translated to a different place, the new location mean of the SMSB can be calculated similarly as $m_{msbp} = (m'_x, m'_y)$. The difference vector of the location mean represents the translation displacement (m'_x, m'_y), where $\begin{cases} m'_x = m'_x - m_x \\ m'_y = m'_y - m_y \end{cases}$.

After obtaining the translation value (m'_x, m'_y), the attacked image can be restored back to the original position by translating back $(-m'_x, -m'_y)$, as in (3) to form the recovery image:

$$\begin{bmatrix} X' \\ Y' \\ 1 \end{bmatrix} = \begin{bmatrix} 1 & 0 & -m'_x \\ 0 & 1 & -m'_y \\ 0 & 0 & 1 \end{bmatrix} \begin{bmatrix} X^a \\ Y^a \\ 1 \end{bmatrix} \tag{3}$$

4.4 Flipping Detection

The mathematical model for a flipping attack can be represented if (X, Y) is the watermarked image, (X^a, Y^a) is the attacked image, and the image size is $M \times N$. A flipping can easily be detected by comparing the eigen vectors. Suppose that we can get the original image's eigen vectors $v = [v_1, v_2]$ and the correspond attacked image's eigen vectors $v^a = [v_1^a, v_2^a]$. If $(v_1^a = -v_1) \wedge (v_2^a = v_2)$ or $(v_1^a = v_1) \wedge (v_2^a = -v_2)$ holds, the image can be detected to be flipped either in vertical or horizontal direction provided that the following condition holds: $|v_1| = |v'_1|$, then $f_1 = b(v_1) \oplus b(v'_1)$, where $\oplus$ is the XOR

$$|v_2| = |v'_2| \qquad f_2 = b(v_2) \oplus b(v'_2)$$

operation and $b(x) = \begin{cases} 1, & \text{if } x > 0 \\ 0, & \text{if } x \le 0 \end{cases}$ representing the sign. By the above conditions the flipping parameter f is obtained as: $f = f_1 \oplus f_2$. The image is flipped if $f = 1$. Otherwise, it is not flipped if $f = 0$. Once the image is detected to be attacked by flipping, it can be flipped back to the correct orientation, as in (4) to form the recovery image:

$$\begin{bmatrix} X' \\ Y' \\ 1 \end{bmatrix} = \begin{bmatrix} -1 & 0 & M \\ 0 & 1 & 0 \\ 0 & 0 & 1 \end{bmatrix} \begin{bmatrix} X^a \\ Y^a \\ 1 \end{bmatrix}, \text{in horizontal}; \quad \begin{bmatrix} X' \\ Y' \\ 1 \end{bmatrix} = \begin{bmatrix} 1 & 0 & 0 \\ 0 & -1 & N \\ 0 & 0 & 1 \end{bmatrix} \begin{bmatrix} X^a \\ Y^a \\ 1 \end{bmatrix}, \text{in vertical} \tag{4}$$

5 Simulations and Results

In the SMSB synchronization image watermarking system, the characteristics in the original image have to be extracted first. In the experiments, the watermarking system proposed in [6] is applied as an example, which is a key based watermarking system embedding the watermark based on block polarity in the DWT domain. In the extraction process, the geometric attacks on images are detected first. After re-synchronization, the normal watermark extraction procedure can be continued.

In the simulations, three commonly used images, Barbara, Lena, and Pepper, are tested as our experimental samples. The RSTF detection for the geometric attacks generated from Matlab and Adobe Photoshop are tested. Fig. 4 shows several geometric attack examples in simulations. Tables 1 to 4 show the synchronization performance, which is represented by the detected geometric parameters. The overall performance of the whole watermarking system is shown in Fig. 5. Table 1 shows the detected rotation angles for the rotation attacks $30°, 45°, 60°$. The error in rotation is negligible and the maximum error is less than 3 degrees. Table 2 shows the scaling attacks in the range of 0.5x ~ 5x. The error in detected scaling ratio is less than 0.01%. Table 3 shows the translation attacks from several randomly selected positions. The error in translation detection is less than one integer pixel. Table 4 shows the flipping attacks including horizontal and vertical directions. All the flipping attacks can be exactly detected without any errors. Based on the watermarking schemes evaluation [14], the applied geometric attacks of rotation, scaling, and flipping are all in the moderate level. In simulations, all attacked images can be recovered to the original positions with limited errors.

Table 5 shows the extracted watermark and the corresponding Normalized Correlation (N.C.) [15] value. With the help of the proposed re-synchronization scheme, the NC values are more than 0.7 in all cases, and the extracted watermark logo is recognizable. Therefore, the proposed re-synchronization scheme can help the original watermarking system overcome the geometric attacks.

Table 1. Rotation detection

Rot.	Barbara	lena	pepper
30	30.43	27.07	30.00
45	45.47	42.19	45.43
60	60.37	56.95	59.88

Table 2. Scaling detection

Scaling ratio	Barbara	Lena	pepper
0.5x	0.4998	0.5024	0.4999
2x	1.9986	1.9926	2.0024
3x	3.0007	2.9905	3.0027
4x	4.0106	3.9996	4.0054
5x	5.0193	5.0044	5.0065

Table 3. Translation detection

Trans.	Barbara	lena	pepper
(12,22)	(12,22)	(12,22)	(11,22)
(25,36)	(25,36)	(25,36)	(24,36)
(28,9)	(28,9)	(28,9)	(27,9)

Table 4. Flipping detection

Flipping detection	Barbara	lena	pepper
Horizontal	Y	Y	Y
Vertical	Y	Y	Y

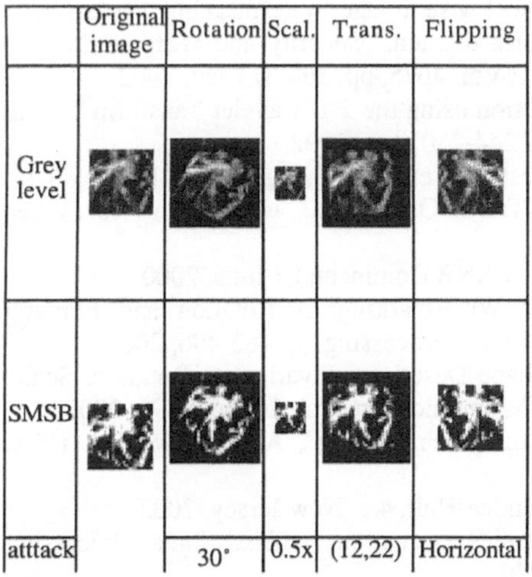

Grey level / SMSB	Original image	Rotation	Scal.	Trans.	Flipping
atttack		30°	0.5x	(12,22)	Horizontal

	barbara	lena	pepper
30°	NCU EE 0.92	NCU EE 0.71	NCU EE 1.00
45°	NCU EE 0.90	NCU EE 0.71	NCU EE 0.95
60°	NCU EE 0.91	NCU EE 0.70	NCU EE 0.97

Fig. 4. Geometric attack examples- Barbara: rotation, scaling, translation, and flipping

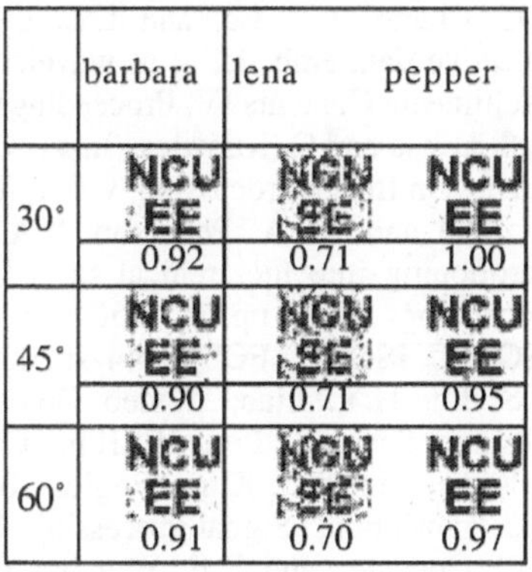

Fig. 5. Extracted watermark and normalized correlation values

6   Conclusions

In the paper, we propose image watermarking synchronization by SMSB plane matching, which is robust to the geometric attacks, especially on rotation, scaling, translation, and flipping. We have successfully applied the Hotelling transform in the DWT domain to obtain the SMSB in spatial/frequency domain for the re-synchronization of the image. Furthermore, it is a standalone re-synchronization scheme that can work with any watermarking system.

References

[1]   J.J.K. O'Ruanaidh, and T. Pun, "Rotation, Scale and Translation Invariant Digital Image Watermarking," Proc. IEEE Int. Conf. on Image Processing, pp. 536 -539, 1997

[2]   S. Pereira, J.J.K. O'Ruanaidh, F. Deguillaume, G. Csurka, and ; T. Pun, "Template Based Recovery of Fourier-Based Watermarks Using Log-polar and Log-log Maps," Proc. IEEE Int. Conf. on Image Processing, pp. 870-874, 1999

[3]   J.J.K. O'Ruanaidh, and T. Pun, "Rotation, scale and translation invariant spread spectrum digital image watermarking", Signal Processing, 66(3): 303-317, May, 1998

[4]   C.Y. Lin, M. Wu, J. A. Bloom, I. J. Cox, M. L. Miller, and Y. M. Lui, "Rotation, Scale and Translation Resilient Watermarking for Images," in IEEE Trans. Image Processing, VOL. 10, NO. 5, May, 2001

[5]   A. Nikolaidis and I. Pitas, "Region- Based Image Watermaking," IEEE Trans. Image Processing, pp. 1726- 1740, VOL.10, NO.11, November 2001

[6] P.C. Chang, T.T. Lu, and L.L. Lee, " Blockwise image watermarking system with selective data embedding in wavelet transform domain," Security and Watermarking of Multimedia Contents IV, Proceedings of SPIE Vol. 4675, pp. 368-377 Jan, 2002

[7] A.S. Lewis and G. Knowles,"Image compression using the 2-D wavelet transform," IEEE Trans. On Image Processing, vol. 1, no.2, pp. 244-250, Apr. 1992

[8] A. Said and W. A. Pearlman, ""A new fast and efficient image codec based on set partitioning into hierarchical trees," IEEE Trans. On Circuits and Systems for Video Technology, Vol.6 pp. 243-250, June, 1996

[9] ISO/IEC, ISO/IEC FCD15444-1: 2000, (draft USNB Comments),7 June, 2000

[10] C.S. Lu, H.Y. Liao, "Video Object-Based Watermarking: A Rotation and Flipping Resilient Scheme," Proc. IEEE Int. Conf. on Image Processing, pp.483-486, 2001

[11] H.K. Kim and J.D. Kim, "Region- Based Shape Descriptor Invariant to Rotation, Scale, and Translation," Signal Processing: Image Communication, Vol. 16, pp.87-93, 2000

[12] R.C. Gonzalez and R.E. Woods, "Digital Image Processing", Addison-Wesley, USA, 1992

[13] Simon Haykin, "Adaptive Filter Theory", Prentice-Hall, 4/e, New Jersey, 2002

[14] Fabien A. P. Petitcloas, "Watemarking schemes evaluation, " IEEE Signal Processing Magazine, Vol. 17, No. 5, pp.58-64. Sep., 2000

[15] I.J. Cox, M.L. Miller, and J.A. Bloom, "Digital Watermarking", Morgan Kaufmann Publishers, 1/e, USA, 2002

Secure Watermark Verification Scheme

Liu Yongliang[1], Wen Gao[1,2,3], Hongxun Yao[1], and Yaxiao Song[1]

[1] Department of Computer Science, Harbin Institute of Technology, China
[2] Institute of Computing Technology, Chinese Academy of Sciences
[3] Graduate School of Chinese Academy of Sciences
ylliu@cti.com.cn

Abstract. Digital watermark is an active research area that has received a considerable attention in multimedia applications. Copyright protection of digital contents, as one of the most important application of digital watermark, works by watermark verification. In traditional watermark authentication scheme, a prover exposed a watermark to be present in a digital data to the verifier. However, an attacker is able to spoil or remove the watermark entirely once classified information is known. Some of previous schemes proposed as solution haven't achieved desirable result really. In this paper, we propose a secure watermark verification scheme based on commitment scheme and zero knowledge protocols in order to solve this problem. There will be no secret information that can be used for removing watermark is disclosed during the verification process. It has considerable advantages over previously proposed schemes in terms of security.

1 Introduction

With the rapid spread of computer networks and the further development of multimedia technologies, digital contents can be accessed easily, and the protection of intellectual property becomes more and more important every day. Digital watermark is proposed as an approach to solve this problem.

Digital watermark is an active research area that has received a great deal of attention in many digital multimedia applications. Many excellent papers have appeared in special issues, conferences and workshops in recent years. The basic idea behind digital watermark is to embed information into a host data so that if the embedded information can be reliably recovered, then this information can specify the affiliation between the data and its original owner. The embedded process involves imperceptibly (for human audio or visual systems) modifying the host data using a secret key and the watermark to produce a watermarked data. The modifications must be done such that reliable extraction of the embedded watermark is possible even under a "reasonable" level of distortion applied to the watermarked data. Some typical distortions that digital watermark schemes are expected to survive include smoothing, compression, rotation, translation, cropping, scaling, resampling, digital to analog and analog to digital conversion, linear and nonlinear filtering. These distortions, whether intentional or incidental, are known as attacks.

Y.-C. Chen, L.-W. Chang, and C.-T. Hsu (Eds.): PCM 2002, LNCS 2532, pp. 477–484, 2002.

Most of previous works concentrated on imperceptibility, robustness, and capacity of watermark scheme, but very little work has been focused on the security of watermark scheme, in particularly on the security of watermark verification scheme. Unfortunately, there is a serious question in watermark scheme in terms of security. In traditional watermark verification scheme, a prover exposed secret information that can be used to remove the watermark in order to prove a watermark presents in a digital data to the verifier. To solve this problem, zero knowledge interactive proof (ZKIP) protocol is proposed [1], [2], [3], [5], [6].

In [1], a graph generated from an image which must has a signature and an isomorphic graph is concealed in this image. The ZKIP for the graph isomorphism is applied to assert the copyright of this image. One problem is that adversary can modify the least significant bits easily, thus prevent copyright owner from showing his ownership of the image. More importantly, the adversary can embed forgery watermark into the image, then he can prove he is "real" copyright owner by ZKIP too.

A protocol for the watermarking decision problem is proposed in [2]. The basic idea is to secretly and verifiably compute the correlation between the watermark and the underlying stego-data: The seller encrypts the watermark W and stego-data using his public key of well-known RSA public key cryptosystem and sends them to the verifier. In a challenge response manner the seller convinces the verifier that the watermark correlates with stego-data. The crucial question that arises is how to ensure the randomness of r.

Adelsbach and Sadeghi give a formal definition of zero knowledge watermark detection protocols based on definitions known from cryptography [3]. For a blind and non-blind version of a well-known class of watermarking schemes as introduced in [4], they propose zero knowledge detection protocols based on commitment schemes. The authors call this protocol a provably secure protocol. But there are at least three problems: (1) Detection disclosed embedded watermark location. (2) Whether authors reasonably define a commitment of A. (3) On what condition we can conclude that the watermark correlates with watermarked image.

Craver presents two schemes for zero knowledge watermark detection in [5]. The first one relies on some permutation of images, where the permutation must be secret. As uncommon intensity values in the image are mapped to uncommon values in scrambled image, giving an attacker a great deal of information by narrowing down the set of original pixels mapping to a scrambled pixel. The same problem also exists in the second one. More recently, Craver et al give a refined protocol [6], but the protocol does not state how to verify the presence of scrambled watermark in the scrambled image.

In this paper, we propose secure watermark verification scheme based on commitment scheme and zero knowledge protocols. It provides copyright proving without revealing any information to remove the watermark. It has considerable advantages over previously proposed schemes in terms of security.

The rest of the paper is organized as follows. In Section 2, we review the commitment schemes. In Section 3, we provide the secure watermark verification scheme. Finally, in Section 4, we give a conclusion and future research direction.

2   Commitment Scheme and Zero Knowledge Proof

2.1   Commitment Scheme

The notion of commitment is at the heart of almost all construction of modern cryptographic protocols. As an informal example, consider the following game [7]:

Suppose Peggy writes a message on a piece of paper, and then places the message in a safe for which she knows the combination. Peggy then gives the safe to Vic. Even though Vic doesn't know what the message is until the safe is opened, we would agree that Peggy is *committed* to her message because she cannot change it. Furthermore, Vic cannot learn what the message is (assuming he doesn't know the combination of the safe) unless Peggy opens the safe for him.

Suppose the message is a bit $b = 0$ or 1, and Peggy encrypts b in some way. The encrypted form of b is sometimes called a *blob* and the encryption method is called a *bit commitment scheme*. In general, a bit commitment scheme will be a function $f : \{0,1\} \times X \to Y$, where X and Y are some sets. An encryption of b is any value $f(b,x)$, $x \in X$. We can informally define two properties that a bit commitment scheme should satisfy:

(1) **Hiding.** For a bit $b = 0$ or 1, Vic cannot determine the value of b from the blob $f(b,x)$.

(2) **Binding.** Peggy can later "open" the blob, by revealing the value of x used to encrypt b, to convince that b was the value encrypted. Peggy should not be able to open a blob as both a 0 and a 1.

If Peggy wants to commit any bit string, she simply commits every bit independently. Two common bit commitment schemes are following [8].

Bit commitment using symmetric cryptography. This bit commitment protocol uses symmetric cryptography: (1) Bob generates a random bit string, R, and sends R to Alice. (2) Alice creates a message consisting of bit she wishes to commit to, b (it can actually be several bits), and Bob's random string. She encrypts it with some random key, K, and sends the result $E_K(R,b)$ back to Bob. That is the commitment portion of the protocol. Bob cannot decrypt the message. So he does not know what the bit is. (3) Alice sends Bob the key. (4) Bob decrypts the message to reveal the bit. He checks his random string to verify the bit's validity. If the message did not contain Bob's random string, Alice could secretly decrypt the message she handed Bob with a variety of keys until she found one that gave her a bit other than the one she committed to. Since the bit has only two possible values, she is certain to find one after only a few tries. Bob's random string prevents her from using this attack; she has to find a new message that not only has her bit inverted, but also has Bob's random string exactly reproduced. If the encryption algorithm is good, the chance of her finding this is minuscule. Alice cannot change her bit after she commits to it.

Bit commitment using one-way function. This protocol uses one-way function: (1) Alice generates two random bit strings, R_1 and R_2.. (2) Alice creates a message consisting of her random strings and the bit she wishes to commit to (it can actually be several bits) (R_1, R_2, b). (3) Alice computes the one-way function on the message and the result, as well as one of the random strings $H(R_1, R_2, b)$, R_1 to Bob. This transmission from Alice is evidence of commitment. Alice's one-way function in step (3) prevents Bob from inverting the function and determining the bit. When it comes the time for Alice to reveal her bit, the protocol continues: (4) Alice sends Bob the original message (R_1, R_2, b). (5) Bob computes the one-way function on the message and compares it and R_1, with the value and random string he received in step (3). If they match, the bit is valid. The benefit of this protocol over the previous one is that Bob does not have to send any messages. Alice sends Bob one message to commit to a bit and another message to reveal the bit. Bob's random string isn't required because the result of Alice's commitment is a message operated on by a one-way function. Alice cannot cheat and find another message (R_1, R_2', b'), such that $H(R_1, R_2', b') = H(R_1, R_2, b)$.. By sending Bob R_1 she is committing to the value of b. If Alice didn't keep R_2 secret, then Bob could compute both $H(R_1, R_2, b)$ and $H(R_1, R_2, b')$ and see which was equal to what he received from Alice.

We will be using commitment scheme to construct secure watermark verification scheme. In the following we use a commitment scheme of [9]: Let $n = pq$ is a safe prime product. We only need that $p = q = 3 \bmod 4$, that $\gcd(p-1, q-1) = 2$ and that $p-1$, $q-1$ do not have too many small prime factors. Let the factorization of n is unknown by Peggy and Vic. We then set $G = Z_n^*$ and set g be is element of large order in G, h is an element of large order generated by g such that both the discrete logarithm of g in base h and the discrete logarithm of h in base g are unknown by Peggy. To commit to an integer $m \in Z_n$, Peggy randomly chooses r in $[0, 2^L n)$, and sends $com(m) = g^m h^r \bmod n$ to Vic, where L is in the order of the bit length of n, r is in secret, n, g and h are public. To open a commitment, Peggy must send m, r such that $com(m) = g^m h^r \bmod n$. Peggy is unable to commit herself to two values m_1, m_2, such that $m_1 \neq m_2$ by the same commitment unless she can factor n or solve the discrete logarithm of g in base h or the discrete logarithm of h in base g. And this commitment scheme statistically reveals no information to Vic. So, this commitment scheme is (statistically) hiding and (computationally) binding.

2.2 Zero Knowledge Proofs

Zero knowledge proof is an active research area in cryptography. The concept of zero knowledge is first introduced by Goldwasser, Micali and Rackoff. Very informally, a zero knowledge proof system allows one person, Peggy, to convince another person, Vic, of some fact without revealing any information about the proof. At the end, Vic is completely convinced of the fact, but doesn't get any useful knowledge about the fact. This shows two things. One, it is impossible for Vic to convince a third party of the proof's validity. And two, it is zero knowledge. Zero knowledge proof must satisfy the following two conditions: completeness and soundness. Limited to length, we only provide the above simple introduction only. The detail to zero knowledge proof is provided in [7] and [8].

3 Watermark Verification Scheme

In this section, we first introduce our basic definitions and notations of watermark schemes. We then provide the secure watermark verification scheme.

3.1 Definitions and Notations of Watermark Scheme

Let $\underline{h}$ denote the host data (image, audio or video) and m denote the watermark message. For watermark message m to be embedded, to make suitable process, we get $w = (w_1, w_2, \ldots, w_N)$ that is the actual watermark sequence to be embedded. Let $\overline{h}$, k_{emb}, k_{extr} be the watermarked host data (it is possible that the watermarked host data is submitted to some attacks), key used for embedding watermark and key used for extracting watermark, respectively. k_{extr} must be kept a secret. For symmetric key watermark scheme, there is $k_{emb} = k_{extr}$. The host data $\underline{h}$ is not necessarily needed during detection process, e.g., blind detection. However, it may be used to improve the robustness. Let $w' = (w_1', w_2', \ldots, w_N')$ be the extracted watermark sequence, where $w_i' = Extr(\overline{h}, [\underline{h}], k_{extr})_i$, $i = 1, 2, \ldots, N$, $Extr(\overline{h}, [\underline{h}], k_{extr})$ denotes extracting watermark based on values of $\overline{h}$, $[\underline{h}]$ and k_{extr}, $[\underline{h}]$ means $\underline{h}$ is optional. In watermark verification the correlation value

$$cr = \frac{<w, w'>}{<w, w>}$$

between the watermark sequence w and extracted watermark sequence w' is used, where $<a, b>$ denotes the scalar product of the two vectors a and b. Given some threshold ε, if $cr > \varepsilon$, then we can think of presence of the watermark w in $\overline{h}$ .. An equivalent version to $cr > \varepsilon$ is

$$<w, w'> - <w, w> *\varepsilon > 0.$$

And its spreading version is

$$(w_1 w_1' + w_2 w_2' + \cdots + w_N w_N') - (w_1^2 + w_2^2 + \cdots + w_N^2)\varepsilon > 0.$$

3.2 Watermark Verification Scheme

In this subsection, we provide watermark verification scheme to prove presence of a watermark in a digital data. This scheme is based on commitment scheme and zero knowledge proof.

Peggy chooses any permutation $\tau \in S_n$, S_n is permutation group on n elements. Peggy scrambles $\overline{h}$ to produce $\tau(\overline{h})$ (if the size of h is larger, block of size n will be scrambled independently). Peggy publishes $\overline{h}$ and $\tau(\overline{h})$, but τ is kept secret. Note that deducing τ from $\overline{h}$ and $\tau(\overline{h})$ is likely to be infeasible, as it would require finding an isomorphism between $\overline{h}$ and $\tau(\overline{h})$. In order to verify $\tau(\overline{h})$ is a scrambled version of $\overline{h}$ by using random permutation τ without revealing any information about τ, we provide a zero knowledge interactive protocol $ZKIP(\tau, \overline{h}, \tau(\overline{h}))$.

Protocol $ZKIP(\tau, \overline{h}, \tau(\overline{h}))$

(1) Peggy chooses a random permutation σ of permutation group S_n on n elements and sends $\sigma(\overline{h})$ to Vic.

(2) Vic chooses at random a bit b, and sends it to Peggy.

(3) If $b = 0$, Peggy sets $\rho = \sigma^{-1}$, else he sets $\rho = \tau\sigma^{-1}$. Peggy sends ρ to Vic.

(4) Vic checks that $\rho(\sigma(\overline{h})) = \overline{h}$ if $b = 0$ or $\rho(\sigma(\overline{h})) = \tau(\overline{h})$ if b=1, and rejects immediately if not.

(5) Peggy and Vic perform these steps k times. If all k checks were completed successfully, Vic accepts $\tau(\overline{h})$ is a scrambled version of $\overline{h}$.

It can be shown easily that the protocol is perfect zero knowledge.

Let n, g, h and ε be the common inputs of Peggy and Vic, where n, g, h can be generated by a trusted third party. We assume ε, the watermark sequence and the extracted watermark sequence are integers. Note that this is not real constraint, because we can scale the sequence appropriately. Now, we give the watermark verification scheme based on commitment scheme.

(1) Peggy first computes $w_i' = Extr(\tau(\overline{h}), [\tau(\underline{h})], \tau(k_{extr}))_i$ and $\tau(w_i)$, $i=1,2,..,N.$. For convenience of denotation, we denote $\tau(w_i)$ with w_i, $i=1,2,..,N$ and denote $\tau(w)$ with w still.

(2) Peggy computes commitments $com(\varepsilon) = g^{\varepsilon}h^{r} \bmod n$, $com(w_i) = g^{w_i}h^{r} \bmod n$ and $com(w_i') = g^{w_i'}h^{r} \bmod n$, then sends $com(\varepsilon)$, $com(w_i)$ and $com(w_i')$ to Vic, $i = 1, 2, \ldots, N$.

(3) Peggy computes $com(w_i w_i')$ and $com(\varepsilon w_i^2)$, then sends them to Vic, $i = 1, 2, \ldots, N$.

(4) Peggy proves Vic that commitment $com(w_i w_i')$ contains number is the product of two numbers contained in $com(w_i)$ and $com(w_i')$, and commitment $com(\varepsilon w_i^2)$ contains number is the product of numbers contained in $com(\varepsilon)$ and square of number contained in $com(w_i)$ using zero knowledge protocol (see [10] or [11]) respectively, $i = 1, 2, \ldots, N$ ..

(5) Peggy proves Vic that both commitment $com(<w, w'>)$ and $com(\varepsilon < w, w >)$ contain numbers are the sum of numbers contained in $com(w_1 w_1')$, $com(w_2 w_2')$, ... $com(w_N w_N')$ and the sum of numbers contained in $com(\varepsilon w_1^2)$, $com(\varepsilon w_2^2)$, ... , $com(\varepsilon w_N^2)$ using zero knowledge protocol (see [10] or [11]) respectively..

(6) Peggy and Vic compute

$$com(<w, w'>-<w, w> \varepsilon) = \frac{com(<w, w'>)}{com(\varepsilon < w, w >)} \bmod n$$

(7) Peggy proves Vic that $com(<w, w'>-<w, w> \varepsilon)$ contains a value ≥ 0 using zero knowledge protocol (see [12]).

The scheme is zero knowledge proof of knowledge. It is easy to see that this proof system satisfies the completeness and soundness properties: (1) completeness: The proof always succeeds if the watermark w is in watermarked data h .. (2) soundness: for cheating Peggy has to break either the soundness of protocols or the binding property of the commitment scheme. However, it is impossible because a cheating Vic can succeed with very small probability and binding is assumed to be computationally impossible.

Note that in the verification scheme we use the scrambled version of $\overline{h}$ and w than $\overline{h}$ and w themselves in order to prevent attacker from underlying attack [6].

4 Conclusion

In watermark verification, it is important to be able to show the presence of a watermark in a digital data without revealing the watermark information. In this paper, we propose a secure watermark verification scheme based on commitment scheme and zero knowledge proof in order to solve this problem. There will be no secret information that can be used for removing watermark that is disclosed during the verification process. It has considerable advantages over previous proposed schemes in terms of security. The disadvantage of the proposed protocol is the larger amount of transmitted information during watermark verification. Thus, our future work will focus on secure scheme with higher efficiency.

References

1. H. Kinoshita.: An Image Digital Signature System with ZKIP for the Graph Isomorphism Problem. Proc. IEEE Conf. Image Processing (ICIP96), vol.3. IEEE Press, Piscataway, N.J., (1996) 247-250.
2. K. Gopalakrishnan, N. Memon, P. Vora.: Protocols for Watermark Verification. Multimedia and Security, Workshop at ACM Multimedia. (1999) 91-94.
3. A. Adelsbach, A. R. Sadeghi, " Zero Knowledge Watermark Detection and Proof of Ownership," Information Hiding: Fourth International Workshop, LNCS 2137, Springer Verlag. (2001) 273-287.
4. I. Cox, J. Kilian, T. Leighton, T. Shamoon.:Secure spread spectrum watermarking for multimedia.. IEEE Transactions on Image Processing, vol. 6. (1997) 1673–1687.
5. S. Craver.:Zero Knowledge Watermark Detection . Information Hiding : Third International Workshop, LNCS 1768, Springer-Verlag, (2000) 101-116.
6. S. Craver, S. Katzenbeisser, "Copyright Protection Protocols Based on Asymmetric Watermarking: The Ticket Concept, " to appear in Communications and Multimedia Security 2001.
7. D. R. Stinson.:Cryptography—Theory and practice. CRC Press, Boca Raton, Fla (1995)
8. B. Schneier.: Applied Cryptography: protocols, Algorithms, and Source Code in C. 2nd ed. New York: John Wiley and Sons (1996)
9. E. Fujisaki, T. Okamoto.:A practical and provably secure scheme for publicly verifiable secret sharing and its applications. Eurocrypt'98, LNCS 1403, Springer -Verlag, (1998) 88-100.
10. J. Camenisch, M. Michels,.:Proving in Zero- Knowledge that a Number is the Product of Two Safe Primes. Eurocrypt'99, LNCS 1592, Springer-Verlag, (2000) 101-116.
11. I. Damgard, E. Fujisaki.:An Integer Commitment Scheme based on Groups with Hiding Order. Preliminary Version.
12. F. Boudot.:Efficient Proofs that a Committed Number Lies in an Interval. Eurocrypt'00, LNCS 1807, Springer-Verlag (2000) 431-444.

A Foveation-Based Rate Shaping Mechanism for MPEG Videos

Chia-Chiang Ho and Ja-Ling Wu

Communication and Multimedia Laboratory,
Department of Computer Science and Information Engineering,
National Taiwan University,
No. 1, Roosvelt Rd. Sec. 4, Taipei, Taiwan
{conrad, wjl}@cmlab.csie.ntu.edu.tw
http://www.cmlab.csie.ntu.edu.tw/cml/dsp/index.html

Abstract. Considering human perceptual property and user specific need can help to reduce the bandwidth requirement for streaming compressed videos over networks. In this paper, we present a foveation-based rate shaping mechanism for MPEG bitstreams. The rate shaper is designed based on an experimental-proven foveation model, and achieve rate reduction by eliminating DCT coefficients embedded in MPEG bitstreams. An efficient rate control mechanism is developed to meet various bitrate requirements, and a real-time implementation is developed to confirm that the proposed scheme is practical for real world usage.

1 Introduction

With rapid increasing of bandwidth of broadband networks and the computation power of general CPU's nowadays, more and more applications depend on transporting videos over networks are developed. The most vital obstacle to achieve real-time video streaming is the heterogeneity problem, which comes from both network and user perspectives. All these heterogeneities require that video bitstreams be available on a continuum of bit-rates, and this raises a new challenge for the design of video coding schemes. In recent years, scalable coding schemes have been proposed to deal with such heterogeneous situations [1][2]. However, scalable coding has it limitation in nature. A different approach is to encode the video with high bitrate and provide some rate reduction mechanism to dynamically adapt the video bitstream to channel condition. In the literature, mechanisms proposed for rate reduction can be divided into two categories: *transcoding* and *rate shaping*. Transcoding refers to some kind of re-encoding. Typical operations of transcoders possibly demand large computation power, especially when motion vector re-estimation and coding mode re-determination are required. Rate shaping, on the contrary, constitutes a light-weighted solution for rate reduction. In a nutshell, rate shaping aims at discarding some information (generally DCT coefficients) resided in the original bitstream and leaving other parts unchanged [3]-[8]. When computation complexity is concerned, rate shaping is obviously more suitable for real-time usage.

Y.-C. Chen, L.-W. Chang, and C.-T. Hsu (Eds.): PCM 2002, LNCS 2532, pp. 485–492, 2002.

Traditional rate shaping schemes try to uniformly minimize the distortion over each region of images. However, in some applications, users focus more on some regions of images and expect better quality in those regions. For example, in a remote education application, students' focus mostly on the teacher, or some specific region of the blackboard and lecture slides. This call for developing new rate shaping scheme adaptive to the content and/or user preference. In this paper, we propose a rate shaping mechanism that makes use of a novel human visual system (HVS) property- foveation, i.e., the decreasing spatial resolution of HVS away from the point of gaze. Reference [9] was a related work. However, it relied on heuristic rules which are determined empirically, without any religious model for foveation.

2   Foveation Model

Modern lossy compression techniques try to discard perceptually unimportant or insensible information under some presumed HVS models. Psychological researches had shown that the capability of human perception over images, measured as sampling density or contrast sensibility, has a non-uniform distribution with respect to spatial location of perceived image segments. Specifically, the sampling density and contrast sensibility decrease dramatically with increasing eccentricity (i.e., viewing angle with respect to the fovea). A foveation model that fits psychological experiment data was proposed in [10] as:

$$CT(f, e) = CT_0 \exp\left(\alpha f \frac{e_2 + e}{e}\right) , \qquad (1)$$

where f is the spatial frequency (cycle/degree), e is the eccentricity (degrees), CT_0 is the minimal contrast threshold, α is the spatial frequency decay constant, and e_2 is the half-resolution eccentricity constant (degrees). The best fitting parameters reported in [10] are $\alpha = 0.106$, $e_2 = 2.3$ and $CT_0 = 1/64$. It was also reported that the same α and e_2 provide a good fit to the data in [12] and a proper fit to the data in [13], with CT_0 equals to 1/75 and 1/76, respectively.

For any given points $\bar{x} = (x, y)$ in a digital image, the corresponding eccentricity with respect to the foveation point $\bar{x}_f = (x_f, y_f)$ can be calculated as:

$$e(x, y) = \tan^{-1}\left(\frac{\sqrt{(x - x_f)^2 + (y - y_f)^2}}{WD}\right) , \qquad (2)$$

where D is the viewing distance measured in image width W (pixels). Note that this calculation is still valid when the image is displayed with scaling, providing that the scaling ratio is the same for both horizontal and vertical directions.

In this paper, we relate the foveation model to the visibility of the DCT basis functions, so that a foveation filter that acts on DCT coefficients resided in MPEG bitstreams, can be developed.

For a $N \times N$ DCT kernel, the (m, n)-th basis function can be written as:

$$B_{m,n}(j, k) = C_{m,n} \cos\left(\frac{(2j+1)\pi m}{2N}\right) \cos\left(\frac{(2k+1)\pi n}{2N}\right), \quad j, k = 0, \cdots, N-1 , \tag{3}$$

where $C_{m,n}$ is a constant. For each $B_{m,n}$, the corresponding spatial frequency $f_{m,n}$ can be calculated by following equations (after [14]):

$$f_{m,n} = \sqrt{f_{m,0}^2 + f_{0,n}^2} , \tag{4}$$

$$f_{m,0} = \frac{m}{2Nw_x} \quad \text{and} \quad f_{0,n} = \frac{n}{2Nw_y} , \tag{5}$$

where w_x and w_y are the horizontal width and the vertical height of one pixel in degrees of visual angle, respectively. In this paper, we approximate w_x and w_y by the following equation:

$$w = w_x = w_y = \frac{\tan^{-1}(1/2D)}{W/2} . \tag{6}$$

It should be noted that double-orientated $B_{m,n}$ (i.e., both m and n are nonzero) can be viewed as a sum of two frequency components with the same spatial frequency as in equation (4), but with different orientations [14]. And the angle between these two components is

$$\theta_{m,n} = \sin^{-1}\frac{2f_{m,0}f_{0,n}}{f_{m,n}^2} . \tag{7}$$

Moreover, a multiplicative factor $1/(r + (1-r)\cos^2\theta_{m,n})$ should be applied to the minimum contrast threshold CT_0 [14], to account for the imperfect summation of the two frequency components and also the reduced sensitivity due to the obliqueness of the two components [15][16]. The value of r is set to 0.6 in our work.

Integrating all these equations yields the following foveation model:

$$CT(f_{m,n}, e) = \frac{CT_0}{r + (1-r)\cos^2\theta_{m,n}} \exp\left(\frac{\alpha(e_2 + e)\sqrt{m^2 + n^2}}{2e_2 Nw}\right) . \tag{8}$$

The *critical eccentricity* $e_c(m, n)$ for a fixed $f_{m,n}$ is found by setting the left side of equation (8) to 1.0 (the maximum contrast) and solving for e:

$$e_c(m, n) = \frac{4Ne_2\tan^{-1}(1/2D)}{\alpha W\sqrt{m^2 + n^2}} \ln\left(\frac{r + (1-r)\cos^2\theta_{m,n}}{CT_0}\right) - e_2 . \tag{9}$$

For one block with center point (x, y), we can thus have the following critical condition for each (m, n)-th DCT coefficient:

$$e(x, y) > e_c(m, n) . \tag{10}$$

That is, if (10) is true, no matter how large the (m, n)-th DCT coefficient is, for human eyes it is indistinguishable from zero.

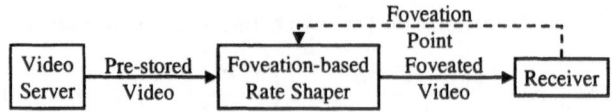

Fig. 1. The system model presumed in this paper.

3   Foveation-Based Rate Shaping

Once the relationship between the foveation model and the sensitivity of DCT coefficients has been established, we are now ready to apply it for rate shaping of MPEG videos. Fig. 1 shows the system model adopted in this paper. When one pre-compressed video is requested for transmission, it is sent to the foveation-based rate shaper for downsizing to meet the available bitrate constraint between the rate shaper and the final receiver. The rate shaper may be located in the bottleneck of the network, or be co-located with the video source. The available bandwidth can be estimated either by sender-based, receiver-based, or hybrid methods [17], and the choice among them is outside the scope of this paper. However, we do propose a rate control algorithm to meet the available band-width estimated. A back channel is assumed between the rate shaper and the receiver, to transmit control signal (most important of all, the foveation point) in-between. In our experiments, foveation point is specified explicitly by the mouse click activated by the user. Since our foveation filter is block-based, the actual foveation point used is the center of the block at which the user specified point located, and we denote the block as the *foveation block*. Collaboration with other kind of user interfaces, such as an eye tracker, has no contradiction to the foundational idea proposed in this paper.

3.1   Foveation-Based Rate Shaping by Coefficient Elimination

Foveation-based rate shaping is based on the critical condition (10). The bitrate of one coded block is reduced by eliminating a series of DCT coefficients at the end of that block, in zigzag scanning order. The number of DCT coefficients kept is called the *breakpoint* (borrowed from [3][4], originally for the constrained DRS problem), corresponding to the first (m, n) pair, in reverse zigzag order, that doesn't qualify the critical condition (10).

Computation complexity is always an issue for real-time rate reduction mechanisms. To ease heavy computation incurred by checking (10), we can calculate critical eccentricities in advance, and generate *breakpoint maps* for different viewing distances. In this way, the required computation at runtime is minimized.

Breakpoint Maps. The image width W is derived from parsing the sequence header of the input bitstream. The viewing distance D is restricted to be of integer values, for example, $D = \{k \mid k \in N, 1 \leq k \leq 8\}$ for normal viewing distances. The foveation block is set to be the top-left block in one frame, and the foveation point is the center of this block. By calculating $e_c(m, n)$'s for all (m, n) pairs, the breakpoint of every block for different viewing distances can be found by comparing the corresponding eccentricity to $e_c(m, n)$'s. These breakpoints are stored in array form, i.e., $BK[D][b_x][b_y]$, and we call breakpoints for different viewing distances as different *breakpoint maps*. By this way, at runtime, the required breakpoints can be retrieved by table look-up, with some index shifting. It can be observed that critical eccentricities are symmetric horizontally and vertically with respect to the foveation point. So if the foveation block is specified at location (B_x, B_y), the breakpoint of one block at (b_x, b_y) is just $BK[D][|b_x - B_x|][|b_y - B_y|]$.

3.2   Foveation Mismatch Problem

The foveation process described in the last subsection has no difference between blocks with different coding types. Thus for predicted blocks (those blocks in P- or B-type macroblocks), we are actually foveating the prediction error. This possibly leads to the foveation mismatch problem discussed as follows. In the original video, assume one block M with location (b_x, b_y) is used to predict another block $M' = M + E$ with location (b'_x, b'_y), where E represents the prediction error. For simplicity, we assume here M is coded in intra mode, and take method 1 as an example. In our work, the block M will be foveation filtered with its corresponding breakpoint value BK_a. Let we denote the filtered data as M_a. Now considering foveation filtering of the block M'. For an ideal foveation, we expect to reconstruct $M_b + E_b$, that is, M' foveation filtered with its breakpoint value BK_b. However, in our work, we actually reconstruct $M_a + E_b$. If BK_a is not the same as BK_b, the foveation mismatch problem occurs. Fortunately, we found that this is not a big issue according to two observations of MPEG compressed videos. First, most motion vectors are very small– this is confirmed by many researches and is due to signal nature of typical videos. Second, due to complexity issue of typical video encoders, the motion vector is limited in a small region, for example, not exceeding two macroblock wide (± 32 pixel). So, for most predicted blocks, the difference between BK_a and BK_b is zero or ignorable.

3.3   Rate Control

Rate control is required to generate a suitable rate-shaped bitstream to fit the available bandwidth estimated. In our work, rate control is achieved by properly increasing the minimum contrast threshold, CT_0. We restrict the modified CT_0, denoted as CT_1, to be some fixed values:

$$CT_1(k) = CT_0 + kS, \quad k = 0, 1, \ldots, K , \tag{11}$$

where S is the step size. Adding a dimension for CT_1, the breakpoint maps in our experiments take forms of $BK[D][k][b_x][b_y]$.

Rate control requires a rate model. Here we choose the ρ-domain rate model proposed in [18], for its simplicity, efficiency and easy integration with the

Table 1. Variable for the rate control scheme used in this paper.

Notation	Meaning (unit)
R_S	The bitrate of the source bitstream (bps).
R_T	The target bitrate of the new bitstream (bps).
r_S	The bitcount of one specific frame F_t in the source bitstream (bits).
r_T	The target bitcount of the frame F_t in the foveated bitstream (bits).
B	The size of encoding buffer (bits).
B_{t-1}	The number of bits in the buffer before processing the frame F_t (bits).
γ	The target buffer fullness ratio (%).
θ_t	The frame dependent constant in the rate model for the frame F_t.
Z_t	The count of zero coefficients in the frame F_t.
$z_t(k)$	The count of zero coefficients when applying the foveation model with $CT_1(k)$ to the frame F_t.
M_{total}	The number of blocks in one frame.

foveation model adopted. Based on the insight that the number of zeros plays an important role in transform coding of images and videos, it was observed in [18] a linear relation between R and ρ (the percentage of zeros among the quantized transform coefficients). This linear relation can be modeled as:

$$R(\rho) = \theta(1 - \rho) , \qquad (12)$$

where θ is a frame dependent constant. In our work, since the input is a compressed MPEG bitstream, the value of θ for each coded frame can be easily found by partial decoding.

Let's come back to our foveation model. For a fixed viewing distance D, there is a one-to-one relationship between the CT_1 and ρ. In this way, we relate the foveation model with the rate model. Before presenting the rate control scheme used in our work, we define necessary variables and list them in table 1.

The rate control method of applying foveation-based rate shaping to frame F_t is briefed as follows.

1. (Initialization) Set r_S, Z_t and all $z_t(k)$'s to zero.
2. Decode one block into DCT coefficients, and increase r_S, Z_t and each $z_t(k)$ accordingly (with breakpoint maps). Iteratively performing this step until all blocks are processed.
3. The frame-dependent constant ρ_t is found as $r_S/(1 - Z_t/M_{total})$. And the target bitcount r_T is calculated proportionally to the ratio of target and source bitrate, with adjustment according to the buffer fullness:

$$r_T = r_S(R_T/R_S) - B_{t-1} + B\gamma . \qquad (13)$$

4. The target percentage of zero is derived as $\rho = 1 - (r_T/\theta_t)$. The intended value of CT_1 is found by:

$$CT_1^* = \arg\min_{CT_1(k)} |\rho M_{total} - z_t(k)| . \qquad (14)$$

5. The frame is foveation-rate-shaped with the breakpoint map corresponding to CT_1^*.

Fig. 2. Snapshots of foveated videos for the sequence *akiyo* (MPEG-2 format, 704×576, 30 fps, 1024kbps). The foveation block is specified around the nose. D is set to 6, and CT_1's used (from left to right) are 0.015625, 0.165625 and 0.315625, respectively.

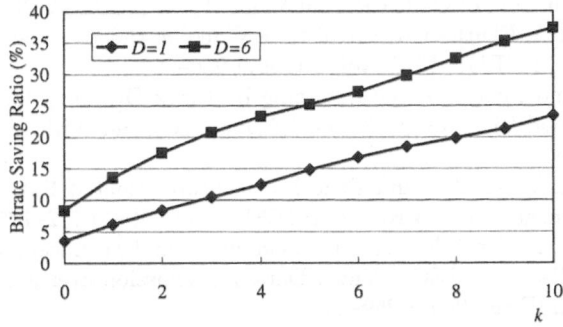

Fig. 3. Tradeoff between CT_1 and the rate saving ratio for the sequence *akiyo*. The stepsize S used here is 0.03, i.e., $CT_1 = CT_0 + 0.03k$.

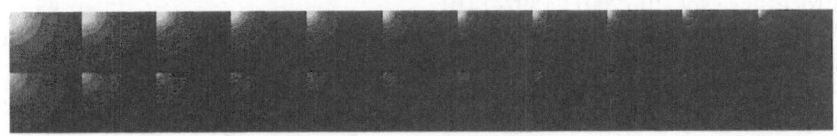

Fig. 4. Breakpoint maps for *akiyo*. The value of D is set to 1 and 6 for upper and lower row, respectively. The value of CT_1 increases from left to right. Note that breakpoint values are scaled up into the range $[0, 255]$ for display here.

4   Experimental Results

We test the proposed foveation-based rate shaping method using some well-known sequences. Fig.2 show snapshots of foveated videos of the sequence *akiyo*. Fig.3 shows the relationship between CT_1 and the bitrate saving ratio. For CT_1 close to CT_0, the quality distortion introduced in the periphery regions (regions far away from the foveation center)is invisible. Larger bitrate reduction caused by larger CT_1 will incur visible block effects in periphery regions, representing a tradeoff between bitrate and periphery distortion. As mentioned previously, the proposed rate shaper is of low complexity because breakpoints for each block are calculated in advance. Fig.4 shows an example of calculated breakpoint maps.

References

1. Information Technology-Generic Coding of Moving Pictures and Associated Audio: Video. ISO/IEC 13818-2 (1995)
2. Coding of Audio-Visual Objects– Part-2 Visual. ISO/IEC 14496-2 (1999)
3. Eleftheriadis and D. Anastassiou: Constrained and General Dynamic Rate Shaping of Compressed Digital Video. Proc. ICIP'95 IEEE, vol. 3. (1995) 396–399
4. Eleftheriadis and D. Anastassiou: Meeting Arbitrary QoS Constraints Using Dynamic Rate Shaping of Coded Digital Video. Proc. NOSDAV'95. (1995) 95–106
5. S. Jacobs and A. Eleftheriadis: Real-time Video on the Web Using Dynamic Rate Shaping. Proc. ICIP'97 IEEE, vol. 2 (1997) 250–253
6. W.-J. Zeng and Bede Liu: Rate Shaping by Block Dropping for Transmission of MPEG-precoded Video over Channel of Dynamic Bandwidth. Proc. ACM Multimedia'96 (1996)
7. W.-J. Zeng, Baining Guo and Bede Liu: Feature-oriented Rate Shaping of Precompressed Image/Video. Proc. ICIP IEEE, vol.2 (1997) 772–775
8. N. Celandroni, E. Ferro, F. Potorti, A. Chimienti and M. Lucenteforte: DRS Compression Applied to MPEG-2 Video Data Transmission over a Satellite Channel. Proc. ISCC'00 IEEE (2000) 259–266
9. T. H. Reeves and J. A. Robinson: Adaptive foveation of MPEG Video. Proc. ACM Multimedia'96 (1996) 231–241
10. W. S. Geisler and J. S. Perry: A Real-Time Foveated Multiresolution System for Low-bandwidth Video Communication. Proc. SPIE, vol. 3299 (1998)
11. Z. Wang and A. C. Bovik: Embedded Foveation Image Coding. IEEE Trans. Image Processing, vol. 10 (2001) 1397–1410
12. W. S. Geisler: Visual Detection Following Retinal Damage: Predictions of an Inhomogeneous Retino-cortical Model. Proc. IEEE, vol .2674 (1996) 119–130
13. M. S. Banks, A. B. Sekuler, and S. J. Anderson: Peripheral Spatial Vision: Limits Imposed by Optics, Photoreceptors and Receptor Pooling. J. Opt. Soc. Amer., vol. 8 (1991) 1775–1787
14. J. Ahumada Jr. and H. A. Peterson: Luminance-model-based DCT Quantization for Color Image Compression. Proc. SPIE, vol.1666 (1992) 365–374
15. G. C. Phillips and H. R. Wilson: Orientation Bandwidths of Spatial Mechanisms Measured by Masking. J. Opt. Soc. Amer., vol. 1 (1984) 226–232
16. B. Watson: Detection and Recognition of Simple Spatial Forms. O. J. Braddick and A. C. Sleigh (Ed.), Physical and Biological Processing of Images, Springer-Verlag, Berlin (1983)
17. D.-P. Wu, Y.-W. Thomas Hou, and Y.-Q. Zhang: Transporting Real-Time Video over the Internet: Challenges and Approaches. Proc. IEEE, vol. 88, No. 12, (2000) 1855–1875
18. Y. K. Kim, Z. He and S. K. Mitra: A Novel Linear Source Model and a Unified Rate Control Algorithm for H.263/MPEG-2/MPEG-4. Proc. ICASSP'01 IEEE, vol. 3 (2001) 1777–1780

A Stereo Image Coding Using Hierarchical Basis*

Han-Suh Koo and Chang-Sung Jeong

Department of Electronics Engineering, Korea University
1-5ka, Anam-dong, Sungbuk-ku, Seoul 136-701, Korea
{esprit@snoopy,csjeong@charlie}.korea.ac.kr

Abstract. With the increase of interesting about stereoscopy, stereo coding techniques are raising issues. Because stereo image pair has many different features compared with monocular image sequences, stereo coding problem should be discussed separately from compression of monocular sequences. In this paper, we propose an improved technique to code a target image patch with specially designed block vector set. Multiresolutional basis vectors are designed to present a hierarchical architecture to adapt our system to a transmission condition or user's request easily. Some block vectors that are independent to reference image help to represent edges or occlusions effectively. We will show that our scheme provides enhancements in not only quality of decompressed image but processing time.

1 Introduction

With the increase of interesting about applications related to 3D, compression techniques of stereo sequence become an issue [1]. Because a lot of techniques for compression of monocular image sequences have been developed and they are used by various systems, coding of stereo sequences should be compatible to these systems. Therefore stereo image coding techniques become the centerpiece in manipulation of stereo sequences and researches are focused on the compression of stereo image pair.

To code stereo images, block-based disparity compensation schemes whose ideas are derived from the motion compensation have been proposed [2,3,4]. However it is expected to get better result if stereo image coding is handled in different manner from compression of monocular image sequences. The property between stereo images and monocular image sequences are different because disparity between stereo pair is distant compared with typical motion vector of monocular image sequences and occlusions may appear in stereo images [5]. Projection-based filtering schemes have been proposed because they are more suitable to stereo pairs for properties described above. A set of basis vectors can help to represent target image correctly [6]. When these approaches are combined with block-based schemes, they can obtain a compromise between good

---

* This work was supported by Grid middleware center(ITRC), Grid middleware research project(KISTI) and BK21 program.

compensation ability and low coding bit rate [7]. Because low-resolution images may be requested in multimedia systems under bad transmission condition, the ability to control the resolution level of decoded image is required. So we designed a stereo coding algorithm, namely the *hierarchical subspace projection* (HSP) scheme, using multiresolutional basis that have the hierarchical property. By HSP scheme, decoder can use basis as many times as it require. Specially designed block vectors which are independent to reference image improve the compensation ability of edges and occlusions.

This paper is organized as follows. In section 2, stereo coding approaches are described briefly. We present our HSP algorithm using hierarchical basis in section 3 and review the experimental results of our algorithm in section 4. Finally we give a conclusion and future work in section 5.

2   Stereo Coding

To compress stereo image sequence, monocular compression techniques can be applied to each channel separately. But these approaches are inefficient because it is wasteful to use double the bandwidth for compression of similar two sequences. So, in most cases, canonical monocular compression techniques are applied to one image as reference image, and prediction and compensation using reference image patches are applied to the other one as target image.

Block-based disparity compensation has been used for motion-compensation. This approach is simple and shows low encoding overhead. But blocky effects and lack of compensation ability are accepted to be inevitable in some degree.

The projection-based filtering approach is one of the alternatives. When this approach is combined with block-based scheme, the defects of block-based scheme can be relieved. This approach is suitable for stereo images that have many occlusions, for it can use either the information from reference image or clues prepared outside the image.

3   Stereo Image Coding Using Hierarchical Basis

3.1   Projection Based Filtering

As most stereo image coding schemes are based on the block-based algorithm, our system divides target image into non-overlapping blocks of size $K \times K$. Each block t_L in target image is fully represented by a linear combination of the vectors in subspace $\mathbf{B} = \{\mathbf{b}_l\}_1^L$ and estimation error vector $\mathbf{e}_L$.

$$\mathbf{t}_L = a_1\mathbf{b}_1 + a_2\mathbf{b}_2 + \cdots + a_L\mathbf{b}_L + \mathbf{e}_L \qquad (1)$$

If basis is selected properly, error vector will ineffective to target vector. In our algorithm, the dimension of subspace $\mathbf{B}$ is equal to the number of image resolution level and one vector is determined at each level. To construct the subspace $\mathbf{B}$, reference image and target image are resized into L levels. The image corresponding to level L is the original size one, and the width and height of image

$$\mathbf{x}_{11} = \begin{bmatrix} 1 & 1 & \cdots & 1 & 1 \\ 1 & 1 & \cdots & 1 & 1 \\ \vdots & \vdots & \cdots & \vdots & \vdots \\ 1 & 1 & \cdots & 1 & 1 \\ 1 & 1 & \cdots & 1 & 1 \end{bmatrix}$$

$$\mathbf{x}_{21} = \begin{bmatrix} 1 & 1 & \cdots & 1 & 1 \\ 2 & 2 & \cdots & 2 & 2 \\ \vdots & \vdots & \cdots & \vdots & \vdots \\ K-1 & K-1 & \cdots & K-1 & K-1 \\ K & K & \cdots & K & K \end{bmatrix} \qquad \mathbf{x}_{22} = \begin{bmatrix} 1 & 2 & \cdots & K-1 & K \\ 1 & 2 & \cdots & K-1 & K \\ \vdots & \vdots & \cdots & \vdots & \vdots \\ 1 & 2 & \cdots & K-1 & K \\ 1 & 2 & \cdots & K-1 & K \end{bmatrix}$$

$$\mathbf{x}_{23} = \begin{bmatrix} K & K & \cdots & K & K \\ K-1 & K-1 & \cdots & K-1 & K-1 \\ \vdots & \vdots & \cdots & \vdots & \vdots \\ 2 & 2 & \cdots & 2 & 2 \\ 1 & 1 & \cdots & 1 & 1 \end{bmatrix} \qquad \mathbf{x}_{24} = \begin{bmatrix} K & K-1 & \cdots & 2 & 1 \\ K & K-1 & \cdots & 2 & 1 \\ \vdots & \vdots & \cdots & \vdots & \vdots \\ K & K-1 & \cdots & 2 & 1 \\ K & K-1 & \cdots & 2 & 1 \end{bmatrix}$$

$$\mathbf{x}_{31} = \mathbf{x}_{21} \odot \mathbf{x}_{22} \qquad \mathbf{x}_{32} = \mathbf{x}_{21} \odot \mathbf{x}_{24} \qquad \mathbf{x}_{33} = \mathbf{x}_{23} \odot \mathbf{x}_{22} \qquad \mathbf{x}_{34} = \mathbf{x}_{23} \odot \mathbf{x}_{24}$$

Fig. 1. External Vector Set $\mathbf{X}$

shrinks to half as the level descends. Because the relationship between the original image and sub-images can be represented as quad-tree relation, the intensity of sub-image corresponding to low resolution is the average of corresponding four pixels in children nodes. To match the blocks at each resolution level, $K \times K$ sized vectors are selected from candidate vector set $\mathbf{C}_l$. Candidate vector set $\mathbf{C}_l$ can contain an internal vector from reference image of corresponding level and external vectors from vector set $\mathbf{X}$ externally predefined. However, external vectors are included only when mismatching is happened between image blocks. After block matching and selection of proper block, we expand these low resolution image into original size. Because low resolution image contains principal texture information and plays important role in coding of original image, this is preferentially used as basis vector. The $K \times K$ sized block of each level possesses $(2^{L-l}K)^2$ pixels at original size actually. Therefore, one block in level l determines 4^{L-l} basis vectors of the original size image level L. By means of hierarchical property, improvements of bit rate and processing time can be achieved.

3.2   Selection of Basis Vectors

The basis vector space $\mathbf{B}$ consists of internal basis vectors and external basis vectors. Internal basis vectors are dependent on the reference image block and external basis vectors are predefined and stored at each side of encoder and decoder. Basis vector is selected from candidate vector set $\mathbf{C}_l$. The number of elements in basis vector and the size of image patch covered by this vector are same in the highest level, but they are not in other levels.

To select basis vectors, image block vector is tested prior to external vectors. Disparities assigned to each image block are estimated by block matching scheme at each level. Firstly, for two images of the lowest level, disparity of (i,j)th block $\mathbf{d}_{i,j:l}|_{l=1}$ is estimated within the search range s. To estimate the disparity of upper level, offset of disparity $\Delta\mathbf{d}_{i,j:l}|_{l=2}$ is found in the range of s whose reference point is the disparity of previous level $\mathbf{d}_{i,j:l}|_{l=1}$. Disparity of each level is estimated in the same rule as $\mathbf{d}_{i,j:l} = 2\mathbf{d}_{\lfloor\frac{i}{2}\rfloor,\lfloor\frac{j}{2}\rfloor:l-1} + \Delta\mathbf{d}_{i,j:l}$.

For the search range at lower level affects higher level, the total size of search range at level l is $S_l = (2^l - 1)s$. If decoder knows the disparity vector at level L and offset of disparity $\Delta\mathbf{d}_{i,j:l}$ of each level, the disparity vector of any level can be estimated. The blocks indicated by disparities at each level are included to corresponding vector set $\mathbf{C}_l$ as a candidate of basis vector, for internal basis vector aims to represent the information of block of target image.

Predefined edge blocks can be used to improve the ability to compensate occlusions that cannot be seen in the reference image or edges for which suitable internal basis block cannot be selected [7]. In this paper, we define external vector set $\mathbf{X}$ containing nine vectors as shown in figure 1. The zero-order vector $\mathbf{x}_{11}$ is designed to represent the uniform surface. Another four vectors $\mathbf{x}_{21}$, $\mathbf{x}_{22}$, $\mathbf{x}_{23}$, and $\mathbf{x}_{24}$ are first-order vectors, and they are used to represent the intensity variation of vertical and horizontal directions. The others, $\mathbf{x}_{31}$, $\mathbf{x}_{32}$, $\mathbf{x}_{33}$, and $\mathbf{x}_{34}$ are second-order vectors for diagonal intensity variations. The entries of matrix that consist of second-order vector are results from the inner product of first-order vectors. These external basis vectors that have entry's smooth distribution are suitable for the representation of occlusion that is invisible in reference image because surfaces of most natural objects have smooth intensity variation. Abrupt change of intensity that can be seen at edge can be represented by border of external vectors. Also PSNR of decoded block that do not have appropriate correspondence because of complex texture can be improved by external vector. External vectors should be used in case of certain block matching failure because they are not inherent to image themselves and excessive use of them may degrade the quality of decoded image.

3.3   Stereo Image Coding Using Multiresolutional Basis

To build subspace $\mathbf{B}$ for each block of target image, internal basis candidate vector $\mathbf{r}_1$ from reference image that is indicated by disparity of the lowest level is included to candidate vector set $\mathbf{C}_l$, i.e. $\mathbf{C}_l|_{l=1} = \{\mathbf{r}_1\}$. This block vector is applied with block vector $\mathbf{t}_1$ from target image of corresponding level to estimate projection coefficient $a_{1:l}|_{l=1}$ for the lowest level. This coefficient is estimated using the formula for calculating projection coefficient $a_{m:l}$,

$$a_{m:l} = \arg\max_{\mathbf{c}_n \in \mathbf{C}_l} \left| \frac{< \mathbf{t}_l, \mathbf{c}_n >}{\|\mathbf{c}_n\|^2} \right|. \tag{2}$$

The error vector $\mathbf{e}_l$ gotten between target block and estimated intensity is $\mathbf{e}_l = \mathbf{t}_l - a_{l:l}\mathbf{r}_l$. The error vector at level $l=1$ is calculated to test the suitability for this

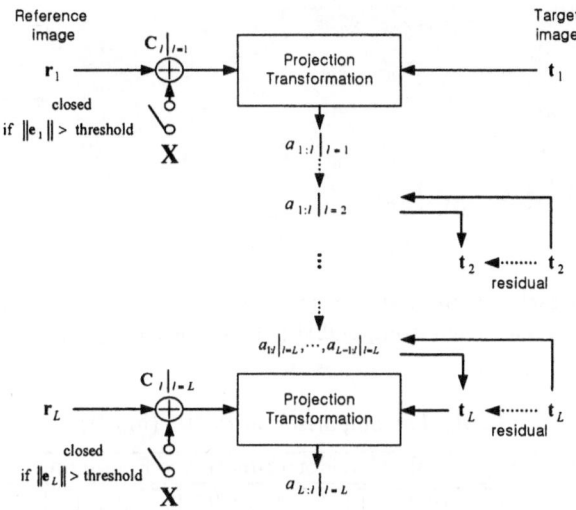

Fig. 2. HSP scheme

block vector. If norm of error vector $\|\mathbf{e}_1\|$ is greater than the quality criterion, we consider that orthogonality between block vector $\mathbf{r}_1$ and block of target image is too great to use as vectors of subspace $\mathbf{B}$ and should test other vectors. The criterion for accepting a block vector $\mathbf{r}_l$ as a container of basis vectors is changeable to the condition of image. By experiment, we found that about 15dB is proper as threshold for general stereo images. If block vector from reference image is not sufficient to be a basis vectors for target image block, projection coefficient should be re-estimated using formula (2) after external vector set $\mathbf{X}$ is added to candidate vector set $\mathbf{C}_l$, i.e. $\mathbf{C}_l|_{l=1} = \{\mathbf{r}_1\} \cup \mathbf{X}$.

To find second basis vector, the next level is considered. Vector $\mathbf{r}_2$ of level 2 comes from the block of reference image indicated by $\mathbf{d}_{i,j:2}$. Projection coefficients estimated at previous level is not valid anymore, because target block has enlarged and detailed contents. Projection coefficients $a_{1:l}|_{l=2}$ for each four blocks with which held by one block of previous level in common are re-estimated with $\mathbf{t}_2$ using formula (2). In the re-estimation of $a_{1:l}|_{l=2}$, candidate vector set $\mathbf{C}_l|_{l=1}$ has only one vector $\mathbf{c}_1$ selected as basis vector container at the process of level 1. For processing residual, $\mathbf{t}_2$ is modified by,

$$\mathbf{t}_l \Leftarrow \mathbf{t}_l - \sum_{m=1}^{l-1} a_{m:l} \mathbf{c}'_m. \tag{3}$$

In this formula, $\mathbf{c}'_m$ is corresponding partial part of $\mathbf{c}_m$ and the target vector $\mathbf{t}_2$ substitutes its entries for residuals from previous level to estimate projection coefficient $a_{2:l}|_{l=2}$. As $\mathbf{r}_2$ is not orthogonal to the corresponding block of previously determined basis vector, vector $\mathbf{r}_2$ is converted into an orthogonal vector using Gram-Schmidt process [8]. Because every nonzero finite-dimensional vector space has an orthogonal basis, we can apply this concept up to level L. After

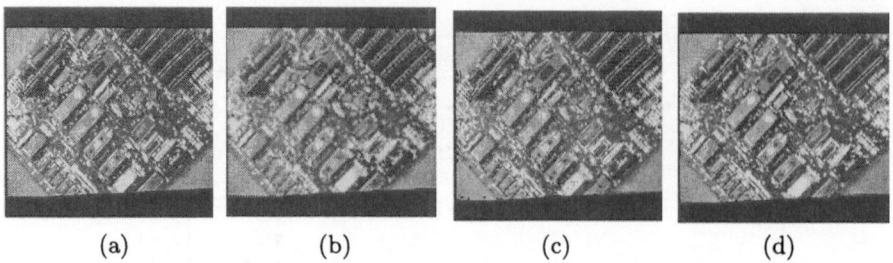

(a)   (b)   (c)   (d)

Fig. 3. Results of each scheme (Apple); (a) Original target image (b) Decoded image using SPT (c) Decoded image using SOSU (d) Decoded image using HSP

Table 1. Comparison in PSNR (in dB)

Algorithm	Apple	Ball	Corridor	Fruit	House	Pentagon	Average
SPT	21.08	18.99	18.58	21.19	24.49	25.11	21.57
SOSU	22.14	21.15	17.33	19.51	26.12	25.60	22.00
HSP-I	24.15	19.24	24.71	19.71	26.24	26.67	23.45
HSP	24.27	20.61	25.31	20.55	26.24	26.67	23.94

orthogonalization, projection coefficient $a_{2:l}|_{l=2}$ is estimated using formula (2). We emphasize the low frequency components by choosing low level basis preferentially for the low frequency components are more important than the high frequency components [3]. Through the quality test of $\mathbf{e}_2$, application of external basis candidate vector space should be determined. If the quality test fails, external vectors that are orthogonalized by basis vectors of previous level are included into $\mathbf{C}_l|_{l=2}$ and newly calculated projection coefficient $a_{2:l}|_{l=2}$ is estimated. With the same manner to level L, target block of level L and each basis vector container produce projection coefficient of each level. After all the calculation is completed up to level L, L basis vectors and corresponding projection coefficients are determined for each blocks of original sized target image. The information to be transferred to decoder are disparity vectors, indices of basis vector space $\mathbf{B}$, and projection coefficients of each resolution $a_{1:l}|_{l=L}, \cdots, a_{l:l}|_{l=L}$. Spatial scalability at decoder is supported by adoption or rejection of transferred information. The entire scheme described in this subsection is shown in figure 2.

4   Experimental Result

As our algorithm is based on projection schemes, we will compare with other similar approaches, such as SPT scheme and SOSU scheme [6,7]. Because we compared the performance of distinctive parts of each scheme, they are substitutive with each other and results given in this paper may be different from those of each work.

In figure 3, we compare the quality of decoded image with stereo image pair. The size of this image is 512×512 with 256 gray levels intensity. In all of our experiments, the dimension of vector space is limited to three and the size of block is chosen to be 8×8 to compare each scheme in similar condition. Figure 3(a) is an original target image. Figure 3(b), 3(c), and 3(d) are decoded images applying SPT, SOSU, and HSP scheme respectively. Compared with other schemes, SPT scheme blurs surfaces. This results from the fixed three bases. Because HSP and SOSU scheme use basis from reference image, they make up for the weak point of SPT scheme. Compared with HSP scheme, SOSU scheme seems to preserve details well. But we learned that SOSU scheme brings about more blocky effects than other schemes do. Our result shows smooth surfaces because larger low-resolution blocks represent low frequency information. This causes some blurring of surfaces. However quantitative analysis of PSNR shows that improvement in blocky effects exceeds degradation by blurring. SPT scheme showed 21.08dB, SOSU scheme showed 22.14dB, and HSP scheme showed 24.27dB for this image. We set the threshold for using external block set to 15.00dB in all of our experiments.

We compared three schemes with various stereo images. The results of each images and average performance are presented in table 1. In ball image and fruit image, the results of HSP scheme are not good as SOSU scheme and SPT scheme, respectively. Because texture of ball image in figure 4 is very complex, blurring property in low resolution of HSP scheme degrades PSNR. The texture of fruit image that possesses some fruits is very simple. This situation minimizes the defect of blurring and SPT scheme shows good performance. However average performance of our scheme exceeds the others except for these extreme cases. In table 1, HSP-I represents the results without external basis. Difference between HSP-I and HSP illustrates that external basis are effective in most cases. Also external basis are not used in some cases, such as house image and pentagon image, because low resolution internal blocks substitute for the role of them.

Figure 4 shows the effects of external basis set. Figure 4(a), 4(b), and 4(c) illustrate the use of external vector set on the original target image. White blocks at each image indicate the position of external basis. In case of failure of matching between block r_l and t_l, external vector set is included in candidate set. This situation arises when blocks contain edge, occlusion, or complex texture. With the help of external basis, we get the gain of 1.37dB compared with the result without external basis. Figure 4(d) shows that mismatched blocks are compensated with external basis.

Multiresolutional basis presents hierarchical structure for disparity vectors, projection coefficients, and block vector indices. We can get the effect of using larger block vector by shrinking the image. Figure 5 illustrates HSP's spatial scalability. Though encoder sends all of information about target image, decoder can discard some information selectively. Figure 5(a) is an original target image. Each block in figure 5(b) is decoded with coefficient $a_{1:l}|_{l=L}$ and corresponding basis vector. Figure 5(c) uses more information of $a_{2:l}|_{l=L}$ and its basis, and 5(d)

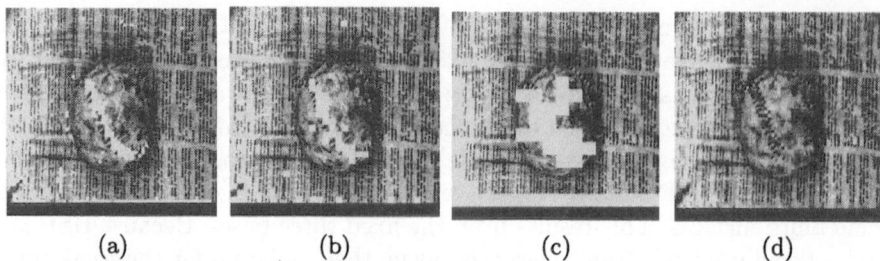

| (a) | (b) | (c) | (d) |

Fig. 4. External blocks (Ball); (a) In high resolution image (b) In mid resolution image (c) In low resolution image (d) Decoded target image

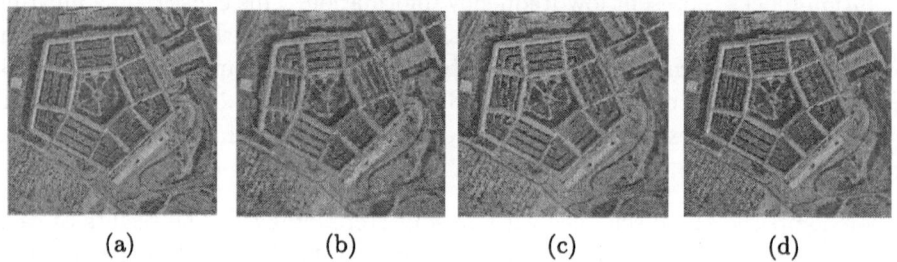

| (a) | (b) | (c) | (d) |

Fig. 5. Spatial Scalability (Pentagon); (a) Original target image (b) Decoded image under level 1 (c) Decoded image under level 2 (d) Decoded image under level 3

Table 2. Processing Time (in second)

Average time	SPT	SOSU	HSP
Encoding	14.72	23.60	2.52
Decoding	0.17	7.69	0.61

uses all of transferred information. The PSNR of figure 5(b), 5(c), and 5(d) are 23.09dB, 24.88dB, and 26.67dB, respectively.

Average processing times for images tested in table 1 are shown in table 2. Tests are performed with P3-500Mhz system. As shown in table 2, HSP scheme shows very fast encoding time. In projection-based schemes, encoding time is mainly dependent on the number of candidate vectors to be a basis. According to each contribution, we assigned 3 candidate vectors to SPT scheme, 126 candidate vectors to SOSU scheme, and 10 candidate vectors to HSP scheme for one basis. Because one basis corresponds to many blocks and external basis is conditional, HSP scheme shows better processing time than others. Decoding time is mainly dependent on the number of bases to reconstruct one block because cost of orthogonalization is considerable. As for decoding time, HSP and SPT scheme are superior to SOSU scheme. Our results show that HSP scheme shows faster encoding time and good decoding time.

5   Conclusion and Future Work

In this paper, we have proposed a new algorithm to code the stereo image using projection-based approach. To select the basis vector, we proposed the method to use hierarchical basis vector. This scheme is to find basis vectors by block matching in various resolution images. For blocks that do not have correct matching, predefined external vectors can be used. By experiments, we showed that our system achieved much improvement. PSNR and processing time can be improved by appropriate selection of hierarchical basis. Also our scheme can adapt to a transmission condition or user's request easily. These advantages enable our scheme to be more suitable for real-time multimedia system. And we are interested in expanding our system to Grid computing environment for future work.

References

1. J. Konrad, "Visual communications of tomorrow: natural, efficient, and flexible," IEEE Communications Magazine, vol. 39, iss. 1, pp. 126-133, Jan. 2001.
2. W. Woo and A. Ortega, "Overlapped block disparity compensation with adaptive windows for stereo image coding," IEEE Trans. Circuits and Systems for Video Technology, vol. 10, no. 2, pp. 194-200, Mar. 2000.
3. M. G. Perkins, "Data Compression of Stereopairs," IEEE Trans. Communications, vol. 40, no. 4, pp. 684-696, Apr. 1992.
4. S. H. Seo, M. R. Azimi-Sadjadi, and B. Tian, "A Least-squares-based 2-D filtering scheme for stereo image compression," IEEE Trans. Image Processing, vol.9, no. 11, pp. 1967-1972, Nov. 2000.
5. O. Faugeras, "Three-Dimensional Computer Vision; A Geometric Viewpoint," Massachusetts Institute of Technology, 1993.
6. H. Aydinoglu and M. H. Hayes, "Stereo image coding: a projection approach," IEEE Trans. Image Processing, vol. 7, no. 4, pp. 506-516, Apr. 1998.
7. S. H. Seo and M. R. Azimi-Sadjadi, "A 2-D filtering scheme for stereo image compression using sequential orthogonal subspace updating," IEEE Trans. Circuits and Systems for Video Technology, vol.11, no. 1, pp. 52-66, Jan. 2001.
8. H. Anton and C. Rorres, "Elementary Linear Algebra : Applications version," John Wiley & Sons, 1994.

A Method on Tracking Unit Pixel Width Line Segments for Function Approximation-Based Image Coding

Fumio Kawazoe[1], Kazuo Toraichi[2], Paul W.H. Kwan[3], and Koichi Wada[2]

[1] Doctoral Program, Graduate School of Systems and Information Engineering,
University of Tsukuba, 1-1-1, Tennodai, Tsukuba-City, Ibaraki, 305-8573 JAPAN
zoe@wslab.is.tsukuba.ac.jp
[2] Institute of Information Sciences and Electronics, University of Tsukuba,
1-1-1, Tennodai, Tsukuba-City, Ibaraki, 305-8573 JAPAN
{toraichi, wada}@is.tsukuba.ac.jp
[3] Doctoral Program, Graduate School of Engineering, University of Tsukuba,
1-1-1, Tennodai, Tsukuba-City, Ibaraki, 305-8573 JAPAN
kwan@wslab.is.tsukuba.ac.jp

Abstract. In this paper, we propose a novel method on tracking unit pixel width line segments for function approximation-based image coding. This method is applied prior to function approximation of line segments in image coding. Compared to conventional methods, our method overcomes the problems introduced by inaccurately tracking unit pixel width contours that appear normally in images of fine details such as maps and circuit diagrams. These problems include the inability to reproduce thin segments of uniform width and the separation of segments at visually unnatural places due to image enlargement. As an illustration of its effectiveness, we apply our method on a blank map image followed by image coding via function approximation.

1 Introduction

With the continual introduction of new models of output devices that include high resolution display monitors and printers, the need for processing digital images to cope with these improved functionalities becomes essential. Because pixel-based image coding methods such as JPEG, GIF, and PNG normally cause jaggy-noises on Affine-transform image enlargement, a number of methods that could transform images in pixel-based coding into function approximation-based coding automatically by tracking contours of a target image prior to approximating the extracted contours have been proposed [1][2][3].

In our earlier work, we had introduced methods on coding fonts, illustrations, and logo marks with high accuracy using a class of functions called the Fluency functions [2]. Fluency functions were proposed by a co-author of this paper, and can be characterized by a parameter m that denotes the times of continuous differentiability of these functions. These functions are composed by piecewise polynomials of degree (m-1)

Y.-C. Chen, L.-W. Chang, and C.-T. Hsu (Eds.): PCM 2002, LNCS 2532, pp. 502–509, 2002.

with only (m-2) times continuous differentiability [4]. In the function approximation approach, a contour is approximated according to its shape. The Fluency functions of m=2, m=3, and m=∞ are used in representing straight lines, second degree curves, and arcs respectively.

A major problem with existing methods on approximating contours of an image is the difficulty in reproducing a thin line segment with a uniform width. To address this problem, a method that can approximate the axis of a thin line segment rather than its contour is preferable. However, conventional methods assume contours of more than 1 pixel in width. As such, it is difficult to approximate an image that has line segments of 1 pixel in width accurately.

When axes of segments of 1 pixel in width are being tracked, patterns that might not occur when tracking thicker width segments appear. A problem with conventional methods is that disruption of a line segment occurs when the function approximated image is being enlarged. In this paper, we propose a method for tracking 1 pixel width contours and apply it to approximate a blank map image using the Fluency functions. In our experiments, we illustrate how the proposed method tracks a contour of 1 pixel in width and verify its effectiveness on a portion of the test images.

The proposed method can track segments of 1 pixel in width without causing disruptions to continuous segments at visually unnatural places. As a result, the map images can be approximated and enlarged with little loss of its visual quality.

2　Method Description

2.1　Problems with Conventional Contour Tracking Methods

Existing contour tracking methods can largely be classified into two types, namely (1) tracking by the boundary of a pixel, and (2) tracking by the center of a pixel. Ideally, both types of methods should not affect image accuracy when a coded image is reconstructed to its original scale. However, visual incongruities normally occur when the approximated image is enlarged. The cause of such problem is that both types of methods cannot maintain the connection of segments when tracking a contour of 1 pixel in width. Fig. 1 shows a binary image with a continuous segment of 1 pixel in width. After applying method of Type (1) and (2), the extracted segments are approximated. Fig. 2 (1-a to 2-c) shows portions of a function approximated image (in Fig. 1) enlarged 5 times using a Type (1) and Type (2) method respectively.

First, let us consider the problems exhibited by a method of Type (1). In this method, both sides of the same pixel are determined as belonging to a different line segment. As such, both sides of the same line segment would be approximated by different functions. The result is that the width of the segment of concern is not uniformly enlarged as shown in Fig. 2 (1-a, 1-b, and 1-c). Furthermore, at the crossing, positions of the four corner points are clearly out of place.

Next, we consider the problem exhibited by a method of Type (2). In this method, the tracking is based on the chain-code technique [5] for which the tracking direction is not natural at diverging points or cross points. When a function approximated image

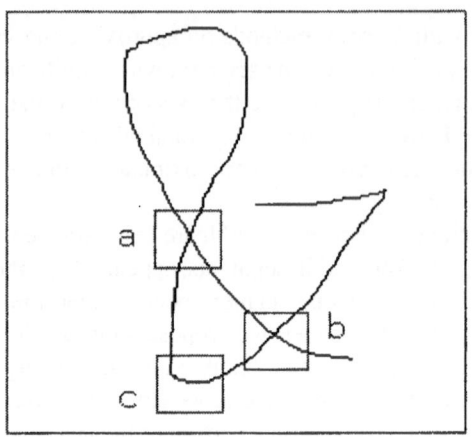

Fig. 1. The original image

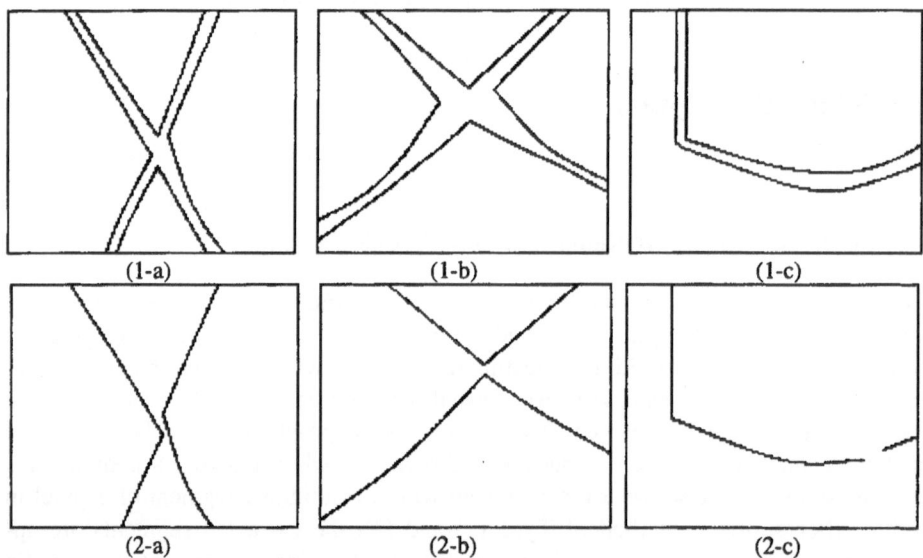

Fig. 2. An enlarged portion of the reconstructed image (in Fig. 1) tracked by conventional methods
[a, b, and c denote an enlarged area, while 1 and 2 correspond to Type (1) and Type (2) method]

with contours tracked by this method is enlarged, certain reconstructed segment will be disrupted. Fig. 2 (2-a, 2-b, and 2-c) illustrate this problem with examples of unnatural connections. In addition, since contours were tracked as shown in Fig. 3 (a), there

exists the additional problem that a disruption occurs at both ends of a thick line when
the image is enlarged.

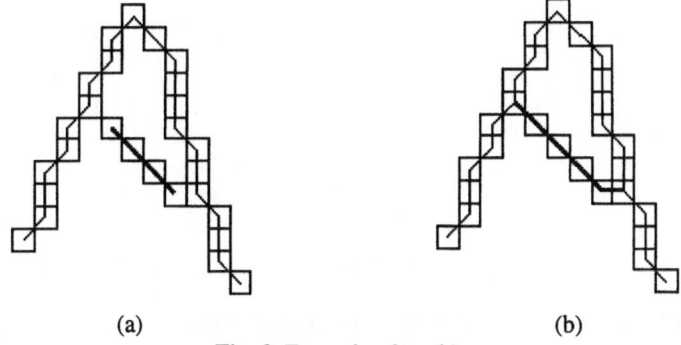

(a)   (b)

Fig. 3. Example of tracking

2.2 Requirements for the Proposed Tracking Method

For an input image having line segments of 1 pixel in width, we require that the function approximated image satisfies the following requirements namely, (1) the width of
the decoded segments must be uniform, and (2) the four corner points at a crossing
must form a parallelogram correctly. Because an image of a map or a circuit diagram
is usually composed of thinner segments than logo marks or illustrations, when processing these images, requirements (1) and (2) ensure that the accuracy of the decoded
image is maintained.

Next, in order to ensure that disruptions of segments do not occur when enlarging a
function approximated image at diverging points and cross points, it is desirable to
obtain the tracking result as shown in Fig. 3 (b). Moreover, the direction of tracking
should be natural at a diverging point or a cross point so that requirement (2) can be
satisfied. In order for a line segment that contains a diverging point or a cross point to
be considered as a single line in the decoded image, it has to be tracked appropriately
prior to function approximation.

3 Implementation

In this section, the successive steps in our method on tracking unit pixel width contours will be presented.

An input image I is composed of segments of 1 pixel in width. For each pixel
$x = (i, j) \in I$, let $I(x)$ be a function that takes the value 0 or 1. Also, the 8-
neighborhood and 4-neighborhood functions for a pixel x_0 are defined as follows
(refer to Fig. 4):

$$n^{[8]}(x_0) = \{x_c ; c \in S\}, \ S = \{1,2,3,4,5,6,7,8\},$$
$$n^{[4]}(x_0) = \{x_c ; c \in S_1\}, \ S_1 = \{1,3,5,7\}.$$

Here, c is called a direction code.

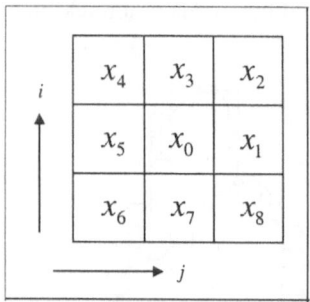

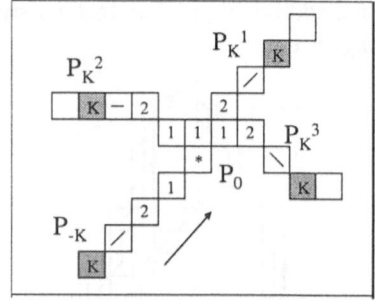

Fig. 4. The neighbors of x_0 **Fig. 5.** Determine the tracking direction at a cross point

To address the problem of a disruption occurring at the crossing of a segment with itself, one end of the segment is chosen as the start point of tracking. At every diverging point or cross point, repeated trackings are allowed.

Next, we will explain how to determine the tracking directions at a diverging point or cross point in detail. For ease of explanation, we will use Fig. 5 as an example.

At the current tracking point '*', if $I(x_0) = 1$ and

$$\sum_{c \in S} I(x_c) - \sum_{c \in S} I(x_c)I(x_{c+1}) + \sum_{c \in S_1} I(x_c)I(x_{c+1})I(x_{c+2}) \geq 3, \tag{1}$$

is satisfied, the following algorithm to search for P_K will be carried out.

Let P_K be a point of distance K from '*'. The tracking direction is determined by inferring the relationships among the positions of P_K, '*', and P_{-K}.

Algorithm

Step I. Assign a label $L(x)$ that indicates the distance between '*' and x for every x that satisfy $I(x) = 1$. This distance is computed by the 8 neighborhood function.

Step II. Let P_0 be x_0 as in Fig. 4. Assign to D as the direction code for P_1 from '*'. ($D \in \{1,2,3,4,5,6,7,8\}$)

Step III. Denote every x that satisfies $L(x) = 2$ and has a direction code D or $(D \pm 1)$ from P_1 by P_2. Similarly, every x that satisfies $L(x) = k+1$ and has a direction code D or $(D \pm 1)$ from P_k be P_{k+1}.

Step IV. After executing Step III, all P_K's that are reachable from the set of P_1's are discovered. Denote the set of P_K's as $\{P_K{}^n\}_{n=1}^{N}$. Here, N denotes the number of P_K's discovered. The C-style pseudo code for Step I to Step IV is shown in Fig. 6.

Step V. Evaluate the digital curvature as

$$Q^n = a_K{}^n \cdot b_K / (|a_K{}^n||b_K|) \quad (n = 1,2,\cdots,N), \tag{2}$$

where

$$P_k = (x_k, y_k),$$
$$a_K{}^n = (x_K{}^n - x_0, y_K{}^n - y_0),$$
$$b_K = (x_{-K} - x_0, y_{-K} - y_0).$$

Here the symbol '$\cdot$' denotes the inner product of two vectors.

Step VI. The $P_K{}^n$ that minimizes Q^n is chosen as the next chain-code tracking point.

As shown in the C-style pseudo code, using recursion, all P_K's can be located. In the case of Fig. 5, $P_K{}^1$ and $P_K{}^2$ are added to $\{P_K{}^n\}_{n=1}^{N}$. However, $P_K{}^3$ is not added because the search goes forward to only direction D or $(D \pm 1)$.

Next, we choose the most suitable $P_K{}^n$ from $\{P_K{}^n\}_{n=1}^{N}$ in order to perform the most natural tracking using Step V and Step IV.

In these two steps, if the $P_K{}^m$ that satisfies the conditions [$Q^n = Q^m$ or $R^m < Q^m$] and $P_K{}^n \neq P_K{}^m$ exists, the tracking is finished at P_0.

R^m is defined by the following equations.

$$R^m = c_K{}^m \cdot d_K / \left(\left| c_K{}^m \right| \left| d_K \right| \right)$$
$$(n = 1, 2, \cdots, N), \quad (3)$$

where

$$c_K{}^m = (x_K{}^m - x_1{}^m, y_K{}^m - y_1{}^m),$$
$$d_K = (x_K - x_1{}^m, y_K - y_1{}^m).$$

By performing the steps above, we can track segment of 1 pixel in width while maintaining the junction naturally at a diverging point or a cross point. Upon applying these steps to the example in Fig. 5, $P_K{}^1$ is chosen as the next chain-code tracking point.

Because repeated trackings are allowed at a diverging point or a cross point, the most natural direction is maintained by performing left to right tracking after the bottom to top tracking has completed.

```
[BEGIN C-style pseudo code]

n = 0;        // the number of P_K found
for(c = 1; c <= 8; c++){
    if( L(x_c) == 1 ){
        D = c;    // the direction code of P_1 from 쳐'
        P_k = x_c;
        FindP(P_k, D, 1);
    }
}

FindP(x_0, D, k){
    k++;    // increase the distance of x_0 form 쳐'
    for(c = 1; c <= 8; c++){
        if( L(x_c) == k &&
            ( c == D || c == D+1 || c == D-1) ){
            if(k < K){
                P_k = x_c;
                FindP(P_k, D, k);  // recursion
            }
            else if(k == K){
                n++;    // the number of P_K found
                P_K^n = x_c;  // Add P_K to {P_K^n}_{n=1}^{W}
            }
        }
    }
}

[END C-style pseudo code]
```

Fig. 6. The C-style pseudo code for showing how $\{P_K{}^n\}_{n=1}^{N}$ are extracted

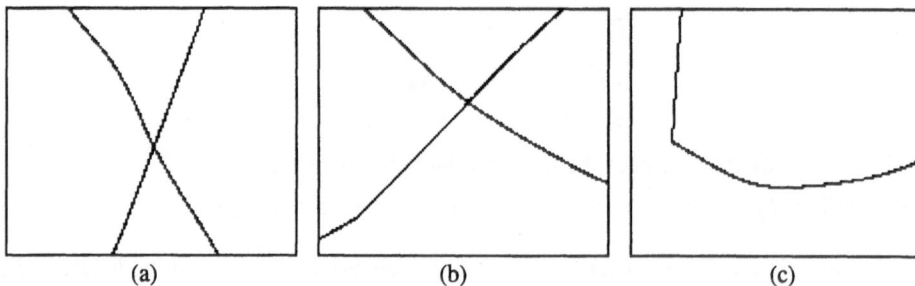

Fig. 7. An enlarged potion of the reconstructed image (in Fig. 1) tracked by the proposed method

4 Experiments

In this section, the effectiveness of the proposed method is illustrated by applying it to the image shown earlier in Fig. 1. A portion of the approximated image after enlargement is shown in Fig. 7. The segments were tracked by the proposed method. In each of (a), (b), and (c), it is clear that disruptions found in Fig. 2 did not occur. Moreover, using the proposed method, we can obtain an enlarged image that maintains the correct connection at a diverging point and a cross point. The proposed tracking method is able to overcome the problems described in subsection 2.1.

In Fig. 7, all points of the image are recognized as belonging to one segment. A diverging point and a cross point appeared twice in the extracted segment.

Next, we applied the proposed method to a blank map image of Taiwan. Fig. 8 (a) shows the original map image, 8 (b) an enlarged portion of the image tracked by the proposed method, 8 (c) the one tracked by a conventional method [6], and 8 (d) one in the BMP format for comparison. In each figure, the scaling ratio used is four. In the image in 8 (c), disruptions appeared at the intersecting points of segments while image 8 (b) does not. Moreover image 8 (b) maintains the original shape of the contour with high precision and without the jaggy-noises that appears in image 8 (d).

From the experimental result, the effectiveness of the proposed method for tracking segment of 1 pixel in width is demonstrated.

5 Conclusion

In this paper, we have described a method on tracking unit pixel width contours for function approximated-based image coding. Our method addressed the problems associated with tracking unit pixel width contours encountered by existing methods.

In our experiment, we apply the proposed method to both synthetic images and a blank map image to show how the tracking is performed. This method satisfies the requirements as given in section 2.2, and it is effective as a preprocessing step for function approximation of images having segments that are of 1 pixel in width.

Further research will focus on judging the direction of tracking by taking a broader view than simply the digital curvature that uses only three determined points. These would involve judging by the shape of objects as well as by considering the curvature of the entire point sequence.

(a) The original image

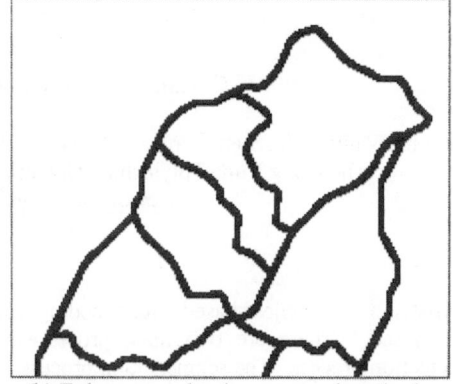

(b) Enlargement by the proposed method

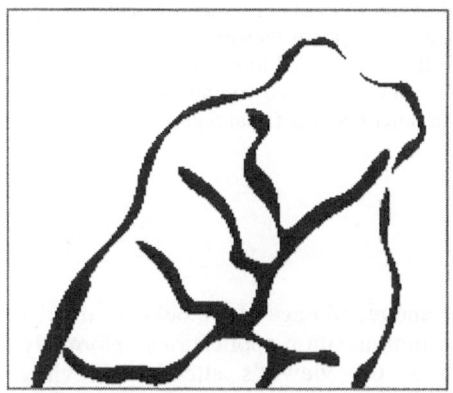

(c) Enlargement by a conventional method[6]

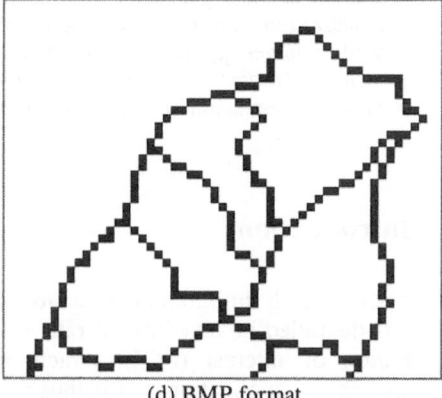

(d) BMP format

Fig. 8. A blank map image of Taiwan

References

1. Sklansky, J. and Gonzalez, V.: Fast polygonal approximation of digitized curves. Pattern Recognition, Vol.12, pp.327-331 (1980)
2. Kazuo Toraichi: On a Method of Automatically Compressing Fonts with High Resolution. Pattern Recognition, Vol.26, No.2, pp.227-235 (1993)
3. Yi Xiao, Ju Jia Zou, and Hong Yan: An adaptive split-and-merge method for binary image contour data compression. Pattern Recognition Letters 22 pp.299-307(2001)
4. Masaru Kamada, Kazuo Toraichi, and Ryoichi Mori: Periodic Spline Orthonormal Bases. Journal of Approximation Theory, Vol.55, No.1, pp.27-34 (1988)
5. Rosenfeld, A., Kak, A.C: Digital Picture Processing. Academic Press, Vol.2, New York (1982)
6. Koichi Mori, Koji Yamauchi, Koichi Wada, and Kazuo Toraichi: High Quality Digital Document System Using Function Approximation of Image Contours. I.I.E.E.J Vol.28, No. 5, pp627-635(1999) (in Japanese)

Object Assisted Video Coding for Video Conferencing System

K.C. Lai, S.C. Wong, and Daniel Lun

Centre for Multimedia Signal Processing, Dept. of Electronic & Information Engineering,
The Hong Kong Polytechnic University, Hung Hom, Hong Kong
enscwong@polyu.edu.hk

Abstract. An object-based video coding for video conferencing system is proposed. There are two main processes: segmentation process and face detection process. The segmentation process is used to segment each frame of a video sequence into two non-overlapping regions, namely foreground and background. A novel face detection technique based on chrominance and the contour of the segmented region is applied to the foreground region. Smaller quantization step is used for the facial region to improve viewer's perception while a larger quantization step is used for the background to compensate the coding efficiency. The remaining regions are kept in normal coding quality to prevent degradation of important information other than the facial regio.

1 Introduction

Due to bandwidth limitation, the quality of the encoded image of a block-based video codec is degraded in very low bit-rate video communication applications. Normally, the region of interest (ROI) attracts most of the viewer's attention in video communication applications. It is thus worthwhile to enhance the quality of ROI and sacrifice the quality of the other regions. Based on this observation, Segmentation-based video codec has been proposed in the literature [1-7].

In video communication applications, video is mainly head-and-shoulder images. The facial region is often the ROI of the viewers. Therefore, the facial region is encoded in higher quality by sacrificing the quality of the other regions. As the non-facial regions are usually of less significant to viewer's perception, the overall subjective quality of the image is perceptively improved. Many researchers have used this approach. Eleftheriadis and Jacquin proposed an algorithm to detect facial region using a model-assisted coding method [1]. Chai and Ngan [2] presented a foreground/background video coding scheme, using a skin-colour face detection approach. C. W. Lin et al. [3] described skin-colour face detection and tracking scheme using a Gaussian probability model and a double integral projection method.

Although face-based video codec has been pursued with impressive results, these hybrid algorithms still suffer from some inherent problems. Some of them are not fully compatible with existing video coding standard; extra information of ROI is required to send to the decoder side. Others may be too complicated that are not suitable for real-time application. However, the major shortcoming of these

Y.-C. Chen, L.-W. Chang, and C.-T. Hsu (Eds.): PCM 2002, LNCS 2532, pp. 510-517, 2002.
© Springer-Verlag Berlin Heidelberg 2002

algorithms is that only facial region are consider as the ROI, other regions such as the moving objects, for instance a moving hand, may be degraded, although it is a ROI.

Instead of segmenting facial region, some research activities have been focused on the segmentation of moving regions [4-7]. Displace frame difference (DFD), motion vector, hausdorff distance, intensity, texture and color information have been used for the segmentation. However, they are either too sensitive to noise, or still too computational intensive for real-time applications.

In this paper, we present an object assisted video codec. Edge information is select as the main criteria for segmentation. A colour-based face detection scheme is performed in the foreground regions. More bits are allocated to the facial region and less to the background regions. The non-facial regions of the foreground are kept in normal quality to prevent degradation of ROI other than the facial region.

2 Proposed Algorithm

The proposed algorithm is divided into two main processes: segmentation process and face detection process.

2.1 Segmentation Process

As our algorithm is designed for block-based video codec, segmentation process is performed at 8x8 blocks. Each block of the frame is divided into foreground and background by using edge information. Different edge detectors, such as Laplacian operators, are tested and have a good performance in generating the edge information for classification. However, the huge computational demand is a common problem of them. We propose a simpler edge detector to obtain binary edge information of the block. We first scan all the pixels insides a block into a 1-D array according to Hilbert scan [8] as shown in figure 1, denoted by $I_R(x)$. High-pass filter is used to generate the binary edge information of the block according to equation 1.

$$E_R(x) = \begin{cases} 1, & |I_R(x) - I_R(x+1)| > T \\ 0, & \text{otherwise} \end{cases} \qquad (1)$$

where $E_R(x)$ is the binary edge map of the block in Hilbert scan order. Although the resulting edge map is much rough than other edge detectors, experimental results show that it is fast and accurate for isolating the background.

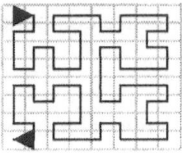

Fig. 1. Hilbert scan

2.1.1 Foreground/Background Segmentation

The segmentation process is divided into two stages. We compare the binary edge map of the current frame with two binary edge maps. One of the binary edge maps is calculated using the previous frame and the other edge map is updated adaptively and will be defined subsequently.

We use the "Edge Mean Absolute Difference, *EMAD*" in equation (2) to compare the block at position (i, j) of the current frame and the reference frame.

$$EMAD_{Ref}(i, j) = \frac{1}{NM} \sum_{x=0}^{NM-1} \left| E_{R(i,j)}^{Curr}(x) - E_{R(i,j)}^{Ref}(x) \right| \tag{2}$$

where $N \times M$ is the total number of pixels of a block, and $E_{R(i,j)}^{Ref}$ and $E_{R(i,j)}^{Curr}$ are the binary edge maps of the reference and current block (i, j) in Hilbert scan order respectively. $EMAD_{previous}(i, j)$ can be used to isolate the moving object form the static background. However, the static background covered by the moving object in the previous frame may sometimes be wrongly classified as part of the moving object. Therefore, an adaptive edge map denoted by $EMAD_{Model}(i, j)$ is introduced. The binary edge map of the first frame of the sequence acts as the initial adaptive edge map. The adaptive edge map is updated in blocks according to $EMAD_{previous}(i, j)$. If more than a number of consecutive frames of $EMAD_{previous}(i, j)$ are smaller than a threshold, the corresponding block of the adaptive edge map $EMAD_{Model}(i, j)$ is updated. If $EMAD_{previous}(i, j)$ and $EMAD_{Model}(i, j)$ are greater than a predefined threshold, then block (i, j) is identified as a foreground block. Otherwise, it is identified as a background block. Figure 3 and 4 show the foreground/background segmentation results after segmentation and regularization processes. It is clear that the moving blocks of the moving region are segmented from the static background. Besides, important regions other than the facial region, such as the moving hand of figure 4b, are preserved.

2.2 Face Detection Process

Once the foreground region of the frame is segmented, the facial region will be detected from it. In a video compression system, colours are usually separated into luminance and chrominance components (Y, Cr, Cb) to exploit the fact that human eyes are less sensitive to chrominance variation. Some researches [2-3] pointed out that although skin colours differ from person-to-person, and race-to-race, they are distributed over a very small area on the chrominance plane. Therefore, skin colours are relatively consistent in chrominance components.

2.2.1. Colour Segmentation

The first stage of the face detection algorithm uses the colour information. The foreground is divided into skin-colour and non-skin colour regions. The skin-colour regions can be identified by the presence of a certain set of chrominance (Cr and Cb) values. We use the ranges of $C_r \in [133, 173]$ and $C_b \in [77, 127]$ to detect the skin-colour regions, as these boundaries have been tested in [2] to be very robust against different types of skin colour. With reference to equation (3), we partition the frame into non-overlapping blocks at position (x, y) of 4 x 4 pixels, and then count the number of skin-colour pixels (P_{skin}) within the block. If the number of skin-colour pixels $(Count_{skin})$ inside the block is greater than a threshold (T_1), it is a skin block; otherwise, it is a non-skin block. Figure 3(a) shows results of the skin colour segmentation.

$$BK_{skin}(x,y) = \begin{cases} 1, & \text{if } Count_{skin}(x, y) > T_1 \\ 0, & \text{otherwise} \end{cases}$$

$$Count_{skin}(x,y) = \sum_{i=0}^{3}\sum_{j=0}^{3} P_{skin}(4x+i, 4y+j) \qquad (3)$$

$$P_{skin}(x, y) = \begin{cases} 1, & \text{if } C_r \in [133, 173] \,\&\, C_b \in [77, 127] \\ 0, & \text{otherwise} \end{cases}$$

2.2.2 Shape Constraints and Contour Extraction

Just like colour, the shape of human faces is unique and consistent. In [1], the contour of human face is approximated using an ellipse with an aspect ratio in a narrow range of (1.4, 1.6) and tilt in a range of (-30°, +30°) [9].

In our face detection algorithm, skin blocks are grouped into different skin-colour regions according to the contour of the skin blocks. The contour of the skin blocks is identified using equation 4. If all the horizontal and vertical adjacent blocks of a skin block are also skin block, it is a block inside a skin colour area. In contrast, it is an isolate skin block and should be ignored. For the remaining cases, if two or more adjacent diagonal blocks of a skin block are skin blocks, we consider that skin block as the contour skin block. Figure 3b shows the contour (CT_{skin}) of the skin blocks.

$$CT_{skin}(x, y) = \begin{cases} 1, & \text{if } (1 \le N_N(x, y) < 4) \,\&\, (N_D(x,y) \ge 2) \\ 0, & \text{otherwise} \end{cases}$$

$$N_N(x, y) = BK_{skin}(x, y-1) + BK_{skin}(x-1, y) + \\ BK_{skin}(x+1, y) + BK_{skin}(x, y+1)$$

$$(4)$$

$$N_D(x, y) = BK_{skin}(x-1, y-1) + BK_{skin}(x-1, y+1) + \\ BK_{skin}(x+1, y-1) + BK_{skin}(x+1, y+1)$$

where $N_N(x, y)$ is the number of horizontal and vertical adjacent blocks of skin block (x, y) that are in skin colour, and $N_D(x, y)$ is the number of diagonal adjacent blocks of skin block (x, y) that are in skin colour.

Once the contour is extracted, we classify the region enclosed inclusively inside the contour as a face candidate. In this manner, we obtain a set of face candidates as shown in figure 3(b). We will use the method of eliminations to qualify the remaining face candidate(s) as face region(s).

The orientation and aspect ratio of a face can roughly be obtained by fitting an ellipse to its face outline. If the orientation and aspect ratio of a face candidate exceeds the ranges of (1.4, 1.6) or (-30°, +30°) respectively [9], it is eliminated from the set of face candidates. Consider figure 2, the orientation of the ellipse can be calculated if both the coordinates of 'c' and 'a' are known, where 'c' is the center of the ellipse and 'a' is the intersection point between the major axis of the ellipse and the ellipse itself. We approximate the point 'a' as a point on the contour, which has longest distance between itself and the center. Therefore

$$\tan \vartheta = \frac{x_a - x_c}{y_a - y_c} \tag{5}$$

where $a : (x_a, y_a)$, $c : (x_c, y_c)$. The center of a face candidate can be calculated by averaging positions of its contour.

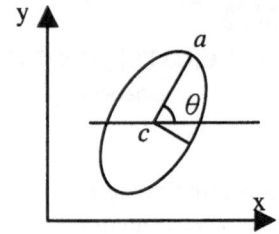

Fig. 2. Orientation of the face region.

2.2.3 Ellipse Fitting

For a face candidate, if its contour can be fitted with an ellipse, it is considered as the face region of the frame. The equation of an ellipse centered at $c : (x_c, y_c)$ is represented using the following equation:

$$\left(\frac{x - x_c}{a}\right)^2 + \left(\frac{y - y_c}{b}\right)^2 = 1 \tag{6}$$

where its rotation function is given as:

$$\begin{aligned} x &= x'\cos\alpha - y'\sin\alpha \\ y &= x'\sin\alpha + y'\cos\alpha \end{aligned} \tag{7}$$

The contour of a face candidate is joined by blocks of 4x4 pixels. We use a fix aspect ratio (1.5:1) of the ellipse (a:b). The fitting criterion has to be focused on the percentage of points that the ellipse passes through the contour of the face candidates. If the percentage is greater than a threshold, the face candidate is considered as the face region of the moving objects. Figure 3(c) shows the face detection results with the fitting ellipse. Figure 4 shows other ellipse fitting results. Since the face block is of 4 x 4 pixels, we should convert it back to macroblock size of the video codec before encoding. For those macroblock, which involve some face blocks, we consider it as ROI and are encoded in higher quality.

(a) F/B and colour segmentation   (b) Contour extraction   (c) Ellipse fitting

Fig. 3. Output of the face segmentation in different steps.

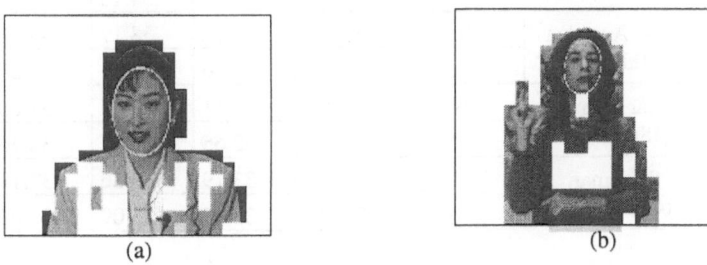

(a)   (b)

Fig. 4. Ellipse fitting results.

3 Experiment Results

In our experiment, the macroblock layer bit allocation scheme of TMN8 is employed in our proposed method. Different weighting factors, α as shown in equation (8), are used for face regions, non-face foreground regions and background regions.

$$
\alpha = \begin{cases} 1 + 0.5 * \dfrac{N_{BG}}{N_{Face}}, & \text{Face Region} \\ 1, & \text{Non-Face Foreground} \\ 0.5, & \text{Background} \end{cases} \tag{8}
$$

where N_{BG} is the number of background macroblock and N_{Face} is the number of face macroblock.

Table 1 shows the experimental results and indicates that the proposed algorithm can effectively enhance the visual quality of a face region at the cost of introducing some degradation on the background. The performance improvement in PSNR on face region ranges from 0.55 to 0.86 dB for the four test sequences. On the other hand, the quality of the non-face foreground is retained with the proposed algorithm. Figure 5 compares the results between TMN8 and the proposed method.

Table 2 compares the speed of TMN8 and the proposed method using a PC (Pentium III 500). It is clear from the table that although extra segmentation and face detection processes are introduced in the encoding process, the change in encoding frame rate is very small. Extra computational power is saved from motion estimation as zero motion vectors are used for background blocks. As the percentage of background blocks increase, the proposed method can even faster than the original codec in encoding sequences like "Claire" and "salesman". Therefore, the proposed method is suitable for real-time applications.

Table 1. Comparisons of averaged PSNR of the proposed method (PM) and TMN8.

	PSNR	Overall	Face	FG	BG
Claire (24kbps)	TMN8	38.41	31.86	34.30	44.50
	PM	37.82	32.73	34.13	42.99
Miss America (24kbps)	TMN8	39.16	33.78	38.17	44.48
	PM	38.70	34.56	38.13	44.27
Car phone (48kbps)	TMN8	33.43	32.11	31.55	37.68
	PM	33.05	32.65	31.45	36.96
Salesman (48kbps)	TMN8	35.26	33.19	33.26	37.13
	PM	34.19	33.87	33.09	35.08

Table 2. Comparisons of processing speeds between TMN8 and the proposed method using a PC Pentium III 500.

	Frames per second	
	PM	TMN8
Claire	23.27	23.26
Miss America	20.28	20.41
Car phone	17.18	18.52
Salesman	23.04	22.73

4   Conclusion

In this paper, an object-based segmentation codec is proposed. The moving objects are first segmented using edge-based moving object detection. They are divided into skin-colour and non-skin-colour regions. By using the characteristic of the face outline, the contour of the skin-colour region is enclosed with an ellipse. The face region of the moving object is therefore detected. Fewer bits are assigned to the static background. The free up bits are used for encoding the face-region of the moving object. The non-face regions of the moving objects are kept in normal quality. The experimental results show that the proposed algorithm can effectively enhance the visual quality of face regions without degrading the quality of other moving parts of a frame. Furthermore, the algorithm is compatible to block-based video codec standards and suitable for real time applications.

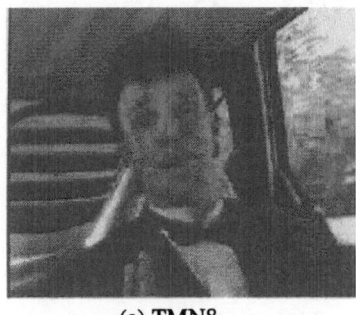

(a) TMN8   (b) Proposed method

Fig. 5. A comparison between TMN8 and the proposed method.

Acknowledgement. This research is supported by the Project Account Code G-V972, The Hong Kong Polytechnic University.

References

1. Eleftheriadis and A. Jacquin, "Automatic face location detection and tracking for model-assisted coding of video teleconferencing sequences at low bit-rate," *Signal processing: Image Communication*, Vol. 7, No. 4-6, pp. 231-248, Nov. 1995.

2. D. Chai and K. N. Ngan, "Face segmentation using skin-color map in videophone application," *IEEE Trans. Circuits Syst. Video Technol.*, vol. 9, No. 4, 551-564, Jun. 1999.

3. Chia-Wen Lin; Yao-Jen Chang; Yung-Chang Chen, "Low-complexity face-assisted video coding," *Proc. IEEE Int. Conf. Image Processing*, pp 207-210, 2000.

4. Thomas Meier and King N. Ngan, "Automatic Segmentation of Moving Objects for Video Object Plane Generation", *IEEE Tran. On Circuits and System for VT*, Vol. 8, No. 5, Sept. 1998.

5. R. Fablet, P. Bouthemy and M. Gelgon, " Moving Object Detection in Color Image Sequences using Region-level Graph Labeling", Image Processing, 1999. *ICIP 99. Proceedings. 1999 International Conference on*, Vol. 2, Page(s): 939 -943 vol.2

6. Lili Qiu; Li Li, "Contour extraction of moving objects", Pattern Recognition, 1998. *Proceedings. Fourteenth International Conference on*, Volume: 2, 1998, Page(s): 1427 - 1432 vol.2

7. C. H. Lin and J. L. Wu, "Content-based rate control scheme for very low bit-rate video coding", *IEEE Tran. On Consumer Electronics*, Vol. 43, No2, May 1997.

8. F. Pinciroli, C. Combi, G. Puzzi, M. Negretto, L. Portoni, and G. Invernizzi, " A Peano-Hilbert derived algorithm for compression of angiocardiographic images," *in Proc. 18th Annu. Conf. Computers Cardiology*, 1992, pp. 81-84.

9. V. Govindaraju, R. K. Srihari, and D. B. Sher, "A computational model for face location," *in Proc. Third Int. Conf. Computer Vision*, 1990, pp. 718-721.

Inter-subband Redundancy Prediction Using Neural Network for Video Coding

Ivan Lee[1] and Ling Guan[2]

[1] School of Elec. and Info. Eng.
University of Sydney
Sydney, NSW 2006, Australia
[2] Department of Elec. and Comp. Eng.
Ryerson Polytechnic University
Toronto, Ontario, Canada M5B 2K3

Abstract. High performance video codec is mandatory for multimedia applications such as video-on-demand and video conferencing. Recent research has proposed numerous video coding techniques to meet the requirement in bandwidth, delay, loss and Quality-of-Service (QoS). In this paper, we present our investigations on inter-subband self-similarity within the wavelet-decomposed video frames using neural networks, and study the performance of applying the spatial network model to all video frames over time. The goal of our proposed method is to restore the highest perceptual quality for video transmitted over a highly congested network. Our contributions in this paper are: (1) A new coding model with neural network based, inter-subband redundancy (ISR) prediction for video coding using wavelet (2) The performance of 1D and 2D ISR prediction, including multiple levels of wavelet decompositions. Our result shows a short-term quality enhancement may be obtained using both 1D and 2D ISR prediction.

1 Introduction

Video technology plays an essential role in multimedia applications, and tremendous research was taken place to encode video signals effectively for the storage. It was not until recently that wired and wireless communication has become matured for video applications, and growing attentions were taken to investigate the combination of video technology and communication for the best perceptual quality.

Among many novel proposals for the video communication systems, layered coding or Fine-Granular-Scalability (FGS) algorithms were one of the most popular approach studied by numerous individuals. In particular, MPEG-4 has integrated such technique as part of its standard [1]. These approaches aim to deliver the video with the highest perceptual quality with unknown channel capacity. The underlying concept of the FGS system is to encode the video signal into a base-layer and multiple enhancement-layers, and each layer is associated with a different priority using protocols such as DiffServ [2]. While the encoded

Y.-C. Chen, L.-W. Chang, and C.-T. Hsu (Eds.): PCM 2002, LNCS 2532, pp. 518–525, 2002.
© Springer-Verlag Berlin Heidelberg 2002

bitstream is transmitted over the packetized network, whenever the channel capacity falls below the required bitrate, the enhancement-layer packets with lower priority will start dropping to ensure minimal impact on the video quality.

Apart from the discrete cosine transform (DCT) based coding technique found in MPEG-4, another popular video coding technique applies wavelet technology. Wavelet-based coding technique has proven several benefits for image compression: (1) better perceptual quality [3]. (2) multi-resolution decomposition provides a simple resizing capability. Embedded zero trees (EZW) [4] and set partitioning in hierarchical trees (SPIHT) [5] both propose layered coding based on the wavelet technique. These 2D image coding techniques can be extended to include the time space for encoding the video [6]. EZW and SPIHT aim for better compression ratio by utilizing the spatial self-similarity. Our approach, on the other hand, is aiming for restoring the best perceptual quality while assuming higher resolution subbands are lost.

The usage of non-linear neural network function to predict the inter-subband redundancy has shown a bit-rate improvement for wavelet-based image compression [7]. Our work take a step further to study a similar model for video compression. Our previous work has presented a layered video codec using the ISR prediction technique, to transmit over the peer-to-peer streaming network [8]. This paper emphasizes the investigation of the source coding technique using the ISR prediction.

This paper is organized as follows: Section 2 outlines the scalable video coding technique using the ISR prediction. Our investigations on the ISR prediction using 1D and 2D information, different number of training frames, with multi-level wavelet decomposition, are presented in section 3 and 4. Section 5 concludes our observations and points out the possible use of the ISR prediction technology.

2 Inter-subband Redundancy for Wavelet-Based Image/Video Coding

Our investigation was originated from the observation of the self-similarity between the wavelet subbands. To illustrate the correlation, we firstly decompose a frame of the Akiyo sequence using the Daubechies 4-tap filter. As shown in Fig. 1, the matching subbands $\{LH1, LH2\}$, $\{HL1, HL2\}$ and $\{HH1, HH2\}$ represent horizontal, vertical, and diagonal details, respectively. Each of these pairs presents a high correlation, which we refer to as the "Inter-Subband Redundancy" (ISR).

Because each wavelet decomposition down-samples to obtain the edge-detail subband and the smooth-detail subband, it is irreversible to obtain the original signal when the edge-detail subband is missing. We assume a non-linear relationship for the ISR. Upon finding this non-linear relationship, it is possible to construct a novel image/video coding technique using the combination of the ISR prediction and the residual encoding. Fig. 2 illustrates the concept of the proposed encoder. A frame is firstly decomposed using wavelet filters. The low-frequency components are transmitted, while the high-frequency components are

1st level decomposition   2nd level decomposition

Fig. 1. Multi-resolution wavelet decomposition of the Akiyo sequence. (Note: the intensity level is rescaled for visualization.)

predicted using the ISR function. The residuals introduced by the ISR prediction are encoded and transmitted at a lower priority. The main objective of our proposed technique is to enhance the quality of the video frames while the high frequency edge details are missing, and the details of our proposed technique may be found in the following subsection.

Like FGS-based codecs, our proposed algorithm does not require prior knowledge on the channel capacity, and low priority subbands may be dropped at any point on the transmission path, while introducing minimal impact on the video quality. Another major design consideration of this coder is its ability to recover the loss under a congested network: When all high-frequency components are lost, the proposed ISR prediction technique will be able to recover the edge details from its built-in restoration capability.

2.1   ISR Prediction Using Back Propagation

Previous section has demonstrated the self-similarity between the matching subbands. Consider the scenario that a video frame is decomposed

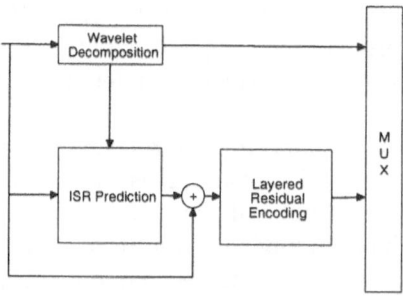

Fig. 2. Block diagram for the video codec with ISR prediction

into $LL1, LH1, HL1$, and $HH1$, and all the high-frequency components $LH1, HL1, HH1$ are missing. Our experiment concluded that finding the ISR between $LL1$ and its high-frequency components is rather inefficient, given that $LL1$ presents the low-pass filtered information. To provide higher similarity between the input and the predicted output, it is obvious that applying a high-pass filter on $LL1$ should provide the edge details. In our observation, the ISR between the matching subbands produced much better training result. (For example, using $LH2$ to predict $LH1$ is better thanusing $LL1$ to predict $LH1$.) We conclude that the ISR prediction should firstly decompose the $LL1$ into $LL2, LH2, HL2$, and $HH2$. Next, the ISRs for each matching subbands are trained independently.

Neural network was chosen to study the ISR due to its non-linear characteristics. As a proof of concept, we use the Back Propagation algorithm. Using $LH1$ prediction for example, each row in $LH2$ is treated as the input, and the matching rows in $LH1$ are treated as the target. Let $C_{col,row}$ represents the wavelet coefficients, $P_{col,row}$ represents the ISR prediction, and the residual, $R_{col,row} = C_{col,row} - P_{col,row}$. The ISR based video codec aims to minimize the residual $R_{col,row}$.

Our network model consists of one hidden layer, which has the dimension four times the size of the input. We train the network with first one or more video frames, and the obtained network model is used to simulate the subsequent frames. The performance of the simulation result is measured according to the reconstructed video quality, and we study the relationship between the performance of the network and the number of the training frames.

3   1-Dimensional ISR Prediction

For 1D ISR prediction, each row of the low frequency subbands $LH2$ and $HH2$ are taken as the input to predict $LH1$ and $HH1$, respectively. Let n_{col} denotes the column size. Let F denotes the ISR prediction function, which firstly decompose the video frame using wavelet filter, and then train the neural network using the matching subbands as the input and the target, to minimize the mean square error (MSE) as shown in equation 1.

$$MSE(row) = \frac{\sum_{col}(C_{row,col} - F(C_{row,col}))^2}{n_{col}} \tag{1}$$

Similarly, each column of the low frequency subband $HL2$ is used to predict $HL1$. Let n_{row} denotes the row size, the MSE is shown in equation 2.

$$MSE(col) = \frac{\sum_{row}(C_{row,col} - F(C_{row,col}))^2}{n_{row}} \tag{2}$$

Fig. 4 shows the quality of the ISR prediction judged in terms of the Peak Signal to Noise Ratio (PSNR) levels. The comparisons are made between the reconstructed frames with and without the ISR prediction. Samples of the reconstructed frames can be found in Fig. 3. The frame with the ISR prediction results better edge details, with a cost of distorted smooth details. A possible avenue for future work is to design a smoothing filter to further visually enhance the predicted frame quality.

The results demonstrate that a successful ISR prediction will restore the video quality under a lossy streaming environment. When all the high-frequency components $LH1, HL1, HH1$ are lost during the transmission, Fig. 4 shows that the ISR prediction produces better video quality, as long as the predicted time-frame is close to the reference timeframe. The PSNR level decays over time due to the growth of the accumulative inter-frame differences over time. There-fore, it is possible to use more video frames as the training input, to construct a more generalized network function to predict the future frames. Our experiments shown in Fig. 4 proves that when more frames are taken for the training input, the network performs better ISR prediction in the long run.

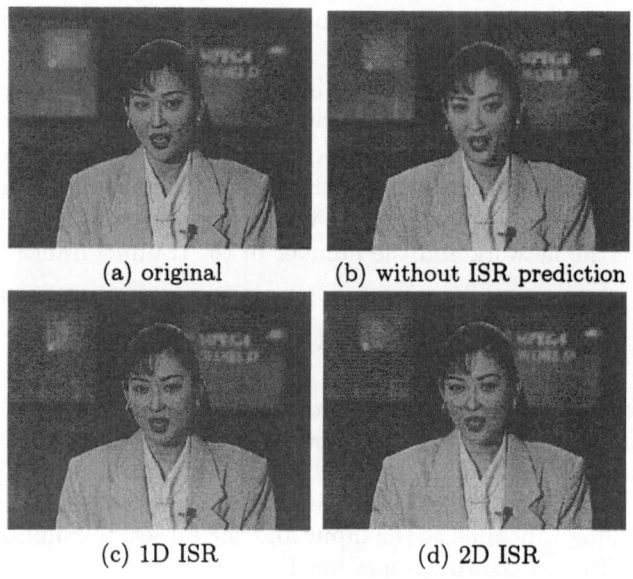

(a) original   (b) without ISR prediction

(c) 1D ISR   (d) 2D ISR

Fig. 3. Example of reconstructed frames with and without ISR prediction

So far we have presented the ISR prediction for the first level wavelet decom-position. The same technique can be applied to multi-level wavelet decompo-sition. Considering a frame decomposed into $LL2, LH2, HL2, LH1, HL1, HH1$ subbands, and only $LL2$ is successfully transmitted. The ISR prediction result is shown in Fig. 5. The plot shows the video quality (measured in PSNR) is improved. Once again, the quality decays over time, and the decay improved when more frames are used for the neural network training. Samples of the re-constructed frames are shown in Fig. 8. We observed a great enhancement for the edge details with the ISR prediction.

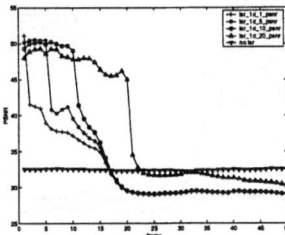
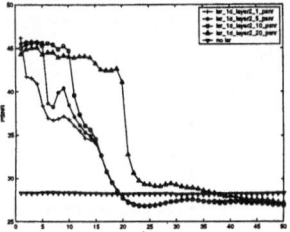

Fig. 4. PSNR of reconstructed frame using 1D ISR prediction for different number of training frames (Note: *isr_1d_1_psnr* denotes the PSNR value for 1D ISR prediction using 1 frame as the training input. *no_isr* denotes the PSNR value without ISR prediction. Same naming rule applies to other figures with PSNR plots)

Fig. 5. PSNR of reconstructed frame using 1D ISR prediction for different number of training frames, with 2nd level wavelet decomposition

Our observation of the ISR prediction leads to an innovative technique for scalable image/video encoding. The low frequency components can be coded using conventional techniques such as DCT-based codec with motion compensation. The ISR technique can also lead to the codebook design, for constructing a high-performance quantization for the high-frequency components.

4   2-Dimensional ISR Prediction

We extended our study on the ISR prediction using 2D blocks from the low frequency subbands to predict the corresponding block from the high frequency subband. The underlying assumption of this approach is that the edge details of a video frame appear continuous as a 2D image, although 2D discrete wavelet transform (DWT) does not guarantee such attribute. This is because DWT does not consist of a 2D filter, instead, a vertical filter and a horizontal filter are applied to the frame sequentially.

Let row_8, col_8 denotes the 8-by-8 blocks from the low frequency subband, and n_{row_8, col_8} denotes the size of the matching block from the high frequency subbands. The goal of the neural network is to minimize the MSE, which is shown in equation 3:

$$MSE(row_8, col_8) = \frac{\sum_{row_8, col_8}(C_{row,col} - F(C_{row,col}))^2}{n_{row_8, col_8}} \qquad (3)$$

Fig. 6 shows the performance of the 2D ISR prediction measured in PSNR. Similar to the 1D ISR prediction, the PSNR value drops over time. With a larger training database (more frames used as training data), the PSNR result behave better in the long run. In comparison to the 1D ISR prediction, the 2D

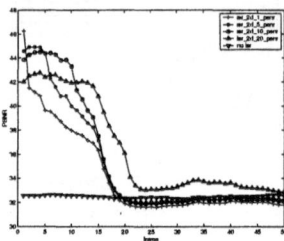
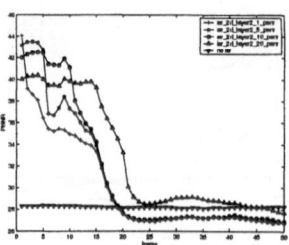

Fig. 6. PSNR of reconstructed frame using 2D ISR prediction for different number of training frames

Fig. 7. PSNR of reconstructed frame using 2D ISR prediction for different number of training frames, with 2nd level wavelet decomposition

ISR prediction appear to provide less precision for the simulating the training frames, but provide a higher restructed quality over non-training frames. This observation is likely due to the fact that 2D ISR prediction is attempting to study the edge details in the 2D image block, which is less tied up to the mathematical wavelet relation (since 2D wavelet decomposition consists of firstly a horizontal 1D wavelet decomposition followed by a vertical 1D wavelet decomposition). Samples of the reconstructed frames can be found in Fig. 3.

Similar to the 1D case, we extend our 2D ISR prediction with second level wavelet decomposition, and the resulted PSNR plot can be found in Fig. 7. Once again, the plot presents similar attribute as the 1D ISR case, that a better image quality with sharper edge details are reconstructed, as shown in Fig. 8.

5   Conclusions

In this paper we presented an innovative video coding technique using wavelet while applying the neural network model for predicting the inter-subband redundancy. Our observation shows that:

1. ISR may be predicted using the neural network model, which can help enhancing the video quality without the high frequency components.
2. The ISR prediction can be applied to multi-layer wavelet decomposition.
3. The quality enhancement of the ISR approach decays due to the accumulative inter-frame differences over time. Therefore, the model could potentially be improved by integrating the inter-frame information in the design, for example, motion vectors.
4. The 1D ISR prediction directly reflects the mathematical model, and produces better training results. The 2D ISR prediction, on the other hand, investigates the 2D image property, and hence results better prediction result for non-trained frames.

The importance of our investigation is that the ISR can be incorporated with the conventional video codecs. For example, using DCT-based codec with motion compensation to encode the low-frequency subband, and use this as the reference frame for the ISR training.

(a) original   (b) without ISR prediction

(c) 1D ISR   (d) 2D ISR

Fig. 8. Example of reconstructed frames with and without ISR prediction, with second level wavelet decomposition

References

1. W. Li, "Overview of fine granularity scalability in MPEG-4 video standard", *IEEE Transactions on Circuits and Systems for Video Technology*, vol. 11, no. 3, pp. 301–317, March 2001.
2. S. Blake, D. Black, M. Carlson, E. Davies, Z. Wang and W. Weiss, "An Architecture for Differentiated Services", *RFC 2475*, Internet Engineering Task Force, December 1998.
3. "JPEG-2000", http://www.jpeg.org, 2000.
4. J.M. Shapiro, "Embedded image coding using zerotrees of wavelet coefficients", *IEEE Trans. on Signal Processing*, 41:3445-3462, 1993.
5. A. Said and W. A. Pearlman, "A new fast and efficient image codec based on set partitioning in hierarchical trees", IEEE Trans. Circuits and Systems for Video Technology, 6:243-250, 1996.
6. B. Kim and Z. Xiong and W. Pearlman, "Very low bit-rate embedded video coding with 3D set partitioning in hierarchical trees", *IEEE Trans. Circuits and Systems for Video Technology*, Submitted October 1997.
7. C. Burges, P. Simard and H. Malvar, "Improving wavelet image compression with neural networks", *Microsoft Research Tech. Rep.*
   http://citeseer.nj.nec.com/500015.html
8. I. Lee and L. Guan, "A Scalable Video Codec Design for Streaming Over Distributed Peer-to-Peer Network", GLOBECOM 2002, in press.
9. "ITU-T Recommendation H.263, Video Coding for Low Bitrate Communication", 1996.

Building the Software Infrastructure for Smart Classroom: From Open Agent Architecture (OAA) to Smart Platform

Yanhua Mao, Weikai Xie, Yuanchun Shi, Guangyou Xu, and Xin Xiang

Institution of Human Computer Interaction and Media Integration, Department of CS,
Tsinghua University, Beijing, 100084, P.R. China
maoyanhua@tsinghua.org.cn, xwk@media.cs.tsinghua.edu.cn,
shiyc@tsinghua.edu.cn,
xgy-dcs@mail.tsinghua.edu.cn, xiang_xin@263.net

Abstract. Smart Classroom is a Smart Space developed to enhance tele-education practice. This paper describes the considerations of bringing forward Smart Platform as the software infrastructure of Smart Classroom system, abandoning the former implementation based on OAA. As a multi-agent system for Smart Space, Smart Platform encompasses following features: spontaneous discovery of runtime environment, automatic management and resolving of agent dependencies, combination of delegated communication and peer-to-peer communication, etc. In addition, a surrogate agent on Smart Platform and Metaglue from MIT is now being developed to inter-connect Smart Classroom with MIT's Intelligent Room to extend their functionality.

Keywords: Smart Space, Software Classroom, OAA, Smart Platform

1 Introduction

Smart Space (or Intelligent Environment)[1], which integrates large numbers of distributed hardware and software into a physical space, within which the human activities could be supported, has been attracting a lot of efforts.

Smart Space usually involves many distributed computation and perception modules to provide its multi-modal and context-aware behaviors. Although different Smart Space projects have different applications with different perceptual technologies, there is still a common need to have an efficient solution to connect, coordinate and manage numbers of hardware and software modules. That's why software infrastructure is regarded as one of the most important issues for developing Smart Spaces.

We began the Smart Classroom [2] project around early 2000, which is a tele-education oriented system. In this system, teacher gives classes in an enhanced classroom – Smart Classroom. The most important feature is that, the user interface of the system for teachers is the classroom itself – a multi-modality enabled environment instead of a desktop computer like that in most current tele-education systems.

Y.-C. Chen, L.-W. Chang, and C.-T. Hsu (Eds.): PCM 2002, LNCS 2532, pp. 526-533, 2002.

In the first stage of our Smart Classroom project, we attempted to build the classroom system based on Open Agent Architecture (OAA)[3], a multi-agent system from SRI. However, we found OAA could not meet our demands satisfactorily. After systematically analyzing the shortcomings of OAA based on our demands, we designed our own software infrastructure: Smart Platform [4]. We focus on how to connect the software and hardware modules in the Smart Space and make them collaborate with each other efficiently. The performance and the usability of the software infrastructure are also taken into consideration.

In this paper, first, we briefly analyze the deficiencies of OAA as the supporting Software Infrastructure of Smart Space (SISS). Then we present the architecture and the advanced features of Smart Platform. Some evaluation results of Smart Platform and a comparison of the performance between OAA and Smart Platform are also given.

2   The Attempt on OAA

2.1 Building the Classroom Based on OAA

In the first stage of our research, we adopted OAA, a multi-agent system from SRI, as the SISS for our classroom.

In OAA, every agent finds and registers its services to Facilitator while starting up. When an agent needs to use a certain service, it sends its request to Facilitator, which is forwarded to corresponding agents according to the registration information. This communication model is called "delegated computing" in the terminology of OAA.

All the software modules are encapsulated into OAA Agents. With the help of Facilitator, the software modules can collaborate with each other while being loosely coupled. The low level communication is taken care of by the OAA program library.

2.2 The Deficiencies of OAA

Here we point out the deficiencies of OAA without further explanation. Later in Section 4 we will discuss these deficiencies and present our solution in Smart Platform.

First, configuration file is needed on each computer that involves in the Smart Space so as to locate the Facilitator when an agent startups. Thus movement of the Facilitator from one host to another will definitely result in changing the configuration files on all the computers in the environment.

Second, although delegated communication (by Facilitator) makes the agents loosely coupled, this communication model is not competent for all the situations, especially those where QoS is important.

Last but not least, all the OAA agents have to be run manually. Module cannot be automatically loaded when needed. It is also impossible for the code to be moved from one host to another so as to balance the burden of computers that participates in the SISS.

3 Architecture of Smart Platform

Here we give an overall description of the architecture of Smart Platform. The rationale of the design will be presented in later section.

Generally speaking, Smart Platform is also a multi-agent system. It runs upon networks-connected computers, masking the boundary of the involved computers and providing a uniform running environment and highly structured communication models for the software modules run on it.

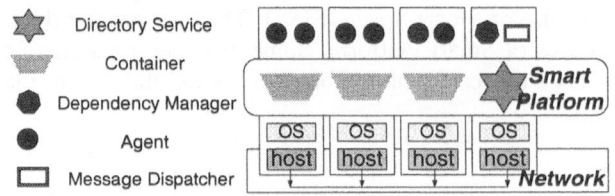

Fig 1. The architecture of Smart Platform

The runtime environment is composed of three kinds of components, which are Agent, Container and DS: (1) An Agent is the basic encapsulation of the software modules in the system;(2) Each computer participating in the runtime environment will host a dedicated process called Container, which provides system-level services for the agents that run on the computer and manages them as well. It makes the details of other parts of the system transparent to agent and provides a simple communication interface for agent;(3) There is one global dedicated process called DS in the environment. The DS mediate the "delegated communication" between agents and provide services such as directory service, dependency resolution.

The structure of the DS (initially represents the abbreviation of Directory Service) can be divided into three subcomponents; each provides a different set of services: (1) The *Directory Service* provides services such as agent registration and query. (2) The *Message Dispatcher* implements the message-oriented communication service for the agents in Smart Platform. (3) The *Dependency Manager* is responsible for the management and resolving of the agent dependencies.

Some development kits are provided in the platform to enhance its usability, which are the Monitor Agent who serves as the monitor and the debugger of Smart Platform, agent development library (both C++ and java version) and a Custom AppWizard for MS VC++ 6 to automatically generate the skeleton code for a new agent. A standard setup program for MS Windows platform, which is now available at our web site [5], is also developed to ease the installation and configuration of Smart Platform.

4 Features of Smart Platform

With the preliminary knowledge described in Section 2 and 3, here we present our consideration on the basic features and characteristics that a SISS should possess based on our first stage attempt on the adopting of OAA in Smart Classroom. All these features have been built into Smart Platform.

4.1 Spontaneous Discovery of Runtime Environment

As we have discussed in Section 2.2, one deficiency of OAA is that developers must manually configure each computer to participate in the Smart Space, which is very inconvenient and lack of scalability, especially when computation device capable of wireless connection moves from one Smart Space to another.

When a Container starts, it should find and establish connection with the DS, just like an OAA agent should find and register to the OAA Facilitator. Here the so-called spontaneous discovery of runtime environment mechanism will facilitate this process. (1) The DS keeps listening on a predefined multicast address. (2) While startups, Container sends a ping packet to this multicast address. (3) On receiving the ping packet, the DS answers in a message containing the unicast address where it can be connected. (4) On receiving the reply packet, Container begins to establish a connection with the DS on the reported address and register to it. (5) Whenever loses connection with the DS, Container starts this procedure again until the DS is found.

Besides the advantage that has been stated before, we have found this mechanism very useful during the development of our Smart Classroom in the cases that new computers need to join in the environment and that we have to restart the DS from time to time as well.

4.2 Hybrid Inter-agent Communication Scheme

The communication model of OAA is essentially a publish-subscribe one. The OAA Facilitator plays the role of the transmission center in this model. There are certain advantages of this communication model. For instance, it makes the agents loosely coupled with each other. One-to-many communication is also very easy to be implemented in this mode. Another advantage is that the numbers of connections that need to be maintained are linear with the number of the agents in contrast with that in the direct communication mode (establish a connection between every two agents).

But this communication model is not applicable for all the cases. It is obvious that the transmission center is the bottleneck of this architecture. And this results in the delivery latency, especially its variation, of any single connection is hard to guarantee. However, the Smart Space does need some kind of communication, which should have guaranteed QoS. For example, in our Smart Classroom, the SameView Agent may need to get the position of the laser pointer from the Laser Pointer Tracking Agent every 100 milliseconds. However, in the implementation based on OAA, the latency varies between several to a dozen seconds in our practice. We have to establish an extra, dedicated UDP path for the two agents. This difficulty leads us to the decision of including this kind of communication as a basic communication model in Smart Platform. This is how the hybrid inter-agent communication scheme of Smart Platform comes from.

The Message Dispatcher, a subcomponent of DS, takes charge of the dedicated communication (message-orient). This kind of communications is grouped into message groups. Agent publishes messages related to the same topic to a message group and the Message Dispatcher transmits them to those agents that subscribe this message group. The Directory Services subcomponent of the DS serves the so-called peer-to-peer communication (stream oriented) in Smart Platform. In order to send its stream-oriented data, an agent should register a stream-oriented message group and obtains a multicast address, which can be queried by recipients. The stream-oriented communication is implemented with RTP [6] over UDP multicast so as to provide real-time high bandwidth communication. The one-to-many scheme is nevertheless needed in this kind of communication; for example, multiple computer vision modules may need the video stream captured by a single camera simultaneously. The UDP multicast here helps to support the one-to-many model. It can save the bandwidth of the network in this case.

The message-oriented ones may occasionally happen and usually have high-level semantics. They are sensitive to the loss of messages; whereas their requirements on the delivery latency is moderate, as long as it is within a reasonable boundary. In contrast, the stream-oriented ones may constantly occur. Their semantic level usually is relatively low and the drop of data units up to several is usually tolerable. But they are sensitive to the variation of the delivery latency. According to the analysis above, the communication that occurs in Smart Space is divided into two catalogs. Developers should apply proper one according to their specific requirement.

4.3 Agent-Dependency Resolving and Dynamic Code Loading

An agent may use the services provided by another agent. If certain services cannot be satisfied, an agent may refuse to work or exhibit different behavior. We call this relationship as agent dependency. Smart Platform can facilitate the management and resolving of these dependencies.

When an agent joins the computation environment, it must announce the services it provides and the services it depends on. Smart Platform will store this information in a persistent storage. If an agent starts up asking for a service and the agent, which provide this service happens not to be working, Smart Platform will use the stored knowledge to locate the agent and automatically launch it. This feature is called "Agent Dependency Resolution". The satisfying or lose of the agent dependency is informed to the agent through the two overidables of CAgent: OnDependSatisfied and OnDependLost. Agent can adjust its behavior in these two overidables accordingly.

This feature is achieved by the Dependency Manager subcomponent of the DS together with Containers. Dependency Manager takes charge of resolving agent dependency, while the Container deal with the dynamic code loading. When a certain agent needs to be launched, Dependency Manager notifies the Container on the computer where the agent last ran. On receiving this notification, the Container launches the proper agent. The introduction of Container gives us a centralized point to manage the agents run on the same host, while OAA does not has a counterpart. We are also studying the burden balance mechanism of Smart Platform. The DS can act as the cauterized manager, which balances the burden of the computers in the environment, with the dynamic code loading/unloading ability of Container.

As a by-product of this feature, launch only some key agents may put the whole system into a running state, as long as the developers have carefully designed the inter-agent dependencies. We found this feature help us a lot during the development of Smart Classroom, as we have to restart the whole system from time to time.

4.4 XML Based ICL (Inter-agent Communication Language)

OAA adopt a message format based on Prolog, which has traditionally been used to solve the logic problems in AI. The message format is not so efficient because of its complex implementation. Moreover, it is relatively difficult to grasp, not self-describing and has no adequate extensibility. All these deficiencies lead us to design a more efficient and easy-to-use ICL

After a careful study, XML is chosen as the base of the ICL for Smart Platform for its following advantages. (1) The good extensibility of XML contributes greatly to the extensibility of Smart Platform. Developers can start with a rough message structure and add detailed fields later without impacting prior works. (2) XML is user-friendly for its readable format and self-describing capability, which is very helpful when prototyping the system or debugging the system. (3) Developers can formally define valid messages in XML DTD to the validity of a message exchanged in runtime in the later version of Smart Platform, for we have noticed that the mistyping of message by developers accounted for a great part of bugs found in a distributed system.

During the design phase of Smart Platform, we also thought of binary encoded ICL. We have to admit that the XML based ICL is slightly inefficient compared with the binary based one. But the advantages stated above and the rapid growth of today's computer power and network bandwidth convince us this deficiency is neglectable.

4.5 Open Wire-Protocol

We build Smart Platform with a set of well-designed and open wire-protocol both between agent and Container and between Container and DS. The wire-protocol describes the events that take place in Smart Platform and the messages that transacted between agents. An entity is considered as a valid agent, Container or DS as long as it complies with the corresponding wire-protocol, no matter what its underlying hardware and software platform are, how it is implemented or what programming language it used.

This feature is designed to tackle with the issue of supporting heterogeneous platforms and agent developing languages. OAA also tackles this issue by means of its wire-protocol. However, the wire-protocol of OAA is not opened. Other software infrastructures, such as Metaglue from MIT [7], resort to Java to achieve the same goal. But we think it is not an efficient approach to build a Smart Space in the sense of performance for it is very common for a single perceptual software module in a Smart Space to use up the resources of the most powerful PC of today.

Another point we'd like to mention here is that the wire-protocol is also based on XML to exploit the advantages stated in Section 4.4.

5 Experiments

The effectiveness of the Smart Platform has been validated by its real use in our Smart Classroom project. The software and hardware modules in Smart Classroom are encapsulated into Smart Platform Agents.

An informal usability study was also made by means of training other members of Smart Classroom, who has different research backgrounds, to use the Smart Platform.

Most of them can understand the principles of Smart Platform and learned how to use the Agent Development Library in no more than an hour. With the help of the development kits presented in Section 3.2, half of them can develop Smart Platform Agent without further help.

5.1 Performance Evaluation

The performance of Smart Platform is also taken into consideration during the design and development of it. We conduct an experiment to evaluate the throughput and delivery latency of Smart Platform in contrast with OAA.

The experiment is carried out on seven networked computers (PIV 1.8G/256M RAM) connected by a dedicated 100M Ethernet LAN. DS (Facilitator) is placed on Computer A. A Ping Agent and a Pong Agent reside on Computer B and C respectively, while the other four computers are used to run Background Agents, who publish messages in a rate according to Poisson process, to simulate the background load of the system. The Round-Trip Time (RTT) between the Ping and Pong Agents is measured to represent the deliver latency of the system. (The deliver latency can be roughly thought as half of the RTT.) Figure 2 illustrated the result of the experiment.

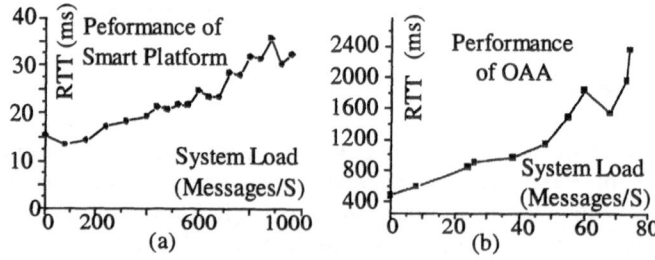

Fig. 2. RTT and throughput performance of Smart Platform (a) and OAA (b)

The experiment shows that the RTT of Smart Platform grows from 13 ms to 36 ms almost linearly with the increase of the background load of the system from 0 to 960 Messages/S. The maximum throughput of the system is also showed as about 960 Messages/S, where the CPU load of the computer where DS is running has reached 100%. It is also showed that the RTT of OAA rides from 500ms to 2400ms as the background payload increases from 0 to 80 Messages/S.

6   Conclusion and Future Work

In this work, we have designed and implemented Smart Platform, a SISS, based on former attempt on OAA in Smart Classroom system. We systematically considered the demands and the characteristics of a SISS, mostly from the deficiencies of OAA, and built Smart Platform with its advanced features. A set of user-friendly development kits are also developed to allow non-expert developers of distributed computing to create their Smart Space application on Smart Platform. The application of Smart Platform in Smart Classroom project has proved its effectiveness.

6.1 Future Work

The issues of service discovery, resource management, burden balance and context-awareness computing in the Smart Space are to be studied in the near future.

Another interesting topic related to the interoperation of heterogeneous SISSs (Smart Platform and the Metaglue from MIT), which arose in the effort to interconnect Smart Classroom with the Intelligent Room [8] at MIT, AI Lab, is now carried through with the cooperation of researchers from MIT, AI Lab. Some scenarios are brought forward to explore some more interesting applications for both systems. Instead of modifying the architecture of both SISSs to make them interconnected with each other, a dual-citizenship surrogate agent based approach is proposed by us. As Figure 3 illustrates, this dual-citizenship agent behaves like a surrogate or a bridge between the two SISSs.

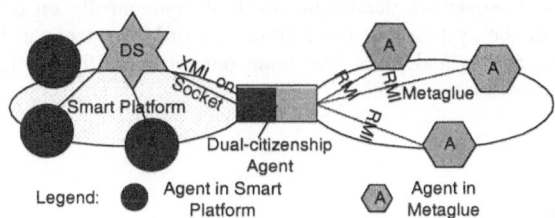

Fig. 3. The proposed approach to interoperate Smart Platform and Metaglue

References

1. http://www.nist.gov/smartspace/
2. W.K. Xie, Y.C. Shi, G.Y. Xu, D. Xie, "Smart Classroom - an Intelligent Environment for Tele-education" In Proceedings of The Second Pacific-Rim Conference on Multimedia (PCM 2001), Pages 662-668, Beijing, China. Springer LNCS2195.
3. SRI. OAA web site: http://www.ai.sri.com/~oaa
4. C.H. Jiang, "The Design and Implementation of Smart Classroom and Its Software Platform," thesis for Master degree, Tsinghua University, May 2001.
5. http://media.cs.tsinghua.edu.cn/smart_platform
6. http://www.ietf.org/rfc/rfc1889.txt
7. M.H. Coen, B. Phillips, N. Warshawsky, et al. "Meeting the computational needs of intelligent environments: The Metaglue system," In Proceedings of MANSE'99, Pages 210-213, Dublin, Ireland, 1999
8. M.H. Coen, "The future of human-computer interaction, or how I learned to stop worrying and love my intelligent room", in IEEE Intelligent System, Pages 8-10, March/April 1999.

Self-Guided Adaptive and Interactive Hypermedia Courseware System

Wang Yao, Liu Wenyu, He Daan, and Zhu Guangxi

E&I Engineering Department, Huazhong University of Sci. & Tech.
Wuhan, Hubei, 430074 P.R. China.
Wangyao_mail@263.net

Abstract. This paper presents the structure and features of a Self-Guided Adaptive and Interactive Hypermedia Courseware (SAIHC) and SAIHC system. The main focus of this system is to provide an individualized-learning environment. Courseware documents are built dynamically on the fly, by the interaction of the system and the learners. In order to achieve this goal, we design some agents and tools. We hope our works will help to set up the Chinese courseware standard.

1 Introduction

Along with the development of the Internet and multimedia, there is more and more multimedia courseware available on the network, and more and more colleagues and people are realizing the importance of the courseware for the distance learning and the engineering training.

Due to the lack of uniform course standards, which impedes the share and communication of education resource, there are many countries around world dedicate in developing modern distance education technology standard research. Distance education technology in China has entered a new stage based on network. However, without any technology standards, different network education systems have their own style and framework. This, of course, will result in repeating works and the waste of resource and financing. And these systems cannot communicate with the international network education systems. The effects are very negative.

Chinese Ministry of Education pays great attention on the construction of network education technology standard. Specialists from eight universities are called in to form the Chinese e-Learning Technology Standardization Committee (CELTSC) on the standardization research. After one-year hardworking, eleven criterions are set down. Meanwhile, it should be also noticed that the standardization is a long-term task and requires repetitious tryout and modification. The work presented in this paper is an effective attempt on multimedia courseware standardization. And it may assert positive effects on the construction of Chinese multimedia courseware standard.

Recent multimedia courseware systems are mainly divided into the following folders:

1. Traditional distance learning system. In this system course materials are presented primarily in a sequential manner according to the author's perception, while the focus is solely on delivering multimedia contents to end-users.

Y.-C. Chen, L.-W. Chang, and C.-T. Hsu (Eds.): PCM 2002, LNCS 2532, pp. 534–539, 2002.

2. Self-guided adaptable courseware system called Multimedia Interactive Telelearning System (MITS) [1]. The key features of this system include [2]: *Self-guided*, it allows learners to choose courses and control learning speed; *Adaptable*: it allows courseware database to dynamically generate the personalized courseware documents according to users' needs; *Enhanced Web presentation*: along with synchronized SMIL multimedia presentations playback, the system provides real-time continuous media streaming; *Platform-independent*: the system is based on Java application so users can access it from anywhere using any platform as long as the browser is Java-enabled.

3. Self-paced and adaptive courseware (SAC) system [3]. The main focus of SAC is to formulate a model that encompasses the important requirements of supporting an adaptive learning courseware environment. This courseware develop an interactive and adaptive learning system that is able to individualize a student learning style, with the ultimate objective of maximizing its learning experience and effectiveness. According to [4], this kind of courseware can be divided in three parts: Course Nodes (CN), Course Unit (CU), and Course Material (CM).

Based on the above research, we suggest some requirements of the courseware system to be adapted to modern distance learning; it must be self-guided, adaptive, interactive and hypermedia-based. With these features we designed a Self-Guided Adaptive and Interactive Hypermedia Courseware System (SAIHC).

The rest of this paper is organized as follows: Section 2 describes the main features of SAIHC; Section 3 introduces this courseware's structure; Section 4 provides a system proposes for SAIHC; Section 5 concludes with the system description and discusses some future orientations.

2   Key Features of SAIHC System

The SAIHC system is developed to be a Self-Guided Adaptive and Interactive Hypermedia Courseware System, in order to adapt to any students with the diverse background, knowledge and learning style. So it has some basic and key features. Now we will describe these features.

Hypermedia-based: Studies have shown that computer-based multimedia can help people learn better than traditional classroom lectures or in single media style [5] and [6]. Education hypermedia systems provide a flexible style of accessing information and learning that is different from the strategies used by traditional linear systems [7]. So modern distance learning systems must provide a vast array of media materials to support the transfer of information, which include: audio files, video files, graphic files, digital movies, hypertext, and so on. Another important thing is the structure of these materials, which will be introduced in the next section.

Self-Guided: It is reasonable to assume that each student may want the courseware designed according to his or her unique learning style. As it is not possible to copy with handing all requirements at once, the courseware must be self-guided. That is why the courseware documents are built dynamically and adaptable to individual students' needs and preferences.

In order to be self-guided, system must be aware of users' individuality. Just like [3] the system builds user model and adaptive agent. The adaptive agent captures the educational background of individual student via pre-admission test and system enrolment history; it also keeps track of evolving aspects of the user, such as preferences and domain knowledge, which is used to guide the user learning. The structure of adaptive agent can be seen in Figure 1.

To be self-guided, the user track analyses tool and guide tool are very important. The input data of the analyses tool include: user background, system enrolment history, user custom, study status and so on. While the output is the study guides. With these guides, adaptive agent can decide the courseware content, which can realize different contents for different people.

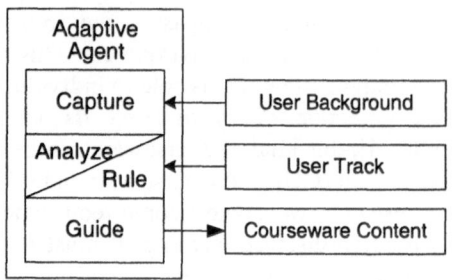

Fig. 1. Structure of Adaptive Agent

Adaptive: In our system, the adaptive feature is different from the above. As we all know, the current best-effort Internet does not offer any quality of service (QoS) guarantees to AV stream. Various network characteristics make the AV streaming applications more challenging than traditional Internet application like email and the Web [8]. Thus, we must design an efficient and adaptive media stream delivery system. The access methods are different for different user, so they have different network characteristics. For example if a user only has 56Kbps bandwidth, it is impossible for him or her to reach video stream. So the system must have the feature that provide the best media combination method according to different users' network status and choices, such as combination of audio, video and text or only text. This special requirement must be taken into consideration in our system. Because only with this feature, the distance learning can be available at any time, in any place, and with any online device.

Interactive: In a learning environment, the interactive feature is very important. But traditional learning methods lay emphasis on the students' passive reception of information, whereas in a SAIHC system the role of the learner becomes very active during the learning process. One can choose the difficulty level and the correlative knowledge. So the structure of a SAIHC is not linear, and it may be interrupted by system questions or user choices, and then continue along any possible path.

3   Structuring of SAIHC

In this section, we propose the structure of SAIHC; first, we define some terms.

Multimedia Material (MM) is the basic element that may be used in hypermedia courseware, and it consists of Internet standard formats like text, audio or video.

Courseware Material (CM) describes the material used in the courseware; it is not the real material but the citation of multimedia material. For example, an image material: <img id="smile" src="http://www. hotwired.com/images/thing"/>.

Learning Subject (LS) is the set of several courseware materials and learning objectives. It organizes different courseware materials, marks their time sequences by SMIL (Synchronized Multimedia Integration Language) [9], and marks the learning goal by their attributions.

Learning Subject Attribute (LSA) describes some attributes of the learning goal, such as definition information (theme, and key words etc.), version information (Author, Corporation and sharing grade etc.), difficult grade, related learning goal, forward learning goal, recommended following learning goal and so on.

Learning Subject Interactive Unit (LSIU) is a main unit of courseware except learning object. Through an interactive unit (for example a select question), the user study status can be real-timely obtained by the LSIU. The manner of how a user answers and makes his (or her) selections can show its current study status, which can be referred to the system's guide.

Then we suggest the structure of SAIHC as Fig. 2 shows. From this figure, we can see that several learning subjects and LSIU compose each courseware. Each learning subject is composed by several courseware materials and a LSA. Each material corresponds to one element (object) in the media materials database, and LSA describes the basic information of this subject. The system can realize self-guided purposes by LSA. It should be noticed that the courseware is not all the same during the study. It can be dynamically generated and organized by LSIU. For example, it can select the next subject content by user's selection of difficult level, through which it can realize to dynamically generate or change the content of the hypermedia courseware. Meanwhile, through the related information in LSA, user can pause current study and refer to related area. However, to avoid weakening study goal because of too many related information, each related point do not have next grade of related point. As a result, the hypermedia here is not a real net structure, but a convergent structure based on courseware contents. The advantage of this structure is: (1). To realize self-guided and interactive specialty. Because the LSIU can dynamically change the content of courseware, system can be adaptive to user's requirements with different knowledge background and different study habit. (2). To realize the Hypermedia-based specialty, and to limit the hypermedia from study circumstance aspect. (3). To make the courseware reusable.

4   System of SAIHC

Based on [4] Modular Training System (MTS) and [2] Multimedia Interactive Telelearning System (MITS), we design a 3-Tier Application Model architecture. The first tier is implemented through the browser, which is concerned with presentation of the courseware. The middle tier provides some agents and tools; include user behavior agent, behavior analysis agent, self-guided agent, courseware searcher, access controller, courseware constructor, and so on. The tiered architecture of SAIHC system is illustrated in Figure 3.

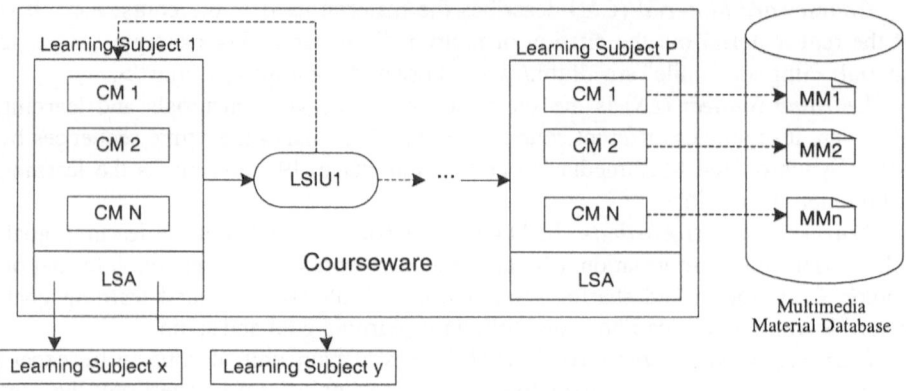

Fig. 2. Structure of SAIHC

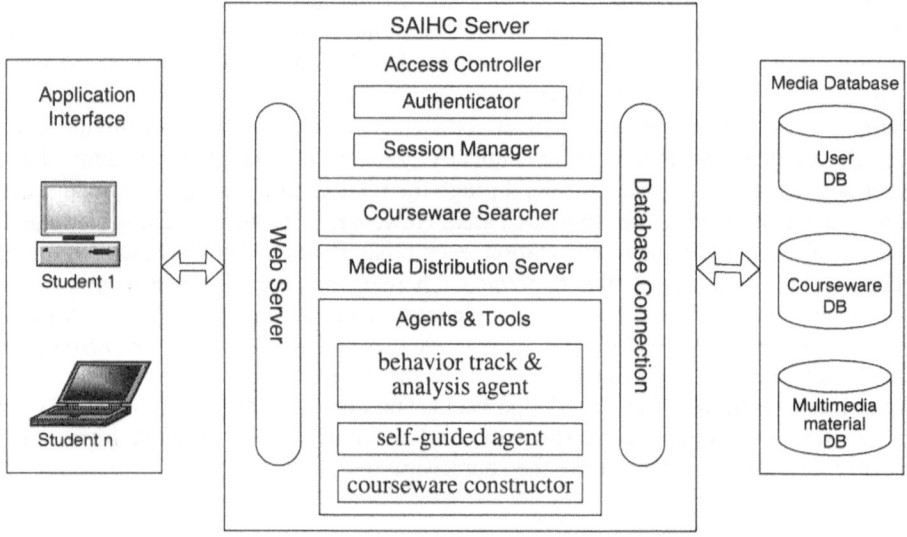

Fig. 3. Tiered Architecture of SAIHC system

5   Conclusion

In this paper, we have presented a Self-Guided Adaptive and Interactive Hypermedia Courseware and SAIHC System. This system is self-guided for learners and hypermedia-capable in storing and delivering courseware over the Internet. The features of self-guided and interactive can help learners achieve a good learning experience, and the feature of adaptive provides the continuous and scalable AV streams to the learners.

Presently, China has not brought forward the standard of courseware. So much more works must be done in the future two years. We will discuss our system and improve it continually.

References

1. Z. Zhang & A. Karmouch. "Multimedia Courseware Delivery Over the Internet", Proc. of IEEE Canadian Conf. Elec.& Computer Engineering '98, Waterloo, Canada, May 24-28,1998.
2. Lei Yuan et al. Self-guided multimedia courseware system over the Internet, Proc. of IEEE Canadian Conf. Elec.& Computer Engineering '99, Edmonton, Alberta, Canada, May 9-12,1999.
3. Chan et al. SAC: a self-paced and adaptive courseware system, Advanced Learning Technologies, Proceedings. IEEE International Conference on, 2001 Page(s): 78–81, 2001.
4. Wang, T. & Hornung, C. The Modular Training System (MTS). A system architecture for Internet-based learning and training, Virtual Systems and Multimedia, 1997. VSMM '97. Proceedings. International Conference on, Page(s): 166 –173, 1997.
5. Uden, L. et al. Multimedia Design Framework for courseware. Advanced Learning Technologies. IWALT 2000. Proceedings. International Workshop on, 2000 Page(s): 85 – 86, 2000.
6. L.J. Najjar. Multimedia Information and Learning, Journal of Multimedia and Hypermedia, 5(2), 129-150, 1996.
7. Chuen-Tsai Sun. An Environment for Learning through Hypertext construction. 29th ASEE/IEEE Frontiers in Learning Conference, Nov.10-13, San Juan, Puerto Rico, 1999.
8. Dapeng Wu et al. Streaming video over the Internet: Approaches and Directions. IEEE Transactions on circuits and systems for video technology. Vol.11, No.3.March, 2001.
9. W3C Recommendation. Synchronized Multimedia Integration Language (SMIL) 2.0 Specification. 9.Aug.2001, *http://www.w3.org/TR/REC-smil.*

Combining Hybrid Media Tools for Web-Based Education

Wouseok Jou, Kangsun Lee, Jonghoon Chun, Hyunmin Park, Hyuksoo Jang, and Soonjung Bahng

Division of Computer Science and Engineering, MyongJi University, San 38-2
Namdong, YongIn, Kyunggido, Korea 449-728
red@mju.ac.kr,

Abstract. In recent years, due to the improvement in network speed, it has become possible to deliver diverse multimedia applications in near real time, and remote education is an area that can most benefit from such developments. In this way, large number s of people have the opportunity to learn anywhere and at any time. With remote education, the proper use of multimedia components is an essential factor for achieving higher learning efficiency. However, the main prevailing tools used for contents creation do not explicitly provide a detail-level interface for combining possible media components. Most importantly, an interface that can coordinate the synchronization between hybrid media is required. In this paper, we present two additional types of teaching media, namely slides and handwriting. Moreover, we present an encoder interface that can combine these media with the conventional video streaming format.

1 Introduction

With the advent of the Internet era, web-based remote education system has gained its importance over the last few years. Because of its inherent advantage, in that the training can take place in any place and at any time and even to a very large number of students, the remote system is starting to replace many of the conventional off-line classes. As a result, many colleges and universities are beginning to replace their regular courses with remote ones, often in the form of a lecture consortium [1,2]. Undoubtedly, the most important factor in education is learning efficiency. In contrast with conventional off-line training, distant learners can easily lose their sense of presence. They easily lose their identity as a member of the class, their attention wanders during the lecture, and finally they may become demotivated. The use of proper media objects is very important for increasing training efficiency. In off-line classes, the instructor can continuously keep the students alert during the lecture. In the remote class, however, direct interaction is not possible. Even if their learning motivation is strong, students cannot be expected to remain concentrated on the lecture for a relatively long period of time. To regain the students attention, we must resort to presentation methodology. We must amplify their sense of presence to

Y.-C. Chen, L.-W. Chang, and C.-T. Hsu (Eds.): PCM 2002, LNCS 2532, pp. 540–547, 2002.

the extent that they feel as if they were in an off-line class. All of the audio-visual experiences that are present in the off-line class must also be provided to the remote students. Different media components can continuously stimulate the students interests. In fact, we can provide more than that which can be provided in the typical off-line classes. In this paper, we present an encoder system which accommodates the slides and handwriting media, and Interfaces these media with the Windows media encoder (hereafter referred to as WME).

2   Literature Review

Remote education methodology has evolved in accordance with available media characteristics [1]. In the earlier stages, uni-directional broadcasting using radio and television was a popular method. Then, with the dissemination of CDs, stand-alone CAI tools became prevalent. More recently, the success of Internet technology has brought diverse computer application tools into the remote educational domain [2,3,4]. The use of multimedia technology for effective presentation is essential in the field of remote education [5]. For instance, in comparison with text-based presentations, using both text and animation can greatly increase the level of understanding [6]. Each mono-medium has its own role. The audio for imagination, video for the recognition of behavior, graphics for delivering concept, and text for precise information [7]. In the remote educational area, various methods for combining these different media have been developed and commercialized. One of the most common software packages used in Korea is DAIS [8]. However, in spite of the prevalence of this tool, it has a critical weakness in that the different media cannot be combined into one. In text mode, the movie is not visible, and vice versa. Microsoft Corporation is probably the major software provider in this area. WME can be used to create multimedia contents in advanced streaming format(hereafter referred to as ASF) [9]. This tool allows the creation of illustrated presentations by embedding graphics and script commands. Nevertheless, the integration of these different media requires precise control of the timing of each mono-medium [10,11,12,13], and WME does not provide an API for detail level control.

3   Encoder Architecture

The Educational System Board (hereafter referred to as ESB) encoder pilots a mixture of multimedia tools for cyber education. In this section, we will describe its presentation structure, handwriting media, encoding interface, media synchronization, and a typical encoding logic.

3.1   Presentation Structure

The media must be chosen to be adequate for the domain. For example, to present a course on how to play tennis, graphics and video are more suitable than texts. By the same token, multimedia components must be carefully chosen based on the nature of the educational topic. Each course has its own characteristics, and the presentations structure has to be designed to suit the individuals needs. However, an effective presentation of the general theoretical aspects should always be a prerequisite for all of the courses. The ESB system supports the multimedia requirements for the general theoretical courses. Multimedia objects comprising the ESB system are shown in Fig 1-(a), and a summary of the media components corresponding to each region is shown in Table 1. Usually, a lecture can be subdivided into several sessions, each of which covers a specific topic. Region 1 provides basic information about the session. The course logo or title can be displayed here. The audio-visual movie stream is displayed in Region 2. Not only voices, but also facial expressions and gestures have crucial importance in learning. Hence they are a must, even if this costs mass storage and requires enormous communication bandwidth. During the lecture, the students may want to rewind and replay the movie, or skip a familiar portion. Such navigational tools, provided by the Windows media player (hereafter referred to as WMP) appear in Region 3. Based on feedback from students, displaying the elapsed time or the elapsed number of slides since the beginning of the lecture is an important requirement. This additional information appears in Regions 3 and 4.

Table 1. Media Type and Components in Fig. 1-(a)

Region	Media Type	Description
1	Text	Course Title, Subtitle
2	Movie	Audio and Video
3	User Interface	Navigation Buttons,Sound Adjustment,Elapsed Time
4	Text	Current Slide Number
5	Text,Hyperlink	Table of Contents,Links to Reference Sites
6	Text, Graphic, Handwriting	Slides,Handwriting Stream

Region 5 can actually be configured depending on content-specific needs. For instance, some variation of the ESB system uses this area to list the slide titles. When clicking on an item in the list, the corresponding slide is displayed. At the same time, the movie in Region 2 is synchronized with the new slide. The provision for this list or table of contents provides them with a simultaneous overview of the entire contents. Depending on the requirements, this area can also be used for hyperlinks related to the lecture contents. Region 6 is the slide window. In the ESB system, the slides can contain texts and graphics. During slides preparation, the graphic images in bitmap or postscript format can be pasted or imported into the slides by an activeX [14] control. In this region, we wish to superposition another layer of handwriting medium.

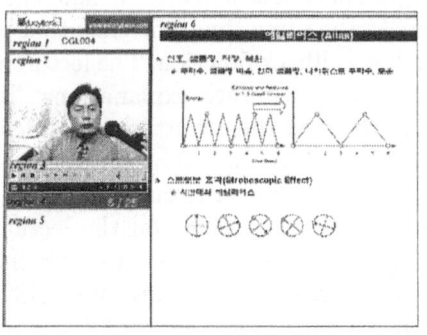
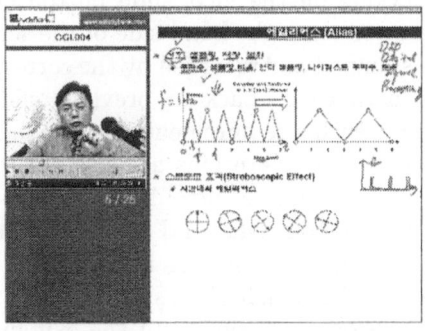

(a) Layour Structure

(b) Overlaying Handwritten Image

Fig. 1. Presentation Module of the ESB System

3.2 Handwriting Media

No matter how perfect the slide materials are, instructors always tend to add additional writings during the lecture. The ESB system allows the instructors to write or draw additional data in the slide area. Fig. 1-(b) shows the result of overlaying handwriting on top of the slide. A drawing tablet is used for inputting the handwriting during the lecture. The handwriting is not displayed all at once. It is not a static image. Rather, the gradual writing sequence is visible. In terms of logical graphic inputs [15], the image drawn by the tablet is treated as a stroke. During the encoding stage, sequential coordinate values are traced, time-stamped, and stored as activeX data objects. During the presentation stage, the objects are decoded and displayed in complete synchronization with the movie stream.

3.3 Encoding Interface

Encoding is the logical counterpart of presentation. The ESB encoding module enables us to use different types of mono-medium. Basic input types include the movie stream of the lecture scene, the slides, and the handwriting stream. Fig. 2-(a) shows the layout and control buttons for the ESB encoding module. The title fields reminds the instructor of the name of the current lecture topic. The record time field shows the total time elapsed since the start of the encoding. The line width button allows the lecturer to select the proper line width of the stylus pen. The color selection button allows the lecturer to select the appropriate pen. This selection can be changed at anytime during the lecture, so that different items can be emphasized with different colors. Sometimes the lecturer may want to erase all handwriting generated so far, in order to start from scratch. The erase button satisfies just such a demand.

Clicking on the next slide button changes slides. As a result, a new slide appears on the right-hand side of the screen. At the same time, the click time is time-stamped and recorded by the corresponding callback function. The lecturers often need to go back to previous slides so as to reiterate explanations. To facilitate such a requirement, the previous and the next slides button was added. These clicking operations are also treated as events, and are time-stamped for later presentation. Control buttons to specify the encoding environment appears near the bottom left-hand corner of the screen. When clicking on the lecture selection button, the user is requested to indicate where in the directory the slide materials reside. The start and end button marks the beginning and ending of the encoding session, and the exit button is used to close current encoding session.

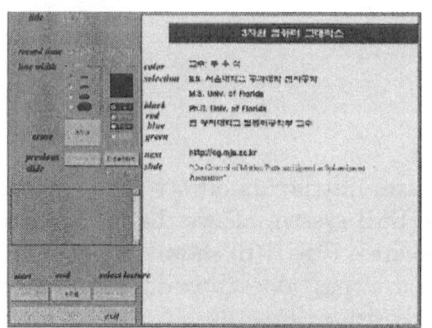
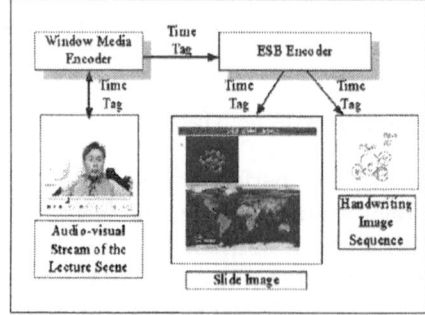

(a) Layout Structure   (b) Conceptual Interface

Fig. 2. Encoding Module of the ESB System

3.4   Media Synchronization

One of the major features of the ESB system is its accommodation of slides and handwriting. However, synchronization is the key issue here, since all of the media comprising the presentation module must work together. That is, both the slide flipping and the handwriting stream must be synchronized with the movie stream controlled by WME.

WME is relatively limited as regards the supplementary media. XML tags in the ASX file can only be used for the high-level integration of short multimedia titles. The custom script commands have limited capability for controlling the synchronization details. In fact, each item of data in the ASF data units carries a time stamp that specifies when that data should be rendered. Nevertheless, WME does not allow the modification or control of its timing logic either at the source code or the API level. To solve this problem, we treat the ESB encoder as being independent from WME. This is shown in Fig. 2-(b). We let WME process data in its own way, and do not interrupt its flow. Similarly, the ESB encoder handles its own media objects. As in the object-oriented paradigm, each media encoder works as an independent unit. The only information that requires to be communicated is the timing data linking the different media objects. This can be readily accessed via public variables.

The most crucial part of the synchronization is that concerning the start time. As shown in Fig. 3-(a), the WME timer assigns its own time stamp to the movie stream. Between the time interval t_{-1} and t_1, WME loads relevant code segments, and initializes relevant parameters. When these operations are finished, the first frame of the movie is time-stamped to zero at time t_1, and the stamp value increases thereafter. The ESB encoder must determine the exact time t_1 in order to synchronize its own media with WME encoder.

The WME timer value can be accessed by passing the message function "Encoder.Statistics. EncodingTime to WME. If we attempt to obtain the WME time immediately after time t_0, it will normally return a zero value. This happens because WME has not yet finished initialization, and the value of the public variable EncodingTime is as yet undefined. To overcome this, we can continuously loop and monitor the variable until the first time-stamp is recorded. However, in this case, it is not guaranteed that we will poll it at the time $t_1 = 0$. Rather, we may end up polling it near time $t = t_r$ whereupon the returned timer value will be t2. The time delay between $t = t_r$ and $t = t_{wt}$ must also be considered. If we request the WME timer value at $t = t_r$ and the value t_2 is returned in t_{wt}, the actual WME timer value has already increased by the amount of the delay. However, at this early stage of encoding, the WME has not yet begun interaction with the other modules. Therefore, the update of the timer value happens near real time. This time delay has proven to be less then 1ms in our test environment. Similarly, there is a time delay induced when calling the timeGetTime function of the windows system, but it is also negligible compared with tgap. In general, we can safely assume that $t_r = t_2 = t_3 = t_{wt} = t_{st}$. Using this assumption, we can now backtrack the start time of the WME encoder. Because the windows system timer returns the total cumulative time elapsed since the time $t_0 = 0$, we can subtract t_{gap} from t_3, and set the result as the start time of our ESB encoder. We assume that this time best approximates to the start time of WME.

3.5 Typical Encoding Logic

An ASF object is composed of three types of objects; header, data, and index object. Data units inside the data object have two types of tags, namely presentation time and send time. The presentation time means the time stamp required for synchronized rendering, and the send time resolves the synchronization problem with respect to any possible delay caused by the network transmission. The ESB encoder uses a simplified version of this scheme. The data size of the slides and the handwriting is relatively tiny compared with that of the WME movie stream. Therefore, instead of tagging the send time, we pre-download the entire

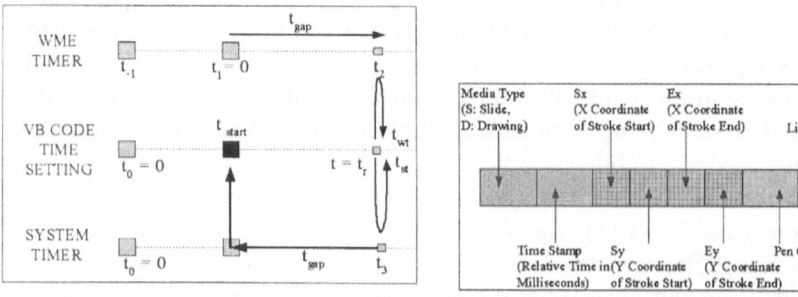

(a) Synchronization Timing   (b) Data File Format

Fig. 3. Timing and Format of the ESB System

ESB encoding file before the presentation starts. Fig. 3-(b) shows the file format used in the ESB encoder. The slide and the handwriting data are treated identically. In fact, the slide data records only the flipping time, so that the corresponding slide can be loaded during the presentation. To speed up the downloading, the file can be prepared in binary format or compressed.

The presentation of the encoding file is entirely event-driven. In practice, the media consistency must also be maintained at this level. For instance, the movement of the slide bar in the movie window will cause WMP to advance or rewind to the movie frame with the changed index marker. At the same time, the ESB encoder must reposition its own media in accordance with this new timing position. To do this, the slide corresponding to this time must be searched and reloaded. In addition, the handwriting strokes drawn up to this time are applied cumulatively beginning from the start of the corresponding slide.

3.6   Implementation Environment

The ESB encoder wars developed using Visual Basic language in the MS Windows environment. It was embedded into the HTML in the form of an activeX data object. A Dell systems Power Edge 4400 equipped with an Intel Xeon PIII CPU and RAID level-5 storage was used as the encoding server. The studio facility includes the server, a TOA DM1200 directional microphone, a SONY VX 2000 digital camcorder, a Watcom PL400 LCD tablet, and an Osprey WM Pro500 digital capture card. The encoding parameters related to audio-visual quality were optimized for a bandwidth of 100Kbps. Server co-location service provided by KIDC(Korea Internet Data Center) offers reliable 100Mbps network bandwidth nationwide. Remote education service with the ESB platform is now commercialized with more than 20,000 members, and about 100 courses are currently offered.

4 Conclusion

In this paper, we described how the WME-based remote educational tool could be expanded to accommodate additional media, namely the use of slides and handwriting. The ESB encoder controls these types of media in close accordance with the media produced by the WME. In this paper, we explained the presentation structure and the encoding environment of the ESB encoder. Synchronization between the different media originating from different encoders was required, and the method used for tracing and synchronizing the exact start time was explained. In addition, typical encoder logic and file formats were suggested. In terms of service quality, there are numerous factors to consider in the integrated pipeline of encoding, transmission, and presentation. In the near future, methods for optimizing these factors must also be established. In addition, different strategies must be developed for different training courses.

References

1. Kim, W. et al. Real-time Interactive Education System in Distributed Environment. *Journal of Korean Multimedia Society*, 3(5):506–515, 2000.
2. Hiltz, S.R. The Virtual Classroom: Using Computer Mediated Communications for University Teaching. *Journal of Communication*, 36(2):95–102, 1986.
3. Franklin, N.Y. and Warren, W.R. *A Guide to System Planning and Implementation.* Indiana University Press, 1995.
4. Corrigan, D. *The Internet University: College Courses by Computer.* Cape Software Press, 1996.
5. Bates, A.W. *Technology, Open Learning, and Distance Education.* Routledge Studies in Distance Education. Routledge, London, 1995.
6. Mayer, R.E. and Anderson, R.B. Animations Need Narrations: An Experimental Test of a Dual-coding Hypothesis. *Journal of Educational Psychology*, 83:484–490, 1991.
7. Alty, J.L. Multimedia. In Diaper, D. and Hammonds, N., editor, *People and Computer IV.* Cambridge, 1991.
8. Dawoo Corporation. *What Is DAIS?* Dawoo Corporation, Seoul, Korea, 1998.
9. Microsoft Corporation. *Inside Windows Media.* Que Publishing, 1999.
10. Steinmetz, R. and Nahrstedt, K. *Multimedia: Computing, Communications, and Application.* Innovative Technology Series. Prentice Hall, New Jersey, 1995.
11. Hodges, M.E. and Sasnett, R.M. *Multimedia Computing: Case Studies from MIT Project Athena.* Addison Wesley, 1990.
12. Anderson, D.P. and Homsy, G. A Continuous Media I/O Server and It's Synchronization Mechanism. *IEEE Computer*, 24:51–57, 1991.
13. IBM Corporation. *IBM Multimedia Presentation Management Programming Reference and Programming Guide 1.0.* IBM Corporation, 1992.
14. Deitel H.M., Deitel P.J. and Nieto, T.R. *Internet & World Wide Web: How to Program.* Prentice Hall, 2001.
15. Hearn, D. and Baker M.P. *Computer Graphics.* Prentice Hall, 1997.

X-WALTZ: The Framework of an Interactive Multimedia Math E-learning

Long Chyr Chang, Pi-Shin Wey, and Heien-Kun Chiang

Department of Information Management, Da-Yeh University
112 Shan-Jeau Rd. Dah-Tsuen, Chang-Hwa, Taiwan, 51505, R. O. C.
{long, pswey, chiang}@mail.dyu.edu.tw

Abstract. Current e-Learning systems are still lacking support of providing standard and good tools for sharing and exchange multimedia information on the Web. For math e-Learning, current math representation often uses image and vector methods such as FLASH or QUICKTIME. Unfortunately, they lack clarity and open standard, which limit their potentials in content sharing and exchange. In addition, they do not provide effective mechanisms that enable them to deliver multimode multimedia presentations to fit users' needs and preferences. In this paper, we propose a framework called X-WATLZ[1], which aims to provide an interactive multimedia e-Learning environment for learners to learn math anywhere, anytime with any computing device such as PC or PDA. The X-WALTZ contains six components: learning management, content management, interaction management, activity management, content delivery, and Math Web Service systems. Our implementation is based on the open standard XML, SVG, MATHML, and related technologies. Some implementation issues and results are also discussed.

1 Introduction

It has been over thirty years since people began using computers for educational purpose. For many years, instructional computing was filled with excitement and promise for the potential of great educational improvement through computer-based instruction. Although there have been a lot of studies in applying computer technology to instruction, actual improvement in learning is less dramatic [1]. In the early 1990s, Internet technologies have fundamentally transformed the entire technological and economical landscapes. Nowadays, hundreds of millions of people use the World Wide Web (WWW) to pursue activities as diverse as trading, dating, entertaining, researching, and of course, learning. Since then, we have laid out our hope with respect to using computers and web-based network communication technologies to

---

[1] This research was supported in part by National Science Foundation (NSC 89-2745-P-212-001), and in part by the Advanced IA Technology Development Project of Institute for Information Industry and sponsored by MOEA, R.O.C.

Y.-C. Chen, L.-W. Chang, and C.-T. Hsu (Eds.): PCM 2002, LNCS 2532, pp. 548–555, 2002.
© Springer-Verlag Berlin Heidelberg 2002

deliver and facilitate learning. Internet-enabled learning, also called e-Learning, opens a new vision for successful learning [13].

According to Rosenberg's definition [13], e-Learning refers to "the use of Internet technologies to deliver a broad array of solutions that enhance knowledge and performance". This definition is based on three fundamental criteria: (1) E-Learning is networked, which can instantly update, store/retrieve, distribute, and share instruction or information; (2) E-Learning is deliverable to any network-capable computing devices using standard Internet technology; (3) E-Learning focuses on the broadest view of learning, which integrates the scopes of web-based online instruction and content management. In other words, the Web based e-Learning paradigm is about online instruction, content management, their interdependency, and their interaction [10,13].

In some ways, the Web and related network communication technologies have both advanced and hindered the growth of effective e-Learning systems. They advance it by making computer networks easily accessible to people to proceeding learning at anytime, anywhere, with any forms of devices. However, they hinder it by not providing standard and good tools for exchanging and sharing multimedia information during e-Learning [1]. The current state of e-Learning is still in its infant stage, facing issues of providing effective supports to enhance online instruction and content management. For math e-Learning, the fundamental issues are not different from other learning subjects. However, due to the abstract nature of math notations and contents, the online math representation is usually lack of semantic meanings and is difficult to understand for human as well as computers. Many experts suggest that math contents should be illustrated and even presented in situated multimedia learning space so that students can learn interactively or collaboratively with fun. This raises another issue of how to seamlessly integrate currently available technologies in a standard form to facilitate the representation, exchange, and sharing of reusable and interactable math contents. For instance, current popular image-based methods for representing math equations have difficulties in: (1) efficient Web transmission, (2) automatic screen size adjustment, and (3) human editing or machine interpretation [6,7]. Even popular vector-based FLASH/QUICKTIME formats are still suffered various limitations, such as (1) lacking an open standard, (2) lacking interoperability, and (3) lacking machine-to-machine direct translation [8]. As a result, math contents in many e-Learning systems cannot be easily integrated, shared and exchanged. Apparently, we need better techniques and tools to circumvent the above-mentioned difficulties.

For many years, the W3C (World Wide Web Consortium) has been working on XML (Extensible Markup Language) related technologies to facilitate information exchange among different systems. It has gained overwhelming supports from software industries and business sectors. In particular, two XML-based new comers known as SVG (Scalable Vector Graphics) and MATHML (Mathematics Markup Language) [12,17] have gained great attention among academics and information industries in representing multimedia math contents. The main advantages of using SVG or MATHML over previous approaches lie in their ability in encoding math expressions and semantics, in presenting math contents on the Web, and in enhancing the sharing, interactivity, collaboration among online learners with diverse computing devices. Furthermore, current rapid development of wireless network, multimedia, and mobile devices, such as PDAs or Smartphones or Webpads, has brought a new way of communication among users. Mobile businesses as well as mobile learning are becoming next wave of computing and communication paradigms. Altogether, these emerging paradigms provide a new opportunity for building a platform- and device-independent environment for students to learn math interactively in multimedia fashion using any computing devices from anywhere at anytime.

In this paper, we propose an interactive multimedia math e-Learning framework called X-WALTZ, inspired by the success of WALTZ which is a collaborative Pythagorean theorem learning space for junior high school students in Taiwan [2]. Based on XML and its related technologies, X-WALTZ intends to support Web-based mechanisms that enable interactive, sharable, reusable, and dynamic multimedia math instruction. In addition, it also supports personalization and customization to fit users' learning or computing preferences. The ultimate goal of this project is to let users learn math as fun as playing online video game. The rest of this paper is organized as follows. Section 2 discussed experience and lesson learned from WATLZ project. Section 3 discusses the background of XML, SVG, MATHML technologies, and related research in detail. Section 4 presents the framework of XWALTZ. Section 5 explains X-WALTZ implementation issues. Section 6 concludes the research and summarizes future research directions.

2 WALTZ Project Experiences

The WALTZ project had proceeded from 1999 to 2001. The main goal of WALTZ was to develop a web-based interactive and adaptive math-learning environment based on the CIA (Content/Interaction/Adaptivity) learning model according to the theory of constructivism. WALTZ was capable of supporting discovering, project-based, and collaborative learning in 2D/3D shared virtual learning space. It was structured into two major parts: (1) Online Pythagorean Theorem Learning, including Pythagorean theorem instruction, collaborative learning, virtual gaming, and online testing, and (2) Online Learning Supports, including user navigation, chat room, personal math learning tools, FAQ, site map, Pythagorean theorem learning resources, and e-mail. Two experiments (WALTZ prototype's usability test and Pythagorean Theorem multimedia instruction's effectiveness test) were conducted to test the performance of the WALTZ. The first experiment's results showed that the system's usability was good in terms of efficiency, effectiveness, and user satisfaction. Complaints from testers were mostly related to the difficulties in controlling VR player in virtual game, and in sharing ideas in 2D Collaborative Learning Space [5]. The results of the second test revealed that the system did not have significant influence on students' learning outcomes, but all the teachers and students who participated in this experiment gave very high mark in the satisfaction of system's multimedia instructional design [3].

Technically, WATLZ lacked an open standard to present math contents, which hindered the reusability and interoperability of its content in e-Learning systems. What we had learned from the WALTZ experience was that although virtual reality presents a paradigm for constructing a situated and interactive leaning environment for learners to manipulate online subjects, it still has a long way to go for supporting effective math learning.

3 Backgrounds and Related Research

One well-known effort in standardization of learning contents is the SCORM specifications [4] developed jointly by the Advanced Distributed Learning Initiative (ADL), IEEE, IMS, AICC and ARIADNE in 2000. Built upon XML technologies, the SCORM intends to support "RAID" features: reusability, accessibility, interoperability and durability so that learners can access high quality learning materials whenever and wherever they need. Since then, many e-Learning frameworks for dedicated applications are proposed and more features such as extensibility, scalability, security, and adaptability are raised [14]. Khan [9] proposed a framework of e-Learning to guide the design, development, evaluation, and implementation of e-Learning environments. The framework has eight dimensions: institutional, pedagogical, technological, interface design, evaluation, management, resource support, and ethical. However, none of these frameworks suggests how math e-Learning should be built.

XML is a self-descriptive well-formed structure. The advantages of using XML over HTML or other data formats in e-Learning framework are well known [8,14,15]. Its powerfulness and attractions lie in its simplicity and allowing separation of content and presentation. Thus it can provide a flexible model for multimode delivery of content according to users' preferences. In addition, it can facilitate learning resource searches, exchange and sharing since it can be easily parsed. For math contents, the drawbacks of traditional representation methods such as image methods and vector graphics methods have been recognized by W3C for many years [16,17]. Two XML new standards (MATHML and SVG) toward math and multimedia presentation have been formulated to facilitate effective communication and presentation of math contents on the Web. MATHML actually is a low-level specification for describing machine-to-machine mathematics communication. Without such presentation, human will have great difficulties in communicating math contents with math software agents on different platforms. ActiveMath [15] project is one of pioneers in math e-learning system that can provide math services using symbolic algebraic systems such as Maple or Mathematica. They also intend to implement some "RAID" features of SCORM. However, there is no multimedia interactivity for their math contents. On the other hand, SVG is a future star for open two-dimensional graphics on the Web. The SVG graphics is readable, interactive, and dynamic. It can be animated, pointed, roomed and panned. In addition, it can be progressively rendered to fit any size of display screen without suffering resolution-loss. Today, many SVG tools and browsers are being developed for PC, PDA and cellular phones. Both MATHML and SVG all have advantages of XML technologies. In addition, they offer many benefits including (1) dynamic interactivity, (2) searchability, (3) time and space efficiency, (4) extensibility, (5) accessibility, (6) interoperability, (7) internationalization, (8) distributed authoring, (9) progressive rendering, and (10) readability [8]. These benefits enable us to build a highly interactive multimedia math e-Learning environment so that users can learn math with their choice of computers such as PC or PDA anywhere, anytime.

4   The Framework of X-WALTZ

X-WALTZ focuses on providing better interactive multimedia environment for learning math. The ultimate goal is to let users learn math, either collaboratively or not, as fun as playing Nintendo Game-Boy video machine anywhere, anytime. Since e-Learning actually is a self-paced learning through Internet, learners might want to access learning material whenever and wherever they need using any computing devices available. In addition, if a poor learner found difficult in math problems, he might need help from others. A Math Web Service that can solve his/her problem immediately might be a handy solution. Otherwise, he might want to communicate math problems with others through chat, forum or math whiteboard. Therefore, personalization, customization, performance, interaction and math service support are important for users so that they can learn happily with their pace anytime anywhere. In short, X-WALTZ is designed to meet the following key requirements:

1. Accessibility (providing access math contents on an anytime, anywhere basis);
2. Interoperability (seamless flow of math contents via the Internet, regardless of systems);
3. Reusability (ensuring that learning content can be easily reused by others);
4. Flexibility (the ability to display different styles of math contents according to user's needs);
5. Interactivity (learning math by interaction via multimedia interface);
6. Collaboration (ability to learn math with others through forum or synchronous mechanisms);
7. Integration (ability to integrate math contents from different e-Learning systems);

The framework of X-WATLZ is designed based on the lessons gained from WALTZ project. It supports WALTZ's CIA (Content, Interaction, and Adaptivity) learning model and Constructivism learning theory. One main feature of X-WALTZ framework is that it supports math multimedia interaction in two ways: asynchronous and synchronous. To facilitate interoperability, reusability, and flexibility of the e-learning system, the X-WALTZ is built upon open standard XML technologies. Figure 1 illustrates the X-WALTZ framework and its interaction with other e-learning components. Following are key components of X-WALTZ.

Learning management system (LMS): The LMS is the central part of the X-WATLZ framework. It integrates various processes and tools to provide content authoring and integration, multimedia interaction, learning activity management and dynamic delivery of math contents. In addition, the LMS incorporates links to math

Web Service mechanism that integrate external math engines for computing math. It coordinates with the following systems:

Content management system (CMS): The content system contains authoring and integration supports. The authoring sub-system supports various distributed tools that enable math content developers, teacher, or students to design math contents with math problems, equations (MATHML), graphics (SVG), solutions and other information (i.e. difficult levels, type, category) in XML format. The integration sub-system allows teachers or content developers to share content and its components over the network.

Interaction management system (IMS): The interaction systems provide asynchronous mechanism such as chat or math forums and synchronous mechanism, such as math whiteboard, slideshow, for learners to interact math contents with other students or teachers.

Activity management system (AMS): The activity management systems manage learning activities including online registration, notification, evaluation, assessment, testing, and performance tracking. It also records learners' profile to support personalization and customization.

Content delivery system (CDS): The delivery sub-system contains transformer and presentation engine that can transform math content to appropriate format such as SVG, XML, X3D, and PDF. It can dynamically deliver multimedia math contents to users according to learners' needs and preferences.

Math Web Service System (MWS): It provides mechanisms for learners to communicate their math problems (represented in MATHML) with math software agents to solve their problem on the fly. The math software agent actually is a Web Service [11] with remote math engines that can receive SOAP (Simple Object Access Protocol) messages and compute the result and return solutions back to learners.

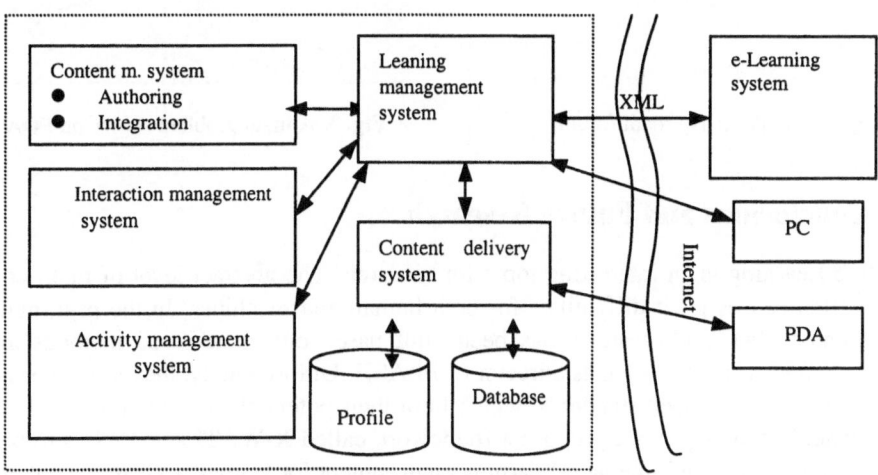

Fig. 1. The X-WALTZ framework

5   Implementation Issues

The implementation of X-WALTZ framework is built according to the XML, MATHML, SVG and other related technologies. Currently, we are focusing on the following components: (1) authoring tools (2) math forum (3) dynamic multimedia presentation and testing and (4) mobile SVG collaborative systems. For authoring and math forum, we provide DTD (Document Type Definition), and integrated tools for writing math equation and SVG graphics. For dynamic multimedia presentation and testing, we support transformers and presentation engines that can deliver multimode dynamic multimedia contents according to user's need and preference. Figure 2 shows a math forum that contains multimode (SVG/X3D) representations of math messages. One of the advantages of using such design is that users can interact with math objects designed by message posters. Figure 3 shows a math problem presented in PDA using SVG. One nice feature about SVG in PDA is that users can point and zoom the area of interests without suffering image quality-loss. We are currently developing PDA collaborative systems, which enable users to use PDA as a collaborative platform for sharing information anywhere anytime.

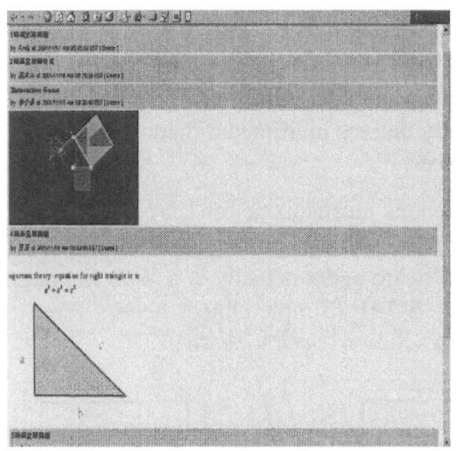

Fig. 2. An interactive math forum   **Fig. 3.** A math problem shown on PDA

6   Conclusions and Future Research

Math e-Learning is an interesting topic for research. The abstract level of math contents often causes great difficulties for both human and machines. In the past, many multimedia CAI math systems has been built based on image-based methods and vector graphics systems such as Director or FLASH. Unfortunately, they are either not effective or lack of open standards, which limit their potentials in content sharing and exchange. In this paper, we propose a framework called X-WATLZ that aims to provide an interactive multimedia e-Learning environment for learners to learn anywhere, anytime with any computers such as PDA. The framework is based on the lessons we learned in developing WATLZ, which is based on CIA learning model and Constructivism learning theory. X-WALTZ supports content authoring, integration, interaction and activity management, delivery and math Web Service. Our current implementation is based on the XML, SVG and MATHML technologies. We are developing following components (1) authoring tools, (2) math forum, (3) dynamic multimedia testing and presentation, and (4) mobile SVG collaboration system. The result is very promising. However, there are still some problems in using PDA as a platform of learning math. The interface design of collaboration system in PDA needs to be explored in depth in order to provide a friendly, easy-using math environment for PDA-based learners. Our current implementations focus mainly on multimedia authoring and presentation of math contents using SVG and MATHML. In the near future, we will develop more useful tools that allow learners to use PDAs as collaborative platforms for e-Learning.

References

1. Alessi, S. M., Trollip, S. R., Multimedia for Learning: Methods and Development, 3rd ed, Boston: Allyn and Bacon (2001)
2. Chang, L. C., Chiang, H. K., Wey, P. S., "WALTZ: A Web-based Adaptive/Interactive Learning and Teaching Zone," Proc. of the ICCE/ICCAI Conference (2000), 1442-1448
3. Chang, L. L., The Presentation Design of Web-based Junior High School Mathematics Multimedia Instruction System, Master Thesis, Da-Yeh University, R.O.C. (2001)
4. Cox, K., "ADL and SCORM," In Web Tools Newsletter, July 10 (2000)
5. Deng, Y. C., The Usability-Criteria Interface of Web-Based Math Instruction System for Junior High Students, Master Thesis, Da-Yeh University, R.O.C. (2001)
6. Foster, K.R., "Mathtype 5 with MathML for the WWW," IEEE Spectrum, Vol. 38, Issue: 12, Dec. (2001), pp. 64
7. Hagler, M., "Mathematics and equations on the WWW," Frontiers in Education Conference, FIE'98, Vol. 2. (1998) 583–586, http://fie.engrng.pitt.edu/fie98/papers/1266.pdf
8. Kamthan, P. "XMLization of Graphics," http://tech.irt.org/articles/js209/
9. Khan, B. H., "A framework for Web-based learning," In B. H. Khan (Ed.), Web-based training. Englewood Cliffs, NJ: Educational Technology Publications (2001)
10. Lee, W.W., Owens. D. L., Multimedia-Based Instructional Design: Computer-Based Training, Web-Based Training, Distance Broadcast Training, CA: San Francisco: Jossey-Bass/Pfeiffer, A Wiley Company (2000)
11. Mougin, P., Barriolade, C. "Web Services, Business Objects and Component Models," Orchestra Networks, Jul. (2001)
12. Pierron, L., Belaid, A., "An XML/SVG platform for document analysis," INRIA-LORIA, Campus scientifique, 239-242, http://www.loria.fr/~abelaid/publi_ps/DLIA_2001.pdf
13. Rosenberg, M. J., e-Learning: Strategy for Delivering Knowledge in the Digital Age, New York: McGraw-Hill Company (2001)
14. Singh, H, "Achieving Interoperability in e-Learning," http://www.learningcircuits.org/
15. "The ActiveMath Project," http://www.activemath.org/
16. W3C, "Mathematical Markup Language (MathML) 2.0," http://www.w3.org/Math (2001)
17. W3C, "Scalable Vector Graphics(SVG) 1.0 Specification," http://www.w3.org/SVG (2001)

Hybrid Learning Schemes for Multimedia Information Retrieval

Wei-Cheng Lai[1], Edward Chang[2], and Kwang-Ting (Tim) Cheng[2]

[1] VIMA Technologies, 3944 State Street, Suite #340 Santa Barbara, CA 93105, USA
wlai@vimatech.com
[2] Electrical & Computer Engineering University of California
Santa Barbara, CA 93106, USA
echang@ece.ucsb.edu

Abstract. Traditional database systems assume that precise query concepts can be specified by users (for example, by using query languages). For many search tasks, however, a query concept is hard to articulate, and articulation can be subjective. Most users would find it hard to describe an image or a music query in low-level perceptual features. We believe that one desirable paradigm for search engines is to mine (i.e., to learn) users' query concepts through *active learning*. In this paper, we formulate the query-concept learning problem as finding a binary classifier that separates relevant objects from those that are irrelevant to the query concept. We propose two hybrid algorithms, *pipeline learning*, and *co-training*, that are built on top of two active learning algorithms. Our empirical study shows that even when the feature dimension is very high and target concepts are very specific, the hybrid algorithms can grasp a complex query concept in a small number of user iterations.

1 Introduction

A database system cannot answer a query without knowing the query criteria (i.e., *query concept*). For querying a relational database, a query concept is conveyed via query languages. For querying with an Internet search engine, a concept is conveyed through keywords. For querying a multimedia database, however, a query concept is hard to articulate in query languages, and articulation can be subjective. For instance, in an image search, it is difficult for a user to describe desired images using low-level features such as color, shape and texture. In addition, different users may perceive the same image differently (i.e., subjectively). Even if an image is perceived similarly, users may use different vocabulary (i.e., different combinations of low-level features and keywords) to depict it. In order to make query formulation easy and personalized, it is both necessary (for capturing abstract and subjective concepts) and desirable (for alleviating difficulties from specifying complex query concepts) to build intelligent search engines that can quickly learn users' query concepts.

Y.-C. Chen, L.-W. Chang, and C.-T. Hsu (Eds.): PCM 2002, LNCS 2532, pp. 556–563, 2002.

For learning complex and subjective query concepts with a small amount of training data, we have proposed two *active learning* algorithms—MEGA and SVM$_{Active}$. For the detailed algorithms and extensive experimental results of MEGA and SVM$_{Active}$, please refer to [1,2,3]. In this paper, we present hybrid approaches to improve the effectiveness of these base algorithms. We regard the problem of learning a query concept as learning a binary classifier that separates the data objects relevant to the query criteria from the irrelevant ones. The learning task faces three challenging steps:

1. Initialization. The learner must quickly identify some positive and some negative examples to obtain a fuzzy boundary separating the objects relevant to the query concept from irrelevant ones.
2. Refinement. The learner must then refine the classification boundary with a minimum number of labeled instances (i.e., with minimum rounds of relevance feedback).
3. Ranking. When the binary classifier is learned with sufficient confidence, the learner must quickly return the top-k objects that are relevant to the query concept.

Our proposed hybrid schemes for tackling the above challenges are as follows:

1. *Pipeline training.* We combine the strengths of MEGA (finding initial relevant objects to the concept) and SVM$_{Active}$ (refining the class boundary), to show that using MEGA first and then switching to SVM$_{Active}$ can enable the learner to learn a concept substantially faster and more accurately than the individual algorithms can.
2. *Recursive subspace co-training.* This approach aims to remedy the training-instance scarcity problem by dividing the feature space into subspaces and conducts recursive training in these subspaces. The initial training data can in different subspaces infer different negative-labeled instances. The inferred negative-labeled instances can be added to the training data to retrain the binary classifier in all subspaces to infer even more negative-labeled instances. This recursive procedure continues until few negative-labeled instances can be further inferred.

Given the same number of feedback rounds (or the same amount of training data), our empirical study shows that these hybrid schemes can learn a query concept with higher accuracy when compared to the base algorithms.

The rest of the paper is organized into seven sections. Section 2 presents our hybrid learning strategies. Sections 3 and 4 report experimental results. Finally, we offer our concluding remarks in Section 5.

2   Hybrid Algorithms

The first challenge of query concept learning is to find some relevant objects so that the concept boundary can be fuzzily identified. Finding a relevant object can be difficult if only a small fraction of the dataset satisfies the target concept. For instance, suppose the desired objects in a one-million-image dataset is 100 (0.1%). If we randomly select 20 objects per round for users to identify relevant objects, the probability of finding a positive sample after five rounds of random sampling is just 10%—clearly not acceptable.

We can improve the odds with an intelligent sampling method MEGA (The Maximizing Expected Generalization Algorithm), which finds relevant samples quickly, to initialize query-concept learning. MEGA models query concepts in k-CNF [4], which can formulate virtually all practical query concepts. MEGA [3] uses k-DNF to bound the sampling space from which to select the most informative samples for soliciting user feedback.

Once some relevant and some irrelevant samples are marked, we can employ SVM$_{Active}$ [2] to refine the class boundary. Intuitively, SVM$_{Active}$ works by combining the following three ideas:

1. SVM$_{Active}$ regards the task of learning a target concept as one of learning an SVM binary classifier. An SVM captures the query concept by separating the relevant images from the irrelevant images with a hyperplane in a projected space, usually a very high-dimensional one. The projected points on one side of the hyperplane are considered relevant to the query concept and the rest irrelevant.

2. SVM$_{Active}$ learns the classifier quickly via active learning. The active part of SVM$_{Active}$ selects the most informative instances with which to train the SVM classifier. This step ensures fast convergence to the query concept in a small number of feedback rounds.

3. Once the classifier is trained, SVM$_{Active}$ returns the top-k most relevant images. These are the k images farthest from the hyperplane on the query concept side.

Although MEGA and SVM$_{Active}$ are effective active learning algorithms, we believe combining their strengths can result in even better learning algorithms. In the rest of this section we propose two such hybrid algorithms:

- Pipeline learning (Section 2.1), and
- Subspace co-training (Section 2.2).

2.1   Pipeline Learning

As depicted in [2], the SVM$_{Active}$ scheme needs at least one positive and one negative example to start. MEGA is not restricted by this seeding requirement, and it is able to find relevant examples quickly by refining the sampling boundary. It is therefore logical to employ MEGA to perform the *initialization* task. Once some relevant images are found, the refinement step can be executed by either MEGA or SVM$_{Active}$.

Thus, we can have three execution alternatives.

1. MEGA only. Use MEGA all the way to learn a concept.
2. SVM_{Active} only. Use random sampling to find the first relevant example(s) and then use SVM_{Active} to learn a concept.
3. Pipeline learning. Use MEGA to find initial relevant objects, and then switch to SVM_{Active} for refining the binary classifier and ranking returned objects.

2.2   Recursive Subspace Co-training

The problem of using a large unlabeled sample pool to boost performance of a learning algorithm is considered under the framework of co-training [5]. A broad definition of co-training is to provide each instance multiple distinct views. We have just shown that distinct views can be provided by different learning algorithms. Here, we propose another co-training method, which provides each training instance distinct views via subspace learning. This method recursively conducts subspace co-training at each feedback iteration in the following steps:

1. Divide the feature space into G subspaces.
2. Conduct parallel training in these G subspaces using labeled training dataset L.
3. Use the G resulting learners to label the unlabeled pool and yield a new set of labeled instances L'.
4. $L \leftarrow L \cup L'$
5. Go back to Step 1 until no more labeled instance can be inferred (i.e., until $L' = \emptyset$).

3   Experiments

We implemented both MEGA and SVM_{Active} in C, $C++$, and tested using an Intel Pentium III^{TM} workstation running Linux. We have implemented an industrial strength prototype [6] with all features discussed in this paper. We tested our prototype with the intent of answering three central questions.

1. Does using MEGA to find the first relevant object(s) and then switching to SVM_{Active} a more effective algorithm than using the two learning algorithms individually?
2. Does the percentage of relevant data affect learning performance? (If we reduce the matching data from 5% of the dataset to 1%, does it take more iterations to learn query concepts?)
3. Do additional heuristics such as co-training help accelerate concept convergence?

3.1 Data

For our empirical evaluation of our learning methods we used a real-world image dataset: a twenty-category image dataset where each category consisted of 200 to 300 images (the total number of images is about 5,000). Images for this dataset were collected from Corel Image CDs and the Internet. Each image as a 144-dimension vector [2].

- *Twenty-category* set. The set consists of images of *architecture, bears, cities, clouds, couples, flowers, insects, ladies, landscape, objectionable images, planets, tigers, tools, waves, elephants, fabrics, fireworks, food,* and *textures.*

To enable an objective measure of performance, we assumed that a query concept was an image category, or a superset or a subset of a category. For instance, a query can be "wild animals" including "tigers", "elephants", and "bears." A query can be "white bears" (a subset of "bears"), or "purple flowers" (a subset of "flowers"). The learners do not have prior knowledge about image categories. Unlike some recently developed systems [7] that contain a semantical layer between image features and queries to assist query refinement, our system does not have an explicit semantical layer. We argue that having a hard-coded semantical layer can make a retrieval system restrictive to some predefined concepts. Rather, dynamically learning the semantics of a query concept is flexible and hence makes the system useful.

3.2 Queries

We separate our queries into two categories: 5% and 1% queries. The matching images for each of the more specific query concepts such as "purple flowers" and "white bears" account for about 1% of the total dataset. More general concepts such as "bears", "flowers" and "architectures" have about 5% matching images in the dataset. For each experiment, we will report results for these two categories of queries separately. In the experiment, we report precisions of the top-10 and top-20 retrievals to measure performance.

4 Results and Discussion

Here we present our analysis of the results, organized with regard to the central questions listed at the start of Section 3.

4.1 MEGA, SVM$_{Active}$, and Pipelining MEGA with SVM$_{Active}$

For top-10 retrieval with 5% matching data (Figure 1(a)), SVM$_{Active}$ clearly outperforms MEGA. The major weakness of SVM$_{Active}$ is in initialization—finding

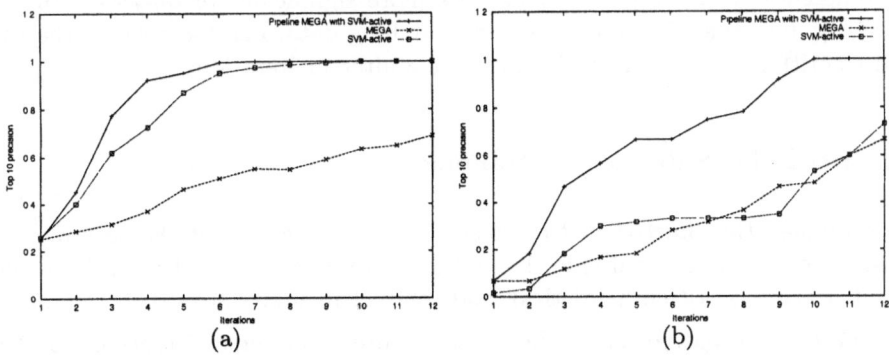

Fig. 1. Precision versus iterations for top-10 retrieval (a) 5% and (b) 1% queries.

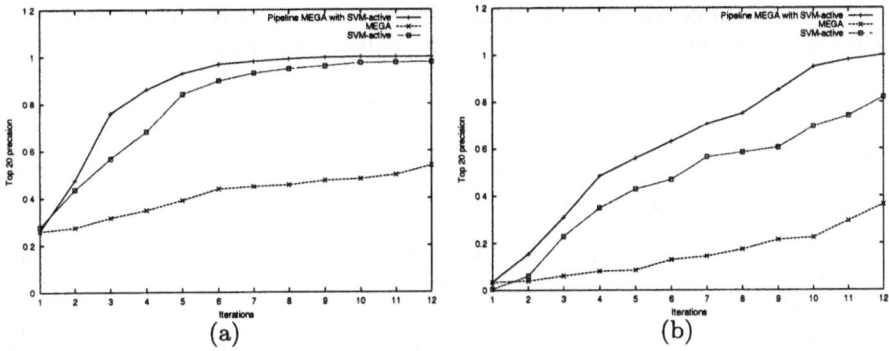

Fig. 2. Precision versus iterations for top-20 retrieval (a) 5% and (b) 1% queries.

the first few positive samples. Such weakness may not seriously affect this experiment, since there is a high probability of finding one of the 5% positive examples through random sampling. For queries with only 1% matching data (Figure 1(b)), such a weakness becomes more significant, because it substantially degrades SVM$_{Active}$'s performance. Especially, its precision in the first two iterations is very low. Overall, the precision of MEGA and SVM$_{Active}$ is similar for 1% queries.

The hybrid algorithm (pipelining MEGA with SVM$_{Active}$) clearly outperforms SVM$_{Active}$ and MEGA when they are used individually. The difference in precision is more significant for queries with 1% matching data than for those with 5% matching data. This trend indicates the strength of the hybrid algorithm in handling more specific query concepts and/or larger datasets. Note that the precision of the hybrid algorithm reaches 80% after 3 and 6 iterations, respectively, for 5% and 1% experiments (Figures 1(a) and (b)). It takes 6 and 10 iterations, respectively, for the algorithm to achieve near-100% precision.

For top-20 retrieval (Figures 2(a) and (b)), the precision of the hybrid algorithm remains the highest, followed by SVM$_{Active}$ and MEGA. As expected, the differences in their performances are more significant for queries with 1% matching data than for those with 5% matching data. For 1% queries, the hybrid algorithm achieves near-100% precision after 11 iterations.

4.2   Recursive Subspace Co-training

We examined the effective of the subspace co-training scheme. For conducting subspace co-training, we divide the features into 20 subsets (please refer to [8] for our feature-partition heuristics), and conduct recursive subspace training.

Figures 3(a) and (b) show the curves of precision versus iterations for 1% queries with and without co-training. Co-training indeed improves the precision for both top-10 and top-20 retrievals. On average, the co-training scheme achieves $7 - 15\%$ higher precision over the pipeline scheme. For a 1% query, the recursive subspace co-training scheme can reach 70% precision for a top-10 retrieval, and 60% for a top-20 retrieval, after the fourth feedback iteration.

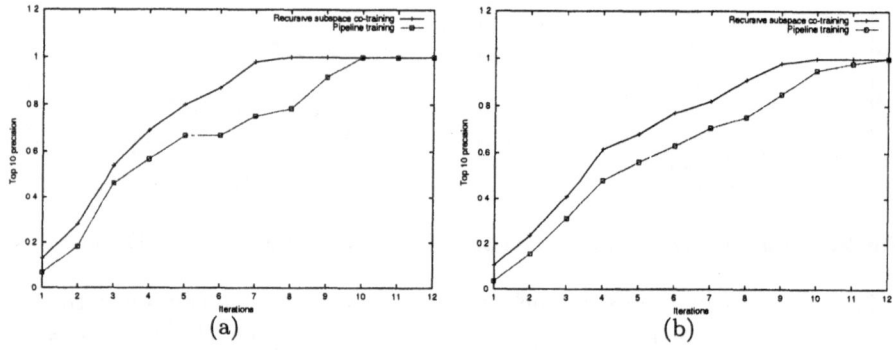

(a)   (b)

Fig. 3. Precision versus iterations for (a) top-10 retrieval and (b) top-20 retrieval for 1% matching objects with and without co-training.

4.3   Observations

Our experiments have answered the four questions that we stated in the beginning of Section 3.

1. MEGA and SVM$_{Active}$ can learn complex query concepts in high-dimensional spaces in a small number of user iterations. Compared to some recent schemes proposed by the database community such as Mindreader [9] and Falcon [10], MEGA and SVM$_{Active}$ perform substantially better.

2. The hybrid scheme that uses MEGA to find the first relevant object(s) and then switches to SVM$_{Active}$ works significantly better than using the two learning algorithms individually.
3. When the matching data is scarce, the number of iterations required to learn a concept increases.
4. We show co-training is a good strategy for accelerating concept convergence.

5   Conclusion

This paper proposes using hybrid active learning schemes to quickly capture complex and subjective query concepts. We have proposed using MEGA to first find objects relevant to the query concept, and then switch to SVM$_{Active}$ once some relevant objects are found. Our experimental results show that this pipeline approach outperforms MEGA and SVM$_{Active}$ when they are used individually. We have also proposed using co-training to find more useful negative-labeled instances to accelerate the progress of learning. All these hybrid schemes show improved learning performance over the based algorithms.

References

1. Beitao Li, Edward Chang, and Chung-Sheng Li. Learning image query concepts via intelligent sampling. *Proceedings of IEEE Multimedia and Expo*, August 2001.
2. Simon Tong and Edward Chang. Support vector machine active learning for image retrieval. *Proceedings of ACM International Conference on Multimedia*, pages 107–118, October 2001.
3. Edward Chang and Beitao Li. Mega — the maximizing expected generalization algorithm for learning complex query concepts (extended version). *Technical Report http://www-db.stanford.edu/~echang/mega-tois.pdf*, November 2000.
4. Michael Kearns, Ming Li, and Leslie Valiant. Learning boolean formulae. *Journal of ACM*, 41(6):1298–1328, 1994.
5. A. Blum and T. Mitchell. *Combining Labeled and Unlabeled Data wih Co-Training.* Proceedings of the Workshop on Computational Learning Theory, 1998.
6. Edward Chang, Kwang-Ting Cheng, and Lisa Chang. PBIR — perception-based image retrieval. *ACM Sigmod (Demo)*, May 2001.
7. James Wang, Jia Li, and Gio Wiederhold. Simplicity: Semantics-sensitive integrated matching for picture libraries. *ACM Multimedia Conference*, 2000.
8. Beitao Li, Wei-Cheng Lai, Edward Chang, and Kwang-Ting Cheng. Minig image features for efficient query processing. *Proceedings of IEEE Data Mining*, November 2001.
9. Y. Ishikawa, R. Subramanya, and C. Faloutsos. Mindreader: Querying databases through multiple examples. *VLDB*, 1998.
10. Leejay Wu, Christos Faloutsos, Katia Sycara, and Terry R. Payne. Falcon: Feedback adaptive loop for content-based retrieval. *The 26th VLDB Conference*, September 2000.

Lecturer Position Detection for Distribution System Using High Resolution Partial Images

Haruo Yago, Tomohide Takano, Keisuke Terada, and Nobuyuki Tokura

OPTOWAVE LABORATORY Inc.
3-1 Hikari-no-oka, Yokosuka-shi, 239-0847, Japan
{yago,k-terada,tokura}@owl.co.jp

Abstract. Most distance learning or teaching systems use just regular television equipment, so the receiver is limited to passively watching the incoming low-resolution video stream. We have created a high-resolution image transfer system that creates a virtual copy of the sender's environment, captured by multiple high-resolution still cameras, within the receiver's computer. The receiver can peruse the virtual copy and zoom in to read what the lecturer has written on the board whenever desired. This paper shows how to reduce the transmission bandwidth required; the system periodically updates the images held in the receiver's computer when necessary by sending only the images in which a significant change is detected and that show the lecturer's most recent position. A simple method of detecting the lecturer's position accurately is introduced and we discuss the impact of sound localization on service acceptance.

1   Introduction

In recent years, ADSL, CATV, and FTTH have begun to be more widely adopted and the Internet is being used more often to link homes, schools, and companies so as to form a high-throughput telecommunication network. This trend has increased interest in using multimedia communication to link remote sites.

Most of the systems currently being used to establish remote lectures, lessons, or group discussions utilize ordinary video cameras that are manually directed by staff members[1-3]. Several methods that offer automatic camera control by detecting the position of people have been proposed. People can be tracked by the use of infrared cameras[4]. Another approach used foot switches placed along the person's expected track. Pattern matching systems have also been proposed, but the computing load is excessive. Change detection based on a comparison of the gradient vectors of two frames was proposed for general use[5], but such a complicated method is not required for our system. One proposed method examined compressed video data to realize position detection[6]. Unfortunately, its detection sensitivity was insufficient to clearly distinguish the person from the background if both had similar overall colors. A more basic problem with existing systems is that the receiver is basically stuck with a low performance terminal and can only see what the camera is currently pointing at. Moreover, the use of regular cameras places severe limitations on what

Y.-C. Chen, L.-W. Chang, and C.-T. Hsu (Eds.): PCM 2002, LNCS 2532, pp. 564-572, 2002.

detail can be perceived by the receiver. This problem is often exacerbated by the compression applied to the video stream to reduce the bandwidth requirements.

Our approach is quite different since we emphasize the utility of the receiver. That is, the communication session is intended to "inform" the receiver and so his ability to control what he sees and the depth of detail offered are paramount. We have already described the basic details of our new system[1][7,8]. It consists of several high-resolution still cameras at the sender's side. The still image streams are passed to the receiver over a high-speed network [9]. At the receiver side, the images are combined and made available to the receiver as one contiguous high-resolution image, a virtual copy of the sender's environment. One obvious problem, the excessive bandwidth requirement, was eased by selective transmission. Since only one of the cameras was capturing an image that contained the lecturer at any one time, it was unnecessary to continually send the images of the other cameras.

This paper extends our original system by creating a person position detecting method that uses interframe differences. First, our position detection method is explained. Its effectiveness in reducing the volume of data transmitted is then elucidated using field trial results. We then discuss the function of sound localization.

2   High Resolution Virtual Copy System

Since this system takes a sequence of still pictures, the time available for lecturer position detection equals the image interval. To reduce the processing time and cost, we restrict position detection to two scan lines in each image as shown in Figure 1.

The bottom line should be set to run across the midsection of the lecturer while the top line runs across the position where we can expect the writing on the whiteboard to be.

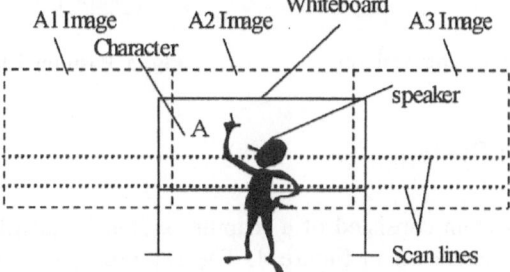

Fig. 1. Image feature detection lines

For each camera, we determine the difference information as follows. The images are shown in Figure 2.

1) Compare the color (R,G,B) values of all pixels on the two scan lines in the current image to those in the reference image and to those in the immediately previous image. The difference value, the difference between the results of the two comparisons, is compared to a threshold.

---

[1] JGN(Japan Giga-bit network) project JGN-P12520

2) If the difference value exceeds the threshold, the current image is sent to the clients.

3) The difference values of all cameras are compared and the largest difference value is taken as indicating the lecturer's position.

4) If the lecturer walks outside the field of view of all the cameras, his/her position is taken to be the last segment occupied.

A flow chart of person detection is shown in Figure 3.

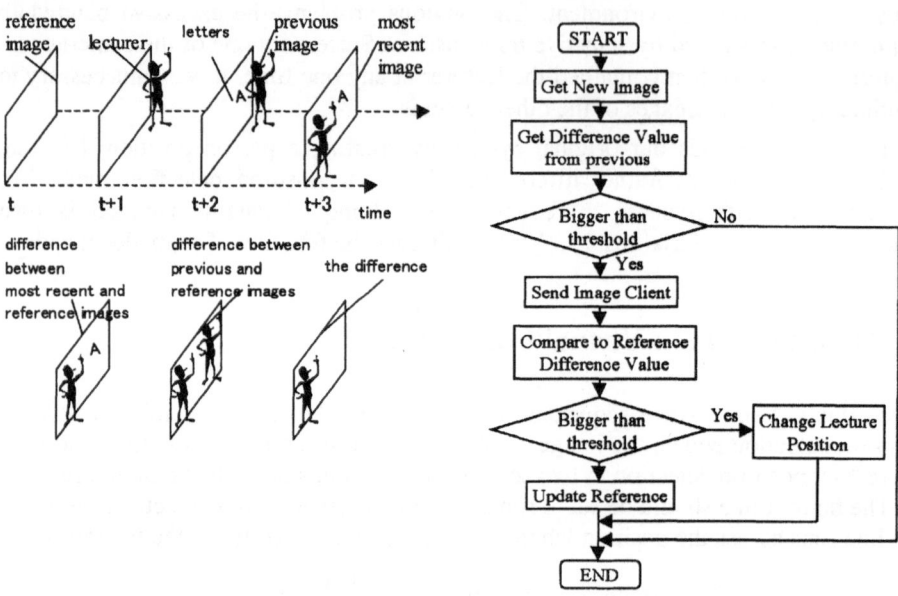

Fig. 2. Detecting lecturer position   **Fig. 3.** Position detection flow chart

3 Experimental System

The experimental system consisted of a "capture system", "distribution system", and "end use systems", as shown in Figure 4. The capture system consisted of three 3 million pixel, color still cameras (A), and an image processing machine (B). The distribution system consisted of a communication machinewith multicasting ability (C), a distribution network (JGN[9]), and a communication machine at the receiving side (D). The end use systems were a PC (E) for individual use and a projector system (F) for group use. The specifications are given in Table 1.

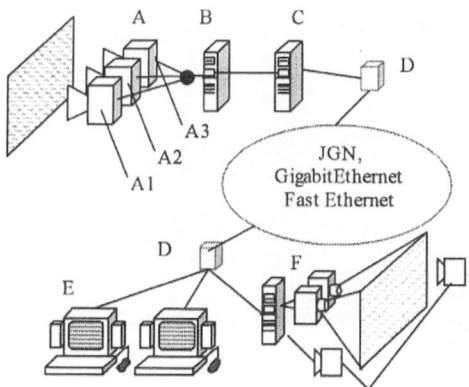

Fig. 4. System architecture

Table 1. Experimental system specifications

Item	Contents
Image capture	3 digital camera each with 3.3 million pixel resolution. Image format is JPEG.
Camera-PC interface	USB1.1
Audio in	Mono, FM quality
Transmission (Picture, Audio)	UDP for voice and TCP/IP for images Multicast (IGMP), JGN/ATM-Ethernet conversion[2]
Image display	Image cycle = 6 seconds (target:1sec)
Audio out	Sound localization possible
Record	Images can be recorded

4 Experiments and Results

4.1 Condition

Tests were conducted to confirm the effectiveness of the system in minimizing the volume of data transmitted by actually using the system to follow three lectures. The first, at Aichi Prefectural University, was held in a dark hall (less than 10 lx); the cameras were 11 m from the board and the area captured was 2.5 m by 11 m; lecture duration was 70 minutes. The second, at the University of Tokushima, was held in a fairly bright hall (300 to 400 lx); the cameras were 4 m from the board and the captured area was 1.5 m by 6m; lecture duration was 90 minutes. The third, at Optowave Lab. Inc., was held under the same condition as Tokushima; lecture duration was 20 minutes. The scenes of lecture are shown in Figure 5.

---

[2] JGN project JGN-G11015

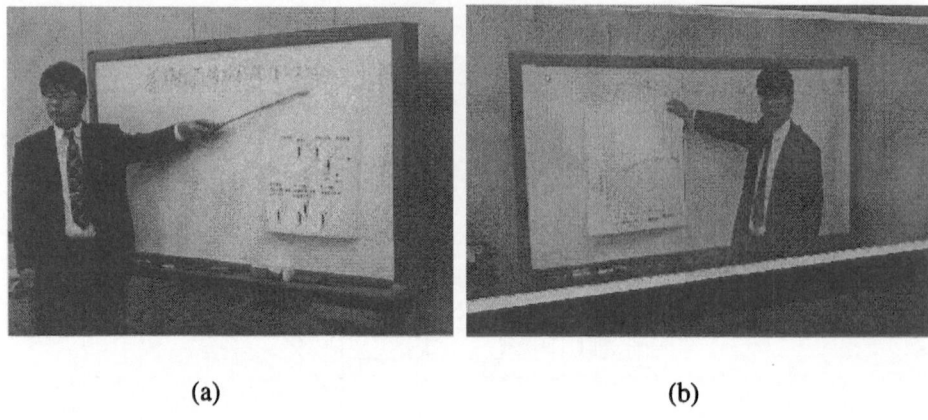

(a)   (b)

Fig. 5. Scene of lecture (a; lecture at Optowave lab., b; projected image of projector system)

4.2 Position Detection

To determine the threshold level that yields accurate lecturer detection, the noise level was measured as shown in Figure 6. The histogram indicates that the threshold must be more than 20 (color level). A man of average height whose clothes included a white business shirt was then placed in front of the whiteboard.

To maximize the difficulty of this test we placed the scan line across his shirt. The difference plots are shown in Figure 7. The plots clearly indicate that the system can clearly differentiate the white shirt and other parts from the whiteboard since many color difference values can be seen.

The subject was then asked to walk from 2 m on the left side of the whiteboard to 2 m on the right side (thus crossing the field of view of all cameras). The maximum color level differences (among all channels) over 8 consecutive image cycles are plotted in Figure 8 for 2 different lecturer position methods.

One method, as shown in Figure 8(a), detected the change in size of the jpeg

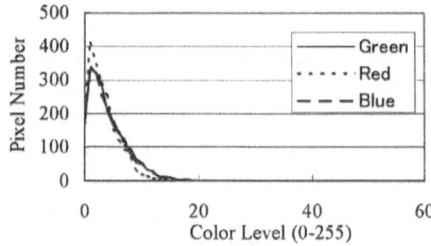

Fig. 6. Background noise

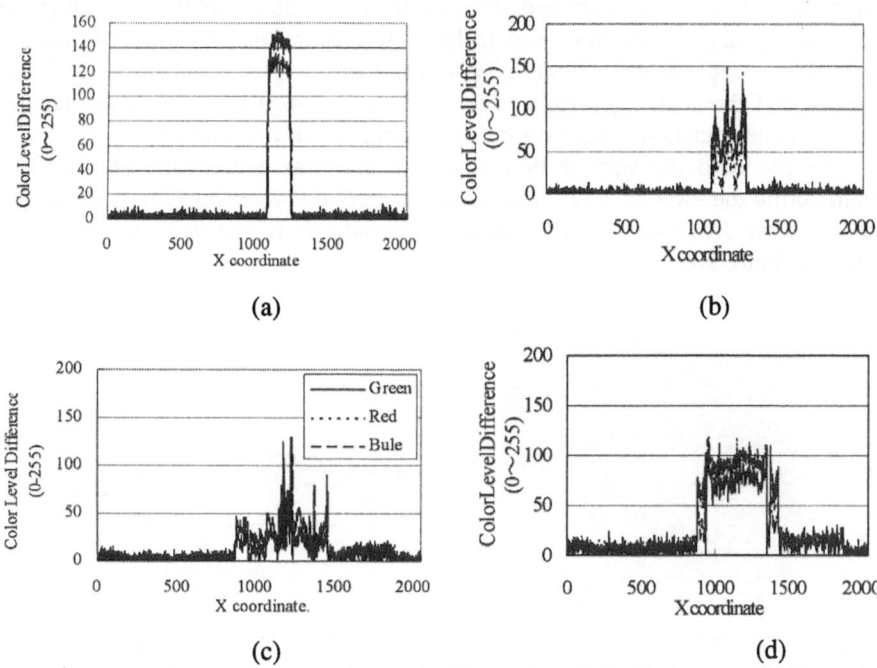

Fig. 7. Color level differences across lecturer's shirt (a; head (black), b; face (flesh), c; shirt (white), d; trousers (gray))

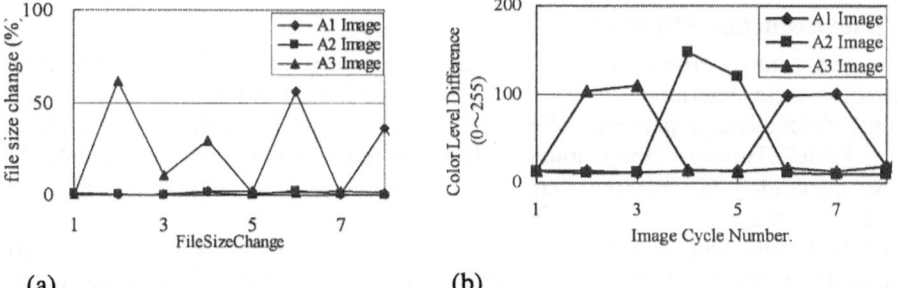

Fig. 8. Position detection over 8 image cycles (a; file size change, b; difference from previous images)

(compressed) files. Unfortunately, the lecturer was not detected at A2 image area. Since the white board and lecturer's shot have almost same color, their boundary was not clear.

The other method, as shown in Figure8(b), detected the difference from previous images for all areas. It is clear that the system with this method could well track the subject as he moved.

4.3 Detection Accuracy

To optimize scan line position and threshold level for lecturer position detection, we calculated the detection accuracy from the 20 minute lecture at Optowave using the color levels (0 to 255) of the R, G and B channels. Seven different lines across and around the lecturer were examined. The results are plotted in Figure 9. The position numbered equally spaced from legs to head. It appears that the available threshold levels of the experimental capture system, which ranged from 40 to 150 in all channels, and the scan lines yield position detection accuracies of more than 80%. This system can detect the lecture's position using any of the scan lines.

We recorded the volume of image data that was actually transferred by the system during the three lectures. The system detected lecturer position from two scan lines as shown in Figure 1. The threshold dependency of the detection accuracy is plotted in Figure 10.

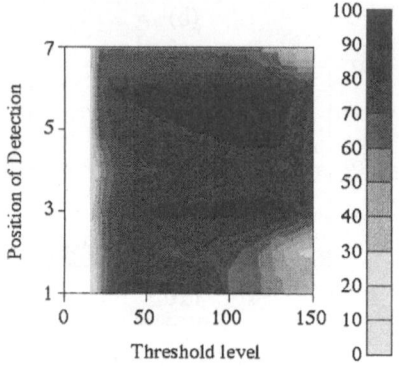

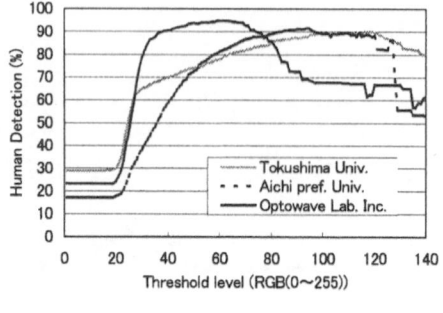

Fig. 9. Position Detection Accuracy   **Fig. 10.** Detection Accuracy

4.4 Data Reduction Efficiency

Since each camera produced an image that occupied about 400 kB and the color differences were determined every 6 seconds, the Aichi, Tokushima and Optowave lectures yielded image data sets of 849 MB, 1030 MB and 473MB, respectively as shown Table2. However, the amount of data transferred was reduced, since only the images containing the lecturer were sent to the clients. The reduction results are shown in Table 2.

The lecture hall at Tokushima Univ. and Optowave lab. experienced many changes in lighting and lecturer's movement, and so the level of reduction was not as good as that seen in the Aichi lecture. Since Aichi hall was larger than the other halls, the Aichi lecturer generally occupied the same image area. The detection accuracy, 90%, is good enough to reduce traffic.

Table 2. Reduction in image data volume

	Full set	Sent	Reduction	Detection(by file size)
Aichi pref. Univ.	849 MB	84 MB	90.4%	89.5% (4.2%)
Tokushima Univ.	1030 MB	344MB	66.6%	89.5% (53.7%)
Optowave Lab. Inc.	473 MB	139MB	70.6%	94.6% (60.9%)

4.5 Sound Localization

While it is possible to use a stereo audio system, we found that such systems pick up too much background noise. Accordingly, we adopted a pin microphone. Since the receiver side has multiple loudspeakers, the question is how to control sound localization at the receiver side. The sound volume balance of both channels was set to the lecturer's position. In order to investigate the optimal transition time for sound localization, we presented 11 audience subjects with a clip from the Tokushima lecture in which the lecturer moved to from one end of the stage to the other while varying the time over which the sound location was correspondingly moved (0, 1, 2, and 4 seconds). The subjects were asked to award each combination one of the following five scores.

5) Very lifelike.
4) Lifelike but with slight feeling of incongruity.
3) Acceptable with feeling of incongruity.
2) Annoying.
1) Worse than no movement.

The results, shown in Table 3, indicate that rapid movement of the sound location is desired

Table 3. Subjectivity evaluation on movement speed of sound location.

Movement time of sound location (sec)	0	1	2	4
Average score	3.1	2.9	2.6	2.4

5 Discussion

The experimental system detected the color level differences every 6 seconds, which is far from the desired interval of 1 second. The main problem is the USB1.1 interface of the current cameras; it takes 4 seconds to download each image to the position detection machine. Alternative interfaces such as USB2.0 and IEEE1394 exist, but equipment costs are much higher. Given the rapid growth in computing power, the position detection stage does not appear to be a significant problem.

6 Conclusion

This paper has reported the extension of our high-resolution image transfer system through the addition of a lecturer position detection system. This system is accurate, inexpensive, and allows the volume of transmitted image data to be greatly reduced. Since our proposed system is composed of PCs, commercially available digital cameras, and minor software packages, this system is inexpensive.

Acknowledgment. The authors wish to thank Mr. Katsumi Kusuba who provided the distribution and end-use systems, the members of the TAO supporting JGN, and Aichi Pref. Univ., Tokushima Univ., Saga Univ. and Iwate Pref. Univ. for opening their facilities.

References

[1] D. Zotkin et al., "An audio-video front-end for multimedia applications," Proceedings of IEEE International Conference on Systems. Man and Cybernetics 2000, vol.2, pp.786-791, 2000.

[2] S Sabri, "Video Conferencing Systems", Proceedings of the IEEE, vol.73, no.4, pp.671-688, Apr.1985.

[3] D. K. Norman et. al., "Behavioral and User Needs for Teleconferencing", vol.73, no.4, pp. 688-699, Apr.1985.

[4] K. Tanaka et al.,"Study of Efficient Data Transmission Technique on Teleconference System", Proceedings of the 1999 engineering sciences society conference of IEICE, D-15-2, pp.226 Sep.1999.

[5] Liyuan Li and Maylor K. H. Leung,"Integrating Intensity and Texture differences for Robust Change Detection",IEEE Trans. Image Processing, Vol.11, No.2,P.105,2002

[6] http://www.dpreview.com/news/9905/99051801 digitaresults.asp

[7] H.Yago et al., "High Resolution Partial Images Distribution System for Distance Learning via High Speed Networks", to be published in the proceedings of ICITA 2002.

[8] K. Kusuba et al.,"Construction of High Resolution Partial Images Distribution System on High Speed Networks", Technical report of IEICE, Vol.100 No.102 IE2000-11, pp.15-20, May 2000.

[9] Japan Gigabit Network http://www.jgn.tao.go.jp/

Boosting Speech/Non-speech Classification Using Averaged Mel-Frequency Cepstrum Coefficients Features

Ziyou Xiong and Thomas S. Huang

Department of Electrical and Computer Engineering,
Beckman Institute for Advanced Science and Technology,
University of Illinois at Urbana-Champaign,
405 N. Mathews Av., Urbana, IL, 61081,
zxiong,huang@ifp.uiuc.edu

Abstract. AdaBoost is used to boost and select the best sequence of weak classifiers for the speech/non-speech classification. These weak classifiers are chosen the simple threshold functions. Statistical mean and variance of the Mel-frequency Cepstrum Coefficients(MFCC) over all overlapping frames of an audio file are used as audio features. Training and testing on a database of 410 audio files have shown asymptotic classification improvement by AdaBoost. A classification accuracy of 99.51% has been achieved on the test data. A comparison of AdaBoost with Nearest Neighbor and Nearest Center classifiers is also given.

1   Introduction

Robust speech/non-speech classification is useful in the pre-processing stage for speech recognition. This is because the non-speech signal can be discarded so as not to degrade the performance of speech recognition. It is also useful in content-based audio retrieval[1][2] where the database is composed of human speech and other sound such as music, natural sound. When the task is to find the speech uttered by a certain person, the discrimination of speech/non-speech can filter out the non-speech signals before selecting the speech that belongs to the specific person.

AdaBoost[3][4] is used to boost the classification performance of a set of simple learning algorithms and has been shown to be successful in many applications[5][6]. Since there are many audio features[7][8] proposed to do speech/non-speech classification but each has its advantage and disadvantage, boosting from several classifiers each of which is built from a small set of features is promising in giving a more robust strong classifier.

Y.-C. Chen, L.-W. Chang, and C.-T. Hsu (Eds.): PCM 2002, LNCS 2532, pp. 573–580, 2002.

AdaBoost
Inputs: training examples $(\mathbf{x}_1, y_1), \cdots, (\mathbf{x}_n, y_n)$ with $y_i \in \{0, 1\}$ and the number of iterations T.
Initialize weights $w_{1,i} = \frac{1}{2m}, \frac{1}{2l}$ for $y_i = 0, 1$ respectively, where m and l are the number of negative and positive examples respectively, with $l + m = n$.
Train Weak Classifiers.
for $t = 1, \cdots, T$
1. **Normalize** the weights, $w_{t,i} = \frac{w_{t,i}}{\sum_{j=1}^{n} w_{t,j}}$ so that w_t is a probability distribution.
2. For each feature j, train a weak classifier h_j. The error is evaluated with respect to w_t, $\epsilon_j = \sum_i w_{t,i} |h_j(x_i) - y_i|$.
3. Choose the best weak classifier, h_t, with the lowest error ϵ_t.
4. **Update** the weights: $w_{t+1,i} = w_{t,i} \beta_t^{1-e_i}$ where $\beta_t = \frac{\epsilon_t}{1-\epsilon_t}$ and $e_i = 0$ if x_i is classified correctly, $e_i = 1$ otherwise.
Output: The final strong classifier is: $h(x) = sign(\sum_{t=1}^{T} (\alpha_t(h_t(x) - \frac{1}{2})))$ where $\alpha_t = \log \frac{1}{\beta_t}$.

Fig. 1. AdaBoost algorithm

2   Problem Definition and Algorithms

The problem of speech/non-speech classification can be stated as follows.

Given a set of sound files each of which is recorded from either human speech or any non-speech sound, learn a classifier that classify any un-heard sound file into speech/nonspeech mostly correctly.

The problem is hard in a machine learning point of view. The general concept of "human speech" is hard to be represented using any numerical quantity due to variabilities such as accent, age, sex, emotion etc. The sound files are of different length but most of the times equal length of features are desired to design a learning algorithm. In order for this problem to be put into the Probably Approximately Correct(PAC)[9][10] learning framework, an unknown but fixed probability distribution is assumed for the features of both the given set of sound and the un-heard sound file(s).

Mel-scale Cepstrum coefficients(MFCC)[11] are extracted from audio files. MFCC have been widely used in automatic speech recognition due to its relatively low sensitivity to the variability problem in human speech. To deal with the problem that sound files have different lengths, we propose to use the mean and variance of the MFCC of all the audio frames of an audio sample as features. Hence the number of features is fixed irrespective of the length of the sound file. More discussion on MFCC and features can be seen in Section (3).

As MFCC are used to deal with the variability problem in the feature level, AdaBoost helps to deals with the problem in the classifier design level. AdaBoost is an adaptive algorithm to boost a sequence of weak classifiers by dynamically changing the weights associated with the examples based on the errors in the previous learning so that more "attention" will be paid to the wrongly classified examples. The pseudo-code of AdaBoost is shown in Fig. 2.

How to choose an easy and fast weak learner is detailed in Section (4).

3   Feature Extraction

3.1   Pre-processing of Sound Files

Before feature extraction, an audio signal(8-bit Next/Sun *.au format) is pre-
emphasized with parameter 0.97 and then divided into overlapping frames each
of which is of 256 samples with 25%, i.e, 64 samples overlapping for pair of
consecutive frames. Each frame is then hamming-windowed by $w_i = 0.5 - 0.46 \times cos(2\pi i/256), 0 \le i < 256$. No detection of silent frames is performed. Instead, a
small positive number ϵ is embedded in the calculation of MFCC's to take into
account the existence of silent frames as an inseparable part of the total sound
file.

3.2   Mel-Frequency Cepstrum Coefficients

For each tone with an actual frequency, f, measured in Hz, a subjective pitch
is measured on a so called "Mel-scale". Mel-scale is a gradually warped linear
spectrum, with coarser resolution at high frequencies with a reference point of
a perceived pith of 1000 Mels for a 1 kHz tone, 40 dB above the perceptual
hearing threshold. The Mel-frequency sub-band energy is defined accordingly.
MFCC are based on discrete cosine transform(DCT). They are defined as:

$$c_n = \sqrt{\frac{2}{K}} \sum_{k=1}^{K} (\log S_k \times \cos[n(k - \frac{1}{2})\frac{\pi}{K}]), \quad n = 1, \cdots, L, \tag{1}$$

where K is the number of the subbands and L is the desired length of the
cepstrum. Usually $L \ll K$ for the dimension reduction purpose. $S_k's, 0 \le k < K$
are the filter bank energy after passing the k_{th} triangular band-pass filter. The
frequency bands are decided using the Mel-frequency scale(linear scale below
1kHz and logarithmic scale above 1kHz).

4   Proposed Approach

Two decisions have to be made before AdaBoost is called. One is the final feature
representation of each x_i's and the other is what the weak learner should be.

4.1   How to Choose the Final Features

For each sound, MFCC are calculated for all the overlapping audio frames. The
mean and variance of all the frames are concatenated into a 26-element vector
as the feature vector representation of the sound. By using the statistical mean
and variance values, the number of features is constant no matter how long the
audio files are.

4.2   How to Choose the Weak Learner

The weak learner is chosen to be a threshold function along one feature axis. What the weak learner learns is the optimal threshold with lowest classification error along that axis. Formally this threshold function is defined as follows:

$$\forall j \in \{1, \cdots, 26\}, h_j(\mathbf{x}) = \begin{cases} 1 & \text{if } x_j \geq \theta_j \ ; \\ 0 & \text{otherwise.} \end{cases}$$

where θ_j is the optimal threshold for the j_{th} weaker learner. In practice, the interval between the minimum and maximum value of x_j is divided into a certain number of sub-intervals. The optimal threshold is associated with the best interval at which the classification error is minimum. Several different numbers of sub-intervals that have been experimented are 50, 100, 1000.

5   Experiments

5.1   Audio Database, Training Set, and Test Set

An audio database of 410 sounds from Muscle Fish is used for the experiments. The database can be obtained from **http://www.musclefish.com/ cbrdemo.html**. This database has been used in many other systems as well. The 410 sounds are classified into 16 different classes. The names of the audio classes are altotrombone(18), animals(9), bells(7), cellobowed(47), crowds(4), female speech(35), laughter(7), machine sounds(11), male speech(17), oboe(32), percussion(99), telephone(17), tubularbells(19), violinbowed(45), violinpuzz(40) and water(7) where the numbers in the parentheses indicate the number of audio clips available in the classes. Of these, 52 are positive examples(female speech(35)+male speech(17)) and all the others are negative examples(non-speech).

The training set is composed of sound #1, #3, $\cdots$, #409 and the test set is composed of sound #2, #4, $\cdots$, #410. The positive examples and negative examples are evenly divided into the training and the test set.

5.2   Results

In order to see the performance of AdaBoost over the iterations, a temporary "final" strong classifier is constructed at the end of the body of the "**for**" loop in AdaBoost algorithm for each iteration, i.e, the classifier uses the best weak learner learned so far up to the current iteration. This classifier is used to test on both the training set and the test set. 30 iterations are used to see the convergence pattern of AdaBoost. Different number of sub-intervals have been used to train the weak learner. These numbers are 5, 10, 50, 100, 200, 500. The classification error rates are put into the following tables for the 5 selected iterations. All the data over 30 iterations is plotted in the Fig.2.

The following observations can be made from Fig. 2 and Table 1 and Table 2.

Table 1. Classification error rate on the Training Set after 5 selected iterations (row-wise) and with different number of sub-intervals for learning the weak learner(column-wise).

	1	2	10	20	30
5	0.1902	0.1219	0.0146	0.0146	0.0048
10	0.1073	0.1219	0.0048	0	0
50	0.1463	0.1463	0	0	0
100	0.1414	0.0926	0.0048	0	0
200	0.1317	0.0926	0.0048	0	0
500	0.1317	0.0926	0	0	0

Table 2. Classification error rate on the Test Set after 5 selected iterations (row-wise) and with different number of sub-intervals for learning the weak learner(column-wise).

	1	2	10	20	30
5	0.1902	0.1414	0.0195	0.0243	0.0195
10	0.1024	0.1414	0.0292	0.0243	0.0243
50	0.1365	0.1609	0.0195	0.0146	0.0048
100	0.1365	0.1073	0.0243	0.0243	0.0243
200	0.1365	0.1073	0.0292	0.0097	0.0097
500	0.1365	0.1023	0.0343	0.0195	0.0097

- AdaBoost drives classification error rates down on both the training set and the test set dramatically over the iterations. One example is the error rate jumps down from roughly 15% at the 1_{st} to less than 1% at the 30_{th} iteration for the training set with 5 subintervals used for learning the weak learner. More examples can be seen from the "dip" at the beginning of the curves on each sub-figure in Fig. 2 and the the comparison between the numerical data in both tables.
- In four sub-figures(number of sub-intervals being 50, 100, 200, 500) in Fig. 2, the error rates on test data still decrease even though those on training data have become 0. This is in agreement with the fact that AdaBoost tends not to over-fit, as having been explained in [4].
- Although performance of the weak learner depends on the number of sub-intervals used to find the best threshold, the difference is small. When 5 sub-intervals are used, the strong learner gives an error rate of 0.019512(or 1.9512%). In comparison with 500 sub-intervals, the strong learner has error rate of 0.009746(or 0.9746%). The computation for the 5 sub-interval case can be almost 100 times faster.
- The classification performance on the test set is consistently worse than the that on the training set. The fact that all the curves denoted by stars('*') lie below those denoted by straight lines is consistent with the intuition that the hypothesis learned from the training set performs better on training set than test set.

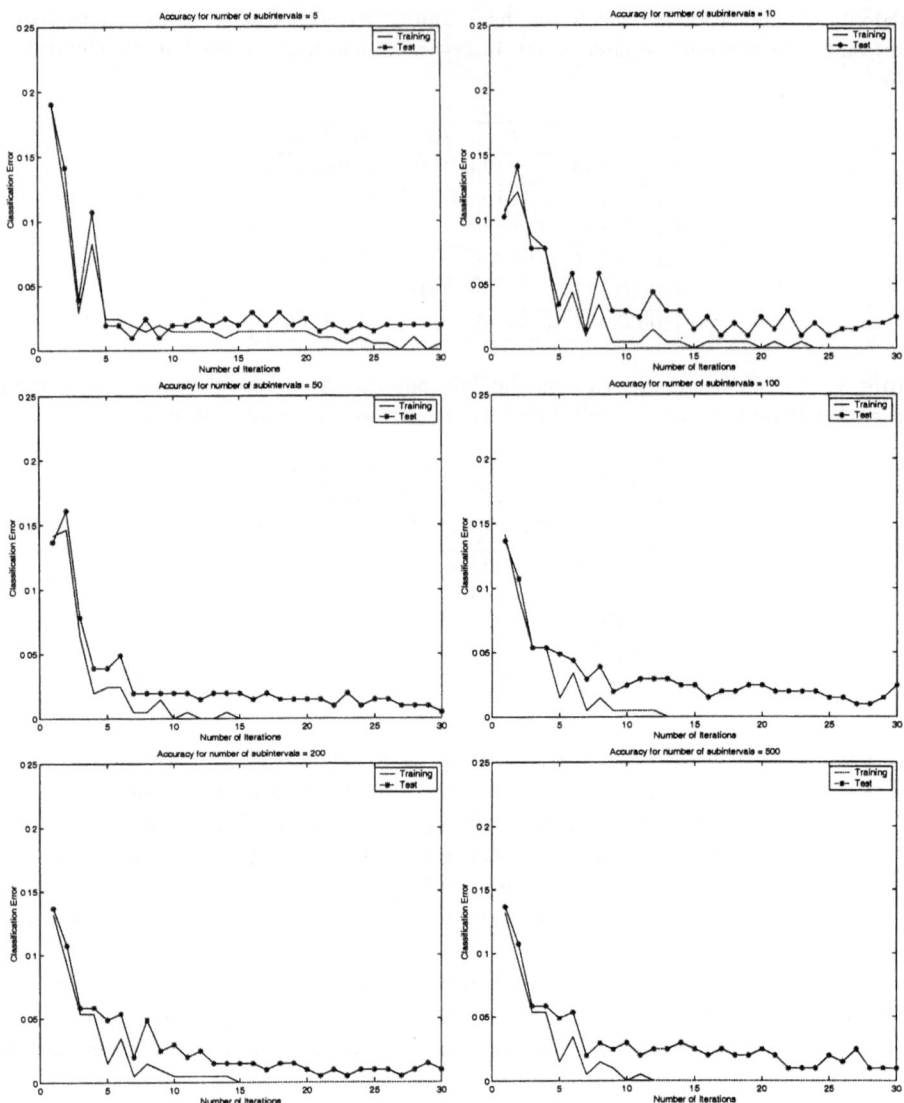

Fig. 2. Error rates on Training Set(by line) and Test Set(by stars) for 6 different number of sub-intervals(5, 10, 50, 100, 200, 500) over 30 iterations.

6   Comparison with Nearest Neightbour(NN) and Nearest Center(NC)

The audio files in the test set are also classified using the NN classifier and NC classifier.

For NN using the same set of features, each test sound file is classified as positive or negative according to its NN's label. Both the Euclidean distance and Mahalanobis distance have been used.

For NC, the centroid of the positive examples and that of the negative examples are computed and used as the prototypes with which each test sound file is compared. Hence classification label is assigned accordingly. The results are shown in Table 3.

Table 3. Error Rate(ER) comparison of AdaBoost, NN Euclidean(NN-E), NN Mahalanobis(NN-M) and NC.

	Boosting	NN-E	NN-M	NC
ER	0.0048	0.019	0.019	0.887

Table 3 shows that AdaBoost performs better than both Nearest Neighbor(NN) classifier with either Euclidean distance or Mahalanobis distance and Nearest Center method. NN with either Euclidean distance or Mahalanobis distance achieves more than 98.05% accuracy while the best AdaBoost in all the experiments is 99.95%. In fact Nearest Center is shown not to be suitable for this classification task.

The experiments show the advantage of AdaBoost over Nearest Neightbour(NN) classifier in this data set. Its property of boosting weak classifiers into strong classifier can be desirable in many other applications where NN may not be suitable.

7   Related Work

The most closely related work may be [12] where the same database is used for a multiple-class classification and a comparison between AdaBoost and Support Vector Machines(SVM) is given. Focus in our studies has been on the classic AdaBoost on the simple two class classification problem which can be complement to their work in understanding AdaBoost on audio classification problem.

8   Conclusion

AdaBoost is used to boost and select the best sequence of weak classifiers which are the simple threshold functions for the speech/non-speech classification problem. Statistical mean and variance of the Mel-frequency Cepstrum Coefficients(MFCC) over all overlapping frames of each audio file are used as audio features to deal with the problem that audio files are of different length. Training and testing on a database of 410 audio files have shown rapid classification improvement of AdaBoost over the iterations. A classification accuracy of 99.51% has been achieved on the test data set after a strong learner is constructed from 30 weak learners. The strong learner is a better classifier than the NN classifiers.

References

[1] E. Wold, T. Blum, D. Keislar, and J. Wheaton, "Content-based classification, search and retrieval of audio," *IEEE Multimedia Magazine*, vol. 3, no. 3, pp. 27–36, 1996.

[2] S.Z. Li, "Content-based classification and retrieval of audio using the nearest feature line method," *IEEE Tran on Speech and Audio Processing*, September 2000.

[3] Y. Freund and R.E. Schapire, "A short introduction to boosting," *Journal of Japanese Society for Artificial Intelligence*, vol. 14, no. 5, pp. 771–780, September 1999, (Appearing in Japanese, translation by Naoki Abe.).

[4] Y. Freund and R.E. Schapire, "A decision-theoretic generalization of online learning and an application to boosting," *Journal of Computer and System Sciences*, vol. 55, no. 1, pp. 119–139, 1997.

[5] M. Rochery, R. Schapire, M. Rahim, N. Gupta, G. Riccardi, S. Bangalore, H. Alshawi, and S. Douglas, "Combining prior knowledge and boosting for call classification in spoken language dialogue.," *International Conference on Accoustics, Speech and Signal Processing(ICASSP)*, 2002.

[6] P. Viola and M. Jones, "Robust real-time object detection," *Second International Workshop on Statistical and Computational Theories of Vision - Modeling, Learning, Computing and Sampling*, July 2001, Vancouver, Canada.

[7] L. Lu, H. Jiang, and H.J. Zhang, "A robust audio classification and segmentation method," *Proc. ACM Multimedia*, 2001.

[8] E. Scheirer and S. Malcolm, "Construction and evaluation of a robust multifeature speech/music discriminator," *Proc. ICASSP-97*, April 1997, Munich, Germany.

[9] T. Mitchell, *Machine Learning*, McGraw Hill, 1997.

[10] L.G. Valiant, "A theory of the learnable," *Communication of A.C.M.*, vol. 27, pp. 1134–1142, 1984.

[11] L. Rabiner and B.-H. Juang, *Fundamentals of Speech Recognition*, Prentice Hall, 1993.

[12] G. Guo, H.J. Zhang, and S.Z. Li, "Boosting for content-based audio classification and retrieval: An evaluation," *Proceedings of 2001 Intl' Conf on Multimedia Exposition(ICME01)*, 2001.

Statistical Analysis of Musical Instruments

Namunu Chinthaka Maddage[1], Changsheng Xu[1], Chin-Hui Lee[2], Mohan Kankanhalli[2], and Qi Tian[1]

[1] Lab for Information Technology, 21 Heng Mui Keng Terrace
Singapore 119613
{maddage, xucs, tian}@lit.a-star.edu.sg
[2] Dept of Computer Science, National University of Singapore
Singapore 117543
{chl, mohan}@comp.nus.edu.sg

Abstract. One important field in the research of computer music concerns the modeling of sounds. In order to design computational models mirroring as closely as possible a real sound and permitting in addition transformation by altering the synthesis parameters, we look for a signal model based on additive synthesis, whose parameters are estimated by the analysis of real sound. In this paper we present model-based analysis of musical notes generated by the electric guitar. Both time domain and frequency domain feature analysis experiments have been performed to select the appropriate parameters and the features for the musical signal analysis. Finally, non-parametric classification technique i.e. Nearest Neighbor Rule has been utilized to classify musical notes with this best set of parameters of the musical features.

1 Introduction

Music content analysis in general has many practical applications, including structured coding, database retrieval systems, automatic musical signal annotation, and as a musicians' tools. A subtask of this, automatic musical instruments identification is of significant importance in solving these problems and is likely to provide useful information also in the sound source identification applications, such as speaker recognition. However musical signal analysis has not been able to attain as much commercial interests as for instance, speaker and speech recognition.

First attempts in musical instrument recognition operated with a very limited number of instruments. De Poli and Prandoni used mel-frequency cepstrum coefficients calculated from isolated tones as inputs to a Kohonen self-organizing map, in order to construct timber spaces [1]. Kaminsky and Materka used features derived from an rms-energy envelope and used neural network or a k-nearest neighbor rule classifier to classify guitar, piano, marimba and accordion tones over a one octave band [2].

The recent works have already shown a considerable level of performance, but have still been able to cope with only a limited amount of test data. In [3], Martin reported a system that operated on single isolated tones played over full pitch ranges of 15 orchestral instruments and uses a hierarchical classification framework. Brown [4] and Martin [5] have managed to build classifiers that are able to operate on test

Y.-C. Chen, L.-W. Chang, and C.-T. Hsu (Eds.): PCM 2002, LNCS 2532, pp. 581–588, 2002.

data that include samples played by several different instruments of a particular instrument class, and recorded in environments, which are noisy and reverberant. However, recent systems are characterized either with a limited context or with a rather unsatisfactory performance.

Since 8-prominent musical notes in an octave generate the musical score, in this paper we experiment to find out the best selection of both musical features and their dynamic parameters, which could be the foundation for further research work on music signals. We utilized both time domain and frequency domain features to characterize the different properties of middle scale musical notes generated by an electric guitar (low noise & high amplification string type instrument)

2   Musical Scales

A musical scale is a logarithmic organization of pitch based on the octave, which is the perceived distance between two pitches when one is twice the frequency of other. For example, middle C (C4) has frequency 261.6 Hz; the octave above (C5) is 523.2 Hz and above that is soprano high C (C6) at 1046.4 Hz. The octave below middle C (C3) is 130.8 Hz, and below that, at 65.4 Hz is C2.

Although the octave seems to be a perceptual unit in humans [6], pitch organization within the octave takes different forms across cultures. In western music, the primary organization since the time of Bach has been the equal-tempered scale, which divides the octave into twelve equally spaced *semitones*. The octave interval corresponds to a frequency doubling and semitones are equally spaced in a multiplicative sense, so ascending one semitone multiplies the frequency by the twelfth root of 2, or approximately 1.059. The smallest pitch difference between two consecutive tones that can be perceived by humans is about 3 Hz.

3   Feature Extraction and Experimental Setup

Feature selection is important for music content analysis. Selected features should reflect the significant characteristics of different kinds of musical signals. We have selected some of the features (Figure 1) to find out how good are they for musical signal processing.

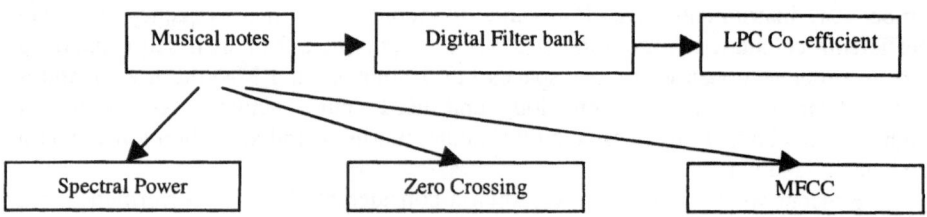

Fig. 1. Block diagram of feature extraction

3.1 Musical Notes

In our experiments musical notes (middle scale) are played on an electric guitar with 4-pickup amplification and recoded at 44.1KHz sampling rate, stereo channels and 16 bits per sample. All the signals are fully attenuated after –30dB. Figure 2 shows the recoded & normalized musical signals C, D, E, F, G, A, B, C+ ("+" stands for the high C notation) and their time durations are 7426, 7426, 7426, 7390, 5078, 4169, 3192 and 4220 milliseconds.

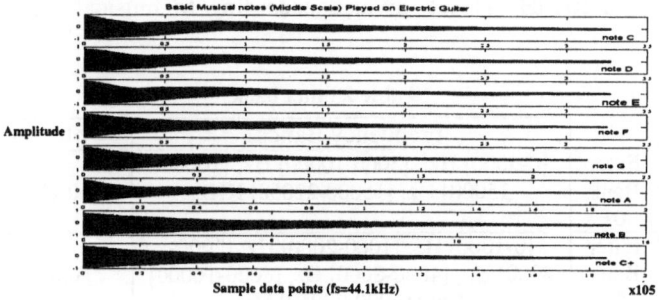

Fig. 2. Musical Notes

3.2. Distance Equation

$$\text{Average Distance Between Musical Notes} \Big\} = \frac{1}{a}\underset{b}{\sum}\underset{c}{\sum}\underset{d}{\sum}\big|X - Y\big| \qquad (1)$$

a = *(No of filter banks) x (No of frames)x(No of Coefficients)*

b = *Summation over total number of frames*

c = *Summation over total number of filter banks*

d = *Summation over coefficients*

Table 1. Distance of musical notes

	C	D	E	F	G	A	B	C+
C		O	O	O	O	O	O	O
D			O	O	O	O	O	O
E				O	O	O	O	O
F					O	O	O	O
G						O	O	O
A							O	O
B								O
C+								

Equation (1) calculates the average distance between musical notes sequence given above in the Table 1. X & Y are the feature vectors of musical notes and we calculate the distances between musical notes (C-D, C-E, C-F...B-C+). When average distances related to either diff-filter banks or diff-order of features are higher, then musical notes are comparatively far from each other in that filter or feature order. (i.e. Identical Musical Note Features).

3.3 Digital Filter Bank

Designing a good digital filter bank to generate distinct LPC Coefficients is a very important task [8]. Equally spaced frequency bands [Table 2- Filter bank 01] of filter bank are usually used in speech recognition systems [7]. Our experimental results show filter bank 01 is not good for music signal analysis (ie- Avg distance is 0.43and it is the lowest). Since distinct musical information lies between 0-5000Hz frequency range, we use music knowledge to design logarithmic filter bank (02 & 03) where frequency range 0-1000Hz is sub divided according to musical scales [Table 2- Filterbank 03].

Table 2 Filter banks

	Frequency Bands	Distances
Filter Bank 01	[0-5000] Hz; [5000-10000] Hz; [10000-15000] Hz; [15000-22050] KHz;	0.43
Filter Bank 02	[0-1000] Hz; [1000-2000] Hz; [2000-4000] Hz; [4000-8000] Hz; [8000-16000] Hz; [16000-22050] Hz;	0.67
Filter Bank 03	[0-220.5] Hz; [220.5-441] Hz; [441-661.5] Hz; [661.5-882] Hz; [882-1103] Hz; [1103-2205] Hz; [2205-4410] Hz; [4410-8820] Hz; [8810-17640] Hz; [17640Hz-22050] Hz;	1.08

Table 2, shows the calculated average distance [eq^n (1) & Table 1] between musical notes of three filter banks and LPC order 5 has been selected in making feature vector in each filter bank. Since test results show filter bank 03 has the maximum distance (i.e. 1.08), which means calculated LCP-Coefficients through this filter bank are identical to each musical note. Hence filter bank 3 has been used for finding LPC order in section 3.4

3.4 Linear Prediction Coefficients (LPC)

The basic idea behind linear predictive analysis is that a music sample can be approximated as a linear combination of past music samples. By minimizing the sum of the squared differences (over finite interval) between the actual music samples and the linear predictive ones, a unique set of predictor coefficients can be determined. The importance of linear prediction lies in the accuracy with which the basic model applies to musical signals [10-11]. Selecting the order of LPC coefficients such that set of the values are as identical as possible to each musical note, is tough challenge, when the signal is complex. Unlike musical signals, in speech recognition, the order (6-10) is enough to distinguish the speech signals.

In Figure 3, we have plotted our experiment results of the average distance [eq^n (1) & Table 1] vary with the order of LPC. Order 12 is the best set found where the average distance (i.e-1.87) is higher than other LPC orders.

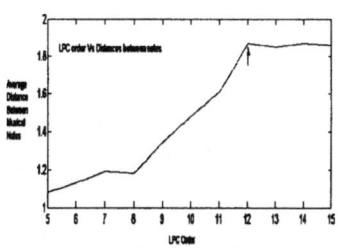

Fig. 3. LPC order vs. distances of musical notes

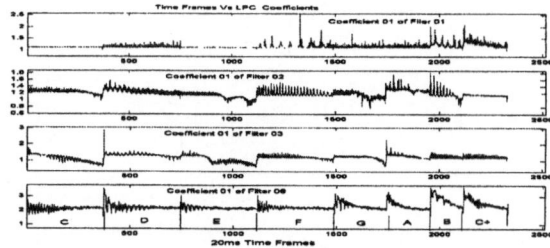

Fig. 4. LPC coefficients vs. time frames

Figure 4 shows how coefficient 01 of LPC order 12 of digital filter 1,2,3 & 8 of filter bank 03 varies with 20ms time frames. Mean values of all musical notes in coefficient 01 of filter 01 are above 1.00 and the variances in note C+ and B are much higher than the other notes. Note C & E are having lowest variance and both mean and variance are nearly same in each other. So distinguishing note C and E using coefficient 01 of filter 01 is difficult. Mean values of Coefficient 01 of filters 2, 3 & 8, of all musical notes are around 1.1~2.05 and variances are around 0.07~0.36. Since the variation of these coefficients identical to each musical note, they are more significant in distinguishing musical notes

3.5 Mel-Frequency Cepstrum Coefficients (MFCC)

The Mel-frequency Cepstrum has proven to be highly effective in automatic speech recognition and in modeling the subjective pitch and frequency content of audio signals[11]. The mel-cepstral features can be illustrated by the Mel-Frequency Cepstral Coefficients (MFCCs), which are computed from the FFT power coefficients. The power coefficients are filtered by a triangular band pass filter bank. The filter bank consists of K=19 triangular filters. They have a constant mel-frequency interval, and covers the frequency range of 0Hz – 20050Hz. Our test results show that order 9, which gives the maximum avg-distance [eq^n (1) & Table 1] (0.1378) over the order range (2 to25), is the best order for the frequency domain analysis.

The variation of Coefficients 01, 02, 03 and 04 of Mel-frequency Cepstrum according to time frames with the order of 09 is shown in Figure 5. Note G, A, B, and C+ have got higher variance than other notes in coefficient 01 and C+ has the highest variance among them (i.e.- 1.21). Mean values of coefficient 01 of all the notes are in the range of –0.023 to –0.105. Although coefficient 02, 03 & 04 of note C+ shows good variance, coefficient 01's variance is higher than coefficient 02, 03 & 04, which is significant in note classification.

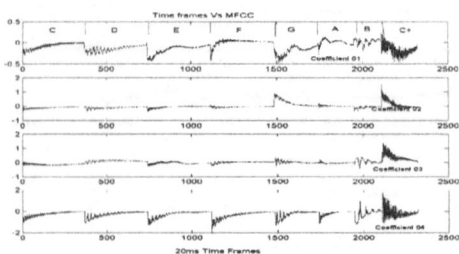

Fig. 5. MFCC vs. time frames

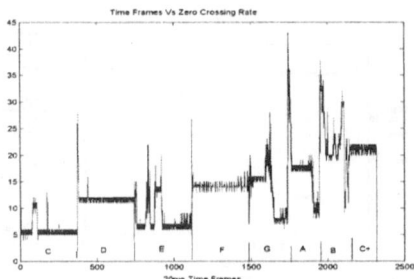

Fig. 6. Zero crossing rate vs. time frame

3.6 Zero Crossing Rates

The rate at which zero crossing occurs is a simple measure of the frequency content of a signal. The number of zero crossings (number of times the sequence changes sign) is also a useful feature in music analysis. Zero crossing rate is usually suitable for narrowband signals, but music signals include both narrowband and broadband components [11].

This feature is directly proportional to harmonic structure of the musical notes. It can be seen in Figure 6 that C and C+ have the lowest and highest average rates of zero crossing, because these notes have lowest and highest fundamental frequencies. The starting frames of all the notes have high ZCR, because of the attacking times are nearly zero and are just like the impulse responses where frequency tends to infinity. Since note E and G have strong harmonics below the fundamental frequencies, they have comparatively lower average ZCR than note D and F.

3.7 Spectral Power (SP)

For a music signal $s(n)$, each frame is weighted with a Hamming window $h(n)$, Where N is the number of samples of each frame. The spectral power of the signal $s(n)$ is calculated according to equation (2). Since order 12 gives the maximum average distance [eq[n] (1) & Table 1] between musical notes (i.e 14.78) in the order range (2 to 25), we have used order 12 as the best spectral power order for our further experiments.

$$S(k) = 10 \log_{10}\left[\frac{1}{N} \left\| \sum_{n=0}^{N-1} s(n)h(n)\exp\left(-j2\pi\frac{nk}{N} \right) \right\|^2 \right] \tag{2}$$

Variations of first 4 coefficients of order 12 of spectral power with time frames are shown in Figure 7. Coefficient 01, 02 & 03 varies negative direction in all the notes. But coefficient 04 is more significant because all the notes have higher variance than notes in first 3 coefficients

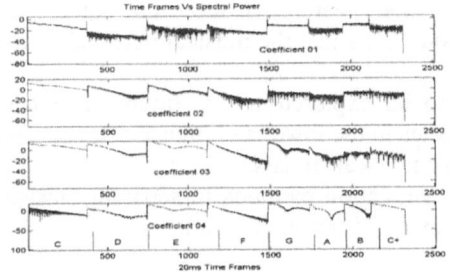

Fig. 7. Spectral power coefficients vs. distance

Table 3. Musical notes classification results

Musical Notes	Correct Classification on Testing Data Set			
	X	Y	Z	Avg %
C	81.35	86.15	89.54	85.68
D	88.12	84.26	87.92	86.77
E	86.24	87.38	83.84	85.82
F	88.58	91.61	92.52	90.90
G	83.43	89.43	86.37	86.41
A	85.27	82.93	88.17	85.46
B	89.39	93.31	85.23	89.31
C+	93.14	90.33	92.44	91.97

4   Classification of Musical Notes

Since it is not usually possible to determine a specific form (either Gaussion or something else) for the distribution of features of musical notes and even chosen form doesn't fit one of the estimable formulations, we design a classifier [9] using non-parametric learning techniques assuming labeled training data set is available for each class of musical notes. (i.e.- k-nearest neighbor rule)

The posteriori probability $P(\omega_i \mid X)$ where ω_i is the class of musical note and X is feature vector, related to Nearest Neighbors Rule which by pass probability estimation and directly gets to decision function. Let $H_n = \{x_1, x_2, \ldots x_n\}$ be labeled training set and let x' be the labeled sample nearest to x. *1-NN Rule* assigns x to the label associated with x' Evaluate $d(x, \omega_j) = ^{min} I_{i=1 \ldots Nj} \|x-x_i\|$ Then choose class m if $d(x, \omega_m) < d(x, \omega_j)$ for all j.

We use same musical notes played by 10 people at 10 different times under the same auditory environment for the classification test. So there are 374000, 374000, 374000, 370000, 254000, 209000, 160000 and 211000 sample frames of musical notes C, D, E, F, G, A, B, and C+ respectively for the training and testing. Sample data frames of each musical note are equally divided in to 3 parts and 2 parts are taken as label training samples and 1 part is taken as testing. (See Fig-8).

For each frame, we have calculated linear prediction, mel-frequency cepstral coefficients, zero crossing rate and spectral power to form a feature vector $V_i = (LPC_i, MFCC_i, ZCR_i, SP_i)$ $i=1,2,3,\ldots\ldots N$ Then we calculated the Euclidian distances between training and testing samples and labeled test frames according to 1-NN rule.

The average correct classification of musical notes using 1-NN rule is over 85% and results have been noted down in Table 3.

$$X \ 1/3 \ \mid \ Y \ 1/3 \ \mid \ Z \ 1/3$$

Fig. 8. Sample frames of Musical note

5 Summary and Future Work

We have presented a statistical analysis of a musical instrument, which is the electric guitar. We have designed digital filter bank for musical feature analysis. Our test results show the orders of LPC, MFCC and spectral power are 12, 9 and 12 respectively for distinguishing the musical note features from each other. Our classification results of non-parametric method shows that the musical notes are piece wise linearly separable.

There are several directions that need to be explored in the future. The first direction is, to do analysis of more musical notes in the lower and higher octaves. The next task is, to do testing on mixed polyphonic musical signals.

The third direction is to test different classification methods to separate musical notes that belong to same instruments and to that of different instruments.

References

1. De Poli, G. & Prandoni, P. "Sonological Models for Timbre Characterization". Journal of New Music Research, Vol 26 (1997), pp. 170-197, 1997.
2. Kaminskyj, I. & Materka, A. "Automatic source identification of monophonic musical instrument sounds" Proceedings of the 1995 IEEE international Conference of Neural Networks, pp. 189-194, 1995.
3. Martin, K, D. "Musical Instruments Identification: A pattern recognition Approach". Presented at the 136th meeting of the Acoustical Society of America, 1998.
4. Brown, J.C. "Computer Identification of Musical Instruments using pattern recognition with cepstral coefficients as features." J. Acoust. Soc. Am. 105(3) 1933-1941.
5. Martin, K. D. "Sound source Recognition: A Theory and computational Model". PhD thesis, Massachusetts Institute of Technology, Cambridge, MA, 1999.
6. D. Deutch. Octave Generalization and Tune Recognition, Perception and Psychophysics, Volume 11, Number 6, pages 411-412, 1972.
7. Markel, J.D., and Gray, A. H., "Linear Prediction of speech " Springer-Verlag, New York, 1976.
8. Ellis, G.M., "Electronic Filter Analysis and Synthesis" Artech House, Boston, USA, 1994.
9. Richard O. Duda, Peter E. Hart, David G. Stork, "Pattern Classification" Second Edition 2001, A wiley-Interscience publication.
10. L.R. Rabiner / R.W. Schafer "Digital processing of Speech Signals" Prentice-Hall Signal Processing Series 1978.
11. John R. Deller,Jr., John H.L. Hansen, and John G. Proakis "Discrete-Time Processing of Speech Signals", IEEE press, New York 2000.

Text-to-Visual Speech Synthesis for General Objects Using Parameter-Based Lip Models

Ze-Jing Chuang and Chung-Hsien Wu

Department of Computer Science and Information Engineering,
National Cheng Kung University, Tainan, Taiwan, R.O.C.
{bala, chwu}@csie.ncku.edu.tw

Abstract. This paper presents four parameter-based 3-dimension (3D) lip models for Chinese text-to-visual speech synthesis. This model can be applied to general objects with lip-like meshes. Three main components will be described in this paper: the generation of weighted parameter sequence of lip motions for each Mandarin syllable, the definition and construction of parameter-based lip models, and the synchronization of speech and facial animation. The result shows that the system produces a promising and encouraging speech and facial animation output.

1 Introduction

In the past years, facial animation systems tended to focus on the simulation of human faces while they were not applicable to non-human objects. But in some cases, it is necessary to design an animation system for non-human objects. Text-to-visual speech synthesis system, also called talking head, is an integration of a facial animation (FA) system and a text-to-speech (TTS) conversion system. It requires easy creation of individual models, easy replacement of virtual characters, visually pleasing facial animation quality, and modest computing requirement.

There are lots of previous works in early periods, and most of them focused on the simulation of human face. Waters [1] developed a muscle model to simulate facial animation. Thalman [2] developed an abstract muscle model animation system. The approach used only few parameters to simulate basic facial expressions. Afterward, many approaches focused on the synchronization of images and speech [3]. There are some innovations on the construction of 3D models. Pighin [4] proposed a delicate method to reconstruct the 3D head model from a set of images. In [5], the face model can be obtained using laser-based cylindrical scanners.

In this paper, we pursue the goal of creating a Chinese text-to-visual speech system. The system diagram is shown in Fig. 1. Three main components will be described in this paper. Firstly, 408 Chinese syllables are analyzed and grouped into 105 categories based on the characteristics of the corresponding lip motions. Then the video footage of a real speaker is recorded with some black markers on the pre-defined facial feature points. The image-processing technique is applied to extract the movement of each facial feature points from image sequence. Finally, the motion of facial segment is obtained through the transformation from the feature movement. For each lip model, we define the transformation from the original lip-motion features to the parameters of the lip models. These parameters contain the rotation angle, bend

Y.-C. Chen, L.-W. Chang, and C.-T. Hsu (Eds.): PCM 2002, LNCS 2532, pp. 589–597, 2002.
© Springer-Verlag Berlin Heidelberg 2002

angle, and offset distance. The synchronization process is performed using a two-thread method. The syllable durations generated from the TTS system are used to control the number of frames and the corresponding lip parameter is placed at the key time frame. The experimental results show that the speech and animation output is encouraging and satisfactory.

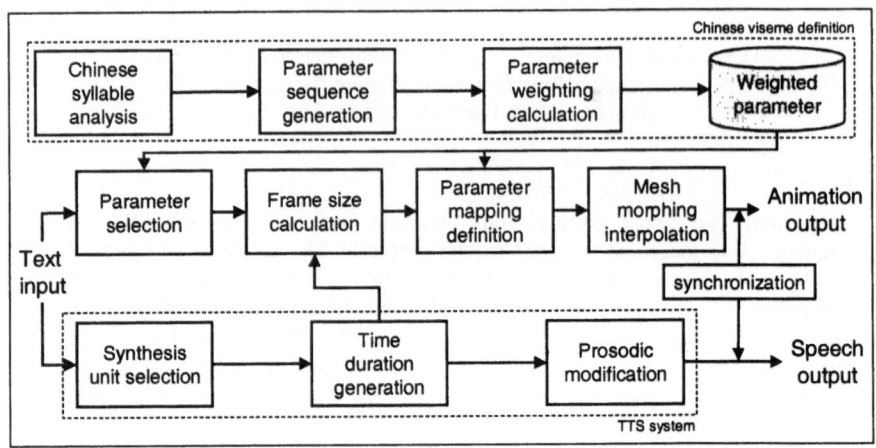

Fig. 1. System diagram

2 Generation of Parameter Sequence for Mandarin

There are 16 vowels and 21 consonants in Mandarin Chinese. These vowels are clustered into 3 different categories based on acoustic phonetics. The 21 consonants are also classified according to the place of articulation. It is important that every vowel has a unique lip shape but, different to vowels, the consonants in the same category have similar lip shapes. So we can reduce the number of lip shapes necessary to represent all Mandarin syllables. Based on the above classification of vowels and consonants, 105 categories of lip motions are defined to represent the lip motions of all 408 Mandarin syllables.

For the recorded video of a speaker with some black markers on the facial feature points, a simple feature tracking method is applied to trace the black markers in the image sequence. Given a feature point with location (x_t, y_t) in frame t, the location of this feature point in frame $t+1$ is decided by:

$$(x_{t+1}, y_{t+1}) = \operatorname*{argmin}_{(x_t+u,\, y_t+v)} \left[\sum_{i=\frac{-m}{2}}^{\frac{m}{2}} \sum_{j=\frac{-m}{2}}^{\frac{m}{2}} \left[I(x_t+i,\, y_t+j) - I((x_t+u)+i,\, (y_t+v)+j) \right]^2 \right], \quad -\frac{b}{2} \leq u \leq \frac{b}{2}, -\frac{b}{2} \leq v \leq \frac{b}{2} \quad (1)$$

where $I(x, y)$ indicates the intensity of pixel (x, y). (x_{t+1}, y_{t+1}) is the new location of feature point in frame $t+1$, m is the mask width and b is the block size that contains the possible location of the feature point in frame $t+1$. We assume that the feature points change smoothly in a short time duration so that only a region of size b is necessary for tracking.

After the parameters have been calculated, the interpolation weight of each parameter has to be defined. For the parameter sequence of a Mandarin syllable, $P =$

$\{p_1,...,p_n\}$, every element p_i is a location set of the corresponding feature points. $W = \{w_1,...,w_n\}$ is the parameter weight vector; every element w_i indicates the significance of element p_i. The weight w_i is calculated according to the change rate from p_{i-1} to p_{i+1}:

$$w_i = \begin{cases} 3 & \text{, for } i = 1 \text{ or } n \\ Round\left(3\left(\log_{\pi+1}\left(\theta_i+1\right)\right)^{1/3}\right) & \text{, other wise} \end{cases}$$

(2)

where variable θ_i is the included angle between lines $(p_i - p_{i-1})$ and $(p_{i+1} - p_i)$ and the function $Round()$ is a round-off function.

3 Definition of Lip Models

In this definition, the lip type is defined by its shape and flexibility. This induces four types of lip models as listed in Table 1. The corresponding appearance of lip models is shown in Fig. 2. Row (a) and row (b) in Fig. 2 indicate the closed mouth and open mouth, respectively.

Table 1. Four lip models.

Lip Model	Lip Shape	Flexibility
Type-I	Squared	Inflexible
Type-II	Squared	Flexible
Type-III	Cylindrical	Inflexible
Type-IV	Cylindrical	Flexible

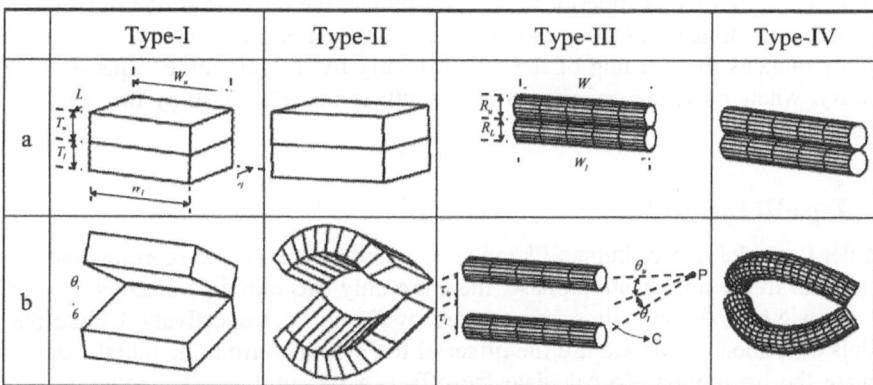

Fig. 2. The appearance of four lip models.

3.1 Type-I Lip Model

The typical appearance of type-I lip model is the simplest. The two squares in this model indicate the supramaxillary and submaxillary of the mouth. Symbols W, T, and L are the initial parameters and represent width, thickness, and length of each square, respectively. The subscripts u and l indicate the supramaxillary and submaxillary. Owing to the inflexibility of both squares, the only motion for type-I lip model is rotation. The mouth motion can be controlled by only two parameters: the rotation angles of supramaxillary, θ_u, and submaxillary, θ_l. For convenience, the angle θ_u is defined positive when the supramaxillary rotates upward. Oppositely, the angle θ_l is defined positive when the submaxillary rotates downward.

3.2 Type-II Lip Model

The only difference between type-I and type-II lip models is the flexibility. This difference results in an entirely different appearance. The square here has the same initial parameters with type-I model, but they are changeable when it is talking. There are three kinds of motions in this lip model: rotation, superior bend, and anterior bend.

The rotation angles are defined the same as those in type-I model. The flexibility in this model is shown in **Fig. 3**. The bend motion shown in **Fig. 3(a)** can be divided into two components: superior bend in **Fig. 3(b)** and anterior bend in **Fig. 3(c)**. The corresponding bend angles are defined as σ_u and δ_u respectively. In submaxillary part, the definition of bend motion and parameters are the same, and we use symbols σ_l and δ_l to represent the angles of superior bend and anterior bend, respectively.

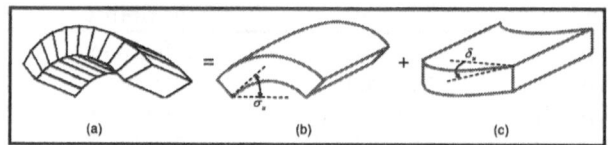

Fig. 3. The division of bend motion in the supramaxillary square.

In practice, rotation and superior bend can simulate the opening of the mouth. So we use a linear combination factor η to model the opening of the mouth. When $\eta = 0$, this model simulates the opening of the mouth totally by the rotation of squares. On the contrary, when $\eta = 1$, the opening of the mouth is modeled only by the bend of the squares.

3.3 Type-III Lip Model

In order to model a more human-like mouth, cylinders are used to represent the lips of the mouth. In the initialization phase, there are only two initial parameters: the radius and the width of the cylinders, represented by R and W, respectively. Unlike the lip models described above, we use the offset of the cylinders from the initial location to indicate the lip motion. To calculate the offset, we assume that the rotation of chin section causes the offset of the lips. The relation between lip offset and chin rotation can be formulated as:

$$\tau_u = Dis(C, P) \times \tan(\theta_u)$$
$$\tau_l = Dis(C, P) \times \tan(\theta_l)$$

$$(3)$$

where τ_u and τ_l represent the offsets of upper lip and lower lip respectively and points P and C indicate the pivot of rotation and the initial location of lips. $Dis(C, P)$ indicates the distance between points C and P.

3.4 Type-IV Lip Model

Type-IV lip model is the most similar to that of human being. Two cylinders form the upper and lower lips. The ends of the two cylinders are fixed and form the corner of the mouth. Because of the fixedness of the corner, there is no offset parameter in this model. The definition of bend motion is the same as that in type-II lip model.

4 Mathematical Definition of Motions

4.1 Talking-Head System Driven by the Original Features

We built a feature-based talking-head system that integrates a text-to-speech system with a lip-motion synthesis system. Firstly, we define 11 feature points around the outer lip line and the pivot of chin rotation, which is shown in Fig. 4. Under the assumption of the symmetric property of human face, we control only 6 feature points in half the face. Secondly, Chinese characteristics are analyzed and used to group syllables with similar lip motions. According to the observation, we group the lip shape sequences for the 408 Mandarin syllables into 105 sequence categories. Finally, the video footages were recorded with some black markers on the facial feature points of the speaker. By applying the feature tracking technique and normalization, we obtain a feature sequence for each category.

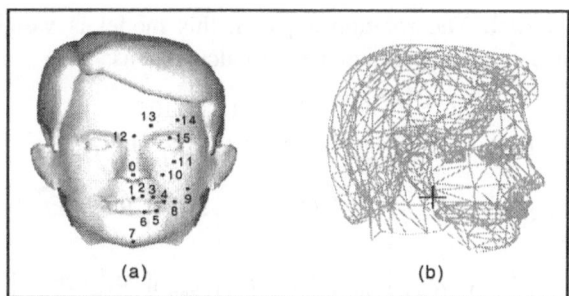

(a)   (b)

Fig. 4. (a) The 6 feature points around the outer lip line. (b) The profile view of head. The black cross indicates the pivot of rotation of the chin segment.

In the following formulas we define some symbols in the talking-head system.

$$S_i = \{F_1^i, F_2^i, ..., F_n^i\}, \quad 1 \le i \le 105 \tag{4}$$

$$F_j^i = \{fp_1^{ij}, fp_2^{ij}, fp_3^{ij}, fp_4^{ij}, fp_5^{ij}, fp_6^{ij}\}, \quad 1 \le j \le n \tag{5}$$

where S_i indicates the set of feature sequences of viseme i. There are n frames in set S_i. F_j^i represents the set of feature points in the j-th frame of S_i, and fp_r^{ij} is the feature of the r-th feature point in F_j^i. In particular, S_0, F_0^0 and fp_r^{00} indicate the corresponding features for the initial closed mouth.

4.2 Transformation from Feature Point Movement to Lip-Model Parameter

We have collected the parameter sequence of original feature points. Some transformations are needed to transform the feature points to the parameter sequences of different lip models.

Type-I lip model. Type-I model is the simplest lip model and contains two motion parameters. The initial parameters are manually modified to ensure that the two squares can fit the mesh. The transformation is defined in the following:

$$I_i = \left\{ \Theta_1^i, \Theta_2^i, ..., \Theta_n^i \right\}, \quad 1 \le i \le 105 \tag{6}$$

$$\Theta_j^i = \left\{ \theta_u^{ij}, \theta_l^{ij} \right\} = \left\{ T_1\left(F_j^i \right), T_2\left(F_j^i \right) \right\} \tag{7}$$

$$T_1\left(F_j^i \right) = \tan^{-1}\left(\frac{fp_2^{ij} - fp_4^{ij}}{d} \right) - \tan^{-1}\left(\frac{fp_2^{00} - fp_4^{00}}{d} \right) \tag{8}$$

$$T_2\left(F_j^i \right) = \tan^{-1}\left(\frac{fp_4^{ij} - fp_6^{ij}}{d} \right) - \tan^{-1}\left(\frac{fp_4^{00} - fp_6^{00}}{d} \right) \tag{9}$$

where I_i is the parameter set of viseme i. As described above, there are n frames in viseme i. Symbol Θ_j^i, containing two parameters θ_u^{ij} and θ_l^{ij}, indicates the j-th parameter set in I_i. Rotation angels θ_u^{ij} and θ_l^{ij} are estimated by functions $T_1(F_j^i)$ and $T_2(F_j^i)$ respectively. Parameter d in Equations (8) and (9) is the distance from pivot to the lip tip.

Type-II lip model. The rotation angle in this model is weighted by a linear combination factor $(1-\eta)$. The parameter set is calculated as:

$$I_i = \left\{ \Theta_1^i, \Theta_2^i, ..., \Theta_n^i \right\}, \quad 1 \le i \le 105 \tag{10}$$

$$\Theta_j^i = \left\{ \theta_u^{ij}, \theta_l^{ij}, \sigma_u^{ij}, \sigma_l^{ij}, \delta_u^{ij}, \delta_l^{ij}, W_u^{ij}, W_l^{ij}, T_u^{ij}, T_l^{ij} \right\} \tag{11}$$

$$\theta_u^{ij} = T_1'\left(F_j^i \right) = (1-\eta)\left[\tan^{-1}\left(\frac{fp_2^{ij} - fp_4^{ij}}{d} \right) - \tan^{-1}\left(\frac{fp_2^{00} - fp_4^{00}}{d} \right) \right] \tag{12}$$

$$\theta_l^{ij} = T_2'\left(F_j^i \right) = (1-\eta)\left[\tan^{-1}\left(\frac{fp_4^{ij} - fp_6^{ij}}{d} \right) - \tan^{-1}\left(\frac{fp_4^{00} - fp_6^{00}}{d} \right) \right] \tag{13}$$

The second parameter is the bend angle σ. The bend angle σ_u is defined by the feature points 1 to 4, and the bend angle σ_l is defined by feature points 4 to 6. Based on feature point 4, the offsets of other feature points are calculated as:

$$\Delta_r^{ij}(x) = \left(fp_4^{ij}(x) - fp_r^{ij}(x) \right) - \left(fp_4^{00}(x) - fp_r^{00}(x) \right)$$
$$\Delta_r^{ij}(y) = \left(fp_4^{ij}(y) - fp_r^{ij}(y) \right) - \left(fp_4^{00}(y) - fp_r^{00}(y) \right), \quad 1 \le r \le 6 \tag{14}$$

The variables $fp_r^{ij}(x)$ and $fp_r^{ij}(y)$ indicate the x- and the y-coordinates of the feature point fp_r^{ij}, respectively. By assuming that the curve of the square is an arc, we can calculate the bend angle as:

$$\left\{ \sigma_u^{ij}, \sigma_l^{ij} \right\} = \left\{ T_3\left(F_j^i \right), T_4\left(F_j^i \right) \right\}$$

$$T_3\left(F_j^i \right) = \eta \cdot \sin^{-1}\left(\frac{\Delta_1^{ij}(x) \cdot \left(\Delta_1^{ij}(y) + \Delta_2^{ij}(y) \right)}{\Delta_1^{ij}(x)^2 + \left(\Delta_1^{ij}(y) + \Delta_2^{ij}(y) \right)^2 / 4} \right) \tag{15}$$

$$T_4\left(F_j^i\right)=\eta\cdot\sin^{-1}\left(\frac{\Delta_6^{ij}(x)\cdot\left(\Delta_5^{ij}(y)+\Delta_6^{ij}(y)\right)}{\Delta_6^{ij}(x)^2+\left(\Delta_5^{ij}(y)+\Delta_6^{ij}(y)\right)^2/4}\right)$$

(16)

Another bend angle δ is defined in a similar way. Unlike the bend angle σ, δ is calculated from the lip raise in z-coordinate. We assume that the raise of lip relates to the width of mouth, that is:

$$\Delta_r^{ij}(z)=\frac{\Delta_r^{ij}(x)-\Delta_r^{00}(x)}{10}$$

(17)

where symbol $\Delta^{ij}(z)$ indicates the anterior lip raise. From Equation (15), we calculate the bend angle δ as follows.

$$\left\{\delta_u^{ij},\delta_l^{ij}\right\}=\left\{T_5\left(F_j^i\right),T_6\left(F_j^i\right)\right\}$$

$$T_5\left(F_j^i\right)=\sin^{-1}\left(\frac{2\Delta_1^{ij}(x)\cdot\Delta_1^{ij}(z)}{\Delta_1^{ij}(x)^2+\Delta_1^{ij}(z)^2}\right)$$

(18)

$$T_4\left(F_j^i\right)=\sin^{-1}\left(\frac{2\Delta_1^{ij}(x)\cdot\Delta_6^{ij}(z)}{\Delta_1^{ij}(x)^2+\Delta_6^{ij}(z)^2}\right)$$

(19)

The last two parameters are the width and the thickness of the squares. Because of the flexibility, the width of the square is increased and the thickness is reduced when the square bends. The width of the square is defined by the bend angle

$$\left\{W_u^{ij},W_l^{ij}\right\}=\left\{T_7\left(F_j^i\right),T_8\left(F_j^i\right)\right\}$$

$$T_7\left(F_{ji}\right)=\frac{\sigma_u^{ij}\times W_u^{00}}{2\sin\sigma_l^{ij}}\times\frac{fp_4^{ij}-fp_1^{ij}}{fp_4^{00}-fp_1^{00}}$$

(20)

$$T_8\left(F_{ji}\right)=\frac{\sigma_l^{ij}\times W_l^{00}}{2\sin\sigma_l^{ij}}\times\frac{fp_4^{ij}-fp_1^{ij}}{fp_4^{00}-fp_1^{00}}$$

(21)

According to the equality of volume of squares, the thickness can also be easily calculated as:

$$\left\{T_u^{ij},T_l^{ij}\right\}=\left\{T_7\left(F_j^i\right),T_8\left(F_j^i\right)\right\}$$

$$T_9\left(F_{ji}\right)=T_u^{ij}\times\frac{W_u^{00}}{W_u^{ij}}=T_U^{ij}\times\frac{2\sin\sigma_u^{ij}}{\sigma_u^{ij}}\times\frac{fp_4^{00}-fp_1^{00}}{fp_4^{ij}-fp_1^{ij}}$$

(22)

$$T_{10}\left(F_{ji}\right)=T_L^{ij}\times\frac{W_l^{00}}{W_l^{ij}}=T_L^{ij}\times\frac{2\sin\sigma_l^{ij}}{\sigma_l^{ij}}\times\frac{fp_4^{00}-fp_1^{00}}{fp_4^{ij}-fp_1^{ij}}$$

(23)

Type-III lip model. In type-III model, instead of rotation, we use an offset to control the lip motion. The parameter set is defined as

$$I_i=\left\{\Theta_1^i,\Theta_2^i,...,\Theta_n^i\right\}, \quad 1\le i\le105$$

$$\Theta_j^i=\left\{\tau_u^{ij},\tau_l^{ij}\right\}=\left\{T_{11}\left(F_j^i\right),T_{12}\left(F_j^i\right)\right\}$$

(24)

$$T_{11}\left(F_j^i\right)=\Delta_1^{ij} \tag{25}$$

$$T_{12}\left(F_j^i\right)=\Delta_6^{ij} \tag{26}$$

As shown in Equations (23) and (24), the transformation is performed by simply copying the offset values of feature points 1 and 6.

Type-IV lip model. The parameter set of type-IV model is similar to the parameter set of type-III model, except the rotation value. We define the parameter set as follows:

$$I_i=\left\{\Theta_1^i,\Theta_2^i,...,\Theta_n^i\right\}, \quad 1\le i\le105$$

$$\Theta_j^i=\left\{\sigma_u^{ij},\sigma_l^{ij},\delta_u^{ij},\delta_l^{ij},W_u^{ij},W_l^{ij},R_u^{ij},R_l^{ij}\right\} \tag{27}$$

All parameters are equally defined as type-III model except the parameter R. Since type-IV model is flexible, the radius of the cylinder is changeable when it is bending. The radius is calculated according to the equality of cylinder volumes when bending and defined as follows.

$$\left\{R_u^{ij},R_l^{ij}\right\}=\left\{T_{13}\left(F_j^i\right),T_{14}\left(F_j^i\right)\right\}$$

$$T_{13}\left(F_{ji}\right)=R_U^{ij}\sqrt{\frac{W_u^{ij}}{W_u^{00}}}=R_u^{ij}\sqrt{\frac{2\sin\sigma_u^{ij}}{\sigma_u^{ij}}\times\frac{fp_4^{00}-fp_1^{00}}{fp_4^{ij}-fp_1^{ij}}} \tag{28}$$

$$T_{14}\left(F_{ji}\right)=R_L^{ij}\sqrt{\frac{W_l^{ij}}{W_l^{00}}}=R_l^{ij}\sqrt{\frac{2\sin\sigma_l^{ij}}{\sigma_l^{ij}}\times\frac{fp_4^{00}-fp_1^{00}}{fp_4^{ij}-fp_1^{ij}}} \tag{29}$$

5　Simulation Results

According to the four lip models, we selected four 3D characters for simulation: a sparrow, a dinosaur, a robot, and a human. We applied these models to the lip motion of the word "shou" (hand) in Chinese. The linear combination factor $(1-\eta)$ in type-II model is set to 0.5. The system was implemented on a Pentium IV PC with 512 Mb memories and an on-board graphic chip.

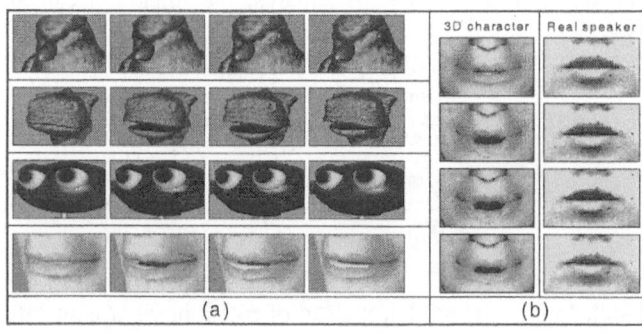

Fig. 5. (a)The image sequence of the syllable "shou" for different objects. (b) Lip motion comparison

The simulation results are shown by the sequence of images in Fig. 5.(a). The models of type-I to type-IV are presented from the first row to the last row. Fig. 5.(b) shows a comparison of lip-motion sequence between real speaker and a 3D character. In each syllable, there are more than 4 video frames in a parameter sequence.

6 Conclusion

In this paper, we analyzed the characteristics of Mandarin Chinese and defined 105 categories of lip motions for Chinese syllables. We also proposed four parameter-based lip models for lip motion simulation of general objects and demonstrated the usage of different lip models by the simulation of different objects. With these lip models, the lip animations in these objects are well synthesized.

References

1. Keith Waters: A Muscle Model for Animating Three-Dimensional Facial Expression. ACM SIGGRAPH Computer Graphics, Vol. 21 Issue 4, New York (1987) 17-24
2. N. Magmenat Thalmann, E. Primeau, D. Thalmann: Abstract Muscle Action Procedures for Human Face Animation. Visual Computer 3, no. 5, (1988) 290-297
3. Gaspard Breton, Christian Bouville, Danielle Pele: FaceEngine: A 3D Facial Animation Engine of Real Time Applications. ACM SIGWEB, New York (2001) 15-22
4. Frederic Pighin, Hamie Hecker, Dani Lischinske, Pichard Szeliske, David H. Salesin: Synthesizeng Realistic Facial Expressions from Photographs. ACM SIGGRAPH Computer Graphics, New York (1998) 75-84
5. Cyberware Laboratory, Inc: 4020/RGB 3D Scanner with Color Digitizer. Montiery, California 1990

Speaker Verification from Coded Telephone Speech Using Stochastic Feature Transformation and Handset Identification

Eric W.M. Yu, Man-Wai Mak, and Sun-Yuan Kung*

Center for Multimedia Signal Processing
Dept. of Electronic and Information Engineering
The Hong Kong Polytechnic University, China

Abstract. A handset compensation technique for speaker verification from coded telephone speech is proposed. The proposed technique combines handset selectors with stochastic feature transformation to reduce the acoustic mismatch between different handsets and different speech coders. Coder-dependent GMM-based handset selectors are trained to identify the most likely handset used by the claimants. Stochastic feature transformations are then applied to remove the acoustic distortion introduced by the coder and the handset. Experimental results show that the proposed technique outperforms the CMS approach and significantly reduces the error rates under six different coders with bit rates ranging from 2.4 kb/s to 64 kb/s. Strong correlation between speech quality and verification performance is also observed.

1 Introduction

Due to the proliferation of electronic banking and electronic commerce, recent research has focused on verifying speakers' identity over the telephone. A challenge of telephone-based speaker verification is that transducer variability could result in acoustic mismatches between the speech data gathered from different handsets. The sensitivity to handset variations means that handset compensation techniques are essential for practical speaker verification systems.

Feature transformation is a possible approach to resolving the mismatch problem. This approach includes cepstral mean subtraction (CMS) [1] and signal bias removal [2], which approximate a linear channel by the long-term average of distorted cepstral vectors. However, they do not consider the effect of background noise. The codeword-dependent cepstral normalization (CDCN) [3] is a more general approach that accounts for the effect of background noise. However, it works well only when the noise level is low.

* This work was supported by The Hong Kong Polytechnic University, Grant No. A442 and RGC Project No. PolyU 5129/01E. S. Y. Kung is on sabbatical from Princeton University, USA. He is currently a Distinguished Chair Professor of The Hong Kong Polytechnic University.

Y.-C. Chen, L.-W. Chang, and C.-T. Hsu (Eds.): PCM 2002, LNCS 2532, pp. 598–606, 2002.

A technique that combines stochastic feature transformation and handset identification was proposed in [4] for the compensation of channel mismatch in telephone-based speaker verification. It was demonstrated that the technique can significantly reduce verification error rate.

As a result of the popularity of digital communication systems, there has been increasing interest in the automatic recognition of resynthesized coded speech [5], [6], [7]. For example, speaker verification based on GSM, G.729, and G.723.1 resynthesized speech was studied in [6]. It was shown that the verification performance generally degrades with coders' bit rate. As the perceptual quality of coded speech generally decreases with coders' bit rate, the verification performance decreases with decreasing perceptual quality of speech. To improve the verification performance of G.729 coded speech, techniques that require knowledge of the coder parameters and coder internal structure were proposed in [6] and [7]. However, the performance of these improved techniques is still poorer than that achieved by using resynthesized speech.

As [6] and [7] focus on using coder parameters and pitch information for speaker verification, channel compensation was limited to CMS and RASTA processing. This paper, on the other hand, applies a more advanced channel compensation technique [4] for speaker verification over a digital communication network. As the technique operates directly on the coded telephone speech, no access to the coder parameters and structure will be required. In order to study the performance on coded speech with a wide range of compression ratios, six coders (G.711, G.726, GSM, G.729, G.723.1, and LPC) were employed to generate the coded speech.

Unlike [4], where LP-derived cepstral coefficients (LPCC) were used as features, we employed mel-frequency cepstrum coefficients (MFCC) [8] as the feature vectors in this work. Speaker verification results based on uncoded and coded corpora are presented. Results using CMS as channel compensation are also shown for comparison.

2   Stochastic Feature Transformation

Stochastic matching [9] is a popular approach to speaker adaptation and channel compensation. Its main idea is to transform distorted data to fit the clean speech models or to transform the clean speech models to better fit the distorted data. In the case of feature transformation, the channel is represented by either a single cepstral bias ($\mathbf{b}$) or a bias together with an affine transformation matrix (A). In the latter case, the component-wise form of the transformed vectors is given by

$$\hat{x}_{t,i} = f_\nu(\mathbf{y}_t)_i = a_i y_{t,i} + b_i \tag{1}$$

where $\mathbf{y}_t$ is a D-dimensional distorted vector, $\nu = \{a_i, b_i\}_{i=1}^D$ is the set of transformation parameters, and f_ν denotes the transformation function. Intuitively, the bias $\{b_i\}$ compensates the convolutive distortion and the parameters $\{a_i\}$ compensate the effects of noise.

In this work, we will consider the bias term only (i.e. $a_i = 1$ for all i) because our previous results [4] have shown that the zero- and 1st-order transformations achieve a comparable error reduction.

Given a clean GMM speech model

$$\Lambda_X = \{\omega_j^X, \mu_j^X, \Sigma_j^X\}_{j=1}^M \tag{2}$$

derived from the clean speech of several speakers (ten speakers in this work) and distorted speech $\mathbf{y}_t$, $t = 1, \ldots, T$, the maximum likelihood estimates of ν can be obtained by maximizing an auxiliary function

$$Q(\nu'|\nu) = \sum_{t=1}^T \sum_{j=1}^M h_j(f_\nu(\mathbf{y}_t)) \cdot \log \{\omega_j^X p(\mathbf{y}_t|\mu_j^X, \Sigma_j^X, \nu')\}$$

$$= \sum_{t=1}^T \sum_{j=1}^M h_j(f_\nu(\mathbf{y}_t)) \cdot \log \{\omega_j^X p(f_{\nu'}(\mathbf{y}_t)|\mu_j^X, \Sigma_j^X) \cdot |J_{\nu'}(\mathbf{y}_t)|\} \tag{3}$$

with respect to ν'. In (3), ν' and ν represent respectively the new and current estimates of the transformation parameters, T is the number of distorted vectors, $\nu' = \{b_i'\}_{i=1}^D$ denotes the transformation, $|J_{\nu'}(\mathbf{y}_t)|$ is the determinant of the Jacobian matrix whose (r, s)-th entry is given by $J_{\nu'}(\mathbf{y}_t)_{rs} = \partial f_{\nu'}(\mathbf{y}_t)_s / \partial y_{t,r}$, and $h_j(f_\nu(\mathbf{y}_t))$ is the posterior probability given by

$$h_j(f_\nu(\mathbf{y}_t)) = P(j|\Lambda_X, \mathbf{y}_t, \nu) = \frac{\omega_j^X p(f_\nu(\mathbf{y}_t)|\mu_j^X, \Sigma_j^X)}{\sum_{l=1}^M \omega_l^X p(f_\nu(\mathbf{y}_t)|\mu_l^X, \Sigma_l^X)} \tag{4}$$

where $\{\omega_j^X\}_{j=1}^M$ are the mixing coefficients in Λ_X and

$$p(f_\nu(\mathbf{y}_t)|\mu_j^X, \Sigma_j^X) = (2\pi)^{-\frac{D}{2}} |\Sigma_j^X|^{-\frac{1}{2}}$$

$$\cdot \exp\{-\tfrac{1}{2}(f_\nu(\mathbf{y}_t) - \mu_j^X)(\Sigma_j^X)^{-1}(f_\nu(\mathbf{y}_t) - \mu_j^X)\}. \tag{5}$$

Ignoring the terms independent of ν' and assuming diagonal covariance (i.e. $\Sigma_j^X = \text{diag}\{(\sigma_{j1}^X)^2, \ldots, (\sigma_{jD}^X)^2\}$), (3) can be written as

$$Q(\nu'|\nu) = \sum_{t=1}^T \sum_{j=1}^M h_j(f_\nu(\mathbf{y}_t)) \left\{ -\frac{1}{2} \sum_{i=1}^D \frac{(y_{t,i} + b_i' - \mu_{ji}^X)^2}{(\sigma_{ji}^X)^2} \right\} \tag{6}$$

In the M-step of each EM iteration, we maximize $Q(\nu'|\nu)$ to obtain

$$\mathbf{b}' = \frac{\sum_{t=1}^T \sum_{j=1}^M h_j(f_\nu(\mathbf{y}_t))(\Sigma_j^X)^{-1}(\mu_j^X - \mathbf{y}_t)}{\sum_{t=1}^T \sum_{j=1}^M h_j(f_\nu(\mathbf{y}_t))(\Sigma_j^X)^{-1}} \tag{7}$$

where $f_\nu(\mathbf{y}_t) = \mathbf{y}_t + \mathbf{b}$, μ_j^X and Σ_j^X, $j = 1, \ldots, M$, are the mean vectors and covariance matrices of an M-center Gaussian mixture model (Λ_X) representing the clean speech.

3   Handset Selector

Unlike speaker adaptation where the transformation parameters can be estimated during recognition, in speaker verification we need to estimate the transformation parameters before verification takes place. This is because we do not know the claimant's identity in advance. If the transformation parameters are estimated based on claimant's speech obtained in a single verification session only, all the transformed vectors, regardless of the claimant's genuineness, will be mapped to a region very close to the claimed model in the clean feature space. As a result, the claimant will likely be accepted regardless of whether he/she is a genuine speaker or an impostor.

Therefore, to apply stochastic transformation to telephone-based speaker verification, we need to derive one set of transformation parameters for each type of handsets. During verification, the transformation parameters corresponding to the most likely handset are used to transform the distorted features. This can be achieved by applying our recently proposed handset selector [10]. Specifically, each handset is associated with one set of transformation parameters; during verification, an utterance of claimant's speech is fed to H GMMs (denoted as $\{\Gamma_k\}_{k=1}^{H}$). The most likely handset is selected according to

$$k^* = \arg \max_{k=1}^{H} \sum_{t=1}^{T} \log p(\mathbf{y}_t | \Gamma_k) \tag{8}$$

where $p(\mathbf{y}_t | \Gamma_k)$ is the likelihood of the k-th handset. Then, the transformation parameters corresponding to the k^*-th handset are used to transform the distorted vectors.

4   Experiments and Results

Uncoded and Coded Corpora: In this work, the HTIMIT corpus [11] and six coded HTIMIT corpora containing resynthesized coded speech were used to evaluate the feature transformation technique. The HTIMIT corpus was obtained by playing a subset of the TIMIT corpus through a set of telephone handsets (cb1-cb4, el1-el4, and pt1) and a Sennheizer head-mounted microphone (senh). Speakers in the corpus were divided into a speaker set (50 male and 50 female) and an impostor set (25 male and 25 female). Each speaker was assigned a personalized 32-center GMM that models the characteristics of his/her own voice. For each GMM, the feature vectors derived from the SA and SX sentence sets of the corresponding speaker were used for training. A collection of all speakers in the speaker set was used to train a 64-center GMM background model ($\mathcal{M}_b$). The handset "senh" was used as the enrollment handset.

To evaluate the performance of the feature transformation technique on the coded HTIMIT corpora, six different codecs were employed in this work: G.711 at 64 kb/s, G.726 at 32 kb/s, GSM at 13 kb/s, G.729 at 8 kb/s, G.723.1 at 6.3 kb/s, and LPC at 2.4 kb/s. Six sets of coded corpora were obtained by coding the speech in HTIMIT using these coders. The encoded utterances were then decoded to produce resynthesized speech. Feature vectors were extracted from each of the utterances in the uncoded and coded corpora. The feature vectors were 12-th order mel-frequency cepstrum coefficients (MFCC) [8]. These vectors were computed at a frame rate of 14 ms using a Hamming window of 28 ms.

Feature Transformation: The uncoded clean utterances of 10 speakers were used to create a 2-center GMM (Λ_X) clean model (i.e. $M = 2$ in (2)). Using this model and the estimation algorithms described in Section 2, a set of coder-dependent feature transformation parameters ν were computed for each handset in each coded corpus. In particular, the utterances from handset "senh" were considered as clean and were used to create Λ_X, while those from other 8 handsets (cb1-cb4, el1-el3, and pt1) were used as distorted speech. As the experimental results in [4] show that the difference in error rates is not significant among stochastic transformations with zero-th, 1-st and 2-nd order, we used zero-th order transformations for all handsets and coders in this work.

Coder-Dependent Handset Selectors: Six handset selectors, each of them consisting of ten GMMs $\{\Gamma_k^{(i)}; i = 1, \ldots, 6 \text{ and } k = 1, \ldots, 10\}$, were constructed from the SA and SX sentence sets of the coded corpora. For example, GMM $\Gamma_k^{(i)}$ represents the characteristics of speech derived from the k-th handset of the i-th coded corpus. As we assume that in most practical situations the receiver will know the type of coders being used (otherwise it will not be able to decode the speech), there will not be any error in choosing the handset selector. The only error that will be introduced is the incorrect decisions made by the chosen handset selector. This error, however, is very small, as demonstrated in the latter part of this paper.

Verification Procedures: During verification, a vector sequence $\mathbf{Y}$ derived from a claimant's utterance (SI sentence) was fed to a coder-dependent handset selector corresponding to the coder being used by the claimant. According to the outputs of the handset selector (8), a set of coder-dependent transformation parameters was selected. The features were transformed and then fed to a 32-center GMM speaker model ($\mathcal{M}_s$) to obtain a score ($\log p(\mathbf{Y}|\mathcal{M}_s)$), which was then normalized according to

$$S(\mathbf{Y}) = \log p(\mathbf{Y}|\mathcal{M}_s) - \log p(\mathbf{Y}|\mathcal{M}_b) \tag{9}$$

where $\mathcal{M}_b$ represents the background model. The normalized score $S(\mathbf{Y})$ was compared with a threshold to make a verification decision. In this work, the threshold for each speaker was adjusted to determine the equal error rate (EER). Similar to [12], the vector sequence was divided into overlapping segments to increase the resolution of the error rates.

Verification Results: The experimental results are summarized in Tables 1, 2, and 3. A baseline experiment (without using the handset selectors and feature transformations) and an experiment using CMS as channel compensation were

Table 1. Equal error rates (in %) achieved by the baseline approach (without handset selectors and feature transformation) on speech corpora coded by different coders. The enrollment handset is "senh".

Codec	Equal Error Rate (%)								
	cb1	cb2	cb3	cb4	el1	el2	el3	pt1	senh
Uncoded (128 kb/s)	4.85	5.67	21.19	16.49	3.60	11.11	5.14	11.74	1.26
G.711 (64 kb/s)	4.88	5.86	21.20	16.73	3.67	11.08	5.21	12.04	1.34
G.726 (32 kb/s)	6.36	8.71	22.67	19.61	6.83	14.98	6.68	16.42	2.66
GSM (13 kb/s)	6.37	6.10	19.90	15.93	6.21	17.93	9.86	16.42	2.35
G.729 (8 kb/s)	6.65	4.59	20.15	15.08	6.18	14.28	6.71	11.93	2.67
G.723.1 (6.3 kb/s)	7.33	5.49	20.83	15.59	6.56	14.71	6.58	14.03	3.30
LPC (2.4 kb/s)	10.81	10.30	29.68	24.21	8.56	19.29	10.56	14.97	3.43

Table 2. Equal error rates (in %) achieved by the cepstral mean subtraction (CMS) approach on speech corpora coded by different coders. The enrollment handset is "senh".

Codec	Equal Error Rate (%)								
	cb1	cb2	cb3	cb4	el1	el2	el3	pt1	senh
Uncoded (128 kb/s)	4.00	3.02	10.69	6.62	3.36	5.16	5.67	5.67	3.67
G.711 (64 kb/s)	4.06	3.07	10.73	6.70	3.43	5.26	5.74	5.84	3.75
G.726 (32 kb/s)	5.65	4.42	11.78	8.00	5.61	7.95	6.97	9.07	5.12
GSM (13 kb/s)	5.25	4.10	11.32	8.00	4.95	7.04	7.47	7.58	4.73
G.729 (8 kb/s)	5.43	4.37	11.81	7.98	5.16	7.38	7.32	7.21	4.69
G.723.1 (6.3 kb/s)	6.40	4.60	12.36	8.53	6.11	8.50	7.31	8.28	5.62
LPC (2.4 kb/s)	6.34	5.51	14.10	9.22	6.35	8.95	8.95	9.55	4.57

Table 3. Equal error rates (in %) achieved by combining 0th-order stochastic transformation with coder-dependent handset selectors on speech corpora coded by different coders. The accuracy achieved by the handset selectors is also shown. The enrollment handset is "senh".

Codec	Equal Error Rate (%)									Handset Selector Accuracy (%)
	cb1	cb2	cb3	cb4	el1	el2	el3	pt1	senh	
Uncoded (128 kb/s)	1.63	1.27	9.65	4.47	1.41	3.58	3.37	3.08	1.09	97.92
G.711 (64 kb/s)	1.52	1.26	9.57	4.53	1.41	3.53	3.33	3.21	1.17	98.02
G.726 (32 kb/s)	2.55	2.55	11.66	6.05	2.74	6.19	4.17	5.82	2.29	97.73
GSM (13 kb/s)	3.13	2.44	11.13	7.10	3.10	6.34	6.29	5.58	2.67	96.91
G.729 (8 kb/s)	3.94	3.27	9.99	6.63	4.18	6.17	6.20	4.70	2.89	96.39
G.723.1 (6.3 kb/s)	3.94	3.42	10.74	6.83	4.49	6.70	5.80	5.71	3.41	96.27
LPC (2.4 kb/s)	5.68	5.93	17.33	11.05	7.14	10.50	9.34	8.89	3.95	94.39

also conducted for comparison. All error rates are based on the average of 100 genuine speakers. Average EERs of the uncoded and coded corpora are plotted in Figure 1. The average EER of a corpus is computed by taking the average of all the EERs corresponding to different handsets of the corpus.

The results show that the transformation technique achieves significant error reduction for both uncoded and coded corpora. In general, the transformation approach outperforms the CMS approach except for the LPC coded corpus. From the results in Table 1, we observe that the error rates of LPC coded corpus are relatively high before channel compensation is applied. An informal listening test reveals that the perceptual quality of LPC coded speech is very poor, which means that most of the speaker's characteristics have been removed by the coding process. This may degrade the performance of the transformation technique.

Nowadays, G.711 and GSM coders are widely used in fixed-line and mobile communication networks respectively, and G.729 and G.723.1 have become standard coders in teleconferencing systems. These are the areas where speaker verification is useful. LPC coders, on the other hand, are mainly employed in applications where speaker verification is not very important (e.g., toys). As the feature transformation technique outperforms CMS in areas where speaker verification is more important, it is a better candidate for compensating coder- and channel-distortion in speaker verification systems.

It is obvious from the last column of Table 1 and Table 2 that CMS degrades the performance of the system when the enrollment and verification sessions use the same handset (senh). When the transformation technique is employed under this matched condition, the handset selectors are able to detect the most likely handset (i.e. senh) and faciliate the subsequent transformation of the distorted features. As a result, the error rates become very close to the baseline.

As observed from the experimental results, verifcation based on uncoded telephone speech performs better than that based on coded telephone speech. However, since the distortion introduced by G.711 is very small, the error rates of uncoded and G.711 coded corpora are similar.

In general, the verification performance of the coded corpora degrades when the bit rate of the corresponding codec decreases (Figure 1). However, the performance among the GSM, G.729, and G.723.1 coded speech does not obey this rule occasionally for some handsets. After CMS was employed for channel compensation, the error rates were reduced for all the uncoded and coded corpora while a stronger correlation between bit rates and verification performance can be observed among the GSM, G.729, and G.723.1 coded speech. Using the transformation technique, the error rates are reduced further while correlation between bit rates and verification performance becomes very obvious among the coded speech at various bit rates. As the perceptual quality of the coded speech is usually poorer for lower rate codecs, we conclude that a strong correlation between the coded speech quality and the verification performance exists.

Comparing with the results in [4], it is obvious that using MFCC as features is more desirable than using LPCC. For example, when MFCC are used the average error rate for the uncoded speech is 9.01%, whereas the error rate increases to 11.16% when LPCC are used [4].

5   Conclusions

A new channel compensation approach for verifying speakers from coded telephone speech has been presented. The proposed approach combines stochastic transformation with handset identification. Results show that the transformation technique outperforms the CMS approach and significantly reduces the error rates of a baseline system. The error rate achieved by the transformation technique correlates with the bit rate of the codec and hence reflects the perceptual quality of the coded speech. In this work, we also observed that MFCC outperform LPCC in representing speakers' characteristics.

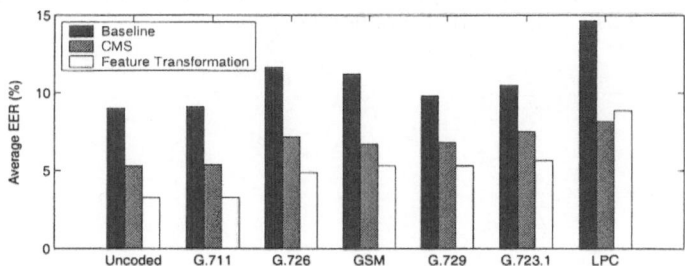

Fig. 1. Average EERs achieved by the baseline, CMS, and transformation approaches. Note that the bit rate of coders decreases from left to right, with "uncoded" being the highest (128 kb/s) and LPC the lowest (2.4 kb/s).

References

1. B. S. Atal, "Effectiveness of linear prediction characteristics of the speech wave for automatic speaker identification and verification," *J. Acoust. Soc. Am.*, vol. 55, no. 6, pp. 1304–1312, 1974.
2. M. G. Rahim and B. H. Juang, "Signal bias removal by maximum likelihood estimation for robust telephone speech recognition," *IEEE Trans. on Speech and Audio Processing*, vol. 4, no. 1, pp. 19–30, Jan 1996.
3. A. Acero, *Acoustical and Environmental Robustness in Automatic Speech Recognition*, Kluwer Academic Pub., Dordrecht, 1992.
4. M. W. Mak and S. Y. Kung, "Combining stochastic feautre transformation and handset identification for telephone-based speaker verification," in *Proc. ICASSP'2002*, 2002.
5. J. M. Huerta and R. M. Stern, "Speech recognition from GSM coder parameters," in *Proc. 5th Int. Conf. on Spoken Language Processing*, 1998, vol. 4, pp. 1463–1466.
6. T. F. Quatieri, E. Singer, R. B. Dunn, D. A. Reynolds, and J. P. Campbell, "Speaker and language recognition using speech codec parameters," in *Proc. Eurospeech'99*, 1999, vol. 2, pp. 787–790.
7. T. F. Quatieri, R. B. Dunn, D. A. Reynolds, J. P. Campbell, and E. Singer, "Speaker recognition using G.729 codec parameters," in *Proc. ICASSP'2000*, 2000, pp. 89–92.

8. S. B. Davis and P. Mermelstein, "Comparison of parametric representations for monosyllabic word recognition in continuously spoken sentences," *IEEE Trans. on ASSP*, vol. 28, no. 4, pp. 357–366, August 1980.

9. A. Sankar and C. H. Lee, "A maximum-likelihood approach to stochastic matching for robust speech recognition," *IEEE Trans. on Speech and Audio Processing*, vol. 4, no. 3, pp. 190–202, 1996.

10. K. K. Yiu, M. W. Mak, and S. Y. Kung, "A GMM-based handset selector for channel mismatch compensation with applications to speaker identification," in *2nd IEEE Pacific-Rim Conference on Multimedia*, 2001, pp. 1132–1137.

11. D. A. Reynolds, "HTIMIT and LLHDB: speech corpora for the study of handset transducer effects," in *ICASSP'97*, 1997, vol. 2, pp. 1535–1538.

12. M. W. Mak and S. Y. Kung, "Estimation of elliptical basis function parameters by the EM algorithms with application to speaker verification," *IEEE Trans. on Neural Networks*, vol. 11, no. 4, pp. 961–969, 2000.

Recognition of Visual Speech Elements Using Hidden Markov Models

Say Wei Foo[1] and Liang Dong[2]

[1] School of Electrical and Electronic Engineering
Nanyang Technological University, Singapore 639798
eswfoo@ntu.edu.sg
[2] Department of Electrical and Computer Engineering
National University of Singapore, Singapore 119260
engp0564@nus.edu.sg

Abstract. In this paper, a novel subword lip reading system using continuous Hidden Markov Models (HMMs) is presented. The constituent HMMs are configured according to the statistical features of lip motion and trained with the Baum-Welch method. The performance of the proposed system in identifying the fourteen visemes defined in MPEG-4 standards is addressed. Experiment results show that an average accuracy above 80% can be achieved using the proposed system.

1 Introduction

Lip reading, which is also referred to as speech reading, is the technique of retrieving speech content from visual clues. As early as 1970's, researchers had studied the bimodal aspects of human speech. The "McGurk effect" indicated that the perceived sound existed in both audio signal and visual signal[1]. And even earlier, Sumby and Pollack proved that visual clues could lead to better perception of speech especially under noisy environment[2]. However, the ability of lip reading was long regarded as the privilege of our human being because of the complexity of machine recognition. Only in recent years did lip reading become an interested area of multimedia processing due to the development of pattern recognition tools and modern computing techniques. In 1988, Michael Kass *et al* developed snake-based method to dynamically track lip boundaries[3]. Tsuhan Chen and Ram R. Rao studied the audio-visual integration in multimodal communication[4]. Bregler *et al* used the time-delayed neural network (TDNN) for visual speech recognition[5]. The efforts made by the researchers chiefly serve two objectives: i) Providing an informative description for the lip motion, and ii) Designing a sequence recognition algorithm with strong logic capacity. The first task is associated with image processing and feature extraction, whose purpose is to obtain sufficient features for speech analysis. The second task involves configuration and training of certain mathematic tool, e.g. neural network or HMM. However, the progress in both areas is not smooth due to the difficulties in information extraction from lip motion. In many bimodal speech

Y.-C. Chen, L.-W. Chang, and C.-T. Hsu (Eds.): PCM 2002, LNCS 2532, pp. 607–614, 2002.
© Springer-Verlag Berlin Heidelberg 2002

processing systems, the visual channel only serves for performance enhancement for an existing acoustic speech recognizer. In this paper, we introduce a novel HMM-based subword classifier and investigate the possibility of visual-only speech analysis. The dynamics of lip motion is systematically studied and the HMMs are configured accordingly. Experiment results show that if the HMMs are well tuned, high recognition rate of individual visual speech element can be achieved.

2   Features of Lip Motion

While we are speaking, our lip is driven by some facial muscles to move in continuous 3D space. In most cases, only the frontal projection is processed for speech analysis. The boundary of the lip (2D) or the surface of the lip (3D) can be very complicated under fine resolution. However, not all of the details are helpful for speech reading. For example, a human speech reader knows what a person is speaking from a distance. What he sees is merely a coarse shape. Computer-aided lip reading should also not pay too much attention on the details but focuses on the "skeleton" of the lip, such as the width and height.

Lip motion is chiefly the up-and-down shift of the upper lip and lower lip. The movement of the other parts, e.g. the lip corner, is somewhat subject to it. Such motion is simple at the first glance. However, it is difficult to be applied to speech analysis because of the following reasons.

i) the movement of the lip is slight compared with its geometric measures during natural speaking. For example, if the width of a speaker's mouth is 6cm in its relaxed state, the variance is usually between 5.5 to 6.5cm during speaking. This fact indicates that the statistical features of lip motion concentrate around some stable states.

ii) the movement of the lip varies slowly over time. Compared with the speech signal, which has significant frequency components up to 4kHz, the lip motion is a very low-frequency signal. It indicates that the information conveyed by lip motion is limited.

iii) the basic visual speech elements corresponding to English phonemes, namely visemes, have too many similarities with each other. Most visemes experience the same process during production: starting from closed mouth, proceeding to half-opened mouth and ending with closed mouth again. Such similarity is easy to observe in our daily experience and is reported in many experiments.

iv) the visemes are liable to be distorted by their context. For example, the visual representation of the vowel /ai/ is very different in the words *hide* and *right*. The preceding letter and the posterior letter will both influence the lip states of the studied viseme to certain extent. A viseme will therefore demonstrate polymorphism under different context.

The above factors make it a challenging job for visual-only speech recognition. In the following sections, we will discuss the measures taken in our system to solve some of the issues.

3   Components of a Lip Reading System

The flow chart of the proposed viseme-level lip reading system is illustrated in Fig. 1.

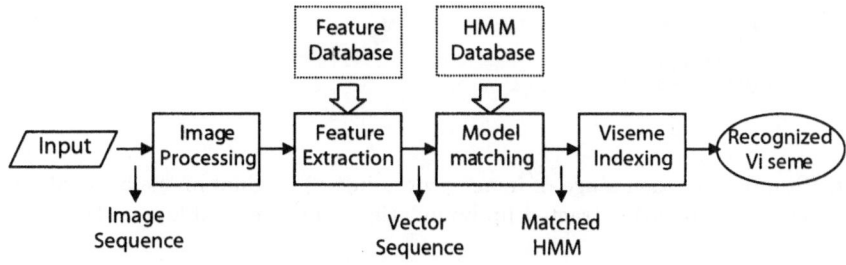

Fig. 1. Flow chart of a viseme-level lip reading system

3.1   Image Processing for Lip Reading

The purpose of image processing is to track the movement of the lip during articulation. In recent years, much research has been conducted on dynamical lip tracking. The term "dynamical" means that the optimal lip state is jointly determined by the past states (or state templates) and currently observed state. Compared with the conventional image segmentation methods that are individual-image-oriented, the dynamical approach has the advantage of offering good continuity and accuracy. For example, the snake method developed by M. Kass *et al*[3] and the deformable template method developed by Yuille *et al*[6]. In our system, the deformable template approach is adopted.

The raw data describing the visemes are image sequences sampled at 25Hz. A typical image is shown in Fig. 2a. The image reveals the lip area of the speaker during speaking. Before implementing lip tracking, the approximate position of the lip is located based on the contrast of brightness. Under normal illumination, the hole (mouth) between the lips is darker than the surface. A proper threshold can then be chosen from the histogram of brightness and the mouth is isolated. After that, the hue-saturation factors, which are relatively insensitive to changes in the absolute brightness, are extracted to highlight the lip area and erase the unnecessary parts of the image. Fig. 2b illustrates the segmented lip area after the processing. The deformable templates are then applied to track the lip boundaries. The principle of the method is to adapt the template to match the target object. During the process, the parameters are adjusted to minimize certain cost function. A detailed discussion of the method is presented in Hennecke's report[7]. The difference between our experiments and Hennecke's work is that eight Bezier curves are adopted in our templates while parabolas and quartics are used in[7]. Fig. 2d shows the extracted boundaries and Fig. 2c gives the actual lip area. It manifests that the obtained contour maintains the basic shape of the lip but neglect the trivial undulations along the boundaries.

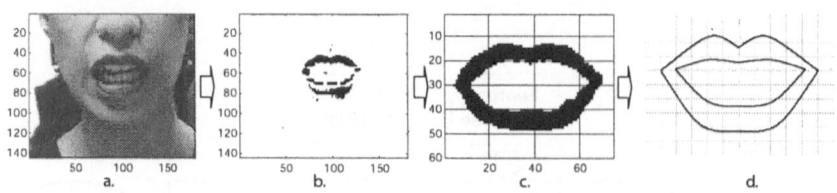

Fig. 2. Results after each stage of image processing: a) original image b) localized lip area c) actual lip area d) extracted lip boundaries using deformable templates

3.2   Extraction of Geometric Measures

The factors describing the movement of the lip include geometric features and frequency features. Because the visual signals indicating the lip movement are usually sampled at relatively low frequency ($\leq$50Hz), the spectral features are not very useful for speech decoding. What is important is the geometric measures that determine the shape of the lip at each moment. When the 3D movement of the lip is projected onto 2D plane, it usually involves translation, scaling, changing of curvatures and sometimes rotation.

i) *Changes in Size.* The height, width of the lip, as well as the "interior" size of the lip, such as thickness vary during the course.

ii) *Translation.* It indicates the shift of some points in relate to a reference point, such as the horizontal movement of the mouth corner. Translation can be looked as a linear shift. It only affects the position of the lip bows without deforming their shape much. For example, if we open our mouth slowly, there will be chiefly translation but minor deformation.

iii) *Change of Curvature.* Human lip is arc-shaped in itself. As a result, the curvature determines the shape of the lip bows. While we are speaking, this parameter changes accordingly. For example, when we round our lip to articulate the phonetic sound /o/ and stretch our lip to articulate /i/, the curvatures are very different.

Based on the above analysis, some elaborate measures are drawn from the eight Bezier fitting curves. As illustrated in Fig. 3a, parameter $S_1 \sim S_3$ give the thickness of various parts of the lip, $P_1 \sim P_3$ indicate the positions of some key points of the lip, and T denotes the length of the tongue if it is visible. In Fig. 3b, $C_1 \sim C_4$, which are the heights between the controlling points of the Beziers and the lip corner, measure the curvatures of the boundaries. These eleven parameters uniquely determine the shape of the lip and are chosen to build the feature vectors used in our lip reading system.

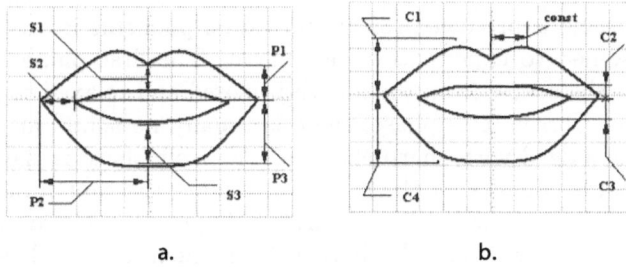

a.   b.

Fig. 3. Geometric measures of the lip: a) thickness and position   b) curvatures
S_1: thickness of the upper bow S_2: thickness of the lip corner S_3: thickness of the
lower bow P_1: position of the upper lip P_2: position of the corner P_3: position of the
lower bow C_1: curvature of the upper-exterior boundary C_2: curvature of the upper-
interior boundary C_3: curvature of the lower-interior boundary C_4: curvature of the
lower-exterior boundary T: length of the tongue (invisible here)

The eleven extracted features are all continuous and are correlated with each
other to some extent, although the relationship is too complex to be generalized. The collected feature vectors are put through normalization and principal
component analysis. They are finally clustered into groups using K-*means* algorithm. For the experiment conducted in this paper, 32 clusters are used in the
database. The vectors in each cluster is assumed to be Gaussian distributed. For
example, $G(\mu_k, \sigma_k)$ is the probability density function (pdf) of the k-th cluster,
where μ_k is the mean vector and σ_k is the variance of Euclidean distance.

3.3   Configuration of the HMMs

Continuous HMMs are adopted to model the individual viseme in the pro-
posed system. Let $\{S_1, S_2, \cdots S_N\}$ be the state set and $G(\mu_1, \sigma_1), G(\mu_2, \sigma_2), \cdots$
$G(\mu_M, \sigma_M)$ denote the M Gaussian mixtures that are generated in the previous
section, an HMM is determined by the following three components:
i) The probability array of the initial state: $\pi = [P(s_1 = S_i)]_{N \times 1}$ $(1 \leq i \leq N)$
and $\sum_{i=1}^{N} P(s_1 = S_i) = 1$, where s_1 is the first state in the state chain.
ii) State transition matrix: $A = [P(s_{t+1} = S_j | s_t = S_i)]_{N \times N}$ $(1 \leq i, j \leq N)$ and
$\sum_{j=1}^{N} P(S_j | S_i) = 1$, where s_t is the t-th state and $s_t + 1$ is the $t + 1$-th state.
iii) In continuous case, the output probability distribution $b_i(o_t)$ is obtained from
1, where o_t is the t-th observed symbol and c_{il} is a non-negative coefficient.

$$b_i(o_t) = \sum_{l=1}^{M} c_{il} G(o_t, \mu_l, \sigma_l) \quad \text{with} \quad \sum_{l=1}^{M} c_{il} = 1 \tag{1}$$

In the Baum-Welch estimation, the final HMM is closely associated with the
selection of the model type, number of states and the initial estimations of π,
A and B. In our system, these parameters are set according to the dynamics
of the lip motion. Investigation on human speaking habit reveals that while an

independent viseme is produced (or an individual phoneme is articulated), the lip can be assumed to experience three phases. The first phase is the initial phase, which is the course from the mouth is closed and relaxed to get ready to make the sound. During this phase, there is usually no sound articulated and the lip is characterized with sharp changes. The next phase is the articulation phase, which is the course that the lip poses to make the sound until the sound is made. The change of the lip shape during this phase is not so violent as the previous phase and there is usually short stable moment in this phase. The third phase is the end phase. The mouth will restore from the articulation state to relaxed state. Among these phases, the articulation phase is the most important for recognition because the difference between visemes chiefly lies there and it is relatively independent to the context. The initial phase and end phase are transitional phases. They may change to a great extent under different contexts. Fig. 4 illustrates the three phases and the corresponding acoustic signal when the phonetic sound /u/ is uttered.

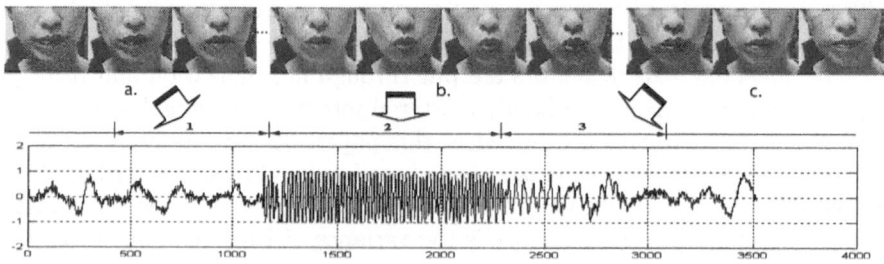

Fig. 4. The three phases of viseme production: a) Initial phase b) Articulation phase c) End phase

Three-state left-right HMMs (Fig. 5) are adopted to model the visemes in our system. This design has the following advantages: First, the states of HMM may have some physical significance because they are associated with the three phases of viseme production. Second, such structure is convenient to be applied to connected-viseme recognition. Complex state chain can be constructed by connecting the viseme models and at the same time, adding more variance to the initial and end states and less variance to the articulation states. However, such three-state frame is not a fixed standard. For diphthongs such as /oi/ or combination of phonemes, if there exists more articulation phases, more articulation states of the HMM should be designated.

The initial value of the transition matrix A is set according to the durations of the phases of viseme production. Given an image sequence of a viseme, the approximate initial phase, articulation phase and end phase can be manually partitioned from the image sequence and the acoustic signal (like those did in Fig. 5). The frame number of each phase is counted. And a set of forward probabilities (the probabilities of jumping to the next phase) and iteration probabilities (the

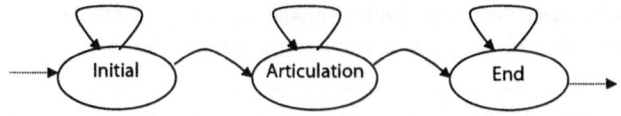

Fig. 5. The three-state left-right HMM of a viseme

probabilities of the phase repeats itself) are computed. These value are then adopted as the initial values of the coefficients in A.

The initial value of $b_i(o_t)$ is also set according to the statistics of a phase. The distribution density function of each phase is estimated by counting and averaging the appearance of the observation symbols in it. After that, some pdf bases $G(\mu_l, \sigma_l)$ and coefficients c_{il} are chosen to fit the density curve. The initial value of $b_i(o_t)$ is then calculated from 1.

With the above initial settings in hand, the HMMs for all the visemes are trained with the Baum-welch method (A detailed description about the Baum-welch method please refer to[8] and[9]). During recognition, the input observation is measured by all the HMMs, the one that gives the greatest likelihood is chosen as the class of the viseme.

4   Performance of the System

Experiments are conducted to evaluate the performance of the proposed system. The task is to identify the fourteen visemes defined in MPEG-4 multimedia standards[10]. For each viseme, 40 samples are drawn to train the HMM and another 100 samples are used to test the performance. To demonstrate the advantages of the HMMs configured with the proposed strategy, the recognition results of the HMMs with other two commonly used configurations - uniform configuration (the initial values in B gives uniform distribution) and random configuration (the initial values in B gives random distribution) are listed for reference. In the experiment, the 100 testing samples are drawn from independent production of single viseme. The classification rate of the HMMs is listed in Table 1.

For the independent visemes, the average classification accuracy is well above 80%, especially for the vowels, where the accuracy is nearly 100%. This rate is normally well above the uniformly or randomly configured HMMs. It indicates that the proposed configuration strategy is effective to improve the discriminative ability of the HMMs.

5   Conclusion

For the lip reading system investigated in this paper, the continuous HMMs are carefully configured according to the features of lip motion. Experimental results of recognition indicate that such management is helpful in improving the performance of the classifier. The application of the proposed method on

Table 1. Classification accuracy (independent visemes) of the proposed HMM M_1, uniform-configured HMM M_2 and random-configured HMM M_3

Visemes	M_1	M_2	M_3	Visemes	M_1	M_2	M_3
1 p, b, m	87%	65%	76%	8 n, l	81%	61%	65%
2 f, v	96%	90%	85%	9 r	82%	59%	73%
3 T, D	89%	48%	63%	10 A:	99%	84%	90%
4 t, d	65%	70%	59%	11 e	92%	87%	78%
5 k, g	76%	73%	74%	12 I	100%	92%	75%
6 tS, dZ, S	90%	87%	56%	13 Q	93%	91%	87%
7 s, z	96%	94%	86%	14 U	93%	97%	89%

identifying independent visemes is successful with average classification accuracy above 80%. The potential of single HMM under the Baum-Welch estimation is well developed. For further improvement of the discriminative ability of the HMMs to distinguish visemes under various contexts, new training method such as maximum mutual information (MMI) estimation or the use of multiple-HMM classifier would be explored.

References

1. H. McGurk and J. MacDonald: Hearing lips and seeing voices, Nature, (1976) 748-756
2. W. Sumby and I. Pollack: Visual contributions to speech intelligibility in noise, J. Acoust. Soc. Amer. (1954)
3. M. Kass, A. Witkin and D. Terzopoulus: Snakes: Active contour models, International Journal of Computer Vision, (1988) 321-331
4. Tsuhan Chen and Ram R. Rao: audio-visual Integration in Multimodal Communication, Proc. IEEE, Vol. 86, No.5, (1998) 837-852
5. C. Bregler and S. Omohundro: Nonlinear manifold learning for visual speech recognition, Proc. IEEE ICCV, (1995) 494-499
6. Alan L. Yuille, David S. Cohen and Peter W. Hallinan: Feature extraction from faces using deformable templates, IEEE Computer Society Conference on Computer Vision and Pattern Recognition, (1989) 104-109
7. M. E. Hennecke, K. V. Prasad and D. G. Stork: Using deformable templates to infer visual speech dynamics, Technical report, Ricoh California Research Center, (1994)
8. L. R. Rabiner: A tutorial on Hidden Markov Models and selected applications in speech recognition, Proc. IEEE, Vol. 77, No. 2, (1989) 257-286
9. Y. Wu, A. Ganapathiraju and J. Picone: Report for Baum-Welch Re-estimation of Hidden Markov Model, Institute for Signal and Information Processing, (1999)
10. M. Tekalp and J. Ostermann: Face and 2-D mesh animation in MPEG-4, Image Communication J. (1999)

Robust and Inaudible Multi-echo Audio Watermarking

Dong-Yan Huang[1] and Theng Yee Yeo[2]

[1] 11 Science Park Road, Singapore Science Park II
Singapore 117685
dongyan@ime.a-star.edu.sg
[2] Dept of Electrical Engineering, National University of Singapore,
10 Kent Ridge Crescent, Singapore 119260

Abstract. A novel echo embedding technique is proposed to overcome inherent trade-off between in-audibility and robustness in conventional echo hiding. It makes use of masking model to embed two echoes by both positive and negative pulses (closely located) and high energy to host audio signals. Subjective listening tests show that the proposed method could improve robustness to operations of noise addition, re-sampling, cropping, filtering and MP3 coding without perceptual distortion.

1 Introduction

Efficient distribution, reproduction, and manipulation have led to rapid growth of digital multimedia, but this has also increased the need for protection of digital data concerning intellectual property rights. Digital watermarking is a technique to hide copyright or other information into digital data [1]. To be effective in the protection of the ownership of intellectual property, a number of criteria should be satisfied for a watermarking technique. The watermark should be inaudible even to golden ears, robust to manipulation and common signal processing operations, resistant to collusion and forgery attacks. The early research topic is emphasized on the problem of in-audibility of watermark: to embed the watermark into the audio signal without degraded host audio quality. The reason is that the applications do not involve in signal distortion or tampering. However, the purpose of copyright control, robust to signal processing operations and resistant to tampering attacks has become important research topic. It is recognized that robustness to signal processing operation and resistance to tempering require watermarks having large energies to be embedded in perceptual significant region of audio signal. However, this requirement is contrary to the need for the watermarks to be imperceptible.

Audio watermarking techniques currently focus mainly on two aspects:s pread-spectrum-based coding, and echo coding [1],[3]. Especially, Bobey , *et al* [5] explicitly make use of MPEG psycho-acoustic model I to obtain the frequency masking values to achieve good in-audibility for spread spectrum watermarking scheme. However, the high quality of audio compression technique exploits also these characteris-

Y.-C. Chen, L.-W. Chang, and C.-T. Hsu (Eds.): PCM 2002, LNCS 2532, pp. 615–622, 2002.

tics. It is possible to make the embedding pseudo random sequence trivial and indetectable for the watermarking decoder part.

Echo hiding embeds data into a host audio signal by introducing an echo. The nature of the echo is to add resonance to the host audio and is not to make embedding signal as additive noise. It is possible to embed the signal to audio while having the same statistical and perceptual characteristics [3]. But the robustness of watermarking requires high energy echo to be embedded which increases audible distortion. Xu *et al* [2] proposed a multi-echo embedding technique to reduce the possibility of echo detection by third parties. But the technique can not increase the robustness because the audio timbre is changed with the sum of pulse amplitude [6]. Oh *et al* [6] proposed echo kernel comprising multiple echoes by both positive and negative pulses with different offsets (closely located) in the kernel, of which the frequency response is plain in lower bands and large ripples in high frequency. Even they are perceptually less important for most of music, but these large ripples can be audible as disagreeable noise for some music sometimes.

In order to further improve the in-audibility of Oh's echo embedding technique, the frequency masking are exploited to adjust the decays of echo kernel. The corresponding watermarking technique will be compared to the existing echo hiding schemes and is evaluated in terms of audibility, computational efficiency and detection accuracy. In Section II, the echo hiding technique is reviewd. The echo kernel design based on masking threshold is presented in Section III. Simulation results are presented in Section IV. Finally, Section V gives a brief conclusion.

2 Echo Hiding Technique

Echo hiding embeds data into a host audio signal by introducing an echo. The offset (or delay) between the original and the echo is so small that the echo is perceived as added resonance. The four major parameters are initial amplitude, decay rate, "one" offset and "zero" offset (illustrated in Fig.1).

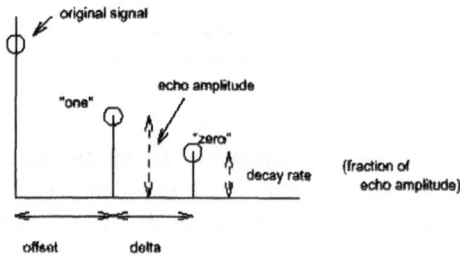

Fig. 1. Adjustable paprameters

The encoding process can be represented as a system that has one of two possible system functions. In the time domain, the system functions are discrete time exponential differing only in the delay between impulses. For simplicity, only two impulses are chosen, one to copy the original signal and one to create an echo.

Processing a signal through any kernel in Fig .1 will result in an encoded signal. The delay (δ_i) between the original signal and the echo is dependent on the kernel being used, δ_1 if the "one" kernel is used and δ_0 if the "zero" kernel is used.

The original signal is divided into smaller portions for encoding more than one bit. Each individual portion can then be considered each as an independent signal and echoed with the desired bit. The final encoded signal (containing several bits) is composite of all independently encoded signal portions. A smooth transition between portions encoded with different bits should be considered to prevent abrupt changes in the resonance of the final (mixed) signal.

Information is embedded into a signal by echoing the original signal with one of two delay kernels. A binary one is represented by an echo kernel with a δ_1 second delay while a binary zero is represented by a δ_0 second delay. Therefore, extraction of the embedded information is to detect the spacing between the echoes. The magnitude of the autocorrelation of the encoded signal's cepstrum can be examined at two locations:

$$F^{-1}(\ln_{complex}(F(x))^2) \tag{1}$$

where F represents the Fourier Transform, F^{-1} the inverse Fourier Transform. In each segment, the peak of the auto-cepstrum detects embedded binary data.

3   Echo Kernel Design Based on Perceptual Model

3.1 Nature of Echo

In order to better understand the role of echo in watermarking, we study the echo produce process. The single echo phenomenon happens when there is a big object between source and receiver, which receive two multipath components with differential delay. In this case, the model of the channel transfer function can be described as [7]:

$$c(f) = 1 + be^{-j2\pi f \delta_0} \tag{2}$$

where b is called a shape parameter, and δ_0 is the relative delay between the direct and the multipath components. This simplified model can be used to study the echo for human perception. The study [6] shows that a single clear echo is heard when the time delay is about 50 ms, while one of the change of timbre in the sound is perceptible as the time delay is short of 2ms, usually called coloration. These facts can be clearly explained in the ear model theory [6].

As we consider the temporal masking, that stronger masker render the following weaker signals inaudible during 50-200ms with exponentially decays. It is normal to choose small value of offset of echo kernel, which locates in the coloration region. However, too small value of offset of echo kernel is not easily detected by cepstrum method. Through perceptual analysis in frequency domain for echo located in coloration region and a number of tests for echo offset, an echo kernel comprising closely located positive and negative pulses is proposed [6]. The frequency response of this echo kernel can be described as:

$$c(f) = 1 + be^{-j2\pi f\delta_0} - be^{-j2\pi f(\delta_0+\Delta)} \tag{3}$$

where $\Delta \to 0$ and we can derive Eq.(3) with this condition and we get:

$$|c(f)|^2 = 1 + b^2(\sin 2\pi f\Delta)^2 - 2b\sin(2\pi f\Delta)\sin(2\pi f\delta_0) \tag{4}$$

We can observe from Eq. (4) that this echo kernel has a plain response in lower bands and large ripples in higher bands. However, the second and third terms lead the distortion of music as b is too big.

With the same analysis, we can study the feasibility of multiple echoes method proposed by Xu et al [2]. Instead of using a single echo, four smaller echoes with different offsets are embedded to the host audio signal. In this case, echo kernel can be model as:

$$c(f) = 1 + b_0 e^{-j2\pi f\delta_0} + b_1 e^{-j2\pi f\delta_1} + b_2 e^{-j2\pi f\delta_2} + b_3 e^{-j2\pi f\delta_3} \tag{5}$$

The timbre of music is considerable changed. Such distortion of audio signal can not be acceptable for musicians even it reduce the possibility to remove the watermark by the third parties. This method is not robust to signal processing operations.

In order to enhance robustness and in-audibility of Oh's method, we propose to use MPEG-1 psycho-acoustic model I to adjust the decay.

3.2 Masking

Using a constantly high decay rate in all audio segments will definitely fail in some segments (i.e. noisy or ringing effects for certain sound clips) because some segments have low signal energy (or even completely silent), consist of decaying signals or are simply problematic for one reason or another. As such, masking is performed to determine the maximum decay rates of the impulses in the kernel for the echoes to be inaudible. The masking block diagram is shown in Fig 2.

Signal energy for all audio segments is computed using the formula below and those segments with higher signal energy are encoded first.

$$E_{rms} = \sqrt{1/N \sum_{i=1}^{N} s_i^2} \tag{6}$$

Signal energy is compared with a threshold T, and segments with low signal energy are skipped. Our experiments indicate that $T = 0.01$ works well for the test clips.

Next, the signal is amplified to have at least desired amplitude of 0.95 and the scale factor is passed to the de-emphasis block to rescale the signal back to its original level later.

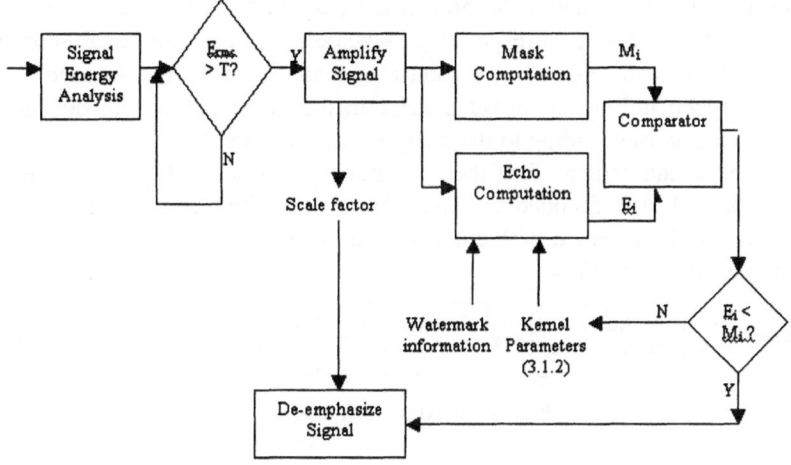

Fig. 2. Masking block diagram

After the signal is amplified, the decay rate in each audio segment is adaptively modified by masking. This means that the echo is compared with a mask to determine if the echo components are well-masked (i.e. 80% of the echo components below the mask).). Depending on the masking method being selected, the method of mask computation is MPEG-1 psychoacoustic model I [4]. The mask is computed in the frequency domain for 26 critical bands. For each segment, decay rate is adjusted such that frequency components of the echo from 1kHz to 5kHz of echo are below the mask computed from original host wave. Fig. 3 clearly shows that the echo components in the specified frequency region are below the computed mask.

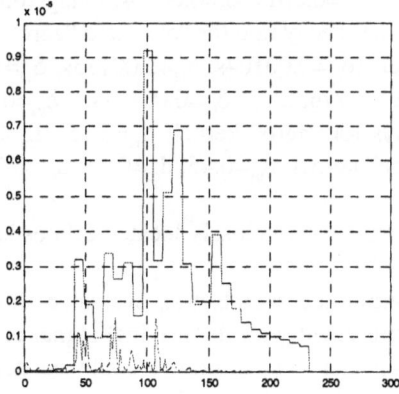

Fig. 3. Masking using psychoacoustic

3.3 Watermark Decoding

Watermark decoding is carried out by checking the peak detection on the autocepstrum. As the offsets will be passed to the decoder, the problem become "one" and "zero" estimation. For single echo hiding, the magnitude of the autocepstrum is examined at the two locations corresponding to the delays of the "one" and "zero" kernel respectively. If the autocepstrum is greater at δ_1 than it is at δ_0, it is decoded as "one". For multiple echo hiding, all peaks present in the autocepstrum are detected. The number of peaks corresponding to the delay locations of the "one" and "zero" kernels are then counted and compared. If there are more peaks at the delay locations for the "one" echo kernel, it is decoded as "one". The two positive and negative closely located echoes can be detected with autocepstrum method by counting two peaks. The decoding is illustrated in Fig.4.

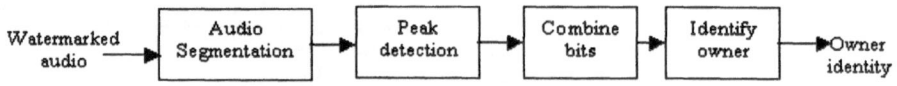

Fig. 4. Decoder block diagram

4   Experimental Results

In order to evaluate the performance of the proposed method, sujective listening tests, computation efficiency and various rubusteness tests such like the operations of noise addition, re-sampling, cropping, filtering and MPEG Layer 3 coding are conducted over different music like classic music, pop music, chinese folk music, and capella music.

The original audio is divided into independent segments using a data rate of 4 bps.
The single echo kernels, the multiple echo kernels, proposed echo kernels parameters are given below:

- Single echo kernels (δ_1=0.001s, δ_2=0.0013s, delay for "one" and "zero" kernels; $d_1 = 0.5$, $d_2 = 0.5$, decay rate for "one" and "zero" kernels);
- Multi echoes kernels (δ_{11}=0.00104s, δ_{12}=0.00183s, δ_{13}= 0.00220s, δ_{14}=0.00262s, delays for "one" kernel; δ_{01}=0.00127s, δ_{02}=0.00133s, δ_{03}=0.00136s, δ_{04}=0.00238s, delays for "zero" kernel; d_{11}=0.15, d_{12}=0.45, d_{13}=0.40, d_{14}=0.50, decay rates for "one" kernel; d_{01}=0.45, d_{02}=0.35, d_{03}=0.20, d_{04}=0.35, decay rates for "zero" kernels);
- The two positive and negative closely located echoes have the same magnitude b=1.5 and $\Delta = 0.05$.

The quality of the watermarked signals was evaluated through informal listening tests. The listeners were presented with the original signal and the watermarked signals and reported as to whether any difference could be detected between the two signals. The informal listening tests show a significant improvement in audio quality. By adaptively modifying the decay rate in each audio segment, the inaudibility of the watermark for all echo hiding encoding options was improved. Adaptive data attenuation and Oh's method work well on most segments, but the psychoacoustic model gives better results.

To estimate the computational efficiency for each echo hiding method, the computational time for each method is obtained from the audio watermarking software using a Pentium III 550 MHz computer with PC-133 128 Mb RAM and 20.4 GB ATA66 / 7200rpm. A summary of the computation time for each method is tabulated below.

Table 1. Computation time summary

	PopSong	SaxoMusic	ErHu-Music	AcapSong	Speech-Clip
Psycho (single)	124.90	110.35	124.41	12.75	35.48
Psycho (multiple)	189.66	186.47	183.62	21.86	52.95
Psycho (pos +Neg.)	146.95	134.13	152.60	16.64	42.06

The detection accuracy is calculated using the formula:

Recovery accuracy = (no of bits correctly decoded)x100%/(no of bits placed)   (7)

Detection accuracy summary for PopSong , SaxoMusic, ErHuMusic and AcapSong with different echo embedding methods is shown in Table 2.

Table 2. Detection accuracy summary

	Pop-Song	Saxo-Music	ErHu-Music	ACap-Song	Ave
Psycho (single)	92.38%	93.81%	87.62%	86.90%	88.24%
Psycho (multiple)	92.38%	85.71%	85.24%	85.71%	85.52%
Psycho (Pos.+Neg.)	94.21%	93.14%	90.13%	88.57%	89.73%

The detection accuracy results demonstrate that the proposed watermarking technique is robust to common signal processing operations.

The detection accuracy summary for various malicious attacks such like noise, re-sampling, cropping (five short pieces of duration 0.1s), filtering (a butterworth 15-tap low-pass filter, with a cutoff frequency equal to 1/8 the Nyquist frequency), and MP3 coding/decoding with a bit rate of 112 kbits/s is shown in Table 3 .

The results show that detection accuracy is dependent on signal characteristics and structure. PopSong, a segment of popular song, has very high signal energy with no gaps of silence, so an excellent average detection accuracy of over 90% is achieved. The watermark is so easily recoverable even after common signal processing operations. As seen in Table 3, the proposed watermarking methods are more robust to cropping (detection accuracy = 99.29%), noise addition (accuracy = 89.24%) and re-sampling (accuracy = 84.67%) than the other common signal processing operations because filtering and MPEG coding/decoding remove much more signal information. This is especially true if the autocorrelation between signals is low.

Table 3. Detection accuracy for various distortions

	Closed-loop	Noise	Resample	Crop	Filter	MPEG
PopSong	100.00%	94.29%	92.38%	100.00%	85.24%	76.17%
SaxoMusic	100.00%	92.74%	83.93%	100.00%	74.88%	73.93%
ErHuMusic	99.52%	85.40%	81.43%	98.10%	78.41%	66.98%
ACapSong	97.62%	84.52%	80.95%	94.05%	66.67%	67.86%
Average	99.29%	89.24%	84.67%	98.04%	75.55%	71.24%

5 Conclusion

Pure echo hiding, one of the methods for copyright protection, is problematic because the echoes are audible and the detection accuracy of the embedded watermark is low. Multiple echos method proposed by Xu *et al* [2] can not increase the robustness to malicious operations. The results presented in this paper have shown that the proposed method to multi-echo hiding (two positive and negative closely located echoes) improves inaudibility and robustness to common signal processing operations. By adaptively modifying the decay rate in each audio segment, a significant improvement in audio quality is achieved. The results show that detection accuracy is highly dependent on additional signal processing performed. 100% accuracy can be achieved if there is no additional signal processing. The proposed methods are more robust to cropping, noise addition and re-sampling than the other operations of filtering and MPEG coding/decoding.

References

1. W. Bender, D. Gruhl, N. Morimoto, A.Lu, "Techniques for data hiding", *IBM Systems Journal,* vol 35, Nos 3 &   4, pp. 313-336, 1996.
2. C. Xu, J. Wu, Q. Sun, K. Xin, "Applications of Watermarking Technology in Audio Signals*", Journal Audio Engineering Society,* vol. 47, No. 10, 1999 October.
3. D. Gruhl, A. Lu, W. Bender, "Echo Hiding", *in Proc. Information Hiding Workshop (University of Cambridge, U.K., 1996),* pp. 295-315.
4. "Information Technology – Coding of moving pictures and associated audio for digital storage up to about 1.5 Mbits/s", ISO/IEC IS 11172, 1993.
5. L. Boeny, A. H. Tewfik, and K. N. Hamdy. Digital watermarks for audio signals. In *Proc. of Multimedia 1996,* Hiroshima,1996.
6. H.O Oh, J.W. Seok, J.W. Hong, D. H. Youn, "New Echo Embedding Technique for Robust and Imperceptible Audio Watermarking", CD-ROM, *International Conference on Acoustic, Speech and Signal Processing,* May 9-13, 2001, Salt lake City, Utah, U.S.A.
7. J.G. Proakis, Digital Communications, 4th Edition, *McGraw-Hill,* New York, 2001.

Kernel-Based Probabilistic Neural Networks with Integrated Scoring Normalization for Speaker Verification

Kwok-Kwong Yiu[1], Man-Wai Mak[1], and Sun-Yuan Kung[2]*

[1] Center for Multimedia Signal Processing
Dept. of Electronic and Information Engineering
The Hong Kong Polytechnic University, China
[2] Dept. of Electrical Engineering
Princeton University
USA

Abstract. This paper investigates kernel-based probabilistic neural networks for speaker verification in clean and noisy environments. In particular, it compares the performance and characteristics of speaker verification systems that use probabilistic decision-based neural networks (PDBNNs), Gaussian mixture models (GMMs) and elliptical basis function networks (EBFNs) as speaker models. Experimental evaluations based on 138 speakers of the YOHO corpus and its noisy variants were conducted. The original PDBNN training algorithm was also modified to make PDBNNs appropriate for speaker verification. Experimental evaluations, based on 138 speakers and the visualization of decision boundaries, indicate that GMM- and PDBNN-based speaker models are superior to the EBFN ones in terms of performance and generalization capability. This work also finds that PDBNNs and GMMs are more robust than EBFNs in verifying speakers in noise environments.

1 Introduction

Speaker verification aims to verify the validity of a claimed identity through voice. Text-dependent approaches, such as dynamic time warping (DTW) and hidden Markov models (HMMs) [1], explore the static and temporal characteristics of speakers. On the other hand, text-independent approaches, such as vector quantization (VQ) [2] and Gaussian mixture models (GMM) [3], assume independence among feature vectors and make use of distortion measures or probabilistic estimates. Most of these approaches, however, use data from the target speakers only to train the speaker models. As a result, discriminative information from anti-speakers will not be embedded in the speaker models.

Discriminative information can be utilized during model training and evaluation. For the former, supervised learning algorithms are used to discriminate

* This work was supported by The Hong Kong Polytechnic University, Grant No. G-W076. S. Y. Kung is on sabbatical from Princeton University. He is currently with The Hong Kong Polytechnic University.

Y.-C. Chen, L.-W. Chang, and C.-T. Hsu (Eds.): PCM 2002, LNCS 2532, pp. 623–630, 2002.

within-class data from out-of-class data. For the latter, likelihood ratio [4] or scoring normalization [5] are applied during evaluation.

Neural networks are one of the approaches that allow discriminative information to be embedded in the speaker models. For example, the elliptical basis function networks proposed in [6] include the cluster centers of anti-speakers' speech in their hidden layer. It was shown that EBFNs perform better than radial basis function networks (RBFNs) and VQ. The neural tree networks (NTNs) are another type of networks that use discriminative training, and research has shown that NTNs are superior to VQ in speaker recognition tasks [7].

One of the main challenges in speaker recognition is to recognize speakers in adverse conditions. Noise is commonly considered as additive components to the speech signals. Speaker models trained by using clean speech signals are usually subject to performance degradation in noisy environments. The present study compares the speaker verification performance of three kernel-based speaker models under clean and noisy environments. They are Gaussian Mixture Models (GMMs), Elliptical Basis Function Networks (EBFNs) and Probabilistic Decision-Based Neural Networks (PDBNNs) [8]. The comparison aims to demonstrate the effect of supervised learning on the speaker models (least squares learning on EBFNs and reinforced learning on PDBNNs). For example, by comparing GMMs against PDBNNs, the importance of reinforced learning can be highlighted.

Three problem sets have been used in this study. These include a large-scale speaker verification experiment, speaker classification based on 2-D speech features and speaker verification using noisy variants of the YOHO corpus.

2   Speech Corpus and Pre-processing

The YOHO corpus [9] was collected by ITT Defense Communication Division. The corpus features "combination lock" phrases, 138 speakers (108 male, 30 female), inter-session variability, and high-quality telephone speech (3.8kHz/clean). These features make YOHO ideal for speaker verification research. In this work, Gaussian white noise with different noise power was added to the clean YOHO corpus. Both the clean and noisy YOHO corpora were used in the experimental evaluations.

LP-derived cepstral coefficients were used as acoustic features. For each utterance, the silent regions were removed, and the remaining signals were pre-emphasized. Twelfth-order LP-derived cepstral coefficients were then computed using a 28 ms Hamming window at a frame rate of 14 ms.

3   Enrollment Procedures

Each registered speaker was assigned a personalized network (GMM, EBFN or PDBNN) modeling the characteristics of his/her own voice. Each network was trained to recognize the speech derived from two classes—speaker class and anti-speaker class. To this end, two groups of kernel functions (one group representing the speaker himself/herself while the other representing the speakers in the anti-speaker class) were assigned to each network. We denote the group corresponding to the speaker class as the speaker kernels and the one corresponding to the anti-speaker class as the anti-speaker kernels. For each registered speaker, a unique anti-speaker set containing 16 anti-speakers was created. This set was used to create the anti-speaker kernels. The anti-speaker kernels enable us to integrate scoring normalization [10] into the networks, which enhances the networks' capability in discriminating the true speakers from the impostors.

4   Verification Procedures

Verification was performed using each speaker in the YOHO corpus as a claimant, with 64 impostors being randomly selected from the remaining speakers (excluding the anti-speakers and the claimant) and rotating through all the speakers. For each claimant, the feature vectors of the claimant's utterances from his/her 10 verification sessions in YOHO were concatenated to form a claimant sequence. Likewise, the feature vectors of the impostor's utterances were concatenated to form an impostor sequence.

The feature vectors from the claimant's speech $\mathcal{T}^c = \{\boldsymbol{x}_1, \boldsymbol{x}_2, \ldots, \boldsymbol{x}_{T_c}\}$ was divided into a number of overlapping segments containing $T(< T_c)$ consecutive vectors. For the t-th segment ($\mathcal{T}_t \subset \mathcal{T}^c$), the average normalized log-likelihood

$$z_t = \frac{1}{T} \sum_{\boldsymbol{x} \in \mathcal{T}_t} \{\phi_S(\boldsymbol{x}) - \phi_A(\boldsymbol{x})\} \tag{1}$$

of the PDBNN and GMM speaker models was computed, where $\phi_S(\boldsymbol{x})$ and $\phi_A(\boldsymbol{x})$ represents the log-likelihood function of the speaker and anti-speaker respectively [8]. Verification decisions were based on the criterion:

$$\text{If } z_t \begin{cases} > \zeta & \text{accept the claimant} \\ \leq \zeta & \text{reject the claimant} \end{cases} \tag{2}$$

where ζ is a speaker-dependent decision threshold (see Section 5 below for the procedure of determining ζ). A verification decision was made for each segment, with the error rate (either FAR or FRR) being the proportion of incorrect verification decisions to the total number of decisions. In this work, T in Eqn. (1) was set to 500 (i.e., 7 seconds of speech), and each segment was separated by five consecutive vectors.

For the EBFN-based speaker models, verification decisions were based on the difference between the scaled network outputs [6]. Again, computing the difference between the two outputs is equivalent to normalizing the score in GMMs. Thus, we integrate scoring normalization into the network architecture.

5   Threshold Determination

The procedures for determining the decision thresholds of PDBNNs, GMMs and EBFNs are different. For GMM and EBFN speaker models, the utterances from all enrollment sessions of 16 randomly selected anti-speakers were used for threshold determination [11]. Specifically, these utterances were concatenated and the procedure described in Section 4 was applied. The threshold ζ was adjusted until the FAR fell below a pre-defined level. In this work, we set this level to 0.5%.

To adopt PDBNNs to speaker verification, three modifications on the PDBNN's training algorithm have been made. First, we modified the likelihood computation such that only one threshold per speaker is required. Specifically, instead of comparing the network's loglikelihood against its corresponding threshold as in the original PDBNNs, we compared a normalized score against a single decision threshold as in Eqns. (1) and (2).

In the second modification, we changed the frequency at which the threshold is updated. As our speaker verification procedure is based on a segmental mode (see Section 4), we modified the globally supervised training to work on a segmental mode as follows. Let $\mathcal{T}_n$ be the n-th segment extracted from speaker's speech patterns $\mathcal{X}_S$ or from anti-speakers' speech patterns $\mathcal{X}_A$, the normalized segmental score is computed by evaluating

$$S(\mathcal{T}_n) = S_S(\mathcal{T}_n) - S_A(\mathcal{T}_n) = \frac{1}{T} \sum_{x \in \mathcal{T}_n} \{\phi_S(x) - \phi_A(x)\}.$$

For each segment, a verification decision was made according to the criterion:

$$\text{If } S(\mathcal{T}_n) \begin{cases} > \zeta^{(j)}_{n-1} & \text{accept the claimant} \\ \leq \zeta^{(j)}_{n-1} & \text{reject the claimant} \end{cases} \tag{3}$$

where $\zeta^{(j)}_{n-1}$ is the decision threshold of the PDBNN speaker model after learning from segment $\mathcal{T}_{n-1}$ at epoch j. We adjusted $\zeta^{(j)}_{n-1}$ whenever misclassification occurs. Specifically, we updated $\zeta^{(j)}_{n-1}$ according to

$$\zeta^{(j)}_n = \begin{cases} \zeta^{(j)}_{n-1} - \eta_r l'(\zeta^{(j)}_{n-1} - S(\mathcal{T}_n)) & \text{if } \mathcal{T}_n \in \mathcal{X}_S \quad \text{and} \quad S(\mathcal{T}_n) < \zeta^{(j)}_{n-1} \\ \zeta^{(j)}_{n-1} + \eta_a l'(S(\mathcal{T}_n) - \zeta^{(j)}_{n-1}) & \text{if } \mathcal{T}_n \in \mathcal{X}_A \quad \text{and} \quad S(\mathcal{T}_n) \geq \zeta^{(j)}_{n-1} \end{cases} \tag{4}$$

where η_r and η_a are respectively the reinforced and anti-reinforced learning parameters (more on next paragraph), $l(d) = \frac{1}{1+e^{-d}}$ is a penalty function, and $l'(d)$ is the derivative of $l(\cdot)$.

In the third modification, we introduced a new method to compute the learning rates. Specifically, the reinforced (anti-reinforced) learning rate η_a (η_r), is proportional to the rate of false rejections (acceptance) weighted by the total number of impostor (speaker) segments:

$$\eta_r = \frac{FRR^{(j-1)}}{FAR^{(j-1)} + FRR^{(j-1)}} \frac{N_{\text{imp}}}{N_{\text{imp}} + N_{\text{spk}}} \eta$$

$$\eta_a = \frac{FAR^{(j-1)}}{FAR^{(j-1)} + FRR^{(j-1)}} \frac{N_{\text{spk}}}{N_{\text{imp}} + N_{\text{spk}}} \eta$$

where $FRR^{(j-1)}$ and $FAR^{(j-1)}$ represent respectively the error rate of false rejections and false acceptances at epoch $j-1$, N_{imp} and N_{spk} represent respectively the total number of training segments from impostors and the registered speaker, and η is a positive learning parameter. This modification aims at increasing the convergence speed of the decision threshold.

6 Pilot Experiments

The architecture of GMMs, EBFNs and PDBNNs depends on several free parameters, including the number of speaker kernels, the number of anti-speaker kernels, and the number of anti-speakers for creating a speaker model. To determine these parameters, a series of pilot experiments involving 30 speakers from the YOHO corpus were performed. Equal error rates (EERs) were used as the performance indicators.

Table 1. Average equal error rates based on 30 GMMs with different numbers of (a) speaker kernels (where the number of anti-speakers and the number of anti-speaker kernels were set to 16 and 160 respectively), (b) anti-speakers (where the number of speaker kernels and anti-speaker kernels were set to 40 and 160 respectively) and (c) anti-speaker kernels (where the number of speaker kernels and anti-speakers were set to 40 and 16 respectively).

No. of speaker's kernels	EER (%)
10	2.78
20	1.51
40	0.77
80	0.57
160	0.48

(a)

No. of antispeakers	EER (%)
4	2.02
8	1.30
16	0.77
32	0.48
64	0.81

(b)

No. of anti-speaker kernels	EER (%)
40	0.83
80	0.83
160	0.77
320	0.75
640	0.79

(c)

Based on the results in Table 1, we used 40 speaker kernels, 160 anti-speaker kernels, and 16 anti-speakers for creating a speaker model in the rest of the experiments. Note that we have selected a sub-optimal number of anti-speakers in order to reduce the computation time in creating the speaker models. As the EBFNs, GMMs and PDBNNs use the same set of kernels, it is not necessary to repeat the above experiments for EBFNs and PDBNNs.

7 Large-Scale Experiments

Table 2 summarizes the average FAR, FRR, and EER obtained by the PDBNN-, GMM- and EBFN-based speaker models. All figures and results were based on the average of 138 speakers in the YOHO corpus. The results, in particular the EER, demonstrate the superiority of the GMMs and PDBNNs over the EBFNs. The EER of GMMs and PDBNNs are the same since their kernel parameters are identical.

Table 2. Average error rates achieved by the GMMs, EBFNs and PDBNNs based on 138 speakers in the YOHO corpus. The pre-defined FAR for GMMs and EBFNs was set to 0.5%.

Speaker Model	FAR (%)	FRR (%)	EER (%)
GMMs	8.01	0.08	0.33
EBFs	15.24	0.50	0.48
PDBNNs	1.10	1.87	0.33

Table 3. Performance of the PDBNN, GMM and EBFN in the 2-D speaker classification problem.

	PDBNN/GMM		EBFN	
	Train	Test	Train	Test
EER(%)	4.12	24.61	6.86	27.17

In terms of FAR and FRR, Table 2 demonstrates the superiority of the threshold determination procedure of PDBNNs. In particular, Table 2 clearly shows that the globally supervised learning of PDBNNs can make the average FAR very small during verification, whereas the ad hoc approach used by the EBFNs and GMMs is not able to do so. Recall from our previous discussion that the pre-defined FAR was set to 0.5%; however, the average FAR of EBFNs and GMMs are very different from this value.

To illustrate the difference among the PDBNN-, GMM- and EBFN-based speaker models, we extracted the first and second cepstral coefficients of speaker 162 and those of his anti-speakers and impostors to create a set of two-dimensional (2-D) speech data. A PDBNN, a GMM and an EBFN (all with 2 inputs and 6 centers) were trained to classify the patterns into two classes—similar to the enrollment procedure in the speaker verification experiments. Therefore, except for the reduction in feature dimension, the training methods, learning rate and verification methods are identical to the speaker verification experiments described previously.

Table 3 compares the performance of three speaker models, and Figure 1 shows the test data, decision boundaries, function centers, and contours of basis function outputs formed by these models. The decision boundaries are based on the equal error thresholds obtained from the corresponding data set. It is evident from Figure 1(a) that the decision boundaries formed by the EBFN enclose two regions, which belong to the speaker class, with a large amount of test data; whereas, the complement region, which belongs to the impostor class, extends to infinity. On the other hands, the decision boundaries created by the GMM and PDBNN extend to infinity in the feature space for both speaker class and impostor class. Both the decision boundaries (Fig. 1) and the EERs (Table 3) suggest that the GMM and PDBNN provide better generalization than the EBFN. These results also agree with what we have found in Table 2. The poor

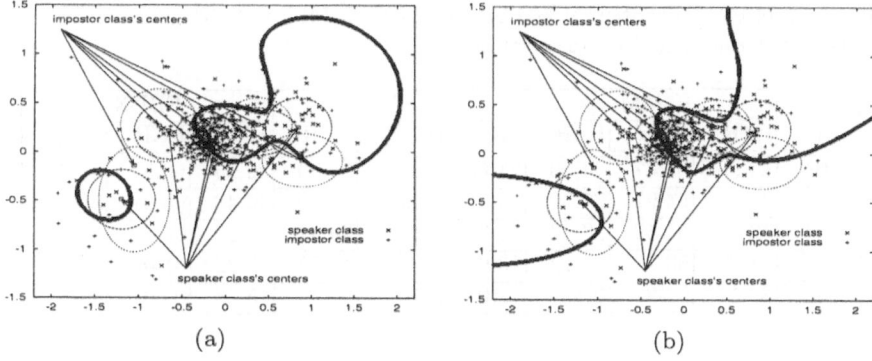

Fig. 1. Speaker classification based on 2-D speech features. The figures plot the decision boundaries, function centres and contours of constant basis function outputs (thin ellipses) produced by (a) EBFNs and (b) GMMs and PDBNNs. Markers 'x' and '+' represent respectively the speaker's data and impostor's data.

performance in EBFNs may be caused by the least squares approach to finding the output weights. As the EBFNs formulate the classification problem as a function interpolation problem (mapping from the feature space to 0.0 or 1.0), overfitting will easily occur if there are too many hidden nodes but too few training samples.

To test the robustness of different speaker models against noise, zero-mean Gaussian noise was added to the YOHO speech so that the resulting corrupted speech has an SNR of 10dB, 6dB, 3dB and 0dB. Tables 4 summarize the average FAR, FRR, and EER obtained by the GMM-, PDBNN- and EBFN-based speaker models under different SNRs. The results show that the error rates of all models increase as the noise power increases. Such performance degradation is mainly caused by the mismatches in training and testing environments.

Evidently, the EERs of PDBNNs and GMMs are smaller than those of EBFNs under different SNRs. Although PDBNNs and GMMs provide better generalization, the performance of PDBNNs and GMMs are still unacceptable at low SNR. In addition to additive noise, telephone speech may also be distorted by the handsets and the telephone channel. We are currently investigating compensation techniques [12] that aim to recover speech signals distorted by both additive and convolutive noise.

8   Conclusions

This paper addresses the problem of building a speaker verification system using kernel-based probabilistic neural networks. The modeling capability and robustness of these pattern classifiers are compared. Experimental results, based on 138 speakers and visualization of decision boundaries indicated that GMM- and PDBNN-based speaker models outperform the EBFN ones. Results also show that our modifications on the PDBNN's supervised learning not only makes

Table 4. Average error rates (in %) obtained by the GMM, PDBNN and EBFN speaker models at different signal-to-noise ratios.

SNR	GMM			PDBNN			EBFN		
	FAR	FRR	EER	FAR	FRR	EER	FAR	FRR	EER
0 dB	43.98	55.47	34.00	21.63	76.34	34.00	30.95	66.57	37.51
3 dB	43.52	54.91	27.30	19.52	77.53	27.30	30.48	65.91	30.32
6 dB	42.51	53.59	20.32	17.03	77.53	20.32	29.97	65.16	22.45
10 dB	41.20	50.70	12.79	13.67	76.38	12.79	29.22	61.06	14.58
clean	8.01	0.08	0.33	1.10	1.87	0.33	15.24	0.50	0.48

PDBNNs amenable to speaker verification tasks but also makes their performance more predictable. This work also finds that PDBNNs and GMMs are more robust than EBFNs in recognizing speakers in noisy environments.

References

1. C. Che and Q. Lin. Speaker recognition using HMM with experiments on the YOHO database. In *Eurospeech*, pages 625–628, 1995.
2. F. K. Soong, A. E. Rosenberg, L. R. Rabiner, and B. H. Juang. A vector quantization approach to speaker recognition. In *Proc. ICASSP 85*, pages 387–390, 1985.
3. D. A. Reynolds and R. C. Rose. Robust text-independent speaker identification using Gaussian mixture speaker models. *IEEE Trans. on Speech and Audio Processing*, 3(1):72–83, 1995.
4. A. Higgins, L. Bahler, and J. Porter. Speaker verification using randomized phrase prompting. *Digital Signal Processing*, 1:89–106, 1991.
5. A. E. Rosenberg, J. Delong, C. H. Lee, B. H. Juang, and F. K. Soong. The use of cohort normalized scores for speaker verification. In *Proc. ICSLP'92*, pages 599–602, 1992.
6. M.W. Mak and S.Y. Kung. Estimation of elliptical basis function parameters by the EM algorithms with application to speaker verification. *IEEE Trans. on Neural Networks*, 11(4):961–969, 2000.
7. K. Farrell, S. Kosonocky, and R. Mammone. Neural tree network/vector quantization probability estimators for speaker recognition. In *Proc. Workshop on Neural Networks for Signal Processing*, pages 279–288, 1994.
8. S. H. Lin, S. Y. Kung, and L. J. Lin. Face recognition/detection by probabilistic decision-based neural network. *IEEE Trans. on Neural Networks, Special Issue on Biometric Identification*, 8(1):114–132, 1997.
9. Jr. J. P. Campbell. Testing with the YOHO CD-ROM voice verification corpus. In *ICASSP'95*, pages 341–344, 1995.
10. C. S. Liu, H. C. Wang, and C. H. Lee. Speaker verification using normalized log-likelihood score. *IEEE Trans on Speech and Audio Processing*, 4(1):56–60, 1996.
11. W. D. Zhang, M. W. Mak, and M. X. He. A two-stage scoring method combining world and cohort model for speaker verification. In *Proc. ICASSP'2000*, June 2000.
12. M. W. Mak and S. Y. Kung. Combining stochastic feautre transformation and handset identification for telephone-based speaker verification. In *Proc. ICASSP'2002*, 2002.

An On-the-Fly Mandarin Singing Voice Synthesis System

Cheng-Yuan Lin[1], J.-S. Roger Jang[1], and Shaw-Hwa Hwang[2]

[1] Dept. of Computer Science, National Tsing Hua University, Taiwan
{gavins,jang}@cs.nthu.edu.tw
[2] Dept. of Electrical Engineering, National Taipei University, Taiwan
kk5911@seed.net.tw

Abstract. An on-the-fly Mandarin singing voice synthesis system, called SINVOIS (singing voice synthesis), is proposed in this paper. The SINVOIS system can receive the continuous speech of the lyrics of a song, and generate the singing voice immediately based on the music score information (embedded in a MIDI file) of the song. Two sub-systems are designed and embedded into the system. One is the synthesis unit generator and the other is the pitch-shifting module. In the first one, the Viterbi decoding algorithm is employed on a continuous speech to generate the synthesis unit for singing voice. And the PSOLA method is employed to implement the pitch-shifting function in the second one. Moreover, the energy, duration, and spectrum modifications on the synthesis unit are also implemented in the second part. The synthesized singing voice sounds reasonably good. From the subjective listening test, the MOS (mean opinion score) of 3.1 are obtained for synthesized singing voices.

1 Introduction

Text-to-speech (TTS) systems have been developed in the past few decades and the most recent TTS systems can produce human-like natural sounding speech. The success of TTS systems can be attributed to their wide applications as well as the advances in modern computers. On the other hand, the research and developments of singing voice synthesis are not as mature as speech synthesis, partly due to its limited application domains. However, as computer-based games and entertainments are becoming popular, interesting applications of singing voice synthesis are emerging, including software for vocal training and synthesized singing voices for virtual singers, and so on.

In a conventional concatenation-based Chinese TTS system, the synthesis unit is taken from a set of pre-recorded 411 syllabic clips, representing the distinct base syllables in Mandarin Chinese. A concatenation-based singing voice synthesis system works in a similar way, except that we need to synthesize the singing voice based on a given music score and lyrics of a song.

Y.-C. Chen, L.-W. Chang, and C.-T. Hsu (Eds.): PCM 2002, LNCS 2532, pp. 631-638, 2002.

This work was supported in MOE Program for Promoting Academic Excellent of Universites under the grant number 89-E-FA04-1-4.

The lyrics are converted into syllables and the corresponding syllable clips are selected for concatenation. Then the system performs pitch/time modification and adds other desirable effects such as vibrato and echoes to make the synthesized singing voice more naturally sounding.

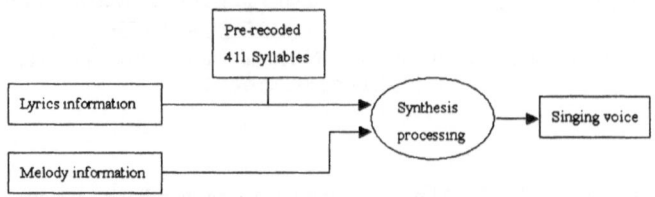

Fig. 1. The figure demonstrates flow chart of conventional singing voice synthesis system

However, such conventional singing voice synthesis systems cannot be used to produce personalized singing unless one has to record the 411 base Mandarin syllables in advance, which is a time-consuming process. Therefore, we propose the use of speech recognition technology as a front end of our SINVOIS system. In other words, to create a personalized singing voice, the user needs to read the lyrics, sentence by sentence, to our system. Our system then employs forced alignment via Viterbi decoding to detect the boundary of each character, as well as its consonant and vowel parts. Once these parts are identified, we can use them as synthesis units to synthesize a singing voice of the song, retaining all the timbre and co-articulate effects of the user.

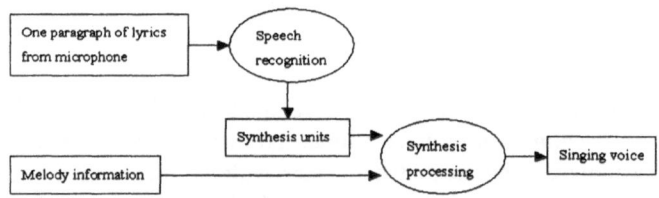

Fig. 2. The figure demonstrates flow chart of SINVOIS system.

2   Related Work

Due to limited computing power, most previous approaches to singing voice synthesis employ acoustic models to implement the human voice production. These include:

1.   The SPASM system by Perry Cook [4]
2.   The CHANT system by Bennett et al. [1]
3.   Frequency modulation method by Chowning [3]

However, performance of the above methods is not acceptable since the acoustic models cannot produce natural sounding human voices. Recently, the success of concatenation based text-to-speech systems motivates the use of concatenation for singing voice synthesis. For example, the LYRICOS system by Macon et al. [8][9] is a typical example of concatenation-based singing voice synthesis system. The SMALLTALK system by OKI company [6] in Japan is another example that adopts PSOLA [5] method to synthesize singing voices. Even though these systems can produce satisfactory performance, they cannot produce personalized singing voices on the fly for a specific user.

3   Generation of Synthesis Unit

The conventional method of synthesis unit generation for speech synthesis derives from a database of 411 syllables that was recorded previously by a specific person who possesses clear tone. Once the recordings of 411 base syllables are available, we need to process the speech data according to the following steps:

1. End-point detection [13] based on energies and zero crossing rates are employed to identify the exact position of the speech recordings.
2. Search the pitch marks of each syllable, which are positions at the time axis indicating the beginning of a pitch period.
3. The consonant part and the vowel part of each syllable are also labeled manually.

For best performance, the above three steps are usually carried out manually, which is a rather time-consuming process. In our SINVOIS system, we need to synthesize the singing voice on the fly; hence all three steps are performed automatically. Moreover, we also need to identify each syllable boundary via Viterbi decoding.

3.1   Syllable Detection

For a given recording of a lyric sentence, each syllable is detected by force alignment via Viterbi decoding [11][12]. The process can be divided into the following two steps:

1. Each character in the lyric sentence must be labeled with a base syllable. This task is not as trivial as it seems since we need to take care of some of the character-to-syllable mappings that are one-to-many. A maximum matching method is used in conjunction with a dictionary of about 90,000 terms to determine the best character-to-syllable mapping.
2. The syllable sequence from a lyric sentence is then converted into bi-phone models for constructing a single-sentence of a linear lexicon. Viterbi decoding [11][12] is then employed to align the frames of the speech recording to the bi-phone models in the one-sentence linear lexicon, such that a best state sequence of the maximal probability is found. The obtained optimal state sequence indicates the best alignment of each frame to a state in the lexicon. Therefore we can cor-

rectly identify the position of each syllable, including its consonant and vowel parts.

Of course, before the use of Viterbi decoding, we need to have an acoustic model in advance. The acoustic model used here contains 521 bi-phone models, which are obtained from a speech corpus of 70 subjects to achieve speaker independency. The complete acoustic model ensures the precision in syllable detection.

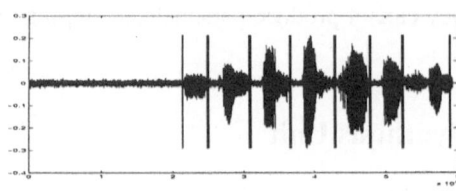

Fig. 3. The figure demonstrates a typical result of syllable detection.

3.2 Identification of Pitch Mark

Pitch marks are the positions where complete pitch periods start. We need to identify pitch marks for effective time/pitch modification. The steps involved in pitch mark identification are listed next:

1. Use ACF (autocorrelation function) or AMDF (average magnitude difference function) to compute the average pitch period T_0 of a given syllable recording.

2. Find the global maximum of the syllable waveform and label its time coordinate as t_m; this is the position of the first pitch mark.

3. Search other pitch marks to the right of t_m by finding the maximum in the region $[t_m + 0.9 * T_0, t_m + 1.1 * T_0]$. Repeat the same procedure until all pitch marks to the right of the global maximum are found.

4. Search the pitch marks to the left of t_m and the region should be $[t_m - 1.1 * T_0, t_m - 0.9 * T_0]$ instead. Repeat the same procedure until all pitch marks to the left of the global maximum are found.

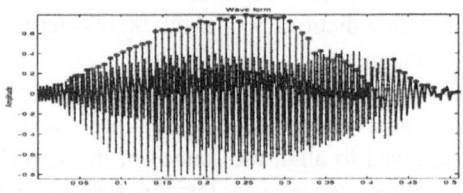

Fig. 4. The figure shows the waveform after pitch marks (denoted as circles) are found.

Once pitch marks are found, we can perform necessary pitch/time modification according to the music score of the song, and add other desirable effects for singing voices. These procedures are introduced in next section.

4 Pitch Shifting Module

In this section we will introduce the essential operations of SINVOIS that include pitch/time scale modification and energy normalization. Afterward we further to do fine tuning such as echo effect, pitch vibrato, co-articulation effect to make the singing voice more natural.

4.1 Pitch Shifting

Pitch shifting of speech/audio signals is an essential part in speech and music synthesis. There are several well-known approaches to pitch shifting:

1. PSOLA (Pitch Synchronous Overlap and Add) [5]
2. Cross-Fading [2]
3. Sinusoidal Modeling [10]

In our system, we adopt the PSOLA method to achieve a balance between quality and efficiency. The basic concept behind PSOLA is to multiply a hamming window centered at each pitch mark of the speech signal. If we want to shift up pitch, the distance between neighboring pitch marks will be decreased. On the contrary, if we want to shift down pitch, the distance between neighboring pitch marks should be increased. We might want to insert some zeros between two windowed signals if a pitch-down operation with less than 50% of the original pitch frequency is desired.

4.2 Time Modification

Time modification is used to increase or decrease the duration of a synthesis unit. We use a simple linear mapping method for time modification in our system. The method can duplicate or delete fundamental periods, as shown in the following diagram:

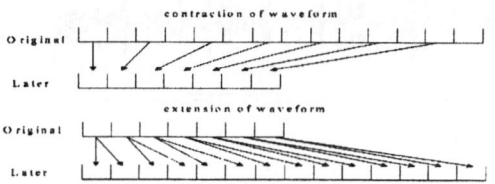

Fig. 5. The figure shows contraction and extension of waveform.

4.3 Energy Modification

The concatenated singing voice occasionally results in unnatural sound since each synthesis unit has diverse level of energy (intensity or volume). Therefore, we can simply adjust the amplitude in each syllable such that the energy is equal to the average energy of the whole sentence. The energy normalization procedure is described as follows:

1. Compute the energy of each syllable in the recorded lyric sentence, $E_1, E_2, \ldots\ldots E_N$, where N is the number of syllables.

2. Compute the average energy $E_{ave} = \dfrac{1}{N}\sum_{k=1}^{N} E_k$.

3. Multiply the waveform of the k -th syllable by a constant $\left(\sqrt{10}\right)^{E_{ave}/E_k} = 3.16^{E_{ave}/E_k}$.

4.4 Other Desirable Effects

Results of the above synthesis procedure constantly contain some undesirable artificial-sounding buzzy effects. As a result, we adopt the following formula to implement the echo effect:

$$y[n] = x[n] + ay[n-k]$$

Or in its z-transform:

$$H(z) = \frac{Y(z)}{X(z)} = \frac{1}{1 - az^{-k}}$$

The value of k controls the amount of delay and it can be adjust accordingly. The echo effect can make the whole synthesize singing voice more genuine and softer. Besides the echo effect, the inclusion of vibrato effect [8] is an important factor to make the synthesized singing voice more natural. Vibrato effect can be implemented according to the sinusoidal function. For instance, if we want to alter the pitch curve of a syllable to a sinusoidal function in the range [a b] (for instance, [0.8, 1.2]), we can simply do so by rescaling and shifting the basic sinusoid $\sin(\omega t): \dfrac{\sin(\omega t) * (b-a)}{2} + \dfrac{a+b}{2}$, where ω is the vibration angular frequency and t is the frame index.

The following two figures demonstrate the synthesized singing voice. The first plot is without vibrato effect; the second plot shows that pitch curve with vibrato.

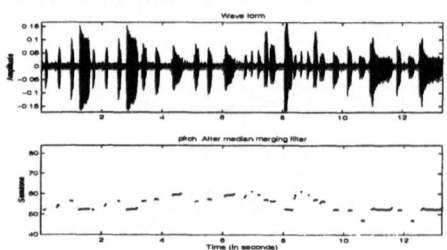

Fig. 6. The upper part of figure shows time-domain waveform and lower part of figure shows the corresponding pitch curve without vibrato.

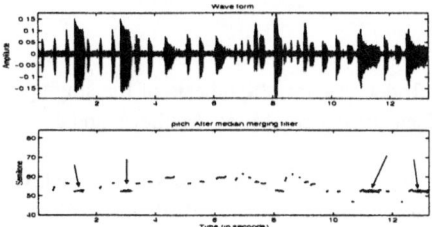

Fig. 7. The upper part of figure shows time-domain waveform and lower part of figure shows the corresponding pitch curve with vibrato.(the direction of an arrow)

5 Results and Analysis

The performance of our SINVOIS system depends on three factors: the outcome of force alignment via Viterbi decoding, the result of pitch/time modification, and the special effects of singing voice. We have 15 persons try 15 different Mandarin Chinese pop songs and obtain a 95% recognition rate on syllable detection. We adopt a test of MOS (mean opinion score) [7] to obtain subjective assessments of our system. In the test, we have ten persons to listen to the fifteen synthesized singing voice and each person has to give a score for each song. The score ranges from 1 t o 5, with 5 representing the best grade for naturalness. The following table shows the MOS score.

Table 1. The average score of MOS test for 15 different songs.

Song	1	2	3	4	5	6	7	8	9	10	11	12	13	14	15
MOS	3.0	3.1	3.5	2.4	3.8	2.6	2.9	3.0	3.7	2.9	3.4	2.8	3.3	2.6	3.5

From the above table, it is obvious that the synthesized singing voices are acceptable, but definitely not satisfactory enough to be described as natural sounding. The major reason is that the synthesis units are obtained from recordings of "speech" instead of "singing".

6 Conclusions and Future Work

In the paper, we have described the development of a singing voce synthesis system called SINVOIS (singing voice synthesis). The system can accept a user's speech input of the lyric sentences, and generate a synthesized singing voice based on the input recording and the song's music score. The operation of the system is divided into two parts: one is the synthesis unit generator via Viterbi decoding, and the other is time/pitch modification and special effects. To assess the performance of SINVOIS, we designed an experiment with MOS for subjective evaluation. The experiment results are acceptable. However, the fun part of the system also comes from the personal recording, which can be used for on-the-fly synthesis that can retain personal features.

References

[1]   Bennett, Gerald, and Rodet, Xavier, "Synthesis of the singing voice," in Current Directions in Computer Music Research (M. V. Mathews and J. R. Pierce, eds.), pp. 19-44, MIT Press, 1989.

[2]   Chen, S.G. and Lin, G.J., "High Quality and Low Complexity Pitch Modification of Acoustic Signals," Proceedings of the 1995 IEEE International Conference on Acoustic, Speech, and Signal Processing, May, Detroit, USA, 1995, p2987-2990.

[3]   Chowning, John M., "Frequency Modulation Synthesis of the Singing Voice," in Current Directions in Computer Music Research (Max. V. Mathews and John. R. Pierce, eds.), pp. 57-63, MIT Press, 1989.

[4]   Cook, P.R., "SPASM, a real time vocal track physical model controller and singer, the companion software synthesis system, "Computer Music Journal, vol. 17, pp.30-43, spring 1993.

[5]   F. Charpentier and Moulines, "Pitch-synchronous Waveform Processing Technique for Text-to-Speech Synthesis Using Diphones," European Conf. On Speech Communication and Technology, pp.13-19, Paris, 1989.

[6]   http://www.oki.com/jp/Cng/Softnew/English/sm.htm

[7]   ITU-T, Methods for Subjective Determination of Transmission Quality, 1996, Int. Telecommunication Unit.

[8]   Macon, Michael W. and Jensen-Link, Leslie and Oliverio, James and Clements, Mark A. and George, E. Bryan, "A Singing voice synthesis system based on sinusoidal modeling," Proc. of International Conference on Acoustics, Speech, and Signal Processing, Vol. 1, pp. 435-438, 1997.

[9]   Macon, Michael W., and Jensen-Link, Leslie and Oliverio, James and Clements, Mark A. and George, E. Bryan, "Concatenation-based MIDI-to-Singing Voice Synthesis," 103rd Meeting of the Audio Engineering Society, New York, 1997.

[10]   Macon, Michael W., M. W. Macon, "Speech Synthesis Based on Sinusoidal Modeling," PhD thesis, Georgia Institute of Technology, October 1996.

[11]   Ney, F., and Aubert, X., "Dynamic programming search: from digit strings to large vocabulary word graphs," in C. H. Lee, F Soong, and K. Paliwal, eds., Automatic Speech and Speaker Recognition, Kluwer, Norwell, Mass., 1996.

[12]   Rabiner, L., and Juang, B-H., Fundamentals of Speech Recognition, Prentice-Hall, Englewood Cliffs, N.J., pp. 339-340, 1993.

[13]   Yiying Zhang, Xiaoyan Zhu, Yu Hao, Yupin Luo, "A robust and fast endpoint detection algorithm for isolated word recognition", IEEE International Conference on Volume: 2 , 1997 , Page(s): 1819 -1822 vol.2

Popular Song Retrieval Based on Singing Matching

Yazhong Feng, Yueting Zhuang, and Yunhe Pan

Department of Computer Science, Zhejiang University, Hangzhou, China
fengyz_zju@263.net, yzhuang@cs.zju.edu.cn,
panyh@sun.zju.edu.cn

Abstract. An approach to retrieval popular song by singing matching is presented in this paper. Vocal singing is the dominant part in popular song, after extracting singing from monaural or stereo recording of popular song by independent components analysis, MFCC feature is calculated on it, self-similarity sequence is constructed on this feature, recurrent neural network is employed to remember the self-similarity sequence, self-similarity sequence is also constructed on input singing, the weights of recurrent neural network are used as indices on music database, retrieval list is generated by correlation degree of self-similarity sequence. Preliminary experiment result shows the effectiveness of our approach.

1   Introduction

Content-based music information retrieval (MIR) is attracting more and more attentions in recent years. Since the first QBH (Query by humming) system is introduced [1], researchers have developed several techniques to retrieval music by its content [2][3][4][5]. Most of these techniques deal with music in MIDI, and melody contour is the popular music representation scheme in the published literatures, string matching is borrowed to evaluate the similarity of the input melody contour (converted from humming or singing) with that stored in music database, some researchers employ melody and rhythm information simultaneously in their MIR system.

We concentrate our research on popular song retrieval, which will defiantly find applications in future. Our approach differs from other existing ones on that we retrieval songs by matching input singing directly with singing extracted from popular songs. The key techniques we use are singing extraction and self-similarity sequence based on MFCC.

2   Related Work

Extracting singing from raw audio is a key technique in our song retrieval system. There are many contributions to singing extraction, some refer themselves to prior knowledge about music, e.g. [6] presents a method for separation of singer and piano sounds using musical score knowledge, [7] introduces a technique for coding the

Y.-C. Chen, L.-W. Chang, and C.-T. Hsu (Eds.): PCM 2002, LNCS 2532, pp. 639–646, 2002.
© Springer-Verlag Berlin Heidelberg 2002

singing voice using Linear Predictive Coding and prior knowledge of the musical score to aid in the process of encoding; some work on singing locating not singing separating, e.g. [8] locates the portions of musical track during which the vocals are present, it design a singing detector based on Hidden Markov Model to classify speech-like sounds in music. Our approach of singing extraction is to some extent an application of independent component analysis (ICA) [9] on raw audio source separation. Some works were also reported about the application of ICA to audio sources separation, [10] extents ICA and propose a method of independent subspace analysis (ISA) for separating individual audio source from single-channel mixture.

3   Our Approach

In MIR literatures, query by singing is by no means a new approach, usually acoustic input is pitch-tracked, segmented into notes and converted into three or five level melody contour, melody contour is also extracted from all the music in database, music retrieval is equivalent to melody matching. Most of MIR systems deal with monophonic music for the reason that it is extremely difficult to extract melody from polyphonic music. Our approach does not try to segment notes at all, nor do we extract melody from music, we employ statistic model, say ICA, to extract singing directly from popular song, input singing and extracted singing are all converted to self-similarity sequence, which is a curve in two-dimension space, music retrieval is equivalent to comparison of curves, the feature we use to calculate self-similarity sequence is MFCC.

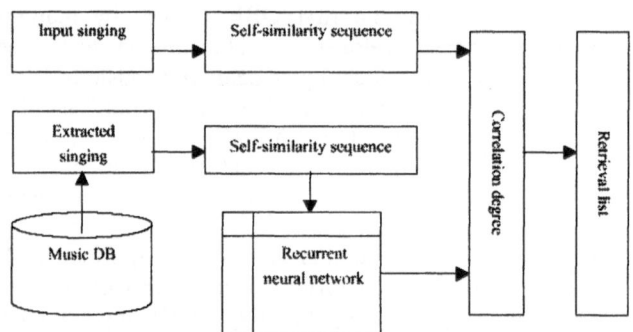

Fig. 1. Diagram of our song retrieval system.

The reason why we employ ICA to extract singing from raw audio recordings is that, at first, its proper application gives successful separation of source signals without their explicit knowledge, so no false assumption about the song's structure will decrease the reliability of singing extraction; the second, when singing is regarded as a signal source, ICA can extract it as an individual from the ensemble, not a collection of segments. Our experiment music database is composed of raw audio popular song, indices on it are the weights of recurrent neural network, similarity of query singing with song in database is represented by their correlation degree [5].

4   Singing Extraction from Raw Audio

ICA is a statistical and computational technique for revealing hidden factors that underlie sets of random variables, measurements, or signals. It can be seen as an extension to principal component analysis and factor analysis. It is capable of finding the underlying factors or sources when these classic methods fail completely.

Though ICA is widely used in music/speech discrimination [11], speaker identification and speech recognition [12], few work is reported on singing extraction to my knowledge, the application of ICA to singing extraction is straightforward and the result is so good that it is worthy of doing more research on this direction.

4.1   Independent Component Analysis

Assume that N linear mixtures $x_1, x_2, \ldots, x_N$ of M independent components are observed,

$$x_j = a_{j1}s_1 + a_{j2}s_2 + \ldots + a_{jM}s_M, \, j = 1, 2, \ldots, N, \tag{1}$$

in ICA model, assume that each mixture x_j as well as each independent component s_k is a random variable instead of a time signal. Without loss of generality, assume that both the mixture variables and the independent components have zero mean. Use vector-matrix notation for $\mathbf{x} = [x_1, x_2, \ldots, x_N]^T$ and $\mathbf{s} = [s_1, s_2, \ldots, s_M]^T$, so that (Eq. 1) can be rewritten as,

$$\mathbf{x} = \mathbf{As}, \tag{2}$$

where $\mathbf{A}$ is a full rank $N \times M$ scalar matrix. If the multivariate probability density function (pdf) of $\mathbf{s}$ can be written as the product of the marginal independent distributions, that is

$$p(\mathbf{s}) = \prod_{i=1}^{M} p_i(s_i), \tag{3}$$

and the components of $\mathbf{s}$ are such that at most one source is normally distributed, then it is possible to extract the sources from the mixtures. The goal of ICA is to find a linear transformation $\mathbf{W}$ of the dependent sensor signals $\mathbf{x}$ that makes the outputs as independent as possible.

4.2 Extracting Singing from Stereo Popular Song

The number of independent components is assumed to be equal to that of observed variables in classic ICA ($M = N$), FastICA [13] can be employed to perform ICA. The application of FastICA is straightforward in our approach.

Let $\mathbf{x} = (x_1, x_2)^T$ be stereo music, $\mathbf{s} = (s_1, s_2)^T$ be audio resource, x_1, x_2 is right and left channel recording of music respectively, s_1, s_2 is singing and accompaniment respectively. To define the singing extraction problem, (Eq.2) is rewritten as

$$\mathbf{s} = \mathbf{W}\mathbf{x}, \tag{4}$$

where $\mathbf{W} = \mathbf{A}^{-1}$, $\mathbf{W} = (w_1, w_2)^T$ is basis filter matrix of $\mathbf{x}$, FastICA learning rule finds a direction, i.e. a unit vector $\mathbf{w}$ such that the projection $\mathbf{w}^T\mathbf{x}$ maximizes nongaussianity. After $\mathbf{W}$ is determined, singing (here, s_1 or s_2, ICA can not tell us which one is singing) is extracted. Experiments show that FastICA performs very well in extracting singing from popular song except that drum blurs the singing in some cases.

4.3 Extracting Singing from Monaural Popular Song

Several algorithms [10][14][15] deal with source separation from single recording by ICA, we extends [14] to extract singing from monaural popular song recording, for single channel recording $\mathbf{Y}$, we assume that

$$\mathbf{Y} = \mathbf{Y}_1 + \mathbf{Y}_2 \tag{5}$$

$$\mathbf{Y}_i = \lambda_i \mathbf{x}_i \tag{6}$$

where $\mathbf{Y}_i = \{y_i(t) | t \in [1, T]\}$. In [14], it is forced that

$$\lambda_1 + \lambda_2 = 1, \tag{7}$$

we use an exponential power density for resource $\mathbf{s}$, which is zero mean [16], e.g.

$$p(\mathbf{s}) \propto \exp(-|\mathbf{s}|^q), \tag{8}$$

at every time point $t \in [1, T - N + 1]$, a segment $y_1(t)$ of contiguous N samples is extracted from $\mathbf{Y}_i$, we infer the independent source to be $s_1(t) = \frac{1}{\lambda_1}\mathbf{W}_1 y_1(t)$, The final learning rule is:

$$\Delta y_1(t) \propto \sum_{n=1}^{N} [\lambda_2 \varphi(s_{1t_n})^T w_{1n} - \lambda_1 \varphi(s_{2t_n})^T w_{2n}], \tag{9}$$

where $\varphi(s) \propto -|s|^{q-1} sign(s)$, w_{in} is the nth column vector of $\mathbf{W}_i$. Because $y = y_1 + y_2$, we have $\Delta y_2(t) = -\Delta y_1(t)$. λ_i should be simultaneously adjusted with $y_i(t)$, according to [14], we have

$$\lambda_1^* = \frac{\sqrt{|\psi_1|}}{\sqrt{|\psi_1|} + \sqrt{\psi_2}}, \lambda_2^* = \frac{\sqrt{\psi_2}}{\sqrt{|\psi_1|} + \sqrt{\psi_2}},$$

(10)

where $\psi = \sum_{t=1}^{T_N} \sum_{k=1}^{N} \varphi(s_{tk}) w_k y_t$ .When $\Delta y_i(t)$ converges to zero, the adaptation process is complete, thus independent sources are extracted.

5 Self-Similarity Sequence

Music is generally self-similar; when singing, lay people tends to singing in his own way or introduce some errors such as, tempo variation, insertion or deletion of notes, but they also tend to keep the same kind of error in one epoch of singing, that is, input acoustic singing is self-similar. These evidences support our using of self-similarity sequence to represent input singing and song in music database in our song retrieval system. To form a self-similarity sequence from an audio segment, we extract its MFCC feature and calculate the self-similarity matrix on these MFCCs, self-similarity sequence is then derived from the self-similarity matrix, Figure 2. is the procedure.

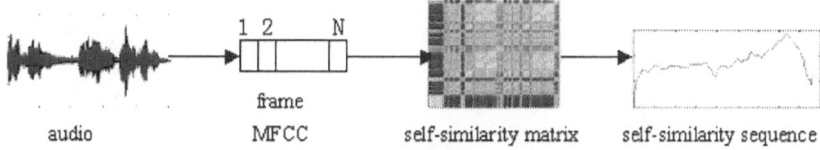

frame

audio   MFCC   self-similarity matrix   self-similarity sequence

Fig. 2. The procedure for driving self-similarity sequence.

5.1 Mel-Frequency Cepstral Coefficients (MFCC)

MFCC has been used to model music or audio, [17] builds a retrieval system based on a cepstral representation of sounds, a music summarization system based on cepstral features is presented in [18], [19] reveals that the use of Mel scale for modeling music is at least not harmful in speech/music discrimination.

5.2 Self-Similarity of Music

[20] represents acoustic similarity between any two instants of an audio recording in a 2D representation, which is called similarity matrix, we borrow this idea to form the self-similarity sequence in our approach, define

$$s(i, j) = \frac{v_i \bullet v_j}{\|v_i\|\|v_j\|},$$
(11)

as the element of self-similarity matrix S of an audio segment, where v_i is the feature vector of ith frame, $i, j \in [1, N]$, there are N frames in this segment.

5.3 Self-Similarity Sequence

We employ MFCC of an audio segment as the feature and define the self-similarity sequence of this segment of audio as

$$ss(i) = \frac{\sum_{j=i}^{N} diag(S, j-1)}{N+1-i}, i \in [1, N],$$
(12)

for every time point i, $ss(i)$ is the mean diagonal sum in self-similarity matrix S.

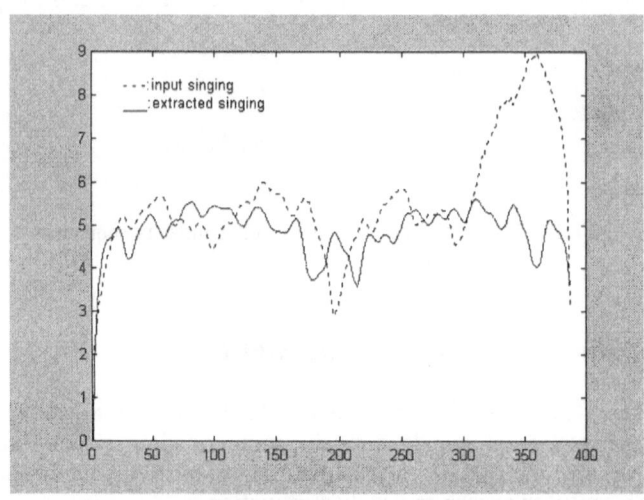

Fig. 3. The solid curve is the self-similarity sequence of extracted singing from 15s segment in song "Happy Birthday to You"; the dashed curve is the self-similarity sequence of male singing of the same song.

Self-similarity sequence is a fault-tolerant representation of music because of its not using the exact acoustic input or music information but retain their latent structures. In our system, self-similarity sequence is used to represent song in our music database, input singing is also converted to self-similarity sequence. Figure 3. shows two self-similarity sequences of the same song, their shapes are similar except some time-delay points.

6   Indexing on Music Database

After singing is extracted from a song in database and being converted into self-similarity sequence, recurrent neural network (RNN) [21] is employed to remember this sequence, for each piece of music, we train a corresponding RNN. We do not know in previous which part of a piece of song users will singing, so the system must be robust enough for users to singing any part of the song. Recurrent neural network is of strong ability in time series prediction [21], the RNN in our system has four layers: input layer, output layer, hidden layer and context layer, and the node size is 1, 1, 10, 10 respectively, the weights between different layers store what information the network remembers. The weights of RNN act as indices on music database, it is obvious that index size $index$ is linear to the size of music database.

$$index = |W_1| \times |W_2| \times |W_3| \times |W_4| \times size(music - database) \qquad (13)$$

where $W_i, i = 1,2,3,4$ are the weights of RNN. When feeding self-similarity sequence of input singing to RNNs, we obtain a corresponding sequence from output layer, calculate the correlation degree [5] of the input and output, the bigger the correlation degree is, the more similar the input is with the song represented by this RNN.

7   Experiment Result

We test our approach on a database of 120 pieces of popular song; its performance is listed in Table 1.

Table 1. System Performance

Resolution	Successful Rate
Top1	79%
Top3	86%

The database is rather small, but is enough to test our idea. The inaccuracy may result from bad singing extraction because of too many drum sound and improperly selected features used to calculate self-similarity sequence.

Our preliminary work reveals that ICA is a promising technique for separating singing from songs, but further research should be done to improve its performance. Performance evaluation of singing extraction by ICA is a non-trivial problem, but it is beyond the scope of this paper.

Self-similarity is an interesting character of music, if there are features more appropriate for self-similarity sequence is still open for future discussions.

References

1. Ghias, A., J. Logan, D. Chamberlain, and B. Smith: Query by humming-musical information retrieval in an audio database. ACM Multimedia, San Francisco (1995).
2. McNab, R., L. Smith, I. Witten, C. Henderson, and S. Cunningham: Towards the digital music library: Tune retrieval from acoustic input. Dig. Lib.(1996).
3. Downie, J.S.: Music retrieval as text retrieval: Simple yet effective. Proc. of SIGIR(1999)297-298.
4. Kosugi, N., et al.: A practical query-by-humming system for a large music database. Proc. of ACM Multimedia, Los Angeles, CA(2000).
5. Feng, Y.Z., Y.T. Zhuang, and Y.H. Pan: Query similar music by correlation degree. Proc. of IEEE PCM(2001)885-890.
6. Meron, Y. and K. Hirose: Separation of singing and piano sounds. Proc. of 5th int. conf. on spoken language proc., Sydney, Vol. 3. (1998)1059-1062.
7. Kim, Y.E.: Structured encoding of the singing voice using prior knowledge of the musical score. Proc. Of IEEE Workshop on App. of Sig. Proc. to Audio and Acou., New Paltz, New York(1999).
8. Berenzweig, A.L. and D.P.W. Ellis: Locating singing voice segments within music signals. IEEE Workshop on Apps. Of Sig. Proc. to Acous. and Audio, Mohonk NY(2001).
9. Hyvärinen, A. and E. Oja: Independent component analysis: algorithms and applications. Neural Networks,13(4-5)(2000)411-430.
10. Casey, M.A. and A.Westner: Separation of mixed audio sources by independent subspace analysis. Proc. of ICMC, (2000)154-161.
11. Williams, G. and D. Ellis: Speech/music discrimination based on posterior probability features. Proc. Eurospeech99, Budapest(1999).
12. Lee,J-H. Jung, H-J. Lee, T-W. and Lee, S-Y: Speech coding and noise reduction using ICA-based speech features. Proc. of Int. Workshop on Independent Component Analysis, Helsinki (2000)417-422.
13. Hyvärinen, A.: Fast and robust fixed-point algorithms for independent component analysis. IEEE Tran. on Neural Networks 10(3)(1999)626-634.
14. Jang, G.J., T.W. Lee, Y.H. Oh: Blind Separation of Single Channel Mixture Using ICA Basis Functions. 3rd Int. Conf. on Independent Component Analysis and Blind Signal Separation. San Diego, California, USA. (2001)595-600.
15. Roweis, S.: One Microphone Source Separation. Neu. Inf. Proc. Sys. 13 (2000)793-799.
16. Lewicki, M.S.: A Flexible prior for independent component analysis. Neural Computation (2000).
17. Foote, J.T.: Content-Based Retrieval of Music and Audio. Multimedia Storage and Archiving Systems II, Proc. of SPIE, Vol. 3229(1997)138-147.
18. Logan, B.T. and S. Chu: Music Summarization Using Key Phrases. Proc. of IEEE Int. Conf. on Acoustic, Speech, and Signal Processing, (2000).
19. Logan, B.T.: Mel Frequency Cepstral Coefficients for Music Modeling. Proc. of Int. Syp. on Music Inf. Ret. (2000).
20. Foote, J.: Visualizing Music and Audio using Self-Similarity. Proc. of ACM on Multimedia, (1999).
21. Elman, L.J.: Finding Structure in Time. Cognitive Science, 14(1990)179-211.

Improving Audio Watermark Robustness Using Stretched Patterns against Geometric Distortion

Ryuki Tachibana

Tokyo Research Laboratory, IBM Japan,
1623-14, Shimotsuruma, Yamato-shi, Kanagawa-ken 242-8502, Japan
ryuki@jp.ibm.com
http://www.trl.ibm.com/projects/RightsManagement/datahiding/index_e.htm

Abstract. One of the problems for audio watermarks is robustness against signal processing causing de-synchronization of the pseudo-random sequences. To tackle the problem, we previously introduced an audio watermarking method using a two-dimensional pseudo-random array, which is robust against pitch shifting and random stretching to some extent. In this paper, we explain a modification to the detection algorithm to improve the robustness against excessive distortion. The method uses multiple pseudo-random arrays each of which is stretched assuming a certain amount of distortion. Since most of the detection process for the multiple arrays is shared, the additional computational cost is limited.

1 Introduction

Robustness of image watermarks against geometric distortion has been gathering increasing attention recently [1,2]. When the image is rotated, translated, or scaled, the mis-synchronization of the embedded pseudo-random sequence (PRS) and the PRS which the detection algorithm uses prevents the detector from properly correlating the PRSs, and leads to serious damage on watermark detection.

Similarly, there is a class of audio signal processing which effects on audio watermark as geometric distortion effects on image watermark. Audio processing such as pitch shifting, random stretching, and wow-and-flutter changes the time and frequency property of the embedded PRS, and is hence difficult for watermark to survive. To tackle this problem, several audio watermarking techniques modifying magnitudes in the frequency domain were proposed in the past two years [3,4,5]. We introduced an audio watermarking method that is robust against pitch shifting and random stretching up to ±4% without any exhaustive search for the scale change in [6]. However, it was still difficult for the method to survive excessive geometric distortions. [7,8] solved the problem by performing multiple correlation tests. One possible problem with the multiple correlation tests is that that may increase the false alarm rate.

In this paper, we modify the detection algorithm of [6] and improve the robustness against excessive geometric distortions. While multiple correlations are

Y.-C. Chen, L.-W. Chang, and C.-T. Hsu (Eds.): PCM 2002, LNCS 2532, pp. 647–654, 2002.

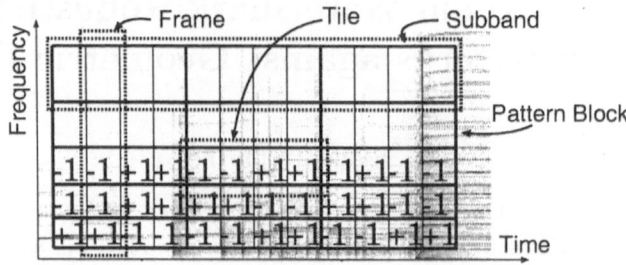

Fig. 1. A pattern block consists of tiles, which are segmented areas in the time-frequency plane of the content. The embedding algorithm modifies magnitudes in the tiles according to pseudo-random numbers assigned to the tiles. The numbers in the figure are examples of the pseudo-random values. Although a DFT frame overlaps with the next frame, that is not expressed in the figure

calculated also in the paper, the proposed algorithm chooses one correlation by the strength of a synchronization signal. Because the strength of the synchronization signal and that of the message signal are independent, the false alarm rate is preserved. Furthermore, because the same synchronization signal, which was necessary for the original detection algorithm to search the head of the message, is used for the scale selection, this method does not decrease the data payload.

2   The Previous Method

In this section, we summarize the method introduced by [6].

The method can embed a multiple-bit message in the content by dividing it to short messages and embedding each of them in *a pattern block*. The patter block is defined as a two-dimensional segmented area in the time-frequency plane of the content (Fig. 1), which is constructed from the sequence of power spectrums calculated using short-term DFTs. A pattern block is further divided into *tiles*. We call tiles in row a *subband*. A tile consists of four consecutive overlapping DFT frames. A pseudo-random number is selected corresponding to each tile. If the pseudo-random value assigned to a tile is positive, the embedding algorithm increases the magnitudes of frequency bins of the first two frames in the tile and decreases those of the last two frames.

The detection algorithm calculates the magnitudes for all tiles of the content and correlates them with the pseudo-random array by applying the following steps.

1. Windowing DFT
   The magnitude $a_{t,f}$ of the f-th frequency in the t-th frame of a pattern block of the content is calculated by the DFT analysis of a frame of the content. A frame overlaps the adjacent frames by a half window.
2. Normalization
   The magnitudes are then normalized by the average of the magnitudes in the frame. A normalized magnitude is

$$\widehat{a}_{t,f} = \frac{a_{t,f}}{\frac{1}{N_{PCM}/2} \sum_{f=1}^{N_{PCM}/2} a_{t,f}} . \tag{1}$$

The difference between the logarithmic magnitudes of a frame and the next non-overlapping frame is taken as $P_{t,f} = \log \widehat{a}_{t,f} - \log \widehat{a}_{t,f+2}$.

3. Magnitudes of tiles

The magnitude of a tile located at the b-th subband of the t-th frame in the block is calculated by

$$Q_{t,b} = \frac{\sum_{f=f_b^L}^{f_b^H} P_{t,f}}{f_b^H - f_b^L + 1} , \tag{2}$$

where f_b^H and f_b^L are the highest and lowest frequencies in the b-th subband, respectively.

4. Watermark strength

The detected watermark strength for the j-th bit in the tile is calculated as the cross-correlation of the pseudo-random numbers and the normalized magnitudes of the tiles by

$$X_j = \frac{\sum_{k=1}^{D_B} \omega_{j,k}^B (Q_{t,b} - \overline{Q})}{\sqrt{\sum_{k=1}^{D_B} \{\omega_{j,k}^B (Q_{t,b} - \overline{Q})\}^2}} , \tag{3}$$

where $\overline{Q} = \frac{1}{D_B} \sum_{k=1}^{D_B} Q_{t,b}$, D_B is the number of tiles assigned for a bit, and $\omega_{j,k}^B$ is the k-th pseudo-random number of the j-th bit corresponding to the tile at the b-th subband in the t-th frame. Similarly, the synchronization strength is calculated by

$$S = \frac{\sum_{k=1}^{D_S} \omega_k^S (Q_{t,b} - \overline{Q})}{\sqrt{\sum_{k=1}^{D_S} \{\omega_k^S (Q_{t,b} - \overline{Q})\}^2}} . \tag{4}$$

Because this detection algorithm calculate the difference of magnitudes of a frame and the next non-overlapping frame per tile, the pattern block regarding detection can be illustrated as Fig. 2.

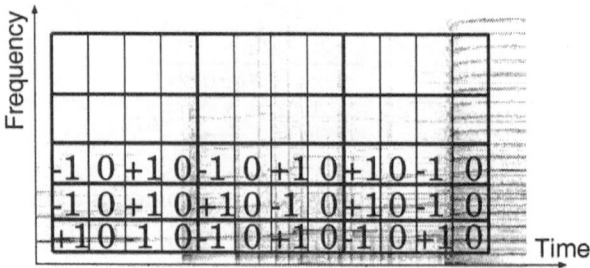

Fig. 2. A detection pattern block. The detection algorithm uses, for calculating correlation, the difference of magnitudes of a frame and the *next non-overlapping* frame. In other words, the frames *overlapping* with the above-mentioned frames are not used for the correlation. Hence, we can consider the pattern block used by the detection algorithm as illustrated in this figure.

3   Improving Robustness

In this section, we explain a method to improve the robustness of the audio watermarking method against pitch shifting and random stretching. In the experiment, we used a software system that can embed and detect a 64-bit message in 30-second pieces of music. Its details and parameters that are not explained below are same as explained in [6]. All the following graphs are experimental results using ten 100-second music samples. The watermark strength data plotted in the figures or shown in the table are measured after the accumulation of doubly-encoded watermarks. *Pitch shifting* is performed using linear interpolation without anti-alias filtering. *Random stretching*[1] is a transformation that changes the length of the total content to a different length by omitting or inserting a random number of sample blocks from 50 up to 500 samples per block.

When the content is distorted by pitch shifting or random stretching, the time and frequency location of the embedded tiles are displaced. Accordingly, our idea for improving robustness is to detect watermark using multiple patterns each of which is stretched in advance assuming a certain amount of distortion. As for random stretching, because it changes the length of the content, watermark is expected to be detectable using a pattern that is also stretched with respect to time(Fig. 3). The watermark strength using the pattern that is stretched at the rate of r_t is calculated by

$$X_j = \frac{\displaystyle\sum_{k=1}^{D_B} \omega_{j,k}^B (Q_{\lfloor r_t t + 0.5 \rfloor, b} - \overline{Q})}{\sqrt{\displaystyle\sum_{k=1}^{D_B} \{\omega_{j,k}^B (Q_{\lfloor r_t t + 0.5 \rfloor, b} - \overline{Q})\}^2}}. \tag{5}$$

---

[1] *Random sample cropping* can be considered as random stretching with the target length smaller than 100%.

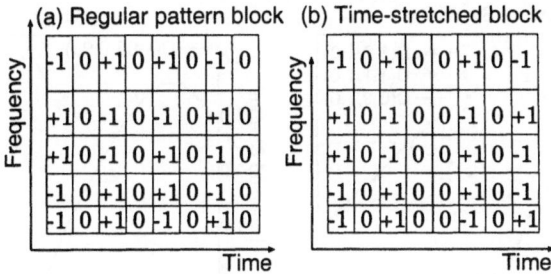

Fig. 3. Pattern block stretched with respect to time

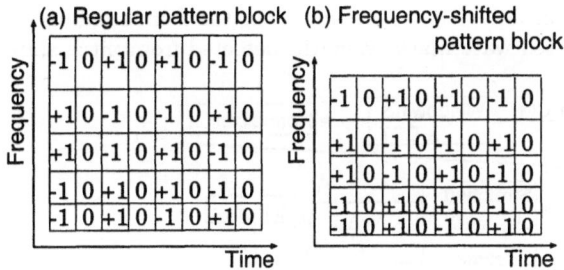

Fig. 4. Pattern block stretched with respect to frequency

To detect watermark from a sample whose pitch is shifted at the rate of r_f, we correspondingly shift the subbands (Fig. 4) as $f_b^{L'} = r_f f_b^L$ and $f_b^{H'} = r_f f_b^H$. Moreover, since linear pitch shifting changes the duration of the block as well as its frequency, we also stretch the pattern using Eq. 5.

In this way, we define a *stretched detector*, $D(r_t, r_f)$, which matches best to a time expansion rate, r_t, and a frequency shifting rate, r_f. Figure 5(a) and Figure 5(b) show mean watermark strengths detected by $D(0.90, 1.00)$, $D(0.935, 1.07)$, $D(1.00, 1.00)$, $D(1.075, 0.93)$, and $D(1.10, 1.00)$ from distorted content. While the strength detected by the regular detector, $D(1.00, 1.00)$, decreases as the content is severely distorted, the stretched detectors have their maximum strengths approximately at their assumed distortion rates.

These experiments indicate that if several stretched detectors detect watermark in the music sample using differently stretched patterns in parallel, and an appropriate stretched detector is selected, we can detect watermark even from an excessively distorted music sample by some of the stretched detectors. In this way, the detection flow becomes as shown in Fig. 6. The selection of a stretched detector is done approximately every 30 seconds based on the *accumulated synchronization strength*,

$$A^{(i)} = \frac{1}{\sqrt{N_S}} \sum_{n=1}^{N_S} S_n^{(i)}, \tag{6}$$

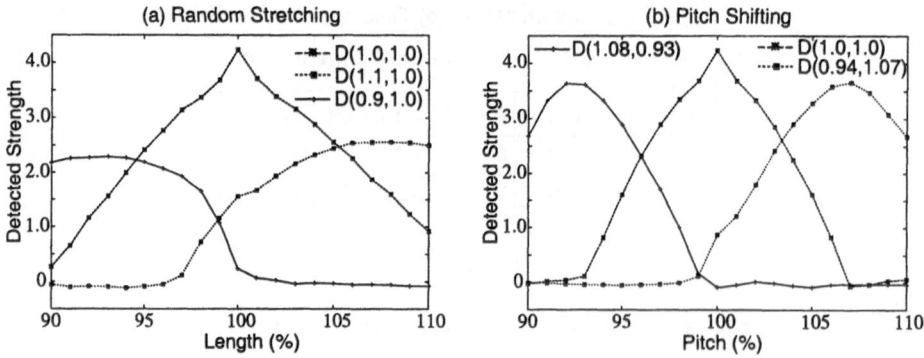

Fig. 5. (a) Mean of detected watermark strengths from randomly stretched samples. (b) Mean of detected watermark strengths detected from pitch-shifted samples

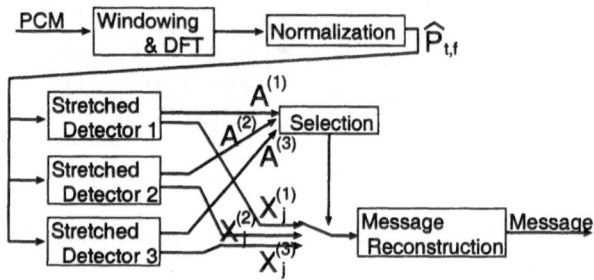

Fig. 6. Detection flow with three stretched detectors

where i is the index of stretched detectors, n is the index of synchronization signals detected in the 30-second period, and N_S is the number of synchronization signals detected in the period. After the stretched detector that gives the maximum $A^{(i)}$ is selected, the watermark strengths detected from the stretched detector are used for the message reconstruction.

The mean of $A^{(i)}$ detected from five stretched detectors are shown in Fig. 7(a) and Fig. 7(b). It can be seen in Fig. 7(b) that, for example, $D(1.08, 0.93)$ is selected for the pitch-shifting rate ranging from 90% up to 96%.

Consequently, the mean strengths by the selected stretched detectors become as shown in Fig. 8(a) and Fig. 8(b), and are enough high for every degree of tested distortion. Corresponding bit error rates are also shown in the figures.

Table 1 shows (1) the means of the detected strengths, (2) the bit error rates (BER) which are plotted in Fig.8(a) and Fig.8(b), and (3) the correct detection rates (CDR) at which correct 64-bit message was detected. CDR over 80% were seen for every one of the tested degradation. The error correction and detection algorithm and the counting of weak bits successfully avoided detection of an incorrect message.

Performance. We also measured the detection speed using a PC with 600 MHz Pentium III running Windows NT. While, when the detector uses only a

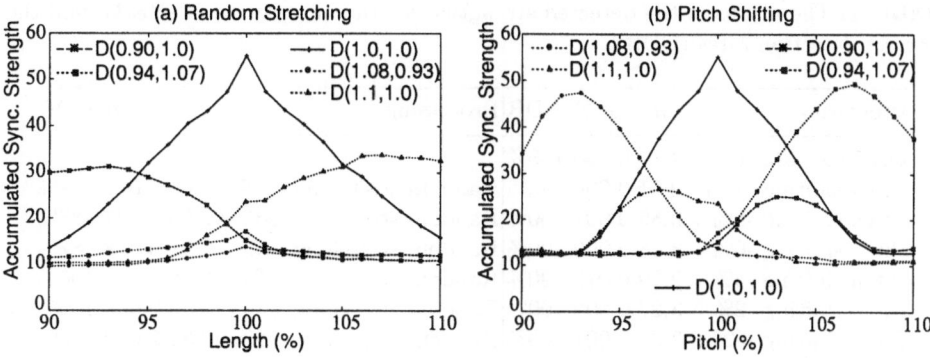

Fig. 7. (a) Mean of accumulated sync. strengths detected from randomly stretched music samples. (b) Mean of accumulated sync. strengths detected from pitch-shifted music samples

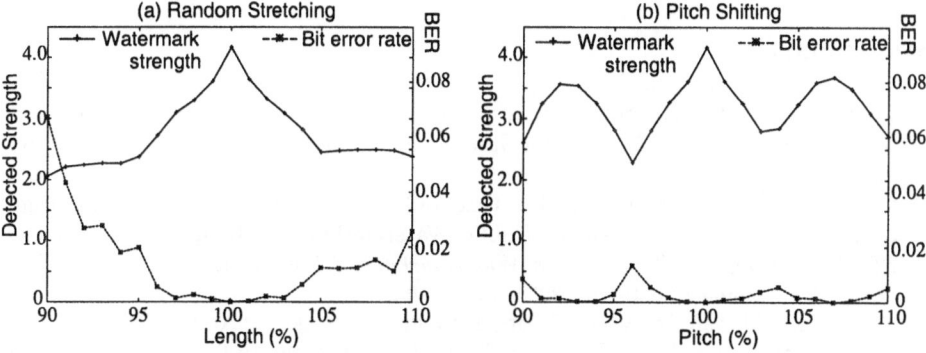

Fig. 8. (a) Mean of detected strengths and bit error rate(BER) for randomly stretched samples. (b) Mean of detected strengths and BER for pitch-shifted samples

regular detector, detection takes 7.72% of the length of the content, when the detector uses five stretched detectors, it is performed within 8.96% of the length of the content. That is only 16% increase for four more stretched detectors. This is because the Fourier transform and calculation of the normalized magnitudes take most of the processing time, and the stretched detectors can share this part of calculation. Therefore, using stretched detectors in a detector is much faster than simply using multiple detectors.

4   Summary

We improved robustness of our previous audio watermarking method by using multiple stretched pattern blocks. With the improvement, robustness against pitch shifting and random stretching up to ±10% was achieved with only 16% additional computational time. Further improvement is required to shorten the duration of content required to carry a message.

Table 1. The means of the detected strengths (μ), the bit error rates (BER), and the correct detection rates (CDR)

Processing	μ	BER	CDR	Processing	μ	BER	CDR
Original watermark	4.17	0.000	100%				
Pitch shifting -10%	2.61	0.008	96%	Random stretching -10%	2.06	0.067	83%
Pitch shifting -8%	3.56	0.001	100%	Random stretching -8%	2.25	0.027	87%
Pitch shifting -6%	3.25	0.000	100%	Random stretching -6%	2.27	0.018	87%
Pitch shifting -4%	2.29	0.013	90%	Random stretching -4%	2.72	0.005	100%
Pitch shifting -2%	3.27	0.002	100%	Random stretching -2%	3.30	0.003	100%
Pitch shifting +2%	3.25	0.001	100%	Random stretching +2%	3.32	0.002	100%
Pitch shifting +4%	2.85	0.005	100%	Random stretching +4%	2.82	0.006	100%
Pitch shifting +6%	3.59	0.001	100%	Random stretching +6%	2.48	0.012	93%
Pitch shifting +8%	3.49	0.001	100%	Random stretching +8%	2.49	0.015	93%
Pitch shifting +10%	2.71	0.005	100%	Random stretching +10%	2.38	0.026	87%

References

[1] M. Kutter, "Watermarking resisting to translation, rotation, and scaling," in *Proc. of SPIE Int. Conf. on Multimedia Systems and Applications*, 1998, vol. 3528, pp. 423–431.

[2] C-Y. Lin, M. Wu, J.A. Bloom, I.J. Cox, M.L. Miller, and Y-M. Lui, "Rotation, Scale, and Translation Resilient Public Watermarking for Images," in *Proc. of SPIE Int. Conf. on Security and Watermarking of Multimedia Contents II*, San Jose, USA, January 2000, vol. 3971, pp. 90–98.

[3] J. Haitsma, M. van der Veen, F. Bruekers, and T. Kalker, "Audio Watermarking for Monitoring and Copy Protection," in *Proc. of ACM Multimedia*, Marina del Rey, USA, November 2000, pp. 119–122.

[4] C-P. Wu, P-C. Su, and C-C. J. Kuo, "Robust and efficient digital audio watermarking using audio content analysis," in *SPIE Int. Conf. on Security and Watermarking of Multimedia Contents II*, San Jose, USA, January 2000, vol. 3971, pp. 382–392.

[5] D. Kirovski and H. Malvar, "Robust spread-spectrum audio watermarking," in *IEEE International Conference on Acoustics, Speech, and Signal Processing*, Salt Lake City, Utah, USA, May 2001, pp. 1345–1348.

[6] R. Tachibana, S. Shimizu, T. Nakamura, and S. Kobayashi, "An audio watermarking method robust against time- and frequency-fluctuation," in *SPIE Conf. on Security and Watermarking of Multimedia Contents III*, San Jose, USA, January 2001, vol. 4314, pp. 104–115.

[7] D. Kirovski and H. Malvar, "Spread-spectrum audio watermarking:requirements, applications, and limitations," in *IEEE Forth Workshop on Multimedia Signal Processing*, Cannes, France, October 2001, pp. 219–224.

[8] D. Kirovski and H. Malvar, "Robust covert communication over a public audio channel using spread spectrum," in *4th Int. Workshop on Information Hiding*, Pittsburgh, USA, April 2001, vol. LNCS 2137, pp. 354–368.

A Digital Audio Watermarking Using Two Masking Effects

Yong Hun Kim, Hwan Il Kang, Kab Il Kim, and Seung-Soo Han

NPT Center
Myongji University
Division of Electrical and Information Control Engineering
San 38-2, Namdong, Yongin, Kyunggido 449-728, South Korea
Kikki2u@kebi.com, {hwan,kkl,shan}@mju.ac.kr

Abstract. In this paper, a new digital audio watermarking algorithm is presented. The proposed algorithm embeds watermark by eliminating some frequency information of audio signal based on human auditory system (HAS). This algorithm is a blind audio watermarking method, which does not require any prior information during watermark extraction process. In this paper, two masking effects are used for audio watermarking, frequency-domain masking effect and time-domain masking effect. This algorithm finds watermarking position using time-domain masking effect and embeds/detects the watermark using frequency-domain masking effect. Detection of embedded watermark is obtained by finding the eliminated frequency using band-pass filter. By using the two masking effects, the degradation of the audio quality can be minimized. It is confirmed that the proposed algorithm has robustness against various attacks such as cropping, down sampling, time stretch, MPEG1-layer3, and MPEG2-AAC compression with good audio quality.

1   Introduction

With the rapid spread of computer networks and the further progress of multimedia technologies, security and legal issues of copyright protection have become important. Digital watermark is one promising technique for effectively protecting the copyright of digital contents. The important properties of the digital watermarking are the less degradation of the watermarked data, the robustness of the watermark against modification of the contents, resistance to intentional removal of or tampering with the watermark, and the reliability of extracted watermark data. In case of audio watermark, standard work is in progress by SDMI (secure digital music initiative). A digital audio watermarking technique is a challenging job because of the difficulties within noble characteristics of digital audio signal. Compared to video signal, audio signal can be represented as small number of samples per time. It represents that there is no enough room for watermark information, compared to video signal. Another problem in audio watermarking is that the HAS (Human Auditory System) is more sensitive than the HVS (Human Visual System). This makes audio watermarking very difficult. Many researchers have developed audio watermarking methods. In echo hiding, the echo signal is inserted into the original audio signal [1]. Some algorithms

Y.-C. Chen, L.-W. Chang, and C.-T. Hsu (Eds.): PCM 2002, LNCS 2532, pp. 655-662, 2002.
© Springer-Verlag Berlin Heidelberg 2002

use the patchwork method [2]-[3], and spread spectrum is one of the most general audio watermarking method [4]-[5]. Spread spectrum technique is designed to encode a stream of information by spreading the encoded data across as much of the frequency spectrum as possible. This allows the signal survival excellent, even if there are interferences on some frequencies. But it has a fatal weakness in asynchronous attack. A solution to overcome such a problem is one of the most difficult matters in audio watermarking method. In the algorithm proposed in this paper, the degradation of sound quality can be minimized using some characteristics of HAS and the synchronization can be obtained by utilizing zero-crossing rate (ZCR) and energy of audio signal. This algorithm also uses conventional all-pass filter followed by modulation, which was proposed by Ciloglu et. al. [6]. This algorithm also reduces computation complexity, achieves high speed by both limiting position of insertion and filtering. The robustness of this algorithm was tested by applying several attacks such as quantization, time stretch, cropping, MPEG1 layer3, MPEG2 AAC compression. And the comparison between this algorithm and spread spectrum algorithm is performed in robustness test against asynchronous attack.

2 Proposed New Audio Watermarking Method

The algorithm proposed in this paper uses HAS and psychoacoustics model [7]. This algorithm embeds watermark into audio signal by using two masking effects. The watermark embedding area was selected by using time domain pre-masking effect. When extracting the embedded watermark, the first process is synchronization, which means finding the watermarked area by searching pre-masking area. This is the most difficult part in audio watermark detection. After the area was found, the watermark is embedded by removing some frequencies.

2.1 Background

2.1.1 Psychoacoustic Model

Proposed method is to seek and remove some frequencies, which exist in original audio signal but not sensible to human ears, using HAS characteristic and masking effect. To find these frequencies, absolute threshold of hearing, critical band analysis, simultaneous-temporal masking effects are utilized. Frequency characteristic of human auditory system is an essential factor of MPEG audio encoder.

Absolute threshold of hearing.
Absolute threshold of hearing represents minimum limitation to perceive sound in noiseless environment [8]. It can be approximated by following non-linear function [9].

$$T_q(f) = 3.64(f/1000)^{-0.8} - 6.5e^{-0.6(f/1000-3.3)} \tag{1}$$
$$+ 10^{-3}(f/1000)^4$$

The frequency range of 2~5kHz is more sensitive than other frequency range. This range includes a lot of audio data than the others. If the watermark is embedded in this frequency range, the embedded watermark causes the degradation of audio quality.

Masking effect
Masking effect is related to the limitation of certain sound according to the noise and distortion. Audio masking is the effect by which a faint but audible sound becomes inaudible in the presence of another louder audible sound. Masking effect is consisted of temporal masking in time domain and simultaneous masking in frequency domain. In simultaneous masking, a critical band is defined as a frequency range that masking effect occurs, and this band is changed according to the amplitude of frequency. The bandwidth of the critical band is about 100Hz when the center frequency is less than 500Hz, and 20% of center frequency if the center frequency is lower then 500Hz. The following equation is the function of critical band [10].

$$BW_c = 25 + 75[1 + 1.4(f/1000)^2]^{0.69} (Hz) \tag{2}$$

Simultaneous masking is divided into two, tone-masking-noise and noise-masking-tone. Tone-masking-noise is phenomenon that noise become masking in center of critical band [11]. This phenomenon is used in this paper and some frequencies are removed with band rejection filter. Temporal masking refers to both pre- and post-temporal masking. Pre-masking effects are weaker signals inaudible before the stronger masker is turned on, and post-masking effects are weaker signals in audible after the stronger masker is turned off. In this paper, the watermark is embedded using both simultaneous masking and pre-temporal masking.

2.1.2 Digital Filter Design

Digital filter is used in process of both watermark embedding and extraction. The following digital filter equation is applied to extract specific frequency.

$$y_k = \sum_{m=0}^{M} a_m x_{k-m} + \sum_{n=1}^{N} b_n y_{k-n} \tag{3}$$

Equation (4) is the frequency characteristic of the digital filter.

$$\left| H(e^{jwt}) \right| = \sqrt{\{H_R(e^{jwt})\}^2 + \{H_I(e^{jwt})\}^2} \tag{4}$$

2.1.3 ZCR(Zero-Crossing Rate) and Energy Analysis

By applying appropriate size of window to the audio signal in time domain, the audio signal is divided into several frames and the ZCR and energy of each frame are obtained. These two factors are usually used for start/end point detection in speech recognition. In this paper, these two factors are used to search regions to embed/extract watermark. The frames with high-ZCR with low-energy are selected as pre-temporal masking regions. In Fig. 1, the 68th frame shows high ZCR followed by low energy. This region is selected as a good point to embed watermark.

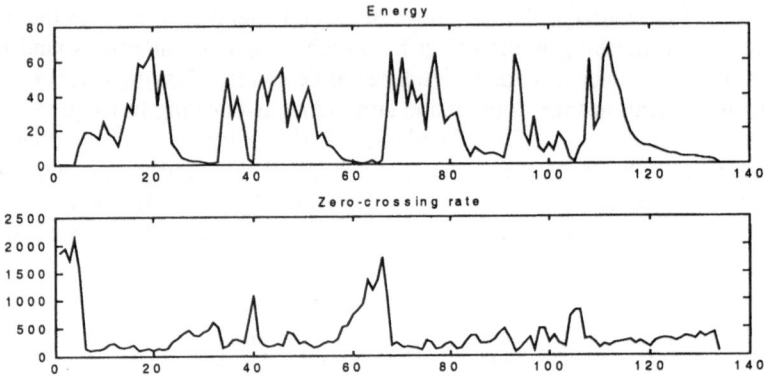

Fig. 1. ZCR and energy analysis. Pre-temporal masking appears most remarkably in the 68th frame.

2.2 Watermark Embedding

STEP1: The audio signal is divided into frames of the same length. There is time-overlap between two frames and the size of time-overlap is pre-determined. The length of window is calculated by subtracting time-overlap from frame length.
STEP 2: Window is shifted to calculate the ZCR and energy.
STEP3: The pre-temporal masking area was selected by analyzing ZCR and energy level of the frame. The algorithm calculates average ZCR and energy level. The ZCR and energy level are normalized using the maximum value within each frame. If a frame with high-ZCR and low-energy is followed by a frame with low-ZCR and high-energy, then the former frame is selected as a candidate for watermark embedding frame. Among the selected candidate frames, one frame with the highest ratio of ZCR to energy level is selected.
STEP4: Because the band reject filter has non-linear phase characteristic, a zero-phase filter was applied to both before and after the band reject filer to compensate phase.

STEP5: Watermark embedded in the frequency within the selected frame, which cannot be heard by human ears with simultaneous masking effect, was removed by applying IIR band rejection filter.

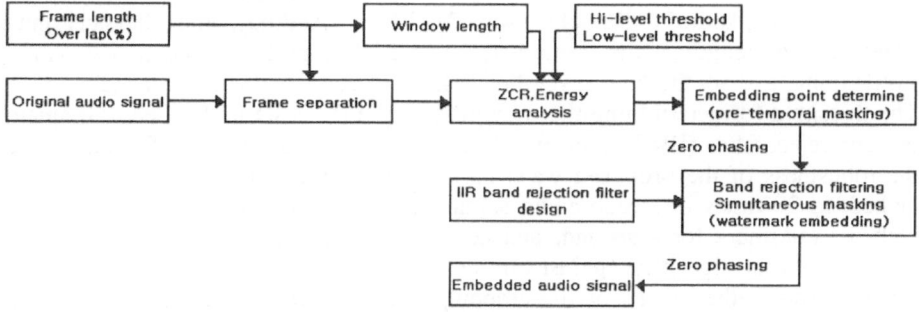

Fig. 2. Watermark embedding procedure.

2.3 Watermark Extractions

Proposed watermark extraction process is similar to embedding process, but band pass filter is used for watermark extraction instead of band rejection filter. In extraction process, band pass filter is applied to find rejected frequency, which is removed during watermark embedding process. If the watermark is properly embedded, then the rejected frequencies should not appear after the band pass filter. If the rejected frequency is detected, the frequency can be separated easily by multiplying proper scaling factor. If the multiplied value is greater than pre-defined threshold, it is assumed that there is no watermark. The first two figures (Fig.3 (a),(b)) shows the original audio signal and watermarked audio signal in frequency domain. Since there is no watermark in the original signal, some frequencies appear after band pass filtering (Fig.3 (c)). However, the result of band pass filtering shows no frequency with watermarked audio signal (Fig.3 (d)), which means that there is a watermark.

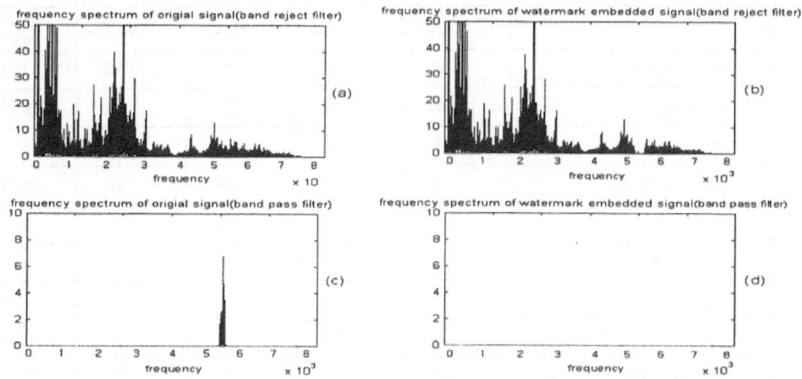

Fig. 3. Frequency spectrum of band rejection filter and band pass filter

3 Experimental Results

Experiments were performed according to the requirements of SDMI [12]. The audio signals under test were 16 bits mono signal sampled at 44.1kHz. The audio samples include Rock (Audio1), Ballade (Audio2), Metal (Audio3), and Classical music (Audio4). The length of the frame was set to 2,205 samples. We used 2% window overlapping, and set the high-level threshold to 35 and the low-level threshold to 10. The threshold for determining the watermark existence is set to 45. Center frequency of band reject filter (IIR-Elliptic filter) and band pass filter is set to 5.5kHz. To test the robustness of the proposed watermarking algorithm, 1 bit watermark code was embedded 30 times into each audio signal. Repeated process was performed which embeds watermark for 4 seconds and no watermark for next 4 seconds. To test the robustness of the algorithm against various types of attacks.

Table 1 shows the results of the cropping, quantization, down sampling, MPEG1 layerIII, MPEG2 AAC compression, time stretch, and echo addition attacks. the watermark detection rate is more than 92%. This algorithm is also robust against cropping and down sampling, but after the quantization process, the watermark extraction ratio is just above 56%. This should be improved in future work. Table 2 shows the results of the performance comparison between proposed watermarking method and spread spectrum method, which is proposed by Cox. et. al. Spread spectrum algorithm spreads data in frequency domain using by DCT (discrete cosine transform). An obvious weakness appears in spread spectrum algorithm with asynchronous attacks (time stretch, MPEG1 layerIII and MPEG2 AAC). Comparatively, proposed method shows robust results in asynchronous attacks.

Table 2 shows the results of the performance comparison between proposed watermarking method and spread spectrum method, which is proposed by Cox. et. al. Spread spectrum algorithm spreads data in frequency domain using by DCT (discrete cosine transform). An obvious weakness appears in spread spectrum algorithm with asynchronous attacks (time stretch, MPEG1 layerIII and MPEG2 AAC). Comparatively, proposed method shows robust results in asynchronous attacks. (time stretch, MPEG1 layerIII and MPEG2 AAC). Comparatively, proposed method shows robust results in asynchronous attacks.

Table 1. Watermark detection results for the attacks.

	Audio1	Audio2	Audio3	Audio4	Detection rate
No manipulation	30	30	30	30	100%
Cropping	28	27	28	29	93.3%
Quantization	18	12	19	19	56.6%
Down sampling	30	30	29	28	97.5%
MPEG1 layer 3	28	27	28	28	92.5%
MPEG2 AAC	27	29	30	28	95%
Time stretch (+5%)	30	29	28	30	97.5%
Time stretch (-5%)	29	30	30	29	98.3%
Echo addition	28	27	29	28	93.3%

Table 2. A performance test compare proposed watermarking method with spread spectrum method

	Proposed method detection rate	Spread spectrum method detection rate
No manipulation	100%	100%
Cropping	93.3%	94.2%
Quantization	56.6%	50.3%
Down sampling	97.5%	87.3%
MPEG1 layer 3	92..5%	34.5%
MPEG2 AAC	95%	30.1%
Time stretch (+5%)	97%	4.3%
Time stretch (-5%)	98%	3.2%
Echo addition	93.3%	90..8%

We also calculated SNR (Eq. 5) to evaluate the watermarked audio quality. If SNR is above 60 dB, it is generally hard to detect the degradation of the audio quality by human ears.

$$SNR = 20(\log_{10} \frac{Signal}{Noise}) \quad (dB) \tag{5}$$

In this experiment, SNR is kept at least above 60dB at each music which watermark embedded.

4   Conclusions

In this paper, we proposed an HAS and psychoacoustics model based new algorithm for audio watermarking. This algorithm utilizes absolute threshold frequency of hearing, critical band analysis, ZCR-energy analysis, and two masking effects to embed watermark. This is a kind of blind watermarking method that does not require original signal for watermark extraction. By applying several attacks proposed by SDMI, the robustness of the proposed algorithm is tested, and showed good performance in synchronization and other audio signal manipulation with minimal audio quality degradation.

Acknowledgment. Authors would like to thank Korea Ministry of Science and Technology, and Korea Science and Engineering Foundation for their support through ERC program.

References

1.   Say Wei Foo, Theng Hee Yeo, and Dong Yan Huang "An adaptive audio watermarking system," Electrical and Electronic Technology, 2001. TENCON. Proceedings of IEEE Region 10 International Conference, vol.2, (2001) 509 -513

2. W, Bender, D .Gruhl, N. Morimoto, and A. Lu "Techniques for data hiding," IBM Systems Journal, vol.35, no. 3&4, (1996) 313- 336
3. H. Kii, J. Onishi, and S. Ozawa, "The digital watermarking method by using both patchwork and DCT," Multimedia Computing and Systems, 1999. IEEE International Conference on, vol.1 (1999) 895-899
4. Cox, I. J., Kilian, J., Leighton, T.,and Shamoon, T., "Secure spread spectrum watermarking for multimedia," IEEE Trans. on Image Processing, vol.6, (1997) 1673-1687
5. L. Boney, A. Twefik, and K. Hamdy, "Digital watermarks of audio signals," Europ. Signal processing. Conf., Trieste, Italy (1996)
6. Tolga Ciloglu, and S. Utku Karaaslan, "An Improved All-Pass Watermarking Scheme for Speech and Audio," Proceeding of the 2000 IEEE international Conference on Multimedia and Expo, vol.2, (2000) 1017-1020
7. ISO/IEC IS I1I172, Information technology – coding of moving pictures and associated audio for digital storage up to about 1.5Mbits/s
8. Fletcher, "Auditory Patterns," Re. Mod. Phys., (1940) 47-65
9. Terhardt, E. "Calculating Virtual Pitch," Hearing Research, vol.1, (1979) 155-182.
10. Zwicker, E. and & Fastl, "Psychoacoustics Facts and Models," Springer-Verlag (1990)
11. Hellman, R. "Asymmetry of Masking between Noise and Tone," Percep.and Psychphys vol.11, (1972) 241-246
12. http://www.julienstern.org/sdmi/files/sdmiF/
13. Laurence Boney, Ahmed H. Tewfik, and Khaled N. Hamdy "Digital Watermarks for audio signals," Multimedia'96 IEEE, (1996)

On the Possibility of Only Using Long Windows in MPEG-2 AAC Coding

Cheng-Hsun Yu[1] and Shingchern D. You[2]

[1] Department of Computer and Communications,
National Taipei University of Technology,
1, Sec. 3, Chung-Hsiao East Rd.,
Taipei 106, Taiwan
[2] Department of Computer Science and Information Engineering,
National Taipei University of Technology,
1, Sec. 3, Chung-Hsiao East Rd.,
Taipei 106, Taiwan
you@csie.ntut.edu.tw

Abstract. The MPEG-2 AAC standard uses both long and short windows. However, the use of short windows complicates the implementation of decoders as well as encoders. In this paper, we propose a method based on the modification of the amplitude of the time-domain signal to replace the function of short windows. Compared with the use of short windows, the proposed approach is relatively easy to implement. The subjective experiments show that the proposed approach is a promising alternative in coding transient signals.

1 Introduction

Perceptual audio coding is the mainstream of audio coding now. Audio coding standards such as MPEG-1 [1], MPEG-2 [2],[3], and AC-3 [4], all are in this category. In the MPEG-2 standard, two audio coding schemes are available, namely part 3 [2] and part 7 [3]. The part 3 is designed to be MPEG-1 back compatible (BC); while the part 7 is not. That is the reason that the part 7 was originally known as MPEG-2 NBC standing for Non-Back Compatible. The part 7 was finally named as MPEG-2 Advanced Audio Coding (AAC). Subjective (listening) experiments showed that the coding quality of AAC was better than that of MPEG-2 BC [5]. Therefore, the development of MPEG-4 natural audio coding [6] was largely based on the AAC coding scheme.

2 The Window Switching Mechanism

According to the AAC standard, a certain number of PCM samples in a channel, dependending on the signal type, are multiplied by a window function, and the results are taken a Modified Discrete Cosine Transform (MDCT) for time to frequency conversion (or subband analysis). To achieve perfect reconstruction (PR),

Y.-C. Chen, L.-W. Chang, and C.-T. Hsu (Eds.): PCM 2002, LNCS 2532, pp. 663–670, 2002.

the second half of PCM samples covered in the previous window are in the first half of the current window scope. For stable signals, long windows are used to increase the coding gain. A long window covers 2048 samples, or equivalently 1024 spectral lines after MDCT operation. These spectral lines, after quantization, are packed in one block of bitstream. For coding transient signals, short windows each having 256 samples are applied to have better time resolution. Eight such short windows are used consecutively to obtain eight sets of 128 spectral lines to be packed in a coded block. In order to smoothly change the window type from a long window to a short window, an intermediate window called start window is used. Also, a stop window is used for switching from a short window to a long window. Both start and stop windows covers 2048 PCM samples, and then 1024 spectral lines are obtained after the MDCT operation. The psychoacoustic model in the encoder determines whether the signal in the present block is stationary or transient. In the following, when we refer to a "block," we mean either 1024 spectral lines or the corresponding 2048 PCM samples. In this description, we may say that two consecutive blocks are overlaped by 50 %.

2.1   Coding with Short Windows

The concept of critical bands indicates that some adjacent spectral lines should be grouped together to form scalefactor bands. Spectral lines in the same scalefactor band use the same scalefactor, which is proportional to the quantization step size. In the long window case, the encoded bitstream of a block contains one scalefactor per scalefactor band. In the short window case, the bitstream of a block can have up to eight sets of scalefactors, one per short window. So, at most there are 112 scalefactors in the bitstream of a block at sampling rate of 48 ks/s. Compared with 49 scalefactors in the long window case, a block coded with short windows allocates more bits for scalefactors, and thus fewer bits for spectral lines. Therefore, lower coding gain is observed. At higher bit rate, the influence is small. However, the coding quality is then affected at lower bit rates. In fact, during listening experiments we found that a piece of music coded at 32 kb/s in main profile by only long windows in many instances had a higher quality than its counterpart coded with both long and short windows using ISO's reference program. The quality gets worse especially when short windows are un-necessarily used.

To reduce the number of coded scale factors when short windows in use, several adjacent windows may share the same set of scalefactors. This technique is known as window grouping. In addition, to efficiently encode the eight sets of spectral lines, they are re-ordered before performing the Huffman coding. While window grouping and spectral line re-ordering improve the coding efficiency when short windows are in use, still the quality of coded signals decreases at lower bit rates as mentioned previously. More over, the use of window grouping and spectral re-ordering complicates the implementation. Besides that, special care has to be taken for blocks using start windows and stop windows. A rough estimation shows that about 5 % of the C source code in the ISO's AAC program are written for dealing with block switching and short windows.

2.2   Reasons for Using Short Windows

Knowing the basic operation of the window switching, we now consider the reasons for using short windows. Basically, there are two reasons. One is to reduce the pre-echo noise. In such audio coding as MPEG-1 Layer 3 (MP-3), using short windows to control pre-echoes is a typical approach. However, the case is not necessary true for AAC coding. The gain-control tool in Scalable Sampling Rate (SSR) profile and the Temporal Noise Shaping (TNS) tool in all profiles may also be used to control pre-echoes [7]. The second one is to provide a higher time resolution for transient signals. This is done by using one set of scalfactors per window so that the quantization step size can be changed in a shorter time instance. As a transient signal usually has a large change of waveform in a short time, the fast change of scalefactors in a short period of time is understandable. For example, Fig. 1a is a transient signal and Fig. 1b is the coded result using short windows at 32 kb/s. It can be seen that the coded result is not distorted. However, if the same signal is coded with only long windows, then severe distortion is observed, as shown in Fig. 2a. This can serve as an evidence of the necessity of using short windows. Although the evidence is persuasive, it may not be as strong as we thought at the first glance. Fig. 2b shows the same transient signal coded at 64 kb/s with only long windows. This time the coded signal does not have severe distortion. With the increase of bit rates, whether or not to use short windows does not greatly affect the coding quality. In the extreme case, perfect reconstruction (one reason for using MDCT) can be obtained for arbitrarily long windows if enough bits are available. Therefore, short windows are mainly useful at lower bit rates. However, as we mentioned previously, unnecessarily switching to short windows may result in lower coding quality at lower bit rates. Therefore, the use of short windows should be limited.

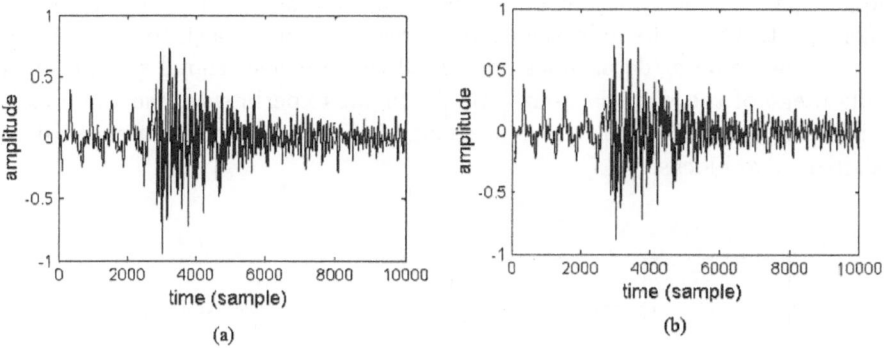

Fig. 1. (a) The transient signal under test. (b) The coded results via short windows

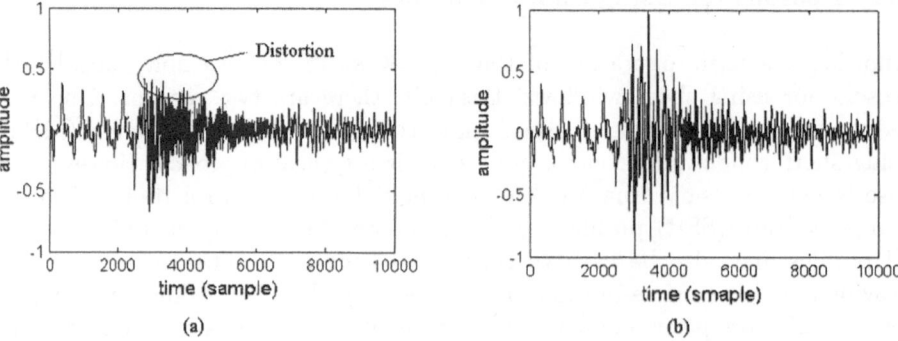

Fig. 2. (a) The coded results via long windows at 32 kb/s. Note the distortion in the waveform. (b) The coded results via long windows at 64 kb/s. The distortion is not obvious

3   The Proposed Method

Based on the above discussion, we know that it is possible to use only long windows in audio coding at higher bit rates. However, at lower bit rates we need to overcome the distortion problem, such as the one shown in Fig. 2a. One possible approach, as shown in Fig. 3, is to use gain change in place of short windows. In this approach, we encode all PCM samples using only long windows. For samples to be encoded with short windows in ISO's standard, we reduce their values before encoding. Then, the normal encoding process is carried out with additional information recorded in the bitstream indicating that the gain is altered. During decoding, the reduced gain is compensated. In order not to make the gain change audible, it is gradually reduces from 1 to g_r from the stationary part to the transient part. The gain remains g_r until the end of the transient part. Then, the gain smoothly increases from g_r back to 1, as shown in Fig. 4. The value g_r determines how small the transient signal should be. A suitable range of the value is from $\frac{1}{4}$ to $\frac{1}{10}$. In the experiments, the value g_r is chosen to be $\frac{1}{8}$. In addition, the gain change is carried out only if a transient signal spans two blocks.

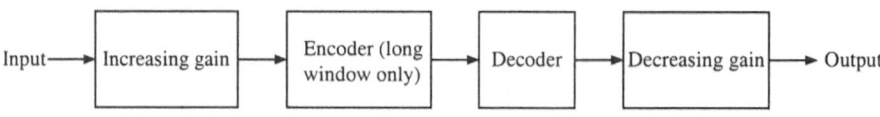

Fig. 3. The proposed approach

The encoding process is carried out as follows: The input PCM samples are analyzed by the psychoacoustic model to determine the coding strategy. If the

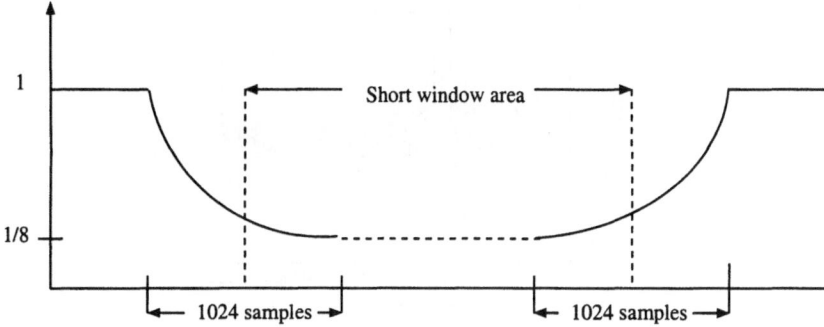

Fig. 4. Gain adjustment in the encoding process

model indicates to use long window in the current block, then nothing is changed. When the model indicates that a start window is to be used in the current block, we then look ahead the analysis results from the model for the next two blocks to see if both should use short windows. If so, the gain is changed from current block but the long window is still in use. The gain remains at the lower value until the stop window is supposed to be used.

4   Experiments and Results

The experiments were conducted in two parts. The first part was to encode the signal shown in Fig. 1a to see if the proposed approach could reduce the distortion. The second part was a subjective comparison between the original (short window) method and the proposed method. The proposed approach was implemented by using the ISO's reference program with modification.

4.1   Results of Coding Transient Signal

The coded results for the transient signal is shown in Fig. 5. From the figure, it can be seen that the coded signal is no longer distorted, unlike the one in Fig. 2a. In order to understand why the proposed approach solves the distortion problem, the bit allocation for each scalefactor band in both signals are given in Fig. 6. It is clear that the bits are allocated evenly across the scalefactor bands in the proposed approach. On the other hand, the same signal coded by long windows exhibits a significant variation in bit allocation, and some low-frequency bands do not have any bits. That is the reason that coding with only long windows has a severe distortion.

4.2   Results of Subjective Experiments

Three subjective experiments were also carried out. The comparison counterpart was encoded by the ISO's reference program. Due to lacking of experienced audiences, we used a simplified CMOS (Comparative Mean Opinion Score) method

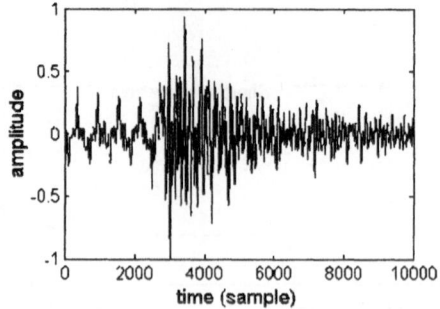

Fig. 5. The coded results using the proposed approach

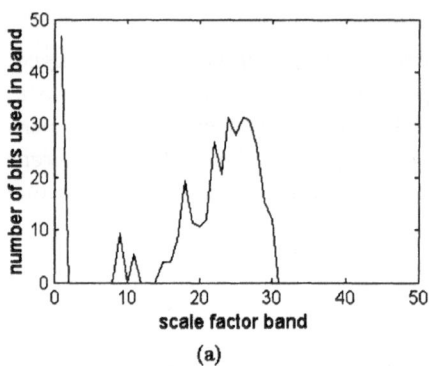
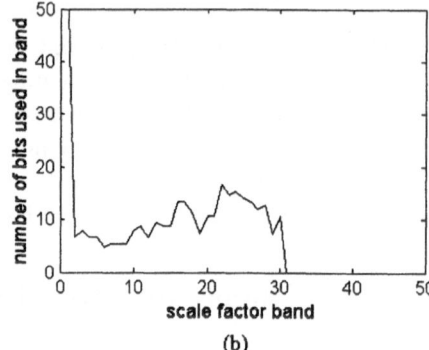

Fig. 6. The number of bits used in each scalefactor band. (a) The original long window case. (b) The proposed approach

Table 1. Signals used in the experiments

else	Soft music (female vocal)	bird	Piano with accompany
heavy	Heavy metal music	sampg	Soft music (male vocal)
rock	Rock and roll	harp	Harpsichord
michael	Pop music	orchestra	Waltz orchestra

in the experiments. Fifteen grad students were asked to give opinions after listening to three pieces of music arranged in Ref/A/B format, where Ref was the original signal, and A and B were the two coded results. The opinions are: A is better than B, A is equal to B, and A is worse than B. The signal coded by the proposed method was randomly assigned to either A or B. Besides, the audiences had no knowledge about which one was coded by the proposed method. The signals for comparison were eight pieces of music containing many strong attacks (transient signals). The contents of the signals are listed in Table 1. In the first experiment, signals were coded at 32 kb/s with a window switching threshold of -1000, the default value in the ISO's reference program. The results are in

Table 2. Experimental results for coding at 32 kb/s with threshold of -1000

Music name	Proposed approach better	Both equal	Short window better	Average score
else	15	0	0	1.00
heavy	15	0	0	1.00
rock	15	0	0	1.00
michael	15	0	0	1.00
bird	15	0	0	1.00
sampg	15	0	0	1.00
harp	15	0	0	1.00
orchestra	15	0	0	1.00

Table 3. Experimental results for coding at 32 kb/s with threshold of 400

Music name	Proposed approach better	Both equal	Short window better	Average score
else	3	6	6	-0.2
heavy	7	7	2	0.33
rock	3	8	4	-0.06
michael	5	9	1	0.26
bird	2	12	1	0.06
sampg	4	9	2	0.13
harp	8	3	4	0.26
orchestra	0	14	1	-0.06

Table 4. Experimental results for coding at 64 kb/s with threshold of 400

Music name	Proposed approach better	Both equal	Short window better	Average score
else	4	10	1	0.20
heavy	6	7	2	0.26
rock	3	10	2	0.06
michael	0	14	1	-0.06
bird	1	13	1	0.00
sampg	2	9	4	-0.13
harp	3	11	1	0.13
orchestra	0	15	0	0.00

Table 2. It can be seen that in this case the proposed approach performs much better. However, after a deeper study, we found that the thrshold value used in the first experiment was not adequate because short windows were used too often. Therefore, the second experiment also used 32 kb/s but with the switching threshold of 400, a value subjectively determined to be better. The results are in Table 3. Based on the results, we observe that the proposed approach performs

slightly worse than the standard method on some signals. But the difference is small and acceptable, considering that the coding quality is not very good at 32 kb/s. Also, results of the above experiments show that the performance of the standard method is sensitive to the switching threshold. A similar experiment was also carried out at 64 kb/s with the switching threshold of 400. The results are in Table 4. Overall speaking, the coding quality of the proposed approach is acceptable without the use of short windows. In addition to ease of implementation, the proposed approach is not sensitive to the window-switching threshold.

5   Conclusions

In the paper, we propose a method based on the time-domain signal modification as an alternative to short windows. Compared with the standard AAC coding, the proposed approach uses only long windows and simple time-domain gain modification. Therefore, in terms of implementation, the proposed approach is advantageous to the standard AAC coding. The subjective experiments showed that the proposed approach had a coding quality almost equal to the standard method in coding test signals.

References

1. ISO/IEC: Information Technology - Coding of Moving Pictures and Associated Audio for Digital Storage Media at up to About 1.5 Mbit/s - Part 3: Audio. IS 11172-3 (1993).
2. ISO/IEC: Information Technology - Generic Coding of Moving Pictures and Associated Audio Information - Part 3: Audio. 2nd edn. IS 13818-3 (1998).
3. ISO/IEC: Information Technology - Generic Coding of Moving Pictures and Associated Audio Information - Part 7: Advanced Audio Coding (AAC). IS 13818-7 (1997).
4. Advanced Television Systems Committee: Digital Audio Compression Standard (AC-3). Doc. A/52, (1995).
5. Bosi M., et al: ISO/IEC MPEG-2 Advanced Audio Coding. Journal of Audio Eng. Soc. 45 (1997) 789 - 812.
6. ISO/IEC: Information Technology - Coding of Audio-visual Objects - Part 3: Audio, Subpart 4 General Audio Coding. IS 14496-3 (1999).
7. Herre J., Johnston J. D.: Enhancing the Performance of Perceptual Audio Coders by Using Temporal Noise Shaping (TNS). 101st Conference of the Audio Engineering Society, Los Angeles, CA (1996) pre-print 4384.

A Call Admission Control Algorithm Based on Stochastic Performance Bound for Wireless Networks*

Wei-jen Hsu[1] and Zsehong Tsai[2]

[1] Chunghwa Telecom
wjhsu@cht.com.tw

[2] Department of Electrical Engineering, National Taiwan University
ztsai@cc.ee.ntu.edu.tw

Abstract. In this paper, we derive stochastic performance bounds under the assumption of exponentially bounded burstiness (EBB) traffic model and exponentially bounded fluctuation (EBF) channel model. Then we propose a measurement-based call admission algorithm providing statistical service level agreement (SLA) guarantee for accepted flows based on the QoS prediction equations for both single and multiple priority services. Our call admission control algorithm is characterized by tunable tradeoff between channel utilization and SLA violation probability.

1 Introduction

Wireless access technologies have become a competitive solution for the access network in recent years. Unfortunately, high packet error rate and sporadic service outage due to channel impairments have been a challenge for network engineers to deploy wireless network with QoS guarantee or to provide satisfactory streaming media services. Thus, systematic approaches to provide QoS guaranteed service on error-prone wireless channels have become an important research issue.

Most performance bounds currently available in literature can be classified into two broad categories, namely deterministic bound [2] and stochastic bound [1]. Directly providing deterministic QoS guarantee in the wireless environment is either infeasible or can be with extremely high cost. The performance bound we seek in wireless environment falls in the category of probabilistic forms or the so-called stochastic bound.

We believe that stochastic bounds fit better in terms of theoretical tightness and validity in the wireless environment. Its applicability in the call admission control is also better. (We use the term "call admission control" for the mechanism deciding whether we accept a new traffic flow.) When deterministic bounds are used as call admission criteria, the system utilization is usually lower than that if stochastic bounds are used. To provide acceptable quality of multimedia service to users, a small probability of SLA violation events may be tolerable, thus providing stochastic bound is sufficient.

Although measurement-based admission control has been largely available in the literature [4][5][6], we propose one characterized by low operation overhead. In addi-

---

* Most of this work is done when W. Hsu was with National Taiwan University.
This work is partially sponsored by MOE under grant 89E-FA06-2-4-7.

Y.-C. Chen, L.-W. Chang, and C.-T. Hsu (Eds.): PCM 2002, LNCS 2532, pp. 671-679, 2002.

tion, not many of these previous works on measurement-based admission control include the discussion about wireless environment, as we emphasize in this work.

This paper is organized as follows: Stochastic performance bounds in wireless network under FCFS and prioritized access queueing disciplines are derived in section 2. Based on these bounds, we proposed a measurement-based call admission algorithm for wireless access networks in section 3. Simulation results are given in section 4. We conclude the paper in section 5.

2   Performance Bounds in Wireless Networks

2.1   Network Model

We consider the network environment in which end terminals access the Internet through a shared wireless channel, as illustrated in Fig 1. In such an environment, the shared wireless channel serves as a substitute for point-to-point wire link.

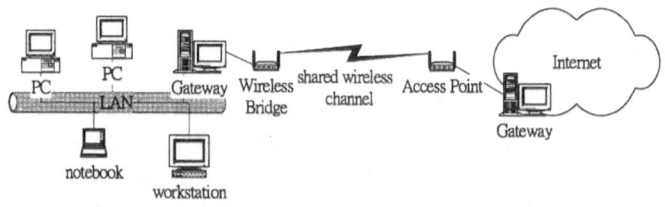

Fig. 1. Illustration of shared wireless channel

We consider two different scheduling algorithms: the FCFS (First Come First Serve) queueing discipline and prioritized access. We derive stochastic bounds for the corresponding queue size and queueing delay for each flow, under either service discipline.

In this paper, we adopt the EBB source model and EBF channel model. Please refer to [1] for its definition and notation. Most traffic models used in modeling data sources, such as IPP sources, MMPP sources, or on-off sources, can be substituted by EBB sources after choosing appropriate pre-factor and decay-factor. Detailed mathematical treatment of such transform can be found in [3].

As well as EBB sources can be used to substitute most source models, EBF channel can be used to substitute most channel models, such as on-off channel, finite state Markov channel, and channel with non-zero, time-varying packet loss probability. Hence, we use it to model the error prone wireless channel. Interested readers can refer [8] for detailed discussions.

2.2 Performance Bounds under FCFS Queueing Discipline

We now consider the FCFS queueing model with traffic sources modeled by $(\lambda_i, A_i, \alpha_i)$-EBB processes, where i is the index of source. The channel is modeled as $(\mu-\varepsilon, B, \beta)$-EBF, where μ is the ideal channel rate, ε is the error rate.

Theorem1. Queue size process $Q(t)$ of the shared FIFO queue is upper bounded by an exponentially bounded process (EB process)

$$Q(t) \sim (\frac{\sum\limits_{\text{for all } i} A_i + B}{1 - e^{-\zeta(\mu-\varepsilon-\sum\limits_{\text{for all } i}\lambda_i)}}, \zeta) \text{-EB} \quad \text{where} \quad \frac{1}{\zeta} = \sum\limits_{\text{for all } i} \frac{1}{\alpha_i} + \frac{1}{\beta} \quad . \tag{1}$$

Theorem2. Queueing delay process $D(t)$ of each EBB flow at the shared FIFO queue is upper bounded by an EB process as follows.

$$D(t) \sim (\frac{\sum\limits_{\text{for all } i} A_i + B}{1 - e^{-\zeta(\mu-\varepsilon-\sum\limits_{\text{for all } i}\lambda_i)}}, \zeta(\mu-\varepsilon)) \text{- EB} \quad . \tag{2}$$

where ζ is the same as in Eq.(1).

The proofs of theorems are similar to those in [1] and are omitted for sake of limited space. Interested readers can refer [8] for details.

2.3 Performance Bounds under Prioritized Service Queueing Discipline

In this section, we consider the prioritized service queueing discipline. The traffic source i of class n is modeled by $(\lambda_{ni}, A_{ni}, \alpha_{ni})$-EBB process. The channel is again modeled as $(\mu-\varepsilon, B, \beta)$-EBF. Packets belong to each class is put into a separated queue. Under this service discipline, whenever the server is ready to provide service, it serves the backlogged queue with the highest priority. Each class receives service only when higher priority classes have no backlog in queues at all. By the duality between data traffic and error in channel in [1], the equivalent channel model seen by a non-highest priority class is a channel with higher error rate that combines the actual channel error process and the traffic processes of higher priority classes.

Theorem3. Under prioritized access queueing discipline, the stochastic bounds in Theorem1~Theorem2 still apply, with the modification in channel parameters depending on incoming flow's priority class as follows.
(i).The queue size of class n is an EB process and its parameters are abbreviated as

$$Q_n(t) \sim (\frac{A'_n + B}{1 - e^{-\zeta(\mu-\varepsilon-\Lambda_n)}}, \zeta) \quad . \tag{3}$$

where

$$\Lambda_n = \sum_{\substack{\text{for all flow } k \text{ with same} \\ \text{or higher priority than class n}}} \lambda_k \quad , \quad A'_n = \sum_{\substack{\text{for all flow } k \text{ with same} \\ \text{or higher priority than class n}}} A_k \quad , \quad \frac{1}{\zeta} = \sum_{\substack{\text{for all flow } k \text{ with same} \\ \text{or higher priority than class n}}} \frac{1}{\alpha_k} + \frac{1}{\beta} \; . \tag{4}$$

(ii). The queueing delay of each EBB flow of class n is an EB process a satisfying

$$D(t) \sim (\frac{A'_n + B}{1 - e^{-\zeta(\mu - \varepsilon - \Lambda_n)}}, \zeta(\mu - \varepsilon - \Lambda_n)) \; . \tag{5}$$

where Λ_n, A'_n, ζ are defined as above.

3   Measurement-Based Call Admission Control under Wireless Channel

In this section, we present an algorithm that makes call admission decision based on queue size statistics at the entrance node of wireless channel. The objective of our algorithm is maintaining statistical guarantee on queueing delay of incoming packets.

3.1 Call Admission Control for Single-Priority Class

To achieve the goal of maintaining statistical delay bound, an intuitive way is book-keeping statistics about queueing delay of each packet and using it for call admission decision. But doing this may introduce serious packet manipulation overhead. Thus, we propose a procedure to make call admission decisions based on queue size statistics, which can be gathered easier, while maintaining the QoS target specified in terms of delay.

First, we have a target QoS requirement specified in terms of delay (for example, more than 99% of packets encounter delay less than 50ms) and name it as *Target Point (TP)*. Once we specify the *TP* in delay domain, we can find the corresponding *TP* in queue size domain according to the Eq.(1) and Eq.(2). Namely, the decay-factor of queue size and decay-factor of delay are directly related by a proportional factor μ-ε, which is the average service rate of the wireless channel.

We make call admission decision according to a simple guideline: Bookkeeping statistics about queue size and summarize it into a *System state Line (SL)*, as illustrated in Fig. 2. The leftmost point on *SL*, which is the probability of having non-zero queue size, is called *Starting Point (SP)*. As a new flow requests for service, we estimate the increment by which *SL* will shift upward according to the new flow's characteristics. If the shifted *SL* still remains below *TP*, we accept the new flow; otherwise, we reject it. A similar approach can be found in [4].

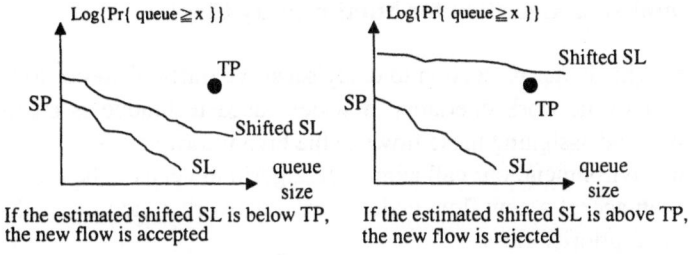

Fig. 2. Making call admission decision based on shifted *SL* and *TP*

When network is a time-varying system, statistics about earlier history provides less valuable information for making current decision. As a result, we have to make earlier data stand less weight in queue size statistics. A generally used technique in such situation is auto-regressive weighted average. Based on this method, we update the *SL* periodically.

The next step in making call admission decision is estimating *SL* shift. *SL* shift can be divided into two parts: The shift of *SP* and change of *SL* slope, corresponding to changes in pre-factor and decay-factor in Eq.(1), respectively. The change of slope is simpler to estimate, since decay-factor of queue size is only related to decay-factor of input flows and channel (See Eq.(1)). The decay-factors of existing flows and the channel are aggregated in decay-factor of current *SL*. We denote the estimated slope of current *SL* as m_{cnt}, the decay-factor of the new flow requesting service as α_{new}, and the estimated slope of shifted *SL* as m_{sfd}. Then we use the relation in Eq.(6) to estimate the decay-factor after the new flow joins the system, which is also the slope of the shifted *SL*.

$$1/m_{sfd} = 1/m_{cnt} + 1/\alpha_{new} \cdot \tag{6}$$

The actual shift of *SP* is somewhat complicated to estimate. Thus, we use approximation technique to find upper bound of shift of *SP*. The *SP*, corresponding to Prob{queue size ≥ 0}, also indicates the system utilization. If a new flow joins in, the system utilization increases by λ/μ, where λ is the average rate of new flow, μ is the ideal channel rate. Thus we can estimate the shift of *SP* by Eq.(7).

$$SP_{new} = SP_{old} + \lambda/\mu \cdot \tag{7}$$

An important feature of our call admission control algorithm is that we adjust *TP* according to system utilization. Specifically, we choose a *Warning Level* of system utilization. If the estimated system utilization (SP_{new}) is under this level, we use original *TP* as call admission threshold. But if shifted *SP* is higher than this *Warning Level*, *TP* is moved down along the probability axis by multiplying a *Protection Factor*, which is less than 1. Different choices of *Warning Level* and *Protection Factor* can be made to achieve tradeoff between channel utilization and SLA violation probability.

3.2   Call Admission Algorithm for Multi-priority Classes

In order to provide better protection to delay sensitive traffic flows or to flows considered important by network operators, a widely used technique is creating multiple priority classes and assigning these flows to the high priority class.

In such an environment, our call admission algorithm needs to be modified to check whether we can accept a new flow under current network condition, without violating the SLA of *each* priority class.

From Theorem3, we see that the admission of a flow has no impact on performance of flows with higher priority, but influences the performance of flows with the same or lower priority. When admitting a flow of a specific class, we should check whether SLA for each of the lower priority classes can be sustained.

To enable such a check, we maintain separate *SL* curve for each priority class. The *SL* of highest priority class collects the statistic of highest priority queue size, which is the only visible queue to the highest priority flows. The *SL* of second highest priority class collects the statistic of the sum of the highest priority queue size and the second highest priority queue size, which is the equivalent queue size for second highest priority flows, and so on. In this case, the SLA and *TP* can be different in each priority class. When a new flow requests to join, we must check all the *SL*s it influences and make sure that after the estimated shift, each of these *SL*s remains below the corresponding *TP*. If any of these checks fail, we conclude that SLA guarantee for some priority class may fail with the admission of the new flow and we reject the new flow.

4   Simulation Results

In this section, we present some simulation results indicating that our call admission algorithm provides an effective mechanism leading to high system utilization while keeping SLA violation probability low. The *Warning Level* and *Protection Factor* introduced in section 3 make the call admission algorithm adjustable to match different requirements in various operation environments.

4.1   Simulation Environment

The simulation environment is illustrated in Fig. 3. During simulation, the users make random selections among 14 video clips stored in the VoD server. The video streams are modeled by EBB processes, and its parameters are known. The video traces are packet patterns of movie previews encoded in Real Media format. We assume the queueing delay at the shared FIFO queue is the major part of end-to-end delay and neglect other factors, i.e. Congestion occurs only at the wireless channel. A rejected request is assumed to leave the system without changing the future request arrival pattern.

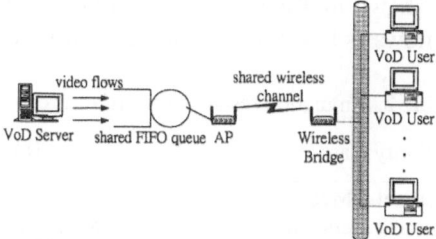

Fig. 3. The simulation environment

4.2 Adjustable Policy of the Call Admission Algorithm

In all following simulation cases, the target QoS guarantee in SLA for video flows is stated as "Less than 1% of packets encounter queueing delay more than 50ms." The parameters used in simulation cases are summarized in Table 1(a). We test the call admission algorithm under the on-off channel model with alternating, exponentially distributed channel-on and channel-off periods with mean 0.99 and 0.01 second, respectively. We adapt this model to characterize the sporadic service outage in wireless channels. Simulation results are listed in Table 1(b).

Table 1. Simulation parameters and results using Real Media format video traces

(a) Simulation Parameters

Simulation case	Warning Level	Protection Factor
Loose	1.0	N/A
Step-1	0.7	0.01
Step-2	0.6	0.01
Step-3	0.5	0.01

(b) Results of on-off channel

Simulation case	SLA violation prob.	Average channel utilization
Loose	99.09%	0.875
Step-1	29.12%	0.850
Step-2	5.07%	0.803
Step-3	2.29%	0.759

From the results above, we see a tradeoff between channel utilization and SLA violation probability for accepted flows. The SLA violation probability can be effectively reduced at the cost of lower channel utilization. The most desirable policy depends on the operator's considerations and is different case by case. However, if we do not adjust *TP* according to utilization (the *Loose* case in simulation), the resulting SLA violation probability is unacceptable. This shows the need of using *Protection Factor*.

4.3 Mixing Video Traffic with Data Traffic

Next, we validate the applicability of our call admission algorithm for multiple priority classes. When delay sensitive video traffic flows and TCP flows are multiplexed in a single queue, the bursty nature of TCP flows causes performance degradation of video traffic flows, as shown in Table 2(a). A solution for this problem is assigning delay insensitive TCP flows as low priority and video traffic flows as high priority.

Table 2. Simulation results with LAN trace injected

(a)   Single priority class

Simula-tion case	SLA violation prob.	Average channel utiliza-tion	Mean delay of LAN trace packets
Loose	99.29%	0.892	465.3ms
Step-1	42.78%	0.866	302.2ms
Step-2	22.79%	0.824	110.6ms
Step-3	7.17%	0.767	22.9ms

(b) 2 priority classes

Simula-tion case	SLA violation prob.	Average channel utiliza-tion	Mean delay of LAN trace packets
Loose	27.96%	0.862	980.8ms
Step-1	2.67%	0.836	336.8ms
Step-2	2.16%	0.800	406.2ms
Step-3	0%	0.744	75.1ms

In the simulation case, we choose one of the LAN traces available at [7] as representative of data traffic flows from the Internet. Target QoS guarantee for video flows are the same as that in section 4.2. No call admission control is used for the data traffic and no QoS guarantee is provided to it. It is a "background traffic" that always exists during the simulation. We use the on-off channel model and simulation results are summarized in Table 2(b).

We see that the SLA violation probability of video flows is not adversely influenced by data traffic if prioritized access queueing discipline is used, but the mean delay of LAN trace packets is obviously larger. The average channel utilizations in these simulation cases are similar in comparison to those in Table 1. If the TCP flows can tolerate higher queueing delay, setting them as low priority can be a viable solution toward providing QoS for delay sensitive video flows in a general-purpose network environment.

5   Conclusions

In this paper, we first derive stochastic performance bounds for key performance metrics under FCFS and prioritized access queueing disciplines. Then, base on the bound equations, we propose a call admission algorithm, which performs on-line measurement of current network condition. With the call admission algorithm, the network operator can provide statistical SLA guarantee to accepted users. The call admission algorithm can be modified for multi-priority queueing discipline, in which important or delay sensitive flows are better protected by assigning them as high priority flows.

Simulation studies show that there is a tradeoff between system utilization and SLA violation probability. The parameters of our call admission algorithm can be adjusted to match different operator requirements. If video traffic and data traffic are multiplexed in single FIFO queue, some additional mechanism, such as prioritized access of channel at the data link or MAC layer, is required if one wants to provide statistical SLA guarantee to video flows in a general-purpose network.

We conclude that the stochastic bound approach for QoS control is suitable to be used for loss tolerant multi-media traffic or other Internet applications in the wireless access networks.

References

1. K. Lee, "Performance Bounds in Communication Networks with Variable-rate Links," *Proceedings of the conference on Applications, technologies, architectures, and protocols for computer communication*, pp. 126 – 136, 1995.
2. R. Cruz, "A Calculus for Network Delay, part I: Network Elements in Isolation," *IEEE Trans. Information Theory*, vol. 37, no. 1, pp.114-131, Jan. 1991.
3. W. Fischer and K. Meier-Hellstern, "The Markov-Modulated Poisson Process (MMPP) Cookbook," *Performance Evaluation*, vol. 18, pp.149-171, 1992.
4. M. Venkatraman, N. Nasrabadi, "An Admission Control Framework to Support Media-Streaming over Packet-Switched Networks," *ICC 1999*, vol. 2, pp. 1357-1361, 1999.
5. T. Lee, M. Zukerman and R. Addie, "Admission Control Schemes for Bursty Multimedia Traffic," *INFOCOM 2001*, vol. 1, pp.478-487, 2001.
6. Y. Bao and A. Sethi, "Performance-driven Adaptive Admission Control for Multimedia Applications," *ICC 1999*, vol. 1, pp. 199-203, 1999.
7. http://www.acm.org/sigs/sigcomm/ITA/, The Internet Traffic Archive.
8. Wei-jen Hsu, *Performance Bounds and Call Admission Control Algorithm in Wireless Access Networks*, Master Thesis, National Taiwan University, 2001.

Management of Multiple Mobile Routers for Continuous Multimedia in Mobile WLANs[1]

Eun Kyoung Paik and Yanghee Choi

School of Electrical Engineering and Computer Science, Seoul National University
Seoul 151-744, Korea
{eun, yhchoi}@mmlab.snu.ac.kr

Abstract. Network mobility architecture was designed with mobile routers enabling continuous connection to the Internet. This paper proposes the mobile WLAN architecture that provides wide bandwidth for the users in the moving hot spot while the whole WLAN changes its point of attachment to the Internet. To serve mobile WLANs with continuous wideband, this paper focuses on the multiple mobile routers and their management in the manner of attaining larger wireless access area and seamless mobility. With the proposed architecture, WLAN users are able to enjoy multimedia applications while moving.

1   Introduction

The success of public accessed Wireless Local Area Network (WLAN) in hot spot areas encourages the new service requirement for the users on the moving public vehicles. Public WLAN enables large volume of multimedia over wireless link, but does not support smooth mobility. The lack of mobility is caused by the small cell size of WLAN.

To provide continuous multimedia communication services for the group of mobile users on the fast mobile vehicles, a *network mobility* mechanism is deployed with new challenges. Terminal/user/service mobility provides mobile communications, but still has limitations for serving passengers on the fast moving vehicles.

In this paper, IEEE 802.11b WLAN organizes the *mobile network* with m*obile routers* (MRs) to provision broadband wireless link. This paper will focus on the *multiple MRs* to enlarge wireless access coverage, thus support seamless mobility. With the proposed architecture, WLAN provides continuous wide bandwidth even though it changes its point of attachment to the Internet.

If the network mobility is served with traditional Mobile IP [1] protocol, mobility management of nodes in the moving network introduces new problems. Since lots of mobile nodes move at once, mobility management becomes explosive, thus smooth handoff becomes more difficult. Mobile IP also introduces a nested encapsulation problem when it serves network mobility.

[1] This work was supported by the National Research Laboratory project of Ministry of Science and Technology, Korea.

The remainder of the paper is organized as follows. In section 2, the basic network mobility architecture is described. Section 3 introduces multiple mobile routers deployment architecture and its management scheme. Section 4 summarizes the implementation issues and analyzes the expected results - wireless coverage enlargement and seamless mobility. Finally, section 5 concludes with future work.

2   Network Mobility and Previous Work

This section describes the basic concept of network mobility [2] and previous work. Network mobility enables a mobile network to maintain Internet connectivity while it moves. A mobile network is composed of one or more MRs and *mobile network nodes* (MNNs) connected to the MR. Fig. 1 shows the basic network mobility architecture. In Fig.1, mobility of the mobile network is transparent to the MNNs inside of it. The MR takes actions, e.g. binding update to the home agent, on behalf of the MNNs when the network changes its point of attachment to the Internet.

Numerous solutions are proposed for network mobility to aggregate mobility management. Ernst suggests prefix scope binding updates [3] based on Mobile IPv6 [4], in which the MR binds the prefix of its COA to its home address for the routing to the MNNs inside the mobile network. It has several constraints, however. First, the mobile network has only one MR and the MR has only one egress interface. Second, all MNNs are fixed nodes to the mobile network. MNNs can not move from/into the mobile network so that this solution can not be utilized for the large vehicle situation where many passengers with MNNs get on/off.

Hierarchical Mobile IPv6 mobility management [5] is scalable with its hierarchical architecture, but it is not originally designed for mobile networks but MN's routing optimization. It only supports visiting mobile nodes of mobile networks.

The United State Coast Guard (USCG), National Aeronautics and Space Administration (NASA) and Cisco also built a test-bed [6]. It was aimed at the deployment trial of mobile IP and mobile routers in a real network. Any of the above solution, however, does not support multiple MRs efficiently.

3   Management of Multiple Mobile Routers

This section introduces the proposed management architecture of multiple MRs. Multiple MRs provide continuous multimedia for the group of mobile users with mobile networks. To manage multiple MRs, our architecture composes the *consensus* of mobile routers and selects a *representative mobile router* (RMR) that represents all the other MRs on the mobile network.

Among the MRs, the mobile network selects a MR, called RMR, which can listen to the wireless link. In the proposed scheme, one MR at a time communicates with the access router (AR) directly. To achieve that, RMR selection scheme elects the most appropriate MR based on the wireless link availability. Then the selected MR becomes the RMR, and the others become candidate MRs.

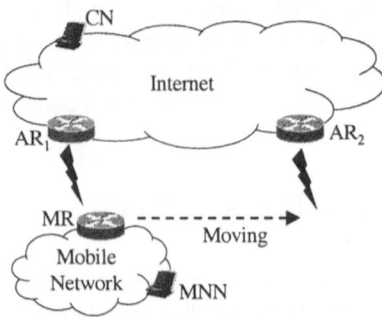

Fig. 1. Network mobility concept. The mobile network changes its point of attachment to the Internet from the old access router (AR_1) to the new access router (AR_2) as it moves

Fig.2 shows the role of the RMR in the architecture of multiple MRs. In Fig.2, MR_1 is the RMR when it is in the wireless coverage area of AR_1. It relays messages to the other MRs as RMR. As the mobile network moves, MR_1 goes away from the AR_1. Then, MR_n approaches to the AR_2 and becomes the new RMR for relaying.

Large networks have the tendency to move along predictable direction and rarely take unpredictable paths, thus the RMR can be adaptively selected according to the direction. As the RMR goes away from the AR, the opposite side MR prepares to be the RMR. In Fig. 2, for example, as MR_1 goes away from the AR_1, MR_n prepares to be the RMR with AR_2.

After selecting the RMR, three types of routings are examined: (1) the routing from the correspondent node (CN) outside of the mobile network to the RMR, (2) the relaying between the RMR and MRs, and (3) the routing from the RMR to the MNNs inside of the mobile network. When a CN sends a packet to a MNN, the RMR is the default router of ARs. When a MNN send a packet to a CN, the RMR becomes the default router of MRs. Following sections describe the RMR and the routing in detail.

3.1 Mobile Router Consensus and Selecting Representative Mobile Router

To operate the RMR-oriented management of multiple MRs, the RMR and the other MRs communicate among themselves for the consensus. Since any MR can be the RMR as the mobile network moves, consensus of MRs should be dynamically maintained. For the consensus, the RMR propagates *propose* and *decide* signal to the other MRs in the mobile network and the *management information base* (MIB) is maintained by the mobile network.

The RMR selection and release loop is shown in Fig. 3. Initially, all MRs are in the candidate state. When a MR hears the router advertisement message of any AR, it sends a *propose* signal as shown in Fig. 4. Then, it receives the *decide* signal and becomes a new RMR by updating the binding of its home agent. Now it implements mobility management functions on behalf of the mobile network.

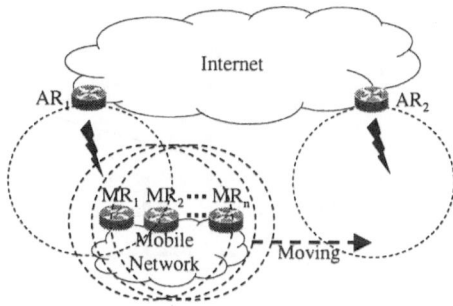

Fig. 2. Wireless link coverage enlargement with multiple mobile routers. MR_n is not directly attached to the Internet, but it can maintain connection to the Internet through the MR_1

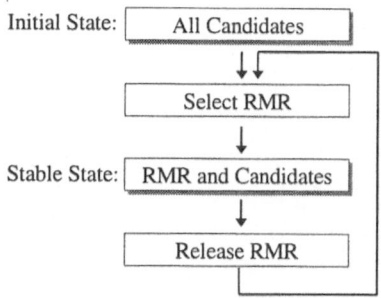

Fig. 3. Representative mobile router (RMR) selection and release loop

As the RMR goes away from the AR, it broadcasts the *release* signal so that the next RMR can be selected. Upon receiving the release signal, any MR who listens the router advertisement of AR proposes to be the new RMR and the old RMR becomes one of the candidate MRs. When more than one MRs propose to be a new RMR, the present RMR decides as coordinator based on the MIB. The MIB provides the information of the moving direction of the mobile network and the relational location of each MR. With the information, the best RMR can be selected.

3.2 Routing toward Mobile Networks

The RMR manages mobility of the MNNs behind it. The routing mechanism is based on Mobile IPv6 [4] and prefix scope binding updates [3], but it is extended to support multiple MRs. We assume that a mobile network consists of one IP subnet, and all MRs in a mobile network have the same network prefix and home agent.

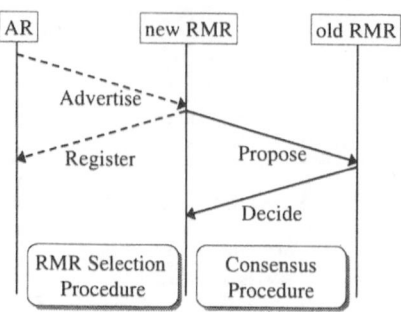

Fig. 4. Representative mobile router selection and consensus of mobile routers. When the current RMR broadcasts *release* message, RMR selection (router advertisement and register) and consensus (propose and decide the RMR) procedures are performed. After the procedure, the new RMR sends binding update to the home agent

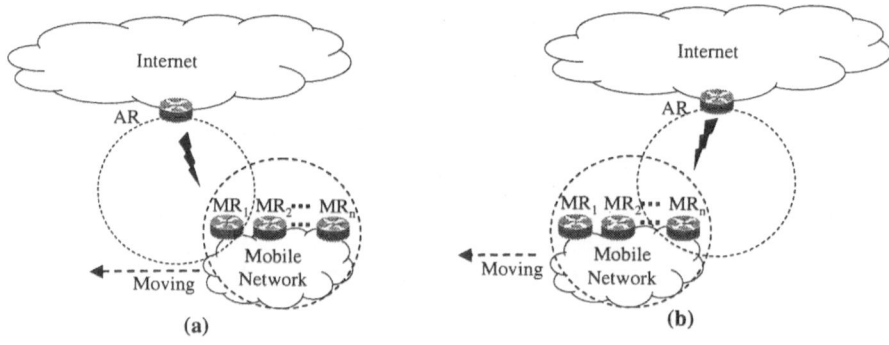

Fig. 5. Routing by mobile router when a mobile network moves. (a) At first, MR_1 gets in the coverage of AR and becomes the RMR. It sends the prefix scope binding update. (b) As the mobile network moves, MR_1 leaves away from the AR and MR_n becomes the new RMR. Then, messages can be routed through MR_n without new binding update. Since MR_1 and MR_n have the same prefix, the AR can forward packets correctly

If the new RMR is selected with a new AR, it sends a prefix scope binding update to its home agent as the MR in [3] does. The RMR of our scheme extends the function of the MR in [3] to propagate the routing information to the other MRs for replication. This extension eliminates the binding update when the new RMR is selected with the registered AR (Fig. 5). Since all MRs have the same prefix, the RMR does not have to update the prefix binding. The prefix scope binding is valid as long as one of the MRs are reachable from the registered AR.

For MNNs, network mobility is transparent. So, MNNs do not have to react to the network mobility and care of routing from outside the mobile network.

3.3 Routing inside Mobile Networks

After receiving the packets, the RMR routes them to the designated MNN. Routing inside a mobile network is based on the routing information replication. In this way, all routing information are replicated to the other MRs, thus all MRs in a mobile network have the same routing table entry.

For existing MNNs, RMR receives the packets designated them for further forwarding. Since the MRs replicate the same routing information, packets are routed to the designated MNNs correctly even though any MR becomes the RMR.

For a new MNN, a new mobile node comes into a mobile network, it gets a new IPv6 address using stateful address autoconfiguration and the correspondent MR updates its routing table as well as propagates the updated information to the other MRs. The proposed architecture uses stateful IPv6 address configuration by DHCPv6 with the prefix of the MRs.

3.4 Routing from Mobile Networks toward the Internet

Routing from a MR or a MNN of a mobile network is straightforward. MRs know the RMR thus forward data to it, which is reachable by the Internet via an AR.

4 Evaluation

The target service scenario for the evaluation is the case of public vehicles. A large vehicle such as a train, a ship, or an airplane with lots of passengers requires continuous connection to the Internet for providing wireless multimedia communication.

4.1 Environments

Access Routers and Mobile Routers. In the case of implementing mobile network with WLAN, ARs will be implemented with access points (APs). The APs will be equipped with routing functions. MRs will also be implemented with APs equipped with routing functions and operate as ad hoc mode bridges.

Connection of Mobile Routers. For the consensus, communication between MRs should be defined according to the physical characteristics of MRs. MRs can be connected to each other with wired or wireless links. MRs connected with wired links are stable. On the contrary, MRs connected with wireless links can dynamically adapt to the change of environment. The MRs connected with wireless link should have egress network interfaces out of the railroad cars and ingress network interfaces inside them.

Mobile Router Positioning. Multiple MRs should be positioned in the manner of effective management. We divide the requirement of positioning multiple MRs into two parts: balancing coverage, and avoiding frequency interference by architectural material, e.g. metal. First, coverage balancing should be achieved with optimizing the number of MRs in terms of space and mobile nodes attached to them.

Second, our first deploying candidate vehicle is a train with a line of railroad cars connected with each other. A wireless link cannot be reached from one railroad car to another, for its material characteristics. So, each railroad car should have its own MR and the mobile network of the train handles multiple MRs. This architecture is also applicable to the vehicles with metal partitioning inside them.

4.2 Analysis

Originally, we have two motivations for deploying multiple MRs. One is distributed architectural philosophy and the second is physical constraints of WLAN. From the point of distributed computing, multiple MRs provide consensus and additional gain of fault tolerant reliability. The physical constraints are related to the positioning of MRs.

Advantages. Multiple MRs provide following advantages:

- *Wireless coverage enlargement* by relaying
- *Bandwidth extension* by selecting the best RMR
- *Seamless mobility* by dynamic selection and release of the RMR

Fig. 2 shows the effect of coverage enlargement. In Fig. 2, MR_1 relays as RMR when it is in the coverage area of AR_1. Then MR_n, outside of the AR_1's coverage can access the WLAN.

The proposed architecture provides coverage gain efficiently when the length of a mobile vehicle is long enough in comparison to the WLAN cell size. In our examination, in the case of subway trains, the length of a vehicle is about 200 meters, while the coverage of IEEE 802.11b is 200 to 300 meters in diameter. So, the scheme is expected to result in expanding the wireless link coverage area with dynamic relaying. As a result, users enjoy up to 11Mbps multimedia services while moving with the vehicle.

Drawbacks. As most centralized systems do, the RMR-oriented approach may lead to load centralization on the RMR. But the approach reduces the delay of multiple registrations of MRs with ARs. In addition, it has advantage of simple implementation and centralized management in comparison to the architecture that allows multiple MRs to connect to the Internet simultaneously. Moreover, single home address assigned to a network interface can not bind with multiple network interfaces of multiple MRs in current mobile IPv6 implementations. So there is a tradeoff between the load balancing and implementation/management efficiency.

5 Conclusion

This paper introduced the architecture of mobile WLAN, which enables continuous multimedia services. To meet the requirement, we deployed multiple MRs with RMR-oriented management scheme. It is expected to be applicable to serve large volumes of wireless data to the group of mobile users on fast moving public vehicles such as trains, buses, and aircrafts. It can be further extended to the integrated system with cellular mobile systems to get larger access area.

We are planning to build a test-bed of mobile WLAN based upon the described issues. With the test-bed, traffic characteristics will be investigated to make it a real architecture. Our main interest on the traffic pattern is divided into three parts: (1) traffic between MNNs and CNs outside the mobile network, (2) traffic between MNNs in one mobile network and MNNs in other mobile networks, and (3) traffic between MNNs in the same mobile network.

After the first stage of the test-bed is completed, security mechanism should be strengthened for the WLAN which is originally developed for private systems thus has a weak security system.

References

1. C. Perkins, "IP Mobility Support," IETF RFC 2002, Oct. 1996.
2. T. Ernst and H. Lach, "Network Mobility Support Terminology," IETF Internet Draft, draft-ernst-monet-terminology-00.txt, Feb. 2002. work in progress.
3. T. Ernst et. Al, "Mobile Networks Support in Mobile IPv6 (Prefix Scope Binding Updates)," IETF Internet Draft, draft-ernst-mobileip-v6-network-03.txt, Mar. 2002. work in progress.
4. D. B. Johnson and C. Perkins, "Mobility Support in IPv6", IETF Internet Draft, draft-ietf-mobileip-ipv6-16.txt, April 2000. work in progress.
5. Soliman et. Al, "Hierarchical MIPv6 mobility management (HMIPv6)," IETF Internet Draft, draft-ietf-mobileip-hmipv6-05.txt, Jul. 2001. work in progress.
6. D. Shell, J. Courtenay, W. Ivancic, D. Stewart, T. Bell: "Mobile IP & Mobile Networks Promise New Era of Satellite and Wireless Communications," *Second Integrated Communications, Navigation and Surveillance Technologies Conference & Workshop*, April 29 - May 2nd, 2002.

VoIP Quality Evaluation in Mobile Wireless Networks

Pei-Jeng Kuo[1,2], Koji Omae[1], Ichiro Okajima[1], and Narumi Umeda[1]

[1] NTT DoCoMo, Inc., R&D Center, Wireless Laboratory , 3-5 Hikarinooka,
Yokosuka, Kanagawa, Japan
{peggykuo, Omae, Okajima, Umeda}@mlab.yrp.nttdocomo.co.jp
[2] Current Contact: peggykuo@alum.mit.edu

Abstract. Managing voice service quality over both IP-based wired and wireless networks has become a challenge, especially in a heterogeneous network environment. This paper discusses the issues that affect voice quality in a mobile wireless network. We compare the wireless Voice over IP (VoIP) quality performance using a combination of voice codecs and three mobility management protocols (MMP), which are Mobile IPv6 (MIP), Hierarchical Mobile IPv6 (HMIP) and the proposed Hierarchical Mobile IPv6 with Buffering Extension. The evaluation is based on ITU-T recommended MOS (Mean Opinion Score) and E-Model factors. Time varying impairments are also considered. Our evaluation shows that the proposed MMP provides a higher voice quality performance especially for low bit rate voice codecs.

1 Introduction

Traditionally, cellular systems deliver wireless voice services via circuit based connections similar to wired public phone system. The fact is changing due to rapid development of the IP (Internet Protocol) and VoIP technology. Real time services over IP-based wired or wireless environment can dramatically reduce the cost and complexity of system and enable the possibility of communication anytime, anywhere. While VoIP technology is maturing commercially in wired telephone networks, VoIP applications over wireless network is also emerging. As high-transmission data rate is now possible in wireless systems, real-time high quality voice and video services are highly expected, which are very sensitive to quality degradation due to network instability. This paper discusses the issues that affect voice quality especially in a mobile wireless network. Different mobility management protocols, which conduct the packet routing tasks, are evaluated with computer simulations. The evaluation is based on ITU-T recommended MOS (Mean Opinion Score) and E-Model factors, while time varying impairments are also considered. In Sec. 2, brief introduction of mobile wireless network is given. In Sec. 3, issues and proposed models for VoIP quality evaluation are described. Sec. 4 provides special highlight for the impact of those issues on the mobile network condition. The network simulation results can be seen in Sec. 5. Sec. 6 concludes this paper.

Y.-C. Chen, L.-W. Chang, and C.-T. Hsu (Eds.): PCM 2002, LNCS 2532, pp. 688–695, 2002.
© Springer-Verlag Berlin Heidelberg 2002

2 Mobile Wireless Networks

Next generation wireless networks are designed to enable high-performance streaming multimedia content such as streaming video and audio to mobile users. There are many factors to be considered in a wireless environment in terms of transmitting performance, for example, channel interference, radio fluctuation and handoff effects. The Quality of Service (QoS) requirements for streaming audio and video over a wireless network are dramatically different from the requirements for the transmission of standard TCP data, such as FTP and emails. While making a call from cellular phone, for example, many people consider the radio fluctuation and channel interference the cause of bad conversation quality. However, in a mobile wireless network, when the mobile terminal changes its point of connection, some packets can be lost or delayed during the handoff period. These packet loss or delay can be apparent and significantly degrade the perceived quality of realtime data. Many MMPs have been proposed in literature to perform more efficient handoffs, however, most evaluations are done with non-realtime data transmission. In this paper, we focus on the facts of real-time UDP data stream and VoIP quality evaluation over different MMPs.

3 Voice Quality Evaluation

3.1 Voice Quality Issues in IP Network

VoIP quality can be influenced by many factors, such as equipment, environment, and an individual's subjective perception. As customers choose different services subjectively, finding suitable VoIP evaluation criteria is essential to service providers. In a traditional network, voice is transmitted through dedicated circuit switch channels. When moving to packet-based networks, there are many factors that can determine the voice quality perceived by end users. Among those, the most important factors are codec, packet delay, packet loss and packet jitters. Nowadays, many compression techniques called *codecs* are available that require less bandwidth while preserving voice quality. The most used codecs today are those standardized by organizations such as ITU-T, for example, G.711, G.723 and G.729. Table 1 summarizes the packet properties of major codecs. *Packet loss* is a common problem on packet networks. TCP traffic such as FTP or email retransmits lost packets when they do not arrive within a certain time. However, it is not practical for real-time traffic such as voice or video since they are time sensitive. In some VoIP implementations, vendors leave a gap in the voice stream or fill the gaps with noise when packets are lost. Some vendors repeat the last voice sample before the lost packet. A better strategy is to interpolate the missing gap based on buffered history voice samples. This technique is called Packet Loss Concealment (PLC). An *end-to-end delay* of VoIP includes codec delay, packetization delay, propagation delay and jitter buffer delay. In general, a *lower bit rate codec* require longer algorithmic delay. Because of network congestion, load balancing or other reasons, packets sent to the network often traverse different routes and sometimes arrive at their destination out of order, this is called *packet jitter*. For real time applications, it makes no sense to play out packets when they are out of order. Normally, most implementations hold the incoming packets in a certain buffer period and wait for the slower packets, then reorder the packets into correct sequence before playing out. This jitter buffer adds end-to-end delay and impairs voice quality.

Table 1. Voice codecs and properties

Codec	Bit Rate	Payload	pps	Quality
G.711	64kbps	160Byte	50pps	Excellent
G.729	8kbps	20Byte	50pps	Good
G.723.1	6.3kbps	24Byte	32.8125pps	Good

3.2 Subjective Measurement: Mean Opinion Score (MOS)

Users often have the impression that VoIP quality is not as good as the public switched telephone network (PSTN) due to the lack of an ensured Quality of Service. Voice quality judgment is subjective since it is evaluated based on listeners' impression of perceived speech clarity. VoIP service providers have to find a balance between users' satisfaction and provisioning cost. In ITU-T P.800, a numerical representation of voice quality measurement called MOS (Mean Opinion Score) is described. MOS is a subjective voice quality assessment; test subjects judge the quality of the voice perceived by a conversation or speech samples transmitted through the system and then rank the voice quality by a 5 score scale. The scores of perceived voice quality from 5 to 1 represent "Excellent", "Good", "Fair", "Poor" and "Bad". The MOS score reflects the perceived quality change, which is useful information while planning voice quality. However, it is subjective and depends on human opinions. In addition, performing a MOS test can be time-consuming and costly. Hence, there is a lot of interest in devising objective tests.

3.3 Objective Measurement: E-model

ITU-T Recommendation G.107 describes a computation model for predictive voice analysis, called "E-Model". It is based on equipment impairments and the primary output is a scalar called "R Factor". The R-factor is calculated based from various impairments and can then be transformed into estimates of customer opinion for planning purposes. The R factor is calculated as $R = R_o - I_s - I_d - I_e + A$, where R_o is the basic signal-to-noise ration, I_s indicates simultaneous impairment, I_d is the impairment factor caused by delay, I_e represents the equipment impairment factor and A is the impairment compensation factor, which can adjust the overall R according to user's expectation. From the resulting R-factor, Mean Opinion Score (MOS) can be obtained. Detailed explanation of E-Model can be found in [8].

3.4   Time Varying Impairments

In ITU-T Recommendation G.108, G.113 and G.114, provisional planning values of the I_e and I_d are given based on several experiment data. Default values of parameters for other R factor components Ro, Is and A are also provided.   There are also some time varying impairments which were not originally considered in the E-Model.   In 1998, AT&T conducted a MOS experiment and found that by moving a burst of noise from the beginning, to the middle and the end of a call, the resulting MOS score changes from 3.8, to 3.3 and 3.2. This shows that people tend to remember recent quality impairment and hence give a lower MOS score if the bad event happens closer to the end of a voice sample.   In the France Telecom ITU SG12 Contribution, an asymmetric effect between degradation and improvement of voice quality was discussed.   It is found that the listeners take longer time to reflect in instantaneous MOS judgments when the voice quality changes from bad to good, while the reflection time is much shorter reversely.   Another AT&T MOS experiment shows that when packet loss happens in bursts, the resulting MOS score is lower than random loss pattern. The result can be found in [4] and are provided as ITU-T provisional values in burst loss conditions.

3.5   Extended E-model

In [2], an extension to the E-Model called VQmon is proposed by Telchemy Inc., which incorporates time varying effects mentioned above.   In VQmon algorithm, the E-Model can be simplified as function of I_d and I_e while adapting the provided default parameter values of Ro, Is and A.   To calculate I_e, VQmon separates a voice sample into gap and burst events by a 4-state Markov model.   A gap state is defined as an event where consecutive packets are received, and a burst state is considered when consecutive packet loss occurrs.   Based on the provisional values recommended by ITU-T, I_e values for burst and gap condition can be calculated and represented as I_{eb} and I_{eg} respectively. The average I_e can be calculated after asymmetric perception effect described above is applied according to transition calculations described in [2]. Lastly, the recency effect is modeled with exponential decays consideration from the last burst event.   Detailed explanation of the extended E- model can be found in [5]. In terms of I_d, the default values of for selected one-way delay times are listed in ITU-T Rec. G.107.   And in [3], a linear expression to calculate I_d from one-way delay can be found.

4   VoIP Performance in Mobile Networks

In literature, most provisional data for E-Model and hence MOS scores are gathered or calculated in wired network test environments.   As described in the previous sections, the I_e and I_d values are different for the various voice codecs. For a lower bit rate codec, the default equipment impairment I_e is higher and the one-way delay is normally longer due to algorithmic coding time.   Also, a lost packet contains more

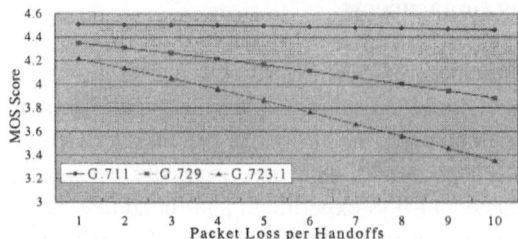

Fig. 1. Comparison of packet loss per handoff and MOS score for three major codes

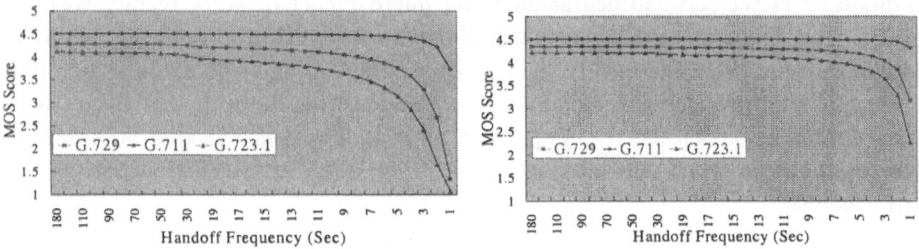

Fig. 2. MOS vs. handoff frequency for three codecs with (a)8 and (b)3 packets loss per handoff

syllables and hence can further degrade the voice quality with a lower bit rate codec. Unfortunately, current VoIP services are usually implemented with lower bit rate codecs due to bandwidth limitations. In terms of wireless VoIP condition, bursty packet loss happens whenever handoff occurs; this effect can further exaggerate the degradation.

In light of these considerations, we reconstruct an E-Model calculation, which combines the provisional values provided in [8, 9, 10] with time varying effects adjustments described in [2, 3, 4, 5]. The reconstruction calculation has a specific emphasis on the handoff effect, which has significant impact on perceived VoIP quality in wireless mobile networks. We separate the voice transmission into burst and gap conditions according to the VQmon algorithm described in [5]. For the instantaneous I_e factor, we adopt the linear expression used in [3] for three codecs, G.711, G.729 and G.723.1. In our simulated wireless mobile network, we assume all packet losses happen during handoffs. Hence the default values of burst and gap packet loss percentages are 100 and 0 respectively. The gap and burst length in VQmon model are calculated based on handoff frequency and consecutive packet loss value during each handoff, which differ for different MMPs. The time delay since last burst event in VQmon is set to be 5s. The Advantage Factor, A, in E-model is set to 10 according to default value for "mobility in a geographical area or moving in a vehicle" condition

Figures 1, 2(a) and 2(b) show the results from our simulations. Fig.1 compares the packet loss number per handoff with MOS score for three major codecs G.711, G. 729 and G.723.1. Fig. 2(a) and 2(b) plot handoff frequencies versus MOS scores. In Fig.1, the handoff frequency is set to 8s and one-way delay is set to be 50 msec. In Fig.2(a) and 2(b), the packet losses per handoff are 8 and 3 respectively. From Fig.1, we can see that, the number of packet loss per handoff has a greater impact on the predicted MOS score for a low bit rate codec. When it exceeds 7 for the case of G.723.1, the resulting voice quality could be unacceptable for most users. In Fig.2(a) and (b), the G.711 voice quality remains acceptable even with higher handoff frequency. However, when the packet loss per handoff is 8, voice quality for both G.729 and G.723.1 degrade significantly if the handoff frequency is shorter than 5s. When the packet loss per handoff is 3, the voice quality of a low bit rate codec remains acceptable even when handoff frequency is 2s.

5   Computer Simulation

5.1   Simulation Topology

The topology of our simulation is illustrated in Fig. 3. The simulation consists of real-time UDP voice traffic from Correspondent Host (CH) to Mobile Host (MH). We use three different codecs, G.711, G.729 and G.723.1 for our traffic. We partition the network into Internet and local network domains and the time delays are 50 msec and 10 msec respectively. A 2s frequency is selected to simulate the frequent handoffs in a mobile wireless environment. The wireless and wired transmission rates are 20 and 100Mbps in our simulation. Detailed architecture of the simulation can be found in [11].

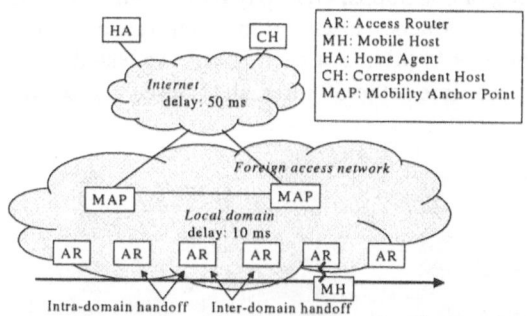

Fig. 3. Simulation Network Topology (Source: Omae et al., Feb 2002)

5.2   Simulated Mobility Management Protocols

We tested three mobility management protocols in our primary simulations. *Mobile IPv6* [6] is an IETF (Internet Engieneering Task Force) proposed MMP, which allows mobile node (MN) moves between access routers (AR) while retaining the same Home Address. When MN moves to a foreign network, it can get a temporary Care of Address (CoA). Home Agent (HA) in home network takes care of Home Address and binding updates (BUs) registration of CoA. When a packet from Correspondent Host (CH) is sent to a MN, it will route to MN's HA and be transmitted to MN's CoA.

Hierarchical Mobile IPv6 (HMIPv6) [7], also proposed by IETF, introduces a Mobility Anchor Point (MAP) function and minor extension to the MN. MAP serves in the local domain and receive all the packets sent to MH. When MH changes its point of attachment, it only needs to send BU of its new address to MAP. MAP will forward and encapsulate the packets to MN and hence behalf as a local HA for MN. In MIPv6, packets sent between AR handoff and MN's BU will be lost by misrouting; the introduction of MAP can reduce the latency due to handoffs between ARs since it requires less time for BUs to arrive a local MAP than a remote HA. *Hierarchical Mobile IPv6 with Buffering Extension* [11], our proposed MMP, is an extension of HMIPv6, which adds buffering function in the MAP of HMIPv6. In this extension, a 1-bit B-flag in the BU packet for buffering request (BU with B set) is added. Before changing to a new AR, MH will send a BU with B set to MAP. When MAP receives the BU, it will return a binding acknowledgement (BA) and start buffering received packets. When the BA arrives MH, MH starts to perform the handoff and then obtain a new CoA. After the BU of a new CoA is sent to MAP, MAP will send all the buffered packets during handoff to MH's new CoA. The packet loss during handoffs can be eliminated in this extension. Details of the three protocols can be found in [6], [7], [11] respectively.

5.3   Simulation Results

We firstly test VoIP network performance for the three MMPs with G.729 traffic. The packets sending rate is 50pps, UDP payload length is 32Bytes including a 12 Byte RTP header, handoff frequency is 2s and the total traffic last for 3 minutes. The traffic direction is from CH to MH. For each MMP, we tested two scenarios with the AR handoff disconnection time set to 50 msec and 0 msec respectively.

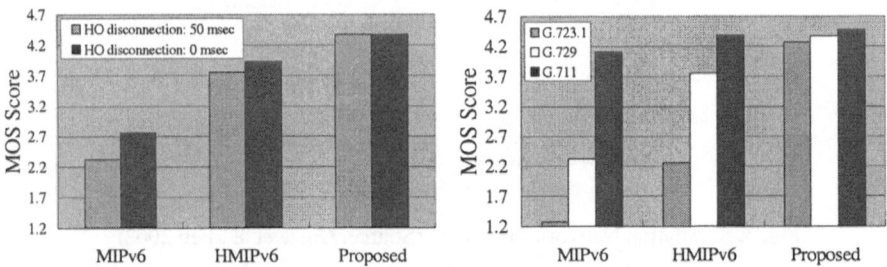

Fig. 4. Voice Quality Performance vs. (a) MMPs and (b) Voice Codecs

Fig.4(a) is the result of above simulation. The proposed MMP eliminates packet loss during handoffs and result in a very high MOS score. The voice quality transmitted with HMIPv6 gives MOS scores of 3.87 and 3.75 with 0 and 50 msec handoff disconnection time respectively, still within the acceptable range. With MIPv6, the MOS score is lower than 3 and the predicted voice quality is poor. From Fig.4(a), when the disconnection period between AR handoff is close to zero, the packet loss per handoff is reduced, resulting in better voice quality. We also simulated the same

MMPs for G.711 and G.723.1 traffic. Fig.4(b) shows the results. For higher bit rate codec, G.711, high quality VoIP performance can be achieved even with MIPv6. Upgrading from MIPv6 to the proposed MMP only slightly improves the resulting MOS score from 4.11 to 4.48. However, with lower bit rate codec, G.723.1, our proposed MMP results in a significant improvement over MIPv6 and HMIPv6. The MOS score of 1.27 for MIPv6 and 2.25 for HMIPv6 is dramatically improved to 4.27 with our proposed MMP. For G.729, which is often used in VoIP implementations, our proposed MMP also improves the voice performance from a MOS score of 3.75 for HMIPv6 to the "best" level of 4.37.

6 Conclusion

In this paper, a VoIP quality evaluation model based on the ITU-T MOS score and E-model is described. Time varying impairments such as burst packet loss and recency effects that can significantly degrade VoIP quality are adjusted with E-model extensions based on Telchemy's VQmon model and AT&T's linear model. Here we focus on mobile network situations, in which emphasis on handoff performance and bursty packet loss are considered as special case for the above model. Three MMPs - MIPv6, HMIPv6 and our proposed HMIPv6 extension with buffering are evaluated in our simulation network. We compared the performance of the three MMPs for the major voice codecs G.711, G.729 and G.723.1. The result shows that our proposed MMP can significantly improve VoIP quality, especially for low bit rate codecs.

References

[1] I. Okajima et al., "Network Architecture for Mobile Communications Systems Beyond IMT-2000", *Personal Communications,* Oct. 2001.

[2] A. Clark, "Passive Monitoring for Voice over IP Gateways", *TIA Cont.,* Feb 2001.

[3] R. G. Cole et al., "Voice over IP Performance Monitoring", *AT&T prep.,* Sep 2000.

[4] AT&T, "Results of a Subjective Listening Test for G.711 with Frame Erasure Concealment", *T1 W G Contribution,* T1A1.7/99-016, May 1999.

[5] A. Clark, "Extensions to the E-Model to incorporate the effects of time varying packet loss and recency", T1A1.1/2001-037, Apr2001.

[6] H, Soliman, et al., "Hierarchical MIPv6 Mobility Management", draft-ietf-mobileip-hmipv6-05.txt, Jul 2001. (work in progress)

[7] D.B. Johnson, et al., "Mobility Support in Ipv6", draft-ietf-mobileip-ipv6-16.txt, Mar 2002. (work in progress)

[8] ITU-T Rec.G.107, "The E-Model, A Computational Model for use in Transmission Planning", May 2000.

[9] ITU-T Rec.G.108, "Application of the E-Model: A Planning Guild", Sep 1999.

[10] ITU-T Rec.G.113, "Transmission impairments due to Speech Processing, Appendix I: Provisional Planning Values for the Equipment Impairment Factor I_e", Feb 2001

[11] K. Omae, et al., "Hierarchical Mobile Ipv6 Extension for IP-based Mobile Communication System", *T R of IEICE,* IN 2001-178, Feb 2002.

Connection Removal Algorithms for Multimedia CDMA Wireless Networks

Jui Teng Wang

Institute of Communication Engineering
National Chi Nan University, Nantou, Taiwan
teng@atm.cm.nctu.edu.tw

Abstract. We study in this paper connection removal algorithms for multimedia CDMA wireless networks. In our study, users can have different data rates as well as different quality of service (QoS) requirements characterized by bit energy-to-interference ratios. In the distributed power control algorithm, connection removal mechanism is invoked if, after a pre-specified number of iterations of power control, QoS requirements are not satisfied. We prove in this paper that, if the transmitter power levels are not reset after a connection is removed, then a feasible power set can be found faster and the power levels employed are smaller. Performances of some connection removal criteria for multimedia CDMA wireless networks are also studied. Three connection removal criteria, i.e., smallest CIR, smallest normalized CIR and largest CIR requirement, are evaluated.

1 Introduction

Multimedia applications over wireless networks, especially CDMA wireless networks [8]-[10], have recently attracted much attention from researchers. Different from single-service networks, multimedia networks have to deal with users which have different data rates and different quality of service (QoS) requirements. The QoS requirement of a multimedia application may include maximum packet delay and bit error rate. Maximum packet delay can be guaranteed with the help of connection admission control and (re)transmission scheduling. In this paper, we focus on guarantee of bit error rate in a CDMA network. We assume that bit error rate requirement can be mapped into an equivalent bit energy-to-interference ratio requirement. It is acceptable because, given a transmission technology, bit error rate can be derived from bit energy-to-interference ratio.

In CDMA wireless networks, all users share the same frequency band and thus the interference sets a limit on system capacity. Therefore, it is important to use power control technique to reduce the interference and allow as many receivers as possible to obtain satisfactory reception. Several centralized and distributed power control algorithms had been proposed [1]-[5] to achieve the goal. In centralized power control, a network center can compute the optimum power levels for all users simultaneously. However, it requires measurements of all the link gains and communication overhead between network center and base stations and thus is

Y.-C. Chen, L.-W. Chang, and C.-T. Hsu (Eds.): PCM 2002, LNCS 2532, pp. 696-703, 2002.
© Springer-Verlag Berlin Heidelberg 2002

difficult to realize in a large system. Distributed power control, on the other hand, uses only local information to iteratively adjust the transmitting power of each individual user. It is much more scalable than centralized power control. However, the speed for finding a feasible power set, i.e., a power set which can meet the QoS requirements, may be a big concern. As reported in [4], the fully distributed power control (FDPC) algorithm finds a feasible power set faster than similar algorithms.

For distributed power control, one connection is removed if, after a pre-specified number of iterations of power control (which are counted as a round), QoS requirements are not satisfied. The initial power levels for the next round hence need to be determined when connection removal mechanism is invoked. We prove that in the FDPC algorithm, if the transmitter power levels are not reset after a connection is removed, then a feasible power set can be found faster and the power levels employed are smaller.

For real applications, it is important to adopt an efficient removal criterion to determine the priority of removal. In this paper, we study and compare the performance of some connection removal criteria for the FDPC algorithm. Three connection removal criteria, namely, smallest CIR (SC), smallest normalized CIR (SNC) and largest CIR requirement (LCR), are evaluated. The SC criterion removes the connection with the smallest CIR and was employed in [2], [4] for single type of service. In the SNC criterion, the connection with the smallest normalized CIR (i.e., CIR divided by the CIR requirement) is removed. In the LCR criterion, the connection with the largest CIR requirement is removed, if there are multiple such connections, the one with the smallest CIR is removed. The SC criterion considers only CIR values, while the SNC and LCR criteria take into account both CIR values and CIR requirements. Our simulation results reveal that the SNC and LCR criteria result in better performance than the SC criterion in a multimedia environment.

The rest of this paper is organized as follows. Section 2 describes the investigated system model. Connection removal algorithms are studied in Sections 3. Numerical examples are presented in Section 4. Finally, we draw conclusion in Section 5.

2 System Model

We consider the reverse link of a CDMA wireless network. As mentioned previously, users are allowed to have different data rates and QoS requirements in terms of bit energy-to-interference ratios. We treat the link gains as constant during the operation of power control. It is possible in the wireless local loop (WLL) system, wireless local area networks (WLAN) and other personal communication systems, where the users are still or move slowly relative to the speed of power control algorithm.

We assume that there are N active base stations in the network with K_i users connected to base station i, $1 \leq i \leq N$. Notice that K_i is constant during the process of power control. The pair (i,k) is used to denote the kth user connected to the ith base station. Consider user (i,k). Let P_{ik}, r_{ik} and G_{ik} represent its transmitting power, data rate and processing gain, respectively. Also, let η_i denote the thermal noise for the receiver of the ith base station and W denote the spread bandwidth. As a result, since $G_{ik} = W / r_{ik}$, the received bit energy-to-interference ratio for user (i,k) is given by

$$E_{ik} \equiv \left(\frac{E_b}{I_0}\right)_{ik} = \frac{P_{ik}L_{(i,k)i}/r_{ik}}{\left(\sum_{n=1}^{N}\sum_{l=1}^{K_n}P_{nl}L_{(n,l)i} - P_{ik}L_{(i,k)i} + \eta_i\right)/W} \tag{1}$$

$$= \frac{P_{ik}L_{(i,k)i}G_{ik}}{\sum_{n=1}^{N}\sum_{l=1}^{K_n}P_{nl}L_{(n,l)i} - P_{ik}L_{(i,k)i} + \eta_i},$$

where $L_{(n,l)i}$ represents the link gain between user (n,l) and base station i. To minimize transmitting power, a user is connected to base station i if the link gain between the user and base station i is greater than that between the user and base station j for all $j \neq i$.

After some manipulations, (1) can be rewritten as

$$\sum_{n=1}^{N}\sum_{l=1}^{K_n}P_{nl}L_{(n,l)i} + \eta_i = P_{ik}L_{(i,k)i}\left(1 + G_{ik}/E_{ik}\right), \tag{2}$$

$$1 \leq i \leq N \text{ and } 1 \leq k \leq K_i.$$

Let Q_{ik} denote the QoS requirement, i.e., the minimum bit energy-to-interference ratio requirement, of user (i,k). For all the users to meet their QoS requirements, we must find a power set $\mathbf{P} = \{P_{ik}\}$ ($1 \leq i \leq N$, $1 \leq k \leq K_i$) such that $P_{ik} > 0$ and

$$E_{ik} = \frac{P_{ik}L_{(i,k)i}G_{ik}}{\sum_{n=1}^{N}\sum_{l=1}^{K_n}P_{nl}L_{(n,l)i} - P_{ik}L_{(i,k)i} + \eta_i} \geq Q_{ik} \tag{3}$$

for $1 \leq i \leq N$ and $1 \leq k \leq K_i$.

As in [3], such a power set is called a feasible power set. Given a configuration specified by $\mathbf{K} = \{K_i\}$ ($1 \leq i \leq N$) and $\mathbf{L} = \{L_{(n,l)i}\}$ ($1 \leq n \leq N$, $1 \leq l \leq K_n$), if there exists a feasible power set $\mathbf{P} = \{P_{ik}\}$, then this configuration is said to be feasible. Otherwise, it is said to be infeasible.

3 Connection Removal Algorithms

In this section, we first describe the FDPC algorithm and then propose the connection removal algorithms based on it. Throughout this section, $\mathbf{P}^0 = \{P_{ik}^0\}$ denotes the initial transmitter power set. Also, $\mathbf{P}^m = \{P_{ik}^m\}$ and $\mathbf{E}^m = \{E_{ik}^m\}$ denote the transmitter power set and the set of received bit energy-to-interference ratio in the mth discrete time, respectively.

FDPC Algorithm

$$\mathbf{P}^0 = \left\{ P_{ik}^0 \right\}$$

and

$$P_{ik}^{m+1} = a_{ik}^m * P_{ik}^m,$$

where

$$a_{ik}^m = \frac{\min(E_{ik}^m, Q_{ik})}{E_{ik}^m}. \qquad \square$$

After a pre-specified number (say L) of iterations of the FDPC algorithm, if no feasible power set is found, one user is removed. For convenience, every L iterations are counted as a round and the round number is denoted by n. Moreover, for the simplicity of notations, we let Ω represent the set of all connections and renumber the users so that user (i,k) is mapped to connection j, where $1 \le i \le N$, $1 \le k \le K_i$ and $1 \le j \le \sum_{i=1}^{N} K_i$. Hence, we have $P_j^m = P_{i,k}^m$ for all i, k, j and m. The removal algorithm can be described as follows.

Step 1: Let $n=1$, $\Omega = \{1,2,..., \sum_{i=1}^{N} K_i\}$ and $P_j^0 = P_{max}$ for all connections j.

Step 2: Execute at most L iterations with the FDPC algorithm.

Step 3: Stop if a feasible power set is found. Else, remove connection u from Ω according to some connection removal criterion.

Step 4: Let $n=n+1$, $\Omega = \Omega - \{u\}$ and $P_j^0 = P_j^L$ for all connection $j \in \Omega$. Go to Step 2.

In step 4, the power levels remain unchanged after removal, so the above algorithm is called the non-reinitialized removal (NRR) algorithm. On the contrary, the removal algorithms in [2], [4] reset the power levels to the initial values after removal, thus we call them the reinitialized removal (RR) algorithms. In the following, we compare the performance of the NRR algorithm with that of the RR algorithm. We assume that the connection removed by both NRR and RR algorithms are the same in every round. Under such assumption, we prove that the NRR algorithm performs better than the RR algorithm.

Let $\mathbf{P}_r^{n,m} = \left\{ P_{r,j}^{n,m} \right\}$ and $\mathbf{E}_r^{n,m} = \left\{ E_{r,j}^{n,m} \right\}$ denote respectively the transmitter power set and the set of bit energy-to-interference ratio in the mth iteration of round n for the RR algorithm. Similarly, let $\mathbf{P}_{nr}^{n,m} = \left\{ P_{nr,j}^{n,m} \right\}$ and $\mathbf{E}_{nr}^{n,m} = \left\{ E_{nr,j}^{n,m} \right\}$ represent those sets for the NRR algorithm.

Lemma 1: Assume that a connection has to be removed at the end of round n. If $E_{nr,j}^{n,L} \ge Q_j$, then $E_{nr,j}^{n+1,0} \ge Q_j$ for all j and n.

Lemma 2: Assume that, at the beginning of round n, the following two conditions hold

    (i) $P_{nr,j}^{n,0} \le P_{r,j}^{n,0}$ for all connections j, and

    (ii) $E_{nr,j}^{n,0} \ge Q_j$ if $E_{r,j}^{n,0} \ge Q_j$ for any connection j.

We have, for all iterations $m \leq L$ of round n,

(iii) $P_{nr,j}^{n,m} \leq P_{r,j}^{n,m}$ for all connections j, and

(iv) $E_{nr,j}^{n,m} \geq Q_j$ if $E_{r,j}^{n,m} \geq Q_j$ for any connection j.

The proofs of the above lemmas can be found in [5]. The meaning of Lemma 2 is that if, at the beginning of a round, the power levels employed in the NRR algorithm are smaller than or equal to those employed in the RR algorithm and, moreover, connection j satisfies its QoS requirement in the NRR algorithm if it is so in the RR algorithm, then the same conditions hold after every iteration of the round. On the basis of Lemmas 1 and 2, we obtain the following theorem.

Theorem 1: It holds for all n that,

(i) $P_{nr,j}^{n,m} \leq P_{r,j}^{n,m}$ for all j and m, and

(ii) if $E_{r,j}^{n,m} \geq Q_j$, then $E_{nr,j}^{n,m} \geq Q_j$ for all j and m.

Proof: We prove Theorem 1 by mathematical induction. For $n = 0$, $P_{nr,j}^{0,0} = P_{r,j}^{0,0}$ and $E_{nr,j}^{0,0} = E_{r,j}^{0,0}$ for all j, thus according to Lemma 2, (i) and (ii) are true. Assume that the theorem is true for $n = N$. Consider the case $n = N+1$, since $P_{r,j}^{N+1,0} = P_{max}$ and $P_{nr,j}^{N+1,0} = P_{nr,j}^{N,L}$ for all j, and $P_{ik}^{m+1} \leq P_{ik}^{m}$ for all i, k, and m (the property of the FDPC algorithm), it is clear that $P_{nr,j}^{N+1,0} \leq P_{r,j}^{N+1,0}$ for all j.

For the FDPC algorithm, when $E_{ik}^{m} < Q_{ik}$, it holds that $P_{ik}^{m+1} = P_{ik}^{0}$ for all i, k, and m, thus, if $E_{nr,u}^{N,L} < Q_u$ for some connection u, then we have $P_{nr,u}^{N,L} = P_{max}$. Since $P_{nr,u}^{N+1,0} = P_{r,u}^{N+1,0} = P_{max}$ and $P_{nr,j}^{N+1,0} \leq P_{r,j}^{N+1,0}$ for all j, if $E_{r,u}^{N+1,0} \geq Q_u$, we also have $E_{nr,u}^{N+1,0} \geq Q_u$.

On the other hand, if $E_{nr,u}^{N,L} \geq Q_u$, then according to Lemma 1, it holds that $E_{nr,u}^{N+1,0} \geq Q_u$. So, if $E_{r,u}^{N+1,0} \geq Q_u$, we also have $E_{nr,u}^{N+1,0} \geq Q_u$.

On the basis of the above discussions and Lemma 2, we conclude that (i) and (ii) are true for $n = N+1$.

This completes the proof of Theorem 1

A consequence of theorem 1 is that the NRR algorithm employs smaller power levels and finds a feasible power set faster than the RR algorithm. Numerical results presented in the following section show that the NRR algorithm may result in a much smaller outage probability than the RR algorithm.

In addition to the determination for the power levels, another important issue for the removal algorithm is the choice for the connection removal criterion. Listed below are three possible connection removal criteria. Let CIR_j, Γ_j, E_j, Q_j and G_j represent the carrier-to-interference ratio, the CIR requirement, the bit energy-to-interference ratio, the QoS requirement and the processing gain for the jth connection, respectively, we have $CIR_j = E_j / G_j$ and $\Gamma_j = Q_j / G_j$.

(1) Smallest CIR (SC) criterion

Remove connection $u \in \Omega$ which has the smallest CIR among all connections in Ω (i.e., $CIR_u \leq CIR_j$ for all $j \in \Omega$, $j \neq u$).

(2) Smallest normalized CIR (SNC) criterion

Remove connection $u \in \Omega$ which has the smallest normalized CIR among all connections in Ω (i.e., $(CIR_u / \Gamma_u) \leq (CIR_j / \Gamma_j)$ for all $j \in \Omega$, $j \neq u$).

(3) Largest CIR requirement (LCR) criterion

Remove connection $u \in \Omega$ which has the smallest CIR requirement among all connections in Ω. If there exist multiple such connections, the one with the smallest CIR is removed.

The idea of the above three criteria is to remove a connection which is unlikely to meet its CIR requirement. For the SNC criterion, the connection which has the largest difference (in dB) between its CIR requirement and current CIR is removed.

4   Numerical Results

In this section, we study an integrated voice/data CDMA wireless network which is composed of 19 hexagonal cells. The radius of the cell is 1 Km and a base station is located in the middle of each cell. We adopt the FDPC algorithm in the considered network and assume that the locations of the users are uniformly distributed over the cell area. The initial power level is set to 1 W and the thermal noise is 10^{-15} W. An user is connected to the base station with the largest link gain to minimize its transmitting power level and the number of iterations L for removal algorithms is chosen to be eight. The spread bandwidth W is set to 1.25 MHz. The data rate and QoS requirement of voice users are 9.6 Kbps and 7 dB, respectively. Data users send data at 38.4 Kbps with 9 dB QoS requirement. The same characteristics were used in [8]. Numerical results are obtained by means of computer simulation for 10000 independent configurations.

The link gain $L_{(n,l)i}$ is modeled as $L_{(n,l)i} = A_{(n,l)i} / d_{(n,l)i}^{\alpha}$, where $A_{(n,l)i}$ is the attenuation factor, $d_{(n,l)i}$ is the distance between user (n,l) and base station i, and α is a constant that models the large scale propagation loss. The attenuation factor models power variation due to shadowing. $A_{(n,l)i}$, $1 \leq i, n \leq N$ and $1 \leq l \leq K_n$, are assumed to be independent, log-normal random variables with 0 dB expectation and σ dB log-variance. The parameter value of σ in the range of 4-10 dB and the propagation constant α in the range of 3-5 usually provide good models for urban propagation [6]. In our simulations, we choose $\alpha = 4$ and $\sigma = 8$ as in [7].

In Fig. 1, we plot the outage probability against the number of voice users (no data user present) for the NRR and RR algorithms. The outage probability is defined as the ratio of the number of removed connections to the number of total connections. In the NRR and RR algorithms, the connection with the smallest received initial CIR is first removed. It can be seen that the NRR algorithm results in a much smaller outage probability than the RR algorithm. In this figure, the curve for NRR* represents the outage probability for the NRR algorithm in which the connection removed in round n is the one which has the smallest CIR after one iteration of the round. It can be seen that outage probabilities for NRR and NRR* algorithms are close to each other.

In Fig. 2, we plot the average number of iterations needed to find a feasible power set for different removal criteria. Finding a feasible power set faster also means that the removal algorithm has smaller outage probability. It can be seen that the LCR criterion finds a feasible power set faster than the SNC criterion, which in turn finds a feasible power set faster than the SC criterion. The reason is that the connection with a larger CIR requirement needs more iterations to reduce its received interference so that its CIR requirement can be satisfied. Therefore, by removing the connection with a larger CIR requirement, one can usually decrease the number of iterations needed in finding a feasible power set. We also perform simulations for data applications with various other bit rates and CIR requirements. The results are consistent, i.e., the LCR criterion performs better than the SNC criterion, which in turn has a better performance than the SC criterion. However, the difference becomes smaller as the CIR requirement of data applications gets closer to that of the voice applications.

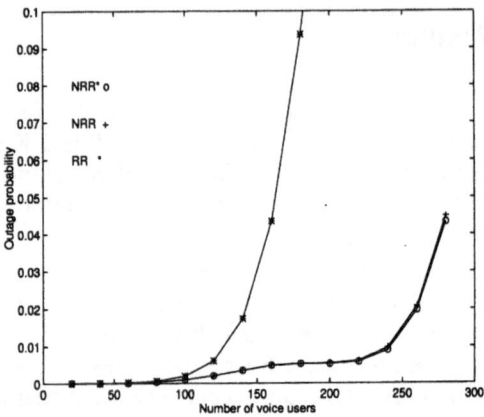

Fig. 1. The outage probability against the number of voice users for the NRR and RR algorithms.

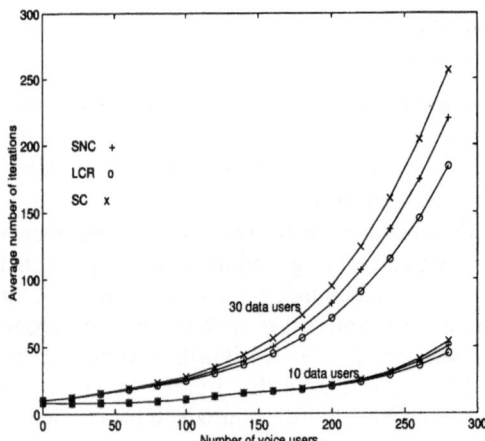

Fig. 2. Average number of iterations to find a feasible power set against number of users for different number of data users.

5 Conclusion

We have studied in this paper connection removal algorithms for multimedia CDMA wireless networks. We prove in this paper that in the FDPC algorithm, the non-reinitialized removal algorithm finds a feasible power set faster and employs smaller power levels than the reinitialized one.

The proposed removal criteria aim to speed up the process in finding a feasible power set and reduce the outage probability. From our numerical results, the LCR criterion results in better performance than the other removal criteria. Since different types of connections are likely to have different bandwidth requirements, other removal criteria which can maximize bandwidth utilization or minimize some cost function worth to be further studied.

References

1. Zander, J.: Performance of optimum transmitter power control in cellular radio cellular systems. IEEE Trans. Veh. Technol., Vol. 41, No. 1. (1992) 57-62
2. Zander, J.: Distributed cochannel interference control in cellular radio systems. IEEE Trans. Veh. Technol., Vol. 41, No. 3. (1992) 305-311
3. Yates, R. D.: A framework for uplink power control in cellular radio systems. IEEE J. Select. Areas Commun., Vol. 13, No. 7. (1995) 1341-1347
4. Lee, T. H., Lin, J. C.: A fully distributed power control algorithm for cellular mobile systems. IEEE J. Select. Areas Commun., Vol. 14, No. 4. (1996) 692-697
5. Wang, J. T., Lee, T. H.: Non–reinitialized fully distributed power control algorithm. IEEE Communications Letters, Vol. 3, No. 12. (1999) 329-331
6. Lee, W. C. Y.: Elements of cellular mobile radio. IEEE Trans. Veh. Technol., Vol. VT-35. (1986) 48-56
7. Gilhousen, K. S., Jacobs, I. M., Padovani, R., Viterbi, A. J., Weaver, L. A. Jr., Wheatley, III, C. E.: On the capacity of a cellular CDMA system. IEEE Trans. Veh. Technol., Vol. 40, No.2. (1991) 303-312
8. I, C-L., Sabnani, K. K.: Variable spreading gain CDMA with adaptive control for true packet switching wireless networks. Proc. ICC' 95. 725-730
9. Wu, J., Kohno, R.: A wireless multimedia CDMA system based on transmission power control. IEEE J. Select. Areas Commun., Vol. 14, No. 4. (1996) 683-691
10. Wyrwas, R, Zhang, W., Miller, M. J., Anjaria, R.: Multiple access options for multi-media wireless systems. Wireless Communications-Future Directions, Kluwer Academic Publishers. (1993) 305-317

Integration of GPRS and Wireless LANs with Multimedia Applications

Hong-Wei Lin[1], Jyh-Cheng Chen[1,2], Ming-Chia Jiang[1], and
Ching-Yang Huang[2]

[1] Department of Computer Science
[2] Institute of Communications Engineering
National Tsing Hua University, Hsinchu, Taiwan

Abstract. This paper presents a gateway approach for the integration
of GPRS and wireless LANs (WLANs). The proposed architecture leverages Mobile IP as the mobility management protocol over WLANs. The
interworking between GPRS and WLANs is achieved by a gateway which
resides on the border of GPRS system. The design goal is to minimize the
changes in GPRS and WLANs as that both systems are widely available
in the markets already. By deploying the gateway, users can seamlessly
roam among two systems. This paper also presents a testbed based on
the architecture and design principles. Empirical experiments with multimedia applications are conducted to analyze the testbed performance
in terms of handoff latency and throughput.

1   Introduction

The number of mobile users grows rapidly in recent years. They not only require
traditional voice service but also aspire multimedia service with high bandwidth
access. General Packet Radio Service (GPRS), a wireless data system based on
the GSM architecture, is designed to serve highly mobile subscribers with sophisticated high-power radio. Cell diameters can exceed $10\ Km$. The current
available data rate is on the range of $20 - 170\ Kbps$. On the other hand, by
utilizing short range and low power radio wireless LANs (WLANs) are mainly
deployed in indoor environment for low mobility and high speed applications.
The bit rate of IEEE 802.11b can achieve $11\ Mbps$, while IEEE 802.11a and
ETSI (European Telecommunications Standards Institute) HIPERLAN/2 are
defining standards with $50\ Mbps$. It is likely that both of them will coexist and
complement each other in the future. Users might want to use GPRS virtually
anywhere to access to the Internet. They nevertheless would like to leverage the
high-speed access of WLANs whenever it is possible. In addition, many organizations provide free WLAN access for their employees/students within their
own buildings/campuses. However GPRS and WLANs are based on different
networking technologies. The integration of them, especially seamless roaming,
thus becomes a critical issue.

   IP (Internet Protocol), which is already a universal network-layer protocol for wireline packet networks, is a promising universal network-layer protocol to integrate heterogeneous wireless systems. GPRS introduces two special

Y.-C. Chen, L.-W. Chang, and C.-T. Hsu (Eds.): PCM 2002, LNCS 2532, pp. 704–711, 2002.

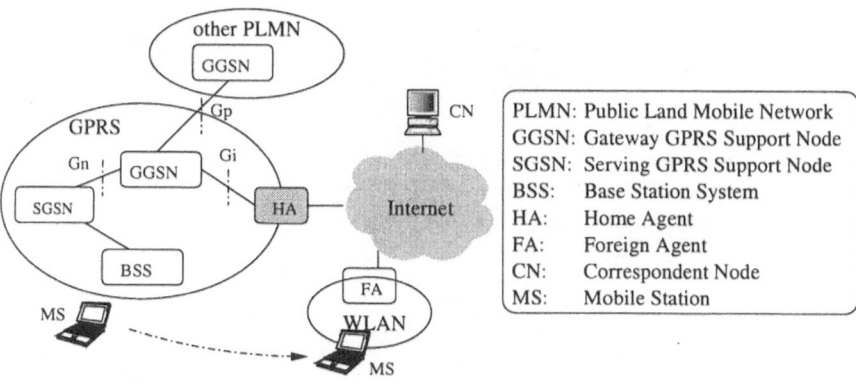

Fig. 1. Architecture of the gateway approach

nodes, GGSN (Gateway GPRS Support Node) and SGSN (Serving GPRS Support Node), and GTP (GPRS Tunneling Protocol) to provide IP services [1,2]. WLANs however primarily focus on physical layer and link layer without considering IP layer. To enforce mobility in WLANs among different IP subnets, Mobile IP [3], the protocol developed by the IETF (Internet Engineering Task Force) to support IP mobility, is a natural choice. Based on this principle, the primary issue in the integration of GPRS and WLANs is in the integration of Mobile IP with the mobility management defined in GPRS.

This paper presents a *gateway approach* to integrate GPRS and Mobile IP such that users can seamlessly roam among these two systems. As that both GPRS and WLANs are mature systems and available in the markets already, the design goal is to minimize the necessary modifications in both systems. We propose to design a gateway which will reside on the border of GPRS and WLAN systems. By simply deploying this gateway, the integration of GPRS and WLANs can be achieved without changing existing infrastructures. Based on the design principles, a testbed consisting of most GPRS and Mobile IP components has been implemented to demonstrate the feasibility of the proposed approach. Empirical experiments are conducted to analyze the testbed performance.

2   Gateway Approach

Mobility management is a primary task for the integration of heterogeneous networks. Since both GPRS and WLANs are widely deployed already, an efficient way to integrate them should reduce the impact on the existing systems as much as possible. We thus propose a gateway approach to effectively integrate Mobile IP and GPRS such that the operations of mobility management in both systems should be able to function as what they are as possible. A gateway which is placed in the conjunctional point of GGSN and the external packet data network is responsible for the integration. A gateway is a logical entity which could be

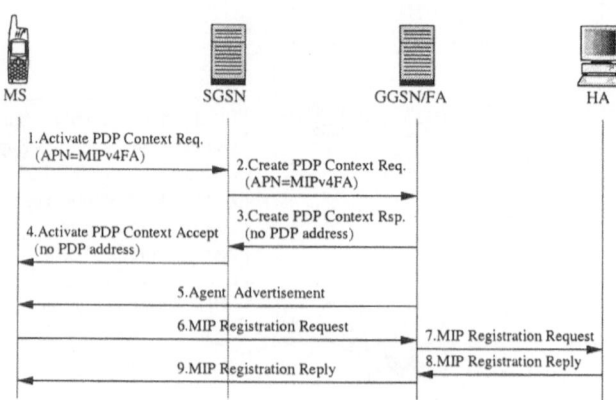

Fig. 2. PDP context activation with MIP registration

implemented stand-alone or as an addition to the gateway GGSN which connects to external networks. Since a user might have his/her home network in either GPRS or WLAN networks, the gateway should be able to function like a HA (Home Agent) and FA (Foreign Agent)*. Fig. 1 shows the architecture when the gateway serves as a HA. The following sections first present the cases when a user has home network in WLANs and GPRS, respectively, followed by the discussion of the requirements in MS.

2.1   Home in WLANs

When the home network of a user is in WLANs, the correspondent node (CN) sends its traffic to the WLAN system regardless of the mobile station's (MS) anchor point. The home network should be able to tunnel traffic to the MS's current location. In this scenario, the gateway should function like a FA. In 3GPP technical specification [4], it defines an architecture such that Mobile IP can be optionally supported to provide mobility management for inter-system roaming. In this architecture, a gateway GGSN is enhanced with FA functionality. Although the location of HA is out of the scope of this specification, we envision that there is a HA for each MS in WLANs. To identify a MIP (Mobile IP) request, the access point name (APN) is utilized to select the specific network service. Fig. 2 illustrates a PDP (packet data protocol) context activation with MIP registration procedure. The MS sends an activation with *MIPv4FA* as the APN, which instructs the SGSN to forward the request to the GGSN with FA service. The MIP registration will be performed after the PDP context activation is completed. After that, packets destined to the MS's home IP address will be intercepted by HA and then be forwarded to the FA located in GPRS network. FA decapsulates the packets and the gateway GGSN will transmit datagrams

---

* Please note the major consideration here is Mobile IPv4 as that the integration of GPRS and WLANs is a timely issue and IPv4 is the one widely deployed now.

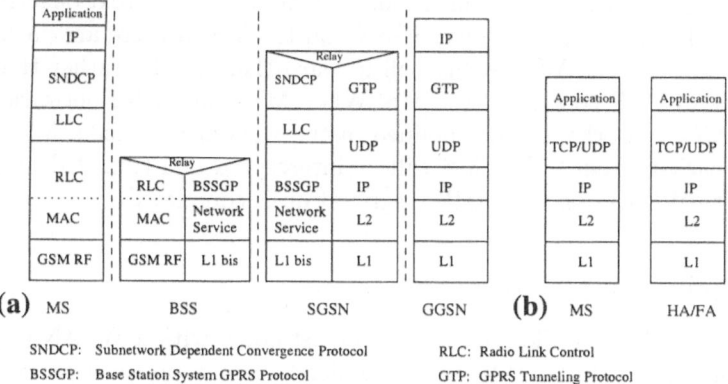

SNDCP: Subnetwork Dependent Convergence Protocol   RLC: Radio Link Control
BSSGP: Base Station System GPRS Protocol   GTP: GPRS Tunneling Protocol

Fig. 3. Dual protocol stacks in MS

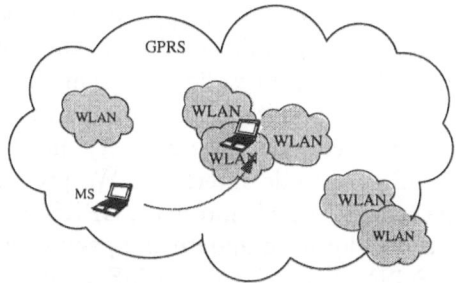

Fig. 4. Radio coverage of GPRS and WLANs

based on GTP tunneling to the target SGSN. They finally will reach the MS in the way defined in GPRS [4].

2.2   Home in GPRS

The GGSN/FA approach described above is the way defined in 3GPP specification for roaming between PLMN (Public Land Mobile Network) and other packet data networks. It presumes that there is an external network which is the home network of the MS. Many users however may have subscribed to GPRS but do not affiliate with any WLANs. It is possible that this type of users will roam to WLAN systems but still want to be reachable by their home GPRS network. Architecture indicated in Fig. 1 is proposed for this scenario. The gateway plays a role as HA and connects to GGSN through the standard Gi interface.

When both MS and CN are inside GPRS, packets from CN to MS will pass through BSS, SGSN and finally arrive at GGSN. GGSN will route them to the suitable SGSN by looking up the PDP context of the MS. Once a MS moves to WLANs, the MS will send MIP registration message to its HA (the gateway). The gateway then will send a message to inform the GGSN that the MS is out of the GPRS network. GGSN thus needs to initiate PDP context deactivation to delete the PDP context in GGSN, SGSN and the MS. If there are packets from GPRS network to the MS, GGSN will forward them to HA rather than SGSN due to lack of PDP context of the MS. When MS is in GPRS network and CN is in WLANs, it works as what defined in the standards. Once a MS roams to WLANs, packets from CN to MS will be intercepted and tunneled by HA (the gateway) to WLANs once the MIP registration is completed.

2.3   Requirements for MS

In addition to GPRS radio interface, MS must equip with a WLAN-compatible radio interface. Evidently, MS should understand the protocol stacks of both systems as illustrated in Fig. 3. Fig. 3(a) represents the user plane of GPRS, while Fig. 3(b) shows a conventional Internet protocol stack, in which Layers 1 and 2 are based on a WLAN system. Fig. 4 displays a typical radio coverage of GPRS and WLANs. Usually WLANs is applied for indoor applications while GPRS is utilized for outdoor usage. The choice of radio interfaces may involve many factors such as availability of the radio, type of application, and billing, etc. It is also possible to utilize both systems for data transmission simultaneously. Nevertheless, this paper only considers the mobility management issues caused by switching between different radio interfaces. We propose that even though packet transmission is through WLAN interface, GPRS radio should be enabled for control messages, such as location update and paging, as long as MS is under GPRS radio coverage. SGSN thus still regards MS as reachable so that the high cost and long latency for reattaching when MS switches back to GPRS can be minimized. Besides, the circuit-switched network service is still available for voice phone calls. Basically they do not interfere with each other because of different radio frequency.

3   Testbed and Experimental Analysis

The implementation of a testbed aims to realize the proposed idea and perform various experiments. In the testbed, a GPRS system consisting of HLR, BSS, SGSN and GGSN is purchased from ITRI (Industrial Technology Research Institute). MSC is not implemented because the experiments focus on packet-switched network. Due to the regulation of spectrum allocation, instead of GPRS BTS (base transceiver station) IEEE 802.11b is applied to emulate the GPRS radio. As shown in Figs. 5–6, it indeed is a GPRS system except of radio interface. It is reasonable to validate our approach because the integration is mainly based on higher layers. In addition to GPRS core network, a HA providing Mobile IP service for GPRS network is connected to GGSN via Gi interface. There are two foreign networks in WLANs thus two FAs are presented. Furthermore, we also implement a simplified SIP [5] user agent in the testbed. The SIP user agent executes IP signaling to establish real-time multimedia sessions between two end nodes. Both MS and CN are equipped with cameras. They can not only talk

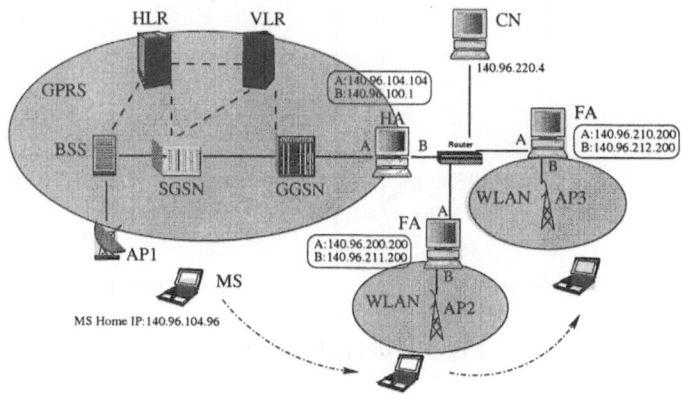

Fig. 5. Testbed architecture

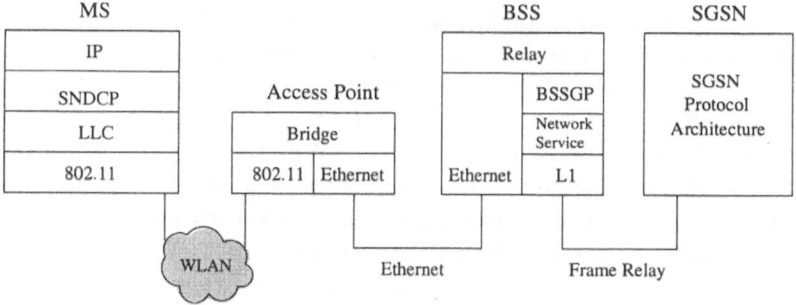

Fig. 6. Radio emulation in GPRS system

to each other, but also see each other and use whiteboard to exchange information. Please note the case when MS has its home in WLANs is not implemented because it is well-defined in 3GPP specification already.

Based on the testbed architecture, various experiments are performed. To switch between two systems, we implement two policies: *WLAN-preferred* and *user-trigger*. In WLAN-preferred mode, the link quality is tracked. It changes to WLAN access if WLAN system is available. The link quality is tracked as well in user-trigger mode. On the other hand, the decision for switching systems is based on user command and the availability of radio interface. The placement of AP1 (access point 1) AP2 in Fig. 5 is close such that MS could be in the coverage of both GPRS and WLAN systems. In experiments initially AP1 is turned on and AP2 is off. MS thus attaches to GPRS and data is received and sent via GPRS radio interface. Once AP2 is on, MS changes to WLAN (AP2) for high bandwidth service by *WLAN-preferred* mode because the WLAN radio is now available. MS then moves to AP3 and follows the same path back to AP1. The *user-trigger* mode is enforced to switch back to the GPRS radio.

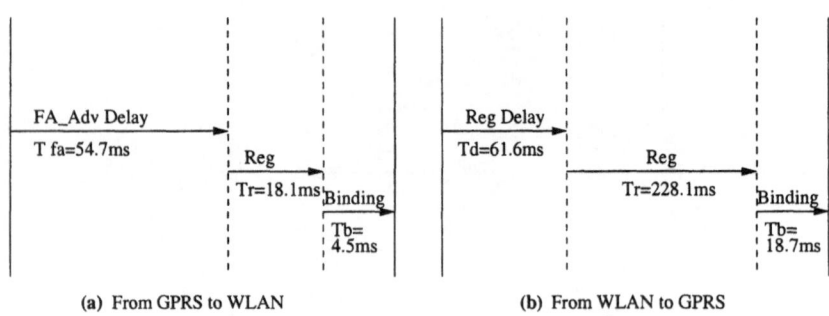

(a) From GPRS to WLAN   (b) From WLAN to GPRS

Fig. 7. Handoff latency

Fig. 7 indicates the handoff latency between GPRS and WLAN systems. In this experiment, CN continuously sends *ping* packets to MS with an interval of 1 *ms*. Fig. 7(a) shows that the average delay to detect FA advertisement is 54.7 *ms*. The average time for MS to receive ack from the HA after MS sends MIP registration message is 18.1 *ms*. Finally, it costs an average of 4.5 *ms* for MS to receive packets from CN again after the binding update in HA is done. The average handoff latency from GPRS to WLAN totally is 77.3 *ms*. Relatively, Fig. 7(b) presents the handoff latency from WLAN to GPRS. As mentioned above the handoff is triggered by user, and the average delay is 61.6 *ms* to send out the registration request. The average delay is 228.1 *ms* for the MS to receive ack from the HA. After that, the average latency is 18.7 *ms* for MS to receive packets from CN again. By comparing them, we notice that the handoff latency from WLAN to GPRS is larger then the latency from GPRS to WLAN. This is because GPRS employs much more complex architecture and protocol stacks. As shown in Figs. 5–6, in GPRS network packets would need to go through several nodes with more protocol stacks to reach the HA.

Due to space limitation, in addition to handoff latency this paper presents only the throughput of video application in Fig. 8. Experimental results discussed here are part of the multimedia conference initiated by SIP signaling. The video codec is based on H.263. Initially, MS obtains an averaged throughput of 56 *Kbps* in GPRS network. After roaming to WLAN, the traffic is conditioned by a *Traffic Controller (TC)* with 200 *Kbps*, 400 *Kbps* and 600 *Kbps*, respectively. When MS first moves from GPRS to WLAN system, the video quality is drastically improved because of high bandwidth of WLANs. The data rate dramatically drops in handoffs which are marked by vertical dotted-line. Even though there is no retransmission because of UDP packets, the video coding techniques help recover loss of small amount of packets by other correctly received packets.

4   Summary

The integration of GPRS and WLANs should benefit both operators and users. From operators' point of view, minimizing modification in existing systems is a

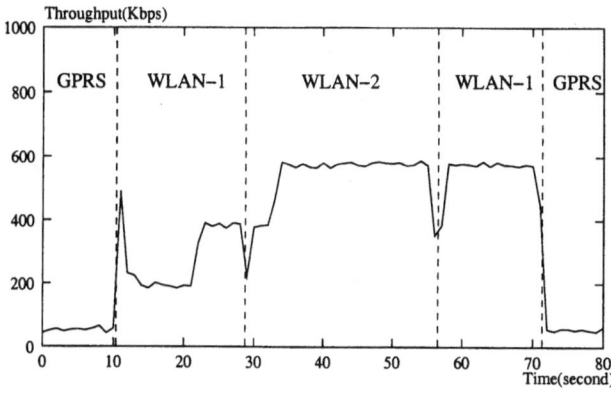

Fig. 8. Throughput of video application

key factor for success. The *gateway approach* proposed in this paper provides a solution for this goal. A testbed is constructed to validate the proposed approach. Various experiments are carried out to examine the design principles and analyze the performance. The results show that the gateway approach could achieve the intended goal and provide a solution to integrate the mobility management in GPRS and WLANs. Future work includes billing strategy and integration in security.

Acknowledgment. J.-C. Chen's work was sponsored in part by MOE Program for Promoting Academic Excellent of Universities under the grant number 89-E-FA04-1-4, Taiwan Cellular Corp. under the contract of PCSF-91-002, National Science Council under the grant number 91-2213-E-007-039 and 91-2213-E-007-046, and Industrial Technology Research Institute under the contract of T2-91034-11.

References

1. 3GPP TS 23.060: Gernal Packet Radio Service (GPRS); Service description; Stage 2 (2002)
2. 3GPP TS 29.060: Gernal Packet Radio Service (GPRS); GPRS Tunneling Protocol (GTP) across the Gn and Gp Interface (2002)
3. Perkins, C.: IP mobility support. IETF RFC 3220 (2002)
4. 3GPP TS 29.061: Packet Domain; Interworking between the Public Land Mobile Network (PLMN) supporting packet based services and Packet Data Network (PDN) (2002)
5. Handley, M., Schulzrinne, H., Schooler, E., Rosenberg, J.: SIP: session initiation protocol. IETF RFC 2543 (1999)

Lecture Notes in Computer Science 2532

Edited by G. Goos, J. Hartmanis, and J. van Leeuwen

Lecture Notes in Computer Science 2532
Edited by G. Goos, J. Hartmanis, and J. van Leeuwen

Springer-Verlag Berlin Heidelberg GmbH

Yung-Chang Chen   Long-Wen Chang
Chiou-Ting Hsu (Eds.)

Advances in Multimedia
Information Processing –
PCM 2002

Third IEEE Pacific Rim Conference on Multimedia
Hsinchu, Taiwan, December 16-18, 2002
Proceedings

 Springer

Series Editors

Gerhard Goos, Karlsruhe University, Germany
Juris Hartmanis, Cornell University, NY, USA
Jan van Leeuwen, Utrecht University, The Netherlands

Volume Editors

Yung-Chang Chen
National Tsing Hua University
Department of Electrical Engineering
Hsinchu, Taiwan
E-mail: ycchen@ee.nthu.edu.tw

Long-Wen Chang
Chiou-Ting Hsu
National Tsing Hua University
Department of Computer Science
Hsinchu, Taiwan
E-mail:{lchang/cthsu}@cs.nthu.edu.tw

Cataloging-in-Publication Data applied for

Bibliographic information published by Die Deutsche Bibliothek
 Die Deutsche Bibliothek lists this publication in the Deutsche Nationalbibliografie;

detailed bibliographic data is available in the Internet at <http://dnb.ddb.de>.

CR Subject Classification (1998): H.5.1, H.3, H.5, C.2, K.6, H.4, I.4, I.3

ISSN 0302-9743
ISBN 978-3-540-00262-8   ISBN 978-3-540-36228-9 (eBook)
DOI 10.1007/978-3-540-36228-9

http://www.springer.de

© Springer-Verlag Berlin Heidelberg 2002
Originally published by Springer-Verlag Berlin Heidelberg New York in 2002

Typesetting: Camera-ready by author, data conversion by PTP-Berlin, Stefan Sossna e. K.
Printed on acid-free paper   SPIN 10871500   06/3142   5 4 3 2 1 0

Preface

The 2002 IEEE Pacific Rim Conference on Multimedia (PCM 2002) is the third annual conference on cutting-edge multimedia technologies and was held at Tsing Hua University, Hsinchu, Taiwan, December 16–18, 2002. Hsinchu City, located about 70 km to the south of Taipei, is known as Taiwan's Silicon Valley, where hundreds of successful hi-tech companies, two major national universities, several research centers, and the Industrial Technology Research Institute (ITRI) are clustered to form and reinforce the "Science-Based Industrial Park." The conference complemented this wonderful setting by providing a forum for presenting and exploring technological and artistic advancements in multimedia. Technical issues, theory and practice, and artistic and consumer innovations brought together researchers, artists, developers, educators, performers, and practitioners of multimedia from the Pacific Rim and around the world.

The technical program featured a comprehensive program including keynote speeches, tutorials, special sessions, regular paper presentations, and technical demonstrations. We received 224 papers and accepted 154 of them. We acknowledge the great contribution from all of our committee members and paper reviewers who devoted their time to reviewing submitted papers and providing valuable comments for the authors.

PCM 2002 could never have been successful without the support and assistance of several institutions and many people. We sincerely appreciate the support of the National Science Council and the Ministry of Education of Taiwans, ROC. The financial sponsorships from the Institute of Applied Science & Engineering Research of Academia Sinica, Sunplus Technology Co., Ltd., the Institute for Information Industry, Chunghwa Telecom Laboratories, AIPTEK International, Inc., the MOE Program for Promoting Academic Excellence of Universities, and Opto-Electronics & Systems Lab/ITRI are also gratefully acknowledged. Our sincere gratitude goes to our advisory committee chairs: Prof. Sun-Yuan Kung of Princeton University, Dr. Bor-Shenn Jeng of CHT Labs of Taiwan, and Prof. H.Y. Mark Liao of Academia Sinica of Taiwan. Deep thanks go to the IEEE Signal Processing Society and the Circuits and Systems Society for technical co-sponsorship.

December 2002

Yung-Chang Chen
Long-Wen Chang
Chiou-Ting Hsu

IEEE
*Networking
the World™*

Third IEEE Pacific Rim Conference

on Multimedia

Advisory Committee Chairs:
Sun-Yuan Kung   Princeton University, USA
Bor-Shenn Jeng   Chunghwa Telecom Labs, Taiwan
H.Y. Mark Liao   Academia Sinica, Taiwan

Conference Chair:
Yung-Chang Chen   National Tsing Hua University

Program Chair:
Long-Wen Chang   National Tsing Hua University

Poster/Demo Chair:
Shang-Hong Lai   National Tsing Hua University

Tutorial/Special Session Chair:
Chung-Lin Huang   National Tsing Hua University

Local Arrangements Chair:
Chaur-Chin Chen   National Tsing Hua University

Publicity Chair:
Fenn-Huei Simon Sheu   National Tsing Hua University

Proceedings Chair:
Chiou-Ting Hsu   National Tsing Hua University

Registration Chair:
Tai-Lang Jong   National Tsing Hua University

USA Liaison:
Jenq-Neng Hwang   University of Washington

Japan Liaison:
Kiyoharu Aizawa   University of Tokyo

Korea Liaison:
Yo-Sung Ho   Kwangju Institute of Science and Technology

Hong Kong Liaison:
Bing Zeng   Hong Kong University of Science and Technology

Web Master:
Chao-Kuei Hsieh   National Tsing Hua University

Organizers

National Tsing Hua University, Taiwan

Sponsors

IEEE Circuits and Systems Society

IEEE Signal Processing Society

National Science Council, Taiwan

Ministry of Education, Taiwan

Institute of Applied Science & Engineering Research, Academia Sinica

Sunplus Technology Co., Ltd.

Institute for Information Industry

Chunghwa Telecom Laboratories

AIPTEK International Inc.

MOE Program for Promoting Academic Excellence of Universities (MOE 89-E-FA04-1-4)

Opto-Electronics & Systems Laboratories, Industrial Technology Research Institute

Table of Contents

Mobile Multimedia

Digital Watermarking and Data Hiding

Motion Analysis

Multimedia Retrieval Techniques

Image Processing

Multimedia Security

Image Coding

Multimedia Learning

Audio Signal Processing

Wireless Multimedia Networks

Multimedia Processing Techniques

Image Segmentation

Multimedia Streaming

Multimedia Systems in Internet

Distance Education with Multimedia Techniques

Internet Security

Computer Graphics and Virtual Reality

Object Tracking Techniques

Face Analysis

MPEG 4

Adaptive Multimedia System Architecture for Improving QoS in Wireless Networks

Amit Mahajan, Padmavathi Mundur*, and Anupam Joshi**

Department of Computer Science and Electrical Engineering
University of Maryland, Baltimore County, Baltimore, MD 21250, USA
{amitml, pmundur, joshi}@csee.umbc.edu

Abstract. In this paper, we present an adaptive end-system based architecture for improving QoS in wireless networks. The proposed system adapts to fluctuating network resources by transmitting lower fidelity streams, chosen based on user preferences. Adaptation based on user preference leads to selection of data that satisfies both the network (avoids congestion) and user (better perceptual value). The system does not have any dependency on the underlying network, making its implementation possible in any wireless network.

1 Introduction

With the growth of bandwidth available in wireless networks, it is feasible to stream multimedia rich audio/video content to mobile clients. The available bandwidth has increased from 9.6 Kbps-14.4 Kbps (2G - GSM and TDMA wireless networks of 1990s) to 64 Kbps (3G networks). Increasing bandwidth is a necessary first step for accommodating real-time streaming applications, however it is not sufficient due to unpredictable and large bandwidth fluctuations experienced in wireless networks. Some minimum *quality of service (QoS)* must be provided to support smooth audio/video playback. Fluctuations in network resource availability due to channel fading, variable error rate, mobility, and handoff, makes QoS provisioning more complex in wireless networks.

In this paper, we present an adaptive end-system based architecture for improving QoS in wireless networks. We use layered-encoding feature provided by ISO (MPEG) and ITU (H.26x) video standards to achieve graceful adaptation in case of bandwidth variation. The adaptation is based on user preference in order to increase the perceptual value of the multimedia stream by making better use of available bandwidth. The end-system based architecture consists of modules at the two ends of the networks, namely the mobile client and the multimedia server. Thus, the system does not have any dependency on the underlying network, making its implementation possible in any wireless network. After the connection is established with a multimedia server, the client periodically sends feedback about bandwidth availability to the server. The server stores multiple copies of streaming data encoded at different fidelity levels. Based on the feedback and user preference, the scheduler at the server dynamically selects the appropriate copy of audio/video stream. The adaptation to the available bandwidth also provides means of

* Dr. Mundur and student supported in part by a grant from Aether Systems, Inc.
** Dr. Joshi supported in part by NSF award IIS 9875433

Y.-C. Chen, L.-W. Chang, and C.-T. Hsu (Eds.): PCM 2002, LNCS 2532, pp. 712–719, 2002.
© Springer-Verlag Berlin Heidelberg 2002

avoiding the network congestion. User preferences are specified in terms of user-level QoS parameters such as resolution and frame-rate, to keep the interface simple for the user. We propose *perceptual-value based analysis* to obtain the value of data received at mobile client.

The paper is organized as follows. Related work in adaptive mobile architectures is presented in Section 2. In Section 3 we describe the architecture of the proposed adaptive system. We present the simulation environment and results in Section 4. The conclusion of the paper is given in Section 5.

2   Related Work

Several projects address the issue of bandwidth variation in wireless networks by providing an adaptive architecture. The MobiWeb project [1], is based on the proxy model in which the proxy layer at the base station (BS) intercepts TCP or UDP streams and applies the appropriate filter. Bandwidth reservation and priority scheme are used to provide continuous smooth audio/video stream. The Odyssey system [2] uses similar proxy based approach to provide smooth audio/video streaming. The system includes client components to request lower fidelity of data. Proxy based system in [3] utilizes MPEG standard features to achieve smoother video delivery. The system uses Resource Reservation Protocol (RSVP) to reserve bandwidth for high priority real-time packets. The PRAYER [4] framework is based on QoS-unaware servers and QoS-aware clients. A concept similar to home network in Mobile IP is used to achieve QoS by dynamic adaptation. Most of the proposed solutions follow proxy based approach, and also rely on the underlying network to provide services like bandwidth reservation and priority routing. Though the approach is transparent to the applications, lack of support from any intermediate network or node can render the architecture useless. For example, in case priority routing is not supported by a router on the transmission path the whole scheme will fail. Moreover, proxy based solutions have scalability problems [5], especially in case of computation intensive proxy functionality like transcoding. Most systems do not use video standard (MPEG and H.26x) features and user preference to maximize the perceptual quality of video. We propose an end-system based architecture which does not depend on either the proxies or the underlying network for additional services.

3   Adaptive Multimedia System Architecture

The block diagram of our end-system based adaptive system is shown in Figure 1. We first list the factors dictating our design and then describe each of the system component.

End-System Based Design. The end-system based architecture consists of modules only at the two ends of the networks, namely the mobile client and the multimedia server. Using the mechanism explained next, the client components have the best knowledge of bandwidth available and user preferences. Client's current knowledge of bandwidth is sent to the server. The server will periodically send some control packet at higher bandwidth than reported by the client. Depending on the rate at which the client is able to receive data, any decrease or increase in bandwidth will be detected by the client.The server components have the best knowledge of the levels of data fidelity stored in the

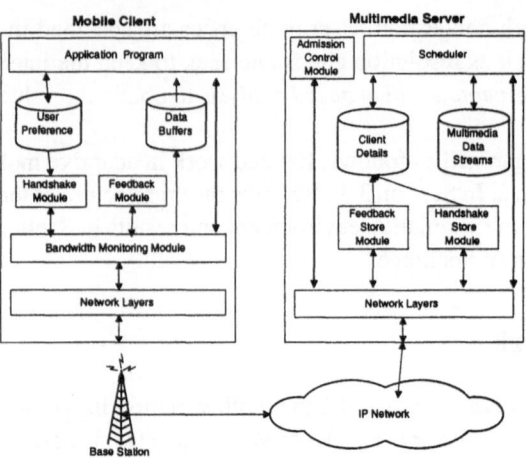

Fig. 1. Adaptive Multimedia System Architecture

database. Hence a system with participation of both client and server components should yield better results. The two end-systems (client and server) can be relatively easily modified and updated. With the current size of the Internet, it is a quantum task to effect any change in the network. Based on this intuition we have designed the system which does not have any dependency on the underlying network.

Video Standard Features. The MPEG and H.26x video standards [6] offer a generalized scalable framework supporting temporal, spatial, and SNR scalability. SNR scalability allows video streams to be divided into two types of layers - base layer and enhancement layer. Multiple enhancement layers can be used to improve the quality of multimedia playback. This division offers a means of gracefully degrading the quality when the bandwidth and other resources are limited and change frequently (Figure 2). With the declining cost of storage, the multimedia server can easily store multiple streams of data encoded at different fidelity levels.

Perceptual-Value Based Analysis. In our perceptual-value based analysis we determine the value of data based on user perception and not on quantity of data received. For example, viewing the slides is more important in the case of presentation, and hearing the speech is more important in the case of news. The properties of streaming data received: audio quality, resolution, color, and frame-rate, are compared with the user preferences to compute the perceptual-value. Larger perceptual-values are assigned for data that match user expectations. *Expected Data (ED)* is multimedia data (audio, base layer, and enhancement layer) user expects based on user-preference provided to the system. *Received Data (RD)* is multimedia data actually delivered to the client. *Received-Expected Match Ratio (REMR)* is defined as ratio of bytes matching the user-preference ($B_{RD \cap ED}$) and bytes of RD (B_{RD}), and is used to determine how closely does the RD match the user-preference.

$$REMR(\%) = \frac{B_{RD \cap ED}}{B_{RD}} * 100$$

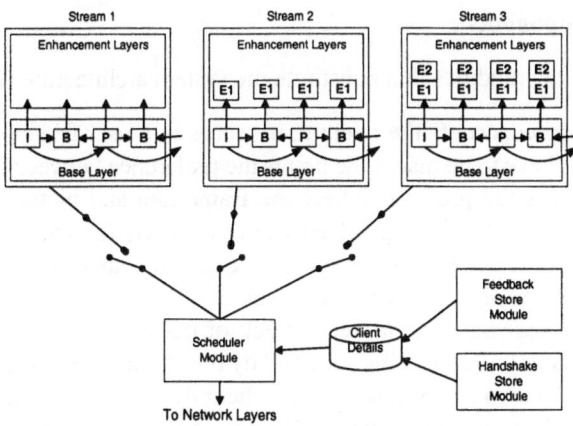

Fig. 2. Scheduling Base and Enhancement Layers

Perceptual value (PV) of the data received is the aggregate number of bytes that match the user-preference.

$$PV = \Sigma B_{RD \cap ED}$$

For example, for viewing a presentation user preference chosen is video resolution and when bandwidth falls to 32 Kbps, ED is enhancement video layer and base video layer (Table 1). When user preference are not considered RD is audio layer and base video layer . The intersection of RD and ED is base video layer and with equal bandwidth for each layer, REMR value of 50% is achieved. When adaptation takes user preference into consideration, RD is enhancement video layer and base video layer, which results in REMR value of 100%. Comparison between RD and ED is done for various user preferences to obtain the complete Perceptual-Value Table 1 for 32 Kbps bandwidth. Similar tables can be obtained for other bandwidth values.

Table 1. Perceptual-Value of Data Received for 32 Kbps

Preference	Expected	No user preference		With user preference	
	Data	Received Data	REMR (%)	Received Data	REMR (%)
Audio	Au+BL	Au+BL	100%	Au+BL	100%
Frame-rate	BL+2EL (@ 12 fps)	Au+BL (@ 25 fps)	50%	BL+2EL (@ 12 fps)	100%
Resolution	BL+EL	Au+BL	50%	BL+EL	100%

Au: Audio Layer   BL: Base Video Layer
EL: Enhancement Video Layer   fps: frames per second

3.1 System Components

The following are the modules that constitute the system architecture (Figure 1).

- *Client Application* accepts the client preferences in a user friendly interface. Two simple choices have to be made: the first is the preference between audio and video, and the second is the preference between frame rate and picture resolution. The client application stores these preferences in a database for later use.
- *Handshake Module* accesses the preference database and sends the information in MSG_HANDSHAKE message to the server.
- *Bandwidth Monitoring Module* keeps track of current network state by keeping track of the amount of data being received by the client. The information is used to determine the bandwidth available to the client device. It periodically invokes the services of feedback module to update the server about the bandwidth variation.
- *Feedback Module* is periodically invoked by bandwidth monitoring module to update the server (by MSG_FEEDBACK message) about the bandwidth available to the mobile client.
- *Admission Control Module* decides whether the multimedia server has sufficient free resources to service a new request from a client. Based on available resources, the server decides to accept or reject the connection request.
- *Handshake Store Module* processes the MSG_HANDSHAKE message received from client during the initialization phase. It then stores the client preferences received in the message in the *client details* database.
- *Feedback Store Module* processes the MSG_FEEDBACK message received from the client and stores the bandwidth availability value in the *client details* database.
- *Scheduler Module* uses data from client details database to select appropriate stream of multimedia data. Both client preferences and bandwidth available to the client are used to decide the appropriate stream. The scheduler also prepares data packets for transmission to the client. Figure 2 shows the scheduler modules switching between three streams of multimedia data based on *client details* which include user preference and bandwidth available.

The server and client interaction starts with the connection initialization phase in which the client requests streaming data from the server. The server accepts or rejects the request based on admission control. In the handshake phase the user preferences are transferred to the server and stored in client details database for future use. The handshake message, MSG_HANDSHAKE, has four bits for user preferences (audio, video, resolution, and frame rate). The available bandwidth is monitored by the client and reported to the server. The feedback message, MSG_FEEDBACK, has four values of 1 byte each for bandwidth over the previous 30 seconds (Bw30), 60 seconds (Bw60), 120 seconds (Bw60) and 180 seconds (Bw180). Thus, the size of MSG_HANDSHAKE is 29 bytes and of MSG_FEEDBACK is 32 bytes, with IP header 20 bytes and UDP header 8 bytes. The server adapts the fidelity of data in the adaptation phase and transmits the adapted video stream.

Overhead on Mobile Client. Mobile devices have limited capabilities in terms of power, computation power, memory, and storage. Hence it is important to discuss the overhead of the proposed architecture. Minor changes are required in the application program and the network layer, hence the overhead introduced is negligible. User preference needs two bits of storage and memory, one bit to indicate choice between audio and video, and second bit to store choice between resolution and frame-rate. Handshake module requires few (around 50) cycles and one network packet to send the information to the server, and does not require extra storage or memory. Bandwidth Monitoring module is invoked for each received packet to calculate the current bandwidth available to the client. It stores the bytes received during the past few seconds to calculate the bandwidth available. Hence, the memory requirement is 16 bytes, four bytes each for Bw30, Bw60, Bw120, and Bw180. Computation overhead of both Feedback module and Bandwidth Monitoring module is less than 100 cycles. Hence, the system does not have much of overhead on the mobile client.

4   Simulation

To test the performance of the system architecture described in Section 3, we implemented the modules in network simulator-2 (NS-2) for simulation experiments. The setup consists of grid of 1000m by 1000m. The base stations have range of 50m and can provide maximum bandwidth of 64 Kbps to mobile clients. Base stations are placed such that mobile client can communicate with minimum one base station at any point in the topology. We used simulated H.263 streams over RTP and UDP protocols to perform the experiments. In the simulation model, multimedia server stores various combination of the audio, base video, and two enhancement video layers. Each layer requires 16 Kbps of bandwidth, and hence, the best quality stream (one audio, one base and two enhancement layers) can be streamed at 64 Kbps. We randomly vary the bandwidth available in the new cell within the range of 16-64 Kbps to mimic the real life scenario. Each simulation of 500 seconds is repeated ten times to obtain the average values used in the graphs. Randway Algorithm is used to generate mobility patterns for the client node. Three scenarios were executed on top of a simulated dynamic wireless environment. In the first scenario, no feedback mechanism is used and the server streams data at 64 Kbps. When available bandwidth declines, the client will experience long starvation periods. During the starvation periods no data is presented and the user experiences pauses or gaps in playback. Such a scenario is also observed in the standard media players and the status shown during the pause or gaps is "buffering" or "waiting for data". Playback time is defined as the amount of time for which audio/video is played to the user and used as a metric in the simulation experiments. In the second scenario, feedback mechanism is employed without using user preferences. The server is able to adapt to the bandwidth variation and selects appropriate stream for the client. In the third scenario, both feedback mechanism and user preferences are used to dynamically schedule data transmission resulting in better perceptual values of received data for the client. Since with feedback, we are considerably reducing the starvation period, the audio/video playback is smoother for the user.

Figure 3 shows playback time corresponding to the simulation of the three scenarios. Without feedback, the playback time is considerably reduced because of the mismatch in the playback rate and the reduced bandwidth. Less playback time means more starvation resulting in breaks during playback. Feedback increases the playback time because the server is able to adapt to lower fidelity multimedia stream matching the transmission bandwidth and the playback rate. The overhead of using client preferences causes slight reduction in the playback time as shown in Figure 3. Without feedback multimedia data is played for 21% - 26% of time (see Table 2). With feedback the playback time increase to 87% - 98% of the time. Figure 4 shows perceptual-values for the three scenarios with the user preference as video and resolution. Feedback with user preference results in maximum perceptual-value for the corresponding data received among all the three scenarios. Figure 5 shows perceptual-values for the three scenarios with the user preference as video and frame-rate. The results are similar to the previous simulation. In the above two scenarios, adaptation with user preference has shown improvement of 47%-56% over adaptation without user preference. Figure 6 shows perceptual-values for the three scenarios with the user preference as audio. As the default adaptation is now same as the one explicitly chosen, the results of the two scenarios are similar. Still there is marked improvement from the base case which does not use feedback for adaptation.

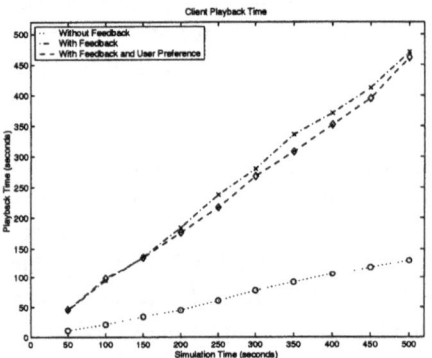

Fig. 3. Client Playback Duration

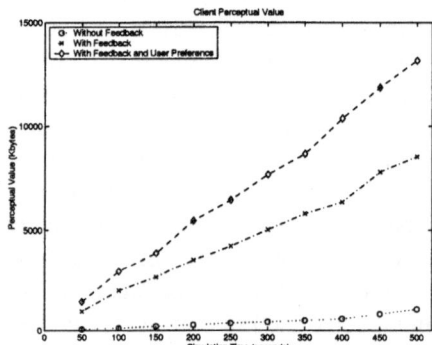

Fig. 4. Perceptual-value of Data with Video and Resolution as user preference

Table 2. Average playback percentage of time

Time (s)	Without Feedback	With Feedback Without User Preference	With Feedback With User Preference
100	21.0	95.0	98.0
200	22.5	92.0	88.0
300	26.0	93.33	89.33
400	26.5	92.75	88.0
500	26.2	94.2	92.4

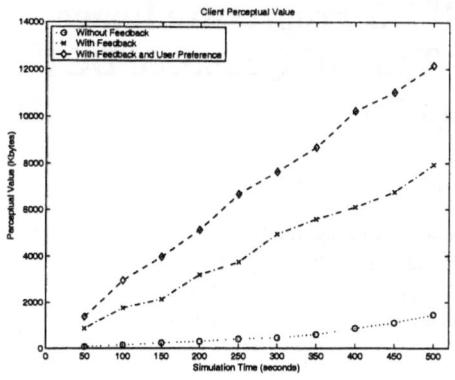 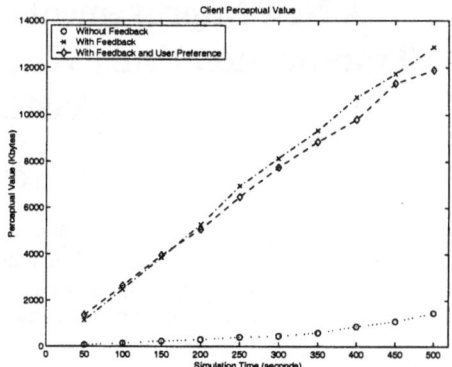

Fig. 5. Perceptual-value of Data with Video and Frame-rate as user preference

Fig. 6. Perceptual-value of Data with Audio as user preference

5   Conclusion

Significant improvement in playback time and perceptual-value of data are obtained by using the proposed adaptive multimedia system. Improvement of 47%-56% in perceptual values have been observed over the traditional adaptation techniques. The system does not have much of overhead which makes it suitable for less resourceful mobile client. The "perceptual-value based" system takes the user preference into account resulting in better adaptation. Our system does not have any dependency on the underlying network, making its implementation possible in any wireless network including the future 3G wireless networks. The system adapts to both the user preferences and network resources to improve the perceptual value of the data delivered to the user. To test the proposed system in real life conditions, we are working to implement it on test bed with actual wireless devices.

References

1. Margaritidis, M., Polyzos, G.: MobiWeb: Enabling adaptive continuous media applications over 3G wireless links. IEEE Personal Communications Magazine **7** (2000) 36–41
2. Noble, B., Satyanarayanan, M.: Experience with adaptive mobile applications in odyssey. Mobile Networks and Applications **4** (1999) 245–54
3. Bahl, P.: Supporting digital video in a managed wireless network. IEEE Communications Magazine Special Issue on Wireless Video **36** (2000) 94–102
4. Bharghavan, V., Gupta, V.: A framework for application adaptation in mobile computing environments. Computer Software and Applications Conf., Bethesda, MD (1997)
5. Joshi, A.: On proxy agents, mobility, and web access. ACM/Baltzer Journal of Mobile Networks and Nomadic Applications (MONET) **5** (2000) 233–41
6. Puri, A., Eleftheriadi, A.: MPEG-4: An object-based multimedia coding standard supporting mobile application. Mobile Networks and Applications **3** (1998) 5–32

A New Improvement of JPEG Progressive Image Transmission Using Weight Table of Quantized DCT Coefficient Bits

Tung-Shou Chen and Chen-Yi Lin

Department of Information Management
National Taichung Institute of Technology
No. 129 Sec. 3, San-min Road, Taichung, Taiwan 404, R.O.C.
tschen@ntit.edu.tw   eva_38@mail2000.com.tw

Abstract. Traditional JPEG progressive transmission transmits quantized DCT coefficients one by one, and does not consider the importance among the bits in each transmission stage. Thus the reconstructed image quality at earlier stages is not acceptable. This phenomenon does not match the requirements of progressive image transmission. In this paper, we propose a new method to improve the reconstructed image quality of JPEG progressive transmission. We assign each bit of quantized DCT coefficients a weight number, and collect all weight numbers into a weight table. The weight table is fixed for all blocks and all images in the proposed method, and is owned in both sender and receiver. Next, the sender and receiver transmit and receive the data bits based on the weight table. Compared to JPEG, the experimental results show that the method can significantly improve the reconstructed image quality at each transmission stage, especially for the first and the second stages.

1 Introduction

Image is one of the most important multimedia that includes video, document, music, and so on. However, the storage memory of the digital image is always very large and the transmission time of the network is always very long because of the digital image's storage memory. Thus, we use the progressive image transmission (PIT) [1-4] idea to alleviate this trouble.

In general, the progressive image transmission divides the original image's transmission into several stages. The sender sends the image to the receiver via several stages and the reconstructed image is changed from blurred to clear stage by stage. If the reconstructed image quality is good enough, the receiver can interrupt the transmission. Otherwise, the full-resolution image can be completely reconstructed.

To achieve the above objective, PIT must conform to the following four basic demands:

(1) The original image is divided into several stages for transmission.
(2) The image information contained in the first and second stages.
(3) The most important image information is transmitted in the first stage.
(4) The image information of prior stage is reused in the later stage.

In recent years, much research has explored progressive image transmission. These methods can be classified into two categories: spatial domain and frequency

Y.-C. Chen, L.-W. Chang, and C.-T. Hsu (Eds.): PCM 2002, LNCS 2532, pp. 720-728, 2002.

domain. Most improvements for PIT in the spatial domain [1-4] use the relation between any pixel and near pixels. But the image's compression effect is not better in the spatial domain than in the frequency domain.

The image data in the frequency domain can be classified into three sections: low frequency, middle frequency, and high frequency. In general, DCT coefficients in low frequency are the most important, and DCT coefficients in high frequency are the least important. Thus, we employ the characteristics in the frequency domain to achieve the image compression's objective and speed up the image transmission in the network.

ISO and CCITT organizations establish traditional JPEG [5-6] that is one of the international standard image's formats. Progressive coding is one of traditional JPEG's compressive modes. It is specially designed to PIT. In the progressive coding's procedure, first, the original image is partitioned into non-overlapping square blocks after color space transform and sampling. Next, every block produces 64 DCT coefficients after FDCT. Last, the sender transmits the quantized DCT coefficients and the receiver reconstructs the image according to Zig-Zag order.

Traditional JPEG divides original image information into ten transmission stages. The sender transmits quantized DCT coefficients one after another, and does not consider the importance among the quantized DCT coefficient bits in each transmission stage. Thus, the reconstructed images quality at the receiver and the beginning stages are usually not satisfactory. In this paper, we shall propose a new progressive image transmission technique to improve the above-mentioned defect. In this new method, we decide a weight number for each quantized DCT coefficient bit according to the importance of the bit. The weight number is larger if the DCT coefficient bit is more important. In other words, the weight number is smaller if the DCT coefficient bit is more unimportant. Last, we collect all the weight numbers into a weight table.

The weight table is fixed for every block in the proposed method, and is held in both the sender and receiver. The sender transmits the data bits and the receiver restructures the image based on the weight numbers from the weight table. The data bits in the prior stages are reused in the later stages. Thus, the image quality in each transmission stage is from blurred to clear.

The remainder of the paper is organized as follows. Section 2 reviews the procedures of the traditional JPEG. Section 3 describes our proposed method for PIT. The experimental results are shown and discussed in Section 4. Finally, the conclusions are given in Section 5.

2   Traditional JPEG

Progressive coding of JPEG image compression models is specially designed for PIT. After color space transform and sampling of the original image, an image is partitioned into non-overlapping square blocks. Every block contains 8×8 pixels, so each block produces 64 DCT coefficients after Forward Discrete Cosine Transformation (FDCT), as shown in Figure 1 (a). Next, all quantized DCT coefficients of a block are divided into ten transmission stages according to their importance. Last, the sender transmits quantized DCT coefficients one by one in each block to the receiver in each stage. The receiver restructures the image based on the receiving image information.

The order of the transmitted DCT coefficient is based on the Zig-Zag scan order, as shown in Figure 1 (b). In other words, DC in each block will be transmitted to the receiver in first stage. AC1 in each block will be transmitted to the receiver in second stage. Other DCT coefficients' method is the same as described previously. Here DC, AC1, AC2, and the other DCT coefficients are all the quantized results.

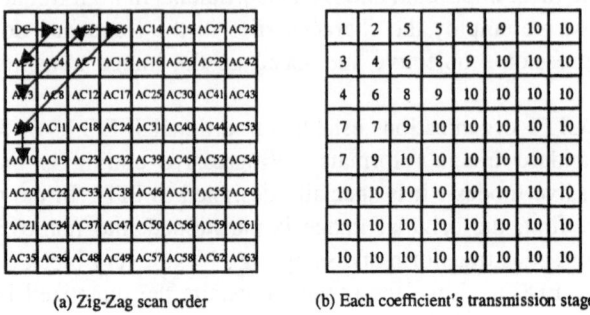

(a) Zig-Zag scan order   (b) Each coefficient's transmission stage

Fig. 1. The scan order and transmission stage of DCT coefficients

In first stage, the sender transmits DC in each 8×8 block to the receiver. After the receiver receives DC in each 8×8 block, the receiver restructures the image block by inverse quantization, inverse discrete cosine transformation (IDCT), inverse sampling, and inverse color space transform.

In second stage, the sender transmits AC1 in each 8×8 block to the receiver. After the receiver receives AC1 in each 8×8 block, the receiver collects the DC and AC1 coefficients of each block and restructures each image block by inverse quantization, IDCT, inverse sampling, and inverse color space transform. From in third stage to tenth stage, the receiver's decoder procedure is the same as in first and second stages. Thus, the restructured image is changed from blurred to clear stage by stage in the receiver side.

3 Our Method

When restructuring an image in traditional JPEG the DC coefficient is more important than the AC1 coefficient, the AC1 coefficient is more important than the AC2 coefficient, and so on. Thus, the sender transmits the DC coefficient in first stage, the AC1 coefficient in second stage, and so on.

However, traditional JPEG's transmission order does not consider that the most significant bits (MSBs) of the AC1 coefficient may be more important than the least significant bits (LSBs) of the DC coefficient, and MSBs of the AC2 coefficient may be more important than LSBs of the AC1 coefficient. In other words, MSBs of the AC2 coefficient may be more important than LSBs of the DC coefficient.

That is to say, LSBs of low frequency coefficient cannot be ensured more important than MSBs of middle frequency coefficient, and LSBs of middle frequency coefficient cannot be ensured more important than MSBs of high frequency coefficient. In this paper, we propose a new method to improve the reconstructed image quality of JPEG progressive coding. We assign each bit of quantized DCT coefficients a weight number based on the results of the reconstructed image quality, and collect all weight numbers into a weight table. The weight table is fixed for all blocks, and is contained in both the sender and receiver. Therefore, the sender and receiver transmit and receive the data bits based on the weight table.

3.1 Designing and Training of a Weight Table

3.1.1 Gathering Statistics of Quantized DCT Coefficient Lengths

After color space transform, sampling, FDCT, and quantization, each DCT coefficient's length is not the same as each other. Thus we must beforehand gather statistics of the longest bit numbers of each quantized DCT coefficient.

We collect several training images, process them by color space transform, sampling, FDCT, and quantization, and gather the longest bit length of each quantized DCT coefficient. In Table 1, we apply L_{DC} to be the longest bit length of DC coefficient, L_{AC1} to be the longest length of AC1 coefficient, and so on.

Table 1. The longest bit length of each quantized DCT coefficient

Coefficient	The length (bits)
DC	L_{DC}
AC1	L_{AC1}

3.1.2 Training Procedure of Weight Numbers

We use the following two rules to generate the value of the weight number for each bit of each quantized DCT coefficient:

Rule 1: In the same bit position of quantized DCT coefficients, DC is more important than AC1, AC1 is more important than AC2, and so on.

Rule 2: In a quantized DCT coefficient, MSBs are more important than LSBs.

These two rules are intuitive and correct. In Figure 2, by **Rules 1-2**, we suppose that the first bit of DC coefficient is the most important bit for each block. Next, the first bit of DC and one of other DCT coefficient bits are combined and reconstructed the original image. The mean square (MSE) value of the reconstructed image compared with the original image is then calculated respectively for each quantized DCT coefficient bit. The second important bit is chosen based on the MSE value. First, the MSE value from the first two bits of DC is compared with the MSE value from the combination of the first bit of DC and the first bit of AC1. We choose the smaller one. For example, the MSE value is 825 from the first two bits of DC, and the MSE value is 2876 from the first bit of DC and the first bit of AC1. Obviously, the MSE value from the first two bits of DC is smaller. For this reason, the second important bit in quantized DCT coefficients is the second bit of DC. Note that we do not have to check the MSE value from the combination of the first bit of DC and the other bit of AC since it does not satisfy the above two rules.

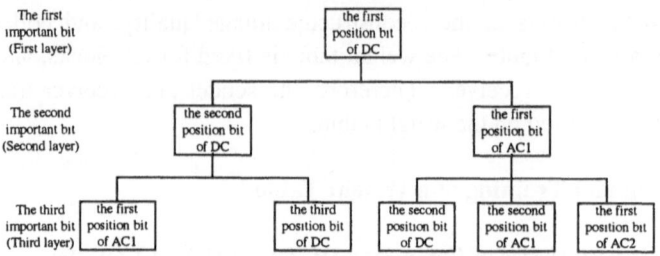

Fig. 2. The flowchart of the weight number generation

After the first two important bits are determined, we intend to choose the third important bit. Because the first two important bits are the first two bits of DC, the third important bit may be the third bit of DC or the first bit of AC1. The MSE value from the first three bits of DC is compared with that from the combination of the first two bits of DC and the first bit of AC1. We also choose the smaller one.

In the proposed method, we apply the corresponding MSE value to the weight number for each coefficient bit. The MSE value is 825 from the first two bits of DC, and the MSE value is 2876 from the first bit of DC and the first bit of AC1. The smaller one is 825. Thus we apply 825 to be the weight number of the second bit of DC coefficient. Note that a more important bit shall have a larger weight number because the MSE value shall be smaller when there are more bits received.

Changing the order for each bit of quantized DCT coefficients is not allowed after some weight numbers are decided. For example, now the first important bit is the first bit of DC, and the second important bit is the second bit of DC. When the first two important bits are decided, we have to find out the third important bit continuously based on the first two bits. We do not consider the other combinations. After the above processes, each quantized DCT coefficient bit shall have a weight number, and all of them will be combined as a weight table.

3.2 The Sender and Receiver

The weight table is fixed for all blocks in the proposed method, and is owned in the sender and receiver. The sender transmits the data bits based on the weight numbers in the weight table, as shown in Figure 3. In the first stage, the proposed method transmits the most important bits of quantized DCT coefficients to the receiver. In the second stage, the proposed method transmits the most important bits of the other quantized DCT coefficient bits to the receiver, and so on. All of the bit choices are based on the weight numbers in the weight table from bigger to smaller and from important to unimportant. After receiving image information, the receiver restructures the image according to the weight numbers in the same weight table, as shown in Figure 4. Note that the data of prior stages is reused in the later stage. Thus, the restructured image is changed from indistinct to clear stage by stage.

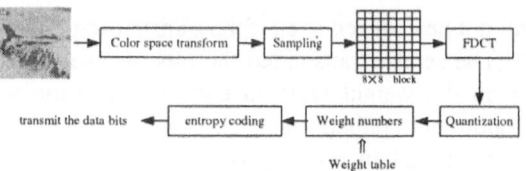

Fig. 3. Flowchart of the sender side

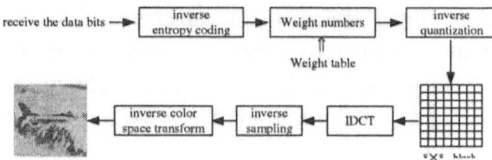

Fig. 4. Flowchart of the receiver side

4 Experimental Results

We used "Airplane", "Baboon", "Girl", "Lena", and "Zelda" to be our training images for gathering the longest bit length of quantized DCT coefficients. Each of the images we used has three different sizes. They are 128×128, 256×256, and 512×512 pixels. Each pixel has 256 gray levels. We gathered the longest bit length for each quantized DCT coefficient in these images after color space transform, sampling, FDCT, and quantization. We found that the total bit lengths of each block does not exceed 196 bits, and DC, AC1, and AC2's longest lengths are 7 bits, as shown in Table 2.

Table 2. The longest bit length of each coefficient

Coefficient	The length (bits)
DC	7
AC1	7
AC2	7

For training, the weight table, "Airplane", "Baboon", and "Lena" were applied in our experiments to the other training images. Each of the images has also 128×128, 256×256, and 512×512 three different sizes. These images are also gray-level. According to the reconstructed image quality, each quantized DCT coefficient bit was given a different weight number. Finally, we collected all weight numbers into a weight table, as shown in Table 3.

Table 3. The weight table in our experiments

Weight number	Each quantized DCT coefficient bit						
Coefficient	0(MSB)	1	2	3	4	5	6(LSB)
DC	17907	8017	5314	4633	4456	3967	3653
AC1	4362	4120	3859	3634	3300	2956	2146
AC2	3650	3223	2867	2702	2506	2285	2146

From the proposed method mentioned above, the weight table was trained and owned in both the sender and receiver. In Table 3, the weight table is fixed, the weight numbers will not be changed even if the transmitting image does not belong the training image set. The sender transmitted the bits of quantized DCT coefficients to the receiver based on the weight table in each transmission stage from bigger to smaller and from important to unimportant.

The test images applied in our experiments were "Airplane", "Baboon", and "Lena". They were all gray-level images and digitized with three different kinds of resolutions; 128 × 128, 256 × 256, and 512 × 512 pixels. At some specific compression ratio, the reconstructed image quality at each PIT transmission stage using the proposed method was compared with that of the traditional JPEG as shown in Tables 4-6. That is, the PSNR values of 128 × 128, 256 × 256, and 512 × 512 pixels in the each PIT transmission stages of JPEG and the proposed method are listed in Tables 4-6, respectively.

In these tables, we see that the reconstructed image qualities of the proposed method are obviously much better than traditional JPEG. Especially, in the first stage of each table using the new method, the average values of image qualities are 0.4dB, 0.35dB, and 0.34dB more than those using traditional JPEG.

Table 4. The PSNR values of our experimental results for 128×128 images

Stage	Transmission bit rates	Adoptive method	Airplane	Baboon	Lena
1	0.0357	JPEG	20.130034	21.660652	19.559876
		Our method	20.77596	21.7034626	19.775084
2	0. 0357	JPEG	21.499162	22.304895	20.173897
		Our method	21.875858	22.678302	20.986147
3	0. 0357	JPEG	22.457592	23.748742	22.139424
		Our method	22.645535	23.780796	22.735904
4	0.0612	JPEG	23.488768	24.539967	24.172576
		Our method	23.869343	24.653728	24.204061

Table 5. The PSNR values of our experimental results for 256×256 images

Stage	Transmission bit rates	Adoptive method	Airplane	Baboon	Lena
1	0.0357	JPEG	21.303633	21.163072	21.269782
		Our method	21.890646	21.23505	21.362587
2	0. 0357	JPEG	22.529886	21.704462	21.827357
		Our method	23.133965	21.860896	22.978621
3	0. 0357	JPEG	23.810986	22.515882	24.385829
		Our method	24.128311	22.542798	24.853557
4	0.0612	JPEG	25.045084	23.196532	26.387808
		Our method	25.406656	23.194601	26.38576

Table 6. The PSNR values of our experimental results for 512×512 images

Stage	Transmission bit rates	Adoptive method	Airplane	Baboon	Lena
1	0.0357	JPEG	23.217154	20.480526	23.958124
		Our method	23.803254	20.546331	24.144847
2	0. 0357	JPEG	24.588955	21.026023	24.750164
		Our method	25.37675	21.104891	25.854579
3	0. 0357	JPEG	26.540641	21.635429	27.515024
		Our method	26.807837	21.667851	28.026334
4	0.0612	JPEG	28.101502	22.27046	29.968377
		Our method	28.479035	22.346068	29.992329

In order to show the improvement of the visual quality for the reconstructed images, in this section, we also display some experimental results of traditional JPEG and the proposed method after the first and the second transmission stages. The original image of "Airplane" with a resolution of 256 × 256 pixels is shown in Figure 5. The reconstructed images after the first two stages are illustrated in Figures 6-7. In each of these figures, (a) and (b) represent the reconstructed images respectively by traditional JPEG and the proposed method. Note that there are many indistinct regions in Figures 6 (a) and 7 (a) which have been circled. For example, in Figure 6 (a), we cannot separate the top of airframe from the background. However, the images in Figures 6 (b) and 7 (b), which are reconstructed by the proposed method, are quite clear so that the airframe can be obviously recognized. Besides the first two stages, in the next eight stages, the image quality of the proposed method is still better than that of traditional JPEG.

Fig. 5. The original image: Airplane

(a) JPEG(PSNR : 21.303633)   (b) Our method (PSNR : 21.890646)

Fig. 6. The reconstructed image after the first transmission stage

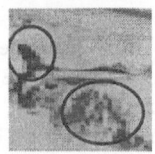 

(a) JPEG(PSNR : 22.529886)   (b) Our method(PSNR : 23.133965)

Fig. 7. The reconstructed image after the second transmission stage

The proposed method has three drawbacks. One is that the weight table has to take up some storage space. Two is that the proposed method costs more training time for training the weight table and traditional JPEG does not. Note that the training procedure belongs to the preprocessing of the proposed method. The third drawback is that the reconstruction time of the proposed method is 4.33 seconds more than that of traditional JPEG in our experiments. However, it is worth these few seconds because the reconstructed image quality of the proposed method is more impressive than that of traditional JPEG.

5 Conclusions

The reconstructed image quality of traditional JPEG at earlier stages is not acceptable. In this paper, we propose a new method to improve the reconstructed image quality of JPEG progressive transmission. We use MSE value to decide the weight number of each bit of quantized DCT coefficient according to its importance. We collect all weight numbers into a weight table. The weight table is fixed for all blocks and all images in the proposed method, and is owned in both the sender and receiver. After the generation of the weight table, the sender and receiver transmit and receive the quantized DCT coefficient bits based on the weight table.

The proposed method spends more time in training the weight table, and the execution time of the image reconstruction in the proposed method in the receiver side is 4.33 seconds more than that of traditional JPEG. However, this is acceptable especially for a slow transmission environment, such as the wireless communications. The experimental results show that the proposed method can significantly improve the reconstructed image quality at each transmission stage compared with JPEG, especially for the beginning stages. Besides, the visual quality of the reconstructed images using the proposed method is more impressive than that of JPEG.

References

1. C. C. Chang, F. C. Shiue, and T. S. Chen, "A New Scheme of Progressive Image Transmission Based on Bit-Plane Method," Proceeding of Fifth Asia-Pacific Conference on Communications and Fourth Opto-electronics and Communications Conference (APCC/OECC'99), Beijing, China, Oct. 1999, pp. 892-895.
2. C. C. Chang, J. C. Jau, and T. S. Chen, "A Fast Reconstruction Method for Transmitting Images Progressively," IEEE Transactions on Consumer Electronics, Vol. 44, No. 4, Nov. 1998, pp. 1225-1233.
3. K. L. Hung, C. C. Chang, and T. S. Chen, "A Side-Match Reconstruction Method Using Tree-Structured VQ for Transmitting Images Progressively," IEICE Transactions of Fundamentals of Electronics, Communications and Computer Science, Nov. 1999, pp. 213-228.
4. T. S. Chen and C. C. Chang, "Progressive Image Transmission Using Side Match Method," Information Systems and Technologies for Network Society, World Scientific Publishing Co. Pte. Ltd, 1998, pp. 191-198.
5. W. B. Pennebaker and J. L. Mitchell, JPEG: Still Image Data Compression Standard. New York: Van Nostrand Reinhold, 1993.
6. W. M. Lam and A. R. Reibman, "Self-Synchronizing variable- length codes for image transmission," in Proceedings of IEEE Int. Conf. Acoust,. Speech, Signal Processing, 1992, pp. III-447-III-480.

MediaView: A Semantic View Mechanism for Multimedia Modeling[1]

Qing Li[1], Jun Yang[1,2], and Yueting Zhuang[2]

[1] City University of Hong Kong, HKSAR, China
itqli@cityu.edu.hk, yangjun@acm.org
[2] Zhejiang University, Hangzhou, China
yzhuang@cs.zju.edu.cn

Abstract. The semantics of multimedia data, which features context-dependency and media-independency, is of vital importance to multimedia applications but inadequately supported by the state-of-the-art database technology. In this paper, we address this problem by proposing *MediaView* as an extended object-oriented view mechanism to bridge the "semantic gap" between conventional databases and semantics-intensive multimedia applications. This mechanism captures the dynamic semantics of multimedia using a modeling construct named *media view*, which formulates a customized context where *heterogeneous* media objects with similar/related semantics are characterized by *additional properties* and user-defined *semantic relationships*. View operators are proposed for the manipulation and derivation of media views. The usefulness and elegancy of *MediaView* are demonstrated by its application in a multi-modal information retrieval system.

1 Introduction

Owning to the expanding Web, recent years witness a phenomenal growth of multimedia information in a variety of types, such as image, video, animation. The vast volume of multimedia data creates the challenge of manipulating them in an organized, efficient, and scalable way, preferably, using a database approach. In the database community, however, although a great number of publications have been devoted to the presentation, indexing, and querying of multimedia (see, e.g., [2]), relatively little progress has been achieved on the semantic modeling of multimedia, which is of primary importance to various multimedia applications. A typical multimedia application, say, authoring of electronic lecture notes, is more likely to query against the semantic content of data, e.g., "*find an illustration of the three-schema database architecture*", rather than to query against the primitive data features, e.g., "*find all the images in JPEG format with size over 200KB*". Therefore, it is critical for a database to model the semantics of multimedia data in order to effectively support the functionality of semantics-intensive multimedia applications. Unfortunately, most existing data models are unable to capture precisely the semantic aspect of multimedia, which features the following two unique properties:

- *Context-dependency*. Semantics is not a static and inherent property of a media object. (In this paper, a media object refers to an object of any type of modality,

---

[1] The work described in this paper was supported, primarily, by a strategic research grant from City University of Hong Kong (Project No. 7001384), and partially by a grant from the Doctorate Research Foundation of the State Education Commission of China.

Y.-C. Chen, L.-W. Chang, and C.-T. Hsu (Eds.): PCM 2002, LNCS 2532, pp. 729–736, 2002.
© Springer-Verlag Berlin Heidelberg 2002

such as an image, a video clip, or a textual document.) Rather, the semantic meaning of a media object is influenced by the application (user) that manipulates the object, the role it plays, and other objects that interact with it, which collectively constitute a specific context around this object. As an example, consider the interpretations of van Gogh's famous painting "Sunflower", the leftmost image in Fig.1 (a) and Fig.2 (b). When it is placed with the other two images in Fig.1 (a), which are other paintings of van Gogh, the meaning of "van Gogh's paintings" is suggested. When the same image is interpreted in the context of Fig.2 (b), however, the meaning of "flower" is manifest. Moreover, a media object may acquire context-specific properties when interpreted in a certain context. For example, as a painting, the "Sunflower" can be described by "artist" and "year", whereas as a flower it can have attribute like "category".

(a)   (b)

Fig. 1. (a) Context of "van Gogh's paintings". (b) The context of "flower"

- **Media-independency**. Media objects of different types of modality (i.e., multi-modal objects) may suggest the related semantic meaning. For instance, the concept of "three-schema database architecture" can be expressed by a textual document, an image illustration, a PowerPoint slide, or a combination of them.

The dynamic nature of multimedia is fundamentally different from that of the traditional alphanumeric data, whose semantics is explicit, unique, and self-contained. This distinction explains the failing of applying traditional data models to characterize the semantics of multimedia data. For example, in a conventional (strongly typed) object-oriented model, each object statically belongs to exactly one type, which prescribes the attributes and behaviors of the object. This obviously conflicts with the context-dependent nature of a media object, which needs to switch dynamically among various types depending on specific contexts. Moreover, a conventional object model can hardly model the media-independency nature, which requires media objects of different types to have some attributes and methods defined in common.

The incapability of semantic multimedia modeling severely undermines the usefulness of a database to support semantics-intensive multimedia applications. This problem, referred to as the "semantic gap" between databases and multimedia applications, constitutes the major motivation of *MediaView* as an extended object-oriented view mechanism. As illustrated in Fig. 2, *MediaView* bridges this "semantic gap" by introducing above the traditional three-schema database architecture an additional layer constituted by a set of modeling constructs named *media views*. Each media view, defined as an extended object view, formulates a *customized context* in which the dynamic and elusive semantics of media objects are properly interpreted.

To cope with the dynamic semantics of multimedia, *MediaView* builds the following extensions to the traditional object-oriented view mechanisms (e.g., [1], [3]): (1) A media view can accommodate *heterogeneous* media objects (i.e., objects belonging to different classes) as its members. (2) Objects included as the members of a media view are endowed with *additional properties* that are specific to that media view. (3) Objects in a media view are interconnected by user-defined *semantic relationships*. A media view serves as a container that accommodates semantically related objects and describe them by additional properties and semantic relationships. The basic concepts of media view are defined in Section 2. The operations of media views, such as creation, deletion, and manipulation, are provided as a set of *view operators*, which are described in Section 3. Moreover, in Section 4 we demonstrate how a real-world application, namely multi-modal information retrieval, can be elegantly modeled by media views. The conclusion of the paper is given in Section 5.

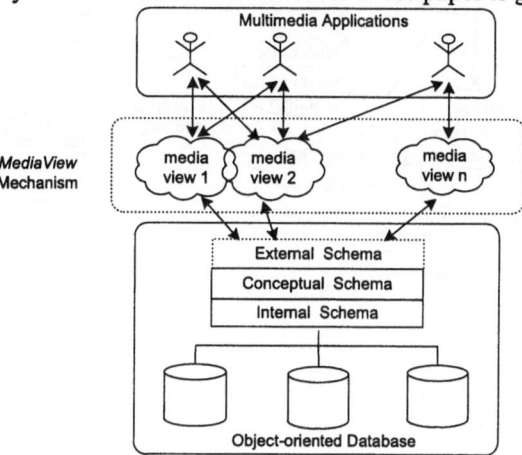

Fig. 2. *MediaView* as a "semantic bridge"

2   Fundamentals of *MediaView*

MediaView is essentially an extension built on top of a standard object-oriented data model. In an object model, real-world entities are modeled as objects. Each object is identified by a system-assigned identifier, and has a set of attributes and methods that describe the structural and behavioral properties of the corresponding entity. Objects with the same attributes and methods are clustered into classes, as defined below:

Definition 1. *A* **class** *named as C_i is represented as a tuple of two elements:*

$$C_i = <O_i, P_i>$$

1.   *O_i is the extent of C_i, which is a set of objects that belong to C_i. Each object o O_i is called an instance of C_i .*

2.   *P_i is a set of properties defined by C_i. Each property p P_i is an attribute or a method that can be applied to all the instances of C_i.*

In contrast, a media view as an extended object-oriented view is defined as follows:

Definition 2: *A* **media view** *named as MV_i is represented as a tuple of four elements:*

$$MV_i = <M_i, P_i^v, P_i^m, R_i,>$$

1.   *M_i is a set of objects that are included into MV_i as its members. Each object o M_i belongs to a certain source class, and different members of MV_i may belong to different source classes.*

2. P_i^v is a set of view-level properties (attributes and methods) applied on MV_i itself.

3. P_i^m is a set of member-level properties (attributes and methods), which are applied on all the members of MV_i.

4. R_i is a set of **relationships**, and each r R_i is in the form of $<o_j, o_k, t>$, which denotes a relationship of type t between member o_j and o_k in MV_i.

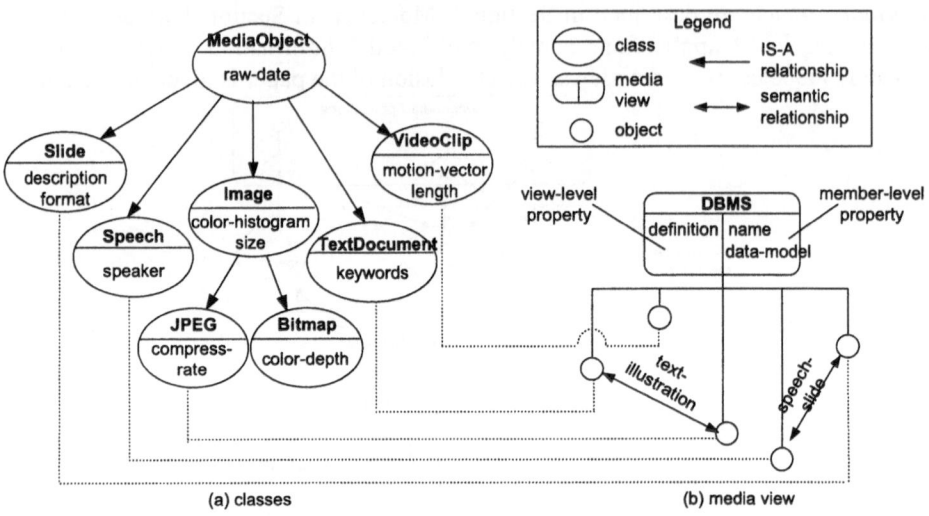

Fig. 3. Examples of classes and a media view

The relationship between classes and a media view is exemplified in Fig.3. As shown in Fig.3 (a), a set of classes is defined to model media objects of different types, such as *Image*, *VideoClip*, and *Speech*, which are connected into a conceptual schema. From the properties defined in these classes, one can see that they emphasize on the primitive features of media objects, such as the color of images, keywords of text document, which have uniform interpretation irrespective of specific contexts. Although such emphasis is not mandatory, by doing so the conceptual schema is able to provide a context-independent foundation based on which a variety of customized contexts can be formulated.

Fig.3 (b) illustrates an example media view called *DBMS*. Each member of this media view is a media object that is about a specific DBMS product, such as a JPEG image illustrating a DBMS, a slide as the demonstration of a DBMS, etc. Note that all these objects are not created by this media view, but are selected from heterogeneous source classes in Fig.3 (a). However, these objects obtain a set of new (member-level) properties when they become the members of *DBMS,* such as the name of the DBMS product. Different from the properties defined in their source classes, their properties in the media view focus on the semantic aspects of media objects. Moreover, a view-level property, *definition*, is used to describe the global property of the media view itself (i.e., the definition of a DBMS). Different types of semantic relationships exist between the view members. For example, the "speech-slide" relationship between the *Speech* object and the *Slide* object denotes that the speech accompanies the slide.

3 View Operators

To support manipulations of media views, we have devised a set of view operators, whose definitions[2] are presented as follows.

1. *CREATE-MV (N: mv-name, VP: set-of-property-ref, MP: set-of-property-ref): mv-ref.* This operator creates a media view (*MV*) named as *N*, which takes the properties in *VP* as its view-level properties, and those in *MP* as its member-level properties. When executed successfully, it returns the reference to the created media view, which has no members and relationships initially.

2. *DELETE-MV (MV: mv-ref).* This operator deletes a media view specified by *MV* from the database. All the members of *MV*, their properties (value) defined in *MV*, and all the relationships in *MV* are also deleted. Note that the member itself as an instance of its source class is not deleted from the database.

3. *GET-ALL-MV():set-of-mv-ref.* This operator retrieves all the media views currently in the database. The return value is a set of references to these media views.

4. *ADD-MEM (MV: mv-ref, O: object-ref).* This operator adds the object referred by *O* as a member of the media view referred by *MV*. All the member-level properties for *O* are set to their default values.

5. *REMOVE-MEM (MV: mv-ref, O: object-ref).* This operator excludes the object *O* from the media view *MV*, with all its relationships and properties in *MV* deleted.

6. *ADD-RELATION (MV: mv-ref, O1: object-ref, O2: object-ref, R: relationship-type): relationship-ref.* This operator establishes a relationship of type *R* between objects *O1* and *O2*, which are the members of the media view *MV*. If the operator is applied successfully, the reference to the relationship object is returned.

7. *REMOVE-RELATION (MV: mv-ref, O1: object-ref, O2: object-ref[, R: relationship]).* If the last argument is not specified, this operator removes all their relationship(s) between objects *O1* and *O2* in the media view *MV*. Otherwise, it only deletes the relationships of the type specified by *R*.

8. *GET-ALL-MEM (MV: mv-ref): set-of-object-ref.* This operator retrieves all the (heterogeneous) objects as the members of the media view *MV*.

9. *HAS-MEM (MV: mv-ref, O: object-ref): boolean.* This operator tests if object *O* is a member of the media view *MV*.

10. *GET-RELATED-MEM (MV: mv-ref, O: object-ref[, R: relationship]): set-of-object-ref.* This operator returns all the objects that have relationship of any type (if the last argument is absent) or of type *R* (if the last argument is given) with object *O* in the media view *MV*.

11. *GET-ALL-RELATION (MV: mv-ref): set-of-relationship-ref.* This operator retrieves all the relationships in the media view *MV*.

12. *GET/SET-VIEW-PROP (MV: mv-ref, P: property-ref): value.* This operator retrieves (or sets) the value of the view-level property *P* of media view *MV*.

13. *GET/SET-MEM-PROP (MV: mv-ref, O: object-ref, P: property-ref, V: value).* This operator retrieves (or sets) the value of the member-level property *P* of object *O* in media view *MV*.

---

[2] In the definition of view operators, the suffix "-ref" represents the reference to object, which is actually a variable holding the *Oid* of an object. For example, *mv-ref* is the reference to a media view, *relationship-ref* is the reference to a relationship, etc.

The set of view operators defined above provides the basic functions of media views, while more sophisticated operations can be implemented as a combination of these basic ones. For example, a search for objects that are related with a specific object in any media view can be handled by applying *GET-ALL-MV()* and *GET-RELATED-MEM ()* in a combined fashion.

4 Real-World Application: Multi-modal Information Retrieval

To show the usefulness and elegancy of *MediaView*, we introduce a real-world application in which media views are found to be a natural and suitable modeling construct. The application comes from our on-going research project on a multi-modal information retrieval system, *Octopus* [4]. In this section, we describe several specific media views created as the data model of *Octopus*, and demonstrate how a variety of retrieval functions are implemented using view operators.

4.1 Data Model

Octopus is proposed to provide search functionality in multimedia repositories ranging from web to digital libraries, where data are typically of multiple types of modality. The basic search paradigm supported by *Octopus* is query-by-example, that is, a user forms a query by designating a media object as the sample object and the system retrieves all the media objects relevant to it. For example, using the poster (an image) of the movie "Harry Potter" as the sample, we expect to receive media objects such as a textual introduction of the movie, a "highlight" video clip, and the music of the movie. Essential to such a multi-modal retrieval system is the relevance between any two media objects, which is evaluated from the following three perspectives:

1. **User perceptions**. Two media objects are regarded as relevant if users have the same/similar interpretation of them, e.g., annotating them with the same keywords.
2. **Contextual relationship**. Media objects that are spatially adjacent or connected by hyperlinks are usually relevant to each other.
3. **Low-level features**. Low-level features (e.g., color of images) can be extracted from media objects to describe their visual/aural characteristics. Intuitively, media objects are considered relevant if they possess highly similar low-level features.

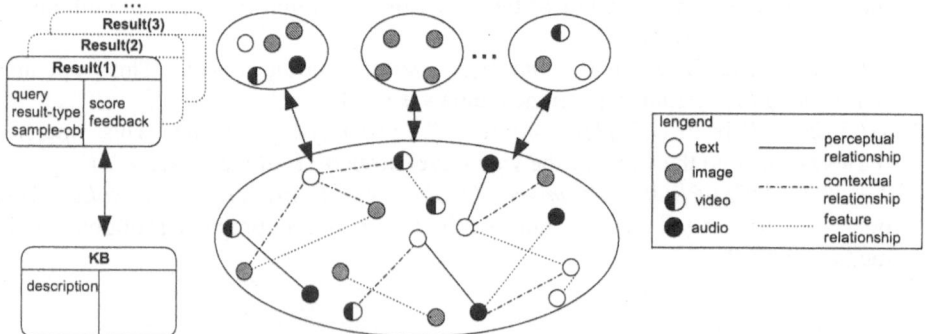

Fig. 4. Media views created for *Octopus*

As shown in Fig.4, a media view called *KB* is created to model the relevance between any two media objects in the database of *Octopus*. The members of *KB* are media objects such as images, videos, audios, which are modelled as instances of heterogeneous source classes (see Fig.3). Three types of relationships (*perceptual*, *contextual*, and *feature*) are defined to represent the inter-object relevance from the aforementioned three perspectives. A weight can be associated with each relationship as its property to indicate the strength of the relevance.

KB provides an integrated knowledge base on the relevance among media objects, based on which user queries can be processed by analysing the various relationships contained in it. For each query, a media view named *Result(n)* is created to accommodate the results of the query, where n is the serial number. As shown in Fig.4, the global aspect of the query is described by its view-level properties, such as the sample object used, while member-level properties are assigned on each object to describe its characteristics as a query result, such as its relevance score, and users' feedback opinion towards it (relevant, neutral, or irrelevant).

4.2 Implementation of Retrieval-Related Functions

Octopus provides a variety of retrieval-related functions, such as search, relevance feedback, navigation, learning, all of which are realized by applying view operators over the media view *KB* and *Result(n)*, as summarized in Table 1.

Table 1. Pseudo-codes of the algorithms of various retrieval functions implemented in *Octopus*.

Query (S, K, o_S)
S: a set of objects as the query result
K: the number of iterations for
   propagation
o_S: the sample object
 	
1. S:= {o_S}
2. For n= 1 to K
3.   T: = {}
4.   For each object o in S
5.   T:=T ∮GET-RELATED-MEM("KB",o)
6.   S := S ∮T
	Navigate (o)
	o: the object currently been viewed
	   by the user
	
	1. S:=GET-RELATED-MEM("KB", o)
	2. Present all the objects in S to
	   the user, from which the user
	   can choose an interested object
	   and navigate to it
	3. Go to Step 1

Feedback (S, R, N, K)
S: a set of objects as the query
   results
R: a set of relevant examples
N: a set of irrelevant examples
K: the number of iterations for
   propagation
 	
1. For n=1 to K
2.   T: = {}
3.   For each object o in R
4.   T:=T ∮GET-RELATED-MEM("KB", o)
5.   R:=R ∮T
6.   T:={}
7.   For each object o in N
8.   T:=T ∮GET-RELATED-MEM("KB", o)
9.   N := N ∮T
10.S:= R-N
	Learning ()
	Result(n) (n=1,...,N): a set of media
	views for query results
	
	1. S: = GET-ALL-MEM ("KB")
	2. For any two objects o_i,o_j in S
	3. For n = 1 to N
	4. mv := Result(n)
	5. If HAS-MEM(mv,o_i) && HAS-MEM
	(mv,o_j) && GET-MEM-PROP(mv, o_i,
	"feedback")="Relevant" && GET-MEM-
	PROP(mv,o_j,"feedback")="Relevant"
	6. ADD-RELATION("KB", o_i, o_j,
	         "perceptual")

- **Query**: The media objects relevant to a sample object specified in a user query are found by "propagating" via the relationships in *KB*. Starting from the sample object, we traverse to other media objects in *KB* through relationships (up to a specific number of iterations) and identify these objects as relevant results. We can designate the type(s) of relationship used in propagation by specifying it in *GET-RELATED-MEMBER* (Step 5). Moreover, the modality of query results can be controlled by distinguishing the source class of each object (i.e., image, videos, etc). All the retrieval results, together with the user's possible feedback opinions towards them, are stored in the media view *Result(n)* created for the query.

- **Navigation**. Navigation among the media objects can be facilitated by using the various relationships in *KB* as the natural routes for navigating from one media object to related objects.
- **Relevance feedback**. Relevance feedback is a mechanism used to refine the retrieval results by giving evaluations to the previously retrieved results, typically, by designating some results as relevant or irrelevant examples. The algorithm *Feedback* presents a simple algorithm for relevance feedback. Specifically, we perform propagation based on relevant and irrelevant examples respectively, resulting in a set of "positive" results and a set of "negative" results. The final results are obtained by removing the "negative" results from the "positive" ones.
- **Learning from feedbacks**. Besides exploring the knowledge in *KB* to facilitate search and navigation, new knowledge can be derived from user feedbacks recorded in *Result(n)* and incorporated into *KB*. The algorithm *Learning* suggests an intuitive way to do that: if two objects are relevant examples for the same query (i.e., they appear in the same *Result(n)* with property *feedback* being "relevant"), we add a perceptual relationship between them in *KB*. More sophisticated techniques can be used for knowledge discovery based on media views.

4   Conclusions

The *MediaView* mechanism presented in this paper builds a bridge across the "semantic gap" between conventional databases and multimedia applications, the former of which are inadequate to capture the dynamic semantics of multimedia, whereas data semantics plays a key role in the latter. This mechanism is based on the modeling construct of *media view*, which formulates a customized context where *heterogeneous* media objects with related semantics are characterized by *additional properties* and *semantic relationships*. View operators have been developed for the manipulation of media views. The application of *MediaView* in a multi-modal information retrieval system has been described to demonstrate its usefulness.

References

1. Abiteboul, S., Bonner, A.: Objects and Views. Proc. ACM Conf. on Management of Data (1991) 238-247
2. Apers, P., Blanken, H., Houtsma, M. (eds.): Multimedia Databases in Perspective. Springer, London (1997)
3. Rundensteiner, E.A.: MultiView: A Methodology for Supporting Multiple Views in Object-Oriented Databases. Proc. 18th Int. Conf. on Very Large Database (1992) 187-198
4. Yang, J., Li, Q., Zhuang, Y.T.: Octopus: Aggressive Search of Multi-Modality Data Using Multifaceted Knowledge Base. Proc. 11th Int. Conf. on World Wide Web (2002) 54-64

The Connection between Pyramidal Algorithm and Wavelet Series

Sun Wu, Youzhao Wang, and Zhengchang Wu

Institute of Advanced Digital Technologies & Instrumentation,
Zhejiang University, Hangzhou 310027,China
sun_wu@cbeis.zju.edu.cn

Abstract. Wavelet Series (WS) and Pyramidal Algorithm (PA) are both widely used in many fields. The values of WS can be obtained by its inner product definitions while approximation and detail coefficients of PA are computed with a pyramidal construction based on convolutions with filters. When the initial inputs of PA are signal samples, the connection between PA and WS is analyzed detailedly in this paper. And simple formulas are also given to obtain exact values of scaling and wavelet functions on a certain point.

1 Introduction

Continuous Wavelet Transform (CWT) and WS have proven to be powerful tools for signal processing applications. The scale and time parameters of CWT are still continuous variables. So, there is heavy computational redundancy in CWT. Its scale and time parameters can be sampled with the dyadic grid to form WS. The inner productions of WS are

$$c_{j,k} = \int x(t)\phi_{j,k}(t)dt . \tag{1}$$

$$d_{j,k} = \int x(t)\varphi_{j,k}(t)dt . \tag{2}$$

where scaling function $\phi_{j,k}(t) = 2^{-\frac{j}{2}}\phi(2^{-j}t - k)$,wavelet function $\varphi_{j,k}(t) = 2^{-\frac{j}{2}}\varphi(2^{-j}t - k)$. $c_{j,k}$ and $d_{j,k}$ are approximation and detail coefficients, respectively.

But it is not easy to calculate the inner product definitions above in general. Thanks to the fast PA, an efficient implementation comes true for biorthogonal(or orthogonal) wavelet bases and discrete signal sequences .

As a basis of PA, the two-scale relations [1], [2] are well known as

$$\phi_{j,0}(t) = \sum_k h(k)\phi_{j-1,k}(t) . \tag{3}$$

Y.-C. Chen, L.-W. Chang, and C.-T. Hsu (Eds.): PCM 2002, LNCS 2532, pp. 737-742, 2002.

$$\varphi_{j,0}(t) = \sum_k g(k)\varphi_{j-1,k}(t). \tag{4}$$

where $h(k)$ and $g(k)$ are the low pass and high pass filters, respectively.

For a discrete signal sequence, PA can be used to compute approximation and detail coefficients for biorthogonal(or orthogonal) bases:

$$c_{j,k} = \sum_{n'} h(n'-2k)c_{j-1,n'}. \tag{5}$$

$$d_{j,k} = \sum_{n'} g(n'-2k)c_{j-1,n'}. \tag{6}$$

Samples of the signal are usually taken as the initial inputs of PA:

$$c_{J,k} \approx 2^{\frac{J}{2}} x(2^J k). \tag{7}$$

The approximate values of $c_{j,k}$ and $d_{j,k}$ can be calculated by approximations (7) in the finest subspace V_J and iterating with the filters according to the two-scale relations, which is called Natural Sampling (NS) in Johnson and Kinsey's algorithm [3].

In this paper, the connection between NS and WS is analyzed in detail. It is found out that NS can be considered to compute the approximations of the inner product definitions (1) and (2). At the same time, simple formulas are given to obtain exact values of scaling and wavelet functions on a certain point.

2   The Connection

2.1   Natural Sampling

Assume $n'-2k = n$, (5) can be rewritten as follows:

$$c_{j,k} = \sum_n h(n)c_{j-1,n+2k}. \tag{8}$$

For the explanation below, we add subscript $j-1$ for n in (8):

$$c_{j,k} = \sum_{n_{j-1}} h(n_{j-1})c_{j-1,n_{j-1}+2k}. \tag{9}$$

Using (9) repeatedly, we obtain the iterative convolution process of NS:

$$
\left.
\begin{aligned}
c_{j,k} &= \sum_{n_{j-1}} h(n_{j-1}) c_{j-1,\, n_{j-1}+2k} \\
c_{j-1,\, n_{j-1}+2k} &= \sum_{n_{j-2}} h(n_{j-2}) c_{j-2,\, n_{j-2}+2n_{j-1}+2^2 k} \\
&\cdots\cdots\cdots\cdots \\
c_{J+1,\,(n_{J+1}+2n_{J+2}\cdots\cdots+2^{J-2-J} n_{j-1}+2^{J-1-J} k)} &= \sum_{n_J} h(n_J) c_{J,\,(n_J+2n_{J+1}+\cdots\cdots 2^{J-1-J} n_{j-1}+2^{J-J} k)}
\end{aligned}
\right\} \tag{10}
$$

From (7), the approximations in subspace V_J are

$$
c_{J,\,(n_J+2n_{J+1}+\cdots\cdots 2^{J-1-J} n_{j-1}+2^{J-J} k)} \approx 2^{\frac{J}{2}} x(2^J k + s) \ . \ \left(s = \sum_{i=J}^{j-1} 2^i n_i\right) \tag{11}
$$

Inserting (11) into the iterative process of (10), we obtain a formula of NS:

$$
\begin{aligned}
c_{j,k} &\approx \sum_{n_{j-1}, n_{j-2}, \cdots, n_J} h(n_{j-1}) * h(n_{j-2}) * \cdots * h(n_J) * 2^{\frac{J}{2}} * x(2^J k + s) \\
&= \sum_{n_{j-1}, n_{j-2}, \cdots, n_J} (h(n_{j-1}) * h(n_{j-2}) * \cdots * h(n_J) * 2^{-\frac{J}{2}}) * 2^J * x(m).
\end{aligned} \tag{12}
$$

$$
(m = 2^J k + s)
$$

The formula (12) formulates the connection between the approximation coefficient and the discrete signal sequence $x(m)$, which has something in common with the inner product definition (1).

In (11) and (12), to each m and s correspond to a series of (k, s) and $(n_{j-1}, n_{j-2}, \ldots n_J)$, respectively. So, a fixed point $x(m)$ corresponds with a series of coefficients $h(n_{j-1}) * h(n_{j-2}) * \cdots * h(n_J)$. Summing up all the coefficients of $2^J * x(m)$ for a certain m in (12), we define the sum by $\phi^J_{j,k}(m)$:

$$
\phi^J_{j,k}(m) = 2^{-\frac{J}{2}} \sum_{n_{j-1}, n_{j-2}, \cdots, n_J} h(n_{j-1}) * h(n_{j-2}) * \cdots * h(n_J) . \tag{13}
$$

$\phi^J_{j,k}(m)$ can be called the scaling function's approximation of order $|j - J|$. The reason of such naming can be seen in the following reasoning:

1.   Substituting (13) to (3), we obtain

left-hand side of (3)= $\phi_{j,0}^{J}(m^{l})$

$$= 2^{-\frac{J}{2}} \sum_{n_{j-1}, n_{j-2}, \cdots, n_{J}} h(n_{j-1}) * h(n_{j-2}) * \cdots * h(n_{J}). \tag{14}$$

right-hand side of (3)= $\sum_{k} h(k) \phi_{j-1,k}^{J}(m^{r})$

$$= 2^{-\frac{J}{2}} \sum_{k} h(k) \sum_{n_{j-2}, n_{j-3}, \cdots, n_{J}} h(n_{j-2}) * h(n_{j-3}) * \cdots * h(n_{J}) \tag{15}$$

where the superscripts l and r of m correspond to the left-hand and right-hand sides of equation (3), respectively. The same notation rule is used in variable t of (16), s of (18) and n of (19).

2.For two-scale relation (3), it is obvious that

$$t^{l} = t^{r}. \tag{16}$$

Because continuous variable t of (3) corresponds to discrete variable m of (12), we get

$$m^{l} = m^{r}. \tag{17}$$

According to the definition of m in (12), for m^{l} of (14) and m^{r} of (15), we have

$$2^{j} * 0 + s^{l} = 2^{j-1} k + s^{r}. \tag{18}$$

$$\Rightarrow \sum_{J}^{j-1} 2^{i} n_{i}^{l} = 2^{j-1} k + \sum_{J}^{j-2} 2^{i} n_{i}^{r}. \tag{19}$$

$$\Rightarrow 2^{j-1} n_{j-1}^{l} + \sum_{J}^{j-2} 2^{i} n_{i}^{l} = 2^{j-1} k + \sum_{J}^{j-2} 2^{i} n_{i}^{r}. \tag{20}$$

$\Rightarrow$ The solution of $(n_{j-1}^{l}, n_{j-2}^{l}, \cdots, n_{J}^{l}) \equiv$ the solution of $(k, n_{j-2}^{r}, \cdots, n_{J}^{r})$ $\quad$ (21)

3.From (21), we obtain
(14) $\equiv$ (15).

that is to say, $\phi_{j,k}^{J}(m)$ also satisfies two-scale relation (3) just as $\phi_{j,k}(t)$. Further,

when $J \to -\infty$, discrete sequence $\phi_{j,k}^{J}(m) \to$ continuous function $\phi_{j,k}(t)$.

In addition, adding all the coefficients of $x(2^j k + s)$ in (12), we get

$$\sum_{n_{j-1}, n_{j-2}, \cdots, n_J} h(n_{j-1}) * h(n_{j-2}) * \cdots * h(n_J) * 2^{\frac{J}{2}} = 2^{\frac{J}{2}} [\sum h(n)]^{(j-J)} = 2^{\frac{j}{2}}.$$

(22)

2.2 Results

The inner product definition (1) can be rewritten as

$$c_{j,k} = \lim_{\Delta t \to 0} \sum_m \phi_{j,k}(m\Delta t) * \Delta t * x(m\Delta t).$$

(23)

Further, (23) can be simplified as

$$c_{j,k} = \lim_{\Delta t \to 0} \sum_m \phi_{j,k}(m) * \Delta t * x(m).$$

(24)

Comparing (24) with (12), 13, and 22, we get their correspondence which is listed in Table 1. In Table 1, initial resolution 2^J corresponds to step width Δt, which is a common sense. $\phi^J_{j,k}(m)$ is an approximation of $\phi_{j,k}(m)$.

Table 1. Correspondence between Natural Sampling and Wavelet Series

Formula (12),(13),(22)	Formula (24)
2^J	Δt
$x(m)$	$x(m)$
$\phi^J_{j,k}(m)$	$\phi_{j,k}(m)$
$\sum_{n_{j-1}, n_{j-2}, \cdots, n_J} h(n_{j-1}) * \cdots * h(n_J)$ $*2^{\frac{J}{2}} = 2^{\frac{j}{2}}$	$\int \phi_{j,k}(t)dt = 2^{\frac{j}{2}}$

It can be seen that if NS is used to calculate $c_{j,k}$, we actually compute the approximation of its inner product definition using (25):

$$c_{j,k} \approx \sum_m [\phi^J_{j,k}(m) * x(m)] * \Delta t.$$

(25)

When the initial resolution 2^J changes according to the sequence $2^{j-1}, 2^{j-2}, 2^{j-3}, \cdots$, from the angle of NS, this change means $c_{j,k}$ is computed on finer and finer initial resolution while for inner definition (1), it means the step width decreases by half every time to approach the theoretical value of $c_{j,k}$ little by little.

In addition, (13) is a simple formula to obtain the approximation of scaling function on a certain point. Usually, the scaling function's theoretical value can be obtained by equations derived from the two-scale relation (3) in the case of compactly supported bases [4]. The iterative convolution of $h(k)$ [5],[6] is also used to approach the value of scaling function .The advantage of (13) is that if a point is specified, its value can be obtained independently while in the previous two methods, values of some other points need be calculated, too.

In this paper, only the case of approximation coefficient and scaling function is studied. However, it is straightforward to extend the reasoning and results to detail coefficient and wavelet function.

3 Conclusion

In this paper, the connection between NS and WS is studied in detail. It is found out that NS can be considered to compute the approximations of the inner product definitions. At the same time, simple formulas are given to obtain exact values of scaling and wavelet functions. They can obtain approximations of the two functions on a certain point independently in comparison with the previous two methods.

References

1. Mallat, S.: A Theory for Multiresolution Signal Decomposition: The Wavelet Representation. IEEE Trans.Patt .Anal.Machine Intell.,Vol.11,No.7, (1989) 674-693
2. Mallat, S.: Multiresolution Approximation and Orthonormal Bases of Trans.Amer.Math. Soc., Vol.315, (1989) 69-87
3. Johson, B.R., Kinsey, J.L.: Quadrature Prefilters for the Discrete Wavelet Transform. IEEE Trans. Signal Processing , Vol.48, No.3,(2000) 873-875
4. Daubechies, I.: Ten Lectures on Wavelets. Philadephia,PA:siam, Vol.61,(1992)
5. Daubechies,I.: Orthogonal Bases of Compactly Supported Wavelet. Comm.on Pure and Appl.Math., Vol.41, (1988) 909-996
6. Yang, F.S.: Analysis and Application of Wavelet Transform. Science Publishing House P.R.China (2000)

A Hybrid Motion Data Manipulation: Wavelet Based Motion Processing and Spacetime Rectification

Feng Liu, Yueting Zhuang, Zhongxiang Luo, and Yunhe Pan

Department of Computer Science and Engineering
Microsoft Visual Perception Laboratory of Zhejiang University
Zhejiang University, Hangzhou, 310027, P.R.China
lffred@yahoo.com.cn yzhuang@cs.zju.edu.cn zdlzx@263.net
panyh@sun.zju.edu.cn

Abstract. In this paper, we present a hybrid approach to motion data manipulation. Motion signal is decomposed into multi-resolution levels with wavelet analysis. The coarse level represents the globe pattern of a motion signal while the fine levels describe the individual styles. Special motion style can be highlighted through enhancing the corresponding level content and can be fused into other motions by texturing them with related fine levels. And multiple motions can be synthesized by multi-resolution blending to create new motions somehow like to the blended motions. Motion signals implicitly preserve constraints to keep realistic. However, the above manipulations may inviolate some constraints and result in the unrealistic artifact. Spacetime rectification is proposed to reserve the essential constraints. Our experiment shows the effectiveness of this hybrid motion data manipulation approach.

1 Introduction

Recently, the increasing demand for powerful and intuitive animation systems has led to the development of new techniques. The motion capture system [1] provides tools for real-time animation, with extremely realistic results: human motion is captured and mapped onto animated characters, and the generated animation preserves the unique characteristic of the actor.

However, problems appear when we modify the captured data. Even if the modification is trifling, the whole motion capture procedure should be repeated. The powerful motion editing systems are demanded. These systems should provide easy and effective tools to modify motion data, including interactive editing, blending, stitching, smoothing and so on.

The goal of this research is to provide an efficient approach to motion editing. The motion signal is firstly decomposed into many resolution levels. The special motion feature can be highlighted through enhancing related level contents. And motions can be characterized with special styles by texturing them with corresponding fine levels. Also multiple motion signals can be synthesized by multi-resolution blending to create a series of new motions somehow like to the blended components. At last, spacetime

Y.-C. Chen, L.-W. Chang, and C.-T. Hsu (Eds.): PCM 2002, LNCS 2532, pp. 743–750, 2002.

rectification is proposed to preserve the essential constraints hidden in original motion signals to guarantee the resulting motion be realistic.

The remainder of this paper is organized as follows: in the following section, we will give a review on motion editing techniques. In Section 3, we describe wavelet analysis based motion manipulation methods in detail, including motion enhancement, motion style texturing and multiple motion synthesis. In Section 4, we elaborate spacetime motion rectification. And we show the experimental result in Section 5 and conclude the paper in the last section.

2 Related Work

Gleicher [2] suggested a constraint base method for editing a pre-existing motion such that it meets new needs yet preserves the original quality as much as possible. A similar technique for adapting an animated motion from one character to another was also suggested [3]. J.Lee [4] proposed a hierarchical approach to interactive motion editing. Popovic and Witkin [5] presented a physically based motion editing algorithm, which considers some physical attributes as constrains, besides those specified by users; meanwhile, to improve the efficiency of computation, it first handles the reduced motion model and then deals with the complete one.

Bruderlin and Williams [6] apply techniques from image and signal-processing domain to designing, modifying and adapting animated motion. Witkin and Popovic [7] introduced the idea of motion warping. Brand and Hertzmann [8] proposed a style machine, which produces new motion containing the desired feature by learning motion patterns from a highly varied set of motion capture sequences.

More recently, Lee [9] developed a multiresolution analysis method that guarantees coordinate invariance for use in motion editing operations. Pullen and Bregler[10] presented a motion capture assisted animation, which allows animators to keyframe motion for a subset of degrees of freedom of a character and use motion capture data to synthesize motion for the missing degrees of freedom and add texture to those keyframed. In the work of Li et al [11], motion data was divided into motion textons, each of which could be modeled by a linear dynamic system. Motions were synthesized by considering the likelihood of switching from one texton to the next.

3 Wavelet Based Motion Analysis and Manipulation

The posture of an articulate figure can be specified by its joint configurations together with the orientation and position of Root [12]. And motion can be regarded as a posture sequence. Using the multiresolution property of wavelet, motion signal S can be decomposed into many resolution levels as follows:

$$S = A_J + \sum_{j=1}^{J} D_j, J \in Z. \tag{1}$$

where A_j is the approximation, and D_j is the detail at level j. A_j conveys the overall trend of a motion, while D_js represent the mode, style and even the emotional contents of a motion.

3.1 Motion Enhancement

The coarse content of motion represents the main pattern and the fine contents correspond to some special motion styles. With the information at some resolution levels processed, the corresponding feature of a motion can be highlighted or weakened. For example, with high resolution contents enhanced, the corresponding details of motion can be highlighted. Whereas the transformation of low resolution content will change the basic attributes of a motion. In contrary to the Fourier transform in which the variations affect all the motion (as it is local only in frequency domain but not in time domain), the wavelet transform is local both in time and frequency domain. So editing a special part of the motion is possible without destroying the other parts. The main steps of motion enhancement algorithm are outlined below:

1) Apply discrete wavelet transform (DTW) to motion signal S_0 to decompose it into the coarse and fine coefficients and then apply inverse discrete wavelet transform (IDTW) to get the approximation and a series of details as Equation 1.
2) Enhance each component with multiple factors, and get the approximation and details of new motion signal S_n.
3) Reconstruct the new motion signal S_n as Equation 1.

Given a normal walk, we can modify the step size through adjusting the approximation of the original motion signals of joint Hip and Knee and edit arm motions through adjusting the approximation of the original motion of joint Shoulder analogously (See Fig. 3(a)). Moreover, enhancing the details of the motion of joint Knee, the quiver in the walk can be highlighted and thus a jittering walk is produced (See Fig. 3(b)).

3.2 Motion Style Texture

The approximation of a motion signal represents the overall trend, while the detailed parts indicate the individual styles. Texturing a given approximation with different detailed parts from other motions, a family of motion somehow like to each other is produced.

Motion synchronization processing is conducted beforehand. For example, to texturing a run motion with the style of a sexy walk, they must be in phase. Here we employ the motion time warping algorithm to align the original motions as follows:

$$f(t) = g(h(t)). \tag{2}$$

Where $h(t)$ is the time warping function, usually a linear subsection function, and $g(t), f(t)$ are the motion before and after warping. Given two motions, the animator takes one as the reference and specifies several temporal corresponding points to determine $h(t)$. Then warp another motion as Equation 2, and the resulting motion is in phase with the reference one (See Fig. 1).

Due to the discrete expression of motion signal, two cases must be handled in performing re-sampling. When $h'(t)$ is less than 1, we must be able to determine what happens in between the individual samples. Otherwise, we must handle properly when throwing away information, since we will have fewer samples with which to encode things, and the problem called *alias* will occur. The former case can be easily handled by interpolation. For the latter, another motion can be selected as the reference to decrease $h'(t)$.

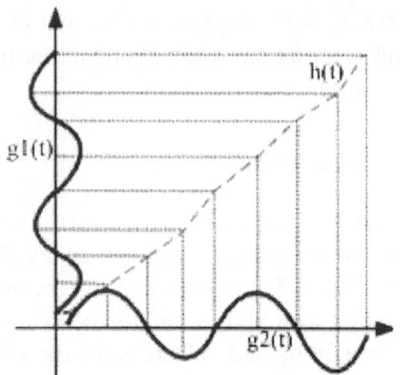

Fig. 1. Motion time warping. Taking $g2(t)$ as the reference, the time warping function $h(t)$ can be determined. Let $f(t)=g1(h(t))$, $f(t)$ and $g2(t)$ are synchronized

We describe the motion style texturing algorithm in the following steps:

1) Choose a dominating motion S_d, and a texture motion S_t.
2) Synchronize motions through motion time warping.
3) Apply DTW to the dominating motion signal S_d to decompose it into the coarse and detail coefficients and then apply IDTW to get the approximation A_{dJ} and a series of details D_{di}. Similarly, D_{ti}, the detailed parts of the texture motion S_t, can be extracted.
4) Texture the approximation A_{dJ} with the detailed parts D_{tj} and D_{dj}. Let S_n be the resulting motion signal, w_j be the texturing weight of detailed part j, the resulting motion signal S_n can be reconstructed as follows:

$$S_n = A_{dJ} + \sum_{j=1}^{J} w_j D_{tj} + (1 - w_j) D_{dj}, J \in Z .$$ (3)

3.3 Motion Synthesis

Motion blending is a useful operation, in which multiple motions are interpolated to create a motion family somehow like to the blended ones. Using the multiresolution property of wavelet analysis, we can perform blending at different resolution levels using different blending operators. For extrapolation among motions is unsuitable here, the empirical blending operators is between -0.5 and 1.5. Since wavelet transform is local both in time and frequency domain, each blending operation is independent.

The main steps of the multiresolution blending operation are outlined below:

1) Synchronize the blended motions using motion time warping algorithm.
2) Apply DTW to the blended motion signal S_i to decompose it into the coarse and detail coefficients and then apply IDTW to get the approximation A_{iJ} and a series of details D_{ij}.
3) Blend motions independently at each resolution level with rational operators and get the approximation and details of the new motion.

4) Reconstruct the resulting motion signal S_n as Equation 1.

Applying the above algorithm to blend a sneaking walk and a normal run, we can obtain a sneaking run shown as Fig. 4.

4 Spacetime Constrained Based Motion Rectification

The above motion data manipulations provide an easy and effective tool for motion editing. However, it can not guarantee the resulting motion to be realistic. This is because editing on a motion may inviolate the constraints hidden in the motion data and thus destroy the harmony and physical correction. The constraints mainly focus on the following two points:

1) The postures should be physical correct.

2) The transformation between postures should be rational.

These are spatial and temporal constraints. To make up the damaged, essential spacetime constraints [2] can be imposed on motion data. Then establish objective functions to prescribe how to accomplish the resulting motion. At last, solve the constraint optimization problem for the rectified motions. The main step of the motion rectification algorithm is outlined below:

1) Impose formulized spacetime constraints on motion signals;

2) Establish objective functions;

3) Solve the constraint optimization problems using inverse kinematics and numerical optimization methods.

Spacetime constraints are special spatial and temporal restrictions on motion, aiming at preserving essential properties of motions while meeting new requirements. For example, to avoid the body's slipping we prescribe that a foot touch the ground while walking. Both kinematics and dynamics attributes of motion can serve as constraints. However, kinematical constraints are the preference due to the complexity of dynamics. Those constraints are usually specified during a period of time and they can be decomposed into the discrete kinematical constraints on individual frames through sampling. We satisfy the constraints on each frame so as to meet the constraints over the whole period of motions.

Objective functions aim at how to accomplish a motion. In resolving the continuous motion, after specifying objective functions for character movement, the system is able to select the exclusive solution from a set of reasonable ones. Considering different parameters often have vastly different effects, we adopt a weighted sum-of-squares of the parameters. The objective can be seen as an approximation to the function that minimizes the difference from ideal position. The following two measurements can serve as objective functions:

1) Minimizing the difference of position between ideal joints and practical joints;

2) Minimizing the difference of movement before and after motion edition.

Both forward and inverse kinematics can be employed to solve the problem of spacetime constraints optimization. Using forward kinematics, animators need to specify the values of all motion parameters directly to move a character, while inverse kinematics (IK) allows moving the position or orientation handles attached to points

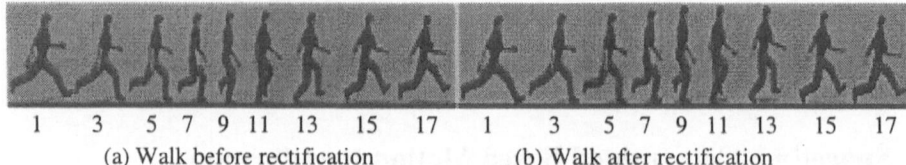

| 1   3   5   7   9   11   13   15   17 | 1   3   5   7   9   11   13   15   17 |

(a) Walk before rectification   (b) Walk after rectification

Fig. 2. Motion rectification

on a character's body and lets the computer figure out how to set the joint angles to achieve the goals. Inverse kinematics can relieve the heavy work of animators in contrary to forward kinematics degree. We combine IK with numerical optimization methods to improve the computational efficiency.

4.1 Sample

When we enhance or weaken the approximation of a walk motion, and create new motions with various steps (See Section 3.1), the unexpected problem occurs:

1) Sometimes the foot gets into the ground, for example frame 9, 11, 13 in Fig.2 (a); and sometimes the foot hangs in the air, as frame 1, 3, 17 shown in Fig.2 (a).

2) Slipping occurs during walking with big steps.

The violation against that at least one foot should contact the ground during walking, causes the above problem 1) and the violation against that the location of the foot contacting the ground remain unchangeable results in the problem 2). So we restrict that the foot contact the ground during walking, and remain still during half cycle of motion. And these are imposed on motion as spacetime constraints. And we define the objective function on minimizing the difference of movement before and after motion editing. Solve this constraint optimization problem and we get the rectified motion shown in Fig.2 (b).

5   Result

We devise an equalizer based on motion enhancement algorithm to aid animators to edit motions. Given a normal walking motion(See Fig. 3(c)), we enhance the approximations of the motion of joint Hip, Knee and Shoulder, and create a new walking with large steps shown in Fig. 3(d). And if the details of motion signals are enhanced, jittering in the motion is highlighted (See Fig. 3(e)). (All the resulting motions shown have been rectified using the method in Section 4).

The style of a sexy walk is embodied mainly by the twisting of joint Hip. We select a run as the dominating motion and extract its approximation. Then texture it with the details of the motion signal of joint Hip from a sexy walk and create a sexy running motion (See Fig. 5(b)). Also we can texture it with details from other motions and characterize it with corresponding styles shown in Fig. 5(d).

If multiple motions are synthesized by multiresolution blending, new motions somehow like to the blended are created. For example, if we blend a running motion with a series of walking motions with different style respectively, corresponding new motions are synthesized (See Fig. 4).

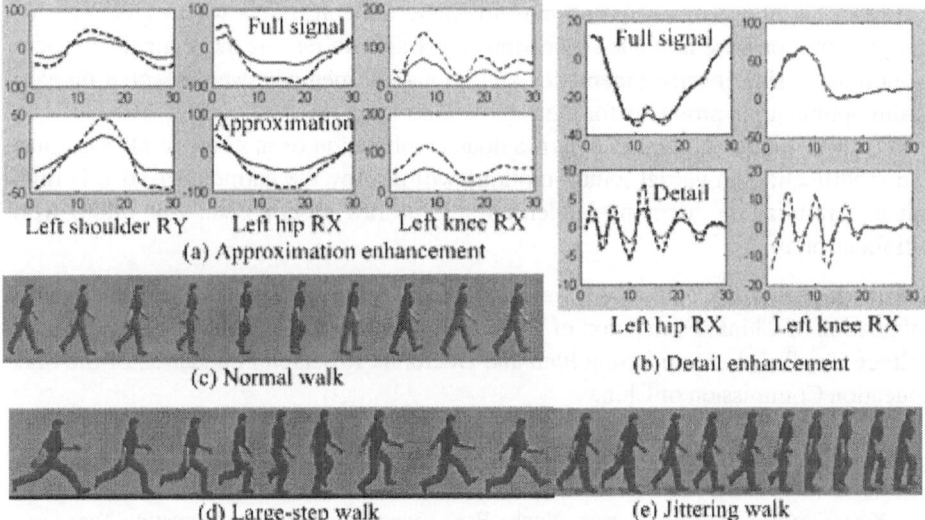

(a) Approximation enhancement

(b) Detail enhancement

(c) Normal walk

(d) Large-step walk

(e) Jittering walk

Fig. 3. Motion enhancement. The solid line represents the input signal and the dashed line is the output signal

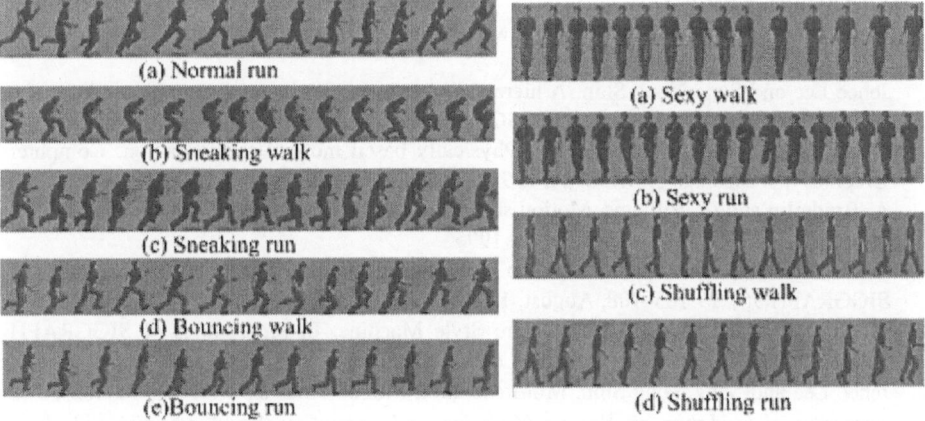

(a) Normal run

(b) Sneaking walk

(c) Sneaking run

(d) Bouncing walk

(e)Bouncing run

(a) Sexy walk

(b) Sexy run

(c) Shuffling walk

(d) Shuffling run

Fig. 4. Motion synthesis

Fig. 5. Motion texturing

6 Conclusion

Motion editing is the key technique to improve the reusability of motion capture data. The goal of this research is to provide an easy and effective tool to adapt the pre-existing motion data to new application. Using the powerful multiresolution property, we decompose the motion signals into many resolution levels, and get the approximation and details. Unlike the Fourier transform, the wavelet transform is local both in time and frequency domain, we can manipulate the contents at each resolution levels independently. We propose some useful approaches to motion editing, including motion enhancement, motion style texturing and motion synthesis by blending. Considering that the above manipulation may inviolate the constraints which guarantee the reality of motions, we introduce spacetime constraints to resume the damaged property of motions. Using inverse kinematics and numerical methods, we can solve the constraint optimization problems for the rectified motions.

However, human motion is a harmonious combination of motions of all the joints. The modification on partial joints' motions will destroy the harmony. And it is difficult to formulize the harmony hidden among the raw motion data. Our future work will focus on it.

Acknowledgement. This work is sponsored by the National Natural Science Foundation of China, Foundation of Education Ministry for Excellent Young Teacher, College Key Teacher Supporting Plan and Doctorate Research Foundation of the State Education Commission of China.

References

1. Xiaoming Liu, Yueting Zhuang, Yunhe Pan. Video Based Human Animation Technique. ACM Multimedia'99 10/99 Orlando, FL, USA, pages 353-362, 1999.
2. Michael Gleicher. Motion editing with spacetime constraints. In Michael Cohenand David Zeltzer, editors, 1997 Symposium on Interactive 3D Graphics, pages139–148. ACM SIGGRAPH, April 1997.
3. M.Gleicher. Retargeting motion to new characters. Computer Graphics (Proceedings of SIGGRAPH 98), 32:33-42, July 1998.
4. Jehee Lee and Sung Yong Shin. A hierarchical approach to interactive motion editing for human-like figures. Proceedings of SIGGRAPH 99, pages 39-48, August 1999.
5. Zoran Popovic and Andrew Witkin. Physically based motion transformation. Computer Graphics (Proceedings of SIGGRAPH 99, Los Angeles, August 8-13, 1999).
6. A. Bruderlin and L. Williams. Motion signal processing. Computer Graphics (Proceedings of SIGGRAPH 95), 29:97–104, August 1995.
7. A. Witkin and Z. Popovic. Motion warping. Computer Graphics (Proceedings of SIGGRAPH 95), 29:105–108, August, 1995.
8. Matthew Brand and Aaron Hertzmann. Style Machine. In Proceedings of SIGGRAPH 2000, July 23-28, 2000. New Orleans, Louisiana, USA.
9. Jehee Lee and Sung Yong Shin, Multiresolution Motion Analysis with Applications, *The international workshop on Human Modeling and Animation*, Seoul, pp. 131-143, June 2000.
10. Pullen, K., and Bregler, C. 2002. Motion capture assisted animation: Texturing and synthesis. In *Proceedings of SIGGRAPH 2002*.
11. LI, Y., Wang, T., and Shum, H.-Y. 2002. Motion texture: A two-level statistical model for character synthesis. In *Proceedings of SIGGRAPH 2002*.
12. F. Sebastian Grassia, Motion Editing: Mathematical Foundations, in course: Motion Editing: Principles, Practice, and Promise, in Proceedings of SIGGRAPH 2000, July 23-28, 2000. New Orleans, Louisiana, USA

Foreground Segmentation Using Motion Vectors in Sports Video

Ling-Yu Duan, Xiao-Dong Yu, Min Xu, and Qi Tian

Laboratories for Information Technology, Agency for Science, Technology and Research,
Singapore, 119613
{lingyu, xdyu, xumin, tian}@lit.org.sg

Abstract. In this paper, we present an effective algorithm for foreground objects segmentation for sports video. This algorithm consists of three steps: low-level features extraction, camera motion estimate, and foreground object extraction. We employ a robust M-estimator to motion vectors fields to estimate global camera motion parameters based on a four-parameter camera motion model, followed by outliers analysis using robust weights instead of the residuals to extract foreground objects. Based on the fact that foreground objects' motion patterns are independent of the global motion model caused by camera motions such as pan, tilt, and zooming, we considers those macro-blocks as foreground, which corresponds to the outliers blocks during robust regression procedure. Experiments showed that the proposed algorithm can robustly extract foreground objects like tennis players and estimate camera motion parameters. Based on these results, high-level semantic video indexing such as event detection and sports video structure analysis can be greatly facilitated. Furthermore, basing the algorithm on compressed domain features can achieve great saving in computation.

1 Introduction

Segmentation of dynamic objects in a scene, often referred to as *"foreground segmentation"* or *"background subtraction"*, is one of the major areas in computer vision research. With the rapid advancement of multimedia computing techniques, semantic event detection and analysis is becoming an important aspect of the multimedia understanding problem. "An event represents a change in the (combined) state of one or more objects" [1]. In most natural scenes, there is a significant number of moving objects. It is the analysis of their trajectories and interaction with the feature of the scene that allows us to classify and recognize interesting events. Hence, foreground segmentation is fundamental to event detection and analysis.

Typically, foreground segmentation algorithms operate in the pixel domain [2-6]. That is, the visual features (e.g. color, shape, texture, motion, etc.) are extracted from the image pixels. In the case of compressed video sequences, a time-consuming decompression process is unavoidable prior to the application of any pixel-domain techniques. This has led to the proliferation of compressed domain segmentation techniques [7-9].

Due to inherent game rules and television field production formalities, sports video features remarkable structured constraints. Of particular interest is exploring how to

Y.-C. Chen, L.-W. Chang, and C.-T. Hsu (Eds.): PCM 2002, LNCS 2532, pp. 751–758, 2002.

effectively segment foreground with the help of domain constraints in sports video. Since the photographer's motivation is to incorporate movement into every scene, rather than show a static object in panorama, the camera often swivels to follow action. In addition, the camera might move through space to keep moving objects in the frame. Therefore, the primary work is to implement efficient foreground segmentation under the presence of some kind of camera motion.

J.M. Odobez and P. Bouthemy [11] have developed two robust estimators to estimate parametric motion models, namely multi-resolution least-mean-squares estimator and robust multi-resolution estimator. They take advantage of M-estimator to solve the minimization of the cost function from the model-based displacement frame difference. Such algorithms provide an efficient first stage for the detection of moving objects in image sequences. However, the algorithms operate in pixel domain and cannot achieve satisfactory computational efficiency directly in compressed video. In [12], M-estimator is applied to decoded P-frame motion vector fields and thus the estimated global motion is used for motion-driven browsing in video databases. R.Wang, H.J.Zhang, and Y.Q. Zhang [7] try to separate moving objects in the dynamic scene wherein moving objects are considered as outliers in the iterative least square estimation using unfiltered motion vectors only. Although the regression diagnostics is introduced, the success of this method depends tightly upon the quality of the initial least square estimation. This algorithm also implies another assumption that the projections of moving objects occupy only a small part of the image due to the weakness of least square estimator. J.H. Meng and S.F. Chang [10] find the global parameter using the least square estimation and detect moving objects by thresholding the residuals after global motion compensation.

In this paper, we propose a fast algorithm for segmenting foreground under the presence of camera motion. This algorithm takes advantage of motion vectors to recover camera motion model and segment foreground by investigating outliers during robust regression procedure. We assume that the foreground does not follow camera motion. Differing from traditional approaches [7][10], the proposed algorithm detects outliers through evaluating the robust weights resulting from M-estimator.

This paper is organized as follows. In Section 2, we present the parametric model of camera motion. In Section 3, we make a brief review of robust M-estimator and its advantages. Section 4 considers the foreground extraction with robust regression. We will show results obtained on tennis video sequences involving camera motion in Section 5. Finally, conclusions and future works will be given in Section 6.

2   Parametric Camera Motion Model

In numerous dynamic scene analysis issues, it is necessary to first recover the motion due to camera movement, and then perform detection and tracking of moving objects in the scene. M. Irani and P. Anandan [13] divide approaches to the problem of moving object detection into two classes: 2-D algorithms which apply when the scene can be approximated by a flat surface and/or when the camera is only undergoing rotations and zooms, and 3-D algorithms which work well only when significant depth variations are present in the scene and the camera is translating. According to the visual grammar of sports video photography, we can represent camera-induced motion in terms of a global 2-D parametric transformation. Among many existing transformations, the affine and eight-parameter models are very popular. However, our scheme takes a four-parameter model to estimate camera rotation, pan, tilt, and zoom. The formulation is as below:

$$\begin{pmatrix} x^{'} \\ y^{'} \end{pmatrix} = \begin{pmatrix} zoom & rotate \\ -rotate & zoom \end{pmatrix} * \begin{pmatrix} x \\ y \end{pmatrix} + \begin{pmatrix} pan \\ tilt \end{pmatrix} + \begin{pmatrix} x \\ y \end{pmatrix} \qquad (1)$$

where (x, y) are the image plane coordinates in the current frame, and (x', y') the transformed coordinates in reference frames.

In MPEG compressed video, block matching is widely used for motion compensation. Although the corresponding motion vectors do not represent the true optical flow, we can exploit them to estimate camera motion parameters. Now let us see how to take P-frame motion field as observation datum and compute camera model with linear regression. Let $V = [v_1, \ldots, v_m]^T$ be the motion vector field, $(v_x^{(n)}, v_y^{(n)})$ the motion vector of the corresponding nth macroblock with center coordinates $(x^{(n)}, y^{(n)})$, then Equation (1) becomes:

$$\begin{pmatrix} v_x^{(n)} \\ v_y^{(n)} \end{pmatrix} = \begin{pmatrix} 1 & x^{(n)} & y^{(n)} & 0 \\ 0 & y^{(n)} & -x^{(n)} & 1 \end{pmatrix} \cdot \begin{pmatrix} pan & zoom & rotate & tilt \end{pmatrix}^T$$

Through imposing this linear model on all N motion vectors, we can obtain an over-determined linear system as follows:

$$Y = H \cdot X + \varepsilon \qquad (2)$$

where:

$$Y = \begin{pmatrix} v_x^{(1)} \\ v_y^{(1)} \\ \vdots \\ v_x^{(N)} \\ v_y^{(N)} \end{pmatrix} \quad H = \begin{pmatrix} 1 & x^{(1)} & y^{(1)} & 0 \\ 0 & y^{(1)} & -x^{(1)} & 1 \\ \vdots & \vdots & \vdots & \vdots \\ 1 & x^{(N)} & y^{(N)} & 0 \\ 0 & y^{(N)} & -x^{(N)} & 1 \end{pmatrix} \quad X = \begin{pmatrix} pan \\ zoom \\ rotate \\ tilt \end{pmatrix}$$

ε is an 2N-by-1 vector of random disturbances.
The ordinary least-squares estimator (OLS) tries to estimate X by minimizing the following sum of squared errors or residuals:

$$\xi = \varepsilon^T \varepsilon = (H \cdot X - Y)^T (H \cdot X - Y)$$

which gives us a closed-form solution as:

$$X = (H^T H)^{-1} H^T Y \qquad (3)$$

Obviously the residuals are useful for detecting failures in the model assumptions, since they correspond to the errors ε_i in the model equation. It can be shown that the OLS estimator produces the optimal estimate X in terms of minimum covariance of X. That is, the errors ε_i must be uncorrelated (i.e., $E(\varepsilon_i \varepsilon_j) = \sigma_i^2 \delta_{ij}$) and their variances are constant (i.e., $\Lambda \varepsilon_i = \sigma^2, \forall i \in [1, \ldots, n]$). Unfortunately, the OLS estimators are vulnerable to the violation of the assumption above. Sometimes even when the data contains only one bad datum, the OLS estimator may be completely perturbed. To improve the robustness against departure from the assumption, we resort to robust M-estimators.

3 Robust Estimation

As discussed above, the global motion estimation is related to the problem of estimating parameters from noisy data. A parameter estimation problem is usually formulated as an optimization one. As have been stated before, OLS estimator can suffer from weak havoc due to even one or two outliers in a larger set. However, the MPEG vectors do not always correspond to the true motion and problem arises if the projections of moving objects occupy a small part of the image or partially unstructured scenes are present. To reduce the influence of outliers we apply M-estimator technique, derived from maximum likelihood theory. We now briefly review this technique.

M-estimator is defined as

$$\hat{\Theta} = \arg\min_{\Theta} \sum_i \rho(y_i - M(\Theta, X_i), \sigma) \qquad (4)$$

where ρ is a symmetric, positive definition function with a unique minimum at zero, and is chosen to be less increasing than square; Θ is the parameter vector to be estimated; M denotes the parametric model. To help analyze the robust of M-estimators, the influence function $\psi(x)$, namely the derivative of the ρ function, is introduced. For example, for the least squares with $\rho(x) = x^2/2$, the influence $\psi(x) = x$, that is, the influence of a datum on the estimate increases linearly with the size of its error. This confirms the non-robustness of the least square estimate. Then a bounded influence function is the first constraint to meet for a robust M-estimator. Readers are referred to [15] for other robustness constraints. There are a few commonly used influence functions such as bisquare, fair, huber, cauchy, welsch, tukey [15]. Our scheme employs the Tukey's biweight function because it even suppresses the outliers other than reduce the effect of large errors. This function is plotted along with its associated influence function in Fig. 1, where the ρ, ψ functions are given by:

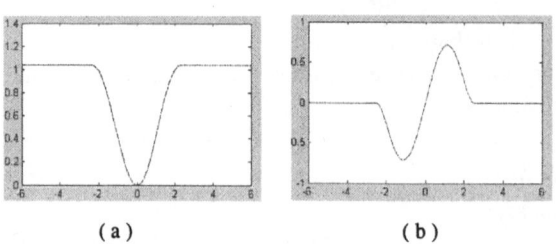

(a)   (b)

Fig. 1. Tukey's biweight functions: (a) function ρ, and (b) influence function ψ (C=2.5)

$$\rho(x,C) = \begin{cases} \frac{C^2}{6}\left(1-\left[1-(x/C)^2\right]^3\right) & \text{if } |x|<C, \\ C^2/6 & \text{otherwise.} \end{cases} \quad (5)$$

$$\Psi(x,C) = \begin{cases} x[1-(x/C)^2]^2 & \text{if } |x|<C, \\ 0 & \text{otherwise.} \end{cases} \quad (6)$$

4 Foreground Extraction

In this section, we will discuss foreground segmentation with the robust weights resulting from M-estimator.

4.1 Robust Weights

The proposed scheme takes iterative re-weighed least squares method to solve the M-estimation problem. See Equation (7). Combining with Equation (4), we find that a necessary condition for minimization is ensuring the derivates of the error measure with respect to each component Θ_j of the parameter vector Θ to be null. We get Equation (8). Thus, the weights at each points X_i are given by Equation (9). Readers are referred to [14] for more details.

$$\sum_i \rho(r_i) = \sum_i \frac{1}{2}w_i r_i^2, r_i = y_i - M(\Theta, X_i) \quad (7)$$

$$\sum_i \Psi(r_i)\frac{\partial r_i}{\partial \Theta_j} = \sum_i w_i r_i \frac{\partial r_i}{\partial \Theta_j} = 0 \quad (8)$$

$$w_i = \frac{\psi(r_i)}{r_i} \quad (9)$$

Table 1. Least-squares Leverage vs. Tukey estimator's Robust Weight

Point Index	1	2	3	4	5	6	7	8	9	10
Leverage	0.35	0.25	0.18	0.13	0.1	0.1	0.13	0.18	0.25	0.35
Robust Weight	1	1	0	0.97	1	0.98	1	0.5	0.94	0

Please note outliers indexed by 3 & 10.

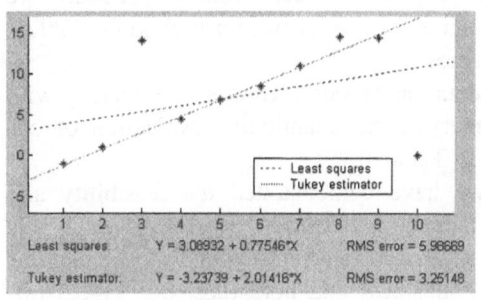

| Least squares | Y = 3.08932 + 0.77546*X | RMS error = 5.98669 |
| Tukey estimator: | Y = -3.23739 + 2.01416*X | RMS error = 3.25148 |

Fig. 2. A simple performance comparison of least-squares and Tukey's estimator

The weights should be recomputed after each iteration. Refer to Fig. 1, the Tukey's biweight function is able to reduce and further suppress the outliers. Once the parameter estimates settle, the resulting robust weights W_i can be used to detect the outliers.

Now let us see an one-dimension example. First we generate a sample data set following the equation $y = -3 + 2 \cdot x$ plus some random noise. We then change two y values to simulate outliers. We use both least-squares and Tukey estimator to estimate the straight line fit. In least-squares process, 95% confidence interval is taken. In Tukey estimator process, tunning constant C is chosed to be 4.6851 for 95% asymptotic efficiency on the standard normal distribution of the Tukey's biweight function. See Fig. 2 for the fitting result. Table 1 shows the comparison of the influence of a given observation on regression, i.e. leverage measure [16] for Least-Squares and robust weight measure for Tukey estimator.

4.2 Foreground Extraction

Once we obtain the parametric description of camera motion, the remaining work is to segment foreground independent of global motion. Instead of evaluating residual against fitted model, We investigate such motion independency by qualifying the final robust weights (Refer to Table 1). The motivation comes from a statistical observation. That is, parametric statistics derive results under the assumption of a priori probability distribution (e.g. normal distribution, exponent distribution) which a parametric modelling implies. However, such assumption are never exactly true. Thus, we think it is appropriate to pinpoint potential outliers by using influence measures, namely robust weights. Starting from this criteria, the detection of independent motion is performed by comparing robust weights with a predefined threshold C:

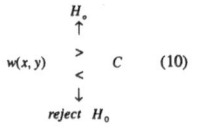

Here, H_0 denotes the hypothesis associated with the camera motion class contrary to the independent local motion class.

By assuming that foreground do not follow global camera motion, we can extract foreground by composing those macroblocks with accompanying outlier local motion.

5   Experimental Results and Discussions

We tested the proposed foreground segmentation algorithm using tennis video data collected by the Dazzle Digital Video Creator MPEG1-encoder. To evaluate the effectivity of our method, we carried out experiments in three kinds of frames involving camera movement, those extracted from the long shot (LS), the medium shot (MS), and the medium closeup (MCU) [17], respectively. From lack of space, we will only report results obtained with two representative frames for each kind. Table 2 summarizes the details of representative frames.

Fig. 3 illustrates the foreground segmentation process. Through comparing with least square fit given 80% confidence interval, the quantitative evaluation of our proposed algorithm is performed as shown in Table 3.

From the series of samples above, we have demonstrated the feasibility and efficiency of our proposed foreground segmentation algorithm. See Fig. 3 (e)(f), it is worth noticing that under the presence of relatively large foreground independent of camera motion, our method shows great robustness and potentials. See Fig. 3 (a). However, due to some "bad" motion vectors produced in low-textured regions without motion, the segmented foreground might be contaminated. An alternative is to perform spatial filtering on the original results. Note that with the change of sports category and shot class, the foreground of interest is different in the occupied image part's size. Hence, the proposed approach must be combined with domain constraints in sports video towards a systematic foreground segmentation scheme.

6 Conclusions

We have proposed a foreground segmentation algorithm for sports video. The experimental results show that robust weights-based outlier analysis is effective for detecting foreground objects, even when foreground occupies relatively large part of the image. Due to the fact that sports video is highly structued, it is quite straightward to indentify the segmtented foreground objects as individual tennis players.

Although a robust M-estimator exhibits great capability in reducing the influence of numerous outliers, the global motion estimation results may be poor when the expected global motion does not dominate with respect to the local motion. In that case, we cannot obtain interesting foreground according to final robust weights. This phenomenon often occurs in extreme closeup (ECU) shots when the subject is isolated entirely from its surrounding environment. Thus, one of the remaining goals is to effectively diagnose the failure of robust regression and to use other means to extract the foreground objects.

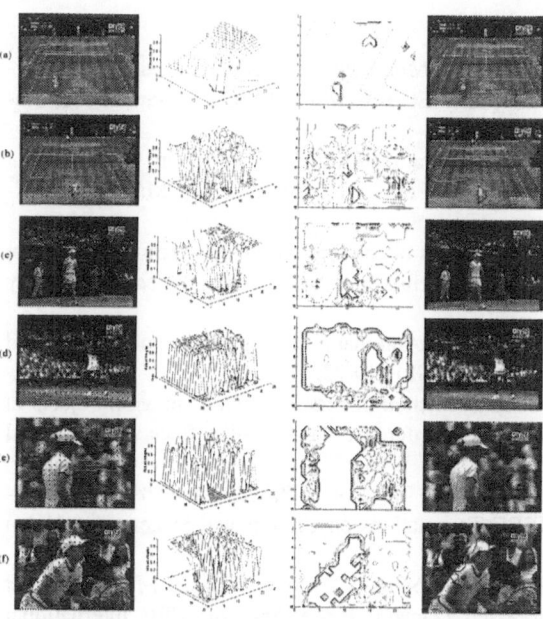

Fig. 3. Foreground segmentation results of six representative frames: (a) Frame 1829, (b) Frame 3161, (c) Frame 109, (d) Frame 2289, (e) Frame 2465, and (f) Frame 1121. (Left to right: the original frames along with motion vectors fields, 3-D wireframe meshes of robust weights, 2-D contour plots representation of robust weights, and the resulting foreground mask outlined by red curves.)

Table 2. Details of representative frames

Shot Type	LS		MS		MCU	
Frame Type	P-	P-	P-	P-	P-	P-
Frame No	1829	3161	109	2289	1121	2465

Table 3. Comparison of the Tukey estimator with the least square fit given 80% confidence Interval

Frame No	(Pan, Zoom, Rotate, Tilt)	Method		RMS Error
		Least squares fit given 80% confidence interval	Tukey Estimator	
1829	(-0.1785, -0.0116, 0.0185, 0.3214)	√		1.8495
	(0, 0, 0, 0)		√	0.2546
3161	(-1.8319, -0.0218, 0.0121, 0.1855)	√		3.8089
	(-1.8287, -0.0021, -0.0135, -0.1520)		√	1.4516
109	(1.2341, -0.0652, -0.0045, 0.4496)	√		3.4573
	(1.1698, -0.0278, -0.0156, 0.0352)		√	0.7943
2289	(-4.7336, 0.3711, -0.0890, -8.5876)	√		6.5638
	(-10.5636, 0.7739, -0.0001, -12.6743)		√	1.5891
1121	(0.1859, 0.0020, 0.1352, 5.3103)	√		3.3725
	(1.2248, -0.0398, 0.0432, 3.0585)		√	1.6831
2465	(14.3925, 0.0264, 0.2345, 4.3381)	√		13.6682
	(31.2046, 0.0172, 0.0167, 0.9271)		√	2.4924

References

1. International Organization for Standardization, Multimedia Content Description Interface - Part 5 Multimedia Description Schemes, ISO/IEC JTC 1/SC 29/WG 11, March 2001, Singapore (2001)
2. D.W.Murray and B.F.Buston: Scene Segmentation From Visual Motion Using Global Optimization, Vol.9, No.2. IEEE Transactions on Pattern Analysis and Machine Intelligence (1987) 220-228
3. T.Meier and K. Ngan: Automatic segmentation of moving-objects for video object plane generation, Vol.8. IEEE Transactions on Circuits and Systems for Video Technology (1998) 525-538
4. A.Neri, S.Colonnese, G.Russo, and P. Talone: Automatic moving object and background separation, Vol.66, No.2. Signal Processing (1998) 219-232
5. R. Mech and W. Wollborn: A noise robust method of segmentation of moving objects in video sequences, Vol.4. IEEE International Conference on Acoustics, Speech, and Signal Processing (1997) 2657-2660
6. D. Zhong, S.F. Chang: An Integrated Approach for Content-Based Video Object Segmentation and Retrieval, Vol.9, No.8. IEEE Transactions on Circuits and Systems for Video Technology (1999) 1259-1268
7. R. Wang, H.J. Zhang, and Y.Q. Zhang: A Confidence Measure Based Moving Object Extraction System Built For Compressed Domain. Proceedings of IEEE International Symposium on Circuits and Systems (2000) 21-24
8. A. Yoneyama, Y. Nakajima, H. Yanagihara, and M. Sugano: Moving Object Detection and Identification from MPEG coded data, Vol.2. Proceedings of International Conference on Image Processing (1999) 934-938.
9. Sukmarg O., Rao K.R.: Fast Object Detection and Segmentation in MPEG Compressed Domain, Vol.2. TENCON 2000 Proceedings (2000) 364-368.
10. J.H. Meng, S.F. Chang: CVEPS – A Compressed Video Editing and Parsing System, Proceedings ACM Multimedia (1996) 43
11. J.M. Odobez and P. Bouthemy: Robust Multisolution Estimation of Parametric Motion Models, Vol.6, No.4. Journal of Visual Communication and Image Representation (1995) 348-365
12. A.Smolic, M. Hoeynck and J.R. Ohm: Low-complexity Global Motion Estimation from P-Frame Motion Vectors for MPEG-7 Applications, Vol.2. International Conference on Image Processing Proceedings (2000) 271-274
13. M. Irani and P. Anandan: A unified approach to moving object detection in 2d and 3d scenes, Vol.20, No.6. IEEE Transaction on Pattern Analysis and Machine Intelligence (1998) 577-589
14. Holland, P.W., and R.E. Welsch: Robust regression using iteratively reweighted least-squares, A6. Communications in Statistics: Theory and Methods (1977) 813-827
15. William J.J. Rey: Introduction to Robust and Quasi-Robust Statistical Methods, Springer, Berlin, Heidelberg (1983)
16. Chatterjee, S. and A. S. Hadi: Influential Observations, High Leverage Points, and Outliers in Linear Regression. Statistical Science (1986)
17. Bob Burke, Frederick Shook: The Visual Grammar of Moving Picture Photograph, Chapter 3, in Television Field Production and Reporting, Longman Publisher USA (1995)

Color Image Segmentation Using Anisotropic Diffusion and Agglomerative Hierarchical Clustering

Daehee Kim[1], Yo-Sung Ho[1], and B.S. Manjunath[2]

[1] Kwangju Institute of Science and Technology
1 Oryong-dong Puk-gu, Kwangju, 500-712, Korea
{kimdh, hoyo}@kjist.ac.kr
[2] University of California
Santa Barbara, CA 93106-9560, USA
manj@ece.ucsb.edu

Abstract. A new color image segmentation scheme is presented in this paper. The proposed algorithm consists of image simplification, region labeling and color clustering. The vector-valued diffusion process is performed in the perceptually uniform LUV color space. We present a discrete 3-D diffusion model for easy implementation. The statistical characteristics of each labeled region are employed to estimate the number of total clusters and agglomerative hierarchical clustering is performed with the estimated number of clusters. Since the proposed clustering algorithm counts each region as a unit, it does not generate oversegmentation along region boundaries.

1 Introduction

Image segmentation refers to the operation of partitioning an image into separate regions, each of which is homogeneous with respect to some image features. Most image segmentation algorithms have been proposed for gray-scale images, while segmentation of color images has received much less attention from the scientific community until recent years.

Fast and accurate segmentation is necessary for authoring multimedia content and for high-level image analysis, such as object recognition, image understating, and scene interpretation. If we can achieve good object segmentation in generic images, it will enrich the current MPEG-4 and MPEG-7 standards. While MPEG-4 enables object-based functionalities, MPEG-7 is related to content-based indexing and retrieval of multimedia databases.

In this paper, we propose a new segmentation algorithm for color images that is applicable to various types of images. The proposed algorithm consists of three operations: image simplification, region labeling, and color clustering. According to Skarbek's classification [1], our proposed algorithm can be classified as a mixture of pixel-based segmentation and region-based segmentation. In this paper, we propose a discrete 3-D diffusion model with a shock filter and a new clustering method that does not require any priori known information. These subtasks are explained in detail in the following sections.

Y.-C. Chen, L.-W. Chang, and C.-T. Hsu (Eds.): PCM 2002, LNCS 2532, pp. 759–766, 2002.

2 Image Segmentation

2.1 Morphological Simplification

Since images have several objects of homogeneous regions and too specific small structures are not interesting in semantic analysis, we can initially perform structure simplification and region texture simplification. In order to simplify image structures, the morphological open-close and close-open operations by reconstruction filters are used in the RGB color space independently [2].

In this paper, we employ the morphological opening and closing operations by reconstruction filters to preserve object boundaries during image simplification. These filter pairs can remove fractional regions that are smaller than a certain size and contours of the remaining objects in the image are well-preserved [2]. The opening and closing operations by reconstruction filters can be described by partial reconstruction. Once unwanted details in the texture of the regions are removed, the image is homogenized in terms of region textures.

2.2 Anisotropic Diffusion

In order to simplify region textures, we can apply an image smoothing operation in homogeneous regions, but not across region boundaries. This requirement can be satisfied with an anisotropic diffusion filter or a scale-space filter [3]. The diffusion is carried out in the perceptually uniform LUV color space [4].

If each component in the LUV color space is diffused independently, it evolves with different smoothing directions and intensities. Therefore, the vector-valued diffusion is performed in the 3-D LUV color space by

$$\frac{\partial \mathbf{I}(x,y,t)}{\partial t} = div(\rho(x,y,t)\nabla \mathbf{I}(x,y,t)) \tag{1}$$

where $\mathbf{I}(x, y, t)$ is a vector in the LUV color space and ρ is the diffusion or conduction coefficient.

For the scalar case, the gradient of the gray level is used as an edge estimator and the conduction coefficient is defined as a decreasing function of the magnitude of gradient to prevent diffusion from affecting region boundaries. Therefore, a vector image diffusion process needs to define the local variation of $\|d\mathbf{I}\|^2$ [5].

$$\|d\mathbf{I}\|^2 = \begin{bmatrix} dx_1 \\ dx_2 \end{bmatrix}^T \begin{bmatrix} g_{11} & g_{12} \\ g_{21} & g_{22} \end{bmatrix} \begin{bmatrix} dx_1 \\ dx_2 \end{bmatrix} \text{ where } g_{ij} = \frac{\partial \mathbf{I}}{\partial x_i} \cdot \frac{\partial \mathbf{I}}{\partial x_j} \tag{2}$$

The two eigenvalues of $[g_{ij}]$ are the extrema of $\|d\mathbf{I}\|^2$ and the orthogonal eigenvectors η and ξ are the corresponding variation directions.

Sapiro-Ringach proposed an anisotropic vector diffusion PDE [6]:

$$\frac{\partial \mathbf{I}}{\partial t} = g(\lambda_+ - \lambda_-)\mathbf{I}_{\xi\xi} \tag{3}$$

Eq. (3) includes the second derivative of a vector in the tangential direction to the maximal variation and a decreasing function of the difference between two eigenvalues. However, since the tangential direction is continuous and vector-valued images are on the digitized grid, a bilinear or geometrical interpolation is needed; however, such an interpolation operation may introduce additional image burring or distortion. In addition, calculation of eigenvalues increases computational complexity.

The scalar-valued diffusion also requires gradient and tangential directions [7]. In order to alleviate these problems, Perona-Malik's resistor model [3] can be employed; however, this model was originally developed for scalar-valued images. In this model, each pixel is connected to four neighboring pixels with resistors whose resistances increase as the pixel differences of each connection increase.

In this paper, we extend Perona-Malik's resistor model to vector-valued images. Since the diffusion equation relates the amount of the temporal variation to the amount of the spatial variation, it is more reasonable to employ the eight-connected resistor model rather than the four-connected model. In addition, we describe resistances between each connection with the local variation $\|d\mathbf{I}\|$ in Eq. (2) for vector-valued images. The local variation can be expressed as the sum of two eigenvalues of $[g_{ij}]$, which can be calculated by

$$\|d\mathbf{I}\|^2 = \sum_{n=1}^{3}\|\nabla I_n\|^2 \tag{4}$$

where n represents each space of the LUV color space.

Therefore, the discretized 3-D diffusion equation of Eq. (1) is described by

$$\mathbf{I}_{y,x}^{t+1} = \mathbf{I}_{y,x}^{t} + \frac{1}{8}(r_N d\mathbf{I}_N + r_S d\mathbf{I}_S + r_E d\mathbf{I}_E + r_W d\mathbf{I}_W) \tag{5}$$

$$+ \frac{1}{8\sqrt{2}}(r_{NW} d\mathbf{I}_{NW} + r_{SW} d\mathbf{I}_{SW} + r_{NE} d\mathbf{I}_{NE} + r_{SE} d\mathbf{I}_{SE})$$

where N, S, E, W are the subscripts for the north, south, east, and west directions, respectively. r_x is a admittance function of each direction, and $d\mathbf{I}_x$ represents eight neighbor differences, defined by

$$
\begin{aligned}
d\mathbf{I}_N &= \mathbf{I}_{y-1,x} - \mathbf{I}_{y,x} & d\mathbf{I}_S &= \mathbf{I}_{y+1,x} - \mathbf{I}_{y,x} \\
d\mathbf{I}_E &= \mathbf{I}_{y,x+1} - \mathbf{I}_{y,x} & d\mathbf{I}_W &= \mathbf{I}_{y,x-1} - \mathbf{I}_{y,x} \\
d\mathbf{I}_{NW} &= \mathbf{I}_{y-1,x-1} - \mathbf{I}_{y,x} & d\mathbf{I}_{NE} &= \mathbf{I}_{y-1,x+1} - \mathbf{I}_{y,x} \\
d\mathbf{I}_{SW} &= \mathbf{I}_{y+1,x-1} - \mathbf{I}_{y,x} & d\mathbf{I}_{SE} &= \mathbf{I}_{y+1,x+1} - \mathbf{I}_{y,x}
\end{aligned}
\tag{6}
$$

In order to compensate for differing distances to pixel's neighbors, we scale the differences of the diagonal directions by $1/\sqrt{2}$.

Although we employ an anisotropic diffusion based on the resistor model, there are some leakages at the region boundaries. In order to address this problem, a shock filter that enhances blurred edges can be included in the entire diffusion equation. A shock filter for scalar-valued images [7] is given by

$$\frac{\partial I}{\partial t} = -\text{sign}(\nabla^2 I)|\nabla I| \tag{7}$$

For vector-valued images, a vector-valued shock filter should be also controlled by the local variation in the LUV color space because of the same reason in Eq. (1).

$$\frac{\partial \mathbf{I}_{Shock}}{\partial t} = -(1 - r(\|\nabla \mathbf{I}\|)) \begin{pmatrix} \text{sign}(\nabla^2 I_L) \|\nabla I_L\| \\ \text{sign}(\nabla^2 I_U) \|\nabla I_U\| \\ \text{sign}(\nabla^2 I_V) \|\nabla I_V\| \end{pmatrix} \qquad (8)$$

where r is an admittance function.

The discretized version of Eq. (8) is implemented using the difference of each connection and the weighted sum of the differences in the same way as in Eq. (5). The final diffusion equation is given by

$$\frac{\partial \mathbf{I}(x, y, t)}{\partial t} = div(r\nabla \mathbf{I}) + \alpha \frac{\partial \mathbf{I}_{Shock}}{\partial t} \qquad (9)$$

where α is inversely proportional to the number of iterations to guarantee system stability against the enhancement of a shock filter. The operation of Eq. (9) makes texture more homogeneous.

3   Region Labeling and Clustering

Some color segmentation algorithms have performed clustering in a color space directly; however, those algorithms show coarse segmentation results near object boundaries, because those algorithms use only the color histogram and the similarity measure; it does not consider the region information of objects.

In order to alleviate these problems, we employ a gradient-based watershed algorithm and obtain partitioned regions of the simplified image, resulted from Section 2. The watershed algorithm is region-growing and region-labeling algorithm that assigns a unique label to each region. Various watershed algorithms have been proposed in the literatures. In this paper, we use an immersion-based watershed algorithm because it is simple and computationally efficient [8]. The color gradient image, the input image to the watershed step, is generated by $\|d\mathbf{I}\|$.

Our goal here is to find the best representative clusters in the LUV color space and to preserve the boundaries of objects. Most clustering algorithms need a priori information, such as the number of clusters and the initial mean vectors, or a certain threshold value given by input parameters [9, 10, 11]. Furthermore, segmentation results of clustering algorithms are often dependent on the initial conditions.

In the proposed method, we estimate the number of color clusters based on the region information. The proposed clustering algorithm consists of two steps: estimation of the number of clusters, and agglomerative hierarchical clustering.

In order to estimate the number of clusters required, we assume that each vector component in each region resulted from the watershed algorithm obeys a Gaussian distribution $N(\mu_i, \sigma_i)$, where i indicates one component among the LUV color space. This assumption is valid because a vector in the each diffused region has a small Euclidian distance to the mean vector in the corresponding region. Under the hypothesis H_o that two points are in the same region, the difference d_i between two points in the same region obeys a zero mean Gaussian distribution $N(0, \sqrt{2}\sigma_i)$.

$$p(d_i \mid H_0) = \frac{1}{\sqrt{4\pi\sigma_i^2}} \exp\left(-\frac{d_i^2}{4\sigma_i^2}\right) \tag{10}$$

Since the Euclidian distance is a good representation of the color distance in the LUV color space that is perceptually uniformly distributed, we consider the normalized following test statistic.

$$\theta = \sum_{i=1}^{3} \frac{d_i^2}{2\sigma_i^2} \tag{11}$$

where i is the index for each space of the LUV color space. In Eq. (11), the test statistic θ has a χ^2 probability density function with three degrees of freedom.

$$p(\theta \mid H_0) = \frac{1}{\sqrt{2\pi}} \theta^{\frac{1}{2}} \exp\left(-\frac{\theta}{2}\right) \tag{12}$$

With the known distribution $p(\theta|H_0)$, the decision whether or not two points are in the same region can be made by a significance test [12]. For this purpose, we specify a false alarm rate α.

$$\alpha = \Pr(\theta > \theta_{th} \mid H_0) = 0.1 \tag{13}$$

In Eq. (13), if the interval $[0, \theta_{th}]$ is a $100(1-\alpha)$ confidence interval for the parameter θ, the hypothesis H_0 is rejected if and only if θ is not in the interval $[0, \theta_{th}]$. In practice, the relationship between α and θ_{th} is in look-up tables [12]. In this work, we set θ_{th} to be 6.25 because we select the false alarm rate α to be 0.1.

If we obtain n partitioned regions from the watershed algorithm, we assign a central vector to each region. A central vector is a representative vector of each region, which is the average vector of a corresponding region. The test statistic θ is now evaluated by the differences between the central vector of a certain region to be tested and the central vectors of the reference regions where the test statistic θ is normalized by variances of the reference regions. Whenever it exceeds θ_{th}, this region is declared as this region is not homogeneous to the previous reference regions. Thus, the estimated number of clusters increases by one.

Fig. 1 shows the estimation procedure to find the number of clusters. The reference regions are updated and the final number of the reference regions is the estimated number of clusters. All regions obtained by the watershed algorithm are sorted with the region size in the descending order. The largest region is the initial reference region T_1 and each region $\mathcal{R}_i$ is represented with the mean vector m_i. In Fig. 1, each region T_j is the reference region, c is the estimated number of clusters and n is the number of regions obtained from the watershed algorithm.

After the number of clusters is estimated, we merge the regions generated from the watershed scheme by an agglomerative hierarchical clustering algorithm [9]. As described in Fig. 2, this procedure is terminated when the estimated number of clusters is obtained and it returns the final color clusters.

Therefore, the final color clusters can segment images based on colors and regions and the proposed clustering algorithm does not require any a priori information. Since this clustering algorithm reflects the shape of the region, it does not generate oversegmentation along region boundaries.

Algorithm 1: Estimation of number of clusters
  begin initialize n, $\mathbf{T}_1 \leftarrow R_1$, $R_i \leftarrow \{\mathbf{m}_i\}$, $c \leftarrow 1$, $i \leftarrow 1$
    do $i \leftarrow i+1$
      find nearest $\mathbf{T}_j$ to R_i among c reference regions based on Euclidian Distance
      compute θ
      if($\theta > \theta_{th}$)
        $c \leftarrow c+1$, $\mathbf{T}_c \leftarrow R_i$
      else
        merge $\mathbf{T}_j \leftarrow R_i$ and $\mathbf{T}_j$
        recompute $\mathbf{m}_j$ on $\mathbf{T}_j$
        recompute variances of each space on $\mathbf{T}_j$
    until $i=n$
    return c
  end

Fig. 1. Estimation of Number of Clusters

Algorithm 2: Clustering based on Region
  begin initialize c, $c^* \leftarrow n$, $R_i \leftarrow \{\mathbf{m}_i\}$
    do $c^* \leftarrow c^*-1$
      find nearest clusters, say, R_i and R_j based on Euclidian Distance
      merge R_i and R_j
    until $c = c^*$
    return c clusters
  end

Fig. 2. Agglomerative Hierarchical Clustering

4   Experimental Results

In order to evaluate our proposed algorithm, we have performed computer simulations on many different kinds of images. Fig. 3 shows the simulation results from the MOTHER AND DAUGHTER image. After we have applied morphological filtering, anisotropic diffusion, watershed, estimation of number of color clusters, and agglomerative hierarchical clustering operations on the sequence, Fig. 3©, Fig. 3(e), Fig. 3(g) and Fig. 3(h) are obtained by the proposed algorithm.

While Fig. 3(b) is the diffused image by Eq. (9) without the morphological filtering, Fig. 3(c) is the diffused image after morphological filtering. In Fig. 3(c), we can ignore specific detail image structures, which are not interesting for semantic image analysis because of small regions. Fig. 3(d) and Fig. 3(e) are output images by the watershed algorithm on the diffused image without morphological filtering and with morphological filtering, respectively. We note that Fig. 3(e) shows a much simpler output than Fig. 3(d).

Fig. 3(f) shows the segmentation result based on the clustering using a color histogram [10]. Fig. 3(f) demonstrates oversegmentation at region boundaries because the clustering algorithm has directly been applied on the diffused or low-pass filtered images in a certain color space and the diffused or low-pass filtered images can generate the mixed colors along the region boundaries. On the other hand, the final result of our proposed scheme does not generate oversegmentation at region boundaries and it can ignore the unwanted details, as shown in Fig. 3(g).

Algorithm 1 estimates that the MOTHER AND DAUGHTER image has twelve color clusters and Algorithm 2 makes twelve color clusters. Fig. 3(h) displays the segmented image that is represented by the final twelve color clusters.

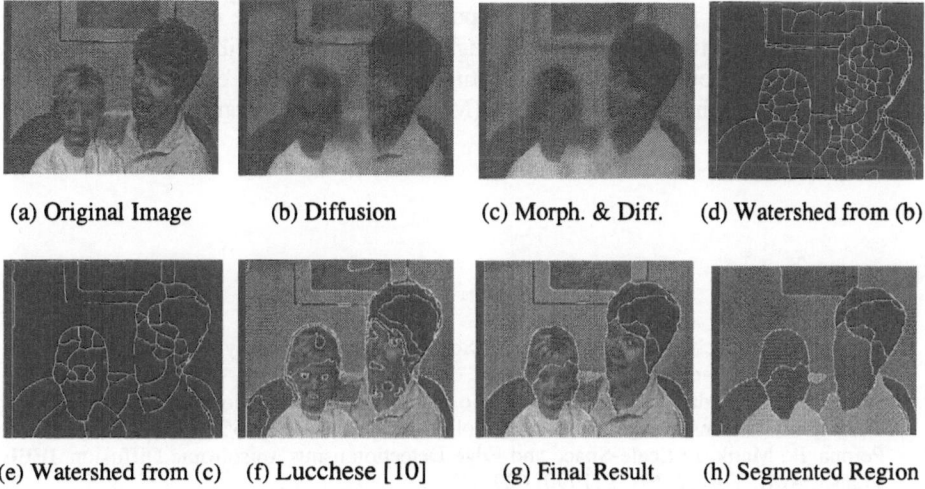

(a) Original Image   (b) Diffusion   (c) Morph. & Diff.   (d) Watershed from (b)

(e) Watershed from (c)   (f) Lucchese [10]   (g) Final Result   (h) Segmented Region

Fig. 3. Result for MOTHER AND DAUGHTER

The proposed algorithm works well on other types of images, as shown in Fig. 4. In addition, unlike the previous works [10, 11], this algorithm operates without any color quantization and is independent on the positions of the initial mean vectors.

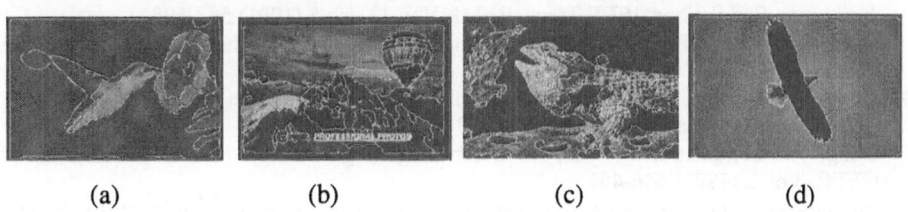

(a)   (b)   (c)   (d)

Fig. 4. Segmentation Results for Various Images

5   Conclusions

In this paper, a new region-based color segmentation algorithm has been presented. The proposed algorithm consists of image simplification, region labeling and color clustering. In order to take advantage of the perceptually uniformly distributed LUV color space, we perform the vector-valued diffusion process in the LUV color space. In addition, statistical characteristics of each labeled region are employed to estimate the number of total clusters and agglomerative hierarchical clustering is performed with the estimated number of clusters. Therefore, the proposed clustering algorithm does not require any a priori information. The proposed algorithm is also stable because it does not need any initial conditions for the clustering operation. Since the proposed clustering algorithm reflects the shape of the region, it does not generate oversegmentation along region boundaries.

Acknowledgement. This work was supported in part by the Korea Science and Engineering Foundation (KOSEF) through the Ultra-Fast Fiber-Optic Networks (UFON) Research Center at Kwangju Institute of Science and Technology (K-JIST), and in part by the Ministry of Education (MOE) through the Brain Korea 21 (BK21) project.

References

1.   Skarbek, W., Koschan, A.: Colour Image Segmentation – A Survey. Technical Report 94-32, Technical University of Berlin (1994)
2.   Salembier, P., Pardas, M.: Hierarchical Morphological Segmentation for Image Sequence Coding. IEEE Trans. Image Processing, Vol. 3, No. 5 (1994) 639-651
3.   Perona, P., Malik, J.: Scale-Space and Edge Detection using Anisotropic Diffusion. IEEE Trans. PAMI, Vol. 12, No. 7 (1990) 629-638
4.   Plataniotis, K.N., Venetsanopoulos, A.N.: Color Image Processing and Applications. Springer, New York (2000)
5.   Zenzo, S.D.: A note in the Gradient of a Multi-Image. CVGIP, Vol. 33 (1986) 116-125
6.   Sapiro, G., Ringach, D.L.: Anisotropic Diffusion of Multivalued Images with Applications to Color Filtering. IEEE Trans. Image Processing, Vol. 5, No 11, (1996) 1582-1585
7.   Guichard, F., Moisan, L., Morel, J.-M.: A Review of P.D.E. Models of Image Processing and Image Analysis. Journal de Physique IV, Vol. 12 (2002) 137-154
8.   Vincent, L., Soille, P.: Watersheds in Digital Spaces: an Efficient Algorithm based on Immersion Simulations. IEEE Trans. PAMI, Vol. 13, No.5 (1991) 583-598.
9.   Duta, R.O., Hart, P.E., Stork, D.G.: Pattern Classification. John Wiley & Sons Inc., Singapore (2001)
10. Lucchese, L., Mitra, S.K.: Unsupervised color image segmentation. Proc. IEEE Workshop on Multimedia Signal Processing (1998) 33-38
11. Deng, Y., Manjunath B.S., Shin, H.: Color Image Segmentation. Proc. of IEEE Conf. on CVPR, Vol. 2 (1999) 446-451
12. Montgomery, D.C.: Design and analysis of Experiments 5th Edition. John Willy & Sons Inc., New York (2001)

Extraction of Text Regions and Recognition of Characters from Video Inputs

Jong Ryul Kim and Young Shik Moon

Department of Computer Science and Engineering, Hanyang University,
1271 Sa-Dong, Ansan, Korea
{jrkim, ysmoon}@cse.hanyang.ac.kr

Abstract. In this paper, a new algorithm for extracting and recognizing characters from video, without a priori knowledge such as font, color, size of characters, is proposed. From input videos with complex backgrounds at low resolution, continuous frames with identical text region are automatically detected to compose an averaged frame. Using boundary pixels of a text region as seeds, we apply region filling to remove backgrounds from characters. Then color clustering is applied to remove remaining backgrounds. For the recognition of characters, simple features such as white run and zero-one transition from the center, are extracted. These features are compared with a pre-defined character feature set to recognize the characters. Experimental results tested on various news videos show that the proposed method is effective in terms of caption extraction rate and character recognition rate.

1 Introduction

Caption information in news videos can be very useful for video indexing and retrieval since it usually suggests or implies the contents of the video very well. Therefore, if the caption information is utilized in news video indexing, users can easily search and retrieve the news they want [1], [2], [3]. For example, the caption information in news video exactly shows the contents of the news. Especially the highlighted title is the representative information of the news.

Many algorithms for text frame extraction have been proposed. Jeon et al. proposed a method of extracting the geopolitical features of characters by multi-level presentation[5]. Jain et al. used the periodic difference of brightness shown in the character string[4],[6]. Also, many researchers have recently proposed solutions to this problem using the vertical, horizontal, and diagonal edges in DCT block in the compression domain[8],[9]. But, the drawback of these methods is that a priori knowledge is required. Since characters in news video have complex backgrounds at low resolution, using the common OCR(Optical Character Recognition) to recognize the characters may not be directly applied to this application. For that reason, an image enhancement process to eliminate complex backgrounds is needed to effectively recognize characters in news video. Kwak et al. proposed a method to detect the text frame to remove the background by means of logical AND operation on two consecutive frames with the underlying

Y.-C. Chen, L.-W. Chang, and C.-T. Hsu (Eds.): PCM 2002, LNCS 2532, pp. 767–774, 2002.

principle that the same frame appears over several frames and there is no change of text region[2].

In this paper, we propose a method to automatically detect the text frame from news video, to extract the text region in the frame, and to effectively recognize the characters in text region. The proposed method is composed of three parts, including text frame extraction, character region extraction, and character recognition. First, in the process of text frame extraction to detect identical frames with a caption from video input, an edge image of text frame is projected in horizontal and vertical direction. If the number of character regions, positions, sizes, and distributions, are similar to the values of the previous frame, we decide the current text frame has the same text region. In the process of text region extraction, we eliminate backgrounds from the text region using multi-level background elimination and verification such as boundary region filling, and color clustering on the temporally averaged edge image. In the process of character recognition, we extract relatively simple features such as white run and zero-one transition from the center, and compare these values with the pre-defined feature sets.

2   The Proposed Method

2.1   Text Frame Extraction

Since the caption characters have various types of color, font, and size, the decision for existence and nonexistence of caption characters is very difficult. But, since characters in video sequence appear over several consecutive frames, this characteristic is highly utilized in the text frame extraction.

The proposed method of text frame extraction finds a text frame if an identical text appears over several frames. This text shot also implies an interval between the first frame and the last frame with abrupt change in the distribution of text region. Fig.1 shows the overall process of text frame extraction.

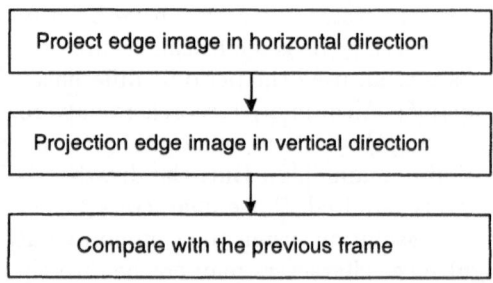

Fig. 1. The process of text shot extraction

2.2   Text Region Extraction

In the text region extraction, we enhance the quality of image using a temporal average of all edge images within a text shot. Then, the text region in a frame is passed through three background elimination steps. The first step of background elimination removes the background by using region filling. The result is verified according to the distribution of each character region using K-means color clustering. Finally, noises are removed in the third step. The overall process of text region extraction is shown in Fig.2.

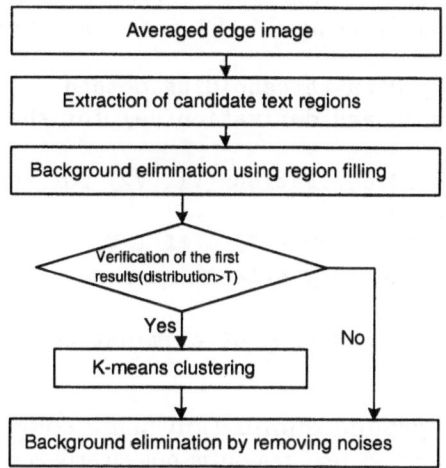

Fig. 2. The process of text region extraction

Background elimination using region filling.   The first background elimination step is region filling using boundary pixels of a text region as seed points. Equation (1) is used to decide the distance between two colors in region filling process.

$$Dist = (R_1 - R_2)^2 + (G_1 - G_2)^2 + (B_1 - B_2)^2 \tag{1}$$

where R_1, G_1, B_1 is the color of seed point and R_2, G_2, B_2 is the color of arbitrary pixel in the text region. The results of the first elimination step are shown in Fig.2.2.

Verification of first elimination step.   The next step for background elimination is to verify the result of the first background elimination. The reason why we perform the verification step is that there are remaining background regions which are not eliminated around characters and in isolated regions. To verify whether an additional elimination step is required or not, we first calculate the total distribution of a text region. If the separation of character and background can be clearly done, the second step is not necessary. Otherwise, the

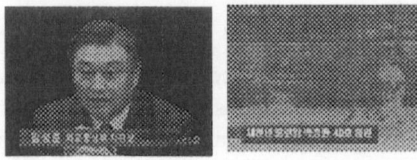

Fig. 3. Results of backgound elimination using region filling

second background elimination step is performed. The details of this verification process are shown in the following. T1, T2, and Te are threshold values.

```
1. Determine 'K' by Otsu thresholding method.
2. Calculate the standard derivation(Ve) for the total
   text region.
3. Calculate standard derivations(V1, V2) for two regions
   divided by K value.
4. If (( V1 > V2 * T1 || V2 * T2 ) && ( Ve < Te )
      skip the second step of elimination
   else
      perform the second step of elimination
```

Second step of background elimination using color clustering. If the distribution in the extracted text region is not clearly separable after the first background elimination, an additional background elimination is required. The second step of background elimination is performed to eliminate the remaining backgrounds from characters by using the K-means color clustering.

When the K-means algorithm with K=2 is performed, the input vector of clustering is each color value. Also, for a better clustering performance, the centers of clusters are selected by two local max colors in color histogram($8 \times 8 \times 8$). After the second step of background elimination, the number of elements in the character region cluster is relatively higher than those of background cluster. Fig.2.2(a) is the result of color clustering to all characters after region filling. As shown in Fig.2.2(a), strokes of characters indicated by circles are removed. In Fig.2.2(b), strokes survive in the result of the second elimination by selectively applying the elimination according to the verification step. The result of the second background elimination is shown in Fig.2.2.

| (a) Background elimination to all characters | (b) Background elimination to selected characters |

Fig. 4. Results of second elimination

Fig. 5. The result of second background elimination

2.3   Recognition of Caption Characters

Since the caption characters in video sequence have various font types and the exact shape of characters may not be maintained after background elimination, it is not easy to get a feature set to recognize each character. In the proposed character recognition method, features are directly extracted from video including various font types.

Feature extraction. Fig.2.3 shows a binary image of text region, where backgrounds are eliminated for feature extraction. The character regions are normalized to 30 × 30 , in order to handle the variation of character sizes. Each rectangular box in Fig.2.3 represents a syllable in Korean language. One syllable consists of two or more characters. The features used in recognition process are

Fig. 6. Region segmentation and normalization for each syllable

shown in Fig.2.3. One set of features consists of white runs from top, bottom, left and right. The other set includes zero-one transition in 8 directions from the center.

The reason we use relatively simple features is to process the huge number of characters and various font types in reasonable computation time.

Classification. The recognition is carried out on each syllable and the classification is basically done by using the minimum distance classifier. We classify total of 588 syllables in Korean language, and 5 different font types for each syllable is considered. To train the classifier, we use 3-5 samples for each syllable and font type. The feature vectors are extracted from training samples and the average value is computed and saved. To recognize an unknown syllable, the feature vector is extracted and compared with each pre-defined feature vector, as in Equation(2).

$$Bestmatch = \min_{\alpha}(\min_{\beta}(\sum_{i=0}^{N} \omega_i (d_{\alpha\beta i} - u_i)^2)) \qquad (2)$$

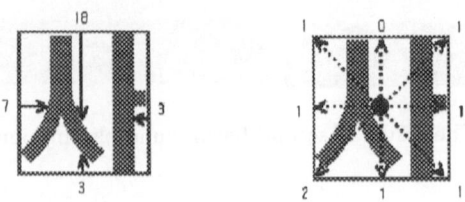

(a) White-run   (b) Zero-one transition from center

Fig. 7. Features for character recognition

where α includes all 588 syllables, β includes 5 font types, $\alpha\beta i$ is the i-th feature of known syllable α and font type β, u_i is the i-th feature of unknown syllable, ω_i is a weight for the i-th feature, and N is the dimension of the feature vector. Fig.2.3 is the result of character recognition using white run and zero-one transition from center. The values in parenthesis in Fig.2.3 indicate the font type and the difference value.

Fig. 8. Results of character recognition

3   Experimental Results and Performance Analysis

For an experiment, we use news and sports sequences of KBS(Korea Broadcasting System), MBC(Moonhwa Broadcasting Company), and SBS(Seoul Broadcasting System) among Korean broadcasting stations. The input videos are in the NTSC format, which are MPEG-1 encoded for experiment.

To analyze the performance, we measure the rate of text frame extraction and the rate of character recognition. Experiments have been carried out using IBM Pentium-III 800 Mhz computer system and Visual C++6.0 compiler. Table 1 shows the summary of news video clips used in the experiment. Fig.3 shows some news video samples used in the experiment.

We first evaluate the performance of text frame extraction based on the rate of correct extraction and the rate of erroneous extraction using Equation (3) and Equation (4).

$$CER = NCE/NTF \qquad (3)$$

Table 1. News videos used in the expriemnt

	Length	The number of text frames	The number of characters
KBS	2 hour 36 minute	397	4,822
MBC	1 hour 54 minute	243	3,170
SBS	1 hour 30 minute	236	3,082

Fig. 9. News video samples

$$EER = (NME + NFE)/NTF \qquad (4)$$

where CER(Correct Extraction Rate) is the rate of correctly extracted text frames, EER(Erroneous Extraction Rate) is the rate of erroneous extraction. NCE(Number of Correct Extraction) is the number of correctly extracted text frames, NME(Number of Missed Extraction) is the number of missed extraction frames, NFE(Number of False Extraction) is the number of false extraction frames. Finally, NTF(Number of Text Frames) is the total number of text frames in the video sequences. Table 2 summarizes the performance in terms of frame extraction rate.   Another performance measure is CRR(Character Recognition

Table 2. Frame extraction rate

Number of text frames	Number of correct extraction	Correct extraction rate	Number of missed extraction	Number of false extraction	Erroneous extraction rate
876	830	94.8%	27	19	5.2%

Rate). CCR is measured for 2 cases as shown in Table 3.   As shown in Table 3,

Table 3. Character recognition rate

	No. of Frame	No. of characters	No. correct recognition	CCR
In case of NTF	876	11,074	8,460	76.4%
In case of NCE	830	10,298	8,460	82%

the rate of character recognition is 76.4 percent from the viewpoint of overall character recognition system. But, if only the correctly extracted frames are considered, the rate of character recognition is 82 percent. If we use high quality video inputs such as MPEG-2, the performance will be improved further.

4   Conclusion and Future Works

In this paper, we propose a method to automatically detect text frames from news videos, to extract text regions in the frame and to effectively recognize the characters in the text region without a priori knowledge such as font type and size. Experimental results show that the rate of text frame extraction is 95 percent and the rate of character recognition is 82 percent for the extracted text frame. This performance will be improved if high equality video inputs such as MPEG-2 are used.

Future works include the automatic decision of threshold values used in the verification process and the improvement of character recognition rate using more characters in the training phase.

Acknowledgement. This work was supported by grant No. R01-2000-00281 from the Basic Research Program of the Korea Science and Engineering Foundation.

References

1. K. J. Choi, H. L. Byun and I. B. Lee: Study on image enhancement method for theshoding. IEEK conference of Image Processing and Image Understanding, (1998) 176–181.
2. S. S. Kwak, S. M. Kim, Y. W. Choi and K. S. Jung: Image enhancement to efficient recognition for video caption. IEEK conference of Image Processing and Image Understanding, (2000) 342–347.
3. U. Gargi, S, Antani and R. Kasturi: Indexing Text Event in Digital Video Database. Proceeding of 14th International Conference of Pattern Recognition, (1998) 916–919.
4. A. K. Jain and B. Yu: Automatic Text Location in Images and Video Frames. Pattern Recognition, vol. 31, no. 12, (1998) 2,055–2,075.
5. B. T. Jeon, Y. L. Bae and T. Y. Kim: Generalized Method for Character and Video Caption Extraction. KISS Journal, vol. 27, no. 6, (1996) 632–641.
6. A. K. Jain and Y. Zhaong: Page Segmentation Using Texture Analysis. Pattern Recognition, vol. 29, no. 5, (1996) 743–770.
7. H. Kuwano, Y. Taniguchi and H. Arai: Telop-on-demand : Video Structuring and Retrieval Based on Text Recognition. IEEE International Conference of Multimedia and Expo, (2000) 759–762.
8. Y. Zhong, H. Zhang and A. K. Jain: Automatic Caption Localization in compressed Video. IEEE Transaction on PAMI, vol. 22, no. 4, (2000) 385–392.
9. Y. K. Park, S. K. Kim, W. Y. Yu, J. C, Kim and J. H. Lee: Character Extraction and Recognition in MPEG-II news video. IEEK conference of Signal processing, (1998) 117-120.

Target Tracking via Region-Based Confidence Computation with the CNN-UM

Hyong-suk Kim[1], Hong-rak Son[1], Young-jae Lim[2], and Jae-chul Chung[3]

[1]School of Electronics and Information Eng., Chonbuk National Univ.
hskim@moak.chonbuk.ac.kr,hrson@orgio.net
[2]Spatial Imagery Information Research Team, Computer & Software Laboratory,
Electronics and Telecommunications Research Institute
[3]4th System Development Communication Electronics Department,
Agency for Defense Department.

Abstract. A target tracking algorithm with the region-based confidence computation on the CNN-UM is proposed. The CNN-UM is an analog parallel computational system which handles regions easily with its region creating capability, parallel processing in the region and regional constraining capability. If the probability for each feature is created in each region, the total confidence of a target can be computed with a fusion algorithm employing products of weighted sums of feature probabilities. The cell-wise target decision in the region can be performed depending on the confidence value at each cell. By virtue of the analog parallel computational structure of the CNN-UM, the computation speed is very fast. On chip experimental results are included in this paper.

1 Introduction

Image frames usually contain large amount of data to be processed. Since such image frames are processed in serial manner in the conventional digital computer, the processing speed does not reach to the human vision requirements. Therefore, the human like parallel processing is needed for real time processing of many image applications. The CNN (Cellular Neural/Nonlinear Networks) is invented from such necessity [1][2]. It is an integration of many simple dynamic cell units which have continuous inputs, continuous states, continuous outputs and continuous processing time. Cells lying inside a "sphere of influence" called the cell neighborhood interact each other and the resulting architecture is a cellular lattice. Therefore, CNN is an analog parallel computational structure, where cells are disposed at nodes of 2-D grid.

Selecting its weighting templates from its template library [6], the various types of image processing are possible. By constraining the region with its input, regions of interests are easily created and handled through parallel processing of the CNN.

Presenting some value to a point on a CNN cell array and propagating it for a fixed period of time with a diffusion template, the region with arbitrary size or with arbitrary value is easily created. Also, parallel and identical processing of cells in a region achieves the region-based processing in CNN. Roska et al. developed such CNN as engineering model called CNN-UM (CNN Universal Machine) [3][8] which is an efficient system to perform many sophisticate image processing [4][5]. Recently, the CNN-UM is implemented into a chip [7] though it is still under evolution.

The proposed target tracking idea is with the probability fusion on the regions of influence for features using the region-based processing of CNN-UM. The probability of the target existence is created depending on the representativeness of the feature for the target, the reliability and the strength of the features. Since region of influence for some specific feature is not confined to the segment border but to the predefined geometric range in the proposed algorithm, the decision performance is not degraded by the possible segmentation error.

2   Cellular Neural Network-Based Image Processing

CNN is a massively parallel computational structure as in Fig. 1(a). In the CNN, a processing unit called a cell is disposed at each node of 2-D grid. At each cell, there are 3 different sets of information sources: one from outputs of its neighboring cells through weighted connections called A template, the other from its and its neighbor's inputs through another set of weighted connections called B template, and another one from its own bias value z. In the CNN, each cell has identical dynamic operation as in (1).

$$\frac{dx(i,j)}{dt} = -x(i,j) + \sum_{kl \in N_r} A(ij,kl) y_{kl} + \sum_{kl \in N_r} B(ij,kl) U(k,l) + z_{ij} \tag{1}$$

where $x(i,j)$ is the state of the cell (i,j). $A(ij,kl)$ and $B(ij,kl)$ are the templates(weights) between cell (i,j) and cell (k,l). Also, Z_{ij} is the bias value of cell (i,j).

The output of the cell (i,j), $y(i,j)$ is

$$y(i,j) = f(x(i,j)) \tag{2}$$

where f is a nonlinear output function defined as in Fig. 1(b).

Since every CNN cell has same weighted connections and dynamic mechanism, every cell is doing identical behavior as long as input and sate value are the same. However, if different template sets are employed, different processing results are obtained even though same input or initial state values are given. Abundant sets of templates for different type of image processing have already been developed [6].

3   Region-Based Confidence Computation through the Fusion of Feature Probabilities

To enhance the confidence for a target on a dim surveillance image, as much evidence or clue should be utilized as possible. Even though the individual evidences of the target are not strong enough, integration of the evidences in conjunction with their probabilities will strengthen the confidence for the target detection. If a feature of a target is detected at a specific image location, the target or other features' existence probability around it will be raised. The region of nonzero probability caused by a specific feature is called the region of influence. For example, if a feature F1 is detected as in Fig. 2, the confidence of the target existence at the region of influence of F1 will be high. If another feature F2 exists near by, it creates another region of influence centered by F2. In this situation, the probability of target existence in common area of F1 and F2 is even higher than that with the single feature. Such probability should be computed with the fusion of two probabilities. We call the outcome of the fusion the confidence value of the target.

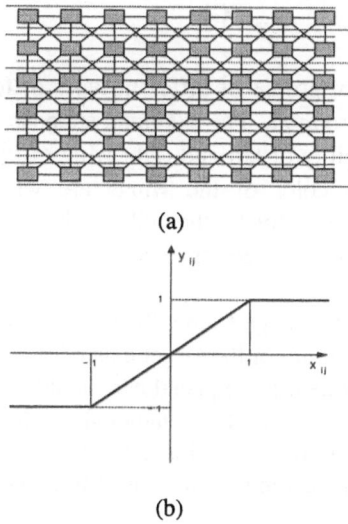

(a)

(b)

Fig. 1. Cellular Neural Networks(CNN). (a) Cell disposition of the CNN. (b) Nonlinear output function of a CNN cell.

The proposed strategy to compute the confidence of a target is through products of the weighted summations of the involved feature probabilities. For this, features, which influence the point (i,j), can be classified into several groups depending on their way of fusion.

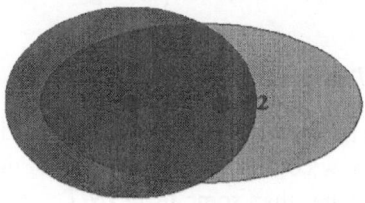

Fig. 2..Regions of feature influences.

Let G be the set of all features and k_{ij} be the subset of G as

$$k_{ij} \in G \qquad (3)$$

The set G can be subdivided into subgroups, where the confidence value computation is performed through weighted summation and multiplication for intra and inter group computation, respectively. Let p_{mn} be the probability of feature n in the mth group. Then, the confidence value $C_t(i,j)$ at the cell (i,j) is

$$c_t(i,j) = f(p(k_{mn}), k_{mn} \in G) \qquad (4)$$
$$= (w_{11}p_{11} + w_{12}p_{12} + w_{13}p_{13} + ...)(w_{21}p_{21} + w_{22}p_{22} + ...)..$$
$$= \prod_{m=1}^{M} \sum_{n=1}^{N_m} (w_{mn}p_{mn}, p_{mn} \in G)$$

where M is the number of groups of different types of features and N_m is the number of features in a given group m. For example, suppose that we want to detect airplane target. Let the probability of left and right wing of the airplane be p_1 and p_2, respectively. If the possible color of the wings are white or gray and the their probabilities are p_3 and p_4, respectively, the body of the target should be detected only at the region of gray or white. Therefore, confidence of the target is computed as $C_t = (p_1 + p_2)(p_3 + p_4)$.

If a target is detected on an image frame, the tracking of it at the subsequent frame is easier task since the probability of the target existence at the neighboring area of the previous target location will be high. Special care should be taken to search the target around the previous target location. More challenging situation is the target detection at the beginning of the target presence. This is the target initiation problem. To initiate a new target on a screen, accumulation of the confidence is employed to obtain reliable confidence value.

Let the accumulation parameter be ξ with the range of [0, 1] and $\chi(i,j)(k)$ be the temporally accumulated confidence of a target at the pixel location (i,j) at the kth frame. Then, $\chi(i,j)(k)$ is accumulated with (5).

$$\chi(i,j)(k) = \chi(i,j)(k-1) + \xi c(i,j)(k) \qquad (5)$$

However, if $\chi(i,j)(k)$ is still keeping high value at the location on the old trajectory which the target has passed before, targets will be initiated repeatedly at same points. To avoid such problem, (5) is modified employing decay factor λ ranged [0, 1] as in (6).

$$\chi(i,j)(k) = \lambda(\chi(i,j)(k-1) + \xi c(i,j)(k)) \qquad (6)$$

The confidence level is reduced through being multiplied by the factor of λ at every image frame as long as a new confidence value, c, is not updated. When the value of $\chi(i,j)(k)$ grows until it is higher than some level $INIT_{TH}$ as in (7), a new target is initiated at (i,j).

$$\chi(i,j)(k) \geq INIT_{TH} \qquad (7)$$

4 On-Chip Experiment

The proposed moving target tracking algorithm has been implemented and tested on a 64x64 CNN-UM chip. Since the CNN-UM chip is not matured enough to show the terra Hz speed as claimed in [3], the experiment is focused on the functionality checking of the CNN-UM chip for the target tracking. The features employed for this experiment are inter-frame gray value difference, inter-frame target existence, and speed of the target. The dynamic range of [-1, 1] is used to express the confidence and the strengths of features. To fuse the available features for this practical situation, a reduced form of the confidence computing in (5) is used as.

$$c(i,j) = 2 p_s(i,j) p_d(i,j) \big(p_n(i,j) + \chi(i,j) - 0.5 \big) \tag{8}$$

where $p_s(i,j)$, $p_d(i,j)$ and $p_n(i,j)$ are the probabilities of target existence caused from the features of speed, inter-frame gray value difference, and inter-frame target existence, respectively. Note that the constants for subtraction and the multiplication are for converting the probability values to the confidence range of [-1, 1]. The parameters used for λ and ξ are all 0.9. Also, $INIT_{TH}$ and C_{TH} are all 0.8.

For the new target, $p_n(i,j)$ in (8) is zero since no target exists on the previous frame. In this situation, the target is initiated through the development of $\chi(i,j)$ using the spatio-temporal accumulation of target confidence with (6). The confidence value used in this spatio-temporal accumulation is obtained through the fusion of the inter-frame gray value difference and the speed features.

Fig. 3(a) shows an example of the inter-frame difference feature. Thresholding the absolute value of image difference produces the approximative shape of the target. Such shape of the target is utilized to compute the speed of the target through calculating the displacement of the targets on two neighboring image frames. The size of the displacement is proportional to its speed. Obtaining the speed in this way, the region of influence for the speed feature is created by diffusing speed feature to its neighbor area for 50 τ (time constant) as in Fig. 3(b). The inter-frame target existence feature is the target location on the previous frame as in Fig. 3(c). After converting the features into probabilities and computing its confidence through fusion of these features, the confidence is accumulated along the time axis to get better reliability. Fig. 4 shows an example of initiation and tracking of a target. With the repeated appearance of target, its confidence value grows gradually via the temporal accumulation as in Fig. 5. When the confidence value is matured enough as in the third frame of Figure 5, the target begins to be detected as in Fig. 4.

The confidence decaying effect has also been tested with temporary missing target tracking. If the target disappears as in the 2nd and 3rd frames of Fig. 6, its confidence is decayed as shown in 3rd and 4th frames of Fig. 7. However, since such confidence value is not decayed out completely during the short time disappearance of the target, it is detected again very soon after the target reappears as in Fig. 6.

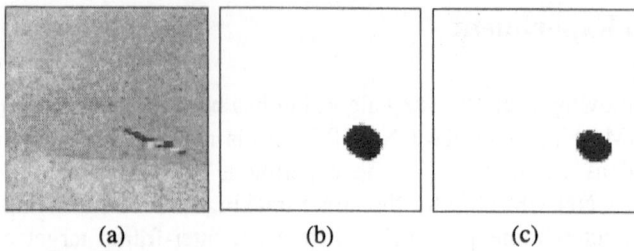

(a)   (b)   (c)

Fig. 3. An example of regions of influence for (a)inter-frame gray value difference (b)speed of the target (c)inter-frame target existence.

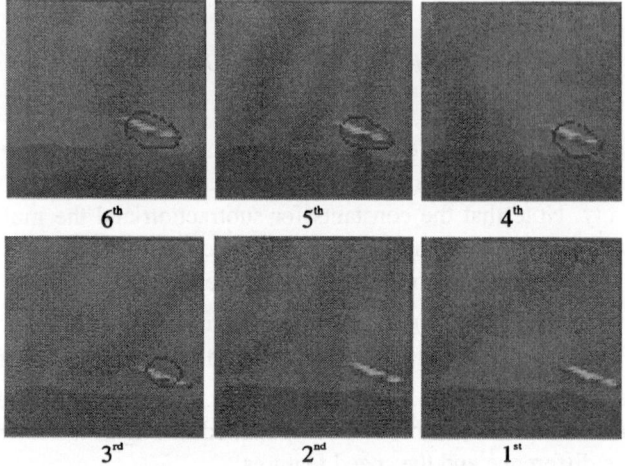

6th   5th   4th

3rd   2nd   1st

Fig. 4. First 6 frames of original image sequence overlapped by the boundary of detected target.

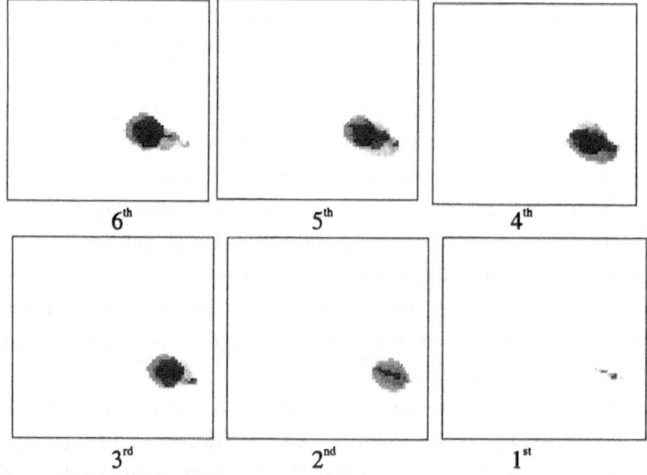

6th   5th   4th

3rd   2nd   1st

Fig. 5. Accumulation of the confidence value for the initiation of a target.

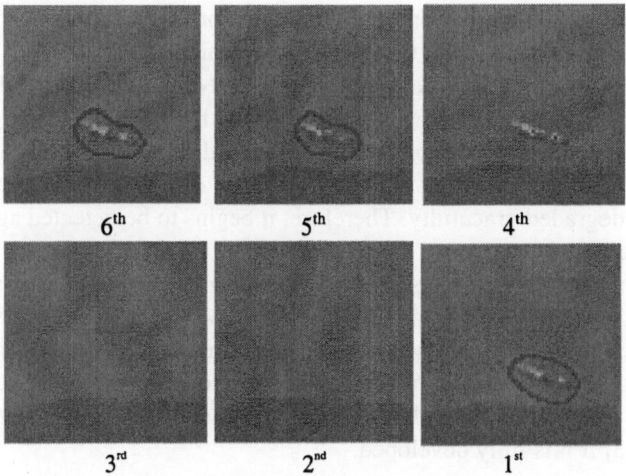

Fig. 6. An image sequence with a temporary missing target and its detection.

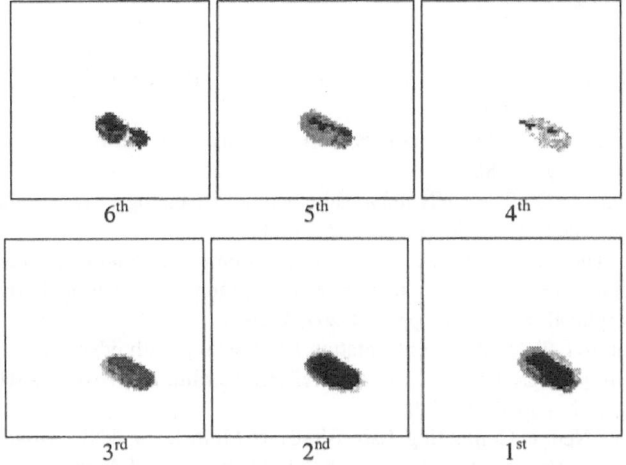

Fig. 7. Accumulated confidence for the image sequence with a temporary missing target.

5 Conclusion

The region-based confidence computation algorithm of the target existence with CNN-UM has been proposed and utilized for moving target tracking. On the dim target image under surveillance environment, fearures are often noisy and unclear. Integration of all the possible clues about target is required to enhance the confidence of the target. The strategy used in this paper is with the region-based probability fusion of target existence for multiple features. Though the computation of CNN is done individually at each cell, the region-based computation is performed with the parallel computation of the cells and with the regional constraints in CNN-UM.

In the target tracking experiment on the real CNN-UM chip, several desirable aspects of the proposed algorithm are disclosed. When the target appears repeatedly, the algorithm initiates the target automatically through the temporal accumulation of the confidence value. Under the situation that the target disappears temporary, the confidence value is degraded gracefully. Therefore, it begins to be detected again very soon if the target reappears.

The proposed algorithm detects the target automatically and tracks successfully for all 100 frames used in the experiment. Since the experiment is performed on a CNN-UM chip which is still under-development, the computation speed is still 10 frames per second. However, by virtue of the analog parallel computational structure of the CNN-UM, the computation speed is expected to reach to terra operations per second as claimed in [3] if it is fully developed.

References

1. Chua, L. O., Yang, L.: Cellular neural networks: theory. IEEE Tr. on Circuits Systems, vol.35, pp. 1257-1272, 1988.
2. Chua, L. O., Yang, L.: Cellular neural networks: applications. IEEE Tr. on Circuits Systems, vol. 35, pp. 1273-1290, 1988.
3. Roska, T., Chua, L. O.: The CNN universal machine: an analogic array computer. IEEE Tr. on Circuits Systems II, CAS-40, pp. 163-173, 1988.
4. Rekeczky, C., Tahy, A., Vegh, Z., Roska, T.:CNN-base spatio-temporal nonlinear filtering and endocardial boundary detection in echocardiography. International Journal of Circuit Theory and Applications, vol. 27, pp. 171-207, 1999.
5. Czuni, L., Sziranyi, T.: Motion segmentation and tracking with edge relaxation and optimization using fully parallel methods in the Cellular Nonlinear Network Architecture. Real-Time Imaging, vol.7, pp.77-95, 2001.
6. Analogical and Neural Computing Lab. SimCNN-Multi-layer CNN Simulator for Visual Mouse Platform: Reference Manual version 2.2, Computer and Automation Institute (MTA SzTAKI) of the Hungarian Academy of Sciences, 1998.
7. Espejo, S., Domínguez-Castro, R., Liñán, G., Rodríguez-Vázquez, A.: A 64x64 CNN universal chip with analog and digital I/O. Proc. 5th Int. Conf. on Electronics, Circuits and Systems (ICECS-98), Lisbon, Portugal, pp. 203-206 1998.
8. Roska, T., Zarándy, A., Zöld, S., Földesy P., Szolgay, P.:The computational infrastructure of analogic CNN computing - Part I: The CNN-UM chip prototyping system. IEEE Trans. on Circuits and Systems I: Special Issue on Bio-Inspired Processors and Cellular Neural Networks for Vision, (CAS-I Special Issue), Vol. 46, No.2, pp. 261-268, 1999,

Improved Scheme for Object Searching Using Moment Invariants

K.L. Lau, W.C. Siu, and N.F. Law

Centre for Multimedia Signal Processing, Department of Electronic and Information
Engineering, The Hong Kong Polytechnic University, Hung Hom, Hong Kong
kllau@eie.polyu.edu.hk, { enwcsiu, ennflaw}@polyu.edu.hk

Abstract. For multimedia retrieval application, shape is always a conspicuous
element of an object. Moment-based approaches are widely used for shape description due to its translation, scaling and rotation invariance. Moment invariants are defined in the continuous domain. However, when considering the
digital images in practice, quantization errors are introduced. Thus, the moment
invariants calculated might not be truly invariant. This paper presents an analysis of quantization effects on four moment-based approaches of both regular and
irregular objects. From the analysis, the scaling errors for all approaches are
large when the scaling factor is less than 0.5. Moreover, the rotational errors are
big for the objects rotated other than the multiples of 90°. Our experimental results show that Dudani moment invariants suffer the largest error for overall
sensitivity, while Affine moment invariants show the smallest. Furthermore,
this error analysis has also been applied successfully to object searching applications using a threshold selection scheme.

1 Introduction

Multimedia is the use of computers to process and/or transmit media information
including text, audio, image and video. One of the major areas of interest is multimedia information searching. For these applications, shape can capture the prominent
elements of an object. Using a set of moment invariants is one of the most popular
approaches employing shape descriptors that has been widely used for object identification, character recognition [1], etc. The formulation of integrals moments can ensure the moment invariants are independent of translation, scaling, and rotation of
objects. However, in practice, moments have to be calculated on digital images and
the discrete summations have to be used instead of the continuous integrals. Then, the
moment invariants calculated might not be truly invariant. This paper presents an
analysis of quantization effects on four popular moment-based approaches (Hu [2],
Affine [3-4], Dudani [5] and Improved [6] moment invariants). Teh [7] and Salama
[8] used only rectangular objects to illustrate error. This paper extends their work by
considering both regular and irregular objects. We propose to apply this error analysis
to object search applications. In fact, the analysis is useful for deciding the threshold
value so that all scaled and rotated objects can be retrieved successfully.

Y.-C. Chen, L.-W. Chang, and C.-T. Hsu (Eds.): PCM 2002, LNCS 2532, pp. 783-790, 2002.
© Springer-Verlag Berlin Heidelberg 2002

2 Moments and Quantization Problem

We first define the moment invariants. Let R be the region of object. The $(p+q)^{th}$ order central moments for binary-valued image is defined as,

$$\mu_{pq} = \iint_R (x-\bar{x})^p (y-\bar{y})^q \, dxdy \text{ , for } p, q = 0,1,2,\dots \tag{1}$$

A set of seven Hu moment invariants [2] is derived. Features characterized by I_1 to I_7 are independent of translation and rotation, but not scale. They are $I_1 = \mu_{20} + \mu_{02}$,

$I_2 = (\mu_{20} - \mu_{02})^2 + 4\mu_{11}^2$, $I_3 = (\mu_{30} - 3\mu_{12})^2 + (\mu_{03} - 3\mu_{21})^2$, $I_4 = (\mu_{30} + \mu_{12})^2 + (\mu_{03} + \mu_{21})^2$,

$I_5 = (\mu_{30} - 3\mu_{12})(\mu_{30} + \mu_{12})[(\mu_{30} + \mu_{12})^2 - 3(\mu_{21} + \mu_{03})^2] +$ $I_6 = (\mu_{20} - \mu_{02})[(\mu_{30} + \mu_{12})^2 - (\mu_{21} + \mu_{03})^2] +$ and
$(3\mu_{21} - \mu_{03})(\mu_{21} + \mu_{03})[3(\mu_{30} + \mu_{12})^2 - (\mu_{21} + \mu_{03})^2]$, $4\mu_{11}(\mu_{30} + \mu_{12})(\mu_{21} + \mu_{03})$

$I_7 = (3\mu_{21} - \mu_{03})(\mu_{30} + \mu_{12})[(\mu_{30} + \mu_{12})^2 - 3(\mu_{21} + \mu_{03})^2] + (3\mu_{12} - \mu_{03})(\mu_{21} + \mu_{03})[3(\mu_{30} + \mu_{12})^2 - (\mu_{21} + \mu_{03})^2]$.

The quantization problem is occurred when the double discrete summations are replaced from eqn. (1) for approximation. μ_{pq} becomes,

$$\mu_{pq} = \sum_R \sum (i-\bar{i})^p (j-\bar{j})^q \tag{2}$$

where $\bar{i} = m_{10}/m_{00}$, $\bar{j} = m_{01}/m_{00}$.

Using eqn. 2, the moment invariants might not be strictly invariant when the image is rotated or scaled. The errors always occur due to sampling and quantizing of the continuous image for digital computation.

3 Scaling Property for Moment-Based Approaches

Hu [2] moment invariants use η_{pq} to achieve scaling invariant. η_{pq} is defined as $\eta_{pq} = \mu_{pq}/\mu_{00}^{\gamma}$ where $\gamma = [(p+q)/2]+1$. Therefore, ϕ_1 to ϕ_7 become $\phi_1 = I_1/\mu_{00}^2$, $\phi_2 = I_2/\mu_{00}^4$, $\phi_3 = I_3/\mu_{00}^5$, $\phi_4 = I_4/\mu_{00}^5$, $\phi_5 = I_5/\mu_{00}^{10}$, $\phi_6 = I_6/\mu_{00}^7$ and $\phi_7 = I_7/\mu_{00}^{10}$.

Affine moment invariants [3-4] were derived by using the Affine transformation. Therefore, the invariants, ζ_1 to ζ_4, can be obtained as $\zeta_1 = \frac{1}{\mu_{00}^4}(\mu_{20}\mu_{02} - \mu_{11}^2)$,

$\zeta_2 = \frac{1}{\mu_{00}^{10}}(\mu_{30}^2\mu_{03}^2 - 6\mu_{30}\mu_{21}\mu_{12}\mu_{03}$ $\zeta_3 = \frac{1}{\mu_{00}^7}(\mu_{20}(\mu_{21}\mu_{03} - \mu_{12}^2)$
$+ 4\mu_{30}\mu_{12}^3 + 4\mu_{03}\mu_{21}^3 - 3\mu_{21}^2\mu_{12}^2)$, $- \mu_{20}(\mu_{21}\mu_{03} - \mu_{21}\mu_{12}) + \mu_{02}(\mu_{12}\mu_{30} - \mu_{21}^2))$ and

$\zeta_4 = \frac{1}{\mu_{00}^{11}}(\mu_{20}^3\mu_{03}^2 - 6\mu_{20}^2\mu_{11}\mu_{12}\mu_{03} - 6\mu_{20}^2\mu_{02}\mu_{21}\mu_{03} + 9\mu_{20}^2\mu_{02}\mu_{12}^2 + 12\mu_{20}\mu_{11}^2\mu_{21}\mu_{03} + 6\mu_{20}\mu_{11}\mu_{02}\mu_{30}\mu_{03}$
$- 18\mu_{20}\mu_{11}\mu_{02}\mu_{21}\mu_{12} - 8\mu_{11}^3\mu_{30}\mu_{03} - 6\mu_{20}\mu_{02}^2\mu_{30}\mu_{12} + 9\mu_{20}\mu_{02}^2\mu_{21}^2 + 12\mu_{11}^2\mu_{02}\mu_{30}\mu_{12} - 6\mu_{11}\mu_{02}^2\mu_{30}\mu_{21} + \mu_{02}^3\mu_{30}^2)$

Dudani [5] moment invariants make use of the radius of gyration β, $\beta = \sqrt{\mu_{20} + \mu_{02}}$, to normalize I_1 to I_7. Thus, M_1 to M_7 become $M_1 = I_1/\beta m_{00} = \sqrt{I_1}/m_{00}$, $M_2 = I_2/\beta^4$, $M_3 = I_3 m_{00}/\beta^6$, $M_4 = I_4 m_{00}/\beta^6$, $M_5 = I_5 m_{00}^2/\beta^{12}$, $M_6 = I_6 m_{00}/\beta^8$ and $M_7 = I_7 m_{00}^2/\beta^{12}$.

Improved moment invariants [6] are applied to the shape boundary rather than the region. η_{pq} is defined as $\eta_{pq} = \mu_{pq}/\mu_{00}^{\gamma}$, where $\gamma = p+q+1$. ψ_1 to ψ_7 become $\psi_1 = I_1/\mu_{00}^3$, $\psi_2 = I_2/\mu_{00}^6$, $\psi_3 = I_3/\mu_{00}^8$, $\psi_4 = I_4/\mu_{00}^8$, $\psi_5 = I_5/\mu_{00}^{16}$, $\psi_6 = I_6/\mu_{00}^{11}$ and $\psi_7 = I_7/\mu_{00}^{16}$.

4   Quantization Due to Scaling

4.1   Regular (Rectangular) Object

We first consider the case of a rectangular object with length a and width b in Fig. 1 (a). The scaled version of Fig. 1 (a) with a scaling factor of r is shown in Fig. 1 (b).

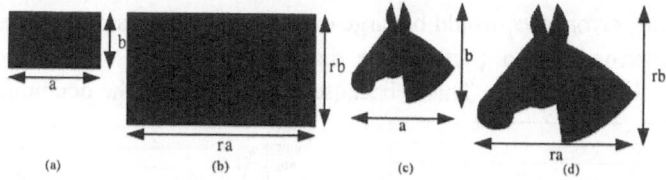

(a)　　　　(b)　　　　(c)　　　　(d)

Fig. 1. (a) Regular object, (b) its scaled version, (c) Irregular object and (d) its scaled version

Hu Moment Invariants. Expressions for ϕ_1 to ϕ_7 are now obtained for both continuous integral (eqn. 1) and discrete summation (eqn. 2) cases. We have,

Case 1: Continuous Integral	Case 2: Discrete Summation
$\phi_1 = \frac{a^2+b^2}{12ab}$, $\phi_2 = \left(\frac{a^2-b^2}{12ab}\right)^2$, ϕ_3 to $\phi_7 = 0$ (3)	$\phi_1 = \frac{a^2+b^2-2/r^2}{12ab}$, $\phi_2 = \left(\frac{a^2-b^2}{12ab}\right)^2$, ϕ_3 to $\phi_7 = 0$ (4)

The scaling quantization effect has a bigger effect on ϕ_1 than ϕ_2. When r tends to 0, the numerator of ϕ_1 in eqn. 4 will be significantly smaller than that in eqn. 3. Therefore, the difference becomes significantly large. If r is large enough, the value, $-2/r^2$, becomes very small and can be ignored. Then, the difference of ϕ_1 tends to 0.

Affine Moment Invariants. ζ_1 to ζ_4 are calculated for both cases. We have,

Case 1: Continuous Integral	Case 2: Discrete Summation
$\zeta_1 = \frac{1}{144}$, ζ_2 to $\zeta_4 = 0$ (5)	$\zeta_1 = \frac{1}{144} - \frac{(a^2+b^2)}{144r^2a^2b^2} + \frac{1}{144r^4a^2b^2}$, ζ_2 to $\zeta_4 = 0$ (6)

The difference of ζ_1 in these two cases is significantly large. Consider the discrete case, ζ_1 involves three parameters (length a, width b, and scaling factor r), while ζ_1 in continuous case is a constant. When changing in r (for fixed a and b), ζ_1 becomes large as r increases. Therefore, the error in ζ_1 would be large when the r tends to 0.

Dudani Moment Invariants. M_1 to M_7 can be found for both cases. We have,

Case 1: Continuous Integral	Case 2: Discrete Summation
$M_1 = \left(\frac{a^2+b^2}{12ab}\right)^{\frac{1}{2}}$, $M_2 = \left(\frac{a^2-b^2}{a^2+b^2}\right)^2$, M_3 to $M_7 = 0$ (7)	$M_1 = \left(\frac{a^2+b^2-2/r^2}{12ab}\right)^{\frac{1}{2}}$, $M_2 = \left(\frac{a^2-b^2}{a^2+b^2-2/r^2}\right)^2$, M_3 to $M_7 = 0$ (8)

r is present in the numerator of M_1 (eqn. 7.1), while it is present in the denominator of M_2 (eqn. 8.2) for discrete cases. The error in M_2 is larger than that in M_1, since the denominator in M_2 involves a power of 2 and the nominator in M_1 takes square root. Besides, as r increases, the value of M_1 decreases, while M_2 increases.

Improved Moment Invariants. We have to transform the objects (Fig. 1 a-b) into the boundary-based objects by detecting their edges with one-pixel width. We have,

Case 1: Continuous Integral	Case 2: Discrete Summation

$$\psi_1 = \frac{a^2+b^2}{12a^2b^2}, \ \psi_2 = \left(\frac{a^2-b^2}{12a^2b^2}\right)^2, \quad (9) \qquad \psi_1 = \frac{a^2+b^2-2/r^2}{12r^2a^2b^2}, \ \psi_2 = \left(\frac{a^2-b^2}{12r^2a^2b^2}\right)^2, \quad (10)$$

$$\psi_3 \text{ to } \psi_7 = 0 \qquad\qquad\qquad \psi_3 \text{ to } \psi_7 = 0$$

There are big differences for both numerator and denominator of ψ_1. Both parts involve r. Thus, error in ψ_1 would be large even if r showed a small change. Moreover, when considering ψ_1 and ψ_2 from the discrete summation case, the error in ψ_2 is smaller than the error in ψ_1. This is because ψ_2 contains r at the denominator only.

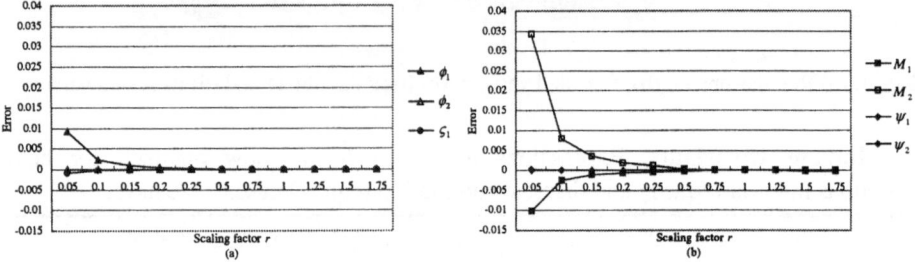

Fig. 2. Plot of error against scaling factor for rectangular objects for a) Hu and Affine moment invariants and b) Dudani and Improved moment invariants

Experimental Analysis. In our experiment, we generated a set of rectangular objects with $a=120$, $b=60$ pixels, and let r change between 0.05 and 1.75. Fig. 2 shows a plot of errors against r. From this figure, it is seen that all four approaches show a similar trend. Errors tend to zero as r increases, but errors become large when r decreases. When r reaches 0.5, the errors are essentially equal to zero. This means, if the size of the target object is half of the original size, the error due to scaling would not be significant using either of these four approaches. However, when r is as small as 0.05, Dudani moment invariants are affected heavily by the scaling.

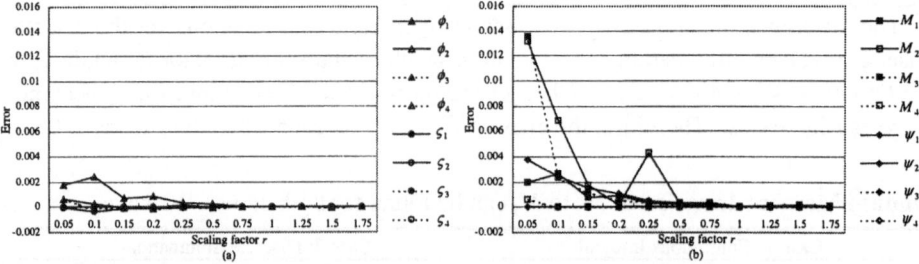

Fig. 3. Plot of error against scaling factor for irregular objects for a) Hu and Affine moment invariants and b) Dudani and Improved moment invariants

4.2 Irregular Horse-Shaped Objects

Fig. 3 shows the results of horse-shaped objects with $a=187$, $b=167$ pixels as shown in Fig. 1c, and r is between 0.05 and 1.75. Note that we consider the first four elements, since their values are larger than 10^{-7}. Comparing Fig. 2 and 3, the general trends are similar. This indicates that four approaches are robust to quantization error when r ranges from 0.5 to 1.75. However, the improved moment invariants suffer a higher error due to the scaling of irregular objects as compared to regular objects.

5 Quantization Due to Rotation

5.1 Regular (Rectangular) Object

We give results of our studies on quantization effects due to rotation. Fig 4 shows regular and irregular objects and their rotated version. Let the angle of rotation be θ,

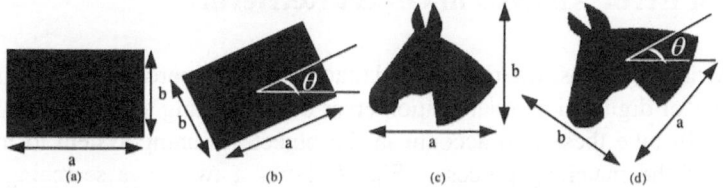

Fig. 4. (a) Regular object, (b) its rotated version, (c) Irregular object, (d) its rotated version.

Experimental Analysis. Fig. 5 shows the error curves of a set of rectangular objects, with $a=120$, $b=60$ pixels, and θ ranging from $0°$ to $180°$. It can be seen from Fig. 5 that they form an "M" shape. None of the four approaches has error at the angles where $\theta = 0°$, $90°$ and $180°$. In fact, ψ_1 suffers the largest rotational error at angles between $40°$ and $50°$ and between $130°$ and $140°$. The second and the third most sensitive measures of error due to rotation are M_1 and M_2.

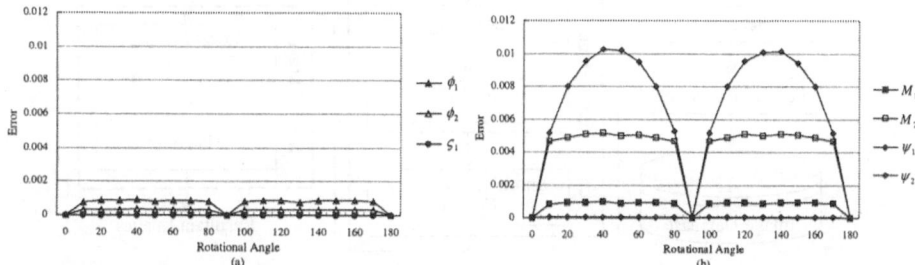

Fig. 5. Plot of error against the angle of rotation for rectangular objects for a) Hu and Affine moment invariants and b) Dudani and Improved moment invariants

5.2 Irregular Horse-Shaped Objects

Experimental Analysis. A set of irregular objects with $a=187$, $b=167$ pixels for θ ranges from $0°$ to $180°$ is examined. Similar to the observations in Section 5.1, all curves in Fig. 6 show an "M" shape. The most sensitive measure of error due to rotation is M_2. The second and the third most sensitive measures are M_1 and ϕ_1.

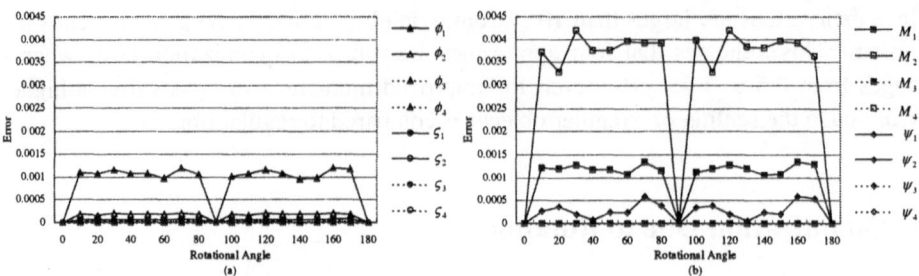

Fig. 6. Plot of error against the angle of rotation for irregular objects for a) Hu and Affine moment invariants and b) Dudani and Improved moment invariants

6   Use of Error Analysis in Object Retrieval

In the previous sections, we have proved that these four approaches suffer from different degrees of digitization/ quantization error due to scaling and rotation. In this section, we will take these into account in the object searching system to improve the accuracy of the matching process. Fig. 7 shows a two-stage searching algorithm. The first stage aims at producing a fast listing from the whole database to select those objects with similar global characteristics; while the second stage obtains the local information. The advantage is to prevent from matching on the whole database for every query submission. This can reduce the computational complexity, resulting in an efficient and effective searching algorithm. However, to achieve better accuracy for retrieving scaled and rotated objects, a threshold selection is crucial.

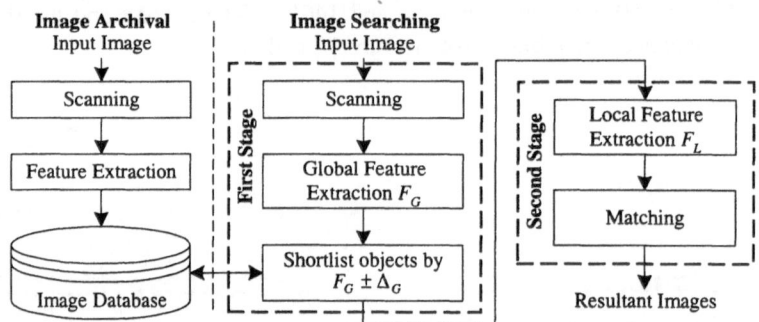

Fig. 7. A two-stage object searching model

We have tested this selection method for the approach with the biggest quantization effect: Dudani moment invariants. F_G be the feature vector of the first stage, i.e.,

$$F_G = \begin{pmatrix} M_1 & M_2 & \cdots & M_7 \end{pmatrix}^T \tag{11}$$

and the threshold Δ_G be the error limit, i.e.,

$$\Delta_G = \begin{pmatrix} \lambda_1 & \lambda_2 & \cdots & \lambda_7 \end{pmatrix}^T \tag{12}$$

where λ_i is the maximum error due to the quantization effect on corresponding M_i.

Fig. 8. Some example objects in the test database

We search relevant objects within the range, $F_G \pm \Delta_G$, so that a range of possible objects can be retrieved. If Δ_G equals zero, only one object will be selected at this stage, which is not desirable. If Δ_G is set to a large value, we cannot guarantee low computational complexity and too many irrelevant objects may be retrieved. In order to achieve a high retrieval rate and at the same time to have a low computational complexity, the threshold, Δ_G, can be obtained by using the analysis in this paper, which takes consideration of the quantization effect of scaling and rotation.

A set of the experimental databases was setup: 1000 images of 100 classes containing digitally scaled and rotated objects. Each class contained 5 scaling factors (0.05, 0.15, 0.25, 0.5, and 0.75) and 5 rotational angles (0°, 23°, 45°, 68° and 90°). Fig. 8 shows examples of the test objects. Two query objects as shown in Figs. 1a and 1c were submitted to the system. For the rectangular object, Figs. 2 and 5 show that the highest error of M_1 for Dudani approach is 0.012; while M_2 is 0.035 (defined as Set 1). Then we put $\Delta_G=(0.012 \quad 0.035)^T$, while $M_3 - M_7$ are zero. For the horse-shaped object, the highest errors of the first four elements of Dudani approach are 0.003, 0.014, 0.014 and 0.001 (defined as Set 5) respectively, deduced from Fig. 3 and 6. Then we put $\Delta_G=(0.003 \quad 0.014 \quad 0.014 \quad 0.001)^T$, while $\lambda_5 - \lambda_7$ are ignored as $M_5 - M_7$ are smaller than 10^{-7}. We also tested the cases for bigger Δ_G. Sets 2, 3 and 4 (resp. sets 6, 7 and 8) were obtained by multiplying Set 1 (resp. Set 5) with 2, 5 and 10 respectively.

Table 1. Results of different selections

Δ_G	Number of object retrieved in the same class	Number of object retrieved in the other classes
Rectangular objects		
Set 1	10	0
Set 2	10	7
Set 3	10	94
Set 4	10	589
Horse-shaped objects		
Set 5	10	0
Set 6	10	35
Set 7	10	193
Set 8	10	287

Table 1 shows the results of these eight sets of selection. When we set Δ_G to the highest error (Set 1 and 5), it can guarantee that all scaled and rotated objects in the same class, not other classes, are selected in the retrieval. However, when Δ_G is set to a larger value (Set 4 and 8), many objects from other classes are retrieved. In fact, if Δ_G is wrongly selected, the retrieval result will include objects from other classes and thus the computational complexity of the matching increases significantly. Therefore, the error analysis provides a way of choosing the threshold and is useful for ensuring that the two-stage approach is invariant to translation, scaling and rotation.

7 Conclusion

This paper has presented an analysis of quantization error for four moment-based approaches. They are Hu moment invariants, Affine moment invariants, Dudani moment invariants and Improved moment invariants. Analytical expressions in continuous and discrete domains have been derived and experimental results have also been found for regular (rectangular) and irregular objects undergoing scaling and rotation changes.

We have found that the error due to scaling increases as the object size decreases. The Dudani moment invariants tend to have a larger error than that of the other three moment-based approaches. Moreover, the error due to rotation increases as the object is rotated with an angle other than $\theta = 0°$, $90°$ and $180°$.

In order to ensure the shape descriptor is invariant to translation, scaling and rotation, we can apply the analysis of the quantization effects to scaling and rotation for selecting the threshold for an object searching system. From our experimental work, it is proved that all scaled and rotated objects can be retrieved correctly by setting the threshold to the value of the error.

Acknowledgement. This work is supported by the Centre for Multimedia Signal Processing, the Hong Kong Polytechnic University. K.L. Lau acknowledges the research studentships provided by the University.

References

1. Wong, W.H., Siu, W.C.: Generation of Moment Invariants and their Uses of Character Recognition. Pattern Recognition. 16 (1995) 115–123
2. Hu, M.K.: Visual Pattern Recognition by Moment Invariants. IRE Trans Inform Theory. IT-8. (1962) 179–187
3. Flusser, J., Suk, T.: A Moment-based Approach to Registration of Images with Affine Geometric Distortion. IEEE Trans. on Geoscience and Remote Sensing, 32, 2, (1994), 382-387
4. Flusser, J., Suk, T.: Pattern Recognition by Affine Moment Invariant. Pattern Recognition. 26, 1, (1993), 167-174
5. Dudani, S.A., Breeding, K.J., Mcghe, R.B.: Aircraft Identification by Moment Invariants. IEEE Trans. on Computers. C-26, 1, (1977), 39-45
6. Chen, C.C.: Improved Moment Invariants for Shape Discrimination. Pattern Recognition. 26, 5, (1993), 683-686
7. Teh, C.H., Chin, R.T.: On Digital Approximation of Moment Invariants. Computer Vision, Graphics, and Image Processing. 33, (1986), 318-326
8. Salama, G.I., Abbott, A.L.: Moment Invariants and Quantization Effects. IEEE Computer Society Conf. on Computer Vision and Pattern Recognition. (1998), 157-163

Segmenting People in Meeting Videos Using Mixture Background and Object Models

Dar-Shyang Lee, Berna Erol, and Jonathan J. Hull

Ricoh Innovations, Inc.
2882 Sand Hill Road, Suite 115, Menlo Park, CA 94025, U.S.A.
{dsl,berna,hull}@rii.ricoh.com

Abstract. We have developed a meeting recorder system which captures a panoramic video of a meeting room. Segmentation of people from this video is required for tracking and retrieval applications. However, the application scenario makes it difficult to rely on the usual solution of static background initialization and purely motion-based tracking for segmenting people. In this paper, we describe a novel framework for segmenting people in these videos using adaptive Gaussian mixtures for both background and object modeling. Based on a Bayesian formulation of the problem, results of object segmentation provide feedback to the background segmentation module. Experimental results on real meeting videos are presented.

1 Introduction

Object segmentation is an important component of many multimedia systems with applications ranging from content-based retrieval to object-based coding. Although it has been the subject of intensive study, fully automatic object segmentation is still considered an open problem. In our application, we are interested in tracking humans in videos captured by a single omni-directional camera. The realistic setting of our application makes it infeasible to rely on static background subtraction because some people will always be present when a recording is started. In this paper, we propose a solution using an adaptive mixture background model coupled with a mixture-based object model.

We have developed a meeting recorder prototype which captures a panoramic view of a meeting room. The capture device consists of an omni-directional camera equipped with four microphones. The camera can be positioned anywhere on a table and there are no specified seating locations for the participants. Recording is controlled manually via a VCR-like interface provided on a small touch-screen panel. Captured videos are dewarped to produce a full panorama of the meeting room. Analysis of the four-channel audio input allows us to identify the direction of speakers, and a special playback tool is used to provide a regular perspective view of the meeting which automatically centers on the speaker based on the results of the

Y.-C. Chen, L.-W. Chang, and C.-T. Hsu (Eds.): PCM 2002, LNCS 2532, pp. 791–798, 2002.

analysis.   To improve the accuracy of view selection and to facilitate person identification, people segmentation is needed.

We propose a two-module system for tracking people using an adaptive background model and a blob-based object model. The background segmentation module identifies regions of interest that the object segmentation module classifies into individual objects. While this is the typical approach to most tracking systems, our system differs in that an adaptive mixture model is used for both the background and the object model. We also provide a Bayesian formulation of the background segmentation problem which allows the results of object segmentation and other domain-specific priors to be incorporated.

There has been a significant amount of work on tracking humans àssuming various sensor inputs and environmental constraints [5],[6],[15]. The context of our application is similar to that of [13], where a single Gaussian recursive filter is used for background modeling and three clusters in the color space are used for object modeling. Our work differs in the background and object models used. Given the multimodal nature of the background process, a mixture model is more appropriate than a single Gaussian recursive filter [3],[11], and more efficient than the non-parametric approach of [1].

For background segmentation, we extend the work of [11] using an improved adaptive learning scheme and provide a Bayesian formulation of the segmentation problem.   The generalized framework offers a guideline for incorporating domain-specific priors and feedback from the object model. Our object model is based on the blob representation of [15], where a person is composed of several blobs, and each blob is represented as a Gaussian distribution of spatial and color features. This representation was extended to handle multiple people and occlusions in [7]. However, in both applications, foreground is determined after background subtraction with static initialization.   The existence of an image of the empty room was also assumed.

The rest of the paper is organized as follows.   In Section 2, we provide a short description of our meeting recorder system to set the context for this work. In Section 3, we describe our framework for people tracking.   Each of background and object segmentation modules is described in a subsection. Experimental results are shown in Section 4 followed by conclusions.

2   Meeting Recorder System

Recently, several multimedia systems have been proposed to facilitate the recording of meetings [2],[14]. Our meeting recorder system is designed with portability and compatibility with commercial hardware in mind. The hardware configuration consists of a special capture device, a touch screen monitor, as shown in Figure 1, and a PC. The capture device is composed of an omni-directional camera in the center and 4 microphones positioned at corners of the base.

The camera has a parabolic mirror that captures a panoramic view of the meeting in a single *doughnut* video stream. The video, along with digitally mixed stereo audio, is sent to a video capture card and recorded as an MPEG-2 file. Encoding is done at 640x480 at 30fps. Although several other panoramic video capture systems based on multiple cameras have been proposed [2],[10], we chose a simpler design to avoid dealing with multiple video streams. This makes it feasible to replace the capture PC with a commercial digital video recorder for portability.

Before the audio signals are digitally mixed and sent to the video capture card, they are processed in real-time to determine the direction of speakers. A software filter receives four-channel audio and calculates the sound source direction between 0 and 360 degrees whenever human speech is detected. The results are post-processed to produce a sequence of virtual camera parameters used by our meeting viewer to automatically center on the speaker during playback. However, users can manually control the view using pan, tilt, and zoom operations.

The data on speaker directions is also used in combination with skin detection to extract face images of meeting participants. Background images are extracted from the video to identify the meeting location. This information is displayed in a meeting description document in HTML format along with user-added annotations. The audio is further analyzed to detect significant events. Based on motion analysis performed on the compressed data stream, events involving large spatial activities are identified. All the information associated with the meeting is written to a meta file. The video and meta file are archived and made available on a database server. The system has been used regularly since the beginning of 2002. As a result, we have collected more than 60 meetings and have over 50 hours of video. Additional details of the system are described in [8].

3   Algorithm Description

Our proposed solution consists of a background segmentation and an object segmentation module, as shown in Figure 2. The background segmentation module identifies regions of interest which can be further segmented and tracked by the object module.

In the background segmentation module, a Gaussian mixture is constructed for each pixel in the image to model the distribution of values observed at that pixel over time, effectively color quantizing the observations to discrete processes. A constraint for this quantization process is that it learns in an online mode and is adaptable over time. Each process corresponds to a distinct cluster and can be classified as foreground or background based on its color or other domain-specific attributes. Segmentation is then achieved by classifying a pixel value according to the class of the underlying process to which it belongs.

In the object segmentation module, regions identified as foreground are matched against a list of objects represented as blobs. New objects are created for regions that do not match any existing object. Object parameters are updated using the results of this classification. Information on the updated objects is used to improve the background model. Since objects are represented by spatially and chromatically coherent blobs, processes similar to the object are less likely to be background. We describe each module in a subsection below.

3.1   Background Segmentation

For background segmentation, the decision at every pixel location over time is to separate observations resulting from a foreground process from those belonging to a background process. From a statistical pattern recognition perspective, this decision should be based on $P(B|x)$, where B represents the background class and x is the pixel value. Considering the multimodal nature of pixel values observed at a location over a time window, a Gaussian mixture is appropriate for modeling the distribution [3],[11].

$$P(x) = \sum_{k=1}^{K} P(x|G_k)P(G_k) = \sum_{k=1}^{K} w_k \cdot g\left(x, \mu_k, \sigma_k^2\right) \tag{1}$$

where G_k denotes the k-th Gaussian constituent, and $g(x, \mu_k, \sigma_k^2) \equiv g_k(x)$ is the normal density function computed at x.

Assuming all observations coming from a single Gaussian process belong to either foreground or background, the original posterior probability can be reformulated as

$$P(B|x) = \frac{\sum_{k=1}^{K} P(x|G_k)P(G_k)P(B|G_k)}{\sum_{k=1}^{K} P(x|G_k)P(G_k)} \tag{2}$$

The segmentation problem is decomposed as two independent problems of estimating the distribution of all observations at a single pixel, $P(x)$, as a Gaussian mixture, and estimating the probability of each Gaussian in the mixture being background, $P(B|G_k)$. The first problem corresponds to the quantization in Figure 2, and the second problem corresponds to the classification of each process as foreground or background.

The problem of density estimation using Gaussian mixtures is well studied. The constraint for our application is that an online, instead of batch, learning algorithm is needed and the model must adapt to distribution changes over time. We follow an adaptive filtering algorithm in [11] with a few modifications. The most significant change is that an adaptive learning rate schedule is introduced for each Gaussian to improve convergence. In addition to the normal weight, mean and variance parameters, a new parameter c_i is added to count the number of data points that have directly contributed to the update of the i-th Gaussian. We have found that using a separate learning rate for each Gaussian based on this number instead of using a fixed learning rate for all Gaussians in the mixture dramatically improves the convergence speed and approximation results [9].

Unlike the previous problem of density estimation where the objective and desired algorithm behaviors are well defined, estimating $P(B|G_k)$ is largely heuristic and application dependent. Since background is typically observed more often and displays less variation in value, we approximate $P(B|G_k)$ with $b_k'^{,\iota} = w_k'^{,\iota} \cdot (E_\sigma / \sigma_k'^{,\iota})$ where E_σ is the expected value of the variance for a background Gaussian. We estimate this by averaging the variance of the top 25% of Gaussians in the entire image that have the largest $P(B|G_k)$. The decision could also depend on other sensor inputs such as depth [4] if it were available. We also apply domain-specific priors and neighborhood constraints. To enhance the detection of humans, a strong bias is placed against skin color being background. Skin tone is detected using a single Gaussian distribution in the normalized red-green color space 12. Finally, background estimates at neighboring locations reinforce each other. If the mean of a Gaussian at position (r,c), $\mu_k^{r,c}$, evaluates to be background with a high probability at its neighboring positions (r',c'), then its estimate $b_k^{r,c}$ is also incremented. This local reinforcement helps propagate established background models to regions where background is not well recognized as background. The object models described in the next section also provide feedback to this module.

3.2   Object Segmentation

At the end of the background segmentation process, every pixel position is classified as foreground or background. After smoothing out small noise and performing connected component analysis, regions of interest are identified. The goal of the object segmentation module is to match up these regions with a list of existing objects, or create new objects if necessary. Since the human body is highly deformable, we use a blob-based representation [7],[15].

A blob is simply a set of points sharing certain spatial and visual characteristics. Each object is composed of a set of blobs. This is naturally modeled as a Gaussian mixture of an augmented feature vector X consisting of the spatial coordinate (r,c) and the color components (R,G,B). The probability that a point belongs to an object O_j is

$$P(O_j \mid X) = \sum_{k=1}^{K} w_{j,k} \cdot g_{j,k}(X) \tag{3}$$

Every foreground pixel in a region of interest is matched against the list of existing objects. If most pixels in a region belong to the same object, then all foreground pixels in that region are assigned to that object, and the object model is updated. If the majority of pixels do not match any object well enough, then a new object is created. At the end of object classification, we obtain an object segmentation map where each pixel is labeled with an object ID or as background.

Object parameters are updated using the batch EM algorithm on all the samples in its support map. The parameters learned at time t are used as initial values for the update at time $(t+1)$. When an object is first created, one iteration of an online learning algorithm is used to initialize the Gaussians before applying batch learning.

Objects identified by this module are used to enhance the background segmentation module. If a blob corresponding to the torso has been identified, then Gaussian constituents in nearby background models that look similar to that blob are unlikely to be background. The background model is periodically updated by evaluating its Gaussians against the current list of objects. If $\mu_k^{r,c}$ matches an object well, computed by Eq.(3), its probability of being background is decremented. This feedback improves detection of stationary parts of the body that otherwise would be treated as background and in turn improves the object model.

4   Experiments

The proposed algorithm was tested on meetings recorded at our lab. For the background models, we used K=3 with a temporal retention α=0.99. Since $b_k^{\prime\prime}$'s are expensive to compute, they are updated on every tenth frame. For the object segmentation module, K=5 and α=0.999. To obtain reasonable initial segmentation, object models are not created until 30 frames into the video. Both modules are implemented based on Microsoft's DirectShow. The system runs at 10 Hz with a 360x50 panoramic video on a 2GHz Pentium4 PC.

Segmentation results of a frame 10 seconds into a meeting video are shown in Figure 3. Fig.3(a) shows the video frame. From the motion history in Fig.3(b) it can be seen that all except the person on the right had relatively little motion since frame 0. Fig.3(c) shows a representation of the background model. The person on the right was easily detected as foreground and has become invisible in the background model. For the other three people, regions behind their heads that have not been completely occluded are showing through. Fig.3(d) shows regions of interest extracted by the background segmentation module. The rightmost person is well segmented since a good background estimation was achieved at that position. The bodies of the two people on the left were not segmented correctly because there was little motion. After image processing and object classification, the segmented object map is shown in Fig.3(e). Both people on the right were segmented correctly. However, there were holes in the two people on the left, which indicates that image processing can be improved. Fig.3(f) shows the object models that were constructed. The head and torso were well represented in position and color for the middle two persons. Although the models were not as good for the other two people, they were segmented correctly mainly by spatial proximity.

In summary, the preliminary results were very encouraging. We found that background segmentation worked well. A significant improvement was gained from our proposed adaptive rate algorithm for online mixture learning. We experimented with different selection criterion for Gaussian reassignment, various retention factors, and different color space representations. However, we did not notice any significant difference. One area for future investigation is the development of a more systematic approach to estimate $P(B|G_k)$. It is difficult to determine the relative importance of various priors and heuristics used in the background classifier. A strategy for training is needed.

The object segmentation algorithm can also be a subject of future investigation. Results obtained by simultaneously training background and object models depend on the object motion. While it handles moving objects quite well, it tends to break up hands from bodies if the person stays stationary for a while. This can be improved by incorporating priors into the object models and better object grouping. In addition, morphological processing can help fill up small holes. We are currently investigating these issues and preparing a more thorough evaluation using ground truth data.

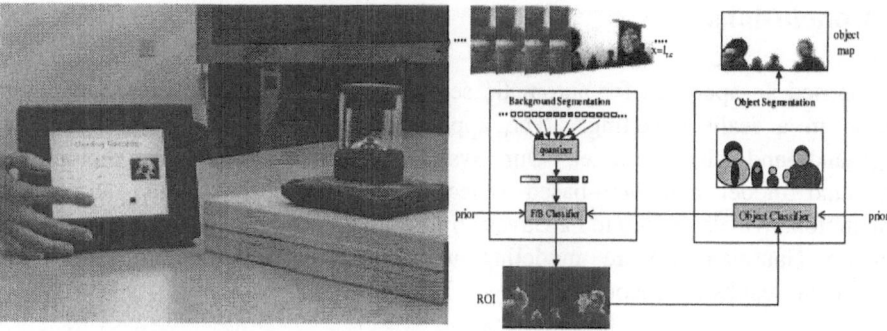

Fig. 1. A meeting recorder prototype consisting of an omni-directional camera with 4 microphones at its base (right) and a touch-screen controlled interface on the left. The recording PC is not shown.

Fig. 2 A segmentation system consisting of two tightly coupled modules for background and object segmentation. The background segmentation module models each pixel with a Gaussian mixture and classifies each Gaussian constituent as foreground or background.

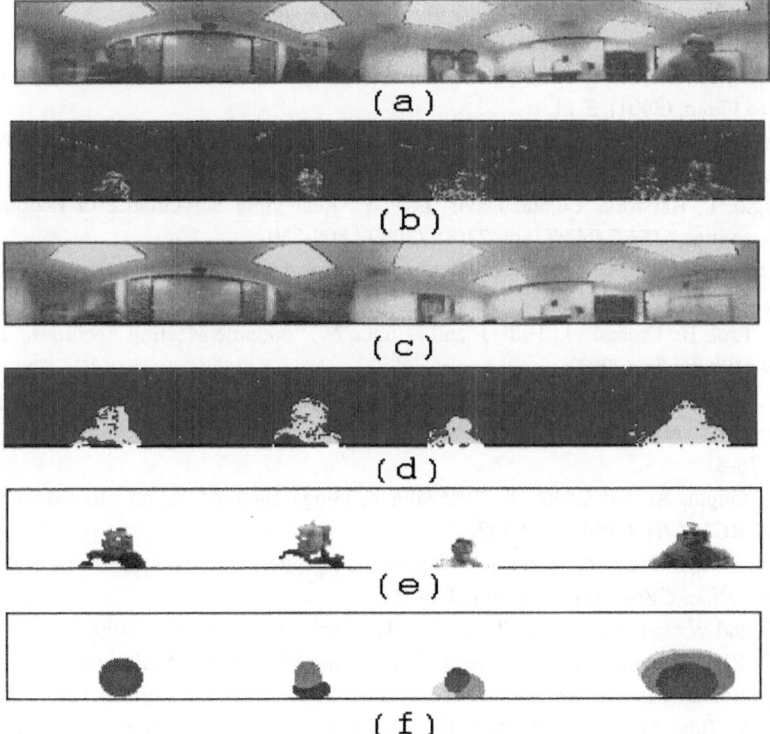

(a)

(b)

(c)

(d)

(e)

(f)

Fig. 3. From top to bottom showing (a) the original panoramic video frame, (b) motion history prior to this frame, (c) a representation of the background model, (d) segmented foreground region, (e) foreground region after object segmentation, and (f) the object model.

5   Conclusions

We proposed an approach for automatic segmentation of people in meeting videos captured in a realistic setting. The application scenario calls for an adaptive background and object model. Our system simultaneously learns a mixture background model and blob-based object models for background and object segmentation. We also presented a Bayesian formulation of background segmentation based on Gaussian mixture modeling with an improved learning algorithm. Experimental results are encouraging.

References

1. Elgammal, A., Harwood, D. and Davis, L., "Non-parametric model for background subtraction," *Proc. 6th European Conference on Computer Vision*, (2000).
2. Foote, J. and Kimber, D., "FlyCam: Practical panoramic video and automatic camera control," *Proc. of Int. Conf. on Multimedia & Expo*, vol.3, (2000), 1419-1422.
3. Friedman, N. and Russell, S., "Image segmentation in video sequences: a probabilistic approach," *Proc. 13th Conf. Uncertainty in Artificial Intelligence*, (1997).
4. Harville, M., Gordon, G. and Woodfill, J., "Foreground segmentation using adaptive mixture models in color and depth," *ICCV Workshop on Detection and Recognition of Events in Video*, (2001), 3-11.
5. Gavrila, D. M., "The Visual Analysis of Human Movement: A Survey," *Computer Vision and Image Understanding*, vol. 73(1), (1999), 82-98.
6. Haritaoglu, I., Harwood, D. and Davis, L., "W4: Real-Time Surveillance of People and Their Activities," *IEEE PAMI*, vol. 22(8), (2000), 809-830.
7. Khan, S. and Shah, M., "Tracking People in Presence of Occlusion," *Proc. of ACCV*, (2000).
8. Lee, D., Erol, B., Graham, J., Hull, J. and Murata, N., "Portable Meeting Recorder," *Proc. of ACM Multimedia*, (2002).
9. Lee, D., "A Bayesian Framework for Background Segmentation Based on Adaptive Gaussian Mixtures," *Proc. of Conf. On Systemics, Cybernetics and Informatics*, vol. 14, (2002), 76-81.
10. Rui, T., Gupta, A. and Cadiz, J., "Viewing meetings captured by an omni-directional camera", *ACM CHI*, (2001), 450-457.
11. Stauffer, C. and Grimson, W.E.L., "Adaptive background mixture models for real-time tracking," *Proc. CVPR*, vol. 2, (1999), 246-252.
12. Yang, J. and Waibel, A., "A Real-Time Face Tracker," *Proc. of WACV*, (1996), 142-147.
13. Yang, J., Zhu, X., Gross, R., Kominek, J., Pan, Y. and Waibel, A., "Multimodal People ID for a Multimedia Meeting Browser," *Proc. of ACM Multimedia*, (1999), 159-168.
14. Waibel, A., Bett, M., Metze, F., Ries, K., Schaaf, T., Schultz, T., Soltau, H., Yu, H. and Zechner, K., "Advances in automatic meeting record creation and access", *Proc. of ICASSP*, (2001), 597-600.
15. Wren, C., Azarbayejani, A., Darrel, T. and Pentland, A., "Pfinder: Real-Time Tracking of the Human Body," *IEEE PAMI*, vol. 19(7), (1997), 780-785.

A Framework for Background Detection in Video

Laiyun Qing[1,2], Weiqiang Wang[2], Tiejun Huang[1], and Wen Gao[1,2]

[1] Graduate School of Chinese Academy of Sciences, Beijing, P. R. China, 100039)
[2] Institute of Computing Technology, Chinese Academy of Sciences, Beijing, P. R. China, 100080)
{lyqing, wqwang, tjhuang, wgao}@ict.ac.cn

Abstract. This paper presents a framework for background detection in video. First, key frames are extracted to capture background change in video and reduce the magnitude of the data. Then we analyze the content of the key frames to determine whether there is an interesting background in them. A time-constrained clustering algorithm is exploited for key frame extraction. Background detection in the key frame is done with color and texture cues. The illumination varies much in natural scenes. To deal with the varying illumination, color is modeled with three sub-models: strong light, normal light and weak light. The connectivity of background pixels is used to reduce the computing cost of texture. Experimental results show that background can be detected simply and efficiently under the framework.

1 Introduction

Automatic event detection in video becomes more important with increasing volume of digital video. Many projects on event detection focus on tracking foreground, such as face and car [1][2][3]. The main information used is motion between images. But in some cases, you would like to find a clip of football game in a long video program. Maybe a good retrieval representation in this case is the grass background plus a football. In this paper, we focus on such background detection and propose a framework for background detection. We select grass as an example, because grass can be the background for many events such as football games, golf games and wild animals.

Unlike foreground, background has many different attributes: little active motion, no definite shape and large area. Therefore the technique used to detect background is a little different.

Because backgrounds change usually results in large visual content change between frames, key frame can be applied to capture this change and reduce the magnitude of the data to be processed. A time-constrained clustering technique is exploited to extract the key frames. Then color cues and texture cues are used to detect the interesting background in them.

Varying illumination is a main obstacle to detect background in natural scenes. To deal with this situation, color under varying illumination is modeled with three typical light conditions: strong light (sunny), normal light (cloudy) and weak light (in shadow).

Y.-C. Chen, L.-W. Chang, and C.-T. Hsu (Eds.): PCM 2002, LNCS 2532, pp. 799-805, 2002.
© Springer-Verlag Berlin Heidelberg 2002

Texture computing is complex and time consuming. If this is done for every pixel, the time is beyond endurance. The pixels in backgrounds usually connect with each other and this connectivity can be used as a cue to reduce the texture computing cost. If one pixel is declared as a pixel in background, the adjacent pixels with similar color are also declared as background pixels.

The rest of this paper is organized as follows. Key frame extraction is described in section 2. In section 3, background detection in the key frames is discussed. Experimental results are given in section 4. The paper is ended with a summary and discussion.

2   Key Frame Extraction

Key frame is appropriate to capture background change. The existing approaches for key frame extraction [4][5] are usually applied after shot boundary detection. We directly extract key frames on raw video stream without shot segmentation, which makes the system works very effeciently. The technique for key frame extraction is time-constrained clustering, based on Zhuang et al s' [4] but in a sliding time window. The size of the window is denoted as T.

The color histogram of the DC image of the video frame is selected as visual feature. The color histogram used here is $64*64=4096$ bins of Cb, Cr in YCbCr color space. The similarity between two frames is defined as:

$$sim(f_1, f_2) = sim(H_1, H_2) = \frac{1}{N} \sum_{k=1}^{4096} \min(H_{1,k}, H_{2,k}) \tag{1}$$

Where N is the number of the pixels in the DC image, H_1 and H_2 are the histograms of the DC images of f_1 and f_2 respectively.

The clustering algorithm in the sliding time window is summarized as follows:

1. Initialization: $f_1 \rightarrow C_0$, f_1 is the center of the cluster C_0, $1 \rightarrow numCluster$;
2. Get the next frame f_i, if the video stream ends, the clustering procedure stops;
3. Calculate the similarity $sim(f_i, c_k)$ between f_i and the center of every last T clusters C_k, where c_k is the center of cluster C_k, and get the maximal similarity $MaxSim$, $MaxSim = max(sim(f_i, c_k))$ ($k = numCluster-1$, $numCluster-2$, $numCluster - T$ And $k>=0$);
4. If $Maxsim< \delta$, f_i can not be putted into any cluster in the sliding time window, Go to 5; Otherwise put f_i into the cluster C_j, $j = argmax_k(sim(f_i, c_k))$, Go to 6;
5. If the time window is full, shift out the oldest cluster C_{old}. If C_{old} is large enough, the frame which is closest to the center of C_{old} is selected as a key frame. Create a new cluster $C_{numCluster}$ and put f_i into it, f_i is the center of the new cluster, $numCluster = numCluster +1$, Go to 2;
6. Adjust the center of the cluster C_j which f_i belongs to: assume original center is c_j', w is the number of frames in it, then the new center is: $c_j = \frac{w}{w+1} c_j' + \frac{1}{w+1} f_i$, Go to 2.

In the algorithm, the parameter δ controls the density of the clustering. The change of background usually causes large visual content change, thus δ is a small float. Another parameter T is the size of sliding window, which means that only the clusters in the sliding window are compared. $T=1$ is used for most of the video programs, which is something like shot segmentation, except that visual content comparison is done between the frame and the center of every cluster instead of the previous frame. In some other video programs, there are a lot of shots with similar content, for example in sports news video, camera is shifted between the reporter and the game. If one key frame is enough for the similar shots, T can be a larger integer.

3 Background Detection

After key frames have been extracted, every key frame is treated as an image. Once the interesting background is detected in the key frame, all clips that the key frame represents are declared to include the interesting background.

Color and texture are important cues for background detection, while the shape is not exploited since generally it doesn't exhibit any definite shape. In this paper, we select grass as an example for its common. The background model is a per-pixel model with color and texture features. If the proportion of background pixels in a key frame is larger than a threshold τ, the key frame is declared to have the background.

3.1 Color Model

It's natural to think that grass is green and its color locates in a subspace of the color space. Here we select *HSV* color space. Grass usually appears in natural scenes where illumination varies very much. The color of grass looks different under varying illumination. Some images with grass under different illumination are illustrated in Fig. 1.

Fig. 1. Different color of grass under varying illumination

To deal with the varying illumination, color is modeled with three typical light conditions: strong light (sunny), normal light (cloudy) and weak light (in shadow). Each sub-model is represented with four statistical parameters: maximum, minimum, mean and standard deviation. These parameters are obtained by taking statistical analysis on the color of the pixels in grass background under corresponding illumination.

A pixel is declared as a candidate background pixel if the distance between the color of the pixel and either center of the three sub-models is less than a threshold d.

The distance metric can be Euclidean distance, Mahalanobis distance or angle between the two color vectors. Because the value ranges of three components in color vector are different ($h\in [0,360]$, $s,v\in [0,1]$), the value range should be normalized before calculating Euclidean distance and angle distance.

3.2 Texture Model

We select Gabor wavelet transform coeffecients [6] as texture features for its success in many applications such as texture classification and object segmentation.

Given an image $I(x,y)$, its Gabor wavelet transform is defined as:

$$w_{mn} = \iint I(x, y) * g_{mn} (x - x_1, y - y_1)dx_1 dy_1 \tag{2}$$

Where $g_{mn}(x - x_1, y - y_1)$ is the mother Gabor wavelet, $m=0, 1, ..., S-1$, S is the number of scales, $n = 0, 1, ..., K-1$, K is the number of orientations.

The feature vector of the pixel (x,y) is $W_{mn} = \|w_{mn}\|$. But we find that W_{mn} is not good enough for grass and non-grass classification. As illustrated in Fig. 2, the appearance of grass varies much while there are some other textures similar with grass.

(a) Different grass textures

(b) Non-grass textures similar with grass

Fig. 2. Grass textures and non-grass textures

To let the algorithm be more robust, we use the coefficients W_{mn} in another way:
- Coefficients of different frequency scaled with different factors

The coefficients of high, middle and low frequency, W_{mn} are scaled with different factors s_1, s_2, s_3 ($s_1 > s_2 > s_3$) and labeled as W_{mn}', because higher frequency components have better discrimination.

- Mean and standard deviation of the coefficients in a neighbor region, $\mu_{m,n}$ and $\sigma_{m,n}$ are used as feature vector

$$\mu_{mn} = \frac{1}{N} \iint | W_{mn} (x, y) | \, dxdy \tag{3}$$

$$\sigma_{mn} = \frac{1}{N} (\iint (W_{mn} (x, y) - \mu_{mn})^2 \, dxdy)^{1/2} \tag{4}$$

Where N is the number of pixels in the neighbor region.

After the feature vector has been extracted, it is inputted into a SVM (Support Vector Machines) classifier. We select 1000 train vectors in which 500 positive samples and 500 negative samples are included. Kernel function and its parameters are important for a SVM but there is no good guide to how to select them in theory. We did this by experiments. The two employed rules are: the precision on train samples and the number of support vectors. We tried four kernel functions: linear, polynomial, RBF and Sigmoid. Polynomial kernel function is selected as the final function according to the above rules. The function is:

$$K(\mathbf{x}, \mathbf{y}) = [10 * (\mathbf{x} \cdot \mathbf{y})]^2 \tag{5}$$

We can see that texture computing is complex and time consuming, even with few scales and orientations ($S=3$, $K=4$ in this paper). The time can't be endurable if texture computing is done for every pixel. Since the pixels in backgrounds connect with each other, this connectivity can be used as an important cue to reduce the times of texture computing.

For a pixel i to be processed, the *nColorMask[i]* and *nTexureMask[i]* is used to indicate if it satisfies the color model and the texture model respectively. If *nColorMask[i]=1*, texture feature will be extracted for the pixel and inputted into the SVM classifier. If the classifier declares that the pixel is a background pixel, then *nTexureMask[i]* is set to 1. For every pixel j connecting with pixel i, directly or indirectly, if *nColorMask[j]=1*, *nTexureMask[j]* is also set to 1 and considered as a background pixel. In the ideal condition that all the pixels in background connect with each other, only one successful texture verification is needed.

The method has also solved the problem of the border in texture windows. We can't compute texture features of the pixels in the region of four borders in an image. If the frame size is not large enough compared with the window size, the problem is more serious. The SVM classifier may discard the pixels on the boundary of background since some of their neighborhoods are not background pixels. With the connectivity, all the pixels in the borders can be found.

4   Experimental Results

4.1   Experimental Results on Image Database

o validate the effectiveness of the background pixel model, we have done experiments on the images databases, Corel Image Lib, which includes natural scenes, buildings, human beings, animals and computer-generated textures. The numbers of train pixels of the three types of grass are 21025, 15417 and 9053 respectively. These pixels are from 50 images. Experiments show that modeling illumination in three typical conditions is efficient. Most grass pixels are detected correctly, no matter under strong light or in shadow. Some images are illustrated in Fig. 3, in which grass pixels are marked with white while non-grass pixels are marked with black. The distance used in the experiment is Euclidean distance and h,s,v are scaled into the range [0,360]. The parameters are $d=7$ and $\tau =0.1$, where d is the minimum distance between the pixel and the trained centers and τ is the proportion of background pixels.

(a) The original pictures

(b) Color masks of (a)

Fig. 3. Grass detected under varying illumination with color model

4.2   Experimental Results on Videos

In the experiments, video streams are MPEG-2 compressed. We process only I frames to speed up the calculation procedure. Key frames are extracted as described in section 2, where $\delta = 0.42$ and $T=1$. Here we select three video streams: Golf, Football and West. The two formers are sports games and the last one is about grasslands in the west of China.

The experimental results are given in Table 1. We can see that all the grass clips are in the key frames. Only one key frame with grass is declared as wrong non-grass because its color becomes yellow under too strong sun light. Two of the key frames without grass are declared to have grass because parts of them are green sweatshirt and green trees, which are similar with grass not only in color but also in texture.

Table 1. Experimental results on video.

Video ID	Fs	Ks	Gs	KGs	M	N
Golf	3053	15	11	11	10	4
Football	6162	46	31	31	31	14
West	2410	38	32	32	32	5

Note:
Fs: the number of the frames
Ks: the number of the key frames
Gs: the number of the clips with grass
KGs: the number of the key frames with grass
M: the number of the correctly detected clips with grass
N: the number of the correctly detected clips without grass

5 Summary and Discussion

In this paper, we propose a framework to detect the interesting background in video. Key frames are exploited to efficiently capture background change in video. Color cue and texture cue are used to detect the interesting background in the key frames. The color under varying illumination is modeled with the three sub-models: strong light, normal light and weak light. The connectivity of background pixels is used to reduce the texture computing cost.

The proposed method is suitable for the background that has one dominant color. If the background has more than one color, the per-pixel model is not appropriate any more. For a more complex texture, if it is periodically repeated, a standard tile can be computed automatically using [7], then the comparison can be done between standard tiles. Because backgrounds generally have no active motion, the motion of cameras is the main factor to affect the precision. If the motion of the camera is large and the visual content of frames changes much, it can be captured by key frames.

We hope that combining foreground and background cues will improve the performance of event detection in video.

References

1. http://www.ai.mit.edu/projects/cbcl/res-area/object-detection/object-detection-video.html
2. Javed O. and Shah M.: Tracking And Object Classification For Automated Surveillance. ECCV2002, Copenhagen, Danmark, (2002)
3. Cucchiara R., Grana C., Piccardi M., and Prati A.: Detecting Objects, Shadows and Ghosts in Video Streams By Exploiting Color and Motion Information. ICIAP01, Palermo, Italy, (2001) 360-365
4. Zhuang Y., Rui Y., Huang T. S. and Mehrotra S.: Adaptive key frame extraction using unsupervised clustering. ICIP'98, Chicago, IL, (1998)
5. Toklu C. and Liou S. P.: Automatic keyframe selection for content-based video indexing and access. Proc. of SPIE, vol. 3972, (2000) 554-563
6. Manjunath B. S. and Ma W. Y.: Texture features for browsing and retrieval of image data. IEEE Transactions on PAMI, 18(8), (1996) 837-842
7. Liu L. and Collins R. A computational model for repeated pattern perception using frieze and wallpaper groups. In IEEE Computer Vision and Pattern Recognition, (2000)

High Speed Road Boundary Detection with CNN-Based Dynamic Programming

Hyongsuk Kim, Seungwan Hong, Taewan Oh, and Junsu Lee

Division of Electronic and Information Engineering,
Chonbuk National Univ, Republic of Korea.
hskim@moak.chonbuk.ac.kr, hong0404@orgio.net,
{control,junsu0759}@mail.chonbuk.ac.kr

Abstract. Analogic CNN-based road boundary detection algorithm for fast and optimal driving of autonomous vehicle is proposed. The CNN is a massively connected analog parallel array processor. In the previous study, the dynamic programming which is an efficient algorithm to find the optimal path is implemented with the CNN algorithm [1]. Due to the parallelism of the CNN structure, the processing speed of the CNN-based dynamic programming is expected to be very fast. The proposed study is an extension of previous optimal path finding algorithm for high speed road-boundary detection. If the road-edge images are utilized as the space variant weights and if the goal and the start lines are positioned at the top and the bottom of the image, respectively, the optimal path finding concept can be exploited for the road boundary detection. The proposed road boundary algorithm is described and simulation results are included.

1 Introduction

Road boundary detection is one of the most important tasks in the autonomous vehicle technology. Due to its strong need of safety and fast driving speed, the autonomous vehicle requires the robust computation and the high speed processing. Many researchers have elaborated to enhance the robustness in finding the true road boundary using the model based approach [5][6][7][8]. However, it is not easy to obtain the precise geometrical road models [8]. To enhance the processing speed, the road boundary detection techniques rely mostly on the simplified algorithm [9][10] at the sacrifice of its robustness. The proposed road boundary detection algorithm involves the technique to achieve both of the robustness and fast processing using CNN-based dynamic programming approach.

Dynamic Programming (DP) [11] is an efficient solution for finding the optimal path which involves the combinatorial computation complexity. Since it is inherently the algorithm for the parallel processing in which each node in the computational array performs identical function, the CNN (Cellular Neural Networks) is an ideal hardware model to implement the DP with simple analog processing of locally connected cells [2][3]. Roska et al. developed its realistic engineering model called CNN-UM [4] and

Y.-C. Chen, L.-W. Chang, and C.-T. Hsu (Eds.): PCM 2002, LNCS 2532, pp. 806–813, 2002.
© Springer-Verlag Berlin Heidelberg 2002

Rodriguez et al. [12] implemented it into chips. Also, Kim et al. have shown that DP algorithm is able to be implemented with the nonlinear template of the CNN [1]. Knowing that the road boundary can be detected efficiently with DP and the processing can be speed-up with the parallel processing of CNN with nonlinear templates, the idea of the CNN implementation of DP for the high speed road boundary detection is formulated.

2 Principle of CNN

CNN is a massively parallel computational structure as in Fig. 1(a). In the CNN, a processing unit called cell is disposed at each node of 2-D grid. At each cell, there are 3 different sets of information sources: one from outputs of its neighboring cells through weighted connections called A template, the other from its and its neighbor's inputs through another set of weighted connections called B template, and another one from its own bias value z. In the CNN, each cell has same dynamic operation as in (1).

$$\frac{dx(i,j)}{dt} = -x(i,j) + \sum_{k,l} A(ij,kl) y_{kl} + \sum_{k,l} B(ij,kl) U(k,l) + z_{ij} \tag{1}$$

where $x(i,j)$ is the state of the cell (i,j). $A(ij,kl)$ and $B(ij,kl)$ are the templates(weights) between cell (i,j) and cell (k,l). Also, Z_{ij} is the bias value of cell (i,j).

The output of the cell (i,j), $y(i,j)$ is

$$y(i,j) = f(x(i,j)) \tag{2}$$

where f is a nonlinear output function defined as in Fig. 1(b).

Since every CNN cell has same weighted connections and dynamic mechanism, every cell is doing same behavior as long as input and sate value are the same. However, if different template sets are employed, different processing results are obtained even though same input or initial state values are given. Abundant set of templates for different type of image processing have already been developed [6].

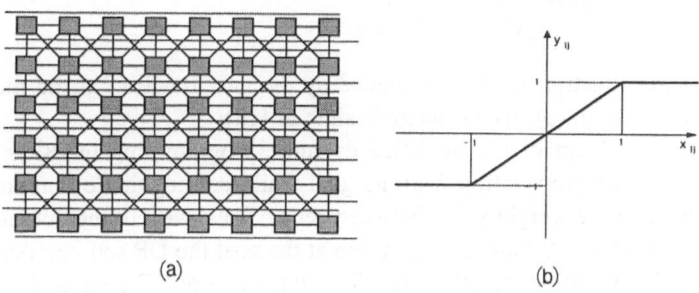

(a)   (b)

Fig. 1. Cellular Neural Networks(CNN). (a) Cell disposition of the CNN. (b) Nonlinear output function of a CNN cell.

3   Implementation of the DP with CNN Nonlinear Templates

The Dynamic Programming(DP) is a global optimization algorithm to compute the optimal path through taking the locally minimum operation at each node.

Let $D(i,j)$ and $D(k,l)$ be the shortest distance to the goal from the current node (i,j) and from its neighboring node (k,l), respectively. Then, $D(i,j)$ is

$$D(i, j) = \min\left\{ d_{ij,kl} + D(k,l) , (k,l) \in R(i, j)\right\} \qquad (3)$$

where $d_{ij,kl}$ is the shortest distance between the node (i,j) and (k,l), and $R(i,j)$ is the set of neighboring nodes of (i,j). If an arithmetic cell is arranged to compute (3) at each node, the processing of (3) is confined to the local operation of *min* and *summation*. Since the *min* circuits is known to be more complicated than *max* circuits for the practical implementation [14]. Some arrangement of (3) to employ *max* operation instead of *min* is necessary.

Let's $y(i,j)$ be the complement value of $D(i,j)$ from a dummy constant I_{max} for the cell at (i,j) as

$$y(i,j) = I_{max} - D(i,j) \qquad (4)$$

Plugging $D(i, j)$ of (4) into (3) and rearranging its result,

$$y(i, j) = \max \left\{ y(k,l) - d_{ij,kl} ; (k,l) \in R(i, j)\right\} \qquad (5)$$

Since the I_{max} given at the goal should be bigger than any other values coming from its neighbor cells, (5) becomes

$$y(i, j) = \max\left\{ u(i, j) , (y(k,l) - d_{ij,kl}, (k,l) \in R(i, j))\right\} \qquad (6)$$

where $u(i,j)$ is provided as the input of the node (i,j) defined as in (7).

$$u(i,j) = \begin{cases} I_{max} & ; if \ (i,j) \ is \ a \ goal \ position \\ 0 & ; otherwise \end{cases} \qquad (7)$$

Since the *min* function in (3) is replaced by the *max* function in the modified dynamic programming in (8), Its hardware is simpler [14].

The physical concept of the modified dynamic programming in (8) is associated with the information propagation from its goal while its magnitude is reduced by the amount of the distance weight value between cells. Thus, we call the output of the cell the Distance Potential (DP) and the I_{max} given at the goal the DP source. Also, the area with non-zero DP is called the DP field. Thus, the value of DP source (I_{max}) should be as big as possible to maintain the meaningful distance information (non-zero) at the long distance cell.

The nonlinear function of the *max* and the linear function of subtraction are involved in operation(6). Therefore, it is not easy to be directly implemented with CNN template since high nonlinear functions are involved. The proposed strategy to implement the functions (6) with CNN is associated with the decomposition of it into several simple functions. Arranging them to be processed by cells at different layer, the computing outcome of a cell can be shared by other cells, which allows the network structure to be compact. Adding y_{ij} to both side of (6), (6) becomes

$$2y_{ij} = \max\left\{ y_{ij} + y_{kl} - d_{ij,kl} \ , \ (k,l) \in R(i,j) \right\} \tag{8}$$

or

$$y_{ij} = \max\left\{ \frac{y_{ij} + y_{kl} - d_{ij,kl}}{2} \ , \ (k,l) \in R(i,j) \right\} \tag{9}$$

Let the *max* in (6) be processed by a cell on a layer called Distance Computation layer and the terms inside of the parenthesis be processed by a cell on the other layer called Intermediate layer. Then,

$$y_{DC}(i,j) = \max\left\{ y_I(i,j) \right\} \tag{10}$$

and

$$y_I(i,j) = \frac{1}{2}(y_{DC}(i,j) + y_{DC}(k,l)) - \frac{d_{ij,kl}}{2} \tag{11}$$

where $y_I(ij)$ and $y_{DC}(ij)$ are the output of the cell (i,j) in the I layer and DC layer, respectively. The structure to find the optimal path through such processing is as in Figure 2. The cells of I layer are placed at the locations corresponding to the links between the nodes and the metric information is provided externally to its input. The cells in DC and PF layer have connections only with their adjacent cells in I layer.

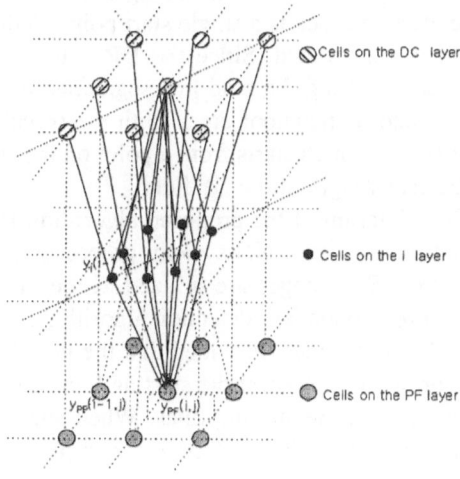

Fig. 2. Connections of a cell in the proposed multi-layer CNN structure.

Thus, the *max* computation in (10) can be performed with the interaction between the cells in DC layer and I layer.

Path decision criterion can also be more simplified utilizing the cells in the I layer as

$$y_I(i, j) = y_{DC}(i, j) \tag{12}$$

The average operation and the subtraction in (11) can easily be performed with the linear template [13]. The nonlinear operation of *max* in (10) and comparison in (12) can be implemented with nonlinear templates in [1].

4   Road Boundary Detection with CNN-Based Dynamic Programming

With the CNN on which the DP is implemented, the optimal path on the space variant weight space can be found through the parallel processing. The principle under this algorithm is the determination of the most likely boundary lines to reach the goal. Though there are usually many noisy line segments on the road edge image, human vision system determines the most likely lines for the road boundary through the integration of various clues (line segments). Same function as the optimality of human vision system is implemented on CNN. Utilizing the globally optimal path finding capability of the CNN-based DP, the optimal road boundary lines are determined.

To find the optimal road line on the image as in Fig. 3(a), some arrangement is needed as following. Let the goal point and the start point in optimal path finding in [1] be extended to a line as shown at upper part of the image and two shorter ones at the bottom in Fig. 3(b). If equally high DP source values are assigned to all goal points, all the points on the goal line act as a single goal point. Also, the connected multiple points on the start lines act as a single start point. With the given DP value at the goal, the DP field is constructed. Since the DP value is arranged to propagate without significant reduction along the road line segments, the DP field remains high along the line segments and its neighbor area. With the principle of the optimal path finding, the optimal road line which starts from a point on the start line heads to the direction of the most highest strength of the DP field.

Fig. 4 shows the flow diagram of the proposed algorithm. If the road image is presented on the proposed multiplayer CNN system, preprocessing of edge extraction is performed at the first step. Such edges are utilized as the distance weights (distance metric) for the proposed road boundary detection algorithm. The next step is the presentation of the goal and starting lines. Provided that the goal line is given at the CNN input, the DP field is constructed. Also, if the starting lines are given, the optimal road boundary lines are grows from the starting lines. When such the optimal lines reach the goal line, the optimal road-boundary detection is completed.

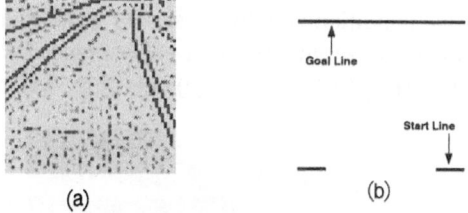

(a)   (b)

Fig. 3. (a) An example of the road edge image (b) and goal/ start lines

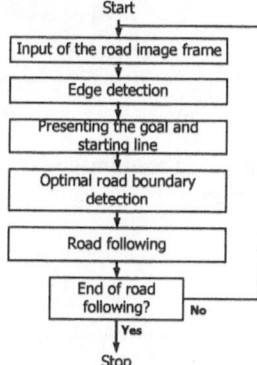

Fig. 4. Flow diagram of the proposed algorithm

5 Simulations

Simulations of the road boundary detection has been done about the several different conditions of road images including the paved, the unpaved, and the snowy road. The image size used for the simulation is 59x59. The edge images are provided as the input of the I layer for the simulation. The goal and the start lines are also provided at inputs on the DC layer and the PF layer of the multiplayer CNN, respectively.

The first road image frame for the simulation is the one of the paved road as in Fig. 5(a). After running edge detection template [13] on the CNN road image, the edge lines are detected as in Fig. 5(b), where many noisy edge segments as well as the true edge lines appear. This is the typical edge image of the normal road image. Presenting the edge image as the distance weight of the CNN, and providing goal and starting lines as in Fig. 3(b), the DP field is propagated and constructed as in Fig. 5(c). The Fig. 5(d) shows the optimal road boundary obtained with the proposed algorithm. The light weighted lines at the lower part of the road boundary is to be ignored since the boundary line below the contacting point to image boundary is meaningless.

The same simulation has been done on the unpaved road with tire trace as in Fig. 6. On the edge image, edges of the tire trace, tree shadows and many noises as well as true road boundary lines appear. Extracting only the true road boundary lines among such messy line segments is difficult. The DP field propagated from the goal line is shown in Fig. 6(c) and the true road boundary lines obtained is as in Fig. 6(d).

One quite different road condition is with the snowy weather as shown in Fig.7(a). With the same simulation as above, the resultant edge image, DP field and the determined road boundary lines are as in Fig. 7(b), 7(c), and Fig. 7(d), respectively.

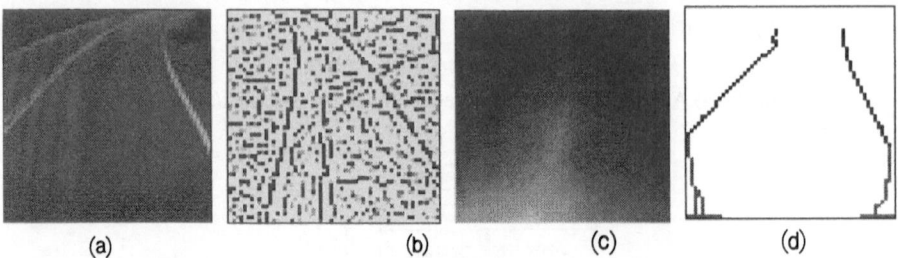

(a)   (b)   (c)   (d)

Fig. 5. Road boundary detection on the paved road image (a) paved road image (b)edge image (c) DP field (d) determined road boundaries

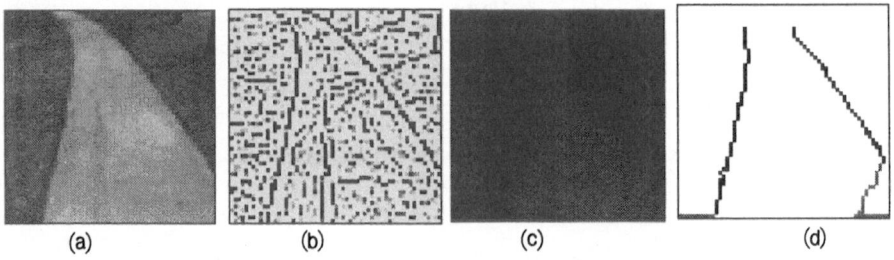

(a)   (b)   (c)   (d)

Fig. 6. Road boundary detection on the unpaved road image (a) unpaved road image (b)edge image (c) DP field (d) determined road boundaries.

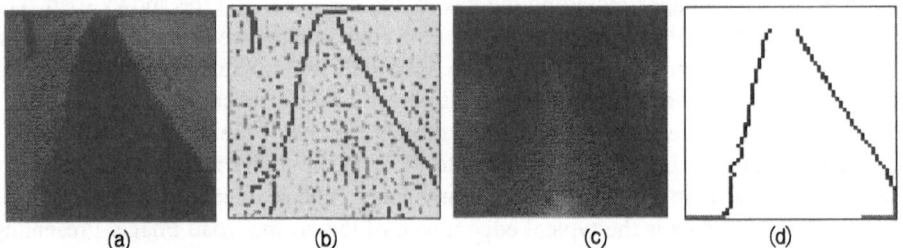

(a)   (b)   (c)   (d)

Fig. 7. Road boundary detection on the snowy road image (a) snowy road (b)edge image (c) DP field (d) determined road boundaries.

6   Conclusion

Fast processing and robust detection of road boundary are very important tasks in the autonomous vehicle technology. The proposed road boundary detection algorithm suggests a solution to resolve the technical bottleneck of the autonomous vehicle by combing the high speed parallel processing of the CNN and the optimal path finding capability of the dynamic programming. The proposed idea is an application of the previous study [1] to the optimal road boundary detection via some special arrangement with the goal and start lines.

Simulation results show that the proposed algorithm is able to detect reasonable road boundaries about all the tested images including the paved, unpaved, and snowy road by exploiting the clues on the road maximally.

Though the proposed algorithm with non-linear templates of CNN is tested on the software simulator, the successful implementation of the linear CNN chips gives a light for the implementation of the nonlinear CNN.

References

1. Kim, H., Son, H., Roska, T.,Chua, L.O.: Optimal path finding with space- and time-variant metric weights with Multi-layer CNN. International Journal of Circuit Theory and Applications, vol. 30, pp.247-270, 2002, 2.
2. Chua, L.O. and Yang, L.: Cellular neural networks: theory. IEEE Tr. on Circuits Systems, vol.35, pp. 1257-1272, 1988.
3. Chua, L.O. and Yang, L.: Cellular neural networks: applications. IEEE Tr. on Circuits Systems, vol. 35, pp. 1273-1290, 1988.
4. Roska, T. and Chua, L.O.: The CNN universal machine: an analogic array computer. IEEE Tr. on Circuits Systems II, CAS-40, pp. 163-173, 1988.
5. Crisman, J.D. and Thorpe, C.E.: SCARF: A color vision system that tracks roads and intersection. IEEE Trans. Robotics and Automation, vol. 9, pp. 49-58, 1993.
6. Kluge, K.C.: Extracting road curvature and orientation from image edge points without perceptual grouping into features. Proceedings of the Intelligent Vehicles Symposium, pp. 109-114, 1994.
7. Pomerleau, D. and Jochem, T.: Rapidly Adapting Machine Vision for Automated Vehicle Steering. IEEE Expert, vol, 11, No. 2, pp. 19-27, 1996.
8. Tsao, J., Hall, R.W. and Shladover, S.E.: Design options for operating automated highway systems. Proceedings of the IEEE-IEE Vehicle Navigation and Information Systems Conference, pp. 494-500, 1993.
9. Broggi, A.: Robust real-time lane and road detection in critical shadow conditions," Proceedings of International Symposium on Computer Vision, pp. 353 –358, 1995.
10. Jeong, S., Kim, C., Lee, D., Ha, S., Lee, D., Lee, M. and Hideki Hashimoto.: Real-time lane detection for autonomous vehicle. Proceedings of IEEE International Symposium on Industrial Electronics, vol 3, pp. 1466 –1471, 2001.
11. Bellman, R.: Dynamic Programming, Princeton, NJ: Princeton Univ. Press, 1957.
12. Espejo, S., Domínguez-Castro, R., Liñán, G. and Rodríguez-Vázquez, A.: A 64x64 CNN universal chip with analog and digital I/O. Proc. 5th Int. Conf. on Electronics, Circuits and Systems (ICECS-98), Lisbon, Portugal, pp. 203-206 1998.
13. Analogical and Neural Computing Lab, SimCNN-Multi-layer CNN Simulator for Visual Mouse Platform:Reference Manual version 2.2. Computer and Automation Institute (MTA SzTAKI) of the Hungarian Academy of Sciences, 1998.
14. Soumyanath, K. and Borkar, V.S.:An analog scheme for fixed-point computation-part II: application. IEEE Trans. on Circuits and Systems-I: Fundamental Theory and Applications, vol.46, no. 4, pp. 442-451, 1999.

A New Error Resilient Coding Scheme for H.263 Video Transmission*

Li-Wei Kang and Jin-Jang Leou**

Department of Computer Science and Information Engineering,
National Chung Cheng University,
Chiayi, Taiwan 621, Republic of China
{lwkang, jjleou}@cs.ccu.edu.tw

Abstract. For entropy-coded H.263 video frames, a transmission error in a codeword will not only affect the underlying codeword but also may affect subsequent codewords, resulting in a great degradation of the received video frames. In this study, a new error resilient coding scheme for H.263 video transmission is proposed. At the encoder, for an I frame, the important data of each macroblock are extracted and embedded into another macroblock within the I frame by the proposed odd-even data embedding scheme for I frames. For a P frame, a rate-distortion optimized coding mode selection approach is employed. The important data for each GOB (group of blocks) are extracted and embedded into the next frame by using the proposed macroblock-interleaving GOB-based data embedding scheme. At the decoder, after all the corrupted macroblocks within a video frame are detected and located, if the important data of a corrupted macroblock can be extracted correctly, the extracted important data will facilitate the employed error concealment scheme to conceal the corrupted macroblock; otherwise, the employed error concealment scheme is simply used to conceal the corrupted macroblock. Based on the simulation results, the proposed scheme can recover high-quality H.263 video frames from the corresponding corrupted video frames up to video packet loss rate = 30%.

1 Introduction

For entropy-coded H.263 video frames [1]-[2], a transmission error in a codeword will not only affect the underlying codeword but also may affect subsequent codewords, resulting in a great degradation of the received video frames. To cope with the synchronization problem, each of the two top layers of the H.263 hierarchical structure, namely, picture and group of blocks (GOB), is ahead with a fixed-length start code. After the decoder receives any start code, the decoder will be resynchronized regardless of the preceding slippage. Although the propagation effect of a transmission error can be terminated when any start code is correctly received, a transmission error may affect the underlying codeword and its subsequent codewords within the corrupted GOB. Moreover, because of the use of motion-compensated interframe coding, the effect of a transmission error may be propagated to the subsequent video frames.

---

*   This work was supported in part by National Science Council, Republic of China under Grants NSC 90-2213-E-194-044 and NSC 90-2213-E-194-039.
** Author to whom all correspondence should be addressed.

Y.-C. Chen, L.-W. Chang, and C.-T. Hsu (Eds.): PCM 2002, LNCS 2532, pp. 814-822, 2002.

In general, error resilient approaches include three categories [3], namely: (1) the error resilient encoding approach [4]-[5], (2) the error concealment approach [6]-[9], and (3) the encoder-decoder interactive error control approach [10]. The foregoing error resilient approaches [3]-[10] concentrate on limiting error propagation and using the correctly received information to estimate corrupted video data. If the information of neighboring blocks are not available or the video contents between a corrupted block and its neighboring blocks are very different, the concealed results of the foregoing error resilient approaches are not good enough. Recently, several error resilient coding approaches based on data embedding are proposed [11]-[13], in which some important data useful for error concealment at the decoder can be embedded into video frames, when they are encoded at the encoder. At the decoder, the embedded data for the corrupted blocks are extracted and used to facilitate error concealment performed at the decoder. Yin, Liu, and Yu [11] embedded the block type and edge direction index of a block within an image into the DCT coefficients of another block of the image by using the odd-even embedding scheme. Song and Liu [12] proposed a data embedding scheme for error-prone channels, in which some redundant information for protecting motion vectors and coding modes of macroblocks in one frame is embedded into the motion vectors in the next frame. However, if either the next frame of a corrupted frame is also corrupted or the total number of corrupted GOBs in a corrupted frame is larger than 2, the performance of the system will degenerate greatly. In this study, a new error resilient coding scheme for H.263 video transmission is proposed.

This paper is organized as follows. Error concealment for H.263 video transmission is given in Section 2. The proposed error resilient coding scheme for H.263 video transmission is addressed in Section 3. Simulation results are included in Section 4, followed by concluding remarks.

2 Error Concealment for H.263 Video Transmission

In this study, both the best neighborhood matching (BNM) algorithm [6] and the spatial error concealment algorithm in TML-9 [7] are employed together to conceal H.263 intra-coded I frames. In the BNM algorithm, each corrupted block of size $N \times N$ is extracted from the video frame together with its neighborhood as a range block of size $(N + m) \times (N + m)$. Within a range block, all the pixels in the corrupted region belong to the lost part, and the others belong to the good part. After a range block is extracted, an $H \times L$ searching range block centralized with the range block within the video frame is generated. Each $(N + m) \times (N + m)$ block in the searching range block with no lost pixels may be a candidate domain block for recovery of the lost part of the range block, i.e., the corrupted block. For each candidate domain block, the mean square error (MSE) between the good part of the range block and the corresponding good part of the candidate domain block is evaluated. The candidate domain block with the minimum MSE will be determined as the best domain block, which is used to conceal the lost part of the range block by copying its corresponding central part to the lost part of the range block. On the other hand, for the spatial error concealment algorithm in TML-9 [7], each pixel value in a corrupted macroblock is formed as a weighted sum of the closest boundary pixels of the selected four-connected neighboring macroblocks.

Here, a corrupted macroblock within an H.263 I frame will be concealed by the spatial error concealment algorithm in TML-9 if (1) the immediately bottom macroblock of the current corrupted macroblock is correctly received, and (2) $|m_T - m_B| > Q \times \sigma_T$ and $|m_T - m_B| > Q \times \sigma_B$, where m_T, m_B, σ_T, and σ_B are the means and the standard deviations of the pixel values in the top and bottom macroblocks, respectively, of the corrupted macroblock and Q is a prespecified constant. If any of the two conditions is not satisfied, the corrupted macroblock within an H.263 I frame will be concealed by using the BNM algorithm.

On the other hand, the BNM algorithm [6] is originally developed for still images and in this study, the "motion-compensated" BNM algorithm proposed in [9] is used to conceal corrupted macroblocks in each H.263 P frame.

3 Proposed Error Resilient Scheme for H.263 Video Transmission

3.1 Error Resilient Coding for H.263 I Frames

Because the human eyes are more sensitive to the luminance component than the chrominance component, in this study, the four quantized DC values for the Y component of each macroblock in an H.263 I frame are extracted as important data, which are identically quantized by a quantization parameter Q_{DC}. Q_{DC} is set to 64 and 5 bits are required to represent each DC value, i.e., 20 bits are required to represent the four corresponding DC values.

Here, the extracted important data for a macroblock within an H.263 I frame will be embedded into the DCT coefficients of another macroblock, called the masking macroblock, in the same I frame. A macroblock and its masking macroblock should be as far as possible so that both the two corresponding macroblocks will be seldom corrupted at the same time. Here, a macroblock and its masking macroblock should not be in the same GOB and the masking macroblocks of the macroblocks of a GOB should not be in the same GOB. For a macroblock, $MB(i, j)$, $0 \leq i \leq 10$, $0 \leq j \leq 8$, in an H.263 QCIF I frame, its masking macroblock $MB(p,q)$ within the same I frame is determined as:

$$
(p,q) = \begin{cases} (i,(i+j+2) \bmod 9) & \text{if } 0 \leq i \leq 5, \\ (i,(i+j-4) \bmod 9) & \text{if } 6 \leq i \leq 10. \end{cases} \tag{1}
$$

To perform data embedding in H.263 I frames, the odd-even embedding scheme [11] operates on the quantized DCT coefficients. If the data bit to be embedded is "0," the selected quantized DCT coefficient will be forced to be an even number. If the data bit to be embedded is "1," the selected quantized DCT coefficient will be forced to be an odd number. Additionally, only the quantized DCT coefficients larger than a prespecified threshold, T_I, are used to embed data bits. If the data bit to be embedded is b_j, and the selected quantized DCT coefficient is C_i, the odd-even data embedding scheme operates as:

$$C_i = \begin{cases} C_i +1 & \text{if } |C_i| > T_l,\ C_i \bmod 2 \neq b_j,\ \text{and } C_i > 0, \\ C_i -1 & \text{if } |C_i| > T_l,\ C_i \bmod 2 \neq b_j,\ \text{and } C_i < 0, \\ C_i & \text{otherwise.} \end{cases} \quad (2)$$

Note that for a macroblock within an H.263 I frame, if the extracted important data of its macroblock cannot be embedded completely into its masking macroblock, the "remaining" important data of the macroblock can be embedded into the corresponding macroblock in the next frame, with the threshold T_l being replaced by another threshold T_P.

At the decoder, for each corrupted macroblock within an H.263 I frame, its masking macroblock is determined accordingly. If the masking macroblock is correctly received, the embedded data for the corrupted macroblock can be extracted. Then, each corrupted macroblock is firstly concealed by the employed error concealment scheme. The Y component of the firstly "concealed" macroblock is transformed to four sets of DCT coefficients by the 8×8 discrete cosine transform (DCT), and the four firstly "concealed" DC values are replaced by the four corresponding extracted DC values from the corresponding masking macroblock. The resulted four sets of DCT coefficients are transformed back to pixels by the 8×8 inverse DCT to obtain the secondly-concealed macroblock. The resulted secondly concealed macroblocks are processed by a blocking artifact reduction scheme proposed in [14]. Note that if the masking macroblock of a corrupted macroblock is also corrupted, the corrupted macroblock is concealed only by the employed error concealment scheme.

3.2 Error Resilient Coding for H.263 P Frames

For H.263 inter-coded P frames, similar to [4], a rate-distortion (RD) optimized macroblock coding mode selection approach is employed, which takes into account the network condition, including the video packet loss rate, the quantization parameter used in the encoder, the error concealment scheme used at the decoder, and the data embedding scheme used in the encoder. The Lagrangian function for macroblock encoding mode selection is given by:

$$J = (1 - p)D_{qw} + pD_c + \lambda R, \quad (3)$$

where p denotes the probability of corruption of a macroblock, D_{qw} denotes the distortion induced by quantization and data embedding, D_c denotes the distortion induced by transmission errors and error concealment for a P frame, R denotes the bit rate used to encode the macroblock, $\lambda = 0.85 \times (Q/2)^2$, and Q denotes the quantization step size used for the macroblock, which has been shown to provide good RD tradeoffs [4]. Here the mode (intra, inter, or skip) minimizing Eq. (3) is selected. Additionally, a maximum intra-coded refresh period, T_{max}, is imposed [5]. Inserting intra-coded macroblocks with a maximum refresh period can not only limit the temporal error propagation, but also provide a larger capacity (larger DCT coefficients) for embedding important data. In this study, the error rate of the network is defined as the video packet loss rate and a video packet is equivalently one complete GOB [4]. Hence, the probability of corruption of a macroblock used in Eq. (3) is equivalently the video packet loss rate.

For H.263 inter-coded P frames, two bits are used to represent the coding mode of a macroblock. Because the motion vector for each macroblock includes two components, i.e., MV_x and MV_y, if the search range for motion vectors is ±15 with half-pixel accuracy, six bits are needed for each motion vector component. Hence, the important data for each macroblock in a P frame will range from two to at most fourteen bits, depending on the mode of the macroblock is intra-coded, inter-coded, or skipped. To reduce the size of the important data required to be embedded, based on the experimental results obtained in this study, for an inter-coded macroblock, if either (1) both components of the motion vector are identically zero, or (2) the MSE (mean square error) between the concealed macroblocks using the actual motion vector and the estimated motion vector is smaller than a threshold T_M, the motion vector of the inter-coded macroblock should not be embedded in its masking macroblock. Here the odd-even data embedding scheme is employed, in which the thresholds for intra-coded and inter-coded macroblocks are T'_I and T_P, respectively. The important data extracted from the current P frame will be embedded into the next frame.

Because the smallest synchronization unit in H.263 video frames is a GOB, by adopting the even-odd block-interleaving technique proposed in [15], a macroblock-interleaving GOB-based data embedding scheme is proposed for H.263 P frames, which is described as follows.

Assume that two non-adjacent GOBs in frame k are denoted by GOB A and GOB B, respectively. The important data for the two GOBs are extracted. The data extracted from the even-number macroblocks of GOB A and the data extracted from the odd-number macroblocks of GOB B are interleaved by the even-odd order and concatenated to a mixed bitstream and then the bitstream is embedded into its masking GOB in the next frame (frame $k + 1$) by using the odd-even data embedding scheme. On the other hand, the data extracted from the odd-number macroblocks of GOB A and the data extracted from the even-number macroblocks of GOB B are also interleaved by the even-odd order and concatenated to another bitstream, and the bitstream is embedded into another masking GOB in the next frame. The distance between two masking GOBs in the next frame of the two interleaved GOBs (GOB A and GOB B) in the current frame should be as far as possible so that two or more successive corrupted video packets in the next frame will not induce two corrupted masking GOBs in the next frame.

At the decoder, for each corrupted macroblock in a corrupted GOB, its corresponding pair of masking GOBs are found first, and the important data of the corrupted macroblock is extracted from the corresponding pair of masking GOBs if the pair of masking GOBs is correctly received. Then

(1) if the coding mode of the corrupted macroblock is "*skip*," the macroblock is concealed by copying the corresponding macroblock in the previous reconstructed frame;

(2) if the coding mode of the corrupted macroblock is "*inter*" and its motion vector information is recovered completely from the corresponding pair of masking

GOBs, the macroblock is concealed by copying the motion compensated macroblock in the previous reconstructed frame;

(3)   if the coding mode of the corrupted macroblock is *"inter"* and its motion vector (i) is not embedded, (ii) can not be embedded completely at the encoder, or (iii) cannot be recovered completely, the macroblock is concealed by using the employed error concealment scheme for H.263 P frames; and

(4)   if the coding mode of the corrupted macroblock is *"intra,"* the employed error concealment scheme for H.263 P frames is also employed.

Traditionally, the order of concealing consecutive corrupted macroblocks is in a raster scan manner. If all the eight neighboring macroblocks of a corrupted macroblock are received correctly or well-concealed, the concealed results of the corrupted macroblock will be better. Thus, before concealing a corrupted macroblock, its 8-connected neighboring macroblocks will be checked first. If some of its 8-connected neighboring macroblocks of the corrupted macroblock are also corrupted, and these corrupted neighboring macroblocks can be concealed only with important embedded data extracted from its masking macroblock(s), these corrupted neighboring macroblocks will be concealed first. Finally, the corrupted macroblock can be concealed by using the employed error concealment scheme for H.263 P frames with more neighboring macroblock information.

In this study, for a corrupted GOB, if only one of its masking GOB is corrupted, the even (or odd) macroblocks of the corrupted GOB can be concealed using the important data extracted from the "good" masking GOB first. Then the odd (or even) macroblocks can be concealed by the employed error concealment scheme with more neighboring macroblock information. Because the corresponding two masking GOBs are seldom corrupted simultaneously, the concealed results of the proposed macroblock-interleaving GOB-based data embedding scheme will be better than that of the conventional approaches.

4   Simulation Results

Four QCIF test video sequences *"Carphone," "Coastguard," "Foreman,"* and *"Salesman"* with different video packet loss rates, denoted by *VPLR*, are used to evaluate the performance of the proposed scheme (denoted by proposed). Here a video packet is equivalently one complete GOB [4]. All video sequences are coded at frame rate 10 frames/second (fps) with bit rates 48kbps and 64kbps using the H.263 test model TMN-11 rate control method [2] and the peak signal to noise ratio (PSNR) is employed in this study as the objective performance measure. In this study, the constants Q in Eq. (1) and T_I in Eq. (3) are set to 0.4 and 55, respectively. In the BNM algorithm and the employed error concealment scheme for H.263 P frames, N, m, H, and L are set to 16, 2, 30, and 30, respectively, for the Y component, and 8, 2, 15, and 15, respectively, for the C_B and C_R components. In the employed macroblock coding mode selection scheme, T_{max} is set to 10 and in the proposed data embedding scheme for H.263 P frames, T'_I, T_P, and T_M are set to 15, 1, and 10, respectively.

To evaluate the performance of the proposed scheme, six existing error resilient coding and error concealment approaches for comparison [2], [7]-[8], [12] are implemented in this study. They are: (1) zero-substitution, which simply replaces all pixels in a corrupted macroblock by zeros (denoted by Zero-S); (2) the zero motion vector technique, which copies the corresponding macroblock in the previous reconstructed frame (denoted by Zero-MV); (3) the error concealment method described in the H.263 test model TMN-11 (denoted by TMN-11) [2]; (4) concealment by selection, in which a neighbor matching criterion is employed to select a motion vector from a set of motion vector candidates to conceal a corrupted macroblock (denoted by Selection)

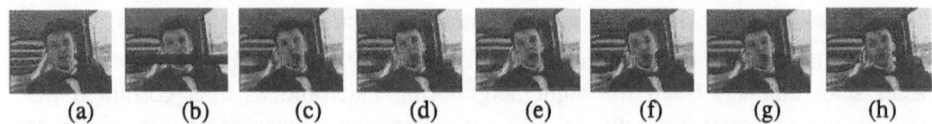

(a)   (b)   (c)   (d)   (e)   (f)   (g)   (h)

Fig. 1. The error-free and concealed H.263 video frames (the Y component) of an I-frame (the first frame) within the "*Carphone*" sequence at frame rate 10 fps with the video packet loss rate = 10% and bit rate = 48kbps: (a) the error-free frame; (b)-(h) the concealed frames by Zero-S, Zero-MV, TMN-11, Selection, IBR, DEVCS, and the proposed scheme, respectively.

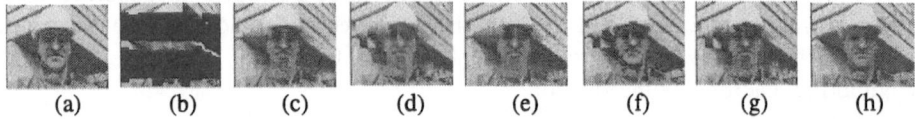

(a)   (b)   (c)   (d)   (e)   (f)   (g)   (h)

Fig. 2. The error-free and concealed H.263 video frames (the Y component) of a P-frame (the fourteenth frame) within the "*Foreman*" sequence at frame rate = 10 fps with the video packet loss rate = 30% and bit rate = 48kbps: (a) the error-free frame; (b)-(h) the concealed frames by Zero-S, Zero-MV, TMN-11, Selection, IBR, DEVCS, and the proposed, respectively.

[8]; (5) the intra block refresh technique in the encoder supported by TMN-11, in which an intra refresh rate is set to 10, and the error concealment method described in TMN-11 is used (denoted by IBR) [2]. (6) the data embedded video coding scheme in [12] (denoted by DEVCS). For simplicity, the error concealment method for I frames supported by TML-9 [7] is employed in the approaches (2)-(6) for comparison.

In terms of the average PSNR of a video sequence, denoted by $PSNR_{seq}$ in dB, the simulation results for the "*Foreman*" sequence with different video packet loss rates of the six existing approaches for comparison and the proposed scheme (denoted by proposed) are listed in Table 1. As a subjective measure of the quality of the concealed video frames, the error-free and concealed frames (the Y component) by the six existing approaches for comparison and the proposed schemes are shown in Figs. 1-2. Note that the average degradation of the proposed scheme with data embedding (compared with the original H.263 algorithm) is about 0.5 dB, which is comparable with that in [12].

Table 1. The simulation results, $PSNR_{seq}$ (dB), for the "*Foreman*" sequence at frame rate = 10fps with bit rate = 48kbps, and different video packet loss rates of the six existing error resilient coding and error concealment approaches for comparison and the proposed scheme.

VPLR	Without data embedding						With data embedding	
	Zero-S	Zero-MV	TMN-11	Selection	IBR	DEVCS	Only employed error concealment	Proposed
0%	28.32	28.32	28.32	28.32	28.13	27.35	27.91	27.91
10%	6.88	23.39	23.42	23.55	25.80	23.46	25.28	26.27
20%	5.20	21.56	21.58	22.46	24.25	21.56	24.19	26.02
30%	5.03	20.98	21.02	21.13	23.70	21.01	23.66	25.23

5 Concluding Remarks

Based on the simulation results obtained in this study, several observations can be found. (1) Based on the simulation results shown in Table 1 and Figs. 1-2, the concealment results of the proposed scheme are better than that of the six existing approaches for comparison. (2) Based on the simulation results shown in Table 1, the relative performance gains of the proposed scheme over the existing approaches for comparison increase as the video packet loss rate is increased, i.e., the performance of the proposed scheme is "slightly" better than that of the six existing approaches for comparison when video packet loss rate is relatively low, whereas the performance of the proposed scheme is "much" better than that of the six existing approaches for comparison when video packet loss rate is relatively high.

Compared with the six existing approaches for comparison, the proposed scheme is more robust for noisy channels with burst video packet loss. That is because for low video packet loss rate cases, burst video packet loss will seldom occur and the important data, such as the motion vector of each corrupted macroblock, can be well estimated. On the other hand, for high video packet loss rate cases, burst video packet loss will frequently occur, and the important data cannot be estimated accurately. Within the proposed scheme using the macroblock-interleaving GOB-based data embedding technique, the important data are usually available. Additionally, using macroblock-interleaving, on the average, each corrupted macroblock will have more neighboring information, resulting in better concealed video frames. The proposed scheme is simple, very efficient, and can be easily adopted in various network environments and applicable to many other block-based video compression standards, such as MPEG-2, with some necessary modification.

References

1. ITU-T. Recommendation H.263: Video coding for low bit rate communication (1998)
2. ITU-T/SG16 Video Coding Experts Group, "Video codec test model near-term, version 11 (TMN11)," Document Q15-G16 (1999)

3. Wang, Y., Wenger, S., Wen, J., Katsaggelos, A. K.: Error resilient video coding techniques. IEEE Signal Processing Magazine. **17**(4) (2000) 61-82
4. Cote, G., Kossentini, F.: Optimal intra coding of blocks for robust video communication over the Internet. Signal Processing: Image Communication. **15**(1999) 25-34
5. Frossard, P., Verscheure, O.: AMISP: A complete content-based MPEG-2 error-resilient scheme. IEEE Trans. on Circuits and Systems for Video Technology. **11**(9) (2001) 989-998
6. Wang, Z., Yu, Y., Zhang, D.: Best neighborhood matching: an information loss restoration technique for block-based image coding systems. IEEE Trans. on Image Processing. **7**(7) (1998) 1056-1061
7. ITU VCEG, H.26L Test Model Long-Term Number 9 (TML-9) draft 0 (2001)
8. Valente, S., Dufour, C., Groliere, F., Snook, D.: An efficient error concealment implementation for MPEG-4 video streams. IEEE Trans. on Consumer Electronics. **47**(3) (2001) 568-578
9. Kang, L. W., Leou, J. J.: A new hybrid error concealment scheme for MPEG-2 video transmission. (submitted for publication)
10. Girod, B., Farber, N.: Feedback-based error control for mobile video transmission. Proceedings of the IEEE. **87**(10) (1999) 1707-1723
11. Yin, P., Liu, B., Yu, H. H.: Error concealment using data hiding. Proc. of IEEE Int. Conf. on Acoustics, Speech, and Signal Processing. **3**(2001) 1453-1456
12. Song, J., Liu, K. J. R.: A data embedded video coding scheme for error-prone channels. IEEE Trans. on Multimedia. **3**(4) (2001) 415-423
13. Bartolini, F., Manetti, A., Piva, A., Barni, M.: A data hiding approach for correcting errors in H.263 video transmitted over a noisy channel. Proc. of IEEE Fourth Int. Workshop on Multimedia Signal Processing. Florence, Italy (2001) 65-70
14. Chuah, C. S., Leou, J. J.: An adaptive image interpolation algorithm for image/video processing. Pattern Recognition. **34**(12) (2001) 2383-2393
15. Zhu, Q. F., Wang, Y., Shaw, L.: Coding and cell-loss recovery in DCT-based packet video. IEEE Trans. on Circuits and Systems for Video Technology **3**(3) (1993) 248-258

A Bit-Plane Coding Scheme of MPEG-4 FGS with High Efficiency Based on the Distribution of Significant Coefficients

Kenji Matsuo, Koichi Takagi, Atsushi Koike, and Syuichi Matsumoto

KDDI R&D Laboratories Inc.
2-1-15 Ohara Kamifukuoka Saitama 356-8502 JAPAN
matsuo@kddilabs.jp

Abstract. MPEG-4 FGS video coding can perform video transmission with adaptation to channel bandwidth variation on the network. However, binary zero-run-length coding used by FGS decreases its coding efficiency in the lower bit-plane. In this paper, we propose a new coding scheme improving coding efficiency in the lower bit-plane. Based on the distribution of a significant coefficient, each bit is classified into two groups. At the same time, information that raises picture quality higher than any other coefficient is coded first. Simulation results show that this proposed scheme improves the coding efficiency up to more than 1.06%, and achieves 0.2dB gain in terms of average PSNR.

1   Introduction

On networks, such as the Internet, radio and so forth, transmission quality is not guaranteed, so channel bandwidth varies every moment influenced by congestion, transmission delay and additive noise. When video is transmitted on such networks, it is important to prevent variation from adding perceptual noise to the video in order to offer the highest quality of video always [1]. In MPEG [2, 3], SNR scalable coding scheme and data partitioned coding scheme are specified, and their hierarchical coding schemes give high tolerance against channel bandwidth variation to video transmission. The hierarchical coding scheme constitutes two layers, one is the base layer that is composed of the essential video information, and the other is the enhancement layer that is composed of the additive information to enrich the picture quality. Even if some coded data in the enhancement layer is not obtained because of channel bandwidth variation, the bare quality of video can be obtained by decoding only the coded data in the base layer. However, conventional hierarchical coding schemes discard all coded data in the enhancement layer at this time, so they cannot offer picture quality in proportion to the amount of received data.

For this reason, we studied the fine granularity scalability (FGS [4, 5]) scheme defined in MPEG-4 Visual Ver.2 [6] as a coding scheme to control the picture quality in proportion to the amount of received data. However, according to a report on a core experiment in an MPEG meeting [7], the picture quality of FGS is about 2.0dB lower than standard MPEG-4 with a single layer, like the other hierarchical coding schemes.

Y.-C. Chen, L.-W. Chang, and C.-T. Hsu (Eds.): PCM 2002, LNCS 2532, pp. 823-830, 2002.

One reason is that division into two layers decreases the accuracy of motion compensation and estimation. The FGS scheme has to use a decoded picture of the base layer as a reference frame not to propagate drifting noises. Its picture is low quality, so the accuracy of motion compensation becomes worse, and mean square error increases. However, some coding schemes has already been proposed to solve this problem [8, 9], and it is reported that their PSNR performance are actually improved. Another reason is that the efficiency of the bit-plane coding in the enhancement layer becomes extremely poor in the lower plane.

In this paper, to improve the coding efficiency of FGS, we describe the coding scheme of FGS briefly in Chapter 2, and clear up the problems of the bit-plane coding scheme used in the enhancement layer of FGS. In Chapter 3, in consideration of this problem, we propose a new bit-plane coding scheme based on the distribution of the significant coefficients. In Chapter 4, the simulation results show that the proposed coding scheme achieves the better video quality performance than conventional FGS schemes, even when channel bandwidth is varied. In addition, we analyze the effectiveness and performance of the proposed coding scheme quantitatively by simulations.

2 The FGS Functionality

The FGS encoder is shown in Figure 1. The base layer part is exactly the same as MPEG-4 with a single layer. In the enhancement layer, the residue between the original picture and the reconstructed picture in the base layer is transformed with 8x8 DCT, and coded by bit-plane coding. First, find the maximum value of all the absolute values of the residues, and decide the minimum number of bits, N, needed to represent its value in binary format. At the same time, N is the number of bit-planes for the enhancement layer. Next, the coefficients in the block are arranged in zig-zag-scan order, and each coefficient is represented by N binary symbols, '0' and '1'. Later, (RUN, EOP) symbol is generated one after the other by binary zero-run-length coding from the MSB plane, and is coded using variable length code.

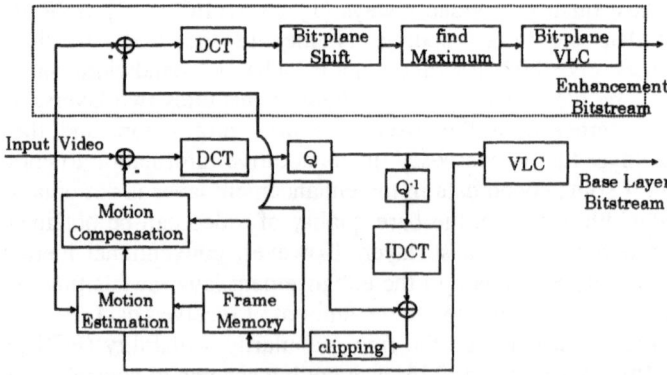

Fig. 1. Block diagram of the FGS encoder

Zig-zag-scan order gives top priority to low frequency coefficients in the structure of coded data. The features of a natural picture are taken into consideration, high frequency coefficients are almost 0 or values near 0. So, the probability that the high frequency coefficients have '0' symbol in the upper plane is much higher, the zero-run continued very long, and good coding efficiency is achieved by the binary zero-run-length coding method. On the contrary, the probability of a binary symbol of '0' or '1' becomes random in the lower bit-plane, and coding efficiency using binary zero-run-length becomes extremely lower. Therefore, it is important for the new coding scheme to prevent the coding efficiency falling even in the lower bit-plane.

3 Proposed Coding Scheme

3.1 Division into Two Bit Groups

We propose a new bit-plane coding scheme for FGS enhancement layer to prevent coding efficiency falling in the lower bit-plane. First, each bit is classified into a significant bit group and a refinement bit group as a boundary on a significant bit. Here, the significant bit is the top of the bit whose symbol is 0 when an absolute value of DCT coefficient is represented by binary expression. That is, any bits that are in an upper position from the significant bit are '0' symbol. The significant bit and upper bits are classified as the significant bit group, and bits lower than the significant bit are classified as the refinement bit group. All bits belong to either the significant or refinement bit group. It is very important that optimum coding methods are applied to each bit group respectively, because the occurrence probabilities of symbols differ in the two groups.

Therefore, first, for the significant bit group, the binary zero-run-length coding technique used in FGS is applied. One reason is that any bits upper from the significant bit are all '0' symbols, and symbol '0' continued for a long length. Another reason is that the run-length of symbol '0' could become longer because of removal of the refinement bits whose symbols appear at random. Next, for the refinement bit group, fixed length coding is applied. In the refinement bit group, symbol '0' or '1' appears at random. However, the occurrence probability of a symbol does not become exactly equal, and symbol '0' occurs slightly more frequently than symbol '1'. The reason is as follows. The DCT coefficients in the enhancement layer are the residue values between the original picture and the decoded picture in the base layer. Generally, a residual signal tends to follow Laplacian distribution, so DCT coefficient whose absolute value is close to 0 has higher occurrence probability. For example, when the absolute value is expressed by 2 bits, 2 and 3 exist, and 2 often occurs compared with 3. Similarly, when the absolute value is expressed by 3 bits, there are four coefficients such as 4, 5, 6 and 7, and the appearance probability of 4 is higher than 5, and the probability of 5 is higher than 6, and the probability of 6 is higher than 7. Eventually, when the absolute value of the DCT coefficient is expressed by the same number of bits, the coefficient that has many '0' symbols by binary expression occurs with a higher probability. For these reasons, symbol '0' appears with higher probability than symbol '1' in the refinement bit group. We

Table 1. Occurrence rate of symbol '0'
(A) Occurrence rate of symbol '0' in refinement bit group
(B) Rate of refinement bit group occupied to a plane

plane	0	1	2	3	4	5	6
(A)	---	0.95	0.74	0.62	0.58	0.56	0.56
(B)	0.00	0.01	0.06	0.16	0.29	0.43	0.59

measured the number of '0' symbols in refinement bit group at every plane and the results are shown in Table 1. Occurrence rate of symbol '0' exceeds 0.5 at all bitplanes in the refinement bit group and its tendency becomes remarkable in the upper plane. In consideration of the above result, fixed length entropy coding using Huffman codes is applied as coding technique in the refinement bit group. The results of elementary experiment, when composition symbol length of Huffman codes is set to about 4, the coding efficiency is good. So, Huffman codes with composition symbol length 4 are applied as the coding technique in the refinement bit group. If the rest of the refinement bits are less than 4 bits at the last of block, then the symbols are not coded and outputted as it is.

An example of the proposed coding method for the enhancement layer described above is shown in Figure 2. Clearly, refinement bits occupy most of the plane as the coding progresses in the lower plane. As compared with FGS coding, decline in the coding efficiency in the lower plane can be prevented using not binary zero-run-length but Huffman coding for the refinement bit group.

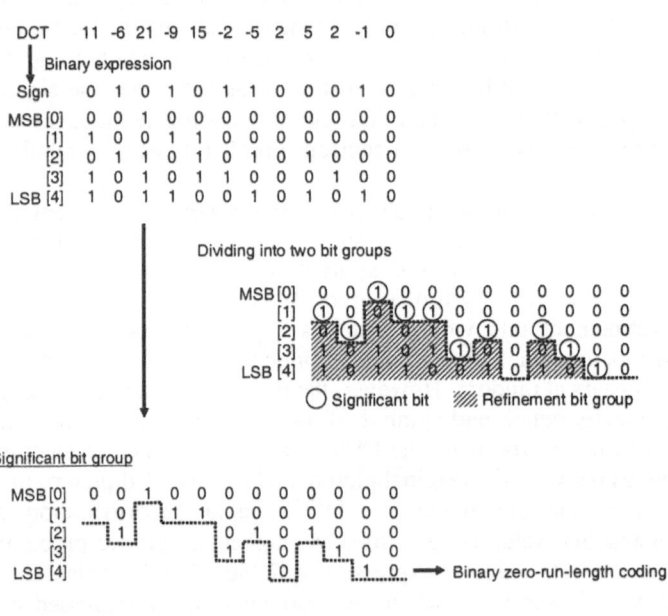

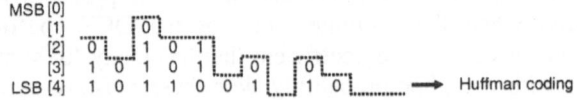

3.2 Transmission Order

In this chapter, we describe a transmission order that offers a high quality picture according to the amount of received data without dropping the coding efficiency of the coding scheme proposed in the previous chapter. Here, it is necessary to carefully consider the meaning of the information that a significant bit group and a refinement bit group have respectively. DCT coefficients in the enhancement layer are initialized to 0 before decoding, and if coding data representing a '1' symbol is not decoded at all, the value of the DCT coefficient is still 0. That is, DCT coefficients in the enhancement layer will have a meaningful value for the first time when its significant bit is decoded, since all the bits upper from the significant bit are '0' symbols. Put another way, the DCT coefficient is still 0 when its significant bit is not decoded. Therefore, the significant bit is the most important bit for deciding the rough value of its DCT coefficients in the enhancement layer, and has the highest contribution to the subjective quality of the picture. On the contrary, the refinement bits are additive information to refine the value of the DCT coefficient. By transmitting the significant bit group ahead of the refinement bit group, the decoder can receive the information in order having high contribution to subjective quality of picture, and the relationship between subjective quality and transmission rate is improved.

4 Simulation Results

The computer simulation was performed in order to show the effectiveness of the proposed coding scheme. Experiment parameter is shown in Table 2.

Table 2. Condition of simulation

GOV structure	IBBPBBP....
Frame rate	30 fps
Test sequence	Stefan, Foreman
Resolution	352x288 (CIF), YUV4:2:0
Number of frames	60 frames
Base layer rate	288 kbps (H.263, Q=30)
Enhancement layer rate	256, 512, 768, 1024, 1280, 1536, 1792, 2048, 2304, 2560 kbps

4.1 Coding Efficiency

To investigate the coding efficiency of the proposed coding scheme, the average amount of coded bits in the enhancement layer is measured and shown in Table 3. For comparison, the average amount of coded bits of FGS is also measured, and the improvement rate of the proposed coding scheme is shown in Table 3. Here, the VLC table used in the proposed coding scheme is optimized, because division into two bit groups makes the zero-run length shorter. Quantization value is set to 30 in the base

Table 3. Average amount of coded bits

Plane	FGS		Proposed		Improvement
0	3289	(3289)	3227	(3227)	1.89%
1	28411	(31700)	28301	(31528)	0.39%
2	50597	(82297)	50893	(82421)	-0.59%
3	69404	(151701)	68754	(151175)	0.94%
4	85712	(237413)	84578	(235753)	1.32%
5	109044	(346457)	107595	(343348)	1.33%
6	130910	(477367)	128956	(472304)	1.49%

layer, therefore 7 bits is needed to represent residue value in the enhancement layer by binary. The amount of coded bits at every bit-plane is shown at each row in Table 3, and the cumulative value from the 0th bit-plane to its bit-plane is shown in parenthesis. Coding efficiency of the proposed scheme is improved by 1.06% as a whole, and this result shows that its scheme using Huffman codes to refinement bit group solves the problem that the coding efficiency of the binary zero-run-length becomes worse at the lower bit plane. Comparison for each bit-plane shows that the improvement rate is higher at the lower bit-plane than at the upper bit-plane except for the 0th bit-plane having no refinement bits. Since most bits are included in the significant bit group at the upper bit-plane, division does not work effectively and there is little difference between the proposed coding scheme and the conventional FGS scheme. In addition, at the 2nd plane the amount of coded bits increases, division loss has occurred. To prevent division loss, it is effective to decide whether two bit groups should be divided or not at the upper bit-plan according to the probability of symbol '0' in the refinement bit group.

4.2 Performance on Picture Quality

The relationship between transmission rate and picture quality is shown in Figure 3, and we discuss its performance. Performances on FGS and MPEG-4 with single layer are shown for comparison. From Figure 3, the proposed coding scheme is the same picture quality as FGS at 0 ~ 1024 kbps rate, but the proposed coding scheme improves by about 0.2 dB better PSNR gain than FGS at 1024 kbps or higher rate. The reason difference does not appear at a low rate is that there is no difference of decoded information between the proposed coding scheme and FGS since most information received at a low rate includes only significant bit group and hardly includes the refinement bit group. Here, the number of decoded planes at each transmission rate assigned to the enhancement layer is measured, and the average between all frames is shown in Table 4. For example, at 512 kbps rate, it is comparatively low, the average number of decoded planes is 2.13. This means that 0th and 1st bit-planes are decoded completely and 13% of the 2nd bit- plane is decoded. Only 0th and 1st bit-planes to which the significant bit group occupies most or all are decoded at low rate, and the proposed method doesn't show the effectiveness of division into two bit groups. On the other hand, at the middle or high rate, bit-plane coding has division profits, so the proposed method shows better performance on

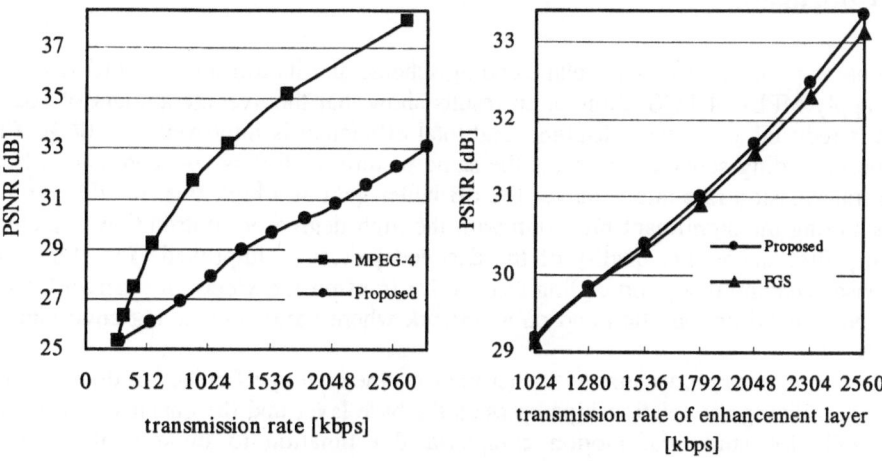

Fig. 3. PSNR performance

PSNR than FGS. In addition, from Figure 3, the proposed coding scheme is 5 dB worse than MPEG-4 with a single layer because of using the hierarchical coding functionality. The reason is that the reference frame used in motion compensated estimation is picture decoded in the base layer with low quality because of using the hierarchical scheme, and the accuracy of motion compensation becomes worse, and the prediction error increases. However, the proposed bit-plane coding method is independent of motion compensated prediction, so another method of motion compensated prediction can de applied to further improve the coding efficiency.

4.3 Subjective Quality of Decoded Picture

The proposed coding scheme reduces the block noise subjectively compared with FGS. Especially, the block noises appearing around the boundary between grass and wall are reduced, and the gradation on the grass becomes smooth. Since the proposed coding scheme codes the coefficients in the significant bit group first, the difference between the proposed coding scheme and FGS appears as subjective quality.

Table 4. Average number of decoded bit-plane

Rate (kbps)	FGS	Proposed
512	2.12	2.13
1024	2.67	2.70
1536	3.09	3.09
2048	3.36	3.40
2560	3.63	3.71
∞	7.00	7.00

5 Conclusion

The paper proposes a new bit-plane coding scheme and its transmission order, which can apply MPEG-4 FGS. Simulation results show that the average amount of coded data is reduced at a lower bit-plane, and total efficiency is improved by 1.06%. The proposed coding scheme maintains the same picture quality as conventional FGS at low transmission rate and achieves 0.2 dB better gain at a high rate. In addition, by transmitting the significant bit group with the high degree of contribution to picture quality first, subjective quality of the decoded picture is improved. Therefore, the proposed scheme is a good coding scheme for transmit the video on a network with channel bandwidth variation and on a network where various receiving environment exists.

In future research, we aim to further improve the coding efficiency of the bit-plane coding, utilizing the relationships between the base layer and the enhancement layer. We will also study the motion compensated estimation to improve the coding efficiency of the hierarchical coding scheme.

Acknowledgements. The authors would like to thank T. Asami, President of KDDI Research and Development Laboratories and Y. Matsushima, Executive Vice President of KDDI Research and Development Laboratories. This research was conducted under a project by the Telecommunications Advancement Organization (TAO) in Japan.

References

1. S. Sakazawa, Y. Takishima, M. Wada, and Y. Hatori, "Coding control scheme for a multi-encoder system," in Proc. 7th Int. Workshop Packet Video, Mar. 1996, pp. 83–88.
2. ISO/IEC 13818-2:1996, "Generic coding of moving pictures and associated audio information: Video"
3. ISO/IEC 14496-2:2001, "Coding of audio-visual objects --- Part 2: Visual"
4. ISO/IEC 14496-2:2001/Amd.2, "Coding of audio-visual objects --- Part 2: Visual AMENDMENT 2: Streaming video profile"
5. "FGS Verification Model Version 4.0," ISO/IEC MPEG 51st meeting, N3317, Noordwijkerhout, Mar., 2000.
6. "Description of Core Experiments in FGS," ISO/IEC MPEG 50th meeting, N3096, Maui, Dec. 1999.
7. Xiaoyan Sun, Feng Wu, Shipeng Li, Wen Gao and Ya-Qin Zhang, "Macroblock based progressive fine granularity scalable video coding," IEEE International Conference on Multimedia and Expo (ICME), 461-464, Tokyo, Aug. 2001.
8. Feng Wu, Shipeng Li, Ya-Qin Zhang, "A framework for efficient progressive fine granular scalable video coding," IEEE trans. on Circuits and Systems for Video Technology, vol. 11, no3, 332-344, Mar. 2001

A VBR Rate Control Using MINMAX Criterion for Video Streaming

Chih-Hung Li[1], Chung-Neng Wang[2], and Tihao Chiang[1]

[1] Dept. and Institute of Electronics Engineering, National Chiao Tung University (NCTU),
Hsinchu, 30050, Taiwan
{chihon, tchiang}@cc.nctu.edu.tw
[2] Dept. of Computer Science and Information Engineering, NCTU, Hsinchu, 30050, Taiwan
cnwang@csie.nctu.edu.tw

Abstract. In this paper, we present a frame-level rate control scheme based on a modified linear Rate-Distortion model to achieve minimal maximum (MINMAX) distortion for frame-dependent quantizers. The MINMAX distortion measure is used because the worst visual quality often dominates the overall perceptual quality. In our approach, we first perform the iterative offline analysis of the rate-distortion behavior for the original sequences on a video server. Such compactly stored information enables the encoder to select quantization parameters in real-time during streaming process. Our results show that our algorithm obtains higher minimum PSNR values than the TM5 rate control while the average PSNR is similar. We also use the same technique to optimize statistical multiplexing for a multi-channel transmission application.

1 Introduction

For most video coding standards such as ITU-T H.261, H.263/H.263+, ISO/IEC MPEG-1, MPEG-2 and MPEG-4, the rate control scheme is critical in maintaining the video quality for each encoder. For video streaming applications, the content providers need to provide a guaranteed quality-of-service (QoS) according to the channel bandwidth. Thus, it is challenging to design a high quality rate control scheme that adapts to the unpredictable and varying channel bandwidth and extensive video content for streaming video over the Internet or wireless channels.

Most bit allocation methods focus on obtaining minimum average (MINAVE) distortion for a given bit budget [1]-[5]. The rate–distortion (R-D)-based techniques were proposed by H. Everett aim at the best possible quality for a given channel rate and buffer size [5]. The bit allocation methods using the Lagrange multiplier techniques require expensive modeling of the R-D characteristics for each coding unit [2]-[3] with large delay [4].

A less computational expensive approach is to use an approximation model to describe the R-D behaviors without actual encoding. Many model based approaches have been proposed including quadratic models [6], piecewise linear models [1], and linear models [8]. Among these models, the linear source model proposed by He et al. provides a simple and accurate modeling. In [8] the R-D behavior is modeled with a linear relationship between bit rate and percentage of zero quantized DCT coefficients. A linear model and a non-linear behavior obtained through pre-coding can

Y.-C. Chen, L.-W. Chang, and C.-T. Hsu (Eds.): PCM 2002, LNCS 2532, pp. 831-838, 2002.

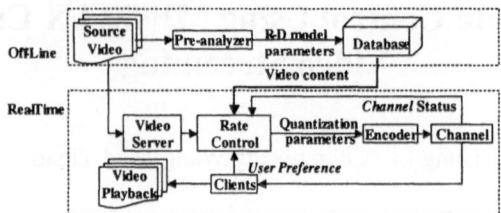

Fig. 1. Block diagram of video streaming system based on model-based approach.

jointly describe the non-linear R-Q behavior. However, the linear model in [8] did not consider the inter-frame dependency of the whole sequence. Consequently, it is challenging for the existing rate control scheme to provide constant quality and minimum PSNR variation.

To satisfy both constant quality and minimum PSNR requirements simultaneously, the main issue is on how to obtain minimum maximum (MINMAX) distortion for a given bit rate [7]. This can be achieved by selecting the best quantizers for both the reference and predicted frames. Thus, we present a frame level linear model considering the inter-frame dependency. The linear model is derived from the pre-analysis of the whole sequence under MINMAX criterion. The parameters of the linear model for each sequence are archived in the server's database for future use. Based on the stored model parameters, the streaming server can dynamically adapt to varying channel bandwidth and extensive video content at encoder.

This paper presents a rate control scheme to adjust quantization parameters (QP) for each coding unit under MINMAX criterion to stream video over the Internet or wireless channels. The overall video service system is shown in Fig. 1. Based on this system, the maximum PSNR difference of the frames is within a range of 1.5 dB.

2   R-D Characteristics Modeling

For video server or digital storage media, source video can be encoded off-line but requires best video quality. It can be justified to allow more complexity and delay to achieve an optimized set of encoding parameters. Thus, a sophisticated pre-analysis and optimized rate control algorithms are permissible for the best performance.

As shown in Fig. 1, we propose a constant quality MINMAX criterion based bit allocation approach, which is referred to as CQMM (Constant Quality with MINMAX). The proposed CQMM off-line segments the video sequence into a number of groups and develops a linear model to describe the R-D characteristics for each group. Based on such a R-D model, we can real-time encode the video using the stored parameters for any channel bandwidths.

2.1   Pre-analysis and R-D Models

A.   Video Segmentation Based on Constant Quality Requirement

The video sequence tends to contain similar contents within a shot or a segment of video, which is now referred to as the video coding unit (VCU). In each VCU, all the frames have similar R-D behaviors. To get accurate model parameters, the input video

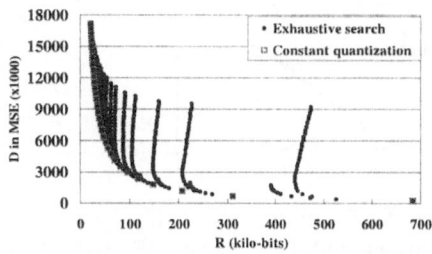

Fig. 2. R-D performance of the constant quantization approach and the encoding schemes use all pairs of the QPs.

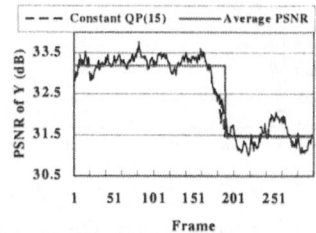

Fig. 3. Illustration of a PSNR profile that has two different PSNR levels used to segment Carphone_CIF sequence with two shots into two VCUs.

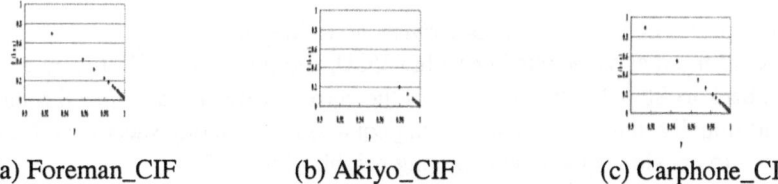

(a) Foreman_CIF   (b) Akiyo_CIF   (c) Carphone_CIF

Fig. 4. Linear relationship between the coding bitrate and the percentage of zero quantized DCT coefficients ρ.

is segmented into several distinct units after the first pre-encoding. Thus, the pre-analysis can be simply performed for each VCU instead of each frame.

Additionally for each frame in every VCU, the Lagrange multiplier technique should yield similar QPs. To support such an argument, we use an exhaustive set of QPs to encode two successive frames of a video sequence. The R-D points in Fig. 2 show that the constant QP scheme performs near the optimal case for a wide range of bitrate. Similar phenomenon occurs even when there is dependency between successive frames. Thus, we present a new bit allocation algorithm that can achieve constant QPs, which performs close to the optimum case.

To encode the frames in a VCU with almost constant QPs also means a near constant quality for the reconstructed pictures, which is consistent with the observations in Fig. 3. Thus, we can locate the boundaries between the consecutive shots based on PSNR profiles by coding with constant QP. The video segmentation method with the PSNR profile can segment the sequence into several VCUs by

1. Pre-encoding the input sequence using constant QP, where is set as q. Set the index of the current VCU as zero, $i=0$.
2. Initially, for VCU$_i$, set the frame number and the average PSNR value of the coded frames as zero: $N_i = 0$, and $P_{i,average} = 0$, for $i=1..M$, where M is the total number of VCUs in this sequence. The symbol $P_{i,average}$ stores the average PSNR value of the current VCU as computed by

$$P_{i,average} = N_i^{-1}\left(P_{i,average} + P_{current}\right).$$ (1)

3. Compute the PSNR value of the current frame after pre-encoding.

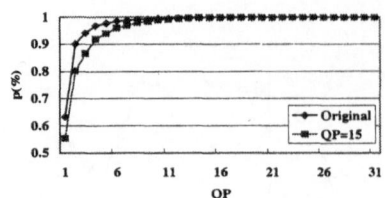

Fig. 5. ρ-Q mapping derived with one pre-coding using anchor QP of value 15. The mismatch from the actual ρ-Q data increases as QP is smaller than 15.

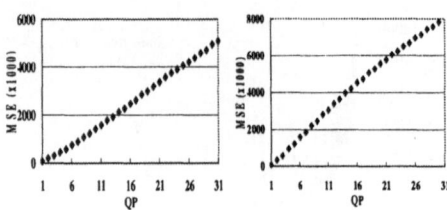

Fig. 6. The linear relationship between the MSE and QP. Left: Akiyo_CIF. Right: Foreman_CIF. Both are 100-frame video sequences.

If $\left| P_{current} - P_{i,average} \right| \leq 1.0$, increase the frame counter N_i by one and update the average PSNR by   (1). Otherwise, go to Step 4.

4. Record the real frame number within VCU_i and proceed to VCU_{i+1} by $i = i + 1$.

5. Go back to Step 2 until all frames of the current sequence are gone through.

Additionally, the goal of maintaining equal quality among successive frames is now reduced to provide equal quality among neighboring VCUs.

B.   R-D Models for Rate Control

To quantify the R-D behaviors of each VCU, the three models formulated as R-ρ, ρ-Q, and Q-D functions are obtained in pre-analysis processes by pre-encoding the input sequence several times.

Based on the MPEG-4 reference encoder, we fist encode the test sequences using 31 possible QP values over the whole sequence, and we can get 31 points on the R-ρ plane. In Fig. 4, we plot the linear relationship between the bit rate in kbps and the percentage of zero for several test sequences as referred to [8]. It's interesting that the linear relationship exists at the sequence level.

1. Linear interpolation of ρ-Q mapping

Unlike the linear ρ-Q mapping in [8], the simulation results in Fig. 5 exhibit a nonlinear relationship because the reference frames with different QPs have different residuals for the current frame, which yields different statistical distributions of the DCT coefficients. Consequently, linearity does not exist at sequence level. To address this problem, we need to encode the input sequence with all combinations of QPs to get accurate ρ-Q mapping that requires high complexity. To strike a balance between complexity and coding efficiency, we propose an approximation by encoding with only a few QPs and linear interpolation. To describe the ρ-Q relationship, 7 out of 31 possible QPs instead of one QP (=15) are used to describe the ρ-Q mapping. With the 7 anchor data points, the estimation errors of the ρ-Q relationship are now reduced to less than 10%.

2. Distortion model

I Fig. 6 the distortion measured in Mean Square Error (MSE) is proportional to QP despite the inter-frame dependency. With such linear relationship, the Q-D mapping can be found by linear interpolation. A similar method has been used in [2].

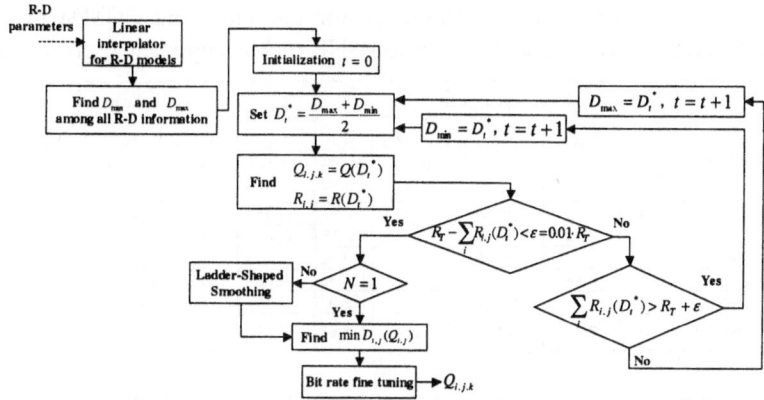

Fig. 7. Flow chart of CQMM rate control. The value k indicates the total amount of QPs used in the encoder.

2.2 CQMM: VBR Rate Control under MINMAX Criterion

Our constant quality rate control under MINMAX criterion is shown in Fig. 7.

A. Optimal VBR Rate Control

Based on the R-D parameters of all VCUs, the encoder takes the following three requirements using the MINMAX criterion. For a sequence, there are M VCUs and N_i is the total number of frames for VCU$_i$. Thus, this sequence has N frames with $N = N_1 + N_2 + \cdots + N_M$.

Let $Q_{i,j}$ be the QP used for the j-th frame of the i-th VCU (VCU$_i$). With $Q_{i,j}$, let $R_i(Q_{i,j})$ and $D_i(Q_{i,j})$ be the rate and distortion for each VCU$_i$, respectively. To minimize the variation in quality, we shall minimize the following function,

$$\eta = D^{\max} - \overline{D} \text{ , subject to } \sum_{i=1}^{M} R_i(Q_{i,j}) = R_T \text{ .} \tag{2}$$

Where R_T denotes the target bit rate. In addition, the maximum distortion $D^{\max}$ and the average distortion $\overline{D}$ are defined by $D^{\max} = \max\{D_{i,j}(Q_{i,j})\}$ with $i=1..M$,

$j=1..N_i$, and $\overline{D} = \dfrac{1}{MN} \sum_{i=1}^{M} \sum_{j=1}^{N_i} \left(D_{i,j}(Q_{i,j}) \right)$, respectively.

B. Rate Control Algorithm

When we obtain R-D data for each VCU, we can perform the rate control algorithm with MINMAX criterion. The goal is to compute the QP for each VCU such that they all have the same PSNR.

To get the optimal VBR rate control with each frame as a separate VCU, there are k^N possible solutions for an N-frame sequence. As we use identical QP for every frame of a VCU and treat each VCU independently. Thus, as the sequence has M

Table 1. Comparisons of coding efficiency for the TM5 and CQMM rate control schemes through the average and minimum PSNR of Y component at given bitrates.

Target Bitrate (kbps)	Method	Mother_Daughter_CIF					Carphone_CIF				
		Avg. PSNR (Y)	Δ Avg. PSNR (Y)	Min PSNR (Y)	Δ Min PSNR (Y)	Real Bitrate (kbps)	Avg. PSNR (Y)	Δ Avg. PSNR (Y)	Min PSNR (Y)	Δ Min PSNR (Y)	Real Bitrate (kbps)
92	TM5	39.14		36.60		92.17	33.45		28.76		91.99
	CQMM	39.86	0.72	39.57	2.97	92.35	32.63	-0.82	31.87	3.11	93.06
112	TM5	39.74		37.38		112.32	34.24		29.86		112.00
	CQMM	40.58	0.84	39.79	2.41	114.85	34.00	-0.24	33.13	3.27	112.39
128	TM5	40.12		37.94		128.32	34.75		30.52		128.00
	CQMM	41.05	0.93	40.68	2.74	128.63	34.52	-0.23	33.84	3.32	127.96

VCUs, the complexity is reduced to k^M, where M is much smaller than N since the video typically has a limited number of shots. However, the complexity is still high.

Although there is temporal dependency between neighboring VCUs, the characteristic of each VCU tends to dominate in an average manner. The averaged bit rate of the current VCU does not significantly depend on how the previous VCU is encoded. Thus, the encoding is now simplified to the selection of QPs for a VCU. Consequently, the complexity is now reduced to $k*M$ encoding.

In summary, we propose a low complexity rate control scheme using constant QP for each VCU. With the derived R-D model, the rate control scheme can achieve the constant quality for each VCU by selecting the same distortion. The remaining issue is on how to adjust QP for each VCU such that there is the smallest PSNR variation.

C. Ladder-Shaped Smoothing Method

Since we allocate bits to the neighboring VCUs independently, there is noticeable PSNR drop at the transition regions between the VCUs. To optimize under MINMAX criterion, we propose a ladder-shaped smoothing method for the rate control with multiple VCUs. Whenever there is a transition in quality like the PSNR drop during 170th-190th frames in Fig. 3, QPs are decreased gradually in the transition interval.

D. Bitrate Fine Tuning

To meet the bit rates and achieve equal quality, the PSNR profile is fine-tuned by
1. With the estimated R-Q function for each VCU and target bitrate R_T, the derived QP for every VCU satisfies

$$\sum_{i=1}^{M} R_i(Q_{i,j}) < R_T \text{ and } D_{i,j}(Q_{i,j}) < D^{\max}, i = 1..M .$$

The number of motion bits is assumed to be independent to the QP values.
2. Find the VCU with the maximum distortion and calculate the difference ratio

$$r = \left[R_T - R_i(Q_{i,j}) \right] \left[R_i(Q_{i,j} - 1) - R_i(Q_{i,j}) \right]^{-1} \tag{3}$$

3. Decrease the QPs of the first $\lfloor r \cdot N_i + 0.5 \rfloor$ frames by 1, where N_i is the total frame number of VCU_i and the operator $\lfloor a \rfloor$ gives the nearest integer smaller than a.

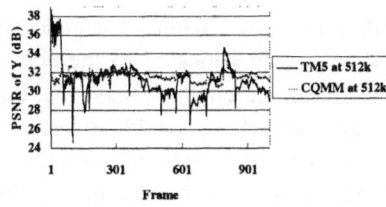
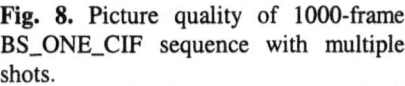
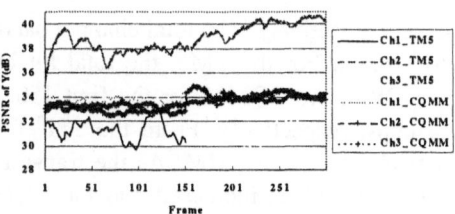

Fig. 8. Picture quality of 1000-frame BS_ONE_CIF sequence with multiple shots.

Fig. 9. PSNR comparisons of reconstructed pictures with the two rate control schemes and three sequences under channel variation.

E. Complexity Reduction

In Fig. 7, the R-D parameters are extracted by applying 7 times pre-coding with QP of values 1, 5, 10, 15, 20, 25, and 31. To further reduce the complexity, the binary search algorithm is adopted to derive the optimal R-D models by only 3 times pre-coding. The pre-analysis can be done with high complexity for only once and then the R-D characteristics are stored. For practical video service, a hardware encoder can real-time encode a video at any target bit rates using the R-D parameters without any extra rate control scheme.

3 Experimental Results

To show the performance of our proposed CQMM rate control algorithms, the TM5 [9] rate control is used for comparisons. The test sequences are in CIF formats. As for the time-varying channel conditions, we examine both rate control approaches by changing the channel numbers and the bandwidths available. As shown in Table 1 and Fig. 8, the CQMM algorithm outperforms the TM5 in providing the equal quality video.

For the video sequences with several scenes such as Foreman, the CQMM can provide smaller variation in quality among the successive frames as compared to that encoded by TM5. Furthermore, CQMM algorithm gets a significant improvement on the minimum PSNR at the cost of a small drop in the average PSNR. For the video sequences consisting of stationary scenes such as Mother_Daughter, both the average PSNR and minimum PSNR obtained by CQMM are better than those encoded by TM5. Similar results are found in Fig. 8. The noticeable variation in PSNR values through TM5 is because it decides the QPs without looking ahead. Thus, the CQMM algorithm can maintain the quality at a guaranteed level for various video contents and bit rates.

Our algorithm also can be applied to the multi-channel application. For the TM5, the total bit budget is equally divided among each channel with no consideration of video contents while the CQMM can have a look ahead. Thus, the CQMM can automatically adapt the QPs based on the archived R-D parameters, which allows it to limit the variation in quality for each channel. To examine the robustness of the multi-channel bit allocation algorithms under the time-varying channel conditions, the results are given in Fig. 9, where three channels encode Foreman, Mother_Daughter and

Carphone, respectively. The total channel bandwidth is 192kbps. Channel 1 is ended at the 151st frame. For the TM5, the total bit budget is equally allocated to the active channels. With the CQMM for the first 150 frames, the three channels have 48, 80, and 64 kbps, respectively. From the 151st frame, the channel bandwidth is decided automatically by the CQMM. As the transmission in Channel 1 ends, the remaining channel bandwidth is increased and the CQMM can enhance the picture quality by adapting the parameters for the remaining frames of the VCUs. The adaptation is based on the similar R-D behaviors for the frames in each VCU. Therefore, the CQMM approach can adapt the picture quality when the channel number is changed.

4 Conclusions

In this paper, a new and near-optimal VBR rate control using MINMAX criterion was proposed to minimize the maximum distortion of frames in a video sequence. In the proposed CQMM scheme, the parameters for modeling the R-D behaviors are offline measured once using pre-analysis. With the parameters archived in the database at the server side, we can find the optimal QPs to generate the bitstream in real-time. Thus, the CQMM approach can provide constant quality based on a modified linear R-D model at sequence level. Additionally, the complexity of modeling the R-D behaviors is reduced using only a few encoding and interpolating the remaining data points. The complexity of exhaustive search for the final R-D relation is improved by binary search.

Based on the similarity of the R-D behaviors for each VCU, the proposed CQMM rate control can adapt the R-D models by normalizing the parameters with the ratio of the number of remaining frames over the actual number of frames in a VCU.

References

1. Lin, L.J., Ortega, A.: Bit-rate control using piecewise approximated rate–distortion characteristics. IEEE Trans. Circuits Syst. Video Technol., Vol. 8, No. 4, (1998) 446-459.
2. Lee, W.Y., Ra, J.B.: Fast algorithm for optimal bit allocation in rate-distortion sense. Electronics Letters, Vol. 32, (1996) 1871-1873.
3. Ding, W., Liu, B.: Rate control of MPEG-2 video coding and recording by rate-quantization modeling. IEEE Trans. Circuits Syst. Video Technol., Vol. 6, (1996) 12-20.
4. Kim, T., Roh, B., Kim, J.: An accurate bit-rate control for real-time MPEG video encoder. Signal Processing: Image Communication, Vol. 15, (2000) 479-492.
5. Everett, H.: Generalized Lagrange multiplier method for solving the problem of optimum allocation of resources. Operation Research, Vol.11, (1963) 399-417.
6. Chiang, T., Zhang, Y.-Q.: A new rate control scheme using quadratic rate distortion model. IEEE Trans. Circuits Syst. Video Technol., Vol. 7, No. 1, (1997) 246-250.
7. Schuster, G.M., Melnikov, G., Katsaggelos, A.K.: A review of the minimum maximum criterion for optimal bit allocation among dependent quantizers. IEEE Trans. Multimedia, Vol. 1, (1999) 3-17.
8. He, Z., Kim, Y. K., Mitra, S. K.: Low-delay rate control for DCT video coding via ρ -domain source modeling. IEEE Trans. Circuits Syst. Video Technol., Vol. 11, No. 8, (2001) 928-940.
9. Test Model 5, ISO-IEC/JTC1/SC29/WG11, Draft, (1993).

Implementation of Real-Time MPEG-4 FGS Encoder

Yen-Kuang Chen and Wen-Hsiao Peng

Microprocessor Research Labs, Intel Corporation

Abstract. While computers become faster than they used to be, software implementation of the latest video codec in real time is still a challenging topic. This paper presents our techniques in optimizing the speed of MPEG-4 Fine Granularity Scalability (FGS) video encoders. First, zigzag scans are slow processes in video encoding and decoding. While state-of-the-art processors utilize hardware data prefetchers to reduce memory latency, non-sequential addresses in the zigzag scan may destroy the trackability of hardware prefetching. The problem is even more serious in MPEG-4 FGS where we need multiple scans in bit-plane coding. More than 30% of CPU time is for bit-plane encoding in an MPEG-4 FGS encoder (including base layer and enhancement layer). In this work, we rearrange the layout of the image structure so that zigzag scans are in sequential memory locations. After the rearrangement, there are prefetch reads and we see 80% speed-up in bit-plane encoding. Second, variable length encoder (VLC) incurs a huge number of unpredictable conditional branches. While modern processors can execute tens of instructions in their pipeline, a mis-predicted branch will decrease the efficiency of the pipeline. The problem is severer in MPEG-4 FGS where we need multiple bit-plane VLC's. More than half of the CPU time for MPEG-4 FGS enhancement layer encoder is on bit-plane VLC's. In this work, we also design a bit-plane VLC algorithm, which has fewer unpredictable branches. The new design reduces mis-predicted branches by 2.4x. After these changes, overall speed-up in our MPEG-4 FGS software encoder is 1.4x without any assembly and MMX technology optimization.

1 Introduction

Due to bandwidth constraints of communication channels, video data are often compressed prior to transmission on a communication channel. Encoding and decoding video signals are computationally intensive processes. While the state-of-the-art microprocessor offers us more computations per second than it used to be, (1) memory speed is much slower than the microprocessor, and (2) branch mis-prediction penalty is larger than it used to be. In order to implement the latest codecs in software, we must avoid slow memory accesses and branch mis-predictions in the applications. In this work, we first rearrange the storage layout of the video/image data during compression so as to utilize the hardware data prefetch, which takes some pressure off longer memory latency. Second, we re-design the run-length encoder so as to reduce the branch mis-prediction rate.

Y.-C. Chen, L.-W. Chang, and C.-T. Hsu (Eds.): PCM 2002, LNCS 2532, pp. 839–846, 2002.
© Springer-Verlag Berlin Heidelberg 2002

The structure of an MPEG-4 FGS encoder [2, 3] is shown in Fig. 1. Similar to many image or video encoding processes, which have discrete cosine transform (DCT), quantization, a zigzag scan, and variable length coding VLC, the FGS enhancement layer encoding process has the following:

1. DCT
2. (Optional shifting operation of selective enhancement & frequency weighting [2])
3. Zigzag scan
4. Multiple bit-plane extraction and VLC

One uniqueness of the enhancement layer encoder is bit-plane extraction and VLC of the bit-planes, as shown in Fig. 2.

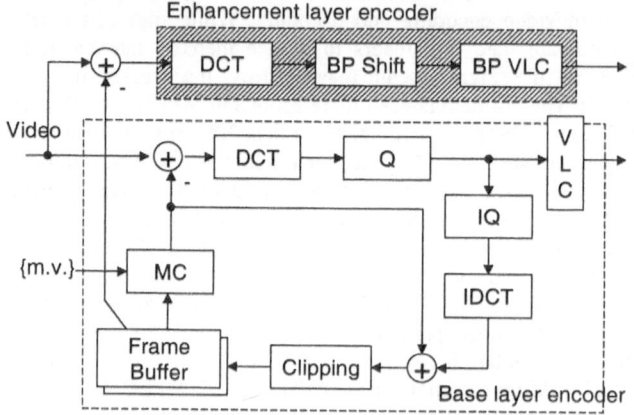

Fig. 1. The structure of an MPEG-4 FGS encoder.

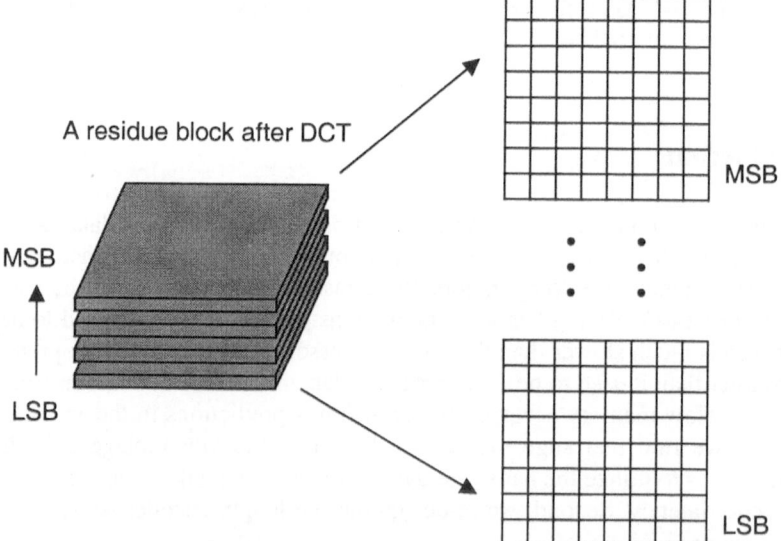

Fig. 2. Bit-plane coding in MPEG-4 FGS. A residue block after DCT is coded using bit-plane coding from MSB to LSB.

One critical performance factor, which appears in FGS codec, is the large amount of randomized zigzag data addressing.

Zigzag scans map the 8x8 matrix to a 1x64 vector, which groups low frequency coefficients in top of vector. Fig. 3(a) shows a normal storage of a block in the raster scan order, where we put horizontal data together first. When we need to scan the data in the zigzag scan order (as shown in Fig. 3(b)), we will access data in the order at location 1, 2, 9, 17, 10, 3, 4, 11, 18, 25, etc.

Fig. 4 shows a straightforward implementation of the bit-plane extraction and encoding in C programming language. In this implementation, for each bit-plane encoding, we need a zigzag scan, which causes performance problems.

The first problem is that we need extra steps to generate the addresses because the addresses are not sequential. If we scan the data only once, one extra step is acceptable. On the other hand, encoding MPEG-4 FGS enhancement layers takes multiple scans. In this case, multiple extra steps become a bigger overhead.

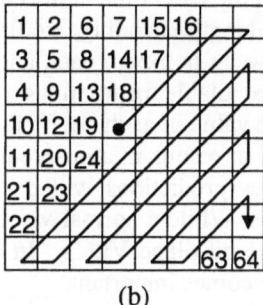

(a)   (b)

Fig. 3. (a) Normal raster scan order, where horizontal data are stored together. (b) Zigzag scan pattern.

```
for (different bit-plane) {
    bit_mask = 1<<bit-plane;
    for (different blocks) {
        while (position<=EOPposition) {
            /* (1) Data in block_buffer is of the raster scan order. */
            /*     However, the data is accessed in the zigzag scan order */
            /* (2) Conditional branch at bit level, difficult to predict */
            if (block_buffer[zigzag[position]] & bit_mask) {
                EOP=(position==EOPposition)?1:0;
                Coding <RUN, EOP, Sign>;
                RUN=0;
            }
            else {
                RUN++;
            }
            position++;
        }
    }
}
```

Fig. 4. A straightforward implementation of bit-plane extraction and encoding. This implementation must translate the array address for each bit-plane extraction. Also, there will be a different branch path when the extracted bit is non-zero.

Another problem of storing data in the raster scan order while processing data in the zigzag scan order is that random accesses of data make it harder for hardware to prefetch data. Intel Pentium 4 processors introduced hardware prefetchers, which load the data into the second-level cache before the application needs the data [1]. More precisely, the prefetchers check whether there are linear data access patterns and retrieve data if a linear access pattern is detected. If data are prefetched into the cache, then it takes less time for applications to get the data. In this case, larger memory latency is not as critical as it used to be. Unfortunately, hardware prefetchers work less effectively if the application processes data in the zigzag scan order while data are stored in the raster scan order. In this work, to make hardware prefetchers work efficiently, we rearrange the data.

Another critical performance factor is the VLC. Normally, VLC takes about 10% of the CPU time in the entire encoding process (wherein a fast motion estimation algorithm is used). Nonetheless, FGS have multiple bit-plane VLC's and takes more than half of the CPU time in the enhancement layer encoding process.

In run length encoding, we first locate the non-zero coefficients. Then, we count the 0's between non-zero data, and encode the number of 0's with the non-zero data. Currently available instructions do not permit efficient determination of this run length. The value of each coefficient bit must be tested individually with a conditional operation that results in a mispredicted branch each time a non-zero data is extracted. Branch miss predictions will decrease the pipeline efficiency and slow down the applications. While a normal video encoder has one VLC, an MPEG-4 FGS encoder has multiple bit-plane VLC's. In this case, a VLC algorithm with fewer conditional branches becomes important.

The reference software uses a straightforward implementation to obtain the RUN symbol. The implementation counts RUN's between non-zero bits one by one. For each non-zero bits, we need a branch, as shown in Fig. 4. That is, bit-plane extraction will introduce conditional branches. Currently, 11.2% of the conditional branches in the VLC are mispredicted. Branch misprediction penalty would be huge in future architectures with deeper pipeline. Thus, it is important to design a bit-plane extraction and VLC of runs without conditional branches.

2   Zigzag Scan In-Order Approach

We should perform only one zigzag scan for all bit-plane extraction and VLC's. Because the outputs of DCT are usually in the raster-scan fashion, the inputs of VLC are normally in the raster-scan manner as well. In order to access coefficients in the zigzag scan order, there are some address calculations required. Currently, in the reference software, the zigzag scan is combined with bit-plane VLC. Thus, for a 6-bit-plane FGS encoding, we need 6 zigzag scans and 6-bit-plane VLC's. Fig. 5 (a) shows the situation described above. After DCT, we store DCT coefficients in the raster scan order at point [a]. Then, we convert them into 32-bit integers at point [b]. When we extract bit-planes for VLC, we work on the raster-scanned buffer. Thus, we need a zigzag scan for each bit-plane extraction.

To reduce extra zigzag scans, our implementation pre-scans the data in the zigzag scan order and stores the data in the sequential order. So, only one address calculation for each coefficient is needed. Fig. 6 shows the pseudo code of the proposed implementation, which works the same as that in Fig. 4. While this approach can significantly reduce the number of calculations needed, additional memory buffer is needed. Hence, we combine the pre-zigzag scan into other buffer-copy operations (between [a] and [b] in Fig. 5 (a). Fig. 5. (b) shows our implementation that has only one internal buffer copy.

3 Branchless VLC

To reduce conditional branches, we should perform logic operations. There are two main stages in the new approach. Instead of counting the runs of zero bits, we first extract the positions of non-zero bits into a buffer. Then, we encode the runs using the difference of the positions in the buffer.

During the first stage, we transform conditional branches into logic operations. As shown in Fig. 7, we won't write the correct values into *ones_position* nor increase the *ones_counter* unless the Boolean variable *oneorzero* is equal to one. In this case, the condition branches only happen at the end of the both loops.

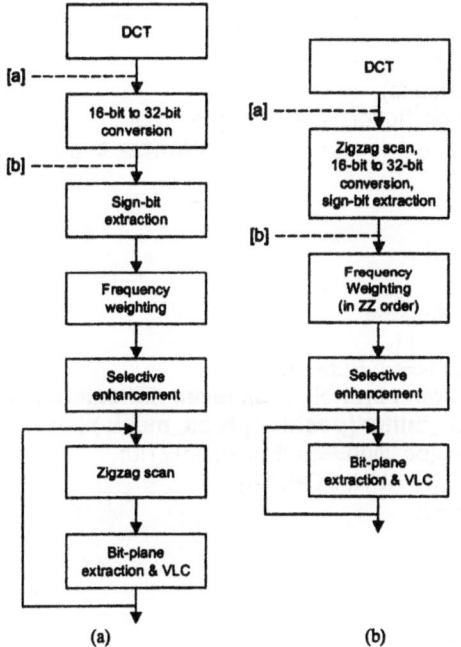

Fig. 5. FGS enhancement layer encoding processes

4 Results

Besides reducing the address calculations in the zigzag scan, making memory accesses predictable improves the performance as well. This is because current hardware prefetchers have limited capabilities. Originally, we zigzag scan DCT blocks when we extract the bit planes. When the data stored in the raster-scan order, zigzag-scanning a DCT block will access memory randomly. After we re-organize our memory layout, accesses to the DCT coefficients are sequential. Thus, it is easier for hardware to predict our memory access pattern and prefetch data effectively. Using special hardware monitors, we found that the number of "reads non-prefetch" drops by 50%. "Reads non-prefetch" counts read requests to the main memory, but the subset that are not due to prefetches. Seeing 50% fewer counts indicates that the hardware prefetchers have launched these other cases. That is, our goal of getting hardware prefetchers to trigger more was achieved. Table 1 shows that our FGS encoder is 40% faster after the new memory organization. Table 2 shows the CPU time breakdown of each module before & after our changes (on 1.6GHz Pentium 4 systems). The bit-plane extraction module is 80% faster. In this case, our code is about 1.4x faster than the MPEG-4 reference software without any assembly and MMX technology optimization.

```
// Part I:
for (different blocks) {
    for (different positions)
        /*Data in block_buffer' is of zigzag in order*/
        block_buffer'[position] = block_buffer[zig_zag[position]];
}

// Part II:
for (different bit-plane)
{
    bit_mask = 1<<bit-plane;
    for (different blocks) {
        while (position<=EOPposition) {
            /*Conditional branch at bit level, difficult to predict*/
            if ( block_buffer'[position] & bit_mask ) {
                EOP=(position==EOPposition)?1:0;
                Coding <RUN, EOP, Sign>;
                RUN=0;
            }
            else {
                RUN++;
            }
            position++;
        }
    }
}
```

Fig. 6. The proposed implementation of bit-plane VLC. The zigzag scan is performed first before the bit-plane extraction.

Moreover, the new VLC algorithm greatly reduces mispredicted conditional branches by 2.4x in the VLC module, as shown in Table 3. Thus, the overall algorithm has 3.9% misprediction rate instead of 7.7%. While currently we see only 1.6% speed-up, in a CPU with 50-pipeline stages, the new algorithm will have 15% speed-up. This is because the number of mispredicted conditional branches drops by more than 50%.

5 Summary

In this paper, we analyze the performance bottleneck of the software implementation of MPEG-4 FGS encoders and present four basic optimization techniques:
1. Take redundant operations out of the loops.
2. Combine multiple slow, data-dependent operations together in one step.
3. Make memory accesses predictable.
4. Reduce conditional branches

Mostly, putting data in the zigzag scan order makes memory accesses predictable and improves performance. This is because we can utilize hardware prefetchers to reduce memory latency.

```
// Part II:
for (different bit-plane) {
    bit_mask = 1<<bit-plane;

    for(different blocks) {
        /* First stage: bit-plane extraction */
        ones_position[0]=-1;
        ones_counter=1;
        while (position<=EOPposition) {
            ones_position[ones_counter] = position;
            oneorzero = (block_buffer' [position] & bit_mask)||0;
            /* No conditional branch at bit level */
            ones_counter += oneorzero;
        }
        ones_position[ones_counter] = position;

        /* Second stage: VLC the bit-plane */
        /* Conditional branch at symbol level, easy to predict */
        for (symbol=1; symbol<ones_counter+1; symbol++) {
            RUN=ones_position[symbol]-ones_position[symbol-1]-1;
            EOP=(symbol==ones_counter)?1:0;
            Coding <RUN, EOP, Sign>;
        }
    }}
```

Fig. 7. New algorithm with fewer conditional branches. We use logic operations to put ones' positions into an array. Then, we just encode the runs without conditional branches. The number of mispredicted branches in the new algorithm is independent of the number of ones in the bit-plane. There are two mispredicted branches in the new algorithm.

Our technique to have the zigzag scan immediately after the DCT not only can be applicable to encoders, but also to decoders. In decoders, we should not perform the zigzag scan until we accumulate all bit-planes together.

Table 1. Speed of the FGS encoder (enhancement layer only) of CIF images at 1.6GHz Pentium 4.

Sequences	Raster-scan	New memory	Speed up
Akiyo	30.9 (fps)	43.5 (fps)	1.41x
Foreman	23.4 (fps)	33.7 (fps)	1.44x

Table 2. CPU time of each module in the FGS encoder (enhancement layer only).

	Akiyo		Foreman	
	Raster-scan	New memory	Raster-scan	New memory
Bit-plane extract	54%	40%	59%	44%
Put bits	11%	19%	12%	20%
Encode symbols	5%	13%	6%	12%
Sign-bit extract	13%	12%	10%	10%
Forward DCT	8%	11%	6%	10%

Table 3. Performance comparisons of the FGS VLC algorithms.

		Old algorithm	New algorithm	Speed up
Overall Application	Cycles (millions)	9,923	9,772	1.02x
	Misprediction rate	7.7%	3.9%	
	Mispredicted cycles	12.9%	6.1%	
VLC Module Only	Mispred. branches (millions)	51.5	21.3	
	Misprediction rate	11.2%	5.2%	
Future Projection	M Cycles (50 stage pipeline)	11,851	10,317	1.15x

References

[1] Intel Corp., Intel Pentium 4 Processor Optimization Reference Manual, Order Number: 248966-04, 1999-2001.
[2] "Streaming video profile---Proposed Draft Amendment," ISO/IEC JTC1/SC29/WG11, N3315, Mar. 2000.
[3] W. Li, "Overview of Fine Granularity Scalability in MPEG-4 Video Standard," IEEE Trans. on CSVT, vol. 11, no. 3, Mar. 2001, pp. 301 –317.
[4] H. Jiang, "Using Frequency Weighting in Fine-Granularity-Scalability Bit-plane Coding for Natural Video", ISO/IEC JTC1/SC29/WG11, M5489, 1999.

MPEG-4 Video Streaming with Drift-Compensated Bitstream Switching

Yeh-Kai Chou, Li-Chau Jian, and Chia-Wen Lin

Department of Computer Science and Information Engineering
National Chung Cheng University
Chiayi 621, Taiwan
cwlin@cs.ccu.edu.tw
http://www.cs.ccu.edu.tw/~cwlin

Abstract. Bandwidth variations is one of the major problems in providing QoS guaranteed services for the current Internet users. The FGS coding scheme is considered an efficient and effective solution to solving the bandwidth variation problem. However, its coding efficiency is significantly lower than the non-scalable coder when the supporting bit-rate range is wide. Streaming video with multiple-bitstream switching may provide a more efficient solution for rate adaptation for users with a large degree of heterogeneity than using a single bitstream. In this paper, we propose a receiver-driven drift-compensated switching method for rate adaptation in heterogeneous video multicasting applications. Our proposed method can achieve significant performance improvement in case of packet loss or network congestion.

1 Introduction

With the proliferation of online multimedia content (e.g., electronic documents, emails, news, entertainment and commercial video clips, etc.), the popularity of multimedia streaming technology, and the establishment of video coding standards, people are able to ubiquitously access and retrieve various multimedia contents via the Internet, promoting networked multimedia services at an extremely fast pace. Real-time multimedia, as the name implies, has timing constraints. For example, video sequences must be played out frame by frame. If the client cannot receive the video data in time, the playout process will pause or collapse, and then annoys the human visual system. In addition to the time constraint, video streaming over the Internet presents several challenges, such as high storage-capacity and throughput in the video server and high bandwidth in the network to deliver a large number of video streams.

Bandwidth variation is one of the primary characteristics of "best-effort" networks, and the Internet is a prime example of such networks. Scalable coding plays a crucial role in delivering the best possible quality over unpredictable "best-effort" networks by trading the streaming video quality with the changing network conditions. The newly established MPEG-4 Fine-Granularity Scalable (FGS) [5], has several out

Y.-C. Chen, L.-W. Chang, and C.-T. Hsu (Eds.): PCM 2002, LNCS 2532, pp. 847–855, 2002.

standing features of low complexity, supporting a wide range of user bit-rates rather than some discrete rates, and packet-loss resilience, making it especially suitable for video streaming applications. It thus has been adopted as the coding tool in the MPEG-4 streaming video profile [5]. However, the benefits come with the cost of poorer coding efficiency, especially when the bit-rate rage is wide. As a result, a single FGS bitstream may not achieve best tradeoff among cost, flexibility, and performance for users with different requirements and capacities. Therefore streaming video with multiple FGS bitstreams has been proposed to serve users with a large degree of heterogeneity [1-3]. However, direct switching from one bitstream to another directly will result in drifting errors, which can lead to significant quality degradation.

In this paper, we present a receiver-driven congestion control scheme which can support video multicasting with multiple FGS bitstream switching. Our proposed system can estimate the TCP throughput by detecting the packet loss ratio and measuring the round-trip delay values in a receiver-driven manner, and then perform the congestion control for heterogeneous video multicasting accordingly. Besides, in order to serve users who may have fluctuated bandwidth such as modem or ADSL, we proposed a drift-compensated bitstream switching scheme to reduce the drift error when performing switching for rate adaptation. Furthermore, by combining the receiver-driven multicasting mechanism and the proposed multiple bit-stream switching, our proposed system can achieve significant performance improvement in case of packet loss or network congestion.

2   Drift-Compensated Bitstream Switching

In streaming video applications, the server may provide several bitstreams with different bitrates for ech client to switch over the bistreams to choose the bitstream which matches the client's channel bandwidth the most for rate adaptation. For instance, clients with high channel bandwidths can subscribe to higher-rate bitstreams for better video quality, while low-bandwidth clients need to subscribe to lower-rate bitstreams with worse perceptual visual qualities. There are some issues with such bitstream switching we have to concern about. When the available channel bandwidth drops, clients have to switch from one higher-rate bitstream to another lower-rate one (a "switching-down" process), and vice versa. Both the switching-up (from a lower-rate to a higher-rate) and switching-down (from a high-rate to a lower-rate) processes will introduce drifting errors as will be explained below.

We assume that the streaming video server just provides two bit-streams of different bit-rates (can be extended to more than two bitstreams) for clients to choose: one is encoded at a higher bit-rate R_h, and the other is encoded at a lower bit-rate R_l. These bitstreams are offline-encoded and stored at the server side. Besides these two bitstreams, we propose to use two extra drift-compensation bitstreams based on the concept of "SP" frames in [3] and drift-compensation frames in [4].

The way how we encode the drift-compensation bitstreams goes as follows. Let H represent the higher-rate bistream, L the lower-rate one, D^{HL} the drift-compensation bitstream used for switching from H to L, and D^{LH} the drift-compensation bitstream used for switching from L to H. D^{HL} and D^{LH} are generated using the following equations.

$$D_n^{HL} = \text{Pred}(H_{n-1}, L_n) \qquad (1)$$

and

$$D_n^{LH} = \text{Pred}(L_{n-1}, H_n) \qquad (2)$$

where H_n and L_n stand for the nth frames of bitstreams H and L, respectively; Pred(A,B) represents an inter-frame prediction process that frame B is predicted from the reference frame A. Fig. 1 shows the process of generating the D^{HL} bitstream, where the drift-compensation frames D_n^{HL} are encoded using an MPEG-4 coder (without the IDCT and inverse quantizer) with L_n as the input and the H_{n-1} stored in the frame memory (instead of L_{n-1}) as the reference. The D^{LH} bitstream can be obtained using a similar manner, while H_n is used as the input and L_{n-1} is stored in the frame memory as the reference for prediction.

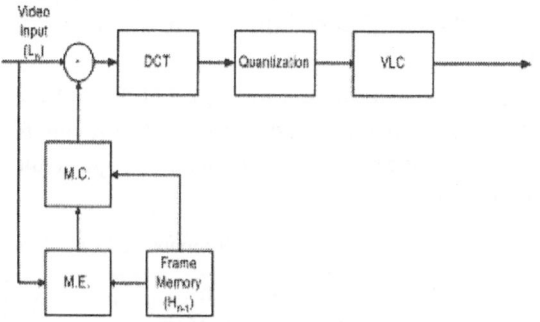

Fig. 1. An example of generating the D^{HL} bitstream

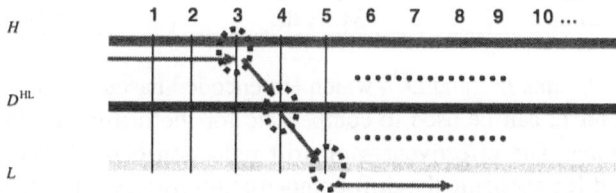

Fig. 2. An example of drift-compensated high-to-low-rate bitstream switching

When a client requests the server to perform bitstream switching, the drift-compensation frames are used for switching between H and L. For example, if a switching down operation (i.e., switching from H to L) at frame n is requested, the server will send frames as ..., H_{n-1}, D_n^{HL}, L_{n+1}, ..., instead of ..., H_{n-1}, L_n, L_{n+1}, ... as illustrated in Fig. 2 with frame 4 as the switch-point. With our proposed algorithm, the server will send one drift-compensation frame to replace the frame at the switch-point in the new bitstream to switch to. In the example shown in Fig. 2, after sending frame 4 of H, the server sends frame 4 of D^{HL} (the switch-point) followed by frame 5 of L, leading to a sequence as $..., H_2, H_3, D_4^{HL}, L_5, L_6,...$ After completing the switching process, the server will keep sending frames of the new bitstream. Similarly, the switching from L to H at frame n can be done by sending $..., L_{n-1}, D_n^{LH}, H_{n+1}, ...$ from the server.

Table 1 shows the average PSNR comparison of drift-compensated and direct bitstream switching between 512 kbps and 1024 kbps. The two bitstreams are encoded with a frame rate of 30 fps and GOP size of 30 frames using an MPEG-4 encoder with TM5 rate control. The quantization parameter used for encoding the D^{HL} drift-compensation bitstream is 11. There are 3 switching operations (switching down, then switching up, and finally switching down again) in the experiments in Table 1. The PSNR performance is evaluated by comparing the frames decoded from the drift-compensated and direct-switched bitstreams which are received at the client with that obtained from the drift-free (i.e., with perfect switching) sequence that is composed of corresponding frames directly decoded from the higher-rate (512 kbps) and lower-rate (1024 kbps) bitstreams.

Due to the temporal prediction used for encoding P- and B-frames, the drifting errors will propagate from the switch-point to the following frames until the next I frame is reached. This error propagation can lead to significant quality degradation if the drift is not well controlled.

Table 1. PSNR performance of using drift-compensated switching and direct switching

Sequence	PSNR with drift-compensated switching	PSNR with direct switching
Coastguard	35.68 dB	34.31 dB
News	34.89 dB	30.33 dB
Singer	34.81 dB	30.49 dB

The two bitstreams D^{HL} and D^{LH}, which are encoded based on the reconstructed images from H and L, can be used to compensate for the drifting errors caused by bitstreams switching. The effectiveness of drift reduction depends on the quantization parameters used for encoding the drift-compensation frames [4]. The finer the quantization step-size, the less the drift, but the higher the sending bit-rate and the storage cost. If D^{HL} and D^{LH} are losslessly encoded, there won't be any drift errors. Because the storage costs are much lower, and continuously decreasing nowadays, the increase on the storage cost for the drift-compensation bitstreams is not an important issue. Moreover, since D^{HL} and D^{LH} are all off-line encoded, the extra complexity required in the streaming video server is to decide which frames from which bitstreams should be transmitted when performing bitstream switching. This bitstream management cost is not high. The most attractive feature of the proposed method is that, like direct switching scheme, it just requires a standard video decoder to decode the switched bitsteams. Compared with the "seamless switching" scheme in [1] which involves a high-complexity non-standard decoder, the decoder complexity is reduced drastically, leading to a great cost reduction since the number of clients is usually high.

3 Receiver-Driven Video Multicasting with Drift-Compensated Bitstream Switching

3.1 Client Channel Bandwidth Estimation

In order to multicast FGS coded video bit-stream over heterogeneous networks, we should truncate the FGS enhancement layer into one or more sub-layers and transmit each to different multicast groups. In the case of truncating fixed bit-rates of enhancement layer into multicast groups, clients may receive unbalanced quality video in each frame. The advantage of separating one bit-plane into one group in the FGS enhancement layer is that clients can have an average visual quality of each frame. In our work, the server transmits one base layer and two or more enhancement sub-layers (MSB, MSB-1, etc.) to different multicast groups respectively. As a result, the clients can subscribe to one or more multicast groups with different levels of video quality according to their own capacity, bandwidth, and quality requirement.

In order to detect packet loss and calculate the packet loss ratio, we use the RTP (Real-time Transport Protocol) [9] on top of UDP to add the sequence number in the packet header. The clients keep tracking on the sequence number and frame number, to calculate the channel statistics and identify the lost frames and packets so as to calculate the packet loss ratio in an interval as follows:

$$P_k = \frac{L_k}{C_k} \tag{3}$$

where C_k is the interval with a constant number of packets and L_k is the number of lost packets in the interval C_k.

The clients can use the time-stamp of RTP to estimate RTT. First of all, assuming that the clocks of server and clients are well synchronized, the packets are time-stamped at the server side and sent to the Internet. The clients then receive these packets and report the receiving time. As a result, the RTT value can be estimated by subtracting the time-stamp of server from the receiving time of clients as described below.

$$RTT_i = 2 \times (t_i^c - t_i^s) \tag{4}$$

$$\overline{RTT}_k = \frac{1}{C_k} \sum_i^{C_k} RTT_i \tag{5}$$

where RTT_i denotes the round-trip time of packet i, t_i^c and t_i^s are respectively the time-stamps at the client and the server, and $\overline{RTT}_k$ denotes the average RTT in the interval C_k.

The TCP-friendly rate adaptation is necessary for multimedia applications to prevent congestion and unfair resource utilization in the Internet. Equation-based congestion control mechanisms [6,7] use the TCP throughput model [8] to adjust the transmission rate by estimating the TCP throughput R_{TCP} with the following equation.

$$R_{TCP} = \frac{MTU}{RTT\sqrt{\frac{2p}{3}} + RTO\sqrt{\frac{27p}{8}} p(1+32p^2)} \tag{6}$$

where *MTU* is the maximum transmission unit, *RTO* is the retransmission time out, and *p* is the estimated packet loss rate.

3.2 Receiver-Driven Multiple Bitstream Switching

In our system, clients can decide which layers to subscribe to according to the initial set-up information. After receiving the video sequence for a period of time, clients may suffer from packet loss and/or insufficient bandwidth with their subscription level, i.e., these clients should leave some higher-level multicast groups they are subscribing to. For example, if one client subscribes to three multicast groups (one base layer and two enhancement layers) in the beginning and it turns out to detect packet loss by checking the sequence numbers of packets, this client will leave the highest-level multicast group to prevent packet loss. If the client still suffers from packet loss due to deficient bandwidth then it is also going to leave the second enhancement layer. Now the client only subscribes to one multicast group (base layer), if packet loss occurs at this moment, the client cannot leave the latest multicast group, otherwise, the connection will be broken. Therefore, we add a multicast group with a lower bit-rate base layer to the system, and then clients are able to switch to the lower bit-rate layer from original base layer by leaving the original multicast group to the lower one.

To avoid the drift caused by direct switching down (from higher-rate to lower-rate) or switching up (from lower-rate to higher-rate), we propose to add a drift-compensation bit-stream to reduce the drift errors. For example, if a client finds the bandwidth is not enough according to the channel throughput estimation when receiving the third frame and the client must switch down. In order to solve the drift problem, the client has to receive the fourth frame of the switching bit-stream and then the fifth, sixth, seventh frames of the lower-bit-rate bit-stream respectively. Fig. 3 illustrates the switching down example.

For video multicasting with multiple-bitstream switching, we must ensure that the drift-compensation frames be received properly by the clients while switching. For example, as shown in Fig. 3, the 4th drift-compensation frame must be received before switching to the 5th frame of the lower-rate bitstream. Therefore, we propose to delay the drift-compensation frames by some time-slots in transmission so that the client can receive the correct video data to decode and display.

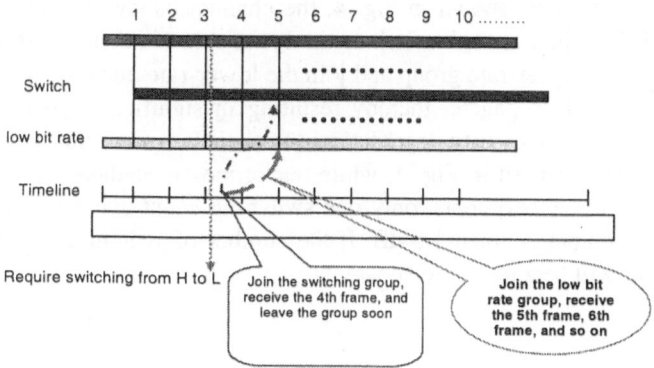

Fig. 3. Delayed switching bit-stream for multicasting

4 Experimental Results

Two CIF (352x288) video sequences, "News" and "Singer," were encoded with a GOP size of 14, at two bit-rates: 256 kbps and 128 kbps, respectively. The bit-rate of one base layer plus the MSB bit-plane of the enhancement layer is bout 300 kbps. The bit-rate of the base layer plus the first two enhancement sub-layers (MSB and MSB-1 bit-planes) is about 700 kbps. In the beginning, the clients subscribe to the higher-bit-rate base-layer and several enhancement sub-layers if their bandwidth is enough. Then the receiver-driven congestion control mechanism starts to estimate the network conditions, including the packet loss ratio, *RTT*, and compute the TCP throughput by Eq. (6). When a client observes the estimated available bandwidth is lower than its current subscription level, it will leave one higher enhancement sub-layer to avoid packet loss or congestion.

By incorporating the drift-compensated switching algorithm presented in Section 3, the proposed system can further adapt to large bandwidth variations, while remaining reasonable visual quality. Furthermore, since our proposed system is capable of estimating the channel throughput, the clients can subscribe to the drift-compensation frames and the next bit-stream to switch to prior to switching when the estimated available bandwidth is close to the switching threshold. Since each frame is ensured to be prepared for decoding by grabbing in the buffer beforehand, the decoded video with the proposed method would be much smoother than the direct switching scheme.

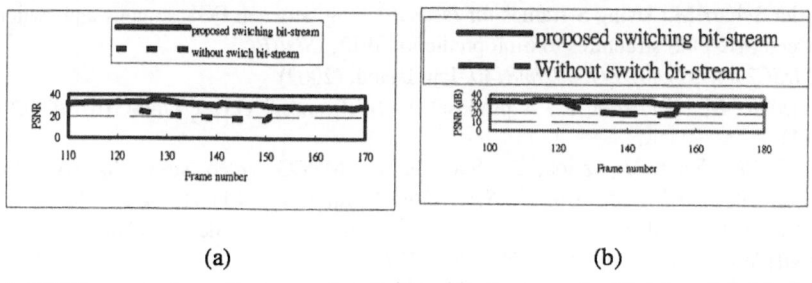

(a)   (b)

Fig. 4. PSNR comparison of proposed switching bit-stream and without switch bit-stream (a) "News" sequence (b) "Singer" sequence.

In our experiments shown in Fig. 4, the channel bandwidth for one client is not enough and the client should switch to the lower-rate bitstream at frame #120. If the client leaves the higher-rate group and join the lower-rate one directly, drift errors will be introduced and propagate, thereby resulting in significant quality degradation as explained above. The quality degradation due to drift errors with the direct switching scheme can be observed in Fig. 4, while our proposed method can mitigate the drift drastically. In the experiments, only one switching event was triggered. The average PSNR improvement is about 1.5 dB. If the number of switching events is higher, the improvement will become more apparent.

5 Conclusions

In this paper, we proposed an MPEG-4 video streaming system with both unicast and multicast support. The proposed system can provide network adaptation with receiver-driven congestion control by estimating the network conditions and bandwidth capacity. In the proposed system, the values of *RTT*, packet loss ratio, and packet size are used to compute the TCP throughput. Using the information carried in the RTP (real-time transport protocol), the *RTT* and packet loss ratio can be estimated efficiently. With the estimated TCP throughput, clients are able to adjust their subscription levels by joining or leaving some multicast groups according to the estimated bandwidth. In addition to the congestion control mechanism, we also presented a drift-compensated bitstream switching scheme to allow users to switch up and down over different-rate bitstreams with minimized drift errors. We also integrated the proposed switching scheme into our receiver-driven multicasting platform so that users can adapt to large network variations more efficiently. In the experiments, we showed that our proposed schemes can solve network congestion efficiently and achieve significant video quality improvement.

References

1. Sun, X., Wu, F., Li, S., Gao, W.: The framework for seamless switching of scalable bit-streams, *ISO/IEC JTC1/SC29/WG11/MPEG2002/m8214*, Jeju Island (2002)
2. van der Scharr M.: Using S-frames for fast switching between FGS streams and switching between MC-FGS structures to limit prediction-drift, *ISO/IEC JTC1/SC29/WG11/MPEG2002/m8140*, Jeju Island, (2002)
3. Karczewic, M., Kurceren, R.: A proposal for SP-frames," ITU-T Q6/SG16, VCEG-L27 (2001)
4. Lin, C.-W., Youn, J., Zhou, J., Sun, M.-T.: MPEG video streaming with VCR-functionality, *IEEE Trans. Circuits Syst. Video Technol.* 3 (2001) 415 -425
5. Li, W.: Overview of Fine Granularity Scalability in MPEG-4 video standard, *IEEE Trans. Circuits Syst. Video Technol*, 3 (2001) 301-317
6. Floyd, S., Pahdye, J., Widmer, J.: Equation-based congestion control for unicast applica-tion," *SIGCOMM* (2001)

7. Kim, Y., Kim, J., Kuo, C.-C. J.: Smooth and fast rate adaptation mechanism (SFRAM) for TCP-friendly Internet video, *Proc. Packet Video Workshop* (2000)
8. Padhye, J., Firoiu, V., Towsley, D.: Modeling TCP throughput: a simple model and its empirical validation, *UMASS CMPSCI Technical Report, TR98-008*, (1998)
9. Kikuchi, Y., Nomura, T., Fukunaga, S.: RTP payload format for MPEG-4 audio/visual streams, *Request for Comments (proposed standard) 3016. IETF*, (2000)

Flexible and Efficient Switching Techniques between Scalable Video Bitstreams

Xiaoyan Sun[*][1], Feng Wu[2], Shipeng Li[2], Wen Gao[1], and Ya-Qin Zhang[2]

[1] Department of Computer Application, Harbin Institute of Technology, Harbin, 150001
{xysun, wgao}@jdl.ac.cn
[2] Microsoft Research Asia, Beijing, 100080
{fengwu, spli, yzhang}@microsoft.com

Abstract. In this paper, we first describe a seamless switching scheme for scalable video bitstreams that fully takes advantage of both the high coding efficiency of non-scalable bitstreams and the flexibility of scalable bitstreams. Small bandwidth fluctuations are absorbed by the scalability of the bitstreams, while large bandwidth fluctuations are tolerated by switching between scalable bitstreams. Flexible and efficient switching techniques are investigated as the focus of this paper. A flexible method is proposed to switch from current scalable bitstream to one operated at lower rates at any frame without any overhead bits. Since additional bits are necessary in the proposed scheme when switching from a scalable bitstream operated at lower rates to one operated at higher rates, an efficient method is proposed to greatly reduce the amount of overhead bits. Experimental results show that the seamless switching scheme with the proposed switching techniques significantly outperforms both the approach with a single scalable bitstream and the approach of switching among multiple non-scalable bitstreams.

1 Introduction

With the steady growth of the access bandwidth, more and more Internet applications start to use streaming audio and video contents [1][2]. Since the Internet is inherently a heterogeneous and dynamical best-effort network, channel bandwidth usually fluctuates in a wide range from bit rate below 64kbps to well above 1 Mbps. This brings great challenges to video coding and streaming technologies in providing a smooth playback experience and best available video quality to the users. To deal with the network bandwidth variations, two main approaches, namely, switching among multiple non-scalable bitstreams and streaming with a single scalable bitstream, have been extensively investigated in recent years.

In the first approach, a video sequence is compressed into several non-scalable bitstreams at different bit rates. Some special frames, known as *key frames*, are either compressed without prediction or coded with an extra switching bitstream [3]-[5]. Key frames provide access points to switch among these bitstreams to fit in the available

---

[*] This work has been done while the author is with Microsoft Research Asia.

Y.-C. Chen, L.-W. Chang, and C.-T. Hsu (Eds.): PCM 2002, LNCS 2532, pp. 856-864, 2002.

bandwidth. The advantage of this method is the high coding efficiency with non-scalable bitstreams. However, due to limitation in both the number of bitstreams and switching points, this method only provides coarse and sluggish capability in adapting to channel bandwidth variations.

In the second approach, a video sequence is compressed into a single scalable bitstream, which can be truncated flexibly to adapt to bandwidth variations. Among numerous scalable coding techniques, MPEG-4 Fine Granularity Scalable (FGS) coding has become prominent due to its fine-grain scalability [6]. Since the enhancement bitstream can be truncated arbitrarily in any frame, FGS provides a remarkable capability in readily and precisely adapting to channel bandwidth variations. However, low coding efficiency is the vital disadvantage that prevents FGS from being widely deployed in video streaming applications. Progressive Fine Granularity Scalable (PFGS) coding scheme [7][8] is a significant improvement over FGS by introducing two prediction loops with different quality references. But since only one high quality reference is used in enhancement layer coding, most coding efficiency gain appears within a certain bit rate range around the high quality reference. Generally, with today's technologies, there is still a coding efficiency loss compared with the non-scalable case at fixed bit rates.

A seamless switching scheme is described in this paper to significantly improve the efficiency of scalable video coding over a broad bit rate range by using two scalable bitstreams. Each scalable bitstream has a base layer coded at a certain bit rate to best adapt to the channel bandwidth variation within a certain bit rate range. The scalable bitstream can be seamlessly switched from one to another according to the variation of the channel bandwidth for better coding efficiency. We will refer to switching from a scalable bitstream operated at lower bit rates to one operated at higher bit rates as *switching up* and the reversion as *switching down* hereafter in this paper. This basic idea about the seamless switching scheme was first proposed in [9], this paper focuses the researches on the switching techniques.

The key problem we try to solve in this paper is how to flexibly and efficiently switch up and down between scalable bitstreams. There are different requirements for switching down and switching up, respectively. When channel bandwidth somehow drops, switching down should be operated rapidly to reduce packet loss ratio and maintain smooth video playback. Therefore, two basic requirements should be met in switching down: (1) the scalable bitstreams could be switched down at any frame; (2) overhead bits should be avoided during switching down since they will increase network traffic and may further deteriorate network conditions.

When channel bandwidth increases, a delay is usually needed for the server to make a reliable decision for switching up. Moreover, network condition also allows additional bits to be transmitted in this case. Therefore, the method adopted in the proposed scheme is to attach an extra bitstream in some frames for switching up. In order to avoid drifting errors, the extra bitstream is usually formed by losslessly compressing the mismatches between the reconstructed frames with different bitstreams. However, this would cause huge overhead bits in these frames. A new method referred to as *switching frame* (SF) is proposed in this paper to greatly reduce the amount of overhead bits for switching up.

This paper is organized as follows. Section 2 briefly describes the proposed seamless switching scheme. The methods for switching down and switching up are discussed in Section 3 and Section 4, respectively. Experimental results are given in Section 5. Finally, Section 6 concludes this paper.

2 The Seamless Switching Scheme

Either MPEG-4 FGS or PFGS coding can be used in the proposed scheme. For better coding efficiency, the macroblock-based PFGS (MPFGS) is chosen as the basic scalable video codec in this paper [8]. The MPFGS codec compresses a video sequence into two bitstreams. In each frame, the base layer bitstream is first generated by traditional non-scalable coding technique, and then the residue between original/predicted DCT coefficients and dequantized DCT coefficients of the base layer forms the enhancement layer bitstream with bit-plane coding technique. The bit rate of the base layer is the lower bound of the channel bandwidth covered by this scalable bitstream. The enhancement layer bitstream provides fine-grain scalability to adapt to channel bandwidth variations.

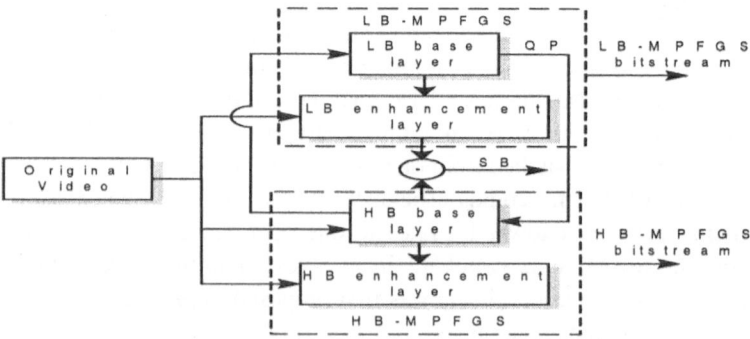

Fig. 1. The sketch of the proposed seamless switching scheme with two MPFGS encoders.

The proposed seamless switching scheme for two scalable video bitstreams is sketched in Fig. 1. There are two MPFGS encoders outlined by the dashed boxes in this figure. The upper one is denoted as LB-MPFGS because of the low bit rate base layer, whereas the bottom one is denoted as HB-MPFGS accordingly. The middle part between the two MPFGS encoders is used to generate a *switching bitstream* (SB) for switching up. To ensure that the MPFGS bitstreams are able to be seamlessly switched from one to the other, the base layer bitstreams of the two MPFGS are actually generated dependently. Firstly, the same motion vectors are applied to both HB-MPFGS and LB-MPFGS. Secondly, the video encoded at the LB-MPFGS base layer is the reconstructed base layer of HB-MPFGS instead of the original video. Finally, the quantization parameters of the LB-MPFGS base layer are encoded into both HB-MPFGS and LB-MPFGS base layer bitstreams. The block diagram of the proposed seamless switching scheme and the MPFGS coding technique are given in [8][9], respectively. How to switch down and up between MPFGS bitstreams is discussed in the next two sections.

3 Switching Down between Scalable Bitstreams

The technique proposed for switching down is similar to transcoding bitstreams from high bit rate to low bit rate. Given that the bit rate of the base layer in HB-MPFGS is much higher than that in LB-MPFGS, the reconstructed high quality base layer of HB-MPFGS, instead of the original video, is input into the LB-MPFGS base layer encoder. In other words, the signal encoded at the LB-MPFGS base layer is the difference between the reconstructed HB-MPFGS base layer and the temporal prediction. This is the key point for achieving the switching down in any frame without any overhead bits.

When the HB-MPFGS bitstream is being transmitted to the client, the reconstructed HB-MPFGS base layer, which is the image to be encoded at the LB-MPFGS base layer, is available at both the encoder and the decoder. When network bandwidth drops below the bit rate of the HB-MPFGS base layer, the HB-MPFGS bitstream has to be promptly switched to the LB-MPFGS bitstream. Since the network can hardly tolerate more overhead bits in this case, the main problem here is how to precisely recover the reconstructed LB-MPFGS base layer in the current frame without an extra bitstream. In the proposed method, the reconstructed LB-MPFGS base layer is directly calculated from the current reconstructed HB-MPFGS base layer, provided that the temporal prediction and quantization parameters of the LB-MPFGS base layer are available.

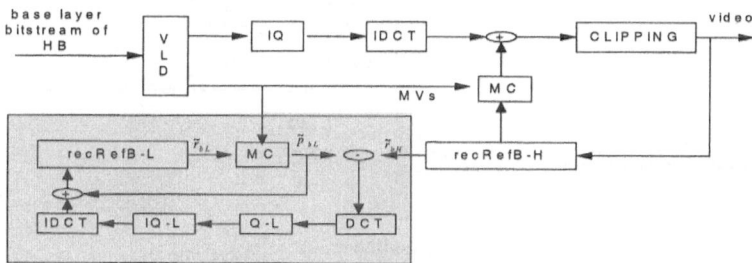

Fig. 2. The HB-MPFGS base layer decoder

The quantization parameters of the LB-MPFGS base layer can be readily encoded into the HB-MPFGS bitstream. If the quantization parameters are adjusted at frame level, only five extra bits are necessary for each frame. Even if the quantization parameters are adjusted at macroblock level, the number of overhead bits is still relatively quite small in the HB-MPFGS base layer bitstream. The temporal prediction for the LB-MPFGS base layer is constantly computed at the HB-MPFGS base layer decoder. Fig. 2 illustrates the HB-MPFGS base layer decoder, where the gray part is for this purpose. This would increase the complexity of the HB-MPFGS decoder merely, but it would not incur any new overhead bits.

When scalable bitstream is just switched up to HB-MPFGS, the prediction $\tilde{P}_{bL}$ in Fig. 2 is available in LB-MPFGS. After the next frame is decoded in HB-MPFGS, the reconstructed reference $\tilde{r}_{bH}$ is also available. Since the quantization parameters of LB-

MPFGS are encoded in the HB-MPFGS base layer bitstream, the reconstructed reference $\tilde{r}_{bL}$ is calculated as shown in Fig. 2. Furthermore, since the same motion vectors are used at both MPFGS decoders, the HB-MPFGS can readily get the next prediction $\tilde{P}_{bL}$ after motion compensation.

The prediction $\tilde{P}_{bL}$ and the quantization parameters of the LB-MPFGS base layer are always available in HB-MPFGS. Thus the most virtue of this method is that the proposed technique can switch down in any frame. Furthermore, no extra overhead bits are needed when switching down from HB-MPFGS to LB-MPFGS bitstreams.

4   Switching Up among Scalable Bitstreams

The proposed scheme switches up for one MPFGS bitstream to the other by attaching an extra bitstream in some frames. Since the extra switching bitstream is usually generated with lossless method, this would cause huge overhead bits in these frames. Therefore, the SF technique similar to that in [5] is proposed to greatly reduce the overhead bits for switching up.

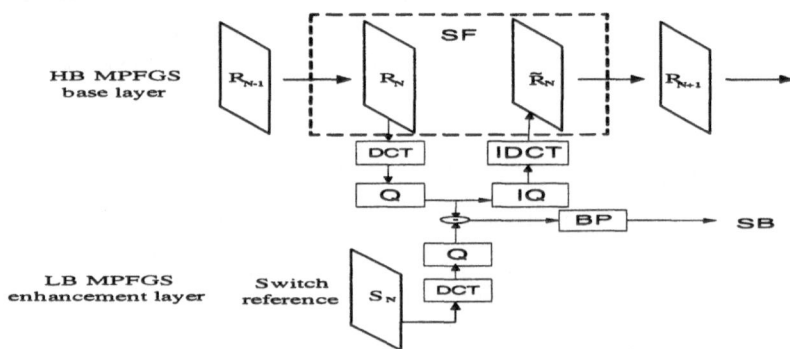

Fig. 3. The switching frame (SF) coding

As shown in Figure 3, assume that the Nth frame is one point for switching up. Normally the switching up happens when the available channel bandwidth is high enough to cover the HB-MPFGS base layer bit rate. S_N is the reconstructed image from the LB-MPFGS enhancement layer at the corresponding bit rate. R_N is the reconstructed image at the HB-MPFGS base layer. For the traditional method, the difference between them is compressed losslessly into the switching bitstream.

In the SF method, both S_N and R_N are first transformed into DCT domain and quantized with the same quantization parameter. The difference between two sets of quantized DCT coefficients is compressed with the bit plane coding technique to form the switching bitstream. In this case, the sum of the dequantized S_N and the difference encoded in the switching bitstream is equal to the dequantized $\tilde{R}_N$. Therefore, to avoid drifting errors at the HB-MPFGS base layer, the reference for the next frame coding is $\tilde{R}_N$ instead of R_N in the switching frame.

Since the quantization is introduced in the SF method, the overhead bits in the switching bitstream can be greatly reduced by adjusting the quantization parameter. The main concern is the effect of the SF method on the coding efficiency of two MPFGS encoders. Firstly, S_N, which used only for the purpose of switching up, does not directly involve in the LB-MPFGS coding, thus the quantization of $\tilde{S}_N$ will have little effect on the LB-MPFGS coding efficiency. Secondly, using $\tilde{R}_N$ as reference will affect the coding efficiency of HB-MPFGS to some extent. But the switching point is inserted with half a second or one second interval in the most applications. This kind of coding efficiency losses is afforded in HB-MPFGS.

5   Experimental Results

Five different schemes, namely, the seamless switch with lossless SB, the seamless switch with SF, MPEG-4 FGS, MPFGS, the switch between non-scalable bitstreams, are compared in terms of both coding efficiency and channel bandwidth adaptation. The QCIF sequence News and Foreman are used in this experiment with 10Hz encoding frame rate. Only the first frame is encoded as I frame, and the rest of frames are encoded as P frames. TM5 rate control method is used in the base layer encoding. The range of motion vectors is limited to ±15.5 pixel with half pixel precision.

In the seamless scheme with or without the SF method, the bit rate of the LB-MPFGS base layer is 32 kbps. The high quality reference is reconstructed at 64 kbps (base layer plus 32 kbps enhancement layer), and channel bandwidth covered by LB-MPFGS is from 32 kbps to 128 kbps. The bit rate of the HB-MPFGS base layer is 80 kbps including the overhead bits for coding quantization parameters of the LB-MPFGS base layer. The high quality reference is reconstructed at 112 kbps. The channel bandwidth range covered by the HB-MPFGS can be from 80 kbps up to lossless rate. However, the upper bound of the HB-MPFGS bit rate is limited to 160 kbps in this experiment.

Switching between non-scalable bitstreams is extensively used in many commercial streaming video systems. Two non-scalable bitstreams are used in this experiment with the same conditions as in the LB-MPFGS and HB-MPFGS base layers. However, I frames are inserted every ten frames for the purpose of easily switching between bitstreams, since channel bandwidth changes with minimum 1 second interval in this experiment. In the single MPEG-4 FGS and the single MPFGS schemes, the base layer bit rate is same as that in LB-MPFGS. The high quality reference in the single MPFGS bitstream is reconstructed at the bit plane with bit rate over 40kbps. Thus, the most significant coding efficiency gain is biased toward high bit rates.

The effect of the SF technique on the coding efficiency of the HB-MPFGS base layer is first evaluated in Figure 4. The switching points are inserted every ten frames in the HB MPFGS base layer. The quantization parameter of SF is always set to 3 for all sequences. The results in Figure 4 show that the average PSNR loss is below 0.1dB compared with the lossless coding method. However, the average overhead bits in each switching frame are greatly reduced as listed in Table1. Only about 20% overhead bits are needed for the SF technique.

The curves of average PSNR versus bit rate are depicted in Figure 5. Switching between non-scalable bitstreams only provides two different quality levels, while other schemes can flexibly and precisely adapt to channel bandwidth and provide smooth visual quality. Compared with the single FGS and MPFGS bitstream schemes, the coding efficiency of the proposed scheme can be 2.0dB higher than MPFGS and 3.0dB higher than FGS at higher bit rates.

Table 1. Average bits for each frame in the extra bitstream.

News		Forman	
SF	Lossless	SF	Lossless
30351	133090	31840	156212

A dynamic channel is used to verify the performances of four different coding schemes in term of bandwidth adaptation. The overhead bits for switching up are taken into account in the simulation. The bit rate periodically switches from 72kbps to 152kbps. Each cycle starts at 72kbps for 1 second and then switches to 152 kbps for 3 seconds. The curves of PSNR versus frame number are shown in Figure 6. The proposed scheme switches up 3 times and switches down 2 times in order to adapt channel bandwidth fluctuations. Clearly, the proposed scheme with the SF technique can always achieve the best performances among these four schemes at both lower bit rates and higher bit rates.

6 Conclusions

This paper describes a seamless switching scheme for scalable video bitstreams that fully takes advantage of both the high coding efficiency of non-scalable bitstreams and the flexibility of scalable bitstreams. No additional bits are needed in the freely switching down with the proposed technique. Furthermore, the proposed SF technique saves about 80% overhead bits for switching up, meanwhile provides the almost same coding efficiency as that of the lossless coding. The experimental results show that the proposed scheme with the switching techniques can achieve the best streaming performance among numerous schemes.

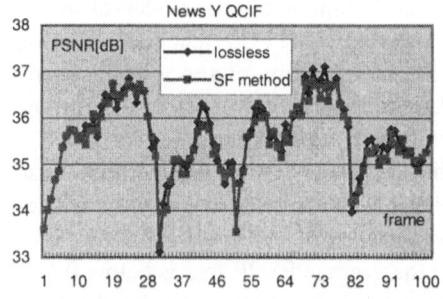 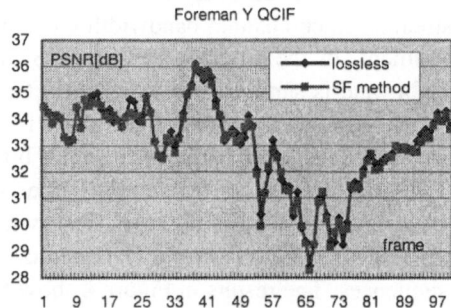

Fig. 4. Coding efficiency comparisons between SF and lossless coding.

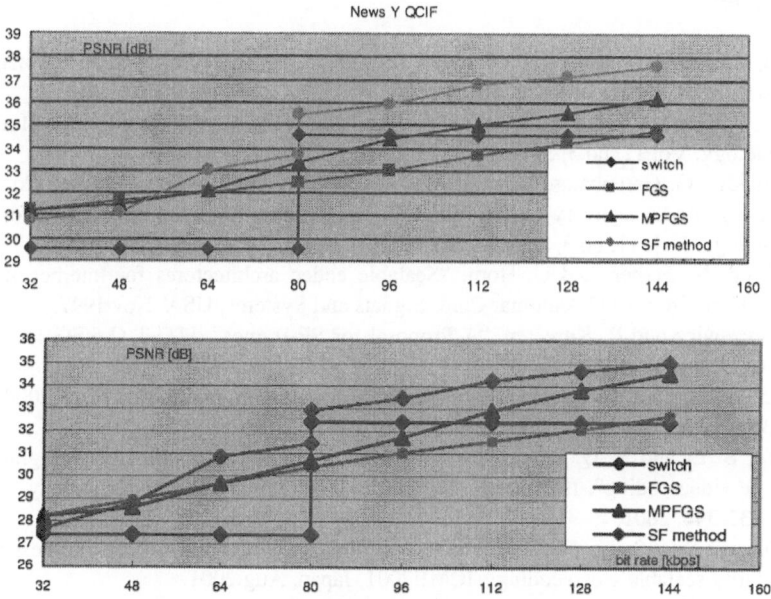

Fig. 5. The curves of average PSNR versus bit rate.

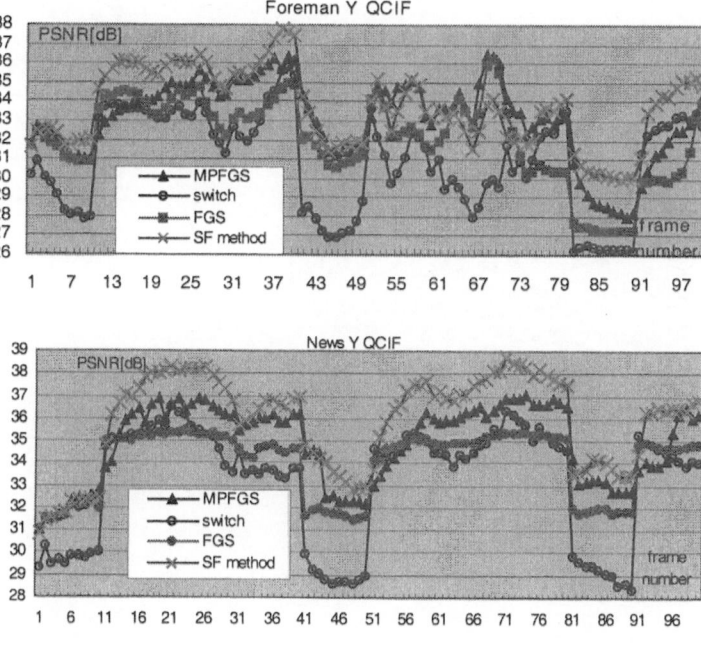

Fig. 6. The curves of PSNR versus frame numbers in which channel bandwidth periodically varies at 72kbps and 152kbps.

References

[1] J. Lu, "Signal processing for Internet video streaming: A review", SPIE in Image and Video Communication and Processing 2000, Vol 3974, 246-258, 2000.

[2] W. Li, "Streaming video profile in MPEG-4", IEEE trans. Circuits and Systems for Video Technology, Vol 11, no 3, 301-317, 2001

[3] G. Conklin, G. Greenbaum, K. Lillevold, A. Lippman and Y. Reznik, "Video Coding for Streaming Media Delivery on the Internet", IEEE trans. Circuits and Systems for Video Technology, Vol. 11, no 3, 269-281, 2001

[4] B. Girod, N. Farber, and U. Horn, "Scalable codec architectures for Internet video on demand", in Proc. 1997 Asilomar Conf. Signals and Systems, USA, Nov 1997.

[5] M. Jarczewicz and R. Kurceren, "A Proposal for SP-frames", ITU-T Q.6/SG 16, VCEG-L27, Germany, Jan 2001.

[6] W. Li, "Fine granularity scalability in MPEG-4 for streaming video", ISCAS 2000, vol 1, 299-302, Switzerland, May 2000.

[7] F. Wu, S. Li and Y.-Q. Zhang, "A framework for efficient progressive fine granularity scalable video coding", IEEE trans. Circuits and Systems for Video Technology, Vol. 11, no 3, 332-344, 2001.

[8] X. Sun, F. Wu, S. Li, W. Gao, and Y,-Q. Zhang, "Macroblock-based progressive fine granularity scalable video coding", ICME2001, Japan, Aug 2001.

[9] X. Sun, F. Wu, S. Li, W. Gao, and Y-Q. Zhang, "Seamless switching of scalable video bitstreams for efficient streaming", submit to ISCAS 2002.

Robust Video Transmission Using RSE-Code-Based FEC*

Tae-Uk Choi and Ki-Dong Chung

Department of Computer Science
Pusan National University
Kumjeoung-Ku, Pusan 609-735, Korea
{tuchoi, kdchung}@melon.cs.pusan.ac.kr

Abstract. The RSE(Reed-Solomon Erasure) code is widely used to prevent packet loss over a lossy network. RSE-code-based FEC does not require additional network delay but needs much additional network bandwidth to transmit redundant data. Thus, an effective redundancy control mechanism is required to minimize the amount of redundancy. In this paper, we propose a redundancy control algorithm for RSE-code-based FEC that can adjust the amount of redundancy depending on network loss conditions as well as the prioirty of frames. Experiments show that RSE-code-based FEC with the proposed redundancy control algorithm considerably reduces the amount of redundancy and keeps the frame loss rate under any threshold.

1 Introduction

Real-time video transmission over the Internet have suffered due to loss, delay and jitter. Packet loss degrades video quality, and excessive network delay lowers user interactivity. As well, because most video compression standards such as MPEG I, II and H.263 use motion estimation and compensation, a small loss in a frame can severely affects video quality and can be propagated to the subsequent frames. Many techniques to prevent error propagation have been proposed. Choi et al.[1] classified these techniques of preventing error propagation into codec-level and network-level schemes. Codec-level schemes such as ET(Error Tracking) and RPS(Reference Picture Selection) prevent error propagation during encoding and decoding frames. Network-level schemes such as FEC and ARQ control the errors during sending and receiving packets.

FEC sends the original data along with the redundant data and tries to recover the lost data from the redundant data when the original data is lost. Because FEC does not require additional network delay, it is preferred in real-time video applications. RSE(Reed-Solomon Erasure) correcting code, such as the one described by McAuley[2], is widely used to generate the redundant packets. However, because RSE-code-based FEC needs much additional bandwidth for

* This work was supported by grant No. R05-2002-000-00345-0 from the Basic Research Program of the Korea Science & Engineering Foundation.

Y.-C. Chen, L.-W. Chang, and C.-T. Hsu (Eds.): PCM 2002, LNCS 2532, pp. 865–872, 2002.

parity packets, an effective redundancy control algorithm is required to reduce the bandwidth overhead.

In this paper, we discuss two strategies of redundancy control for RES-code-based FEC. One is to adjust the amount of parity according to network loss conditions. This means that the number of parity packets increases when the network loss rate is high and decreases when the network loss rate is low. Another is to adjust the redundancy depending on the priority of frames. This means that high-prioirty frames such as I frames have more parity packets than low-priority frames such as P and B frames. Based on two strategies, we propose a redundancy control algorithm for RSE-code-based FEC that can adapts the amount of redundancy according to the network loss conditions as well as the priority of frames.

The rest of the paper is organized as follows. Section 2 analyzes the performance of the RSE code using two statistical models. In Section 3, two strategies of redundancy control are described and the redundancy control algorithm for RSE-code-based FEC is proposed. Section 4 presents experimental results of the proposed algorithm. Lastly, conclusion is drawn in Section 5.

2   Performance of the Reed-Solomon Erasure Code

The RSE encoder takes k data packets $d_1, d_2, ..., d_k$ and produces $n - k$ parity packets $p_1, p_2, ..., p_{n-k}$. The RSE decoder at the receiver side can reconstruct the data packets $d_1, d_2, ..., d_k$ whenever it has received any k out of n packets $d_1, ..., d_k, p_1, ..., p_{n-k}$. The k data packets is referred to as a TG(transmission group), and the n packets is referred to as an FEC block. As well, $RS(n, k)$ denotes the RSE code in which k data packets is encoded into n packets.

2.1   One-State Loss Model

In RSE-code-based FEC, if a receiver can estimate the packet loss rate from the sender to itself, it can request more parity packets than what it actually needs in order to protect frame loss with probabilities that are close to one. To do so, the receiver must be able to calculate the probability of receiving at least k packets out of an FEC block of n packets, or the probability that a TG is received and reconstructed successfully. We represent this value by $P(n, k)$. If the loss is modeled as a temporally independent loss process with packet loss probability p, then $P(n, k)$ is as follows[3]:

$$P(n, k) = \sum_{i=k}^{n} \binom{n}{i} (1 - p)^i p^{n-i} \tag{1}$$

$P(n, k)$ is calculated recursively using equation (2) and (3).

$$P(n, k) = P(n - 1, k) + \binom{n - 1}{k - 1} (1 - p)^k p^{n-k} \tag{2}$$

$$P(n, n) = (1 - p)^n \tag{3}$$

If k is fixed and n is large, $P(n, k)$ is extremely close to one. An appropriate n that satisfies $P(n, k) \geq \eta$ can be determined so that the packets are received with a probability larger than any $\eta(0 \leq \eta \leq 1)$.

2.2 Two-State Loss Model

The previous results assume that losses are not temporally correlated, and will produce inaccurate calculations for networks with burst losses. Burst losses in the Internet can be accurately modeled using the two-state loss model. Fig. 1 shows a state diagram for the two-state Markov model, which was first used by Gilbert[4]. In a Good state (G), errors would occur with low probability P_G while in a Bad state (B), they occur with high probability P_B. The errors occur in bursts with relatively long error-free intervals between them. The model with $P_G = 0$ and $P_B = 1$ is referred to as the simplified Gilbert model.

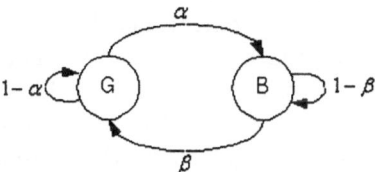

Fig. 1. Gilbert model

Based on the simplified model, a receiver can calculate $D(n, k)$ the probability of receiving k packets out of n packets. Let $D(n, k|B)$ be the probability of sending n packets, receiving k packets and winding up in state B, and $D(n, k|G)$ be the similar probability but that one winds up in state G. Then, $D(n, k)$ is obtained as follows[3]:

$$D(n, k) = D(n, k|G) + D(n, k|B) \tag{4}$$
$$D(n, k|G) = D(n - 1, k - 1|B)\beta + D(n - 1, k - 1|G)(1 - \alpha) \tag{5}$$
$$D(n, k|B) = D(n - 1, k|B)(1 - \beta) + D(n - 1, k|G)\alpha \tag{6}$$

$D(n, k)$ is calculated recursively by using the boundary conditions:

$$D(n, 0|G) = 0 \tag{7}$$
$$D(n, n|G) = \pi_G(1 - \alpha)^n + \pi_B\beta(1 - \alpha)^{n-1} \tag{8}$$
$$D(n, n|B) = 0 \tag{9}$$
$$D(n, 0|B) = \pi_G\alpha(1 - \beta)^{n-1} + \pi_B(1 - \beta)^n \tag{10}$$

The transition probability α and β can be obtained by the mean length of the nonloss period T_R and the mean length of the loss period T_L. Because of the state transition rate of the Markov chain, α is T_R^{-1} and β is T_L^{-1}. π_G indicates the probability that the system initially resides in state G and is calculated by $\pi_G = \beta/(\alpha+\beta)$, and π_B indicates the probability that the system initially resides in state B and is obtained by $\pi_B = \alpha/(\alpha + \beta)$.

There is a probability that a TG can be reconstructed in the receiver. In the two-state loss model, $P(n, k)$ the probability of receiving at least k packets out of n packets is calculated using $D(n, k)$ as follows:

$$P(n,k) = \sum_{i=k}^{n} D(n,i) \tag{11}$$

3   Redundancy Control

3.1   Adapting to Network Conditions

A weakness of FEC is the demand for additional network bandwidth for parity packets. An effective redundancy control algorithm is necessary to reduce the bandwidth overhead. One approach is to adjust redundancy (the number of parity packets) according to network loss conditions. This means that the number of parity packets should increase when network loss rates are high and decrease when network loss rates are low. Fig. 2 shows the system architecture for redundancy control, the FEC encoder produces parity packets using the RSE code. The FEC decoder reconstructs lost data packets using these parity packets. The QoS monitor collects the QoS information including T_R and T_L. The redundancy controller determines the values of k and n based on the feedback of the QoS information.

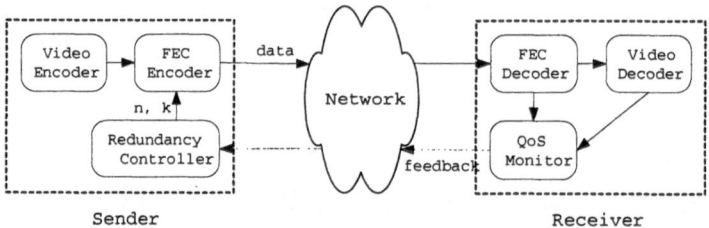

Fig. 2. System architecture for redundancy control

RTCP can be used to get feedback of the QoS information. To measure T_R and T_L, the receiver counts the short-term average of loss periods $\hat{T}_L$ and non-loss periods $\hat{T}_R$ during each RTCP period, and smooth them out using first order auto-regression as shown in (18) and (19). This smoothing gives long-term averages of the loss period and the non-loss period and diminishes oscillation of T_R and T_L.

$$T_R = \lambda \hat{T}_R + (1 - \lambda)T_R \tag{12}$$

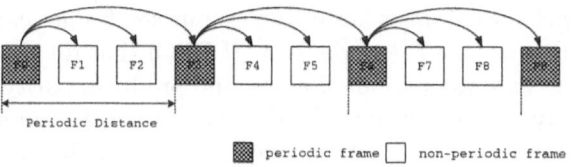

Periodic Distance

◼ periodic frame   ☐ non-periodic frame

Fig. 3. Periodic Referencing

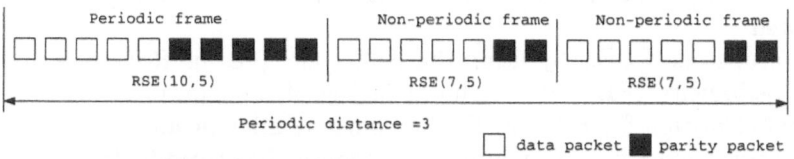

Periodic distance =3

☐ data packet ◼ parity packet

Fig. 4. RSE-code-based FEC with periodicity

$$T_L = \lambda \hat{T}_L + (1 - \lambda) T_L \qquad (13)$$

where, λ is a smoothing factor. In every RTCP period, the transition probabilities α and β, and stationary probability π_G and π_B are recalculated based on the measured T_R and T_L.

In RSE-code-based FEC, each video frame is divided into several data packets, and parity packets are created through the RS encoding. Then, the corresponding FEC block is transmitted to the receiver. Based on the feedback information, redundancy should be controlled by adjusting the parameters n and k to network loss states. The RSE coder proposed by McAuley[2] uses a symbol size m with $m = 8$ or $m = 32$. When packet size $S_{packet} > m$, we need to choose a packet size $S_{packet} = Y \times m$ where Y is an integer. If the packet size S_{packet} is pre-defined and the size of an encoded frame is S_{frame}, k is obtained as follows:

$$k = \lceil \frac{S_{frame}}{S_{packet}} \rceil \qquad (14)$$

After determining k, n can be calculated using (15). If k is fixed, and the tolerable loss rate of a TG is τ at the receiver, the smallest t that satisfies $P(t, k) \geq 1 - \tau$ will be chosen as n.

$$n = \min_{k \leq t \leq \infty} \{t | P(t, k) \geq 1 - \tau\} \qquad (15)$$

where, $0 \leq \tau \leq 1$.

3.2 Adapting to the Priority of Frames

Another approach to control the redundancy is to utilize the priority of video frames. In case of MPEG, if I frames have more parity packets than P frames or B frames, the loss probability of I frames will decrease to prevent error propagation.

In case of H.263, most frames are P frames, but key frames can be chosen to give priority. Choi[1] proposed Periodic FEC (PFEC) that divides video frames into periodic frames and non-periodic frames, and produces parity packets for not all frames but only periodic frames. PFEC can reduce the amount of redundancy much more than FEC while it keeps video quality similar to FEC. Fig. 3 shows the frame referencing method of PFEC. In this method, the effect of losses in non-periodic frames is limited to the period only if the periodic frame in the period has no error. However, if a periodic frame is lost, the error will propagate to the next period. Therefore, a mechanism to protect the periodic frame is required.

We upgrade PFEC by using the RSE code, present RSE-code-based FEC with periodicity (FECwP) as shown in Fig. 4, and propose the redundancy control algorithm for FECwP. FECwP offers a different amount of redundancy to periodic frames than to non-periodic frames. The periodic frames have more parity packets than the non-periodic frames so that they can survive packet losses better than the non-periodic frames. To allow a different amount of redundancy, two tolerable loss rates of a TG is required: one is the tolerable TG loss rate for periodic frames τ_p, and the other is the tolerable TG loss rate for non-periodic frames τ_n. τ_p must be smaller than τ_n. Fig. 5 shows the redundancy control algorithm of FECwP. After each frame is encoded, k is obtained, and then n is determined depending on frame types and network loss conditions.

Procedure Redundancy control()
Begin Procedure
    While (every frame)
        $k \leftarrow \lceil S_{frame}/S_{packet} \rceil$.   /* k is obtained */
        If (periodic frame) $\eta \leftarrow 1 - \tau_p$. /* depending on frame types */
        Else $\eta \leftarrow 1 - \tau_n$.
        $t \leftarrow k$.
        While $(P(t,k) < \eta)$ $t \leftarrow t + 1$. /* depending on network loss states */
        $n \leftarrow t$.   /* n is determined */
    End While
End Procedure

Fig. 5. Redundancy control algorithm for FECwP

4 Experiments

We implemented the prototype system of Fig. 2 to evaluate the proposed redundancy control algorithms. The video encoder and decoder was implemented by modifying a H.263 source. The RSE-code-based FEC schemes and redundancy control algorithms were programmed using C language. The video sequence "akiyo" was used in this experiments which has 176×144 QCIF and

30 f/s. We used the NS-2 simulator[5] to generate various network traffics. We assume that the average encoded frame size is $100 \sim 400$ bytes and packet size is 80bytes.

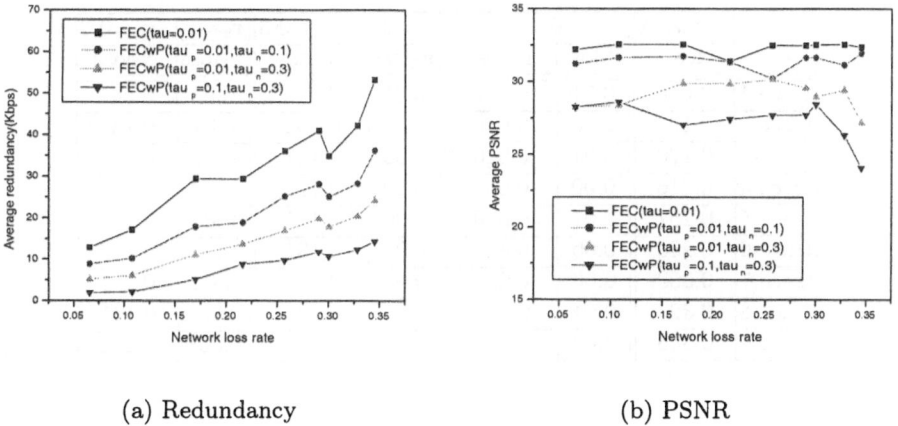

(a) Redundancy   (b) PSNR

Fig. 6. Average redundancy and PSNR in FECwP with redundancy control according to network loss rates

To evaluate FECwP with the redundancy control algorithm, the amount of redundancy, PSNR and the frame loss rate are measured varing τ_p and τ_n. Fig. 6(a) illustrates the average amount of redundancy according to network loss rates. FEC denotes the RSE-code-based FEC that adapts to network loss conditions but does not consider the priority of frames. As network loss rate increses, the amount of redundancy increases in order to protect packets against losses. The average redundancy of FEC is highest since FEC produces parity packets for all frames. The redundancy of FECwP with small τ_p and τ_n values is higher than that with large τ_p and τ_n values. These imply that the less τ_p and τ_n are used, the larger redundancy is produced.

Fig. 6(b) illustrates the average PSNR according to network loss rates. Although network loss rates increase, the PSNR of FEC hardly decreases because it makes more redundancy in relation to network loss rates. However, the PSNR of FECwP with the large τ_p and τ_n values may decrease when the network loss rate is high since the redundancy is too insufficient to recover lost packets. As expected, the PNSR of FEC is the highest, and the PSNR of FECwP with small τ_p and τ_n values is higher than that with large τ_p and τ_n values. These imply that the more redundancy is used, the higher PSNR is obtained.

Table 1 shows the frame loss rates according to network loss rates. P-loss and N-loss denote the loss rate of periodic frames and non-periodic frames respectively. We assume that if a single packet of a video frame is lost, the entire frame is lost. As shown in the table, as the τ_p and τ_n values are small, the frame loss rates of FECwP become minimal. It is also observed that FECwP keeps the loss rates of periodic frames and non-periodic frames under τ_p and τ_n respectively.

Table 1. Average frame loss rates of periodic frames and non-periodic frames in FECwP with redundancy control

	Network loss	$\tau_p{=}0.01$, $\tau_n{=}0.1$		$\tau_p{=}0.01$, $\tau_n{=}0.3$		$\tau_p{=}0.1$, $\tau_n{=}0.3$	
		P-loss	N-loss	P-loss	N-loss	P-loss	N-loss
trace 1	0.066	0.01	0.040	0.01	0.152	0.01	0.141
trace 2	0.108	0.00	0.040	0.00	0.152	0.02	0.131
trace 3	0.170	0.01	0.020	0.00	0.121	0.02	0.152
trace 4	0.216	0.00	0.051	0.00	0.121	0.02	0.131
trace 5	0.257	0.01	0.040	0.00	0.121	0.04	0.101
trace 6	0.290	0.00	0.040	0.00	0.131	0.02	0.172
trace 7	0.300	0.00	0.051	0.00	0.162	0.04	0.111
trace 8	0.327	0.01	0.040	0.01	0.121	0.051	0.141
trace 9	0.345	0.00	0.040	0.00	0.232	0.051	0.222

5   Conclusion

In this paper, we have discussed redundancy control of RSE-code-based FEC to minimize the amount of redundancy. Based on the analysis of network loss process, the number of parity packets in RSE-code-based FEC was obtained. As well, a different amount of parity in FECwP was allowed depending on the frame types. In summary, the proposed redundancy control algorithm offers the followings:

- Adapting to network loss conditions and the priority of frames.
- Reducing the amount of redundancy considerably.
- Preventing the loss of periodic frames effectively.

This technique can be used for real-time video transmission in video telephony and videoconference etc.

References

1. T.U. Choi, M.K. Ji, S.H. Park and K.D. Chung, *An adaptive periodic FEC Scheme for Internet video applications*, Springer LNCS 2170, pp.691-702, 2001.
2. A.J. McAuley, *Reliable broadband communications using a burst erasure correcting code*, in Proc. ACM SIGCOMM, Philadelphia, PA, Sept. 1990.
3. D. Rubenstein, J. Kurose and D. Towsley, *Real-time reliable multicast using proactive forward error correction*, UMASS Tech. Rep. 98-19, 1998.
4. E.N. Gilbert, *Capacity of a burst-noise channel*, Bell System Technology Journal, p.1253, Sept. 1960.
5. *ns - Network Simulator*, See http://www-mash.cs.berkeley.edu/ns/ns.html.

A Peer-to-Peer Communication System

Yong Li[2], Jiang Li[1], Keman Yu[1], Kaibo Wang[3], Shipeng Li[1], and Ya-Qin Zhang[1]

[1] Microsoft Research Asia, 3F Sigma Building, 49 Zhichun Road,
Beijing 100080, China
{jiangli, i-kmyu, spli, yzhang}@microsoft.com
[2] Department of Computer Science, Zhejiang University
Hangzhou 310027, China
liyong_zju@hotmail.com
[3] CIM Institute, Xi'an Jiaotong University,
Shanxi 710049, China
kbwang@msn.com

Abstract. The demand of communicating anywhere, anytime on any device is growing with the development of modern information technology. Current instant messaging services enable people to be aware of each other's presence and to exchange text information. However, almost all of these services are based on client/server architecture. If servers crash, all connections are lost. As an alternative, peer-to-peer architecture basically relies on clients, but existing systems usually emphasize sharing of computing resources and files. In this paper, we propose a peer-to-peer communication system, which combines the advantages of instant messaging services and peer-to-peer networking. In the system, in addition to being aware of each other's presence, users can simultaneously attend multiple multimedia meetings with each meeting allowing multiple attendees. Users have full control over the exchange of real-time text/voice/video information in these meetings.

1 Introduction

The ultimate goal of communication technology is to enable people to exchange information anywhere, anytime, on any device. Currently instant messaging services such as MSN Messenger, AOL Instant Messaging, ICQ and Yahoo Pager provide presence awareness and chat functions to users. Some of them also provide audio and video capabilities. However, their client/server architecture makes them still unreliable sometimes. For instance, MSN Messenger once crashed for almost one week, and the buddy list information for about 10% of users were permanently lost. As an alternative, a peer-to-peer architecture basically relies on clients. It overcomes some drawbacks of client/server systems though it also has its limitations. While SETI@home and Napster are used purely for computing resource sharing and music file sharing, Gnutella, Freenet and Groove also put emphasis on collaborations [1].

Y.-C. Chen, L.-W. Chang, and C.-T. Hsu (Eds.): PCM 2002, LNCS 2532, pp. 873-879, 2002.
© Springer-Verlag Berlin Heidelberg 2002

Gnutella [2] is a file sharing system that uses architecture quite different from Napster. Gnutella does not rely on any central servers to organize the network. It is a fully decentralized pure peer-to-peer system. It uses a message-based, application-level routing strategy. When sending a query, it uses message broadcasting. Message broadcasting is perfectly suitable when more than one participant can provide a valid response to a request. But broadcasting is not a rational method for response. Gnutella creates temporary routing items for the response to be sent back to the requester. Determining node connections when a node takes part in the Gnutella network is an interesting issue. It adopts a hierarchical scheme to reduce links between low-capacity nodes to diminish the burden of these nodes.

Freenet [3] is a peer-to-peer application which permits the publication, replication, and retrieval of data. It also gives a mechanism to prevent both authors and readers of data from being detected by others. In other words, it provides anonymity for users. Freenet creates a very large and geographically distributed hard drive with anonymous access. When inserting a file, a Freenet node will distribute the encrypted file data in several other nodes, and each node saves the file data and creates a routing item for the future request of this file. After a successful insertion, the owner will publish a unique file description. A user who wants to retrieve a file only needs to input the file description. This retrieved message is forwarded until a node which holds the request data returns it. Each node in the path for returning the requested data also caches the data in a local routing table. So the quality of the routing should improve over time.

Groove [4] is a system which provides shared spaces for people who have requirements to collaborate in some work. In Groove, users make immediate and direct connections with other users. It is a virtual space for small group interactions. These interactions include communication media, tools for sharing, and activities. In each shared space, the user can directly invite other members, add new tools, and keep track of activity and changes. Groove is not a pure peer-to-peer system. It uses a central directory server named Groove.net to find other users and then creates connections to them. It also uses a relay service to keep synchronization for each member in a shared space.

To sum up, existing peer-to-peer systems basically emphasize sharing computing resources and files. There is usually no real-time requirement in these systems. However, for communication, the ideal situation is that as soon as a user joins a network, the user can get a connection to the target people and exchange text/voice/video information in real-time even if the user does not has a direct link to that people. The system will take any method to provide links whether intermediate servers are used or not. The objective of our work is just to realize such kind of system.

The paper is organized as follows. The architecture of the peer-to-peer communication system will be described in section 2. A real peer-to-peer system will be shown in section 3. We will conclude the work and indicate future research topics in section 4.

2 System Architecture

How to find other users is a very interesting and challenging issue in pure peer-to-peer applications. As we know, a social network exhibits a small-world phenomenon (popularly known as six degrees of separation) [5, 6, 7]. It means any two individuals in the network are likely to be connected through a short sequence of intermediate acquaintances. Recent work has suggested that the phenomenon is pervasive in networks arising in nature and technology. It indicates that through just five or six intermediaries, you could possibly be linked to millions of others. Small-world phenomenon provides a theoretic basis for the peer-to-peer communication system.

The peer-to-peer communication system is composed of nodes connected to the Internet, where each node acts as both a server and a client of the whole system. In this network, nodes may join the system at any time and may silently leave the system without warning. So each connection among every two nodes is highly dynamic. Each time when a node exits from the network, the failure of the current node must be detected by all his directly connected nodes. At the same time, those routing tables that use the node as a soft router to relay messages must be rebuilt according to the change. Both of these processes should be done in a timely manner.

The query and search schemes of the system are designed based on small-world phenomenon. A client sends request packets to his directly connected buddies, and his directly connected buddies further forward these packets to their directly connected buddies. Most probably after a few rounds of forwarding, an expected buddy can be found.

An efficient routing scheme in the system ensures that users can also exchange messages with indirectly connected buddies via soft routers. In addition to text information, users can also exchange voice/video information via indirect connections. To achieve this, we apply a very low bit rate audio/video codec, namely the portrait video codec [8], in the system. The bit rate of portrait video is so small that it can even be transmitted via an HTTP proxy. This guarantees that the communication can be completed even between two users who are separated by a firewall. Beside this, flexible meeting controls are also provided in the system. Some key components of the system are described as follows.

2.1 The Identification of a User

It is very easy for a server-based system to identify and manage users. Basically, the user ID such as an email address and its corresponding password can be stored in a server. Wherever a user logs on to the server, he can always be identified by his email address and password. However, it is not so easy for a decentralized system to do this. In our design, each user is identified by a universally unique identifier (UUID) which is generated by the system. An algorithm guarantees that the UUID will not be duplicated even if it is generated in different machines. When a user logs on to the system for the first time, the user can either ask the system to generate a UUID for him if he is a new user or imports a file to the system, which records his UUID, his personal information and his buddy list information. Personal information mainly includes username, Internet Locator Service (ILS) servers and the user's ID in these ILS servers. The user needs to input a password to decrypt the file before importing. Certainly, a user can also export his information to a file and bring it to another machine. That allows the user to use different machines to join the peer-to-peer network.

2.2 The Joining of the Peer-to-Peer Network

There are several methods to let a user join the peer-to-peer communication network. (1) A user can input the IP address of a person who is already in the peer-to-peer network. He will find that person if that person is online. The user then adds that person to his buddy list. A request will automatically be sent to that person. If that person accepts, the user is connected to the peer-to-peer network through that person. (2) A user can also browse in an Internet Locator Service (ILS) server, which other persons in the peer-to-peer communication network have also logged on to. (3) A user can also find a person who also belongs to the peer-to-peer communication network through instant messaging services such as MSN Messenger, AOL Instant Messaging, ICQ or Yahoo Pager. The purpose of this method is to get another person's IP address and send a connection request to him.

If a user receives a request from another user for establishing a buddy relation, he can either accept or reject the request. If the request is accepted, then the users' UUID and other personal information are exchanged. Each user is added to the other one' s buddy list.

2.3 Query

Each time a user logs on to a peer-to-peer communication system, the system tries to establish connections with the user's buddies in the background. The system first uses the recorded IP addresses of the user's buddies to connect. For those buddies who use local area network, this method usually works. However, for dialup network buddies, since their IP addresses usually change, the method may fail. As a second method, the system retrieves the recorded ILS server information of the user's buddies and logs on to these ILS servers. If the system finds that the buddies are in these ILS servers, then their IP addresses are gotten. The system then connects these buddies with the new IP addresses. If all the above methods fail, the system sends query packets to all connected buddies. The connected buddies further send these query packets to their connected buddies. If someone is reached, the routing information is sent back to the user who initiated the query. The system then uses the newly acquired IP address to directly connect to the person. If no one is reached, information will only be sent via the acquired routing information in the future.

2.4 Search

The system allows users to search people by certain criteria such as first name, last name, email address, etc. These items are sent to all connected buddies. The connected buddies then return their buddies' information if any to the source node who sent the search packet and further forward the search packet to their connected buddies. When a node receives a packet that contains the returned buddies' information, he first checks if he is the source who originated the search. If he is, he unpacks the packet and retrieves the information in it. Otherwise, he forwards the packet to the former node that sent the search packet to him.

In both query and search operations, we use $p(u, t)$ to denote a packet. The symbol u denotes the unique message identifier of a packet and the symbol t denotes time-to-live value of the packet. Here is the transmission process of a packet: (1) The source node sends $p(u, t)$ to all his directly connected buddies respectively. (2) When a node receives packet $p(u, t)$, it first looks up in its received message table to see whether the packet has been received previously. If true, the packet is discarded. Otherwise, the node records the unique message identifier u of the packet in its received message table and checks whether the node itself is one of the proper receivers. If true, it saves the packet and processes. If the current node is the only node left, the packet is dropped without forwarding. If there are still some other nodes that need to receive this packet, the node checks whether $t > 0$. If true, the node forwards the message $p(u, t\text{-}1)$ to all its directly connected neighbors. Otherwise, the node discards the packet without forwarding.

2.5 Application Level Routing

Routing is a process of sending data from a source node to a destination node through a network path. There must be at least one other node to act as an intermediate in the path. In the traditional routing strategy, the routing process contains two basic steps: (1) searching a reachable path and (2) forwarding packets to the next router. Because there may be several different paths from a given source node to a destination node, it is necessary to find the optimal path. Step (1) is implemented by routing protocols. Routing protocols must select some metrics to determine optimal routing paths and routing information must be updated at certain time intervals.

The routing strategy of the peer-to-peer communication system differs from that of the traditional routers. First, the routing protocol of the system is very simple. Every node in the system acts as a soft router. Routing information is saved in each node independently. No frequent routing information exchange is needed. Second, because a node may leave the peer-to-peer network at any time, it is necessary for those nodes that use the node as their soft routers to detect the departure and rebuild routing tables. In detail, we record a routing item in a routing table in the format: *(Sender, Receiver)* - *(From, To)*, where *Sender* is the identifier of the node who sends the packet; *Receiver* is the identifier of the node who receives the packet; *From* is the identifier of the node who delivers the packet of the sender to the current node; and *To* is the identifier of the node who delivers the packet to the receiver from the current node. Please note routing paths are bidirectional. If either the *From* or *To* is detected to be down, all routing paths that include the *From* or *To* are rebuilt.

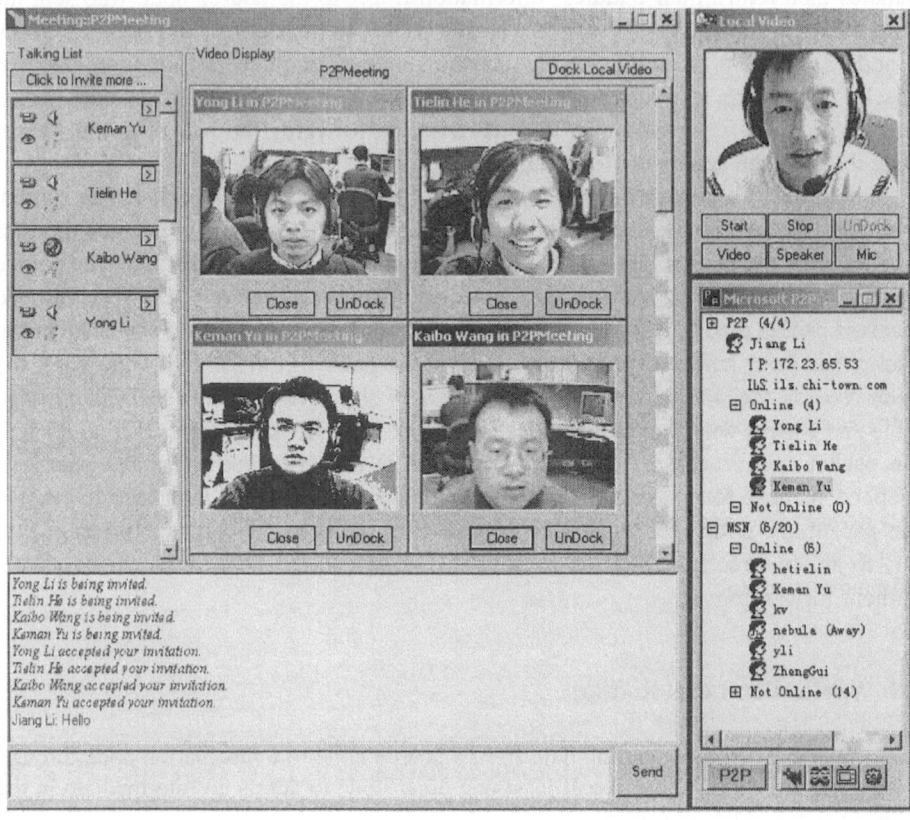

Fig. 1. A meeting in the peer-to-peer communication system.

3 Implementation

As shown in Fig. 1, the main frame of the real peer-to-peer communication system is the buddy list window. It displays the peer-to-peer buddies of the user and the MSN Messenger buddies of the users. We may include AOL Instant Messaging, ICQ and Yahoo pager buddies in the future. The main frame provides tools for users to manage their buddy list, launch meetings that multiple people can attend, initialize local video windows and configure personal and audio/video settings. If a user launches or attends a meeting, he can then decide whether he listens to or watches each attendee, and whether he allows each attendee to hear or see him. The control buttons are shown in the left column of the meeting window. In the bottom of the meeting window, there is a chat window. Each attendee can type in the chat window and send to all the other attendees. If a user wants to only send text to a particular buddy, he can use an instant messaging tool in the system. In the left column of the meeting window, the system also allows users to invite their other buddies to attend an existing meeting.

4 Conclusions

We develop a peer-to-peer communication system. In this system, users are linked through either direct computer to computer connections or indirect peer routing. Users can be aware of each other's presence and initiate or attend various multimedia meetings at the same time. In each of these meetings, a user can control whether he listens to or watches each attendee, and whether he allows each attendee to hear or see him. The peer-to-peer routing and real-time voice/video function are the main features of the system. In addition, the system can also utilize Internet Locator Service and instant messaging services such as MSN Messenger to find buddies. Future research topics would be how to optimize peer-to-peer routing, how to apply multicast technology to multimedia meetings, and how to adaptively transmit audio/video in various bandwidth conditions.

References

1. Andy Oram, Peer-to-Peer:Harnessing the Benefits of a Disruptive Technology, O'Reilly & Associates, Inc., 2001
2. The Gnutella protocol specification, 2000. http://dss.clip2.com/gnutellaProtocolo4.pdf
3. Freenet, http://freenet.sourceforge.net/
4. Introduction to Groove, http://www.groove.net/pdf/ introducinggroove.pdf
5. Jon Kleinberg, "The Small-World Phenomenon: An Algorithmic Perspective". Technical Report, Cornell University Computer Science Department, October 1999
6. D. Watts and S. Strogatz "Collective dynamics of 'small-world' networks". Nature, 393:440-442, June 1998.
7. Robert Matthews, "Six Degrees of Separation" New Scientist Dec 4th 1999.
8. Jiang Li, Gang Chen, Jizheng Xu, Yong Wang, Hanning Zhou, Keman Yu, King To Ng and Heung-Yeung Shum, "Bi-level Video: Video Communications at Very Low Bit Rates". ACM Multimedia Conference 2001, Sep. 30 – Oct. 5, Ottawa, Ontario, Canada, pages 392-400.

A Project Management Model for Multimedia System Development

G. Joubert

Technical University of Clausthal, Department of Computer Science,
Julius Albert Str. 4, 38678 Clausthal, Germany
joubert@informatik.tu-clausthal.de

Abstract. Multimedia systems integrate time dependent and time independent media. This makes their development significantly more complex than that of conventional information processing systems. Standard paradigms for system development do not satisfactorily model multimedia system development processes. In this paper a new flexible project management model for the development of multimedia systems (M-STAGE) is proposed. This model can readily be adapted to meet particular project requirements. It enables improved project, cost and quality control.

1 Introduction

Multimedia systems differ from standard software systems in that time dependent media, such as sound, video clips and animations, must be processed in addition to time independent media, such as text, still images, etc. These aspects must be taken account of in addition to the standard tasks to be executed during software development. Appropriate time dependent data such as animations, videos and sounds must be created within the framework of system development. Furthermore, the synchronisation of time dependent media with time independent and/or (other) time dependent media, data modelling and management of multimedia components and the design and development of specialised user interfaces are additional complicating factors. These additional aspects and tasks can severely impact on project control, duration and costs. They must be properly planned and controlled in addition to the standard project management tasks needed in the case of all software projects.

The development of time dependent media requires the availability of specialised staff in addition to software engineers. Examples are specialists for the preparation of sound samples or video clips, and HCI-specialists for the design of advanced multimedia user interfaces. Such specialists often have backgrounds and work methods, which do not allow for easy integration into teams of software engineers who are used to more formal software engineering work procedures. Experts in the development of multimedia content do not easily adapt to formal project management and execution methods. A more flexible approach, allowing for greater flexibility to accommodate ad hoc changes and decisions, is more amenable to them. The desired flexibility can be achieved in practice through the use of so-called *exploratory* or *trial and error* development models. The considered advantage of a trial and error approach for multimedia system development is that it more readily allows for the handling of unfore

Y.-C. Chen, L.-W. Chang, and C.-T. Hsu (Eds.): PCM 2002, LNCS 2532, pp. 880–887, 2002.
© Springer-Verlag Berlin Heidelberg 2002

seen occurrences. This is especially important when user requirements are vaguely defined. As a result the practical development of multimedia systems has and is largely executed with the use of such methods. This way of working offers several advantages in that no elaborate system requirements analyses are required in advance, users can quickly see and assess the results of first efforts and user interfaces and system functionality can more easily be adapted to changing user preferences.

As is well known from standard software development projects, however, exploratory or informal methods suffer from a number of inherent deficiencies that may prove counterproductive if the overall software life cycle is considered. Systems developed in this way suffer from a lack of structure with resultant high maintenance costs, delivered systems often show up bad or even unacceptable performance, and documentation is usually incomplete, faulty or even non existent. In addition the control of the number and extent of requirement changes by users is difficult. A trial and error approach to software development is thus not desirable from a project management point of view as control of project progress and costs becomes well-nigh impossible.

In order to enable a more structured approach to multimedia systems development the so-called *Multi-Model* approach was proposed in [5]. This model of the development process strives to combine the advantages offered by the exploratory programming paradigm with more conventional models.

2 The Multi-model Approach

According to the *Multi-Model* paradigm a development process can commence in a trial and error fashion in order to facilitate the communication between users and development teams. As greater clarity emerges about the actual functional and non-functional system requirements, development progresses along increasingly formal lines. The global *Multi-Model* approach is depicted in Table 1. Note that the *Multi-Model* is a metamodel for software development, which is based on three standard models, viz. exploratory programming, prototyping and the waterfall model.

It should be noted that within the class of *exploratory methods* a number of different approaches exist of which any suitable one, such as extreme programming, can be used. The *prototyping* stage may in many instances seem superfluous. In the case of not too complex systems, this stage may be skipped. In the case of complex systems the synchronisation and performance issues often do require some form of prototype to reach a more conclusive system specification. The development of a prototype also allows for the creation and testing of time-dependent media, such as video material and animations. The final stage is developed along the stringent and restrictive lines of the *waterfall model*. The focus in this final stage is on developing a high quality and robust system that meets users' requirements. The *Multi-Model* applies equally well to the development of all kinds of multimedia systems, such as systems for supplying information, learning, training, maintenance, service, etc.

Each stage of the *Multi-Model* includes five phases as shown in the first column of Table 1. Within each phase different methodologies, methods and tools as described in the general literature on software engineering [1, 7], can be selected to meet local standards and preferences.

Table 1. Multi-Model: Phases and Development Stages

System Phase	Exploratory Programming Model: Initial System	Prototyping Model: Intermediate System	Waterfall Model: Final System
Feasibility Study	Global Analysis	More Detailed Analysis	Detailed Analysis
Requirements & Data Analysis	Initial Requirements	Prototype: Improved Analysis	Detailed Analysis
System & Media Design		Prototype: Improved Design	Detailed Design
Implementation & Media Production	Interactive Implementation, User Tests	Implementation	Final Implementation
Tests, Integration & Delivery		Integration, User Tests	Integration, Final System Tests & Delivery

3 Multimedia Project Management

In order to properly manage the development of software systems, as well as control progress and the consummation of resources, well-defined project management procedures are required. Many project management models have been developed and are in vogue in particular communities. These were mostly developed prior to the emergence of multimedia technologies and are not well suited to meet the particular requirements of multimedia system development. In addition most of these models concentrate on the development process, ignoring the overall product life cycle. Thus a life cycle or version planning and the planning of system maintenance, is usually ignored. In the case of multimedia systems a life cycle planning is particularly important due to the fast aging of multimedia content such as video clips and sounds. Changes in musical, clothing and hair styles, for example, severely shorten the life cycle of video clips.

The Multi-Model approach supplies a conceptual basis for an improved project planning and management paradigm. In the following section such a new project management model is proposed. It should be noted that a cost estimation method for multimedia systems based on the Multi-Model is available [4, 6].

4   M-STAGE Project Management Approach

The STAGE (STArt-Go-End) project management approach was developed within the framework of a series of software engineering courses [3]. It incorporates standard software project management paradigms [2]. In addition it covers the whole lifecycle planning of a software product. The project management method M-STAGE (Multimedia STAGE) presented in this paper is an extension of the STAGE concepts to cover the project management needs of multimedia system development along the lines of the *Multi-Model* paradigm.

The STAGE method comprises three distinct phases of software development, viz.

- The *Start Phase (SP)* includes the development of a static project plan, resource estimates and planning.
- The *Go Phase (GP)* includes the dynamic controlling- and adaptation activities during project execution.
- The *End Phase (EP)* includes the planning of system delivery, installation and acceptance, user/operator training as well as the planning of system maintenance and the planning of future versions.

These phases are repeated for the development of the next version, etc.

In the case of M-STAGE the same three phases exist, but may be repeated within a single system development activity. This allows for the two dimensional concept of the *Multi-Model* approach to be planned and managed. In order to distinguish between project phases an index i is used with $i = init, inter$ or *final* to differentiate between them. Thus, e.g., the *Start Phase* for *initial, intermediate* or *final* system development is indicated by SP_i, $i=init, inter$ or *final* and similarly for GP_i and EP_i. For the development of a multimedia system up to nine separate phases are thus distinguished. A motivated decision should be taken as to whether some of these phases may be skipped in the case of a particular project.

5   Start Phases

5.1   Initial Stage: Start Phase SP$_{init}$

The first phase SP_{init} is in fact a feasibility study. Alternate strategies for system development must be considered, user requirements clarified, resource estimates made and risks identified. During this stage no media content is developed, but the requirements are defined. To reduce risks and costs the development of expensive media content should preferably be left for the intermediate or final development stages.

Note that also in the case of exploratory software development goals and deliverables must be clearly defined. The focus should be on the essential aspects of the project. For cost estimates refer to [4,6]. Consider at least the tasks given in Table 2.

5.2 Intermediate Stage: Start Phase SP$_{inter}$

The second phase SP_{inter} should be executed if a clearer specification, especially regarding the development of media content, is needed. In simpler projects this phase may be skipped, or it may form the starting point of project development. The main focus of this phase should be to obtain greater clarity regarding user requirements, media content and the development thereof. Consider at least the aspects in Table 3.

Table 2. Tasks for Start Phase SP_{init}

Project Management Tasks	Aspects to be Considered
Identify Goal, Scope and Strategies	Project goals.
	Type of multimedia system: information, marketing, teaching, etc.
	Responsibilities for project execution.
	Interested parties and user groups.
	Alternate realisation strategies.
	Project risks: competitive products, technological risks, non acceptance by (some) users.
Project Infrastructure	Team Structure.
	Communication channels.
	Tools selection: support for exploratory development process, e.g. authoring tool.
Activities and Products (Deliverables)	Identify products (deliverables).
	Identify dependencies between products (deliverables).
	Make activity planning, showing dependencies.
	Define milestones.
Cost (Resource) Estimates	Resources (quantity and expertise) needed for particular activities, including software and media development.
	Adapt activity planning to match resource availability.
Detailed Risk Analysis	Analyse risks for each activity.
	Strategy decisions to reduce risks.
	Adapt planning and resource estimates in view of risks.
Validate and Publish Project Plan	Validate project plan.
	Document and publish project plan.

5.3 Final Stage: Start Phase SP_{final}

The planning and execution of the final phase SP_{final} benefits from the development of the initial and preliminary versions of the system. A clear picture as to the requirements of the final system, the optimal strategies to achieve the stated goals, the resources needed and the risks involved should be available at this point. The main focus of this phase is to build a well-structured, flexible, robust and maintainable system. Consider at least the aspects listed in Table 4.

Table 3. Tasks for Start Phase SP_{inter}

Project Management Tasks	Aspects to be Considered
Identify Goal, Scope and Strategies	Project goals and scope: review and adapt. Evaluate alternate realisation strategies.
Project Infrastructure	Team structure, especially regarding media development. Tools selection: support for media development including audio, video, animation.
Activities and Products (Deliverables)	Identify products (deliverables) for the intermediate system. Identify dependencies between (deliverables). Make activity planning, giving dependencies Define milestones.
Cost (Resource) Estimates	Resources (quantity and expertise) needed for particular activities, including software and media development. In particular estimates with respect to the following must be made: • Artists, e.g. designers, models, performing artists, etc. • Equipment, e.g. video cameras, audio equipment, special rooms, lighting, etc. • Software, e.g. for sound, video and image processing, graphics, animation • Outsourcing of media creation and processing. Adapt activity planning to match resource availability.
Detailed Risk Analysis	Analyse risks for each activity. Strategy decisions to reduce risks. Adapt planning and resource estimates in view of risks.
Validate and Publish Project Plan	Validate project plan. Document and publish project plan.

6   GO Phases

The three phases GP_i are very similar. The main concern is to control progress and quality. Consider at least the following activities in each GP_i:

1. Start present stage of project (Kick-off meeting)
2. Detailed planning of project execution for each activity (progress and resource planning; deliverables; availability of experts; milestones)
3. Progress and Quality control (reviews, tests, etc.) with each milestone
4. Planning review and adaptation: activities and overall project
5. Release of deliverables (configuration management)
6. System integration

6.1 Initial Stage

In the case of exploratory methods more control over unnecessary changes is required, for example, by a CCB (Change Control Board).

Table 4. Tasks for Start Phase SP_{final}

Project Management Tasks	Aspects to be Considered
Identify Goal, Scope and Strategies	Project goals: review, adapt goals for final product. Evaluate alternate realisation strategies.
Project Infrastructure	Team structure. CASE tools selection: support for software development as well as media development including audio, video, animation.
Activities and Products (Deliverables)	Identify products (deliverables) for the system. Identify dependencies between deliverables. Make activity planning, showing dependencies. Define milestones.
Cost (Resource) Estimates	Resources (quantity and expertise) needed for particular activities, including software and media development. Adapt activity planning to match resource availability.
Detailed Risk Analysis	Analyse risks for each activity. Strategy decisions to reduce risks. Adapt planning, resource estimates in view of risks.
Validate and Publish Project Plan	Validate project plan. Document and publish project plan.

6.2 Intermediate Stage

The focus is on media production and integration into a prototype multimedia system. The advantage of separating media production from initial system development is that the particular characteristics of media production can be dealt with separately. Many different approaches to media development exist [8, 9].

6.3 Final Stage

Final system development is based on the results obtained from the initial and intermediate stages. This enables good planning and close control of final system build.

7   END Phases

7.1   Initial and Intermediate Stages

The end phases of the initial and intermediate system development are similar. Thus EP_i , $i = init, inter$, involve the same steps, viz.:
1.   Validation of software and media against specified requirements
2.   Assessment of developed software and media by users
3.   Quality control measures: synchronization, robustness, user interfaces, etc.
4.   Compilation of changes to be implemented during next development stage
5.   Assessment of expended resources

7.2 Final Stage

The end phase of the final system development, EP_{final}, must ensure a clearly defined configuration management, system delivery, etc. Tasks to be executed are e.g.:
1. Integrated system test and delivery
2. Configuration management: delivered systems, components and media content
3. Acceptance tests by users
4. Planning and organization of maintenance tasks
5. Version planning of future releases

8 Practical Experience

The M-STAGE project management method was developed and tested in the case of a number of multimedia projects. These include a university computer science department multimedia information system for use by prospective students and industrial partners, and an internet based real estate marketing system. The different user views required for such applications makes the design of the user interfaces and the multimedia content particularly complex. The step-wise *Multi-Model* approach proved to offer distinct advantages to handle this complexity. The M-STAGE management model is well-suited to plan and control progress and expenditures.

9 Summary

The proposed M-STAGE model offers a framework for managing multimedia system development. The model is readily accepted by practitioners as it models their preferred work procedures. It can easily be adapted to meet specific project requirements.

References

1. B.W. Boehm, Software Engineering Economics, Prentice Hall, Englewood Cliffs (1981)
2. M. Cotterell, B. Hughes, Software Project Management, International Thomson Computer Press, London Boston (1995)
3. G. Joubert, Software Engineering: Project Management, Lecture Series on Software Engineering, Clausthal University of Technology, Germany (2002)
4. S. Lechtenberg, G. R. Joubert, Effort Estimation for Multimedia Information Systems Development, Technologies for the Information Society: Developments and Opportunities, IOS Press, Amsterdam Berlin etc. (1998) 615-622
5. S. Lechtenberg, G. Joubert, A. Bierwirth, A Multimedia Development Model, Advances in Information technologies: The Business Challenge, IOS Press, Amsterdam Berlin etc. (1998) 553-560
6. S. Lechtenberg, Effort Estimation for Multimedia Information Systems' Development, PhD-thesis, Clausthal University of Technology, Germany (1998)
7. I. Sommerville, Software Engineering, Addison-Wesley, Wokingham (UK), Reading (Mass) etc. (1992)
8. R. Steinmetz, Multimedia-Technologie, Springer Verlag, Berlin etc. (1993)
9. T. Vaughan, Multimedia: Making it Work, Osborne McGraw-Hill, Berkeley etc. (1993)

TCP-Friendly Congestion Control Algorithm on Self-Similar Traffic Network

Yuheng Liu, Yan Hu, and Guangzhao Zhang

Dept. of Electronics & Communication Engineering, SUN YAT-SEN University, PR.China
vincent-liu@163.com, hu_yan@263.net, isszgz@zsu.edu.cn

Abstract. This paper proposes a new unicast TCP-Friendly protocol called RAAR-MT, which on-line predicts the tendency of traffic level in the near future and use this predicted information to exert multiple time scale traffic control at receivers. Simulation shows that this protocol can improve the performance in loss rate on self-similar traffic network. Even in traditional short-range dependent environment, the performance will not degrade severely. Compared with TFRC, RAAR-MT has better performance in TCP-Friendliness, intra-protocol fairness and smoothness. RAAR-MT is also a promising avenue of development for congestion control of multicast multimedia traffic since it is not a per-packet acknowledgement and is mainly implemented at receivers.

1 Introduction

TCP is ill-suited for multimedia streaming applications, because halving the sending rate of a multimedia streaming flow is a too severe response to a congestion indication as it can noticeably reduce the flow's user-perceived quality [1]. Per-packet acknowledgment and retransmission mechanisms in TCP are not needed to these applications because of their real-time and loss-tolerant natures. For lack of congestion control mechanism, using UDP to transport multimedia applications will result in unfair bandwidth allocation and congestion collapse for Internet [2].

Since the dominant Internet traffic is TCP-based [1], with rapid growth of multimedia applications in Internet, it's very critical to develop new end-to-end congestion control schemes which are suit to multimedia applications and can share bandwidth fairly with TCP flows. We say a flow is TCP-friendly if its throughput is approximately the same as that of a TCP flow in the same circumstances. Major proposed TCP-friendly transport protocols could be roughly categorized into two classes: AIMD-based such as TEAR [3], RAP [4], RAAR [5], etc. and formula-based such as TFRC [6]. TFRC has been accepted as an IETF draft [13] and submitted to IESG for consideration as a proposed standard.

Research on modern telecommunication networks over the last decade has shown that self-similarity (or Long-Range Dependence, LRD) is a ubiquitous phenomenon spanning across diverse network environments [7]. Park and Tuan [8, 9] have explored the feasibility of exploiting long-rang correlation structure in self-similar network

Y.-C. Chen, L.-W. Chang, and C.-T. Hsu (Eds.): PCM 2002, LNCS 2532, pp. 888-895, 2002.

traffic for congestion control and proposed the Multiple Time Scale Congestion Control mechanism to enhance performance for rate-based feedback control. How to exploit the properties associated with LRD effectively to optimize the performance of TCP-friendly protocols is the major subject in this paper. In this paper, we extend RAAR [5] protocol with multiple time scale control, which can exploit the properties of self-similarity effectively to improve the performance of congestion control.

2   RAAR-MT Algorithm

RAAR (Rate Adaptation at Receivers)[5] is a TCP-Friendly protocol in which most flow control mechanisms are shifted to receivers. Based on RAAR, we perform on-line prediction at receiver and use this predicted information to module the GAIMD rate control mechanism of RAAR in a larger time scale. This extended RAAR protocol is called RAAR-MT, which can adapt the changing of self-similar network traffic more efficiently and thus gain better protocol performance.

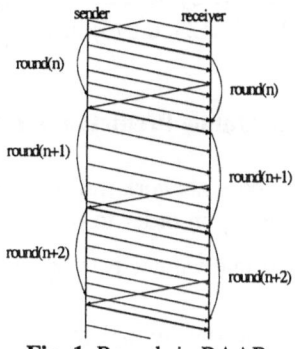

Fig. 1. Rounds in RAAR

2.1   Overview of RAAR

In RAAR, a receiver determines the appropriate receiving rate by GAIMD [10] principle and control the sending rate by feeding back ACK packets containing the rate information to the sender. An ACK packet is needed to send immediately when one of the following events occurs: (1) New evaluated rate is smaller than the current sending rate; (2) RTT timer at receiver expires. Without loss of ACK packets, sender will receive an ACK packet within an interval less than 2RTT. If a sender receives no ACK packet after 2RTO, it will decrease its sending rate. The evaluation of RTO is also carried out at receiver.

In GAIMD control law with per-packet acknowledgement, the window size is increased by α once receiving an ACK packet which indicates no loss events occurs and it is decreased to β of the current value whenever there is any congestion indication, where $\alpha>0$ and $0<\beta<1$. For TCP, $\alpha=1$ and $\beta=0.5$. To get an AIMD-based TCP-Friendly control law, (α, β) should satisfy the following equation [10]:

$$\alpha=4*(1-\beta^2)/3 \qquad (1)$$

In RAAR, only one ACK packet is send within one round (Fig.1). The protocol phase in receiver is initialized to SLOW-START when the first data packet arrives. In this phase, the current rate is increased by pktSize/RTT per packet received in sequence. Once a loss event is detected, the protocol phase is transited to

CONGESTION-AVOIDANCE. In this phase, when a packet arrives, the sending rate is adjusted by a modified GAIMD law:

$$\begin{cases} rate\_ \leftarrow rate\_ + \dfrac{\alpha \cdot k_o}{wnd\_} * \dfrac{pktSize\_}{RTT} * FA\_MT, & \text{if no loss event occurs} \\ rate\_ \leftarrow rate\_ * \beta * FM\_MT, & \text{if loss event occurs} \end{cases} \quad (2)$$

where wnd_ is the evaluated packet number received in a round, k_o is a revised factor in practical measurement. In simulations, it shows that better protocol performance will be attained when $k_o=1/6$. However the optimization of k_o should be further studied in future. FA_MT and FM_MT are two rate control factors in a larger time scale introduced by RAAR-MT. (α, β) is a constant pair, which satisfies Equation (1). We take (0.3125, 0.875) instead of (1, 0.5) to reduce the fluctuations of sending rate.

2.2 Online Prediction for Traffic Level

Suppose network traffic be quantized into m levels. Given the current observed traffic level L_1, in order to predict the traffic tendency, the expectation of traffic level in the next interval needs to be computed by: $\bar{l}' = E(L_2 \mid L_1 = l) = \sum_{l'=1}^{m} l' * P(L_2 = l' \mid L_1 = l)$·

The conditional probability distribution can be got by updating an array Condprob[•][•] of size m*(m+1) on-line. The whole process is segmented into contiguous non-overlapping blocks of length T_s. Condprob[l][$m+1$] is used to keep track of h_l, the number of blocks observed thus far whose traffic level is l. Condprob[l][l'] maintains the count $h_{l'}$, the number of blocks whose traffic level are l' and the traffic levels of the blocks just before are l. Thus, P($L_2=l'$|$L_1=l$) can be attained directly by $h_{l'}/h_l$.

Suppose the current traffic level $L_1=l$. If the traffic level $L_2=l'$ in the next block, Condprob[L_1][L_2] and Condprob[L_1][m+1] are increased by 1, respectively. The traffic level expectation given the condition $L_1=l$, arv_condprob[L_1], is also updated synchronously. Finally, let $L_1 \leftarrow L_2$, continue to observe the traffic level in the next block. The above on-line estimation can be accomplished at receivers with O(1) operations at every update interval T_s, which will not burden the receiver so much.

We employ RTT to estimate the network state, since its fluctuation reflects the congestion level of the network. Let $RTT_{Am}= RTT_{Max}-RTT_{Min}$ and $RTT_{Var}= (RTT_{now}-RTT_{Min})/RTT_{Am}$, where RTT_{Max} and RTT_{Min} are the maximum and minimum RTT measured in the transmission respectively; RTT_{now} is the evaluated RTT in the current interval. Network traffic is quantized into 8 levels by the range of RTT_{Var} (Table 1).

Table 1. The Partition of Traffic Level

Traffic Level	1	2	3	4	5	6	7	8
RTT_{Var} Range	[0, 0.05)	[0.05, 0.20)	[0.20, 0.35)	[0.35, 0.50)	[0.50, 065)	[0.65, 0.80)	[0.80, 0.95)	[0.95, 1]

Fig.2 shows the estimated conditional probability densities according to our on-line prediction algorithm with T_s=2s in simulation. Under LRD environment (α=1.05), the conditional probability densities can be seen to be skewed diagonally from the lower right side toward the upper left side (Fig.2.a). This indicates the probability is very large that traffic level in the next interval is similar to the current traffic level. Under short-range dependent environment (α=1.95), it shows that the shape of the distribution is insensitive to conditioning, i.e. $P(L_2|L_1) \approx P(L_2)$. The simulation results gear to the self-similar theory very well, which indicates our on-line prediction is available.

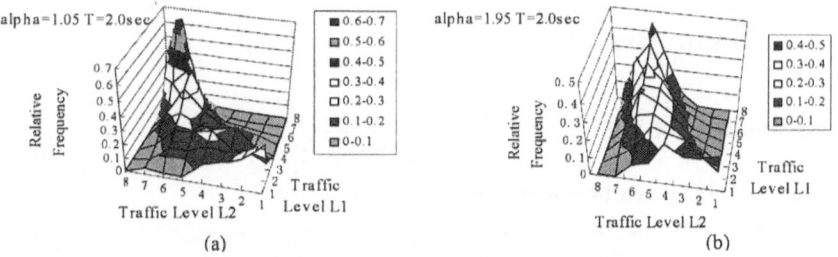

Fig. 2. Conditional Probability Densities Distribution

2.3 Rate Control in Large Time Scale

In RAAR-MT, using the predicted traffic level $\bar{l}'$ to adjust the control factors FA_MT and FM_MT in a larger time scale can bridge a gap that feedback control in a small time scale cannot reflect the tendency of the traffic level in a long term. FA_MT and FM_MT move around 1 guided by the following symmetric control policy:

$$FA\_MT(\bar{l}') = (17 - 2*\bar{l}')/8 \tag{3}$$

$$FM\_MT(\bar{l}') = \begin{cases} 15.0/14.0, [\bar{l}'] = 1 \\ 36.0/35.0, [\bar{l}'] = 2,3 \\ 34.0/35.0, [\bar{l}'] = 4,5 \\ 32.0/35.0, [\bar{l}'] = 6,7 \\ 6.0/7.0, \quad [\bar{l}'] = 8 \end{cases} \tag{4}$$

When $\bar{l}'$ is high, FA_MT and FM_MT will get small to alleviate the congestion degree and reduce the loss rate; when $\bar{l}'$ is low, FA_MT and FM_MT will get large to attain the available bandwidth more efficiently and increase the throughput of the system. FA_MT and FM_MT remain unchanged during a predicted interval T_s.

2.4 Evaluation for RTT and Regulation for Sending Rate

It's easy to get the RTT sample by the timestamp in packets. But single RTT measurement can vary and smoothing of the samples is necessary to prevent unstable protocol behavior. We use an EWMA filter to smooth the RTT samples, i.e. SRTT←α*SRTT+(1-α)*sampleRTT.

To get a compromise between smoothness and responsiveness, we set α=0.95 and regulate the rate_ got from Equation (2) as: $Rate\_ \leftarrow rate\_ * \sqrt{SRTT / sampleRTT\_}$. When network tends to be congested (sampleRTT_>SRTT), we slightly reduce the sending rate; contrariwise, we slightly increase the sending rate. But we can't replace rate_ by Rate_ in the next AIMD computation; otherwise TCP-Friendly performance of the protocol will be affected.

3   Simulation Results

3.1 Simulation Set-Up

We use NS2 [11] as our simulation platform to study the protocol performance of RAAR-MT in self-similar environment. The topology in simulation is shown in Fig.3. The link between R1 and R2 is the bottleneck with bandwidth of 15Mbps

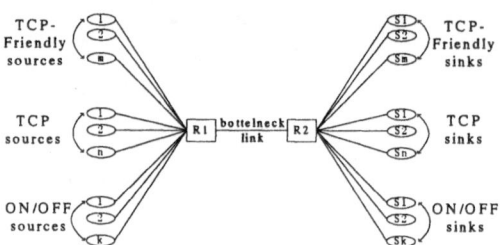

Fig. 3. Topology in Simulation

and propagation delay of 50ms. Bandwidth in other links is 100Mbps. The sum of the propagation delay in each access link on both sides is 5ms. 64 ON/OFF UDP sources, whose ON/OFF times are drawn from Pareto distributions with shape parameter α, construct the self-similar background traffic in which Hurst parameter H=(3-α)/2 [12]. The proportion of mean ON/OFF duration is set to 1:1, and the average sending rate during ON period in each source is 500kbps.We study the steady state protocol behaviors in simulation. All the results are drawn from the last 2/3 period of the experiments. The packet size in all protocols is set to 1kbyte. The flows which behavior we need to observe stats at random times, uniformly distributed between 5 and 10 seconds. The simulation is run for 6000 seconds and the results are averages of 10 runs.

3.2 Performance Improvement in Large Time Scale Traffic Control

We observe the performance gain of RAAR-MT in loss rate with different background traffic features in both Droptail and RED queues. The performance gain is defined as $(Loss_{RAAR}-Loss_{RAAR-MT})/Loss_{RAAR-MT}$, where $Loss_{RAAR}$ and $Loss_{RAAR-MT}$ are the loss rate of RAAR and RAAR-MT respectively. Buffer size of Droptail is set to 100 packets. Minthresh and Maxthresh of RED are set to 20 and 100 packets respectively.

Fig.4 shows that the more long-range dependent the network traffic is, the more performance gain RAAT-MT will get. The performance gain is larger in Droptail than that in RED. In typical self-similar environment (α=1.5), performance gain in Droptail and RED are about 20% and 12% respectively. Even in traditional short-range dependent environment (α=1.95), some performance gain will be still attained. Since it's widely accepted that performance of RED is much better than Droptail, we only study the protocol behaviors with RED scheme in the following simulation.

The performance gain in loss rate is attained by enhancing the tracking ability to the network state of the control mechanism. We measure the tracking ability of protocols by computing the correlation coefficients of their throughput with the background traffic at the bottleneck link with 1sec as the measurement timescale. Under perfect tracking, their correlation coefficient should equal −1. We find that RAAR-MT exhibits better tracking ability than RAAR in Fig.5, which shows that tracking ability for available bandwidth can be improved by introducing large time scale traffic control.

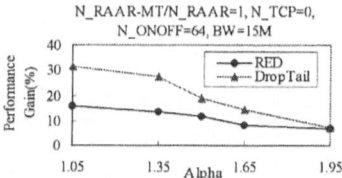
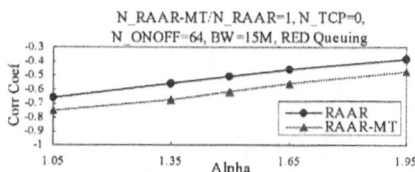

Fig. 4. Performance Gain of RAAR-MT   Fig. 5. Tracking Ability

3.3 TCP-Friendliness

Here we illustrate the fairness of RAAR-MT and TFRC when competing with TCP (SACK) traffic in RED queues under typical self-similar environment (α=1.5).

Fig.6.a uses the inter-protocol fairness index F_P^{inter} [14] as a long-duration metric for the fairness between TCP-Friendly protocol and TCP. It's an ideal fairness when F_P^{inter} =0.5. It shows that F_P^{inter} of RAAR-MT can remain near the ideal fairness in a large measurement range, whereas TFRC will depart from the ideal fairness with the number of competing flows increasing.

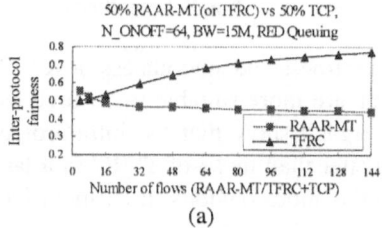
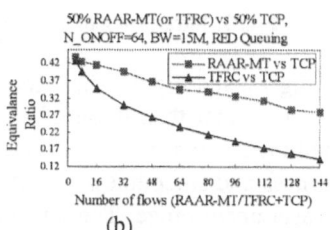

(a)   (b)

Fig. 6. TCP-Friendliness

We use the equivalence ratio [15] in throughput of two flows to evaluate their fairness in smaller timescale. The closer equivalence ratio is to 1, the more "equivalence" the two flows are. The measurement timescale δ is set to 1s in all the simulation experiments. The equivalence ratios shown in Fig.6.b are the results of averaging equivalence ratios of one RAAR-MT (or TFRC) flow and all TCP competing flows. We can observe the similar phenomenon. When the number of competing flows is low, RAAR-MT and TFRC show similar fairness to TCP. With the number of competing flows increasing, the fairness of TFRC to TCP degrades more rapidly.

3.4 Intra-protocol Fairness and Smoothness

Intra-protocol fairness and smoothness are two important performance indexes for transportation protocols. Fig.7 shows the intra-protocol fairness of RAAR-MT, TFRC and TCP with specific RAAR-MT/TCP or TFRC/TCP combinations in terms of equivalence ratio. The equivalence ratios shown in Fig.7 are the results of averaging equivalence ratios of one flow and all the other flows using the same protocol. Fig.8 shows the smoothness of RAAR-MT, TFRC and TCP with specific RAAR-MT/TCP or TFRC/TCP combinations. The smoothness in throughput of a transportation proto-col can be accessed by the coefficient of variation (CoV) [14].

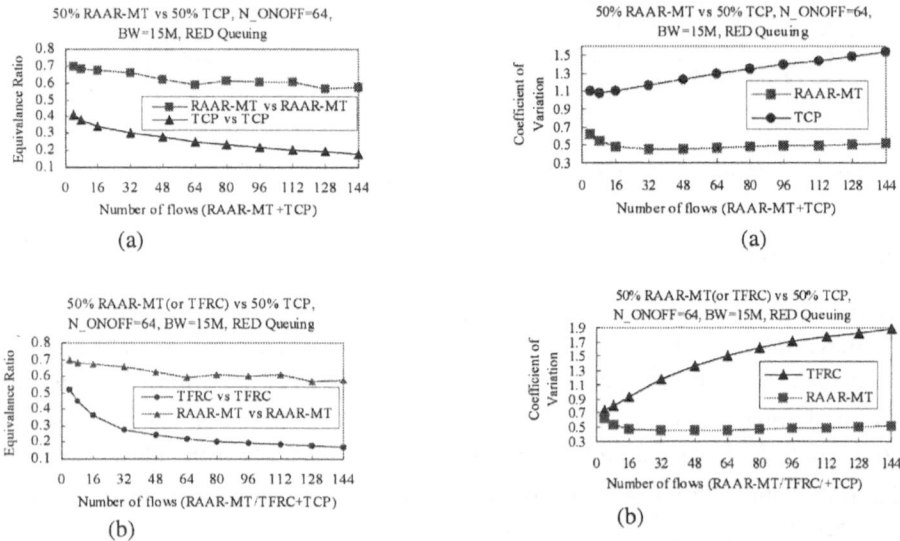

Fig. 7. Intra-protocol fairness   **Fig. 8.** Smoothness

Fig.7.a and Fig.8.a show that the intra-protocol fairness and smoothness of RAAR-MT are better than those of TCP, thus RAAR-MT are more suitable to be used as a multimedia transportation protocol. Fig.7.b and Fig.8.b show that the intra-protocol fairness and smoothness of RAAR-MT are also better than those of TFRC in a large measurement range. The advantage of RAAR-MT is more obvious in an intensively competing environment.

4   Conclusions

This paper proposes a new unicast TCP-Friendly protocol called RAAR-MT, which on-line predicts the tendency of traffic level in the near future and use this predicted information to exert multiple time scale traffic control at receivers. Simulation shows that this protocol can improve the performance in loss rate on self-similar traffic net-work. Even in traditional short-range dependent environment, the performance will not degrade severely. Compared with TFRC, RAAR-MT has better performance in

TCP-Friendliness, intra-protocol fairness and smoothness. The advantage of RAAR-MT is more obvious in an intensively competing environment. The problems of TFRC in high-congested network system have also been reported in [1,3]. We suspect that these problems might be due to the inaccuracy of the throughput formula using in TFRC. In fact it's not an easy job to establish a perfect TCP throughput model that can suit to various network conditions.

It's very attractive to apply RAAR-MT in asymmetric networks such as wireless networks, cable modems, ADSL and satellite networks, since RAAR-MT is not a per-packet acknowledgement mechanism, which can reduce the feedback packets sending in the reverse links lacking bandwidth. With a low frequency of feedback, it helps to solve feedback implosion problems in multicast. Thus, RAAR-MT is also a promising avenue of development for congestion control of multicast multimedia traffic.

References

1. Y. R. Yang, Min S. Kim, and Simon S. Lam. "Transient Behaviors of TCP-Friendly Congestion Control Protocols," Networking Research Laboratory, Department of Computer Sciences, The University of Texas at Austin, Technical Report TR-2000-14, July 2000.
2. S. Floyd, K. Fall. "Promoting the Use of End-to-End Congestion Control," IEEE/ACM Transactions on Networking, August 1999.
3. I. Rhee, V. Ozdemir, Y. Yi, "TEAR: TCP Emulation at Receivers - Flow Control for Multimedia Streaming," Technical report, North Carolina State University, April 2000.
4. R. Rejaie, M. Handley, and D. Estrin, "RAP: An End-to-end Rate-based Congestion Control Mechanism for Realtime Streams in the Internet." Technical Report 98-686, CS-USC, November 1998.
5. Y.Hu, "Study of Multimedia Traffic Transport Congestion Control Protocol in the Internet," Ph.D. Thesis, SUN YAT-SEN University, PR.China, October 2001.
6. S. Floyd, M. Handley, J. Padhye, and J. Widmer, "Equation-Based Congestion Control for Unicast Applications," Proceedings of SIGCOMM 2000, August 2000
7. K. Park, W. Willinger. "Self-similar Network Traffic: An Overview" Self-Similar Network Traffic and Performance Evaluation (ed.), Wiley-Interscience, 2000.
8. K. Park and T. Tuan, "Performance Evaluation of Multiple Time Scale TCP under Self-similar Traffic Conditions", ACM Transactions on Modeling and Computer Simulation, 2000
9. T. Tuan and K. Park, "Multiple time scale congestion control for self-similar network traffic", Performance Evaluation, 1999, 36,359-386.
10. Y.R.Yang and S.S.Lam, "General AIMD Congestion Control," In Proceedings ICNP 2000, Osaka, Japan, November 2000.
11. UC Berkeley, LBL, USC/ISI, and Xerox PARC, The ns Manual (formerly ns Notes and Documentation), March 2001.
12. W. Willinger, V. Paxson and M. S. Taqqu. "Self-Similary and Heavy Tails: Structural Modeling of Network Traffic,", appears on pages 27-53 in the book: "A Practical Guide To Heavy Tails: Statistical Techniques and Applications.", Birkhauser, Boston, 1998
13. M. Handley, J. Pahdye, S. Floyd, and J. Widmer, "TCP Friendly Rate Control (TFRC): Protocol Specification," Internet draft draft-ietf-tsvwg-tfrc-04.txt, April 2002.
14. J. Widmer. "Equation-Based Congestion Control," Diploma Thesis, February 2000.
15. J. Padhye. "Towards A Comprehensive Congestion Control Framework for Continuous Media Flows in Best Effort Networks," Ph.D. Thesis, University of Massachusetts Amherst, March 2000.

Adaptive Call Admission Control for Mobile Multimedia Network

Si-Yong Park, Seung-Won Lee, and Ki-Dong Chung

Department of Computer Science, Pusan National University, Korea
(sypark, bluecity, kdchung)@melon.cs.pusan.ac.kr

Abstract. The rapid growth of the mobile environment has been resulted in servicing not only voice data but also multimedia data. Specially, mobility is a significant feature in mobile environment. In this paper, we propose a multimedia transmission architecture to exploit the mobility in the mobile multimedia network. This architecture can provide seamless communication by overlapping regions among foreign networks in a mobile multimedia network. We propose a bandwidth negotiation policy which a foreign network can admit more requests of new mobile hosts. And the policy can control fairly the differences of allocated bandwidth of foreign networks.

1 Introduction

Current mobile techniques have made possible to service multimedia data in mobile environment. Many network researchers have developed some protocols based on packet switching to provide users efficient services in wired Internet environment. Specially, since IP(Internet Protocol) in wired Internet is not appropriate to support mobility, Mobile IP was proposed by IETF(Internet Engineering Task Force)'s working group. Mobile IP can support the mobility by IP-tunneling. But Mobile IP requires many registration steps. The registration steps accompany with handoff[3]. And the handoff is detrimental to servicing multimedia data continuously. Therefore, we design a multimedia transmission architecture which exploits overlap regions to reduce the overhead of handoff. It is not easy to predict moving directions of a mobile host[2]. Therefore, we consider the architecture that has some overlap regions among foreign networks. In this paper, foreign networks and home networks are a hierarchically structured. A top agent manages several middle agents where each middle agent manages several foreign agents. Foreign networks where mobile hosts may move are managed by a top agent and by middle agents. And many researchers proposed such hierarchical architectures. We propose a bandwidth negotiation policy based on such architectures. Generally bandwidth of mobile environments is less than the bandwidth of wired environment. So, we propose a bandwidth negotiation policy that exploits the small transmission bandwidth. The bandwidth negotiation policy can reduce required bandwidths of foreign networks by mobile hosts in the overlap regions.

University Research Program 2002 supported by Ministry of Information & Communication in South Korea

Y.-C. Chen, L.-W. Chang, and C.-T. Hsu (Eds.): PCM 2002, LNCS 2532, pp. 896-903, 2002.
© Springer-Verlag Berlin Heidelberg 2002

A required bandwidth rate of foreign network in downtown of a city is more than that of foreign network in highway around a city. The bandwidth negotiation policy can control foreign network's bandwidth rates by mobile host's bandwidth in overlap regions.

The rest of this paper is organized as follows. Section 2 reviews the related works in the mobile environment. Section 3 presents a multimedia transmission architecture and seamless multimedia communication. Section 4 describes bandwidth negotiation among foreign networks. In section 5, we show the results of the performance analysis of our proposed policy. Finally we make a conclusion with summary of our research results and refer to the future research.

2   Related Works

Mobile IP consists of home network and foreign networks. Home network is a network, possibly virtual, that has a network address prefix matching the mobile host's home address. Foreign network can be some network, other than the mobile host's home network. And a home agent presents in a home network. A home agent is a router on mobile host's home network that tunnels datagrams for delivery to the mobile host when it is away from home and maintains current location information for the mobile host. A foreign agent is a router on a mobile host's visited network that provides routing services to the mobile host while registered; an agent that detunnels and delivers datagrams to the mobile hosts that were tunneled by the mobile host's home agent; selected as a default router by registered mobile hosts[1].

[6] proposed regional registration. Regional registrations reduce the number of signaling messages to the home network, and reduce the signaling delay when a mobile node moves from one foreign agent to another, within the same visited domain. MRSVP has provided methods to solve overhead of handover and guarantee QoS[4]. Talukdar has provided a bandwidth managing method which divides levels according to congestion states in cells[5]. There are many QoS/fair scheduling approaches wherein all the scheduling activity is logically done at the base station which proposed QoS guarantees in the downlink direction[8,9]. An enhanced Class Based Queuing(CBQ) approach presented in [12] takes into account the channel state of the wireless link before scheduling packets on the link[11].

3   Multimedia Transmission Architecture

We designed a multimedia transmission architecture including overlap regions. We can predict moving directions of mobile hosts by the overlap regions. Mobile hosts in the overlap regions can receive advertisement messages of foreign networks. When mobile hosts move to the other foreign networks, they must pass through overlap regions of foreign networks in the architecture. A foreign domain forms a hierarchical architecture which has several foreign agents and middle agents and a top agent. A top agent has several middle agents. And a middle agent has several foreign agents. In the designed architecture, mobile hosts can move to foreign networks or middle domains. Middle domain consists of several foreign networks which are managed by a middle agent. When a mobile host moves to the overlap region, foreign networks where the mobile host may move will be included in a ghost group. The ghost group is a set of foreign networks where a mobile host may move in. When a mobile host comes out of the overlap region, the corresponding foreign networks will be deleted from the ghost group. Foreign networks in a ghost group start to register and reserve resources before the mobile host enters into the foreign network. When a mobile host moves to the other foreign networks, the foreign networks are managed by the same middle agent or by another middle agent. In case that a mobile hosts moves in an overlap regions between top agents, a top agent where the mobile host did not pass will send a ghost group registration messages to home agent. But moving among foreign networks and middle agents in the same top agent needs not a ghost group registration message. After the home agent makes the top agent register the ghost group, the home agent sends a binding message to a sender. So the sender sends multimedia data packets to a new destination. Figure 1 shows a hierarchical foreign network architecture including overlap regions.

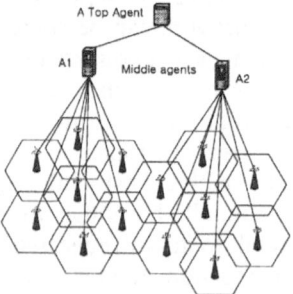

Fig. 1. A Hierarchical Model including overlap Regions

4   Bandwidth Negotiation Policy

Let B_{max}^i be a foreign network i's maximum available bandwidth and B_j^i are the required bandwidths of mobile hosts in the foreign network i. n is a number of mobile hosts in the foreign network i. And the consumption bandwidth rate of the foreign network i is $\sum_{j=1}^{n} B_j^i / B_{max}^i$. A number of new mobile hosts is m. If the foreign network i's bandwidth $B_{max}^i \geq \sum_{j=1}^{n+m} B_j^i$ then a foreign agent in the foreign network i will admit all mobile hosts' required bandwidth. But if the foreign network i's bandwidth $B_{max}^i < \sum_{j=1}^{n+m} B_j^i$, then the foreign agent in the foreign network i will try to exploit the bandwidth negotiation policy.

4.1 Bandwidth Negotiation Steps

In Figure 2, A, B, C are foreign networks and a, b, c are overlap regions. M1 is a new mobile host which is entering the foreign network A. Bandwidth negotiation steps are as follows.

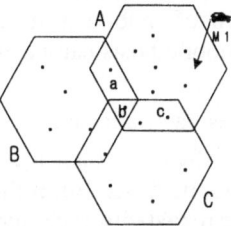

Fig. 2. Distribution of Mobile Hosts in Foreign Networks

First, if the remaining bandwidth in A is not sufficient for M1, the foreign agent in the A sends movement messages to mobile hosts in a, b and c. Second, on receiving movement messages, the mobile hosts send negotiation messages to foreign agents in B and C. Third, if the foreign agents of the B and C accept the negotiation messages, then the foreign agents will begin registrations. After the registration completed, the foreign agents send nego_end messages to the mobile hosts. Fourth, the mobile hosts which successfully negotiated send a nego_ok messages to the foreign agent in A. So, the mobile hosts will be serviced by foreign agents of B, C. Fifth, the foreign agent in A recomputes a consumption bandwidth of A except consumption bandwidths of the mobile hosts which sent nego_ok messages, and reallocates the recomputed bandwidth to mobile hosts in A. Figure 3 shows the bandwidth negotiation steps.

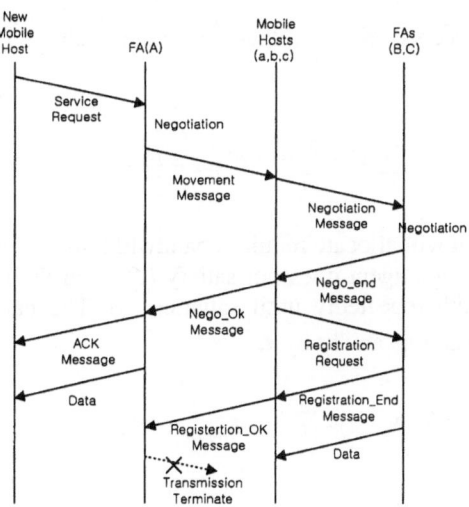

Fig. 3. Bandwidth Negotiation Flow

4.2   Bandwidth Negotiation Policy in a Foreign Network

In section 4.1,it is the worst case when there are no mobile hosts in overlap regions. When new mobile hosts request additional bandwidth to a foreign agent, a sum of the foreign network's consumption bandwidth and the requested bandwidth may exceed the foreign network's maximum available bandwidth. In this case, the foreign agent reduces each allocated bandwidth of mobile hosts in the foreign network, so the required bandwidths to the new mobile hosts can be allocated. These can be stated as follows.

First, the foreign agent reduces each allocated bandwidth of the mobile hosts as much as d. If the reduction satisfies (1), then the foreign agent will allocate the required bandwidths to the new mobile hosts. But if the reduction does not satisfy (1), then the foreign agent will reduce repeatedly each allocated bandwidth of the mobile hosts until (1) is satisfied. Let $B^i_{request}$ be a required bandwidths in a new mobile host, and a number of mobile hosts in the foreign network i is n.

$$\sum_{j=1}^{n}(B^i_j \times d) + B^i_{request} \times d < B^i_{max}$$
$$d : decreasing\ rate.(0 < d \le 1) \tag{1}$$

If a number of mobile hosts in the overlap regions of a foreign network i is m then, the sum of required bandwidths is $\sum_{j=1}^{m} B^i_j$. After the bandwidth negotiation completed, the consumption bandwidth of the foreign network i is $\sum_{k=1}^{n} B^i_k - \sum_{j=1}^{m} B^i_j$. If the foreign agent accepts $B^i_{request}$, then the bandwidth of the foreign agent must satisfy (2).

$$\sum_{k=1}^{n} B^i_k - \sum_{j=1}^{m} B^i_j + B^i_{request} \le B^i_{max} \tag{2}$$

And the foreign agent will allocate required bandwidth to new mobile hosts. But if the bandwidth of the foreign agent does not satisfy (2), then the foreign agent computes its required bandwidth repeatedly until satisfies (3). The bandwidth of the foreign agent will be decreased repeatedly by d.

$$\sum_{j=1}^{n}(B^i_j \times d) - \sum_{k=1}^{m} B^i_k + B^i_{request} \times d \le B^i_{max} \tag{3}$$

If the bandwidth of the foreign agent is decreased by d continuously, then the foreign agent could not guarantee QoS of each mobile host in the foreign network. So we use a threshold α. In the following equations, if calculated values are less than threshold α, then the foreign agent could not allocate the required bandwidths to new mobile hosts.

In case of $m = 0$, $\sum_{j=1}^{n}(B_j^i \times d) + B_{request}^i \leq \alpha$ then $B_{request}^i$ is dropped.

In case of $m > 0$, $\sum_{j=1}^{n}(B_j^i \times d) - \sum_{k=1}^{m}(B_k^i \times d) + B_{request}^i \times d \leq \alpha$ then $B_{request}^i$ is dropped.

5 Performance Evaluation

5.1 Experiment Environments

We designed an experimental model as in Figure 4. Each foreign network has a variable consumption bandwidth rates. The consumption bandwidth rates of the foreign networks are differentiated according to locality. And we simulated based on a foreign network F1.

We simulated two cases of experiments. First experiment shows the values of bandwidths for the foreign network F1. Second experiment compares a normal environment with a proposed environment when a bandwidth negotiation policy is applied. The normal environment uses a simple dropping mechanism. In Figure 4, percentages denote the allocated bandwidth rates of foreign networks.

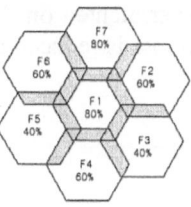

Fig. 4. Virtual Experiment Model

5.2 Performance Evaluation

We experimented on the bandwidths of the F1 according to the normal environment and the proposed environment. The maximum available bandwidth of foreign network is given as 100Mbps. Each required bandwidth of mobile hosts is given as 1Mbps. Rates of mobile hosts in overlap regions is 10% of all hosts. In table 1, EMB is an exceeded amount of maximum available bandwidth in the foreign network F1. TB is the total bandwidth of foreign network F1.

EB is the bandwidth for each mobile host in the foreign network F1. D is a decreasing rate. In case of the normal environment, when EMB is 5Mbps, EB is 0.95Mbps. Each mobile host needs 1Mbps bandwidth but EB needs less than 1Mbps. The foreign agent could not accept the required bandwidths of new mobile hosts. So the foreign agent decreases each bandwidth of mobile hosts in F1. In case of a proposed environment, when mobile hosts in the overlap regions completed the bandwidth negotiation, TB is more than 100Mbps. So the foreign agent allocates 1Mbps to the new mobile hosts. In case that EMB is 80Mbps, the foreign agent drops the new mobile hosts in the normal environment but in the proposed environment, the new mobile hosts will not be dropped.

Table 1. Bandwidths according to exceeded amount of maximum available bandwidth in F1

EMB	Normal environment			Proposed environment		
	TB (Mbps)	EB (Mbps)	D (rate)	TB (Mbps)	EB (Mbps)	D (rate)
1M	99.99	0.99	0.98	101	1	1
5M	99.75	0.95	0.94	105	1	1
10M	99	0.90	0.89	107.8	0.98	0.97
15M	98.9	0.85	0.86	106.95	0.93	0.92
30M	98.8	0.76	0.75	107.9	0.83	0.82
50M	99	0.66	0.65	108	0.72	0.71
80M	98.45	0.55	0.54	107.4	0.60	0.60

Figure 5(a) shows the bandwidth rate of F1 according to the normal environment and the proposed environment. Y axis is a sum of existing mobile hosts' bandwidth in F1. First, we experimented in the normal environment. When the bandwidth rate is more than 100Mbps, the foreign agent in the F1 reduces consumption bandwidths of all mobile hosts. Second, we experimented on the proposed environment. When the time is about 100, the bandwidth rate is reduced to 80(A). The bandwidth negotiation policy begins at A.

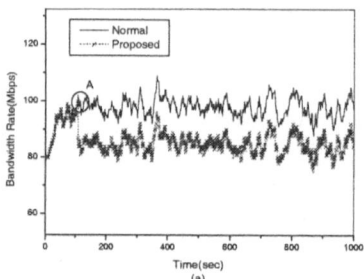 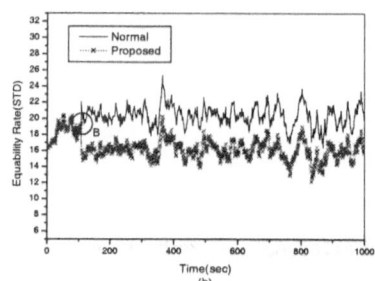

Fig. 5. Bandwidth Rates in Foreign Network F1(a) and Fairness among Foreign Networks(b) according to the Environments(No Dropping)

Figure 5(b) shows whether the consumption bandwidth rates of foreign networks are fair. Each foreign network has different consumption bandwidth rates by locality. In the figure 5(b), we know that the proposed environment is superior to the normal environment. Y axis is a standard deviation of all foreign networks' consumption bandwidth rates. After foreign networks process the bandwidth negotiation policy(B), the proposed environment could control more fairly than the normal environment.

6 Conclusion and Further Works

We propose a bandwidth negotiation policy that can be used on the multimedia transmission architecture. The multimedia transmission architecture shows a hierarchical structure which includes overlap regions. The bandwidth negotiation policy provides that a foreign network could admit more mobile hosts. And the bandwidth negotiation policy controls foreign networks' consumption bandwidth rates more fairly.

In our result of experiments, the bandwidth negotiation policy improves foreign networks' consumption bandwidth rate and can control various consumption bandwidth rates in foreign networks more fairly.

References

[1] Charles E. Perkins, "IP mobility support", RFC2002, 1996.
[2] Suresh Singh, "Quality of Service Guarantees in Mobile computing", Journal of Computer Communication, 1996.
[3] II, Balakrishnam, and V. Padmanabham, S. Seshan and R. katz, "A Comparison of mechanism for improving TCP performance over wireless links", ACM SIGCOMM, Aug, 1966.
[4] A. Talukdar, B. Badrinath, A. Acharya, "MRSVP: A Resource Reservation Protocol for an Integrated Services Packet Network with Mobile Hosts", Technical Report DCS-TR-337, Rutgers University, 1997.
[5] Anup Kumar Talukdar, B. R. Badranath, Arup Acharya, "Rate Adaptation Schemes in Networks with Mobile Hosts", Proceeding of the ACM/IEEE MobiCom, 1998.
[6] Eva Gustafsson, Annika Jonsson, Charles E. Perkins, " Mobile IPv4 Regional Registrations", draft-ietf-mobileip-reg-tunnel-05.txt, 2001.
[7] "Bay area research wireless access network",
      http://http.cs.berkerly.edu/~randy/Daedalus/BARWAN.
[8] M. Naghshineh and A. S. Acampora, "Design and control of micro-cellular networks with QoS Provisioning for data traffic", International Conference on Communications, 1996.
[9] P. Ramanathan and P. Agrawal, "Adapting Packet fair queuing algorithms to wireless networks", Proceeding of the ACM/IEEE MobiCom, 1998.
[10] C. Fragouli, V. Sivaraman and M. Srivastava, "Controlled multimedia wireless link sharing via enhanced class-based queuing with channel-state-dependent packet scheduling", Proc. IEEE INFOCOM, 1998.
[11] Indu Mahadevan and Krishna M. Sivalingam, "Architecture and experimental results for quality of service in mobile network using RSVP and CBQ", ACM/Baltzer Wireless Network, July. 2000.

Providing Multimedia Traffic with Predictability

Yeonseung Ryu

Division of Information and Communication Engineering
Hallym University, Chuncheon, 200-702, Korea
ysryu@hallym.ac.kr

Abstract. Real-time packet schedulers have been studied extensively to
support end-to-end bounded delay for multimedia traffic. Even though
real-time flows are guaranteed by admission control scheme in the packet
scheduler, their schedulability can be violated by arrival of non-real-time
traffic. In this paper, we propose a new packet scheduler scheme to provide real-time traffic with predictability. Proposed scheme also provides
non-real-time traffic with fast service time. We present the schedulability condition considering two packet schedulers and give the admission
control algorithm.

1 Introduction

Recent years have been increasing use of the internet to send and receive multimedia data including streaming playback music and movie, as well as real-time
conferencing. In order to provide end-to-end bounded delay guarantees for multimedia traffic, a number of real-time packet scheduling schemes have widely been
studuied. The real-time packet scheduler should consider non-real-time traffic
since the schedulability of real-time traffic could be violated by non-real-time
traffic. There are some sources that make real-time traffic to behave unpre-
dictably. Usually the nodes in the network periodically receive a number of request messages for the purpose of management. For example, manager software
at management center can periodically send SNMP messages to query MIB data
stored on the node or can send ICMP messages for Ping. The request messages to
setup the real-time flows also could affect the guaranteed transmission of existing real-time traffic if a number of requests arrive at the same time. Therefore,
even though the network switches service only real-time communications, the
real-time flows may experience jitter or loss of data.

A number of real-time packet scheduling algorithms based on *Earliest Deadline First* (EDF) policy have been studied [9,6,4,5,2,12]. EDF is regarded the
best choice for providing delay guarantees since it has been proven to be an
optimal scheduling policy. However, EDF scheduling algorithm cannot deal with
the task systems consisting of a set of real-time tasks and non-real-time tasks
since it assumes that all tasks must have hard deadline requirements. In traditional real-time task scheduling researches, *aperiodic server* schemes have been
proposed for the task system which consists of real-time tasks and non-real-time
tasks to provide non-real-time tasks with fast response time while preserving

Y.-C. Chen, L.-W. Chang, and C.-T. Hsu (Eds.): PCM 2002, LNCS 2532, pp. 904–911, 2002.
© Springer-Verlag Berlin Heidelberg 2002

the schedulability of real-time tasks [11,7]. Aperiodic server schemes create a high-priority periodic server for servicing aperiodic (soft real-time) tasks. Since deadline of aperiodic server is assumed the same as its period, it can be adapted to EDF scheduling scheme.

In this paper, we propose a new packet scheduler scheme which consists of an *EDF scheduler* for real-time traffic and a *Periodic Server (PS) scheduler* for non-real-time traffic. The PS scheduler is a periodic packet scheduler that is responsible for transmitting pending packets of the non-real-time flows. In order not to affect the schedulability of the real-time flows, the PS scheduler is given a reserved time within a period. The PS scheduler is assigned the higher priority than EDF scheduler to provide fast service time to the non-real-time flows. While the PS scheduler is suspending and does not yet spend all its reserved time within the current period, if non-real-time traffic arrives at the node then the PS scheduler is awakened immediately and spends the remaining reserved time servicing them. Since the PS scheduler uses only specified reserved time within one period, it does not violate the schedulability of the real-time flows.

In this paper, we also present the schedulability condition considering PS and EDF scheduler in an integrated manner. With proposed schedulability condition we give an admission control algorithm that can be executed in pseudo-polynomial time. Through simulations we show that proposed admission control algorithm can be applicable to the practical systems with little runtime overhead.

The rest of this paper is organized as follows. In Section 2, we give the details of the system model that services two types of flows: real-time flows and non-real-time flows. We also describe the Periodic Server (PS) method to service non-real-time flows. In Section 3, we give the schedulability condition for our system model and present proposed admission control algorithm. Section 4 presents the experimental results to investigate the practicalness of proposed admission control algorithm. The conclusions of this paper are given in Section 5.

2   System Model

We assume that flow setup protocol such as RSVP is used to provide guaranteed service to the real-time flows. After establishing a flow i, a packet j of flow i arriving at each node has deadline as $D_{i,j} = a_{i,j} + d_i$, where $a_{i,j}$ is arrival time of packet j of flow i and d_i is a local delay bound of flow i, respectively.

We assume that each node has the rate controller, such as RC-EDF (Rate-Controlled EDF) [6] which temporarily buffers the real-time packets to ensure that traffic entering the EDF scheduler queue conforms to traffic constraint function. Using these schemes the maximum traffic arrival to the EDF scheduler is assmued to be bounded by traffic constraint function. Let $A_i[s, t]$ be the amount of traffic (measured in bits/second) from flow i arriving over interval [s, t]. We assume that $A_i[t] = A_i[0, t]$. Let $A_i^*(t)$ be a right continuous subadditive function. $A_i^*(t)$ is said to be an envelope of flow $A_i[t]$, if for all times $s > 0$ and for all $t \geq 0$, we have $A_i[s, t] \leq A_i^*(t - s)$, where $A_i^*(t) = 0$ for all $t < 0$. For example, the traffic constraint function for the (σ, ρ)-model [3] is given by

$A_i^*(t) = \sigma_i + \rho_i t$, where σ_i is a burst parameter and ρ_i is a rate parameter of flow i.

Let $F = \{1, 2, ..., N\}$ denote a set of flows which consists of a set R of real-time flows and a set E of non-real-time flows. Given a set R of real-time flows where each flow $i \in R$ is characterized by a tuple $\{A_i^*, d_i\}$, the set R is schedulable if for all $t \geq 0$ no packet exceeds its local delay bound. In this work, we assume that the real-time traffic is characterized by the (σ, ρ)-model. The (σ, ρ)-model has widely been used in the literature [3,9,5]. However, admission control algorithm which will be presented in next section can be used with any other traffic models.

In each node, there are two packet schedulers: One is an EDF scheduler, which schedules the real-time packets in the order of their assigned deadlines. The other is referred to as a *Periodic Server* (PS) scheduler, which is responsible for servicing non-real-time traffic, including request messages from SNMP agent, RSVP host, and so on. Goals of this work are to:

- guarantee the real-time constraints (end-to-end delay bound) of the real-time flows.
- service the non-real-time flows as soon as possible while not hurting schedulability of the real-time flows that are already guaranteed.

The PS scheduler is a periodic task, which is similar to aperiodic server schemes that were proposed in [11,7]. In order not to affect the real-time flows that are already guaranteed, we need to reserve the capacity of link for the non-real-time flows. The PS scheduler executes periodically and consumes link capacity for a given reserved time within a period. Let T_s and C_s be a period and the amount of reserved time within a period of the PS scheduler, respectively $(C_s < T_s)$.

The priority of the PS scheduler is given higher than the EDF scheduler to service the non-real-time traffics without *starvation*. When the period of the PS scheduler begins, the PS scheduler starts immediately and transmits the non-real-time packets during reserved time interval. If there are no more non-real-time packets to transmit, the PS scheduler stops its work. When the reserved time duration finishes or the PS scheduler completes its work, the EDF scheduler starts its execution. While the PS scheduler is suspending and does not yet spend all its reserved time within the current period, if the non-real-time traffic arrives at the node then the PS scheduler is awakened immediately because its priority is higher than that of the EDF scheduler, and spends the remaining reserved time servicing them. Since the PS scheduler is able to use only specified reserved time within one period, if the PS scheduler spends all its reserved time then it suspends its execution even though it does not yet service all non-real-time traffic.

3   Admission Control Algorithm

In this section, we give the schedulability condition for the system model that consists of the EDF scheduler and the PS scheduler.

Let R be a set of real-time flows, where flow $i \in R$ is characterized by the traffic constraint function. Then the schedulability condition for the set R under EDF scheduler is given as follows [1, 3]:

Theorem 1 *The set R is EDF-schedulable if and only if for all $t \geq 0$*

$$\sum_{i \in R} A_i^*(t - d_i) \leq ct \tag{1}$$

where c is the capacity (maximum rate) of the link (bps).

From Theorem 1, we can obtain the condition that the set R is not schedulable by applying the contrapositive rule to Equation 1. That is, the set R is not schedulable if and only if there exists a time $t \geq 0$ such that

$$t < \frac{1}{c} \sum_{i \in R} A_i^*(t - d_i) \tag{2}$$

Informally the condition states that a deadline violation occurs if there exists a time $t \geq 0$ such that the sum of the time for transmitting the real-time traffic that arrived with deadline before or at time t exceeds the available time in the interval $[0, t]$. Equation 2 also means that there exists an upper bound, written B, of t if the set R is not schedulable. Thus, it follows that the set R is schedulable if there is no time t in the interval $[0, B]$ such that Equation 2 is satisfied.

Next, we discuss the schedulability condition for the set $F = R \cup E$, where E is the set of the non-real-time flows. In our approach the PS is responsible for servicing the non-real-time traffic. The PS executes periodically with higher priority than the EDF scheduler. Let T_s and C_s be a period and the amount of reserved time within a period of the PS, respectively. We use $I(t)$ to denote the maximum amount of time available for PS in the interval $[0, t]$. That is,

$$I(t) = \lfloor \frac{t}{T_s} \rfloor C_s + Min(C_s, t - \lfloor \frac{t}{T_s} \rfloor T_s) \tag{3}$$

where $Min(a, b)$ is the smaller value between a and b.

Since the PS scheduler periodically executes with a priority greater than the EDF scheduler, the available amount of link capacity for the real-time flows is $c(t - I(t))$ in the interval $[0, t]$. If the maximum real-time traffic arrivals with a deadline earlier than or equal to t, i.e., $A_i^*(t - d_i)$, exceeds the capacity of the link available for R, a deadline violation occurs. Thus, Theorem 2 describes the condition that the set F is not schedulable.

Theorem 2 *A set F is not EDF-schedulable if and only if there exist a time $t \geq 0$ such that*

$$t - I(t) < \frac{1}{c} \sum_{i \in R} A_i^*(t - d_i) \tag{4}$$

where c is the capacity of the link.

From Theorem 2, the set F is schedulable if and only if there is no time t in the interval $[0, B]$ such that Equation 4 is satisfied, where B is an upper bound of time t when the set F is not schedulable. We define U as

$$\frac{C_s}{T_s} + \frac{1}{c} \sum_{i \in R} \rho_i \tag{5}$$

We assume $U < 1$. Finally we can give the schedulability condition for the set F as follows:

Theorem 3 *For a given time t, we assign the value of B as followings:*
If $C_s = Min(C_s, t - \lfloor \frac{t}{T_s} \rfloor T_s)$,

$$B = \frac{\sum_{i \in R}(\sigma_i - \rho_i d_i)}{c(1 - U)} \tag{6}$$

Otherwise,

$$B = \frac{(T_s - C_s) + \sum_{i \in R}(\sigma_i - \rho_i d_i)}{c(1 - U)} \tag{7}$$

If for all $t' \in [0, B]$, Equation 4 in Theorem 2 is not satisfied, then the set F is EDF-schedulable.

In order to determine whether the set F is schedulable or not, we only need to find a time in the interval $[0, B]$ such that Equation 4 is satisfied. If there doesn't exist a time t below B such that Equation 4 is satisfied, then the set F is schedulable all the time. Detailed proof for theorems can be seen in [10].

```
ADMISSION_CONTROL_ALGORITHM(
input : set R of real-time flows with (σᵢ, ρᵢ, dᵢ) and the PS parameter (Cₛ, Tₛ)
output : schedulable or not)
1. begin
2.    calculate U;          /* Equ. 5 */
3.    if U ≥ 1 then
4.        return(not schedulable);
5.    endif
6.    calculate B;          /* Equ. 6 and 7 */
7.    for t=1 to B do
8.        calculate I(t);         /* Equ. 3 */
9.        if Equ. 4 is satisfied then
10.               return(not schedulable);
11.       endif
12.   endfor
13.   return(schedulable);
14.end.
```

Fig. 1. Admission Control Algorithm

Using Theorem 3, we can obtain the algorithm for admission control. In Figure 1, we give an algorithm to check the schedulability whenever a new real-time flow joins the packet scheduler. We can easily see that this algorithm can be executed in time $O(Bn)$, where B is the upper bound in Equation 6 or 7, and n is the number of real-time flows. The B is a function of both length and magnitude of the input and hence the complexity of deciding schedulability is pseudo-polynomial time. Since U and B can be computed in time $O(n)$ respectively and hence do not affect the overall complexity of deciding schedulability.

4 Experiments

4.1 Runtime Overhead of Admission Control Algorithm

Since proposed admission control algorithm has pseudo-polynomial time complexity, we need to investigate that it can be used in practical systems with little run-time overhead. We generate a range of traffic patterns that are characterized by the (σ, ρ)-model. In our simulations, we take $\rho = 10^p Kbps$ where p is uniformly distributed in $[1, 3]$. And we take $\sigma = r * \rho Kb$ where r is uniformly distributed in $[0.8, 1.6]$. We take a delay requirement $d = 10^s * 30ms$, where s is uniformly distributed in $[0, 0.52]$, thus d ranging in $[30ms, 100ms]$. The generated traffic patterns include the typical video and audio traffic [8]. We assume the link has a capacity of 155 Mbps.

For PS parameter, we take $T_s = 1000$ ms and $C_s = 100, 300$ and 500 ms. We denote by $U_s = \frac{C_s}{T_s}$ the utilization of PS, thus $U_s = 0.1, 0.3$ and 0.5. U_s means the ratio of time PS is servicing the non-real-time flows to total time. For each U_s, we perform a simulation run. In one simulation run, we generate flows till U in Equ. 5 reaches 1.0 and compute upper bound B using Equ. 6 and Equ. 7. We use the method of independent replications to generate 90% confidence intervals. We are interested in the value of Bn when the number of admitted real-time flows (i.e., n) is at its maximum.

Figure 2 illustrates the results of our simulation. We can find the flex point, called the knee, beyond which B increases rapidly but the increase in n is small. If we limit n to the point less than or equal to the knee, B will be much the smaller value compared with its maximum value and thus we are able to decrease the number of iterations (i.e., Bn) dramatically. To do so, we make the usable link capacity be smaller than the total link capacity. For example, if we want to limit the usable link capacity to 90% of the total link capacity then we modify $U > 0.9$ in line 3 of admission control algorithm. However, if we limit the maximum utilization of link to a smaller value than 100%, the maximum number of flows decreases. In practice, therefore, we consider tradeoff between the maximum number of admitted real-time flows and the runtime overhead of admission control algorithm.

4.2 Responsiveness of Non-real-Time Traffic

Since the priority of the PS scheduler is higher than the EDF scheduler, non-real-time packets are guaranteed for service as soon as possible. However, the

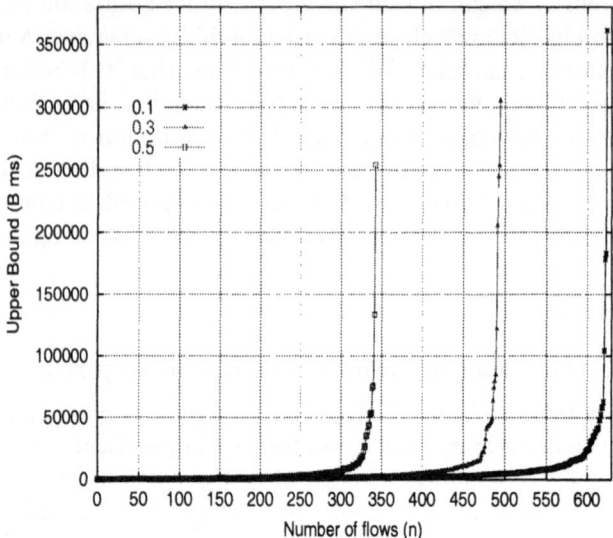

Fig. 2. Experiment result

service time of non-real-time packets could be very large if the utilization of the link reserved for the PS scheduler becomes 100%. Let us assume that interarrival time between non-real-time packets follows an exponential distribution and all non-real-time packets are serviced in FIFO order. In this case, the system can be modeled as $M/D/1$ queueing model. Let λ be arrival rate of non-real-time packets and $E[s]$ be service time per packet, respectively. Then the utilization $u = \lambda E[s]$. In $M/D/1$ queue, the average response time of non-real-time packets $R = E[s] + \frac{uE[s]}{2(1-u)}$. When the utilization of the link is very low, the average response time of packets is almost equal to the service time per packet. When the utilization is very high, i.e., u is close to 1, the denominator goes to zero and R goes to infinity. In fact, R goes to infinity quickly as u gets close to 100%.

Therefore, in order to achieve reasonable responsiveness of non-real-time traffic, we need to restrict utilization below 100%. Recent work of Abdelzaher, et al, also presented that if the utilization is maintained below $\frac{1}{1+\sqrt{1/2}}$, all aperiodic tasks can be completed within certain time limit [1]. There is a tradeoff between the link utilization and the responsiveness of non-real-time traffic.

5   Conclusion

Today's network switches must send and receive *non-real-time traffic* as well as *real-time traffic*. Goal of this work is to provide the real-time flows that are already guaranteed with predictability and to service the non-real-time flows as soon as possible. In proposed scheme, there are two packet schedulers: an *EDF scheduler* for handling the real-time flows and a *Periodic Server(PS) Scheduler* for servicing the non-real-time flows. In order to preserve the schedulability of the real-time flows, the PS scheduler executes periodically and consumes link capacity for a given reserved time within the current period. The PS scheduler is assigned the higher priority than the EDF scheduler to provide fast response time to the non-real-time flows.

We present the schedulability condition considering two packet schedulers and give the admission control algorithm. The computation complexity of proposed algorithm is $O(Bn)$, where B is time limit in Theorem 3, and n is the number of current real-time flows including newly arrived one, respectively. The computation overhead highly depends on the value of B that must be computed using the traffic parameters. However, we show through simulations that the proposed algorithm can be used in practical systems with little runtime overhead.

References

1. T. Abdelzaher and C. Lu. Schedulability analysis and utilization bounds for highly scalable real-time services. In *Real-Time Technology and Applications Symposium*, June 2001.
2. M. Andrews. Probabilistic end-to-end delay bounds for earliest deadline first scheduling. In *IEEE INFOCOM*, 2000.
3. R.L. Cruz. A calculus for network delay, part i:network elements in isolation. *IEEE Transactions on Information Theory*, 37(1):132–141, 1991.
4. Domenico Ferrari and Dinesh C. Verma. A scheme for real-time channel establishment in wide-area networks. *IEEE Journal on Selected Areas in Communications*, 8(3):368–379, 1990.
5. Victor Firoiu, James F. Kurose, and Donald F. Towsley. Efficient admission control for EDF schedulers. In *INFOCOM (1)*, pages 310–317, 1997.
6. Leonidas Georgiadis, Roch Guérin, Vinod Peris, and Kumar N. Sivarajan. Efficient network QoS provisioning based on per node traffic shaping. *IEEE/ACM Transactions on Networking*, 4(4):482–501, 1996.
7. T.M. Ghazalie and T.P. Baker. Aperiodic servers in a deadline scheduling environment. *The Journal of Real-Time Systems*, 9:21–36, 1995.
8. Edward W. Knightly, Dallas E. Wrege, Jorg Liebeherr, and Hui Zhang. Fundamental limits and tradeoffs of providing deterministic guarantees to VBR video traffic. In *Measurement and Modeling of Computer Systems*, pages 98–107, 1995.
9. Jörg Liebeherr, Dallas E. Wrege, and Domenico Ferrari. Exact admission control for networks with a bounded delay service. *IEEE/ACM Transactions on Networking*, 4(6):885–901, 1996.
10. Yeonseung Ryu. Considering non-real-time traffic in real-time packet scheduler. Technical Report, Hallym University.
11. B. Sprunt. *Aperiodic task scheduling for real-time systems*. PhD thesis, Dept. of Electrical and Computer Engineering, Carnegie Mellon University, Pittsburg, PA, August 1990.
12. K. Zhu, Y. Zhuang, and Y. Viniotis. Achieving end-to-end delay bounds by edf scheduling without traffic shaping. In *IEEE INFOCOM*, April 2001.

Dynamic Service Extensibility through Programmable Network in a Mobility Context

Robert Hsieh and Aruna Seneviratne

School of Electrical Engineering and Telecommunications
The University of New South Wales, Sydney, 2052, Australia
roberth@ee.unsw.edu.au, aruna@unsw.edu.au

Abstract. The proliferation of mobile computing devices over the past decade has expedited researches on mobility services and architecture, namely, Mobile IP, Mobile QoS and multimedia content adaptation for limited wireless bandwidth. However, to our knowledge, all of the currently proposed mobility service architectures, such as [3], [7], are restricted to operate within one administrative domain, or a confederation of administrative domains. This paper addresses the following issue: Is it possible to remove the boundary that confines the closeness in service operating environment and be able to extend application-level services in a dynamic, on-demand manner over mobility architecture such as Mobile IP [1]? We present the Dynamic Extensible and Programmable Service Architecture Mobile extension, (DEEPSEA-M), which is aimed at accomplishing the above. Within the mobility context, we discuss issues regarding service extension, security, maintenance and teardown control, as well as detailing an implementation design in achieving DEEPSEA-M framework.

1 Introduction

The emerging trend in Internet mobility research is the offering of value-added services such as low-latency handoff, mobile QoS and content adaptation. What is common with all these service architectures is the introduction of specialized service entities, strategically distributed throughout and inside the network, which provide resource adaptation, service provisioning or control functionalities along the data path. Inevitably, these services are confined in reachability to within a single administrative domain or a confederation of administrative domains / Autonomous Systems (AS). (We use administrative domains and Autonomous Systems interchangeably in this paper.) This, however, is highly undesirable as mobile computing is by nature nomadic. From the network service operator's perspective, the problem is that in order to continue service offering in a new administrative domain, specialized service entities must be present a priori, which is impossible to anticipate with accuracy, not to mention the high set up cost involved. From the service subscriber's perspective, if s/he moves out of the normal service domain into a new administrative domain, the original services can no longer be warranted. It is therefore, DEEPSEA-M's aim in solving the following: Is it possible to extend network service environment in a way that the static service boundary (perhaps formed by a confederation of administrative domains through collaboration) can be extended dynamically and on-demand over the

Y.-C. Chen, L.-W. Chang, and C.-T. Hsu (Eds.): PCM 2002, LNCS 2532, pp. 912–919, 2002.

Internet as well as caters for IP-centric mobile computing devices? Imagine the ability to move anywhere, anytime and anyplace in the world and still maintain the same level of service as if the user is at the home service domain. And more importantly, how does service extensibility operate within the Internet mobility context, where the usefulness of such extensibility is unprecedented. These are the overarching conceptual goals of DEEPSEA-M.

The contribution of this paper is as follows. We define the concept of 'dynamic service extensibility' for value-added services in a mobile networking environment. We address the issue of provisioning of service extension to new administrative domains on-demand and on-the-fly over the Mobile IP architecture. We leverage on our previous work in [5] and illustrated a specific implementation design of our DEEPSEA-M framework. To our knowledge, DEEPSEA-M is unique in that, it explores the intersection between dynamic service extensibility, application-level value-added services and Internet mobility architecture. This paper is structured as follows. Section 2 describes the DEEPSEA-M framework and issues associating with service extension, security, maintenance and teardown. Section 3 presents our implementation design of the programmable execution environment for DEEPSEA-M and we conclude in Section 4.

2 DEEPSEA Mobile Extension

The DEEPSEA-M framework makes two pivotal assumptions about service architectures of the next generation Internet. Firstly, it assumes that the concept of 'resource hiring' will be widely accepted. We formally define resource hiring as the practice where certain certified entities are able to hire from a foreign administrative domain, resources, such as computation power and bandwidth, for an agreed duration, (in the order of hours) with a negotiated price and transacted on-the-fly. The second assumption is that in the foreseeable future, programmable networking devices, such as those described in [4] or [6], will be widely deployed over the Internet, capable of running application programs in transforming data flows. Also, we assume the proliferation of IP-centric mobile device, e.g., GPRS capable mobile handsets, 802.11 equipped laptop computers and Personal Digital Assistants (PDA), as well as wide deployment of necessary supporting network infrastructure.

In demonstrating the inter-operability of DEEPSEA-M with the Mobile IP [1] framework, we decided to take a generic hierarchical Mobile IP model as the basis, as major extension works on Mobile IP are hierarchical based in structure, e.g. [2] and [3]. The hierarchical structure separates mobility into micro mobility (within one domain) and macro mobility (between domains) [2]. To support this, a special network agent entity, *Mobility Anchor Point* (MAP) [2], is placed near the edges of the network, bordering the wireless network. It separates micro from macro mobility, by receiving packets on behalf of the mobile node that it is serving. Thus, when a mobile node moves within a foreign domain, only location update to the MAP is necessary. This hierarchical network structure minimizes the location update signaling with external networks. Our framework utilizes this hierarchical partition in achieving service extensibility by localizing service provision, at the MAP, within the foreign domain where the mobile node is situated.

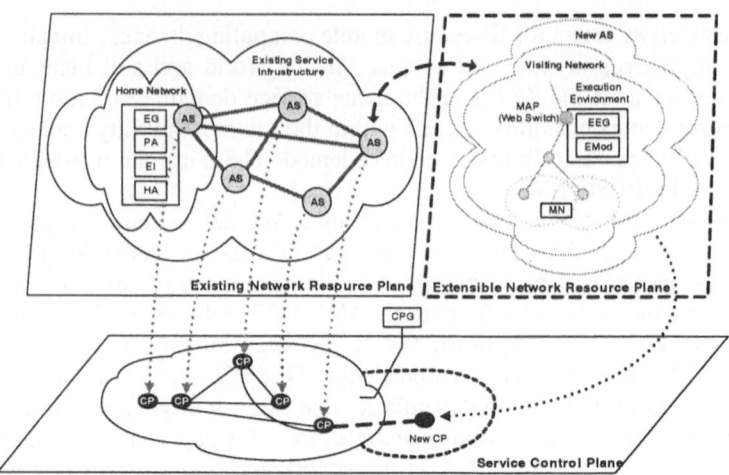

Fig. 1. DEEPSEA-M Framework

2.1 DEEPSEA-M Overview and Extension Scenario

DEEPSEA-M forms a dynamic extensible service framework by defining two logical functional planes and introducing seven generic control entities, as shown in Fig. 1. They are the Network Resource Plane (NRP), the Service Control Plane (SCP), the Control Point (CP), the Control Point Gateway (CPG), the Extension Gateway (EG), the Personal Assistant (PA), the Execution Interpreter (EI), the Execution Environment Gateway (EEG) and the Extension Module (EMod). The Home Agent (HA) and the Mobile Node (MN) entities retain their meaning from the Mobile IP framework.

The NRP consists of raw resources, such as, bandwidth, computation power etc., and is comprised of a confederation of ASs, forming an effective operable service boundary. The SCP consists of management nodes, each associate with a corresponding AS, co-operating together in providing service management, within the defined service boundary of NRP. Within the SCP, a CP is responsible for the local resource management, policing and monitoring of a particular NRP domain, while the CPG is the first point of contact for new administrative domain wishing to join the existing service architecture. It is not our goal to define specific service control architecture for DEEPSEA-M, but rather, we define a generalized requirement where two such control entities, namely the CP and the CPG, must exist within the SCP in making the DEEPSEA-M framework operable.

We define the 'Existing NRP' as the current service infrastructure, while the 'Extensible NRP' as the new domain to be merged with the Existing NRP. Within the Existing NRP, any communication host must belong to a home network. Within the home network, an EG's role is to provide admission control for the dynamic extension of the DEEPSEA-M. The PA is a 'servant' entity that maintains the profile, i.e. bandwidth limitation, communication requirements etc., of its care-of MN. The PA is initially located inside the home network but may migrate, if necessary, in following the MN. The PA is the first point of contact for any MN wishing to request a service extension. Moreover, it actively senses the surrounding network environment in providing its MN with certain level of network awareness, i.e., bandwidth limitation. The deliberate separation of control logic, from the communication host (MN) to a separate entity (PA), is to provide a layer of intelligent indirection. The intelligence is 'stored' inside the network where end hosts are not forced to maintain control states.

In the potential Extensible NRP, we assumed that there is a programmable execution environment, provided by the programmable network platform hardware, containing a run-time environment capable of resource hiring transaction activities, which are managed by the EEG. An EG negotiates with EEG in securing resources for the dynamic deployment of its EMod. The EMod is a specialized control entity, belonging to specific service architecture, used to pledge the new domain with the existing NRP. An EMod essentially represents the new extensible NRP similar to that of the CP entity in the existing NRP infrastructure, within a SCP. The programmable execution environment is situated within the MAP near the MN. As MAP is situated along the data path in managing traffic redirection and network address binding, it is the strategic point in performing tasks relating to dynamic service extension.

Regarding resource negotiation, EEG is responsible in advertising the resource availability. The advertisement, similar to MAP advertisement [2], can be implemented using modified router advertisement message with an optional R bit indicating resource hiring capability and maybe additional bits in indicating the applicable resource negotiation protocol. The role of the Execution Interpreter (EI), located in the home network, is to act as a universal translator, interpreting the resource negotiation protocol in use at the new Extensible NRP. We assume that there are information databases on the Internet, containing the semantics of all available resource negotiation protocols. The EI is able to consult such databases in events where the resource negotiation protocol in use is unknown. We also assume that EEG will actively register and/or update such databases with its protocol information.

In what follows, we illustrate how a transcoding service can be extended dynamically within the context of Mobile IP. The idea of transcoding service is one where with limited resources, how data stream should be 'adapted' to suit the current environment, taking into consideration a balance of pricing, usability and acceptability issues [8]. More specific to our context, we intend to illustrate a transcoding service in converting color images into black and white images, within html files, near the last segment of the data path, i.e. the wireless link where the bandwidth resource is highly scarce. Analogous to micro-macro mobility design, we perform the transcoding service nearer to the MN to achieve maximum effectiveness in bandwidth utilization and assuming that the device is only capable of black and white display.

Fig. 2a shows the typical operational behavior for the service extension within the DEEPSEA-M framework, i.e., i) the migration of the PA and ii) the dynamic service extension. When a mobile node arrives at a new access network, it obtains a new IP address through standard Mobile IP address resolution procedure. After obtaining the network access, it signals its current PA in requesting the same value-added service that it used to receive at its home network. We define the old Personal Assistant (oPA) as mobile node's current PA, while the new Personal Assistant (nPA) as the newly 'migrated' PA for the MN. If the oPA determines that the MN has arrived at a network domain not covered by the existing service architecture, it will trigger the dynamic service extension process. Firstly, the oPA sends an extension request to the

EG located in the home network. The EG, in this case, decides that the oPA should be migrated nearer to the MN, in performing mobile awareness sensing tasks. Therefore, EG will firstly send an assistant replacement request to the oPA and then begin re-

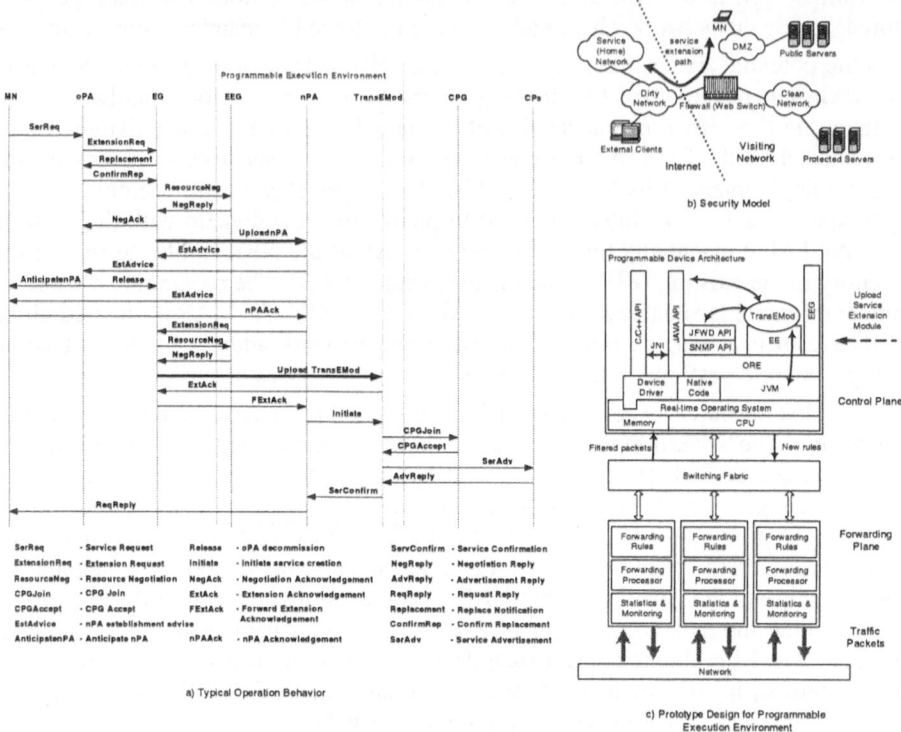

Fig. 2. Operation Scenario, Security Model and Implementation Design

source negotiation with the EEG, specified by the MN via oPA. The programmable execution environment is assumed to situate inside the MAP. (The PA or the MN is responsible for the discovery of the execution environment.) Assuming the requested resource is available, the EG sends a negotiation acknowledgement to the oPA indicating its intent to decommission the oPA as the current PA for the MN. The EG subsequently uploads a nPA to the programmable execution environment. This nPA contains the existing MN's profile and context information which are carried over from oPA via EG as part of the ConfirmRep message prior. The nPA then sends a successful establishment message to the EG as well as the oPA, indicating the completion of the uploading. The oPA then indicates to the EG that it will release the association with the MN and also informs the MN to anticipate for an upcoming association with a nPA The nPA also advices the MN about its existence and receive in reply an acknowledgement message, which signifies the end of the Personal Assistant uploading process. Continuing on, the nPA resumes the role of oPA by sending the service extension request, inherited from oPA, to the EG. The EG then sends a resource negotiation message to the specified EEG. If the resource negotiation is successful, the EG then uploads the Transcoding Extension Module (TransEMod) to the negotiated resource space, inside the programmable execution environment. Upon upload completion, the TransEMod acknowledges the EG with a successful status and the EG forwards the acknowledgement to the nPA indicating a successful extension. Subsequently, nPA sends an initiate message containing the service requirement to the TransEMod. The TransEMod will act as the new CP for the new network domain as well as performing the transcoding services. It will firstly request to join with the existing SCP through the CPGJoin message. An EG possess the knowledge of the location of CPG, and this is passed onto the TransEMod as part of the uploading process. Once the TransEMod is admitted to the SCP, it will begin its service advertising procedure to other CPs and also attempts to offer its service. Other mobile nodes belonging to the same service network will also be able to obtain TransEMod's service if traversing through this foreign domain. Subsequently, TransEMod acknowledges the nPA with a service confirmation message. Finally, the nPA notifies the MN that the requested service is available. The TransEMod have now established a binding with the MN and will transcode any image files into black and white for the MN from then onwards.

2.2 Maintenance, Teardown, and Security

In DEEPSEA-M, the Extension Module (EMod) is responsible for session maintenance and/or monitoring whenever applicable. Similar in concept as Active Network's Active Application [6], this generic entity, EMod, can be persistent where it may keep state within the programmable execution environment, or it maybe ephemeral and die after execution. Through SNMP or specialized network device API such as JFWD [6], EMod will be able to execute monitoring and accounting tasks. This will facilitate proper use of 'hired' resources and determining the appropriate pricing. In service extension maintenance, the EG may need to re-negotiate with the EEG if the current resource is insufficient or service extension is not longer required. The service teardown involves the end host application or the PA initiating the process. The EG finalizes the extension teardown by decommissioning the associate EMod, together with the settlement of the service extension cost, with the resource providers and the end user. We assume that failure of EMod or the hardware providing the programmable execution environment will require the service extension to be reconstructed from scratch.

The DEEPSEA-M assumes a typical security model (Fig. 2b) where a firewall server with 3 interface cards is inserted into the data path. One network interface is connected to the public side of the network. This is the 'dirty' side of the firewall. The other network interface is connected to the side of the network that attaches to resources that need to be protected. This is the 'clean' side of the firewall. The third network interface is connected to the demilitarized zone (DMZ), which is more secure than the dirty side of the firewall but less secure than the clean side. DMZ is typically used for services such as Internet Web servers or temporary guest network access, where public access is required. Essentially, the programmable execution environment together with the EMod entity can be think of as analogous to the firewall.

Logically, we can safely assume that (temporary) network access inside a foreign network is most likely to belong to the DMZ security level for a visiting MN. When roaming in a foreign network, it is unlikely that a MN will be able to gain access to devices in the 'clean' side of the network. Therefore, EMod essentially opens a temporary security wormhole for dynamic services to be reachable inside the foreign network but only within the DMZ security level. This wormhole only allows traffic designated for the specific MN requesting the service extension to go through. Even in events where security has been compromised, only devices or services within the DMZ will be affected, while the clean side of the network still maintains integrity. A suitable security protocol to be used is currently under investigation.

3   Implementation Design

The network hardware platform of our choice is a 'Web' switch. In general, a Web switch include a wirespeed ASIC-based packet forwarding hardware, servicing normal Layer 2/3 switching, and a programmable software component with the flexibility to perform a variety of Layers 4-7 switching services. We choose the Nortel Passport 8600 series LAN switch equipped with the Alteon Web Switching Module as our base hardware platform. This combination achieves a significantly higher level of performance by introducing two separated working planes 'control' and 'forwarding'. The forwarding plane along the data path is implemented, at each port, using WebIC network processing ASIC that combines a L2 packet engine with two RISC processors onto a single chip. The packet engine in each WebIC switches L2 packets in hardware while the network processors support L3-7 switching in software within the control plane. The Oplet Run-time Environment (ORE) [6] provides the environment for dynamic programmability of the switching behavior, at this plane, through EMod oplets.

The ORE supports dynamically injecting customized software services into network devices and provides secure downloading, installation and safe execution of the extension services on the network device. Essentially the control plane is composed of an embedded Java Virtual machine (JVM) and the ORE. Possible ORE services include monitoring, routing, diagnostic, data transforming and other service specific functions, i.e. our transcoding service. ORE services can monitor and change specific Management Information Base (MIB) variables, locally on the device, through the Java MIB API. Moreover, ORE services use the Java Forwarding API (JFWD API) [6] to instruct the forwarding engine regarding the handling of packets. The JFWD API is a uniform, platform-independent portal through which application program can control the forwarding engines of heterogeneous network nodes such as switches and routers. The underlying JVM is also modified to perform accounting for both CPU and memory consumption. Oplets are self-contained downloadable units that encapsulate one or more services, service attributes, authentication information, and resource requirements specification. In our context, EMod is constructed as an oplet.

Fig. 2c depicts the DEEPSEA-M programmable execution environment prototype architecture. The control plane maintains the Java Virtual Machine (JVM), runs ORE, and houses diversified network applications that make up the execution environment of customer's intelligences and value-added services, e.g. TransEMod. Extension of services is initiated at the control plane. In fact, these services can be divided into two further planes, namely, control and data, according to which plane they serve. Control-plane services deal with network management issues such as altering the forwarding behaviors (e.g. forwarding priority) along the data path. While the data-plane services such as data transformation cut through the data path and take in and process particular packets before forwarding them. With respect to our extension example, the TransEMod oplet instructs the web switch in trapping and redirecting images requests, though JFWD, and performs the conversion from color to black and white for images inside html files before merging them back together.

4 Conclusion

This paper presented the design of DEEPSEA-M framework which is a derivative from our previous work in [5]. DEEPSEA-M attempts to broaden the service boundaries of value-added application-level services within mobile networking environment and defines a conceptual method for extension of services in a dynamic on-demand and on-the-fly manner. While Mobile IP is about establishing continual network connectivity, DEEPSEA-M is about establishing universal service availability on top of that. To our knowledge, it is the first unique research work exploring dynamic service extensibility with a mobility emphasis for (adaptive) application-level networking service architectures. We have described our programmable execution environment implementation design for DEEPSEA-M and illustrated in detail the involving steps in dynamic service extension within the hierarchical Mobile IP framework.

References

1. C. Perkins, "IP mobility support," RFC 2002, IETF, October 1996.
2. H. Soliman, C. Castelluccia, K. Malki, and L. Bellier, "Hierarchical MIPv6 mobility management," Internet Draft, IETF, July, 2001. Work in progress.
3. J.-C. Chen, et al., "QoS Architecture Based on Differentiated Services for Next Generation Wireless IP Networks," Internet Draft, IETF, January, 2001.
4. "Nortel Alteon products," http://www.nortelnetworks.com/products/01/alteon/.
5. R. Hsieh and A. Seneviratne, "Dynamic Service Extensibility through Programmable Network," In Proceedings of ICCC, Mumbai, India 2002.
6. R. Jaeger, R. Duncan, F. Travostino, T. Lavian, and J. Hollingsworth, "An Active Network Services Architecture for Routers with Silicon-Based Forwarding Engines," In Proceedings of LANMAN, 1999.
7. V. Rexhepi, G. Karagiannis, and G. Heijenk, "A Framework for QoS & Mobility in the Internet Next Generation," Ericsson Business Mobile Networks B.V., Internet Next Generation Report, 2000.
8. Z.-G. Zhou and A. Seneviratne, "Performance Analysis of Platform Independent Image Transcoders," In Proceedings of ICON, Thailand, 2001.

The Adaptive Feedback Scheduling Framework for Streaming VBR Videos with Wireless ATM ABR Service

Ing-Chau Chang and Ming-Hung Huang

Department of Information Management, Chaoyang University of Technology,
Taichung County, Taiwan, R.O.C.
{icchang, s8854619}@cyut.edu.tw

Abstract. In this paper, we propose a three-layer adaptive feedback scheduling (AFS) framework to guarantee the quality of service (QoS) of the variable bit rate (VBR) MPEG streaming video for the mobile host (MH) in the wireless ATM network. By considering the bit rate variation of the VBR video and the signal attenuation due to the movement of the MH, the AFS algorithm executed in the proxy server periodically schedules next group of picture (GOP) data of all streaming videos to their MHs through the ATM available bit rate (ABR) service. Comparing to three well-known scheduling algorithms by simulations, the AFS approach not only achieves less loss for the moving MHs but also bounds the loss for the fixed MHs.

1 Introduction

In recent years, proprietary streaming technologies such as *Advanced Systems Format* (ASF) of Microsoft and *Real Movie* (RM) of Real Networks win the majority of the market share. For overcoming the proprietary limitations of these technologies, standardized technologies such as the W3C *Synchronized Multimedia Integration Language* (SMIL) [1] and *MPEG-4* [2] are much more flexible on media data formats, access protocols between media servers and players, underlying communication networks, etc. For supporting the streaming video object in the SMIL or MPEG-4 presentation, video data must be transmitted from corresponding video servers and received by the client to continue their playbacks without interruptions. If some video data miss their playback time, which is called as their *deadlines*, these video data cannot be played out on time and should be discarded to avoid delaying the later video at the client. Hence, the *quality of service* (QoS) of the video playback is degraded due to the dynamically changed and unbounded end-to-end network delay and jitter along the transmission path. The client should prefetch the video data earlier from the server to catch up with the playback deadlines. The size of the prefetched video data must be well controlled, especially for resource-limited mobile clients, such as the personal digital assistant (PDA).

In this paper, we first assume the network environment is a hybrid ATM [3] and wireless ATM [4] networks, which is shown in Fig 1. The *mobile host* (MH)

Y.-C. Chen, L.-W. Chang, and C.-T. Hsu (Eds.): PCM 2002, LNCS 2532, pp. 920-927, 2002.
© Springer-Verlag Berlin Heidelberg 2002

communicates with video servers in the wired ATM through a wireless ATM base station. The effective bandwidth perceived by the MH is varied with the distance between it and the base station due to the signal attenuation. Besides as access points for the MHs, these base stations execute functions of the proxy server to prefetch video data from the servers and cache them before conveying them to the MHs. Second, because of the relatively inexpensive cost to the *constant bit rate* (CBR) and *variable bit rate* (VBR) services, the streaming video data is transmitted by two independent *available bit rate* (ABR) connections, one is from the video server to the proxy server and the other is from the proxy server to the MH. Finally, the video object is assumed to be VBR encoded and has different degrees of bit rate *burstiness*, which is defined as the ratio of its peak rate divided by its average rate [5]. Each MPEG video consists of sequence of video clips, which are called as the *group of picture* (GOP). This paper is organized as follows. The related works are summarized in section two. The adaptive feedback scheduling (AFS) framework for conveying the VBR-encoded video with the ABR service is proposed in section three. Simulation results are shown in section four to exhibit excellent loss performances for both the moving and fixed MHs. Finally, section five concludes this paper.

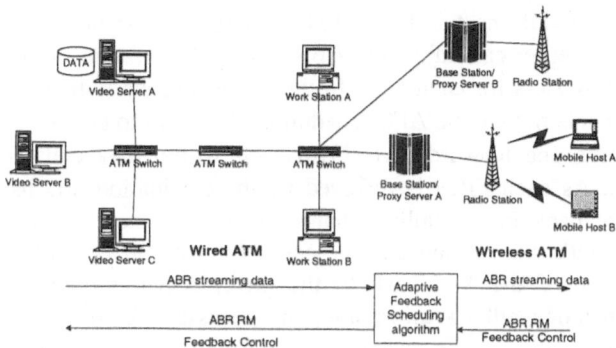

Fig. 1. The video streaming environment.

2   Related Works

Hashimoto et al. proposed the Flexible Multimedia System (FMS) [6] to consider the relationship of the application layer and network layer for attaining better QoS of a multimedia presentation. Wu et al. [7] addressed three techniques, namely scalable video coding, network-aware adaptation of end system, and adaptive QoS supports from networks, to provide graceful degradation during periods of QoS fluctuations for mobile devices. However, these papers only proposed adaptive methodology and system architecture for QoS guarantee and did not clearly propose adaptation algorithms to cooperate with the underlying network protocols. Pang et al. [8] proposed a dynamic Weighted Fair Queuing (WFQ) scheduling in the base station MAC scheduler to combine loss and delay requirements of real-time traffic to implement dynamic priorities. Ito et al. [9] studied effects of four packet-scheduling algorithms, i.e. FIFO, Priority Queuing, Class-based Queuing and WFQ, on media synchronization quality at routers. In [10], the Wireless Access Burst Scheduling (WABS) employs the dynamic polling scheme on a burst basis and fair scheduling algorithms for both real-time and non-real-time traffics to improve the cell loss ratio of rt-VBR services and achieved ABR fairness.

In this paper, both the adaptive AFS framework and its scheduling algorithm on the proxy server, which is executed on the base station, are proposed to guarantee QoS of the streaming VBR video over the relatively inexpensive ABR services on the wireless ATM network. The feedback information for current GOP duration from the MH and the video size of the next GOP duration are combined to derive a dynamic weight for allocating the available ABR bandwidth among all ABR connections.

3 The Adaptive Feedback Scheduling Framework

For supporting streaming videos on this ATM network environment with the ABR service, we propose the *adaptive feedback scheduling* (AFS) framework to guarantee the video QoS. We adopt the wireless TDD (Time Division Duplex) technology proposed in [11] to divide the wireless ATM channel into the uplink and downlink channels. The proxy server can adjust the ABR bandwidth by controlling the number of allocated downlink slots for each MH. In the following, we will first describe the RM feedback mechanism, then the AFS scheduling algorithm to convey all GOP data. The source transmits one forward RM (FRM) cell within data cells for the ABR congestion control. As each FRM is received by the destination, the backward RM (BRM) cell is sent back in the uplink channel to the source to adjust the source transmission rate. With this mechanism, we can use the BRM cell to piggyback the feedback information of the MH back to the proxy server without extra control messages. Two kinds of feedback information are necessary for the AFS framework. One is the timestamp value used to calculate the wireless round trip time ($WRTT_t^i$) of the GOP t for the ith ABR connection to the MH. The other information is the number of eligible received data (RB_t^i) at the display time (DT_t^i) of this GOP t by the MH from the ith ABR connection. We use a time diagram to represent the AFS feedback scheduling process in Fig 2, where the time axis is divided as units of the GOP duration. For minimizing the buffer consumption in the MH, the next GOP data of all streaming connections are scheduled and transmitted in the current GOP duration from the proxy server to their corresponding MH for continuous playback. For the $(t-1)$th duration, the one-way transmission delay TD_{t-1} is defined as half of the maximum $WRTT_{t-1}^i$ value among all streaming connections with Equation 1.

$$TD_{t-1} = \max[\frac{1}{2}WRTT_{t-1}^i], \text{ for all streaming ABRs} \tag{1}$$

The scheduling process of a GOP duration begins when the proxy server has received the feedback BRM cells of all streaming ABR connections, i.e., TD_{t-1} after the display time of the current GOP duration DT_t^i. Equation 2 is used to calculate the scheduling weight, w_t^i, of the tth GOP of the ABR connection i with two terms, $w_t^{i,s}$

and $W_t^{i,f}$. The parameter α, where $0< \alpha <1$, can be adjusted to emphasize the effect of any term. The first term, i.e., $W_t^{i,s}$, denotes the incremental ratio for sizes of two consecutive GOP t and $(t\text{-}1)$ of the connection i. The second term in Equation 2, i.e., $W_t^{i,f}$, is to represent the reciprocal of the normalized effective bandwidth, which is defined as the total size of GOP t (NB_t^i) over the data size received by the MH (RB_t^i). As mentioned above, the effective ABR bandwidth of the MH is varied with the distance between it and the proxy server. Equation 3 and 4 apply the exponential averaging technique, as for predicting the smoothed RTT in TCP on the basis of a time series of past values, to estimate the $W_{t+1}^{i,s}$ and $W_{t+1}^{i,f}$ with constant parameters β and γ ($0< \beta, \gamma <1$) respectively. Therefore, if the size of next GOP is larger than that of current GOP or the received data size is lower than that of the total size sent by the proxy server, the scheduling weight of next GOP is increased, and vice versa.

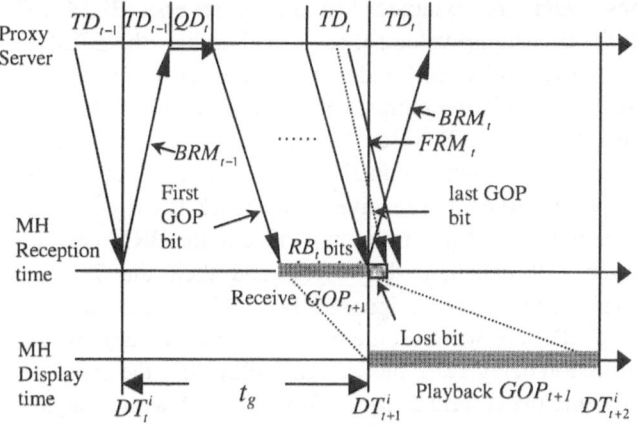

Fig. 2. The time diagram in the AFS.

$$W_t^i = \alpha * W_t^{i,s} + (1-\alpha) * W_t^{i,f}, \; for \; t \geq 1 \tag{2}$$

$$\begin{cases} W_t^{i,s} = \beta * W_{t-1}^{i,s} + (1-\beta) * \dfrac{NB_t^i}{NB_{t-1}^i}, \; for \; t \geq 2 \\[2mm] W_1^{i,s} = 1 \end{cases} \tag{3}$$

$$\begin{cases} W_t^{i,f} = \gamma * W_{t-1}^{i,f} + (1-\gamma) * \dfrac{NB_{t-1}^i}{RB_{t-1}^i}, \; for \; t \geq 2 \\[2mm] W_1^{i,f} = 1 \end{cases} \tag{4}$$

As soon as the scheduling weight for the current GOP of each streaming ABR connection is calculated, the scheduler will allocate available ABR bandwidth to all non-streaming and streaming ABR connections. With Equation 5 where M and N denote numbers of non-streaming and streaming ABR connections and $ABRBW_t^i$ the total available ABR bandwidth, every non-streaming and streaming ABR connection is first allocated with its minimum cell rate (MCR). Further, a calculated percentage of the excess ABR bandwidth, which is defined as the bandwidth by subtracting the sum of MCR of all ABR connections from the total available ABR bandwidth, is allocated additionally to each streaming connection depending on its normalized scheduling weight. The allocated bandwidth NBW_t^i should not be larger than its PCR. The scheduler will reserve $\lceil (NBW^i * t_g)/S \rceil$ downlink slots for connection i and schedule these slots after those of every connection j with its weight $W_t^j > W_t^i$ in this GOP duration t_g, where S is the slot size in bits. It then appends a FRM cell with a current timestamp at the end of these data and transmits them to the MH through the wireless ATM network. The queuing delay QD_t^i of connection i incurred by the scheduler is calculated with Equation 6 as the GOP duration t_g multiplied by the fraction of sum of allocated streaming bandwidth for every connection j with its scheduling weight $W_t^j > W_t^i$ over the total available ABR bandwidth.

As shown in Fig 3, the MH buffers the GOP data for the next duration until their corresponding display time. If some data of this GOP do not arrive at the MH at their display time, these data are assumed lost and a reverse BRM cell is emitted immediately with the timestamp value set as −1. Otherwise, the BRM cell copies the timestamp in the received FRM cell and send it back to the proxy server. The RB value in the BRM cell records the number of the received GOP data at this duration, which may be less than the NB value of this duration because of the degraded effective bandwidth due to signal attenuation in the wireless ATM environment. On the other side, the proxy server will receive all feedback BRM cells emitted from all MHs to calculate the next TD. If the timestamp value in the BRM cell is not equal to − 1, the proxy server will calculate the $WRTT$ and then the TD; otherwise, this timestamp is not valid and should be ignored. For each duration to convey the GOP data of all streaming ABR connections, the duration t_g must be not less than the sum of the previous transmission delay TD_{t-1}, the queuing delay QD_t, the time to emit RB_t over the bandwidth NBW_t and the current transmission delay TD_t with Equation 7.

$$NBW_t^i = \begin{cases} MCR^i, \text{if } i \text{ is a non} - streaming\ ABR\ connection \\ Min\left[\left(\dfrac{W_t^i}{\sum\limits_{j=1}^{N} W_t^j} * \left(ABRBW_t - \sum\limits_{j=1}^{M+N} MCR^j \right) \right) + MCR^i, PCR^i \right] \\ \quad , \text{if } i \text{ is a streaming ABR connection} \end{cases} \tag{5}$$

$$QD_t^i = t_g * \frac{\sum\limits_{j} NBW_t^j}{\sum\limits_{k=1}^{M+N} NBW_t^k} = t_g * \frac{\sum\limits_{j} NBW_t^j}{ABRBW_t} \quad \forall j, W_t^j > W_t^i \tag{6}$$

$$t_g \geq TD_{t-1}^i + QD_t^i + \frac{RB_t^i}{NBW_t^i} + TD_t^i, \text{ for each streaming connection } i \tag{7}$$

If the MH traps into a region where is far from the proxy server, the feedback RB value of this MH is significantly less than its corresponding NB value. If this situation lasts for several GOP durations and other conditions remain unchanged, more and more bandwidth will be allocated to this MH with Equation 4 and less and less remaining ABR bandwidth could be shared among all other MHs adversely. In order to avoid this kind of unfair behavior, we use a counter to count the number of the consecutive GOP durations in which the MH receives less data than the minimum amount of needed data, i.e., $RB < MCR* \; t_g$. If the counter value for a streaming connection grows larger than a predefined threshold TH, the scheduler will not apply Equations 2-4 to calculate its scheduling weight and only allocate its MCR bandwidth to this MH. With this approach, performances of all other MHs will not suffer. As soon as the MH receives more data than its minimum requirement, its counter value is reset to zero and it is scheduled with Equations 1-3 again.

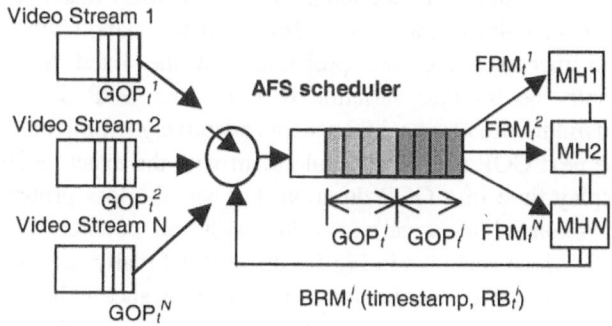

Fig. 3. Scheduling operations of the proxy server.

Simulation Results

In the following simulations, the signal attenuation function is used, where f denotes the signal frequency, β the antenna characteristic, d the distance, P_t the transmitted signal power strength from the proxy and P_r the received power strength by the MH [12]. If f, β and P_t are constants, P_r is reverse proportional to d^{α}. It means the effective bandwidth of the MH follows the same relationship with the distance. We choose α as 2 in this paper. The channel bit rate in the wireless ATM is 6.4 Mbps. We assume N MHs simultaneously play the same VBR video whose bit rate attributes are listed in Table 1. These MHs are divided into two classes; one consists of the moving MHs with the parameter m to denote its distance with the proxy and the other is composed of the fixed MHs. The ABR connection to convey the streaming video defines its PCR as the peak rate and its MCR as the average rate of the video. The values of α, β and γ in Equations 1-3 are set as 0.5 and the counter TH is 20.

$$P_r = \frac{\beta * P_t}{f^2 * d^{\alpha}}, 2 \le \alpha \le 4$$

First, five MHs are assumed to move from $m=0$ to 100 and other five MHs are fixed at $m=30$. For the FCFS, WFQ, WABS and our AFS schemes, their average loss probabilities with respect to different values of m are compared in Fig 4 for the moving MHs and in Fig 5 for the fixed ones. With the increasing m, the loss probability of the moving MHs with our AFS scheme grows slower than the WABS, then the WFQ and finally the FCFS. The reasons are stated as follows. The FCFS and

WFQ schemes allocate static bandwidth to all moving and fixed MHs. They cannot adapt to the instantaneous bit rate variation of the video and the degraded effective bandwidth with the increasing m such that their moving MHs have higher loss probabilities. Oppositely, their loss probabilities for the fixed MHs remain invariant, which is shown in Fig 5, with respect to the m of the moving MHs. Further, the WABS polls each MH and schedules the MH with the longest queue length first to achieve fair share of ABR bandwidth among all connections. With the increasing m, the effective bandwidth for the moving MH will decay rapidly, which results in more serious data loss and shorter queue length after the display deadline. The WABS will allocate more bandwidth to the moving MHs and less bandwidth to the fixed MHs, which in turn increases the loss probability of the fixed MHs. However, by considering both the bit rate variation between two GOP data and the degraded effective bandwidth with m, our AFS scheme adaptively exploits the feedback RB and the size of the next GOP data to schedule them with the exact bandwidth to catch up with their display time in a GOP duration. Further, the loss probability of the fixed MHs can be bounded to a certain value with the counter mechanism with an appropriate TH, which is shown in Fig 5 with $m \geq 80$. Finally, with the smaller TH, the fixed MHs reach a smaller loss bound on a shorter distance m but the loss probability of the moving MHs grows larger than those with the larger TH, which are shown in Fig 6 and 7 respectively.

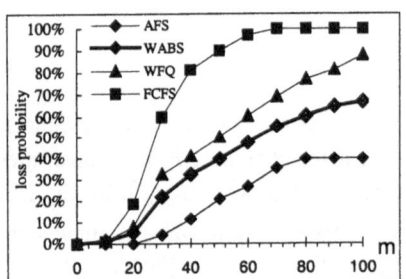

Fig. 4. Loss probabilities of the moving MHs.

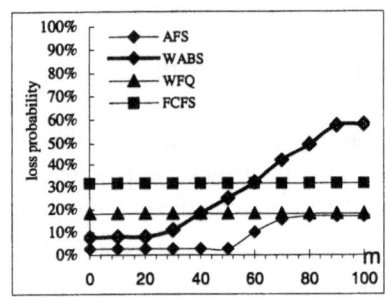

Fig. 5. Loss probabilities of the fixed MHs.

Table 1. Video attributes.

Source	Size	Duration	Peak rate	Min. rate	Average rate
"Rush Hours" MPEG2 40:14-40:34 sec	15.7Mb	20sec	0.9 Mb	0.1 Mb	0.41 Mb

4 Conclusions

Previous researches were rare to discuss how to support the streaming video for the MH by considering both the bit rate variation and signal attenuation in the wireless ATM environment. In this paper, for both the moving and fixed MHs, the AFS framework and its adaptive scheduling algorithm are proposed to provide excellent data loss performances through ABR connections between the proxy server and MHs.

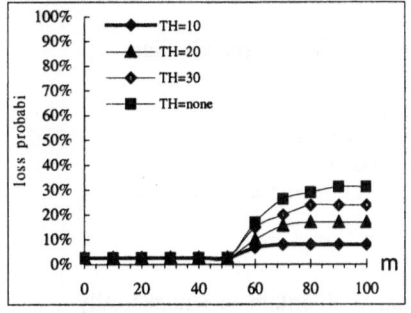

Fig. 6. Loss probabilities of the fixed MHs with different THs.

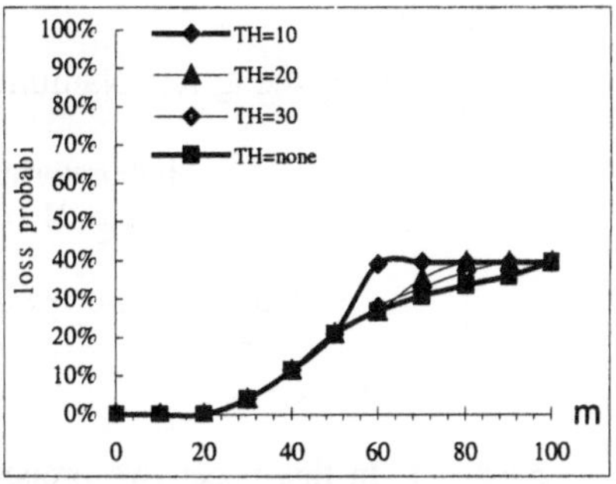

Fig. 7. Loss probabilities of the moving MHs with different THs.

References

1. W3C: W3C Issues Synchronized Multimedia Integration Language (SMIL 2.0) Specification. http://www.w3.org/TR/SMIL20.html (2000)
2. MPEG.ORG: MPEG Starting Points and FAQs. http://www.mpeg.org/MPEG/starting-points.html#mpeg4 (2002)
3. The ATM Forum Technical Committee: Traffic Management Specification Version 4.0. (1996)
4. Wireless ATM. http://www.cis.ohiostate.edu/~jain /cis78897/wireless_atm/index.htm.
5. Fluckiger, F.: Understanding Networked Multimedia: Applications and Technology. Prentice Hall (1995)
6. Hashimoto, K., Shibata, Y., Shiratori, N.: Flexible Multimedia System Architecture with Adaptive QoS Guarantee Functions. IEEE Parallel and Distributed Systems, (2000) 119–126
7. Wu, D., Hou, Y. T., Zhang, Y.Q.: Scalable Video Coding and Transport Over Broad-band Wireless Networks. Proc. of the IEEE, Vol. 89, No. 1, (2001) 6-20
8. Pang, K., Lin, X., Zheng, J., Gu, X.: Dynamic WFQ Scheduling for Real-time Traffic in Wireless ATM Links. IEEE International Conference on Communication Technology, Vol. 2, (2000) 1479-1482
9. Ito, K., Taska, S., Ishibashi, Y.: Effect of Packet Scheduling Algorithms on Media Synchronization Quality in the Internet. IEEE International Conference on Communications, Vol. 9, (2001) 2865-2871
10. Hong, S.E., Kim, S.J.: Wireless Access Burst Scheduling Discipline Supporting Integrated Services in Wireless ATM Networks. IEEE 51st Vehicular Technology Conference, Vol. 2, (2000) 1430 -1434
11. Frigon, J.F., Victor C.M., Chan, C.B.: Dynamic Reservation TDMA Protocol for Wireless ATM Networks. IEEE Journal on Selected Areas in Communications, Vol. 19, No2, (2001) 370-383
12. Howward, S.J., Pahlavan, K.: Autoregressive Modeling of Wide-Band Indoor Radio Propagation. IEEE Trans. on Communication, Vol. 40, No. 9, (1992) 1540-1552

Support Vector Machine Learning for Music Discrimination

Changsheng Xu, Namunu Chinthaka Maddage, and Qi Tian

Laboratories for Information Technology
21 Heng Mui Keng Terrace
Singapore 119613
{xucs, maddage, tian}@lit.a-star.edu.sg

Abstract. In this paper, we propose an effective algorithm to automatically identify and discriminate music content. Linear prediction coefficients, zero crossing rates and mel-frequency cepstral coefficients are calculated to characterize music content. Based on calculated features, support vector machines are applied to obtain the optimal class boundaries between vocal music and pure music by learning from training data. Experimental results of support vector machine learning show good performance in music discrimination and are more advantageous than traditional Euclidean distance based method.

1 Introduction

The rapid development of various affordable technologies for multimedia content capturing, data storage, high bandwidth/speed transmission and the multimedia compression standards have resulted in a rapid increase of the size of digital multimedia data collections and greatly increased the availability of multimedia contents to the general user. Digital music is one of the most important data types distributed by Internet. However, it is still rudimentary for computer to automatically analyze music content, especially to automatically identify and recognize music content. Since lyrics are important information of music, it would be very useful if we can automatically discriminate pure music and vocal music and then detect vocal parts from vocal music. It can be applied to music summarization, classification and content-based music retrieval. The challenge is we can not use speech recognition techniques to detect singing voice from vocal music because singing voice is much more complicated than pure speech.

A number of methods have been done to discriminate music, speech, silence, and environment sound. The most successful achievement in this area is speech/music discrimination, because speech and music are quite different in spectral distribution and temporal change pattern. Saunders [1] used the average zero-crossing rate and the short time energy as features and applied a simple thresholding method to discriminate speech and music from the radio broadcast. Scheirer [2] used thirteen features in time, frequency and cepstrum domains and different classification methods (GMM, BP-ANN, KNN, MAP, etc.) to achieve a robust performance. Both approaches reported accuracy rate for real-time classification over 95%. However, the

Y.-C. Chen, L.-W. Chang, and C.-T. Hsu (Eds.): PCM 2002, LNCS 2532, pp. 928–935, 2002.
© Springer-Verlag Berlin Heidelberg 2002

performance will decrease for above approaches if other audio scenes such as environment sounds are taken into consideration.

Further research works have been done to segment audio data into more categories. El-Maleh [3] proposed a method to classify audio signal into speech, music and others for the purpose of parsing of news story. Kimber [4] proposed an acoustic segmentation approach that mainly applied to the segmentation of discussion recordings in meetings. Audio recordings were segmented into speech, silence, laughter and non-speech sounds by using cepstral coefficients as features and hidden Markov model (HMM) as the classifier. Zhang [5] proposed an approach to divide the generic audio data segmentation and classification task into two stages. In the first stage which was called the coarse-level audio segmentation and indexing, audio signals were segmented and classified into speech, music, song, speech with music background, environmental sound with music background, six types of environmental sound, and silence. In the second stage which was called fine-level audio classification, further classification was conducted within each basic type. Speech was differentiated into the voice of man, woman and child. Music is classified into classics, blues, jazz, rock and roll, music with singing and the plain song, according to the instruments or types. Environmental sounds were classified into semantic classes such as applause, bell ring, footstep, wind-storm, laughter, bird's cry, and so on. Lu [6] proposed a robust two-stage audio segmentation method to segment an audio stream into speech, music, environment sound and silence. The first stage of classification was to separate speech from non-speech based on KNN and LSP VQ classification scheme and simple features such as high zero-crossing rate ratio, low short time energy ratio, spectrum flux and LSP distance. The second stage further segmented non-speech class into music, environment sounds and silence with a rule-based classification scheme and two new features: noise frame ratio and band periodicity.

In this paper, a novel automatic music identification and discrimination approach is presented. In order to discriminate vocal and pure music, support vector machines (SVMs) are applied to obtain the optimal class boundaries between vocal and non-vocal music by learning from training data.

2   Music Feature Selection

Feature selection is important for music content analysis. The selected features should reflect the significant characteristics of different kinds of music signals. In order to better identify vocal and non-vocal music, we consider the features, which are related to vocal signals. The selected features include linear prediction coefficients; zero crossing rates and mel frequency cepstral coefficients.

2.1   Linear Prediction Coefficients

The basic idea behind linear predictive analysis is that a music sample can be approximated as a linear combination of past music samples. By minimizing the sum of the squared differences (over finite interval) between the actual music samples and the linear predictive ones, a unique set of predictor coefficients can be determined. The importance of linear prediction lies in the accuracy with which the basic model applies to vocal signals in music [7]. Figure 1 (a) is an example of linear prediction coefficients for vocal music and pure music. The filter output (200~400) Hz range has got strong musical and vocal information. The mean value is 0.0753 for vocal music and 0.0092 for pure music.

2.2 Zero Crossing Rates

In the context of discrete-time signals, a zero crossing is said to occur if successive samples have different algebraic signs. The rate at which zero crossings occur is a simple measure of the frequency content of a signal. This average zero-crossing rate gives a reasonable way to estimate the frequency of sine wave. The number of zero crossing is also a useful feature in music analysis. Zero crossing rate is suitable for narrowband signals, but music signals include both narrowband and broadband components. Therefore, the short-time zero crossing rate can be used to characterize music signal. Figure 1 (b) is an example of zero crossing rates for vocal music and pure music. It can be seen that vocal music has high zero crossing rates. This feature is also much sensitive to vocals and percussion instruments. Mean values are 188.247 and 47.023 for vocal music and pure music respectively.

2.3 Mel Frequency Cepstral Coefficients

The mel-frequency cepstrum has proven to be highly effective in automatic speech recognition and in modeling the subjective pitch and frequency content of audio signals. The mel-cepstral features can be illustrated by the Mel-Frequency Cepstral Coefficients (MFCCs), which are computed from the FFT power coefficients. The power coefficients are filtered by a triangular band pass filter bank. The filter bank consists of $K=19$ triangular filters. They have a constant mel-frequency interval, and covers the frequency range of 0Hz – 20050Hz. Figure 1 (c) is an example of MFCCs for vocal music and pure music. It can be seen that MFCCs are a good feature for analyzing music because of significant difference between vocal and pure music. The mean value is   –1.025 for vocal music and –0.034 for pure music. When vocals are mixed with music then the variance is very high and for the pure music it is considerably low. It can be seen that MFCCs are more sensitive to percussion instruments, for example, values near 80s, 193s, 350s, and 534s produced by base drum.

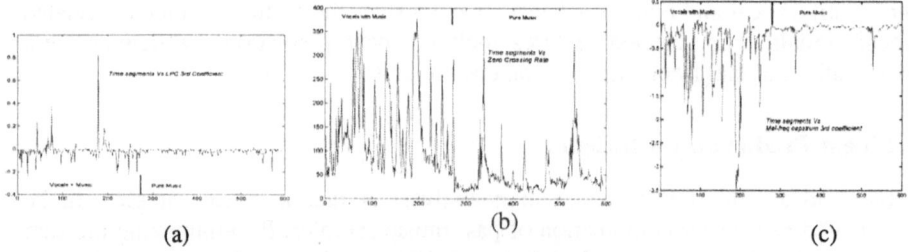

| (a) | (b) | (c) |

Fig. 1. (a) The 3rd LPC coefficient of (200~400) Hz filter; (b) Zero-crossing rates; (c) The 3rd mel-frequency cepstral coefficient. (0-276s is vocal music and 276-592s is pure music)

3 Support Vector Machine Learning

3.1 Linear Support Vector Classifier

Suppose we are given a set of training data $(x_1, x_2, ..., x_n)$ and their class labels $(y_1, y_2, ..., y_n)$, where $x_i \in R^n$ and $y_i \in \{-1, +1\}$, and we want to separate the training data into two classes. We can use SVM to implement this by constructing a hyperplane with maximal margin shown in Figure 2.

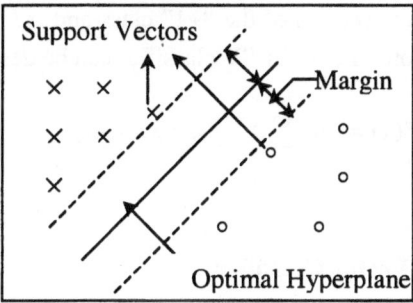

Fig. 2. Linear SVM

The hyperplane can be represented as:

$$<w, x> + b = 0 \tag{1}$$

where $<w, x>$ denotes the inner product between vectors w and x.

To construct the optimal hyperplane, we need to find a pair consisting of a vector w and a constant b such that they satisfy the constraints

$$y_i(<x_i, w> + b) \geq 1, \quad i = 1, ..., l \tag{2}$$

and the vector w has the smallest norm

$$|w|^2 = <w, w> \tag{3}$$

In order to find the optimal hyperplane, we have to minimize the quadratic form (3) subject to the linear constraint (2). This optimization problem can be solved by finding the saddle point of the Lagrange function

$$L(w, b, \alpha) = \frac{1}{2} <w, w> - \sum_{i=1}^{l} \alpha_i \{ y_i [<x_i, w> + b] - 1 \} \tag{4}$$

with Lagrange multiplier $\alpha_i \geq 0$.

According to [8], the optimization problem can be alternatively described as:

Maximize $\qquad W(\alpha) = \sum_{i=1}^{l} \alpha_i - \frac{1}{2} \sum_{i,j=1}^{l} \alpha_i \alpha_j y_i y_j <x_i, x_j> \tag{5}$

Subject to $\qquad \alpha_i \geq 0, \quad i=1,...,l$ $\qquad\qquad$ (6)

and $\qquad \displaystyle\sum_{i=1}^{l} \alpha_i y_i = 0$ $\qquad\qquad$ (7)

The vectors x_i for which $\alpha_i > 0$ are called support vectors. Geometrically, these vectors are the closest to the optimal hyperplane. The solution is calculated as

$$w = \sum_{i=1}^{l} \alpha_i y_i x_i , \qquad b = -\frac{1}{2} < w, [x_+ + x_-] > \qquad (8)$$

where x_+ denotes support vectors of the "+1" class and x_- denotes support vectors of the "-1" class. Therefore, the linear SV classifier can be designed by

$$f(x) = \text{sgn}(\sum_{i=1}^{l} \alpha_i y_i < x, x_i > +b) \qquad (9)$$

3.2 Nonlinear Support Vector Classifier

If the data are linearly non-separable but non-linearly separable, the non-linear SV classifier will be applied. The basic idea is to transform input vectors into a high-dimensional feature space using non-linear transformation Φ, and then to do a linear separation in feature space.

To construct a non-linear SV classifier, inner product $< x, y >$ is replaced by a kernel function $K(x, y)$.

$$f(x) = \text{sgn}(\sum_{i=1}^{l} \alpha_i y_i K(x_i, x) + b) \qquad (10)$$

The SV algorithm can construct a variety of learning machines by use of different kernel functions. Three kinds of kernel functions are constantly used. They are:
(1) Polynomial kernel of degree d

$$K(x, y) = (< x, y > +1)^d \qquad (11)$$

(2) Radial basis function with Gaussian kernel of width $c > 0$

$$K(x, y) = \exp(-\|x - y\|^2 / c) \qquad (12)$$

(3) Neural networks with tanh activation function

$$K(x, y) = \tanh(k < x, y > +\mu) \qquad (13)$$

where the parameters k and μ are the gain and shift.

3.3 SVM Learning and Music Discrimination

We will use non-linear support vector classifier to discriminate vocal and pure music. Therefore, classification parameters should be calculated using support vector machine learning. Figure 3 illustrates a conceptual block diagram of the training process to produce classification parameters of classifier. The training process analyses musical training sample data to find an optimal way to classify musical frames into vocal or non-vocal class. The derived classification parameters are used to identify pure music and vocal music. The music content can be discriminated into vocal and pure music in terms of the designed SV classifier (see Figure 4).

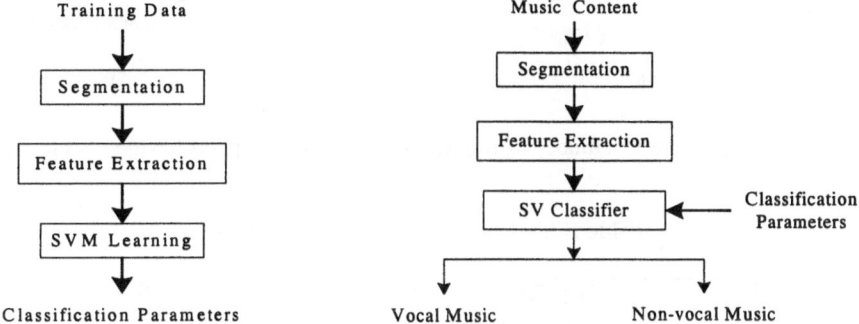

Fig. 3. SVM learning process   **Fig. 4.** Music identification

4   Experimental Results

The music dataset used in music separation experiment contains 100 music samples including 50 vocal music samples and 50 non-vocal music samples. They are collected from music CDs and Internet and cover different genres such as pop, classical, rock and jazz. All data are 44.1kHz sample rate, stereo channels and 16 bits per sample. We select 35 music samples including 5 pop pure music, 5 pop vocal music, 5 classical pure music, 5 classical vocal music, 5 rock pure music, 5 rock vocal music and 5 jazz vocal music. Each sample is segmented into 200 frames and the length of each frame is 8,192 sample points. Therefore, the total number of training data is 7,000 frames including 3,247 vocal frames and 3,753 non-vocal frames. The rest samples are use as a test set.

Radial basis function with $c=2$ is used as the kernel in SVM training and classification. Figure 5 (a) and (b) show the training time and the number of support vectors obtained when training the SVM with 1,000, 2,000, 3,000, 4,000, 5,000, 6,000, and 7,000 frames on a Pentium 4 1.56GHz PC with Windows 2000.

After training the SVM, we use it as the classifier to separate vocal and non-vocal frames on the test set. The test set is divided into three parts. The first part only contains 20 pure music samples (4,000 frames). The second part only contains 20 vocal music samples (4,000 frames). The third part contains 15 pure music samples and 10 vocal music samples (5,000 frames). The test data are tested using SVM and traditional nearest neighbor (NN) method. Table 1 shows a comparison between two methods. It can be seen that SVM achieves a significantly higher accuracy rate than NN.

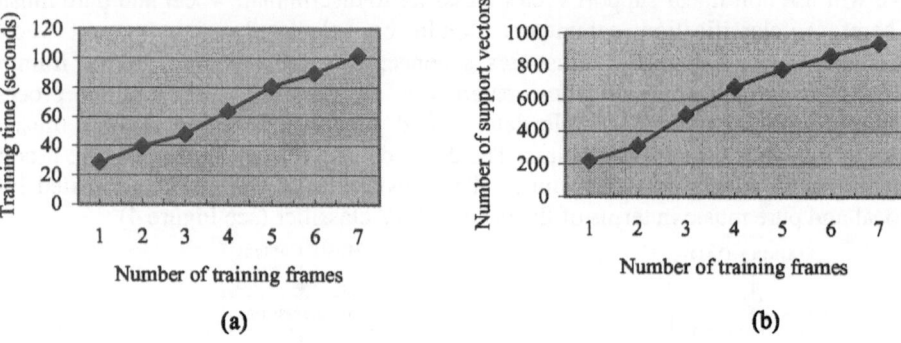

Fig. 5. (a) Training time vs number of frames; (b) Number of support vectors vs number of frames

Table 1. SVM and NN for music separation

	Test Set 1 (error rate)	Test Set 2 (error rate)	Test Set 3 (error rate)
SVM	2.05%	2.87%	3.34%
NN	5.52%	6.45%	7.70%

5 Conclusions

We have presented and demonstrated an automatic discrimination algorithm for pure music and vocal music using support vector machine learning. Linear prediction coefficients, zero crossing rates, and mel-frequency cepstral coefficients are calculated as features to characterize music content. A nonlinear support vector machine learning algorithm is developed to obtain the optimal class boundaries between pure and vocal music by learning from training data. Experiments show the support vector machine learning method has good performance in music discrimination and is more advantageous than traditional Euclidean distance based method.

There are several directions that need to be explored in future. The first direction is to improve the computational efficiency for support vector machines. Support vector machines take a long time in the training process, especially with a large number of training samples. Therefore, how to select proper kernel function and determine the relevant parameters is extremely important.

The second direction we wish to investigate is to make the discrimination result more accurate. To achieve this goal, we need to explore more music features that can be used to characterize the music content.

References

1. J. Sounders, Real-time discrimination of broadcast speech/music, in Proc. ICASSP96, Atlanta, USA, Vol.2, pp.993-996, 1996.
2. E. Scheirer and M. Slaney, Construction and evaluation of a robust multifeature music/speech discriminator, In Proc. ICASSP97, Vol.2, pp.1331-1334, 1997.
3. K. El-Maleh, M. Klein, G. Petrucci and P. Kabal, Speech/music discrimination for multimedia application, In Proc. ICASSP00, 2000.
4. D. Kimber and L. Wilcox, Acoustic segmentation for audio browsers, In Proc. Interface Conference, Sydney, Australia, 1996.
5. T. Zhang and C.-C. Kuo, Video content parsing based on combined audio and visual information, In Proc. SPIE 1999, San Jose, USA, Vol.4, pp.78-89, 1999.
6. L. Lu, H. Jiang and H. J. Zhang, A robust audio classification and segmentation method, In Proc. ACM Multimedia 2001, Ottawa, Canada, 2001.
7. Markel, J.D., and Gray, A. H., Linear Prediction of Speech, Springer-Verlag, New York, 1976
8. Vapnik, V., Statistical Learning Theory, Wiley, 1998.

Dynamic Network Adaptation Framework Employing Layered Relative Priority Index for Adaptive Video Delivery

JongWon Kim[1] and Jitae Shin[2]

[1] Networked Media Lab. Department of Information and Communications,
Kwang-Ju Institute of Science and Technology (K-JIST),
Gwangju, 500-712, Korea, jongwon@kjist.ac.kr
[2] School of Information and Communication Engineering, Sungkyunkwan University,
Suwon, 440-746, Korea, jtshin@ece.skku.ac.kr

Abstract. Delivering high-quality media contents robustly over a wide range of network conditions of the wired/wireless Internet is a highly challenging task. To address this challenging task, the continuous media applications at the edge of network have become more and more adaptive while the best-effort Internet is slowly progressing towards improved networking services. Thus, the role of network adaptation, which dynamically links the quality demand of application contents to the underlying networking services, has become more crucial. In this paper, we present a novel network adaptation approach that efficiently leverages its awareness of both media contents and underlying networks. Detailed discussion on the framework will be covered with deployment scenarios such as the adaptive coordination of source-channel error control for wireless video and the mapping of prioritized video packet to the available network QoS (quality of service) services.

1 Introduction

Realization of high-quality media streaming over the IP Internet faces lots of challenges [1]. Streaming media applications in general have very strict requirements on the network service, thus making the current best-effort (BE) Internet model less than sufficient. They require stable networks and systems, feasible signaling/transport protocols, and network-adaptive applications to achieve acceptable-quality media distribution. From the network side, upcoming QoS (quality of service) networks can alleviates several complications of current best-effort Internet. That is, networks are slowly evolving toward improved QoS services to guarantee loss, delay, and throughput. Enhanced systems are also emerging to support reliable media streaming better. From the protocol side, real-time transport protocol pair (RTP/RTCP) can provide inter-operable/monitored real-time transport channel over the IP network. RTP/RTCP in itself does not guarantee QoS to the streaming applications but acts as a supporter. The key for the successful media streaming, however, is still with the applications at the edge. Recent years the streaming media applications have become more and

Y.-C. Chen, L.-W. Chang, and C.-T. Hsu (Eds.): PCM 2002, LNCS 2532, pp. 936–943, 2002.
© Springer-Verlag Berlin Heidelberg 2002

more adaptive to address the limitation of best-effort Internet [2,3]. Media applications at the server and client systems are required to response to the dynamic fluctuation of underlying networks. Either in a proactive or in a reactive manner, they are controlling sending rate, applying different error controls, and adjusting end-to-end latency. With this *network adaptation*, they are satisfying the requirements of both application itself and involved systems in face of diverse network fluctuations and heterogeneities.

The role of network adaptation is to link the quality demand of application contents to the underlying networking services. For a successful network adaptation, it is highly important to leverage the awareness of both media contents and underlying networks. In our opinion, well-established prioritization (or layering in coarse adaptation case) can play an important role for the efficient network adaptation. That is, via the prioritized media contents, coordination between different priority packets and network service levels can be established efficiently. In this paper, with the layered-RPI (relative priority index), coordinated delivery of packetized video over the given wireless/QoS-enabled networks is investigated under the dynamic network adaptation framework. The proposed framework includes the following components: 1) relative priority generation based on the so-called corruption model and indexing/categorization of streaming video content at the sender, 2) available network adaptation tools to match the fluctuation of the underlying networks, and 3) forward/backward interaction mechanisms assisting the dynamic network adaptation. We introduce two kinds of deployment cases for the proposed framework that focus on the packet-level unequal error protection (UEP): the adaptive coordination of source-channel error control for wireless video [4] and the mapping of prioritized packet to the available QoS service of the differentiated service (DiffServ) network [5].

2 Dynamic Network Adaptation Framework

The proposed dynamic network adaptation framework for the packetized video delivery is illustrated in Fig. 1. The video contents are first pre-processed and layer-encoded. Following the target (albeit assumed) constraints on the bandwidth and buffer, constant quality rate control manipulates the rate composition among the base and enhancement layers in the layered encoding. At the same time they are analyzed with R-D (rate-distortion) and corruption model [6]. Then the encoded video stream with the associated R-D/corruption model parameters is passed to the network adaptation/prioritized packetization module to wait for the delivery. In this module, the encoded stream is first tailored (or transcoded) in the source rate/error-resilience sense to match the given estimated available bandwidth/loss/delay of the underlying network. Then it is packetized with priority (i.e., the layered RPI) before going through the network adaptation at the sending application. Based only on the priority, they are adapted to the network condition in rate/loss/delay sense. That is, the packets are selectively discarded and protected with differentiation. Note that various types of feedbacks are available to guide the required network adaptation. Guided by both end-to-end network feedback (e.g., end-to-end congestion control[1]) and network feedback (e.g., direct congestion indication), the sender application may control the network adaptation. Application-level feedback can also notify about the playout status at the corresponding party and may request the speedup of slowdown of transmission for synchronized playback. Once sent to the network, it may go through network-initiated adaptation, which is also called as network filtering (e.g., with schemes such as priority-based packet dropping and receiver-based layer selection). Finally, the delivered packets are adaptively processed at the receiver to match the receiver capability and user preference.

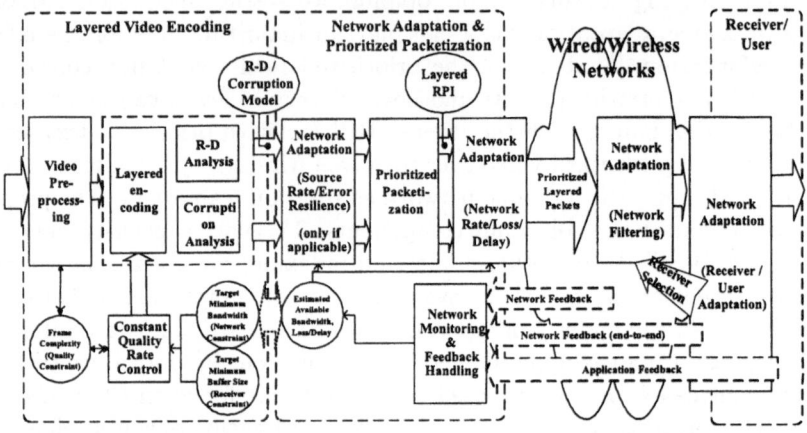

Fig. 1. Packetized video delivery with the dynamic network adaptation.

The proposed network adaptation framework basically assumes the existence of a network or other equivalent options that support prioritized variable-rate delivery of video stream and the associated end-to-end performance and cost (e.g., pricing) models. Since a video codec has several options to trade the compression efficiency for flexible delay manipulation, error resilience, and network friendliness, the coordination (i.e., network adaptation) framework has to provide an simplified interaction process between the video application and the target network. Note that the interaction is taking place at multiple junctions as the media stream is delivered from the sending application, via the underlying network, and to the receiving application. Note that the main purpose of introducing the layered-RPI is to abstract and isolate the coding details from the network adaptation task. By assigning layered-RPI to each video stream in an appropriate manner, the proposed framework can accommodate the demand of each stream to achieve the best end-to-end performance in adapting to the fluctuating networks. Given the prioritization of video stream, the proposed network adaptation can be controlled in both feedforward and feedback sense.

---

[1] TCP-friendly congestion control is required in order to avoid network congestion collapse and share network resources evenly with TCP traffic.

They need to accommodate the fluctuation of the given network in addition to the inherent variability of video stream and receiver/user heterogeneity. Thus, the adaptation should focus on how to dynamically react to sudden changes in the application and network.

2.1   Required Source Prioritization and Layered-RPI

For the streaming video applications, the layered-RPI assignment should reflect the influence of each stream (or down to packet) to the end-to-end quality. Packets will be marked by the content-aware applications in the granularity of session, flow, layer, and/or packet. Among three key parameters for QoS (rate, error, and delay), it is important to associate priority for loss and delay, respectively. Note that the rate (or bandwidth) is linked with the layering itself and the extreme case of this is MPEG-4 FGS (fine-grained scalability) layering.

Most of existing prioritization schemes are in coarse granularities of session, flow, and layer. The per-flow prioritization is promoted under the name of user-based allocation within access networks [7]. Also, lots of prioritization for the UEP is best matched with layer-based differentiation as done in [8] with object-based scalability. For delay, the session-based granularity to account for the delay effect of the source seems a first choice. Since the video application context (e.g., video-conferencing vs video e-mail) plays a crucial role in delay prioritization, RDI (relative delay index) is kept constant for whole session (e.g., session (A) and (B) in Fig. 2).

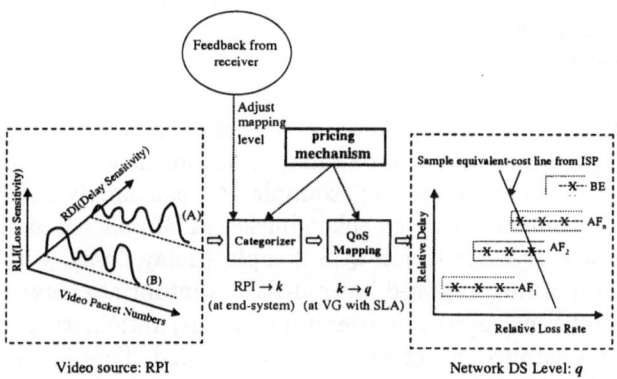

Fig. 2. Source prioritization using RPI and network adaptation (or QoS mapping) for loss and delay.

However, the prioritization can be differentiated down to each packet to enable a fine-grained differentiation. Packet-based prioritization may be adopted to accurately account for the impact of each packet to the end-to-end quality. Especially the loss impact, quantified by RLI (relative loss index), is dependent on the employed video coding scheme. In this work, we consider a motion-compensated prediction-based video compression scheme of MPEG-4 and H.263. At the packet-level, there are dependency relations such as semantic and prediction dependency. The semantic packet-level dependency exists between a packet that includes header parameters and other dependent packets that needs them for decoding. Also, linked by spatial or temporal prediction, the corruption caused by a packet loss can affect the decoding of following packets. This is called the prediction packet-level dependency and we have developed a corruption model to quantify this dependency (i.e., loss impact of a packet) [6]. With the proposed corruption model, the loss impact of each macroblock is explained by taking into account the error concealment, the temporal dependency, and the loop filtering effect. The corruption of macroblocks in a packet is then merged to explain the RLI. For more detailed discussion of this topic, we refer to [6].

2.2   Required Behavior of Network Adaptation

Basically, well-implemented network adaptation can bring benefit to both applications at end and networks by providing better service match at the willingness to pay more complexity. For the network-adaptive applications, the dynamic network adaptation should consider interests of both. That is, the application should get benefit from its network adaptation capability while the network enjoys the benefit of different charging and maximizes the end-user satisfaction. Under a given cost constraint, an efficient network adaptation is trying to match the layered-RPI to the underlying network service level. In this process, the adaptation granularity has to be manipulated intelligibly. The effectiveness is dependent on the accurate association of layered-RPI to each packet, which is one of key investigation issues.

In general, the issue of solving all these network adaptation for rate/loss/delay at the same time is too challenging to be solved simultaneously. Thus, depending on the situation, one may focus on the error and delay control separating the rate control issue. For example, one can simply enforce maximum to the allowed transmitting rate by token bucket (TB) policing in either per-flow or aggregate-flow sense. Then, for QoS 2-tuple {delay, loss}, which is actually the major concern of the proposed layered-RPI, appropriate network adaptation is requested in different degrees by user applications, anticipating different levels of guarantee (or assurance) according to the price paid. That is, each application will demand its loss rate/delay preference by marking the layered-RPI, which is further divided into loss and delay part, respectively. In the proposed network adaptation, each video stream can demand different loss and delay treatment as shown in the left side of Fig. 2. Underlying network will meet these demands with its service provisioning capability. It may provide several differentiated delay and loss levels as shown in the right side of Fig. 2 like the DiffServ network [9]. Or similarly we can envision the effect of FEC/ARQ error controls for the above differentiation.

3 Network Adaptation at End-Systems: Channel-Adaptive Protection for Wireless Video

Reliable video transmission over fading wireless channels relies heavily on a dynamic and coordinated protection effort in response to time-varying channel and source variations. Several adaptive feedback-based systems for rate adaptation, modulation, power control, handoff management, and diversity antenna have been studied recently. Channel adaptation depends on the accuracy of estimated channel status and the underlying time-scale of the estimate [10]. Given the layered-RPI and the estimated channel condition, a proactive network adaptation can be developed as in [4]. A product FEC, which is composed of both Reed-Solomon (RS) and rate-compatible punctured convolutional (RCPC) error correcting codes, is utilized to protect video packets of varying priorities and sizes as well as under instantaneously varying channel. Based on the layered-RPI and the size of each video packet along with the feedback channel state information, network adaptation by the UEP is conducted with the RS/RCPC product code. The resulting channel packet is modulated and transmitted over the underlying wireless channel. At the receiver, the received signal is decoded by the maximum likelihood-based scheme and the long-term fading parameter is estimated. The calculated fading parameter is then fed back via a reliable channel to the sender. To achieve realistic joint source-channel adaptation, special attention will be paid to the channel status feedback in terms of accuracy and delay, the product code tradeoff, and the involved packetization efficiency. As depicted in Fig. 3, source video packets of a variable size from a group of video frames are re-organized into a group of channel packets of a fixed size, which is called the *channel slot*. Since each channel slot consists of fixed-size channel packets, the payload and the redundancy should be negotiated to maintain a fixed total amount. To be more specific, the level of protection is chosen to give the maximum protection to the video packet stream with both bandwidth and packetization constraints. In order to provide the best network adaptation under these constraints, a solution based on dynamic programming is devised and its gain is explored. Please refer [4] for simulation results.

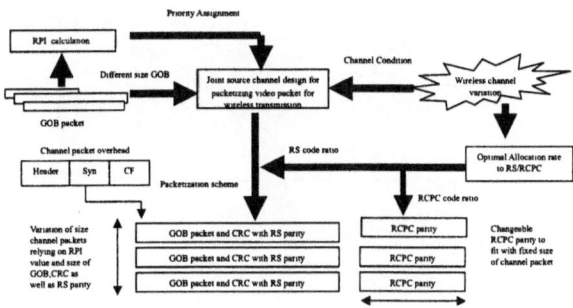

Fig. 3. Feedback-based adaptive network adaptation (error control) for wireless video.

4   Network Adaptation at Networks: QoS-Mapping for Video over DiffServ Network

The emerging DiffServ scheme in IP-QoS methods enables to provide service differentiation in a simple and scalable manner. Especially, the relative DiffServ architecture [11] is an attractive approach that does not require admission control, resource reservations, or signaling. It can provide higher classes receive better services (e.g., lower delay/jitter and lower loss rate) than lower classes. Our approach focuses on the QoS mapping between network-aware streaming applications having k priority categories and q DS levels to achieve efficient network adaptation. We designate the term 'video gateway (VG)' for the traffic conditioning entity at boundary and the VG is responsible for realizing the specialized traffic managements. The QoS mapping covers both layered-RPI prioritization and feedforward/feedback QoS mapping. Each packet is categorized into layer k by RPI at end-systems, without knowing about other applications. An assigned RDI limits the range/ of $k \rightarrow q$ mapping level to meet a certain statistical delay range. We can extract an effective mapping set ($k \rightarrow q$) under total cost constraint in flow/packet granularity [5]. The traffic conditioning is performed via TB-based re-marking by degrading $k \rightarrow q$ mapping level when a flow traffic volume exceed allowed bandwidth in the feedforward control. Feedback-based network adaptation enable the fine-tuned refinement on top of coarse feedforward mapping. Receiver sends a report of delay/packet loss to sender whenever necessary and can ask the adjustment of QoS mapping when it is not satisfied with the received quality or the current quality demands too much price. This feedback mechanism enables the whole network adaptation to be adjusted dynamically and to stabilize the end-to-end QoS within an acceptable range. Please refer [5] for the performance results.

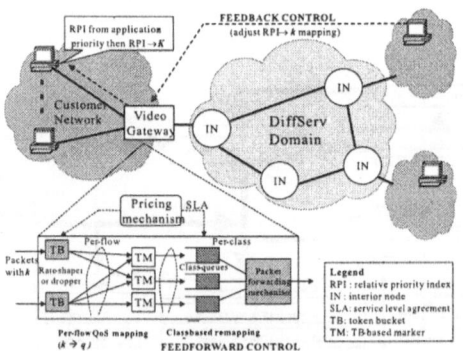

Fig. 4. Feedback and feedforward QoS mapping control for video over DiffServ.

5   Conclusion

We proposed the dynamic network adaptation between categorized packet video and underlying networks. The interaction can be categorized in a variety of ways: feedforward/feedback control and prioritization granularity. We believe this framework can give insight to the desired interaction between the prioritized video applications and the underlying networks.

Acknowledgement. This work is funded in part by the University Research Program supported by Ministry of Information & Communication in Republic of Korea.

References

1. D. Wu *et al.*, "Streaming video over the internet: approaches and directions," *IEEE Trans. on Circuits and Systems for Video Technology*, vol. 11, Mar. 2001.
2. R. Rejaie, M. Handley, and D. Estrin, "Quality adaptation for unicast audio and video," in *Proc. ACM SIGCOMM*, 1999.
3. J. Kim *et al.*, "TCP-friendly internet video streaming employing variable frame-rate encoding and interpolation," *IEEE Trans. on Circuits and Systems for Video Technology*, vol. 10, Oct. 2000.
4. W. Kumwilaisak, J. Kim, and C.-C. J. Kuo, "Reliable wireless video transmission via fading channel estimation and adaptation," in *Proc. IEEE Wireless Communication and Networking Conference (WCNC)*, 2000.
5. J. Shin, J.-G. Kim, J. Kim, and C.-C. J. Kuo, "Dynamic QoS mapping framework for relative service differentiation-aware video streaming," *European Transaction on Telecommunication*, vol. 12, pp. 217–230, May/June 2001.
6. J.-G. Kim, J. Kim, J. Shin, and C.-C. J. Kuo, "Coordinated packet-level protection with a corruption model for robust video transmission," in *Proc. SPIE Visual Communication Image Processing (VCIP)*, Jan. 2001.
7. A. Banchs and R. Denda, "A scalable share differentiation architecture for elastive and real-time traffic," in *Proceedings of 8th IWQoS*, June 2000.
8. Y. T. Hou, D. Wu, B. Li, T. Hamada, I. Ahmad, and H. J. Chao, "A differentiated services architecture for multimedia streaming in next generation Internet," *Computer Networks*, vol. 32, pp. 185–209, Feb 2000.
9. S. Blake, D. Black, M. Carlson, E. Davies, Z. Wang, and W. Weiss, "An architecture for differentiated services," RFC 2475, IETF, Dec. 1998.
10. L. Hanzo, C. H. Wong, and P. Cherriman, "Channel-adaptive wideband wireless video telephony," *IEEE Signal Processing Magazine*, vol. 17, July 2000.
11. C. Dovrolis, D. Stiliadis, and P. Ramanathan, "Proportional differentiated services: Delay differentiation and packet scheduling," in *Proc. ACM SIGCOMM*, (Boston, MA), September 1999.

Peer-to-Peer Support for File Transfer and Caching Mechanism

Jenq-Haur Wang and Tzao-Lin Lee

Department of Computer Science and Information Engineering,
National Taiwan University,
Taipei, Taiwan.
{jhwang,tl_lee}@csie.ntu.edu.tw

Abstract. In existing Internet file transfer mechanism, proxy servers play a major role in load balancing and reducing duplicate file access requests for services like FTP and WWW. However, proxy servers are usually unaware of the availability of cached contents on other peer proxy servers. This is a waste of time since duplicate requests are needed. Unnecessary traffic can be reduced if cooperation and coordination among peer proxies can be utilized. In this paper, peer-to-peer support was incorporated in ordinary file transfer and caching mechanism to reduce unnecessary processing time and storage. Through the location service, hosts requesting file services can dynamically determine if a copy is available and its current location. Work load for file servers will be greatly reduced, and personalization of file transfer configuration can be fully supported.

1 Introduction

With the tremendous growth of the Internet, numerous networking applications such as WWW (World-Wide Web), E-mail, and FTP (File Transfer Protocol) [1] have been widely used. Specifically, file access applications like WWW and FTP have become ubiquitous and central to many people's daily lives. However, in current file transfer mechanism, FTP and Web servers play a critical role since all file access requests require the intervention of these servers. This could result in overloaded server and no service could be provided. Therefore proxy servers have been widely deployed to eliminate unnecessary transfers for file objects already retrieved by other clients.

When a user browses a web page through a proxy server, the URL (Uniform Resource Locator) of requested web page will be checked if a copy is available on proxy server. If so, no further outbound connections are needed since the page is already fetched. If not, the proxy server will act like an agent for the client and make HTTP (HyperText Transfer Protocol) [2] requests to the real web server as indicated in the URL on behalf of the client.

However, communication and coordination among peer proxy servers are still not much used. Proxy servers are usually configured in a hierarchical way where *parent* and *sibling* proxies are manually organized. When a proxy doesn't contain the requested file object (a *cache miss*), it may make Internet Cache Protocol (ICP) [3] requests to see if any of its neighbor proxies has the object. "Neighbor hits" where neighbor proxy has the object may be fetched from either *parent* or *sibling* proxy, but "neighbor misses" must be forwarded only to *parent* proxy. Since parent and sibling

Y.-C. Chen, L.-W. Chang, and C.-T. Hsu (Eds.): PCM 2002, LNCS 2532, pp. 944–951, 2002.
© Springer-Verlag Berlin Heidelberg 2002

relationships must be manually configured in existing implementations like *squid* [4], reutilization of existing cached contents on peer proxy servers can be very difficult. Duplicate file replications among different proxies are still possible and caching efficiency may be further improved.

With the rapid development of various mobile devices, wireless LANs (WLANs) [5] have become more popular as an alternative network access method. In infrastructure mode, mobile nodes can connect to the wired network via access points (APs) as if they have been directly attached. However, since APs are limited in range, mobile nodes may roam into the ranges of different APs. IP roaming problem occurs if different APs are located on different subnets. Mobile IP scheme [6] is one of the most common ways to solve the IP roaming problem.

On the other hand, peer-to-peer technology has been widely deployed in various applications, for example, file sharing software like Napster [7] and ezPeer, instant messaging software like ICQ and MSN, and open source protocol like Jabber [8] and GnuTella [9]. Moreover, the distinction between centralized and decentralized applications has become blurred to leverage the advantages of both. Therefore, an infrastructure for integrating current Internet client-server file transfer mechanism and peer-to-peer file sharing applications was proposed to provide better integrated services. In a mobile environment, each mobile node may act as a peer proxy in which the cached content could be utilized by other nodes. Therefore, our focus is on better utilizing existing proxy caching mechanism and web cache communication and coordination protocols in peer-to-peer applications.

2 Motivation

In this section, the current architecture for file transfer and caching and its shortcomings will be briefly reviewed, and our infrastructure will be proposed as a feasible solution.

In current Internet file transfer mechanism, several protocols are used: HTTP [2] for transferring web pages, FTP [1] for transferring files, and ICP [3] for inter-proxy communication. As shown in Fig. 1, a typical scenario for current file transfer mechanism is illustrated.

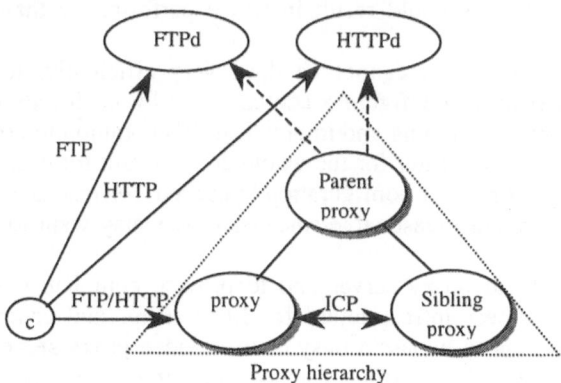

Fig. 1. Shows a typical scenario for file transfer and caching, where a proxy hierarchy is deployed.

As shown in Fig.1, users can browse a web page or access a file with a specific *URL* (*uniform resource locator*) via browser like Microsoft Internet Explorer or Netscape. File access requests are made via either HTTP or FTP directly or through a proxy server. Since common files on the same web site may be requested by different users, proxy server is usually deployed as a cache of similar requests for domain users.

In order to get better performance, more than one proxy servers may be deployed in a hierarchical way. There are many possible deployment schemes for proxy servers with regards to the relative place of a cache between client and server. *Proxy caching* as described above is the most common one. The other possible schemes include *personal proxy server* where cache is on each individual client, *transparent proxy caching* where proxy setting is transparent to clients, *reverse cache* where the focus is on server not clients, and *active caching* where applets are used for caching dynamic documents [10]. In fact, these schemes may be deployed simultaneously with better overall performance.

Proxy server configuration in a browser can be done automatically by protocols like WPAD (Web Proxy Automatic Discovery) [11], through a PAC file (Proxy Auto-Config File Format) [12], or manually configured.

The web caching mechanism works fine, but there are several problems that affect the performance of file retrieval. Firstly, the load on a proxy server is heavy in terms of file storage and time for HTTP/FTP processing. Each proxy server has to deal with every file access request from domain clients. Usually cache hits in proxy server will result in better performance for retrieving file objects. However, in the case of busy proxy server or even server failure, the performance would be worse than without proxy.

Secondly, file objects may have been cached by other peer proxies or personal proxy servers which are unknown to our proxy server. Although inter-cache communication protocols such as ICP [3], WCCP [13], HTCP [14], CARP [15], and Cache Digest [16] have been proposed, they are not widely implemented. Moreover, inter-proxy communication relationships are usually manually configured and dynamic addition and removal of peer proxy can be difficult.

Thirdly, proxy configuration in a browser is usually not versatile enough. In the case of busy server or server failure, no fallback mechanism for bypassing overloaded server is provided. This could result in worse performance than direct connection without proxy.

Fourthly, personalization cannot be done very efficiently in proxy server. For example, it's difficult to configure a content filter for each individual domain user. That would be time-consuming and impractical. It's common to configure on firewall or proxy server a content filter for the whole domain. But for each individual domain user, a finer-grain control of configuration is needed, for instance, a content filter for each user, which is more reasonable since each user may want to filter content from different sources.

In order to offload proxy server and to provide complete customization in file retrieval, a peer-to-peer infrastructure for file transfer and caching was proposed. Specifically, we want to bypass a busy or overloaded proxy server if there are other replications for requested objects. Cached content on peer proxy servers can be utilized for improving cache utilization. Besides, users can have their own configurations for file processing like content filtering.

3 Infrastructure

As shown in Fig.2, an infrastructure for peer-to-peer file transfer is illustrated.

When clients issue HTTP/FTP requests to proxy server, it will first query the location server for possible replications of the given URL. Since peer proxy has registered to location server, its presence and content will be known to location server. After receiving reply from location server, proxy server will issue *redirect* messages to client which will then try to access from the peer proxy.

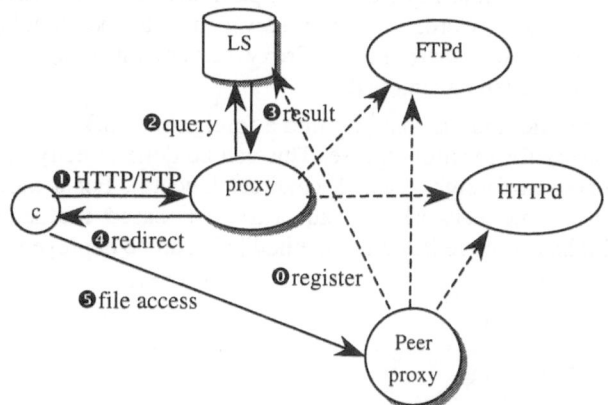

Fig. 2. Shows peer-to-peer support (*redirect* mode) for file transfer and caching.

In this infrastructure, searching for proxy servers can be transparent to users since location service lookups can be done automatically by proxy servers. Besides, the availability of peer proxy can be used as a way of load balancing between servers. Since the latest information for each cache in a domain can be obtained, the most suitable proxy server can be reached and load balancing can be achieved. Fault tolerance mechanism can also be provided in the case of proxy failure. As shown in Fig. 2, key components in the infrastructure include: location servers (LS), proxy servers, and FTP/HTTP servers. The functional description of each component is provided as follows.

3.1 Location Server

Location server is responsible for storing the current location and content index for each peer proxy. These include hostname, current IP address, URLs for cached content, and resource profiles (for example, access control list). Since the peer proxy server may be changing its location or contents frequently, the amount of data update may be quite large. Therefore, Resource Location Records (RLRs) can be stored in a distributed way, for example, one location server for each domain (like DNS server). RLRs for cached URLs on each proxy server are stored in location server of its home domain.

Most of the relevant works in location service are related to geographical positioning of mobile nodes in a wireless network, the location of servers, and location-based services. They mainly focused on the physical positioning of mobile nodes or servers, not the current way of accessing a particular resource, for example, the IP address of currently available peer proxy with the requested data.

As shown in Fig. 3, there are two possible operations for a location server: *update* and *query*. Proxy servers *update* their current location (IP address), URLs and resource profiles for cached content to location server when they are first added, changed, or removed from the domain. On the other hand, peer proxy servers *query* the location server for available replication of a particular URL in order to retrieve resource from it. In other words, location server has to be coupled with the management of resource addition/removal. Proxy servers must do registration/de-registration when being added or removed.

However, when mobile node is roaming into a foreign network, it must register to its home location server for location update. This can be done directly or through the help of location server in foreign network (Indirect Update). For a mobile node to detect it has left its home network, the advertisement based mechanism used in Mobile IP [6] or hint based move detection method [17] can be deployed.

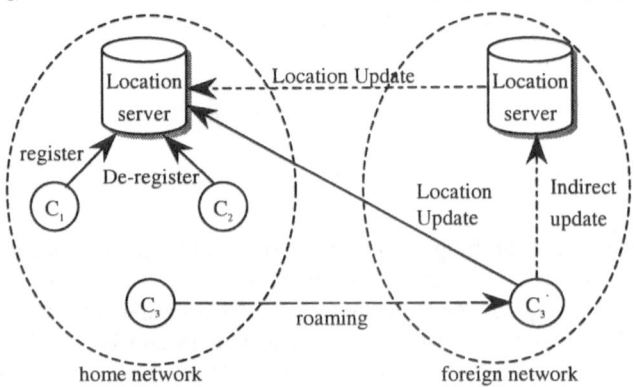

Fig. 3. Shows the operations of location servers.

3.2 Proxy Server

In our infrastructure, each proxy server has to register to its domain location server when the cached contents are added, changed, or removed. The current IP address and the cached contents are indexed by the location server. When a peer proxy needs to search for the availability of a specific URL, a location service query will be issued and the result will be checked to see if redirect is needed.

There are several deployment alternatives for peer-to-peer file transfer and caching. Besides the *redirect* mode depicted in Fig.2, two other schemes are possible, *proxy* mode and *server-to-server copy* mode, which are illustrated as follows.

In *proxy* mode, file access requests from clients are repeated on local proxy where file objects fetched from peer proxy are cached. This "greedy" caching mechanism would require more storage requirement but less penalties for a cache miss will be experienced since as much content as possible will be cached. But it's not suitable for proxy server load balancing since the load of proxy server is heavy.

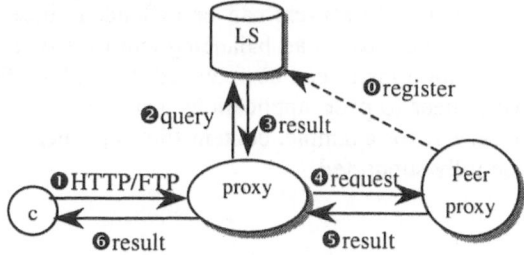

Fig. 4. Shows an alternative deployment scheme (*proxy* mode) for peer-to-peer file transfer and caching.

On the other hand, in *server-to-server copy* mode, file access requests for clients are not redirected to peer proxies. Instead, notifications to both client and peer proxy are issued by local proxy and the real file transmission takes place without the intervention of local proxy. This is illustrated in Fig. 5.

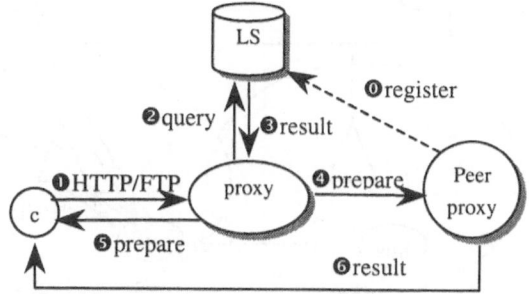

Fig. 5. Shows *server-to-server copy* mode for peer-to-peer file transfer and caching.

This caching mechanism has the advantage of load balancing for *redirect* mode, without much intervention of local proxy.

Note that existing inter-cache communication protocols can still be used in different conditions. For example, ICP [3] can be used for inter-proxy communication protocol, but modifications to ICP are required for supporting mechanisms such as server-to-server copy. On the other hand, cache digests [16] can be used in which full index doesn't have to be built. Only the cache digests for each peer proxy are needed.

Among these alternatives, *redirect* mode is better for load balancing, while *proxy* mode has the advantage of "greedy" caching in local proxy. *Server-to-server copy* mode has the advantage of *redirect* mode without much intervention for local proxy server if inter-proxy communication protocol support is available.

4 Advantages

In our architecture, there are several advantages over current file transfer mechanism. Firstly, file (WWW, FTP, proxy) servers can be offloaded since replication can be found via location service lookups. Load balancing can thus be achieved. Secondly, peer-to-peer support for file transfer can be achieved, and integration of existing file transfer protocols with peer-to-peer applications can be done. Thirdly, personal configuration for file server, for example, content filtering, such as ACL: allow/deny <source URL>, can be fully supported.

5 Security Concerns

When one mobile node is roaming into a foreign network, authentication and authorization is required before it's granted network access. For example, IEEE 802.1x [18] can be used as the network access control mechanism as shown in Fig. 6.

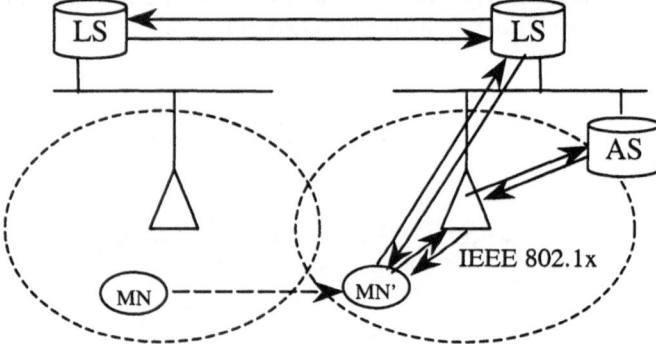

Fig. 6. Shows the authentication and authorization for mobile nodes, where AS is the Authentication Server, and LS is the Location Sever.

On the other hand, for each operation of update and query, authentication and authorization are required to ensure the correctness of each record in location server.

6 Future Work

Most importantly, file authenticity is the most difficult problem. We have to make sure that the file objects registered by peer proxies are indeed the objects as they claim. The authenticity and non-repudiation principle is most important. Besides, conditions for users behind firewall and users inside private network have to be dealt with.

7   Conclusion

In this paper, a peer-to-peer support for file transfer and caching mechanism was proposed. Through the sharing of cached contents of peer proxies in the same domain, we could further improve the cache utilization and reduce unnecessary duplicate file access requests. In addition, load balancing for overloaded proxy servers can be achieved by means of proxy redirecting and server-to-server copy operations incorporated in our scheme.

References

1. J. Postel and J. Reynolds, "File Transfer Protocol (FTP)," *STD 9, RFC 959*, IETF, October 1985.
2. R. Fielding, J. Gettys, J. Mogul, H. Frystyk, L. Masinter, P. Leach, and T. Berners-Lee, "Hypertext Transfer Protocol – HTTP/1.1," *RFC 2616*, IETF, June 1999.
3. D. Wessels and K. Claffy, "Internet Cache Protocol (ICP), version 2," *RFC 2186*, IETF, September 1997.
4. Squid Web Proxy Cache, http://www.squid-cache.org/.
5. Information Technology – Telecommunications and Information Exchange between System – Local and Metropolitan Area Networks – Specific Requirements Part 11: Wireless LAN Medium Access Control (MAC) and Physical Layer (PHY) Specifications, *IEEE Std. 802.11-1999*, 1999.
6. C. Perkins, "IP Mobility Support for IPv4," *RFC 3220*, IETF, Jan. 2002.
7. Napster, http://www.napster.com/.
8. Jabber, http://www.jabber.org/.
9. The GnuTella Protocol Specification v0.4, http://www.clip2.com/GnutellaProtocol04.pdf.
10. G. Barish and K. Obraczka, "World Wide Web Caching: Trends and Techniques," *IEEE Communication Magazine, vol. 38, issue 5*, pp. 178-185, May 2000.
11. P. Gauthier, J. Cohen, M. Dunsmuir, and C. Perkins, "Web Proxy Auto-Discovery Protocol (WPAD)," *Internet Draft*, Internet article at: http://www.web-cache.com/Writings/Internet-Drafts/draft-ietf-wrec-wpad-01.txt, IETF, July 1999.
12. Netscape, "Navigator Proxy Auto-Config File Format," Internet article at: http://wp.netscape.com/eng/mozilla/2.0/relnotes/demo/proxy-live.html, March 1996.
13. M. Cieslak, D. Forster, G. Tiwana, and R. Wilson, "Web Cache Communication Protocol V2.0," *Internet Draft*, IETF, April 2001.
14. P. Vixie and D. Wessels, "Hyper Text Caching Protocol (HTCP/0.0)," *RFC 2756*, IETF, January 2001.
15. V. Valloppillil and K.W.Ross, "Cache Array Routing Protocol v1.0," *Internet Draft*, IETF, February 1998.
16. A. Russkov and D. Wessels, "Cache Digests," *Proceedings of 3rd International WWW Caching Workshop*, April 1998.
17. N. A. Fikouras and C. Goerg, "Performance Comparison of Hinted and Advertisement Based Movement Detection Methods for Mobile IP Hand-offs," *Proceedings of the European Wireless 2000*, Dresden, Germany, September 2000.
18. IEEE Standards for Local and Metropolitan Area Networks: Port based Network Access Control, *IEEE Std. 802.1X-2001*, June 2001.

Exact and Heuristic Algorithms for Multi-constrained Path Selection Problem

Wen-Lin Yang

Department of Information Technology
National Pingtung Institute of Commerce
No.51, Ming-Sheng East Road, Pingtung City,Taiwan
wly@npic.edu.tw

Abstract. The multi-constrained path (MCP) selection problem occurs when the quality of services (QoS) are supported for point-to-point connections in the distributed multimedia applications deployed on the Internet. This NP-complete problem is concerned how to determine a feasible path between two end-points, so that a set of QoS path constraints can be satisfied simultaneously. Based on the branch-and-bound technology and tabu-searching strategy, an optimal algorithm and a heuristic algorithm are proposed in this paper. The experimental results show that our heuristic algorithm not only has very good performance on several different network topologies, but also is very efficient method for solving large-scale MCP problem.

1 Introduction

For real-time multimedia applications deployed on the broadband integrated services networks, various QoS requirements, such as bandwidth, delay, cost, delay jitter, packet loss rate, etc., must be supported in order to provide appropriate service quality [8,9,10]. To provide such QoS-based services, a routing problem concerning how to select a feasible path between two end-points so that all the given QoS constraints can be satisfied simultaneously. This QoS routing problem is often referred as a multi-constrained path selection problem (MCP) [1,2,3,4].

The MCP problem is known to be NP-complete [1]. To cope with the NP-complete, a number of heuristics were developed for MCP problems in the past [1,2,3,4,6]. In [1,2,6], the MCP problem with only two independent constraints was studied, and polynomial-time heuristic algorithms were proposed. For k-constrained routing problem, a limited path heuristic modified from extended Bellman-Ford algorithm was developed in [3], where the simulation results show that this method works well for small meshes. However, since it requires $O(N^2 * \ln N)$ space in each node to store partial paths, the required running space could be enormous for large-scale networks. In [4], a randomized heuristic was proposed for MCP problem with k constraints. For a small real network with 32 nodes, it can find a feasible path in a very high probability. For the MCP problem, a heuristic method may not find a feasible path; even there exists at least one feasible path in the network.

Y.-C. Chen, L.-W. Chang, and C.-T. Hsu (Eds.): PCM 2002, LNCS 2532, pp. 952–959, 2002.

In this paper, a branch-and-bound based optimal algorithm and a tabu-search based heuristic algorithm are presented for the k-constrained QoS routing problem. Based on the simulations conducted in this study, our heuristic method not just performs very well on a number of different network topologies, but also is an efficient method for the MCP problem. The heuristic was developed based on the tabu searching strategy and the branch-and-bound technique. As for the optimal algorithms, our branch-and-bound based method [11] is also much more efficient than the extended-Bellman-Ford method that was proposed in [3,5].

2   The MCP Problem

Consider a network that is modeled by a directed graph $G(V, E)$, where V is a set of nodes and E is a set of links. Each link $(v, u) \in E$ is associated with K positive additive QoS parameters: $w_i(u, v), i = 0, 1, ..., (K - 1)$. For a link e from node u to node v, the notation $w(u, v) = w(e) = (w_0(e), w_1(e), ..., w_{K-1}(e))$ represents K QoS parameters assigned on link e. In addition, for a path P and a QoS parameter i, the path weight $W_i(P)$ is defined as the summation of $w_i(e)$ on every link e along the path P.

Given K constraints C_i, $0 \leq i \leq (K - 1)$, and a pair of nodes S and T representing the source node and destination node respectively, the goal of our MCP problem is to find a path P from S to T such that $W_i(P) \leq C_i$.

3   The Optimal Algorithm

In this section, we present an optimal algorithm for the MCP problem. This algorithm is developed based on the branch-and-bound technique. The optimal algorithm is given in Figure 3, and is used as a kernel function in our tabu-search based heuristic algorithm, which is represented in section 4.

3.1   The Branch-and-Bound Algorithm

In order to solve the MCP problem optimally, a data structure called state-space tree is created from a given network to record all the feasible paths. Based on the state-space tree, a branch-and-bound algorithm is applied to search for a feasible path. The state-space tree is constructed in the following ways.

Let the source node of network G be the root of the state-space tree. As shown in Figure 2, for each state node S_j in the state-space tree, two labels mark it: one is the node number j in the original network and another one is an attribute vector. Let Y_j denote the attribute vector of state node S_j. Let K denotes the number of QoS constraints, and Y_j can then be defined as follows:

1. $Y_j = (obj\_value_j, W_{j,0}, ..., W_{j,K-1})$, $W_{j,i} = \sum_{(u,v)\in(s\rightarrow j)} w_i(u, v)$, $0 \leq i \leq (K - 1)$.

2. The obj_value_j of the attribute vector Y_j is computed based on the following equation:

$$obj\_value_j = \sum_{i=0}^{K-1} [w_i(s \to j) - C_i], \tag{1}$$

where obj_value_j= an integer greater than 0, if $[w_i(s \to j) - C_i] > 0$

In the above equation, we use $w_i(s \to j)$ to represent the summation of $w_i(e)$ on every link e along the path from source node s to node j.

For any state node S_u with node-label u, a new state node S_v is created for each downstream node v, if the link (u, v) is in the network G. In addition, these new state nodes are made to be children of S_u, and they are at the same level in the state-space tree. For any intermediate state node S_j with node-label j, downstream nodes of node j cannot be added in the state-space tree if the $w_{j,i} > C_i$, for some i. Since one of QoS constraints is violated, the path from root to state node S_j is infeasible. As a result, the state node S_j becomes a leaf node in the state-space tree.

By applying the above branching process recursively, the entire state-space tree is then obtained for the MCP problem. The destination node must appear at some of the leaf nodes of the state-space tree. Since the goal of our problem is to find a feasible path that satisfies all the path constraints, we may speed up this searching process by giving priorities to the state nodes that are eligible for branching. That is, the state node j with the smallest obj_value_j should have the highest priority to be selected for branching. This searching strategy is based on an observation that a state node with smaller obj_value would have more chance to lead to a feasible path. A priority heap maintained in Figure 3 is used to keep the state node with the smallest obj_value always on the top of the heap. As shown in lines $14 \sim 15$ of Figure 3, only non-destination state nodes whose obj_values are not greater than zero, are eligible for further branching, and are thus stored into the heap R.

The time complexity of our branch-and-bound algorithm is bounded by $O(d^n)$ where n denotes the number of nodes and d represents the largest node-degree in the network, since at the worst case the height of a state-space tree is at most n and the number of children of any state node could be as large as d.

3.2   The Example

To illustrate our branch-and-bound method for the MCP problem, a numerical example is given in Figure 1 and 2. Based on a six-node network given in Figure 1, the nodes 0 and 5 are assumed to represent the source node and destination node respectively, and the paths between these two nodes must satisfy two QoS constraints, C_0 and C_1, which are no more than 5. A state-space tree is then constructed in Figure 2, where all the state nodes are numbered based on their creating sequence.

For example, state nodes s_4 and s_5 are created earlier than state nodes s_6 and s_7, because the obj_value of s_3 is -6 and the obj_value of s_2 is -7. The branching process occurs on state node s_2 is earlier than state node s_3. After the first feasible path is found ($s_0 \to s_2 \to s_5 \to s_8$), the branching process stops.

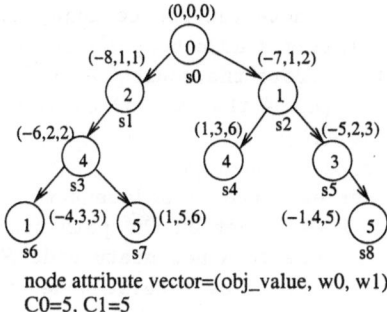

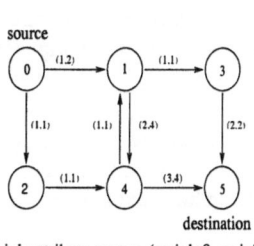

Link attribute vector=(weight0, weight1)

node attribute vector=(obj_value, w0, w1)
C0=5, C1=5

Fig. 1. An example of 6-node net-work

Fig. 2. State-space tree construction based on branch-and-bound algorithm

4   A Tabu-Search Based Algorithm

Since the MCP problem is NP-complete, the optimal algorithm presented in the previous section is only good for networks with a small number of hops between source and destination nodes. For large-scale networks, it may take too much time to traverse the whole state-space tree to find a feasible path.

In this section, a tabu-search based heuristic algorithm is developed to deal with large-scale MCP problems. The main idea of this method is as follows:

(a) Find a good path P as an initial solution.
(b) Select a pair of nodes u and v on P, and delete all the edges between them. Note that the length of this selected partial path between u and v is not greater than a predetermined constant L.
(c) Apply the above branch-and-bound based optimal algorithm to search for a feasible partial path between nodes u and v. Then, rebuild the whole path between original source and destination nodes.
(d) The above path-rebuilding process is then embedded into an iteration loop, which is developed based on the tabu-search technology. A tabu list is imple-mented on a circular queue for storing partial paths, which have been visited recently. Only partial paths not in the tabu list are eligible for rebuilding. The procedure stops after a predefined number of iterations.

The complete heuristic procedure based on the above idea is developed and presented in Figure 4. Note that if the constant L in (b) is made greater than the number of hops of any feasible path between the source and destination nodes, the tabu-search based algorithm becomes an optimal algorithm. Hence, the constant L is adjustable. The time complexity of the heuristic algorithm is bounded by the number of times of branch-and-bound procedure at line 10 being executed. It is $O(d^n * ITERATIONS)$ at the worst case.

1. Let S denote the source node, and T denote the destination node;
2. Initialize a node heap R; Let C_j= the jth constraint, $0 \le j \le (K-1)$;
3. Let S_0 store the source node S and be the root of state-space tree;
4. Let $w_j(u,v)$= the jth QoS parameter on link (u,v); Add S_0 to heap R;
5. While $(R \ne \phi)\{$
6. $S_u = remove\_top(R)$;
7.   For each node v adjacent to node u contained in state node $S_u\{$
8.   if$(v$ is not on the path from S_0 to u and v is unvisited from $u)\{$
9.   Create a new state node S_v for v based on the state node S_u, and let S_v to be a child-node of S_u;
10. $S_v \to branch = YES$; $S_v \to path = S_u \to path + (u,v)$;
11.   Let P_v be the path from S_0 to S_v;
12. $obj\_value_v = \sum_{j=0}^{K-1}[w_j(P_v) - C_j]$, where $obj\_value_v = 1$, if $[w_j(P_v) - C_j] > 1$;
13.   if$(obj\_value_v > 0)$ $\{S_v \to branch$=NO;$\}$
14.   else if $(v = T)\{S_v \to branch$=NO;if$(obj\_value_v \le 0)$ return P_v;$\}$
15.   else$\{$Add v to heap R;$\}$
16. $\}$ $\}$ $\}$

Fig. 3. The optimal algorithm

1. Let S denote the source node, and T denote the destination node;
2. Let C_j= the jth constraint, $0 \le j \le (K-1)$;
3. Let F=$\{\bar{P}|\bar{P}$ is a path from S to T, and $\bar{P}$ is determined by Dijkstra algorithm based on K QoS parameters.$\}$
4. Let $P \in F$, and P contains the longest partial path that satisfies all the constraints;
5. Let a circular queue Q be the tabu list; $k = 0$; L= a small integer;
6. While$(k < ITERATIONS)\{$
7.   Randomly select a partial path R on P where $R \subset P$, $|R| \le L$;
8.   Let $P = P_1 + R + P_2$ and R is a path from node u to node v;
9.   if$(R \notin Q)\{Q = Q \cup R$; $C_j(R) = C_j - C_j(P_1) - C_j(P_2)$, $0 \le j \le (K-1)$;$\}$
10.   Apply the optimal algorithm to find a new feasible path from u to v; Let $\hat{R}$ be this new path;
11.   if$(\hat{R}$ satisfies all sub-constraints $C_j(R), \forall j)\{$
12.   Rebuild a new path $\hat{P}$ from u to v such that $\hat{P} = P_1 + \hat{R} + P_2$;
13.   if$(\hat{P}$ is a feasible path)$\{$return $\hat{P}$;$\}$
14.   else$\{P = \hat{P}$;$\}\}$
15. $k = k + 1$;$\}$

Fig. 4. Tabu-search based heuristic algorithm

5   Simulation Results

In this section, we have several sets of experiments for comparing performance and efficiency between optimal and heuristic algorithms presented in this paper for solving the MCP problem. Two network examples, ANSNET and mesh, are studied in this study, and all the simulations are done with the following experimental parameters: PIII 866 MHz CPU, 512MB RAM, Linux OS, and programs are developed by c++. For all benchmarks, all QoS parameters (the weights) on each link are randomly selected from the range $0 \sim 100$, and the constant L is set to be 12.

5.1   Performance

(a) ANSNET

A network topology shown in Figure 5 is modified from ANSNET [7], which was studied in [3,4]. Under the same experimental environments on ANSNET, for example: the values of QoS parameters on all links are kept the same, 400 distinct pairs of source and destination nodes are randomly selected for performance comparisons. Under 400 runs, success ratio is defined as follows:

Success ratio= number of feasible paths found by optimal algorithm / number of feasible paths found by our tabu-search based heuristic algorithm.

As shown in Table 1, the average success rate is more than 99% for different number of QoS constraints. This experimental results show that our heuristic algorithm is very effective method for the MCP problem.

(b) Mesh

In this set of experiments, the longest path of a mesh is used for evaluate performances. The source and destination nodes are then selected as the way shown in Figure 6. The number of hops between two end-points of the longest diagonal line of an $N \times N$ mesh is at least $2*(N-1)$. In Table 2, based on the same source and destination nodes in an 8×8 mesh, 1000 distinct configurations are generated with different number of constraints. In this paper, a configuration is defined as a set of QoS values assigned on all the links in a mesh. The average success ratio is also more than 99%.

5.2   Efficiency

In order to evaluate the executing speed for the tabu-search based heuristic algorithm, two given nodes (source and destination) located at two end-points of the longest diagonal line of a mesh is used for test. The simulation results are shown in Table 3, where each data entry is measured based on 10 different configurations. For the number of nodes not greater than 100, the executing performance of tabu-search based heuristic is much better than branch-and-bound based optimal algorithm. In addition, the heuristic can efficiently solve the MCP problem for large-scale network. For example, for a 10000-node network in Table 3, it takes only 7.2 seconds to find a feasible path with at least 198 hops.

6   Conclusions

Based on the branch-and-bound technique and tabu-searching strategy, an optimal algorithm and a heuristic are presented for the MCP problem in this paper.

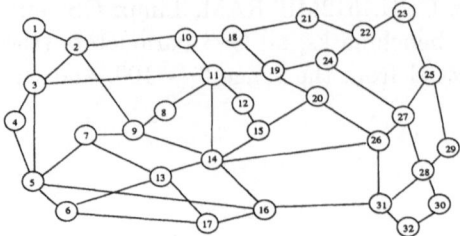

Fig. 5. A network topology

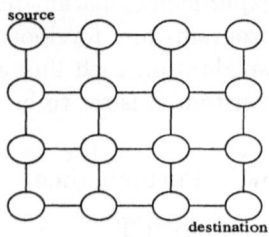

Fig. 6. A 16-node mesh

Table 1. Simulation results for ANSNET

c0/c1/c2/c3	optimal	tabu	success ratio
240/240	335	334	99.7%
200/200	257	257	100.0%
160/120	138	138	100.0%
100/120	88	88	100.0%
Average			99.9%
240/240/240	344	342	99.4%
160/200/240	238	237	99.6%
200/120/160	169	166	98.2%
120/120/120	86	86	100.0%
Average			99.3%
240/240/240/240	281	279	99.3%
200/240/200/160	170	168	98.8%
200/200/160/160	142	141	99.3%
120/160/120/160	86	85	98.8%
Average			99.1%

Table 2. Simulation results for an 8 × 8 mesh

c0/c1/c2/c3	optimal	tabu	success ratio
560/560	934	932	99.8%
560/500	668	662	99.1%
500/500	371	370	99.7%
450/500	145	144	99.3%
560/560/560	547	543	99.3%
560/560/560/560	225	223	99.1%
Average			99.4%

Table 3. Efficiency comparisons based on meshes

#nodes	c0/c1	branch-and-bound (#path/cpu in secs)	tabu-search (#path/cpu in secs)
64	630/630	10/1.8	10/0.1
64	560/560	6/3.1	6/0.1
81	720/720	10/237	10/0.1
81	600/600	5/104.8	5/0.3
100	810/810	10/9976	10/1.2
10000	7000/7000	n/a	10/71.6

The experimental results show that our tabu-search based heuristic is almost as good as the optimal algorithm in terms of performance. As for executing speed, the heuristic is also proved to be a highly efficient method for solving large-scale MCP problems.

References

1. Jaffe, J. M., : Algorithms for finding paths with multiple constraints, Networks, vol. 14 (1984) 95–116
2. Chen, Shiganag, Nahrstedt, Klara, : On Finding Multi-constrained Paths, in Proceedings of the ICC'98 Conference, IEEE (1998) 874–979
3. Yuan, Xin, Liu, Xingming, : Heuristic Algorithms for Multi-Constrained Quality of Service Routing, in Proceedings of the IEEE INFOCOM Conference, IEEE (2001) 844–853
4. Korkmaz, Turgay, Krunz, Marwan, : A Randomized Algorithm for Finding a Path Subject to Multiple QoS Constraints, in Proceedings of the IEEE Global Telecommunications Conference, IEEE (1999) 1694–1698
5. Widyono, R., : The Design and Evaluation Algorithm for Real-time Channels, TR-94-024, International Computer Science Institute, UC Berkeley (1994)
6. Korkmaz, Turgay, Krunz, Marwan, Tragoudas, Spyros, : An efficient algorithm for finding a path subject to two additive constraints, Computer Communications, vol. 25 (2002) 225–238
7. Comer,D.E., : Internetworking with TCP/IP, vol. I, Prentice Hall (1995)
8. Verma, Sanjeev, Pankaj, Rajesh K., Leon-Garica, Alberto, : QoS based multicast routing algorithms for real time applications, Performance Evaluation, vol. 34 (1998) 273–294
9. Korkmaz, Turgay, Krunz, Marwan, : Multi-Constrained Optimal Path Selection, in Proceedings of the IEEE INFOCOM Conference, IEEE (2001) 834–843
10. Orda, Ariel, : Routing with End-to-End QoS Guarantees in Broadband Networks, IEEE/ACM Transactions on Networking, vol. 7, no. 3, (1999) 365–374
11. Yang, Wen-Lin, : Solving the MCOP Problem Optimally, in Proceedings of IEEE Conference on Local Computer Networks, IEEE (2002)

W-CoSIM (Web-Based Hardware-Software CoSimulator) – A Design-Time Simulation Tool for Estimating the Performance of Online Multimedia Applications

Kangsun Lee, Hyunmin Park, Jonghoon Chun, Wouseok Jou, Jaeho Jung, and Youngseok Hwang

Division of Computer Science and Engineering, MyongJi University, San 38-2 Namdong, YongIn, Kyunggido, Korea 449-728
ksl@mju.ac.kr,

Abstract. Internet applications are increasingly being equipped with rich multimedia data. Most e-business development tools are quite good at authoring multimedia contents, however they lack explicit support for estimating the performance of the envisioned multimedia system at design time. W-CoSim (Web-based Hardware and Software Co-Simulator) is an EJB-based simulation tool used for validating the architecture and the performance of online multimedia systems at design time. W-CoSim has four components: Modeler, Translator, Engine and Scenario. Users start from Modeler to describe systems architecture by means of a UML(Unified Modeling Language) deployment diagram, and then specify hardware & software performance parameters such as the size of audio and video data, execution delay and network topology. All information specified in the Modeler are sent to the Translator, and then automatically converted to Java code. Engine and Scenario are responsible to run the Java code and produce results in the form of text and graphs.

1 Introduction

With the popularity of audio and video streaming applications on the World Wide Web, a surge in the volume of multimedia transactions has occurred, resulting in delays and outages as systems and networks become over-loaded [1, 2]. A good web-based multimedia application requires not only good contents but also satisfactory performance, which is determined by such factors as rapid response time and short round trip time. Analysts and designers of online multimedia applications should answer the following typical questions, in order to guarantee the satisfactory performance of their intended systems:

- What is the average response time of the multimedia service during the busiest period?
- What would be the performance of the online web-based multimedia application if the number of customer sessions were to double during the peak period?

Y.-C. Chen, L.-W. Chang, and C.-T. Hsu (Eds.): PCM 2002, LNCS 2532, pp. 960–967, 2002.

- What components of the web-based multimedia system should be upgraded to provide better performance? Database servers? Web servers? Multimedia application servers?

Although these are typical questions to be asked in the case of web-based multimedia applications, most development processes handle these performance issues only during the testing phase or, at worse, only after the application has already been deployed. Therefore, the failure to meet performance criteria usually engenders redesign and reimplementation costs [3]. Quantitative approaches to estimating the performance of web-based multimedia applications are widespread and many such references are to be found [1], however, not many supporting software tools are available, which are specifically designed for evaluating web-based multimedia applications in the early stages of development. Moreover, the unique characteristics of and the typical "what-if" questions associated with web-based multimedia applications are not easily expressed when using software development tools [3,4,5]. In this paper, we present W-CoSim (Web-based Hardware and Software Co-Simulator), a design-time performance prediction tool for web-based multimedia applications. W-CoSim has been developed using the latest web technologies, for example, EJB(Enterprise Java Beans), applets, and servlets. This paper is organized as follows: In Section2, we introduce the W-CoSim architecture. A complete process, from model specification to results generation, using W-CoSim is illustrated in Section 3, by means of an on-line shopping mall example. Section 4 concludes this paper.

2   COSIM Architecture

W-CoSim is composed of Modeler, Translator, Engine and Scenario as shown in Figure   1. Sections 2.1 - 2.3 provide a discussion concerning each of the components.

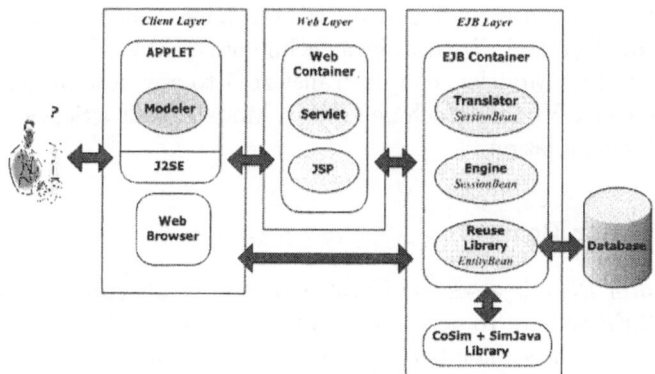

Fig. 1. CoSim Architecture

2.1   Modeler

Modeler provides GUI(Graphical User Interface) to model and simulate a system architecture. The user creates a system architecture, which is represented by a deployment diagram described using UML [6,7,8]. This deployment diagram shows the physical relationships between the software and hardware components in the system to be delivered. A node is a run-time resource, such as a computer, device or memory. Physical relationships among the computational units are represented as links. The UML deployment diagram is useful for visualizing the run-time architecture of web-based multimedia applications. However, we can not obtain performance estimation data directly from this diagram. Some of the information required in order to estimate performance data from the diagram is listed below.

- Node related data : component information (Processing time, Page size, RTT(Round Trip Time), audio and video data size, etc), and hardware information (processor type, memory size, hard disk capacity, etc.)
- Link related data : network type and bandwidth
- Simulation objectives : server utilization and client response time
- General information on simulation : schedule information, simulation time, number of iterations, and confidence interval

The user is required to draw an extended deployment diagram from scratch using Modeler, in order to specify the run-time architecture of the web application along with the performance data to be used for the simulation. Alternatively, users can load an existing deployment diagram from the Reuse Library and refine it according to their specific needs. Further discussion about the Reuse Library is to be found in Section 2.4. Modeler is implemented using JavaBeans and Applet. A JavaBeans component is a reusable software component model of Java [9]. Modeler can be used with any development tool supporting the JavaBeans standard. An applet is a program written in the JavaTM programming language that can be included in an HTML page, much in the same way as an image would be [10]. With a Java technology-enabled browser, the applet's code, generated by Modeler, can be transferred to any system and executed by the browser's Java Virtual Machine (JVM). Modeler calls a Servlet [11] to create a Java file for Simulation.

2.2   Translator Bean

The Translator Bean is a session bean. A session bean represents a single client inside the J2EE server. To access an application that is deployed on the server, the client invokes the session beans methods. The session bean performs work for its client, thereby freeing the client from unnecessary complexity by executing business tasks inside the server [12]. Translator generates Java code equivalent to the extended deployment diagram specified in Modeler. To generate the Java code, Translator uses the XML document received from Modeler. Translator parses this document and verifies it by checking for well-formedness and by validating it against a DTD(Data Type Definition) [13,14] Translator generates Java code by means of the following three steps:

- *(Step1) Model Analysis* : Translator analyzes, classifies, and saves model information in the form of an intermediate language used by the Modeler and the Translator.
- *(Step2) Generation of Simulation Algorithm* : Translator generates the simulation structure in Java, by using the SimJava library[6]. Translator constructs classes for the nodes specified in the deployment diagram, and implements these classes with the use of threads in Java. The scheduling structure (the order in which the simulations should take place) between nodes is determined by analyzing the input/output relationships between the nodes and the links. Links are implemented by means of interactions between the threads.
- *(Step3) Generation of Simulation Objectives* : W-CoSim provides response time, utilization, throughput and transmission time as performance measurements. Translator has a set of methods which it uses to calculate these measurements, and records which method to use for each of the nodes.

SimJava is a process-based discrete event simulation package for Java [15]. It is a collection of entities, each of which runs in its own thread. Since the entities are connected together by ports, they can communicate with each other by sending and receiving event objects. Each node has independence and concurrency, which enables the simulation to be more realistic. W-CoSim extends the SimJava library, so as to construct the simulation codes. More information on SimJava can be found in Reference [15].

2.3   Engine Bean & Scenario

The Engine Bean is a session bean. The Engine runs the Java code generated by the Translator with the specified simulation time. The Engine uses the W-CoSim run-time library (SimJava Library and other utility library) to simulate the execution of the code, and then produces simulation results. Simulation results are summarized by Scenario in the form of a report and associated graphs.

2.4   Reuse Library Bean

The Reuse Library Bean is an Entity Bean. An entity bean represents a business object in a persistent storage mechanism. In the J2EE SDK, the persistent storage mechanism is a relational database. Typically, each entity bean has an underlying table in a relational database, and each instance of the bean corresponds to a row in that table [12]. In the case of W-CoSim, the reuse on can be utilized on three different levels: i.e. the node, link and system archi-tecture levels. Users model their system by 1) browsing reusable components, 2) selecting one and more of these components and 3) modifying them according to their needs. The Reuse Library of W-CoSim guides the user through this process by providing various information on the available reusable components, including implementation languages, processing time, web page size, audio and video size, and processor type.

3   Example: Onling Shopping Mall

In this section, we illustrate how the performance estimation is undertaken using W-CoSim by means of an example. Consider an online shopping mall. This online shopping mall is planning to contain rich multimedia data in order to attract their clients interest. To support these heavy multimedia transactions, the site's architecture consists of three layers. The first one consists of a Web server, which is accessed by Internet clients through a browser. The second layer is an application server that receives transaction requests generated by the Web server. To carry out the transaction, the application server communicates with the database server and requests specific database information. The Web server provides static HTML documents to customers, collects data and transfers them to the application. The application server receives requests from the Web server, parses them and activates the processes that carry out the requested e-business functions(e.g. Purchase, Shopping Cart, Browse, etc). A set of input data for the online shopping mall is given in Table 1.

Table 1. Input Data for the Online Shopping Mall

Server	Processor Demand	IO Demand
Web(WS)	1.32 sec	1.14 sec
Application(WS)	1.42 sec	0.13 sec
Database(DB)	1.18 sec	1.56 sec

Let us suppose that we want to answer the following five questions:

1. What is the average client response time?
2. What is the percentage utilization of the three servers?
3. What would the average client response time be if the server were to be replaced by one which is two times faster?
4. What would the average client response time be if the number of customer sessions were to double during the peak period?
5. How would the average response time increase as a function of the business transaction arrival rate?

Figure 2 shows how the system architecture is specified using W-CoSim.

Users can specify their architecture by means of a UML deployment diagram, either from scratch or with the help of the reuse library, as discussed in Section 2.4. Various performance input data for each of the nodes and links are

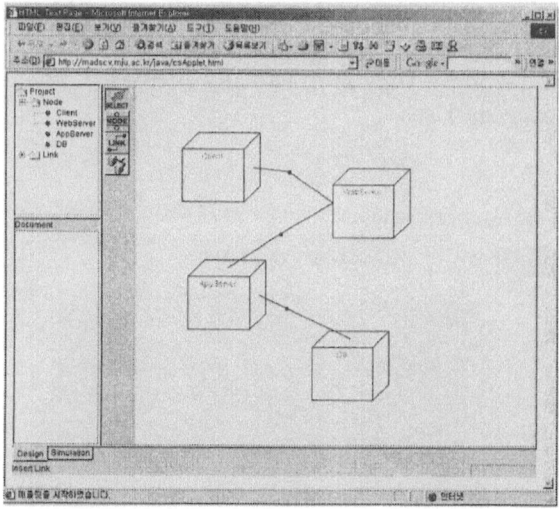

Fig. 2. Deployment Diagram on Modeler

specified in the node specification window and the link specification window. Users specify delay time and frame size in the node specification window. Information on the hardware (process type, memory size, and hard disk capacity) is specified in the hardware specification tab, while information on components (Page size, RTT, Number of Objects, audio and video data size) is specified in the component specification tab. Information on the links is specified in the link specification window, including network delay time, and hardware data (network type and network bandwidth). Simulation orders are specified with the help of the Simulation Wizard. The Simulation Wizard helps a user to correctly specify 1) the simulation orders to be transmitted between the nodes, 2) the simula-tion objectives for the nodes, and 3) simulation duration. In this example, a transaction is instantiated by the Client node, transmitted to the WebServer then to the AppServer and finally to the database. Translator generates Java code upon the successful completion of the Simulation Wizard. The generated Java code is executed on the Engine using the run time library of W-CoSim.

The simulation results can be summarized as follows:

1. What is the average client response time? : 8.46 sec
2. What is the percentage utilization of the three servers? : WS: 20.7%, AS: 13.1%, DB: 22.2%
3. What would the average client response time be if the server were to be replaced by one which is two times faster?: New client response time = 5.13 sec
4. What would the average client response time be if the number of customer sessions were to double during the peak period?: New client response time = 35.96 sec

5. How would the average response time increase as a function of the business transaction arrival rate? : As summarized in Figure 3 and Figure 4, the average client response time is drastically increased when the client inter-arrival time exceeds 1 sec.

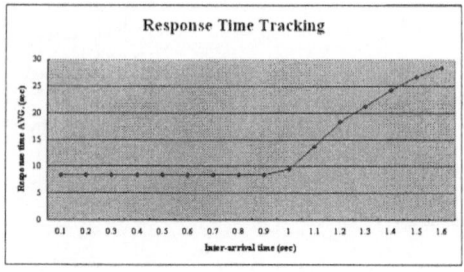

Fig. 3. Response time of the online shopping mall

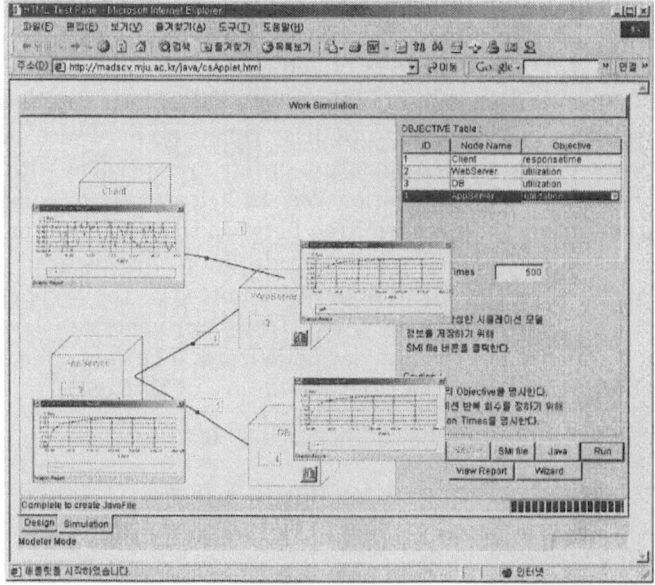

Fig. 4. Scenario

4   Conclusion

In this paper, we introduced W-CoSim, a design-time performance estimation tool for web-based multimedia applications. W-CoSim generates Java code which corresponds to the extended deployment diagram, and then simulates the execution of this code to obtain performance data. In this way, the system architecture of a web application can be validated, based on the performance estimation results provided by W-CoSim, in the early stages of development. Any failure to meet performance criteria is detected prior to the testing phase and well before actual deployment of the application. Consequently, both development costs and time consumed can be substantially reduced by minimizing the risk of having to subsequently redesign and re-implement the multimedia application.

References

1. Daniel A Menasce and Virgilio A. F. Almeda. *Scaling for E-Business*. Prentice Hall, 2000.
2. GNV's WWW User Surveys, http://www.gvu.gatech.edu.
3. Svend Frolind and Pankaj Garg. Design-Time Simulation of a Large-Scaled, Distributed Object System. *ACM Transactions on Modelling and Computer Simulation*, 8(4):374–400, 1998.
4. A. Burns and A.J. Wellings. HRT-HOOD: a structured design method for hard real-time systems. *Real-Time Systems*, 6:72–114, 1994.
5. Kangsun Lee and Paul A. Fishwick. Building a model for real-time simulation. *Future Generation Com-puter Systems*, 17:585 – 600, 2001.
6. James Runbaugh, Ivar Jacobson and Grady Booch. *The Unified Modeling Language Reference Manual*. Addison Wesley, 2000.
7. Jim Conallen. *Building Web Applications with UML*. Addison Wesley, 1999.
8. Craig Larman. *Applying UML and Patterns: An Introduction to Object-Oriented Analysis and Design*. Prentice Hall, 1998.
9. Sun Microsystems: JavaBeans 1.01 API Specification, http://java.sun.com/products/javabeans/glasgow. 2001.
10. Sun Microsystems : Applet Specification, http://java.sun.com/applets/. 2001.
11. Sun Microsystems : JavaTM Servlet 2.3 Specification, http://java.sun.com/products/servlet/. 2002.
12. Java 2 Platform, Enterprise Edition (J2EETM), http://java.sun.com/j2ee/docs.html.
13. Sultan Rehman R. Allen Wyke and Brad Leupen. *XML Programming*. Microsoft press, 2002.
14. W3C (World Wide Web Consortium), http://www.w3.org/XML/.
15. Simjava Library: Writing simulation using the library, http://www.dcs.ed.ac.uk/home/hase/simjava.

Distance Education Based on a Multimedia Mix Provided by a Virtual Organization

Karl Kurbel

VGU - Virtual Global University, School of Business Informatics
and European University Viadrina Frankfurt (Oder), Germany
kurbel@euv-frankfurt-o.de

Abstract. Providing multimedia-based courses over the Internet is a challenging task. Technological requirements are far more exacting than for simple HTML based courses as in traditional web-based teaching. Low-cost multimedia technologies, in particular technologies for video production and delivery over the Internet, have just become available. Established rules and recommendations how to use those technologies effectively are still missing. In this paper, different approaches to the production and delivery of multimedia-based courses are outlined and illustrated by examples. A specific focus is set on videos as the main instructional medium. The examples are taken from real courses that have been produced for an Internet-based study program leading to a master's degree in Business Informatics. This program is provided by a virtual organization. All facets of producing lecture videos require a significantly long phase of learning and getting acquainted with the technology. A learning curve could clearly be observed.

1   Introduction: Is Education Virtual?

The focus of this paper is virtual education and technologies used for that purpose. It is based on experiences from building a virtual study program which is briefly outlined in section 2 below.

The original use of the term virtual as it has developed in information systems research and practice referred to organizations as being virtual [Davidow, Malone 1992]: Organizations, or different organizational units from various organizations, network to form a new organization which is not a real one in the legal sense, yet it behaves like a real one.

Virtual universities seem to match this description to a certain extent. Some of them exist only as virtual organizations, without a legal framework that would establish them as a legal organizational body of its own. Typical examples are combines of universities, institutes or departments that loosely tie up to provide together a number of courses over the Internet [Granow 2001]. Another type of virtual universities are real organizations, yet considered "virtual" because their appearance to the outside world is based on the Internet. An example is the Jones International University (JIU)[1], a fully accredited university in the US. JIU is a real university but courses are taught online only.

---

[1] JIU: http://www.jonesinternational.edu.

Y.-C. Chen, L.-W. Chang, and C.-T. Hsu (Eds.): PCM 2002, LNCS 2532, pp. 968–975, 2002.

The third type of virtual universities are organizations which have features of both real and virtual organizations. An example is the Virtual Global University (VGU)[2]. VGU provides distance education over the Internet, carried by a network of partners, but on the other hand it exists as a private limited company in a legal framework as well.

Section 2 describes the background of the work reported here, an Internet-based master program provided by virtual organization. In section 3, the multimedia technologies used in that program are discussed and illustrated by means of examples. Section 4 covers production and delivery of video-based courses as the technologically most advanced form of instruction. Section 5 summarizes our experiences with multimedia technologies in virtual education.

2 Background of the Work

The work reported in this paper is based on experiences from planning and conducting a virtual master program in Business Informatics. This program was developed by the Virtual Global University (VGU), an organization founded by 17 professors of Business Informatics from Germany, Austria and Switzerland [Kurbel 2000]. It is offered worldwide, leading to the degree of an "International Master of Business Informatics" (MBI).

VGU is a private virtual organization. VGU would not have been able to award an officially recognized master's degree by itself. Instead a cooperation agreement with a "real" university was established. This partner university is the European University Viadrina (EUV) in Frankfurt (Oder), Germany.

While VGU provides expertise and teaching, EUV is responsible for ensuring that the academic and educational standards of the program are maintained at an appropriate level. Ordinances, rules, and regulations for virtual MBI students are equivalent to those for students of EUV's regular face-to-face programs. This cooperation ensures that the master's degree awarded is an official degree fully recognized by German law.

3 Multimedia Techniques Employed in the MBI Program

Many courses and programs in today's virtual education are still text and paper based. We will refer to those as "traditional" virtual courses and programs. In the United States, for example, a large number of virtual educational offers is available but the vast majority of those offers is traditional in this respect. In Europe, more advanced multimedia technologies for higher education have been investigated in research projects and prototypical courses over the past 10 years [e.g. Bodendorf, Grebner 1998]. Advanced tools for cooperative work are also being investigated [Kloeckner 2001].

For the master program underlying this paper, multimedia technologies above the text-based level were intended to play a major role in the instructional design. The

---

[2] VGU: http://www.vg-u.org.

technologies for the MBI courses were chosen depending on the type and on the content of a course. The following instruction modes are used.

3.1 Video Courses

Our first trials to approximate the look and feel of a real lecture in a real classroom were videos taken in a lecture hall and provided for viewing. With powerful video processing and encoding tools (like Media Studio Pro[3], Windows Media Encoder[4]) and easy-to-download video players (e.g. Windows Media Player[5], RealPlayer[6]) available today, video recordings were the primary choice as media type for MBI courses. Watching a lecture recorded in a real or simulated classroom comes close to listening to a real lecture. Slides, blackboard writings and other types of illustrations are recorded along with the speaker.

Video files are not downloaded completely before playing but transmitted in a streaming format. This is clearly an advantage since video files tend to be very large. However, even with a streaming format severe restrictions regarding the data transmission rate are in effect (see section 4). Therefore the size of a video window is normally kept small so that the file to be shown will need less space and the audio and video quality finally reaching the viewer is still acceptable.

The limited size of the window on the monitor's screen is a problem when both the person giving the lecture and the material used for illustration are recorded in one video. While a small window of, say, 9 x 6 cm, is sufficient to see (and hear) the speaker explaining things, it may be to small to allow the user to recognize what is written on the transparencies. For transparencies with large fonts the one-window approach may still be all right. However, when online computer screens are recorded in this way, nothing will be readable for the viewer any more.

3.2 Multimedia Courses Based on Video Plus Presentation Material

The aforementioned problem can be avoided if the person giving the lecture and the material used for illustration are presented separately. Production of this type of video is more complicated since now the two components need to be synchronized. The video showing the speaker is recorded by a digital camera. If the camera is not a digital one, the analogous recording has to be digitalized afterwards for further processing.

When computerized presentations are used, for example Powerpoint slides, a different technique for recording the presentation material can be employed. Since slides do not move like a person speaking does nor change continuously, they can be converted to GIF files. Tools to do so automatically are available today. Since GIF files are smaller than videos, less bandwidth is needed. In return the window size on the screen can be increased significantly.

---

[3] http://www.ulead.com/msp.
[4] http://www.microsoft.com/windows/windowsmedia.
[5] http://www.microsoft.com/windows/windowsmedia.
[6] http://www.real.com.

If a realtime program presentation, for example a demo of a CASE tool or an ERP system, is shown and discussed by the lecturer, a video containing the presentation material can be recorded by means of a screen recorder (e.g. ScreenCorder[7]).

Figure 1 shows a screendump of a video-based course from the MBI program where both the lecturer and the presentation material are recorded and played in separate windows.

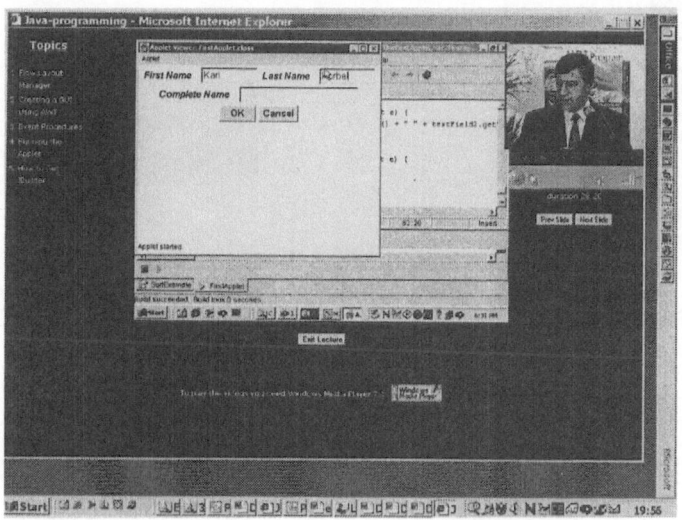

Fig. 1. Video with online screen recording[8]

3.3 Audio-Based Courses with Presentation Material

Video production is a non-trivial task requiring experience and plenty of time. Low transmission rates are hampering delivery of videos over the Internet. One way to bypass part of these problems is to use only an audio track instead of an audio-visual presentation of the speaker on the screen. Sound can be used nicely in combination with Powerpoint slides or other presentations to form something like a "narrated slide show". Like in a real classroom, the speaker explains the things illustrated on transparency or slide; however, he or she is not visible. This is clearly less "lively" than a video accompanying the presentation material but a lot easier to produce.

3.4 Audio-Based Courses with Presentation Material and Text

Just listening to an audio track may be tiring for the viewer. More than in a video-based course, there is some risk that the viewer may miss important points which are discussed by the lecturer but perhaps not stressed sufficiently. For this reason, audio-

---

[7] http://www.matchware.net/screencorder2/default.htm.
[8] Showing Prof. Dr. Karl Kurbel in the MBI course "Java Programming".

based courses can be enhanced by supplementing the lecturer's monologue with text passages transcribing his or her verbal explanations fully or partially. In figure 2, an example from an MBI course employing this technique is given.

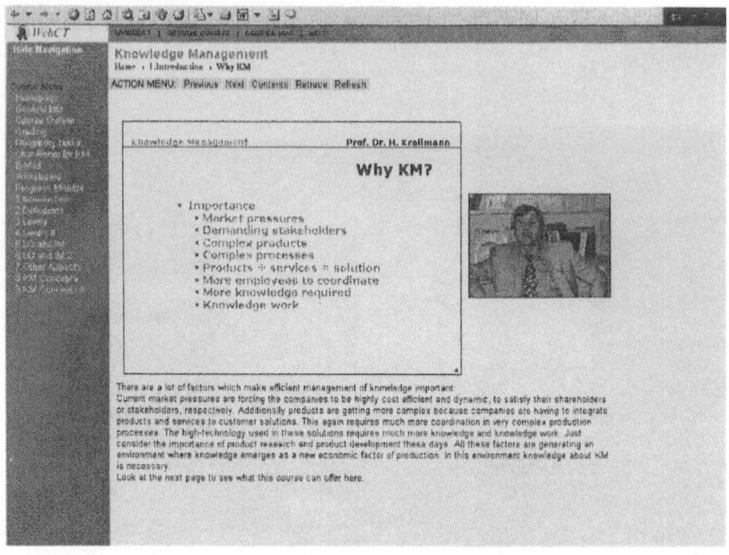

Fig. 2. Audio track, slides and text annotation[9]

3.5 Hypertext-Based Courses

This type of course follows the traditional text-based approach. Structured course material is used as in a conventional distance education program. However, all material is provided electronically and can be viewed with a browser. Hyperlinks connect text, graphics, and exercises in a meaningful way. Video clips and voice annotations may be included as well.

3.6 Textbook-Based Courses with Multimedia Techniques Incorporated

An increasing number of textbooks comprises not only written and printed text but also supportive features provided on the website of the author and/or the publisher [for example, Griffin, Ebert 2002; Laudon, Laudon 2002). Nowadays the support goes far beyond additionnal exercises or examples not given in the book. Some books have a complete learning environment in the Web, providing videos, audio clips, and interactive exercises.

---

[9] Showing Prof. Dr. Hermann Krallmann, Technical University of Berlin, Germany, in the MBI course "Knowledge Management".

Selected courses of the MBI program are based on web-supported textbooks, thus enriching the traditional text-based approach to virtual education with built-in multimedia features.

4   Producing Video-Based Courses for Delivery over the Internet

Since video-based courses are the technologically most advanced ones in VGU's multimedia mix for the MBI program, we will take a closer look at how to make lectures available on video for a global audience.

The fact that students can be distributed worldwide implies not only different time zones but also a variety of different qualities of Internet access. Some people have very fast access but others have to cope with slow dial-up connections.

As a consequence, unless everybody is served with the smallest common denominator (i.e. the least audio and video quality), different versions of the lecture videos have to be designed for different target groups. For VGU's video-based courses the following categories of users are considered.

4.1   Fast Internet Access

The best video and audio quality is obtained by viewers who have an Internet connection of at least 300 kbps (kilobit per second). This is the case with ADSL (asymmetric digital subscriber line) or with computers directly connected to a network by dedicated lines and a LAN (local area network); e.g. in large companies, universities, and the public administration sector.

Normally videos operate with 25 fps. However, through trial and error and during a long learning phase, we found that a frame rate of 12 fps (frames per second) is the best compromise between quality and bandwidth requirements, maintaining both clear focus and smoothness of the lecturer's movements. The screenshot of figure 1 above was taken from a video with these settings.

4.2   Fairly Fast Internet Access

Users with an Internet connection of above 100 kbps are served with a video version that provides still fairly good video quality; however, some mistakes from automatic compression may show. For example, when the lecturer moves fast, the quality of the video decreases. In the worst case (very fast movements), the video may even exhibit small gaps.

The quality of presentation material accompanying the video is not effected. Since mostly GIF files are used, the resolution can be kept at 240 x 180 pixels as in the previous version for 300 kbps.

4.3   Moderate Internet Access

This video version is for students who have an ISDN (integrated services digital network) connection to the Internet, i.e. a transmission rate of 64 kbps. The video quality is a little below the 100 kbps version but still on an acceptable level.

Sensitivity against fast changes of the pictures (e.g. moves of the lecturer) is the same as in the 100 kbps version.

Some reduction in size had to be put into effect regarding the window for presentation material. Powerpoint slides and other material is now displayed at a resolution of 176 x 132 pixels only.

4.4 Slow Internet Access

In order to serve persons with a modem dial-up connection, low-end videos with fewer frames per second, 8 fps, are produced. Although this is only one third of the frame rate of normal Internet videos, the visual appearance is still reasonable if no rapid changes of the pictures occur. Since a lecturer normally stands or sits at a desk but does not jump around when he or she is being recorded, the effect of reducing the frame rate is merely that movements appear slowed down or with delay. The modem speed expected for this version is 56 kbps.

4.5 Very Slow Internet Access

It may be questioned if multimedia-based courses make sense for students who can access the Internet only through a 34 kbps modem -- and how long such connections will survive. However, there are major parts of the world where this type of Internet connection will continue to exist (or yet come into existence).

In our experiments we found the solution to be similar to the variant described in section 3.3 (audio-based courses with presentation material).

By giving up the video component in favor of an audio track we achieved a version with very good quality of sound and presentation material. Although the user is expected to have at least 28 kbps available, this type of course runs even with a transmission rate of 16 kbps.

5 Experiences and Conclusions

Since multimedia technologies at low cost or even for free have just recently become available, reliable experiences and recommendations how to use them are still lacking. Therefore the settings chosen for the above video versions had to be largely gained from trial and error. The same is true for specific tools employed. For example, our video versions are being compressed with the Microsoft Media Video V8 codec. As an alternative, the MPEG-4 V3 codec might be considered. The quality achieved with either codec appeared to be the same at first sight. However, after some trials we found specific parameter settings that gave the Microsoft Media Video V8 codec a clear advantage over MPEG-4.

All facets of producing lecture videos require a significantly long phase of learning and getting acquainted with the technology. A learning curve could clearly be observed. In the beginning of our efforts, the time to produce a sequence of video and audio material for a 90-minute lecture took about one week elapsed time after the video had been recorded, keeping two persons completely engaged. After one year of production and hands-on experience with videos, this time has decreased to two days (still keeping two people occupied).

The multimedia versions outlined above were tested and tried from locations all over the world. The ADSL version basically ran without problems in Germany. It was possible to view the ISDN version in locations in the Middle East (Dubai) and in India, for example. Slow access versions were available all over the world. The author saw the slow-access version (56 kbps) in a normal home in a mid-size town of Central India and was able to listen to the low-end version (28 kpbs), in good audio quality, in a small village of the same area. Nevertheless, coping with small bandwidths and keeping quality at an acceptable level at the same time is a matter of trade-offs.

References

1. Bodendorf, F., Grebner, R., Towards Virtual Universities – ATM-Based Teleteaching in Germany, in: Forcht, K. (Ed.), Information Systems Beyond 2000 – 1998 IACIS Refereed Proceedings, Cancun, Mexico 1998, pp. 67-74.
2. Cadenhead, R., Sams' Teach Yourself Java 2 in 24 Hours, 2nd Edition, Sams Publishing 2000.
3. Davidow, W.H., Malone, M.S., The Virtual Corporation - Structuring and Revitalizing the Corporation for the 21st Century, Harper Colling 1992.
4. Granow, R., Complete Online-Programmes of Study by a Confederation of Campus Universities: Virtual University of Applied Sciences, in: Online Educa Berlin - 7th International Conference on Technology Supported Learning & Training, Book of Abstracts; ICEF Berlin 2001, pp. 81-83.
5. Griffin, R.W., Ebert, R.J., Business, Sixth Edition, Prentice Hall 2002.
6. Kloeckner, K., Preparing the Next Generation of Learning: Enhancing Learning Opportunities by WEB Based Cooperation, in: Proceedings of the Eden 10th Anniversary Conference, Learning Without Limits - Developing the Next Generation of Education; Stockholm, Sweden, 2001.
7. Kurbel, K., A Completely Virtual Distance Education Program Based on the Internet - Case and Agenda of the International MBI Program, in: Hansen, H. R. et al. (Eds.), Proceedings of the 8th European Conference on Information Systems - ECIS 2000, A Cyber-space Odyssey, Vol. 2, Vienna, Austria, pp. 1363-1367.
8. Laudon, K. C., Laudon, J. P., Management Information Systems – Managing the Digital Firm, Seventh Edition, Prentice Hall, 2002.
9. Porter, L.R., Creating the Virtual Classroom - Distance Learning with the Internet, John Wiley & Sons, 1997.

Media-on-Demand for Agent-Based Collaborative Tutoring Systems on the Web

Elvis Wai Chung Leung and Qing Li

City University of Hong Kong {iteleung, itqli}@cityu.edu.hk

Abstract. Currently, guiding students to reach the learning goals through me-dia-on-demand approach in a collaborative learning environment is quite primi-tive in most cyber-courseware systems on the Internet. In particular, these sys-tems do not have powerful multimedia retrieval features for responding student enquiries based on individual student's background and interests. In this paper, we present the architecture and facilities of providing *M*edia-on-demand for an *A*gent-based *T*utoring *s*ystem (MATs). The facilities and capabilities of user profiles, schema, and SMIL are incorporated and utilized by MATs so as to provide a better support to the interactive learning environment in which stu-dent-specific, content-based learning styles can be adequately entertained. A prototype system of MATs manifesting these algorithms has been built in Java, SMIL, using IE and RealOne on the PC platform.

1 Introduction

With the ability to connect people and information around the world, the Internet is already having a significant impact on the traditional education. In the past few years, many education providers have launched a number of online courses on the Web [8,9,10]. Initially many students enrolled in such online courses, however, the drop out rate seems to be quite high. One of the reasons is that these on-line courses do not have an effective multimedia-based tutoring system to help students who are in the learning process and encounter trouble to understand the subjects and/or in problem solving.

1.1 Paper Objective and Organization

To provide an effective multimedia-based tutorship based on user profiles, dynamic generation of case-based solution is one of the possible solutions, which can tailor to students' needs accurately at anytime anywhere. In this paper, we advocate an ap-proach of developing *M*edia-on-demand for an *A*gent-based *T*utoring *s*ystem (MATs). In particular, we present the detailed architecture and algorithms for media-on-demand in eLearning.

Through the designed architecture and algorithms for multimedia-based tutoring system, we aim to address the following main topics in this paper: How to effectively serve individual student's needs in providing multimedia-on-demand for a particular

Y.-C. Chen, L.-W. Chang, and C.-T. Hsu (Eds.): PCM 2002, LNCS 2532, pp. 976-984, 2002.

topic? In fact, the main contribution of this paper is not so much on the performance efficiency side, but to bring out a feasible approach in an innovative way.

The rest of this paper is organized as follows. The review on related work of representative tutoring systems is given in section 2. The agent-based architectural framework for multimedia-based tutoring system is detailed in sections 3. A prototype system is described in section 4. The final section concludes this paper and makes suggestions for further research.

2 Related Work

In this section, we briefly review some representative intelligent tutoring systems on the e-learning domain [14,16].

Andes [11] is a collaborative project started since 1995 between the University of Pittsburgh and the US Naval Academy. It has a modular architecture, and is implemented in Allegro Common Lisp and MS Visual C++. Before execution, a problem author creates both graphical description of the problem and the corresponding coded problem definition. The problem solver uses this definition to automatically generate a model of the problem solution graph. Then an Action Interpreter and a Help System refer to the student model to make decisions about what kind of feedback and help to give the student.

LANCA [15] adopts an intelligent agent's approach to distance learning in a distributed environment. It uses a constructive approach instead of user profiles to assist students in difficulty. Also, it assumes that all the questions and solutions related to the problems and given by a learner should be applicable to other learners, building a common and useful databank. To realize this approach, it uses intelligent agents able to detect the difficulties of the learner and to delegate specific help to be provided.

DT Tutor [12] uses decision-theoretic methods for coached problem solving to select tutorial actions that are optimal given the tutor's beliefs and objectives. It employs a model of learning to predict the possible outcomes of each action, weighs the utility of each outcome by the tutor's belief that it will occur, and select the action with the highest expected utility. GeNIe is an experimental project from the University of Pittsburgh, and it uses SMILE and C++ for building the prototype system. However, it does not yet have suitable user interface, and so has not been evaluated with human students.

Table 1. A comparison between MATs and other systems

Adopted Approach	LANCA	Andes	DT Tutor	MATs
Architecture	Agent-Based	Modular	Decision-theoretic	Web-based, Agent-based
To Model of Student Knowledge/ Problem/Question	Constrictive Approach	Bayesian network	Dynamic belief networks	User profiles, Schema
Represent Suggested Solution Method (Concepts)	Adaptive	Dynamic	Dynamic	Dynamic
Multimedia-on-demand	Static	Static	Static	Dynamic

A comparison between MATs and the above-mentioned systems is shown in Table 1. Compared with the other systems, MATs takes a step forward to providing multi-media-based solutions dynamically.

Purposely, MATs takes the advantage of web technology to place the operation on the Internet. Java (JSP and Servlet) has been used in the middle-tier, while XML and SMIL are used for delivering and presenting the solutions.

3   MATs Architecture and Components

For developing an effective Web-based tutoring system, we need to come up with a question-centered and cooperative architecture to encourage student's learning on the Internet. The concept of collaborative learning is one such possible solution applicable to our system. More specifically, collaborative learning makes use of each member's contribution (such as personal experience, information, and skills) for improving the learning with peers [17]. The most important benefit of collaborative learning is that it creates a learning community which is embodied by *learner networks* and *relationships* for their life-long learning [18].

The overall architecture for MATs is illustrated in Figure 1. As shown in Figure 1, the agent-based architecture for MATs is a collaborative environment that includes *Tutor Agent, Interface Agent, User Profile,* and *Knowledge Domain* [2,4].

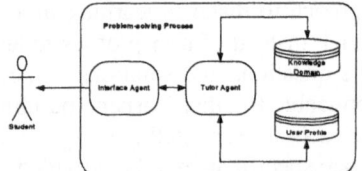

Fig. 1. Agent-based architecture for MATs   **Fig. 2.** 4-state processing of the Interface Agent

3.1   MATs Components

Interface Agent: Its main function is to link students and the Tutor Agent for coached problem solving. It has four states as shown in Figure 2. Normally, the Interface Agent is on the Listening State. When a student makes a request to the Interface Agent for problem solving, the state will be changed to the Processing State for handing the student's input event. Then, it will pass the question to the Tutor Agent, and the Processing State will be changed to Waiting State. Once the Interface Agent receives the return from the Tutor Agent, it will start to present the solution. Then the Processing State will be revisited and the Interface Agent starts to take over the system resources to present the solution for playing the multimedia through SMIL. After the student reads through the solution, MATs will arrive at the Termination State so as to release the hold-up resources and return to the Listening State again.

Tutor Agent: This is the heart of the MATs mechanism. Upon receiving a request from the Interface Agent, the Tutor Agent (TA) connects to the Knowledge Domain and User Profile databases (cf. Figure 1) for providing a solution. More specifically, the TA will search the history to study the peers' contributions related to the given question first. Then the related information (if any) will be merged with the suggested course notes/lessons and sent to the student. Finally, the question and suggested solution will be saved as part of the Knowledge Domain for future use.

User Profile: It is the primary storage for all student-specific information such as study history, personal information, and study status. It provides the relevant information to the Tutor Agent for refining the question and then determining the related concepts for the question. Normally, the user profile will provide the latest student's information on demand.

Knowledge Domain: It is the primary repository for all course notes, peers' contributions, and multimedia lessons. The relevant information will be extracted from the Knowledge Domain in providing solutions for the questions. The retrieval operation will be based on the index server to locate the expected multimedia lessons/course notes for a given question.

4 eLearning Database Application Showcase

In this section, a *Conceptual Model* (CM) for dynamic fetch of multimedia eLearning lessons (on the Internet) is introduced. We also illustrate the structure used in CM that leverages the various mechanisms of the framework's programming model, so as to produce maintainable applications that can be efficiently developed.

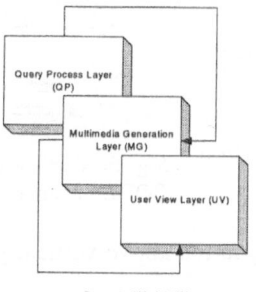

Fig. 3. Conceptual Model

As shown in Figure 3, there are three layers contained in CM, including *Query Process* (QP), *Multimedia Generation* (MG) and *User View* (UV). All layers have its own functions that can handle different tasks and constitute its value to the model. With comparison of delivering multimedia lessons to students, UV should be more static than QP and MG in normal case. Generally, UV is depending on the student's user profile to determine the presentation layout as a frame for multimedia delivery [13]. In contrary, QP and MG are based on every different request to generate the required results. In order to facilitate our discussion, we introduce the following scenario for illustration of how CM works.

Scenario: Assuming an undergraduate student, for his study in a Web design course, needs to know how many relevant homepage design videos (topics) about Flash. As a result of a valid query evaluation process, there are three possible results in delivering multimedia eLearning videos: „Nothing", „Only one video" or „More than one video". Based on this scenario we shall focus on the result set of „More than one video" for our discussions, since the techniques for „Nothing" and „Only one video" are simpler to that of „More than one video".

Based on the above scenario, the detailed processes of each layer are discussed in the following subsections.

4.1 Query Process (QP) Layer

To start the process, QP will collect the HTTP request from a student who wants to retrieve some relevant videos. QP is based on vertical partitioning technique [3] and adopts an indexing search to solve the problems happening in the traditional systems, namely, lack of flexibility resulted from the pre-set model and time-consuming caused by sequential search. As an effective way of using QP, a vertically partitioned OODB schema for eLearning videos is introduced and employed to facilitate efficient search. In this schema, we assume that there are three levels for our search including *Course, Topic, and Section*. Based on the scenario, the parameters for *Course, Topic* and *Section* are „Web design", „Home page design" and „Flash", respectively. As shown in figure 4, an eLearning video course object has a number of topics. In turn a topic object has a number of sections.

An example Vertically Partitioned eLearning Video OODB Schema is in Figure 5.

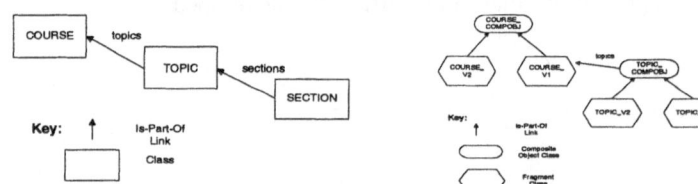

Fig. 4. Example eLearning video OODB Schema.

Fig. 5. Vertically partitioned eLearning Video OODB Schema.

A specification corresponding to the above vertically partitioned eLearning Video OODB Schema is given below:

```
Class COURSE_COMPOBJ {              Class TOPIC_COMPOBJ {               Class SECTION_COMPOBJ {
    Course_v1 ref COURSE_V1;            Topic_v1 ref TOPIC_V1;              Section_v1 ref SECTION_V1;
    Course_v2 ref COURSE_V2;}           topic_v2 ref TOPIC_V2;}             section_v2 ref SECTION_V2; }

Class COURSE_V1 {                   Class TOPIC_V1 {                    Class SECTION_V1 {
    Course_id   char[8];               Topic_id   char[8];                 Section_id   char[8];
    Topics                             Sections                            section_title char[40];}
      Set of   TOPIC_COMPOBJ;}            set of SECTION_COMPOBJ;}

Class COURSE_V2 {                   Class TOPIC_V2 {                    Class SECTION_V2 {
    Course_title   char[40];           Topic_title   char[40];             Description char[256];
    Course_date    date;               prod_date     date;                 duration    char[6],
    Producer       char[20];}          abstract      char[256];            keyword     char[200],
                                       biography     char[256];}           frames      set of FRAME;}
```

Let the class *COURSE* be vertically partitioned into 2 fragments: *COURSE_V1* and *COURSE_V2*, with *COURSE_COMPOBJ*, the composite object to contain the 2 object IDs of the fragments. Fragment *COURSE_V1* contains the instance variables *course_id* and *topics*; fragment *COURSE_V2* contains the instance variables *course_title, course_date* and *producer*. As the OQL query only accesses instance variables in fragment *COURSE_V1*, in query processing, only fragment *COURSE_V1* and composite object *COURSE_COMPOBJ* are being accessed. Similar vertical class partitioning strategy is applied for the classes *TOPIC* and *SECTION*.

The usefulness of vertical partitioning is of two folds: (a) from performance point of view - it reduces irrelevant data accesses by grouping frequently accessed instance variables together to form vertical fragments, and (b) from design/semantic point of view - a vertical fragment is a component object of a more complex object. Finally, QP is responsible for finding out the relevant eLearning videos based on the above schema. Then the result will be handed over to MG (cf. next section) for multimedia delivery.

4.2 Multimedia Generation (MG) Layer

The main functions of this layer are to identify what is the suitable streaming technique to deliver the eLearning video and how to enhance the interactive learning on the Web [1,5]. For our purpose, two streaming techniques are taken into consideration [6,7]. The first technique, HTTP Streaming, is a type of progressive download which HTTP servers are used to deliver the files. Using HTTP streaming, the users may watch when the files are downloading. Because the files need to be downloaded to the users' computer, this is often well suited for short movies that are in small file size.

The second technique, True Streaming, works by first compressing digital media that is well suited for live events or long movies. By using true streaming, there is no need to download the files to the user's computer as the compressed file will be divided into small packets by IP on a streaming media server instead. It does not consume disk space as it is discarded when one part of the playing file finishes streaming. Thus, True Streaming is selected in our design and development. Advantages include the following:
1) the media copyrights are not violated if the files are not placed on the user's hard disk;
2) it can prevent transfer delay;
3) it can manage real-time streaming; and
4) it supports the two-way interactions needed to control media streams, thus, using True streaming is more feasible and cost effectiveness.

Meanwhile, the delivery mode of streaming media also varies. The three most common delivery modes are Live Broadcast, Unicasting, and Multicasting. Broadcasting streaming occurs when the same data source is simultaneously streamed to all users in a network. Unlike broadcasting streaming, the connection between the client and the server in Unicasting is one-to-one. The advantage is that student can control the eLearning video by play, stop, pause, forward and backward. However, the limitation is that the separate media streams for each client consumes a lot of network bandwidth. The last one, Multicasting delivers streams simultaneously one-to-many clients. As a *connectionless* data transmission method, the clients do not need to connect to the server when receiving the streams, and thus, reduces the load placed on the server. In order to get the full control of playing the eLearning video by the student, Unicasting has been selected for MG layer.

In order to enhance the interactive learning on the Web, we adopt Synchronized Multimedia Integration Language (SMIL) for our multimedia delivery. SMIL is suitable for Unicasting streaming techniques. Through SMIL, multimedia data can be not only played on the Internet, but also running in a synchronized manner. For MG's work, it is based on the result set that comes from QP to generate a SMIL file for distribution of eLearning videos. A portion of the SMIL file is given in Figure 6.

Moreover, the Prefetch feature allows to have many different videos pre-set, and then displayed one by one. The waiting time can thus be reduced, and it makes learning to become more efficient. Last but not least, SMIL allows the videos and lecture notes displayed simultaneously on the same screen, either in the same window or under sub-windows. This greatly facilitates students' learning and stimulates their interests.

Fig. 6. SMIL file

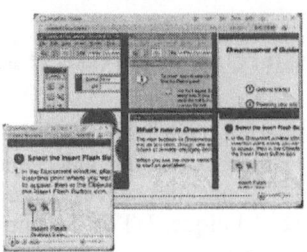

Fig. 7. Sample Screen Shot of the Prototype

4.3 User View (UV) Layer

The last layer, User View, is to manage the possible different scenarios generated by MG. There are two types of player for our consideration. First, the user does not need to pre-install video player. Once the user needs to play a video, the built-in player that is often developed by Java will be transferred from the server to user's browser for playing video. However, the high bandwidth usage is inevitable. Second, the video player is requested to be installed in advance before playing a video. Considering the video playing performance and limited bandwidth usage, we require students to install video player in advance.

We have developed a prototype based on RealOne as the video player and use it to display the retrieved files (tutoring video fragments) through SMIL. As shown in Figure 7, there are totally six results displayed in six subwindows, which actually facilitates and visualizes the student's thinking and selection while the actual screen is displayed for selection. The student can easily pick the one he likes most, and then double click to play the video in a new window (cf. Figure 7).

5 Conclusion and Future Work

In this paper, we have presented an agent-based architecture and a set of facilities that form the core of the MATs mechanism in our e-Learning system on the Web. Among the many desirable features offered by MATs, the following advantages are worth particular mentioning:

- **Multimedia-on-demand.** Based on our proposed architecture and facilities, student can get the multimedia tutoring on demand for their own situation at anytime anywhere. In addition, the previous learning topics/course are consulted for a given question, thus, the learning performance can be enhanced.

- **Active Learning.** The suggested solution is generated based on individual student's question and expectation, which supports the ideas of personalization and interactive learning [1] effectively. The suggested multimedia is transparent to the student for their choices. It is easy for a student to understand what kinds of lessons are suitable for them.

- **Connection-less Approach.** We note that our MATs is a suitable platform for advocating a connection-less approach for the e-Learning environment. In particular, it can reduce the demand on the server support by avoiding a large number of connections with in a particular period.

As an immediate next step of our research, we plan to conduct empirical studies with benchmark queries upon our experimental MATs prototype system.

References

[1]   Jonassen, D.H., Supporting Communities of Learners with Technology: A Vision for Integrating Technology with Learning in Schools. *Educational Technology*, 35(2). 60-63, 1995

[2]   Leung E., and Li Q., Agent-Based Approach to e-Learning: An Architectural Framework, in Kim, W., Ling, T.W., Lee, Y.J. and Park, S.S., *The Human Society and the Internet*, LNCS 2105, pp.341-353, 2001.

[3]   Karlapalem, K. and Li, Q., A Framework for Class Partitioning in Object-Oriented Databases, *Journal of Distributed and Parallel Databases,* 8, 317-350 2000.

[4]   Riley, G., *CLIPS, A Tool for Building Expert Systems.*
      http://www.ghg.net/clips/CLIPS.html.

[5]   Lesser, V. R., *Cooperative Multiagent Systems: A Personal View of the State of the Art,* IEEE Transactions on Knowledge and Data Engineering, vol. 11, no.11, Jan –Feb 1999

[6]   Lawton, George, Industry Trends: Video Streams into the Main Stream. *Computer.* Vol. 33 No.7, 2000

[7]   Alessi H. Peter, *E-Video Producing Internet Video as BroadBand Technologies Converge,* 2000

[8]   Pimentel M. G.C. and Abowd G.D., Ishiguro Y., Linking by Interacting: a Paradigm for Authoring Hypertext, *Proceedings of ACM Hypertext*, May 2000

[9]   Stern M., Steinberg J., Lee H. I., Padhye J. and Kurose J.F., MANIC: Multimedia Asynchronous Networked Individualized Courseware, *Proceedings of Educational Multimedia and Hypermedia*, 1997

[10] Mukhopadhyay S., Smith B., Passive Capture and Structuring of Lectures, *Proceedings of ACM Multimedia*, October 1999.

[11] Gertner A. S. and VanLehn K., Andes: A Coached Problem Solving Environment for Physics in Gauthier G., Frasson C. and VanLehn K., *Intelligent Tutoring Systems*, pp. 133-142, 2000

[12] Murray R. C.and VanLehn J., DT Tutor: A Decision-Theoretic, Dynamic Approach for Optimal Selection of Tutorial Acitons, in Gauthier G., Frasson C. and VanLehn K., *Intelligent Tutoring Systems*, pp. 153-162, 2000

[13] Bradley K., Rafter R. and Smyth B., Case-Based User Profiling for Content Personalisation, in Brusilovsky P., Stock O. and Strapparava C., *Adaptive Hypermedia and Adaptive Web-Based Systems*, pp.63-72, 2000

[14] Trella M., Conejo R. and Guzman E., A Web-Based Socratic Tutor for Trees Recognition, in Brusilovsky P., Stock O. and Strapparava C., *Adaptive Hypermedia and Adaptive Web-Based Systems*, pp.239-249, 2000

[15] Frasson C., Martin L., Gouarderes G. and Aimeur E., LANCA: A Distance Learning Architecture Based on Networked Cognitive Agents, in Goettl B., Halff H., Redfield C., Valerie R. and Shute V., *Intelligent Tutoring Systems*, 594-603, 1998

[16] Sanrach C. and Grandbastien M., ECSAIWeb: A Web-Based Authoring System to Create Adaptive Learning Systems, in Brusilovsky P., Stock O. and Strapparava C., *Adaptive Hypermedia and Adaptive Web-Based Systems*, pp.214-226, 2000

[17] *The Instructional Design for the New Media (IDNM) project.*
http://www.rcc.ryerson.ca/learnontario/idnm/main page/about.htm

[18] Johnson, D.W. and Johnson, R.T. *Cooperative learning: where we have been, where we are going. Cooperative Learning and College Teaching.* Vol 3, No.2, Winter, 1993.

Design a Web-Based Assessment Tool with Multiple Presentation Styles for Language Training

Natalius Huang and Herng-Yow Chen

Department of Computer Science and Information Engineering
National Chi Nan University, Puli, Nantou, Taiwan 545, R.O.C.
natalius@mcll.csie.ncnu.edu.tw, hychen@csie.ncnu.edu.tw,

Abstract. This paper presents the design framework of the proposed web-based assessment tool with multiple presentation styles to meet different goals particularly in language learning. In contrast to most existing assessment systems, we address the learning objects' reusability issues in terms of multimedia presentations. To testify the separation of learning object's presentation from its content, a prototype of assessment tool is elaborately designed to show various presentation features required for different perspectives of language learning: listening, speaking, reading, and writing. The result of this study has also been incorporated into the developed multimedia Chinese tutoring system (http://chinese.csie.ncnu.edu.tw), which is now used to assist overseas students of National Chi Nan University in Taiwan to learn Chinese via World Wide Web.

1 Introduction

Web-based multimedia learning systems have been developed rapidly because of multimedia technologies. A lot of efforts have been focused on distance education for the past few years [1], [2], [3]. Many instructors have used a learning system to put their material into Internet. In order to support their material, the assessment tool is quite necessary. It helps learners to simulate how many portions they have understood. The exercise stored in assessment system must be related with instructors' material to give the effectiveness in learning process.

Multibook [4], [5], [6] aimed to offer different lessons for different users based on reusability aspects of interactive multimedia content and automatic creation of exercises in adaptive hypermedia learning systems. The exercise was represented in a static form. It didn't support different presentation styles. The assessment tool [7] didn't provide multimedia features which can support various contents.

The kind of exercises and the presentation style of each exercise are various types. In other words, each exercise may be represented in different presentation styles. Each presentation style may emphasize different learning goals. Learning goals include the capabilities of listening, reading, speaking and vocabulary spelling. For example, an exercise without playing audio emphasizes the ability of learners' reading. Consequently, the assessment tool must provide different presentation styles for instructors and learners to adapt what kind of learning goals they want to achieve.

Y.-C. Chen, L.-W. Chang, and C.-T. Hsu (Eds.): PCM 2002, LNCS 2532, pp. 985-992, 2002.
© Springer-Verlag Berlin Heidelberg 2002

In order to meet different presentation styles, several aspects must be considered. First, the type of presentation style must be grasped such as doing a section of exercise with time constrained presentation style. This type may be used to evaluate the total time which is very useful for learners to know how long they have wasted to do the exercise. Listening exercises with two types of presentation styles are quite necessary to meet different learning goals. Second, the template of each exercise must be considered. The same template can be used to create another exercises with the same characteristics. The instructors may represent their exercise with red background color to indicate how important this exercise is. Third, user interaction may be involved in presentation. Speaking will need the learners' participation. How to interact with our system is an important thing to be considered. Vocabulary spelling by using typing method also needs learners' interaction.

The existing of multimedia exercise system as an assessment tool requires a transcript as content of resource. A lot of instructors use a transcript to compose and generate multimedia exercise. The transcript that includes multimedia objects may consist of the aggregation of questions to perform a basis of exercise. Each question has many multimedia objects to provide descriptive information about how the exercise should be answered. A suite of selection for each question is required to build a collection of answer. It utilizes many multimedia objects. The evaluative of exercise learning is determined through the corresponding selection answered by students.

This paper addresses a design of assessment tool which provides different presentation style to meet different learning goals. The issue discussed in this paper is illustrated in WSML (Web-based Synchronized Multimedia Lecture) [8] system. It is a distance lecture system that can synchronize the presentation of multimedia lectures, HTML-based Web pages and the HTML navigation events. Now, WSML is being used in our university to support web-based multimedia learning with supporting assessment tool.

The paper is structured as follows: In Section 2, we explain the WSML system. We describe the system architecture in section 3. Content Delivery is given in section 4. The system implementation is described in section 5. Finally, future work and conclusion are given in section 6.

2 WSML System

The Web-based Synchronized Multimedia Lecture system integrates audiovisual lectures, HTML slides, and navigation events to provide synchronous presentations. In our environment, teachers use computers to instruct and this system records the oral guidance along with several navigation events. The navigation events are guided media to assist teachers. These events, such as pen strokes, highlight, dynamic annotation, virtual pointer (cursor), and scrolling, are presented in client side by using state-of-the-art dynamic HTML techniques.

Figure 1 shows the framework of the WSML system. The WSML Recorder records the temporal information of AV lecture and HTML slides with navigation events. The

WSML Event Server receives, deposits, and dispatches those events to clients. The WSML Browser is responsible for synchronous presentation.

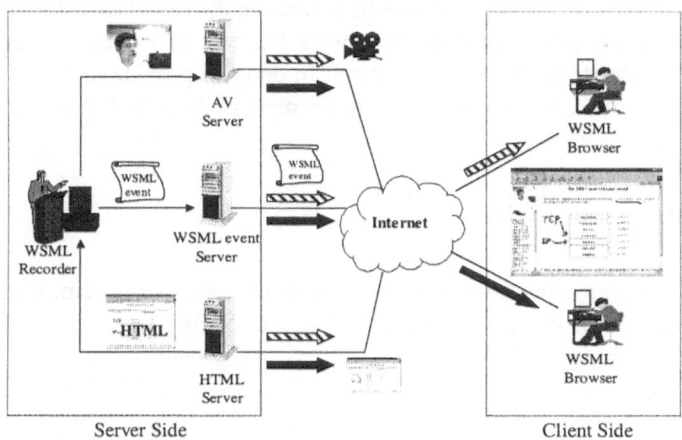

Fig. 1. Framework of WSML System

Navigation events are triggered dynamically to enrich multimedia presentation on web. During audio/video playback, navigation events will be presented at appropriate time and spatial positions. Figure 2 shows the synchronous presentation in the WSML Browser.

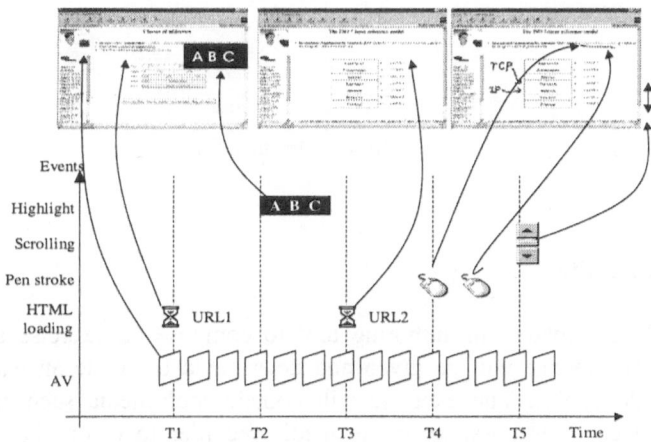

Fig. 2. An Example of Navigation Events

The AV and HTML URL1 are loaded respectively at T1. The AV player then starts playing the AV lecture. And the HTML page is rendered by the embedded HTML browser at the same time. Then, a highlight event over some important words is invoked at T2. At T3, URL2 of a renewed HTML is loaded. At T4, a sequence of pen stroke events is driven to show an ink stroke. At T5, a scrolling offset event is triggered to show the content which is out of screen. These kinds of navigation events provide dynamic guidance rather than static web pages.

After learning multimedia synchronous presentation, the assessment tool is required to compose exercises. Doing an exercise allows learners to examine whether learners have already understood the material or not. In order to provide different presentation style of each exercise, we address a system framework described in the next section.

3 System Framework

Figure 3 shows the system framework of multimedia exercise system. It contains three blocks that have some characteristics. It is described as follows:

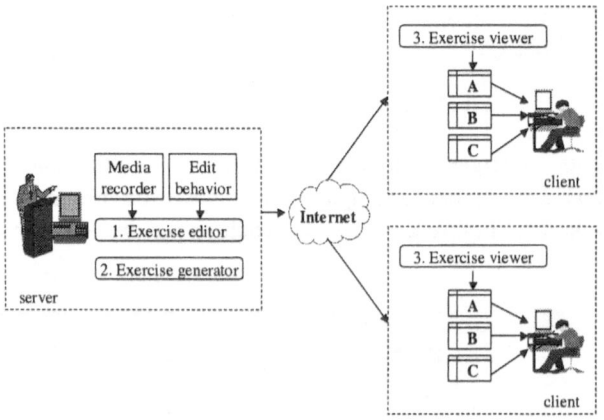

Fig. 3. System Architecture

3.1 Exercise Editor

Exercise editor provides an authoring tool to compose an exercise and templates. Many type of exercise will be given and determined to create an exercise such as single/multiple choice. The exercise will contain multimedia such as text, image, audio and video. It is possible to use media recorder to record instructors' voice. Audio file recorded during composing an exercise may not be played back during presentation. It may display the transcript of instructors' voice to give a different presentation. During composing an exercise, edit behavior is a key important. It can tell the learners how the importance of exercise is. Instructors may use red background-color to indicate it. The templates are created in the exercise editor to meet that different content may use the same template.

3.2 Exercise Generator

After using exercise editor to compose exercises and templates, the system will generate an exercise-learning object. It contains a composite multimedia data that may consist of multiple questions of each exercise and multiple selections of each question. Different kinds of presentation styles that may be used are also indicated. It meets instructors' need to define what more suitable learning goals in a specific exercise are. The exercise generator will backup instructors' exercise as an exercise -learning object.

3.3 Exercise Viewer

The exercise may display in different presentation style or multi-view presentation. Each learner may choose different presentation styles to meet his requirements. Learner may consider that his ability of listening is not good. For this reason, a listening presentation style is suitable for him. With the exercise-learning object, another learner supposes that his ability of reading is not fast enough. He may choose the reading presentation style to get a better learning process.

4   Content Delivery

In this section, we describe the typical scenario of how the content is delivered from server to client side. Figure 4 shows that the content delivery includes several components level to be discussed briefly in the following part illustrated.

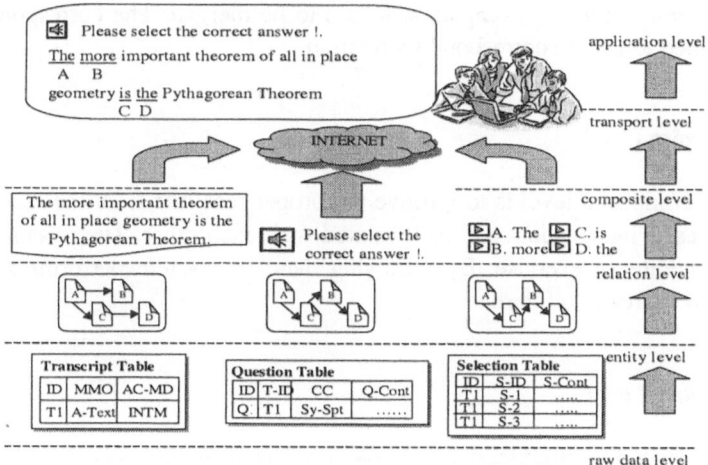

Fig. 4. The Process of Content Delivery

4.1 Raw Data Level

The aggregation of multimedia exercise can be viewed as a collection of one or more multimedia objects stored in the server. It represents the lowest level of granularity of multimedia exercise resources. The server requires a large of physical data size to keep the associated resources. In this level, the resource management is required to maintain the whole resources.

4.2 Entity Level

To provide descriptive information for each exercise, the resource is defined through entity level. An entity is the database representation for a particular object in the real world, generally represented as the "table" in the database environment. The exercise combines the transcript, question and selection table to indicate a particular exercise. The element of each table has a unique ID to identify the resource. In the transcript table, we could retrieve the element of first transcript which has an atomic multimedia object (text). In order to find out the transcript's question, we require a transcript's identifier as an index. With the question's identifier, we get the element of appropriate selections from the selection table.

4.3 Relation Level

Although we know the abstract of exercise, the content of each component isn't fully accessible. In this level, we reference the content of each resource through relation model. The relation is linked via the combination of one or more table in database. The relation may contain a complex structure to be merged. The corresponding queries are defined to get the corresponding relation.

4.4 Composite Level

The goal of composite level is to retrieve the proper resource from the relation level. Each resource is independent and isn't related with each other. The resource is composed to generate an exercise. By retrieving data, the system performs a media to deliver this resource into Internet.

4.5 Transport Level

With the advanced of multimedia technologies, the resource may be streamed into Internet such as audio. Our system uses Real Streaming technologies to achieve the desired result. In this level, the data integration must be established intact through Internet.

4.6 Application Level

The students have a privilege to utilize the exercise given by authors in the application level. The exercise material will be presented exactly as the authors compose the material. The system tracks the evaluation of student's result. It indicates a convenient learning for students who want to review the exercise material.

5 Implementation

Our implementation is described in Figure 5. During composing an exercise, instructors create a new template. This template depicts what the form of exercise is. The creating template will be used later if instructors need to compose another exercise with the same model. After composing a template, the multimedia content of exercise is required. The aggregation of multimedia content will form an exercise-learning object. The exercise-learning object can be described as a black box. If we open it, we could represent multiple presentation styles with the same multimedia content. The right side of figure 5 presents different presentation styles with different learning goals. In the first presentation, learning reading is achieved. The transcript and its question will be displayed. Listening process is represented in the second presentation style. The exercise is presented by playing transcripts' audio. Learners can answer the question after transcript's audio is played back. The last presentation style will help learners to fill up the vocabulary in empty rectangles. After listening transcripts' audio, the ability of learners' vocabulary spelling is tested. Through our implementation, we know that different presentation styles will determine different learning goals. There are a lot of exercises in our system.

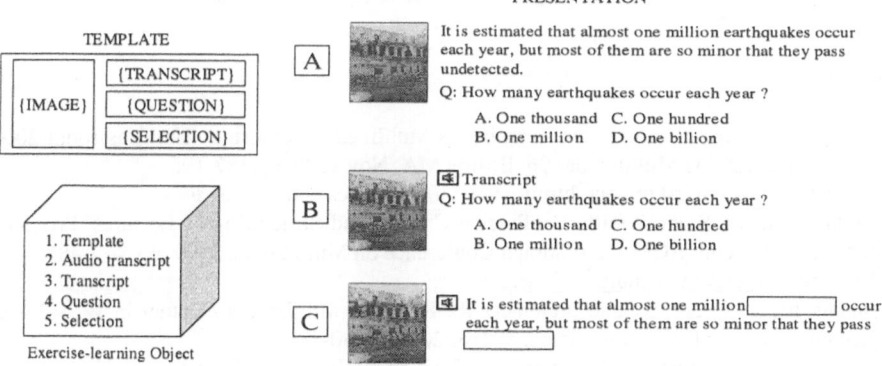

Fig. 5. Exercise-Learning Object with Different Presentation Styles

The students can base on the result (see in figure 6) to predict their average level and degree of understanding. From the instructional perspective, the learning tendency can be found by taking statistics from all of the students that have a learning personal history. From this point of view, the collection of a large amount of students' information is very important to deliver appropriate exercise materials to learners.

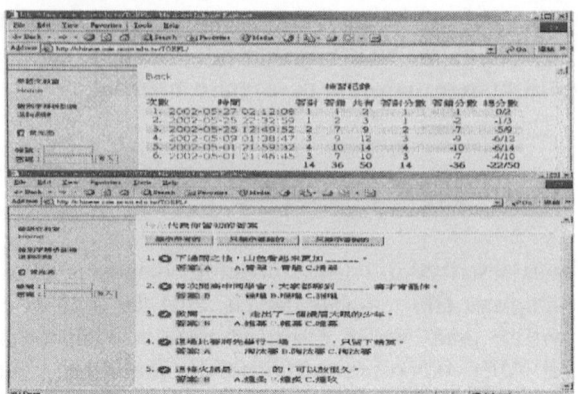

Fig. 6. The Snapshot of Students' Result

6   Conclusion and Future Work

In this paper, we introduce a design web-based assessment tool with multiple presentation styles. Each presentation style provides a different goal of learning. We are currently using our framework to develop other presentation styles with guidance multimedia features such as navigational events described in WSML system. The navigational events will explain how a specific answer is chosen in each question. Instructors can explain more detail to give learners' understanding. In our future work, we aim at extending our framework by powerful tools to define templates to facilitate the exercise-learning object exchange with other learning systems.

References

1.   G. Abowd, et. al., Teaching and Learning as Multimedia Authoring: The Classroom 2000 Project, Proc. ACM Multimedia '96, Boston MA, Nov 1996, pp.187-198.
2.   Education on Demand project, http://www.informedia.cs.cmu.edu/eod/
3.   Mukhopadhyay, S. and Smith, B., Passive Capture and Structuring of Lectures. Proceedings of the Seventh ACM International Conference on Multimedia, 1999, pp. 477-487.
4.   Multibook, http://www.multibook.de.
5.   Saddik A.E., Fischer, S., and Steinmetz R., Reusable Multimedia Content in Web-Based Learning System, IEEE Multimedia, Vol. 8, 2001, pp.30-38.
6.   Fischer S. and Steinmetz R. Automatic Creation of Exercises in Adaptive Hypermedia Learning Systems. In Proceedings of 10th ACM conference on Hypertext 2000, pp. 49-55.
7.   Issac Yihjia Tjai. And Yang J.H.S. Toward Better Assessments in Distance Education, International Conference on Distributed Computing System Workshop, IEEE, 2001.
8.   Chen, H.Y., Chen G.Y., and Hong, J.S., Design of a Web-based Synchronized Multimedia Lecture System for Distance Education. Multimedia Computing and Systems, IEEE International Conference, Vol. 2, 1999, pp.887-891.

Design and Development of a Multimedia Interactive Lab for Distance Learning Applications in the WWW

Yvonne Kam, SoonNyean Cheong, SuFong Chien, and AhHeng You

Multimedia University, Faculty of Engineering, Jalan Multimedia, Cyberjaya,
63100 Selangor, Malaysia
{hskam, sncheong, sfchien, ahyou}@mmu.edu.my
http://www.mmu.edu.my

Abstract. Currently, distance education (DE) courses in Malaysia are only for the non-scientific field since DE lacks the laboratory experimentation indispensable to science. The concept of Virtual laboratory provides a timely solution. This paper describes the development and implementation of a novel, multimedia interactive laboratory (MI-LAB) for online experimentation. The aim of the MI-LAB project is to provide students access via the Internet to various experiments in conceptual physics, simplifying experimentation for home-learners and professionals in a distance teaching environment. MI-LAB's effectiveness is thoroughly demonstrated in the development of the Hall Effect experiment lab aimed at enhancing student's understanding. MI-LAB supplements the physical lab by augmenting student's learning experiences with relevant information, questions, graphs and video demonstrations. This Web approach integrates Flash actionscript to do extensive simulations and interactive animation of physics based experiments in virtual reality. MI-LAB is a low cost, zero maintenance, and risk-free alternative to conventional lab for DE.

1 Introduction

People who don't have the luxury of attending classes as full time students invariably turn to distance education for an alternative that doesn't restrict them to study, at a fixed time, in a fixed place. In the past, distance education consumers were limited to the staple of mail, fax and phone communication. Nowadays, the internet offers so much more in terms of teacher-student interaction and participative learning. Thus, it is just a matter of time for distance education to be adapted to the internet.

While normal web-based implementation may well be fine for courses which have little need for practical training, it is quite insufficient for science and engineering based courses, for which laboratory experimentation is indispensable. The solution may well be virtual laboratories. Virtual laboratories allow distance learners to explore and put into practice theoretical concepts disseminated in the lectures. What's more, two of the biggest problems in distance education are solved simultaneously, temporary availability and practical experience [1]. With the implementation of virtual labs,

Y.-C. Chen, L.-W. Chang, and C.-T. Hsu (Eds.): PCM 2002, LNCS 2532, pp. 993-1000, 2002.

they can perform experiments at any time and location since the labs are available online for 24 hours a day. Equally significant, students can now do experiments by simulation, providing a handy substitute to training in actual conditions.

This article describes a virtual lab developed in MMU that uses dynamic and interactive simulations in a Web-based environment. The paper is organized as follows. Section 2 reviews background and related work. Next, Section 3 presents the design of the system. Section 4 gives an example of a virtual physics laboratory implemented using MI-LAB. Finally, Section 5 concludes the paper.

2 Background and Related Work

Several interactive virtual labs are currently available on the web. In Physics 2000 [2], students can explore elementary physical phenomenon using interactive Java applets. There are categories like Einstein's Legacy and Atomic Lab. Another Java applet based application, ViBE [3] was implemented in Rutgers University for virtual biology experiments. Virtual Labs For Real-Life Scientific Training [4] are currently developing applet-based virtual labs that are interactive three-dimensional scenes. The Bio Interactive Lab [5] by the Howard Hughes Medical Institute is a very advanced virtual biology lab. It contains various learning modules for example bacterial, cardiology and neurophysiology labs. Students can simulate picking up and manipulating apparatus to perform the experiments through clicks of the mouse.

Nevertheless, realism of the lab environment feels lacking in these implementations, as user interaction is mostly restricted to standard web-based methods, like mouse-clicks, buttons and input boxes. To simulate the lab environment, users should be able to imitate real operations i.e. turning knobs, tuning dials, adjusting sliders and so on. We attempt to overcome these shortcomings and provide the user with a more realistic experience through MI-LAB.

Another issue regarding current implementations is that they are not fully platform independent. Some implementations using Java applets sometimes require certain version changes and are platform specific. This is overcome in MI-LAB through the browser-based implementation which is not dependent on any platform.

3 System Design

The main design idea of the system is to use the Web as the communication structure and a Web browser as the user interface. The Web browser provides a platform for transmitting information as well as an environment to run Flash and Director movies. The Web itself provides the infrastructure to exchange the necessary information. The framework for this system is built using a 3 tier web-based architecture (see Fig. 1):

   ϑ   First Tier: Front End - Browser (Thin Client) - a GUI interface lying at the client/workstation

   ϑ   Second Tier: Middle Tier - Application Server - set of application programs

   ϑ   Third Tier: Back End - Database Server

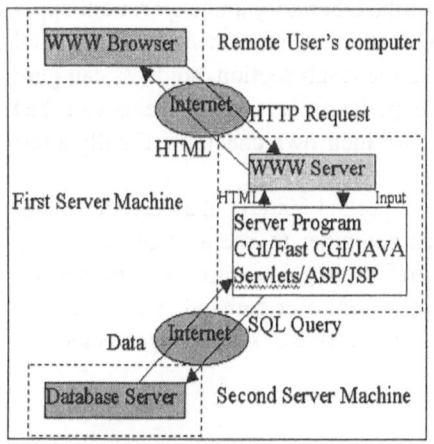

Fig. 1. A 3-tier Structure

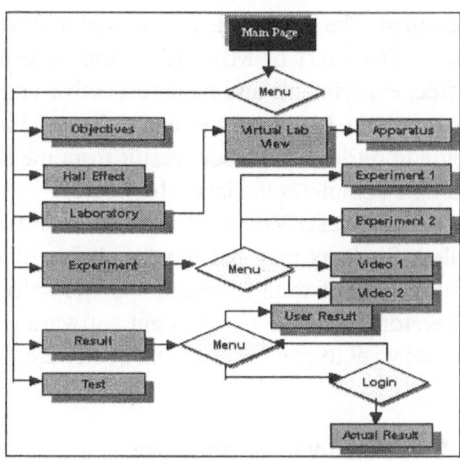

Fig. 2. Process Flow of MI-LAB

The client's request first goes to the Web server, which then sends the required information to the application server. The application server synchronizes and combines with the Web server to process the request made by the client. It then sends the response back to the Web server after taking an appropriate action. The Web server then sends the processed information back to the client. Active Server Pages serve as the back bone technology for receiving and returning processed information to the client.

3.1 Requirements

Web-based implementation for the experiment is necessary for remote experimentation. Another important aspect is to transport the feeling of a real experiment to the remote user. Therefore, we do not want to create a windows GUI with fields to fill in and then click the "OK" button to view the result like some implementations through java applets. For a more realistic experience, we need 3D objects that look like lab apparatus with dials, knobs, buttons, reading windows etc. Two undeniable differences between a real and virtual lab are the experiment environment and the practical experience of handling real apparatus. To minimize the discrepancies, we should provide students with a virtual view around the lab. Likewise, video footage of the actual experiment would help students visualize what they would need and how to perform the real experiment. Multimedia enhances learning through promoting complementarity with classical methods through rapidity of the experiences, the possibility to visualize experiences impossible to see in reality, being the link between modelisation and reality. Thus, it is beneficial to flesh out and bring to life the objective, theoretical background, apparatus, and procedures of the experiments through multimedia. It is also helpful that experimental data should be visualizable in a graph for analysis. Tests should also be a part of performance evaluation.

With this in mind, MI-LAB is organized into 6 sections (Fig. 2). The first section is for the experiment objectives. The second section outlines the theory behind the experiment. The third leads to a virtual 360° view of the laboratory and experiment apparatus. The heart of MI-LAB is the experiment section, which consists of two Hall Effect experiments and their respective videos. In the result section, students can generate graphs based on the data collected in the experiment section. Students can then login to retrieve the model result from the server for their own checking. Finally a test module completes the laboratory setup.

From the user's point of view, there are other important features that have to be fulfilled. Students may not have a choice of which computer to use at their site. They usually do not want to install specific software before they can start the experiments. Therefore, cross-platform client software is an important user demand. Since students do not want to pay for additional software, free client software is advantageous too.

3.2 Framework Architecture

The architecture is based on the Flash Actionscript framework. The main characteristic of Flash actionscript is that it is object-based. The common layers of abstraction comprise the movie layer, object layer, and behaviour layer. The movie is the most commonly used object and is the top level of a flash file. A movie can be made up of multiple objects and other movies. The objects in each movie can be buttons, graphics, sounds i.e. instances of symbols. Symbols are reusable objects that have been created previously. The main benefit of this decomposition is the resulting separation of concerns. The design internally consists of many movies, although the outside world sees a single movie (see Fig. 3).

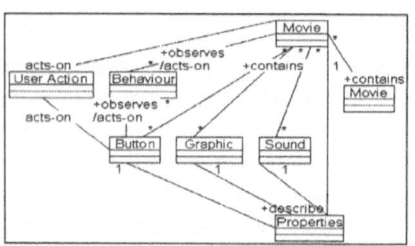
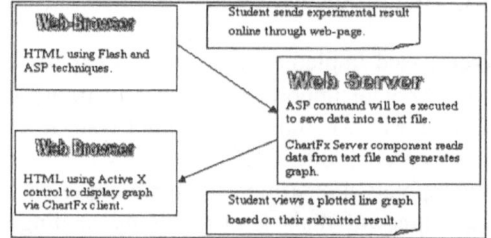

Fig. 3. . Simple conceptual model of a Flash Framework

Fig. 4. Working principle of ChartFX

Movie Layer. An instance of the movie object is actually a mini movie aside from the main movie in which it is contained. It has its own timeline and behaves independently from the main movie. The movie object has its own properties and methods. Examples of the properties that can be set are alpha, height, width, x position, y position, x scale, y scale etc. The main experiment movie is represented by scene. The class diagram is shown in Fig. 5.

Object layer. The objects can be of type movie, graphic, button, text or sound. The components in the level after scene are movie objects. They in turn can contain other objects, for example, all the above contain button and display objects.

Behavior layer. Certain behaviours can be scripted into the objects. For example, the potentiometer object enables mouse dragging by calling startdrag() and stopdrag(). An example implementation is shown below.

Example of a Script used to Describe the Behaviour of an Object

```
on (press){startdrag("",false,0,-75.0,0,75.0);}
on (release, releaseOutside){stopdrag();}
```

4 MI-LAB Implementation

4.1 Client

We chose to implement the media streams in Flash, Dynamic HTML, ASP and Director formats. The reason being that no proprietary software has to be installed and only the most common browser plug-ins (Flash and Shockwave players) are needed to access the application via the Internet. Furthermore, the size of shockwave flash (swf) is relatively small and fast to download.

User Interface. The webpage was developed in Flash with integration of ASP technology. The layout was inserted with interactive JavaScript elements. There is a clear separation between the experimentation interface and the other webpage elements. By constructing the environment in this fashion, the experiment can be replaced with a different one. We can add and change the experiments in MI-LAB by replacing the Flash file with another without the necessity of redesigning the webpage. Thus, we can generate new experiments as goals change, providing the opportunity to practice with classical or advanced strategies in different physics experiments. Since students cannot visualize what the laboratory really looks like with just static images, we incorporated within the webpage, a 360° interactive laboratory view to allow users to see a surround view of the laboratory as if they were physically there. Users can use the mouse to navigate around the laboratory image (Fig. 6).

Experiments. MI-LAB contains a set of objects such as dials, sliders, buttons, electrical instruments, or experiment substances each with specific pre-programmed behaviors. The student interacts with the objects in order to attain a set of given goals, i.e., study of apparatus characteristics, observation of scientific phenomena, measurement of scientific quantities, change of current direction, etc. User immersion is increased with realistic controls and sound effects. When the user makes changes, dynamic simulations are the response. In addition, experiences not obtainable in conventional lab such as mouseover effects, animation etc. are utilized to show invisible but real events, like the movement of deflected electrons. The Flash framework significantly simplifies the development of virtual physics laboratories. The developer's main task is in creating or reusing objects and programming the Behaviors associated with each object. Currently we have implemented two experiments. The two experiments are quantifying the change in Hall voltage w.r.t. change in current, and secondly w.r.t. change in magnetic field (Fig. 7).

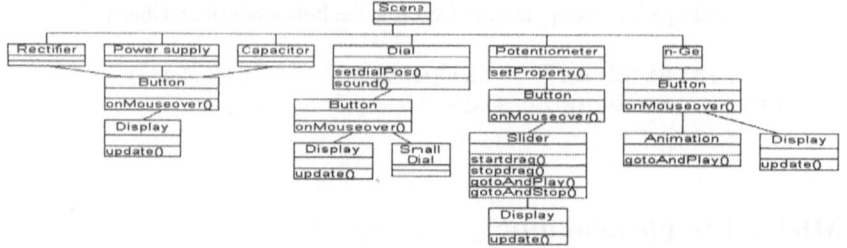

Fig. 5. Class Diagram

Fig. 6. A Virtual View of the Lab

After the experiment page is loaded, the movie starts. The first part of the experiment is to mouseover the experiment setup to find out more about each apparatus. When the mouse is over the n-type Germanium (n-Ge), a larger view will appear showing the animation of electron flow within the n-Ge. In the first experiment, they are required to move the slider on the potentiometer to change the potential across the capacitor. In the second experiment, the student needs to change the current by turning the power supply dial. The corresponding changes in Hall voltage are then recorded.

Real-time Graph Generation. Under the result section, students input their experimental values into text fields. Then, ASP commands will be executed to save the data into a file located at the server. At the same time, ChartFX commands are executed on the server to dynamically generate a graph based on their results (Fig. 4). Next, data will be sent to the client browser through the use of an active X control. These graphs can be printed to prepare lab reports after the exercises. The powerful, easy to integrate, interactive ChartFX is a browser independent, server-side graphing component. It has dynamic template and code generation (ASP, client-side code etc).

ChartFX can generate the Graph from a recordset with the adoResultSet method. The recordset is passed to the method which outputs the graph with the getHtmlTag method. There is a lot of flexibility with ChartFX as we can set properties and methods and have a fair amount of control over the graph.

Example of the Code in Using ChartFX

```
<%
'ChartFX server object
set Chart = Server.CreateObject("ChartFX.WebServer")
```

```
set db = server.createobject("ADODB.connection")
db.open sDSN
sSql = "SELECT * FROM MYTABLE"
set rs = db.execute(sSql)
'pass recordset to the chart's adoResultSet meth
chart.AdoResultset rs
'this generates a full size graph
response.write(chart.GetHtmlTag("100%","100%") )
%>
```

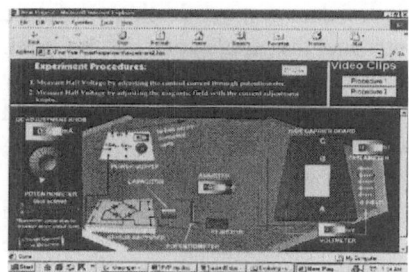   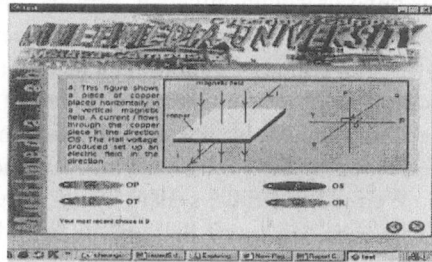

Fig. 7. Experiment Interface   **Fig. 8.** Test Interface

In the resultant chart, users can zoom, rotate, or drag & drop new colors onto the chart elements. They can even change a chart to any of 35 formats.

Test. Evaluation is in the form of an online test. The test interface is interactive and realized in Director and its robust programming language, Lingo. Lingo's conceptual model is like that of Flash in Fig. 2. Lingo is highly standardized, relieving the developer from issues with display, document parsing, etc., and only requiring the developer to program the particular Behavior classes. This interactive test catches student's attention with animation, transition effects, mouse events and sound. Questions pertaining to the lab are asked and a choice of answers is given. The user can choose to skip questions by clicking the Next button to advance or the Back button to reverse. Each answer chosen by the student is retained and the choice highlighted until the next time it is changed (Fig. 8). For the purpose of submitting the test results, there is a text file generated with the answers and score, which is also displayed on screen.

5 Conclusion and Recommendations

Virtual labs can fill a need for hands-on labs for distance education. Their plus points include remote accessibility, cost effectiveness, and improved student interest. We have described the general organization of MI-LAB and the implementation choices made in order to satisfy the requirements of a web-based, multimedia, interactive laboratory based on conventional labs. We have managed to augment the laboratory with video, a charting application, a virtual view of the lab, and performance evaluation. All this was achieved by utilizing cross-platform client software.

In developing our application, we have found that there exist some areas for future enhancement. We find that our lab can be developed to be a Windows application as well as a Web-based application. Nevertheless, both methods have their own limitations; such as non-remote access for windows-based and access delays for Web-based. Thus, to fully utilize the advantages of either side, a hybrid approach that combines both should be developed upon. Secondly, the security features in MI-LAB should be tightened to prevent unauthorized users from performing illegal operations, while enabling user authentication, privacy, and integrity of data communication. In future developments, more interaction between the user and the application is the goal. Switches, contacts, buttons, calculators and so on can be added to the experiment by adding more movie objects to represent them. Furthermore, more interactivity could be implemented, for instance, by allowing the user to connect the circuits by dragging and dropping the circuit elements. Another improvement would be to add help files.

We field tested the system on our university's students and from their feedback and experience, we found that one of main benefits of the MI-LAB approach is that the students are able to work on the lab at their own pace. In addition, the lab provides a means for students to learn in a hands-on environment. The lab lessons also relieved the instructor from the necessity of teaching the lab and therefore allowed more time for teaching. Last, but not least, students were encouraged to learn by themselves since each of them had to experiment with the various controls. Thus, they learnt that they can expand their knowledge without depending on others.

In conclusion, MI-LAB provides an electronic learning resources package accessible from everywhere via the Internet. It is an effective, easy to access, self-learning environment for students. The authors wish to thank MMU for supporting this effort.

References

1. J. Sánchez, F. Morilla, S. Dormido, J. Aranda, and P. Ruipérez, "Virtual and Remote Control Labs Using Java: A Qualitative Approach", *IEEE Control Systems Magazine*, April 2002.
2. M. V. Goldman, "Physics 2000 interactive applets," University of Colorado, Boulder, CO. At: http://www.colorado.edu/physics/2000/TOC.html
3. R. Subramanian and I. Marsic, "ViBE: Virtual Biology Experiments", *Proc. ACM WWW10*, Hong Kong (2001).
4. M. Duguay, "Virtual labs for real-life scientific training," Available online at: www.telelearn.ca/g_access/news/virtual_labs.html
5. Howard Hughes Medical Institute, "Virtual laboratories," At: http://www.hhmi.org/biointeractive/vlabs/index.htm
6. Y. Kam, S. N. Cheong, A. H. You, S. F. Chien, "Web-Based Experimentation Of Physics Concepts: An Alternative to Conventional Laboratory Experiments", *Proc. ICL-Workshop*, Austria (2002).

The System Resource Management in a Distributed Web-Based E-learning Platform

Meng-Huang Lee, Man-Hua Wu, and Wen-Yuan Ko

Department of Information Management, Shih-Chien University,
Taipei, Taiwan
meng@mail.usc.edu.tw

Abstract. In this paper, we propose and implement a system resource management mechanism(content caching to the local site nearby the learners and admission control for learner accesses) in a distributed web-based E-Learning platform, Asian-Mind. For good quality of content accessing, the continuous media course contents are distributed to the course content servers which are closer to the learners according to the course content access popularity. And for guaranteeing the learning quality, learning accesses are admitted by the admission control mechanism in Asian-Mind. Currently, Asian-Mind is successfully used as the network learning platform in the two campuses(Taipei campus and KaoHsiung campus) of Shih-Chien University, Fu-Jen University, and Hi-Net(the largest Internet service provider in Taiwan for the home users). Twenty-four E-learning courses are now available.

1 Introduction

Traditional learning system is up to the trainer. Learners attend a course according to the course time schedule and at a specific classroom. The evolution of distance learning system from synchronous distance learning(video conferencing system) to asynchronous(video-on-demand system), not only lifts the "place" constrain but also the "time schedule" constrain. The learners can learn the course materials at anywhere and anytime. Nowadays, text, audio, and video course materials can be stored efficiently in the computer storage system. And the network bandwidth evolution from narrow band dial up network, to broad-band ADSL and Cable Modem. These improvements make the nowadays' asynchronous learning system possible[1][2][3].

Recently, there are many web-based E-learning platforms proposed[4][5][6] [7][8]. And, although there are many improvements in the network bandwidth and storage capacity. But for a successful E-learning system(it should provide a lot of learning courses and allow a lot of learners accessing the system), system resource(storage capacity and network bandwidth) is still a major problem.

In this paper, we propose and implement a system resource management mechanism(content caching to the local site nearby the learners and admission control for learner accesses) in a distributed web-based E-Learning platform, Asian-Mind. Asian-Mind is a learning management and delivery system that lets you seamlessly integrate your course content, whether you create it yourself or purchase it from other

Y.-C. Chen, L.-W. Chang, and C.-T. Hsu (Eds.): PCM 2002, LNCS 2532, pp. 1001-1008, 2002.

content providers. The web-based platform allows offering distributed learning courses that learners and trainers can access whether they are online or offline. It also provides a flexible framework that can handle any multimedia content, e.g. video, audio, text, Flash, etc.. For good quality of content accessing, the continuous media course contents are distributed to the course content servers which is closer to the learners according to the course content access popularity. And for guaranteeing the learning quality, learning accesses are admitted by the admission control mechanism in Asian-Mind.

Currently, Asian-Mind is successfully used as the network learning platform in the two campuses(Taipei campus and KaoHsiung campus) of Shih-Chien University, Fu-Jen University , and HiNet(the largest Internet service provider in Taiwan for the home users). Twenty-four E-learning courses are available. Based on FAQ, discussion database, real-time virtual classroom, and Quiz database of Asian-Mind, data-mining and knowledge management features will be integrated in the near future.

2   The System Resource Management of Asian-Mind

2.1   Content Caching Policy

Currently, Asian-Mind is used as the network learning platform for the students of Shih-Chien University and Fu-Jen University . The students may access the learning system in the university campus or when they are at home. Although, there are many improvements in current network bandwidth. Good quality video still can not be delivered in the current Internet network. At the local site(e.g. in the university campus), the network is basically connected by the broadband optical fiber architecture. For good quality video accessing, it's reasonable to mirror all the learning content in the campuses of the two universities(for students accessing the system in campuses) and HiNet(for students accessing the system at home) such that video content can be delivered to students by the content server at the nearby of students. For example, if a student is in Taipei Campus of Shih-Chien University, the content is delivered by the content server in Taipei Campus of Shih-Chien University. If a student is at Campus of Fu-Jen University, the content is delivered by the content server in Campus of Fu-Jen University. When a student is at his home, the content can be delivered by the content server which we co-located in HiNet(as shown in Figure 1). But for the large volume needed by the video content, it's impossible to mirror all the learning content in the two university campuses and HiNet. Take a 3 credit hour course for example, the storage volume needed is about 3 Gbytes for 100 kbps quality video streaming. The disk array with 8 disk slots(each is 30 Gbytes) can only store 80 learning course content. For Fu-Jen University, in the Spring of 2002, there are 5372 courses provided. As for Shih-Chih University Taipei Campus, the number is 2192. 80 learning courses are a small ratio. Thus, it is impossible to store all the learning courses on high-speed storage system(e.g. disk array). Therefore, it needs large capacity storage system(e.g.

Tape Library, Juke Box) to store all the learning courses, and cache the most popular courses on the high-speed storage systems[9][10][11][12].

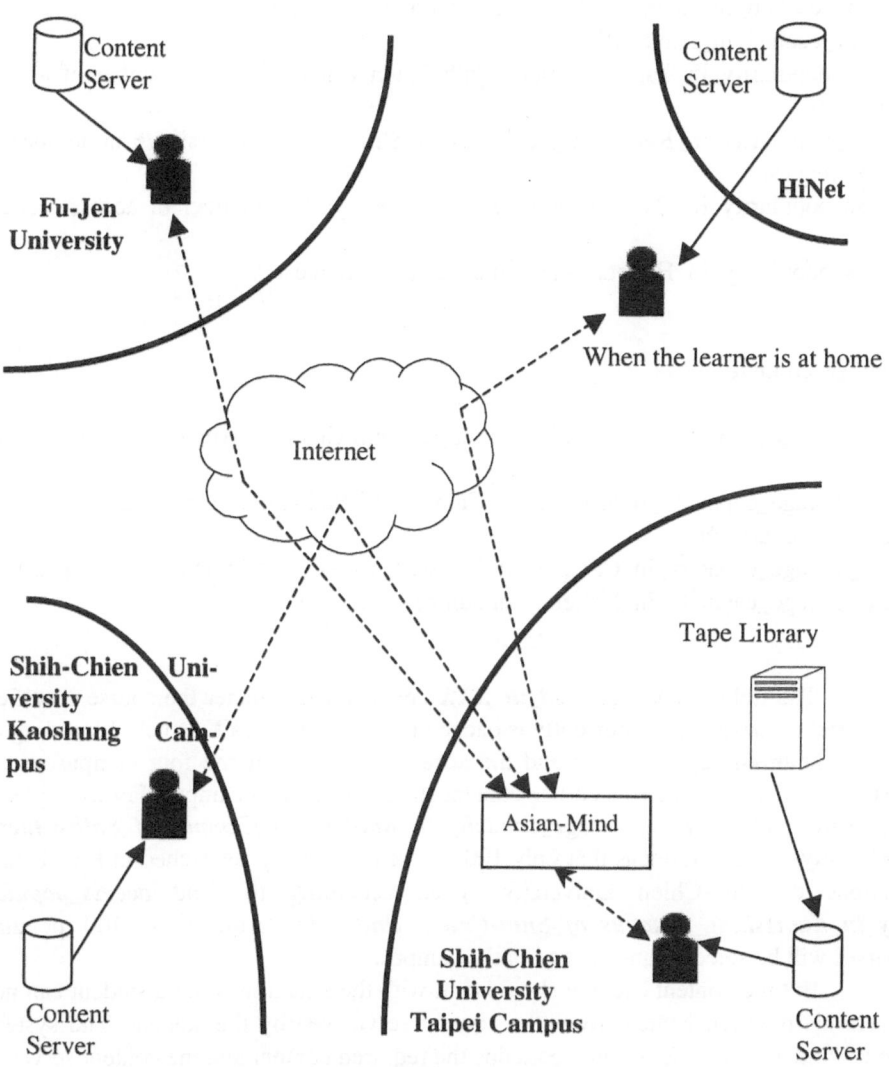

Fig. 1. System Architecture of Asian-Mind

In our system architecture, all learning content are stored at Taipei Campus of Shih-Chien University with Tape Library and disk array. Then we cache the content to the four campuses according to the student access popularity. We maintain two tables (Storage_capacity_table and   Course_popularity_table) for the decision of system caching policy. The attributes of these two tables are as followings.

Course_popularity_table

{

course_name;

already_cached_in_Taipei_Campus_of_Shih-Chien-University; /* yes or no */

already_cached_in_KaoHsiung_Campus_of_Shih-Chien-University; /* yes or no */

already_cached_in_Campus_of_Fu-Jen-University; /* yes or no */

already_cached_in_HiNet; /* yes or no */

access_popularity_in_Taipei_Campus_Shih-Chien University;/* in number of access request */

access_popularity_in_KaoHsiung_Campus_of_Shih-Chien University;/* in number of access request */

access_popularity_in_Campus_of_Fu-Jen- University;/* in number of access request */

access_popularity_in_HiNet;/* in number of access request */

}

Storage_capacity_table

{

max._storage_capacity_in_Taipei_Campus_of_Shih-Chien-University; /* in number of course */

max._storage_capacity_in_KaoHsiung_Campus_of_Shih-Chien-University; /* in number of course */

max._storage_capacity_in_Campus_of_Fu-Jen-University; /* in number of course */

max._storage_capacity_in_HiNet; /* in number of course */

}

The field *already_cached_in_XXX* denotes that whether the course specified in the field *course_name* currently is cached in the campus *XXX* or not. According to the maximum storage capacity and the access popularity of the four campuses, the system can decide whether a course content should cache in a campus. For example, if the value of *max._storage_capacity_in_KaoHsiung_Campus_of_Shih-Chien-University* is 100, it means that only 100 course content can be cached in KaoHsiung Campus of Shih-Chien University. Then according to field *access_popularity_in_KaoHsiung_Campus_of_Shih-Chien University* , the most 100 popular courses will be selected and cached in the campus.

But the content caching should deal with the situation when a student can not access his required content from the content server nearby the student. The system should find a content server that contains the required content and the content server is most nearby the student. In Asian-Mind, a campus_distance_table is used to guide the system to find the most nearby content server that contains the required content. The campus_distance_table is shown in Table 1. The distance in campus_distance_table between two campuses is not geographic meaning, but the network bandwidth meaning. For example, for Shih-Chien University Taipei Campus, the network bandwidth to HiNet is more than to Fu-Jen University, and the network bandwidth to Fu-Jen University is more tan to Shih-Chien University KaoHsiung Campus. If a student in

Shih-Chien University KaoHsiung Campus can not access his required content, the system will automatically check the content server in Fu-Jen University, then HiNet, and finally Shih-Chien University Taipei Campus.

Table 1. Campus_distance_table

	Shih-Chien University Taipei Campus	Shih-Chien University KaoHsiung Campus	Fu-Jen University	HiNet
Shih-Chien University Taipei Campus	0	3	2	1
Shih-Chien University KaoHsiung Campus	2	0	1	3
Fu-Jen University	1	2	0	3
HiNet	1	3	2	0

2.2 Admission Control Policy

Traditionally, admission control issue depends only on the content server data pump capacity. But in system practice, high-speed disk system data pump capacity is more than nowadays' network bandwidth. Although the campus network is basically connected by the broadband optical fiber architecture. But for E-learning applications, network bandwidth is still a major concern. For example, there are 3 optical fiber trunks in Fu-Jen University campus, each one is 155Mbps. But the effective data transmission rate is about 31Mbps.

There are 22,600 students in Fu-Jen University and the bit rate for our learning content is about 100kbps. Only 1,000 students can access the learning system at a time. But for guaranteeing system quality, admission control mechanism depended on campus bandwidth capacity is implemented in Asian-Mind.

In our system, we maintain a Bandwidth_capacity_table for the system admission control.

Bandwidth_capacity_table
```
{
max._bandwidth_capacity_in_Taipei_Campus_of_Shih-Chien-University;
    /* in number of access request */
max._bandwidth_capacity_in_KaoHsiung_Campus_of_Shih-Chien-University;
    /* in number of access request */
max._bandwidth_capacity_in_Campus_of_Fu-Jen-University;
```

```
/* in number of access request */
max._bandwidth_capacity_in_HiNet; /* in number of access request */
}
```

If the number of access request exceeds the maximum bandwidth capacity of a campus, the system will reject the admission of a new access request.

3   Implementation of Asian-Mind

The functions of Asian-Mind are listed in Figure2. There are three groups of users that use Asian-Mind system. One is the learners group in the front end, the others are trainers and system administrators. Learners browse the network pages that are provided and supported by the trainers and system administrators in the back end. With the Multimedia Course Reader, learners can browse any multimedia course materials e.g. video, audio, text, Flash, etc. The FAQ/Course Discussion Board and On-line Discussion Board provide the environment that trainers and learners can share each other. Learners can read any course announcement by trainers from Course Announcement Board. And the learners can take a quiz after the class in Assessment System which randomly selected from the trainers' quiz database. On the back-end, Trainers can build-up their training environment by the Course Announcement System, Quiz Database, Assessment Manager, Member Account Manager, Course Manager. The Course Manager integrates course content, whether you create it yourself or purchase it from other content providers.

In System Resource Manager, Course_popularity_table, Storage_capacity_table and Bandwidth_capacity_table mentioned in previous section are maintained here for system decision of content caching and access admission control. System administrators can specify the maximum system resource (maximum storage capacity and bandwidth capacity) of the four campuses in Storage_capacity_table and Bandwidth_capacity_table respectively. Any learner accesses and content caching situation of the four campuses are logged in Course_popularity_table. Besides, system administrators can specify the period that content caching daemon will be activated to do the content caching according to the log information in Course_popularity_table and maximum system resource specified in Storage_capacity_table and Bandwidth_capacity_table. Currently, the setting of the period is 7 days. Then the content caching daemon is activated every 7 days, and content caching situation of the four campuses is adjusted. Besides, we also provide 2 video quality presentation, one is 100k bps, the other is 256k bps. The learner can choose different video quality presentation according to their network situation. If learners' network is ADSL or Cable Modem, the downstream bandwidth is basically greater than 256k bps. It can provide good video quality presentation.

The database of Asian-Mind is centralized in Taipei Campus of Shih-Chien University. The database includes learner account, FAQ, discussion database, real-time virtual classrooms etc. For the database query and retrieval is not network bandwidth intensive. Database centralization can avoid data inconsistency problem in a distributed system.

All system is build upon the MicroSoft System. The database server is build upon MicroSoft NT server and SQL server. The content servers are build upon the MicroSoft Media server. The interface between learners and servers is MicroSoft Active Server Pages program (ASP).

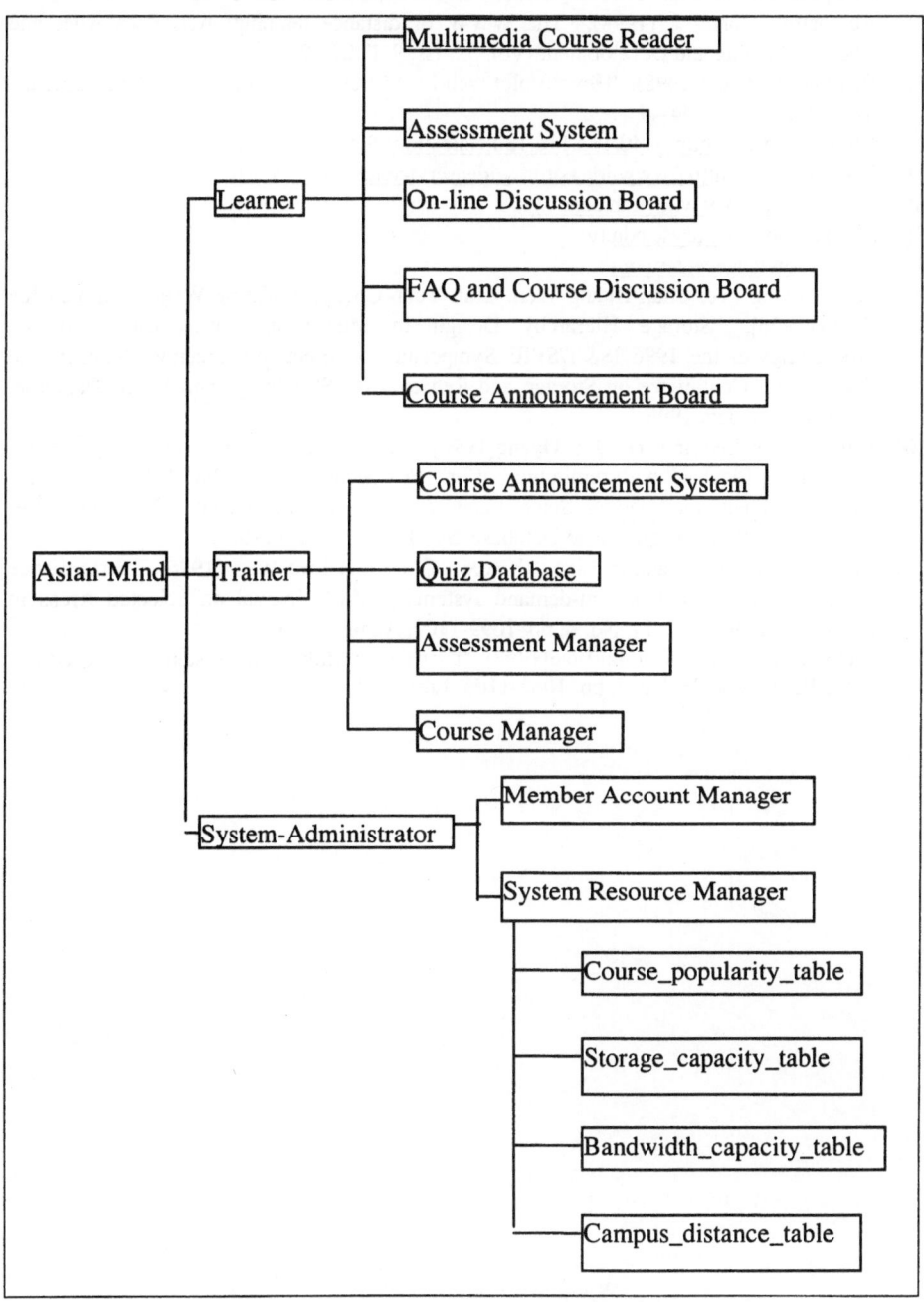

Fig. 2. Functions of Asian-Mind

References

[1]   Karen E. Goeller(1998), "Web-based collaborative learning: a perspective on the future", Computer Network and ISDN Systems, Vol. 30, P. 634-635

[2]   Abernathy, Donna J. (1998), "The WWW of distance learning: who does what and where", Training and Development, Vol. 52, Iss. 9, P. 29-32

[3]   Driscoll, Margaret(1998), "How to plot web-based training, Training and Development", Vol. 52, Iss. 11, P. 44-49

[4]   VICAS (2000)，http://140.112.110.130/education/f9.asp

[5]   IDEA (1999)，http://www.idea.org.tw/ideaservice/home/index.asp

[6]   (2001)，http://www.joyhub.com.tw

[7]   (2001)，http://cu.nsysc.edu.tw

[8]   www.knowledgecenter.com

[9]   Meng-Huang Lee, Chun-Huang Wen, Chih-Yuan Cheng, Fu-Ching Wang, and Yen-Jen Oyang[1996], "Storage Hierarchy Design in Multimedia On-Demand Servers", Proceedings of the 1996 IS&T/SPIE Symposium on Electronic Imaging: Science and Technology, Conference on Storage and Retrieval for Still Image and Video Database, San Jose, CA, Jan. 1996.

[10] Meng-Huang Lee and Yen-Jen Oyang[1996], "Designing a Multiple Disks System for On-Demand Playback with minimum buffer", Proceedings of the 1996 IS&T/SPIE Symposium on Electronic Imaging: Science and Technology, Conference on "Storage and Retrieval for Still Image and Video Database, San Jose, CA. Jan. 1996

[11] Victor O. K. Li , Wanjiun Liao , Xiaoxin Qiu , and Eric Wang[1996], "Performance model of interactive video-on-demand systems", IEEE Journal on Selected Areas in Communications, Vol. 14, No. 6, pp. 1099-1109, August 1996.

[12] Victor O. K. Li and Wanjiun Liao[1997], "Distributed Multimedia Systems", Proceedings of the IEEE, Vol. 85, No. 7, pp. 1063-1108, July 1997.

The Design and Implementation of a Web-Based Discovery-Based Instruction Model

Woochun Jun[1], Le Gruenwald[2], Sungchul Park[3], and Suk-Ki Hong[4]

[1] Dept. of Computer Education, Seoul National University of Education, Seoul, Korea
wocjun@ns.snue.ac.kr
[2] School of Computer Science, University of Oklahoma, Norman, OK 73069, USA
ggruenwald@ou.edu
[3] Seoul Nanwoo Elementary School, Seoul, Korea
edupark1@naver.com
[4] Dept. of Business Administration, KonKuk University, Chungju, Korea
skhong01@kku.ac.kr

Abstract. As the Web is an important medium to deliver multimedia information, the Web can be used to implement various distance learning environments. In order to support distance learning, various instruction models have been developed. In this paper, we present a Web-based instruction model based on discovery-based instruction model. In addition to advantages of the discovery-based model, our model has the following advantages. First, our model utilizes multimedia and simulation materials on the Web so that we can supplement the discovery-based model. Second, our model encourages various types of interaction and students' initiatives so that students can increase their discovery techniques. Third, our model supports various types of discovery-based instruction models based on students' prior knowledge and needs. Finally, our model helps students find rules through their study activities so that they can apply their knowledge to real life. We implement our instruction model and show that our model can be applied to a course in the elementary school.

1 Introduction

With the advent of the new millennium, we are now entering into a knowledge-based society. In a know-based society, the competitiveness of any society is determined by knowledge. Also, in a knowledge-based society, lifelong education as well as distance education should be provided to everyone at anytime, at any place and through various media and methods of education. In this sense, Internet has been an important tool to provide high-quality learning environments.

Among various tools supporting Internet, the advances in the Web technology have affected the traditional teaching-learning method. Web-Based instruction (WBI) has rapidly become an important method for effective teaching-learning. In addition to overcoming the limitations of time and space limitations, it has the following advantages. First, it enables diverse multimedia information to be utilized as study materials. It also makes interactions feasible [1, 2, 3, 4]. That is, it enables dynamic interactions between teachers and students as well as among students themselves. In

Y.-C. Chen, L.-W. Chang, and C.-T. Hsu (Eds.): PCM 2002, LNCS 2532, pp. 1009–1016, 2002.
© Springer-Verlag Berlin Heidelberg 2002

additions, students' problem solving and learning abilities can be improved through the dynamic interactions.

In order for WBI to be successful, various types of instruction models need to be developed. Simply transferring off-line contents to the Web may not be desirable. In this paper, we present a Web-based instruction model. To our best knowledge, the Web-based discovery-based instruction model has not been presented so far. Our model is based on the existing discovery-based instruction model. Our model utilizes the benefits of the discovery-based model. In additions, our model has the following advantages. First, our model utilizes abundant multimedia information on the Web so that we can supplement the discovery-based model. Second, our model encourages various types of interaction and students' initiatives. With the various types of interactions and students' initiatives, students can strengthen their discovering abilities. Third, our model supports various types of discovery-based instruction models based on students' prior knowledge and needs. Finally, our model encourages students to find rules through their studies so that they can apply their knowledge to real life.

This paper is composed of five sections. In Section 2, we present theoretical background, and in Section 3, we explain our instruction model design. Section 4 describes the system implementation and its application to a subject in elementary school. Finally, we conclude our work and discuss future study in Section 5.

2 Theoretical Backgrounds

2.1 Discovery-Based Instruction Model

2.1.1 Principles of the Discovery-Based Model
The discovery-based instruction model, which was originally developed by Brunner, has the following principles [5].

First, it emphasizes the understandings of basic concepts for a subject. These understandings help students apply their ideas to other subjects. Second, it also emphasizes the applicability of study effects. That is, students are required to apply what they've learned to similar subjects. Third, it stresses study processes rather than study outcomes. This encourages students to have creative ideas, and to be more active during their activities. Finally, it requires students to take initiatives all the time. By doing so, students can think, criticize and solve the problems for themselves.

2.1.2 Characteristics of the Discovery-Based Model
Advantages of the discovery-based model are as follows.

First, it enables students to study voluntarily without direct assistance from a teacher. Second, it also enables individualized study efficiently. Third, it can increase students' study abilities for various subjects.

On the other hand, the discovery model may have the following disadvantages.

First, students can deviate from intended study objectives since students are given autonomy from the beginning. Second, students can participate in a class indolently. Third, students may overestimate their personal experiences. Fourth, students are inclined to practical skills rather than basic theories. Fifth, only motivated students participate in the class. Finally, the model has time limit if a course must be dealt with only designated class hour.

2.1.3 Phases of the Discovery-Based Model

The model consists of the following five phases [5,6,7].

a) Phase 1: Materials presentation – Observation

In this phase, students are supposed to observe and reason through the presented study materials. A teacher must observe student's activities and accept their presentations without any prejudice.

b) Phase 2: Supplementary material presentation – Observation

In order to help students understand abstract concepts clearly, a teacher should keep providing supplementary study materials. This phase is to provide more observation opportunities to students and find right concepts through the observation.

c) Phase 3: Inference

In this phase, students are supposed to present what they've observed and the generalized rules through their observation. A teacher is required to lead students to find right rules though asking questions and providing helpful hints.

d) Phase 4: Adjustment

After students induce generalized rules and concepts, a teacher should help students adjust those rules and concepts by presentation or discussion.

e) Phase 5: Application

In this phase, a teacher must help students extend the abstract concepts so that students can apply those concepts to other subjects or real life.

2.2 Related Works

The followings are the similar models or principles with discovery-based model.

2.2.1 Problem Solving Based Enquiry Model [8]

The purpose of this model is to let students find materials on the Web and solve the problem. However, it ignores the learning ability differences among students and lacks the evaluation methods and motivation-supporting techniques. Thus, the supplementary techniques such as providing continuous interactivity, feedbacks and cooperative works among students are required in order to supplement the model.

2.2.2 Constructivism

The basic principles of constructivism are summarized as follows: learner construction of meaning, social interaction to help students learn, and student problem-solving in "real-world" contexts [9,10,11]. The first principle implies that learners construct their own meaning based on their experiences. That is, the constructivism assumes that each person has a unique mental structure that allows him to make meaning based on his experiences. According to constructivism, the study objectives and approaching ways to reach them are not set up in advance. In this case, the Web can provide enough information to learners readily. The second principle means that social interaction provides mediated interpretations of experiences among individuals [11]. In this sense, constructivism encourages both self-directed work and cooperative work. The third principle implies that students can increase problem-solving ability when they are faced with real-world problems.

3   Design of a Web-Based Discovery-Based Instruction Model

3.1   Characteristics of the Proposed Model

The purposes of our model are to provide the following characteristics.

First, our model can let students experience various quests and problems through the Web so that students can increase their problem-solving abilities. Second, our model can assist students to find various data and materials through the Web. That is, our model helps students find rules by providing various types of data and materials. Third, our model can let students encounter materials related with real life. Dealing with those materials encourage students to apply their ideas to real life. Fourth, the casual relation can be formed through the observation and enquiry process. Finally, our model encourages students to extend and clarify the abstract concepts.

3.2   Design Principles

The basic principles of our model are summarized as follows.

First, we design our model to provide various data and materials to students. Second, any concepts and rules that students found are stored in databases so that teachers can monitor students' progresses. Third, in our model, students find their study outcomes any time. For this purpose, all of students' performance records are stored in databases. Fourth, in our model, teachers can help students any time if necessary. We support synchronous and asynchronous communication tools. Finally, we encourage teachers to create problems and store them into databases. On the other hand, teachers can retrieve problems created by himself/herself or others.

3.3   Overall System Structure

In our system, students are required to take initiatives. As a result, students find and search data, observe data, analyze mutual relationships from the data, and induce appropriate rules and concepts. Also, students can check their study outcomes stored in databases any time. The figure 1 shows the overall menu structures of the proposed system.

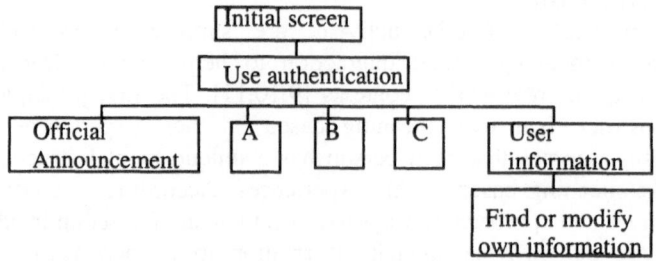

Fig. 1. Overall menu structures of our system

- Module A (Present problems)
An authorized student can select problems and perform their studies. New student is required to fill registration information first. A student can finish his activity after he sends his observation outcomes and answers to questions.

- Module B (Question/Answer)
After study is over, students can ask or exchange their ideas with their teacher or other student via synchronous/asynchronous communication tools. It is known that discussion on cyberspace can increase students' problem-solving abilities [12, 13].

- Module C (Perform discovery-based study)
The module C is a main module of the proposed system. In this module, students are supposed to perform discovery-based study based on the planned procedures. Especially, students are required to select problems based on their level, search the related sites, observe gathered information, solve the problems through observation or experiments, finally enter generalized rules or concepts. If a teacher realizes that students' performances are not satisfactory during observation or quest process, the teacher needs to provide supplementary materials. In this case, the teacher can ask students to discuss each other or find more materials from other students, finally let students enter their generalized rules or concepts. Through this (possibly repetitive) process, a teacher encourages students to form more complete concepts. Finally, students are required to solve the problems and send solutions to database.

- Teacher Module
A teacher can retrieve his/her class information after login. The teacher needs to present problems related with study subjects and check the related sites for students' quest activities. Depending on students' progresses, the teacher needs to identify the generalized rules or concepts for students. Also, the teacher needs to check the results of the formative test and provide another opportunity to students for makeup.

4   Implementation of a Web-Based Discovery-Based Instruction Model

4.1   Systems Development Environment

The systems were developed with PHP, JavaScript, HTML and My-SQL. We use Linux and Apache as operating system and Web server, respectively. In addition, databases were designed with My-SQL. System development environment for this system is shown in Table 1. Our system is implemented in http://comedu.snue.ac.kr/~edupark in Korean. Its English version will be available soon.

Table 1. Development Environment and tools

Items	Specification
Operating System	Linux
Web server	Apache
Database linkage software	MySQL 3.23.33
Web site construction tool and language	- JavaScript -Namo Webeditor 4.0 -EditPlus
Web browser	Internet Explorer 5.0

4.2. Major Screens

1) Problem presentation screen

The problem presentation screen is designed to let a teacher select various problems depending on courses and students' progresses as shown in Figure 2.

2) Standard setting modification screen

The standard setting modification screen is used to allow a teacher to modify initial settings such as number of problems and student's response time, etc. Figure 3 shows the screen.

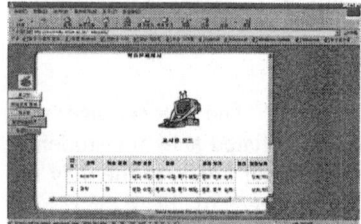

Fig. 2. Problem presentation screen

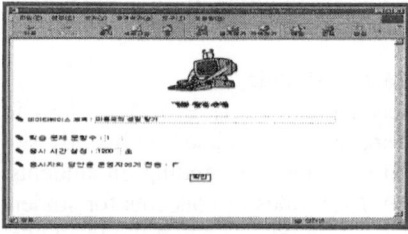

Fig. 3. Standard setting modification screen

3) Making Questions screen

In this screen, a teacher can make questions. The teacher is supposed to provide points and helpful hints for each question. Figure 4 shows the screen.

4) Test score presentation screen

The test score presentation screen shows test score for each student. This screen also presents time limit each student is required to finish the test. Figure 5 shows the screen.

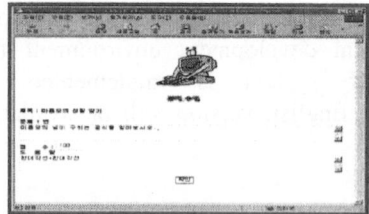

Fig. 4. Making questions screen

Fig. 5. Test score presentation screen

5) Perform discovery-based study screen

In this menu, students are supposed to perform various activities such as quest and search based on the discovery-based study plan. Figure 6 shows the screen.

6) Problem-solving screen

In this menu, students need to solve the problems. The screen shows study title, the remaining time, etc. When necessary, students can send email to their teacher for a question or comment. Figure 7 shows the screen.

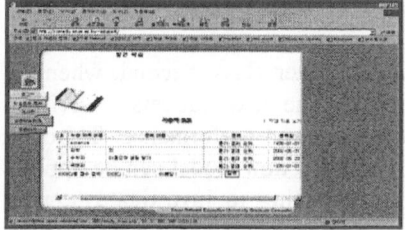

Fig. 6. Perform discovery-based study screen

Fig. 7. Problem-solving screen

7) Sort scores screen

In this menu, a teacher can check the test scores in ascending or descending order for each course or subject. Figure 8 shows the screen.

8) Discussion screen

In this menu, students can discuss using either BBS or online chatting tool. Each student is required to use his or her real name. For BBS discussion, a teacher can moderate students' discussion based on the messages exchanged. Also, a teacher is supposed to monitor students' online chat occasionally. Figure 9 shows the screen.

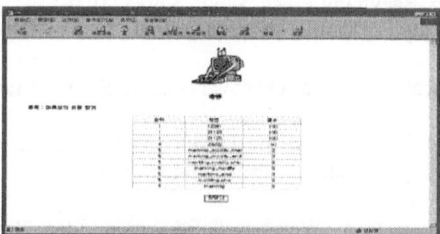

Fig. 8. Sort scores screen

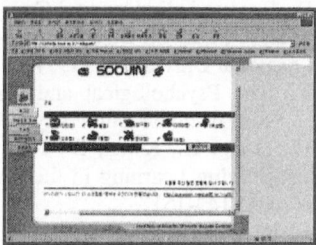

Fig. 9. Discussion screen

5   Conclusions and Further Work

The discovery-based model is originally designed to let students find general rules or concepts when a teacher presents partial concepts or rules to students. In other words, the discovery-based model is an inductive method so that students can induce the general rules or concepts after investigating the partial concepts or rules.

In this paper, we present a Web-based instruction model based on discovery-based instruction model. Our model has the following characteristics. First, our model uses various multimedia data on the Web so that we can supplement the original discovery-based model. Second, our model strengthens students' discovery techniques by stimulating the various types of interactivities and students' initiatives. Third, our model can provide the various types of discovery-based study activities based on students' prior knowledge and needs. Finally, our model helps students find the general rules through their studies so that they can apply their knowledge to real life. We implement our instruction model and show that our model can be applied to a course in the elementary school.

We suggest the following research issues based on our work.

First, in order for our model to be applied in many courses, we need to investigate how to plan students' activities before class as well as after class. Second, when we apply our model to various courses, it is useful to examine how students' individual characteristics such as personalities will affect the students' performance. Third, in general, the main courses to which discovery-based instruction model can be applied are mathematics, social study, and science. It is interesting to investigate how to revise our model in order to be applied for the various courses.

References

1. Choi, J.: A Study on Instruction Strategy to Improve Interactivity in Web-based Instruction, Journal of Educational Technology, Vol. 15, No. 3 (1999) 129 – 154
2. Hwang, S, Han K.: A Design of Web-based Cooperative Learning System Supporting Effective Interactivity, The Proceedings of KAIE, Vol. 6, No. 2 (2001) 74 – 86
3. Lim, I.: A Study on Synthetic model for the Design of Interactive Web-based Instruction", Journal of Educational Technology, Vol. 15, No. 1 (1999) 3-24
4. Lim, J.: Theoretical Bases on Web-based Instruction from a Viewpoint of Interactivity, Journal of Educational Technology, Vol. 15, No. 1 (1999) 29 – 54
5. Lee, H.: Brunner's Educational Curriculum, Baeyoung Press, Seoul, Korea (1988)
6. Kwon, S.: A Study on Discovery-based Study for Mathematics Education, Master Thesis, Seoul National University (1999)
7. Yu, Y.: The Psychological and Theoretical Study on Discovery-based Study, Master Thesis, Seoul National University (1993)
8. Lee, C., Hong, H., Kwak, B., Kim, D.: A Research on the Development of a Site for Problem-Solving Learning in the Elementary Education", Proceedings of KAIE, Vol. 6, No. 1 (2001) 143-151
9. Abbey, B.: Instructional and Cognitive Impacts of Web-based Education, Idea Group Publishing, London, UK (2000)
10. Morrison, G. R., Ross, S. M., Kemp, J. E.: Designing Effective Instruction, 3rd edition, John Wiley & Sons, Inc., New York, NY, USA (2001)
11. Jonassen, D. H., Peck, K. L., Wilson, B. G.: Learning with Technology: A Constructivist Perspective, Prentice Hall, Upper Saddle River, NJ, USA (1999)
12. Khan, B.: Web-based Instruction, Educational Technology Publications, Englewood Cliffs, NJ, USA (1997)
13. Relan, A., Gillani, B.: Web-based Instruction and Traditional Classroom: Similarities and Differences, Educational Technology Publications (1997)

A Quantitative Assessment Method with Course Design Model for Distance Learning

Timothy K. Shih and Lun-Ping Hung

Department of Computer Science and Information Engineering
Tamkang University, Taiwan, ROC
tshih@cs.tku.edu.tw, robin@mail.mine.tku.edu.tw

Abstract. In the information-based New Economy, the benefits and possibilities offered by Information and Communications Technology (ICT) has led to distance learning (DL) become realized. Due to the essence of flexibility provided by DL courses, students who attempt to balance their studies and employment might not put as much efforts as instructor expected into studying. Therefore, from the teaching and learning perspective, instructor needs to construct an effective distance-learning courseware that benefits students in a maximal learning capacity. In this paper, we refer to concept map and influence diagram to construct a courseware diagram that benefits both sides. With the help of our proposed courseware diagram, a maximum student learning performance can be achieved and just-in-time feedback from students can be delivered to instructor.

Keywords: distance learning, influence diagram, courseware diagram.

1 Introduction

Building the basic infrastructure of distance education becomes more solid and advanced. Current development of distance education is as follows: building platform, improving current language, creating new language, setting up standards, developing software engineering, and assessment of learning performance for distance learning. Studies made by researchers in the field of distance education are divided into following groups. Some researchers concentrate on developing adequate platform to support flexible distance learning, such as Intelligent Tutoring System (ITS), Learning Space [1], and SEND [2]. Some researchers dedicate on developing adequate programming language used on Web Browser, such as SMIL (Synchronized Multimedia Integration Language), and XML (Extension Multimedia Language). Some devote to developing the function of sharing and reusing course documents, such as SCORM (Sharable Object Reference Model) [3], IMS (Instructional Management System) [4], IEEE LOM (Learning Object Metadata) [5], ADL (Advanced Distributed Learning) [6]. Some commit themselves to build up Electronic Software for distance learning, such as RM system (Resource Management) [7], and MITS (Multimedia Interactive Telelearning System) [8]. Many of them are working on assessment for distance learning, such as Web based assessment [9]. Our study falls into the last field – measurement of student's learning performance. In our studies, we reference the theory of influence diagram and combine advantages provided by influence diagram to construct our courseware diagram. This paper is organized as follows. The following section, section 2

Y.-C. Chen, L.-W. Chang, and C.-T. Hsu (Eds.): PCM 2002, LNCS 2532, pp. 1017-1024, 2002.

describes our proposed courseware diagram in detail. In section 3, an example of courseware diagram for algorithm class is illustrated. Section 4 introduce the method of developing reduced and expand courseware diagram. Conclusions are presented in section 5.

2 Using Courseware Diagram to Represent Course Design Problem

Influence diagram is very useful for designing distance-learning courses. Due to the nature of designing courses, few adjustments should be made in order to meet the final goal – a maximized student learning result. Transformation from influence diagram to courseware diagram is described in this section.

Nodes used in our courseware diagram are evaluation nodes and course nodes that are very similar to decision nodes and chance nodes used in influence diagram. Decision nodes can represent *evaluation nodes*. And chance nodes can represent *course nodes*. The value node can represent the *final value* of student's learning performance.

There are six possible connections among three types of nodes. However, not all of them are all allowed in our courseware diagram for the sake of the violation of normal practice. Two types of links are prohibited. First, links from course unit to final value unit are prohibited because knowledge value can only be measured by taking exam. Second, links from evaluation node to evaluation node are constrained. Links from course unit to both course unit and evaluation unit and links from evaluation unit to final unit are defined as *informational link* represented as a solid line with arrowhead. Regarding links from evaluation unit to course unit, it is defined as *conditioning link* represented as a dash line with arrowhead.

2.1 Definitions of Courseware Diagram

Definition 1: A *Course Knowledge Weight* (CKW) is a value associated with every course unit. A Course Knowledge Weight reflects the importance of knowledge presented in the course unit. The more important the course unit is, the larger the value of CKW is. Instructor decides the value of CKW. The total value of CKW of all course units is always to be one, meaning 100%. The CKW value for a remedial course is always to be zero because new knowledge presented in a remedial course is nothing. It's reasonable to assign zero to CKW attached to a remedial course unit. An example of a CKW is "CKW=0.1".

Definition 2: An *Acquaintance Degree* (AD) is an accumulated course knowledge weight associated with a course unit. It is represented with a pair of number. An example of AD is "AD [0.4,0.6]". The number on the left shows the learning performance of the worst performed group of students or students who receive relatively lower score on an evaluation up to a certain course unit. The number on the right shows the learning performance of the best-performed group of students or students who receive relatively higher score on an evaluation up to a certain course unit. Acquaintance Degree is deduced by taking an evaluation in order to measure the actual or real learning performance.

Definition 3: *A Group Percentage* (GP) is a pair of values associated with an evaluation unit and indicates the percentage distribution among students who receive lower, average, and higher score in an evaluation. And example of GP is "GP [25,50,25]", meaning students are divided into three groups, 25 percent of students who receive relatively lower and relatively higher score and the rest of students, 50 percent, who receive an average score in an evaluation. The total value of a Group Percentage equals 100. The instructor decides these percentages. Group Percentage cannot be omitted despite whether there is a remedial course followed by an evaluation or not. In our courseware diagram, a very special evaluation node located right in front of the final value node. In real practice, no more regular courses or remedial courses will be given after the last evaluation unit.

Definition 4: *An Discount Rate* (DR) is a value associated with every discount bar placed on conditional links. An example of Discount Rate is "DR=0.9". We assume that student's score on an evaluation reflects the degree of his/her perception on previous taught knowledge. Based on GP assigned by instructor, every group of students gets an average score. The average score for the group of the best-performed students is definitely higher than that of the worst performed students. We assume average score for each group is X, Y, and Z respectively, whereas the relationship among them is X>Y>Z. Student's Acquaintance Degree before an evaluation times Discount Rate gets the actual learning performance received by students.

Definition 5: *An Individual Performance* (IP) indicates an individual's actual performance after a series of courses and evaluations. Like Acquaintance Degree that represents the range of the whole class's performance, Individual Performance represents a single person's actual performance. This number is accumulated by taking courses and deduced by taking evaluations.

In our courseware diagram, there are few restrictions required while designing a course. First, two consecutive evaluation units are not allowed in courseware diagram. Second, parallel learning is allowed in courseware diagram. The meaning of parallel learning can be explained as learning unrelated courses simultaneously within a certain period of time and as a way to differentiate students after taking an evaluation. The most important character of parallel learning is that every course on the path of parallel learning has to be taken by every student because all courses together consist of the whole class. The third restriction is that all paths have to be merged into the final evaluation node prior to the final value node. The reason is obvious. Only one evaluation node can exit before the final value node.

The most important factor in courseware diagram is the value of Acquaintance Degree (AD) indicating the expected best and worst learning performance of entire class along the path of courseware diagram. Another important factor is the value of Individual Performance (IP) indicating individual student's learning performance along the path of courseware diagram. A combination of IP and AD displays one student's performance comparing with entire class.

3 An Example of Constructing Courseware Diagram for Algorithms Course

As an example to show the usage of courseware diagram, we illustrate an example in this section. Figure 1 is a courseware diagram for algorithm class. This class starts with the course of mathematical foundations and ends with the last evaluation unit. On every course unit, there is a Course Knowledge Weight (CKW) attached to it and the total value of all course units is one. Due to the topology of parallel learning, unrelated courses can be embedded in a parallel structure. AD is calculated by adding up previous CKW on the path. So, at sorting course unit and data structure course unit, AD for both courses is 0.2. Before evaluation 1, AD should be 0.3 because there are totally three courses taken by students. These courses are weighted 0.1 for mathematical foundations course, 0.1 for sorting course, and 0.1 for data structure course respectively. The result of evaluation 1 is that 25 percent of best-performed students who receive an average score of 90, 50 percent of average performed students who receive an average score of 70, and 25 percent of worst performed students who receive an average score of 50. Therefore, the discount rate is 0.5, 0.7 and 0.9. AD for these three types of students is deduced to 0.3*50% for worst performed students, 0.3*70% for average performed students, and 0.3*90% for best-performed students. Before move on to the next course, the maximum AD is 0.27 (0.3*90%) and the minimum is 0.15 (0.3*50%). Then, all students have to further their study to advance data structure course (CKW=0.2), advance design & analysis (CKW=0.2), graph algorithm course (CKW=0.1), and Matrix operation course (CKW=0.1). However, graph algorithm and matrix operation courses can be learned simultaneously. These two courses are designed in a parallel learning structure. Advance data structure (0.2), advance design & analysis (0.2), and graph algorithm courses (0.1) that have an accumulated CKW 0.5 are included in evaluation 2 and should be deduced by discount rate (0.5,0.7,0.9). Before taking computing theory course, the maximum AD is 0.45 (0.5*90%) and the minimum is 0.25 (0.5*50%). Then, move on to computing theory course. In evaluation 3, computing theory course (CKW=0.1) and matrix operation course (CKW=0.1) are included and should be deduced by discount rate (0.5,0.6,0.7). Before reaching the final value unit, the maximum AD is 0.14 (0.2*70%) and the minimum is 0.1 (0.2*50%). By adding the maximum and minimum AD obtained in three evaluations, the AD for the final value unit is AD [0.5 (0.15+0.25+0.1), 0.86 (0.27+0.45+0.14)]. In conclusion, the expected students' learning performance is ranged between 0.5 and 0.86.

4 The Method of Developing Reduced and Expand Courseware Diagram

In the following section, we illustrate the transformation process from a reduced diagram to an expanded diagram and the process of reverse transformation. The purpose of two types of transformation is different and each transformation leads to different results and advantages.

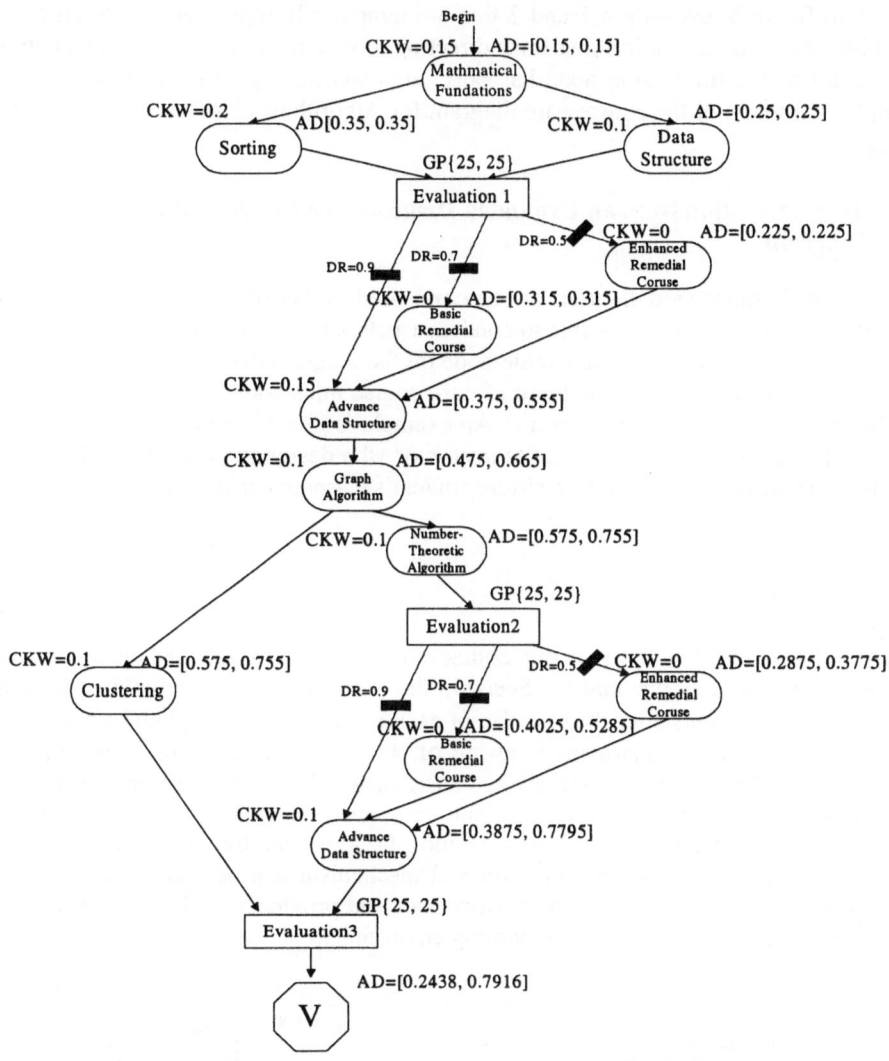

Fig. 1. Courseware Diagram for Algorithms Class

4.1 Transformation from a Reduced Courseware Diagram to an Expanded Diagram

The proposed courseware diagram for algorithm class shown in figure 1 is originally come from a reduced courseware diagram shown in figure 2. The simplest or the very beginning design of courseware diagram starts with a course unit (CKW=1) directing toward the final value node. Figure 3 shows how to develop core courses drawn in bold line that are divided into two types of courses, related courses (or courses arranged in sequence) and unrelated courses (or courses arranged in parallel structure). Expanding the structure of figure 3 leads to the structure shown in figure 4. In figure 5, it shows the place where instructor wishes to put evaluation unit. As shown in figure 5, evaluation 1 and 2 that are temporarily represented with an extra bold line, have three conditioning links directing toward next node but the evaluation node prior to the final value node has only one conditioning link attached to it. A complete structure of the courseware diagram for Algorithms class has already shown in figure 1.

4.2 Transformation from an Expanded Diagram to a Condensed Courseware Diagram

An expanded courseware diagram can be condensed to its original form by following the reverse direction. It is possible to condense a class to leave only core course units, one evaluation unit and one final value node on the diagram due to different demands required by the class. A combination of core course units and expanded course units is allowed in the courseware diagram. An example is given in figure 6. In brief, the proposed courseware diagram benefits instructor who design the class with flexibility and the function of evaluation to measure student's learning performance.

5 Conclusions

There are two key functions in our courseware diagram. First, the instructor can systematically design the class. Second, the instructor can receive just-in-time feedback from students after the exercise of each evaluation. Depending on the result in each evaluation, the instructor is aware of students' learning ability and decides whether to make adjustment for his/her class material. Under instructor's proper control, students' learning performance can be precisely measured and the instructor can cope with students with various education backgrounds by constantly adjusting class material. In conclusion, our proposed mechanism can perform a quantitative analysis based on students' learning performance and provide a flexible course design model for the instructor in distance learning environment.

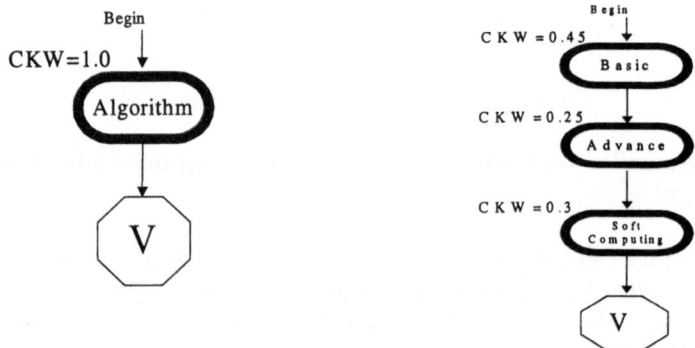

Fig. 2. A reduced courseware diagram for Algorithms class

Fig. 3. An expand structure of figure 4 with core courses

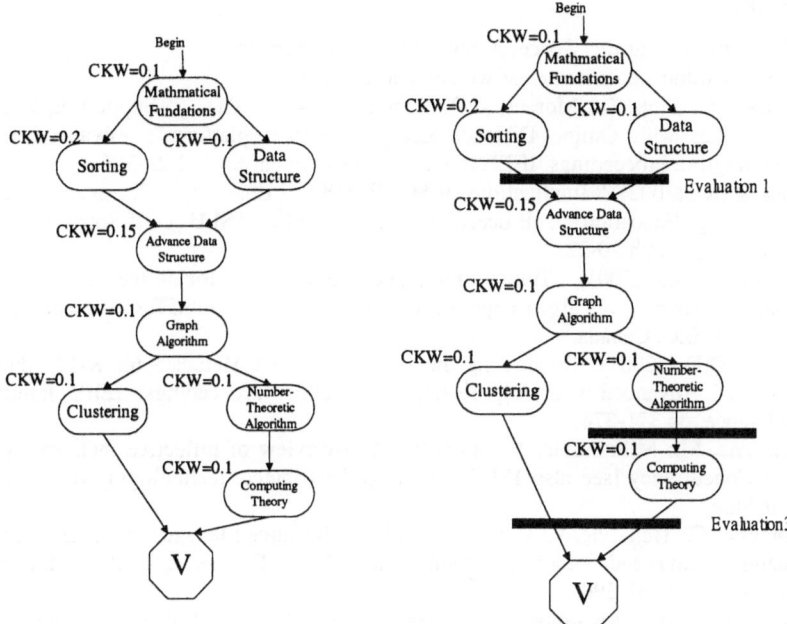

Fig. 4. An expand structure of figure 5 with all course units

Fig. 5. An expand structure of figure 6 with all course and evaluation units

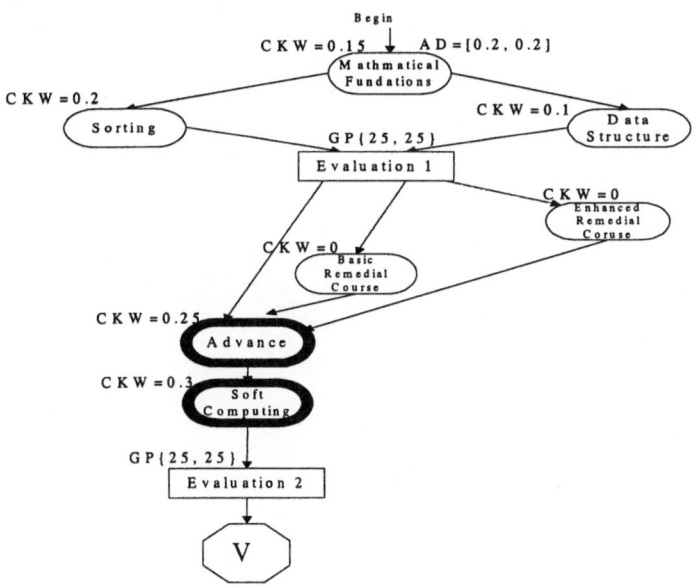

Fig. 6. An example of courseware diagram for a condensed Algorithms class

References

[1] IBM Software Learning Space, A new version of e-learning (http://www.lotus.com/home.nsf/welcome/learnspace)

[2] Correa, J.S.; Fink, D.; Moraes, C.P.; Sonntag, A.A., (2001). " Supporting knowledge communities with Online Distance Learning System platform", Advanced Learning Technologies,. Proceedings. IEEE International Conference, pp. 305 -306.

[3] Jones, E. R., (2002). " Implications of SCORM™ and Emerging E-learning Standards on Engineering Education" , Proceedings of the 2002 ASEE Gulf-Southwest Annual Conference, March 20-22.

[4] Karen Kaminski, (2001). "Transforming an entire institution for online delivery of degree programs: perspectives from experience " Third Annual WebCT Conference June 23, Vancouver, B.C. Canada.

[5] Suthers, D.D., (2001). "Evaluating the Learning Object Metadata for K-12 educational resources" Advanced Learning Technologies, 2001. Proceedings. IEEE International Conference, pp.371-374.

[6] Jovanovic, M.; Milutinovic, V. , (1999). "An overview of reflective memory systems", IEEE Concurrency [see also IEEE Parallel & Distributed Technology], Vol.7, Issue: 2 , April-June.

[7] Kimovski, G.; Trajkovic, V.; Davcev, D.(2001). "Resource Manager for distance education systems", Advanced Learning Technologies, 2001. Proceedings. IEEE International Conference, pp.387-390.

[8] Lei Yuan; Abiza, Y.; Karmouch, A. , (1999). "Self-guided multimedia courseware system over the Internet", Electrical and Computer Engineering, 1999 IEEE Canadian Conference, Vol. 3, pp.1595-1540.

[9] Chetty, M., (2000). "A theme for on-line Web-based assessment [of control engineering students", Engineering Science and Education Journal, Vol. 9, Issue: 1 , Feb.

On (In)security of "A Robust Image Authentication Method"

Takeyuki Uehara and Reihaneh Safavi-Naini

School of Information Technology and Computer Science,
University of Wollongong
Northfields Ave, Wollongong, NSW 2522, Australia
{tu01,rei}@uow.edu.au

Abstract. Image authentication is a challenging area of growing importance. Although a number of image authentication systems have been proposed in recent years but less attention has been paid to their evaluation. In this paper we analyze the JPEG compression tolerant image authentication scheme SARI [1], and show a number of ways of constructing fraudulent images that pass the verification test, hence defeating the system claimed security. We then show methods of modifying the system to make the attacks ineffective.

1 Introduction

Image authentication systems ensure that an image is authentic and is not tampered with. An image authentication system consists of two algorithms, an authentication algorithm which takes an image and some key information and generates an authenticated image, and a verification algorithm that takes a candidate image and the key information and produces a true or a false result.

Lin and Chang [1] proposed an authentication system that tolerates JPEG compression [2] to a designed level. The system uses the property that the relationship between two Discrete Cosine Transform (DCT) [3] coefficients (of the same order) in two image blocks is invariant under JPEG lossy compression. The feature codes generated by the system can be used as a hash value for the image, or encrypted to produce a message authentication code (MAC) for the image. The scheme has been claimed to be capable of distinguishing malicious manipulations from changes to the image that are due to JPEG lossy compression. Radhakrishnan and Memon [4] showed how to construct fraudulent images that are acceptable by this authentication system and proposed a method of protection against this attack. However, the attack is ineffective if the feature codes are encrypted.

In this paper, we present ways of constructing fraudulent images that pass the verification test, and also are visually undetectable. The attacks will work even if the feature codes are encrypted. We also propose a modification to the system to protect against these attacks. In the rest of this paper, first we give an overview of JPEG compression together with a brief description of SARI authentication system, and then present the attacks.

Y.-C. Chen, L.-W. Chang, and C.-T. Hsu (Eds.): PCM 2002, LNCS 2532, pp. 1025–1032, 2002.

2 Preliminaries

2.1 JPEG Compression

The main steps in JPEG [2] are as follows : i) the image is broken into 8×8 pixel blocks, ii) the blocks are transformed using 8×8 DCT, iii) the resulting DCT coefficients are quantized, and iv) the quantized coefficients are entropy coded.

Let $\mathcal{W}$ denote the set of pixel blocks in the image, where $\mathcal{W} = \{p_1, p_2, ..., p_\wp\}$. Then in the transform stage, each pixel block is transformed and produces 64 coefficients. Let $F_p^{(u,v)} \ \forall u, v \in [0, ..., 7]$ and $Q^{(u,v)}$ denote the DCT coefficients of a block p and the quantization table, respectively. Then the quantized value of the coefficient at (u,v) position in block p is given by $T_p^{(u,v)} = rint(\frac{F_p^{(u,v)}}{Q^{(u,v)}})$ where $rint$ is an integer rounding function. The de-quantization of $T_p^{(u,v)}$ is given by $\tilde{F}_p^{(u,v)} = T_p^{(u,v)} \cdot Q^{(u,v)} = rint(\frac{F_p^{(u,v)}}{Q^{(u,v)}}) \cdot Q^{(u,v)}$.

2.2 SARI Authentication System

Lin and Chang [1] proposed an authentication system in which an authenticated image remains authenticated under JPEG lossy compression.

The system is based on the following theorem.

Theorem 1. *Assume $F_p^{(u,v)}$ and $F_q^{(u,v)}$ are DCT coefficients of two arbitrary 8×8 non-overlapping blocks of image X, and $Q^{(u,v)}$ is the quantization table of JPEG lossy compression $\forall u, v \in [0, ..., 7]$ and $p, q \in [1, ..., \wp]$. Define $\Delta F_{p,q}^{(u,v)} = F_p^{(u,v)} - F_q^{(u,v)}$ and $\Delta \tilde{F}_{p,q}^{(u,v)} = \tilde{F}_p^{(u,v)} - \tilde{F}_q^{(u,v)}$.*

Assume a fixed threshold $k^{(u,v)} \in \Re, \forall u, v$, and define $\tilde{k}^{(u,v)} = rint(\frac{k^{(u,v)}}{Q^{(u,v)}})$. Then,

$$\text{if } \Delta F_{p,q}^{(u,v)} > k^{(u,v)}, \ \Delta \tilde{F}_{p,q}^{(u,v)} \geq \begin{cases} \tilde{k}^{(u,v)} \cdot Q^{(u,v)}, & \frac{k^{(u,v)}}{Q^{(u,v)}} \in Z \\ (\tilde{k}^{(u,v)} - 1) \cdot Q^{(u,v)}, & \frac{k^{(u,v)}}{Q^{(u,v)}} \notin Z \end{cases}$$

$$\text{if } \Delta F_{p,q}^{(u,v)} < k^{(u,v)}, \ \Delta \tilde{F}_{p,q}^{(u,v)} \leq \begin{cases} \tilde{k}^{(u,v)} \cdot Q^{(u,v)}, & \frac{k^{(u,v)}}{Q^{(u,v)}} \in Z \\ (\tilde{k}^{(u,v)} + 1) \cdot Q^{(u,v)}, & \frac{k^{(u,v)}}{Q^{(u,v)}} \notin Z \end{cases}$$

$$\text{if } \Delta F_{p,q}^{(u,v)} = k^{(u,v)}, \ \Delta \tilde{F}_{p,q}^{(u,v)} = \begin{cases} \tilde{k}^{(u,v)} \cdot Q^{(u,v)}, & \frac{k^{(u,v)}}{Q^{(u,v)}} \in Z \\ \tilde{k}^{(u,v)} \cdot Q^{(u,v)} \text{ or } (\tilde{k}^{(u,v)} \pm 1) \cdot Q^{(u,v)}, & \frac{k^{(u,v)}}{Q^{(u,v)}} \notin Z \end{cases}$$

The authentication system produces feature codes, each obtained from a particular frequency of a pair of blocks. The pairs of blocks can be chosen using a secret key. Each bit of the feature code is determined by comparing $\Delta F_{p,q}^{(u,v)}$ with $k^{(u,v)}$. The verification system compares $\Delta \tilde{F}_{p,q}^{(u,v)}$ with $\tilde{k}^{(u,v)} \cdot Q^{(u,v)}$ that is derived from the feature codes, and determines the verification result. It can be seen that if a modification of the image does not change $\Delta \tilde{F}_{p,q}^{(u,v)}$, the verification system fails to detect the modification.

3   Attacks

Radhakrishnan and Memon [4] showed a method of finding the secret block pairing if $O(log\wp)$ authenticated images using the same key are found. Once the pairing is discovered, the block pairs can be modified without being detected by the verification system. However an arbitrary modification, most likely, will result in visually detectable artifacts, as had been noted by the original authors [1]. Moreover, encrypting the feature codes will make the attack completely ineffective.

We note that not all modifications result in visually detectable changes. For example, the method used in [5], uses combinations of DCT coefficients such that the central part of a block is modified in a smooth way, while the border of the block is unchanged. In Section 3.1, we describe an attack which generates a fraudulent image with no visual sign of being fraudulent, and succeeds even if the feature codes are encrypted.

3.1   New Attacks

We consider two types of attacks.

1. The image is modified by simultaneously changing a pair of blocks by the same amount. The attack will succeed regardless of the precision of the feature codes and the number of protected coefficients. The modifications include,
   - adding or removing figures, letters and objects to the original image.
   - modifying figures, letters or objects in the original image.
2. If some of the coefficients are not protected, they can be arbitrarily changed.

3.2   Modifying Block Pairs

This attack succeeds if block pairing is known even if all the coefficients are protected and long precision feature codes are used. In Section 3.3 we show how to find the pairing even if the feature code is encrypted. The attack is by modifying quantized coefficients of a JPEG compressed image by an equal amount in pairs of blocks. Figures, letters or objects can be added or removed to pairs of blocks by adding an 8×8 block of quantized coefficients to the quantized coefficients of the pair. This is based on the following proposition.

Proposition 1. *Let D be an 8×8 pixel block, and $G^{(u,v)}$, $u,v \in [0,...,7]$ denote its transformed and then quantized DCT coefficient in (u,v) position. Let $\tilde{F}_p(u,v)'$ and $\tilde{F}_q(u,v)'$ denote the coefficients of the reconstructed blocks corresponding to $T_p^{(u,v)} + G^{(u,v)}$ and $T_q^{(u,v)} + G^{(u,v)}$, respectively, and $\Delta\tilde{F}_{p,q}^{(u,v)}$* ' *denote the difference $\tilde{F}_p^{(u,v)}$* ' $- \tilde{F}_q^{(u,v)}$ '. *Then $\Delta\tilde{F}_{p,q}^{(u,v)} = \Delta\tilde{F}_{p,q}^{(u,v)}$* '.*
   Proof:

$$\Delta\tilde{F}_{p,q}^{(u,v)} = T_p^{(u,v)} \cdot Q^{(u,v)} - T_q^{(u,v)} \cdot Q^{(u,v)}$$

and

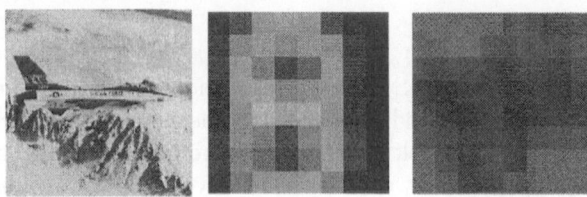

Fig. 1. The original image (left), a pattern "8" (center), and a pattern similar to $\not{\nu}$ (right).

$$\Delta \tilde{F}_{p,q}^{(u,v)}{}' = T_p^{(u,v)}{}' \cdot Q^{(u,v)} - T_q^{(u,v)}{}' \cdot Q^{(u,v)}$$
$$= (T_p^{(u,v)} + G^{(u,v)}) \cdot Q^{(u,v)} - (T_q^{(u,v)} + G^{(u,v)}) \cdot Q^{(u,v)}$$
$$= T_p^{(u,v)} \cdot Q^{(u,v)} - T_q^{(u,v)} \cdot Q^{(u,v)}$$
$$= \Delta \tilde{F}_{p,q}^{(u,v)}$$

Now suppose the attacker has a compressed image and its corresponding feature code. The attack is as follows.

1. The attacker creates the pattern D that is to be added to the block pair p and q.
2. He transforms D, and quantizes the coefficients by $Q^{(u,v)}$ to obtain $G^{(u,v)}$, $\forall u, v$.
3. Then he finds $T_p^{(u,v)} + G^{(u,v)}$ and $T_q^{(u,v)} + G^{(u,v)}$ and de-quantizes the result.

The method will produce visually undetectable changes if the following conditions are satisfied.

C1 To make the block artifacts undetectable, the pixels on the edges of block D should be close to 0. This condition can be ignored if D includes figures or letters with sharp edges at block edges.
C2 The modification should not change the difference between $T_p^{(u,v)}$ and $T_q^{(u,v)}$.
C3 G must be chosen such that the de-quantization and then inverse-transform of the modified coefficients, $T_p^{(u,v)} + G^{(u,v)}$ and $T_q^{(u,v)} + G^{(u,v)}$, do not produce a value outside the valid pixel range (for example, 0 to 255).

Figures 1 and 2 give an example of adding a pattern to an image. We followed the steps above, showing the case of pairing odd number and even number blocks for pattern "8" which is the pairing used in the original paper, and pairing distant location blocks for a pattern similar to $\not{\nu}$.

The pattern D that is added to the image is given in Figure 1. The attack succeeded because the two paired blocks have been smooth. We note that in the case of pattern "8", it is obvious that the same pattern appears twice but in the case of the other pattern, the modification on one of the two blocks (in the background) is not distinguishable. In some cases it might be more difficult to succeed. For example consider removing black numbers from a white license

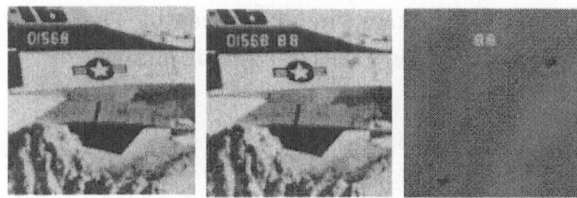

Fig. 2. Close up of the original image (left), the modified image (center), and difference between the original and the modified images (right). The gray region, the darker part, and the brighter part correspond to $\delta^{(i,j)} = 0$, $\delta^{(i,j)} < 0$, and $\delta^{(i,j)} > 0$, respectively.

Fig. 3. The original license plate (left) and removal experiments of "9" (center) and "5" (right).

plate. Assume that the image is gray scale and pixel values are in the range $[0, 255]$, and the black and white pixel values are 0 and 255, respectively. Then to modify the numbers on the plate, some pixels need to be changed from black to white, or from white to black and so 255 has to be added to, or subtracted from these pixels, respectively. If the pixel to be modified is black and the pixel in the corresponding location in the paired block is white, then adding 255 to the pixel in the paired block will violate condition C3.

Let $r_p^{(i,j)}$ and $r_q^{(i,j)}$, $i, j \in [0, ..., 7]$, denote the pixel values of block p and q, respectively, and $\delta^{(i,j)}$, $i, j \in [0, ..., 7]$ denote the pixel values of the modification block.

Then the following must be satisfied.

$$0 \leq r_p^{(i,j)} + \delta^{(i,j)} \leq 255 \text{ and } 0 \leq r_q^{(i,j)} + \delta^{(i,j)} \leq 255 \text{ , } i, j \in [0, ..., 7] \qquad (1)$$

For example, if we want $r_p^{(i,j)}$ to be as bright (ie. large) as possible, we choose the largest possible $\delta^{(i,j)}$ that satisfies condition (1). That is, we choose $\min\{(255 - r_p^{(i,j)}), (255 - r_q^{(i,j)})\}$. If $r_q^{(i,j)}$ is large, then $255 - r_q^{(i,j)}$ is small and so is $\delta^{(i,j)}$. Hence, $r_p^{(i,j)}$ cannot be increased by a large amount. From above, the range of $\delta^{(i,j)}$ is given as follows.

Theorem 2. *The range of $\delta^{(i,j)}$ is given by $[0, \min\{(255 - r_p^{(i,j)}), (255 - r_q^{(i,j)})\}]$ and $[(-1)\min\{r_p^{(i,j)}, r_q^{(i,j)}\}, 0]$ for the brightening and darkening modification, respectively.*

Figure 3 shows the removal of letters from a license plate. Assuming even and odd block pairing, two horizontally neighboring blocks are modified. As an example, two digits were made bright so that it became the same color as the background of the plate.

From above observations, we define a *vulnerable property* as follows.

Vulnerable property : If the range of $\delta^{(i,j)}$, given by Theorem 2, is large, then $r_p^{(i,j)}$ and $r_q^{(i,j)}$ are vulnerable against large modifications.

3.3 Finding Block Pairs

To increase security, block pairings can be kept secret. Suppose the attacker has an authenticated image (image together with its authenticator) and also access to a verification oracle: that is the verification program that inputs an image and its authenticator tag and produces a yes or no answer if the image does match or does not match the authenticator, respectively.

Algorithm 1 : Finding a block pair.
1: The attacker chooses a block p_i to be modified.
2: loop until the pairing block is found.
3:    Choose a block p_k, where $k \neq i$.
4:    Modify p_i and p_k by the same amount.
5:    Give the modified image to the oracle and observe its output.
6:    If it is accepted
7:       Exit the loop.

Note that the attacker does not have to find all block pairs but the ones which he intends to modify.

The cost of finding p_k for a chosen p_i is $\wp - 1$. To find all block pairs, Algorithm 1 is iteratively applied to the blocks. In each iteration, it finds a pair. Initially there are $\wp/2$ pairs to find and in the first iteration it tries at most $\wp - 1$ blocks. Then the number of pairs becomes $\wp/2 - 1$ in the second iteration and it experiments $\wp - 3$ blocks. The number of blocks to be examined at ith iteration is $\wp - (2i - 1)$. There are $\wp/2$ pairs and so the cost of finding all pairs is $\sum_{i=1}^{\wp/2}(\wp - (2i - 1)) = \wp^2/2 - \wp^2/4 = \wp^2/4$.

For example, the 512×512 image lena has 4096 blocks. The cost of finding p_k for a chosen p_i is $4095 \approx 2^{12}$ and that of finding all pairs is 2^{22}, which is considered small in cryptographic systems. If each of 64 frequencies uses different pairing, each pairing can be independently found and in this case, the cost of finding a single, and all pairs for 64 frequencies is $2^{12} \times 64 = 2^{18}$, and $2^{22} \times 64 = 2^{28}$, respectively.

3.4 Attack on Unprotected Coefficients

When only some of the coefficients are protected, the unprotected ones can be arbitrarily modified. Because of visual significance of lower frequencies, it is more likely to choose them for protection. So if the added pattern is obtained by modifying the higher frequency components, the resulting modification will look like spraying the image with black or white dots.

Figure 4 is an example of such attacks.

Fig. 4. The two images will be authenticated with the coefficients 0-10 (left) and 0-59 (right) protected.

4   An Improved System

The attacks in [4] and this paper clearly show that simply hiding the block-pairing will not add security because each feature code can be tied to a single pair of blocks and so the pairing can be found easily. If we allow two pairs to share a block, then modifying one block affects both pairs and so the attacker has to find all the blocks in the two pairs which will increase the cost of the attack. The higher security will be at the cost of longer hash value as blocks are repeated in the pairs. Extending this basic idea allows us to modify the system to provide higher protection against the attacks.

We modify the algorithm by replacing the random pairing method with a new algorithm that constructs pairs which satisfy a number of properties. The properties ensure higher cost of attack, while minimizing the increase in the length of the hash value.

Let $\mathcal{P} = \{p_{a1}, p_{a2}\}$ be a pair of blocks and a let $\mathcal{S}_i = \{\mathcal{P}_1, \mathcal{P}_2, ..., \mathcal{P}_s\}, \forall i$ be sets of pairs.

We call two pairs *linked* if they have a block in common.

We require $\mathcal{S}_i, \forall i$ to satisfy the following properties.

Property 1 : Each pair has exactly one block in common with one more pair. That is for $\mathcal{P}_a \in \mathcal{S}_i$ there exists exactly one $\mathcal{P}_b \in \mathcal{S}_i$ such that $\mathcal{P}_a \cap \mathcal{P}_b \neq \phi$, $\forall a, b, a \neq b$. That is, each pair in $\mathcal{S}_i$ shares one block with another pair. All pairs in $\mathcal{S}_i$ are linked so that the number of pairs for a given number of blocks is minimum.

Property 2 : For $\mathcal{P}_a \in \mathcal{S}_i$ and $\mathcal{P}_c \in \mathcal{S}_j$, $\mathcal{P}_a \cap \mathcal{P}_c = \phi$, $\forall i, j, a, c, i \neq j$. That is, $\mathcal{S}_i$ and $\mathcal{S}_j$ do not share blocks.

Property 3 : $\cup \mathcal{S}_i = \mathcal{W}$. That is, the members of $\mathcal{S}_i$ cover all blocks.

Property 1 ensures that pairs in a subset $\mathcal{S}_i$ are linked and the increase in length of the hash is minimized.

Linking pairs increases the cost of the attack. For example if two pairs share a block, that is $\mathcal{S}_i = \{(p_{a1}, p_{a2}), (p_{a2}, p_{a3})\}$, and assuming an attacker wants to change p_{a1}, then to make the change undetectable, instead of modifying the pair p_{a1}, p_{a2}, he has to modify three blocks p_{a1}, p_{a2} and p_{a3}. A modified version of Algorithm 1 given in Section 3.3 in this case, will have the cost $O(\wp^3)$ which is higher than the original case $(O(\wp^2))$. In general if $\mathcal{S}_i$ contains $s + 1$ blocks with the property that all the pairs linked, the cost of attack will increase to $O(\wp^{s+1})$.

By requiring a block to be in at most two pairs, we ensure that the increase in the length is at its minimum. This means that S_i consists of s pairs and $s+1$ blocks. Assuming all subsets are of the same size, then the number of subsets required to cover $\wp$ blocks of the whole image is $\frac{\wp}{s+1}$ and the total number of pairs in $S_i, \forall i$ is given by $\frac{\wp \cdot s}{s+1}$.

We noted that the increased security is at the cost of longer hash value. By using the above method, the number of pairs increases from $\frac{\wp}{2}$ to $\frac{\wp \cdot s}{s+1}$ and so the ratio of the new hash length to the original length is $\frac{2s}{s+1} = 2 - \frac{2}{s+1}$. For example, if S_i consists of two pairs sharing one block, ie. $s = 2$, the feature code size is $\frac{4}{3}$ times larger than the feature codes generated by the original system. For higher values of s the length gradually increases and gradually approaches a ratio of 2. That is, the length of the hash will be at most twice the original length.

To minimize the increase in the hash length the following two approaches can be used. *Approach 1* : Combine the random block pairing of the original algorithm and the linked block pairing described above. More specifically, *i*) use the random block pairing to form blocks, or *ii*) use the linked pairing algorithm if the pair is a *vulnerable pair*. *Approach 2* : Use the linked block pairing method for regions of interest. For other regions, use random block pairing.

5   Conclusion

We showed methods of modifying authenticated images, which are visually undetectable and pass verification test. We identified vulnerable pairs that can be used to apply large modifications without being detectable. We showed how to modify the system to make it more secure against these attacks.

References

1. Lin, Ching-Yung, Chang, Shih-Fu: Robust Image Authentication Method Surviving JPEG Lossy Compression. Storage and Retrieval for Image and Video Databases (SPIE) (1998) 296-307
2. ITU: JPEG Standard : CCITT Recommendation T.81. International Telecommunication union (1993)
3. Ahmed, N., Natarajan, T., Rao, K.R.: Discrete Cosine Transform. IEEE Trans. on Computers C-23 (1974) 90-93
4. Radhakrishnan, R., Memon, N.: On the Security of the SARI Image Authentication System. Proc. of International Conference on Image Processing vol 3 (2001) 971-974
5. Kuribayashi, Minoru, Tanaka, Hatsukazu: A Watermarking Scheme Based on the Characteristic of Addition among DCT coefficients. Proc. of ISW2000 (2000) 1-14

A Software Protection System for Internet Commerce

Chu-Hsing Lin[1] and Chen-Yu Lee[2]

[1] Department of Computer Science and Information Engineering,
Tunghai University, Taichung 407, Taiwan, R.O.C.
`chlin@mail.thu.edu.tw`

[2] Department of Computer Science and Information Engineering,
National Chiao-Tung University, 300 Hsinchu, Taiwan, R.O.C.
`chenyu@csie.nctu.edu.tw`

Abstract. Copyright protection of software program is crucial for the prosperity of software market. In this paper, we propose a dual software protection scheme. After purchasing a program from merchant, a buyer can exactly install it once. If the buyer redistributed a copy of the program, it could not be installed. Further, if the buyer could break the protection method and redistributed a copy of program, the merchant would be able to identify the traitor.

1 Introduction

Copyright protection of digital data is a crucial issue for software market. Buyers who illegally redistribute copies of digital data he (or she) purchased, disregarding the intellectual property or copyright, are called traitors [11, 9]. The works for copyright protections are twofold: the first one is to protect the software from double installation and the second is to identify the traitor who originally purchased the software. In this paper, we propose a dual protection scheme for copyright programs. After purchasing a program from merchant, a buyer can exactly install it once. If the buyer redistributed a copy of the program, it could not be installed. Further, if the buyer could break the one-time installation method and redistributed copies, the merchant would be able to identify the traitor. The organization of the paper is as follows. In Section 2, we depict the model of the system. The trading subsystem of our scheme appears in Section 3. The idea of one-time installation package is described in Section 4. In Section 5, the identification of a traitor is given. Section 6 is the security analysis. Then the followed section is on the implementation of our scheme. And finally we have a conclusion.

2 The Model of the System Overview

In this section, we first depict the model of the dual software protection (DSP model, in short). The parties involved are: a buyer B, a merchant M, a trusted registration center RC and an arbiter A. Some assumptions are made in our model:

Y.-C. Chen, L.-W. Chang, and C.-T. Hsu (Eds.): PCM 2002, LNCS 2532, pp. 1033-1040, 2002.
© Springer-Verlag Berlin Heidelberg 2002

- The buyer B and the merchant M have registered to a trusted registration center RC (e.g. bank) before the system starts. They have their own certificates and public/private key pairs respectively.
- The merchant can get the timestamp $time_B$ and some environment parameter env_B, explained later, from the buyer's computer.
- The installation procedure runs in a temporary directory of buyer's computer and the directory will be deleted by the package after installation successfully.

The DSP is composed of three subsystems: trading subsystem, one-time installation subsystem, and traitor tracing subsystem. Further, the trading subsystem includes three phases: initialization, one-time account creation, and shopping.

3 Trading Subsystem

To buy a software product, the buyer B first visits the merchant M's website, and generates a purchase information $text$. B selects some secret information and uses them to create a one-time account on RC. RC will verify the information of B and then signs on the account. Afterwards, B is able to purchase a one-time installation package from M by using this account. The one-time installation package is described in the next section. In the following, the trading subsystem is composed of three phases: initialization phase, one-time account creation phase, and shopping phase. Note that in this paper we use the notations: E_{key} and D_{key}, as symmetric encryption and decryption; E_{pk} and D_{sk} as asymmetric encryption/decryption; and Sig_{sk} as a signature scheme using key sk.

3.1 Initialization Phase

In this phase, the buyer B has to prepare some information about his (or her) own identity to be used in the following transactions with M and RC. B sends his (or her) purchasing information $text$ to M and gets back an order identity ID_{text}. In the next phase, B will use the ID_{text} to ask RC to make a signature on this trade.

The steps of initialization are as follows:

Step 1. B visits merchant's website and prepares a purchasing information text. B generates a signature $BSig_{text}$, by using sk_B on $text$, and sends $(text, BSig_{text})$ to the merchant M.

Step 2. M verifies the $BSig_{text}$ and computes $h_{text} \leftarrow hash(text, BSig_{text})$, where hash is an one-way hash function, e.g. SHA-2 [3]. Then he computes the signature $MSig_{text}$, signing on h_{text}, and generates an ID number ID_{text} corresponding to $text$. Finally, M sends $(MSig_{text}, ID_{text}, h_{text})$ to B.

Step 3. B computes $h'_{text} \leftarrow hash(text, BSig_{text})$ and compares h_{text} with h'_{text}. If they are not equal, it means that the merchant receives incorrect purchasing information $text$. Otherwise, this phase is completed successfully.

3.2 One-Time Account Creation Phase

In this phase, the main work is to create a one-time account on RC for this trade. First the buyer selects two random numbers (i, j), and uses j as a key to encrypt the number i by using a symmetric cryptosystem, e.g. AES, Triple-DES. Let the encrypted result be OTA. We use OTA as buyer's one-time account. The buyer then splits j into two parts: j_1 and j_2. Further, B sends ID_{text}, OTA, and j_1 to RC. RC verifies and stores them into its database. The steps of one-time account creation phase are as follows:

Step 1. B selects two large random numbers (i, j) and computes a one-time account $OTA \leftarrow E_j(i)$ by using a symmetric cryptosystem. Then, B splits j into two parts: j_1 and j_2 by using key splitting or secret sharing schemes [2, 6]. Note that OTA is the one-time account of B for this trade.

Step 2. B computes $WdBSig \leftarrow Sig_B (ID_{text}, E_{pk_{RC}} (OTA), j_1, MSig_{text}, h_{text})$, and sends $((ID_{text}, E_{pk_{RC}} (OTA), j_1, MSig_{text}, h_{text}), WdBSig, OTA\_reg)$ to RC, where (pk_{RC}, sk_{RC}) is the public/private key pair of RC and OTA_req is a request of creating a one-time account, which can avoid B's junk messages.

Step 3. RC verifies $MSig_{text}$, $WdBSig$, and stores $(OTA, ID_{text}, j_1, h_{text}, MSig_{text})$ corresponding to B's real identity ID_B in database.

Step 4. RC computes $n \leftarrow hash(OTA)$, $WdRCSig \leftarrow Sig_{sk_{RC}} (n)$ and sends $(n, WdRCSig)$ back to B to acknowledge that the information received is valid.

3.3 Shopping Phase

In this phase, the main work is to verify buyer B's shopping request. First B sends his (or her) one-time account, part of his (or her) secret, RC's signature, and ID of the purchasing order to the merchant M. M verifies and then stores them in a database. After the verification, M begins to prepare the one-time installation package for B. And the procedure will be introduced in the next section. The steps in the shopping phase are as follows:

Step 1. B sends $(n, WdRCSig, ID_{text}, j_2)$ to M.

Step 2. M verifies $WdRCSig$, and then stores (n, ID_{text}, j_2) corresponding to text in a trade database. M sends back an acknowledgement ACK and its signature $MSig_{ACK}$, $(ACK, MSig_{ACK})$, to acknowledge that the information received is valid.

Step 3. M begins to prepare the one-time installation package for B. (in the next section)

4 One-Time Installation Subsystem

4.1 One-Time Installation Package Preparation

At the end of the above subsystem, the buyer B proceeds to download the software product if the merchant M can accept the purchasing information. In other words, the one-time installation subsystem is going to start. In this subsystem, M will generate a one-time installation package. This package is obtained from the setup files of the purchased software with buyer's important information hidden. By the package, the software program can only be installed and executed in the buyer's computer.

First, M gets the client's timestamp $time_B$ and environment parameters env_B from B's computer. M generates an installation key $key_{OTIS} \leftarrow hash(n \text{ xor } time_B)$. Then M uses this key to encrypt the setup files (SF). Further, M hides the data string $(ID_{text} \parallel env_B)$ into the icon of the package by using an invisible watermark technique WAT [10, 12], where $\parallel$ indicates concatenation. Finally, M packs the encrypted setup files (ESF) with a convenient user interface, and then the result is called "one-time installation package." The steps in the one-time installation package preparation are as follows:

Step 1. $Key_{OTIS} \leftarrow hash(n \text{ xor } time_B)$.

Step 2. $ESF \leftarrow E_{Key_{OTIS}}(SF)$.

Step 3. $Icon\_watermark \leftarrow WAT(Icon, (ID_{text} \parallel env_B))$, and $OTIP \leftarrow \{Icon, ESF\}$.

4.2 Package Installation

On the other hand, B needs to install the one-time installation package on-line immediately after downloading it. B's computer sends the icon to M to execute the package. M extracts ID_{text} and env_B, using an operation EXT, from $Icon\_watermark$, and checks the ID_{text} whether it has been used before. If not, M then sends n and env_B back to B, and n is used as the software's serial number. First, the package checks the received env_B. If env_B is the same as that in B's computer, the package will keep running; otherwise, the package is aborted. Then the package generates the installation key key_{OTIS}, by using n and $time_B$, in the same way as that in merchant's key generating procedure. Further, the package uses key_{OTIS} to decrypt ESF and then begins the installation of the bought program. All the installation runs in a temporary directory, and the package will update the file timestamp when completed. The steps in the package installation are as follows:

Step 1. $OTIP$ sends $Icon\_watermark$ to M.

Step 2. M: $(ID_{text} \parallel env_B) \leftarrow EXT(Icon\_watermark)$ and search n by ID_{text} from the database.

Step 3. M sends (n, env_B) to $OTIP$.

Step 4. $OTIP$: $Key_{OTIS} \leftarrow hash(n \text{ xor } time_B)$ and $SF \leftarrow D_{Key_{OTIS}}(ESF)$.

5 Traitors Identification Subsystem

The original setup file is protected under the one-time installation package by using the proposed scheme. We imagine that the buyer B could break it and redistribute the software illegally. Now, the problem is how the merchant M can identify the traitor. It will need the embedded data n and the trade database to obtain the proof of redistribution. And then M presents the proof to ask RC or arbiter A to help identifying the traitor B. Remembering that, when selling the software product, M gets n, which is the important information for B, and M hides it in the icon of the one-time installation package. The steps of identification are as follow:

Step1. M extracts n and ID_{text} from the icon of the copy.

Step 2. M uses n and ID_{text} to find the corresponding j_2 and $text$ from the records in the trade database. If these are related, M sends $proof_1=(n, ID_{text}, text, j_2)$ to RC and asks for identifying the traitor.

Step 3. RC searches its registration database for the value OTA' using ID_{text}. RC computes $n'' \leftarrow hash(OTA')$. By comparing n' with n, if they are equal then RC offers j_1, the identification ID_B of the buyer, his (or her) one-time account OTA', and a signature $TriRCSig \leftarrow Sig_{pk_{RC}}(OTA')$ on OTA' to M. Otherwise, RC will refuse M's request.

Step 4.   By combing j_1 and j_2, M can get the j.

However, if RC refuses to help identifying the traitor, then M can send the $proof_1'=(n, WdRCSig, ID_{text}, text, j_2)$ to the arbiter A. Note that here we assume that the arbiter A is trustworthy. A verifies $WdRCSig$. If it is not matched, A rejects M's request. Otherwise, A sends $proof_1$ to RC and requests $(n, j_1, ID_B, OTA', TriRCSig)$. Then A verifies $TriRCSig$ and computes $n'' \leftarrow hash(OTA')$. By comparing n'' with n, if the same, then A offers j_1, the identification of buyer ID_B, and his (or her) one-time account OTA' to M. Otherwise, A will refuse M's request.

On knowing the real identity of B, M tries to convince arbiter A that B has redistributed the software bought under the description $text$ from M. The trial protocol is summarized as follows:

Step 1. M sends the $proof_2=(j, OTA', ID_B, WdRCSig, TriRCSig)$ to A.

Step 2. A verifies $WdRCSig$ and $TriRCSig$. If matched, the secret OTA' of B responsible for the account on RC is known by M. That is, B has redistributed something.

Step 3. A computes $i \leftarrow D_j(OTA')$, and A asks B whether he (or she) has another valid i also using the same number j in this trade. If it is true, B must show the related information. If B can't do that, then it convinces A that B is guilty for redistributing the copy.

6   Security Analysis

In discussing the security of the proposed method, we divide it into two parts: the securities of the trading subsystem and the one-time installation subsystem. Remember again, i and j are selected as secret information by the buyer B. The security of the merchant M relies on two things. One is n, which is contained in the digital product, and the other is one-time installation package. The security of B relies on i and that is relative to n.

6.1 Security in Trading Subsystem

The security can be discussed from two different points of view: the buyer and the merchant. For merchant, the security problem is focus on illegal redistribution. If the traitor redistributes the software product and M can get the copy luckily then M can extract the secret information n of B, where ID_{text} is the ID of the product used in the purchase. M can get j_2 and $text$. These enable M to ask RC, or in the worst case enforced by A, to identify the traitor. Then M can retrieve $(j_2, OTA', ID_B, TriRCSig)$, and makes the proof presenting to A. Finally, A will arbitrate fairly if the buyer is criminal.

On the other hand, the buyer may concern the problem his/her identity being exposed. In the proposed system, B creates a one-time account by using cryptographic technique. RC just knows (OTA, j_1) and then records them with B's real identity ID_B. B sends n, j_2 and ID_{text} to M. M may use (n, OTA) to get some information from RC. However, M has no information of ID_B. Of course, basically, we have to assume that RC would not collude with M. That is, we have made the assumption RC is trustworthy as in Section 2.

All the information transmission in the subsystem is signed by a signature scheme for the purpose of integration and authentication. It can be resistant against attacks, such as replay attack.

6.2 Security in One-Time Installation Package

For the security of the one-time installation package, it is made a one-to-one relation between the package and the buyer's computer. The security rests on the three points: the system environment parameters, the file timestamp, and the temporary directory for executing the installation.

- System environment parameters: when B downloads the one-time installation package, the envB is hidden in the icon of the package and will be checked before installation. This prevents the package from being distributed elsewhere. The values of the parameters envB will be distinct for different computer hardware and software system environment. If B redistributes the copy to the other people, it will not be able to execute successfully.
- File timestamp: after the installation is completed, the package will update automatically the file timestamp to prevent from being used twice. Since the installation key is generated from n and timeB by using one-way hash function hash. If the file timestamp is not exact, the package will not generate correctly the installation key. Therefore, the package cannot be successfully installed.
- Temporary directory: it creates a temporary directory when the package is going to be installed. All intermediary work is performed in this temporary directory. The directory should be deleted as soon as the installation is completed to prevent from dumpster diving attack [5].

Besides, we consider one case of possible attacks to our system – the merchant impersonation attack – an attacker might try to impersonate the merchant. However, since the installation is required to be on-line, the package need to communicate with the merchant's server to reveal env_B from the icon and gets back the serial number n. If the attacker impersonates the merchant, the package can't get the exact n from the corresponding ID_{text}.

Considering the package again, M hides the important information into the icon by using strong watermark technique [12, 14]. The watermark technique should be selected carefully. It should be strong enough to resist against possible attacks of digital process. However, the watermark is the weakest part in the protection of the package. If the watermark is cracked, it may result in two possibilities. The first possibility is that the cracker moves or damages the information hidden in the icon. In this case, the package will not work correctly. The package requires the exact information hidden in the icon to decrypt ESF. Without correctly decrypted, the package cannot be installed. The second possibility is that if the cracker gets a copy of the package, and changes the hidden information in the icon to some other existing one. It is clearly that the env_B are not matched. Therefore, ESF cannot be decrypted exactly. The third possibility is that if the cracker also copies the package to the other computer in very short time and attempts to install it. In this case, the cracker may be able to pass the check of timestamp $time_B$, but he (or she) still can't pass the check of system environment parameter env_B because the env_B is supposed to be unique in every computer and hard to be changed.

7 Implementation

The system environment parameters env_B mentioned previously should be unique information existing in a buyer's computer. However, it is a problem that how the server can get some information from client's computer such as env_B legally. In practice, there are two different categories depending on whether an assistant program is used. For the first case, we consider the server can get some system information without using assistant programs. There may be only a parameter used, or a set of Internet parameters such as IP address or the other related information. On the other hand, we can use an assistant program to help for collecting unique information inside of a buy's computer. The env_B could be the system hard disk volume number or a set of system information. The buyer has to execute the assistant program to accomplish all the required phases. Through in the communications the merchant is able to obtain certain information about buyer's computer. We worry about that a dishonest merchant would misuse it. In some viewpoint, it seems like to plant a computer worm [4, 1] in buy's computer. However, the cases are different if the owner of the computer is noticed what to do and it is trustworthy.

8 Conclusion

In this paper, we proposed a new model for software protection. The former is for copy prevention and the latter is for traitor identification. In the one-time installation subsystem, a problem is deserved to discuss. As stated in Section 4, the installation will work after everything is checked correctly. At this critical time, the setup file is executing with its very original version in client's computer. In this period of time, the setup file requires some basic protection from the operation system. Till the end of the installation, the temporary directory is deleted. In our system, there exists a weak point that might be able to break our protection scheme. Once the attacker reveals the n from the communication between a legal buyer and the merchant. The attacker can change its computer hardware and system time to be the same as that of the legal user, and create a simulate program on its computer to response the exact (n, env_B) to the package. In this case, it indeed can break the protection scheme. However, when the merchant finds an illegal copy, it can trace and identify the traitor.

We would like to point out that a software protection system developed using pure software technique seems vulnerable. The security can be improved by combining some hardware devices like smart cards [7].

References

1. Denning, P: Computers Under Attack: Intruders, worms, and Viruses. MA: Addision-wesley (1990)
2. H. Feistel: Cryptographic Coding for Data-Bank Privacy. RC 2827, Yorktown Heights. IBM Research, New York. (1970)
3. Draft FIPS 180-2: Secure Hash Standard (SHS). U.S. Doc/NIST. (2001)
4. Hoffman, L.: Rogue Programs: Viruses, Worms, and Trojan Horses. Van Nostrand Rein-hold, New York. (1990)
5. David Icove, Karl Seger, and Willam VonStorch: Computer Crime. O'Reilly & Associ-ates, Inc. (1998)
6. S. C. Kothari: Generalized Linear Threshold Scheme. CRYPTO '84. Springer-Verlag. (1985) 231-241.
7. C. H. Lin and C. Y. Lee: One-Time Installation with Traitors Tracing for Copyright Pro-grams. Proceeding of 35th Annual IEEE International Carnahan Conference on Security Technology. (2001) 149-155
8. Moni Naor, and Benny Pinkas: Threshold Traitor Tracing. CRYPTO '98. Springer-Verlag. (1998) 502-517
9. T. S. Chen, C. C. Chang and M. S. Hwang: A Virtual Image Cryptosystem Based Upon Vector Quamtization. IEEE Transactions on Image Processing, Vol. 7(10), (1998) 1485-1488
10. Benny Chor, Amos Fiat, and Moni Naor: Tracing Traitors. CRYPTO '94, Springer-Verlag. (1994) 257-270
11. S. Craver, N. Memon, B. L. Yeo, and M. Yeung: Can Invisible Watermarks Resolve Rightful Ownership?. Proc. SPIE Storage and Retrieval for Still Image and Video Data-bases V, Vol. 3022. (1997) 310-321

Design of a New Cryptography System

Hun-Chen Chen[1], Jui-Cheng Yen[1], and Jiun-In Guo[2]

[1]Department of Electronics Engineering
National Lien-Ho Institute of Technology, Miaoli, Taiwan, ROC
E-mail: hcchen@mail.nlhu.edu.tw
[2] Department of Computer Science and Information Engineering
National Chung Cheng University, Chiayi, Taiwan, ROC
E-mail: jiguo@cs.ccu.edu.tw

Abstract. In this paper, a new cryptography system is proposed. According to a generation scheme, a binary sequence is generated from a chaotic system. Then, the sequence is used to randomly determine the two parameters *Seed*1 and *Seed*2 and control the signal encryption. Each two neighboring data elements in the input signal are considered whether to swap or not and then XORed or XNORed to *Seed*1 or *Seed*2. The features of the proposed system are high security and low computational complexity. Finally, MATLAB simulation is given.

1 Introduction

Recently, with the great demand in digital signal transmission [1, 2] and the big losses from illegal data access, data security has become a critical and imperative issue. In order to protect valuable data from undesirable readers or against illegal reproduction and modifications, the encryption techniques [3-11] and the watermark embedding schemes [12-14] are proposed, respectively. The former makes the images invisible to undesirable readers and can be applied to protect the frames in the digital versatile disk (DVD) and the cable TV. However, the latter hides the watermark onto an image to declare their ownership and the image is still visible.

Among the proposed encryption techniques [3-11], the basic ideas can be classified into three major types: *position permutation* [5, 6], *value transformation* [7, 8] and *the combination form* [9-11]. The *position permutation* algorithms scramble the data position. It usually has low security. The *value transformation* algorithms transform the data value of the original signal. It has the potential of low computational complexity and low hardware cost. Finally, the *combination form* performs both position permutation and value transformation. It usually has the potential of high security.

In this paper, a new cryptography system is proposed. The encryption algorithm belongs to the category of the combination form. According to a generation scheme, a binary sequence is generated from a chaotic system. The sequence is used to randomly determine the two parameters *Seed*1 and *Seed*2 and control the signal encryption. The neighboring two data elements in the input signal are considered whether to swap or not and then XORed or XNORed to *Seed*1 or *Seed*2. For the verification of the proposed cryptography system, MATLAB simulation is given.

Y.-C. Chen, L.-W. Chang, and C.-T. Hsu (Eds.): PCM 2002, LNCS 2532, pp. 1041–1048, 2002.
© Springer-Verlag Berlin Heidelberg 2002

The paper is organized as follows. In Section 2, the new cryptography system is proposed and discussed. In Section 3, the properties of the system are analyzed. In Section 4, the MATLAB simulation is given. Finally, Section 5 concludes this paper.

2 The New Cryptography System

Let g denote a digital signal of length N, $g(n)$, $0 \leq n \leq N-1$, be the one-byte value of the signal g at n, and g' be the encryption result of g.

Definition 1: The operation $Swapping_w(g(m), g(n))$ is defined to swap $g(m)$ and $g(n)$ if w is equal to 1 or preserve their original positions if w is equal to 0.

Based on the notations and Definition 1, the encryption subsystem of the new cryptography system is proposed in the following.

The Random Seed Encryption Subsystem (RSES)
Step 1: Determine the signal length N.
Step 2: Determine the parameter μ and initial point $x(0)$ of the 1-D logistic map [15, 16], $f_\mu(x) = \mu x(1-x)$, where μ should be selected as the values that can result in chaos and $0 < x(0) < 1$. Evolve successive states from the 1D logistic map by $x(n+1) = \mu x(n)(1-x(n))$, and the preceding 24 bits below the decimal point of the binary representation of $x(n)$, $n = 1, 2, \ldots$, are extracted to constitute the chaotic binary sequence $b(0), b(1), b(2), \ldots$.
Step 3: FOR $k = 0$ To $(N/16 - 1)$ Do

$$Seed1 = \sum_{p=0}^{7} b(24k + p) \times 2^{7-p} ; \tag{1}$$

$$Seed2 = \sum_{p=0}^{7} b(24k + 8 + p) \times 2^{7-p} ; \tag{2}$$

FOR $x = 0$ To 7 Do
$Swap_{b(24k+16+x)}(g(16k+2x), g(16k+2x+1))$;   (3)
END
FOR $y = 0$ To 15 Do
Switch ($2 \times b(24k+y) + b(24k+y+1)$))
Case 3:
$g'(16k+y) = g(16k+y)$ XOR $Seed1$ (4)
Case 2:
$g'(16k+y) = g(16k+y)$ XNOR $Seed1$ (5)
Case 1:
$g'(16k+y) = g(16k+y)$ XOR $Seed2$ (6)
Case 0:
$g'(16k+y) = g(16k+y)$ XNOR $Seed2$ (7)
END
END
Step 4: The result g' is obtained and stop the algorithm.

In Step 2, we generate the chaotic binary sequence $b(\cdot)$ by extracting twenty-four bits from each evolution state of the 1-D logistic map $x(n+1) = \mu x(n)(1-x(n))$. In the chaotic systems [17], there are perfect statistical characteristics such as 1) it has sensitive dependence on initial conditions, 2) there exist trajectories that are dense, bounded, but neither periodic nor quasi-periodic in the state space, 3) the chaotic spectrum is not composed solely of discrete frequencies, but has a continuous and broad-band nature, and 4) the limit set for chaotic behavior is not a simple geometric object like a circle or a torus, but is related to fractals and Canter sets. Since the 1-D logistic map has the plus property of easy realization, it is adopted to generate the unpredictable sequence $b(\cdot)$ in the paper. The sequence $b(\cdot)$ is then used to control the determinaton of parameters $Seed1$ and $Seed2$ in Eqs. (1)(2), whether each two neighboring data elements should be swapped or not in Eq. (3), and how to transform each input signal in Eqs. (4)-(7). Each twenty-four bits from one evolution state control the processing of 16 data elements.

In Step 3, every 16 data elements are regarded as a processing set and they use 24 control bits from one evolution state to perform the signal encryption. Firstly, the $Seed1$ and $Seed2$ are determined by the 1st to 8th bits and the 9th to 16th bits of the 24 control bits as Eqs. (1) and (2), respectively. Secondly, every two neighboring data elements in the processing unit are consider whether to swap or not. If the corresponding bit in $b(\cdot)$ is 1, the the two elements are swapped. Otherwise, the two elements preserve their original positions. Finally, every data elements are XORed or XNORed to $Seed1$ or $Seed2$ according to the corresponding two control bits in $b(\cdot)$. If the two bits are "11", "10", "01", and "00", then the data element is XORed to $Seed1$, XNORed to $Seed1$, XORed to $Seed2$, and XNORed to $Seed2$, respectively. The swapping of neighboring data elements belongs to the type of position permutation and the processing of each data elements XORed or XNORed to $Seed1$ or $Seed2$ belongs to the value transformation. Hence, the RSES belongs to the type of combination form.

The decryption subsystem is the same as the RSES except that the loop containing Eqs. (4)-(7) should be performed before the loop containing Eq. (3). Combining the encryption and decryption subsystems, the new cryptography system (CS) is obtained. and its block diagram is shown in Fig. 1.

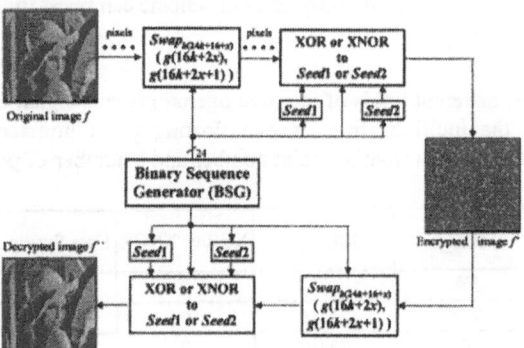

Fig. 1. The block diagram of the proposed cryptography system.

3 Analysis of the RSES

3.1 Security Problem

It is of interest to know if the RSES is easily decrypted or not. The security problem is analyzed in the following.

Proposition 1: For an unknown set of μ and $x(0)$ of the logistic map, the number of possible encryption results is $2^{\lceil N/16 \rceil \times 24}$ if the RSES is applied to a signal of length N, where $\lceil y \rceil$ denotes the smallest integer which is larger than or equal to y.

Proof: Since the signal of length N is partitioned into $\lceil N/16 \rceil$ processing sets and each set requires 24 control bits, it totally requires $\lceil N/16 \rceil \times 24$ bits to encrypt the signal. Hence, the number of possible encryption results is $2^{\lceil N/16 \rceil \times 24}$.

For example, consider an image of size 256×256 pixels. N equals 65536. All the possibilities are 2^{98304} ($\cong 10^{29590}$). Since the chaotic binary sequence is unpredictable [17], it is very difficult to decrypt an encrypted signal correctly by making an exhaustive search without knowing μ and $x(0)$.

Now, we consider the following attack [18]. Assume the encryption procedure, the used keys excepted, is known. That is, the RSES scheme is known except the two keys μ and $x(0)$, and the approach [11] is known except the permutation relation in the transformed domain. If the signal g_{test} and its encryption result g'_{test} are known, could we use the message to decrypt another encrypted signal g'_{new}? In the approach [11], we can obtain the permutation relation by comparing the transformations of g_{test} and g'_{test}. By the relation, we can decode g'_{new} into g_{new} correctly. Hence, this approach cannot resist this kind of attack. However, the proposed RSES scheme contains both the data swapping and value transformation which are randomly controlled by the binary sequence. The keys μ and $x(0)$ cannot be deduced just by comparing g_{test} and g'_{test}. Hence, g'_{new} cannot be decoded correctly and our scheme can resist this kind of attack.

Table 1. Numbers of different kinds of required operations on a signal of length N, where "MUL_1" denotes the multiplication of two floating point numbers and "MUL_2" denotes the multiplication of a floating point number and a number of power of 2.

Step \ Operation	MUL_1	MUL_2	XOR or XNOR	Data Swapping	Addition or Substraction
Step 2	$N/8$	0	0	0	$N/16$
Eq. 1 in Step 4	$N/16$	$7N/16$	0	0	$14N/16$
Eq. 2 in Step 4	0	$7N/16$	0	0	$14N/16$
Eq. 3 in Step 4	0	$5N/16$	0	$N/4$	$17N/16$
Eqs. 4-7 in Step 4	0	N	N	0	$4N$
Total	$3N/16$	$35N/16$	N	$N/4$	$110N/16$

3.2 Computational Complexity

In Step 2, it requires one subtraction and two multiplications to evolve a state from the 1-D logistic map, and the total evolution number is $N/16$. total numbers of subtraction and multiplication are $N/16$ and $N/8$, respectively. In the analysis of Step 3, we made the assumption that $Prob(b(k) = 1) = Prob(b(k) = 0) = 1/2$. Hence, the number of 8-bits memory swap is $N/4$. Besides, the number of basic XOR or XNOR operation is N. The numbers of different kinds of operations when the RSES is applied to a signal of length N are listed in Table 1. From the table, the operation numbers of multiplication, 8-bits memory swap, XOR/XNOR logic operation, and addition/subtraction are $38N/16$, N, $N/4$, and $110N/16$, respectively. Hence, the computational complexity of the RSES is $O(N)$.

4 MATLAB Simulation Results

4.1 Simulated Images and Quantitative Measure

In the simulation, ten images of size 256×256 are used. As representatives, only the images "Cman", "Aero" and "Pepper" are shown in Fig. 2(a) and 2(c), respectively.

The most direct method to decide the disorderly degree of the encrypted image is by the sense of sight. On the other hand, the fractal dimension [19, 20] can provide the quantitative measure. General images typically have a degree of randomness associated with both the natural random nature of the underlying structure and the random noise superimposed on the image. An image f of size $L \times P$ pixels is regarded as a surface with $z = f(x, y)$ in $\mathfrak{R}^3$. To measure how rough the encrypted image surface is, its fractal dimension D is calculated according to the method in [20].

(a)   (b)

(c)   (d)

Fig. 2. (a) Original "Cman", (b) encrypted "Cman", (c) original "Aero", (d) encrypted "Aero".

Let $ndi(k)$ be the average of absolute intensity difference of all pixel pairs with distance values whose integer parts are k. The value of $ndi(k)$ is computed by

$$ndi(k) = \frac{\sum_{x1=0}^{L-1}\sum_{y1=0}^{P-1}\sum_{x2=0}^{L-1}\sum_{y2=0}^{P-1}|f(x2, y2) - f(x1, y1)|}{npn(k)},$$ (8)

where $npn(k)$ is the total number of pixel pairs with distance Δr such that $k \leq \Delta r < k + 1$, and $x1, y1, x2$, and $y2$ must satisfy

$$k \leq \sqrt{(x2 - x1)^2 + (y2 - y1)^2} < k+1.$$

Plot all pairs $(\log(k), \log(ndi(k)))$, and then use a least-squares linear regression to estimate the slope H of the resultant curve. The fractal dimension $D = 3 - H$ can be obtained. In the simulation, the maximal distance k between two pixels in Eq. (8) is set to 60.

In order to apply the RSES, the parameters μ and $x(0)$ in the logistic map must be determined according to Step 2. In the simulation, $x(0) = 0.25$ and $\mu = 3.92$ are set. The encrypted results of the three representative images by the RSES are shown in Figs. 2(b)(d). Moreover, the fractal dimensions of the original images and their encryption results are calculated and listed in Table 2.

According to Fig. 2, the encryption results of the RSES are of complete disorder and can't be distinguished from the original ones. Moreover, from the quantitative measure as shown in Table 2, the fractal dimensions of the original images and the encrypted images range from 2.3996 to 2.7427 and from 2.9954 to 2.9979, respectively. Since the maximal fractal dimension for a 2-dimensional surface is 3.00, the encryption results of the RSES are completely disorderly.

Table 2. The fractal dimensions (fd) of the original and encrypted images.

Image \ Scheme	Cman	Miss	Lenna	Aero	Baboon	Pepper	Oleh	Karen	Einstein	Jet
Original Image	2.5671	2.4739	2.5993	2.7427	2.7178	2.6407	2.3996	2.5932	2.6702	2.7035
Original Image	2.9973	2.9956	2.9966	2.9977	2.9968	2.9968	2.9954	2.9964	2.9969	2.9979

4.2 Demonstration of Parameter Sensitivity

In order to demonstrate that the encryption results of the RSES are very sensitive to μ and $x(0)$, tiny fluctuation in the two parameters is considered. To compare the encryption results under tiny parameter fluctuation, the root mean square difference ($RMSD$) is computed. Let $f'_{\mu_1, x_1(0)}(i, j)$ be the encryption result of the image f under μ_1 and $x_1(0)$ and $f'_{\mu_2, x_2(0)}(i, j)$ be the one under μ_2 and $x_2(0)$. The $RMSD$ used to measure the difference between the two encryption results $f'_{\mu_1, x_1(0)}(i, j)$ and $f'_{\mu_2, x_2(0)}(i, j)$ is defined as

$$RMSD = \left(\frac{1}{L \times P}\sum_{i=0}^{L-1}\sum_{j=0}^{P-1}\left(f'_{\mu_1, x_1(0)}(i, j) - f'_{\mu_2, x_2(0)}(i, j)\right)^2\right)^{1/2},$$ (9)

where f is an image of size $L \times P$ pixels. Firstly, $x(0)$ is fixed to 0.25 and each fluctuation of 10^{-5} in μ is considered. After applying the RSES to "Lenna" under the tiny fluctuation in μ, the $RMSDs$ are listed in Table 3. Secondly, μ is fixed to 3.9 and each fluctuation of 10^{-5} in $x(0)$ is considered. After applying the RSES to "Lenna" under the tiny fluctuation in $x(0)$, the $RMSDs$ are listed in Table 4.

From Table 3, the $RMSDs$ under the tiny fluctuation of 10^{-5} in μ range from 99.605 to 100.227. From Table 4, the $RMSDs$ under the tiny fluctuation of 10^{-5} in $x(0)$ range from 99.615 to 100.505. That is, the root mean squared difference between the two encryption results with the tiny fluctuation of 10^{-5} in μ or $x(0)$ is about 100. It implies that the two results are extraordinarily different. Hence, the encryption result of the RSES is very sensitive to the fluctuation in μ and $x(0)$.

Table 3. The $RMSD$ between the encryption results with $x(0) = 0.25$ and fluctuation of 10^{-5} in μ.

μ	3.92000 vs. 3.92001	3.92001 vs. 3.92002	3.92002 vs. 3.92003	3.92003 vs. 3.92004	3.92004 vs. 3.92005	3.92005 vs. 3.92006	3.92006 vs. 3.92007	3.92007 vs. 3.92008	3.92008 vs. 3.92009	3.92009 vs. 3.92010
$RMSD$	99.605	100.227	100.063	99.8487	100.083	99.960	100.151	100.114	100.128	99.892

Table 4. The $RMSD$ between the encryption results with $\mu = 3.92$ and fluctuation of 10^{-5} in $x(0)$.

$x(0)$	0.25000 vs. 0.25001	0.25001 vs. 0.25002	0.25002 vs. 0.25003	0.25003 vs. 0.25004	0.25004 vs. 0.25005	0.25005 vs. 0.25006	0.25006 vs. 0.25007	0.25007 vs. 0.25008	0.25008 vs. 0.25009	0.25009 vs. 0.25010
$RMSD$	100.475	100.227	99.740	100.157	100.093	100.505	99.973	99.615	99.691	100.468

5 Conclusions

In this paper, a new cryptography system has been proposed. The features of the new system are $O(N)$ computational complexity and high security. The MATLAB simulation results have indicated that 1) the encryption results are completely chaotic by the sense of sight or by the high fractal dimension, and 2) the encryption results are very sensitive to the parameter fluctuation. Finally, it is believed that many digital signal-processing systems can benefit from the integration with the proposed system.

References

1. S. Moni and R. L. Kashyap, "Image communication over a distributed multimedia system," *IEEE Journal on Selected Areas in Communications*, vol. 14, pp. 1472-1483, 1996.
2. Y. Yamamoto, F. Inumaru, S. D. Akers, and K. I. Nishimura, "Transmission performance of 64-Kbps switched digital international ISDN connections," *IEEE Trans. On Comm.*, vol. 42, pp. 3215-3220, 1994.
3. W. Diffie and M. E. Hellman, "Privacy and authentication: an introduction to cryptography," *Proceedings of The IEEE*, vol. 67, pp. 397-427, 1979.

4. M. E. Smid and D. K. Branstad, "The data encryption sstandard: past and future," *Proc. of The IEEE*, vol. 76, pp. 550-559, 1988.

5. J. C. Yen and J. I. Guo, "An efficient hierarchical chaotic image encryption algorithm and its VLSI realization," *IEE Proc. – Vision, Image and Signal Processing*, vol. 147, pp. 167-175, 2000.

6. N. Bourbakis and C. Alexopoulos, "Picture data encryption using SCAN pattern," *Pattern Recog.*, vol. 25, pp. 567-581, 1992.

7. P. Refregier and B. Javidi, "Optical-image encryption based on input plane and Fourier plane random encoding," *Optics Letters*, vol. 20, pp. 767-769, 1995.

8. J. C. Yen and J. I. Guo, "A neural network for signal encryption/decryption and its VLSI architecture," *Proc. of the 10th VLSI Design/CAD Symposium*, NanTou, Taiwan, Aug. 18-21, 1999, pp. 319-322.

9. J. C. Yen and J. I. Guo, "The design of a new signal security system," *The 2002 IEEE International Symposium on Circuits and Systems*, Arizona, USA, May 26-29, pp. IV121-IV124, 2002.

10. C. J. Kuo and M. S. Chen, "A new signal encryption technique and its attack study," *IEEE Interna. Conf. on Security Technology*, Taipei, Taiwan, pp. 149-153, 1991.

11. V. Milosevic, V. Delic, and V. Senk, "Hadamard transform application in speech scrambling", *13th Internal Conference on Digital Signal Processing*, 1997, pp.361-364.

12. C. T. Hsu and J. L. Wu, "Hidden digital watermarks in images," *IEEE Trans. on Image Processing*, vol. 8, pp. 58-68, 1999.

13. B. M. Macq and J. J. Quisquater, "Cryptology for digital TV broadcasting," *Proc. of The IEEE*, vol. 8, pp.954-957, 1995.

14. Z. Xiong and Y. Q. Zhang, "Multiresolution watermarking for images and video," *IEEE Transactions on Circuits and Systems for Video Technology*, vol. 9, pp. 545-550, 1999.

15. C. W. Wu and N. F. Rulkov, "Studying chaos via 1-D maps - A tutorial," *IEEE Trans. on Circuits and Syst. I-Fundamental Theory and Applications*, vol. 40, pp. 707-721, 1993.

16. Schuster, *Deterministic Chaos – An Introd.*, Weinheim: Physik-Verlag, 1984.

17. T. S. Parker and L. O. Chua, "Chaos - A tutorial for engineers," *Proceedings of The IEEE*, vol. 75, pp. 982-1008, 1987.

18. E. Biham, "Cryptanalysis of the chaotic-map cryptosystem suggested at Eurocrypt'91," *Advances in Cryptology - Eurocrypt'91*, pp.532-534, Springer-Verlag, 1991.

19. A. E. Jacquin, "Fractal image coding: A review," *Proceedings of The IEEE*, vol. 81, 1993, pp. 1451-1465.

20. C. C. Chen, J. S. Daponte, and M. D. Fox, "Fractal feature analysis and classification in medical imaging," *IEEE Trans. on Medical Imaging*, vol. 8, 1989, pp. 133-142.

Texture Extraction and Blending without Prior Knowledge of Lighting Conditions

H.L. Chou and C.C. Chen

Opto-electronics & Systems Laboratories
Industrial Technology Research Institute
Hsin-chu, ROC
{hlchou, ChiaChen}@itri.org.tw

Abstract. Texture mapping techniques are widely used in photo-realistic 3D model rendering, but different lighting and viewing parameters create a difference in intensity for neighboring images, so that an edge appears at the boundary where neighboring images are stitched together. We propose an automatic procedure to extract and blend textures. Firstly, textures are extracted from the images and mapped to the triangles of the model. We choose the one with largest resolution if multiple textures extracted from different images are mapped to the same triangle. Secondly, a texture blending procedure is applied. We normalize the images to user-specified base images through overlapping area. Textures are then adjusted to the corresponding textures in the base images, if they exist. Finally, we check the boundary of neighboring textures. Boundary pixels varying discontinuously are averaged, and interior pixels are reassigned colors. Experimental results show that the smooth transition between neighboring textures provide better visual quality than just blending the boundary where neighboring images stitched.

1 Introduction

Texture mapping techniques are widely used in 3D model rendering. In these techniques, images of the real object are captured and mapped onto its geometrical model. To render new images of distinct perspectives, textures are warped to the projections of the polygons of the model. The use of texture mapping techniques not only makes the computer generated images look photo-realistic but also reduces the polygons needed to represent the object. To generate a complete textured 3D model, multiple images are required and mapped. Different lighting and viewing parameters for each image will cause the images projected from the same object surface look different. The edge effects will occur at the boundary where different images stitch.

To remove the boundary effects, expertise skilled at image processing tool, like Photoshop©, are required to edit the textures manually. It is time consuming. Also a talented person in art is needed to get the job done. [3,4,5,6,7] propose to estimate the reflection properties of the model under a controllable lighting environment. The intensity variation influenced by shape of the model, different lighting and viewing conditions can be eliminated if the reflection properties of the model are known. Besides the camera parameters of the images should be known, the lighting condition, i.e. the position of the light, the luminance the light, should be estimated. It makes the texture mapping technique become more complicated and expensive. Without

Y.-C. Chen, L.-W. Chang, and C.-T. Hsu (Eds.): PCM 2002, LNCS 2532, pp. 1049-1056, 2002.
© Springer-Verlag Berlin Heidelberg 2002

knowing the lighting condition, [9] proposes to stitch the images along predefined feature lines by warping the images onto the cylinder. To avoid the boundary edge effects, a multi-resolution image mosaics technique, [10], is proposed to the warped images. Similar works are also found in [11,12,13]. They warp the images onto the cylinder, find out the boundary where two images stitch and blend the pixel intensity around the boundary. 3D model are then projected onto the blended warped images to set their texture coordinates for each triangle. The intensity variation becomes smooth when the boundary of pixels are blended. But those pixels not modified still reveal different coloring if they suppose to be the same. For example, if projections of a surface are black and white on two images respectively, the above blending algorithm will generation a smooth change at the boundary but still look differently on the two sides. Another problem of these methods is that warping images to a simplified model requires resampling the images and losing high frequency information in the original images. [14] improves the texture mapping process by introducing a texture mapping strategy based on particle representation that preserves texture continuity and the quality of the original image. [15] uses the planar homography to estimate an ideal high resolution texture. Sampling theorem is also applied to derive the weights for texture pixel blending.

In this paper, we extract the textures from multiple images, select the one with highest resolution and map it to the triangle of the model. A texture blending procedure is proposed to remove the abrupt intensity change at the boundary and makes the coloring of whole textured model seen smoothly. Our blending procedure is divided as three steps:

a.   The global adjustment of whole image:

Pixel intensity variations of two images are assumed to be the same if they are projected from the same surface point. We select one of the images as the base image. Intensities of other images are adjusted to fit the intensity distribution of the base image. This process causes intensity distributions of the overlapping areas from difference images to get closer. The rest of the image areas are also adjusted making a continuous transition between the boundary of the non-overlapping area and overlapping area of each image.

b.   The local adjustment of individual texture

We shrink the consistent reflection assumption made in the first step to each individual texture. We adjust each individual texture to fit the base image pixel as the process explained in the global adjustment process. There are textures coming different surface with the base image not modified. To smooth the transition between the modified and not modified textures, we apply a blurring operator onto the textures.

c.   Texture boundary blending

After above two steps, colorings of textures are much closer to the base image. However, the boundary across the two neighboring textures still changes differently because textures are adjusted individually. To make the boundary of the texture change smoothly, we blend the pixels by averaging their intensities. Each interior pixel inside the texture is also modified according to the intensity differences of the nearest pixels on three edges.

The rest sections of this paper are organized as follows. Next section is concerned with the texture extraction process. Section 3 discusses the texture blending process we propose. Three texture processing steps are introduced in three subsections, respectively. Two experimental results are shown in section 4. Then the conclusion is described in section 5.

2   Texture Extraction

In this section, we discuss the process of extracting textures from images and mapping them onto the 3D model. We assume the projection matrices, i.e. the intrinsic and extrinsic parameters, of the images are known. Many camera calibration methods are proposed to estimate the projection matrix, one may refer to [16, 17]. To extract the texture, we firstly project the triangles of the mesh onto the images through following equation:

$$
\begin{bmatrix} u \\ v \\ 1 \end{bmatrix} \cong \mathbf{H} \begin{bmatrix} x \\ y \\ z \\ 1 \end{bmatrix} = \begin{bmatrix} h_{11} & h_{12} & h_{13} & h_{14} \\ h_{21} & h_{22} & h_{23} & h_{24} \\ h_{31} & h_{32} & h_{33} & h_{34} \end{bmatrix} \begin{bmatrix} x \\ y \\ z \\ 1 \end{bmatrix}
\tag{1}
$$

where $\begin{bmatrix} u & v & 1 \end{bmatrix}^T$ is the 2D projection of 3D point $\begin{bmatrix} x & y & z & 1 \end{bmatrix}^T$ through the projection matrix $\mathbf{H}$.

For every projection of the triangle on different image, we check the visibility of the triangle. The triangle may be visible from different perspective views. In other words, textures corresponding to the triangle may be more than one. If the triangle is visible from the image, the projection area it occupies is inserted to the texture list. A texture list is established for each triangle to record the possible textures to be mapped. After constructing the texture list for each triangle, we rasterize the candidate textures on the texture list and pick the one having largest resolution as the texture mapped onto the triangle. After that, each triangle of the 3D model is textured with the photo-realistic pixels from the images if it is visible from one of the image perspectives.

3   Texture Blending

The images may be acquired under different conditions, i.e. the lighting condition may be varying, the viewing directions should not be the same, the camera setting may be changed, etc. The inconsistent imaging environment cause the images projected from the same object's surface having different shading appearance. Thus, neighboring triangles having textures from different reveal boundary edge effect. In this section, we propose a procedure for blending the textures mapped to the model. The procedure of blending the textures is divided into three steps from the image-level to the texture-level and then to the pixel-level processing. Firstly, we select one image as the base image, and adjust all other images' intensity statistics distributions to fit the intensity distribution of the base image. Then each single texture is fine-tuned to adapt to specific reflection situation. In the last step, boundaries of the textures are blended for further smoothing the edge visual effect. The interior texture pixels are also updated. Each step of the texture blending process is explained in following subsections.

3.1   Global Adjustment

The first step we apply in the texture blending process is to adjust the image intensity globally. We select one of the images as the base image. Intensities of other images are adjusted to fit the statistics distribution of the base image. Each image is split into two areas: the overlapping area projected from the same surface with a portion of the base image and the non-overlapping area sharing the difference surface with the base image. The overlapping area is used to normalize the whole image. This process causes the intensity distributions of the overlapping areas from difference images being the same. The non-overlapping area of the image is also adjusted at the same time, which makes the boundary of the non-overlapping area and overlapping area change continuously. The normalization process is explained in the case of two images. Let image I_b be the base image, and image I_s be the source image. We adjust image I_s to fit I_b. Suppose surface S of the model is seen in the image I_b and I_s. The pixel intensity observed in the image projected from 3D surface point can be approximated by the Phong reflection model [1] as follows,

$$I_r = K_a I_a + I_i K_d (\mathbf{L} \cdot \mathbf{N}) + I_i K_s (\mathbf{R} \cdot \mathbf{V})^n \tag{2}$$

where $\mathbf{N}$ is the surface normal, $\mathbf{L}$ is the light direction and $\mathbf{V}$ is the viewing direction. The component $K_a I_a$ (ambient) simulates the global illumination, $I_i K_d (\mathbf{L} \cdot \mathbf{N})$ (diffuse term) modeling the light reflection equally in all directions and $I_i K_s (\mathbf{R} \cdot \mathbf{V})^n$ (specular term) results in the high light effects in the image.

   We assume the material property of the model to be Lambertian. It follows that the contribution of specular reflection is zero. Thus, above equation becomes:

$$I_r = C + I_i K_d (\mathbf{L} \cdot \mathbf{N}) \tag{3}$$

Now the projections of point on surface S in image I_b and I_s can be represented as

$$I_r = C + I_i K_d (\mathbf{L} \cdot \mathbf{N}) \tag{4}$$

$$I_s = C' + I_i' K_d (\mathbf{L} \cdot \mathbf{N})$$

respectively. If the surface is planar, $\mathbf{N}$ is the same for all points observed in the image Thus, differences of each pixel pairs from the same surface points should be the same and have the quantity $C' + I_i' K_d (\mathbf{L} \cdot \mathbf{N}) - C - I_i K_d (\mathbf{L} \cdot \mathbf{N})$. Thus, the intensity of image I_s can be adjusted by shifting its mean to the mean of image I_b as follow:

$$I_s'(x_i, y_i) = I_s(x_i, y_i) - \mu_s + \mu_b \tag{5}$$

where μ_b and μ_s are the means of projections of surface S on image I_b and I_s , respectively.

   The goal of this step is to adapt the light condition of the non-overlapping area more close to the base image. The intensity distribution of the overlapping area is used to update the non-overlapping area. After the global adjustment process, we roughly shift the mean intensity of the source image to the reference image under the assumption of the lambertian reflection of the planar surface. But shape of the model is not to be planar and the reflection properties vary from place to place. Thus, we further shrink the assumption to the scale of single texture and make the texture more close to the base image. In the next subsection, we enforce each texture's intensity distribution to the base image if its corresponding triangle is also observed in the base image.

3.2 Local Adaptation

After normalizing the images to the base image, the common areas projected on the images look similar but not identical. It is because that the global adjustment is based on the assumptions of Lambertian reflection and planar surface. In this section, the overlapping area in the image projected from the same surface is further divided into pieces of triangular textures. Textures' intensities are adjusted individually if they satisfy below two conditions:

a.   The texture is not extracted from the base image.
b.   The texture's corresponding triangle is also visible in the base image.

The range of consistent reflection property is narrow down from whole overlapping area to individual textures. We enforce each individual texture to fit the base image pixel as the process explained in the global adjustment process. Performing the texture-level adjustment makes each texture look much closer to the base image. There are still textures in the non-overlapping area not updated yet. They don not share common surface with the base image. To smooth the transition between the overlapping texture and the non-overlapping texture, we apply a blurring operator to the textures for lessening the variations of neighboring textures. It is a kind like pixel level burring operator used in the image processing techniques [2]. We replace the primitive unit from pixel to triangular texture and the intensity quantity used is its mean intensity. The average of the texture's mean intensity with its three neighboring textures' mean intensity is used to adjust the texture pixel intensity. After that, the intensity variation between neighboring textures becomes small.

3.3 Boundary Blending

Applying above two steps makes the texture intensity more consistent with the base image. Since we adjust each texture individually in the second step, the boundary across the two neighboring textures cannot be guaranteed changing smoothly. Thus, in this section we find out the boundary of each texture and the pixels across the boundary in the neighboring textures. If two sides of boundary change abruptly, we blend the pixels by average their intensities. Each interior pixel inside the texture is also modified according to the intensity differences of the nearest pixels on three edges with the weighting set as in equation (8).

$$I'_s(x, y) = I_s(x, y) + \sum_{i=1}^{3} w_i \cdot Id_i \tag{6}$$

where $w_i = \sum \dfrac{1/d_i}{\sum 1/d_j}$, $Id_i = I_s'(x_i, y_i) - I_s(x_i, y_i)$ and $I_s(x, y)$, $I_s'(x, y)$ are the original intensity and updated intensity for the interior texture pixel, respectively and (x_i, y_i) is nearest pixel on the i_{th} edge to current interior texture pixel having the distance d_i.

4 Experiments

Currently, we are developing a template based facial modeling technique. The front view and side view are fed to the system with the selected facial features on the images and model. Then the system will adjust the template facial model and generate a specific person's facial model fitting the appearance in the image. Textures from the front view and side view are extracted and mapped onto the facial model. In this section we use our texture extraction and blending procedure to map the textures onto the facial model. We apply our blending procedure to the color channels (R, G, B) of the image separately. Two experiments are conducted. In the first experiment, we show the process of our texture extraction and blending method step by step. In the second experiment, we compare our result with the results of three other methods.

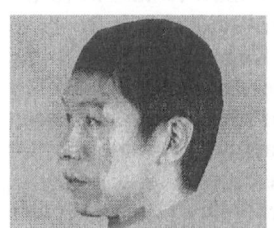 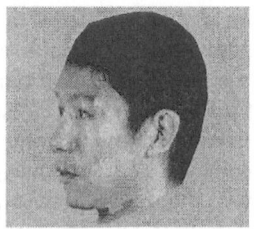 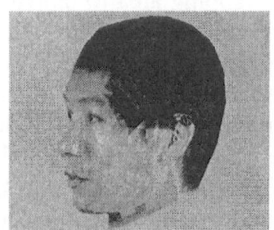

Fig. 1. Original texture mapping appearance.

Fig. 2. Global adjustment (Image level)

Fig. 3. Texture normalization (Texture level)

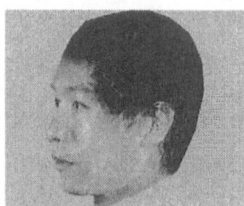 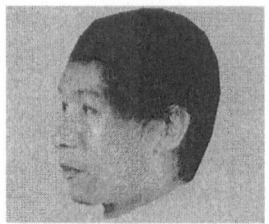

Fig. 4. Influence of surrounding textures.

Fig. 5. Boundary blending (Pixel level)

Experiment 1

In this experiment, we apply our texture blending procedure step by step. The original textures mapped on to the facial model are shown in Fig. 1. One can see the significant intensity change at the cheek. We select the frontal view as the base view, and normalize the side view to the frontal view as described in section 3.1. The result is shown Fig. 2. The color intensities of the two images are getting closer. Fig. 3 and 4 are the results after applying the two sub-steps of the local adjustment process described in section 3.2. In the last step of our method, we blend the boundary of the neighboring textures and update their interior pixels' intensities. The result is shown in Fig. 5. Comparing Fig. 5 with Fig. 1, One may find that the color intensity transition in Fig. 5 is much smoother.

Fig. 6. 3D model textured from original images

Fig. 7. The result of blending the boundary of the images.

Fig. 8. Editing the texture pixels manually.

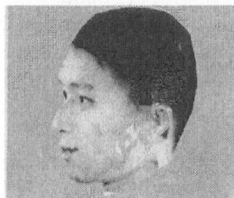

Fig. 9. The result of averaging the textures.

Fig. 10. The result of using our method.

Experiment 2

In this experiment, we compare our method with three other processing procedures. Fig. 6 is the computer-generated-image of the facial model without processing textures. Fig. 7 is the result of blending the texture pixels at the boundary of the two images, one may see that the boundary is blended, but textures besides the boundary still change abruptly. The result of editing textures manually by a Photoshop© expertise, Fig. 8, is pretty good. Fig. 9 is the result by averaging the pixels of textures mapping to the same triangle. Fig. 10 is the result of our method. It presents a visual effect between Fig. 7 and Fig. 8 and better than Fig. 9. Although the texture variation between neighboring textures does look like the one in Fig. 8, but the smooth intensity change does preserved. Also, the color of the textures besides the boundary looks similar.

5   Conclusion

In this paper, we propose a texture processing procedure for texture mapped model rendering. We extract the textures from the images and map them onto the 3D model. We also apply the texture blending process to the textures. We firstly normalize images to fit the intensity distribution of pre-selected based image through the overlapping area. Then the normalization process is narrow down to the size of individual texture level. Neighboring triangle's textures also influence the adjustment of the texture. We perform the pixel level adjustment in the last step. The boundary pixels of two neighboring textures are averaging, and interior texture pixels are updated according to the change of the boundary pixel. The experimental results show that our texture blending procedure provides an acceptable visual effect.

The 3D models we use are not very close to the real ones in the images. Textures normalized to the base image will be wrong if they are not mapped to the same surface correctly. In the future, we will analyze the difference between the texture of source image and its corresponding texture on the base image. If the differences caused by the lighting variations on the observed images and the incorrect texture mapped can be separated, we can use the information to adjust the texture intensity and to refine the shape of the surface.

References

1   A. Watt, 3D Computer Graphics, 3rd Edition, Addison-Wesley, NY, 2000.
2. R. C. Gonzalez and R. E. Woods, Digital Image Processing, Addison-Wesley, NY, 1992.
3. D. Cazier, et. al., "Modeling characteristics of light: A method based on measured data," Pacific Conference on Computer Graphics and Applications, 1994.
4. Y. Sato, M. D. Wheeler, and K. Ikeuchi, "Object shape and reflectance modeling from observation," SIGGRAPH, 1997.
5. S. W. Lee and R. Bajcsy, "Detection of specularity using color and multiple views," Image and Vision Computing, vol. 10, no. 10, 1992.
6. D. S. Lee, Estimating Reflectance Coefficients of An Object from Its Surrounding Images, Master Theisis, NCTU, Taiwan, 1999.
7. S. Genc and V. Atalay, „Texture Extraction from Photographs and Rendering with Dynamic Texture Mapping," Proceedings of Conference on Image Analysis and Processing'99, pp1055-1058.
8. P. J. Burt and R. J. Kolczynski, „Enhanced Image Capture Through Fusion," Proceedings of ICCV'93, pp. 173-182.
9. W. S. Lee, et al., „MPEG-4 Compatible Faces from Orthogonal Photos," Proceedings of ICCA(Computer Animation), pp 186-194, Geneva, Switzerland, 1999.
10. P. J. Burt and E. H. Adelson, „A Multiresolution Spline with Application to Image Mosaics," ACM Trans. Graphics, vol. 2, no. 4, pp. 217-2367, 1983.
11. T. Akimoto and Y. Suenaga, „Automatic Creation of 3D Facial Models," IEEE Trans. Computer Graphics and Applications, vol. 13, pp. 16-22, 1993.
12. Z. Liu and et al., Rapid Modeling of Animated Faces from Video, Technical report, MSR-TR-2000-11, Microsoft Research, Microsoft Corporation, Redmond, 2000.
13. N. Grammalidis, and et al., „Generation of 3-D Head Models from Multiple Images Using Ellipsoid Approximation for the Rear Part," Proceedings of ICIP'2000, pp. 2845-287, 2000.
14. F. Schmitt and Y. Yemez, „3D Color Object Reconstruction from 2D Image Sequences," Proceedings of ICIP'99, vol. 3, pp. 65-69, 1999.
15. L. Wang, et. al., „Optimal texture map reconstruction from multiple views," Proceedings of ICCVPR2001, vol. 1 pp. 785 –790, 2001.
16. Z. Chen, C. M. Wang, and S. Y. Ho, „ An effective search approach to camera parameter estimation using an arbitrary planar calibration object", Pattern Recognition. Vol. 26, No. 5, pp.655-666, 1994.
17. R. I. Hartley, E. Hayman, L. de Agapito, I. Reid, „Camera calibration and the search for infinity," Proceedings of ICCV, vol. 1, pp. 510-517, 1999.

Sharp and Dense Disparity Maps Using Multiple Windows

Jeonghee Jeon[1], Choongwon Kim[2], and Yo-Sung Ho[1]

[1] Kwangju Institute of Science and Technology (K-JIST)
1 Oryong-dong Puk-gu, Kwangju 500-712, KOREA
{jhjeon, hoyo}@kjist.ac.kr
[2] Chosun University
375 Seosuk-dong Dong-gu, Kwangju, 501-758, KOREA
cwkim@chosun.ac.kr

Abstract. In order to minimize boundary overreach, we propose a new stereo matching algorithm for sharp and dense disparity maps for color and gray-level stereo images using adaptive multiple windows. In the proposed method, we consider left-right consistency and unique constraint. Experimental results demonstrate that our algorithm produces sharp and dense disparity maps for color and gray-level stereo image pairs. We point out the disposition order problem of multiple windows and introduce window maps to indicate which window is selected among multiple windows.

1 Introduction

Quality of depth information in stereo images is usually determined by finding corresponding points the same point in two images of the same scene. For this purpose, most stereo matching algorithms use square or rectangle windows of the same size in different images.

Kanade et al. [1][2] proposed an adaptive window for choosing the right support region and also presented a multiple-baseline stereo to determine a single match point in the region of repetitive patterns. Their window has the shape of a square or rectangle according to the local intensity information. Fusiello et al. [3] proposed a method to choose the right support region by the multiple window approach. For each pixel, they perform the correlation operation with nine different windows, and obtain the disparity from the window of the smallest sum of square differences (SSD). The basic idea of this scheme is that a window yielding a smaller SSD is more likely to cover a constant depth region. Klette et al. [4] shows that stereo matching using color information instead of gray-level improves the performance around 25%. Mühlmann et al. [5] presented an efficient implementation method using the RGB information of color stereo images.

However, most window-based stereo techniques have the boundary overreach problem, which is caused by an unsuitable window shape or size [6][7]. In this paper, we introduce special multiple windows to minimize the boundary overreach. We also develop a stereo matching algorithm using left-right consistency, uniqueness constraint, and multiple windows, and point out the disposition order problem.

Y.-C. Chen, L.-W. Chang, and C.-T. Hsu (Eds.): PCM 2002, LNCS 2532, pp. 1057–1064, 2002.

After Section 2 describes conventional stereo matching techniques and similarity measure, a new algorithm using multiple windows to estimate sharp boundaries of objects is explained in Section 3. Section 4 presents experimental results using natural and synthetic, color and gray-level stereo images. Finally, Section 5 summarizes our contributions.

2 Stereo Matching Techniques

In order to measure similarity in stereovision, we usually employ SSD, defined by

$$SSD(x,y,d) = \sum_{(i,j)\in w} \{I_L(x+i,y+j) - I_R(x+i+d,y+j)\}^2 \tag{1}$$

$$SSD(x,y,d) = \sum_{(i,j)\in w} \{ \{R_L(x+i,y+j) - R_R(x+i+d,y+j)\}^2 \\ + \{G_L(x+i,y+j) - G_R(x+i+d,y+j)\}^2 \\ + \{B_L(x+i,y+j) - B_R(x+i+d,y+j)\}^2 \} \tag{2}$$

where I_L and I_R mean left and right images, respectively. d and w are disparity and cells within a window, respectively. In Eq. (2), R, G, and B are color components of each pixel. In Eq. (1) and Eq. (2), matching points can be found at scan line, assuming that stereo images are rectified. The best match for a point in one image can be determined by comparing similarity measures of square windows centered at points that lie on the corresponding scan line in the other image. The location of the smallest measure is selected as the best matching point and is stored as disparity.

In order to detect occlusions, Fua proposed a technique of left-right consistency [8], which is described by Eq. (3) and illustrated in Fig. 1.

$$d_{LR}(x+i,y+j) = -d_{RL}(x+i+d,y+j) \tag{3}$$

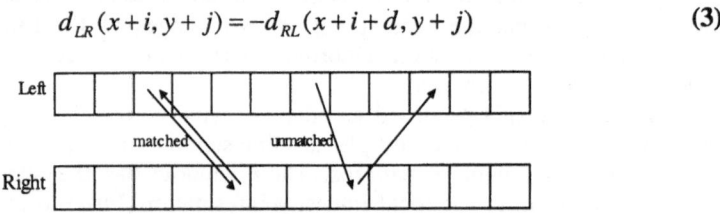

Fig. 1. Left-right Consistency Checking

The principle of the left-right consistency checking is that a valid match point should be equally matched in both left-right and right-left directions. Each point in one image can match at most one point in the other image, and the matched points should have the same disparity in both directions. Therefore, we can easily predict an occluded pixel or region by checking left-right consistency.

The uniqueness constraint means that a given pixel or feature from one image can match only one pixel or feature from the other image [9]. However, if the number of pixels having the same minimum value is two or more, we cannot determine disparity exactly. It could happen in image regions of regular patterns or uniform intensity values. We have described a new method to estimate the single disparity at a region of uniform intensity by expanding the window size [10]. Our method simply expands the window size in four directions to include more pixels if there are multiple local minima within the search range. With the operation, a bulk of multiple local minima is disappeared as the sum of SSD function of multiple-baseline stereo [2].

3 Multiple Windows

The main advantage of using multiple windows is to choose a special window to extract sharp boundaries and estimate more accurate similarity measure compared to the case using a single window [3][11]. The former implies that we can use a pattern of special form, not square or rectangle. In order to detect clear boundaries, we have designed eight windows with characteristics of edges, as shown in Fig. 2.

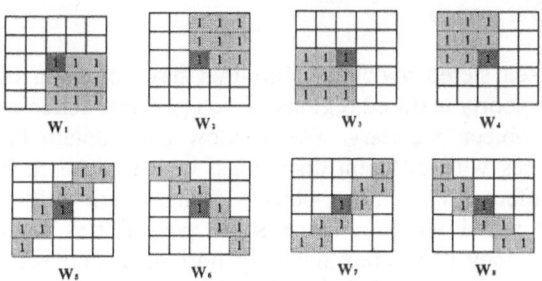

Fig. 2. Multiple Windows

Fig. 2 shows four windows $W_1 \sim W_4$ to detect horizontal, vertical, and corner edges [3][11]. Windows $W_5 \sim W_8$ for diagonal edges are newly introduced. All windows shown in Fig. 2 can be regularly expanded for stereo matching. We notice that the multiple windows have the same number of gray cells if their sizes are the same. All gray cells are considered to calculate similarity of each window and the darker gray cells are pixels that we want to find in other images. The later implies that similarity measure can be calculated as follows.

$$S(x,y,d) = \arg \min_{W=1}^{8} SSD_W (x,y,d) \tag{4}$$

where $S(x, y, d)$ is a similarity function and W is the window index in Fig. 2.

3.1 Disposition Order of Multiple Windows

In Fig. 3(a), the disparity can be easily estimated as d if the minimum of SSD in each window is different. However, as shown in Fig 2(b), we cannot uniquely determine the disparity of the window with the smallest SSD. We call this difficulty as the disposition order problem, which means the priority of windows to estimate a disparity from SSDs. Thus, it should be carefully determined to estimate the right disparity. We have selected the disposition order in Fig. 1. This selection is made from the assumption that boundaries of object in the scene of real world have mostly vertical and horizontal lines.

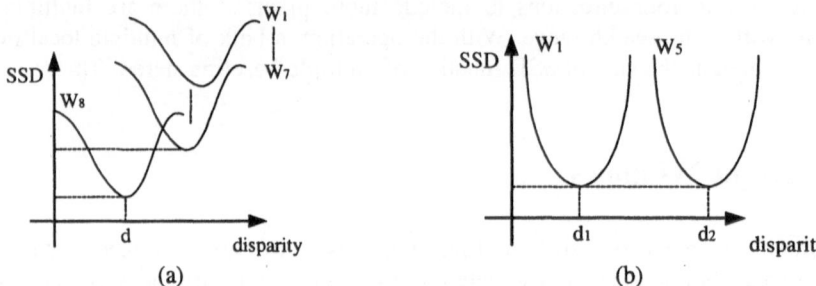

Fig. 3. Disparity in Multiple Windows

3.2 Boundary Overreach

Most window-based stereo matching algorithm have problem of low reliability in occluded areas or poorly textured regions, which generate fattening or thinning of the object along the object boundary. The window can contain both foreground and background surfaces with different disparities, which causes a boundary overreach problem. This affects segmenting objects using depth information [1][11][12]. However, the proposed windows have some possibilities to minimize boundary overreach because they can detect not only horizontal and vertical edges but also diagonal edges in the image and find a disparity using the window with the smallest similarity measure. We show that our algorithm minimizes boundary overreach in spite of expansion of the window size and that the disparity map retains clear boundaries.

3.3 The Proposed Algorithm

In order to estimate the unique matching point, we start with a window of 5×5 pixels. The window can be expanded in four directions according to uniqueness constraint and left-right consistency. All pixels are examined whether uniqueness constraint or left-right consistency are satisfied or not. Unless two conditions are satisfied, the window size is enlarged to include more pixels. A pseudo code for the stereo matching algorithm using new multiple windows to minimize boundary overreach is presented.

```
/*Stereo Matching Algorithm Using Multiple Windows (MW)*/

Input: Left and Right stereo images
Output: Disparity map (Dis)
Parameters: Disparity range (dis_max, dis_min),
            Window size (W_size),
            The number of iteration (I_num)
Initialize: Set all points to "FALSE"(Flag)
     Dis.Flag = FALSE;
```

```
Begin ExpandingWindow( )
      for i= (W_size /2)  to i< I_num  do
            StereoMatching( ); W_size += 2;
      end for i
End ExpandingWindow( ); Display Dis;

Begin StereoMatching ( )
    for x=xmin, y=ymin to xmax, ymax do
      if Dis.Flag == FALSE then Left-Right do
            Compute Similarity Measure (SM) of each MW;
            Find a window with the smallest SM;
            Store Left-Right Disparity(L-RD) of the window;
            Check Uniqueness Constraint (UC) on SMs;
      end Left-Right
      if UC then Right-Left do
            Compute SM of each MW;
            Find a window with the smallest SM;
            Store R-LD of the window;
            Check UC on SMs;
            if L-RD == R-LD then
                  Dis.Flag = TRUE; Dis = L-RD;
            end
      end Right-Left
    end for y, x
End StereoMatching( )
```

4   Experimental Results

In this section, we perform computer simulations to evaluate performance of the proposed algorithm. Test images, color and gray-level as shown in Fig. 4 and Fig. 5, are downloaded from a web site [13]. After performance is evaluated by disparity maps, we examine effects of the disposition order of multiple windows. Window maps indicate which window is used for searching disparity. Finally, we show that the algorithm minimizes boundary overreach and retains a sharp boundary in disparity maps.

4.1   Disparity Maps in Gray-Level and Color Stereo Images

Fig. 4 and Fig. 5 show disparity maps by the proposed algorithm. We use Tsukuba stereo pairs with gray-level and color information. For gray-level images, we compare disparity maps of our algorithm to the symmetric multi-window (SMW) by Fusiello, et al. [3]. The SMW algorithm is an adaptive, multiple windows scheme using left-right consistency to compute disparity and its associated uncertainty. The disparity maps in Fig. 4 show that the proposed algorithm produces improved results in terms of sharp boundaries; however, the SMW algorithm gives a smoother disparity map. The disparity maps of our algorithm assign gray-level values to points of "TRUE" and black to other points of "FALSE". Our disparity maps show steeper boundaries than those of SMW. However, performance of two algorithms cannot be simply compared because the window size of SMW is not known. For the Tsukuba image, by comparing disparity maps of gray-level and color stereo images, we can find that the number of pixels of "FALSE" is reduced and boundaries of narrow objects are improved because of color information.

(a)   Random dot, ground-truth, and disparity maps by our algorithm and SMW

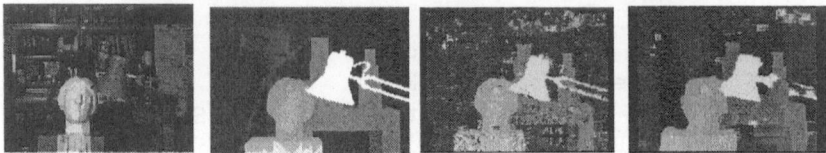

(b) Tsukuba, ground-truth, and disparity maps by our algorithm and SMW

Fig. 4. Gray-level Stereo Images and Disparity Maps

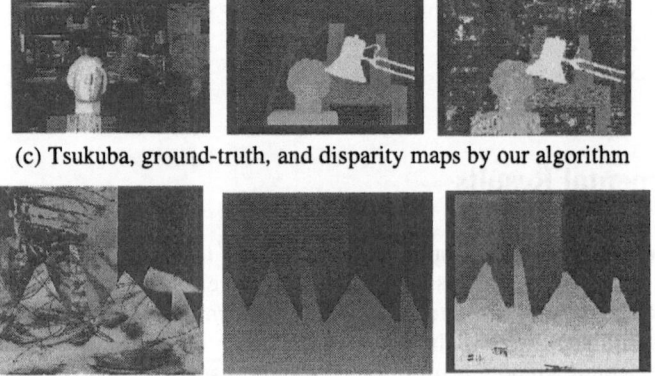

(c) Tsukuba, ground-truth, and disparity maps by our algorithm

(d) Sawtooth, ground-truth, and disparity maps by our algorithm

Fig. 5. Color Stereo Images and Disparity Maps

4.2 Effects of Disposition Order

This section describes the effect of disposition order using disparity and window maps. The window map indicates the selected window. The gray-level bar in Fig. 6(a) shows window maps of Fig. 6(b) and Fig. 6(c). As shown in Fig. 6, changing of the disposition order has an effect on quality of disparity maps. The disparity maps and window maps in Fig. 6 demonstrate that our disposition order is correct.

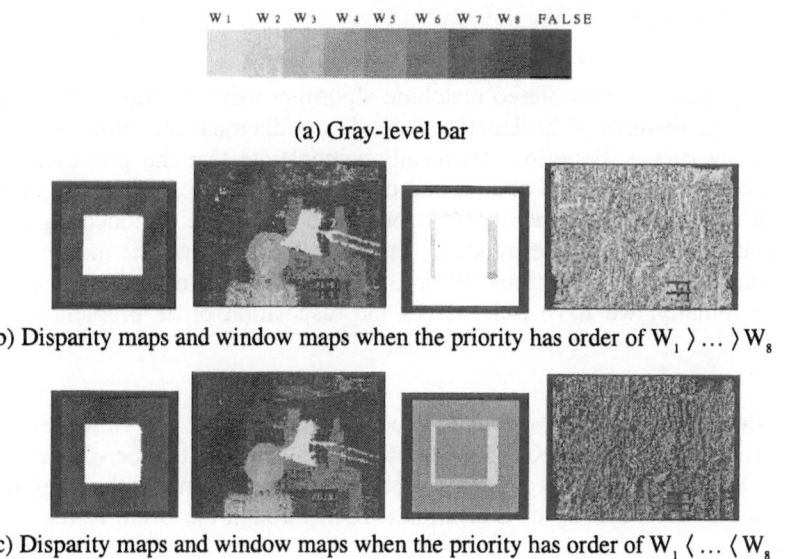

(a) Gray-level bar

(b) Disparity maps and window maps when the priority has order of $W_1 \rangle \dots \rangle W_8$

(c) Disparity maps and window maps when the priority has order of $W_1 \langle \dots \langle W_8$

Fig. 6. Effects of Disposition Order

4.3 Boundary Overreach Problem

In order to experiment boundary overreach, we use two window sizes of 9×9 and 15×15, as shown in Fig. 7, and use only gray-level stereo images. The disparity maps by the proposed algorithm have dense and sharp boundaries irrespective of alteration of window sizes. From Fig. 7, we can observe that our algorithm minimizes boundary overreach.

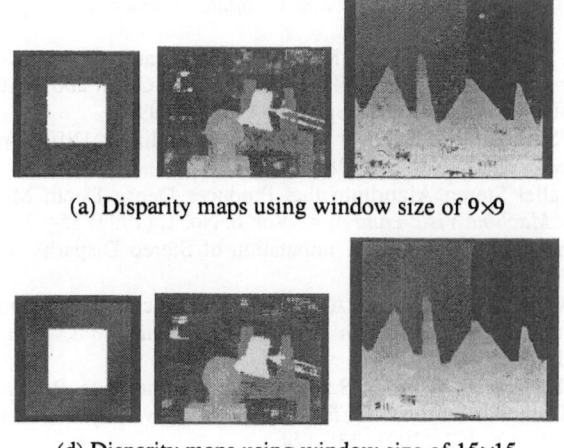

(a) Disparity maps using window size of 9×9

(d) Disparity maps using window size of 15×15

Fig. 7. Boundary Overreach Problem

5   Conclusions

We have proposed a new stereo matching algorithm using multiple windows, which consider edge features of horizontal, vertical, and diagonal directions and minimize boundary overreach. Experimental results demonstrate that the proposed algorithm displays clear boundaries of objects and dense disparity maps. Left-right consistency checking is employed to estimate the depth of objects in the occluded region and the single matching point is determined by uniqueness constraint. The multiple windows are extended in four directions according to uniqueness or left-right consistency checking. Finally, we have pointed out the disposition order problem of multiple windows.

Acknowledgement. This work was supported in part by the Korea Science and Engineering Foundation (KOSEF) through the Ultra-Fast Fiber-Optic Networks (UFON) Research Center at Kwangju Institute of Science and Technology (K-JIST), and in part by the Ministry of Education (MOE) through the Brain Korea 21 (BK21) project.

References

1.   Kanade, T., Okutomi, M.: A Stereo Matching Algorithm with An Adaptive Window: Theory and Experiment. *IEEE Trans. on Pattern Analysis and Machine Intelligence*, Vol. 16, No. 9, (1994) 920-932
2.   Okutomi, M., Kanade, T.: A Multiple-Baseline Stereo. *IEEE Trans. on Pattern Analysis and Machine Intellegence*, Vol. 15, No. 4, (1993) 353-363
3.   Fusiello, A., Roberto, V., Trucco, E.: Efficient Stereo with Multiple Windowing. *Proceeding of CVPR*, (1997) 858-863
4.   Klette, R., Koschan, A., Schlüns, K., Rodehorst, V.: Surface Reconstruction Based on Visual Information. *Tech. Report, Dept. of Computer Science, Univ. of Western Australia*, (1995)
5.   Mühlmann, K., Maier, D., Hesser, J., Männer, R.: Calculating Dense Disparity Maps from Color Stereo Images, an Efficient Implementation. *IEEE CVPR 2001*, (2001)
6.   Otha, Y., H. Tamura: *Mixed Reality*. Springer-Verlag, (1999)
7.   Scharstein, R. Szeliski, R.: Efficient Stereo with Nonlinear Diffusion. *Int. Journal of Computer Vision*, Vol. 28, No. 2, (1998) 155-174
8.   Fua, P.: A Parallel Stereo Algorithm that Produces Dense Depth Maps and Preserves Image Features. *Machine Vision and App.*, Vol. 6, No. 1, (1993) 35-49
9.   Marr, D., Poggio, T.: Cooperative Computation of Stereo Disparity. *Science*, Vol. 194, (1976) 283-287
10.   Jeon, J., Kim, K., Kim, C., Ho, Y-S.: A Roust Stereo Matching Algorithm Using Multiple-Baseline Cameras. *IEEE Pacific Rim Conf. on Communications, Computers and Signal Processing*, Vol. I, (2001) 263-266
11.   Okutomi, M., Katayama, Y., Oka, S.: A Simple Algorithm to Recover Precise Object Boundaries and Smooth Surface. *IEEE Computer Society Conf. on Computer Vision and Pattern Recognition*, Vol. 2, (2001) 138-144
12.   Szeliski, R., Zabih, R.: An Experimental Comparison of Stereo Algorithms. *IEEE Workshop on Vision Algorithms*, (1999) 1-19
13.   http://www.middleburry.edu/stereo

Interpolation of CT Slices for 3-D Visualization by Maximum Intensity Projections

Samuel Moon-Ho Song and Junghyun Kwon

College of Engineering
Seoul National University
Kwanak-gu Shillim-dong San 56-1
Seoul 151-742, KOREA
smsong@snu.ac.kr, jhkwon@vsl.snu.ac.kr

Abstract. Visualization of 3-D volume data through maximum intensity projections (MIP) requires isotropic voxels for generation of undistorted projected images. Unfortunately, due to the inherent scanning geometry, X-ray computed tomographic (CT) images are mostly axial images with sub-millimeter pixel resolution, with the slice spacing on the order of half to one centimeter. These axial images must be interpolated across the slices prior to the projection operation. The linear interpolation, due to the inherent noise in the data, generates MIP images with noise whose variance varies quadratically along the z-axis. Therefore, such MIP images often suffer from horizontal streaking artifacts, exactly at the position of the original slices (*e.g.*, in coronal and sagittal MIPs). We propose a different interpolation technique based on a digital finite impulse response (FIR) filter. The proposed technique flattens the change in noise variances across the z-axis and results in either elimination or a reduction of horizontal streaking artifacts in coronal and sagittal views.

1 Introduction

In contrast to magnetic resonance images (MRI), X-ray CT scanners generate images in the form of axial slices, where the in-slice pixel resolution differs from the distance between adjacent axial slices [1]. Thus, these axial images must be interpolated a realistic and undistorted visualization of the human anatomy. Furthermore, in a typical multi-slice imaging mode, the slice spacing may even change within the 3-D data set. Therefore, for visualization, manipulation, and analysis of such non-isotropic data set, the multi-slice data must be converted so that the voxels are equally spaced (*i.e.*, isotropic) prior to any rendering/projection operation. The non-isotropic data is usually converted to an isotropic set by applying one of the interpolation techniques for the generation of uniformly sampled 3-D images [2].

Interpolations are usually applied before the visualization step, to minimize various interpolation artifacts since interpolation effects (or artifacts) are usually "smoothed-out" by the visualization step that follows [3]. Among a number of visualization algorithms, the maximum intensity projection (MIP) technique has become one of the most popular approaches due to its computational simplicity as well as its visualization power, particularly for vessel structures [4-6]. As mentioned earlier, to

Y.-C. Chen, L.-W. Chang, and C.-T. Hsu (Eds.): PCM 2002, LNCS 2532, pp. 1065-1072, 2002.

obtain MIP images, the 3-D data is preprocessed by a variety of interpolation techniques to improve the quality of the resulting projected image. The linear interpolation technique, due to its computational simplicity, is used most often; however, due to the inherent noise in the data, the linear interpolation cause horizontal streaking artifacts at the position of the original slices when the projection direction is parallel to the axial plane (e.g., for generation of coronal or sagittal views).

In this paper, we focus on the effect of linear interpolation on MIP images and will give a statistical argument for the streaking artifacts. As a remedy for the streaking artifact, we propose a band-limited interpolation technique based on a finite impulse response (FIR) filter. Through a simple statistical analysis for the two techniques, we will compare the two interpolation methods both visually and numerically. As noise in the original 3-D data propagates differently for the two techniques, this will result in different MIP images for the two interpolation techniques. The resulting MIP images obtained by the two techniques will be compared to show the superiority of FIR based interpolation..

2 Formulation

The X-ray CT scanner basically provides samples of the linear attenuation coefficient, which we denote as $f(x, y, z)$. The measurements are taken as samples of $f(x, y, z)$ and we denote the sampling locations as

$$\{x_p\}_{p=0}^{N_x-1}, \{y_q\}_{q=0}^{N_y-1}, \text{ and } \{z_k\}_{k=0}^{N_z-1}, \tag{1}$$

where $N_x \times N_y \times N_z$ denotes number of voxels available in the 3-D data. As most CT scanners provide axial slices with isotropic pixels, we may assume that $x_p = p \Delta x$, and $y_q = q \Delta y$, where $\Delta x = \Delta y$. However, as the slice spacing of axial cuts may be different from the pixel size, and may actually vary even within a single 3-D data set, we still have to work with the arbitrary slice spacing shown as below:

$$\{z_k\}_{k=0}^{N_z-1} = \{z_o, z_1, z_2, \ldots, z_{N_z-1}\}. \tag{2}$$

Thus, assuming the data to be corrupted by additive noise, the following is a model of the measured 3-D data set:

$$g(x_p, y_q, z_k) = f(x_p, y_q, z_k) + n(x_p, y_q, z_k). \tag{3}$$

It is the above data that must be interpolated across the z-axis to generate an isotropic 3-D data set. The exact interpolation may be performed on the above data using the well-known Shannon's interpolation formula [7]. In theory, the exact interpolation may also be implemented using fast Fourier transforms (FFT) with zero padding if the slice spacing does not change within the 3-D data set. Even then, the size of the required FFT may be too large to be implemented on a general purpose computer. In any case, a general solution for the arbitrary slice spacing given in Eq. (2) must resort either to the original Shannon's interpolation formula or its sub-optimal approximation. The original Shannon's interpolation formula requires N_z multiplies per interpolated sample, which is prohibitive for most real-time visualization applications.   The linear interpolation technique, however, requires only two multiplies per interpolated sample [8]

$$g_{lin}(z) = \left(1 - \frac{z - z_k}{z_{k+1} - z_k}\right) g(z_k) + \frac{z - z_k}{z_{k+1} - z_k} g(z_{k+1}), \quad z_k \le z \le z_{k+1}, \tag{4}$$

where we have dropped the in-slice x-y dependence for notational convenience. In the above linear interpolation, two samples are added to form one interpolated sample, with weights that vary along the z-axis. Therefore, the variance in the interpolated sample will vary across the z-axis and can be shown to be [9]:

$$\sigma_{lin}^2(z) = \left(1 - \frac{z - z_k}{z_{k+1} - z_k}\right)^2 + \left(\frac{z - z_k}{z_{k+1} - z_k}\right)^2, \quad z_k \le z \le z_{k+1} \tag{5}$$

The above shows that, linear interpolations, although computationally simple, generate images whose noise variance varies quadratically along the z-axis (see Fig. 1 dashed line).   This variation across the z-axis gives rise to horizontal streaking artifacts in resulting MIP images, as the pixel intensity is known to get amplified during the MIP operation [5].

To alleviate the above variation in the noise variance, we propose a band-limited interpolation, which is essentially an approximation of the exact Shannon's interpolation formula, but with much less computational demand. The idea is to decimate the sequence and insert appropriate number of zeros (up-sampling). The zero-inserted data is then low-pass filtered to reduce the effect of aliasing. The lowpass filtered output is down-sampled to provide the interpolated slices at the desired slice location.

More specifically, the original data $g(z_k)$ is up-sampled by a factor, say M, which is then low-pass filtered (FIR) whose impulse response is $h(n)$. The output of the low-pass filter is then down-sampled by another factor, say N. Thus, the resulting signal becomes the resampled version of the original signal by the factor M/N.

First, assuming the slices to be equally spaced, i.e., $z_k = k\Delta z$, we denote the up-sampled data as $g_0(k)$, i.e., the data with $(M - 1)$ zeros inserted between every samples of $g(z_k)$. The up-sampled data is processed by a low-pass FIR filter and the output of the filter can be expressed as:

$$g_1(n) = \sum_{k=n-(P-1)}^{n} g_0(k) h(n - k). \tag{6}$$

Note that $h(n)$ (FIR filter) is a P-point FIR. As such, exactly $(M - 1)$ out of M multiplies in the above summation become zero.   Thus, upon reindexing $n \to n + P - 1$ and assuming the usual symmetric properties for linear phase FIR filters [7], i.e., $h(n) = h(P - 1 - n)$,

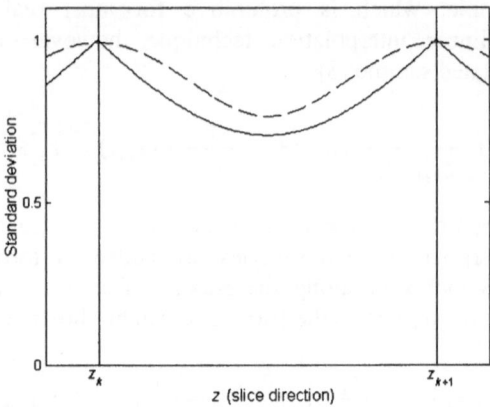

Fig. 1. The comparison of the two variances σ_{lin}^2 and σ_{FIR}^2 (normalized). The peaks occur at the slice boundaries causing horizontal streaking artifacts in resulting MIP images. Solid line: σ_{lin}^2 and dashed line: σ_{FIR}^2

$$g_1(n) = \sum_{k=\left\lceil \frac{n}{M} \right\rceil}^{\left\lfloor \frac{n+P-1}{M} \right\rfloor} g_0(kM)h(kM-n) \tag{7}$$

However, the above output need not be computed for all n as it must be further down-sampled by the factor N. Therefore, for every output point, there are approximately P/M multiplies, as we only compute the output $g_1(n)$ every N samples, for instance, for $n = 0, N, 2N, \ldots$. Putting all this together, the M/N resampling FIR can be mathematically expressed as:

$$g_{FIR}(n) = g_1(nN) = \sum_{k=\left\lceil \frac{n}{M} \right\rceil}^{\left\lfloor \frac{n+P-1}{M} \right\rfloor} g(z_k)h(kM-n) \ . \tag{8}$$

where n denotes samples along the z-axis, and $h(k)$, $0 \leq k \leq P-1$ is a P-point digital FIR filter. Note that $h(\cdot)$, P, and M are design parameters for the problem at hand.

In particular, the FIR filter that we used is a 1024-point filter designed using a Kaiser window with the stop-band attenuation of approximately 75 dBs. As we have selected $M = 256$ (*i.e.*, there are four multiplies per interpolated sample), the variance in the interpolated image essentially rises from the four added samples. Thus, the variance can be shown to vary across the z-axis as follows:

$$\sigma_{\text{FIR}}^2(n\Delta z) = h^2(n) + h^2(n+256) + h^2(n+512) + h^2(n+512), \ 0 \leq n \leq 255, \tag{9}$$

so that $z_k \leq n\Delta z \leq z_{k+1}$.

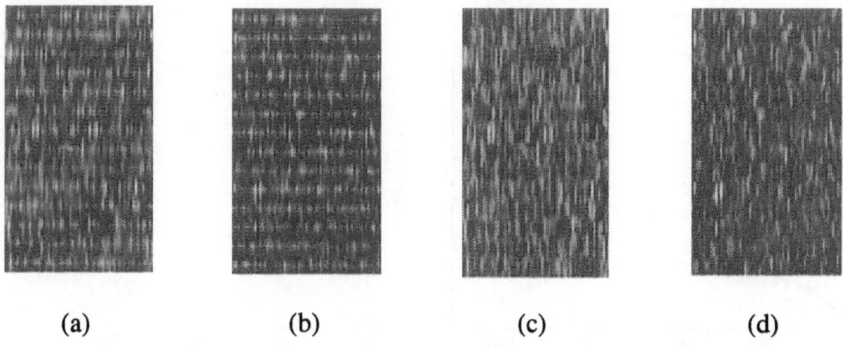

Fig. 2. MIPs of a constant volume data set with additive noise ($\sigma_N = 30$). (a) and (b): linear interpolation with projection depths of 12 and 64, respectively. (c) and (d): FIR interpolation with projection depths of 12 and 64, respectively.

Figure 1 shows the variances σ_{lin}^2 and σ_{FIR}^2 as functions of the slice depth. The figure shows the variation along the z-axis near the slices z_k and z_{k+1}. Notice that the variation of σ_{FIR}^2 is not as severe as σ_{lin}^2. The streaking artifacts in MIPs is due to the non-constant nature (particularly the peaks at slice boundaries) of the variance as the MIP operation is known to amplify these effects. Therefore, the streaking artifacts will be less severe in the FIR interpolated MIP (as opposed to the linearly interpolated MIP) due to its flatter variance. This observation will be verified visually in the next section.

3 Results

The maximum intensity projection (MIP) algorithm casts parallel rays through the image data set, and the greatest intensity along each ray is "projected" in the projection plane. This paper is concerned with the horizontal streaking artifact, which becomes most prominent when the projection direction lies in the axial plane, due to interpolation across axial slices. To demonstrate the effect of non-constant variance in the interpolated image and its manifestation on the resulting MIP image, we present some simple simulation studies. We first generate a non-isotropic constant 3-D data (= 1000) with additive Gaussian noise. The 3-D data is then interpolated across axial slices (either by linear interpolation or the proposed FIR filter) to form an isotropic data set. The MIP image is then generated from this noisy but isotropic 3-D data set with the projection direction in the plane of the axial slice.

Figure 2 shows MIP images with additive noise whose standard deviation $\sigma_N = 30$ using linear ((a) and (b)) and FIR ((c) and (d)) interpolation techniques with projection depths of 12 and 64, respectively. The horizontal streaks are clearly visible in MIPs of linear interpolation; however for the MIP of FIR interpolation, much of the streaking artifacts have been eliminated independent of the projection depth. Note

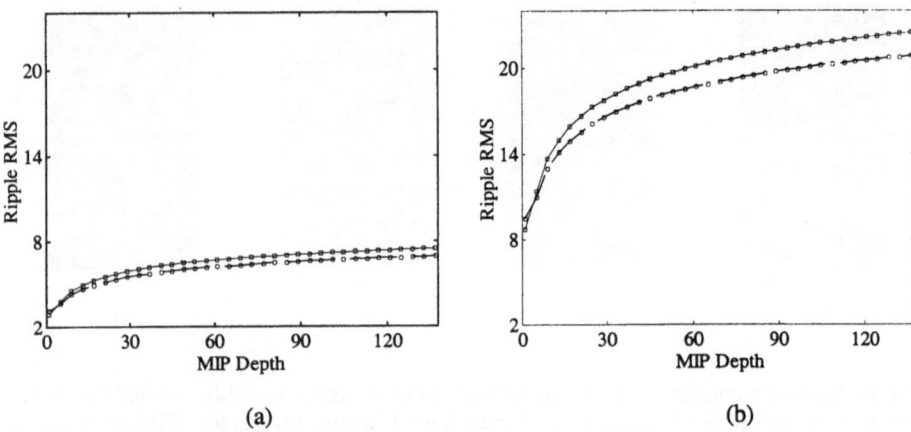

Fig. 3. Ripple RMS vs. projection depth (MIP depth). Solid line: linearly interpolated MIP, dashed line: FIR interpolated MIP. (a) $\sigma_N = 30$ and (b) $\sigma_N = 90$

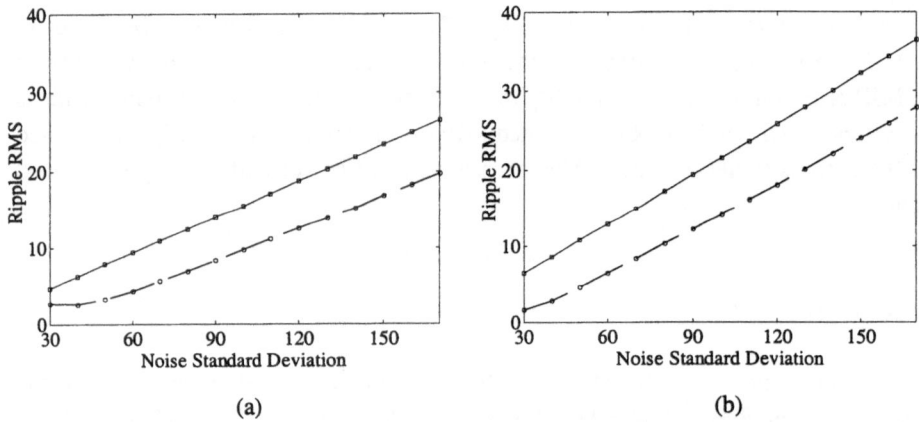

Fig. 4. Ripple RMS vs. standard deviation of the additive noise, σ_N. Solid line: linearly interpolated MIP, dashed line: FIR interpolated MIP. (a) projection depth = 12 and (b) projection depth = 64

that as the projection depth is increased, the streaks become more prominent. This is due to the fact that the MIP operation is known to amplify the pixel intensity while reducing the MIP image variance [5] and this effect would become more prominent as the projection depth is increased. This amplification effect is less prominent for FIR interpolated MIPs due to its flatter noise variance across the axially interpolated data (cf. Fig. 1). This observation has also been made with higher (and lower) levels of additive noise variance $\sigma_N^* = 90$.

The previous visual observation—streaks becoming more prominent as the projection depth increases—can be made more concrete by the following. Figure 3

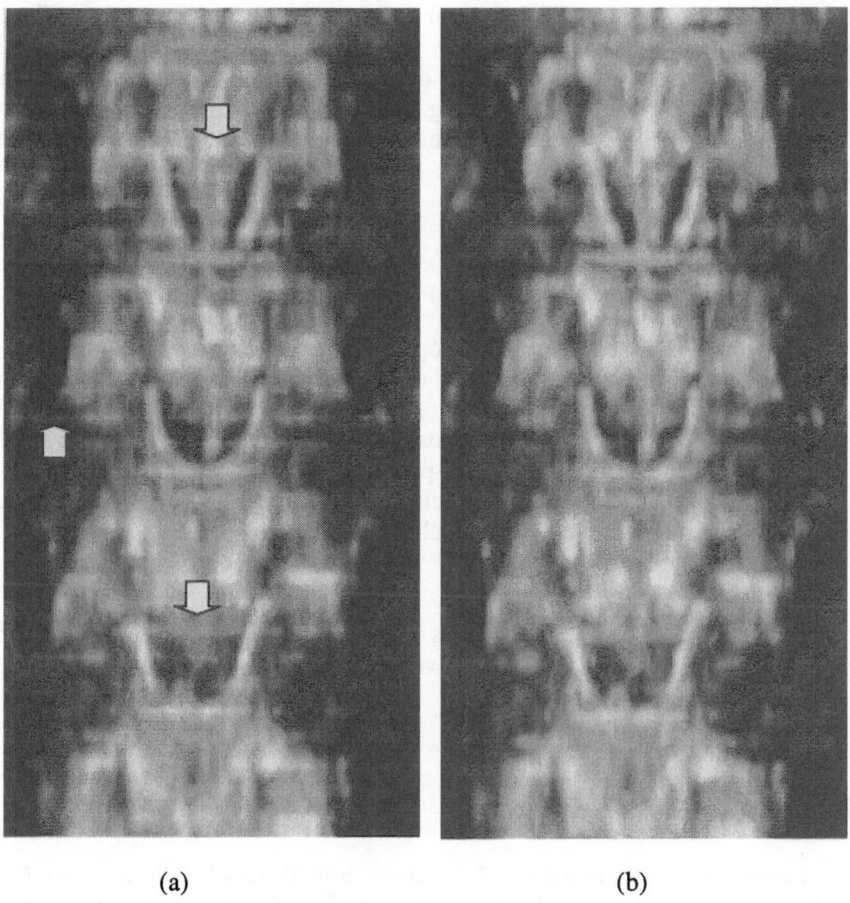

(a)   (b)

Fig. 5. The MIPs of a vertebral column with 3-D EBT data set using (a) linear interpolation and (b) FIR interpolation. The horizontal streak (see white arrow) present in (a) is almost non-existent in (b).

shows the ripple RMS (root-mean-squared of the ripple, or the horizontal streaks) vs. the projection depth for the two noise levels (a) $\sigma_N = 30$ and (b) $\sigma_N = 90$ for linearly interpolated MIP images (solid) and FIR interpolated MIP images (dashsed). Higher ripple RMS values imply more prominent streaking artifact and in all cases, linear interpolated MIP images show higher ripple RMS values.

Figure 4 shows the ripple RMS as a function of the amount of noise present in the data for projection depths of 12 (a) and 64 (b). Notice that the ripple RMS of the FIR interpolated MIP is consistently lower than that of the linearly interpolated MIP.

These observations indicate that the FIR interpolation is superior over the linear interpolation, particularly for visualizations using MIP. Furthermore, it is superior at all projection depths as well as the amount of additive noise.

Figure 5 shows the performance of the two approaches for a real CT data from the Electron Beam Tomography (EBT) system (Imatron, South San Francisco). The MIP images shown are generated from (a) linearly interpolated data and (b) FIR interpolated data. Both images appear to be similar in quality in terms of the image resolution. However, horizontal streaking artifacts (arrows in Fig. 5 (a)) are clearly visible on the linearly interpolated MIP image, where as on the FIR interpolated MIP image, the streaks are almost non-existent.

4   Discussions and Conclusion

As most CT image data sets are non-isotropic, an interpolation step must precede any visualization processing. In this paper, we proposed a band-limited interpolation technique based on a FIR digital filter. The interpolation technique was analyzed statistically and numerically. The proposed FIR interpolation was found to have better statistical characteristics over the popularly used linear interpolation. As a result, the proposed FIR interpolation technique eliminates or considerably reduces the horizontal streaking artifacts in the final MIP image.

Acknowledgement. This research was supported in part by the University Advancement Fund of Seoul National University.

References

1. J. K. Udupa and G. T. Herman (eds.): *3-D Imaging in Medicine.* CRC, Boca Raton (1991)
2. S. M. Goldwasser, R. A. Reynolds, D. A. Talton, and E. S. Walsh, "Techniques for the rapid display and manipulation of 3-D biomedical data," *Comput, Med. Imag., Graph,* Vol. 12(1), (1988) 1-24
3. J. K. Udupa and R. J. Goncalves, "Imaging transforms for visualizing surfaces and volumes," *J. Digital Imag.*,V. 6(4), (1993) 213-236
4. D. G. Brown and S. J. Riederer, "Contrast-to noise ratios in maximum intensity projection images," *Magnetic Reson, Med.,* Vol. 23 (1992) 130-137
5. Y. Sun and D. L. Parker, "Performance analysis of maximum intensity projection algorithm for display of MRA Images," *IEEE Trans. Med. Imag.,* Vol. 18(12), (1999) 1154-1169
6. S. Schreiner and B. M. Dawant, "The importance of ray pathlengths when measuring objects in maximum intensity projection images," *IEEE Trans. Med. Imag.,* Vol. 15(4) (1996) 568-579
7. B. Porat, *A Course in Digital Signal Processing.* Wiley, New York (1997)
8. T. M. Lehmann and C. Gönner, "Survey: Interpolation methods in medical image processing," *IEEE Trans. Med. Imag.,* Vol. 18(11), (1999) 1049-1075
9. A. Papoulis and S. Pillai, *Probability, Random Variables and Stochastic Processes.* McGraw-Hill, New York (2002)

Responsive Transmission of 3D Scenes over Internet

Shu-Kai Yang, Ding-Zhou Duan, and Ming-Fen Lin

Opti-Electronics & Systems Laboratories,
Industrial Technology Research Institute, Hsinchu, Taiwan, R.O.C.
{sagitta,dwin,mingfen}@itri.org.tw

Abstract. The obvious trend of the application on Internet is not only data transferring or providing document browsing, but also providing services and streaming rich media including 3D scenes. In this paper we present a streaming framework for Internet services which is connection saving and responsive to the status of clients. For a scene containing several progressive meshes, our framework refines objects according to their visual importance selectively. Instead of creating streaming connection for each object, our framework assembles a stream containing an interlaced refinement sequence in run-time according to the level-of-detail diagnostics of clients. Exploiting this technology it makes a server able to serve as many clients as possible. It is quite essential for the development of Internet services.

1   Introduction

Since the network connected the hosts over the world, the major use of Internet today has become information and rich-media service or transaction. We all know that the 3D media is the most interactive and editable media [12]. To enable a 3D service over Internet, end users have to have the content ready at client side that includes the scenes, images, and animation descriptions. The most convenient way to distribute just-in-time content is to transmit it over Internet. But downloading 3D scenes is always a long-waiting job for end users. So we propose a framework of transmitting scenes progressively and view-dependently using limited network resources such as bandwidth or number of simultaneous connections of server-side systems.

There are already many works focusing on the progressive streaming of meshes. In this paper we discuss the view-dependent streaming of scenes containing progressive meshes further. For a given scene supposed to be transmitted over Internet, we arrange all scene data in sections according their order of being invoked. In run-time, the streaming server communicates with the client, assembles the stream immediately, and transmits the scene with a single downloading connection. We call the entire framework the *responsive transmission* of 3D scenes. It has two practical features:

1. **Selective refinement**: the transmission of scenes is responsive to the status of clients. With the arrangement of scene data and the communication between client

Y.-C. Chen, L.-W. Chang, and C.-T. Hsu (Eds.): PCM 2002, LNCS 2532, pp. 1073-1079, 2002.

2. and server, we transmit the data that the client actually needs recently such as the refinements of objects near the view of the user.

3. **Connection saving**: both for servers and clients. The numbers of simultaneous connections is quite limited for a single host. It is usually only 64 for a personal computer running a Windows operating system. It we create a stream for every refined object of the scene individually, one server can only serves a few clients simultaneously. If we prepare an interlaced stream consisting of those streams in advance, we lose the advantage of selective refinement. For the reason we assemble the interlaced stream in run-time and keep these two advantages simultaneously.

2 Related Works

There are already many previous works on the modeling [8,11,15] and streaming [1,2,7,13] of multi-resolutional models and the run-time level-of-detail technology [4,10,14]. Mesh-simplification algorithms try hard to preserve the features of given models and reduce the number of polygons [9]. Many simplification criteria have been developed to reach such issues [3,5,6]. After the simplification process, a sequence of simplification operations can be recorded and inverted to a refinement sequence. And the simplified mesh can be refined according to the data of the refinement sequence.

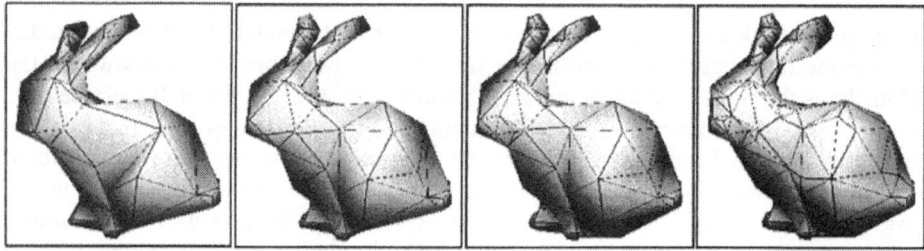

Fig. 1. A progressive mesh sample. A coarsen mesh together with a refinement sequence is called a *progressive mesh*. While a progressive mesh is being transmitted over Internet, the client-side user gets the coarsen mesh which is called the *base mesh* within a short time, then receives the refinement sequence continuously.

In a virtual environment, from the view of a user, there are only a few objects in a scene could be seen when he walks through the scene. Most virtual reality systems will examine the visibility of objects in the scene for such case, and avoid rendering invisible objects to speed up the real-time display for the user. For the example in figure 2, the system only renders the objects inside the viewing frustum. Today visibility-culling algorithms and level-of-detail technology are already essential accelerations of virtual reality systems.

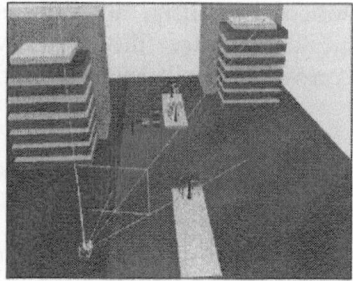

Fig. 2. A visibility culling example. Since the models in a scene could be multi-resolutional, a real-time rendering system can pick different resolutions for visible objects in different distances to the user's current position. And the system renders these objects in different levels of detail to reduce the load of graphics hardware.

Lots of works discuss the modeling and streaming of view-independent progressive meshes. And there are also some works explain the view-dependent modeling of meshes. View-independent streaming does not take the advantage of multi-resolutional modeling fully. And view-dependent modeling only shows its features on some large-scale models such as terrain. So in the paper we describe the view-dependent streaming framework of view-independent progressive meshes. Being responsive means the content of streaming responds to the hardware ability of the client and the viewer's positions.

3 Progressive Scene Stream

According the required order of parts of scene data, we arrange the data in four sections. The stream can be stored as a single stream file or be assembled in run-time. Transmitting the file simply is equivalent to streaming the scene progressively and view-independently.

1. **Scene-graph section**: the scene hierarchy, lights, and viewing settings are transmitted first. The system may create a default display at the client side using built-in models.

2. **Base-mesh section**: coarsen meshes of the objects in the scene are transmitted after the scene-graph section. The spatial rudiment can be reconstructed with the data in these two sections, and the client-side system may be able begin the service.

3. **Appearance section**: the materials and texture images used in the scene are transmitted as the third part of the stream which make the color appearance of the scene been reconstructed.

4. **Refinement section**: the bulk of scene data in the stream is in the last section that consists of all refinements of all models and images. Without the status

information of the client, all refinements are interlaced equably by default. Communicating with the client, the server is able to assemble this section in run time and provides view-dependent selective refinement.

4   Responsive Transmission

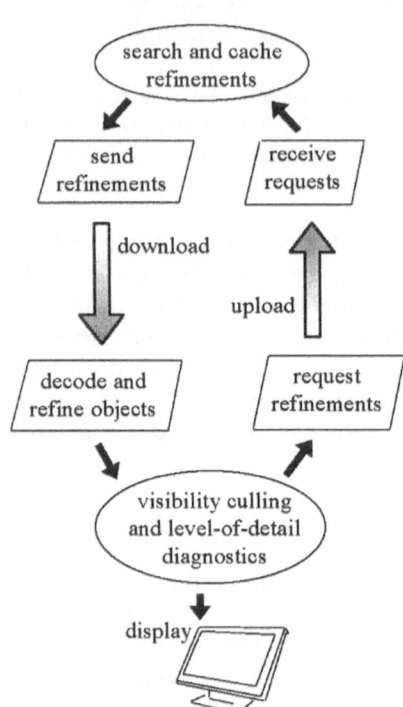

Our responsive-transmission framework depended on the communication between the server and the client. The scene stream files described above are prepared in advance and reassembled in run-time.

4.1   Overview

This framework requires only two connections for each client. Shown in figure 3, the visibility culling and level-of-detail diagnostics of client-side decides the priority of refinements in each frame. The client transmits refinement requests via the uploading connection and receives refinement data from the downloading connection. Different from the level-of-detail technology, there is a flow-control issue of the connections. The uploading and the downloading connections are two asynchronous pipelines to avoid the sending-acknowledgment latency.

4.2   The Streaming Protocol

Fig. 3. The framework of the client and server. The client sends refinement requests according to the viewer's state and receives interlaced refinements data continuously.

A streaming server on Internet can serve several clients simultaneously. The number of simultaneous clients depends on the maximum of connections supported by the server-side operation system. We design a protocol to describe the communication and data transferring between a server and a client. For each scene-stream file stored at the server side, we prepare an index file that indicates the amount and offsets of all refinements in the scene-stream file. This helps the server to find requested refinements in run-time.

The outline of the protocol is demonstrated in figure 4. Since the server boots, it waits for requests of client connection on a fixed port. First, a client sends a connection request using UDP protocol in which the further stream type are indicated.

Then the server replies the address and ports to build downloading and uploading pipelines via UDP, too.

After the message exchange, a downloading pipeline and an uploading pipeline are built. The client sends the scene-stream file name via the uploading pipeline, then the server transmits the refinement information about this file via the downloading pipeline including the amount of meshes and images, and the amount of available refinements.

Then, the server transmits the scene-graph section, base-mesh section, and the appearance section via the downloading pipeline. So a coarsen scene can be constructed at the client side. The user is able to work with the scene now, although the streaming is not finished.

If refinements of the scene objects are available, the client-side system begins two asynchronous threads. In one thread, continuously, when the user walks through the scene, the client-side system performs visibility culling and level-of-detail diagnostics for each display and sends refinement requests via the uploading pipeline. The server receives these requests from the uploading pipeline and transmits refinements via the downloading pipeline. In another thread of the client-side system, the system receives the refinements and refines the objects in the scene until all the refinements are received or streaming is canceled by the user.

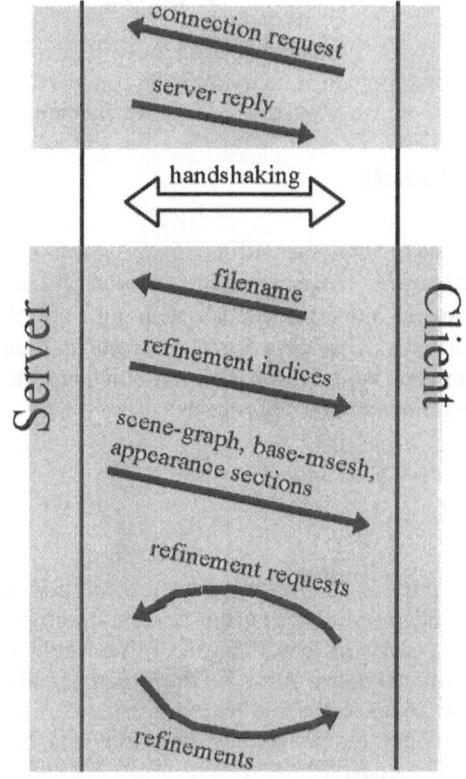

4.3 Refinement Requests

It is not only a resolution-decision problem as the common level-of-detail technology, but also a refinement-priority problem. At the client side, the resolution decision of objects doesn't make sense because the refinements can't be guaranteed to be received in time. We can only decide the priority of the objects that is going to be refined and sends the refinement requests via the uploading pipeline.

We can decide the priority according to some heuristics such as viewing distances or projective areas of the objects in the scene. Besides, we apply a simple flow-control scheme to the uploading pipeline by limiting the refinement requests transferred over Internet simultaneously. If there is not a flow control in the uploading pipeline, the system may sends the requests of all refinements before the user moves his viewing position and   loses the advantage of view-dependent streaming. This flow-control scheme keeps the refinement requesting and displaying symmetrical at the client side.

5   Results

We have implemented a streaming server and a walk-through client to verify the framework. The experimental results on two sample scenes are shown in figure 5 and figure 6. We can see that near and unrefined objects are transmitted first clearly especially in the wire-frame views in figure 5(d-f) and 6(d-f). The level-of-detail heuristics applied in the experiments are the viewing distance, display-area size, and the refinement rate of objects.

6   Conclusion

We present the responsive transmission framework to stream 3D scenes view-dependently, including the stream structure and the streaming protocol. We arrange scene data in sections according their order of been required by the client. Additionally, we describe the communication between a server and a client in this paper to assemble and transmit the stream in run-time. It needs only two connections per client to reach the goal and makes a server able to serve several clients simultaneously.

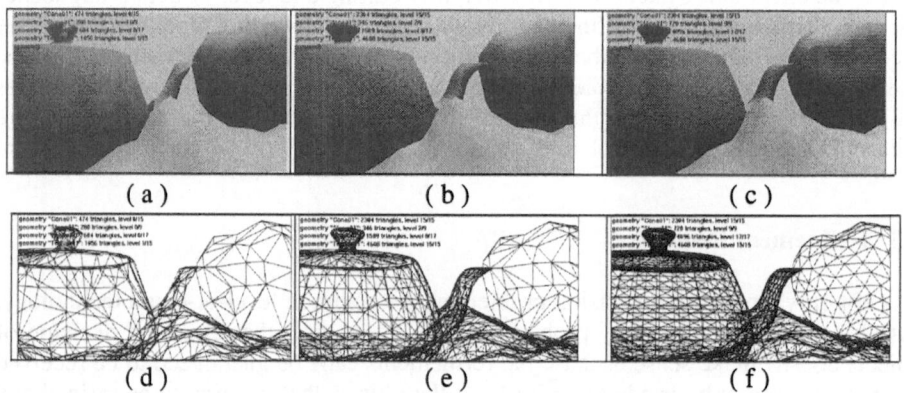

Fig. 5. Responsive transmission of a sample scene.

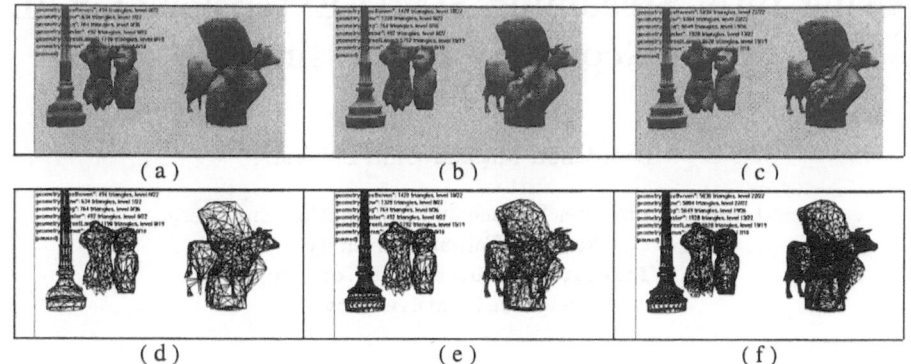

(a)   (b)   (c)

(d)   (e)   (f)

Fig. 6. Responsive transmission of another scene.

References

1. "3D Mesh Objects in MPEG-4", ISO/IEC JTC1/SC29 /WG11 W2802.
2. "MPEG-4 Final Proposed Draft Amendment", ISO/IEC/JTC1/ SC29/WG11 N3383, Jun. 2000.
3. Chang, C.-C., Yang, S-K., Lin, M.-F., and Duan, D.-Z., "Surface Geometry Simplification using Fuzzy Approaches.", proceedings of International Workshop on Advanced Imaging Technology (IWAIT2001), 157-160, Korea, 2001.
4. Chim, J. H. P., Green, M., Lau, R. W. H., Leong, H. V., Si, A., "On Caching and Prefetching of Virtual Objects in Distributed Virtual Environments", proceedings of ACM Multimedia Conference, 171-180, UK, 1998.
5. Garland, M. and Heckbert, P.S. "Surface Simplification using Quadric Error Metrics", Computer Graphics (SIGGRAPH'97 proceedings) , 209-224, 1997.
6. Garland, M. and Heckbert, P.S. "Simplifying Surfaces with Color and Texture using Quadric Error Metrics", proceedings of IEEE Visualization'98, 263-269, 1998.
7. Gueziec, A., Silva, C., Taubin, G. "A Framework for Streaming Geometry in VRML", IEEE Computer Graphics and Applications, special issue on VRML, March-April 1999.
8. Hoppe, H. "Progressive Meshes", proceedings of Computer Graphics (SIGGRAPH'96), 99-108, 1996.
9. Hoppe, H., DeRose, T., Duchamp, T., McDonald, J., and Stuetzle, W. "Mesh Optimization", proceedings of Computer Graphics (SIGGRAPH'93), 19-26, 1993.
10. Hudson, T., Manocha, D., Cohen., J., Lin, M., Hoff, K. E. III, and Zhang, H., "Occlusion Culling using Shadow Frusta", proceedings of 13th Symposium on Computational Geometry, June, 1997.
11. Klein, R., Liebich, G., and Strasser, W. "Mesh Reduction with Error Control", IEEE Visualization '96. Proc., 311-318, 1996.
12. Singhal, S. and Zyda, M., "Networked Virtual Environments", ACM press, Addison-Wesley Inc., ISBN 0-201-32557-8, 1999.
13. Taubin G., Gueziec A., Horn W., Lazarus F. "Progressive Forest Split Compression", proceedings of Computer Graphics (SIGGRAPH'98), 123-132, 1998.
14. Yang, S.-K., and Chuang, J.-H., "Dynamic Shadow Computation for Virtual Environments", proceeding of International Workshop on Advanced Imaging Technology (IWAIT2001), Korea, 2001.
15. Yang, S.-K., Chang, C.-C., Duan, D.-Z., and Lin, M.-F., "A Per-Levelly Controlled Progressive Modeling Algorithm for Streaming and LOD in Virtual Environments", workshop proceedings of the 7th International Conference on Distributed Multimedia Systems (DMS'01), 129-134, Taiwan, 2001.

Using Intel Streaming SIMD Extensions for 3D Geometry Processing

Wan-Chun Ma and Chia-Lin Yang

Dept. of Computer Science and Information Engineering
National Taiwan University
firebird@cmlab.csie.ntu.edu.tw,
yangc@csie.ntu.edu.tw

Abstract. Three dimensional (3D) graphics applications is an important workload running on today's computer system. A cost-effective graphics solution is to use a general processor for 3D geometry processing and a specialized hardware for rasterization. 3D geometry processing is an inherently parallel task. Therefore, many CPU vendors add SIMD (Single Instruction Multiple Data) instruction extensions to accelerate 3D geometry processing. In this paper, we evaluate the performance impact of using the Intel Streaming SIMD Extensions (SSE) for 3D geometry processing. We use SIMD-FP to improve the computational throughput by processing four vertices in parallel. We find that the layout of vertices in memory is important for the effectiveness of SIMD-FP. We also study the effect of using prefetch instructions to improve the memory performance. The experimental results show that using Intel SSE can achieve close to 4x speedup for geometry processing.

1 Introduction

Multimedia applications (e.g. speech, audio/video, image and graphics applications) have become important workloads running on general processors. This type of applications often presents data parallelisms. Therefore, one important architectural enhancement to accelerate multimedia applications is the SIMD (Single Instruction Multiple Data) instruction extensions. In 1996, Intel introduced the MMX technology [3], which packs 8-bit or 16-bit fixed-point data into a 64-bit register and performs arithmetic or logical operations on the packed data in parallel. The MMX works well for applications with integer data type, such as image and video processing. However, several visual and 3D graphics applications are floating-point intensive. To accelerate floating-point computation Intel develops the Streaming SIMD Extensions (SSE) [1] [4]. The key component of the SSE is the SIMD-FP extensions, which can process four single-precision floating-point values in parallel. Another important feature of the SSE is the memory streaming instruction extensions, which allow programmers to prefetch data into a specified level of the cache hierarchy. Most multimedia applications present the streaming data access pattern; that is, data are accessed sequentially

Y.-C. Chen, L.-W. Chang, and C.-T. Hsu (Eds.): PCM 2002, LNCS 2532, pp. 1080–1087, 2002.

and seldom reused. Therefore, prefetching this type of data into the L2 cache is an effective way to improve the memory system performance.

3D graphics is an important workload of nowadays multimedia applications. 3D graphics pipeline contains three stages: 1) database traversal, 2) geometry processing, and 3) rasterization. The first stage reads in the scene models and the second stage transforms 3D coordinates into 2D coordinates. Finally, the rasterization stage converts transformed primitives into pixel values and stores them in the frame buffer for display. For cost consideration, a commodity system usually uses the host processor for geometry processing and a custom hardware to accelerate rasterization. 3D geometry processing has streaming data access pattern and floating-point intensive computation. The vertex information (e.g. coordinate and color) are stored in the floating-point format and read sequentially from the storage. Geometry processing is an inherently parallel task since each vertex can be processed independently. Therefore, 3D geometry processing is one of the targeted applications for the SSE.

Previous studies on the SSE focused primarily on the usage and only analyze the performance effect for application kernels [2]. In this paper, we perform detailed performance analysis of using the SSE on the complete 3D geometry pipeline. We first evaluate the performance impact of using SIMD-FP and the effect of different data layout. We then analyze how much memory stall time can be eliminated through prefetching. Experimental results show that using SIMD-FP along can achieve close to 3x speedup, and arranging the vertices favorable to SIMD computation can further improve performance. We also find that prefetching vertices into the L2 cache one iteration ahead can eliminate most of the L2 cache misses. The overall speedup of using SSE in 3D geometry processing is up to 4x. The paper is organized as follows. Section 2 provides background information on the SSE and 3D geometry processing. Section 3 describes our experimental methodology. Section 4 presents the performance analysis. Section 5 discusses related work. Section 6 concludes this paper.

2   Background

In this section, we describe two main kernels of 3D geometry processing and illustrate how to apply the SSE to speed up the process.

2.1   3D Geometry Pipeline

The 3D geometry pipeline consists of two main kernels:

1. **Transformation:** 3D geometry processing contains three stages of coordinates transformation: viewing, modeling and projection. Each transformation requires a multiplication of a 1x4 vector and a 4x4 matrix. Hence, each transformation needs 12 multiplications and 16 additions.

2. **Lighting:** the lighting stage of the 3D geometry pipeline determines the color of each vertex. For each light source in the scene, the following illumination model is used to calculate the light intensity of a vertex [14]:

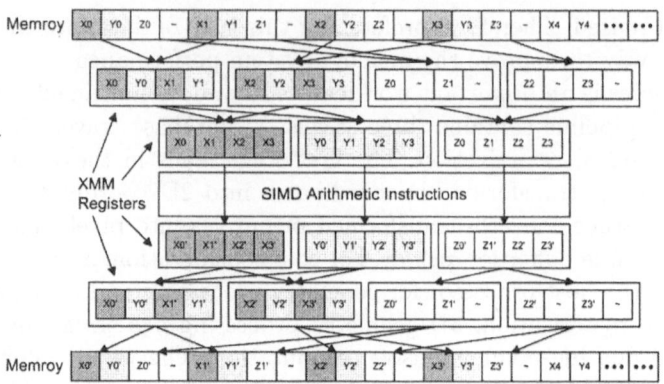

Fig. 1(a). Illustration of using SIMD-FP to process four vertices in parallel using AOS data structure .

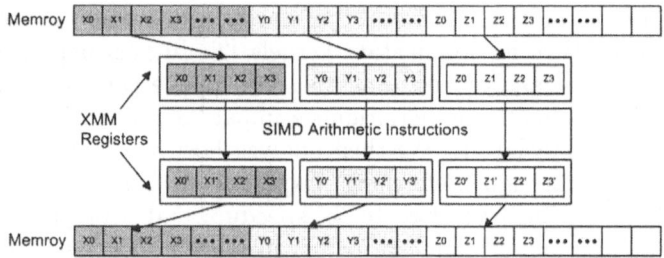

Fig. 1(b). Illustration of using SIMD-FP to process four vertices in parallel using SOA data structure .

$$I = k_a \times I_V + (\frac{1}{d}) \times (k_d \times I_L \times (N \cdot L) + k_s \times I_L \times V \cdot R^{n_s})$$

In this paper, we simplify the illumination model by discarding the specular component of the formula. Therefore, lighting calculation requires one division, 16 multiplications, 6 additions, 3 subtractions and one square root operation assuming single light source.

2.2   Using the SSE

To support the SSE Intel adds eight new 128-bit registers (XMM registers). Thus we can pack four single-precision floating-point operands into a register and use SIMD-FP to operate in parallel on all packed data operands. The most intuitive way to apply the SIMD-FP to 3D geometry processing is to exploit the parallelism between vertices as shown in Figure 1(a). The x (y and z) coordinates of four vertices are first packed into one XMM register. We then apply SIMD-FP arithmetic instructions to the packed data. The computed data is unpacked before stored back to the memory.

struct coordinate	*struct coordinate*

struct coordinate
{
  float x,y,z,w;
}

coordinate vertex[10000];

Fig. 2(a). AOS declaration

struct coordinate
{
  float x[10000]; float y[10000];
  float z[10000]; float w[10000];
}

coordinate vertex;

Fig. 2(b). SOA declaration

As we can see from the illustration, organizing data into the SIMD format incurs significant overhead. To avoid this overhead Intel proposes to transpose the data layout. The conventional approach stores vertices in memory using AOS (array of structures) format (see Figure 2(a)). Intel suggests to store vertices in the SOA (structure of arrays) format (see Figure 2(b)) such that the x (y and z) coordinate of different vertices are stored contiguously in the memory. Therefore, we can reduce the data packing/unpacking overhead for realizing SIMD computation in this new data layout as shown in Figure 1(b). In Section 4, we evaluate the effect of SIMD-FP using both data layout.

3D geometry processing has poor cache performance because of the large working set and streaming access patterns. Therefore, to improve the cache performance we can use the prefetching instructions provided in the SSE to reduce memory stall time. Prefetching hides memory latency by bringing data close to the CPU earlier than demand fetches. The following pseudo code segment shows the usage of prefetch instructions:

```
for i = 0 to # of vertices
    prefetch vertex[i+x];
    process vertex[i]; /* computation on a vertex*/
end loop
```

The variable x controls the prefetching distance; that is how far ahead we need to prefetch data in order to completely hide memory latency. The amount of computation on each vertex and memory latency determines the value of x.

3   Experimental Methodology

We evaluate the SSE on a Pentium 4 processor running Window 2000. The processor and memory configurations are summarized in Table 1. We first implement the 3D geometry pipeline in C and then modify it to use the SSE assembly

Table 1. System configuration

CPU	Intel Pentium 4 1.5GHz	
	L1 Data Cache	4-way, 8K byte
	L2 Cache	8-way, 256K byte
Memory	256M byte 440MHz RAMBUS	

Fig. 3. 3D models used in the experiments.

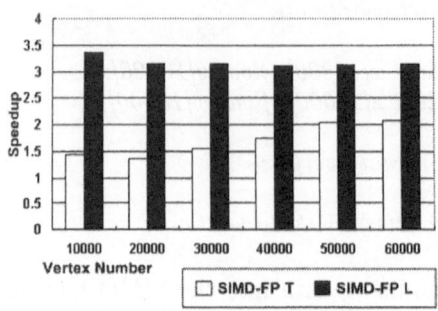

Fig. 4. Speedup from the SIMD-FP implementation for 3D transformation and lighting.

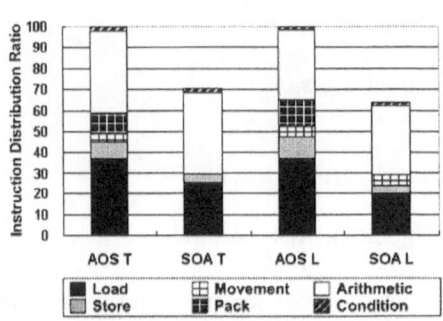

Fig. 5. Instruction distribution in AOS and SOA implementations.

codes. The program codes are compiled by Microsoft Visual C++ 6.0 with Processor Pack 5. The 3D model used in this study is shown in Figure 3. We use mesh re-sampling technique to change the number of vertices in the model. To evaluate the SSE we use two performance profiling tools:

1. **TrueTime** [6]: TrueTime is a performance profiler developed by NuMega. It automatically pinpoints slow codes and accurately reports application and component performance. We use TrueTime to obtain the execution time of different geometry pipeline implementations.

2. **VTune Performance Analyzer** [5]: VTune is a system performance profiling tool created by Intel. This tool is able to monitor several important events, such as mis-predicted branches, cache misses, etc. We use VTune to evaluate the memory system performance.

4   Analysis of Results

In this section, we analyze the performance impact of the SSE instructions on 3D geometry processing. In order to get more insight into the performance increase, we first present the results for transformation and lighting kernels, respectively. The effect of using the SSE on complete geometry pipeline is presented last. We measure the speedup from using only SIMD-FP instructions, evaluate the benefit from using the SOA structure, and finally use prefetch instructions to improve the memory system performance.

Effect of SIMD-FP

The SIMD-FP implementation could achieve the speedup of 4x potentially since we can process four vertices simultaneously. The experimental result shows about 2x and 3x speedup for transformation and lighting as shown in Figure 4. Note that we obtain the speedup using the following formula:

$$\frac{\text{Execution-Time(without SIMD-FP)}}{\text{Execution-Time(with SIMD-FP)}}$$

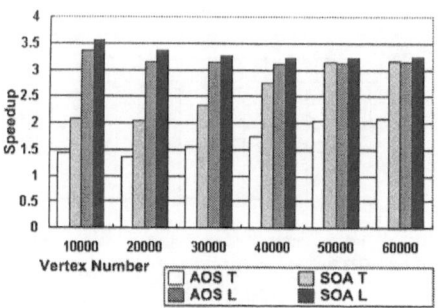
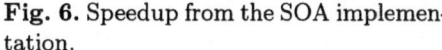
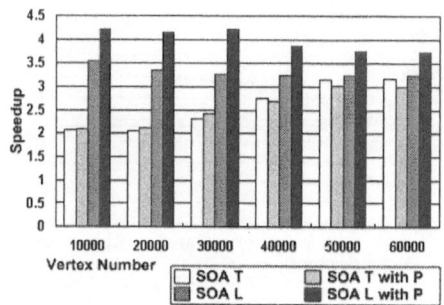

Fig. 6. Speedup from the SOA implementation.

Fig. 7. Speedup from the SOA implementation with prefetching instructions.

The data packing/unpacking overhead undermines the effect of using the SSE. Lighting has higher speedup than transformation because lighting performs more computation on a vertex as described in Section 2. This implies that data manipulation overhead is less significant in lighting compared to transformation. Next, we evaluate how much of the overhead can be eliminated using the SOA structure.

AOS vs. SOA

Figure 5 shows the instruction distribution of transformation and lighting in two different data layouts - AOS vs. SOA. The number of instructions is normalized to the AOS implementation. The results show that SOA reduce 30% of instructions for transformation and 37% for lighting. Note that data packing/unpacking instructions are completely eliminated and the number of load instructions is also reduced significantly. Figure 6 shows the speedup of the kernels using SIMD-FP SOA implementation. The AOS speedup is included for comparison. For transformation, using SOA can achieve the speedup of 3x while AOS can only achieve the speedup of 2x for the largest model. However, SOA shows little performance benefit for lighting even though it reduces 37% of instructions. The computation on lighting requires long latency operations, such as square root and division. Therefore, the number of instructions is not a good indication on the execution time. As mentioned before, the data manipulation overhead is less significant in lighting kernel compared to transformation. So we see less performance gained from using SOA for lighting.

Effect of Prefetching

In this section, we examine the prefetching effect. Because of the streaming access pattern, the vertex data is only prefetched into the L2 cache to avoid the L1 cache pollution. We only prefetch one vertex ahead since it is enough to hide memory latency (in the VTune cache profiling statistics, all the L2 cache misses are eliminated). Figure 7 shows the speed up from prefetching. The results show that prefetching

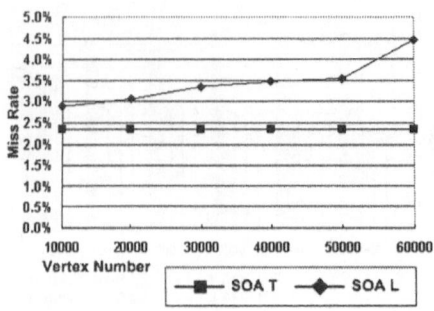

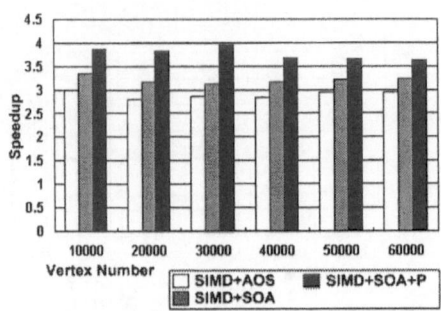

Fig. 8. The L2 cache miss rate of SOA kernels.

Fig. 9. Speedup of the complete geometry pipeline implementation (AOS, SOA, SOA with prefetching).

achieve significant performance improvement for lighting but little for transformation. From the VTune statistics, we find that lighting has higher L2 miss rate than transformation as shown in Figure 8. It indicates that lighting has more memory stall time than transformation, thus prefetching is more effective for lighting. Note that prefetching could incur overhead, such as wasting memory bandwidth and issuing more instructions. That is why prefetching shows negative performance impact for transformation in some testing cases.

Overall Effect on the Complete Geometry Pipeline

The effect of the SSE on the complete geometry pipeline is shown in Figure 9. We assume three light sources in the scene, which is a common setup in 3D applications. The results show that the speedup from using SIMD-FP with the conventional AOS data structure ranges from 2.7x to 3x (the first bar). Using the SOA structure can further improve the performance (3.1x to 3.3x, the second bar). Prefetching shows significant performance improvement for all testing cases. The overall speedup ranges from 3.6x to 3.9x (the third bar).

5   Related Work

Most of papers studying instruction-set extensions for multimedia applications focused on design issues and illustrations of their use instead of performance analysis [7] [8] [10] [11]. Only the speedup of a small code segment (i.e. application kernels) is reported.

Several papers stud the performance aspect of using multimedia instruction extensions. Bharghava et al. [9] evaluated the MMX technology on Pentium-based systems. Daniel Rice [13] and Ranganathan et al. [12] studied the performance of Sun VIS media extensions [8] for image and video workloads. Yang et al. [15] studied the performance impact of using SIMD instructions on 3D geometry processing similar to this work. But their studies were based on simulation and assume a perfect memory system.

6 Conclusion

We evaluate the effectiveness of using the Intel SSE extensions on the 3D geometry pipeline. We observe that:

1. The SSE provides significant speedup for geometry pipeline. The speedup ranges from 3.0x to 3.8x.
2. The layout of vertices in memory is crucial for the effectiveness of SIMD-FP. Using SOA (structure of arrays) can eliminate the overhead of organizing data into SIMD format.
3. Prefetching shows significant performance improvement for lighting. However, for transformation, it shows little performance benefit. Sometimes, the prefetching overhead even outweighs the benefit.

References

1. Intel Pentium 4 and Intel Xeon processor optimization reference manual. *Intel Corporation, order number: 248966-04*
2. Streaming SIMD Extensions -3D transform. *Intel Corporation, order number: 243631-004*, 1999.
3. The IA-32 Intel architecture software developer's manual. *Intel Corporation, order number: 245471*, 1:231–246, 2001.
4. The IA-32 Intel architecture software developer's manual. *Intel Corporation, order number: 245471*, 1: 247–268, 2001.
5. Intel VTune performance analyzer. *Intel Corporation* http://developer.Intel.com/software/products/vtune/vtune60/index.htm.
6. Numega TrueTime,devpartner for visual C++. *Compuware Corporation,* http://www.compuware.com/products/devpartner/visualc/truetimevc.htm.
7. M.P. et al. Altivec technology: Accelerating media processing across the spectrum. *HotChips10*, 1998.
8. M.T. et al. VIS speeds new media processing. *IEEE Micro*, 16(4):10–20, 1996.
9. R.B. et al. Evaluating MMX technology using DSP and multimedia applications. *ACM/IEEE International Symposium on Microarchitecture*, 1998.
10. A. Peleg and U. Weiser. MMX technology extension to the Intel architecture. *IEEE Mirco*, 16(4):42–50, 1996.
11. S.K.Raman,V.Pentkovski,and J.Keshava.Implementing Streaming SIMD Extensions on the Pentium III processor. *IEEE Micro*, 20(4):47–57,2000.
12. P. Ranganathan, S. Adve, and N.P. Jouppi. Performance of image and video processing with general-purpose processors and media ISA extensions. *International Symposium on Computer Architecture*, 1999.
13. D.S. Rice. High-performance image processing using special-purpose CPU instruction set. *Master's thesis, Stanford University*, 1996.
14. J.D. Foley, A.V. Dam, and S.K. Feiner. *Introduction to Computer Graphics Addison Wesley*, 1993.
15. C.-L.Yang, B. Sano, and A.R. Lebeck. Exploiting instruction level parallelism in geometry processing for three dimensional graphics applications. *ACM/IEEE International Symposium on Microarchitecture*, 1998.

Multimodal Gumdo Game: The Whole Body Interaction with an Intelligent Cyber Fencer

Jungwon Yoon[1], Sehwan Kim[2], Jeha Ryu[1], and Woontack Woo[2]

[1]Dept. of Mechatronics, K-JIST
[2]Dept. of Information & Communications, K-JIST
Kwangju, 500-712, Korea
{garden, skim, ryu, wwoo}@kjist.ac.kr

Abstract. This paper presents an immersive multimodal Gumdo simulation game that allows a user to experience the whole body interaction with an intelligent cyber fencer. The proposed system consists of three modules: (i) a nondistracting multimodal interface with 3D vision and speech (ii) an intelligent cyber fencer and (iii) an immersive feedback by a big screen and sound. Firstly, the multimodal interface allows a user to move around and to shout without distracting the user. Secondly, an intelligent cyber fencer provides the user with intelligent interactions by perception and reaction modules that are created by the analysis of real Gumdo game. Finally, an immersive audio-visual feedback helps a user experience an immersive interaction. The proposed interactive system with an intelligent fencer is designed to satisfy comfortable interface, perceptual intelligence, and natural interaction (*I-cubed*) and enhance the life-like impression of fighting actions. The suggested system can be applied to various applications such as education, art, and exercise.

1 Introduction

Nowadays, Virtual Reality (VR) technology is flourishing with the rapid development of high power computer and related technologies. There are wide-range of VR applications such as training, education, entertainment, engineering, medical operation, teleoperation, etc. Especially, edutainment applications are very popular and marketable immediately. However, the lack of natural interface is a main bottleneck of bringing them into widespread use. Therefore, it is necessary to make a natural multimodal interface for the VR applications. In order to enhance the effects of immersive experiences in VR-based edutainment systems, the systems should be *I-cubed*, i.e. the systems have comfortable *interface*, perceptual (or emotional) *intelligence* and natural *interaction* [1].

A number of researchers have reported on interactive systems with autonomous agents. Especially, for the whole body interaction of a user with a virtual environment, the players [2-3] are merged into a virtual environment by head-mounted displays, magnetic sensors and data gloves. Even though the whole body interaction with a

Y.-C. Chen, L.-W. Chang, and C.-T. Hsu (Eds.): PCM 2002, LNCS 2532, pp. 1088-1095, 2002.
© Springer-Verlag Berlin Heidelberg 2002

virtual environment in these systems is possible, these systems still have limitations in providing immersive interactions because the complicated facilities have to be worn or attached on the body and then connected to computers with wires, which tends to distract users from experiencing immersion. The ALIVE system [4] and the KidsRoom [5] used a 2D vision interface in order to extract the user's actions. Note, however, that the 2D vision-based systems in both ALIVE and KidsRoom have limitations in exploiting 3D visual information. Gavrila et al. tried to identify the whole body posture by analyzing multiple-view frames [6]. However, it has limitations in applying it to real-time interactive systems because the posture is analyzed in an interactive post-processing phase. Accordingly, there are only a few *I-cubed* systems providing excitement to a user with the whole body interaction via a comfortable interface and an autonomous agent.

In this paper, we present an immersive multimodal Gumdo simulation game that allows a user to experience the whole body interaction with an intelligent cyber fencer. The proposed system consists of three modules: (i) a comfortable multimodal interface with 3D vision and speech (ii) an intelligent cyber fencer and (iii) an immersive feedback by screen and sound. After taking everything into consideration, the proposed system provides the user with an immersive Gumdo experience with the whole body movement. This paper is organized as follows: In chapter 2, we describe in detail the proposed Gumdo game system in terms of three components; a multimodal interface, fencer intelligence and audiovisual feedbacks. Experimental results and discussions are followed in chapters 3 and 4, respectively.

2 Description of the Proposed Gumdo Simulation System

Gumdo is one of the fencing sports with a bamboo sword and light protective armor. Fencers wear protective equipments covering target areas; head, wrists and abdomen. To make a valid cut, a fencer must strike on the target areas of the opponent with a bamboo sword, while shouting the name of the target areas. The one who strikes the target areas twice among three rounds becomes a winner. In order to properly simulate an immersive Gumdo simulation in a VR setting, first of all a wide range of motion should be covered by a vision interface for detecting a real fencer's full body motion. In addition, a reliable speech interface is needed to express and understand the intension of a fencer. Next, for exciting interaction with a cyber fencer, some realistic intelligence should be provided to the cyber fencer. Finally, a user should experience full immersion with visual, auditory and haptic feedback that can display fighting situation in real-time. Figure 1 shows the block diagram of the proposed Gumdo game system that incorporates all requirements except haptic feedback. Haptic feedback is not considered because it requires a heavy robotic system that may restrict wider full body motion.

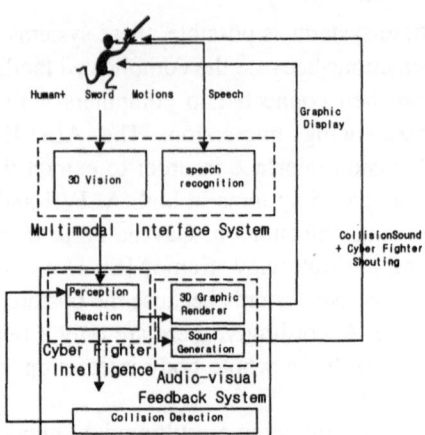

Fig. 1. Block diagram of Gumdo system

2.1 Multimodal Interface (3D Vision & Speech Recognition)

We adopt a non-contact vision-based 3D interface, exploiting depth information without distracting the user while tracking the user in 3D space. To track the movement of the user and the sword in 3D space, we first segment moving foreground from static background after estimating depth information [7]. Next, we separate the sword from the segmented foreground by exploiting two colored markers located at the end points of the sword. Finally, we estimate the line of the sword and the center of the user to track the movements of both of them. Using the moments of the foreground object, the orientation angle of the body about the z-axis is calculated.

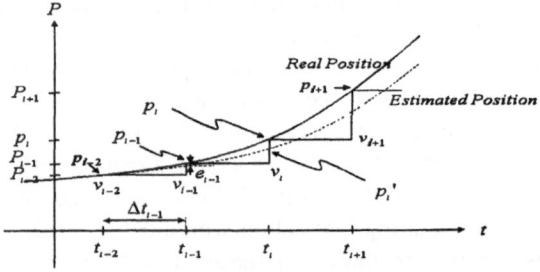

Fig. 2. Compensation of time delay

In general, the real-time tracking of a moving sword in 3D is not easy because some processing time is required to segment and then to estimate its 3D posture [8]. The time-delay due to the processing time has a serious influence on obtaining an accurate 3D position of the sword especially when the movement of the sword is faster than the frame rate of the multiview camera. Therefore, a scheme for compensating for the time delay is proposed. In Fig. 2, the real and estimated positions of the sword are compared. The real 3D position trajectory is represented as a solid line while the estimated one as a dotted line. Based on the past positions prior to t_i, the estimated position of the sword is obtained by:

$$p_i' = p_{i-1} + \alpha v_{i-1} \times \Delta t_{i-1} + f(e_{i-1}), 0 < \alpha < 1 . \qquad (1)$$

where p_i' denotes the estimated position of the sword at time t_i, p_{i-1} is the real position of the sword at t_{i-1}, v_{i-1} is the velocity of the sword from t_{i-2} to t_{i-1}, and Δt_{i-1} the time duration from t_{i-2} to t_{i-1}. The constant α represents a scale factor for determining the ratio of time duration from t_{i-2} to t_{i-1} to estimate the position of the sword at t_i ($0 < \alpha < 1$). The last term $f(e_{i-1})$ is used to compensate for the estimation errors. This function is expressed as a nonlinear function of the error between real and estimated positions. The nonlinear compensator function is usually necessary because the direction of the sword changes abruptly in Gumdo simulation.

The system recognizes three Korean words: "Meo-Ri (HEAD)", "Heo-Ri (ABDOMEN)" and "Son-Mok (WRIST)". The speech inputs in the proposed Gumdo simulation are used for the perception module of the intelligent cyber fencer. The speech inputs are classified into three words based on extracted speech features, LPC (Linear Prediction Coding) cepstrum coefficients [9]. Finally, the positions of both the sword and the user will be transferred to the cyber fencer kernel, combined with the results of speech recognition.

2.2 Cyber Fencer Intelligence

A cyber fencer must have some intelligence for realistic and exciting game with a real-person fencer. The intelligent cyber fencer has perception and reaction modules. The perception module perceives its environment information by internal sensors and external inputs while the reaction module consists of motivation, behavior and motor modules. Fig. 3 shows the schematic diagram of the cyber fencer action. Arrows represent information flows between components.

The perception module should manage intelligently audio-visual inputs from the multimodal interface. The basic actions of the user and the sword can be perceived by observing the motion of the user and the sword in terms of distance and direction as well as by hearing the shout sound. The behavior of the user can be recognized by the body action followed by the sword action. Also, the situation of virtual environment during fighting will be detected by internal sensors such as the percentage of victories and the current position of the cyber fencer inside a fighting field.

The motivation module consists of state and drive. The state refers to the feeling of the cyber fencer and is associated with the action of the cyber fencer. The drive represents the desire of the cyber fencer while fighting with the user. The drive consists of three important elements of Gumdo; *mind, sprit and power*. The *mind* reflects the static condition of the cyber fencer such as the calmness and discernment and shows the ability to recognize the information transferred from the perception module. The *spirit* represents the will of the fencer, i.e. the dynamic conditions of the cyber fencer.

The *power* represents the ability to attack, i.e. the promptitude and tempo of the attack and defense of the fencer. The state is composed of fear that shows the current feeling of the fencer. The fear level of the cyber fencer increases when he meets the human fencer with physical superiority or he encounters unexpected actions from the human fencer.

Given the perception and motivation inputs, the behavior module sends relevant actions to the motor module. The behavior module has two kinds of actions; general and reflective actions. The general action is a set of behaviors to achieve goals. The reflective action is a set of behaviors to protect the attack of the user.

The motor module enables the cyber fencer to match with the user as well as to display the cyber fencer on the screen. The motor module, controlling both the body and the sword motions of the cyber fencer, does real-time motion interpolation to execute Gumdo simulation.

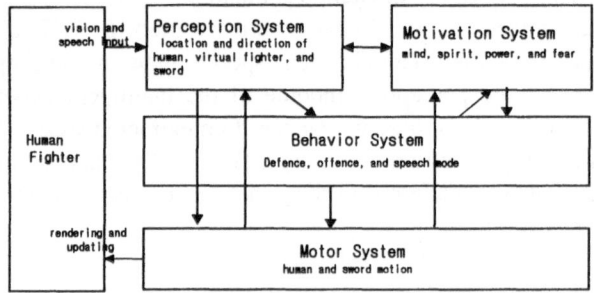

Fig. 3. Schematic Diagram of a Cyber Fencer Action. (adapted from [10])

2.3 Audio-Visual Feedback

For giving immersive feeding to the user, audio-visual feedback is provided with a big screen and sound effects. The geometric model of the cyber fencer consists of a spherical head, a cylindrical upper body, and cylindrical upper and lower arms. The motions of the fencer and the sword models are controlled by a vision interface. For sound effects, we record and play sound from collision impact between two swords, between the sword and one of the targets, fencer's shouting voices, and referee voices that declare start and end of the fighting and that indicate who is the winner after striking. To properly display the collision situation, we detect the collision between two swords or between a sword and one of the target areas: head, wrist and abdomen by considering as collisions between a line and a line or a line and a sphere. In our Gumdo simulation, since the real sword collides with the virtual sword, the sword collision cannot physically stop the motion of the real sword due to the absence of the force feedback. Therefore, the striking passing through the target areas is considered as an invalid striking.

3   Experiment Results

Fig. 4 shows the proposed Gumdo simulation system consisting of multimodal inter-face, artificial intelligence and audio-visual feedback. The proposed system was im-plemented in a Workstation with Pentium III Xeon Dual 1GHz CPUs.

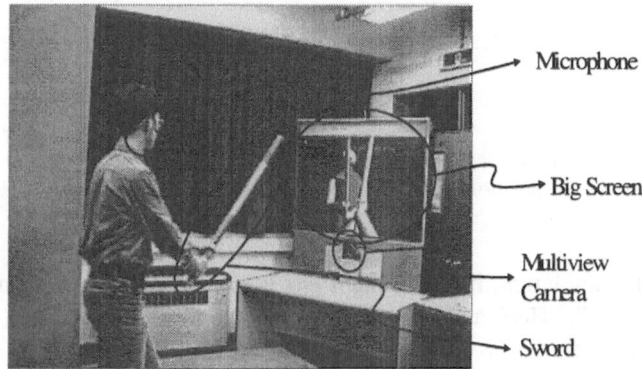

Fig. 4. An immersive Gumdo game with audio-visual feedback

Table 1 shows system specifications of the Gumdo simulation game. The movement range is 2m x 4m and the resolution of the vision system is 5cm/disparity in the range of 3-5m. The speed of the Gumdo simulation game is about 5 Hz due to the time con-sumption in calculating 3D disparity from multiview images. The system recognize 3 words, "Meo-Ri, Heo-Ri , Son-Mok", except the noise.

Table 1. Specifications of the Gumdo system

Parameters	Measurements
Fighting Area	2m (width) * 4m (depth)
Sword Resolution	5 deg (pitch), 5 deg (yaw)
Body Resolution	0.05 m
Bandwidth of System	5 Hz
Speech Recognition	3 words Recognition

In the experiments, we captured a moving sword, which is about 220 cm away from a multiview camera. Through the experiments, we observed that the tracking perform-ance of the user body is not sufficient to enjoy a real fighting with the cyber fencer in the virtual environment since the tracking speed (5Hz) of the sword is a little slow. To overcome the hardware limitations, we adopted a simple but effective motion compen-sation technique. In Fig. 5, we show the motion compensation results considering the processing time-delay. The errors are reduced substantially as shown in Fig. 5 (b).

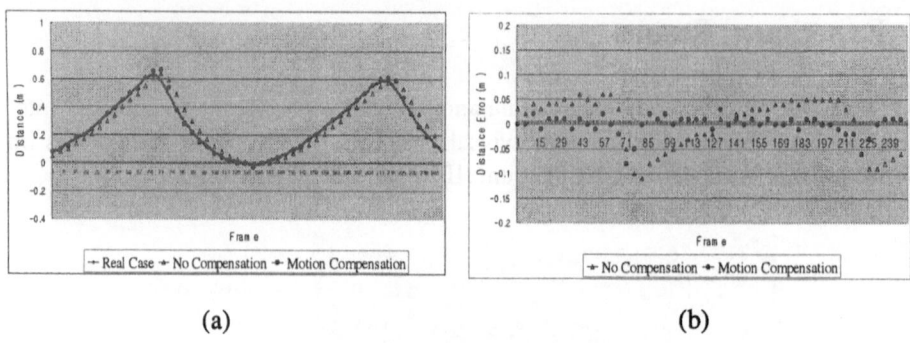

(a)   (b)

Fig. 5. Motion compensation results with the sword moving in x direction, (a) compensation results in x direction, (b) position errors between real case and compensated or uncompensated cases

In the Gumdo simulation, it was enough just to consider the first phoneme of each word, that is, "Meo", "Heo" and "Son" to differentiate three words. Thus, we just used the first phoneme of each word to get cepstrum coefficients for speech samples. For speech recognition, we checked the recognition rates for each of the three words. The speech signal and each Euclidean distance are shown as an example in Table 2. The "Son-Mok" has over 90% success recognition rate because its phonemic structure is so different from the others. Even though there are very different intensities of the "Son-Mok" speech input, the recognition algorithm worked well. However, because "Meo-Ri" and "Heo-Ri" had similar sounds, we had about 80% success recognition rate. When users were trained by experiments, the average success recognition rate was over 90%.

Table 2. The Euclidean distance from the cepstrum coefficient

Pattern Speech \ Euclidean distance	"Meo-Ri"	"Heo-Ri"	"Son-Mok"
"Meo-Ri"	1.9633	2.3052	8.4024
"Heo-Ri"	2.3798	1.6915	6.8680
"Son-Mok"	8.1364	7.8384	2.4082

4   Conclusions and Future Work

In this paper, we proposed a simple immersive Gumdo simulation game that consists of a multimodal interface (3D vision and sound), an intelligent cyber fencer based on perception and reaction modules, and an audio-visual feedback during the fighting between a user and a cyber fencer. The proposed system allows the whole body inter-action with the cyber fencer without distracting the user. The proposed vision system is able to have a wider motion range (2m (width) * 4m (depth)). In addition, we added the speech modality using a wireless microphone to the user to enjoy a natural Gumdo simulation and to interact with the cyber fencer. The proposed interactive system with an intelligent fencer can improve interactions between the user and the cyber fencer in a virtual environment and can enhance the life-like impression of fighting actions. The 5Hz speed of Gumdo game may be slow for applications requiring fast motion. This slow speed may be increased by; higher sampling rate (currently 5Hz) by superior PC, higher rate of communication, use of compensation scheme using extra interpolation, and so on. A remaining challenge is to develop the Gumdo simulation exploiting a force feedback. The force feedback combined with the vision and speech will provide a Gumdo fighting with a full immersion. A photo-realistic avatar in the 3D virtual environment will also provide more realistic experience. In addition, a networked VR game with a real person will be another challenging task.

Acknowledgement. This research was supported by the BK21 research fund from the MOE, Korea.

References

1. W. Woo, N. Kim, K. Wong and M. Tadenuma, " Sketch on Dynamic Gesture Tracking and Analysis Exploiting Vision-based 3D Interface," *in Proc. SPIE PW-EI-VCIP'01*, vol. 4310, pp. 656-666, Jan. 2001.
2. L. Emering, R. Boulic, D. Thalmann, Interacting with Virtual Humans through Body Actions,IEEE Computer Graphics and Applications,1998 , Vol.18, No1, pp8-11.
3. T. Molet, A. Aubel, T. Çapin, S. Carion, E. Lee, N. M. Thalmann, H. Noser, I. Pandzic, G. Sannier, D. Thalmann, "ANYONE FOR TENNIS? ", Presence, Vol. 8, No. 2, pp.140-156, April 1999,
4. Maes P., T. Darrell, B. Blumberg, A. Pentland, 1995. *The ALIVE System: Full-body Interaction with Autonomous Agents*. In Proc. Computer Animation'95, pp 11-18, 1995.
5. F. Bobick, S. S. Intille, J. W. Davis, F. Baird, C. S. Pinhanez, L. W. Campell, Y. A. Ivanov, A. Schutte, A. Wilson, "The KidsRoom: A Perceptually-Based Interactive and Immersive Story Environment ", Presence, Vol. 8, no. 4, pp.369-393, Aug. 1999,
6. Gavrila, L.S. Davis, 1996. *3D Model-Based Tracking of Humans in Action: A Multi-View Approach*. Proc. of IEEE Conf. on CVPR, pp 73-80, June 1996
7. W. Woo and Y. Iwadate, "Object-oriented hybrid segmentation using stereo images," *in Proc. SPIE VCIP*, pp. 487-495, Jan. 2000.
8. S. Kim and W. Woo, "3D Movement Tracking with Asynchronous Multi-cameras for Interactive Systems", *in Proc. SPIE PW-EI-VCIP'02*, vol. 4671, pp. 502-512, Jan. 20-25, 2002.
9. Shuzo Saito, " Fundamentals of Speech Signal Processing", Academic Press, 1985
10. S-Y Yoon, R. C. Burke, B. M. Blumberg, G. E. Schneider, "Interactive Training for Synthetic Characters", *AAAI 2000*.

An Enhanced Transmission Service with 3-Priority Queue Management for Real-Time Interaction in Virtual World

Jui-Fa Chen[1], Wei-Chuan Lin[2], Chi-Ming Chung[1], and Chih-Yu Jian[1]

[1]Department of Information Engineering, TamKang University
alpha@mail.tku.edu.tw
[2]Department of International Business, TakMing College,
wayne@mail.takming.edu.tw

Abstract. In a virtual world, there are many entities moving and each has its own image and action. Due to the bandwidth limitation of the wireless environment, the transmission of image and actions among these entities is a problem. Before transmission, the action and image can be analyzed and converted into several kinds of commands. When the related entity receives the commands from other entities, it can generate the image and simulate the actions of other entities according to these commands. This paper proposes a transmission service to classify the transmitted commands into three kinds of transmission events. Three priority queues are used to transmit these data according to their priority. By this mechanism, some of the data, that are out of date and not to influence the virtual world, could be discarded and also kept the quality of the virtual world. To verify the advantage of this transmission service, an implemented prototype is based on the GSM short message system. The proposed prototype can also be applied in more advanced transmission system such as GPRS. Finally, the proposed prototype compares the time and data lose rate with the transmission mechanism of unique queue and three queues. The results show that the average wait time of the transmitted data packet and the transmission cost are reduced.

Keywords: *Bandwidth, Image, Wireless environment, Virtual world, Priority Queue*

1   Introduction

Many applications are applied on the network just because of its convenience. As the wireless communication provides the mobility of transmission, it can be another platform of a virtual world environment[4]. Before transmission, the action and image can be analyzed and converted into several kinds of commands. The only transmission is to transfer these commands rather than the images and actions. When the related entity receives the commands from other entities, it can generate the image and simulate the actions of other entities according to these commands. However, there are three problems to transmit these commands on the wireless communication

Y.-C. Chen, L.-W. Chang, and C.-T. Hsu (Eds.): PCM 2002, LNCS 2532, pp. 1096–1104, 2002.

system. First, a proper method should decide the command order in the receiving side to ensure the commands are correct. Second, an encoding method should be used to encode the command efficiently for transmission just because the restricted length of data packet. Third, a suitable transmission policy should be proposed to reduce the transmission cost. In this paper, the third problem is solved by classifying the transmitted command into three kinds of transmission events. Three priority queues are used to receive the corresponding events and transmit these data according to their priority. By this mechanism, some of the data, that are out of date and not to influence the quality of virtual world environment, should be discarded. In this way, the cost to transmit image is reduced. Besides, this paper also proposes the mechanisms to handle the command ordering and the encoding problems.

In this paper, section 2 describes the related work of the transmission service. Section 3 proposes a wireless transmission service architecture. Section 4 is the implementation of the proposed transmission service based on the GSM short message system. The proposed mechanism is also compared with other transmission services. Section 5 is the conclusion and the future research.

2   The Related Work

In a virtual world, each entity has its own image and action. However, the transmission of the image and action needs more bandwidth than text. The action and image can be analyzed and converted into several kinds of commands. The transmission is only to transfer these commands rather than the images and actions. The related work of transmitting mobile data in a distributed system is proposed in 1997[5]. Kojo proposed an efficient transmission service for slow wireless telephone links. The transmission architecture named "Mowgli" is used to guarantee the data transmission can be recovered even if the transmission is broken or out of range. There are two kinds of packets such as the control and data packets that are used to transmit data. The control packet has higher priority than the data packet and all the data packets have the same priority. There are two channels corresponding to the control and data packets. The transmission service is designed to be the preemptive multiplexing of data channel based on the channel priority. The channel architecture is shown as Fig 1. In Fig. 1 . If there is no control packet, the data packets are transmitted by the round-robin algorithm. This transmission service can guarantee the control packet can transmit first to get the important control information. However, if there were many control packets in the control channel, some of the data packets should be starved. This paper proposes an enhanced "Mowgli" transmission service to classify the transmission data into three kinds of packets. The data packet of the proposed transmission service, although is the lowest priority, should have the chance to upgrade its priority when it was waiting for a long time. In this way, the transmission service can be in an optimal status.

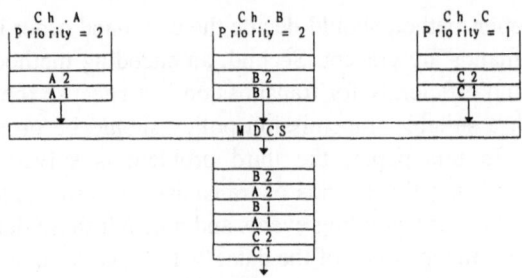

Fig. 1. "Mowgli" Data Channel Architecture

3   The Proposed Architecture

The proposed transmission service architecture is divided into six parts. The first part is the communication between two entities of the virtual world. The second part is the image and action description system. The third part is divided the transmission data into three kinds of transmission events. The forth part explains that there are three priority queues corresponding to the three kinds of transmission events to queue these data. The fifth and sixth parts are the "checkpoint" and "peek " algorithms to reduce the time for transmitting image data. The system architecture is shown as Fig. 2.

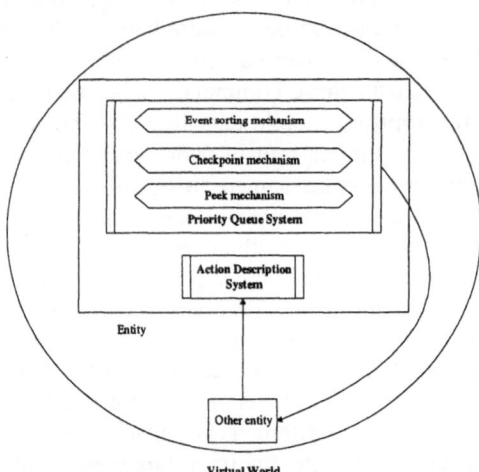

Fig. 2. System architecture

A. The communication between any two entities

The proposed protocol is a packet-based protocol, so it can also be used on packet-based protocol like GPRS[3], etc. In the proposed protocol, the short message service of GSM[6, 7, 8] is used as the transmission protocol for reducing the transmission cost. Because the system provider of GSM can store and re-send the short message when the target user is unavailable, the proposed architecture treats each sending entity as individual "data provider", and each receiving entity as individual "data receiver". The advantage of the proposed architecture is that each mobile entity didn't have to know how many data receivers and where these data receivers are. The data provider entity just has to send data to the short message center. When the other entity receives data from short message center, it doesn't have to communicate with the mobile object individually. The way to transmit data is based on the digital wireless communication system such as GSM or GPRS. However, the cost of transmission data is still higher than expected. Therefore, the proposed transmission service is focused on how to reduce the times to send data and the interval of each data sending.

B.   Image and Action Description System

In a virtual world, each entity has its own image and action. However, the transmission of the image and action needs more bandwidth than text. The action and image can be analyzed and converted into several kinds of commands. The only transmission is to transfer these commands rather than the images and actions. When the related entity receives the commands from other entities, it can base on these commands to generate the image and simulate the actions of other entities. By this method the transmission bandwidth can be reduced and also kept the quality of the virtual world.

In the images description system, there may have many repeated images in a virtual reality world. Even though they are not sent, the repeated images may need many descriptions and resources to restore it from commands. For example, the content of the images is a bird flying in the sky. Those images contain a bird flying in different status and the sky. The sky is the background and always the same. So the needed parts for transmission just the sky in the first image's description once and other images contains the flying status of bird not includes the sky. In this way, the repeated part will not be transferred and save the bandwidth and resources.

The action description system utilizes the "dead-reckoning" algorithm[1] to analyze the difference between two or more actions. The complete description of actions only transferred in the first time, the other transmission information is the difference between actions. When the difference of actions does not exceed the predefined "threshold", the action will be ignored. Only the difference of actions exceeds the threshold, the action will be transferred.

Besides, the image and action description can be used simultaneously. For the example: a bird flying in the sky. The images of this example are the sky and bird, the action is the bird's flying. The images are classified as number. If there is no difference between the first and later images, the system only sent the first image number but not the repeated images. The bird's action is described by the action description system which is applied the dead-reckoning algorithm. Combine these two mechanism, we can describe a virtual world effectively.

C.   The type of transmission data

The transmission data are divided into three kinds of transmission events such as critical event, dead reckoning algorithm event and normal event. The priority of these events is listed from high to low and the system processes these events according to their priority[2].

(1) Critical event

When the behavior of mobile object is out of ordinary (ex: driving over the speed limitation), the system will send a message to the control center. Because the critical event should be sent to control center as fast as possible, it must have the highest priority.

(2) Dead reckoning algorithm event
Control center simulate the path of the mobile object by the dead reckoning algorithm. In this way, the bandwidth of the transmission network can be reduced.

(3) Normal event
If the behavior of mobile object is ordinary and the change of path is not over the predefined threshold, the system would not send any data to the control center. In this case, the control center did not know whether the mobile object is still alive or not. The normal event is just a periodical report. With the report, the control center can know the status of mobile object. If there are critical events or dead reckoning algorithm events in the transmission queues, the normal event may be useless. Therefore, the normal event has the lowest priority.

D.   Three-priority queue policy
There are three-priority queues corresponding to the above three transmission events to store the transmission data. Because the priority of the transmission event is different, the low-priority event may starve. To solve this problem, the proposed transmission service provides "inner packet-type check", "check point" and "peek" algorithms to check the priority of packets and promote the priority of packets. Fig. 3 shows the state transition diagram of the packet in the three-priority queues. The internal transmission decision algorithm is shown in Fig. 4.

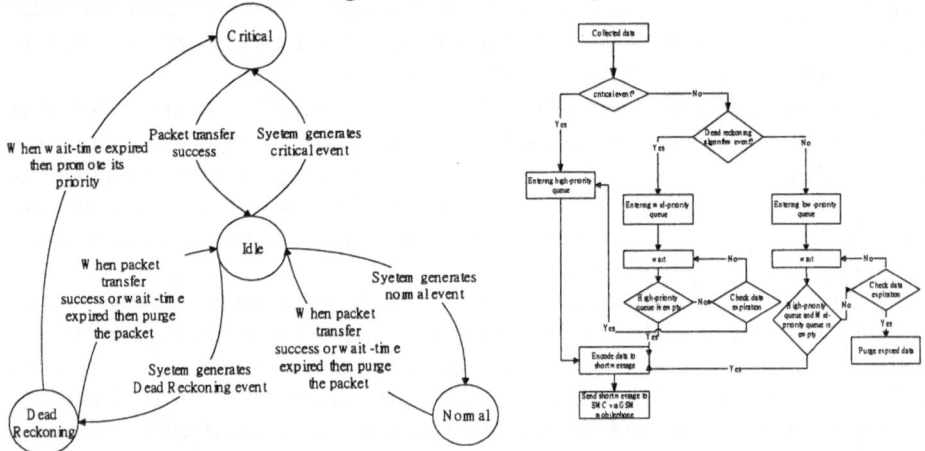

Fig. 3. The state transition diagram

Fig. 4. The transmission decision algorithm

E. Packet processing policy
For preventing the packet with lower priority starvation, the promotion of the lower priority packet should proceed. There are three policies for processing the packet priority promoting provided by the proposed transmission service. These policies are listed followed:

(1) Packet type checking in the same queue

As described in packet structure, the proposed transmission service defined several dead reckoning algorithm types. There may have some packet's types are the same in a queue, the system only needs one of them. The system chooses the newest packet of them. The index_node indicates the type and position of the packet in the queue. With the index_node, the system can find the corresponding packet and its type effectively.

(2) Checkpoint

The checkpoint is a record of packet's generating time. With the checkpoint, the system can get packet's generating time, and not need to analyze the packet. Besides, the system constructs a checkpoint_index to indicate the position of each checkpoint in the queue. The checkpoint and checkpoint_index is shown as Fig. 5.

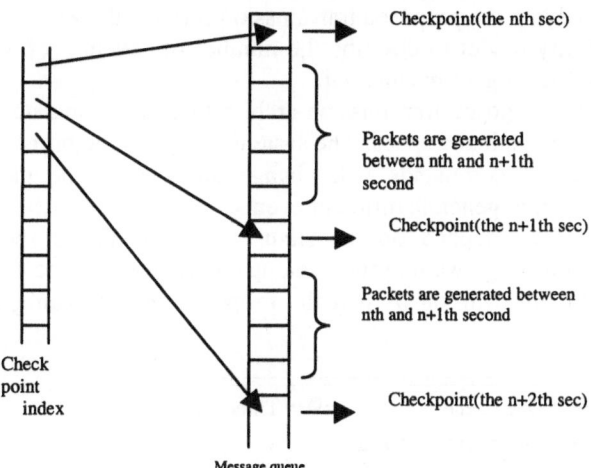

Fig. 5. Checkpoint and checkpoint_index

The algorithm of adding checkpoint into the queue is shown below:

```
Procedure Queue_Manage( )
/* Comments:
  Previous : previous checkpoint time, Now : system time
  target_queue : checkpoint to be insert into which queue
checkpoint_index : checkpoint index
threshold : checkpoint interval */
BEGIN
   struct checkpoint {
   long int time;  struct checkpoint *next;
   };
   struct checkpoint_index {
     long int time;
      struct checkpoint *new_checkpoint, *next;
   };
   while (Now == Previous + threshold)
   BEGIN
      Insert a checkpoint node to target_queue;
      Insert a checkpoing_index to checkpoint_index;
   END
END.
```

E.   Peek

There are some packets that are needed to promote into a higher-priority queue when these packet are waiting for more than a "threshold" time. However, these waiting packets are not always useful for the monitor center. If the packets are useful, it should be promoted to a higher-priority queue. If they are useless, they should be discarded. Peek is a method to take a look at the packet type to check if there is a conflict to decide the packet should be promoted or not.

4   The Implementation and Comparison

Several different kinds of random number generator are useful for simulating different applications. For verifying the proposed transmission service, the Poisson distribution is used as a probability model to describe the number of "events" of a certain type occurring "randomly" during a time interval.

The example of the proposed transmission architecture is to simulate a bird flying in the sky with different path and speed. The system simulates the bird by its different path, so the amount of commands will change along with the path. Different commands make system to generate different events.

The amounts of event depend on the status of entity. Fig 6 shows that the comparison of packet average waiting time among single-queue, three-queue, and the proposed method. In Fig 6, it shows that the proposed method can get the lowest average wait time.

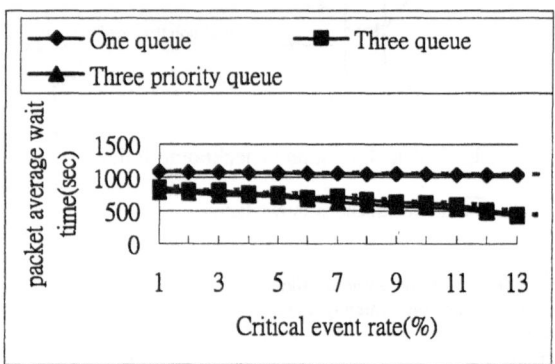

Fig. 6. Comparison of the proposed method and other methods

During the simulation, the probability of producing the total events, which include the proposed three kinds of events, are 40%, 50% and 60%. These simulation data are used for transmission by unique queue, three queues and the proposed three-priority queues mechanism. The test results are shown as Fig. 7. In Fig. 7, it indicates that the more the total event rate, the less packet average wait time.

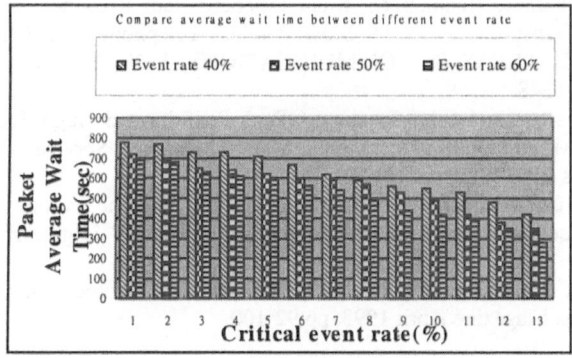

Fig. 7. Compare average wait time between different total event rates

5   Conclusion and Future Work

This paper proposes a transmission service based on the three-priority queues to reduce the transmission cost. The image and action are not real transmitted. They are converted into commands for transmission. The transmitted commands are classified into three kinds of transmission events to distinguish the importance of commands. In this way, the important data are processed first for the sake of interaction of entities. To make sure that the lower priority data are not starvation, the check-point and peek mechanisms are proposed to prevent this phenomenon. These mechanisms are used to decide whether to promote the data from a lower priority queue into a higher priority queue or discard the data that are out of date. The proposed three-priority queues transmission service is implemented and compared with the service of using unique, and three queues to measure the average waiting time of the data packet and the packet data lost rate. In this way, the proposed transmission service is verified to be better than the others.

For future work, a better way of deciding which data packet should be discarded to save the transmission cost will be further investigated.

References

[1] Wentong Cai, Francis B.S. Lee, and L. Chen, "An Auto-adaptive Dead Reckoning Algorithm for Distributed Interactive Simulation", Parallel and Distributed Simulation, 1999. Proceedings. Thirteenth Workshop, pp. 82 - 89, 1-4 May 1999

[2] Jui-Fa Chen, Wei-Chuan Lin, "Distributed Remote Monitoring Architecture Based on GSM System - Using the Car System as a Test Case", Proceeding of PDCAT2000, 2000, May 22-24, pp. 191-196

[3] Roger Dettmer "Mobilising packet data", IEE REVIEW JULY 2001, pp. 9-14

[4] Abracham Silberschatz, Peter B. Galvin, "*Operating System Concepts*," 4th editor, Addison Wesley, 1995, pp479-603

[5] Markku Kojo, Kimmo Raatikainen, Mika Liljeberg, Jani Kiiskinen, and Timo Alanko, "An Efficient Transport Service for Slow Wireless Telephone Links", IEEE JOURNAL ON SELECTED AREAS IN COMMUNICATIONS, VOL. 15, NO. 7, SEPTEMBER 1997, pp. 1337-1348

[6] Guillaume Peersman and Srba Cvetkovic, Paul Griffiths and Hugh Spear, "The Global System for Mobile Communications Short Message Service", IEEE Personal Communcations June 2000, pp. 15-23

[7] G. Peersman, P. Griffiths, H. Spear, S. Cvetkovic and C. Smythe "A toturial overvier of the short message service within GSM", Computing & Control Engineering Journal April 2000, pp. 79-89

[8] Moe Rahnema, "Overview Of The GSM System and Protocol Architecture", IEEE Communications Magazine April 1993, pp.92-100

Enhancing 3D Graphics on Mobile Devices by Image-Based Rendering

Chun-Fa Chang and Shyh-Haur Ger

Department of Computer Science
National Tsing Hua University
Hsinchu, Taiwan, R.O.C.
chunfa@cs.nthu.edu.tw

Abstract. Compared to a personal computer, mobile devices typically have weaker processing power, less memory capacity, and lower resolution of display. While the former two factors are clearly disadvantages for 3D graphics applications running on mobile devices, the display factor could be turned into an advantage instead. However the traditional 3D graphics pipeline cannot take advantage of the smaller display because its run time depends mostly on the number of polygons to be rendered. In contrast, the run time of image-based rendering methods depends mainly on the display resolution. Therefore it is well suited for mobile devices. Furthermore, we may use the network connection to build a client-server framework, which allows us to integrate with non-image-based rendering programs. We present our system framework and the experiment results on PocketPC® based devices in this work.

1 Introduction

With the recent advances in processing power and memory capacity, small portable or handheld devices have emerged as a popular computing platform. Nowadays, typical handheld devices are capable of supporting graphical user interface, audio and video playback, and wireless communication. These new capabilities also open up new areas of applications for handheld devices.

However, rendering three-dimensional (3D) graphics on handheld devices is still considered a formidable task. Because of the vast computational power that is required by 3D graphics applications, even a desktop personal computer or workstation often replies on dedicated hardware and architecture design (such as Intel AGP interface) for 3D graphics to achieve real-time performance. Currently those dedicated hardware supports are still lacking in handheld or mobile devices.

There are actually several implementations of the traditional polygon-based 3D graphics pipeline on mobile devices today. Two examples are the miniGL [6] on Palm OS platform and Pocket GL [8] on Microsoft PocketPC platform. They are both subsets of the popular OpenGL API [7]. Currently their performances are still limited. The performance of Pocket GL is considerably faster than miniGL, mostly due to the fact that the PocketPC devices have more processing power than the Palm devices.

Y.-C. Chen, L.-W. Chang, and C.-T. Hsu (Eds.): PCM 2002, LNCS 2532, pp. 1105-1111, 2002.

Even so, the polygon counts of 3D models that Pocket GL can display at interactive rates are still limited.

This reveals a fundamental issue of the polygon-based 3D graphics pipeline: its rendering time increases linearly with the number of polygons that enter the pipeline. Although we may expect future generations of mobile devices to be equipped with more processing powers, there will also be more complex models with higher polygon counts to be rendered.

In this paper we explore an alternative approach, image-based rendering, to achieve the 3D graphics capability on mobile devices. Unlike the polygon-based 3D graphics pipeline, the rendering time of image-based rendering depends on the screen resolution of the output images rather than the complexity of the input models. This offers a potential advantage for mobile devices that typically have small display areas.

We also present a client-server framework for mobile devices that we equipped with networking capability, e.g., via the IEEE 802.11b based wireless network. Using our framework, a 3D graphics programs (which do not need to use image-based rendering) running on a desktop computer may be integrated with our system to interact with users on mobile devices. This can simplify the process of developing 3D graphics software on mobile devices and offer a way to offload part of the 3D rendering task to the server.

2 The 3D Warping Algorithm

The image-based rendering technique that we use in our work is McMillan's 3D warping method [4][5]. The inputs to 3D warping are depth images, which are 2D color images containing depth information at each pixel. Each depth image also contains a viewing matrix (3×4 as described in [5]) that describes the camera or viewing setup. Figure 1 shows an example where the image on the left shows the color components of the depth image and the image on the right shows the depth components in

Fig. 1. An example of input depth images. **Left**: the color components. **Right**: the depth components.

Compared to the traditional 3D graphics pipeline, 3D warping demands much less computing power. The core of the 3D warping algorithm is the following warping equation:

$$(u_2, v_2) = (\frac{u_1 a + v_1 b + c + \delta_1 d}{u_1 i + v_1 j + k + \delta_1 l}, \frac{u_1 e + v_1 f + g + \delta_1 h}{u_1 i + v_1 j + k + \delta_1 l}) \qquad (1)$$

The warping equation calculates the coordinates (u_2, v_2) on output image for each input pixel at (u_1, v_1). The variable δ_1 is the depth information (or the disparity) of the input pixel. The variables a through l are controlled by the viewing matrices of the input and output images. They are recomputed only when the view of either the input or the output image changes. Therefore they remain constant across pixels of the same output image.

Because the warping equation is computed once for each pixel, the time complexity of 3D warping is $O(n^2)$ where n represents the image resolution in horizontal or vertical direction. It is independent of the scene complexity that is usually measured by the number of polygons in the scene. Although the image resolution refers to the input image here, it is actually more closely related to the output image as demonstrated at [1]. This is good news for the small screen sizes of typical mobile devices. Furthermore, the warping equation is easy to compute as it involves only 20 arithmetic operations[1].

When there is only a single input image, the output image is likely to exhibit the occlusion (or exposure) artifact, which is caused by revealing parts of the 3D scene that are occluded in the input image. To avoid such a problem, the input data format may be extended in a fashion that is similar to the Layered Depth Image [11] or Layered Depth Cube [3]. We implement the Layered Depth Image in our system. However, in order to simplify the discussion, we describe our work as if regular single-layered depth images were used (except when we present the results).

3   System Framework

First, we describe the stand-alone (non-networked) version of our system, which consists of two parts: a model constructor and an interactive warper. Their roles are described in Sections 3.1 and 3.2. Then we describe in Section 3.3 how it is extended to a client-server framework when network connection is available.

3.1   Model Constructor

Usually the 3D models to be displayed are initially provided by the users as a set of polygons. The job of the model constructor is to convert those 3D models into depth images that are amicable to 3D warping. The model constructor can be considered as

---

[1] Note that the two denominators in the warping equation are the same.

a preprocessing step. Therefore it may run on desktop computers rather than on mobile devices. There are many ways to construct the depth images from 3D polygons. In this paper, we modify the POV-RAY ray-tracing program [9] to build the depth images. An alternative is to render the 3D models in OpenGL [7], then combine the resulting frame buffer and depth buffer into a depth image.

The file format of our depth images is simply a concatenation of the image size, the viewing matrix, the color components, and the depth components. No data compression is currently used.

3.2 Interactive Warper

The actual 3D warper runs on mobile devices to accept user input and display the new views interactively. It is an implementation of the 3D warping algorithm that were described in Section 2.

If we traverse the pixels of an input depth image in a particular order, then we can guarantee that the pixels are warped to the output image in back-to-front order. This technique is called the occlusion compatible order by McMillan in [5], and is implemented in our system. Its implementation also means that we do not need the Z-Buffer for hidden surface removal.

The warping equation involves floating-point arithmetic. However most mobile devices do not have floating-point units in their processors. Therefore we use fixed-point number representations in our warping equation, which results in about 350% speedup. (The frame rate improves from about 1.7 frame/second to about 6.0 frame/second in one of our tests.)

When an input pixel is warped to the output image, we simply copy its color to the new output pixel. This could produce gaps between neighboring pixels such as those shown in Figure 2. We can avoid those artifacts by drawing each pixel as a circle that is slightly larger than a pixel, or by using the splatting techniques described in [13] or [10]. However splatting is not currently implemented in our system. We plan to support it in the future using a look-up table method similar to [11].

3.3 Extension to a Client-Server Framework

In Sections 3.1 and 3.2, we have described the stand-alone (non-networked) version of our system. Once the input depth images are constructed, they are loaded to the mobile devices and become static. However this is no longer the case if the networking capability is available on the mobile devices.

When the mobile devices are equipped with networking capability, we can build a client-server framework, where the client is the interactive 3D warper running on mobile devices and the server is a dynamic model constructor running on a more powerful computer such as a desktop workstation. In this framework, the user's interactions with the client are periodically sent to the server via the network. Then the server updates the depth image based on user's current view and transmits the new depth image to the client. The features of this client-server framework are:

1. The client can hide the network latency by performing 3D warping to update the display at interactive rates. Even when the network is down and the server fails to update the input depth image, the client can still work in stand-alone mode.

2. The server may take advantage of the specialized 3D graphics hardware on the desktop workstations.

3. Most importantly, the client-server framework makes it possible to modify an existing 3D graphics program (on desktop computers) to display its results and interact with users on mobile devices.

4 Results

For the stand-alone version, we modify the POV-RAY program to produce depth images for our 3D warper. The depth images are generated on desktop computers and then downloaded to mobile devices where the 3D warper resides. We build and test our 3D warper on Microsoft PocketPC®-based mobile devices, such as the Compaq iPaq H3800 series Pocket PC.

The output images may be displayed via either the GDI functions or the Game API [2] of Windows CE. We opt for the Game API because we found that the GDI functions incur too much operating system overhead.

Figure 2 shows results of the 3D warper using the input model that is shown in Figure 1. The original 3D model contains more than 37,000 primitives, which would be too complicated to be rendered interactively on current mobile devices using the traditional 3D graphics pipeline. However our system is able to render it at the speed of 5.9 to 6.2 frames per second on a 206MHz StrongArm processor based system.

We also implement the layered depth images in our work. Figure 3 shows how the layered depth images reduce the occlusion artifacts.

For the networked (client-server) version, we modify an OpenGL program to continuously generate depth images from the frame buffer (including the depth buffer). The OpenGL program acts as our server and communicates with the client program on an iPaq Pocket PC via IEEE 802.11b based wireless network. Whenever a depth image is ready, the server sends it to the client and queries the client for the current user's view, which is used to generate the next depth image. The client simply uses the most recently received depth image as the input data and performs 3D warping to update the display at interactive rates, regardless how fast the input depth image can be updated. Figure 4 shows the results. The image on the left shows the user changes his/her view on the Pocket PC. The image on the right shows that the server program has updated its view accordingly and the newly generated depth image is now used on the client.

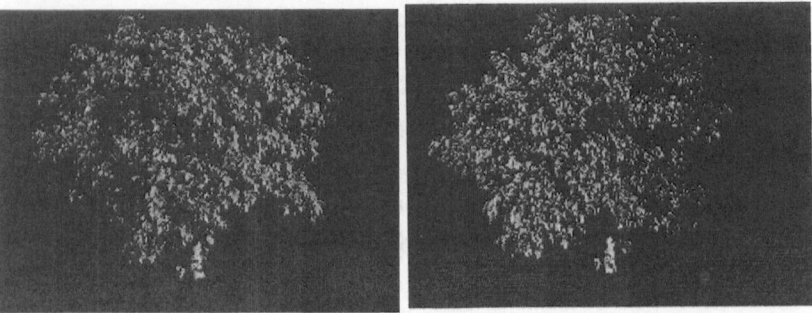

Fig. 2. Output images (in 240×180 resolution) of the 3D warper for three different user's views. The input model is described in Figure 1.

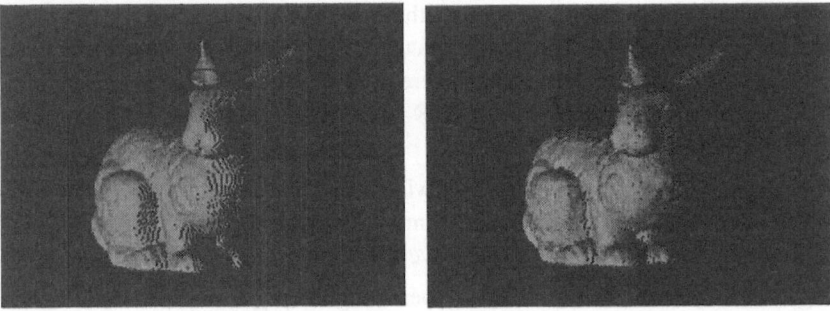

Fig. 3. Using layered depth images can reduce the occlusion artifacts. The image on the left is produced with a regular single-layered depth image. The image on the right is produced with a layered depth image that combines images from four different views.

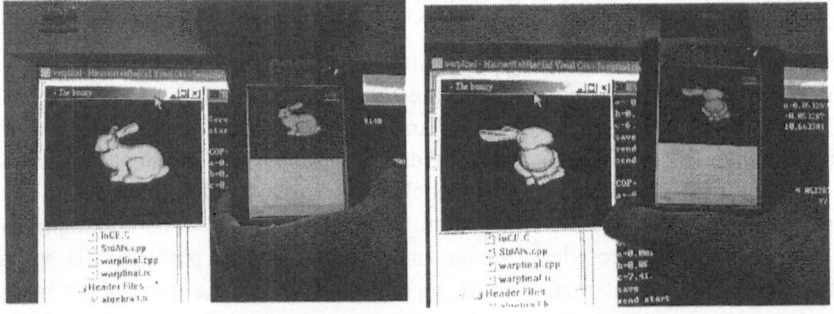

Fig. 4. The networked version of our system at work. The image on the left shows that the user is changing his/her view on the Pocket PC. The image on the right shows that the server program has updated its view accordingly and the newly generated depth image is used on the client.

5   Conclusions and Future Work

We have presented an alternative approach to accomplish 3D rendering on mobile devices. It takes advantage of the smaller display areas of mobile devices and is capable of rendering complex 3D models because its performance does not degrade for 3D models with large polygon counts.

This work also represents the first step in our ongoing effort to build a client-server 3D rendering framework for mobile devices in networked environment. In the future, we hope to release a library that will requires only minimal effort to port any existing 3D rendering program such as those written in OpenGL or DirectX to interact with users on mobile devices, without the users noticing that most of the rendering is actually done on a remote server.

Acknowledgement. We would like to thank Professor Shi-Nine Yang for pointing out some interesting 3D graphics applications on mobile devices. Thanks also to Zhe-Yu Lin and Yi-Kai Chuang for various help in programming. This work is supported by R.O.C. DOE Grant 89-E-FA04-1-4 (Program for Promoting Academic Excellence of Universities) and NSC Grant 91-2213-E-007-032.

References

1.   Chun-Fa Chang, Gary Bishop and Anselmo Lastra. "LDI Tree: A Hierarchical Representation for Image-Based Rendering". In *SIGGRAPH 1999 Conference Proceedings*, pages 291–298, August 1999.
2.   The Game API website: http://www.pocketpcdn.com/sections/gapi.html
3.   Dani Lischinski and Ari Rappoport. "Image-Based Rendering for Non-Diffuse Synthetic Scenes". *Rendering Techniques '98 (Proc. 9th Eurographics Workshop on Rendering)*, June 29–July 1, 1998.
4.   Leonard McMillan and Gary Bishop. "Plenoptic Modeling: An image-based rendering system". In *SIGGRAPH 95 Conference Proceedings*, pages 39–46, August 1995.
5.   Leonard McMillan. *An Image-Based Approach to Three-Dimensional Computer Graphics.* Ph.D. Dissertation. Technical Report 97-013, University of North Carolina at Chapel Hill, Department of Computer Science, 1997.
6.   MiniGL by Digital Sandbox, Inc. The miniGL website: http://www.dsbox.com/minigl.html
7.   OpenGL website: http://www.opengl.org
8.   PocketGL website: http://www.sundialsoft.freeserve.co.uk/pgl.htm
9.   POV-RAY website: http://www.povray.org
10. Szymon Rusinkiewicz and Marc Levoy. "QSplat: A Multiresoluton Point Rendering System for Large Meshes". In *SIGGRAPH 2000 Conference Proceedings*, pages 343–352, July 2000.
11. Jonathan Shade, Steven Gortler, Li-wei He and Richard Szeliski. "Layered Depth images". In *SIGGRAPH 98 Conference Proceedings*, pages 231–242, July 1998.
12. S. Teller and C. Sequin. "Visibility Preprocessing for Interactive Walkthroughs" In *SIGGRAPH 91 Conference Proceedings*, pages 61–70, July 1991.
13. Lee Westover. *SPLATTING: A Parallel, Feed-Forward Volume Rendering Algorithm.* Ph.D. Dissertation. Technical Report 91-029, University of North Carolina at Chapel Hill. 1991.

A Guided Interaction Approach for Architectural Design in a Table-Type VR Environment

Myoung-Hee Kim[1,2], Soo-Mi Choi[2,3], Seon-Min Rhee[1], Doo-Young Kwon[2], and Hyo-Sun Kim[2]

[1] Ewha Womans Univ., Dept. of Computer Science and Engineering, 11-1 Daehyun-dong, Seodaemun-gu, Seoul, Korea
{mhkim, blue}@mm.ewha.ac.kr
[2] Ewha Womans Univ., Center for Computer Graphics and Virtual Reality, 11-1 Daehyun-dong, Seodaemun-gu, Seoul, Korea
{mhkim,smchoi,dykwon, khs3}@mm.ewha.ac.kr
[3] Sejong Univ., Dept. of Software Engineering, 98 Gunja-dong, Gwangjin-gu, Seoul, Korea
smchoi@sejong.ac.kr

Abstract. In this paper, we present a guided interaction approach for architectural design in a table-type VR environment (virtual table). By making it easier to communicate between two or more people in a virtual space, the virtual table is effectively used in architectural visualization, medical visualization, and scientific visualization. However, most applications provide simple functions with easy handling or focus on visualization because accurate interaction on the virtual table is not easy. We developed a table-type VR tool for architectural design using guided 3-D interaction techniques. It consists of *the interactive VR modeler*, *the architectural interpreter* and *the hybrid tracker*. We also introduce architectural design process from the very initial stage to the final one by using our tool.

1 Introduction

Architectural design tends to involve end-users and professional architects with different levels of knowledge [1]. Graphical notations and language are generally used to convey one's ideas to another person or group. However, two-dimensional drawings are not enough to communicate ideas completely. In addition, because most existing screen-based modeling systems require complicated skills to represent the 3-D geometry and various materials of architecture, it is not easy for non-professional end-users to master such systems in short time. The virtual table, a kind of semi-immersive large display, can reproduce operations performed on a table in the real world and it basically makes cooperative tasks easier through face-to-face communication [2]. Such characteristics are very useful for cooperative architectural design.

Stork and Schmalstieg [3] developed a 3-D CAD system called ARCADE. It allows various 3-D transformations by creating object primitives on the virtual table and applying several operations to the primitives. Encarnação [4] developed CADesk for product design. He suggested easier and more diversified interaction techniques in order to use the system in real industrial workplace. Mine [5] explained the difficulty in selecting and handling objects in the virtual space is due to the lack of haptic feed

Y.-C. Chen, L.-W. Chang, and C.-T. Hsu (Eds.): PCM 2002, LNCS 2532, pp. 1112-1119, 2002.
© Springer-Verlag Berlin Heidelberg 2002

back. Szalavari, Gervautz [6], and Dieter [7] proposed an interaction technique using a personal panel with an attached tracker in order to supplement those drawbacks. However, since accurate interaction on the virtual table is not easy, most applications use simple functions with easy handling, or focus on the visualization of 3-D models [8,9]. For that reason, most existing applications using the virtual table do not perfectly support diverse and complicated functions provided by 2-D screen-based CAD tools. In architectural application, the virtual table was used in site planning [10] when the interrelation between several already existing buildings and the surrounding environment should be taken into consideration, or as a kind of application that allows modifying a building's appearance or decoration rather than using the virtual table in construction from the very initial design stages. And most applications target general 3-D primitives rather than architectural primitives for architectural design such as buildings, roofs, windows, doors, etc.

In this paper, we propose an easy and effective tool for architectural design. It provides guided 3-D user interaction in a table-type VR environment. The developed tool consists of *the interactive VR modeler, the architectural interpreter* and the *hybrid tracker*. We also present architectural design process from the very initial stage to the final one by using the proposed tool.

The rest of this paper is organized as follows. The next section describes the system architecture of the proposed table-type VR tool. The third section explains guided 3-D interaction techniques and the fourth section shows architectural design process by using our tool. Conclusions are offered in the final section.

2   A Table-Type VR Tool for Architectural Design

In this section, we present the main function and relations among each component of a table-type VR tool for architectural design. Figure 1 depicts the system architecture of the developed tool.

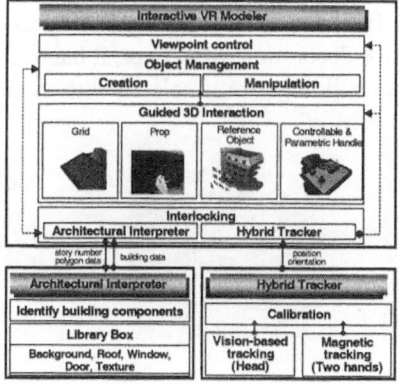

Fig. 1. The components of a table-type VR tool for architectural design and their relations.

2.1 Interactive VR Modeler

The interactive VR modeler offers guided 3-D interaction so that a user can design an architectural 3-D model more easily and intuitively on the virtual table. Likewise, the user can observe the designed model at the different viewpoints according to his/her location.

Viewpoint control: Using the user's location and orientation from the hybrid tracker, the viewpoint of virtual scene is changed. Therefore, the user can see different sides of the model by walking around the virtual table.

Object management: The main function of this component is the creation and manipulation of objects by using 3-D user interaction. First, the user makes 3-D mass as the initial step, and then object transformation is performed to construct a basic shape. It gives knowledge of the building by the architectural interpreter. After this step, the user can decorate each building primitives such as windows, doors, roofs, etc. And the user also can change the color and texture of the model.

Interlocking: This component links the interactive VR modeler with the architectural interpreter and the hybrid tracker.

2.2 Architectural Interpreter

Identify architectural primitives: The architectural interpreter transforms simple 3-D masses into a basic construction form that has architectural knowledge. In the first step, the minimum data (the number of stories and the bottom polygon) essential for the construction is received from the interactive VR modeler. With the data, an architectural model that has hierarchical construction structure is created. In the second step, the created architectural model is traversed to make construction elements. In our VR tool, construction elements are currently limited to the basic ones such as walls, roofs, windows and doors.

Library box: Our tool offers the library box including diverse architectural primitives, colors and textures for decoration. Moreover, it has various backgrounds that are necessary when the created buildings are simulated with its surroundings.

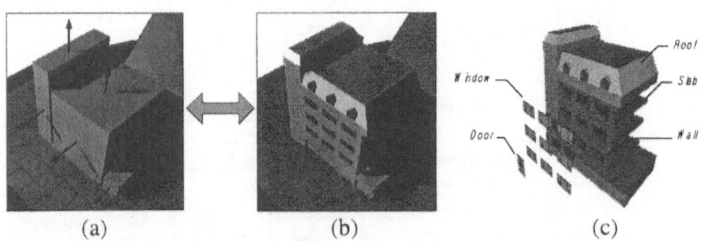

(a)   (b)   (c)

Fig. 2. A building model that has architectural structures. (a) Simple 3-D mass primitives, (b) A building model including architectural structures, (c) Architectural primitives.

2.3 Hybrid Tracker

We used two types of tracking system for viewpoint control and user interaction: vision-based tracking system and magnetic tracking system respectively.

Head tracking with vision-based method: For obtaining the location and orientation of the user's head, we used vision-based tracking method. This method is accurate and convenient for the user to move and walk around the virtual environment because it does not require cables. The camera calibration for calculating user's 3-D position is based on triangulation theorem. In general, a projection-based VR system is used in a very dark environment. In order to reduce its limitation, our VR environment employs three infrared LEDs attached to the user's shutter glasses as a beacon and two cameras with an infrared filter. This is also effective in catching the user's position with stability and easy since the cameras look for only the infrared light.

Hand tracking with magnetic tracker: Hand tracking is essential for manipulating architectural primitives on the virtual table. The magnetic sensors are attached to two interaction tools, a tangible transparent prop and a 6DOF mouse, so the user can interact with virtual objects using the tools.

2.4 Hardware Configuration

In our VR environment, we use the BARCO Baron Projection Table^{TM} as a display device and CrystalEyes3^{TM} shutter glasses from Stereographics with an emitter for stereoscopic display. For our rendering system, we use Silicon Graphics Workstation Zx10 (1GB Intel CPU x 2, IGB RAM) with the Wildcat4210 graphic board. And OpenInventor^{TM} is used as a graphics library.

The vision-based tracking system for head tracking has a Metrox Meteor II-MC/4 frame grabber card and attaches two Sony XC-55 progressive scan cameras with Schneider Optics B+W 093 InfraRed filter. In addition, Asension's Flock of Birds electro- magnetic tracking system is used for two-hands tracking.

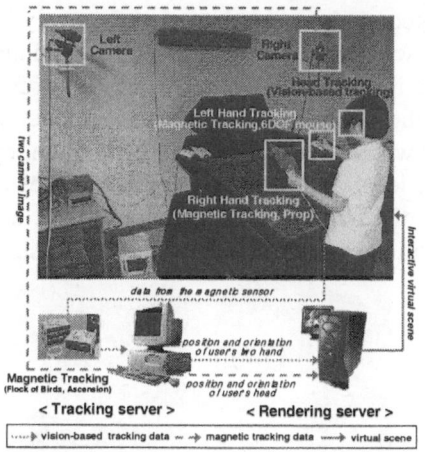

Fig. 3. Hardware configuration of the table-type VR tool.

3   Guided 3-D Interaction Techniques

In this section, we present guided 3-D interaction techniques on the virtual table. We propose grid interaction that is effective in creating architectural primitives and a tangible transparent prop to control basic primitives directly. And we introduce reference objects to find accurate position easily. The reference objects have a function of resizing windows and doors automatically. Also, we introduce a controllable and parametric handle that is able to give numeric input instead of a keyboard, which is very useful for a table-type VR environment without a keyboard.

3.1   Grid Interaction

When the grid is activated horizontal and vertical gridlines are displayed on the virtual table surface. This causes objects to snap to grid intersections between the gridlines. The grid interaction allows the user to create and manipulate objects easily. The work plane can be freely defined in 3-D space according to the user's hand movements by using a prop that is tracked with a magnetic tracking sensor.

3.2   Tangible Transparent Prop

For 3-D modeling, the perpendicular axis of a work plane is commonly used to set the desired direction when transferring an object. By setting up the location and orientation of the work plane, the user can set the desired axis. In our table-type VR environment, the user can set the direction and orientation of the work plane with a tangible transparent prop in a natural way.

3.3   Reference Objects

In a VR environment, geometric constraints can effectively help the user manipulate architectural primitives accurately. When designing a building, the user can add basic building elements to the initial modeling stage, such as roofs, walls, doors, windows, etc. In order to guide the process, our tool produces reference objects through the architectural interpreter with expert knowledge. In addition, by providing information such as type, direction, location and size, the user can select the desired details of building elements from the library. The reference objects also allocate the building element to a precise position by automatically adjusting its size and direction.

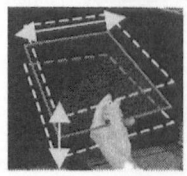 

Fig. 4. Vertical & horizontal manipulation and grid selection using the transparent prop.

3.4 Controllable and Parametric Handle

The user of a 3-D modeling program needs to check the state of currently set-up functions (selected objects, snapping type, types of transformation functions, snapping interval) in the design process. For that purpose, the screen-based 3-D modeling program provides a visual feedback through such major WIMP interface elements as dialogue, menu bar, command icons, status bar, etc. Providing such a visual feedback proves also very effective in working on the virtual table. Our table-type VR tool provides a controllable and parametric handle that provides the direction of objects of currently set-up functions and snapping type. It also allows the use to interactively adjust the input of numerical values such as a moving interval.

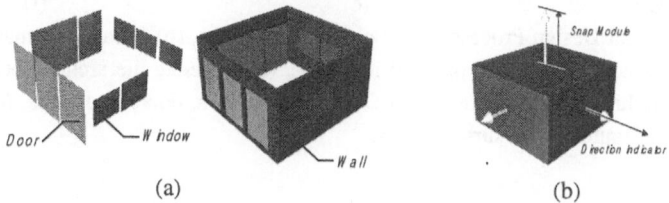

(a)   (b)

Fig. 5. (a) Reference objects - doors, windows, walls, (b) A controllable and parametric handle - manipulation of mass primitive.

4   Architectural Design Process

This section describes an example process that is necessary for designing the appearance of buildings using the afore-mentioned architectural primitives and guided 3-D interaction techniques. The process focuses on designing the appearance of certain buildings. We divided the design process into formation and decoration stages. The formation stage includes the initial massing and conversion steps, whereas the decoration stage includes arrangement of decoration primitives and application of colors and materials. While designing, the user can easily check whether an intermediate design complies with his or her intention. Also, the user can perform simulation by switching modes during the entire design process in order to achieve harmony with the surrounding environment.

4.1   Modeling Step

At modeling stage, geometric models are created in accordance with the initial design idea. Then the models proceed to the next step and transform into more concrete forms. This is done to preserve the user's initial design concept throughout the entire design process. The followings are example steps of modeling stage.

Step 1: The user sets up the form of the floor polygon using grid unit. Using the selected grid unit and the number of stories, we lift up the created floor polygon and create an architectural 3-D mass. A building is created through compounding of sever-

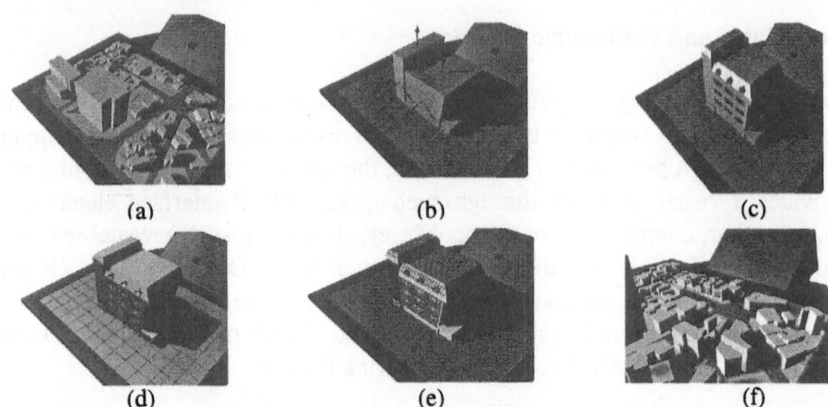

Fig. 6. Architectural Design Process. (a) Choose surroundings, (b) Create 3-D mass using grid interaction and a controllable and parametric handle, (c) Generate hierarchical building structure using the architectural interpreter, (d) Decorate windows, doors and roofs, (e) Set colors and material, (f) Simulate with surroundings.

al masses, and the user creates a desired form with the number of desired masses. Figure 6(b) shows the result of forming one building with three masses.

Step 2: The user transfers each side of the created masses and transforms them into the desired basic building form. After the completion of formation of each mass, the user transfers, rotates, arranges and groups masses in order to construct the overall building form.

Step 3: Grouped objects are automatically transformed one by one into the form of building primitives through the architectural interpreter. The user can create diverse forms by inputting data necessary for transformation (roof type, façade type).

4.2. Decoration Step

At decoration stage, the building is decorated by using subsidiary models, materials and colors with the building structure created at the conversion step of modeling stage. The user watches decoration primitives through the architectural interpreter, selects the desired type of detailed primitives from the decoration library and decorates the building. By using the finishing material library, the user also can modify materials and colors of walls, roofs, floors, etc.

5   Conclusions and Future Works

This paper describes the development of a VR tool that allows non-professionals to participate first-hand in designing buildings using the virtual table, as well as enable collaboration among architecture designers with different levels of professional knowledge. The developed tool provides grid on reference frame for supporting users' 3-D interaction, transparent prop for haptic feedback and direction control, reference objects for an easy tracking of an accurate location at the building decoration stage, and a controllable and parametric handle. Also, the created construction objects allow for an addition of diverse functions as they imply not just a geometry assemblage for a simple visualization, but carry a meaning of construction elements of each and every side (e.g., wall). Such an inside display method enable multiple representations of a building, and supports collaboration among experts in different areas.

Although viewing frustum of the developed system allows to effectively see from above the design process and its results through a bird's eye view, it is not suitable for viewing modeling results in their real size or navigating the inside. Therefore, the future research is expected to expand to a virtual collaboration environment that interoperates with a large projection wall – a type of vertical display equipment – and simultaneously with modeling allows to watch every step and perform simulation.

Acknowledgements. This work was supported in part by the Korean Ministry of Information and Communication under Information Technology Research Center Program and in part by Virtual Reality Research Center Program. It was also supported in part by a grant of the Korea Health 21 R&D Project.

References

1. R.W. Hobbs: Leadership through collaboration, AIArchitect, Vol.3 (1996) 11
2. W.Krueger, C. Bohn, B. Frohlich, H. Schuth, W. Strauss, and G. Wesche: The Responsive Workbench: A Virtual Work Environment, IEEE Computer, Vol.28, No.7 (1995) 42-48
3. ARCADE: http://www.cg.tuwien.ac.at/research/vr/studierstube/arcade/
4. L. M. Encarnação, A. Stork, and D. Schmalstieg: The Virtual Table - A Future CAD Workspace, Proceedings of SME Computer Technology Solutions Conference (1999) 13-19
5. Mark R.Mine, Frederick P., and Brooks Jr: Moving Objects in Space: Exploiting Proprioception In Virtual-Environment Interaction, Proceedings of Computer Graphics, ACM SIGGRAPH (1997) 19-26,
6. Zsolt Szalavári, and Michael Gervautz: The Personal Interaction Panel - A Two-Handed Interface for Augmented Reality, Proceedings of EUROGRAPHICS'97, Budapest, Hungary (1997) 335-346
7. Dieter Schmalstieg, L.Miguel Encarnacao, and Zsolt Szalavari: Using Transparent Props For Interaction with The Virtual Table, Proceedings of ACM Symposium on Interactive 3D Graphics (1999) 26-28,
8. L.Rosenblum, J. Durbin, R. Doyle, and D. Tate: The Virtual Reality Responsive Workbench: Applications and Experiences, Proceedings of British Computer Society Conference on Virtual Worlds on the WWW, Internet, and Networks, (1997)
9. M.Koutek and F.Post: A Software Environment for the Responsive Workbench, Proceedings of the seventh annual conference of the Advanced School for Computing and Imaging (2001) 428-435,
10. Virtual Landscape Design: http://www.cg.tuwien.ac.at/research/vr/studierstube/vt/landscaping/

A Gaze-Direction Controlled Wavelet Packet Based Image Coder

Peter Bergström

Image Coding Group, Dept. of Electrical Engineering
Linköping University, S-581 83 Linköping, Sweden
peter@isy.liu.se

Abstract. An image coding scheme which combines transform coding with a human visual system (HVS) model has been developed. The system include an eye tracker to pick up the point of regard of a single viewer. One can then utilize that the acuity of the HVS is lower in the peripheral vision than in the central part of the visual field. A model of the decreasing acuity of the HVS which can be applied to a wide class of transform coders is described. Such a coding system has a large potential for data compression.
In this paper we have incorporated the model into an image coder based on the discrete wavelet packet transform (DWPT) scheme.

1   Introduction

The field of image coding deals with efficient ways of representing images for transmission and storage. Most image coding methods have been developed for TV-distribution, tele-conferencing and video-phones. Few efforts have been devoted towards coding methods for interactive systems. One example where interactive systems exists is in tele-robotics, where a human operator controls a robot at a distance. Interactive systems usually have only one observer of the transmitted image. In such a system one can include an eye tracker to pick up the point of regard of the viewer.

The human visual system (HVS) works as a space variant sensor system providing detailed information only in the gaze direction. The sensitivity decreases with increasing eccentricity and is much lower in the peripheral visual field. Thus, in a system with a single observer whose point of gaze is known, one can allow the image to be coded with decreasing quality towards the peripheral visual field.

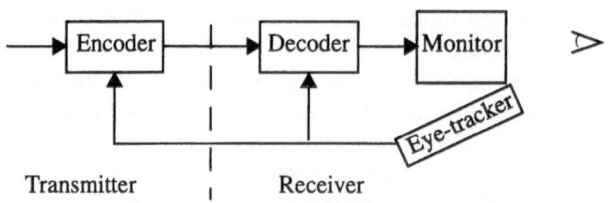

Fig. 1. An eye-movement controlled coding system.

Y.-C. Chen, L.-W. Chang, and C.-T. Hsu (Eds.): PCM 2002, LNCS 2532, pp. 1120–1127, 2002.

In previous works we have incorporated the model of the HVSs acuity described in section 2 into the JPEG coder with good results [2] and a wavelet based coder [3] with not as good results as for the modified JPEG coder. In this work we will apply the HVS model to a coder based on the discrete wavelet packet transform (DWPT) decomposition scheme.

The main steps in the transform coders we have used are transformation, scalar quantization, scanning and finally entropy coding. In the JPEG coder the image is split into 8x8 blocks. Each block is discrete cosine transformed into 64 transform component [10]. In the wavelet based coder the image is decomposed into an octave-band representation [7]. A DWPT decomposition scheme offers an adaptive wavelet decomposition. If a subband will be divided further or not is decided on a cost function. Thus, the resulting decomposition will depend on the image, the decomposition cost function and the filter bank [6, 13]. In the decomposition step in both the DWT and DWPT based coders we have used the Daubechies 9/7 biorthogonal filter bank [1], an excellent filter bank for image compression [9]. The quantizer consists of one uniform scalar quantizer for each subband. A quantization matrix contains the quantization steps. For each image the best quantization matrix is estimated in a rate-distortion sense [7].

The outline of this paper is as follows. Next, the model of the visual acuity will be described. The proposed scheme is presented in section 3 to 6. This is followed by simulation results in section 7. Finally, section 8 draws up the final conclusions.

2   A Visual Acuity Model

Due to the uneven distribution of cones and ganglion cells in the human retina, we have truly sharp vision only in the central fovea. This, covers a visual angle of less than 2 degrees. The ability to distinguishing details is essentially related to the power to resolve two stimuli separated in space. This is measured by the minimum angle of resolution (MAR) [8, 11, 12]. The MAR depends on the eccentricity, which is the angle to the gaze direction. In this work we will use the MAR measured by Thibos [8].

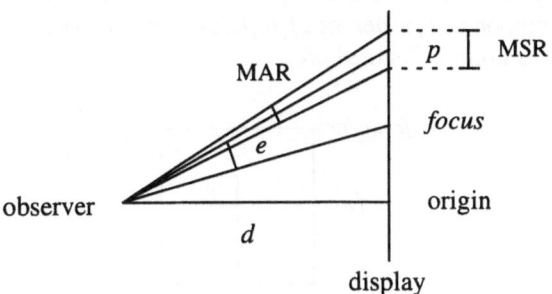

Fig. 2. Viewing situation.

The related size in the image to a MAR value is called the *minimum size of resolution* (MSR). This size depends on the current viewing conditions. We will assume that the display is flat. Figure 2 shows the viewing situation.

With a position tracker and an eye tracker we will get the distance between the observer and the display, denoted d, and the point of regard in the image which will be called the *focus*. From these values, one can calculate the *eccentricity, e,* for any point, p, in the image plane. Furthermore, the minimum size of resolution for the point p is equal to,

$$MSR_{\perp r}(e) = 2\sqrt{d^2 + r_p^2}\tan\left(\frac{MAR(e)}{2}\right) \tag{1}$$

where r_p is the distance between the current point and origin. The MSR in Equation 1 is calculated perpendicular to the r_p-direction. For a computer display the MSR is almost equal for all directions. For larger eccentricities the region which is covered by the MAR will have the form of an oval. However, the $MSR_{\perp r}$ is used since it is the minimum MSR for all directions. This will guarantee that we will not erase visible details.

The MSR-bound can be expressed as a visual frequency constraint. Thus, an image frequency must be less than,

$$f_{vc}(e) = \frac{1}{2 \cdot MSR(e)} \tag{2}$$

if an observer shall be able to perceive it.

3   Eye-Movement Controlled Transform Coder

The DCT, DWT and DWPT schemes will all decompose the image in three signal domains, namely frequency, position and direction. Thus, each transform component represent the energy of the input signal at a certain location in both space and frequency domains.

The energy of a transform component, c_i, is assumed to be located to a corresponding Heisenberg box [5]. A Heisenberg box consist of both an interval in the frequency domain and an interval in the time domain. The lower range of the frequency interval corresponding to component c_i is denoted $f_T(c_i)$ and the point in the space interval which is closest to the focus point is denoted $p(c_i)$.

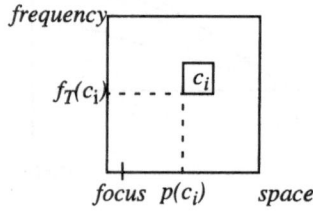

Fig. 3. Visual description of the position $p(c_i)$ and lower frequency range $f_T(c_i)$ corresponding to component c_i

The idea in the eye-movement controlled transform coder method is that since we can not perceive high frequencies in the peripheral visual field, we can set corresponding transform components to zero with insignificant loss of visual quality.

According to section 2, for each position at the display we can estimate the visual frequency constraint, f_{vc}, which is the maximum frequency an observer can perceive at the current position. In addition, each transform component is represented by a frequency, f_T, which is the minimum frequency for which the component will respond and a position which will maximize the f_{vc}-value. Thus, the strategy above can be expressed as,

$$f_{vc}(d, focus, p(c_i)) < f_T(c_i) \quad \Rightarrow \quad c_i = 0 \tag{3}$$

where d is the distance to the observer and *focus* the point on the display which is pointed out by the gaze direction.

4   Space-Frequency Decomposition

To preserve the total number of coefficients the *space-frequency resolution* is maintained constant. Consider a 1-D signal. The space-frequency decomposition in a DCT and a DWT scheme can be illustrated as in Figure 4. Each coefficient is associated with with a Heisenberg box, illustrated as rectangles in the figure.

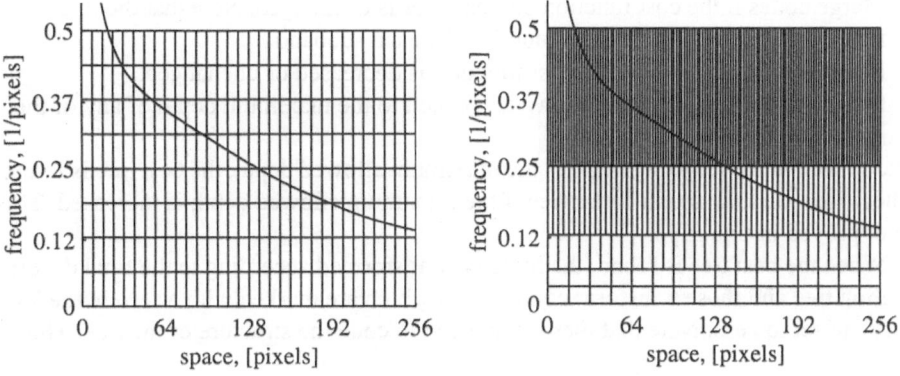

Fig. 4. Space frequency decomposition for a DCT scheme (left) and a DWT scheme (right).

Assume that the viewing conditions are equal to, $d=0.5$m, $is=0.3$m, $ir=512$ pixels, and focus at the centre of the image. Consider the space frequency decomposition along the positive x-axis. Figure 4 shows this space frequency decomposition and the current visual frequency constraint.

According to Equation 1, a component is set to zero if the corresponding Heisenberg box is totally above the visual constraint in a space-frequency decomposition illustration. Consider figure 4, it is then obvious why the acuity based constraint will set fewer components to zero in the DWT scheme than in the DCT scheme.

To maximize the influence of the visual constraint one would like to have an adaptive *space-frequency decomposition* which maximize the number of components which are set to zero.

5   Modified DWPT Coder

In a DWPT scheme the decomposition depends on the cost function which has been chosen. Thus, the number of components which will be set to zero by the visual constraint will also be dependent on the cost function. To maximize the influence of the visual constraint we will define a new cost function. The criterion for the "best" wavelet packet decomposition will be the basis which sets the largest number of components to zero according to the visual constraint. If there exist more than one choice, the decomposition which has the highest space resolution is chosen to minimize the computations and filter spreading. In addition, we will also require that the lowpass branch is decomposed to the maximum depth of the best tree. This since it mostly will increase the compression.

Let a mask, called the VC-mask, have the same size as the image and be one at those components which will be kept and zero otherwise. We define the cost function as the sum of the values in the VC-mask. To find the best decomposition,

1. Start with a full uniform wavelet packet decomposition of the maximum allowed depth. Denote this depth with D_1 and set $i=1$.
2. Calculate the VC-masks for depth D_i and for depth $D_{i+1}=D_i$-1.
   This is done for each decomposition by calculating a f_T-value for each subband and a f_{vc}-value for each component and then applying Equation 4.
3. Merge nodes if the cost function decreases or is unchanged. Note that the total cost function is the sum of the cost function for each subband.
4. Iterate ($i=i+1$) as long as the cost function is decreased or unchanged.
5. Finally, if necessary split the lowpass branch to the maximum depth of any of the resulting branches.

If no branch in the resulting tree has the maximum allowed depth, the best tree is found. Otherwise, one may find a better tree if the maximum allowed depth is increased. This is not proved in this paper.

When the best tree is found, the image is transformed according to the final decomposition tree and those transform components which are marked with a zero in the VC-mask are set to zero. Note that there is no need to code the structure of the tree. This

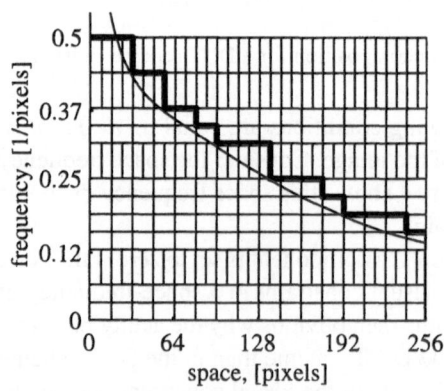

Fig. 5. Example of a wavelet packet decomposition.

since the viewing conditions are known by the decoder. However, since the decomposition tree is dependent on the viewing conditions, a new tree must be calculated each time the focus point is changed.

Figure 5 shows the best wavelet packet decomposition for the same example as in Figure 4. The result is that more components are set to zero in the WP decomposition case than for the two other cases.

6   Reorganized Scan Sequence

After the quantization, the DC subband are treated separately from the rest of the subbands. The AC subbands are zero-tree scanned [7] into one-dimensional signals. These sequences are runlength coded and finally entropy coded. The runlength coder represents each sequence of components with a sequence of symbol pairs, one pair for each non zero component plus one end of block (EOB) symbol [10].

The first symbol in the pair will represent either (R,S), ZRL or EOB. The symbol R represents zero runs of length 0 to 15 and S represents the number of bits to encode the amplitude of the current non zero component. The ZRL symbol represents a runlength of 16 zeros.

When the VC-map is applied some runs of zeros can be increased. This can result in more ZRL-symbols and a more flat distribution of the first symbols. However, these effects can be reduced. The decoder can calculate the VC-map without the need to send any extra information. Thus, let us utilize the knowledge of the positions of the zeros which is caused by the VC-map. The scanned sequence is reorganized so that these zeros are moved to the end of the sequence before the runlength coder. In the decoder these zeros are moved back to their original position before the inverse scan.

Note that there is no guarantee that this reorganization will decrease the final bit rate. In the worst case the bit rate can be increased. However, in all experiments we have done the total bit rate has decreased.

7   Simulation Results

The modified coder described in this paper will be called the MDWPT coder. The corresponding coder which use the same decomposition but does not set any components to zero according to the acuity based model will be called the DWPT coder.

It is well known that there does not exist any objective distortion measure which completely mirrors the perceived image quality [5]. Furthermore, there are no distortion measurement which consider the acuity of the HVS.

We will instead compare the bit rate for the MDWPT coder and the DWPT coder when they use the same quantization matrix. That way all maintained components will be quantized in the same way and the quality in the fovea region will be equal.

Thus, the procedure has been the following. For a given image we estimate the best quantization matrix in a rate-distortion sense which results in a certain bit rate for the DWPT coder [7]. The image is then coded with this quantization matrix in the two coders. The resulting bit rates are denoted R_{DWPT} and R_{MDWPT}. We define the compression gain for the modified coder as,

$$Gain = R_{DWT}/R_{MDWT} \tag{4}$$

Figure 6 shows the results when the images Barbara and Lena are coded. The figure shows the compression gain both when the scan sequences are reorganized according to section 6 and when they are not. The viewing conditions are set to, d=0.5m, is=0.3m, ir=512 and focus in the centre.

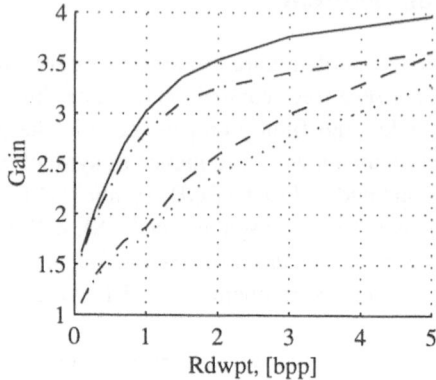

Fig. 6. The compression gain for the images Barbara, with reorganized scan sequence (solid) and without (dashdot), and Lena ,with reorganized scan sequence (dashed) and without (dotted).

As can be seen in the figure the gain by the MDWPT coder depends on the required quality.The reason is that if the required quality is low the quantizer in both coders will set the high-pass components to zero anyway. The gain is also dependent on the frequency content in the peripheral parts of the image. The image Lena is smoother than the image Barbara in the peripheral parts and the gain is therefore less for this image. Furthermore, when the scan sequences are reorganized according to section 6 the gain is increased.

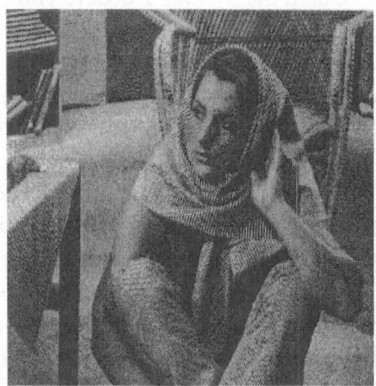 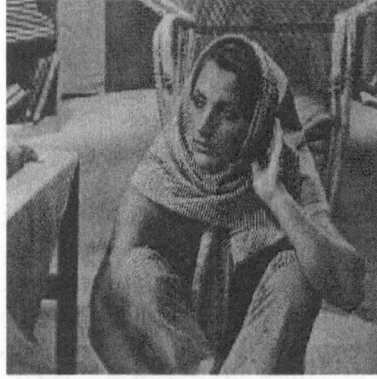

Fig. 7. The image Barbara coded with the DWPT coder (left) and the MDWPT coder (right).

Figure 7 shows the image Barbara coded with the DWPT coder and the MDWPT coder. The same quantization matrix is used in both coders. It will result in a bit rate equal to R_{DWT} = 1.8 bpp and R_{DWPT} = 0.5 bpp. The viewing conditions are as above.

8 Conclusion

The coder described in this paper shows that there is a considerable additional potential for data compression if one takes into account the point of regard of the observer. The gain is dependent on the high frequency content in the peripheral regions of the image and on the quality that is required.

In comparison to the previous works [2, 3] the MDWPT will adapt the space frequency decomposition to the current visual frequency constraint and thereby set the highest number of components to zero and achieve the highest compression gain. The cost is that this requires more computations.

Our future work will be directed towards investigating the real-time performance. Simple visual tests have been done. The observers have then only reported minor artifacts. However, more experiments is necessary too investigate all visual aspects.

A necessary requirement for a system which uses an eye-movement controlled coder is that it can handle the delay introduced by the encoder and the transmission. This is an issue which is not covered in this paper but which will require special attention [4].

References

[1]   M.Antonini, M.Barlaud, P.Mathieu, I.Daubechies, "Image coding using wavelet transform.", IEEE Trans. in Image Process., vol. 1, 1992, pp. 205-220.

[2]   P.Bergström, R.Forchheimer, "An eye-movement controlled DCT-coder.", In Proc. of the SSAB Symposium in Image Analysis, 2000.

[3]   P.Bergström, "An eye-movement controlled DWT-coder.", In Proc. of the IEEE PCM 2001.

[4]   B.Girod, "Eye movements and coding of video sequences.", Visual Com. and Image Proc., SPIE, vol. 1001, 1988.

[5]   N.Jayant, J.Johnston, R.Safranek, "Signal compression based on models of human perception", Proc. IEEE vol. 81, pp. 1383-1422, 1993.

[6]   S.Mallet, "A wavelet tour of signal processing.", Acad. press, ISBN 0-12-466605-1, 1998.

[7]   G.Strang, T.Nguyen, "Wavelets and filter banks.", Wellesley-Cambridge Press, ISBN 0-9614088-7-1, 1996.

[8]   L.N.Thibos, "Retinal limits to the detection and resolution of gratings.", J. Opt. Soc. Am., vol. 4, no. 8, pp. 1524-1529, 1987.

[9]   J.D.Villasenor, B.Belzer, J.Liao, "Wavelet filter evaluation for image compression.", IEEE Trans. in Image Process., vol. 2, 1995, pp. 1053-1060.

[10]   G.K.Wallace, "The JPEG still picture compression standard.", IEEE Tran. on Consumer Electronics, 1991.

[11]   G.Westheimer, "The spatial grain of the perifoveal visual field.", Vision Res., vol. 22, pp. 157-162, 1982.

[12]   F.W.Weymouth, "Visual sensory units and the minimum angle of resolution.", Am. J. Ophthalm., vol. 46, pp. 102-113, 1958.

[13]   M.V.Wickerhauser, "Adapted wavelet analysis from theory to software.", AK Peters, Wellesey, ISBN 1-56881-041-5, 1994.

Qualitative Camera Motion Classification for Content-Based Video Indexing

Xingquan Zhu[1], Xiangyang Xue[2], Jianping Fan[3], and Lide Wu[2]

[1]Dept. of Computer Science, Purdue University, West Lafayette, IN 47907, USA
[2]Dept. of Computer Science, Fudan University, Shanghai, 200433, China
[3]Dept. of Computer Science, University of North Carolina at Charlotte, NC 28223, USA
zhuxq@cs.purdue.edu; {xyxue, ldwu}@fudan.edu.cn;
jfan@uncc.edu

Abstract. Due to the fact that the camera motion usually imply some hints which are helpful in bridging the gap between computationally available features and semantic interpretations, extensive researches have been executed to extract them for various purposes. However, these strategies fail to classify the camera rotation; furthermore, their performance might be significantly reduced by considerable noise or error in extracted features. In this paper, a robust camera motion classification strategy is proposed. We use the mutual relationship between motion vectors for motion classification. Given any two motion vectors in each P-frame, four types of mutual relationships between them are classified, then, a 14-bins feature vector is constructed to characterize the statistical motion information for the P-frame. Finally, the qualitative classification is executed by considering all achieved statistical information.

1 Introduction

Motion characterization plays a critical role in content-based video indexing, since it usually implicates some semantic cues among the video, especially in some specific domains, such as sports video, surveillance system etc. It is also an essential step in creating compact video representation automatically. We can imagine the camera as a "narrative eye": camera pans imitate eye movement to either track an object or to examine a wider view of the scene, freeze frames give the impression that an image should be remembered, close-ups indicate the intensity of impression. To capture these impressions will supply a compact way in video content representation [2-3]. For example, a mosaic image can represent a panning sequence [1]; a single frame represents a static sequence; the frames before and after a zoom can represent the zoom sequence; the targeted object represents a tracking sequence. Thus, an effective characterization of camera motion greatly facilitates the video representation, indexing, clustering and retrieval tasks [8][11-12].

To extract the camera motion, *Ngo et. al* [4] propose a classification method by analyzing temporal segmented slices, however, to distinguish different motion patterns in the temporal slice is a challenge task for videos with cluttered background or object motions. *Srinivasan et. al* [6] introduce a qualitative camera motion extraction method that separates the optical flow into two parts, parallel and rotation, for motion characterization. *Xiong et. al* [5] present a method that characterizes camera motion by spa-

Y.-C. Chen, L.-W. Chang, and C.-T. Hsu (Eds.): PCM 2002, LNCS 2532, pp. 1128-1136, 2002.
© Springer-Verlag Berlin Heidelberg 2002

tial optical flow. However, these last two methods can only be used when the *Focus of Expansion (FOE)* [7] is at the center of the image, and this is not the usual case in generic videos.

On comparing with analyzing the camera motion in decompressed domain, some other methods classify camera motion by utilizing motion features from compressed video stream (e.g., *MPEG* stream) [8-10][12]. In *Tan*'s method [8], a 6-parameters transformation model is used to characterize the motion vectors in each *P*-frame, then, based on acquired transformation parameters, the camera motions is classified into panning, tilting and zooming; In *Kobla* [9] and *Dorai*'s [10] methods, motion vectors in each frame are mapped into eight directions, the values in these eight directions are utilized to develop the motion classifier; however, this voting strategy is sensitive to the noise contained in the motion vectors. Obviously, all methods above fail in detecting the camera rotation. Moreover, due to the considerable noise or error contained in features, their performances are significantly reduced. However, we found the statistical mutual relationship (As shown in Fig. 1) in each frame is relatively noise free. For certain type of camera motion, the mutual relationship in the frame will exhibit a distinct dominant tendency.

In this paper, a qualitative camera motion classification method is proposed. We use statistical mutual relationships between motion vectors in the *P*-frame of *MPEG* stream to address the dominant camera motion. In addition to detecting four types of common motions (pan, tilt, zoom, still), our method can even detect camera rotation.

2 Mutual Relationship between Motion Vectors

To classify camera motions contained in each frame, the mutual relationship between motion vectors is first classified into four categories: approach, parallel, diverging and rotation. Sections below demonstrate that statistical results of mutual relationships will characterize the dominant camera motion in each frame.

Given two points A, B with positions $p_A=(x_A, y_A)$, $p_B= (x_B, y_B)$ and motion vectors $V_A=(u_A, v_A)$ and $V_B=(u_B, v_B)$ in current P-frame P_i, we denote the vector from point A to B by $\vec{V}_{AB}$, and the line cross A and B as $y = \dfrac{y_A - y_B}{x_A - x_B} x + \dfrac{x_A y_B - y_A x_B}{x_A - x_B}$. As shown in Fig. 1, four types of relationships between V_A and V_B could be defined: approach, parallel, diverging and rotation. To classify them, we first distinguish whether V_A and V_B are on the same side (Fig. 1 (A)) or different sides (Fig. 1(B)) of vector $\vec{V}_{AB}$. Based on geometry relationship among points (x_A, y_A), (x_A+u_A, y_A+v_A), (x_B, y_B) and (x_B+u_B, y_B+v_B), it is obvious that if V_A and V_B are on the same side of $\vec{V}_{AB}$, both (x_A+u_A, y_A+v_A) and (x_B+u_B, y_B+v_B) should be above or below the line which crosses point A and B at the same time. Hence, we multiple y_1 and y_2 (y_1 and y_2 are given in Eq. (6)), if the product is no less than 0, we then claim V_A and V_B are on the same side of $\vec{V}_{AB}$; Otherwise, V_A and V_B are on the different side of $\vec{V}_{AB}$.

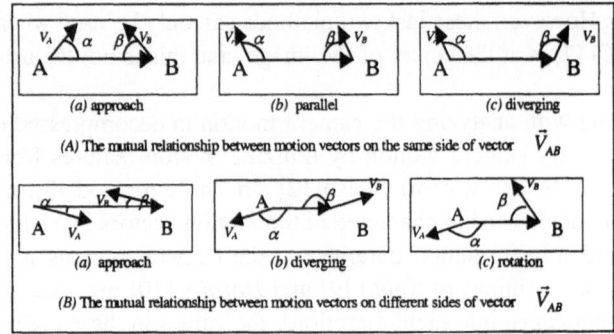

Fig. 1. Mutual relationship between motion vectors

$$\begin{cases} y_1 = y_A + v_A - \dfrac{y_A - y_B}{x_A - x_B} \cdot (x_A + u_A) - \dfrac{x_A y_B - y_A x_B}{x_A - x_B} \\ y_2 = y_A + v_A - \dfrac{y_A - y_B}{x_A - x_B} \cdot (x_A + u_A) - \dfrac{x_A y_B - y_A x_B}{x_A - x_B} \end{cases} \quad (1)$$

As shown in Fig. 1, assume that α denotes the angle between $\vec{V}_{AB}$ and V_A, and β denotes the angle between V_B and $\vec{V}_{AB}$. If V_A and V_B are on the same side of $\vec{V}_{AB}$, their mutual relationship is classified as follows:

- If $\alpha + \beta < 180° - T_{PARA}$, the mutual relationship between them is approach.
- If $\alpha + \beta > 180° + T_{PARA}$, the mutual relationship between them is diverging.
- Otherwise, the mutual relationship between V_A and V_B is parallel.

If V_A and V_B are on different sides of $\vec{V}_{AB}$, they are classified as follows:

- If $\alpha + \beta < T_{CLOSE}$, their mutual relationship is approach.
- If $\alpha + \beta > T_{FAR}$, the mutual relationship between them is diverging.
- Otherwise, the mutual relationship between V_A and V_B is rotation.

In our system, we set T_{PARA}, T_{CLOSE} and T_{FAR} to $15°$, $60°$ and $250°$ respectively. Fig. 2 shows the pictorial experimental results between camera motions and statistical mutual relationships in the frame, it is obvious that:

- If camera pans or tilts, most motion vectors' mutual relationships in the frame are parallel.
- If camera zooms, most motion vectors' mutual relationships in the frame either approach to (zoom out) or diverge from (zoom in) *FOE*.
- If camera rotates, most vertical vectors' (defined in Section 4.4) mutual relationship in the frame either approach to (clockwise rotation) or diverge from (counter-clockwise rotation) *FOE*.

3   Motion Feature Vector Characterization

To characterize camera motion information contained in each *P*-frame, in this section, we construct a 14-bins feature vector by packing four motion histograms sequentially for camera motion classification.

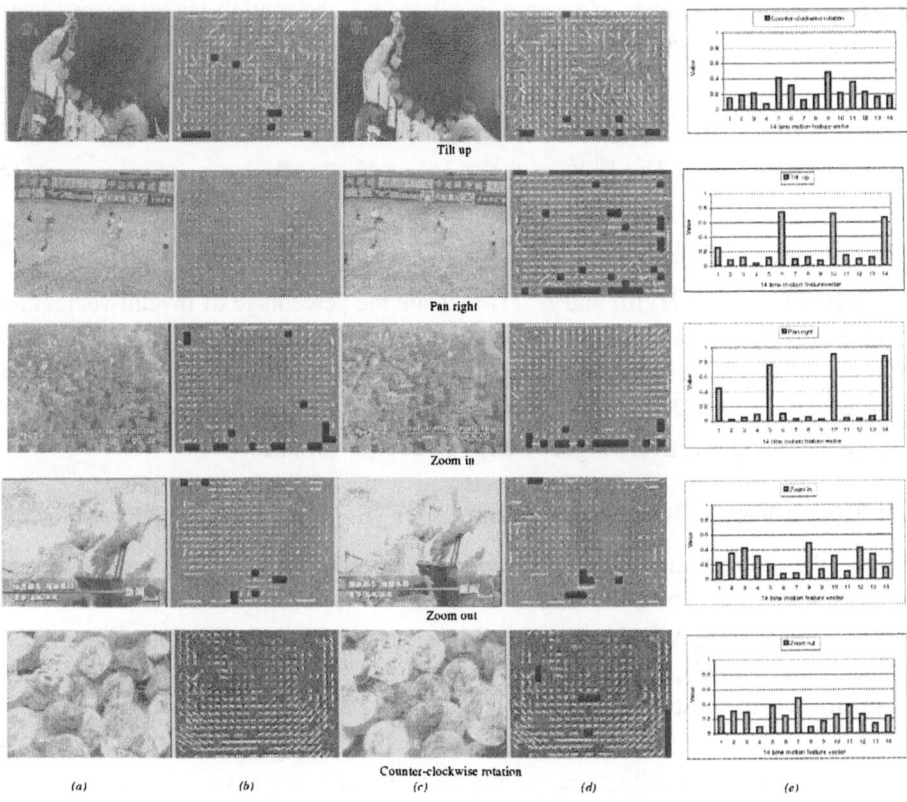

Fig. 2. The relationships between camera motion and motion vectors. The column *(a)*, *(b)*, *(c)*, *(d)* and *(e)* indicate the current *P* frame, the motion vectors in current *P* frame, the succeeded *P* frame, the motion vectors in succeeded *P* frame, and the 14-bins motion feature vector distribution for succeeded *P* frame respectively. The 14- bins feature vector is consisted with histograms H_{me}, H_{mo}, H_{mr} and H_{mvr} from bin 1 to bin 14 sequentially. (The black block in motion vectors indicates the "intracoded macroblock" where motion vector is not available)

3.1 Motion Vector Energy Histogram (H_{me})

For any *P*-frame P_i, assuming it contains *N* macroblocks. We denote AP_i as the aggregation of all available motion vectors (intercoded macroblocks) in P_i, and the number of motion vectors in AP_i is denoted by N_{mv}. Given point A ($P_A=(x_A,y_A)$) in P_i and its motion vector $V_A=(u_A,v_A)$, the energy of V_A is then defined by $\|V_A\|^2 = u_A^2 + v_A^2$. Since motion vectors with smaller energy usually introduce some errors while motion classification, they should be eliminated at first. Assume SP_i denotes the aggregation of motion vectors in AP_i with their energy smaller than a given threshold T_{SMALL}, as shown in Eg. (2), the number of vectors in SP_i is denoted by N_{small}. We then calculate the mean (μ) and variance (δ) of vectors in aggregation $AP_i \cap \overline{SP_i}$. Assume also LP_i denotes the aggregation of vectors in AP_i whose distance to μ is larger than T_{LOC}, as shown in Eq.

(3). We denote the number of vectors in LP_i by N_{loc}, the motion vector energy histogram (H_{me}) is then constructed with Eq. (4).

$$SP_i = \{ V_k \mid \| V_k \|^2 < T_{SMALL} \; ; V_k \in AP_i \} \tag{2}$$

$$LP_i = \{ V_k \mid \| V_k - u \| > T_{LOC} \; ; V_k \in AP_i \} \tag{3}$$

$$H_{me}[0] = (N - N_{mv} + N_{loc}) \Big/ N \; ; \quad H_{me}[1] = N_{small} \Big/ N \tag{4}$$

It is obvious that $H_{me}[0]$ and $H_{me}[1]$ indicate the percentage of invalid vectors and small energy vectors in P_i respectively. In our system, we set $T_{LOC}=1.5\delta$ and $T_{SMALL}=2$. In sections below, we name vectors in aggregation VP_i, which is denoted by $VP_i = AP_i \cap (\overline{SP_i \cup LP_i})$, as the *valid motion vector* of P_i, i.e., the valid motion vectors are those with relatively higher energy and lower variance.

3.2 Motion Vector Orientation Histogram (H_{mo})

Clearly, the orientations of the *valid motion vectors* VP_i in P_i will help us determine the direction of the camera motion. For each vector $v_A = (u_A, v_A)$ in VP_i, assume $D(V_A)$ denote its orientation. We classify all valid vectors' orientations into four categories: (-45°, 45°), (45°, 135°), (135°, 225°) and (225°, 315°). The motion vector orientation histogram is then constructed using Eq. (5)

$$H_{mo}(k) = \frac{\sum\limits_{V_A : V_A \in VP_i, -45°+90°\cdot k < D(V_A) \le 45°+90°\cdot k} 1}{N_{mv} - N_{small}} \quad ; k = 0, 1, 2, 3 \tag{5}$$

It indicates that each bin of histogram H_{mo} represents the percentage of vectors in that direction. Accordingly, they could be used to determine camera motion direction.

3.3 Motion Vector Mutual Relationship Histogram (H_{mr})

Given any two motion vectors in VP_i, their mutual relationship is classified with the strategy given in Section 2. The histogram of the mutual relationships in P_i are then calculated and put into different bins of histogram H_{mr}, with $H_{mr}[0]$, $H_{mr}[1]$, $H_{mr}[2]$ and $H_{mr}[3]$ corresponding to approach, diverging, rotation and parallel, respectively.

3.4 Motion Vector Vertical Mutual Relationship Histogram (H_{mvr})

As Fig. 2 indicates, if the camera motion in current frame is rotation, the mutual relationships of most vectors' vertical lines will approach to *FOE*. Hence, given any motion vector $V_A = (u_A, v_A)$ in VP_i, We denote its *vertical vector* as $V'_A = (-v_A, u_A)$, then the strategy in Section 2 is used to calculate mutual relationship between any two *vertical vectors*. And their histogram is then denoted as vertical mutual relationship histogram H_{mvr} with $H_{mvr}[0]$, $H_{mvr}[1]$, $H_{mvr}[2]$ and $H_{mvr}[3]$ representing approach, diverging, rotation and parallel respectively.

4   Camera Motion Classification

As experimental results in Fig. 2(e) demonstrates, for different types of dominant camera motions, the constructed 14-bin feature vector will have distinct mode for distinguishing. E.g., when camera pan, $H_{mr}[3]$ contains the largest value of all bins in H_{mr}, and the largest bin in H_{mo} will indicate the direction of the panning. For zooming operation, $H_{mr}[0]$ or $H_{mr}[1]$ will have the largest value among four bins of H_{mr}. If the camera rotate, $H_{mr}[2]$ will have the largest value in H_{mr}; and $H_{mvr}[0]$ or $H_{mvr}[1]$ will also have the largest value among four bins in H_{mvr} (corresponding to counter-clockwise rotation and clockwise rotation). Hence, based on the 14-bins vector, our qualitative camera motion classification strategy takes procedure below:

Input: 14-bins motion feature vector in current P-frame P_i.

Output: The motion category (pan left, pan right, tilt up, tilt down, zoom in, zoom out, clockwise rotation, counter-clockwise rotation, still, unknown) P_i belongs to. We denote this judgement as symbolic "$P_i \leftarrow$? ".

Procedure:
1. If $H_{me}[0]$ is larger than threshold T_{UNK}, $P_i \leftarrow$ "unknown", otherwise go to step 2.
2. If $H_{me}[1]$ is larger than threshold T_{STILL}, $P_i \leftarrow$ "still", if not, go to step 3.
3. If $H_{me}[0]+H_{me}[1]$ is larger than threshold T_{UNION}, $P_i \leftarrow$ "unknown", otherwise, go to step 4.
4. Find the maximal value among four bins of H_{mr} with Eq.(6), denote it as H_{mr}^{max}. Meanwhile, we denote the second maximal value in H_{mr} as H_{mr}^{sec} which is also given in Eq. (6). If the ratio between H_{mr}^{sec} and H_{mr}^{max} is larger than threshold T_{REL}, $P_i \leftarrow$ "unknown", otherwise, the steps below is used for classification.
    - If $H_{mr}^{max} = H_{mr}[0]$, then $P_i \leftarrow$ "zoom out"; If $H_{mr}^{max} = H_{mr}[1]$, $P_i \leftarrow$ "zoom in".
    - If $H_{mr}^{max} = H_{mr}[2]$, go to step 6; If $H_{mr}^{max} = H_{mr}[3]$, go to step 5 for refinement.
5. Find the maximal value among four bins of motion vector orientation histogram, H_{mo}, denote it as H_{mo}^{max} which is given in Eq. (7). Then use steps below for pan or tilt classification:
    - If $H_{mo}^{max} = H_{mo}[0]$, $P_i \leftarrow$ "panning left"; If $H_{mo}^{max} = H_{mo}[1]$, $P_i \leftarrow$ "tilting down".
    - If $H_{mo}^{max} = H_{mo}[2]$, $P_i \leftarrow$ "panning right"; If $H_{mo}^{max} = H_{mo}[3]$, $P_i \leftarrow$ "tilting up".
6. Find the maximal value among four bins of vertical mutual relationship histogram, H_{mvr}, denote it as H_{mvr}^{max} which is given in Eq. (8). Then steps below will be used for clockwise or counter-clockwise rotation classification:
    - If $H_{mvr}^{max} = H_{mvr}[0]$, $P_i \leftarrow$ "counter-clockwise rotation"; Else if $H_{mvr}^{max} = H_{mvr}[1]$, $P_i \leftarrow$ "clockwise rotation".
    - Otherwise, $P_i \leftarrow$ "unknown".

$$H_{mr}^{\max} = \arg\max\nolimits_{H_{mr}[k]}\{H_{mr}[k], k=0,1,2,3\}; \quad H_{mr}^{sec} = \arg\max\nolimits_{H_{mr}[k]}\{H_{mr}[k]\,|\,H_{mr}[k]\neq H_{mr}^{\max}, k=0,1,2,3\} \quad (6)$$

$$H_{mo}^{\max} = \arg\max\nolimits_{H_{mo}[k]}\{H_{mo}[k], k=0,1,2,3\} \quad (7)$$

$$H_{mvr}^{\max} = \arg\max\nolimits_{H_{mvr}[k]}\{H_{mvr}[k], k=0,1,2,3\} \quad (8)$$

The thresholds T_{UNK}, T_{STILL}, T_{REL} and T_{UNION} may be determined by experiments, here in our system, we set them as 0.55, 0.5, 0.8 and 0.8 respectively.

5 Experimental Results

Table 1 shows the experimental results produced by our algorithm. We evaluated the efficiency of our algorithm (denoted as A) through an experimental comparison with transformation model based method [8] (denoted as B), since it also works in compressed domain and utilizes only the motion vector of P-frame for classification. Several standard MPEG-I streams (about 11711 frames), which we downloaded from http://www.open-video.org, are used as our test bed. One edited MPEG-I file (about 16075 frames) containing a large number of zooming and rotation motions was also used as a test dataset. For better evaluation, the precision defined in Eq. (9) is used, where n_c, n_f denote the correctly and falsely detected camera motion in the P-frames.

$$Precision = n_c/(n_c + n_f) \quad (9)$$

Table 1. Camera motion classification Result

Camera Motion	Frame Numbers	P-Frame Numbers	Precision (A)	Precision (B)
Pan	7780	2022	0.84	0.82
Tilt	2004	501	0.85	0.81
Zoom	2948	761	0.73	0.65
Rotation	890	233	0.65	
Still	4589	1684	0.87	0.84
Average	20011	5201	0.804	0.756

Among all 27786 frames in the video, the adjacent frames with distinct camera motion (pan, tilt, zoom, rotation, still) are selected as our ground truth. These frames (about 20011 frames) occupy about 72% of the entire video, with about 5201 P-frames contained in the 20011 frames. Our experiment is executed with these 5201 P-frames. From Table 1, we find that, on average, our method has a precision of approximately 80.4%, about 5% higher than transformation model based method [8]. In detecting pure panning and tilting, both methods have about the same precision. However, while there is some abnormal motion vectors caused by objects motion or other reasons or *FOE* is not at the center of the image, the efficiency of transformation model based method is rather reduced, since most motion vectors cannot be characterized by the proposed model. However, our method is a statistical strategy, those abnormal or distorted motion vectors would have not much influence in unfolding the dominant camera motion in the frames, thus, it results in a relatively higher precision. Furthermore, while method B is not able to detect camera rotation, our method produces a precision of 68% in detecting rotation.

6 Conclusion

In this paper, we presented a qualitative camera motion classification scheme which use mutual relationships between motion vectors of P-frame for motion characterization. Experimental results demonstrate the performance of the proposed approach. The novel features that distinguish proposed algorithm from others motion vector based strategies lies in that other methods use the distribution information of single motion vectors, however, we utilize the relationship between two motion vectors for camera motion classification, which is more robust and efficient in characterizing and classifying dominant camera motion from general video data.

Acknowledgement. Xiangyang Xue was supported by NSF of China under contract 60003017, Chinese National 863 project under contract 2001AA114120, Jianping Fan was supported by NSF under contract IIS0208539, Lide Wu was supported by NSF of China under contract 69935010.

References

1. R. Szeliski, "Video mosaics for virtual environments", *IEEE Computer Graphics and Application , pages 22-30 , March 1996.*
2. J. Wang, E. Adelson, "Layer representation for motion analysis", *Proc. IEEE Conf. Computer Vision and Pattern Recognition, pp.361-366, 1993.*
3. H. S. Sawhney, S. Ayer, "Compact representations of videos trough dominant and multiple motion estimation", *IEEE Trans. On PAMI, vol.18, no.8, pp.814-830, 1998.*
4. C.W. Ngo, T.C. Pong, H.J. Zhang and R.T. Chin, "Motion characterization by temporal slice analysis", *In computer vision and pattern recognition, vol. 2, pp.768-773, 2000.*
5. W. Xiong and J. C.-M. Lee: "Efficient scene change detection and camera motion annotation for video classification". *CVIU, Vol.71, No 2, August, pp.166-181 ,1998*
6. M.V. Srinivasan, S. Venkatesh and R. Hosie, "Qualitative estimation of camera motion parameters from video sequences", *Pattern Recognition Vol.30,No. 4, pp593-606,1997*
7. R.C Jain, "Direct computation of the focus of expansion", *IEEE Trans. on PAMI vol.5, No. 1, pp.58-64, Jan, 1983.*
8. Y.-P. Tan, D.D. Saur, S.R. Kulkami, P.J. Ramadge, "Rapid estimation of camera motion from compressed video with application to video annotation", *IEEE Trans. on CSVT, vol.10, No.1, pp.133-146, 2000.*
9. V. Kobla, D.S. Doermann and A. Rosenfeld, "Compressed domain video segmentation", *CfAR technical report CAR-TR-839 (CS-TR-3688), 1996.*

10. C. Dorai, and V. Kobla, "Perceived visual motion descriptors from MPEG-2 for content-based HDTV annotation and retrieval", In *Proceedings of IEEE Third Workshop on Multimedia Signal Processing (MMSP)*, pp. 147-152, Sept., 1999.

11. C.W. Ngo, T.C. Pong, H.J. Zhang, "On clustering and retrieval of video shots", *In proceeding of 8th ACM inter. Multimedia conf., pp.51-60, Ottawa, Canada, Sept., 2001*

12. X. Xue, X. Zhu, Y. Xiao, L. Wu, "Using mutual relationship between motion vectors for qualitative camera motion classification in MPEG video". *Proc. of SPIE: 2th International Conference on Image and Graphics (ICIG), Vol.4875, pp.853-860, Anhui, Aug., 2002.*

Feature-Based Object Tracking with an Active Camera

Young-Kee Jung[1], Kyu-Won Lee[2], and Yo-Sung Ho[3]

[1] Honam University
59-1 Seobong-dong Kwangsan-gu, Kwangju, 506-090, Korea
ykjung@honam.ac.kr
[2] Daejeon University
96-3 YongUn-dong Dong-gu, Daejeon, 300-716, Korea
kwlee@dju.ac.kr
[3] Kwangju Institute of Science and Technology
1 Oryong-dong Puk-gu, Kwangju, 500-712, Korea
hoyo@kjist.ac.kr

Abstract. This paper describes a new feature-based tracking system that can track moving objects with a pan-tilt camera. After eliminating the global motion of the camera movement, the proposed tracking system traces multiple corner features in the scene and segments foreground objects by clustering the motion trajectories of the corner features. We propose an efficient algorithm for clustering the motion trajectories. Key attributes for classifying the global and local motions are positions, average moving directions, and average moving magnitude of each corner feature. We command the pan-tilt controller to position the moving object at the center of the camera. The proposed tracking system has demonstrated good performance for several test video sequences.

1 Introduction

Owing to rapid progress of the computer technology and its applications, computer vision systems are partly replacing our role. In practice, machine vision systems that are composed of computer vision and various kinds of machinery are ripe enough to be used in the industrial field and in our daily life. A popular example of them is the automated surveillance system that watches moving objects in the restricted area or that monitors the traffic condition for the intelligent transportations system. In those applications, object segmentation and object tracking play quite important roles.

Object motion has long been considered as a significant source of information in the natural vision system. Understanding the visual motion is necessary for both distinguishing sources of different motions and identifying moving objects relative to the surrounding environments. Object motion can be recognized by Johansson's moving light display (MLD) [1]. We can use MLD to find trajectories of a few specific points corresponding to connecting joints of the moving object, and can use them as a key to recognition of the object activity. Gould and Shah build a trajectory primal sketch that represents significant changes in motion in order to identify objects using the trajecto-

Y.-C. Chen, L.-W. Chang, and C.-T. Hsu (Eds.): PCM 2002, LNCS 2532, pp. 1137-1144, 2002.
© Springer-Verlag Berlin Heidelberg 2002

ries of a few representative points [2]. In particular, human motion has been studied extensively using model-based approaches [3].

Several motion-based tracking algorithms have been developed with motion energy in the scene. Those can be implemented with a low complexity. However, they are sensitive to noise and difficult to cope with the global motion caused by the camera movement [4].

In this paper, we are concerning with feature-based object tracking in the mobile camera environments [5-6]. We propose a new algorithm for clustering motion trajectories based on corner features. With a video camera mounted on a pan-tilt controller, we can detect motion of the moving object and then command the pan-tilt controller to follow the object such that the object is positioned at the center of the view field.

2   Proposed Tracking Algorithm

As shown in Fig. 1, the proposed tracking system consists of four main functional parts: camera motion estimation, feature detection and tracking, clustering motion trajectories, and control of the pan-tilt camera.

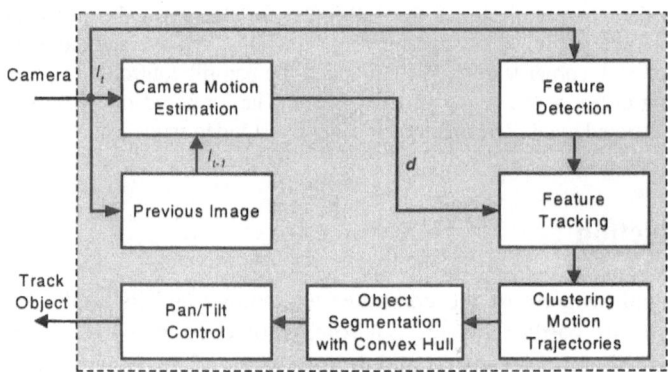

Fig. 1. Proposed Object Tracking Algorithm

In the first part of camera motion estimation, we compute the global motion caused by camera movement by finding the maximal matching position between two consecutive frames using a template-matching algorithm. We have taken a two-level pyramidal approach to reduce the computation cost.

After eliminating the global motion by subtracting the camera movement d from the current feature position, we employ the Kalman filter to predict the search region for each corner point. The 7x7 template, that was extracted when the corner point was detected in the previous frame, is correlated in the search region. After we locate the correlation peak, the feature template of correlation is updated.

We cluster the feature trajectories by grouping the attributes of the feature trajectories that hold similar characteristics. Positions, average moving angles and average moving magnitude of the corner points are used as key attributes for classifying the global and local motions, and regions of moving objects are segmented by forming convex hulls with the classified feature points.

Finally, we command the pan-tilt controller to follow the object such that the object will always lie at the center of the camera.

2.1 Camera Motion Estimation

In order to simplify the analysis of the scene from the mobile camera, we assume that the mobile camera keeps only the translation motion. With this assumption, the camera motion $d(\Delta x, \Delta y)$ is computed by finding the best matching position between the current image $I_t(=I_c)$ and the previous one $I_{t-1}(=I_p)$ using a template-matching algorithm, as shown in Fig. 2.

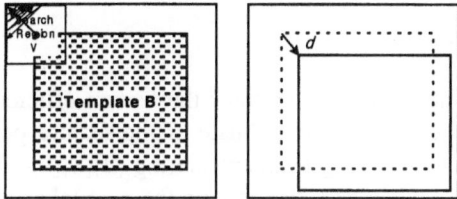

Fig. 2. Camera Motion Estimation

For real-time object tracking, we take a two-level coarse-to-fine pyramidal approach. At the top level, the camera displacement d_s is computed for the pair of 1/3 subsampled images, which is used as the base registration for the next level. For a pair of subsampled images (I_{cs}, I_{ps}), template matching is performed at every pixel location within the search region V_s as follows:

$$\min_{(sx,sy)\in V_s} \sum_{m,n\in B_s} \left| I_{cs}(m+sy,n+sx) - I_{ps}(m,n) \right| \tag{1}$$

where V_s is the search region and B_s is the region for comparison at the top level.

At the bottom level, the camera displacement d is computed for the pair of the original images (I_c, I_p).

$$\min_{(x,y)\in V} \sum_{m,n\in B} \left| I_c(m+y,n+x) - I_p(m,n) \right| \tag{2}$$

$$V = \{(x,y) | sx-1 \leq x \leq sx+1,\ sy-1 \leq y \leq sy+1\} \tag{3}$$

where the search region V is determined by the matching result (sx, sy) at the top level and the comparison region B has nine times of the size of B_s.

2.2 Feature Detection

Since the corner feature is viewpoint invariant and naturally leads to the representation of the object shape, corner points are used as the features in the scene. For corner point detection, we take gradient operations along the x and y directions over the 9x9 window, and compute the second moment matrix Z by taking average of the gradient values [5][6].

$$Z = \begin{bmatrix} g_x^2 & g_x g_y \\ g_x g_y & g_y^2 \end{bmatrix}$$

(4)

where g_x and g_y are the average gradient values along the x and y directions, respectively.

If the matrix Z has two large eigenvalues, the original window contains a corner feature of high spatial frequency. Therefore, we can declare the corner point if $min(\lambda_1, \lambda_2) > \lambda_c$, where λ_1 and λ_2 are two eigenvalues of the matrix Z and λ_c is a predefined threshold value.

2.3 Feature Tracking

Once a corner point is detected, we can track the feature efficiently by predicting the next coordinate from the observed coordinate of the feature point. We design a 2D token-based tracking scheme using Kalman filtering [7][8][9]. The center position of the feature is used as the token $t(k)$. We assume the next token $t(k+1)$ is a sum of the current token $t(k)$ and the token change $\Delta t(k)$. We can define a simplified polynomial motion model by

$$t(k+1) = t(k) + \Delta t(k)$$

(5)

We know that Kalman filtering provides a sequential and recursive algorithm for optimal linear minimum variance (LMV) estimation of the system state $x(k)$. We define the state variable $x(k)$ as a two-dimensional vector, which represents the positional change of the token $\Delta t(k)$.

$$x(k) = \begin{bmatrix} \Delta x\_center(k) \\ \Delta y\_center(k) \end{bmatrix}$$

(6)

Once we define the system model and the measurement model, we apply the recursive Kalman filtering algorithm to obtain LMV estimates of motion parameters [7]. The recursive Kalman filtering algorithm consists of three steps of operations.

At the initialization step, we determine the initial state estimate that is derived from the discrete time derivatives of the feature center locations in the first two frames. We also determine the initial error covariance matrix that represents the deviation of the initial state estimate from the actual initial state. In the state prediction step, we determine a priori LMV estimate and its error covariance matrix for the current state based on the previous state estimate and error covariance. In the measurement update step, we combine the estimated information with new measurements to refine the LMV estimate and its error covariance matrix for the current state. We perform this correction process based on a set of measurement errors using the normalized correlation. The template that was extracted when the corner point was originally detected, is correlated in the search region. After we locate the correlation peak, we can update the system state and the error variance.

2.4 Clustering Motion Trajectories

There are two types of possible motions from the scene of the mobile camera. One is the global motion of the background occurred by camera movement, and the other is the local motion caused by moving objects.

Since we have selected corner points as image features, we can easily obtain a representation of the object shape and other aspects of the background movement. In addition, we can separate two heterogeneous motions by grouping attributes of the corner points according to their spatial and temporal displacements.

The key attributes for classifying the global and local motions are position $C(C_x, C_y)$, average moving direction A_a, and average moving magnitude M_a of the corner points. Each attribute of the feature is computed by the following equations.

$$M_a = \frac{1}{N}\sum_{i=1}^{N} M_i, \; M_i = \sqrt{(C_x(i) - C_x(i-1))^2 + (C_y(i) - C_y(i-1))^2} \qquad (7)$$

where i is the time segment, M_i is the moving distance of the corner point at time i, C_x and C_y are the horizontal and vertical positions of the corner point at current image, respectively, and N is the trajectory length.

$$A_a = \frac{1}{N}\sum_{i=1}^{N} A_i, \; A_i = \arctan\frac{C_y(i) - C_y(i-1)}{C_x(i) - C_x(i-1)} \qquad (8)$$

where A_i is the moving direction of corner point at time i.

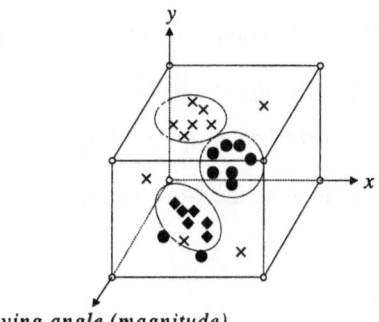

moving angle (magnitude)

Fig. 3. Clustering in Multi-dimensional Feature Space

As shown in Fig. 3, the attributes are arranged in the three-dimensional feature space. We cluster the corner points by grouping the attributes of similar characteristics. After the dynamic range of each attribute is normalized, we cluster the attributes by the K-means algorithm that is extended to three parameters. The full set U of the corner points q is given by

$$U = \{q_0, q_1, q_2, \cdots, q_n\} \tag{9}$$

We compute the first-order moment from the elements of U and denote it as the initial center $\vec{m}_0$. If the standard deviation σ_0 obtained from U and $\vec{m}_0$ is greater than the predetermined threshold, a new center vector of a cluster $\vec{m}_1$ is determined by

$$\vec{m}_1 = \vec{m}_0 + \alpha \sigma_0, \quad \alpha : constant \tag{10}$$

The cluster points are reassigned based on the Euclidean distances, $d(\vec{m}_0, q_k)$ and $d(\vec{m}_1, q_k)$, from $\vec{m}_0$ and $\vec{m}_1$. The criterion for reassignment of the cluster points is described by

$$
\begin{aligned}
C_0 &= \{q_k : d(\vec{m}_0, q_k) \geq, d(\vec{m}_1, q_k)\} \\
C_1 &= \{q_k : d(\vec{m}_0, q_k) <, d(\vec{m}_1, q_k)\} \quad k = 1, 2, 3, \cdots, n
\end{aligned} \tag{11}
$$

where x_0 and x_1 are numbers of elements in the cluster sets C_0 and C_1, respectively.

Consequently, the sets of elements of new clusters are defined by

$$
\begin{aligned}
C_0 &= \{q_{00}, q_{01}, q_{02}, \cdots, q_{0x_1}\}, \, 1 \leq x_0 < n \\
C_1 &= \{q_{10}, q_{11}, q_{12}, \cdots, q_{1x_1}\}, \, 1 \leq x_1 < n \text{ and } x_0 + x_1 = n
\end{aligned} \tag{12}
$$

where x_0 and x_1 are numbers of elements in the cluster sets C_0 and C_1, respectively.

After finding the new first moments $\vec{m}_0'$ and $\vec{m}_1'$ with elements of the sets C_0 and C_1, we perform the reassignment process for the elements classified before by computing $d(\vec{m}_0', q_k)$ and $d(\vec{m}_1', q_k)$ for all elements of the set U. We repeat the process recursively until each standard deviation σ_k is smaller than the specific threshold value. Eventually, the cluster set C_k comprises all the corner points.

$$
\begin{aligned}
C_k &= \{q_{k0}, q_{k1}, q_{k2}, \cdots, q_{kx_k}\}, \\
&1 \leq x_k < n \text{ and } x_0 + x_1 + \cdots + x_k = n
\end{aligned} \tag{13}
$$

where x_k is the number of elements in the k-th cluster.

3   Simulation Results

The proposed tracking system has been tested on several video sequences in indoor environments. The camera is mounted on the pan/tilt driver and the maximum rotation velocity of the camera is about 1.92 rad/sec.

Fig. 4 shows the feature detection results for three eigenvalue thresholds. A high eigenvalue threshold diminishes the number of the detected features. We use 1000 as the eigenvalue threshold λ_c for the tracking system.

(a) 400   (b) 1000   (c) 1600

Fig. 4. Feature Detection for 3 Eigenvalue Thresholds

Three consecutive images of Fig. 5 are captured with two motions. The left panning of camera causes one motion. A moving person occurs the other motion. The camera motion d is computed by finding the maximal matching position using template matching. Subtracting the camera movement d from the current feature position eliminates the global motion. Fig. 5(a) displays the results before global motion compensation. The results after global motion compensation are represented in Fig. 5(b).

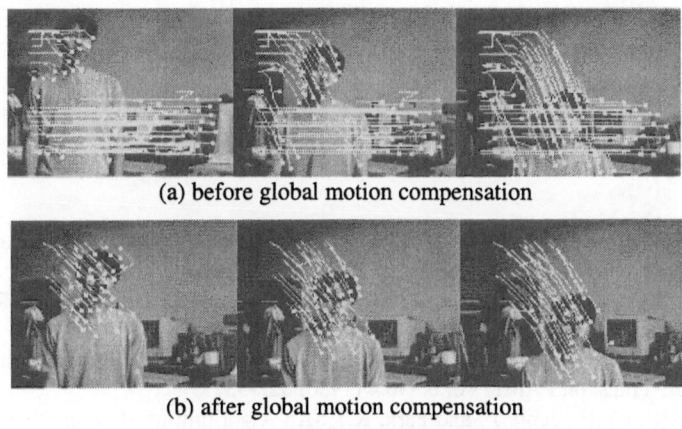

(a) before global motion compensation

(b) after global motion compensation

Fig. 5. Global Motion Compensation

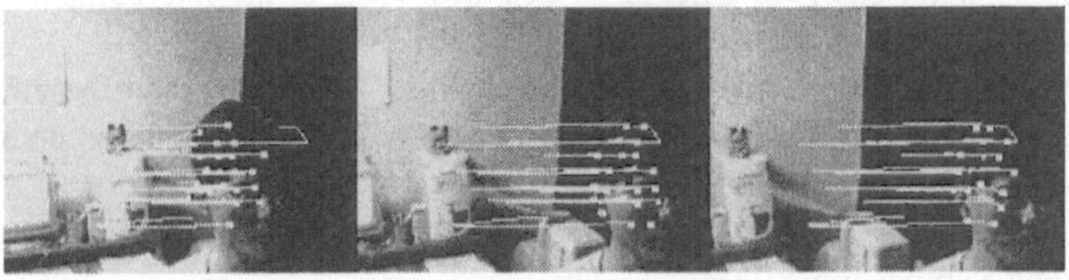

Fig. 6. Tracking Results for The Scene of Right Moving Person. Frames shown here are (top to bottom, left to right) numbers 202, 208, 214

Fig. 6 shows the tracking results for the scene of the person who moved to right direction. As shown in Fig. 6, a number of corners are selected as the active corners. It is seen that there are several feature paths corresponding to the person in the scene. According to the global motion by camera movement is eliminated, the result shows the only local motions of person. The pan-tilt is commanded to move the camera to the centroid of local motion.

4 Conclusions

In this paper, we have proposed an algorithm for moving object tracking with a mobile camera. We use a corner detector to extract features and trace the features using two-dimensional token-based Kalman filtering. Then, the foreground objects are segmented by clustering motion trajectories of the corner features. We have also proposed an efficient clustering algorithm using feature trajectory to obtain a stable local motion. In case of a single moving object, the proposed algorithm shows robust tracking results. In the future, we plan to improve our algorithm by applying active zooming and multiple objects tracking.

Acknowledgement. This work was supported in part by grant NO. R05-2002-000-00868-0 from the Basic Research Program of the Korea Science & Engineering Foundation. This work was also supported in part by KOSEF through UFON and in part by MOE through BK21.

References

1. Johansson, G.: Visual Perception of Biological Motion and a Model for Its Analysis. Perception and Psychophysics, Vol.14 (1973) 201-211
2. Gould, K., Shah, M.: The Trajectory Primal Sketch: A Multi-Scale Scheme for Representing Motion Characteristics. IEEE Conf. of CVPR, (1989) 79-85
3. Rouke, O., Badler: Model-based Image Analysis of Human Motion using Constraint Propagation. IEEE Trans. on PAMI, Vol.3, No.4 (1980) 522-537
4. Lee, K.W., Kim,Y.H., Jeon, J., and Park, K.T.: An Algorithm of Moving Object Extraction Under Visual Tracking without Camera Calibration. Proceedings of ICEIC, (1995) 151-154
5. Forstner, W., Gulch, E.: A Fast Operator for Detection and Precise Location of Distinct Points, Corners, and Centers of Circular of Features. Proc. of the Intercommission Conf. On Fast Processing of Photogrammetric Data, (1987) 281-305
6. Beymer, D., McLauchlan, P., Malick, J.: A Real-time Computer Vision System for Measuring Traffic Parameters. Proc. IEEE Computer Society Conference on Computer Vision and Pattern Recognition, Vol. 12 (1997) 495-501
7. Jung, Y.K., Ho, Y.S.: Robust Vehicle Detection and Tracking for Traffic Surveillance. Picture Coding Symposium, (1999) 227-230
8. Rao, B.S.Y., Durrant-Whyte, H.F., Sheen, J.A.: A Fully Decentralized Multi-Sensor System For Tracking and Surveillance. The International Journal of Robotics Research, Vol. 12 (1993) 20-44
9. McFalane, N., Scholfield, C.: Segmentation and Tracking of Piglets in Images. Machine Vision and Application. Vol. 8 (1995) 187-193

A Depth Measurement System Associated with a Mono-camera and a Rotating Mirror

Jaehong Song[1], Sangik Na[2], Hong-Gab Kim[3], Hyongsuk Kim[2], and Chun-shin Lin[4]

[1] Blue code technology Co. Ltd.
jhsong@mail.chonbuk.ac.kr
[2] School of Electronics and Information Eng, Chonbuk National Univ.
hunter209@mail.chonbuk.ac.kr, hskim@moak.chonbuk.ac.kr
[3] Spatial Imagery Information Research Team, Computer & Software Laboratory,
Electronics and Telecommunications Research Institute
[4] Dept. of Electrical Eng, University of Missouri Columbia U.S.A

Abstract. A novel vision technology to measure the middle-ranged depth with a camera and a plane mirror is proposed. In the image sequence which is taken from a rotating mirror, the speed of pixel movement is higher at the distant objects and slower at the near ones. Utilizing such phenomenon, a new depth measurement scheme is developed and its principle has been investigated. The simpler hardware requirement, the easiness of the pixel matching and the high speed of measurement capability are the advantages of the proposed scheme over the conventional image-based depth measurement technologies. Experimental results are included in this paper.

1 Introduction

The depth information can be measured utilizing information such as sound and light. Though they are the signals of different characteristics, the temporal or spatial difference of signals are commonly utilized to measure the depth. While the ultra-sonic or laser signal utilizes the temporal difference, the image-based depth measurement system utilities the spatial difference of the pixel points. Human vision is the typical one belonging to such type. Even with the shortcoming that the precision of the long distance measurement is poorer than that of the short distance, the image-based measurement system is still very useful in human vision system. One engineering imitation of the human vision system is the stereo vision[1][2][3] which employs two set of fixed camera system. The high price and the calibration difficulties are the problems of the stereo vision.

With two images taken at two different positions by a single camera, the depth information can also be extracted in the similar way of the stereo vision. This is the mono vision system [4][5], which requires much simpler hardware than that of the stereo vision. In the conventional mono vision system, images are taken at two different positions while the camera is moving with the mechanical system like robot arm.

Y.-C. Chen, L.-W. Chang, and C.-T. Hsu (Eds.): PCM 2002, LNCS 2532, pp. 1145-1152, 2002.

Without high mechanical precision of the robot arm, getting the reasonable matching performance is very difficult. Also, depth measurement speed is quite low since the system is associated with the translation movement of the mechanical system [7]. Impact on the camera system during the movement might cause some hazard on the camera system.

The proposed mono camera technology is different from the conventional mono-vision system in that it does not have the difficulty of correspondence problem, the impact on the camera system, and the slow acquisition problem.

2   Relationship between the Depth and the Pixel Speed in the Proposed Mono Camera System

The proposed mono camera system is as shown in Fig. 1. The system is composed of a fixed camera and a rotating plane mirror in front of the camera. While the mirror is rotating and reflecting images, the camera acquires the images from the mirror. With such camera setting, the pixel positions moves at the speed depending on the distance from the camera. Such phenomenon is utilized in the principle of the proposed depth extraction.

Let the crossing point between the lens axis and the plane mirror be O, the depth from O to the object T be R as in the Figure 1. Also, let the angle between the line segment OT and the X axis be ψ. Then, object position R is represented in the polar coordination as $R \angle \psi$. Also, let the focal length from the CCD of the camera be f, the distance from the f to the rotation center of the mirror be d. Also, let the angle of the mirror from X axis be θ_1, and the object in the mirror be T'. Then, the angle between the line segment OT' and the mirror be $\theta_1 + \psi$ and the angle to the X axis becomes $2\theta_1 + \psi$.

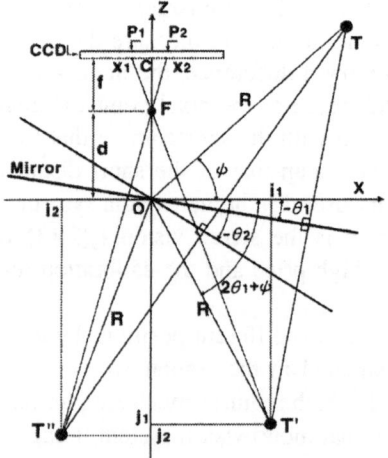

Fig. 1. Proposed rotating mirror-based depth measurement system

If the projection point on the Z axis of the object T' be j_l, then,

$$j_1 = R\sin(2\theta_1 + \psi) \tag{1}$$

Also, if the position on the X axis of the T' be i_l, then,

$$i_1 = R\cos(2\theta_1 + \psi) \tag{2}$$

Let the image point of T' on the CCD be p_l. Then,

$$\frac{p_1}{f} = \frac{-R\cos(2\theta_1 + \psi)}{d + R\sin(2\theta_1 + \psi)} \tag{3}$$

After the differentiation of (3) and some arrangement, (3) becomes

$$\dot{p}_1 = 2\frac{(f + \frac{fd}{R}\sin(2\theta_1 + \psi))}{(\frac{d}{R})^2 + 2(\frac{d}{R})\sin(2\theta_1 + \psi) + \sin^2(2\theta_1 + \psi)}\dot{\theta}_1 \tag{4}$$

Then, the pixel speed is the function of R when the mirror rotates at the speed of $\dot{\theta}_1$ $(=\pi[\text{rad/sec}])$. In other words, the object has long distance if the pixel speed on the CCD is faster, vice versa.

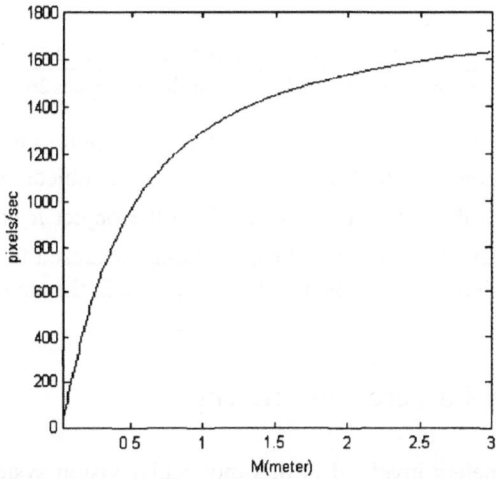

Fig. 2. The relationship between depth and pixel movement speed in the proposed depth measurement system when $\phi=70°$, $\theta=5°$, $f=6mm$, $d=200mm$, $\dot{\theta}=\pi rad/sec$

3   Depth Extraction from the Image Sequence

For the practically useful computation of relationship between the depth and pixel movement, the equation of (4) is modified for the case with larger rotation angle. Let the angle after rotation from $-\theta_2$ by some amount be $-\theta_2$. Then, the equation (3) at $-\theta_2$ becomes

$$\frac{p_2}{f} = \frac{-R\cos(2\theta_2 + \psi)}{d + R\sin(2\theta_2 + \psi)} \qquad (5)$$

It is assumed that the angle θ_1 and θ_2 can be measured externally since they are the rotation angles of the mirror. Also, d is the known value and pixel p_1 and p_2 can be measured on the image. Only R and ψ are unknown.

With the use of (3) and (5), R is expressed as

$$R = \frac{-p_1 d}{f(\cos 2\theta_1 \cos\psi - \sin 2\theta_1 \sin\psi) + p_1(\sin 2\theta_1 \cos\psi + \cos 2\theta_1 \sin\psi)} \qquad (6)$$

and

$$R = \frac{-p_2 d}{f(\cos 2\theta_2 \cos\psi - \sin 2\theta_2 \sin\psi) + p_2(\sin 2\theta_2 \cos\psi + \cos 2\theta_2 \sin\psi)} \qquad (7)$$

From (6) and (7), the relation becomes

$$(p_2 f \cos 2\theta_1 + p_2 p_1 \sin 2\theta_1 - p_1 f \cos 2\theta_2 - p_1 p_2 \sin 2\theta_2)\cos\psi \qquad (8)$$
$$= (p_2 f \sin 2\theta_1 - p_2 p_1 \cos 2\theta_1 - p_1 f \sin 2\theta_2 + p_1 p_2 \cos 2\theta_2)\sin\psi$$

(8) becomes

$$\frac{\sin\psi}{\cos\psi} = \frac{f p_2 \cos 2\theta_1 + p_1 p_2 \sin 2\theta_1 - f p_1 \cos 2\theta_2 - p_1 p_2 \sin 2\theta_2}{f p_2 \sin 2\theta_1 - p_1 p_2 \cos 2\theta_1 - f p_1 \sin 2\theta_2 + p_1 p_2 \cos 2\theta_2} \qquad (9)$$

Therefore, if the point p_2 which is the corresponding point of p_1 and the angles θ_1 and θ_2 are known, then ψ which is the direction of the object can be compute with (9). Plugging ψ into the (6) or (7), the depth to the object R can easily computed. With such measurement scheme, only the uncertainty is caused from the estimation of p_2, which can be obtained through the pixel matching as in the stereo vision system.

4   Calibration of Camera Parameters

The adjustable parameters involved in this monocular vision system are the pixel interval on the CCD and the focal length f as in equations (6)-(9). Let the pixel interval be δ. Then, two pixel positions p_1 and p_2 are

$$p_1 = \delta q_1 \qquad (10)$$

$$p_2 = \delta q_2 \qquad (11)$$

where q_1 and q_2 are the number of pixels from the center of the CCD corresponding to p_1 and p_2, respectively. Plugging (12) and (13) into (8).

$$R = \frac{-q_1 d}{\eta(\cos 2\theta_1 \cos \phi - \sin 2\theta_1 \sin \phi) + q_1 (\sin 2\theta_1 \cos \phi + \cos 2\theta_1 \sin \phi)} \tag{12}$$

where η is defined as the ratio between the focal length and the pixel interval, f/δ. The parameter η is the number of pixel intervals which is equivalent to the length of f. Employing the parameter η, the number of parameters which need to be calibrated is reduced from two to one. The expression with the parameter η is also possible for the direction to the object of (9) as

$$\phi = \tan^{-1} \left[\frac{\eta q_2 \cos 2\theta_1 + q_1 q_2 \sin 2\theta_1 - \eta q_1 \cos 2\theta_2 - q_1 q_2 \sin 2\theta_2}{\eta q_2 \sin 2\theta_1 - q_1 q_2 \cos 2\theta_1 - \eta q_1 \sin 2\theta_2 + q_1 q_2 \cos 2\theta_2} \right] \tag{13}$$

Equations (12) and (13) are expressed by the number of pixels on the image plane instead of the real distance on the CCD. The parameter η can easily be determined by plugging R and ϕ into (12) for known object location.

5 Experiments

The performance of depth extraction is presented with some experiments. Note that the rotating axis of the mirror is adjusted to have the pixel movement vector be parallel to the x-axis of the image plane.

The relation between the object movement on image and the distance is identified through real measurement. The image size used in this experiment 340×240, focal length is 6 mm, and the size of the plane mirror is 110 mm × 60 mm. The distance between the camera and the center of the mirror is 200 mm. Fig. 5(a) is the image with such arrangement before the rotation of the mirror while Fig. 5(b) is that after 5° rotation to the clockwise direction. Observe the center line of the board and the background object indicated by the white arrow. After the rotation, the pixel corresponding to the distant object is translated more than that of close one.

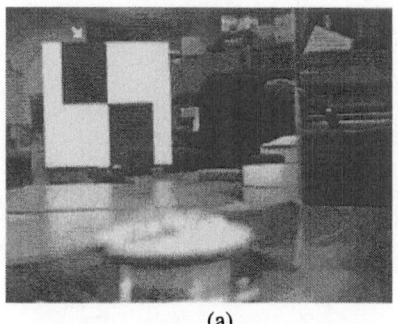 

(a)   (b)

Fig. 3. An example of images acquired through the rotating mirror (a) before rotation (b) after rotation

Fig. 4 shows the disparities at the different objects when distances between the mirror and the camera are 10 cm, 20 cm, and 30 cm. The curve with filled and blank symbols are the objects at the direction of 45° and 90°, respectively. The graphs show that the depth is the function of pixel disparity though its nonlinearity becomes higher as the distance is longer. In contrast to the conventional stereo system, the depth increases as the disparity is larger.

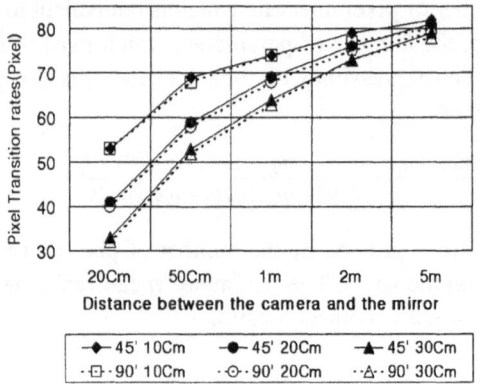

Fig. 4. Pixel transition rates with the different distance between the camera and the mirror

The depth computed with the proposed scheme is compared to the real depth. Fig. 5 is such depth comparison about the objects located at $\psi = 80°$ direction. As shown in the Fig.5, the measurements with the proposed scheme are very close to the real depths within 10 cm at 2.5 m. Fig.6 shows the angular error computed at different distances with the proposed system, when the computed angle is very close to the reference regardless of the depth. Though error grows as the distance, such measurement scheme is still very useful for robots. Since the image is obtained from the mirror which is rotating at fast and constant speed, the measurement speed could be fast. Also, the matching problem is relaxed due to the transition trajectory of the pixel movement is almost constant. Simpler mechanic structure of the proposed system is another advantage.

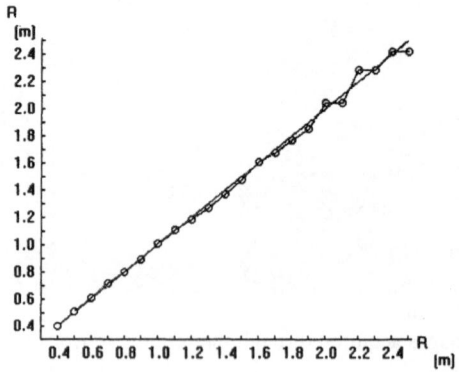

Fig. 5. Comparison of measured distances. The straight line is the real distance and the curved line is the measurement by the proposed system.

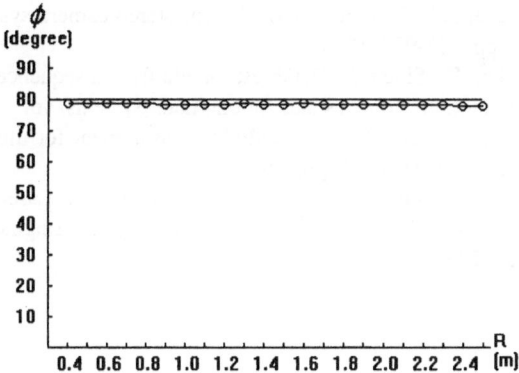

Fig. 6. Angular measurement error. The straight line is the real angle and the curvy line with circular symbols is the one with the proposed system.

6 Conclusion

The proposed depth measurement technology associated with the mono camera and a rotating mirror is proposed. The camera is installed in front of a plane mirror rotating at a constant speed. With this setting, the speed of pixel movement on the camera image is slower at the closer object and faster at the distant object. This is the major difference of the proposed work from the conventional stereo or mono visions systems.

The relationship between pixel disparity in the image sequence and the depth have been investigated for the proposed depth measurement system. The depth obtained with the proposed scheme has the characteristic that the precision is better at the closer distance as in the conventional stereo vision or human vision system. Therefore, it can be useful for the application like robot arm whose working area is confined to couple of meters. Benefits of the proposed system are simpler hardware requirement, the easiness of the pixel matching and higher speed image acquisition than other conventional mono camera-based system.

References

1. Yakimovsky, Y., Cunningham, R.: A System for extracting three-dimensional measurements from a stereo pair of TV cameras. Computer Graphics and Image Processing, vol. 7, pp. 195 - 210, 1978.
2. Eric, W., Grimson, L.: Computational experiments with a feature based stereo algorithm. IEEE Transactions on Pattern Analysis and Machine Intelligence, vol. PAMI-7, no. 1, pp. 17-33, Jan. 1985.
3. Dhond, U. R., Aggarwal, J. K.: Structure from stero- a review. IEEE Trans. on System, Man and Cybernetics, vol. 19, pp. 1489-1510, Nov./ Dec. 1989.
4. Choi, W., Ryu, C., Kim, H.: Navigation of mobile robot using mono-visio and mono-audition. IEEE Computer, vol. 22, No. 6, pp. 46-57, 1989.

5. Goshtasby, A., Gruver, W.: Design of a single-lens stereo camera system. Pattern Recognition, vol. 26, no. 6, pp. 923-937, 1993.
6. Zhuang, H., Sudhakar, R., Shieh, J.: Depth estimation from a sequence of monocular images with known camera motion. Robotics and Autonomous Systems, vol. 13, pp. 87-95, 1994.
7. Marioli, D., Narduzzi, C.: Digital time of flight measurement for ultrasonic sensors. IEEE Trans. Instrum. Meas., vol.41, no. 1, pp. 93-97, 1992.
8. Amann, M. C., Bosch, T., Lescure, M., Myllyla, R., Rioux, M.: Laser ranging: a critical review of usual techniques for distance measurement. Optical Engineering, vol.40, (no.1), SPIE, pp.10-19, Jan. 2001.

Human Behavior Recognition for an Intelligent Video Production System

Motoyuki Ozeki, Yuichi Nakamura, and Yuichi Ohta

IEMS, University of Tsukuba, 305-8573, Japan
{ozeki, yuichi, ohta}@image.esys.tsukuba.ac.jp

Abstract. We propose a novel framework for automated video capturing and production for desktop manipulations. We focus on the system's ability to select relevant views by recognizing types of human behavior. Using this function, the obtained videos direct the audience's attention to the relevant portions of the video and enable more effective communication. We first discuss significant types of human behavior that are commonly expressed in presentations, and propose a simple and highly precise method for recognizing them. We then demonstrate the efficacy of our system experimentally by recording presentations in a desktop manipulation.

1 Introduction

There is now a great demand for audiovisual or multimedia contents in various fields. Content production is, however, a difficult task, which requires both considerable cost and skills. For example, a number of assistants and considerable time for recording and editing are often needed for audiovisual education. Thus, it is widely recognized that automated video production is one of the key technologies on multimedia.

For this purpose, we are investigating a framework for effectively capturing presentations and producing comprehensible videos for teaching/operating /instruction manuals. We have so far constructed the framework's camera system that allows the appropriate video capturing of the targets[1][2]. As the next step, we need a mechanism for emphasizing *the focus of attention* which the members of the audience are expected to recognize.

In this paper, we will first consider the relation between the focus of attention and human behaviors regarding desktop manipulations, and then propose a multimodal method for detecting the focus. We will then present some experiments which demonstrate the performance of our system.

2 Communicating the Focus of Attention

2.1 Research Objective

For desktop manipulation, we assume the following situation as shown in Figure 1:

Y.-C. Chen, L.-W. Chang, and C.-T. Hsu (Eds.): PCM 2002, LNCS 2532, pp. 1153–1160, 2002.

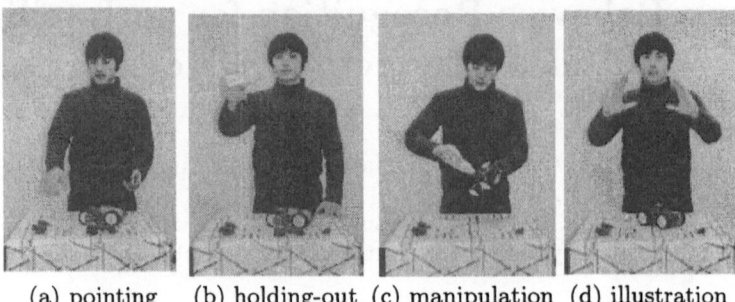

(a) pointing   (b) holding-out (c) manipulation (d) illustration

Fig. 1. Typical types of behavior in presentations

- One person is speaking and presenting desktop manipulation.
- There are virtual audiences, but presenter does not receive questions from them in realtime.

This situation is common to a variety of video presentation contexts, *e.g.,* video manuals or cooking shows. The objective of our research is to realize, in such situations, a *virtual cameraman* who shoots and captures important portions, and to realize a *virtual editor* who selects important shots and edits the videos.

This paper discusses the latter problem: how we can make the most use of a multi-view (multi-angled) video. The key points of this topic regard tagging and editing. Tagging is the problem of describing what information is included in a video at a certain time. Editing is the problem of selecting relevant portions in the sense of time and view, and of making a video suitable for a given purpose.

As one important approach to this topic, we investigated the detection and utilization of a speaker's typical behaviors: detecting a speaker's behaviors which are intended to draw the viewers' attention, tagging in terms of the recognition of those behaviors, and editing by selecting the most appropriate view.

Several related works deal with lectures using automated video capturing or archive systems[3]–[8]. For our purpose, however, different approaches are required:

- The targets that should be captured in desktop manipulations are different from those in lecture scenes. Some targets, such as hands, move fast and in complicated patterns. The combination of simple tracking and simple view switching may result in a shaky and unpleasant video.
- Typical types of behavior that appear in desktop manipulations are different from those of lecture scenes. As we will discuss below, we have to focus on important behaviors that are not considered in the above-mentioned studies.

2.2   System Overview

Figure 2 shows the basic system derived from our research. For realtime measurement of the speaker's position and the object's positions, we currently use

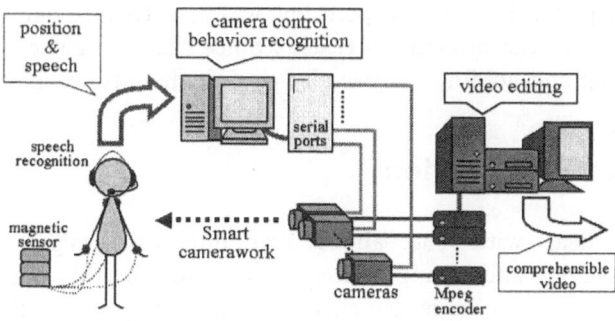

Fig. 2. Overview of the system

magnetic sensors. Pan/tilt cameras are controlled by using the measured positions, and videos taken by those cameras are transmitted, switched, and recorded in MPEG format. For behavior recognition, the system uses a speaker's movements and speech recognition output.

The result of behavior recognition are not only used for tagging the captured videos, but are used for switching to the most appropriate output view. This enables a speaker to give a presentation while checking the status of the system. The switched view can be directly presented to viewers, or the system can edit the recorded video afterward based on the obtained tags.

3   Important Types of Behavior in Desktop Manipulation

The following types of behavior frequently appear in presentations, aimed at drawing the viewers' attention:

Pointing: Pointing with one's hand forces the audience to look at the directed area, as shown in Figure 1(a). This corresponds to *deictic movement* in Ekman's classification [9]. The focus is on the indicated object, location, or direction.

Holding-out: Holding out, or presenting, an object toward the audience, usually at a position higher than the waist and lower than the eyes (Figure 1(b)). The focus is on the held object.

Manipulation: Demonstrating important operations is a typical behavior, as shown in Figure 1(c). It can be a virtual manipulation belonging to *illustrators* in Ekman's classification. The focus is on the manipulation.

Illustration: Illustrating a shape, size, or motion by moving hands draws the viewers' attention to it, as shown in Figure 1(d). This also corresponds to *illustrators* in Ekman's classification. The focus is on the locus or the motion of the hands.

Since discrimination between manipulation and illustration is sometimes difficult in actual presentations and their functions are similar, hereafter we classify them together in this paper. In regard to pointing, we currently deal only with pointing at an object within the presenter's reach[1]. Since this diminishes the difference between pointing and holding-out, we also classify these two behaviors together.

4   Behavior Recognition

We have to deal with the above two important types of behavior, pointing/holding-out and manipulation/illustration. For this purpose, we propose simple and fast methods utilizing using motion and speech clues. If the system detects both speech clues and motion clues within a certain period, the system accepts them as a corresponding behavior. We previously investigated the occurrence between motion clues and speech clues[10], and the statistics showed that they cooccur within 2 seconds in around 90% cases. Since the speech recognition sometimes has a delay longer than 2 seconds, we set the tolerance of the delay to 3 seconds.

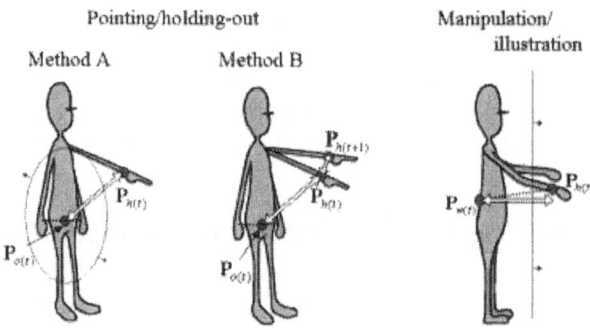

Fig. 3. Behavior recognition

4.1   Motion Clues for Pointing/Holding-out

One of the most distinct features of pointing/holding-out behavior is the arm position: an arm is stretched in front of a speaker. Two other features concern arm motions: a quick stretch of an arm and a sudden stop. We compared two methods, method A and method B, which use arm position, and both arm position and hand motion, respectively.

Using Arm Position (Method A): The system simply detects moments when the arm stretches beyond the threshold. When both hands are stretched and they

---

[1] Pointing at an object beyond the presenter's reach is left for future research, since another research is required for delineating the location of the indicated object.

are close to each other, the system regards the movement as a pointing/holding-out behavior using both hands. If both hands are apart from each other, the system regards the movement as a pointing/holding-out behavior with a single hand whose position is higher than the other's.

Arm Stretch (AS) is calculated using the following equation, as shown on the left in Figure 3.

$$AS_{(t)} = |\mathbf{P}_{h(t)} - \mathbf{P}_{o(t)}|$$

where $\mathbf{P}_h$ is the hand position, and $\mathbf{P}_o$ is the position when the hand is put down.

Using Arm Motion (Method B): If the system focuses only hand position, it can mis-detect other movements to which a speaker does not intend to call attention. To cope with this problem, in method B the system also checks a quick arm stretch and a sudden stop. If the above features are detected for both hands simultaneously, the system regards the movement as pointing/holding-out behavior utilizing both hands.

Arm Stretch Change (ASC), *Pseudo Velocity (PV)*, and *Pseudo Velocity Change (PVC)* are calculated using the following equations, as shown at the center of Figure 3.

$$ASC_{(t)} = AS_{(t)} - AS_{(t-1)}$$
$$PV_{(t)} = |\mathbf{P}_{h(t)} - \mathbf{P}_{h(t-1)}| \ , \ PVC_{(t)} = PV_{(t)} - PV_{(t-1)}$$

4.2   Motion Clues for Manipulation/Illustration

Since a manipulation/illustration movement is originally a simulation or a demonstration of movements or shapes, there is no fixed pattern for it. To deal with this behavior, we are currently using hand position, whether the hands are on/above the desk. It is calculated using the following equation, as shown on the right of Figure 3.

$$|\underline{\mathbf{P}}_{h(t)} - \underline{\mathbf{P}}_{w(t)}| > Th_{wh}$$

where $\mathbf{P}_w$ is the position of the speaker's waist, and $\underline{\mathbf{P}}$ means the horizontal component of $\mathbf{P}$.

4.3   Speech Clues

Speech suggests the presence of an important behavior, and some types of speech also specify the focus of attention. For example, phrases that include a demonstrative pronoun/adjective/adverb, such as "this(is a ...)", "this (switch)", or "this long", frequently appear in speech, and they strongly suggest a focus of attention.

Figure 4 shows the speech clues that we are currently using, and shows the foci of attention suggested by the clues. The balloon located above each arrow gives the words and corresponding movements that trigger the switching. And the focus of attention is shown above each image. Since this system is designed for Japanese, the Japanese words are the targets of speech recognition.

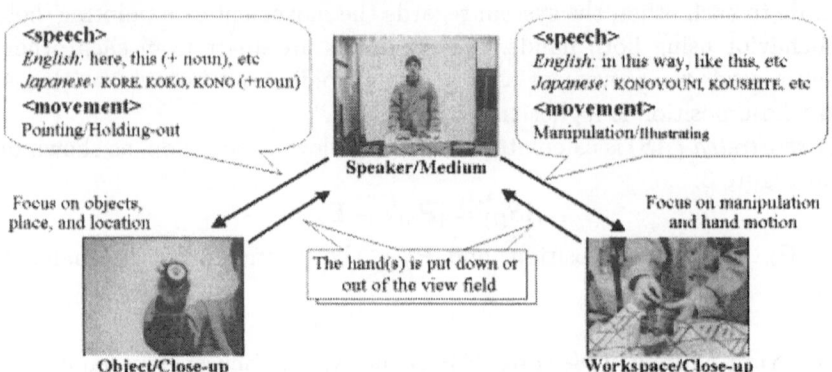

Fig. 4. Typical examples of speech, and video switching condition

5   Experiments

5.1   Evaluation of Behavior Recognition

We examined the performance of our behavior recognition methods by applying our system to real presentations. We gathered 6 students without any professional experience in teaching or giving instructions. Each subject was asked to give a demonstration of the assembly of a toy car. Before the presentation, the subjects were briefed on how the system works, and were asked to express their intentions clearly by means of motion and speech. The subjects were able to see the system's responses by looking at the switched view that indicates the results of focus detection.

Some portions of the video edited according to behavior recognition are shown in Figure 5. In this experiment, three cameras were used, which captured close-up shots of an object held by the speaker, middle shots of the speaker, and close-up shots of the workspace. The switching conditions are illustrated in Figure 4. As we can see in Figure 5, the system properly recognized the focus of attention, producing an effective video.

The left side of Table 1 shows the performance of our system. Without prior training, around 70% of the subjects' behaviors are correctly recognized. All detection failures of method A arose from speech recognition errors. The same can be said for manipulation/illustration.

For the evaluation of our system as a user interface, we asked each subject to fill out a questionnaire after the experiment. Roughly speaking, the subjects had positive impressions of the system. Once we explained the system mechanism, all the subjects were able to quickly adjust to giving presentations on the system. Most of subjects stated that they were not severely constrained by the system and that they were satisfied with the obtained videos. In regard to the detection methods for pointing/holding-out, most of the subjects stated that method A is better than method B because of its better detection rate and fewer constraints.

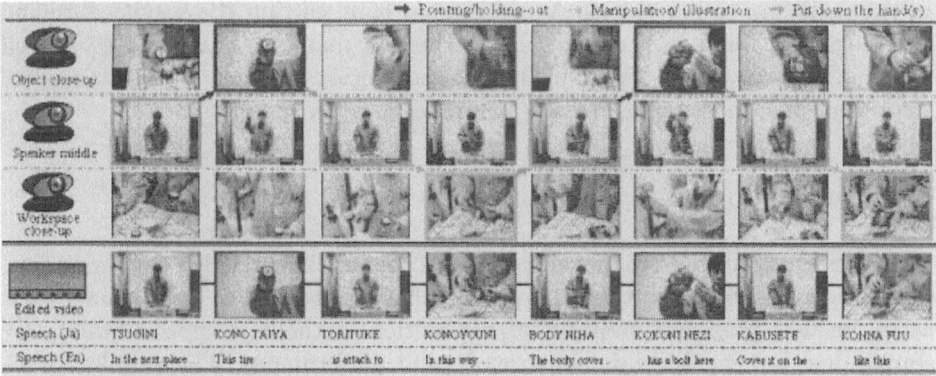

Fig. 5. Example of video switching
The phrases below the images are the transcribed speech. The upper line shows the actual speech in Japanese, and the lower shows the translation into English. The sample movies (mpeg format) can be obtained at
http://www.image.esys.tsukuba.ac.jp/~ozeki/e_movies.html.

Table 1. Recognition result for real presentations (left side) and comparison of automatic editing (right side)

P/H (MA)		P/H (MB)		M/I	
R(%)	P(%)	R(%)	P(%)	R(%)	P(%)
75	94	64	98	75	98

P/H:Pointing/Holding-out
M/I:Manipulation/Illustration
MA(B):using Method A(B) for P/H
R:Recall, P:Precision

Editing Method	Matched frames#(%)			
	P1	P2	P3	Total
Speech only	52.1	57.4	54.9	55.0
Motion only (MA)	71.7	48.9	54.4	57.4
Motion only (MB)	64.1	61.5	47.0	57.2
Motion and Speech	78.8	87.9	80.2	82.6
Random Editing	50.7	46.0	39.0	44.9

5.2 Evaluation of Automatic Editing

We verified our video editing scheme by subjective evaluation. For this purpose, we captured three kinds of desktop manipulations – P1: assembling a toy car, P2: attaching an I/O adopter to a notebook PC, and P3: cooking a sandwich (emulation), each of which are from 50 to 60 seconds long. Three kinds of edited videos created from these data are compared:

- A video manually edited by one of the authors who can clearly recognize the speaker's behavior.
- The automatically edited video that matches best the manually edited video.
- A randomly edited video in which video switching is periodic. The interval is the average of that of the manually edited one. The probability for each shot is close to[2] that of the manually edited video.

The right side of Table 1 shows the results of the comparison. Each figure in the table shows the number of frames in which the same shot is chosen as

---

[2] Since the number of the shots are finite, we cannot arbitrarily set this probability.

in the manually edited videos. As we can see here, editing the results obtained by using speech and motion clues shows the best match to the manually edited video. This proves that our multimodal recognition method is more accurate than other methods such as that which relies only on speech.

6   Conclusion

This paper introduced our novel framework for intelligent video capturing and production. We discussed typical types of behavior intended to draw the viewers' attention and proposed multimodal recognition methods. Experimentally, our simple and fast methods demonstrated good performance. The subjects were generally satisfied with our system and with the obtained videos.

As a goal of our future research, we will attempt to achieve a more detailed behavior recognition. For editing videos in wider variety of ways, much more information is required; for example, the system needs to recognize what a speaker is doing during manipulation/illustration movements.

References

1. M. Ozeki, Y. Nakamura, and Y. Ohta, "Camerawork for intelligent video production – capturing desktop manipulations," *Proc. ICME*, pp. 41–44, 2001.
2. M. Ozeki, M. Itoh, Y. Nakamura, and Y. Ohta, "Tracking hands and objects for an intelligent video production system," *Proc. ICPR*, pp. 1011–1014, 2002.
3. L. He et al., "Auto-summarization of audio-video presentations," *Proc.ACM Multimedia*, pp. 489–498, 1999.
4. S. Mukhopadhyay and B. Smith, "Passive capture and structuring of lectures," *Proc.ACM Multimedia*, pp. 477–487, 1999.
5. Y. Kameda, M. Minoh, et al., "A study for distance learning service - tide project -," *Proc. International Conference on Multimedia and Expo*, pp. 1237–1240, 2000.
6. Y. Kameda, M. Mihoh, et al., "A live video imaging method for capturing presentation information in distance learning," *Proc.International Conference on Multimedia and Expo*, 2000.
7. A. Bobick, "Movement, activity, and action," *MIT Media Lab Preceptual Computing Section*, vol. TR-413, 1997.
8. A. Bobick and C. Pinhanez, "Controlling view-based algorithms using approximate world models and action information," *Proc. Conference on Computer Vision and Pattern Recognition*, pp. 955–961, 1997.
9. P. Ekman and W. Friesen, "The repertoire of nonverbal behavior : Categories, origins,usage,and coding," *Semiotica*, vol. 1, pp. 49–98, 1969.
10. Y. Nakamura et al., "MMID: Multimodal multi-view integrated database for human behavior understanding," *Proc. IEEE International Conference on Automatic Face and Gesture Recognition*, pp. 540–545, 1998.
11. K. Ohkushi, T. Nakayama, and T. Fukuda, *Evaluation Techniques for Image and Tone Quality (in Japanese)*, chapter 2.5, SHOKODO, 1991.

A Robust Algorithm for Video Based Human Motion Tracking

Feng Liu, Yueting Zhuang, Zhongxiang Luo, and Yunhe Pan

Department of Computer Science and Engineering
Microsoft Visual Perception Laboratory of Zhejiang University
Zhejiang University, Hangzhou, 310027, P.R.China
lffred@yahoo.com.cn yzhuang@cs.zju.edu.cn zdlzx@263.net
panyh@sun.zju.edu.cn

Abstract. In this paper, we present a robust algorithm to capture rapid human motion with self-occlusion. Instead of predicting the position of each human feature, the interest-region of full body is estimated. Then candidate features are extracted through the overall search in the interest-region. To establish the correspondence between candidate features and actual features, an adaptive Bayes classifier is constructed based on the time-varied models of feature attributions. At last, a hierarchical human feature model is adopted to verify and accomplish the feature correspondence. To improve the efficiency, we propose a multi-resolution search strategy: the initial candidate feature set is estimated at the low resolution image and successively refined at higher resolution levels. The experiment demonstrates the effectiveness of our algorithm.

1 Introduction

Video based human motion tracking is an important task in video based animation and game, human computer interaction, content based video indexing, etc [1]. A great variety of visual tracking algorithms have been presented, and can be roughly classified into two categories, viz. image based [2] [3] and attribute based [4] [5]. Feature extraction and correspondence are two main steps in attribute-based tracking, which are often supported by prediction. Based on previously detected features and possibly high level knowledge, the state of the objects (appearance, position, etc.) in the next frame is predicted and compared (using some metric) with the states of objects found in the actual image. Prediction introduces an interest-region in both image space and state space and hereby reduces the overall need for processing. Various models [6] are adopted in prediction, including kinematic models, such as that of velocity and acceleration, probabilistic motion models, and even some abstract models, like walking, running and so on.

However, sometimes prediction is misleading when tracking rapid motion with self-occlusion, especially under the condition of small interest-region. A robust algorithm is proposed in this paper to effectively track rapid motion with self-occlusion. Instead of predicting the position of each feature, the interest-region of full body is estimated. Then candidate features are extracted through the overall search in the interest-region. To establish the correspondence between candidate features and actual

Y.-C. Chen, L.-W. Chang, and C.-T. Hsu (Eds.): PCM 2002, LNCS 2532, pp. 1161-1168, 2002.
© Springer-Verlag Berlin Heidelberg 2002

features, an adaptive Bayes classifier is constructed based on the time-varied models of feature attributions. At last, a hierarchical human feature model is adopted to verify and accomplish the feature correspondence. To improve the efficiency, we propose a multi-resolution search strategy: the initial candidate feature set is established at the low resolution image and successively refined at higher resolution levels.

The remainder of this paper is organized as follows: in the next section, we will give an overview of the algorithm. In Section 3, we discuss the feature modeling. And in the following two sections, we describe the multi-resolution candidate feature extraction method and the successive feature correspondence strategy. We discuss the experimental result in Section 6 and conclude this paper in the last section.

2 Algorithm Overview

We define human body as a set of rigid limbs connected by joints, and human motion as the movement of human skeleton, which consists of 16 joints. We design a suit of tight-clothing [7] for the performer. Each joint of the tight-clothing is attached with a patch of different color. Each color block is regarded as a feature as those color blocks are independent. Our algorithm aims at tracking the trajectory of each feature defined above.

The main steps of this algorithm are outlined as follows:
1)   Initialize human feature models and other system parameters.
2)   Establish the candidate feature set of Frame $k+1$ through multi-resolution search.
3)   Determine the sub-candidate-feature set of each feature with adaptive Bayes classifiers, and calculate the match degree of each element in the sub-set.
4)   Verify and accomplish feature correspondence using the hierarchical human feature model.
5)   If the last frame of image sequence is reached, stop; otherwise update system parameters and go to step 2).

3 Feature Modeling

Each feature can be represented by its two attributions, viz. color and motion. And the feature model is defined as $F(P_c, P_m)$ accordingly, where P_c and P_m represent the attribution of color and motion respectively.

3.1 Feature Model

Due to the change of the environment and the motion of body, the illumination is time-varied. Thus induce the variety of each feature's color in the recorded image sequences. Each feature has individual motion, resulting in different illumination

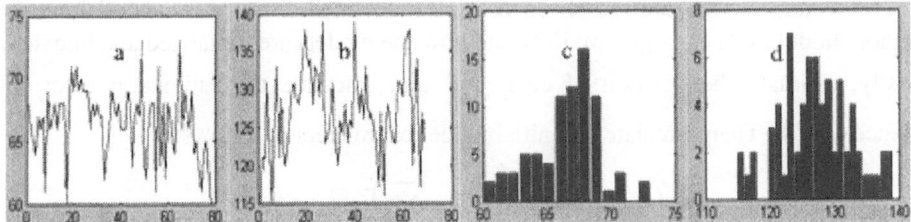

Fig. 1. Color model. *a* and *b* represent the color variation of feature Chest during walking and that of feature LShoulder during jumping each. *c* and *d* are the corresponding color histograms. The motion of feature Chest in *walking* is slow than that of feature LShoulder in *jumping*, which results in small illumination change. And the color with low luminance is less sensitive to illumination variation. So the color variation of Chest is smaller than that of Lshoulder

variety. Even the same illumination variety has different effect on different colors (See Fig. 1). Gauss Distribution is selected to represent the individual feature color.

$$p(c \mid F_i) = \frac{1}{\sqrt{2\pi}\sigma_i} \exp(-\frac{(c-\mu_i)^2}{2\sigma_i^2}).$$ (1)

Where $p(c \mid F_i)$ is the probability density function of the color of feature F_i. μ_i makes the feature distinguish from others and σ_i^2 shows variation of the feature's position and the acuity of feature's color to the illumination change.

Due to short intervals between image sequences, we adopt a local constant acceleration motion model. Assuming that the acceleration between frame k-2, k-1, k, k+1 is constant, $\widehat{P}_{k+1}$, the feature's position in frame k+1, can be calculated from that of the three anterior frames. However, the acceleration of feature's motion is not perfectly constant. The error between the estimated value and the actual value does exist and is uncertain. Experiments show that most of the error values are around a given value, and their distribution is approximate to Gauss Distribution. We adopt Gauss Distribution to describe the error sequence $\{\Delta P_k\}$, where $\Delta P_k = P_k - \widehat{P}_k$. For motion components, along axis X and Y, are independent, the distribution of the estimation error of feature F_i can be represented as follows:

$$p(\Delta P \mid F_i) = p(\Delta x, \Delta y \mid F_i) = \frac{1}{2\pi\sigma_{xi}\sigma_{yi}} \exp - \left(\frac{(\Delta x - \mu_{xi})^2}{2\sigma_{xi}^2} + \frac{(\Delta y - \mu_{yi})^2}{2\sigma_{yi}^2} \right).$$ (2)

3.2 Model Initialization

Initially, users are required to label the features' position in the first K frames. Then clustering is performed to obtain the color block according to the pixel's color and the center and the even color of the clustering block are computed.

The feature models are initialized using the obtained K frames' data. Taking the motion model as an example, we illustrate how the models are initialized and updated. Firstly, estimate the position of each $\widehat{P}_t$ and calculate the estimation error sequence $\{\Delta P_t\}$. Then calculate the initial model parameters as follows:

$$\sigma_{xi}^2(K) = \frac{1}{K}\sum_{t=1}^{t=K}\left(\Delta x_{it} - \overline{\Delta x_i}\right)^2$$

$$\mu_{xi}(K) = \overline{\Delta x_i}$$

(3)

Since P_{T+1}, the feature's position in Frame T+1, is obtained during the tracking, we calculate ΔP_{T+1} and update the model parameters as follows:

$$\sigma_{xi}^2(T+1) = \frac{T}{T+1}\left(\sigma_{xi}^2(T) + \frac{\left(\mu_{xi}(T) - \Delta x_{i,T+1}\right)^2}{T+1}\right)$$

$$\mu_{xi}(T+1) = \frac{T \times \mu_{xi}(T) + \Delta x_{i,T+1}}{T+1}$$

(4)

The model parameters along axis Y can be initialized and updated analogously.

4   Candidate Feature Extraction

To improve the efficiency, we propose a multi-resolution search strategy to extract the candidate features: the initial candidate feature set is established at the low resolution image and successively refined at higher resolution levels. We adopt the well-known Pyramid structure to represent image hierarchically. The basic method to build image pyramid is space down-sampling after low filtering.

We extract initial candidate feature set at the lowest resolution. To reduce the search range, the interest-region of whole body is estimated. Construct the bound rectangle containing all the features in the last frame. Then magnify the rectangle k times as the interest-region ($k \in [1, 2]$). We scan every pixel line by line from top to bottom in the interest-region. Compare the scanned pixel with each feature color. If the color of the scanned pixel is similar enough with one of the feature color, then take it as the seed and perform clustering. At last, calculate the corresponding feature parameters. To avoid repeating scanning the same clustered pixels, a table is maintained, and pixels which have been scanned or clustered are labeled.

The initial candidate feature set is refined through re-clustering at higher resolution levels. Take the position of the initial candidate feature and considering the increase of resolution, magnify it 2 times as the seed for the new clustering. Employ the same clustering to get the clustering block, calculate and update the feature parameters. After all the features are updated, mergence and elimination are performed to refine the candidate feature set. If the clustering block is too small, the corresponding feature is eliminated. If multiple clustering blocks are overlapped, the corresponding features are emerged and feature parameters are updated. The refinement is continued until the number of candidate features is below 16 or the highest resolution is reached.

5 Feature Correspondence

With the candidate feature set obtained, we need to establish the correspondence between the candidate features and actual features. Firstly, construct an adaptive Bayes Classifier to determine the sub-candidate-feature set for each feature. Then select the candidate feature with highest match degree in each sub-set as the feature. At last, verify and accomplish the feature correspondence according to the hierarchical human feature model.

5.1 Feature Match

To establish the feature correspondence, an adaptive Bayes classifier is constructed based on the feature model. Feature is represented by its two attributions, viz. color and motion. We use the feature model in Section 3.1 to estimate the posterior probability of the candidate feature (c_j, p_j) associated with feature F_i and classify the candidate features.

$$P(F_i \mid c_j, p_j) = \frac{p(c_j, p_j \mid F_i)P(F_i)}{\sum_{i=1}^{16} p(c_j, p_j \mid F_i)P(F_i)} (1 \le j \le n). \tag{5}$$

where $P(F_i \mid c_j, p_j)$ is the posterior probability, $p(c_j, p_j \mid F_i)$ is the conditional probability density function, $P(F_i)$ is the prior probability of the occurrence of F_i.

For each feature has the same probability to occur, their prior probabilities are 1/16. As feature's color and motion attribution are independent from each other, $p(c_j, p_j \mid F_i)$ can be calculated as follows:

$$p(c_j, p_j \mid F_i) = p(c_j \mid F_i)p(p_j \mid F_i). \tag{6}$$

$p(c_j \mid F_i)$ and $p(p_j \mid F_i)$ can be calculated according to the feature model in Section 3.1. As the feature model is updated dynamically, this Bayes classifier is adaptive.

As the number of the candidate features is more than that of the actual features, most features have more than one corresponding candidate features. $p(c_j, p_j \mid F_i)$ is calculated as the match degree for each candidate feature. The one with highest match degree is selected as the feature.

5.2 Verify and Accomplish Feature Match

To verify the feature correspondence, we adopt the hierarchical human feature model (See Fig.2), similar with the hierarchical motion representation [8]. The human feature model is regarded as a tree, with joint Pelvis as its Root and other nodes corresponding to the remainder joints of the human model. The human motion is represented by the combination of translation and rotations, viz. the translation of Root and rotation of other nodes around their parent nodes.

A hierarchical human feature table is constructed based on the hierarchical human feature model. This table maintains the relationship of every two adjacent features, and its structure is designed as <P, S, V>, where P is the parent feature, S is the son feature and V is the vector from P to S.

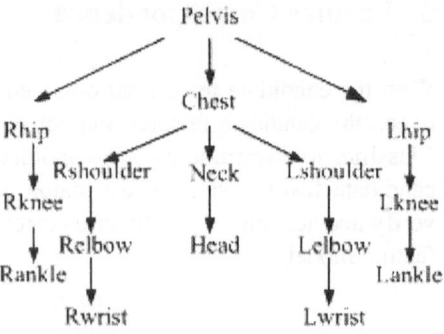

Fig. 2. Hierarchical human feature model

Features with low match degrees are selected as *uncertain features* and the feature with highest match degree as *certain feature*. According to the topology of features registered in the hierarchical human feature table, feature match is verified as follows:

1) Chose one of the *certain features* as the seed feature. Query the records with the seed feature as father feature from the hierarchical human feature table and verify the match of the son feature in the sequent steps.

2) If the son feature has been matched and is not *uncertain feature*, go to Step 6). If the son feature is *uncertain feature*, calculate the vector from the father feature to the son feature. If the difference between this vector and the recorded vector is below the given threshold, go to Step 6); otherwise go to Step 3). If the son feature has not been matched, go to Step 3).

3) Calculate the vector from the father feature to each unmatched candidate feature and compare it to the recorded vector. If the difference is below the given threshold, add the candidate feature to the sub-candidate-feature set of the son feature.

4) If the sub-candidate-feature set is not empty, calculate the match degree of each feature in the sub-candidate-feature set to the son feature according to Equation 6 and select the one with the highest degree as the corresponding feature. Go to Step 6). Otherwise go to Step 5).

5) Estimate the position of the son feature according to Equation 7.

$$P_s = P_f + lR(\theta)$$
$$R(\theta) = [\cos(\theta) \ \sin(\theta)]^T .$$

(7)

where P_s and P_f are the position of the son feature and parent feature each, l is the length of the recorded vector, θ is the direction of the vector and $R(\theta)$ is the rotation matrix.

6) Grant the son feature as *certain feature* and features with the seed feature as the son feature can be verified similarly. If all the features are verified, stop; otherwise select other *certain feature* as the seed feature, go to Step 1).

6 Experiment

The algorithm is implemented in our video based human animation system VBHA, and is tested on a PC equipped with CPU PIII 550 and Memory 128M.Three motion clips, namely *walk*, *jump up* and *jump forward*, are selected for experiment. Self-occlusion is frequency in *walk*, and *jump up* and *jump forward* are rapid.

Firstly, the experiment is conducted without manual correction. The result is shown in Table 1. The miss rate of candidate features is defined as the ratio of the number of features missed from the candidate feature to that of all the features. As shown in Table 1, self-occlusion is frequency in *walk*, resulting in the high candidate feature miss rate. Though *jump up* and *jump forward* are rapid, their candidate feature miss rate is relatively low. All these show that in our algorithm the critical factor for candidate feature missing is self-occlusion, but not motion speed. These demonstrate the effectiveness of the weak prediction and the overall search strategy.

As the adaptive Bayes classifier and hierarchical human feature table are updated dynamically, the previous tracking results have important effect on the successive procedure. If manual correction is introduced into the tracking, the effectiveness of the algorithm can be improved remarkably (See Table 2).

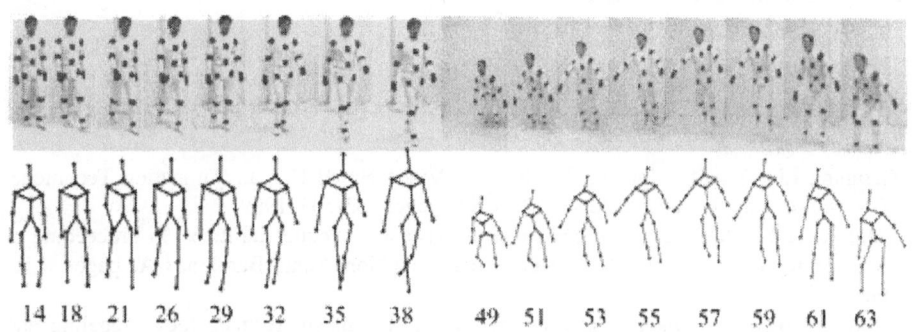

14 18   21   26   29   32   35   38   49 51   53   55   57   59   61   63

Fig. 3. Video and track result. The left sequence shows the original and track result of *Walk* and the right shows the original and track result of *Jump forward*

Table 1. Algorithm performance without manual correction

Motion	Labeled frames(f)	Tracked frames(f)	Miss rate of candidate features	Error rate	Speed (f/m)
Walk	8	120	1.50%	1.85%	76.0
Jump up	8	100	1.00%	1.34%	70.5
Jump forward	6	60	1.25%	1.56%	73.2

Table 2. Algorithm Performance with Manual Correction

Motion	Labeled frames(f)	Tracked frames(f)	Correction rate	Miss rate of candidate features	Error rate
Walk	8	120	0.52%	1.50%	1.65%
Jump up	8	100	0.63%	1.00%	1.24%
Jump forward	6	60	0.73%	1.25%	1.36%

7 Conclusion

Visual human motion track is always a challenge. Current algorithms are not capable of tracking rapid motions with self-occlusion: features with rapid motion are beyond small region search, and the position of the occluded feature is hard to be estimated. Even after occlusion is cleared, the occluded features are difficult to be captured again, for the uncertainty of interest-region. To overcome these problems, we propose a robust algorithm in this paper. Instead of predicting the position of each feature, the interest-region of full body is estimated. Then candidate features are extracted through the multi-resolution search. To establish the correspondence between candidate features and actual features, an adaptive Bayes classifier is constructed based on the time-varied models of feature attributes. At last, a hierarchical human feature model is adopted to verify and accomplish the feature correspondence. The experiment shows the effectiveness of our algorithm.

Acknowledgement. This work is sponsored by the National Natural Science Foundation of China, Foundation of Education Ministry for Excellent Young Teacher, College Key Teacher Supporting Plan and Doctorate Research Foundation of the State Education Commission of China.

References

1. Xiaoming Liu, Yueting Zhuang, Yunhe Pan. Video Based Human Animation Technique. ACM Multimedia'99 10/99 Orlando, FL, USA, pages 353-362, 1999.
2. C.Bregler and J.Malik. Tracking people with twists and exponential maps. In Proceeding of IEEE Conference Computer Vision Pattern Recognition, Santa Barbara, CA, pages 8-15, June 1998
3. P.Fua, A.Gruen, R.Plankers, N.D'Apuzzo, and D.Thalmann. Human body modeling and motion analysis form video sequences, in International Archives of Photogrammetry and Remote Sensing, vol, 32, pages 866-873, Hakodate, Jap, 1998
4. S.S.Intille and A.F.Bobick. Closed world tracking. In Proceedings of the Fifth International Conference on Computer Vision, pages 672-678, Boston, MA, June 20-23,1995, IEEE Computer Society Press
5. J.Rehg and T.Kanade. Model-based tracking of self-occluding articulated objects. In Proceedings of the Fifth International Conference on Computer Vision, pages 612-617, Boston, MA, June 20-23,1995, IEEE Computer Society Press
6. Moeslund, T. B. and E. Granum: 2001, A survey of computer vision-based human motion capture. Computer Vision and Image Understanding 18, 231-268.
7. Luo Zhongxiang, Zhuang Yueting and Liu Feng. Incomplete Motion Feature Tracking Algorithm in Video Sequences. ICIP 2002.
8. F. Sebastian Grassia, Motion Editing: Mathematical Foundations, in course: Motion Editing: Principles, Practice, and Promise, in Proceedings of SIGGRAPH 2000, July 23-28, 2000. New Orleans, Louisiana, USA

Estimating Head Pose from Spherical Image
for VR Environment

Shigang Li and Norishige Chiba

Faculty of Engineering, Iwate University
4-3-5 Ueda, Morioka, 020-8551, Japan
{li, nchiba}@cis.iwate-u.ac.jp

Abstract. In order to estimate a user's head pose at a relative large scale environment for virtual reality (VR) applications, multiple cameras set around him/her are used in conventional approaches, such as a motion capture. This paper proposes a method of estimating head pose from spherical images. A user wears a helmet on which a visual sensor is mounted and the head pose can be estimated by observing the fiducial markers put around him/her. Since a spherical image has a full view, our method can cope with a big head rotation motion compared with a normal camera. Since a head pose at every time is directly estimated from the observed markers, there is no accumulated errors in our method compared with a inertial sensor. Currently, an omnidirectional image sensor is used to acquire the most part of a spherical image in our experiment.

1 Introduction

Mixed Reality includes virtual reality and augmented reality. In virtual environment, virtual 3D world models are made by computer graphics or image-based technologies. Augmented Reality superimposes virtual 3D models on the real world [5]. In order to superimpose the virtual objects on the right place as if they really exist in the real world, it is needed to estimate the relative arrangement of the coordinate system of a real camera and that of a virtual camera. This task is called Geometrical Registration. Computer vision approaches are applied to this aspect widely [5,7,8].

Here, we consider a human wanders around a environment which is wholly or partially replaced virtually. In order to let the human see a virtual scene which is consistent with his head movement, we need to estimate the head pose. What we have to do is to map a real head motion to a virtually changed environment correctly. Inertial sensor mounted on a helmet is used to acquire the information of head motion conventionally. However, it suffers from accumulated error so that human may see a different scene relative to his motion. In this paper, we propose a method of estimating head pose from spherical images. We put fiducial markers around the room which is to be changed virtually, and use an omnidirectional image sensor to observe these markers. A spherical image is transformed from the omnidirectional image sensor.

Why do we use a spherical image?

Y.-C. Chen, L.-W. Chang, and C.-T. Hsu (Eds.): PCM 2002, LNCS 2532, pp. 1169–1176, 2002.
© Springer-Verlag Berlin Heidelberg 2002

- Since we suppose a user wanders in a relative large scale range, multiple cameras set around him/her are used to cover the large range in conventional approaches, such as a motion capture, as shown in Figure 1(a). By using spherical image, the markers around the user are alwayes viewed in it so that the user's head pose can be estimated from a spherical image even he/she moves in a relative large scale range, as shown in Figure 1(b).
- A spherical image has a full view. When a user with a spherical images sensor on his helmet wonders in a room, the fiducial markers can viewed even if there is a big head rotation.
- Motion parallax appears in the opposite direction of camera motion. Using an omnidirectional image, we can acquire all motion parallax in every direction.
- From our living experience, a human being looks around when he/she wants to determine his/her place by using objects surrounding him/her. It is because the error can be reduced from objects in a wider view than in a narrow view as shown in Figure 1(c). A wide view contains more information and makes it possible to select more optimal reference objects [10].

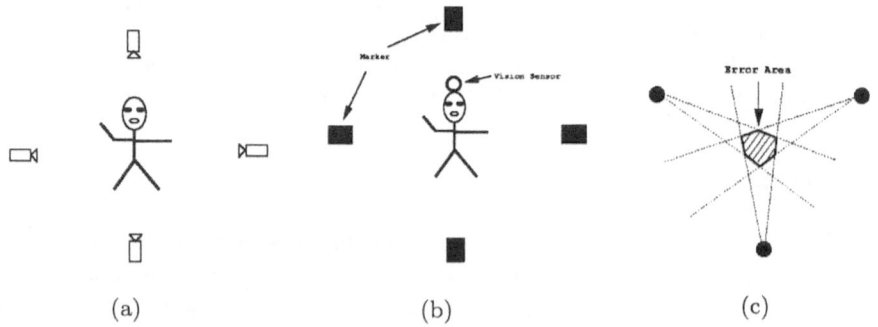

(a)   (b)   (c)

Fig. 1. Using multiple cameras (a), or, a spherical image (b) to cope with a user's movement in a relative large scale range. (c) Position can be determined more accurately by observing surrounding objects.

A spherical image has been used for object recognition [6], motion estimation [13] and etc. . However, it is difficult to obtain a real spherical image sensor with real time rate (30 frame per second); especially, it must be small enough to be wearable in our case. In this paper, we use an omnidirection image sensor to acquire the most part of a spherical image

Omnidirectional image sensors are used widely in telepresence, 3D reconstruction [9,2], autonomous navigation, such as, obstacle avoidance[15]. The omnidirectional images can acquired using a convex paraboloidal mirror [12], a convex hyperbolic mirror [15] and a fish-eye camera or by rotating a camera. Besides the advantage of omnidirectional images in robot navigation, such as obstacle avoidance [15], and construction of 3D model for virtual reality [2,11], it also has advantages in camera motion estimation [10].

Camera motion and environment structure can be computed from image sequences. This problem is called *structure from motion* in computer vision aspect. Estimating camera motion from an omnidirectional sensor is researched widely in robot vision. However, it is difficult to obtain robust and accurate results for estimating structure and motion simultaneously. In [1], method of beacon-based pose estimation (using small bright light bulbs) is proposed to reconstruct 3D interactive walkthrough. In their case, however, only a rotation is considered and the markers are placed only on two straight vertical posts so that the wide view of omnidirectional image cannot be served for a more accurate motion estimation as shown in Figure 1(c). Contrasting with [1,2], there are following characteristics in our research.

- We use an omnidirectional image sensor to acquire the most part of a spherical image. As a different objective, we map head pose to a virtual environment for immersive mixed reality.
- In our case, there are no constraints on the head motion. That is that we estimate three rotational components and three translational components.
- we present a new method of determining head motion from spherical images, which is generated from an omnidirectional image sensor and independent of its type.

The rest of the paper is organized as follows. We give basic assumptions for this research in setion 2. Section 3 present the algorithm of estimating camera pose from omnidirectional images. Section 4 present how to map the estimated motion to virtual environments. Section 5 present our preliminary experimental results. Finally, we conclude and present future work in the last section.

2   Assumptions on Environments

Suppose a user wants to replace his/her room virtually and wanders around a room to see what it will be like. The user wears a helmet mounted with an omnidirectional image sensor as shown in Figure 2(a) and sees the virtually replaced room through a Head Mounted Display. The followings are the basic assumptions for our research.

- The user wanders freely in a virtual reality environments, which can be a flat floor in indoor environments or a vacant land. The user's head motion (almost the same with camera motion) is represented by three rotation components and three translation components.
- We put red patterns on the wall as markers, as shown in Figure 2(b). These markers determine a new plane. We set the world coordinate system, $O - XYZ$, with its X and Y axis parallel with the floor and its Z-axis perpendicular to it.
- In our research, we use an omnidirectional camera sensor, called HyperOmni Vision [15] as shown in Figure 3(a), to acquire the most part of a spherical image. Any other type of omnidirectional image sensor [12] can also be used in our research. Our method is independent of the types of omnidirectional image sensors.

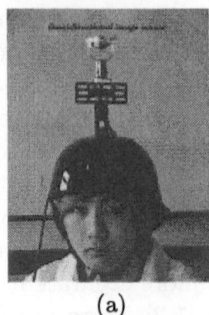
(a)

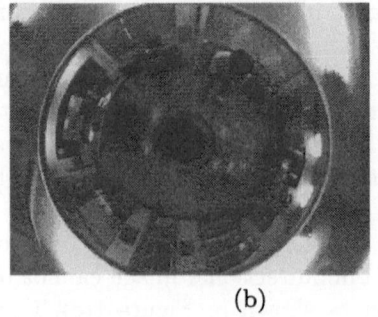
(b)

Fig. 2. (a) Our device (on the left). (b) A sample image acquired from the sensor where the red square patterns used as markers are put surrounding the wall of a room.

3   Estimating Pose Using Markers

3.1   Basic Equations for Spherical Images

We put the markers around the environment. While the head moves, the position of markers in the omnidirectional image changes. In order to cope with a big head motion, we use a spherical image to represent the marker position, which is transformed from an omnidirectional image. Next, we will explain how to estimate the head pose from the virtual spherical image.

As shown in Figure 3(b), suppose the 3D coordinate of a marker at the spherical image coordinate system, O_c, is $M_c = \begin{bmatrix} X_c \ Y_c \ Z_c \end{bmatrix}$. The position projected at the spherical image is $m = \begin{bmatrix} \rho sin\theta cos\phi \ \rho sin\theta sin\phi \ \rho cos\theta \end{bmatrix} = \begin{bmatrix} u \ v \ q \end{bmatrix}$ There is the following relation between the both.

$$m \overset{.}{=} M_c$$

This means that m is equal to M_c apart from a scalar factor.

3.2   Equation for Single Marker

Suppose the coordinate of the marker at the world coordinate system, O_w, is $\tilde{M}_w = \begin{bmatrix} X_w \ Y_w \ Z_w \ 1 \end{bmatrix}$ (Z_w is zero in our case as explained in section 2.). If O_w can be aligned with O_c by a rotational motion, $R = [r_1^T \ r_2^T \ r_3^T]$ (here r_i is the ith row vector of R), and a translation motion, $T = [t_x \ t_y \ t_z]^T$, that is

$$M_c = [R \ T]\tilde{M}_w$$

Thus, our goal (estimating head pose) is to determine the R and T from the marker position measured at the world coordinate system and its position projected on the spherical image.

For one marker, we can have the following two equations.

$$q_i r_1^T M_{wi} - u_i r_3^T M_{wi} + q_i t_x - u_i t_z = 0$$
$$q_i r_2^T M_{wi} - v_i r_3^T M_{wi} + q_i t_y - v_i t_z = 0$$

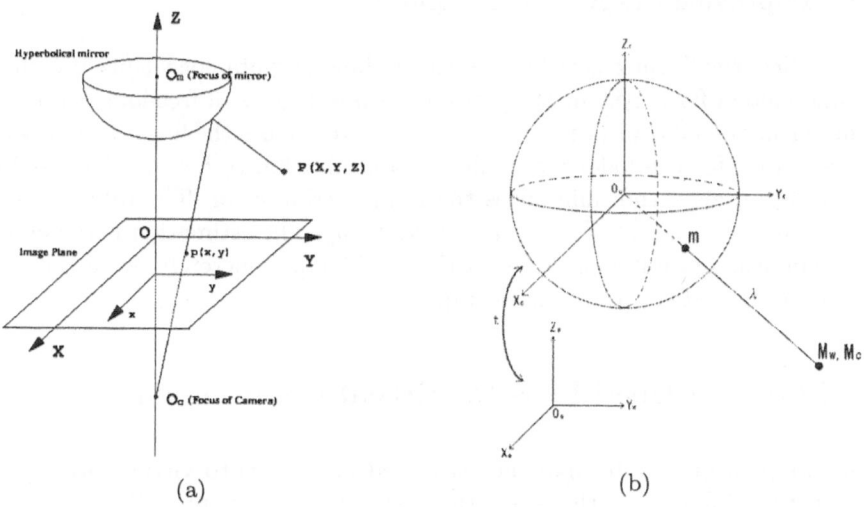

Fig. 3. (a) The HyperOmni Vision sensor. (b) Using a spherical image to represent marker position.

3.3   Equations for Multiple Markers

If we have n markers, we can have the following equations.

$$Bp = 0.$$

Where

$$p = \begin{bmatrix} r_1^T & t_x & r_2^T & t_y & r_3^T & t_z \end{bmatrix}^T$$

and

$$B = \begin{bmatrix} q_1 X_1 & q_1 Y_1 & q_1 Z_1 & q_1 & 0 & 0 & 0 & 0 & -u_1 X_1 & -u_1 Y_1 & -u_1 Z_1 & -u_1 \\ 0 & 0 & 0 & 0 & q_1 X_1 & q_1 Y_1 & q_1 Z_1 & q_1 & -v_1 X_1 & -v_1 Y_1 & -v_1 Z_1 & -v_1 \\ \vdots & \vdots & \vdots & \vdots & \vdots & \vdots & \vdots & \vdots & \vdots & \vdots & \vdots & \vdots \\ q_n X_n & q_n Y_n & q_n Z_n & q_n & 0 & 0 & 0 & 0 & -u_n X_n & -u_n Y_n & -u_n Z_n & -u_n \\ 0 & 0 & 0 & 0 & q_n X_n & q_n Y_n & q_n Z_n & q_n & -v_n X_n & -v_n Y_n & -v_n Z_n & -v_n \end{bmatrix}$$

Since the translation components can only be determined apart from a scale factor from an image, the above equations can be solved if there are more than 6 markers.

Actually, p can be obtained as the eigenvector corresponding to the smallest eigenvalue of $B^T B$. This scale factor can be determined uniquely since the r_1, r_2, r_3 have unit norm.

3.4   Improving the Answer's Accuracy

In practice, the linear algorithm described above is quite noisy since it estimates 12 parameters for a system of equations with 6 degrees of freedom, 3 rotational components and 3 translation components. Here, we use the linear estimate as an initialization for the following nonlinear optimization technique. The nonlinear optimization algorithm minimizes the re-projection error. The rotation matrix is parameterized by ZYX-Euler angles $\theta_1, \theta_2, \theta_3$. The estimation parameters for the nonlinear optimization are $\beta = [\theta_1 \theta_2 \theta_3 t_x t_y t_z]$. Concretely, we use Newton-Raphson method to solve it as in [14].

4   Mapping Head Pose to Virtual Environment

Next we present how to map the estimated head pose to virtual environment. As shown in Figure 4, there are three coordinate systems. W_o indicates the coordinate system of the omnidirectional image sensor for the head pose; W_m indicates that of the real environment determined by the markers' position, and W_v indicates that of the virtual environment. The relation between W_o and W_m, M_{om}, is determined from observed markers' position by the method mentioned above while the relation between the real environment (W_m) and the virtual environment (W_v), M_{mv}, is given by humans. Therefore, we can have the corresponding view of a virtual environment from the estimated head pose using the markers in a real environment.

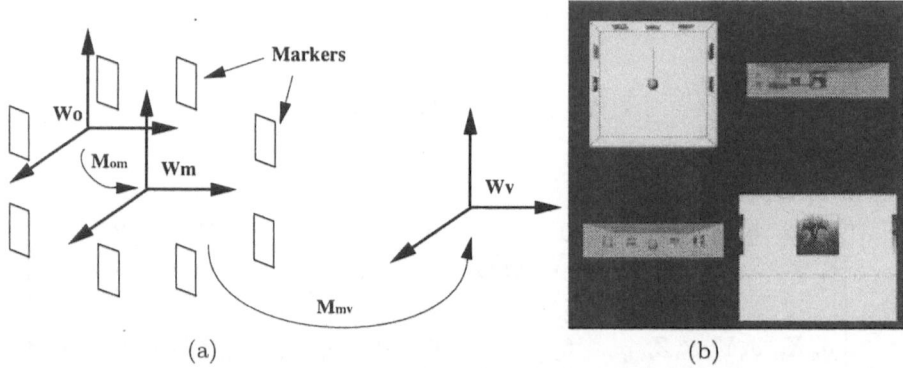

(a)   (b)

Fig. 4. (a) Mapping head pose to a virtual environment. (b)The window of the virtual environment, a gallery, used in our experiment includes a top view (on the upper left), side views (on the upper right and on the lower left) and a view from a virtual camera (on the lower right).

5   Experiments

We carried out an experiment in a real indoor environment. The eight markers, red square patterns, were, put around the wall of our lab with the same height from the floor, as shown in Figure 2(b). The coordinate system of the real environment was set in the plane of the markers with its X and Y axis in this plane and its Z-axis perpendicular to it. The coordinate values of the eight markers were measured by humans. A catadioptric omnidirectional image sensor as in [15] were used, as shown in 2(a). The virtual environment, a gallery, is shown in Figure 4(b).

   We first computed the color constancy of the omnidirctional image. Then, the image was transformed into a binary images. Further, we labeled the binary image and computed the gravity center of pattern as the markers' position, as shown in Figure 5 where the gravity center is indicated by a '+'. Finally, we use the markers' position in the images to estimate the head pose and gave the corresponding view of the virtual environment. The view, which corresponds to the head pose of an observer in Figure 2(b), of the virtual environment was displayed and input to the head mount display of the observer, as shown in Figure5(b). Therefore, when the observer wandered in the room of our lab, he/she can saw the view of the gallery, as if he/she wandered in the gallery.

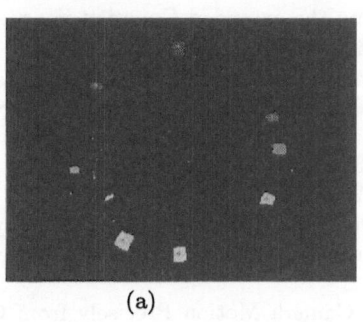

(a)   (b)

Fig. 5. (a) The found marker patterns in the image. (b) The view of the virtual environment displayed according to the corresponding head pose of an observer.

   In order to evaluate the accuracy of of the estimated camera pose, we mounted the sensor on a mobile robot, Nomad200, and moved it around the floor. For the rotation around Z-axis, which is perpendicular to the floor, the measured error by using our method is less than 0.5 degree. As for the other parameters, we have not still evaluated them quantitatively.

6   Conclusions and Future Work

This paper proposes a method for estimating the head pose based upon vision approaches. We put fiducial markers around a room which is to be changed virtually, and use an omnidirectional image sensor to observe these markers.

Evaluating the computation accuracy of the parameters of head pose quantitatively and the usability of our device are our future work.

References

1. Daniel G. Aliaga: Accurate Catadioptric Calibration for Real-time Pose Estimation in Room-size Environment, Proc. of IEEE Computer Vision, 2001.
2. Daniel G. Aliaga and I. Carlbom: Plenoptic Stitching: A Scalable Method for Reconstructing 3D Interactive Walkthroughs, Computer Graphics, ACM SIG-GRAPH'2001.
3. S.E. Chen: QuickTime VR - An Image-Based Approach to Virtual Environment Navigation, Computer Graphics, ACM SIGGRAPH'1995.
4. J. Gluckman and S. Nayar: Ego-Motion and Omnidirectional Cameras, Proc. of Computer Vision, pp.999-1005, 1998.
5. N.Heddley, L.Postner, R.May, M.Billinghurs, H.Kato: Collaborative AR for Geographic Visualization, Proc. of International Symposium on Mixed Reality, pp.11-18, 2001.
6. K. Ikeuchi: Recognition of 3-D objects using the extended Gaussian image, Proc. of Int. Joint Conf. Artif. Intell. 7, pp.595-600, 1981.
7. M.Kanbara, H.Fujii, H.Takemura and N.Yokoya: A Stereo Vision-based Mixed Reality System with Natural Feature Point Tracking, Proc. of International Symposium on Mixed Reality, pp.56-63, 2001.
8. S. B. Kang: Hands-free navigation in VR environments by tracking the head, Human-Computer Studies, vol.49, pp.247-266, 1998.
9. H.Kawasaki, T.Yatabe, K.Ikeuchi and M. Sakauchi: Construction of a 3D City Map Using EPI Analysis and DP Matching, Proc. of Asian Conference on Computer Vision, 2000.
10. S. Li, M. Chiba and S. Tsuji: Estimating Camera Motion Precisely from Omni-Directional Images, IEEE/RSJ/GI Intl. Conf. on Intelligent Robot and Systems, pp.1126-1132, 1994.
11. L. McMillan and G. Bishop: Plenoptic Modeling: An Image-Based Rendering System, Computer Graphics, ACM SIGGRAPH'1995.
12. S. Nayar: Catadioptric Omnidirectional Camera, Proc. of Computer Vision and Pattern Recognition, pp.482-488, 1997.
13. R.C. Nelson: Finding motion parameters from spherical flow fields, IEEE Workshop on Visual Motion, pp.145-150, 1987.
14. C. Sharp, O. Shakernia and S. Sastry: A vision system for landing an unmanned aerial vehicle, Proc. of IEEE International Conference on Robotics and Automation, pp.1720-1727, 2001.
15. Y. Yagi, W. Nishizawa, K. Yamazawa and M. Yachida: Rolling Motion Estimation for Mobile Robot by Using Omnidirectional Image Sensor HyperOmniVision, Proc. of Pattern Recognition, pp.946-950,1996.

An Efficient Algorithm for Detecting Faces from Color Images

Shou-Der Wei and Shang-Hong Lai

Dept. of Computer Science, National Tsing Hua University, Hsinchu, Taiwan
lai@cs.nthu.edu.tw

Abstract. In this paper, we propose an efficient face detection algorithm based on integrating multiple features in face images. The proposed algorithm combines many simple methods to achieve a reasonable detection rate with an acceptable false alarm rate. There are four main components in our face detection algorithm; namely, skin-color filtering, face template search, face verification and overlapped-detection merging. A skin-color filtering process is first applied to eliminate image regions with corresponding color distributions unlikely to be face regions. For regions passing the skin-color test, we find the face candidates by a hierarchical nearest-neighbor search of multiple face templates under a limited range of geometric transformations. Subsequently, the face candidates are further checked via some face verification criteria, which are derived from the face symmetry property and the relatively positional constrains of facial features. Finally, the overlapped face candidate regions are merged to obtain the final face detection results.

1 Introduction

Face detection is usually the first step of many face-processing tasks. These face-processing tasks, including face recognition, face tracking, pose estimation, face feature extraction, and face expression recognition, usually assume the faces in an image have been detected. These face-processing tasks have many applications on surveillance and security.

There are many approaches proposed in the past for face detection [1]. Sung and Poggio[2] developed a distribution-based face detection system. They modeled the probability distributions of face patterns and the non-face patterns that are also close to face templates by mixture of Gaussians. Finally, they used an MLP network to be the face classifier. Rowley et al. [3] trained a multi-layer neural network to detect faces with excellent performance. In their system, there are three types of hidden units to extract facial features, such as eyes, noses, and mouth. Recently, Viola and Jones [4] developed a fast face detection algorithm that can detect faces from images at 15 frames per second. They used a simple type of features that were computed from an integral image, which can speed up the feature computation. They combined a number of automatically selected weak classifiers to accomplish the face detection task. Each

Y.-C. Chen, L.-W. Chang, and C.-T. Hsu (Eds.): PCM 2002, LNCS 2532, pp. 1177-1184, 2002.

classifier was trained from all the face and non-face examples for a feature via an AdaBoost algorithm. Finally, they combined all the classifiers in a cascade structure to increase the detection speed.

Since face is not a rigid object and its appearance is very different due to variations in poses, scales, illuminations and expressions. In this paper, we focus on the detection of frontal faces from color images. An efficient face detection algorithm is proposed by combining multiple face detection components. At first, we apply a skin color segmentation method to find skin-color regions, and then we detect faces on these skin color regions. This pre-filtering process helps to improve the speed of face detection. We collect many face images and use these face samples to compute several representative face templates. To accommodate the variations in illumination, we used the relative image gradient for the feature computation. A hierarchical nearest-neighbor search technique is applied to search the multiple face templates from the skin-color-filtered image regions. Subsequently, a face verification process is used to reduce the number of false detection. Finally, the overlapped regions of candidate faces are merged to obtain the detection results.

2 Skin-Color Filtering

To build the skin-color filter, we collect more than 4000 samples selected from a number of skin regions from a variety of Asian face images. We project these color samples onto the normalized red-green color space. Figure 1(a) shows the skin-color distribution of all these samples. We used rectangles to approximate the skin-color distribution for the performance of speed in skin-color filtering. To improve the accuracy of the skin-color segmentation, we decompose the distribution of these skin-color samples based on their brightness values and model the corresponding distributions by rectangles for different brightness levels. Figures 1(b) and 1(c) show an example of the result applying the skin-color filter.

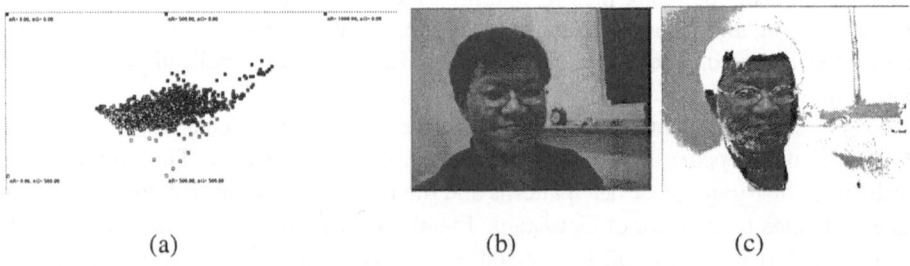

(a)   (b)   (c)

Fig. 1. (a) The distribution of all skin color samples in a normalized color coordinate. (b) An original test image and (b) the result of skin-color filtering.

3   Face Template Search

Our face template search algorithm consists of two phases, namely training phase and execution phase. In the training phase, we compute face features from all the collected face images in the training database and then cluster these extracted feature vectors. The mean of all the feature vectors in each cluster corresponds to a face template. In the execution phase, the system will move a 40x40 window all over the input image to identify if the windowed image is a face or not. Each windowed image is first examined by the skin-color filtering process to see if there are enough skin-color pixels in the window. Only the windows with skin-color pixels greater than a pre-defined threshold are passed from the skin-color filtering test and fed into the next stage.

The training phase involves the generation of templates from face database, enlarging templates to double the size with the step of factor 0.1, and organizing all these templates to Hierarchical Nearest Neighbor Network [5-7]. The templates that we used were trained from the collected face database. Because the sizes of collected faces are different, we first re-size all faces to a 40x40 window, and then compute a feature vector for each face. The feature vector is computed by concatenating the 2D image into a 1D array, subtracting all elements in this 1D array by their mean, and normalizing the mean-subtracted array with its 2-norm. In other words, the feature computation involves an intensity normalization process to alleviate the problem due to lighting variations. This intensity normalization is described by the following equation.

$$f(x,y) = \frac{I(x,y) - \bar{I})}{\sqrt{\sum (I(x,y) - \bar{I})^2} + c} \tag{1}$$

where $f(x,y)$ is the feature, $I(x,y)$ is the windowed image to be determined if it contains a face, and $\bar{I}$ is the mean of $I(x,y)$. The constant c is used to avoid dividing by zero.

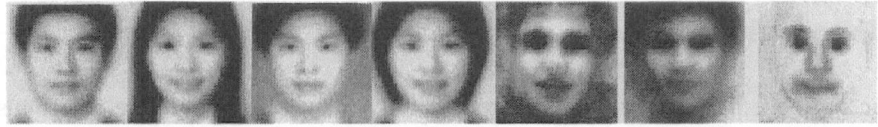

Fig. 2. Some face templates computed from the training face images.

After the feature vectors for all the training face images are computed, we employ the FCM (fuzzy c means) algorithm to classify the extracted features into 16 clusters and the means of these clusters are the face templates. Figure 2 shows some face templates computed by this process.

We adopt the learning-based pattern search strategy for the search of multiple-templates in images [5]. In the learning-based pattern search described in [5], we have used the sub-template window inside the original template for the HNN search. To speed up the face template search, we move the sub-template window on the face template image to extract features for each different sampled translation. The dash window in Figure 3 is sub-template with size of 22x22. The range of translation is from -2 to +2 pixels in x and y directions.

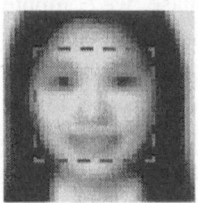

Fig. 3. The dash window on face template is the sub-template window.

For searching faces of different scales, we enlarge the templates to double the template size by the step of factor 10% in the HNNN training phase. We employ a HNN network to facilitate efficient template search of multiple templates under different small geometric transformations. To construct the HNN network, we collect the feature vectors computed from the face images synthesized from all the face templates with selected geometric transformations. The geometric transformation consists of translation, rotation and scaling.

We extract features from the skin-color-filtered face candidate region, and compare the extracted feature vector with the feature vectors in HNNN to find the nearest feature sample. If the comparison is less than a given threshold, the region will be treated as a face candidate again. These face candidates will be verified in the next verification step.

For detecting faces at different scales, the input image is down-sampled by two along x and y directions recursively. The moving window of a fixed size is moved all over the original and down-sampled images to check if it contains a face.

4   Face Verification

After the above face template search process, there may exists many false detections. It is necessary to have a face verification process to reduce the number of false alarms. In this paper, we have applied two different types of verification methods. One is a complete-face comparison procedure and the other is a combination of local face region analysis. We describe the details of these two different verification methods in the following.

4.1   Complete Face Comparison

The HNN search the best match from the hierarchical nearest-neighbor network, which contains the feature vectors of multiple face templates under a number of geometric transformations with the transformation parameters distributed in a limited range. We show an example of face template search in Figure 4. We can get complete image piece from the associated transformation parameters of the matched feature vector in the training database. Then the feature vector computed from the corresponding complete face window can be computed for further verification.

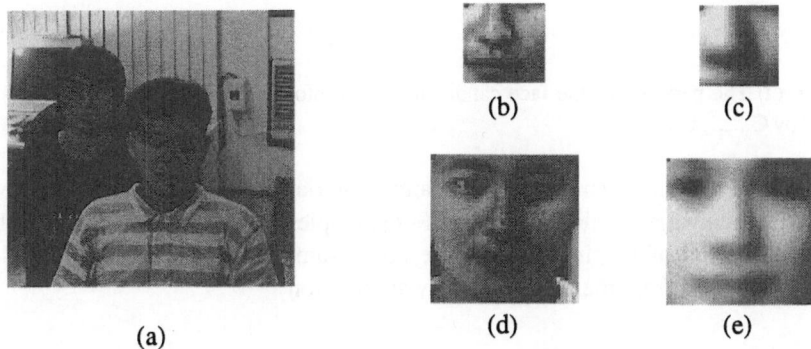

(b)   (c)

(a)   (d)   (e)

Fig. 4. (a) Input Image. (b) A detected face region with the corresponding face template sample shown in (c). (d) & (e) show the images for complete face comparison.

4.2 Local Face Region Analysis

For increasing detection rate, we use loose thresholds in the previous face search procedures to identify faces. The loose thresholds will cause many false alarms. To reduce false alarms, we apply many verification criteria from human face characteristics, like the locations of face features and the symmetry of face. We divided the face candidate region into 9 blocks and calculate the summation of the gray value of pixels in each block. In Figure 5 each block is associated with a variable that indicates the summation of gray values in each block.

The row sums in the 3x3 blocks are denoted by IR1, IR2, and IR3. To be more specific, they are defined as

$$IR_1 = C_0 + C_1 + C_2 \tag{2}$$

$$IR_2 = C_3 + C_4 + C_5 \tag{3}$$

$$IR_3 = C_6 + C_7 + C_8 \tag{4}$$

In addition, we also check the face candidate regions from their edge density distributions. We first apply Sobel edge detection and simple thresholding on the face candidate region to get the edge map. Then we divide the edge map into 6 blocks and 9 blocks, respectively, and compute the total number of edge pixels of each block.

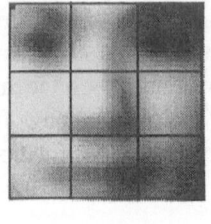

C_0	C_1	C_2
C_3	C_4	C_5
C_6	C_7	C_8

(a)   (b)

Fig. 5. (a) The partition of the face candidate region into 3x3 blocks. (b) These blocks are denoted by C_0, ..., C_8.

We have defined several face verification criteria based on the relationship between the face block variables defined above. For example, one of the criteria is that the ratio between the left and right column edge count sums should be within a fixed range, which is derived from the face symmetry assumption

5 Merging Overlapped Face Candidate Regions

After the step of template matching and verification, some faces are detected with multiple overlapped windows as shown in Figure 6. To define the overlapping between two windows, we compute the center of each box that contain a face and compare it to other boxes. If the distance between the two centers are less than half the box width of either one, then we define there is a significant overlap between the two boxes. When a significant overlap between two boxes is detected, we will eliminate the box that has higher distance with its corresponding template in the complete template comparison result.

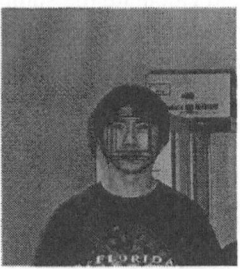

Fig. 6. The face was detected with multiple overlapped windows after the template matching and verification procedure

6 Experimental Results

To build a test set for face detection, we collect about 210 images that contain 342 faces from Internet. Our face templates are trained from the other face data set that contains approximately 1500 face images. We tried different combinations of verification criteria in the face verification procedure in our experiments. Table 1 summarizes the detection precision and total number of false alarms in the experiments of using the proposed algorithm with different combinations of verification criteria. The more criteria are added in the face verification, the less the false alarms are produced. However, the detection rate also decreases with the number of false alarms. A correct face detection is defined when the deviation between the detected face center and manually labeled face center is less than four pixels in both x and y directions. A good compromised setting can achieve more than 80% detection rate with less than half a false alarm per image in average.

Table 1. The results of detecting faces on the test image set with different combination of verification criteria. The total number of faces in the test image set is 342.

Criterion No.	Detected faces	Detection rate	False alarms
1 8 9 10 12	300	87.71	191
1 2 3 8 9 12	279	81.57	132
1 2 3 8 9 10 11 12	277	80.99	93
1 2 3 4 5 8 9 10 11 12	212	61.98	43

Fig. 7. Examples of face detection results by using the proposed algorithm.

7 Conclusions

In this paper, we presented an integrated face detection algorithm. Our face detection algorithm combined many simple methods to achieve reasonable detection rate with acceptable false alarm rates. It is easy to implement our face detection algorithm and the computation involved in our face detection algorithm is not complicated. In this paper, we focused on the detection of frontal faces. Many criteria that we used in face verification are derived from the assumption of face symmetry and the relatively positional constrains of facial features. In our experiments, some false alarms occurred on non-frontal-view faces. In the future, we plan to generalize the current algorithm to detect non-frontal faces by including more face templates under different poses and using more general criteria for non-frontal faces.

Acknowledgements. This research was jointly supported by the Program for Promoting Academic Excellence of Universities (89-E-FA04-1-4), National Science Council (project code: 90-2213-E-007-037), Taiwan, R.O.C., and Ulead Inc.

References

1. Yang, M.H., Kriegman, D., Ahuja, N.: Detecting Faces in Images: A Survey. IEEE Trans. Pattern Analysis Machine Intelligence. 24(1) (2002) 34-58
2. Sung, K.-K., Poggio, T.: Example-based Learning for View-Based Human Face Detection. IEEE Trans. Pattern Analysis Machine Inteilligence 20 (1998) 39-51
3. Rowley, H., Baluja, S., Kanade, T.: Neural Network-Based Face Detection. IEEE Trans. Pattern Analysis Machine Intelligence. 20(1) (1998) 23-38
4. Viola, P., Jones, M.: Rapid Object Detection using a Boosted Cascade of Simple Features. Proc. of Computer Vision and Pattern Recognition. Vol. 1, Kauai, HI. (2001) 511-518
5. Lai, S.-H., Fang, M.: A Hybrid Image Alignment System for Fast and Precise Pattern Localization. Real-Time Imaging. 8 (2002) 23-33

An Illumination-Insensitive Face Matching Algorithm

Chyuan-Huei Thomas Yang, Shang-Hong Lai, and Long-Wen Chang

Department of Computer Science, National Tsing-Hua University
101, Kuang Fu Rd, Sec.2, HsingChu, Taiwan 300 R.O.C
{dr868310,lai,lchang}@cs.nthu.edu.tw

Abstract. Face matching is an essential step for face recognition and face verification. It is difficult to achieve robust face matching under various image acquisition conditions. In this paper, an illumination-insensitive face image-
matching algorithm is proposed. This algorithm is based on an accumulated
consistency measure of corresponding normalized gradients at face contour locations between two comparing face images under different lighting conditions.
To solve the matching problem due to lighting changes between two face images, we first use a consistency measure, which is defined by the inner product
between two normalized gradient vectors at the corresponding locations in the
two images. Then we compute the sum of the individual consistency measures
of the normalized gradients at all the contour pixels to be the robust matching
measure between two face images. To better compensate for lighting variations,
three face images with very different lighting directions for each person are used
for robust face image matching. The Yale Face Database, which contains images acquired under three different lighting conditions for each person, are used
to test the proposed algorithm. The experimental results show good recognition
results under different lighting conditions by using the proposed illumination-
insensitive face matching algorithm.

1 Introduction

Face matching is an essential step for face recognition and face verification. A practical face recognition system should be working under different imaging conditions,
such as head pose variations, different viewing angles, different lighting conditions,
and expression changes. It is a challenging problem to achieve robust face matching
under all kinds of different face imaging variations. In this paper, we particularly
focus on robust face matching under different illumination conditions. Several methods have been proposed to achieve robust face recognition under different illumination
conditions. They can be roughly classified into the feature-based approach
[3,9,13,14,16], the appearance-based approach [1,2,6-8,10,11,17], and a mixed approach [5,15]. In the feature-based approach, face feature points are extracted from
images and matched between different face images. For example, the points of maximum curvature or inflection points are extracted from the Gabor filtered images as the
face feature points. Then, the extracted face feature maps are used to compare the
similarity between different face images by computing the Hausdorff distance between
the corresponding feature point sets. In the appearance-based approach, the eigenface-

Y.-C. Chen, L.-W. Chang, and C.-T. Hsu (Eds.): PCM 2002, LNCS 2532, pp. 1185-1192, 2002.

based methods have been quite popular. Recently, Georghiades et al. [6-7] introduced an illumination cone model to represent images of the same person under all possible illumination conditions. In this work, they assumed a Lambertian surface model for human face. In another approach, an active appearance model [5] or labeled graphs [15] were used to represent and match face images.

In this paper, we propose an integrated method for robust face matching under different lighting conditions. It is based on matching locally normalized gradient vectors at the face contour locations between the input image and three reference face images under different lighting conditions. The rest of this paper is organized as follows. We describe the proposed illumination-insensitive face-matching algorithm in the next section. Then we show some experimental results in section 3. Some conclusions are given in the final section.

2   Proposed Illumination-Insensitive Face Matching Algorithm

The main idea of the proposed face matching method is based on finding the best integrated consistency between corresponding relative gradients of face images along the face edge contours [16]. This contour integral is maximal for a correct face match. In this paper, we generalize the above face matching approach to include multiple face images of the same person under different lighting conditions for more robust face matching. In this new matching algorithm, we compute the maximal matching value of the integrated consistency measure for normalized gradient computed from the multiple face images of the same person at contour locations, thus defining the matching score for the input face image with a specific person. The face pose variation problem has been also very important in many face recognition systems. This problem is partially relieved by the virtual view synthesis techniques [4]. Here we focus on the face image matching under different lighting conditions. Therefore, we assume that there is no change in face poses between face images.

To construct the proposed algorithm, we briefly describe the face matching approach based on the consistency between relative gradients [16]. Let I be a face image, and the pixels of the contour of the face are collected in a set Γ. This contour is extracted from a prototype face image by a standard edge detection method. If the face image and the face contour belong to the same person at the same pose, it is intuitive to assume the contour integral of the consistency measure between corresponding relative gradients of the face images is maximal. The geometric transformation between face images includes translation, rotation, and scaling, denoted by T. The paper [16] proposed the similarity measure based on the above idea. This image similarity measure is given as follows

$$E(I_0,T;I_p)=\frac{1}{|\Gamma|}\sum_{(i,j)\in\Gamma}\left|\frac{\nabla I_0(i,j)}{\max_{(k,l)\in W_{(i,j)}}\left|\nabla I_0(k,l)\right|+c}\bullet\frac{\nabla I_p(T(i,j))}{\max_{(k,l)\in W_{T(i,j)}}\left|\nabla I_p(k,l)\right|+c}\right| \qquad (1)$$

where I_p is the face template image, I_o is the image containing a face to be matched or the search image, and the symbol • is the inner product. Since the absolute value of the normalized inner product is between 0 and 1, the above normalized similarity measure is also between 0 and 1. The larger the value, the more similar the search face image is to the template face image.

To alleviate the problem due to shadow or intensity saturation, we assign smaller weights in the individual similarity measures for points with very bright or very dark intensity values. The modified similarity measure becomes

$$E(I_0, T; I_p) = \sum_{i,j \in \Gamma} \frac{\left| \frac{\nabla I_0(i,j)}{\max\limits_{(k,l) \in W_{(i,j)}} |\nabla I_0(k,l)| + c} \bullet \frac{\nabla I_p(T(i,j))}{\max\limits_{(k,l) \in W_{T(i,j)}} |\nabla I_p(k,l)| + c} \right| \tau(I_p(T(i,j)))}{\sum\limits_{i,j \in \Gamma} \tau(I_p(T(i,j)))} \qquad (2)$$

where the τ is the intensity weighting function given by

$$\tau(I) = \begin{cases} \sin\left(\dfrac{\pi}{2} * \dfrac{I}{I_{Lb}}\right) & \text{where} \quad 0 \le I < I_{Lb} \\ 1 & \text{where} \quad I_{Lb} \le I \le I_{Ub} \\ \cos\left(\dfrac{\pi}{2} * \dfrac{I - I_{Ub}}{255 - I_{Ub}}\right) & \text{where} \quad I_{Ub} < I \le 255 \end{cases} \qquad (3)$$

where I_{Lb} and I_{Ub} denote the lower bound and upper bound of the weight function. For pixels with intensity values closer to zero or 255, we assign smaller weights to them in the similarity measure. The normalization factor in the denominator of eq. (2) is the sum of all the weights at the transformed locations. With the use of this normalization factor, this modified similarity measure is normalized into the interval [0, 1]. The similarity measure given in eq. (2) is the normalized contour integral of the weighted consistency measure along the object contour. This measure is for comparing two images. Since we have multiple face images of the same person captured under different lighting conditions, we can generalize the face matching method as follows. Without loss of generality, we assume that there are three face images of the same person captured with center lighting condition, left lighting condition, and right lighting condition, which are denoted by I_1, I_2, and I_3, respectively. The consistency measure at a contour location is defined for I_0 with I_1, I_2, or I_3 as follows:

$$E_{i,j \in \Gamma}(I_0, T; I_p) = \left| \frac{\nabla I_0(T(i,j))}{\max\limits_{(k,l) \in W_{T(i,j)}} |\nabla I_0(k,l)| + c} \bullet \frac{\nabla I_p(i,j)}{\max\limits_{(k,l) \in W_{(i,j)}} |\nabla I_p(k,l)| + c} \right| \qquad (4)$$

where $p = 1, 2,$ and 3. Thus, we can generalize the previous similarity measure by using the best of the three consistency measure values as follows:

$$E(I_0,T;I_n,n=1,2,3)=\frac{\sum_{i,j\in\Gamma}\max_{n=1,2,3} E_{i,j\in\Gamma}(I_0,T;I_n)\ \tau(I_0(T(i,j)))}{\sum_{i,j\in\Gamma}\tau(I_0(T(i,j)))} \tag{5}$$

In our robust face matching algorithm, we extract face contour by edge detection with non-maximal suppression for each of the template face images in the face database. In addition, we also compute the normalized gradients for the template face images in the database. Then, we compare the input face image I_t with the set of images for each candidate by optimizing the following energy function with respect to the geometric transformation T.

$$\max_{T}\ E\,(\,I_0\,,T\;;I_n\,,n\,=\,1\,,2\,,3\,) \tag{6}$$

Note that this optimization problem can be solved by using the Levenberg-Marquardt algorithm [17] when a good initial guess of the geometric transformation parameters is available. In practice, we first applied a face detection algorithm to find the approximate location and size of the face in the input image. The result of face detection provides a good initial guess of the geometric transformation parameters. Then, the Levenberg-Marquardt algorithm is applied to maximize the similarity measure function for all the template face images. The template face with the highest optimized similarity measure is closest to the input face. Therefore, it is the result of the nearest-neighbor face recognition. In other words, the face recognition can be formulated as the following optimization problem:

$$\arg\max_{k\in F}\ \max_{T} E(I_0,T;I_n^{(k)},n=1,2,3) \tag{7}$$

where $I_n^{(k)}$ is the n-th face template image of the k-th candidate and F denotes the set of all the candidates in the database..

3   Experimental Results

The Yale Face Database is used to examine the robustness of the proposed face matching algorithm against lighting changes. It contains 15 subjects captured under three different conditions, i.e., center-light, right-light, and left-light, for each subject. The images of one subject in the Yale Face Database under the three different lighting conditions are shown in Fig. 2. The face regions of the center-light, right-light, and left-light face images are manually selected as the face template images as shown in Fig. 3. In our implementation, we applied a smoothing operator on the face images before computing the image gradient. This smoothing operation not only reduces the noise effect but also spreads out the support of the gradient function around contour locations. This helps to increase the convergence region in the optimization problem. We used an averaging operator for smoothing in our implementation for its simplicity in implementation.

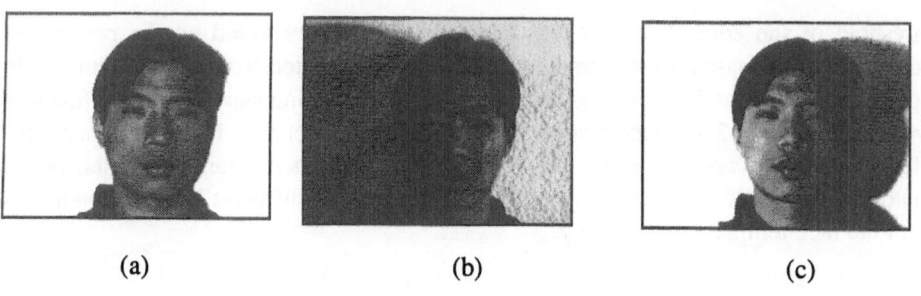

(a)   (b)   (c)

Fig. 1. One face set of the Yale Face Database with (a) center-light, (b) right-light, and (c)left-light.

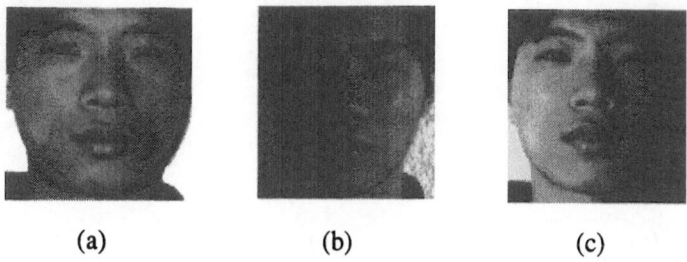

(a)   (b)   (c)

Fig. 2. The face regions are extracted from the face images in Fig. 1 above. These are the face template images used for face matching.

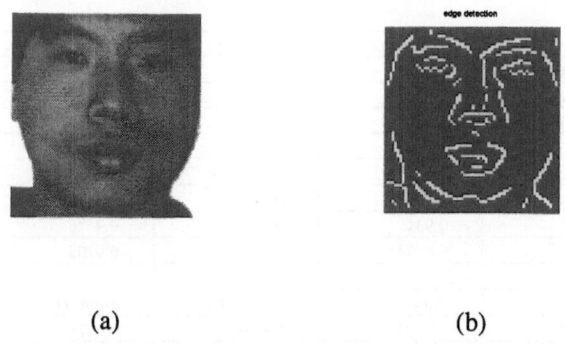

(a)   (b)

Fig. 3. (a) A template face image and (b) the extracted face contour map.

There are several tunable parameters in our implementation, such as the mask size for averaging filter, the window size for finding the local maximum, the threshold for edge detection, the lower bound (I_{Lb}) and upper bound (I_{Ub}) of the weighting function, and the constant c in the similarity measure. For saving the computation time, we down-sampled the face image to a quarter of the original size first. We used a 3×3 average filter, and a 5×5 local window for gradient normalization. For the threshold of the edge detection, we selected it adaptively based on the percentage cutoff in the histogram of the gradient magnitudes computed from the face image. In our experiments, the lower bound and upper bound of the intensity weighting function were set to 60 and 230, respectively. The constant c was set to 5. Fig. 3 depicts a template face image and the extracted contour of this face template. Fig. 4 shows the matching results of the face images of Fig. 2 under three different lighting conditions with the face template given in Fig. 3.

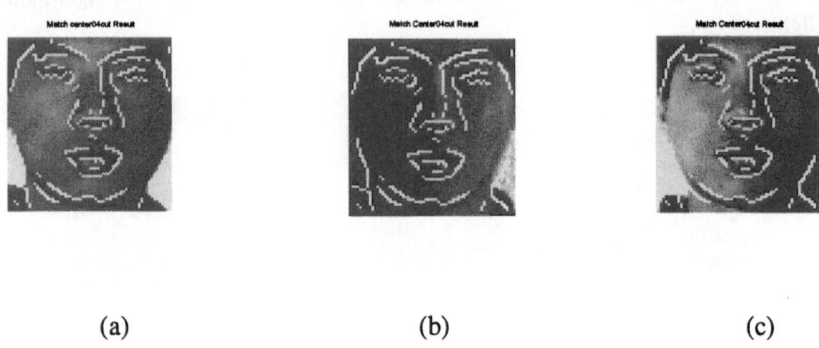

(a)   (b)   (c)

Fig. 4. Face image matching results with one of the face template contour overlaid on the input face images under (a) center-light, (b) right-light, (c) left-light conditions are shown.

Table 1. The matching scores for each lighting condition, such as center: center-light, left: left light, right: right-light for all 45 cases.

	Subject01	Subject02	Subject03	Subject04	Subject05
Center	0.9194	0.9224	0.9219	0.9222	0.9308
Left	0.9237	0.9301	0.9296	0.9457	0.9310
Right	0.9350	0.9234	0.9566	0.9225	0.9279

	Subject06	Subject07	Subject08	Subject09	Subject10
Center	0.9534	0.9741	0.8983	0.9536	0.9335
Left	0.9457	0.931	0.9129	0.9476	0.9767
Right	0.9321	0.9234	0.9416	0.9208	0.9519

	Subject11	Subject12	Subject13	Subject14	Subject15
Center	0.9772	0.9635	0.9274	0.9675	0.9434
Left	0.9278	0.9648	0.9563	0.9129	0.9518
Right	0.9736	0.9754	0.9168	0.881	0.9358

The recognition rate obtained by using our previous face matching algorithm in [16] on this Yale database was 93.33%. By using the proposed method, we can achieve 100% recognition rate. This is because there is one template that is exact one of the test image. Table 1 shows the matching scores of the matching faces with center-light. left-light and right-light, respectively. The score is between 0 and 1, since we normalized the gradients vectors. The closer the matching score is to one, the more similar the input face image is to the face templates. Here we also implemented the naive image matching methods based on sum of absolute grayscale differences inside the template region and along the edge contours, and we obtained 51.11% and 44.44% recognition rates, respectively. Compared with these results, the proposed robust face matching algorithm dramatically outperforms these simple methods.

4   Conclusions

The proposed illumination-insensitive face matching algorithm is based on a normalized consistency measure of weighted relative gradients at corresponding points in face images. The normalized consistency measure is generalized to include multiple face templates of the same person captured under different lighting conditions to improve the matching robustness. A robust image similarity measure was proposed to integrate the normalized relative gradient consistency measures for differently lighted face template images. We formulate the face matching or the face recognition problems as a corresponding optimization problem based on this proposed similarity measure. This similarity measure is computed only at the face contour locations. The computational cost compared to area-based image matching approaches is very low. We applied the proposed illumination-insensitive face matching algorithm to the Yale face database and obtained an excellent matching rate under different lighting conditions. The future research direction is to test the proposed algorithm on a larger face database.

Acknowledgements. This work was jointly supported by the Computer Visual Tracking and Recognition Project (project code: A311XS1213) funded by Ministry of Economic Administration (MOEA), Taiwan, R.O.C. and the National Science Council (project code: 90-2213-E-007-037), Taiwan, R.O.C.

References

1.   Adini, Y., Moses, Y., Ullman, S.,: Face recognition: the problem of compensating for changes in illumination direction. IEEE Trans. Pattern Analysis Mach. Intel., Vol. 19, No. 7 (1997) 721-732

2.   Belhumeur, P. N., Hespanha, J. P., Kriegman, D. J.,: Eigenfaces vs. Fisherfaces: recognition using class specific linear projection. IEEE Trans. Pattern Analysis Mach. Intel., Vol. 19, No. 7 (1997) 711-720

3.   Belongie, S., Malik, J., Puzicha, J.: Matching shapes. Proc. Int. Conf. Computer Vision, (2001) 454-461

4.   Beymer, D., Poggio, T.: Face recognition from one example view. MIT AI Memo No. 1536 (1995)

5.   Edwards, G. J., Taylor, C. J., Cootes, T. F.: Interpreting face images using active appearance models. Proc. Third IEEE Conf. on Automatic Face and Gesture Recognition (1998) 300-305

6.   Georghiades, A. S., Kriegman, D. J., Belhumeur, P. N.: Illumination Cones for Recognition under Variable Lighting Faces. Proc. IEEE Conf. CVPR (1998) 52-59

7.   Georghiades, A. S., Kriegman, D. J., Belhumeur, P. N.: From Few to Many: Illumination Cone Models for Face Recognition under Variable Lighting and Pose. IEEE Trans. Pattern Analysis Mach. Intel., Vol. 23, No. 6 (2001) 643-660

8.   Gros, P.: Color illumination models for image matching and indexing. Proc. Int. Conf. Pattern Recognition, Vol. 3 (2000)576 -579

9.   Hotta, K., Mishima, T., Kurita, T., Umeyama, S.: Face matching through information theoretical attention points and its applications to face detection and classification. Proc. Fourth IEEE Conf. on Automatic Face and Gesture Recognition (2000) 34-39

10.   Mojsilovic, A., Hu, J.: Extraction of perceptually important colors and similarity measurement for image matching. Proc. Int. Conf. Image Processing (2000) 61-64

11.   Mu, X., Artiklar, M., Hassoun, M. H., Watta, P.: Training algorithms for robust face recognition using a template-matching approach. Proc. Int. Joint Conf. Neural Networks (2001) 2877-2882

12.   Press, W. H., Teukolsky, S. A., Vetterling, W. T., Flannery, B. P.: Numerical Recipes in C, 2nd Ediition, Cambridge University Press (1992)

13.   Sengupta, K., Ohya, J.: An affine coordinate based algorithm for reprojecting the human face for identification tasks. Proc. International Conference on Image Processing, Vol. 3 (1997) 340 -343

14.   Takacs, B., Wechsler, H: Face recognition using binary image metrics. Proc. Third IEEE Conf. Automatic Face and Gesture Recognition (1998) 294-299

15.   Wiskott, L., Fellous, J.-M., Kuiger, N., von der Malsburg, C.: Face recognition by elastic bunch graph matching. IEEE Trans. PAMI, Vol. 19, No. 7, (1997) 775 -779

16.   Yang, Chyuan-Huei T., Lai, Shang-Hong, Chang, Long-Wen: Robust Face Matching Under Lighting Conditions. Proc. IEEE International Conference on Multimedia and Expo, Session ThuAmPO1 No. 317 (2002)

17.   Zhao, W.-Y., Chellappa, R.: Illumination-Insensitive Face Recognition using Symmetric Shape-from-Shading. Proc. IEEE Conf. CVPR (2000) 286-293

Facial Expression Analysis under Various Head Poses

Chien-Chia Chien, Yao-Jen Chang, and Yung-Chang Chen

Department of Electrical Engineering, National Tsing Hua University
Hsinchu, Taiwan 30013
ycchen@ee.nthu.edu.tw

Abstract. In this paper, a facial expression analysis method that can allow users to feel free to rotate their heads is proposed; we track facial feature points in synthetic frontal face images called stabilized view, and then translate tracking result into MPEG-4 facial animation parameters for facial expression synthesis. Besides, a pose refinement algorithm is proposed by using error classification method. It can refine the pose error rapidly after pose estimation.

1 Introduction

Facial expression plays a key role for emotion analysis in physiology, brain analysis in neuroscience, and face surgery in medicine [1]. It also serves as a useful medium for intelligent man-machine interface. Since facial expression is different from person to person, early researches only focused on recognizing fundamental expressions such as joy, anger, fear, disgust, sad, and surprise [2]. However, these universal expressions seldom appear in daily oral communications [3] and cannot span the whole facial expression space. Therefore, most researchers seek for low-level expression elements such as facial action units [4] and facial animation parameters (FAP) defined in MPEG-4 standard [5] as a more delicate description. With such a low-level decomposition of facial motions, more delicate facial expression analysis is required. Since the facial expression is mainly contributed by movements of salient facial features, facial expression analysis has been done by monitoring the shape change of facial feature blocks [2], tracking feature points with 2D templates [6], tracking feature shapes with deformable templates [7]. However, these methods have limited ability to handle shape distortion and self-occlusion problems due to global head in-plane and out-of-plane rotations.

Recently, Valente et al. [8] propose to relate facial change (optical flow, texture) and animation parameters by using the user-customized facial model to simulate facial change caused by all possible expression and head rotations. This approach explores the relationships without any user participation. But the large parameter space spanned by all FAPs and head orientations hinders us from thorough examination. Hence, the analysis ability is constrained by limited training data especially for some complicated expressions of the mouth where many FAPs interact together [8].

Y.-C. Chen, L.-W. Chang, and C.-T. Hsu (Eds.): PCM 2002, LNCS 2532, pp. 1193–1200, 2002.

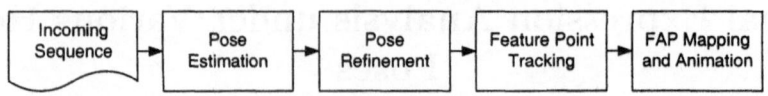

Fig. 1. The conceptual flow diagram of the proposed facial expression analysis scheme.

In this paper, we propose a model-assisted facial feature tracking algorithm for facial expression analysis under various head poses. The conceptual flow diagram is depicted in Fig. 1. The head pose is firstly estimated and refined. And then face images under various poses are mapped to a 3D user-customized facial model with estimated head pose information to generate a synthetic frontal face image (referred to as stabilized view image). In this way, facial expression analysis can be easily carried out by tracking facial features as the head in all images were in frontal up-straight pose. Afterwards, the tracking results are translated to FAPs for facial expression synthesis.

The rest of this paper is organized as follows. Section 2 presents pose estimation and stabilized view generation methods. Section 3 describes a pose refinement algorithm. The expression analysis algorithm is presented in Section 4. Experimental results about pose refinement and expression analysis are provided in Section 5 for performance evaluation. And finally, Section 6 concludes the paper.

2   Pose Estimation

In order to analyze facial expression under various head poses, we estimate head pose at first. With the user-customized facial model generated from two orthogonal views corresponding to user's frontal face and lateral face, the head pose is estimated in an analysis-by-synthesis manner. In the algorithm proposed by Schödl et al. [9], head motion is modeled as a set of points performing 3D affine transform followed by projection to the image plane. As a result, pose estimation is transformed to be an optimization problem, which minimizes the difference between the incoming video and the 2D projection of the head model. The algorithm is extended by using local correlation coefficient as the similarity measure to handle head tracking under non-uniform lighting conditions [10].

With the assistance of the textured facial model, we can generate a synthetic frontal face image called stabilized view image. Firstly, we estimate the 3D head pose. Then facial texture is extracted from the incoming image and mapped to the wireframe 3D facial model by using the planar projection; at this stage, the 3D model is under neutral expression no matter what expression the incoming image is. At the final stage, we rotate the 3D textured facial model into frontal view, and then project the model from 3D space to the 2D image plane. The stabilized view image is a synthetic frontal face image independent of its original head pose. The generation of stabilized view image is shown in Fig. 2.

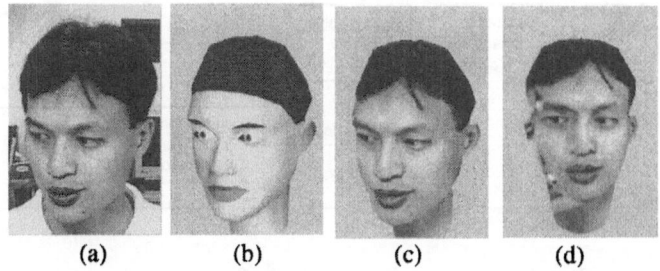

(a)   (b)   (c)   (d)

Fig. 2. Procedures of stabilized view generation. (a) An incoming image, (b) the 3D facial model with estimated pose, (c) texture mapping from the incoming image to the 3D facial model, and (d) the stabilized view generated by rotating back the texture-mapped facial model in (c) to the frontal up-straight pose.

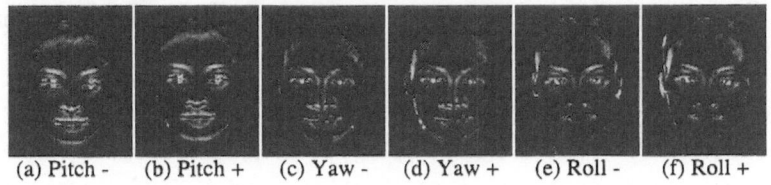

(a) Pitch -   (b) Pitch +   (c) Yaw -   (d) Yaw +   (e) Roll -   (f) Roll +

Fig. 3. Difference images under different pose error directions.

3   Pose Refinement

Stabilized view is very sensitive to head pose. If the estimated pose is not correct, distortion may occur in the stabilized view. Therefore, a pose refinement scheme is required for the following two reasons. Firstly, the accuracy of the pose estimation described in Section 2 is not high enough in some situation, especially when the incoming sequence has very rich expression. Secondly, the pose estimation algorithm proposed in [10] requires iterative process, which is very time-consuming; and the accuracy is directly proportional to its processing time. Consequently, we propose a pose refinement method based on stabilized view, which can rapidly improve the accuracy of the head pose.

From our observation, pose-error information is embedded in the difference image defined as

$$D(x,y) = |SV_{\text{correct\_pose}}(x,y) - SV_{\text{incorrect\_pose}}(x,y)| \qquad (1)$$

where the $SV_{\text{correct\_pose}}(x,y)$ and $SV_{\text{incorrect\_pose}}(x,y)$ are the stabilized view images generated under correct pose and incorrect pose, respectively. As shown in Fig. 3, pose errors in different rotation directions have very unique patterns in difference images. Thereby, the pose-error refinement can be taken as a classification problem. And the Fisherface classification method [12] widely used in face recognition is adopted to classify difference images.

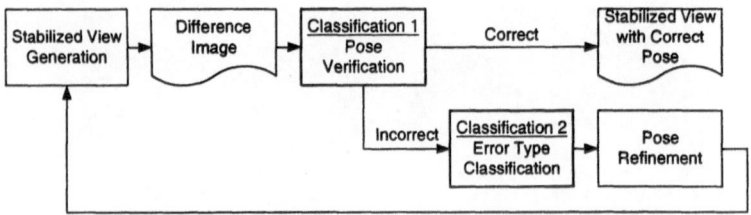

Fig. 4. The flow chat of pose refinement scheme.

Fig. 4 shows the detail procedure of pose refinement scheme. The purpose of the pose refinement is to verify whether the estimated head pose is accurate enough; if the pose is not precise, the pose is refined with the recognized error type. To achieve this purpose, two classification procedures are performed for pose verification and error type classification.

3.1   Pose Verification

Pose verification is a two-class classification problem, the goal of which is to decide whether an estimated pose is precise or not. Through pose verification, if the pose is correct, the facial expression analysis is applied on the stabilized view. On the other hand, if the pose error is judged as not precise enough, another classification procedure is applied on this difference image to determine what kind of pose error occurs, and then correct the pose error.

3.2   Error Type Classification

To classify any kind of pose-error angle is a very complicated problem. We simplify the problem by recognizing the fundamental composition of each pose-error angle, which forms a six-class classification scheme. The six classes represent the six fundamental directions (Pitch+, Pitch-, Yaw+, Yaw-, Roll+, and Roll-) in 3D space; a sample can belong to multiple classes simultaneously if its pose error is a combination of multiple fundamental directions.

In the training phase, duplicates of a training sample with multiple-direction error are put into two or three corresponding classes as their training data. In testing phase, our decision rule is based on Euclidean distance classifier. According to the number of error directions of the testing sample, we select the same amount of classes with the shortest distances as our testing result.

3.3   Practical Procedures for Pose Refinement

Two problems arise when applying the above procedure in practical use. The first problem is that the correct pose is unknown. This can be resolved by requesting the user perform neutral expression with frontal face in the initialization stage.

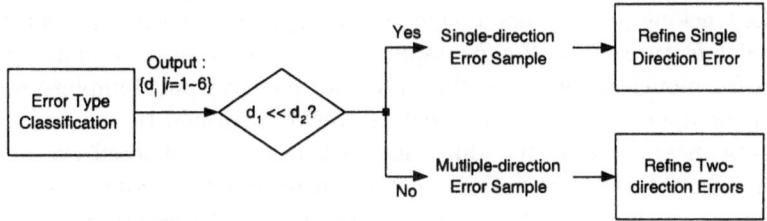

Fig. 5. The decision rule in practical application.

Hence, the stabilized view of the first frame can be taken as the reference image when computing the difference images, i.e.,

$$D'(x,y) = |SV_{\text{first\_frame}}(x,y) - SV_{\text{estimated\_pose}}(x,y)| \qquad (2)$$

where the $SV_{\text{first\_frame}}(x,y)$ and $SV_{\text{estimated\_pose}}(x,y)$ are the stabilized view image of the first frame and the one generated under the estimated pose, respectively.

The other problem in practical application is that the number of pose-error directions is not known. From our observation, if the sample is a single-direction error, the shortest distance to one class mean in the Fisherface space is always much shorter than the other five distances. The decision rule can thus derived as shown in Fig. 5. If we judge that the sample is a single-direction error, we refine it in one direction; if we judge that the sample is not a single-direction error, we compensate errors in two directions with shortest two distances.

4   Facial Expression Analysis

With the stabilized view image generated with refined head pose, face images under various head poses can be treated as they were all in frontal up-straight pose. Therefore, we can adopt any facial expression analysis algorithm designed for frontal face only. Here we use the algorithm proposed in our previous work [11] to accomplish this task by tracking salient facial features such as eyebrows, eye corners, eye centers, mouth corners and mouth shapes. However, some texture distortion may occur especially the head pose is under large out-of-plane rotations. Some facial features may be hidden from view in the original sequence, resulted in texture distortions near these facial features on the stabilized view image. In this case, we estimate their positions instead of tracking them.

4.1   Feature Tracking under Small Rotation

The adopted feature-tracking scheme is divided into two phases. In registration phase, the user performs neutral expression, and thus the facial texture in stabilized view coincides with the facial model. Therefore, we can extract facial feature points from the corresponding locations of the facial model. In this stage, we also register some block matching templates for use in the tracking phase.

In the tracking phase, some image processing techniques are utilized to track these facial features [11]. For example, corner masks and template matching are used for mouth corners tracking; lip color contrast and template matching are used for upper and lower lip centers tracking. In addition, we also detect the eye openness by intensity differences between the registered eye templates and currently detected eye regions. After feature point tracking, a mesh-based mouth-shape tracking algorithm [11] is also applied to describe detail mouth deformation. The tracking results are interpreted by facial animation parameters defined by MPEG-4 to drive a synthetic facial model.

4.2   Feature Tracking under Large Rotation

If a feature point is hidden from view under large rotation, we use a symmetry assumption to estimate its position. A visibility test is performed with assistance of the Z-buffer retrieved from the video frame buffer when rendering the 3D facial model. According to symmetry assumption, the positions of hidden features are estimated from their symmetry counterparts with respect the vertical face center.

5   Experimental Result

5.1   Experimental Result of Pose Refinement

Our experimental data comes from a sequence with various head poses. We select 24 frames, which original head poses are distributed over pitch, yaw, and roll directions. Because we regard the pose error larger than 3 degrees in any axis as unacceptable error for generating stabilized view, we generate some acceptable pose-error samples by permuting 1 degree and -1 degree in each direction; we generate some unacceptable pose-error samples by permuting 3, 5, -3, -5 degrees in each direction.

The accuracy of pose verification given the correct pose achieves 99.23% for acceptable pose error and 96.92% for unacceptable pose error. The accuracy of error type classification achieves 100%, 96.75%, and 93.16% for single-direction, two-direction, and three-direction error, respectively. For practical application, the stabilized view of the first frame is taken as the reference of correct pose. The accuracy of pose verification is 95.19% for acceptable pose error and 98.94% for unacceptable pose error. The accuracy of error type classification achieves 99.65%, 92.71% and 88.87% for single-direction, two-direction, and three-direction error, respectively. Table 1 shows the performance of our pose refinement decision rule shown in Fig. 5 in the first iteration. With such a high classification accuracy, the pose refinement algorithm can correct estimated pose error with few iterations.

5.2   Experimental Result of Expression Analysis

Since the feature tracking is performed on the stabilized view image, it is necessary to translate them back to the original face image for accuracy evaluation.

Table 1. The performance of pose refinement decision rule in the first iteration.

Testing data	Single-direction error	Multiple-direction error
Single-direction error sample	94.93%	5.07%
Two-direction error sample	17.32%	82.68%
Three-direction error sample	12.79%	87.21%

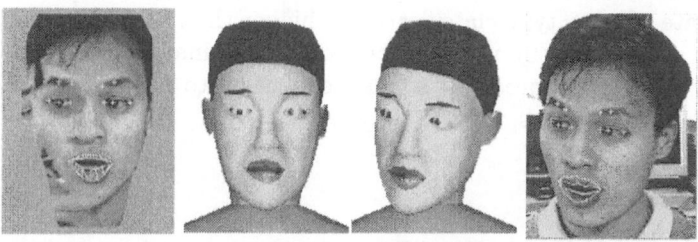

Fig. 6. The FAP-assisted representation of feature point tracking result.

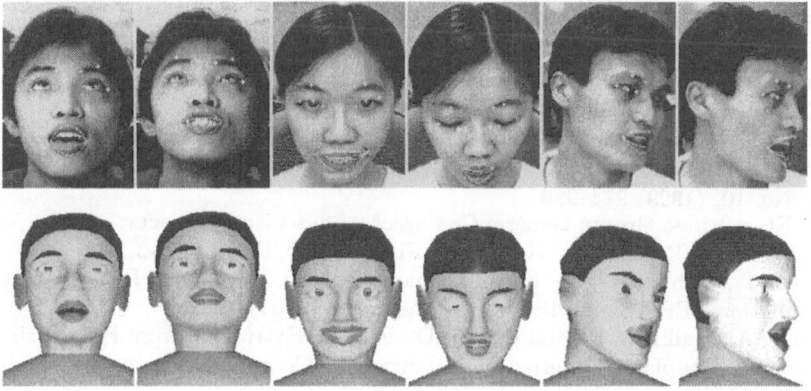

Fig. 7. The feature-point tracking and expression analysis results under different head poses.

This is achieved by firstly translate the tracking results to facial animation parameters (FAPs) to drive a user-customized 3D facial model. And then project vertices corresponding to facial feature points on rotated model onto original image as shown in Fig. 6. More examples are shown in Fig. 7 for different subjects under various head poses. Our method can analyze facial expression under wide range, which is from -60 degrees to 60 degrees in yaw direction, -20 degrees to 30 degrees in pitch direction, and any angles in roll direction. Such a wide range is sufficient to represent any possible orientation in ordinary visual communication.

6   Conclusions

In this paper, we propose a method that can track facial feature point and analyze facial expressions under various head poses. This method translates different orientation problem into frontal face problem, and can work under wide rotation ranges. In addition, a pose refinement algorithm is presented to improve the head pose estimation accuracy for generating reliable stabilized view image for expression analysis. The accurate rate reaches 97% for pose verification, and the accurate rate of error type classification is higher than 91%. And the expression analysis is satisfactory by visual inspection. Preliminary experiment results indicate the proposed approach is a feasible solution to facial expression analysis under various head poses.

References

1. Fasel, B., and Luttin, J.: Facial Expression Analysis and Recognition: A Survey. IDIAP Research Report, IDIAP-RR 99-19, (1999)
2. Yacoob, Y., and Davis, L. S.: Recognizing Human Facial Expressions From Long Image Sequences Using Optical Flow. IEEE Trans. Pattern Analysis Machine Intelligence, Vol.18, No.6, (1996) 636–642
3. Tian, Y. L., Kanade, T., and Cohn, J. F.: Recognizing Action Units for Facial Expression Analysis. IEEE Trans. Pattern Analysis and Machine Intelligence, Vol. 23, No. 2, (2001) 97–115
4. Donato, G., Bartlett, M. S., Hager, J. C., Ekman, P., and Sejnowski, T. J.: Classifying Facial Actions. IEEE Trans. Pattern Analysis and Machine Intelligence, Vol. 21, No. 10, (1999) 974–989
5. MPEG-4 Video Group: Generic Coding of Audio-Visual Objects: Part 2 - Visual. ISO/IEC JTC1/SC29/WG11 N2502, FDIS of ISO/IEC 14496-2, (1998).
6. Goto, T., Kshirsagar, S., and Thalmann, N. M.: Automatic Face Cloning and Animation. IEEE Signal Processing Magazine, (2001) 17–25
7. Yuille, A., Hallinan, P., and Cohen, D.: Feature Extraction from Faces Using Deformable Templates. International Journal of Computer Vision, Vol. 8, No. 2, (1992) 99–111
8. Valente, S., Andres Del Valle, A. C., and Dugelay, J. L.: Analysis and Reproduction of Facial Expressions for Realistic Communicating Clones. Journal of VLSI Signal Processing, Vol. 29, No. 1/2, (2001) 41–49
9. Schödl, A., Haro, A., Essa, I.: Head Tracking Using a Textured Polygonal Model. Workshop on Perceptual User Interfaces. (1998)
10. Chang, Y. J., and Chen, Y. C.: Robust Head Pose Estimation Using Textured Polygonal Model with Local Correlation Measure. In: Shum H. Y., Liao, M., and Chang, S. F. (eds.): Advances in Multimedia Information Processing. Lecture Notes in Computer Science, No. 2195, Springer-Verlag, Berlin Heidelberg New York (2001) 245–252
11. Chou, J. C., Chang, Y. J., and Chen, Y. C.: Facial Feature Point Tracking and Expression Analysis for Virtual Conferencing Systems. Proc. 2001 IEEE Int. Conf. Multimedia and Expo, (2001) 415–418
12. Belhumeur, P. N., Hespanha, J. P., and Kiregman, D. J.: Eigenfaces vs. Fisherfaces: Recognition Using Class Specific Linear Projection. IEEE Trans. Pattern Analysis and Machine Intelligence, Vol. 19, No.7, (1997) 721–732

Region-of-Interest Video Coding Based on Face Detection

Jeng-Wei Chen, Mei-Juan Chen, and Ming-Chieh Chi

Dept. of Electrical Engineering
National Dong Hwa University
Hualien 974, Taiwan
cmj@mail.ndhu.edu.tw

Abstract. The ability to give higher priority to Region-of-Interest (ROI) is the emerging functionality for nowadays video coding. A simple and fast method of face detection is proposed to dynamically define ROI in real time application. We use the color information Cr and RGB variance to determine the skin-color pixels. We don't need extra preprocessing, because these two color spaces are used in most hardware and video codec standards. Then, we use low-pass filters for background to reduce used bits. For video coding system, a region-based video codec based on the H.263+ with the option mode of modified quantization is set up. We adjust the distortion weight parameter and variance at macroblock layer to control the qualities at different regions. From experimental results, the proposed method can significantly improve quality at ROI. Our method is suitable for real time videoconferencing.

1 Introduction

The demand for applications of the digital video communication, such as video conferencing and videophone, has increased considerably. However, the transmission rates over network are very limited. Therefore, very low bit-rate video coding for such applications is an important technology to reduce the data rate of picture sequence without losing much of its subjective quality. Most standards of videoconference system over different networks provide a diversity of codec selection. The Recommendation H.263 [1] is one of the video codec standards and has been successfully adopted in commercial two-way video conferencing applications.

Most implementations of these standards give equal importance to each block. While different blocks within the same picture may be coded with different modes, no one block is more important than another. This model is not appropriate for any ROI (Region-Of-Interest) applications on video sequence. Blocks correspond to some focus areas are more important than blocks in the background or unwanted areas. Allocating more bandwidth towards the quality of areas that user focuses on, while sacrificing background or unwanted areas quality is a better coding strategy for video sequences like video conferencing.

Y.-C. Chen, L.-W. Chang, and C.-T. Hsu (Eds.): PCM 2002, LNCS 2532, pp. 1201–1211, 2002.

Most video conferencing research has been tested on head and shoulders sequences which are the important areas in a frame. The overall perceptual quality at low bit-rates can be improved by encoding the face regions with higher bit-rates than less relevant background regions [2].

There are several methods aim to find structural features that exist even when the pose, viewpoint or lighting conditions vary, and then use these features to detect face region. Detecting human skin-color belongs to this kind. Several color spaces have been utilized to label pixels as skin including RGB [3], normalized RGB [4], HSV (or HSI) [5], YCbCr [2,6], YIQ [7] etc. Although different people have different skin-color, several studies have shown that the major difference lies largely between their intensity rather than their chrominance [8]. So, we can use chrominance information to model skin-color.

In section 2, we describe our method. We show the simulation results in section 3 and make conclusion in section 4.

2   Proposed Methods

In this section, we proposed methods to detect skin-color and enhance the quality of ROI. Fig. 1 is the block diagram of our method. The first stage of our approach is to use color information to define region of interest. To do so, we have obtained a skin-color reference map. We can easily discriminate between region of interest and non-interest via the map. Then, the region of non-interest is processed through a low-pass filter to remove some high frequency component. We combine the region of interest and blurring non-interest. At last, we will adjust parameters of rate control in H.263+ to encode the ROI and region of non-interest for the combined image.

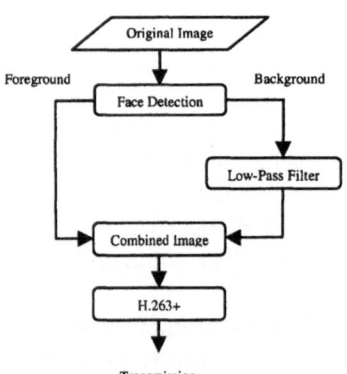

Fig. 1. The block diagram of our method

2.1   Skin-Color Detection

People can make out the skin-color and pseudo skin-color easily in human visual. However, we just get the intensity of the pixels in images. We can't know what the value means. Therefore, it is important to choose the suitable color space for the modeling of human skin-color. RGB is hardware-oriented model and is well known for its color-monitor display purpose [2]. YCbCr is also hardware-oriented model and is used in most video standards like H.263 [1], MPEG1-2 [9, 10] etc. Hence, the use of the same format for face detection will avoid the extra computation required in conversion. And, an effective use of the chrominance information for modeling human skin-color can be achieved in this color space.

Studies indicate that although skin-colors of different people appear to vary over a wide range, they differ less in chrominance than in brightness, specifically the skin-colors from a very compact area in the Cb-Cr space. Therefore, a Gaussian model is utilized for representing the skin-color model with mean and covariance [11]. For real time application, we need easier approach to detect skin-color. The ranges that *Chai* and *Ngan* [2] found to be the most suitable for all the input images that they have used are $R_{Cb} = [77, 127]$ and $R_{Cr} = [133, 173]$. Consider an input image of $M \times N$, for which the dimension of Cb and Cr therefore is $M/2 \times N/2$. Hence, we can get a reference map by following criterion.

$$Map_{Cb}(x, y) = \begin{cases} 255 & , Cb \in R_{Cb} \\ 0 & , Cb \notin R_{Cb} \end{cases} \tag{1}$$

$$Map_{Cr}(x, y) = \begin{cases} 255 & , Cb \in R_{Cr} \\ 0 & , Cb \notin R_{Cr} \end{cases} \tag{2}$$

$$Map_{combined}(x, y) = \begin{cases} 255 & , Cb \in R_{Cb} \cap Cr \in R_{Cr} \\ 0 & , otherwise \end{cases} \tag{3}$$

where $x = 0, 1, \ldots, M/2 - 1$ and $y = 0, 1, \ldots, N/2 - 1$.

We show the reference map in Fig. 2(b)–(d) by using (1)–(3), respectively. Notice that Fig. 2(c) and Fig. 2(d) are almost the same and match all skin-color regions besides some noise pixels that are similar to skin-color. Another set of experimental results in different lighting condition is shown in Fig. 3. We find an interesting problem in our experiment, though *Chai* and *Ngans'* method is well. The face region of Map$_{Cb}$ in Fig. 3(b) is poor, but the Map$_{Cr}$ in Fig. 3(c) is still strong to present the region of skin-color. Deservedly, the face region of Map$_{combined}$ in Fig. 3(d) will be poor, if we use these color information of Cb and Cr. So, we just adopt the color information of Cr to define skin-color. Further, we propose a fast and simple method to remove some noises.

As previously describe, RGB and YCbCr are hardware-oriented models. They have different approaches to represent colors. The color space of RGB is generally used in Windows platform. Hence, we can get color information of RGB easily from any device of capturing image. We can use the information directly without any converting.

From Fig. 3(c), skin-colors and clothes-colors locate at the same range, $R_{Cr} = [133, 173]$, in Cr-component. Nevertheless, these two colors are different in RGB

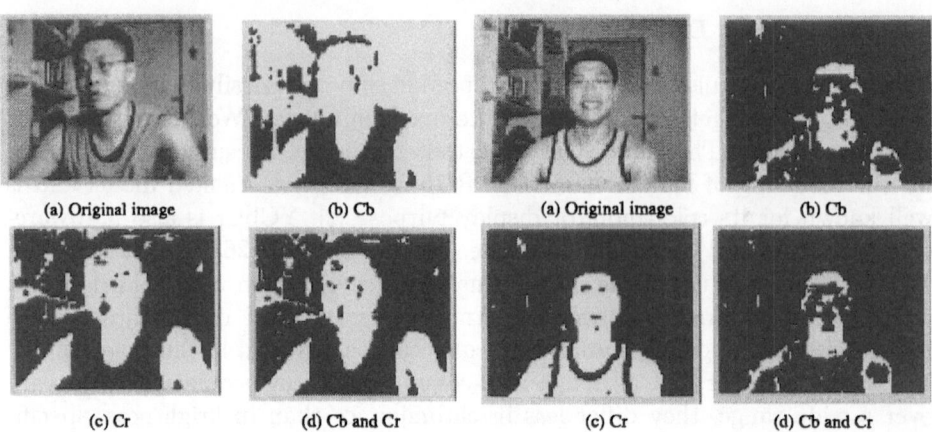

Fig. 2. Results of different reference maps   Fig. 3. Results of different reference maps in different lighting condition

space. In our observation, the distributions of components of R, G and B are different between skin-color and clothes-color. We randomly choose two pixels from clothes and face, and calculate the variance via following equation.

$$Var(\mathrm{X}_{x,y} = E(c^2) - E(c)^2 = \frac{1}{3}\sum_{i=0}^{2}(c_i - \bar{c}_i)^2 \tag{4}$$

where $\mathrm{X}_{x,y}(c_0, c_1, c_2)$ is denoted as the value of RGB locates on (x,y) in image. Equally, c_0 represents the value of R, and c_1 represents the value of G, and c_2 represents the value of B. The variance of clothes-color and skin-color are 6782.3 and 506.7, respectively. It shows that the distribution of clothes-color is larger than the variance of skin-color. The histograms of RGB variance for skin-color pixels of various images are shown in Fig. 4–7.

The statistical results show that the distribution of variances is narrow and consistent. We can utilize the characteristic to remove some noise. Thus, we can set $th1$ and $th2$ as thresholds and use color information of Cr to define skin-color and estimate a reference map. We summarize as follow:

$$Map_{skin\text{-}color}(x, y) = \begin{cases} 255 , Cr \in R_{Cr} \cap Var(\mathrm{X}_{x,y}) \in [th1, th2] \\ 0 \quad , otherwise \end{cases} \tag{5}$$

The reference maps in Fig. 10–12 are produced by using this criterion. The clothes-color is removed, and the results almost correspond to all skin-color pixels. So, we will use the approach to define ROI dynamically.

2.2   ROI Video Coding

TMN8 rate control. H.263+ TMN8 test model suggests the rate and the distortion models which relate bit-rate and distortion in terms of quantization

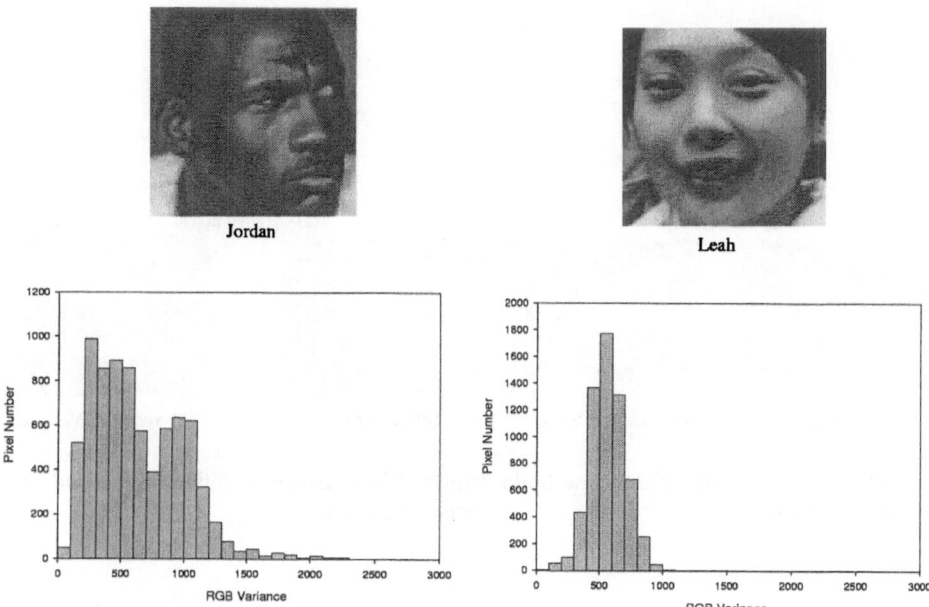

Fig. 4. The distribution of RGB variance of Jordan's face

Fig. 5. The distribution of RGB variance of Leah's face

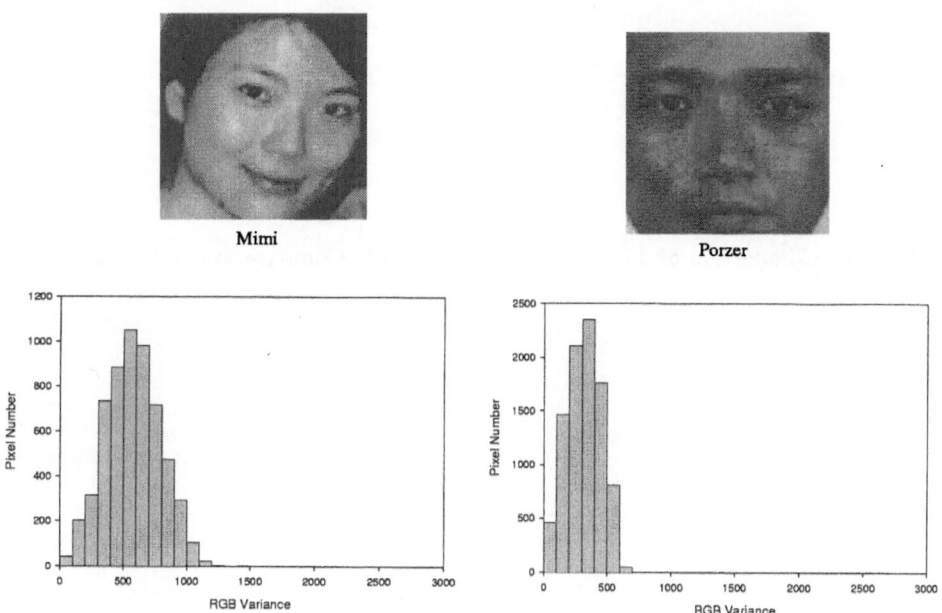

Fig. 6. The distribution of RGB variance of Mimi's face

Fig. 7. The distribution of RGB variance of Porzer's face

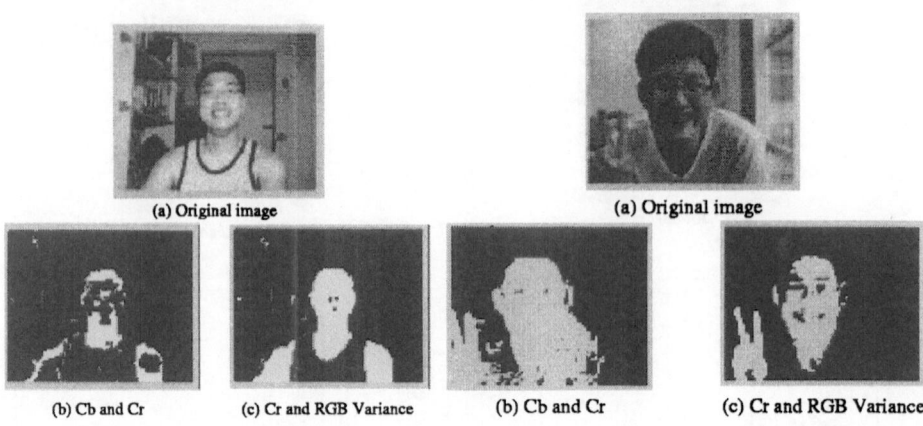

(a) Original image   (a) Original image

(b) Cb and Cr   (c) Cr and RGB Variance   (b) Cb and Cr   (c) Cr and RGB Variance

Fig. 8. Comparison of different methods to detect skin-color

Fig. 9. Comparison of different methods to detect skin-color

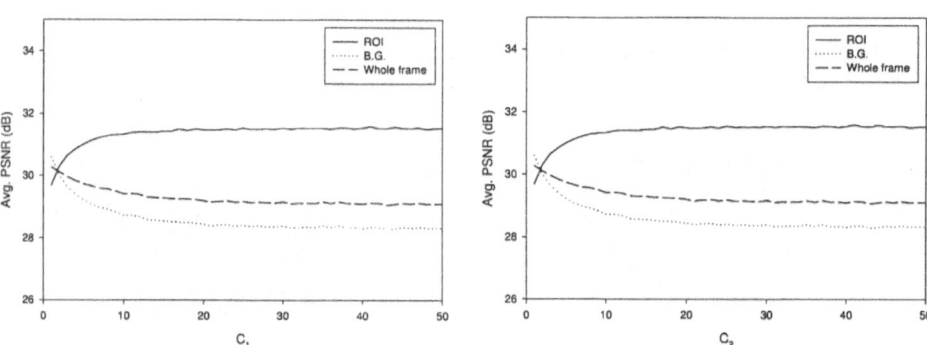

Fig. 10. Comparison of different C_1

Fig. 11. Comparison of different C_2

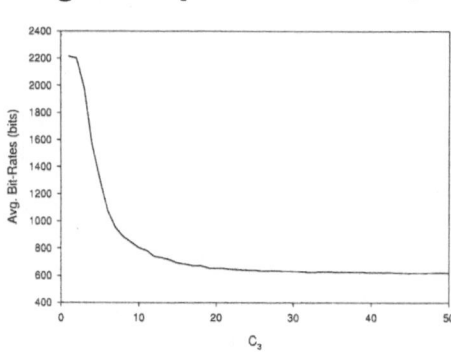

Fig. 12. Comparison of different C_3

parameters and signal variances to estimate the produced bits and distortion of an MB as follows.

$$B_i = A\left(K\frac{\sigma_i^2}{Q_i^2} + C\right) \tag{6}$$

$$D_i = \alpha_i^2 \frac{Q_i^2}{12} \tag{7}$$

where B_i represents the number of bits of the i-th macroblock in a frame. A is the number of pixels in a macroblock (i.e., $A = 16^2$ pixels). The value of K could be set to e/ln2 if the DCT coefficients were Laplacian distributed and independent. But since these assumptions are only approximate, we will adopt K to the statistics of the specific frame during encoding. σ_i represents the i-th macroblock variance of the motion-compensated residual signal. Q_i^2 is the quantization step used for the macroblock. C is the average rate to encode the motion vectors and bit-stream header, and its value is also estimated during encoding. D_i represents the distortion that is introduced by uniformly quantizing its DCT coefficients with a quantizer of step size. α_i is the distortion weight of the i-th macroblock, and is set as (8) for reducing the quantization overhead at lower bit rate.

$$\alpha_i = \begin{cases} 2\dfrac{B}{AN}(1-\sigma_i) + \sigma_i , & \dfrac{B}{AN} < 0.5 \\ 1 & , \; otherwise \end{cases} \tag{8}$$

where B is the target bits in a frame. The optimal quantization step-size can be decided by finding the solution of

$$Q_1^*, \ldots, Q_N^* = \arg\min_{Q_1,\ldots,Q_N} \frac{1}{N}\sum_{i01}^{N} \alpha_i^2 \frac{Q_i^2}{12} \qquad subject \; to \;\; \sum_{i=1}^{N} B_i \le B \tag{9}$$

There is unique solution that can be obtained using Lagrange theory. To do so, the optimized quantization step-size was obtained by the following equation:

$$Q_i^* = \sqrt{\frac{AK}{(B-ANC)}\frac{\sigma_i}{\alpha_i}\sum_{k=1}^{N}\alpha_k\sigma_k} \qquad i = 1, \ldots, N \tag{10}$$

Equation (10) indicates that the optimized quantization step at the i-th macroblock Q_i^* increases with the square root of the macroblock's standard deviation σ_i. Also, the Q_i^*'s increase with the sum of the weighted σ_i's, and decrease when there are more bits available for the frame. In fact, the QP that is used for coding is set to $(Q_i^*/2)$ round to nearest integer in $\{1, \ldots, 31\}$.

Enhancement ROI quality. Based on (10), a simple and fast approach is proposed to enhance the quality of region of interest by the adoption of α_i and σ_i', which are

$$\alpha_i' = \begin{cases} C_1 \times \alpha_i & , if(MB_i \in ROI) \\ \dfrac{\alpha_i}{C_2} & , if(MB_i \notin ROI) \end{cases} \qquad (11)$$

$$\alpha_i' = C_3 \times \sigma_i \quad , if(MB_i \notin ROI) \qquad (12)$$

where C_1, C_2 and C_3 are weighted factors.

α_i can be chosen to indicate the importance or weight of that macroblock's distortion. Larger α_i will get smaller QP to encode the macroblock with more bits. We can set larger value to α_i for the macroblock that belongs to more important objects in the scene or ROI. Hence, C_1 is used to emphasize the important macroblock MBi. Then, we will get smaller QP. And C_2 decreases the value of α_i for background and then gets larger QP to reduce the importance.

σ_i, the standard deviation of i-th macroblock, has the same meaning as variance. It is produced by motion-compensated residual signals. The value of σ_i will be large when the macroblock is complex. As in (10), larger σ_i will get larger Q_i^*. As we know, a complex macroblock, larger σ_i, will produce more bits. Thus, the rate control scheme gives the macroblock larger QP to reduce bits that encoder produces. Similarly, the value of σ_i is smaller when the macroblok is simple. So, the rate control scheme will give smaller QP to maintain the regular bit-rate.

C_3 is used to increase the intensity of σ_i, and we force the rate controller to believe that the i-th macroblock is complex, it will give larger QP to i-th macroblock that is region of non interest. By replacement of α_i' and σ_i' into equation (10), we can use these simple criterias to enhance quality of ROI, and reduce producing bits from background.

3   Simulation Results

We use UBC H.263+ codec(version 3.2) called TMN8 to encode sequences. The objective fidelity criteria are from digital signal processing and information theory and provide us with equations that can be used to measure the amount of error in the reconstructed image. Note that the objective criteria, although widely used, are not necessarily correlated with our perception of image quality. Commonly used objective measure is the Peak-to-Peak Signal-to-Noise Ratio(PSNR).

Fig. 10 shows the comparison of different C_1 for Carphone at 64 Kbits/s. In our knowledge, larger C_1 to ROI block will get better quality. Our experimental results show that quality can't be improved infinitely. And, giving C_1 greater than a threshold will get better quality of ROI than background's. Fig. 11 compares the results for different C_2, and the results are similar to Fig. 10. C_1 and C_2 affect different regions, but they have the similar meanings. The rate controller considers that the region of interest is important, because C_1 emphasizes the region of interest. Similarly, the region of non-interest is not important that the rate controller thinks, because C_2 abates the intensity. Fig. 12 shows that giving larger C_3 will result in fewer bits. Hence, we can utilize the method to reduce bits for encoding background.

Next, we compare different methods in several sequences. The method of without-ROI(WR) codes sequences normally. α's of ROI are multiplied by a factor in the method of Weighted-Alpha(WA). Our method is called "New". We use *Carphone* in 150 frames and the frame size is QCIF format (176×144). The frame rate is 30 fps, and set to the similar average bit-rate. We force I-frame to be coded every 90 frames and set QP to be 10. In our approach, the factors C_1, C_2 and C_3 are set to 450, 2 and 10, respectively, and we use 5 × 5 full filter to I-frame and 3 × 3 cross filter to P-frame. There are 75 frames in *Claire*, and its frame size is QCIF format. The original frame rate of sequence is down to 15 fps, and set to the similar average bit-rate. We force I-frame to be coded every 40 frames and set QP to be 10. The experimental results are shown in Table 1. Our method produces 139 frames in Carphone, which are 0.62 dB higher and more 7 frames than the algorithms of WA. And, there are 0.69 dB higher and 5 frames more than the WA approach in Claire. Fig. 13 and Fig. 14 are experimental results. In (a) and (b) of Fig. 13 and Fig. 14, we can see the number of frames that are skipped is less in our approach. (c) and (d) show subjective comparisons. There are better qualities in face-region by using our method.

Table 1. Comparison of different methods and sequences

		PSNR of ROI (dB)	Average Bit-Rate (bits)	Actually coded frame number
Carphone	WR	30.50	2277	132
	WA	33.04	2278	132
	New	**33.66**	**2268**	**139**
Claire	WR	31.36	1965	55
	WA	31.93	1965	55
	New	**32.62**	**1964**	**60**

4   Conclusion

For face detection, we use Cr-information and a simple and fast criterion to improve the result of detection. The dynamic ROI is defined by the method. Then, we adopt different low-filters to remove high frequency components from region of non-interest, especially I-frame. Hence, it could produce fewer bits and skip fewer frames. In ROI video coding, we adjust the parameters of MB-layer rate control. The approach can enhance the quality of ROI easily and maintain the const bit-rate to avoid buffer overflow. Experimental results show that our method can achieve good quality easily with fewer bit-rates.

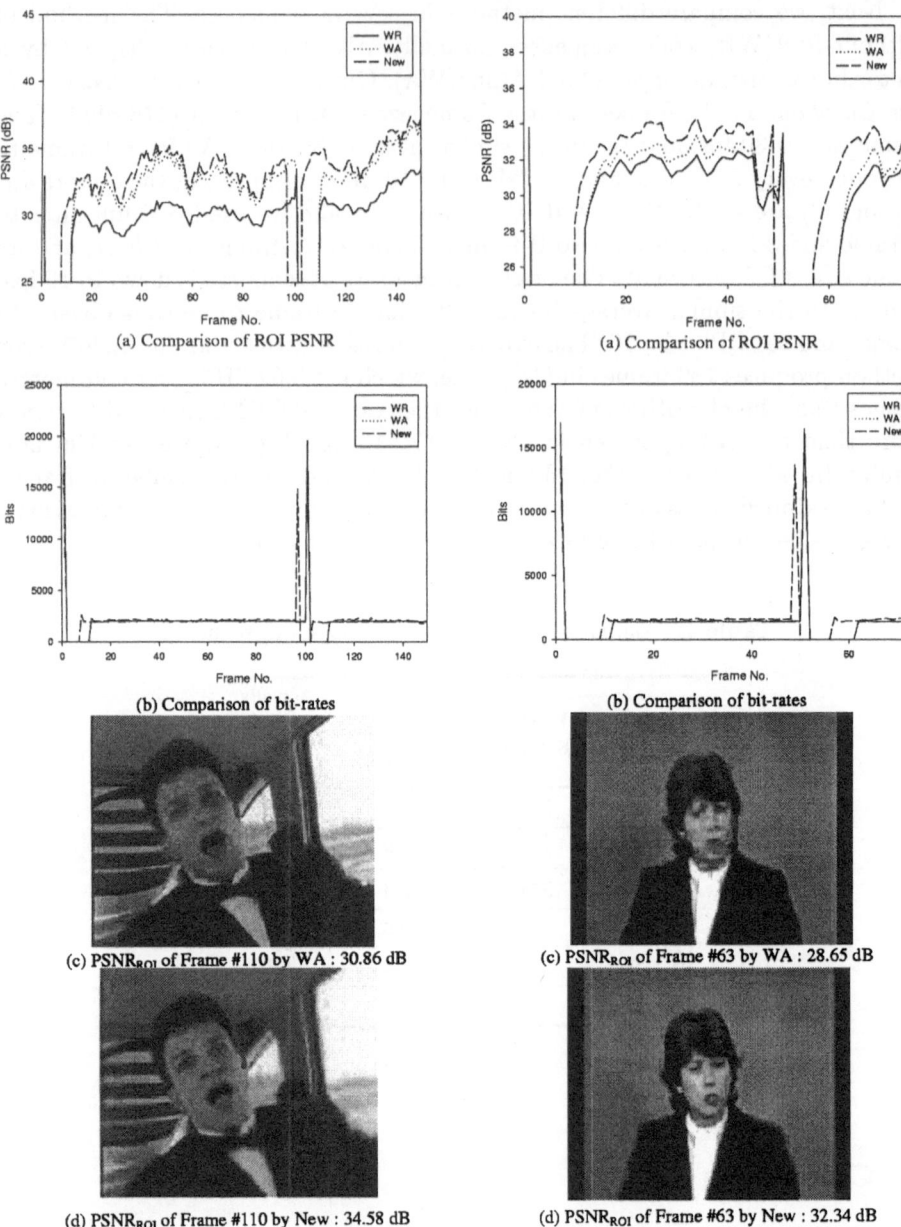

(a) Comparison of ROI PSNR

(a) Comparison of ROI PSNR

(b) Comparison of bit-rates

(b) Comparison of bit-rates

(c) PSNR$_{ROI}$ of Frame #110 by WA : 30.86 dB

(c) PSNR$_{ROI}$ of Frame #63 by WA : 28.65 dB

(d) PSNR$_{ROI}$ of Frame #110 by New : 34.58 dB

(d) PSNR$_{ROI}$ of Frame #63 by New : 32.34 dB

Fig. 13. Results of Carphone

Fig. 14. Results of Clarie

References

1. International Telecommunication Union, "Video coding for low bit rate communication", ITU-T Recommendation H.263 version 2, January 1998.

2. D. Chai and K. N. Ngan, "Face segmentation using skin-color map in videophone applications", *IEEE Trans. On Circuits and Systems for Video Technology*, Vol. 9, No. 4, pp.551–564, June 1999.
3. S. Satoh, Y. Nakamura and T. Kanade, "Name-it: Naming and detecting faces in news video", *IEEE Multimedia*, Vol. 6, No. 1, pp. 22–35, 1999.
4. Q.B. Sun, W.M. Huang and J.K. Wu, "Face detection based on color and local symmetry information", *Proc. 3rd Int'l Conf. Automatic Face and Gesture Recognition*, pp. 130–135, 1998.
5. K. Sobottka and I. Pitas, "Face localization and feature extraction based on shape and color information", *Proc. IEEE Int'l Conf. Image Processing*, pp. 483–486, 1996.
6. D. Chai and K.N. Ngan, "Locating facial region of a head-and-shoulders color image", *Proc. 3rd Int'l Conf. Automatic Face and Gesture Recognition*, pp. 124–129, 1998.
7. J. Yang and A. Waibel, "A real-time face tracker", *Proc. 3rd Workshop Applications of Computer Vision*, pp. 142–147, 1996.
8. Y. Dai and Y. Nakano, "Face-texture model based on SGLD and its application in face detection in a color scene", *Pattern Recognition*, Vol. 29, No. 6, pp. 1007–1017,1996.
9. ISO/IEC JTC1/SC29/WG11, "ISO/IEC CD 11172: Information Technology", MPEG-1 Committee Draft, December 1991.
10. ISO/IEC JTC1/SC29/WG11, "ISO/IEC CD 11172: Information Technology", MPEG-2 Committee Draft, December 1993.
11. C. E. Priebe, "Adaptive mixtures", *Journal of the American Statistical Association*, Vol. 89,No. 427, pp. 796–806, 1994.

An Error Resilient Scheme for MPEG-4 FGS Video over Packet Erasure Channel That Exhibits Graceful Degradation

Chih-Yen Lin[1], I.-Cheng Ting[2], Chyouhwa Chen[1], and Wen-Jen Ho[2]

[1] Department of Electronic Engineering of National Taiwan University of Science and
Technology, D8902101@mail.ntust.edu.tw, cchen@et.ntust.edu.tw
[2] Multimedia Technologies Laboratory of Institute for Information Industry,
{icting,wenjen}@iii.org.tw,

Abstract. The Fine-Granular-Scalability (FGS) video coding framework has been adopted by the MPEG-4 standard as a streaming profile for streaming applications. However, streaming over packet erasure channels (e.g. the Internet) often suffers from arbitrary packet loss characteristics and high packet loss rates that reduce video playback quality in an unpredictable manner. Due to the inherent dependency in the basic FGS bit-stream definition, any packet losses critically affect its playback quality. To improve its resilience to error, we propose two enhancements that remove the dependency in the FGS bit-stream. Our enhancements require marginal computation and redundant information overhead, but significantly improve the error resilience of the FGS scheme. We demonstrate via experiments the effectiveness of our enhancements for Internet streaming applications.

1 Introduction

The Internet provides a world-wide network for computers to be inter-connected for information sharing and exchange. Video streaming over the Internet is a recent and particularly active research area because of its successful deployment in commercial applications and its central role in any applications involving multimedia content. However, streaming video over the Internet runs into several difficult problems, namely variable bandwidth, delay, and delay variations (i.e. delay jitter), and potentially very high packet loss rates. These issues are difficult to contain since the Internet is based on IP, which is an inherently unreliable "best-effort" service.

Currently, popular commercial streaming systems usually deal with bandwidth variations by employing only very simple techniques, such as the SureStream?[5] technology of RealNetwork. The SureStream technique, also termed dynamic stream switching, works as follows. First, the same video content is encoded into multiple, but independent bit-streams at different bit rates. Then, a streaming server can dynamically select and switch to one of the encoded streams that best matches the available bandwidth of a client at a given time. Since there is no relationship between the

Y.-C. Chen, L.-W. Chang, and C.-T. Hsu (Eds.): PCM 2002, LNCS 2532, pp. 1212-1220, 2002.

multiple streams, frequent changing of a client's available bandwidth requires frequent switching of the streams. Furthermore, this stream switching technique is coarse-granular, and requires sophisticated buffering mechanism to deal with the delay jitter of the network. The MPEG-4 FGS[8] has also been designed to address the heterogeneous client bandwidth issue. It solves the problem by using a fine-granular encoding scheme that is much more viable for rate adaptation on the Internet. However, even with the FGS coding technique, the potentially high packet loss rate on the Internet poses significant potential harm to its playback quality. Various approaches have been proposed to address the packet loss issue. For example, many packet loss recovery mechanisms have been proposed to support real-time applications. However, they are far from being able to guarantee perfect recovery[4]. Another approach to guard against errors is forward error correction (FEC), which is widely used for channel coding. FEC adds redundant information to the information to guard against packet losses. However, the degree of protection must be determined a priori based on a estimation of channel loss characteristics. For the constantly changing packet-loss characteristics of the Internet, it is difficult to determine a degree of protection before packets are actually sent. Furthermore, the computation overhead for FEC computation may be too high a price one is willing to pay in some situations.

In this paper, we propose a simple, yet extremely effective error resilient scheme that drastically alleviates the impact of packet losses on the playback quality of MPEG-4 FGS encoded streams, while maintaining the original FGS fine-granular rate adaptation property. Furthermore, our scheme exhibits the desirable graceful degradation property, making our scheme a worthy addition to the FGS framework. This paper is organized as follows. Section 2 reviews the MPEG-4 FGS video coding framework. Section 3 describes our proposed error resilient scheme. Section 4 presents the our simulation environments and experimental results. Section 5 concludes the paper with a summary.

2   MPEG-4 FGS Bit-Plane Coding Review

Figures 1. and 2., respectively, illustrates the encoder and decoder of a typical MPEG4 base layer with FGS enhancement layer[2,3]. The encoder compresses a video sequence into two sub-streams, a base layer bit-stream and an enhancement layer bit-stream. The enhancement layer is based on bit-plane coding of absolute residual value

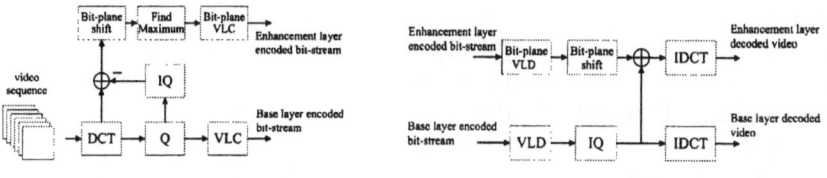

Fig. 1. A MPEG-4 FGS encoder.   **Fig. 2.** A MPEG-4 FGS decoder.

of DCT coefficients. The result is a progressive bit-stream that can be truncated into any number of bits with a corresponding enhancement in quality[1]. Details of the coding of the enhancement layer bit-stream using bit-plane coding is shown in Fig. 3.[2,6,8].

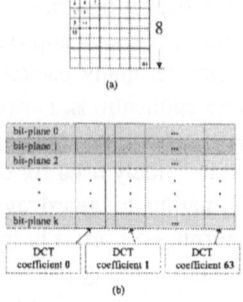

(a)

(b)

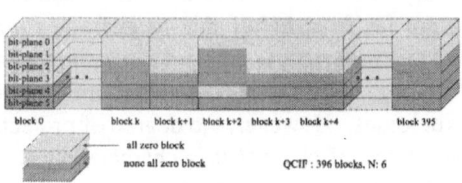

Fig. 3. A bit-plane coding block.   **Fig. 4.** A diagram of bit-plan of QCIF size.

We use a running example, somewhat similar to the one in [6], to illustrate the procedure of FGS bit-plane coding. Assume that the residual values of a block after zig-zag ordering are as follows: {+10,0,-7,0,0,-3,0,+2,+2,0,0,-3,0,0,+1,0,...0,0}. With FGS bit-plane coding, absolute residual values are coded using VLC code. For the example, the values are viewed as the two following sequences:

10,0,7,0,0,3,0,2,2,0,0,3,0,0,1,0,...,0,0 (absolute)

0,*,1,*,*,1,*,0,0,*,*,1,*,*,0,*,...,*,* (sign bits)

To bit-plane encode the values, first, the maximum residual value, -10 in the example, is determined. The maximum value needs 4 bits to represent(1010). Writing the above absolute residual values in binary format, the four bit-planes are shown as follows:

10,0,7,0,0,3,0,2,2,0,0,3,0,0,1,0,...,0,0

1,0,0,0,0,0,0,0,0,0,0,0,0,0,0,0,...,0,0 [MSB]

0,0,**1**,0,0,0,0,0,0,0,0,0,0,0,0,0,...,0,0 [MSB-1]

1,0,**1**,0,0,**1**,0,**1**,**1**,0,0,**1**,0,0,0,0,...,0,0 [MSB-2]

0,0,**1**,0,0,**1**,0,0,0,0,0,**1**,0,0,**1**,0,...,0,0 [MSB-3]

The four level bit-planes can be converted succinctly into (RUN, EOP) symbols as follows:

(0,1)   [MSB]

(2,1)   [MSB-1]

(0,0),(1,0),(2,0),(1,0),(0,0),(2,1)   [MSB-2]

(2,0),(2,0),(5,0),(2,1)   [MSB-3]

These symbols are then coded using variable-length code (VLC). The sign bit for each coefficient is placed in the output bit-stream only once, right after the VLC symbol that represents the most significant bit (MSB) of its absolute value.   In our example, the final coded symbols of the four level bit-planes are shown as follows, along with their sign bits, denoted using bold fonts:

VLC(0,1),**0**   [MSB]

VLC(2,1),**1**   [MSB-1]

VLC(0,0),VLC(1,0),VLC(2,0),**1**,VLC(1,0),**0**,VLC(0,0),**0**,VLC(2,1),**1**   [MSB-2]

VLC(2,0),VLC(2,0),VLC(5,0),VLC(2,1),**0**   [MSB-3]

Note the extreme efficiency and variable length property of this representation for a block. In the FGS bit-stream definition, to increase the computational efficiency in VLC decoding, the whole encoding process is assisted by a VLC table for each bit-plane. For each block, let MSB-plane denote the first bit-plane that is not all zeros. In our example, four VLC tables are used, corresponding to the MSB plane, the MSB-1 plane, the MSB-2 plane, and the MSB-3 plane. Information regarding which VLC table was used in the encoding process is also stored in the bit-stream for the decoding stage.

When a sequence of blocks in a frame are to be encoded, the maximum number of bit-plane used N among all blocks must be determined first. For blocks requiring less than N bit-planes, the bit-planes higher than their MSB-plane consist of all zeros. As a concrete example, a QCIF size video frame is divided into 396 blocks as illustrated in Fig. 4. The value N=6 in the figure indicates every block should be encoded to 6 bit-planes. As shown in the figure, some bit planes are all zeros. Furthermore, each blocks may have different number of significant bit-planes. Bit-planes higher than the MSB-plane consists of only zeros, however, some bit-planes lower than the MSB plane may also be all-zero planes.

To encode the fact that bit-planes higher than the MSB-planes are all zero, rather than using the VLC symbols, another extremely efficient scheme is used in the FGS definition -- **msb_not_reached** bit. The **msb_not_reached** bit is a one bit element to for each bit-plane higher than, and including, the MSB-plane to indicate whether the bit-plane is all zero or not. For planes higher than the MSB plane, **msb_not_reached** bit is set to be 0. When the MSB plane is reached, the **msb_not_reached** bit is set to 1 to indicate that subsequent symbols in the block must be decoded using the VLC table. The decoding process for the block switches to VLC decoding mode. Thereafter, for bit-planes lower than the MSB-plane, the **msb_not_reached** is no longer used. The decoder relies on the VLC tables for each corresponding bit-plane for subsequent decoding.

3 Error Resilient Scheme for FGS

As defined in the original framework, the MPEG-4 FGS framework is extremely efficient and compact. A consequence of this efficiency is the high degree of inter-dependency in its bit-plane. There are two kinds of dependencies in the bit-stream that make it particularly susceptible to decoding errors, (1) the variable length nature of coded information for each block , and (2) association of the sign bit and the **msb_not_reached** bit with the MSB plane only. First, since the coded information for each bit-plane is variable in length, the loss of any single bit renders all subsequent coded information undecodable. Secondly, when the packet containing MSB plane coded information is lost, the following bit-plane will also confuse about its sign of DCT coefficient and which is the corresponding VLC table of such bit-plane.

To overcome the sensitivity of the original FGS to bit errors, the inter-dependency in the coded data must be reduced. Breaking the dependency improves its resilience to error. Our proposed error resilience scheme inserts multiple positional information into the bit-stream to make coded bit-stream decodable in the face of any losses. The scheme involves two components: the resynchronization header and the replication of sign and extend **msb_not_reached** bits [2,6].

3.1 Resynchronization Header

To transmit the encoded bit-stream across the Internet, the bit-stream must first be packetized. The packetization procedure packs as many macro-blocks as possible in the bit-stream into packets up to a predefined packet size. The packetization procedure pads a packet with zeros if not enough room is left for the next macro-block. An important source of errors on the Internet is random losses of data packets. To guard against packet loss errors, the first component of our error resilience scheme involves insertion of a resynchronization header in each packet at the packetization stage. The purpose of the resynchronization header is to synchronize the decoder with the bit-stream when a packet is received. Our resynchronization header is a simple and effective method that enables the decoder to make use of all packets that can be correctly received. The format of the resynchronization header is shown in Fig. 5. The header contains an identification code, a "bit-plane level" indicator, and a "macro block location" pointer. The identification code is used to identify each video packet. The "bit-plane level" is used to denote the bit-plane number of the first macro block contained in the packet. The "macro block location" pointer contains the scanning order number of that first macro block. The resynchronization header makes each packet independently decodable. In the experiments in this paper, the bit-streams are packetized into two size types: 200, and 500 bytes.

3.2 Sign-Bit and Extended_msb_not_reached Bits

In the original MPEG-4 FGS bit-stream definition, the **msb_not_reached** bit is associated with the MSB-plane, and the sign bit is associated with the coded VLC symbol representing the most significant bit of the coefficient, to achieve a very compact representation. With this representation, if the packet containing the MSB-plane coded information is lost, the **msb_not_reached** bit information is also lost. If a packet containing any lower bit-plane is lost, sign bits for a number of coefficients may also be lost. Therefore, any packet loss makes subsequent coded information undecodable. To make subsequent coded symbols decodable even if the packet containing the MSB-plane is lost, both the sign bits and the **msb_not_reached** bit must be duplicated for bit-planes lower than the MSB-plane. In addition, since the VLC encoding of the original (RUN,EOP) representation is bit-plane specific, decoding each coded symbol requires knowledge of which bit-plane the coded symbol belongs to so that the correct VLC table can be selected. The association between coded symbol and its bit-plane has been implicitly represented in the original bit-stream definition.

Note that for each bit-plane higher than and including the MSB-plane in a block, one **msb_not_reached** bit is used to indicate whether that bit-plane contains all zeros or not. We extend the **msb_not_reached** bit into an **extended_msb_not_reached** field, consisting of three bits, for the resolution of the above mentioned difficulties. However, unlike the original **msb_not_reached** bit definition, every bit-plane in a block has one associated **extended_msb_not_reached** field. The first bit contains the original MPEG-4 FGS **msb_not_reached** bit. The next two bits are used to indicate which VLC table to use for decoding the symbols contained in the bit-plane in a block. This design removes the dependency among bit-planes. Therefore, packet losses do not hinders the decoding for information contained in later packets. The added overhead (including the sign bits and **extended_msb_not_reached** field) is about 8~14 % of the original MPEG-4 FGS bit-stream.

Continuing with our previous example, according to our design, the resulting bit-stream is shown as follows. In the example, the bold bits denote the duplicated sign bits.

VLC(0,1),0   [MSB]
VLC(2,1),1   [MSB-1]
VLC(0,0),0,VLC(1,0),1,VLC(2,0),1,VLC(1,0),0,VLC(0,0),0,VLC(2,1),1 [MSB-2]
VLC(2,0),1,VLC(2,0),1,VLC(5,0),1,VLC(2,1), 0   [MSB-3]

In summary, our proposed error resilient scheme combines the resynchronization header with duplicated sign bits and **extended_msb_not_reached** symbol. The error resilient capability is significantly enhanced for streaming MPEG4 FGS video over packet erasure channel. Another important benefit of our proposal is the graceful degradation property if the channel conditions become progressively worse.

3   Experiments and Analysis

The simulation setup is as shown in Fig. 6, involving three main components for simulating a streaming application in the Internet, namely a rate shaping component, a packetization component, and a packet loss simulation components (for the Internet channel model). The rate shaping component simply truncates the bit-stream to a

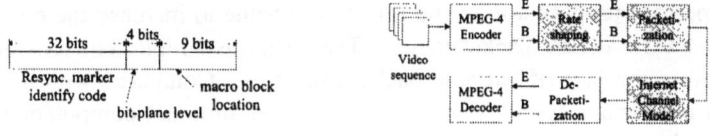

Fig. 5. The format of resynchronization header.   **Fig. 6.** Diagram of simulation set up.

designated bit-rate to simulate the available bandwidth of the Internet. In all experiments, MPEG-4 FGS protected by our error resilient scheme (henceforth called **with_rm**), and the original MPEG-4 FGS scheme (henceforth called **no_rm** scheme) are shaped to the same bit-rate. The operation of packetization is that the with_rm scheme is packetized correspond to video packet size and no_rm scheme is packetized as with_rm packet size and count. The packet loss characteristic is modelled by a two-state Markov model, which has been shown to emulate the actual Internet packet loss behavior well. The average packet loss rates investigated in our experiments are 5%, 10%, 15%, and 20%, representing a wide spectrum of loss behaviors on the Internet.

The video source sequences used in the simulations are the Akiyo, Coastguard and Foreman sequences, which are in CIF format, and totaling 100 frames. The base layer is encoded into one I frame followed by 99 P frames, and the encoded frame rate is 10Hz. The motion vectors are limited to a length of ±32 pixels. The bit rate of the base layer is 128kbps with TM5 rate control. The enhancement layer is encoded using the original FGS coding (no_rm), and FGS with our error resilient coding (with_rm).

The results are shown in Fig. 7. We can make several observations from Fig. 7. First, MPEG4 FGS without protection is extremely sensitive to loss, and is not very responsive to increase in available bandwidth, while the quality of the stream with our protection scheme improves as available bandwidth increases. Second, the with_rm scheme exhibits the graceful degradation property as loss rate increases. The graceful degradation property is important due to the inherent and unpredictable nature of Internet packet losses. We illustrate the increase in PSNR of the with_rm scheme has over the no_rm scheme in Fig. 7. We first observe that performance of the with_rm scheme is better when smaller video packet sizes are used. Secondly, we observe the with_rm scheme performs uniformly better than the no_rm scheme across the spectrum of available bandwidths, except when the available bandwidth is equal to that used by the base layer. This is because the with_rm scheme adds some redundant data. Therefore, in the case when very low bandwidth is available and large video packet size, when a video packet can contain a full video frame, the quality of the with_rm scheme is somewhat poorer compared with no_rm scheme. However, in all the other cases, the performance of the with_rm scheme is substantially better.

5 Conclusion

In this paper, we propose a new and effective scheme to increase the error resilience of MPEG-4 FGS against packet losses. The design is simple, but provides graceful degradation in the face of variable packet loss rates. Compared with the FEC style protection mechanism [9,10], our proposal involves minimal computation and much lower redundancy overhead, while achieving similar protection.

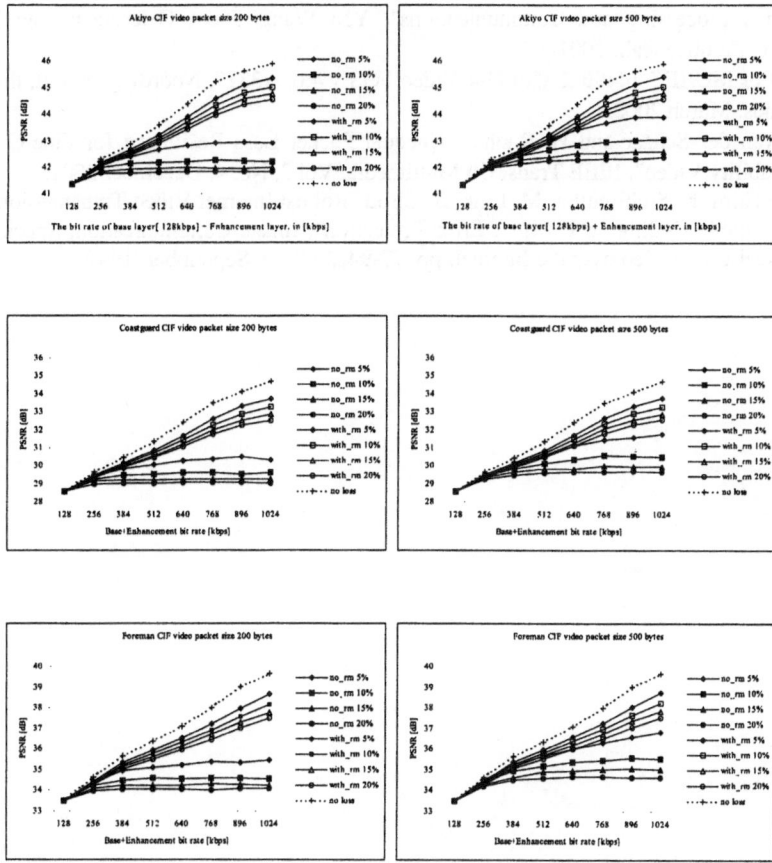

Fig. 7. The PSNR values against to the total bit rate with video packet size 200 and 500 bytes.

References

1. Dapeng Wu, Yiwei Thomas Hou, WenWu Zhu, Ya-Qin Zhang, Jon M. Peha, "Streaming Video over the Internet: Approaches and Directions", IEEE Transaction on Circuits and Systems for video technology, Vol. 11, No.1 February 2001.
2. Weiping Li, "Fine Granularity Scalability Using Bit-Plane Coding of DCT Coefficients", ISO/IEC JTC1/SC29/WG11 MPEG98/M4204,December, 1998.
3. Information Technology - Generic Coding of Audio-Visual Object: Visual ISO/IEC 14496-2 / Amd X , ISO/IEC JTC1/SC29/WG11 N3095, Maui, December 1999.
4. V. Paxson, "End-to-End Internet Packet Dynamic", Proc. ACM SIG-COM'97, France, vol.27, no. 4, p. 13-52, Oct. '97.
5. "SureStream? - Delivering superior quality and reliability", RealNetworks White Papers.
6. Weiping Li, "Overview of Fine Granularity Scalability in MPEG-4 Video Standard", IEEE Transactions on Circuits and Systems for Video Technology, vol.11, no.3, March 2001.

7.   "Video Processing and Communications", Yao Wang, Joern Ostermann, and Ya-Qin Zhang Prentice Hall, 2001.
8.   Text of ISO/IEC 14496-2 MPEG-4 Video FGS v.4.0, N3317, Noordwijkerhout, the Netherlands, March 2000.
9.   M. van der Schaar and H. Radha, "Unequal Packet Loss Resilience for Fine-Granular-Scalability Video", IEEE Trans. On Multimedia, Vol 3, No. 4, December 2001.
10. Uwe Horn, K. Stuhlmuller, M. Link, B. Girod,"Robust Internet Video Transmission Based on Scalable Coding an Unequal Error Protection", Image Communication, Special Issue on Real-time Video over the Internet, pp. 77-94, 15(1-2), September, 1999.

MPEG4 Compatible Video Browsing and Retrieval over Low Bitrate Channel

Chunxi Chen and Zhenrong Yang

Abstract. In this paper, we present an effective approach for video browsing and retrieval on the video server over low bitrate channel. To enable random access, a new stream is generated based on the analysis of the original stream. The random access point is prudently selected with the aim to best fit the user's browsing requirement. By switching between the two streams, the overhead of transporting periodic I-frames can be avoided; furthermore, the user's unconcerned data can be greatly reduced in the transportation. With the transcoding technique, the quality can be improved by nearly 2.2dB. With this algorithm, browsing efficiency, picture quality and disk space occupation can be well balanced.

1 Introduction

For interactive video storage applications that browsing and retrieving video data over low bit rate channel; random access, fast forward and fast reverse are the basic requirements. Among the video compression standards that are in favor of the low bitrate channel, such as MPEG4 [1] and H.263 [2], intra coding is used to enable random access. But intra coding will consume much more bits than inter coding. Thus to frequently insert intra coded frames into the bitstream will increase the bit-rates greatly or reduced the quality significantly at a fixed bitrate. On the other hand, to insert less I-frames in the bitstream will cause the low efficiency in accessing the video sequences randomly.

A good solution to this contradiction is to generate a second bitstream on the video server as [3] mentions. In general, one additional bitstream that consists periodically encoded I-frame is generated. By switching between the two streams, random access can be enabled and the overhead of transforming many I-frames can be avoided. We named it as periodic I-frame generation method in the following sections.

Because of the characteristic of the low bitrate channel, transporting even one frame video data will take up a large portion of the resource. So the efficiency of retrieving data in interest is crucial under this condition. Any redundant or useless video data over such channel will do great harm to the performance of the application. In such cases, just to encode I-frames periodically seems not a good way.

Y.-C. Chen, L.-W. Chang, and C.-T. Hsu (Eds.): PCM 2002, LNCS 2532, pp. 1221-1226, 2002.

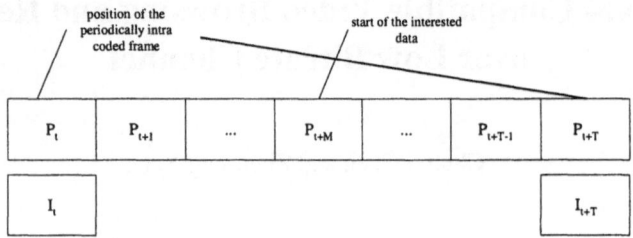

Fig. 1. Periodic I-frames Generation Method

For example, assume the data we want to browse starts from frame P_{t+M} as Figure 1 shows. The position of the nearest I-frame is I_t. Then the user should receive M frames that he is not interested in until P_{t+M} arrives. What if we encode P_{t+M} to I_{t+M} in advance! If the period is T, the worst condition can be that T-1 frames should be received and decoded before the useful data arrives. Furthermore, if an important slice lies in between t and t+T; it will be missed in the fast forward browsing by the periodic I-frames generation method.

In this paper, we propose a more efficient method for video browsing and retrieval over low bitrate channel. The main idea is to generate a new I-stream intelligently (according to the video content) not periodically. Employing the shot detection technique, we first analyze the bitstream for candidate selection and then transform the prudently selected candidate frames into I-streams. Random access can be achieved by the same switching method. Because of the characteristics of the shots and because the selected I-frame candidates usually are the start of the shots, such I-frames are sure to fit the users' browsing and retrieval requirement. The problems mentioned above can be solved consequently. In section 2, we first amplify why adopt shot boundary detection technique in the application and the algorithm we use; then we describe our algorithm and application in detail. In section 3, we show a further quality improvement method by transcoding technique. Further data analysis is carried on there.

2 Selection of Candidate I-Frames

We take advantage of the shot boundary detection technique to select the candidate I-frames instead of using the periodic I-frames generation method to generate the new I-stream.

A shot is composed of a group of frames from a video sequence that have continuity in some sense. Commonly, it represents a continuous sequence of a single action. We can assume that, in most case, if a user is not interested in one frame among a shot, he is not interested in the whole shot. With this assumption, to generate the new I-stream according to shot detection result will improve the efficiency of video browsing and retrieval.

There has been a large number of work on shot detection or named as temporal segmentation. We adopt the technique mentioned in [4]. This is a very fast shot detection method based on the compressed video stream. Because its fastness and good accuracy, it's quite suitable for real-time analysis over low bit-rate channel.

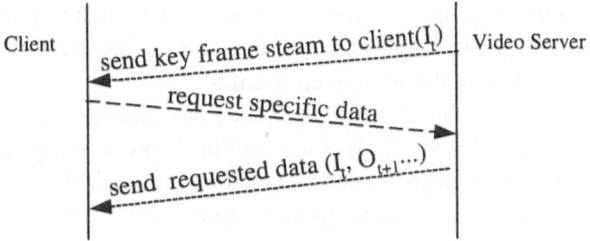

Fig. 2. Data flow between video server and client

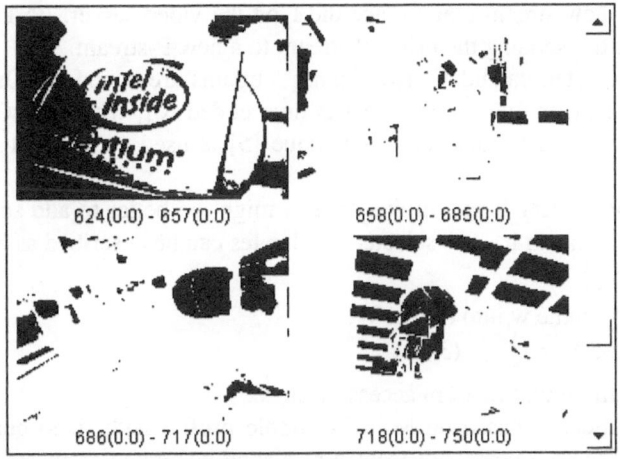

Fig. 3. Key frame shown to the remote user

We propose to store two bit-streams on the video server. One is the original stream, which is I-frame first, and all P-frames afterwards. The other is the I-stream whose generation can be described as

$$I_t = INTRA(O, t, QP) \quad \text{where } t = \text{start of each shot} \quad (2-1)$$

where O represents the original stream and I represents the new generated I-stream. INTRA( ) denotes the operator for transforming the original stream to an I-stream at position t. QP is the quantization parameter.

A sample data flow of the communication between client and video server is described as Figure 2. The I_t is first transmitted to the remote user and shown as the key frame as Figure 3 shows. The user browses the key frame and requests the specific data. The video server then switch to O_t and transmit the rest data to the user. In such cases, transmission of useless video data can be limited to a lowest extent.

3 Further Employing Transcoding Technique

In order to keep the fixed bit rate, we use large QP for encoding the new I-stream. This will reduce the quality significantly. Because of the error propagation, some errors might be amplified in the subsequent frames

One method to improve the quality is to encode one more frame between the new I-frame and the original P-frame. It plays a transitional role to mitigate the great difference between the new and original frame. The idea is incited from [3]. But we focus on the compressed form. So transcoding technique is employed. Combined with (2-1), the algorithm is described as

$$N_t = INTRA(O, t) \tag{3-1}$$

$N_{t+1} = INTER(N, t, O, t+1, QP)$ where t = selected position

where N_t is the new stream that replace the I_t on the video server. INTER( ) denotes the operator for transcoding the original stream to a new P-stream.

For each selected candidate, two frames' streams are encoded. One is the intra coded I-stream N_t with QP=20; the other is inter coded N_{t+1} with QP=10. To accelerate the operation, some transcoding technique [5] is used such as reuse the motion vector etc.

A shot might be very long. In this case, it might be better to add some additional random access points in it. The selected candidates can be described as a set:

$$W = \{w_i\}$$

Then we can add some w_i into the set W:

$$\left(w_i \bmod M = 1\right) \tag{3-2}$$

where M is the minimum random access distance.

Our experiment is based on MPEG4 simple profile with fixed quantization parameters. All the data come out from a sequence generated from an Intel Pentium Processor advertisement with CIF format. We concentrate on the detections of hard cuts that are abrupt changes of content from one frame to another.

The top curve in Fig 4 shows the picture quality of the original stream (O_t from equation 2-1) with QP=10. Frame 718 is a shot position. Using our initially proposed method, we transformed the data at shot position into I-stream with QP=20. By switching to I-stream at shot position, we obtain the picture quality as bottom curve shows. As to the improved algorithm, the quality is shown as the middle curve. The improved algorithm obtains a gain of almost 2.2dB.

We can obtain quality improvement as Figure 4 shows. Almost 2.2dB gain is obtained compared to the basic algorithm and nearly 1dB loss compared to the original one. The space usage is increased because one more frame's stream is generated for each shot. The browsing efficiency remains because the transforming process is still started at the shot boundary, not in advance.

The picture quality data are listed in Table 1.

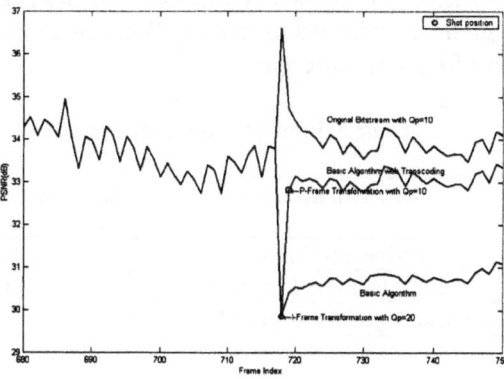

Fig. 4. Picture quality comparison

Table 1. Quality comparison-2

Different methods (Frame 718-750)	Average PSNR (dB)
Original P-stream (QP=10)	34.0059
Basic Algorithm from (2-1)	30.7098
Combined Algorithm with (2-1), (3-1)	32.9450

The data of the additional disk space usage and browsing efficiency are also summarized. Define T as the period for normal I-insertion and A as the total frames in the sequence; I as the average bits for an I-stream; S as the number of the shots; P as the average bits for a P-stream. The disk space occupation can be approximately summarized as:

Table 2. Additional Disk Space Usage Comparisons

Different methods	Additional Disk Space Usage
Periodic I-frames generation method	A/T * I
Basic Algorithm from (2-1)	S * I
Combined Algorithm with (2-1), (3-1)	S*(I+P)

In order to achieve high efficiency for random access, the periodic I-frames generation method requires large disk space. To improve the quality, it can also use the similar technique as (3-1) but with small QP, which will further occupy the disk space. In our method, the number of S depends on the content of the video source. With the control of parameter M in equation (3-2), we can balance the additional stream size to fit the disk space requirement.

The browsing efficiency is defined as how many frames need to be transmitted to the user until the data he is interested in arrives. We assume that the user's browsing requirement will start from a specific shot.

Table 3. Browsing efficiency comparison

Different methods	Browsing effi-ciency
Periodic I-Insertion	(T-1)/2
Basic Algorithm from (2-1)	0
Combined Algorithm with (2-1), (3-1)	0

Because of the restriction of the disk space and quality issue, T can't be too small. For sequence at 30fps, if we have one I-frame every 1 second then T=30. So the efficiency is greatly improved by our algorithm.

4 Conclusion

In this paper, we have presented a MPEG4 simple profile compatible approach for video browsing and retrieval over low bit rate channel. One new stream is generated on the video server to enable random access. The method is oriented to the user's browsing requirement and the channel's characteristic, so that the overhead involved in the transmission of periodic I-frames and the transmission of video data that the user is not interested is avoided or minimized. The quality, browsing efficiency and disk pace occupation can be well balanced by the algorithm.

References

1. ISO/IEC JTC1/SC29/WG11, "Information technology – Generic doing of audio-visual objects – Part2: Visual" 14496-2 FPDAM1, July
2. "Video Coding for low bit rate communication," ITU-T recommendation H.263, 1998
3. N. Farber and B. Girod, "Robust H.263 Compatible Video Transmission For Mobile Access to Video Servers," IEEE Procs. Image Processing, Vol. 2, pp. 73-76, 1997
4. T. Shanableh and M. Ghanbari, "Transcoding of video into different encoding formats", IEEE Conf. ICASSP 2000. Proceedings. Vol. 4, pp. 1927-1930, 2000

Multiple Granularity Access to Navigated Hypermedia Documents Using Temporal Meta-information

Wei-Ta Chu and Herng-Yow Chen

Department of Computer Science and Information Engineering
National Chi Nan University, Puli, Nantou, Taiwan 545, R.O.C.
wtchu@mc11.csie.ncnu.edu.tw, hychen@csie.ncnu.edu.tw

Abstract. Various multimedia document systems that capture, integrate, and synchronously present media have been implemented in many areas. As data volume grows and the diversity of new medium increases, how to efficiently locate the segments of interest is an important issue. To address this problem, this paper presents a framework that facilitates multiple levels of access to navigated hypermedia documents in three different granularities: HTML slide level, navigation event level, and sentence level. In contrast to traditional approaches, hierarchical access structure of navigated hypermedia documents can be exploited by analyzing temporal meta-information captured in the recording stage or computed in the speech-text alignment process. The proposed framework has been applied in the developed "Web-based Synchronized Multimedia Lecture System" for efficient content access.

1 Introduction

The dramatic development of streaming technologies and dynamic HTML techniques encourage multimedia lecturing on web [1-4]. The on-line multimedia lectures that integrate audio/video, text, and various navigation events simulate the chalk-and-board teaching mode in real classrooms. However, the massive multimedia lectures with lengthy audio and various heterogeneous media often impede efficient access and thus decrease the learning efficiency. Therefore, an integrated index that provides multilevel selection and facilitates efficient access to audio/video segments of interest is indispensable for multimedia archives.

Several projects have tackled the issues of multimedia integration and presentation for education purpose on web. The goal of the Cornell Lecture Browser [2] is to automatically produce a structured multimedia document from any seminar, talk, or class without extra preparation by the speaker or changes in the speaker's style. The Classroom 2000 [3] project at Georgia Tech developed an integrated system that automatically captures, integrates, and visualizes multiple media streams. Prepared slide-based lectures with static pen-strokes and corresponding audio/video segments are provided on web.

Both systems deal with presentation and accessible interfaces by exploiting the captured synchronization information between audio and slide events. However, little attention has been paid to taking advantage of the relationship between audio and slide text. In [2], slides and audio/video are incorporated to build a synchronous

Y.-C. Chen, L.-W. Chang, and C.-T. Hsu (Eds.): PCM 2002, LNCS 2532, pp. 1227-1234, 2002.

presentation. Without further analyses among involved media, only an intuitional slide-based timeline with slide change labels is provided for random access. In the Classroom 2000 system [3], slides with static pen strokes and audio/video are available in presentation. Although some different levels of access were also discussed, the audio segments with plenty of information are not utilized to enhance the efficiency and variety of access.

In this paper, on the basis of the Web-based Synchronized Multimedia Lecture system (WSML) [1], we investigate different levels of efficient access by exploiting the timing relationships between audio/video, HTML slide text, and various navigation events that are displayed by state-of-the-art dynamic HTML techniques. In contrast to the Classroom 2000 system, except for the explicit temporal information captured in instructing, the implicit temporal relationships between audio and text are also extracted after applying the speech-text alignment process. Both approaches are then integrated to facilitate efficient access in different granularities.

In the remainder of this paper, Section 2 describes a brief overview of the WSML system. The proposed framework of multiple level access is described in Section 3. In Sections 4, multiple granularity access for navigated hypermedia documents is described. Section 5 states the speech-text alignment technologies that facilitate sentence-level access. Finally, concluding remarks are given in Section 6.

2 The WSML System

The Web-based Synchronized Multimedia Lecture system integrates audiovisual lectures, HTML slides, and navigation events to provide synchronous presentations. In our environment, teachers use computers to instruct and a synchronization recorder keeps track of the oral guidance along with several navigation events. The navigation events, such as pen stroke, highlight, dynamic annotation, mouse track and scrolling, are guided media. Those media objects and navigated events will be presented dynamically in a browser by using state-of-the-art dynamic HTML techniques.

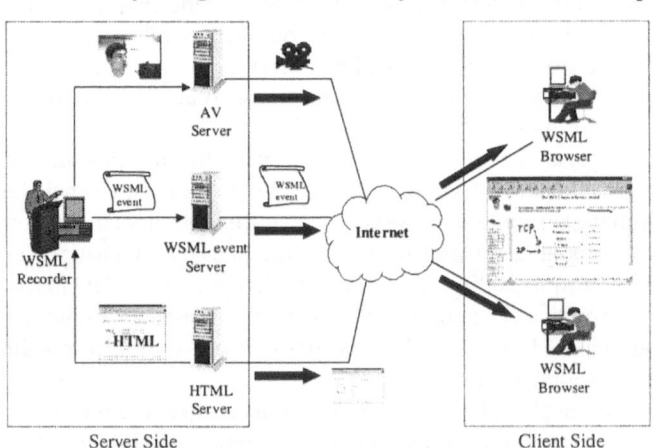

Fig. 1. System framework of the WSML system

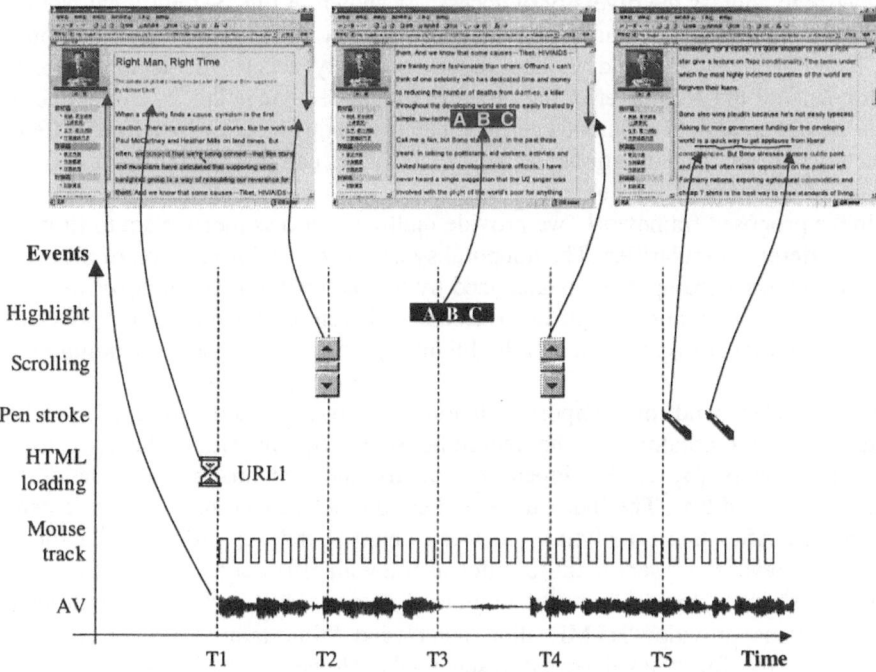

Fig. 2. An example of navigation events

Fig. 1 shows the framework of the WSML system. The WSML Recorder records audio/video along with the associated navigation events on HTML slides. The WSML Event Server receives, deposits, and dispatches those events to clients. The WSML Browser that incorporates synchronization mechanism into a HTML browser is responsible for synchronous presentation. This system records teachers' oral guidance and stores the teaching activities on HTML slides. A vivid teaching experience can be re-constructed in client sides by applying an elaborate synchronization mechanism.

Navigation events are triggered dynamically to enrich multimedia presentation on web. During audio/video playback, navigation events will be presented at appropriate time and spatial positions. Fig. 2 shows the synchronous presentation in the WSML Browser. The AV and HTML URL1 are loaded respectively at T1. The AV player then starts playing the AV lecture. And the HTML page is rendered by the embedded HTML browser at the same time. Then, a scrolling event is triggered at T2 to display the content that is originally out of screen. At T3, a highlight event is displayed to emphasize some words. At T4, another scrolling event is triggered. At T5, a sequence of pen stroke events is driven to show an ink stroke. These kinds of navigation events provide dynamic guidance rather than static web pages.

3 The Proposed Framework

The integration of various media streams really enriches multimedia lectures, but it also burdens users with the complexities of data retrieving. Hence, we propose a framework to address the diversity of access. As shown in Fig. 3, traditional work on web-based multimedia lectures primarily provides a synchronous presentation of slide-based lectures and audio/video. Users can only access the lectures via the control panel of the AV player or the timeline with slide-change labels. Unitary access points are not enough to efficiently retrieve heterogeneous media which have different characteristics and time durations. In most cases, users can just select roughly to seek for parts of a multimedia document.

In the proposed framework, we provide multilevel access mechanism to fit users' need in different granularities. The temporal synchronization information of all events captured in the recording stage is analyzed by the navigation event indexer to create an index table. Navigation event level access is therefore allowed so that users can click any high level event, such as a highlight region, to obtain corresponding audio segments.

On the other hand, the temporal relationship between audio and text is implicit because it is not obtained in the recording stage. In this work, the speech-text alignment process [5] is developed to identify the synchronization relationship between audio and text. The index table is therefore determined to facilitate sentence level access. After these analytic processes, temporal indexes are provided for the multimedia player to present plentiful information with efficient access points.

Fig. 4 shows a logical view of multilevel access. Most web-based multimedia lecture systems provide "HTML slide level" and "timestamp level" access—the coarsest and the finest level access respectively. However, the HTML slide level access is too rough especially when a HTML slide contains too much information. And the timestamp level access is too detailed because in most cases users could not know the exact timestamp of a segment. Both of them cannot meet users' access needs. On the contrary, the "navigation event level" and "sentence level" accesses are very useful to locate some specific subjects. There may exist many navigation events and sentences in one HTML slide. Navigation events are often clues to important information. Thus users can browse and access key information at a glance. Sentence level access provides users with a general view of text access that is important if users want to take repeated practices or few navigation events exist to be accessible entries. Different levels of access will be detailed in next section.

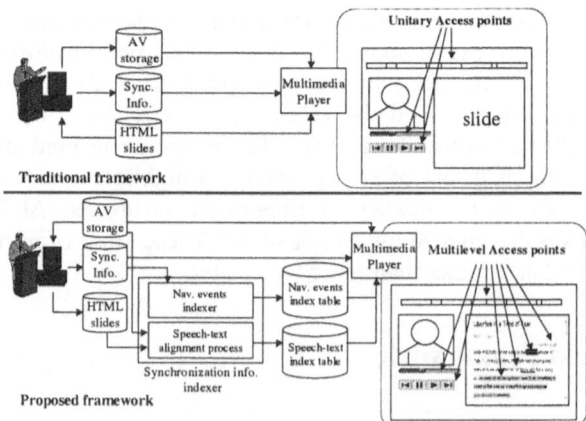

Fig. 3. Comparison of two frameworks

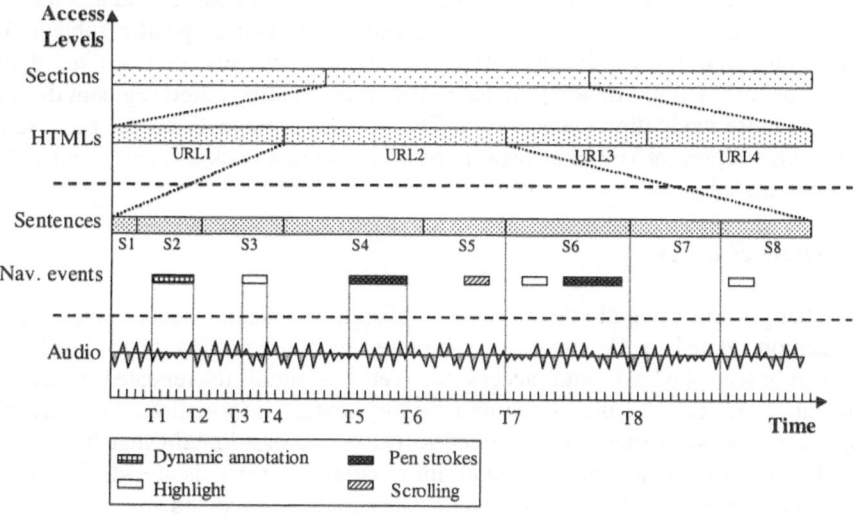

Fig. 4. Logical view of multilevel access

4 Multiple Granularity Access

4.1 HTML Slide Level

The coarsest granularity is the level of each HTML slide. We provide a single entry into a stream that is its beginning. This is similar to playing a tape from beginning to end and there is no way to directly access the details of slides. In the WSML system, the temporal information of URL change is captured by the WSML Recorder and therefore it's simple to present URL changes when playback. As shown in Fig. 4, the HTML level timeline acts as an index to different URLs. Each block means the playback duration of a HTML slide, and the vertical line between two blocks mean URL changes. Users can click any block of this timeline to jump to slides of interest directly.

4.2 Navigation Event Level

The navigation events in the WSML system consist of mouse track, pen stroke, dynamic annotation, highlight, and scrolling events. Related to audio data, each event has temporal information that is determined by the WSML Recorder. Speakers can use the cursor to point out individual elements relevant to the current discussion on HTML slides. Scrolling events will be triggered in a very short moment to show other parts of HTML slides that can't be displayed in the same screen.

Pen stroke, dynamic annotation, and highlight are supplemented media which will be displayed over HTML slides at appropriate time to emphasize some information.

For example, in Fig. 4, an annotation is displayed during T1 to T2, and a pen stroke is written during T5 to T6. Each event is an access point of a specific subject. When viewing the multimedia lecture, users could click on any pen stroke, dynamic annotation, or highlight region to listen to the corresponding audio segment during the time that these navigation events occur. This is a semantic level access because these events often represent key information and users can just click a visual event to locate an important subject.

4.3 Sentence Level

URL changes and navigation events are "explicit timed media" because their temporal information related to AV stream was captured in the recording stage. Furthermore, sentence-based playback and access are very essential to repeated practices or efficient access in a lecture containing lengthy textual information. The speech-text alignment process is therefore designed to perform cross-domain matching between speech and texts. Once the temporal information of texts is decided, any audio segment corresponding to the sentence in slides could be accessed.

5 Speech-Text Alignment

5.1 Alignment Framework

The automatic speech-text alignment process [5] aims to obtain a good speech-text synchronous presentation and to facilitate spoken document access. Fig. 5 shows three major components in this process.

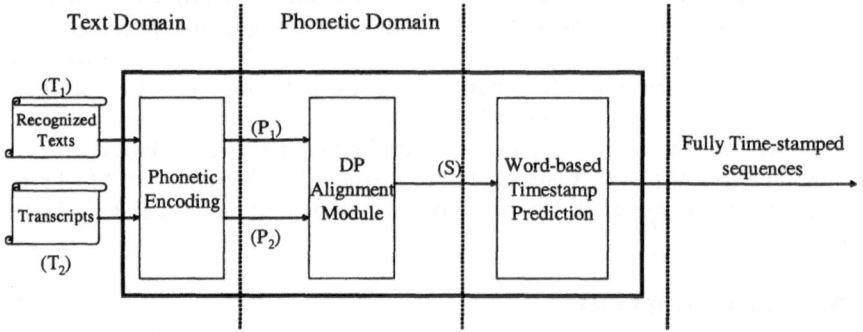

Fig. 5. Automatic speech-text alignment process

First, a speech index engine [6] is exploited to transcribe the input audio into time-stamped recognized text (T_1). After this transformation, the alignment problem between speech and text can be treated as the problem of aligning two text sequences (T_1 and T_2, the real transcript text). However, the recognized text is often imperfect because the recognition performance is often affected by various acoustic conditions, such as background music and noisy environments. For this reason, we translate both text sequences into phonetic sequences (P_1 and P_2) to reduce the influence of spelling differences. Two words that are pronounced similarly would be converted into the same/similar phonetic string by phonetic encoding functions. For example, both *through* and *threw* are converted to *"TH R UW."* Acoustic characteristics are classified and analyzed in phonetic encoding functions [7].

In the phonetic string domain, dynamic programming strategy is used in the second step to find an optimal matching (alignment) between two phonetic sequences (P_1 and P_2). However, phonetic domain string matching differs from traditional exact string matching because we have to consider phonetic characteristics. We define a similarity function that exploits edit distance measurement, a well-known technique of measuring string similarity, to determine whether two phonetic strings are similar. The similar phonetic strings are favorably aligned in the alignment process. Once the alignment is identified, we can obtain a time-stamped sequence (S) where the timestamps of the matched words are determined.

In the third stage, we take advantage of the timestamps of matched words to predict others'. Two closest time-aligned words are selected as predicators, and an interpolation/extrapolation rule is applied to estimate the timestamps of non-aligned words. This automatic alignment module finally generates a fully time-stamped sequence.

5.2 Sentence-Based Random Access

Although word-based access points are also determined in this alignment process, we found that sentence-based access and presentation is more suitable for the retrieval of specific segments. Therefore, we use sentence-based access to describe fine level of access.

Like the temporal relation shown in Fig. 4, we can indicate audio segments after the alignment process. In most cases, users want to just click a sentence to listen to the corresponding audio segments rather than browsing sequentially or blindly tracing the timeline. This interface really improves the access efficiency of a lengthy multimedia lecture.

Fig. 6 shows the integration of multiple streams and different levels of access. Different media are presented at the same time axis. We can locate one medium to retrieve all other media which are in the same time duration. This correlation plays an essential role to facilitate synchronous presentation and direct access.

6   Conclusions

In this paper, we have identified some critical issues on visualized access for rich interactive experiences that contain multiple independent streams. We built the web-based multimedia synchronized lecture system to faithfully present a chalk-and-board teaching environment on web. Several media that include audio/video, HTML slides, and navigation events are incorporated to construct a synchronous presentation. The automatic speech-text alignment process indicates the temporal relationship between audio and the text in HTML slides. By locating one stream, we can also retrieve all other streams by their temporal relationships. Visualized browsing and selection in multiple levels make the multimedia lectures more accessible.

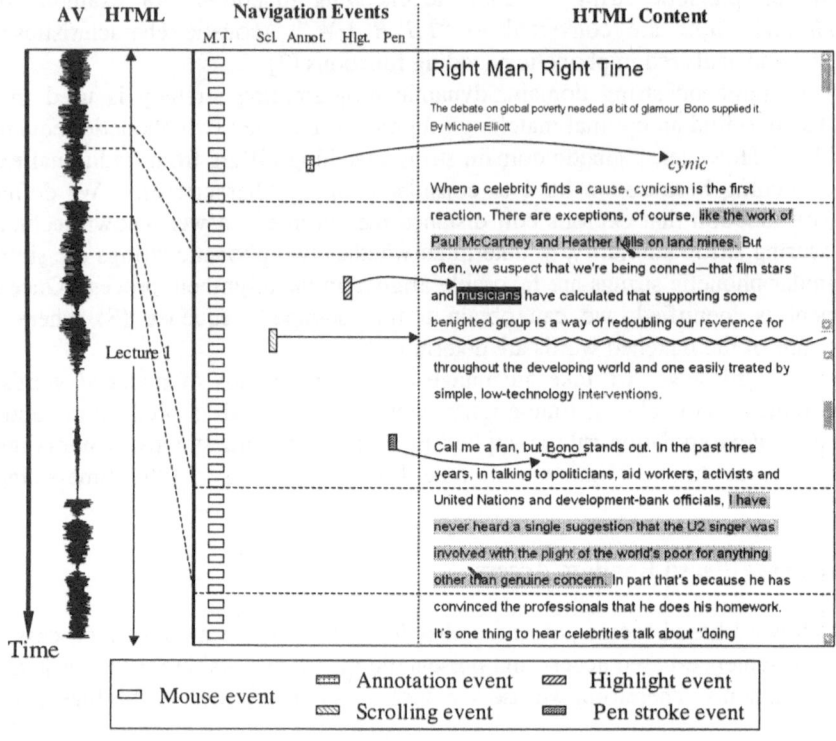

Fig. 6. Cooperation of multiple media

References

1. Chen, H.Y., Chen, G.Y., and Hong, J.S. "Design of a Web-based synchronized multimedia lecture system for distance education," Proceedings of International Conference on Multimedia Computing and Systems, vol. 2, pp. 887-891, 1999.
2. Mukhopadhyay, S. and Smith, B. "Passive Capture and Structuring of Lectures," Proceedings of ACM Multimedia, pp. 477-487, 1999.
3. Brotherton, J.A., and Bhalodia, J.R., and Abowd, G.D. "Automated Capture, Integration, and Visualization of Multiple Media Streams," Proceedings of International Conference on Multimedia Computing and Systems, pp. 54-63, 1998.
4. Roccetti, M. and Salomoni, P. "A Web-based Synchronized Multimedia System for Distance Education," Proceedings of ACM SAC, pp. 94-98, 2001.
5. Chu, W.T., Hsu, K.T., and Chen, H.Y. "Design of an Alignment System for Synchronized Speech-Text Presentation," Proceedings of Distributed Multimedia Systems, pp. 86-93, 2001.
6. Huang, X., Alleva, F., Hon, H.W., Hwang, M.Y., Lee, K.F., and Rosenfeld, R. "The SPHINX II Speech Recognition System: An Overview," Computer Speech and Language, 2(7), pp. 137-148, 1993.
7. The CMU pronouncing dictionary, http://www.speech.cs.cmu.edu/cgi-bin/cmudict

Authoring Temporal Scenarios in Interactive MPEG-4 Contents

Kyungae Cha and Sangwook Kim

Department of Computer Science, Kyungpook National University,
Sankyuk Dong 1370 Daegu, Korea
{chaka, swkim}@woorisol.knu.ac.kr

Abstract. MPEG-4 is an ISO/IEC standard which defines a multimedia system for communicating interactive scenes. An MPEG-4 audio-visual scene is composed of various types of media data that are represented as individual objects. It includes a scene description that refers to the spatio-temporal specifications and behaviors of the individual objects. Particularly in the presentation of an MPEG-4 scene, object-based user interaction is possible within the limit set defined by the author. In this paper, we propose an MPEG-4 scene authoring tool which provides facilitative tools for composing interactive behaviors of the objects. The authoring tool presents a graphical interface for building a temporal scenario of MPEG-4 scenes. It also proposes new means of graphically representing an interactive scenario.

1 Introduction

MPEG-4 provides an object-based approach to describing and composing an audio-visual scene with user interaction.

An MPEG-4 scene is comprised of a set of individual audio-visual objects and the arrangement of the objects, with the scene description specifying the spatio-temporal positions of said objects. The scene description is mapped into a parametric form called Binary Format for Scenes (BIFS)[1,4,7,13,14], which is built on several concepts from the Virtual Reality Modeling Languages(VRML)[5]. In specifying and generating MPEG-4 contents, the author builds a scene description in textual format for both structure and functionality of object composition nodes.

In this paper we present an MPEG-4 contents authoring tool for composing and generating MPEG-4 audio-visual scenes, which provides facilitative tools for composing interactive behaviors of the objects. The traditional timeline model is expanded in order to visualize the temporal scenario and handle the interactive scenario based on the objects. Moreover, we define declarative temporal relationships for providing the specification primitives.

Section 2 describes the defined temporal scenario composition model. Section 3 explains the authoring environment and authoring process of our system, while section 4 shows how the MPEG-4 contents are generated from the visual scene. Section 5 discusses the implementation of the MPEG-4 content authoring system. Section 6 introduces related works, while section 7 presents the conclusion and future plans.

Y.-C. Chen, L.-W. Chang, and C.-T. Hsu (Eds.): PCM 2002, LNCS 2532, pp. 1235-1242, 2002.

2 Temporal Scenario Composition Model

2.1 Temporal Constraints

The temporal behaviors of the objects comprising an MPEG-4 scene are represented by a set of temporal intervals of the objects.

To provide a facile temporal scenario specification tool, we use the timeline model which is simple and provides a graphical representation of a temporal scenario. Moreover the model can specify quantitative relations among objects(e.g., the start time of object m should be set at three seconds after the end time of object n)[3,9]. However, the traditional timeline model doesn't support the specifications of relative temporal relations among objects[2,9,12]. To avoid these restrictions, temporal constraints are defined and provided as the specification primitives of a temporal scenario. The temporal relations are defined vis-à-vis the temporal intervals of the audio-visual objects, based on J.F. Allen's temporal relations[6]. The temporal attribute of an object is specified in the form (st, et), where st and et denote the start and end time of the object, respectively. The dot notation is used to indicate the elements of a tuple. Let O be an object in a scene, thus, the start and end times of O are denoted as $O.st$ and $O.et$, respectively. The implicit temporal constraint of the temporal attributes of object O-- which must be satisfied--can be expressed as $O.st < O.et$.

If O_i and O_j are two audio-visual objects, the temporal relations and corresponding constraints between the two objects are defined as follows :

$Equal(O_i, O_j)$: $(O_i.st = O_j.st) \wedge (O_i.et = O_j.et)$
$Overlap(O_i, O_j)$: $(O_i.st < O_j.st < O_i.et) \wedge (O_i.et < O_j.et)$
$During(O_i, O_j)$: $(O_i.st < O_j.st) \wedge (O_j.et < O_i.et)$
$CoStart(O_i, O_j)$: $O_i.st = O_j.st$
$CoEnd(O_i, O_j)$: $O_i.et = O_j.et$
$Sequence(O_i, O_j)$: $O_i.et = O_j.st$
$After(O_i, O_j)$: $O_i.et < O_j.st$

During authoring time, authors can declare a temporal relation among objects at a certain temporal situation. All the declared constraints among objects are automatically enforced through the authoring process, thereby requiring less repositioning of the timelines of related objects when a temporal scenario modification is occurred.

2.2 User Interactions

User interactions of an MPEG-4 scene involve various action types of media objects, which respond to an end user's event. For example, the author designs the following scenario for the presentation of an advertisement for a clothes sale :

Example 1. If a user clicks a button image object, the rectangle object that shows the color of the product, changes its fill color to show the available colors in turn.

Here, the button image object and the rectangle object refer to the source object and the destination object, respectively. Likewise, the event type and action type are the user's click and the change in the rectangle object's fill color, respectively.

We define user interaction information as an *event object* which is represented as *(destobj_ID, e_Type, a_Type, key_Value)*, where *destobj_ID* denotes the unique number of the destination object ID which is determined when the object is added in the scene. *e_Type* and *a_Type* denote the user event type and the destination object's action type, respectively. *key_Value* is the array of values to be used in changing the parameters of the corresponding object field in response to the user event.

2.3 Object Synchronization

The temporal scenario of a scene is specified by modifying the timelines, which depict the start and end times of the object and declaring the temporal relations among objects.

When the author makes an association between two objects with a relation, the system presents a subset of relations from the set of predefined temporal relations that can be declared at that temporal situation, checking the constraints. Thereby, it is possible to eliminate the need to check constraint consistency from the author(see *example 3* in section 3).

Now assume that the author specifies the following user interaction scenario :

Example 2. If an end user clicks on a text object, e.g., the name of a product, the corresponding image object appears.

In this case, the start and end time of the corresponding image object is not determined at the authoring time. Thus, we define the action types which cause the non-deterministic temporal interval of the corresponding object as *Active* and *Inactive*. These action types mean that if the source object receives an end user's event(such as the user's click), the destination object appears or disappears.

In the case of *Active*, though the temporal interval of a destination object is not known during authoring time, the start of the destination object occurs within the time interval of its source object at presentation time. However the end time of the destination object is definitely unknown, thus the destination object's end time is assumed to be the end of the presentation. Therefore, the temporal relation between a source object(denoted as O_s)and a destination object(denoted as O_d) can be defined as *Overlap(O_s, O_d)*, for a specified *Active* event. In the case of *Inactive*, the end time of a destination object occurs within its source object temporal interval. Thus, the temporal relation between the source and destination objects can be enforced as *Overlap(O_d, O_s)* for the *Inactive* event.

If the text object in *example 2* is denoted as O_1 and the corresponding image object is denoted as O_2, the *Overlap(O_1, O_2)* relation is assigned to the two objects. Moreover, the timeline of the image object is automatically arranged to show the relationship (figure 1 (a)). At this situation, the following *Inactive* event cannot be specified. If the user's click occurs on another text object O_3 whose end time precedes the start time of object O_1, the image object O_2 disappears (figure 1 (b)).

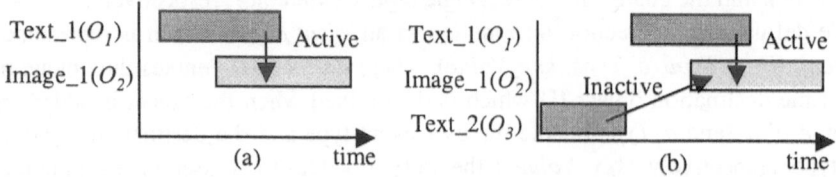

Fig. 1. An example of timelines : (a) Active event specification (b) Active and Inactive event specifications with inconsistency

For the *Inactive* event, the temporal relationship between the object O_2 and O_3 is *Overlap*(O_3, O_2). Based on the above assumption, the temporal constraint of the two text objects is $(O_3.et < O_1.st)$. Moreover, the constraint $(O_1.st < O_2.st)$ must be satisfied in accordance with the relation *Overlap*(O_1, O_2). Thus, the relation $(O_3.et < O_2.st)$ is inferred. As such, the temporal constraint $(O_2.st < O_3.et)$ for *Overlap*(O_3, O_2) cannot be compatible with the constraint for the predetermined relations.

To avoid such inconsistency, the temporal intervals of associated source and destination objects are checked whenever an event object is added. If an inconsistency occurs, the author receives a corresponding report.

3 Temporal Scenario Authoring

We developed a graphical interface for composing a spatio-temporal scenario of MPEG-4 scenes. Figure 2 (a) shows the graphical user interface and a simple example of a scene. Figure 2 (b) illustrates the event scenario authoring interface.

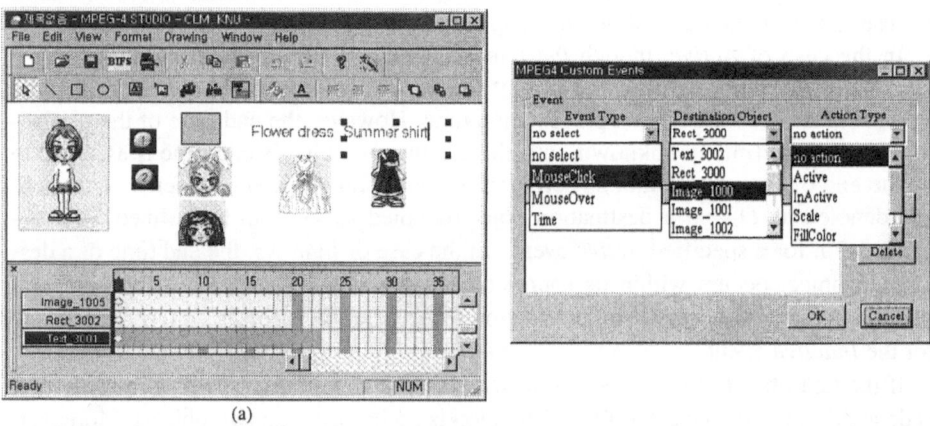

(a)

Fig. 2. Graphical user interface : (a) spatio-temporal composition interface (b) event information authoring interface

Authors select a drawing tool that they want to use in the toolbar. They then insert the selected object in the scene using drag-n-drop. The bottom portion of figure 2 (a) shows the timeline window where the timelines of objects are arranged. Whenever the author adds a new object in the scene, the system automatically assigns the object ID, and the start and end time of the object with default values. A new timeline of the object is also added in the timeline window. The author can directly modify the timelines.

Now consider the following scenario :

Example 3. An image object and a sound object always start at the same time.

When the author modifies the timelines of the two objects like figure 3 (a), {*CoStart, CoEnd, Equal*} constitute the set of possible temporal relations. The system automatically determines the available relationships according to the temporal intervals of the two objects and shows the list of temporal relations to the author. In composing the above scenario, the author declares the *CoStart* relation for the two objects. The timeline of the image object is then automatically updated each time the duration of the sound object is modified (figure 3 (b)).

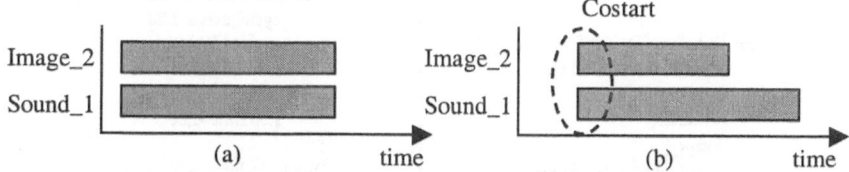

Fig. 3. An example of timeline modification with constraint

Using the dialog interface like figure 2 (b), User interaction scenario specification is done by selecting an event type and destination object, and the attributes of the destination that the author wants the event type to change.

To add user interaction, a selected object is right-clicked to display the shortcut menu. The author can then click any command in the shortcut menu to display the interface. Here, the selected object is referred to as the source object of the interaction information.

As described earlier, the event and action scenario are performed as event objects. The event object for the *example 1* is represented as quadruple (*3000, click, fill color, ((1.00 0.00 0.00), (0.00 0.50 0.00)))* if the rectangle object as the destination has the number 3000 for its object ID. Likewise, the event for *example 2* is specified as quadruple (*1000, click, active, (0,1)*), meaning the destination image object has its object ID of 1000. The *key_Value, 0* and *1* represents the object's inactive or active states, respectively.

The event object is directly linked to the source object as soon as it is created. As such, an event object tuple does not specify its source object ID.

4 MPEG-4 Scene Description Generation

The composed scene in the user interface is represented as a scene composition tree in an internal form. Whenever an object is added, a new object node is created and attached to the scene composition tree.

The scene description generator of our system searches the scene composition tree, in order to generate the MPEG-4 scene description corresponding to the visual scene.

In the scene tree, each object node has its spatio-temporal property values. Using the values written in the object node, the every field in BIFS can be filled.

Figure 4 shows a portion of the BIFS text for describing *example 1*. If an event scenario is specified in the user interface, the event object is attached to the source object as a child node. In BIFS, the interactivity between an end user and the objects is integrated in the form of linked event sources and targets, as well as sensor nodes. We can therefore describe interactivity information by integrating the values of the event object node according to the interactivity information description rules of MPEG-4 scene description.

```
Group {
children [
        DEF Transform2D1000 Transform2D {
            translation -52.00 71.00
            ...
            children [
            Shape {
                appearance Appearance {
                    texture ImageTexture {
                        url 1
                        ... } }
                geometry Bitmap {
                    ...
                    DEF TouchS1000 TouchSensor {
                    enabled TRUE }
            ]
        }
        DEF Transform2D3000 Transform2D {
            translation 0.00 54.00
            scale 1.00 1.00
            ...
                            } }
            geometry Rectangle {
                size 54.00 68.00 }
        }
```

```
DEF TimeSI3000I0 TimeSensor {
    cycleInterval 3.00
    enabled FALSE
    loop TRUE
    startTime 0.00
    stopTime -1.00
}
DEF ColorInter3000I0 ColorInterpolator {
    key [   0.00
            0.33
            0.67
            1.00   ]
    keyValue [ 0.00 0.50 0.00
            1.00 1.00 0.50
            0.00 1.00 0.50
            1.00 0.00 .00 ]
    ...

ROUTE TouchS1000.isActive TO
                TimeSI3000I0.enabled
ROUTE TimeSI3000I0.fraction_changed TO
                ColorInter3000I0.set_fraction
ROUTE ColorInter3000I0.value_changed TO
                Material2D3000.emissiveColor
```

Fig. 4. A portion of the BIFS text for example 1

5 Implementation

The proposed MPEG-4 authoring system was developed using C++ under the Windows 95/98/NT platform. Figure 5 shows the system structure.

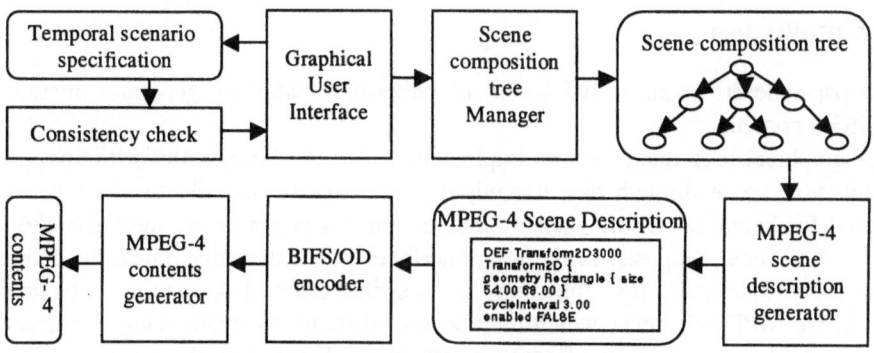

Fig. 5. System Structure

In the graphical user interface, authors compose a multimedia scene and specify a temporal scenario. During this time, the system checks the consistency of the temporal conditions when a scenario modification occurs. The resulting user interface is represented as a scene composition tree, from which the MPEG-4 scene description generator generates the BIFS text corresponding to the visual scene. Finally, the MPEG-4 contents generator multiplexes and generates the MPEG-4 contents.

6 Related Work

J. Song, et al.,[8] presented an interactive authoring tool for building temporal scenario specification. They proposed the elastic time model which considers the temporal length of objects. Similar to ours, their system also foregoes the repositioning of related objects during temporal scenario modification with constraints. Unlike the system of J. Song et al., our system's authoring tool automatically determines a set of possible temporal relations at the temporal condition, considering target objects' temporal durations and proposes the set to the author, when the author wants to declare a temporal relationship among objects. In addition, the system of Song et. al., did not resolve the user interaction issue. On the other hand, our system considers various types of user interactions in building a temporal scenario of multimedia presentations.

N. Hirzalla et al.,[12] proposed an expanded timeline model to represent an active multimedia scenario graphically within the timeline. The timeline splits into various timelines to show a different temporal scenario which can occur according to the user's event. To represent the interactive object in the timeline, the choice object which will make the temporal scenario jump to its destination scenario was defined. However, they didn't consider the inactive scenario which will make an object disappear, as well as other object-based interactions.

Macromedia's Director[11] is a commercial product related to our authoring system. It is a powerful multimedia authoring tool that employs object-based and timeline approaches and provides convenient direct manipulation tools. However, Director does not support declarative temporal relations among objects.

7 Conclusion

This paper describes an MPEG-4 content authoring system that generates interactive MPEG-4 contents.

A graphical user interface was implemented, which allows authors to compose a multimedia scene through direct manipulation. In particular, the timeline was expanded for handling objects whose temporal interval is not determined at authoring time. The scene composed in the user interface is automatically transformed into a form scene description text, thus there is no syntax error. Likewise, a sophisticated interactive MPEG-4 scenes which may be very difficult to create using text description can be generated. In the future, we recommend extending the temporal relation model to provide more various relationships among objects and using a flexible mechanism in checking constraints such as user defined priority.

References

1. A. Puri and A. Eleftheriadis, "MPEG-4: An Object-Based Multimedia Coding Standard Supporting Mobile Applications," *Mobile Networks and Applications*, vol. 3, pp. 5-32, 1998.
2. E. Bertino and E. Ferrari, "Temporal Synchronization Models for Multimedia Data," *IEEE Trans. Knowledge and Data Eng.*, vol. 10, no. 4, pp. 612-631, 1998.
3. E. Bertino, E. Ferrari and M. Stolf, "MPGS:An Interactive Tool for the Specification and Generation of Multimedia Presentations," *IEEE Trans. Knowledge and Data Eng.*, vol. 12, no. 1 pp. 102-125, 2000.
4. ISO/IEC 14496-1:1999 Information technology - Coding of audio-visual objects - Part 1: Systems ISO/IEC JTC1/SC29/WG11 N2501, 1999.
5. ISO/IEC 14772-2 : 1997 VRML97, The Virtual Reality Modeling Languages, 1997.
6. J.F. Allen, "Maintaining Knowledge about Temporal Intervals," *Communications of the ACM*, vol. 26, no. 11, pp. 832-843, 1983.
7. J. Kneip, B. Schmale and H. Möller, "Applying and Implementing the MPEG-4 Multimedia Standard," *IEEE Micro*, vol. 19, no. 6, pp. 64-74, 1999.
8. J. Song, G. Ramalingam, R. Miller and B.K. Yi, "Interactive authoring of multimedia documents in a constraint-based authoring system," *Multimedia Systems*, vol. 7, pp. 424-437, 1999.
9. K.S. Candan, B. Prabhakaran and V.S. Subrahmanian, "CHIMP: a framework for supporting distributed multimedia document authoring and presentation," in *Proc. 4th Conf. ACM International Conference on Multimedia*, Boston, United States, November 18 - 22, 1996, pp. 329-340.
10. M. Vazirgiannis, I. Kostalas, and T. Sellis, "Specifying and Authoring Multimedia Scenarios," *IEEE MultiMedia*, Vol. 6, No. 3, pp. 24-37, July-September 1999.
11. Macromeida, Director, http://www.macromedia.com
12. N. Hirzalla, B. Falchuk, and A. Karmouch, "A Temporal Model for Interactive Multimedia Scenarios," *IEEE Multimedia* , Vol. 2, No. 3, pp. 24-31, Fall 1995.
13. S. Battista, F. Casalino and C. Lande, "MPEG-4: A Multimedia Standard for the Third Millennium, Part 1," *IEEE Multimedia*, vol. 6, no. 4, pp.74-83, 1999.
14. WG11(MPEG), MPEG-4 Overview (V.18 Singapore Version) document, ISO/IEC JTC1/SC29/WG11 N4030, March 2001.

Implementation of Live Video Transmission in MPEG-4 3D Scene

Wen-Hao Wang, Chieh-Chih Chang, and Ming-Fen Lin

Opto-Electronics & Systems Laboratories
Industrial Technology Research Institute
devin@itri.org.tw

Abstract. This paper discusses the implementation of live video transmission in MPEG-4 3D scene. A captured video stream is packetized and time-stamped in MPEG-4 synchronization layer (SL) and transmitted on the channel created by DMIF remote instance. The primary method is to parse the MP4 file and utilize the characteristics of elementary stream (ES) descriptor. The SL configuration and SL header are designed for the live video such that the live media can be properly transmitted and combined with other objects in the original 3D scene. The implemented system has been well verified with the integration version of IM1 3D player and UBC's DMIF.

1   Introduction

MPEG-4 [1] is a binary-encoded and streamable representation of audio-visual objects by means of a scene description (by BIFS [1] [2]) for defining the combination of all objects. This is a well-adapted standard for multimedia applications with features: integration of 2D, 3D, natural, or synthetic objects, synchronization of all streams, streaming, and interactivity. The main implementation for MPEG-4 is IM1 [3], which provides several components: the SL manager, the compositor, and the controller, *etc*. The possible applications [4] of MPEG-4 might be collaborative scene visualization, infotainment, mobile multimedia, visual surveillance, and virtual meeting, *etc*. Most of the applications will benefit from the live video. With the achievement of live transmission, it will become possible to make other applications a successful debut.

The implementation of live video transmission in MPEG-4 3D scene is presented in this paper. In general, an MPEG-4 presentation is created (described in Sec. 3.2) offline as a file (MP4 format [5]) using multiplexing tool. The remote clients access the file with URL format [6] and the MP4 file are delivered by DMIF [6]. Other than files, the presentations can also be stored in the form of SL-packetized streams [7]. A comprehensive discussions and simulations of the IM1 2D player and 3D player can be found in [8]. The implemented system in this paper is based on the IM1 3D player [3] and UBC's implementation [9] due to the reasons: (1) The IM1 3D player does not implement remote DMIF instance, *i.e.*, the client can merely access the local file; (2) The complete DMIF (filter, local and remote instances) are implemented with the 2D

Y.-C. Chen, L.-W. Chang, and C.-T. Hsu (Eds.): PCM 2002, LNCS 2532, pp. 1243-1250, 2002.
© Springer-Verlag Berlin Heidelberg 2002

player by UBC. Therefore, we integrate the IM1 3D player and UBC's DMIF such that MP4 presentation (with 3D objects) can be accessed by remote clients.

The remainder of this paper is organized as follows: In Sec. 2, MPEG-4 System is briefly described. Sec. 3 addresses the client/server architecture of the MPEG-4 System. The principles and the implementation of the live video transmission in MPEG-4 3D scene are presented in Sec. 4. Finally, the conclusions and the future works are given in Sec. 5.

2 MPEG-4 System

MPEG-4 System is specified in standard 14496-1 [1] in which an SDM (system decoder model) is defined and comprehensively described. The main mechanisms of the SDM consist of multiplexing and synchronization of elementary streams. In addition, 14496-1 expounds on interactivity (*client-side interactivity* for local manipulation and *server-side interactivity* using back channel), scene description of how to combine objects, and object descriptors.

MPEG-4, as compared with its predecessor, provides a more flexible way of production of the contents with greater reusability in the viewpoint of authors. *Interactivity* is a brand-new feature to users; it functions by means of routes and sensors mechanism of BIFS. By using this feature, new applications can be developed; *e.g.*, CustomTV [10], which utilizes the interactivity of MPEG-4 and features of MPEG-7 [11] (*i.e.*, indexing and classification of information). The CustomTV can provide the functionalities of selecting programs according to user's preferences. Additionally, other overview of MPEG-4 can be found in [12].

3 MPEG-4 Server

Fig. 1 illustrates the proposed server architecture for transmitting live video (H263 stream) in a 3D scene. The main implementation is based on IM1 architecture which is described in Sec. 3.1. First of all, the MP4 file is created *a priori* as described in Sec. 3.2. Upon request via DMIF, the server will send the relevant MP4 stream to the client. However, the video in one of the 3D objects is still not live; hence, it is required to replace a video object with the live H263 stream which is fed to MPEG-4 MUX from capturing process (as shown in the bottom path of Fig. 1). With such a simple idea, the live video can be seen in one of the 3D objects at the client side. On account that the live video is to be multiplexed with the original streams (*i.e.* BIFS stream and media streams, *etc.*), the captured video must be SL-packetized [15] again with new time stamps and sync layer headers. Therefore, appropriate SL configuration and header are designed for this specific application. Sec. 4 gives the detail discussions regarding the sync layer issue. MPEG-4 System standard does not specify any specific delivery method. Nevertheless, the DMIF [6] is considered as an adequate delivery framework for MPEG-4 transmission. Especially, DMIF plays an important role in session management and content access. The detail access procedure is explained in Sec. 3.3.

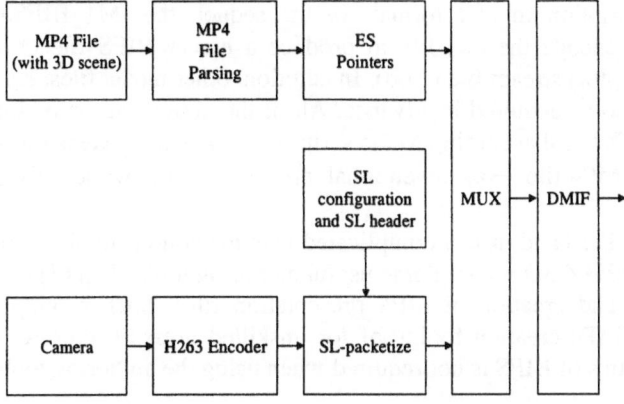

Fig. 1. The proposed MPEG-4 server architecture.

3.1 IM1 Architecture

Many companies contribute to the IM1 core. In general, there are two versions: 2D player and 3D player. All of them can merely open the local MP4 file rather than remote MP4 file since remote DMIF instance is not implemented. UBC [9] is responsible for implementing complete DMIF including DMIF filter, local DMIF instance, and remote DMIF instance. Remote access of 3D scenes is primarily concerned in the simulated application. Thus, the DMIF module of the UBC (2D player) is integrated with the IM1 3D player. Consequently, the 3D scene on remote server can be accessed by clients via the DMIF filter and the remote DMIF instance.

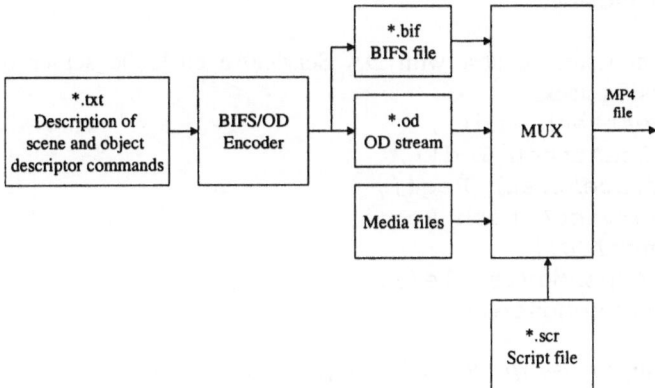

Fig. 2. Procedure of creating an MP4 file.

3.2 MP4 File Creation

The concise illustration of MP4 creation is given in Fig. 2. First, the author must write a scene description in text format. In the sequel, the IM1 BIFS/OD encoder is employed to encode the text file to produce a binary BIFS file (*.bif) and an OD (object descriptor) stream file (*.od). In addition, other media files, *e.g.* H263 or G723 files, must also be acquired in advance. All of the above will be multiplexed together by IM1 "MUX" tool according to the script file (file name extension: scr). At last, we will have the MP4 file — a conventional presentation file without live video.

On the other hand, it is a complicated task for non-professional users to create a complete MPEG-4 3D scene. Some useful authoring tools [13][14] can be utilized for rapid design and creation of MP4 presentation files. Such a template-guided tool would make MP4-creation foolproof for unskilled users. Therefore, comprehending all the semantics of BIFS is not required when using the authoring tools.

3.3 Content Access via DMIF

The user at client side can access the MP4 presentation from the server by the following procedure [1][7]: (1) Client sends URL of the content by using *DA_ServiceAttach()* to request the remote server via DMIF. Because MPEG-4 does not specify how client can get the URL, the client must know the URL *a priori* by means of other ways. (2) With this URL, the server parses (described in Sec. 3.4) the requested MP4 file and returns the IOD (initial object descriptor) to the client. (3) The client requests the server to add channels by *DA_ChannelAdd()* with ES ID (extracted from IOD) as parameter. (4) The server returns the handle of ES to the client. It is noted that the server maintains the mapping between the ES ID's and channel ID's. (5) The client issues *DA_ChannelReady()* to notify the server to send data via the requested channel.

3.4 MP4 File Parsing

After the client issues request with DA_ServiceAttach(), the server performs the following function stacks:

```
DN_ServiceAttach_Ind(),
 DAI_ServiceAttach_Ind(),
  DAI_ServiceAttach_Req(),
   DPI_ServiceAttach_Req(),
    ExtactIOD(),
     MP4OpenMovieFile(),
      parseMovie().
```

As a result, "*ExtractIOD()*" will return the IOD to the client after executing "parseMovie()." The format of MP4 file is illustrated in Fig. 3, which elaborates the interchange structure of MP4 format. The format is composed of object-oriented structures called "atoms" each of which is identified by unique tag and length. The collection of atoms is contained in a "movie atom." The detail description of the MP4 format can be found in [12]. On receiving the IOD, the client can retrieve all ES IDs from the IOD and request the server to create corresponding channel for each ES by DA_ChannelAdd() as described in Sec. 3.3.

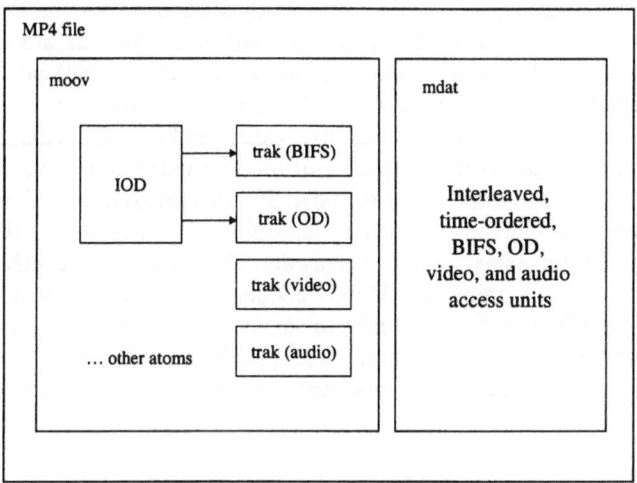

Fig. 3. MP4 file format.

In the designed 3D scene, for example, the live video object is assigned the ES ID = 21. Considering that the live video is desired and the video object (a virtual object) with ES ID = 21 is to be replaced, the ES ID is used to identify the virtual object and redirect the video input stream from an atom to one from live capturing. That leads to a task: the captured video must be SL-packetized [15] again. In the subsequent section, the descriptions of elementary stream and the required SL semantics will be addressed.

4   Sync Layer Semantics for Live Video Stream

ES ID is a unique reference to the elementary stream as stated in the syntax description of "ES_Descriptor" [1]. The values 0x0000 and 0xFFFF are reserved. In the proposed design, the server will SL-packetize and transmit the live H263 video stream instead of sending the original virtual object whenever any client requests a channel to access the object with ES ID = 21. The transmitted live media can then be textured on the original 3D object (as shown in Fig. 4) based on the original arrangement of the virtual object. Consequently, the live video is shown on each facet of the 3D cube of the 3D scene as shown in the 3D player of client side. The SL-packetization is accomplished by appropriate SL configuration. The concerned configuration flags and SL header are elaborated as follows. An ES carries media streams or BIFS stream and each ES is composed of several access units (AUs). The

AU is the smallest entity to be attributed with time stamp. Each AU might be in a single SL packet or be divided into several SL packets. That can be determined by the SL flags: useAccessUnitStartFlag and useAccessUnitEndFlag. If both flags are FALSE, each SL packet corresponds to a complete AU. These flags are set to TRUE in the proposed design. Other SL configuration flags are discussed as follows.

If "useTimeStampFlag" is TRUE, time stamps are used for the synchronization of the ES of the live video. In this case, the live video packets are SL-packetized according to the fixed settings: timeStampResolution and timeScale. In addition, decodingTimeStamp and compositionTimeStamp are set to zero, *i.e.*, a packet is decoded in no time after receiving. Thus, live video can be processed and displayed in a 3D scene properly. However, the quality of the live video cannot be estimated; that would entail rate control at the H263 encoder. If "useTimeStampFlag" is FALSE, the following parameters will be used for synchronization: 1. accessUnitRate: It might correspond to the bit rates of H263 encoder. 2. compositionUnitRate: It might correspond to the bit rates of H263 encoder and other media objects. 3. startDecodingTimeStamp: It can be used to set the time for decoding the first AU. 4. startCompositionTimeStamp. The field "sequenceNumber" should be continuously inserted to SL packets in an incremental way; in case of discontinuity, the loss of an SL packet is expected.

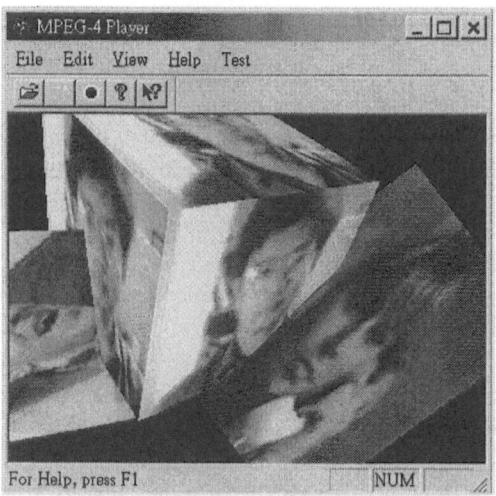

Fig. 4. Live video in 3D scene.

Fig. 4 shows the result of live video transmission in a 3D scene where the live video is displayed on the 3D cube. The following states the procedure to demo the MPEG-4 3D scene: (1) execute the server program at remote side and the 3D player at client side, respectively. (2) In 3D player, open the MP4 file using xdtcp://account: password@IP adress: port_number/cube.mp4. (3) DMIF will process all requests and responses between the client and the server as described in Sec. 3.3. (4) After creating all requested channels, all media streams (file or live) will be transmitted and shown on the corresponding 3D objects. There is no significant discrepancy lie between the quality of the live video and that of the conventional H263 video stream, which is not related to SL-packetization. In addition, more than one client can access the same MP4 file at any time and obtain the same live video. However, the performance degradation will become inevitable if the number of clients increases dramatically.

5 Conclusions and Future Works

The live video transmission in 3D scene is presented in this paper. The main implementation issue is given in Sec. 4 regarding the SL-packetization for live video. Although multiple-clients are acceptable, the bandwidth for transmitting the live video to all clients must be moderately taken into consideration. Furthermore, the multicast DMIF should be exploited for such an application for peer-to-peer scene interactions. MPEG-4 is a multimedia standard, which accommodates many existing media and provides several brilliant features that will lead to a promising development in the new multi-media era. With the advent of MPEG-4, some emerging applications can be anticipated as follows: (1) 3D videoconference (live video textured on 3D facial model), (2) advanced interactive video surveillance, or (3) live show in TV program arranged in a 3D scene. All the above applications need an elementary 3D scene which can be created in advance like templates [13]. To probe further, reference [4] details some possible applications of MPEG-4.

The live video transmission is a preliminary work for further exploitation of related applications. According to our work and the study on MPEG-4, some future works are enumerated as follows:
1. Create template library [13] of specific applications. Authors can customize the templates with objects and attributes.
2. Add new stream type, *e.g.* a progressive mesh, *etc.*
3. Use multiple videos for texturing individual 3D head models in an interactive virtual conference.
4. Use TriMedia processor [16] to enhance MPEG-4 performance.
5. Integrate multicast DMIF for multi-user videoconference or collaboration.
6. In sync layer, pass timing information between all participants in a collaborative environment by means of features of BIFS.

Acknowledgment. This work is a partial result of the project number A311XS1565 conducted by ITRI under sponsorship of the Ministry of Economic Affairs, R.O.C.

References

[1] ISO/IEC 14496-1. ISO/IEC JTC1/SC29/WG11 N2501.
[2] Hosseini, M., and Georganas, N. D.: Suitability of MPEG4's BIFS for Development of Collaborative Virtual Environments. Technical report of Multimedia Communication Research Laboratory. University of Ottawa
[3] Lifshitz Z.: API's for System Software Implementation. ISO/ IEC JTC1/ SC29 M3111.
[4] ISO/IEC JTC1/SC29/WG11 N2724 March (1999)
[5] Text of ISO/IEC 14496-1/PDAM1. ISO/IEC JTC1/SC29/WG11 N22739 March (1999)
[6] ISO/IEC 14496-6. ISO/IEC JTC1/SC29/WG11 N3713.

[7]   Kalva, H., Tang, L., Huard, J.-F., Tselikis, G., Zamora, J., Cheok, L.-T., and Eleftheriadis, A.: Implementing Multiplexing, Streaming, and Server Interaction for MPEG-4. IEEE Trans. CSVT, Vol. 9. 8 (1999) 1299-1312

[8]   Tsai, J.-J.: MPEG-4 Systems and Its Simulation. Thesis of NTU. June (1999)

[9]   Haghighi, K.A., Pourmohammadi, Y., and Alnuweiri, H.M.: Realizing MPEG-4 Streaming over the Internet: a Client/server Architecture Using DMIF. Proceedings of International Conference on Information Technology: Coding and Computing (2001) 23-29

[10] Cosmas, J., Paker, Y., Pearmain, A., Schoonjans, P., Vaduva, A., Dosch, C., Sch fer, R., Erk, A., Mies, R., Bais, M., Sch fer, R., Stammnitz, P., Selinger, T., Klunsoyr, G., Pedersen, L., Bauer, S., Engelsberg, A., Klock, B. and Evensen, G.: CustomTV with MPEG-4 and MPEG-7. IEE. (1999)

[11] Avaro, O. and Salembier, P.: MPEG-7 Systems: Overview. IEEE Trans. CSVT, Vol. 11. 6 (2001) 760-764

[12] ISO/IEC JTC1/SC29/WG11 N4668. March (2002)

[13] Boughoufalah, S., Brelot, M., Bouilhaguet, F., and Dufourd, J.-C.: A Template-Guided Authoring Environment to Produce MPEG-4 Content for the Web. MediaFutures, FLORENCE (2001)

[14] Boughoufalah S., Dufourd, J.-C. and Bouilhaguet, F.: MPEG-Pro, an Authoring System for MPEG-4 with Temporal Constraints and Template Guided Editing. IEEE International Conference on Multimedia and Expo, Vol. 1. (2000) 175-178

[15] Wu, D., Hou, Y.T., Zhu, W., Lee, H.-J., Chiang, T., Zhang, Y.-Q., and Chao, H.J.: On End-to-End Architecture for Transporting MPEG-4 Video over the Internet. IEEE Trans. Circuits and Systems For Video Technology, Vol. 10. 6 (2000) 923 – 941

[16] Stingl, T., Dreier, R., Barheine, O.: Experiences with the Development of an MPEG-4 Oriented PC Multimedia Application. SPIE Optics Conference, Boston. (1998)

Author Index

Lecture Notes in Computer Science

For information about Vols. 1–2456

please contact your bookseller or Springer-Verlag

Vol. 2496: K.C. Almeroth, M. Hasan (Eds.), Management of Multimedia in the Internet. Proceedings, 2002. XI, 355 pages. 2002.

Vol. 2497: E. Gregori, G. Anastasi, S. Basagni (Eds.), Advanced Lectures on Networking. XI, 195 pages. 2002.

Vol. 2498: G. Borriello, L.E. Holmquist (Eds.), UbiComp 2002: Ubiquitous Computing. Proceedings, 2002. XV, 380 pages. 2002.

Vol. 2499: S.D. Richardson (Ed.), Machine Translation: From Research to Real Users. Proceedings, 2002. XXI, 254 pages. 2002. (Subseries LNAI).

Vol. 2501: D. Zheng (Ed.), Advances in Cryptology – ASIACRYPT 2002. Proceedings, 2002. XIII, 578 pages. 2002.

Vol. 2502: D. Gollmann, G. Karjoth, M. Waidner (Eds.), Computer Security – ESORICS 2002. Proceedings, 2002. X, 281 pages. 2002.

Vol. 2503: S. Spaccapietra, S.T. March, Y. Kambayashi (Eds.), Conceptual Modeling – ER 2002. Proceedings, 2002. XX, 480 pages. 2002.

Vol. 2504: M.T. Escrig, F. Toledo, E. Golobardes (Eds.), Topics in Artificial Intelligence. Proceedings, 2002. XI, 432 pages. 2002. (Subseries LNAI).

Vol. 2506: M. Feridun, P. Kropf, G. Babin (Eds.), Management Technologies for E-Commerce and E-Business Applications. Proceedings, 2002. IX, 209 pages. 2002.

Vol. 2507: G. Bittencourt, G.L. Ramalho (Eds.), Advances in Artificial Intelligence. Proceedings, 2002. XIII, 418 pages. 2002. (Subseries LNAI).

Vol. 2508: D. Malkhi (Ed.), Distributed Computing. Proceedings, 2002. X, 371 pages. 2002.

Vol. 2509: C.S. Calude, M.J. Dinneen, F. Peper (Eds.), Unconventional Models in Computation. Proceedings, 2002. VIII, 331 pages. 2002.

Vol. 2510: H. Shafazand, A Min Tjoa (Eds.), EurAsia-ICT 2002: Information and Communication Technology. Proceedings, 2002. XXIII, 1020 pages. 2002.

Vol. 2511: B. Stiller, M. Smirnow, M. Karsten, P. Reichl (Eds.), From QoS Provisioning to QoS Charging. Proceedings, 2002. XIV, 348 pages. 2002.

Vol. 2512: C. Bussler, R. Hull, S. McIlraith, M.E. Orlowska, B. Pernici, J. Yang (Eds.), Web Services, E-Business, and the Semantic Web. Proceedings, 2002. XI, 277 pages. 2002.

Vol. 2513: R. Deng, S. Qing, F. Bao, J. Zhou (Eds.), Information and Communications Security. Proceedings, 2002. XII, 496 pages. 2002.

Vol. 2514: M. Baaz, A. Voronkov (Eds.), Logic for Programming, Artificial Intelligence, and Reasoning. Proceedings, 2002. XIII, 465 pages. 2002. (Subseries LNAI).

Vol. 2515: F. Boavida, E. Monteiro, J. Orvalho (Eds.), Protocols and Systems for Interactive Distributed Multimedia. Proceedings, 2002. XIV, 372 pages. 2002.

Vol. 2516: A. Wespi, G. Vigna, L. Deri (Eds.), Recent Advances in Intrusion Detection. Proceedings, 2002. X, 327 pages. 2002.

Vol. 2517: M.D. Aagaard, J.W. O'Leary (Eds.), Formal Methods in Computer-Aided Design. Proceedings, 2002. XI, 399 pages. 2002.

Vol. 2518: P. Bose, P. Morin (Eds.), Algorithms and Computation. Proceedings, 2002. XIII, 656 pages. 2002.

Vol. 2519: R. Meersman, Z. Tari, et al. (Eds.), On the Move to Meaningful Internet Systems 2002: CoopIS, DOA, and ODBASE. Proceedings, 2002. XXIII, 1367 pages. 2002.

Vol. 2521: A. Karmouch, T. Magedanz, J. Delgado (Eds.), Mobile Agents for Telecommunication Applications. Proceedings, 2002. XII, 317 pages. 2002.

Vol. 2522: T. Andreasen, A. Motro, H. Christiansen, H. Legind Larsen (Eds.), Flexible Query Answering. Proceedings, 2002. XI, 386 pages. 2002. (Subseries LNAI).

Vol. 2525: H.H. Bülthoff, S.-Whan Lee, T.A. Poggio, C. Wallraven (Eds.), Biologically Motivated Computer Vision. Proceedings, 2002. XIV, 662 pages. 2002.

Vol. 2526: A. Colosimo, A. Giuliani, P. Sirabella (Eds.), Medical Data Analysis. Proceedings, 2002. IX, 222 pages. 2002.

Vol. 2527: F.J. Garijo, J.C. Riquelme, M. Toro (Eds.), Advances in Artificial Intelligence – IBERAMIA 2002. Proceedings, 2002. XVIII, 955 pages. 2002. (Subseries LNAI).

Vol. 2528: M.T. Goodrich, S.G. Kobourov (Eds.), Graph Drawing. Proceedings, 2002. XIII, 384 pages. 2002.

Vol. 2529: D.A. Peled, M.Y. Vardi (Eds.), Formal Techniques for Networked and Distributed Sytems – FORTE 2002. Proceedings, 2002. XI, 371 pages. 2002.

Vol. 2532: Y.-C. Chen, L.-W. Chang, C.-T. Hsu (Eds.), Advances in Multimedia Information Processing – PCM 2002. Proceedings, 2002. XXI, 1255 pages. 2002.

Vol. 2533: N. Cesa-Bianchi, M. Numao, R. Reischuk (Eds.), Algorithmic Learning Theory. Proceedings, 2002. XI, 415 pages. 2002. (Subseries LNAI).

Vol. 2534: S. Lange, K. Satoh, C.H. Smith (Ed.), Discovery Science. Proceedings, 2002. XIII, 464 pages. 2002.

Vol. 2535: N. Suri (Ed.), Mobile Agents. Proceedings, 2002. X, 203 pages. 2002.

Vol. 2536: M. Parashar (Ed.), Grid Computing – GRID 2002. Proceedings, 2002. XI, 318 pages. 2002.

Vol. 2537: D.G. Feitelson, L. Rudolph, U. Schwiegelshohn (Eds.), Job Scheduling Strategies for Parallel Processing. Proceedings, 2002. VII, 237 pages. 2002.

Vol. 2540: W.I. Grosky, F. Plášil (Eds.), SOFSEM 2002: Theory and Practice of Informatics. Proceedings, 2002. X, 289 pages. 2002.

Vol. 2546: J. Sterbenz, O. Takada, C. Tschudin, B. Plattner (Eds.), Active Networks. Proceedings, 2002. XIV, 267 pages. 2002.

Vol. 2548: J. Hernández, Ana Moreira (Eds.), Object-Oriented Technology. Proceedings, 2002. VIII, 223 pages. 2002.

Vol. 2549: J. Cortadella, A. Yakovlev, G. Rozenberg (Eds.), Concurrency and Hardware Design. XI, 345 pages. 2002.

Vol. 2550: A. Jean-Marie (Ed.), Advances in Computing Science – ASIAN 2002. Proceedings, 2002. X, 233 pages. 2002.

Vol. 2551: A. Menezes, P. Sarkar (Eds.), Progress in Cryptology – INDOCRYPT 2002. Proceedings, 2002. XI, 437 pages. 2002.

Vol. 2556: M. Agrawal, A. Seth (Eds.), FST TCS 2002: Foundations of Software Technology and Theoretical Computer Science. Proceedings, 2002. XI, 361 pages. 2002.

Vol. 2557: B. McKay, J. Slaney (Eds.), AI 2002: Advances in Artificial Intelligence. Proceedings, 2002. XV, 730 pages. 2002. (Subseries LNAI).

Vol. 2559: M. Oivo, S. Komi-Sirviö (Eds.), Product Focused Software Process Improvement. Proceedings, 2002. XV, 646 pages. 2002.